THE COMPLETE SCHOLARSHIP BOOK

Student Services, Inc.

Published by: **Sourcebooks, Inc.**
P.O. Box 372, Naperville, Illinois 60566
(708) 961-3900
FAX: 708-961-2168

This publication is designed to provide accurate and authoritative information in regard to the subject matter covered. It is sold with the understanding that the publisher is not engaged in rendering legal, accounting, or other professional service. If legal advice or other expert assistance is required, the services of a competent professional person should be sought.

From a Declaration of Principles Jointly Adopted by a Committee of the American Bar Association and a Committee of Publishers and Associations

Every effort has been made to provide you with the best, most up-to-date information on private sector financial aid. However, if you discover an award in this book is listed incorrectly, please contact our research department by mail at: Research Department, Student Services, Inc., 2550 Commonwealth Avenue, North Chicago, IL 60064.

Disclaimer

Care has been taken in collecting and presenting the material contained in this book; however, Student Services, Inc., and Sourcebooks, Inc., do not guarantee its accuracy. This edition contains information relevant to the 1996-97 academic year.

Student Services, Inc., and Sourcebooks, Inc., are private corporations, and are not affiliated in any way with the U.S. Department of Education or any other government agency.

Library of Congress Cataloging-in-Publication Data

The complete scholarship book / Student Services, Inc.
p. cm
Includes index.
ISBN 1-57071-127-5 (pbk.)
1. Scholarships—United States—Directories. 2. Associations, institutions, etc.—Charitable contributions—United States—Directories. 3. Student aid—United States—Handbooks, manuals, etc. I. Student Services, Inc.
LB2338.C653 1996
378.3'4'0973—dc20
96-31154
CIP

Printed and bound in the United States of America.

Paperback — 10 9 8 7 6 5 4 3

Read This First

Congratulations! You hold in your hands the most comprehensive and thoroughly researched publication ever produced on the subject of college financial aid furnished by nongovernment organizations. These philanthropic, private organizations include foundations, corporations, employers, clubs, religious organizations, and civic groups.

About half of the over 5,000 nongovernment financial aid opportunities listed in this book are college-specific—that is, you would have to attend a particular college to receive the award. The other half are independent of any specific institution—you can receive the financial aid no matter which accredited college you attend.

Eligibility Requirements

To win college scholarships from most private donors, the key is to have a particular skill or interest, rather than have financial need. Most private aid is as available to millionaires as it is to paupers.

Eligibility requirements for private aid are often based on one or more of the following criteria:

- Academic performance
- Athletic ability
- College major and career objectives
- Disabilities
- Financial need
- Gender
- Hobbies
- Marital status
- Parental activities
- Participation in the military
- Race and heritage
- Religious affiliation
- The state, city, or county in which you are a resident
- Upcoming school year (freshman, sophomore, junior, senior, graduate, doctorate, postdoctorate)
- Work experience

Types of Assistance

Financial aid for college is offered in three basic forms:

- Grants and scholarships
- Fellowships and internships
- Loans designed especially for students (and parents of students)

Grants and scholarships, sometimes referred to as gift assistance, do not have to be repaid.

Fellowships and internships are monetary awards paid to the student in return for research or work performed according to the guidelines set forth by the sponsor of the award. These are usually awarded to a student so that he or she may gain experience in a particular field of interest.

Student loans, and loans for parents of students, must be repaid. Generally, these loans feature favorable rates of interest and/or deferred payment options.

How to Receive Applications for College Financial Aid from Private Donors

To save time and effort, we suggest that you use a standard form letter when requesting applications and additional information from private donors. Here is a standard form letter which works well:

> Date
>
> <Contact Name at Donor Organization>
> <Name of Donor Organization>
> <Donor's Street Address>
> <Donor's City, State Zip>
>
> Dear Sir or Madam:
>
> Please forward an application and any additional information concerning your financial aid program for postsecondary education.
>
> Sincerely,
>
> <Your Name>
> <Your Address>
> <Your City, State Zip>

Be sure to enclose a self-addressed, stamped envelope with your letter.

How to Use This Book

This book lists over 5,000 different sources of college financial aid from private organizations. Many of the scholarships and awards are available to anyone, requiring you to merely fill out an application form or perhaps submit a short essay.

Other donors, however, target their money toward a specific type of student, often based on your prospective majors, academic interests, skills, and personal background.

To help you quickly and easily find the awards that are most appropriate to you, *The Complete Scholarship Book* provides you with two ways to find your most likely donors:

- Extensive indexes at the end of the book, identifying awards available by major or career objective, ethnic background, gender, religion, marital status, military background of you or your parents, disability, and intercollegiate athletics.
- An icon system which allows you to scan the sources quickly

The Icon System

The icons in this book will allow you to visually identify scholarships which may be appropriate for you based on majors and special criteria.

Majors/Career Objective

College majors have been grouped into nine categories to guide you to general fields of study. The following list includes the most common majors within each category and the icon which will identify them.

Business
Accounting
Advertising/Public Relations
Banking/Finance/Insurance
Business Administration
Economics
Human Resources
Management
Marketing
Sales
Transportation

Education
Childhood Development
Early Childhood Education
Education (General)
Education Administration
Elementary Education
Middle-Level Education
Postsecondary Education

Engineering
Aerospace Engineering
Architecture
Aviation
Civil Engineering/Construction
Computer Science
Engineering (General)
Material Science
Surveying/Cartography
Telecommunications

Fine Arts
Art
Filmmaking
Fine Arts (General)
Graphic Design
Music (General)
Performing Arts
Photography

Humanities
Broadcasting/Communications
Classical Studies
English/Literature
Foreign Languages
Humanities (General)
Journalism
Library/Information Sciences
Philosophy
Religion

Medicine
Dentistry
Health Care Management
Medicine/Medical (General)
Nursing
Pharmacy/Pharmacology/Pharmaceutical
Public Health
Therapy (General)
Veterinary Medicine

Science

Agriculture
Animal Science
Biology
Chemistry
Ecology/Environmental Science
Energy-Related Studies
Geology
Land Management/Design
Marine Sciences
Mathematics
Meteorology
Physics
Science (General)

Social Sciences

African American Studies
Anthropology
Archaeology
Foreign Studies
Geography
Government
History
International Relations
Law
Military Science
Political Science
Psychology
Social Sciences (General)
Sociology
Women's Studies

Vocational

Automotive
Court Reporting
Data Processing
Food Services
Funeral Services
Heating/Plumbing/Cooling Industry
Hotel/Motel Management/Administration
Manufacturing
Real Estate
Textiles
Travel and Tourism
Vocational (General)

Special Criteria

The following categories are the most common criteria on which scholarship awards are based. Look for these icons to help find awards for which you may qualify.

Athletics

Almost all scholarships based on athletics are talent-based. Primarily, these scholarships will only be appropriate for you if you plan to compete at the intercollegiate level or major in physical education.

Disability

Many scholarships are available to individuals who are challenged with a mental or physical disability. Awards marked with this icon include those for the blind, hearing impaired, learning disabled, and physically challenged, in addition to several other disabilities.

Ethnic

This category includes scholarships awarded based on race and heritage. The most common are for African American, Asian American, Hispanic, and Native American students, but the range of available awards is truly global and can get very specific. Consider your family background, and be sure to check with the scholarship provider if you are not sure whether you fit its requirements.

Grade Point Average (GPA)

Three cutoffs have been established for the GPA icons—at 2.5+, 3.0+, and 3.5+. Some scholarships' actual requirements may be somewhere between these numbers, so be sure to read the complete listing for the exact GPA criteria.

Military

Scholarships marked with this icon most often require that either you or one of your parents serve or served in the armed forces. Many of these awards are available to veterans or children of veterans of particular military actions or branches of the service. Also,

many scholarships are for students whose parents were disabled or killed in military action. Items marked with this icon may also denote a major in military science or a related field.

Religion

Religious groups and organizations offer scholarships to students who are involved in religious or church-related activities, attending or coming from a religious school, or are interested in professional religious study.

Women

This icon identifies scholarships which are available to women only. Please note that many other scholarships are not for women only, but will often give preference to women.

Reading the Listings

Each scholarship listing includes the following information:

- Scholarship name
- Amount of the available award or awards
- Deadline for submission of application materials
- Fields/Majors of intended study
- Further information you may need in order to apply
- The award sponsor's address to write for application forms and additional information

Identifying the Icons

Major/Career Objective

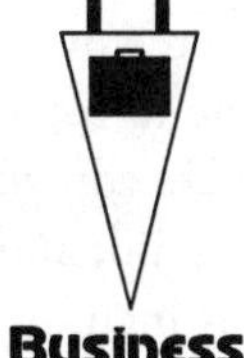
Business

Education

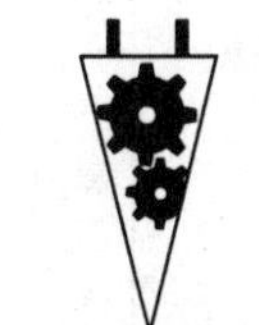
Engineering

Fine Arts

Humanities

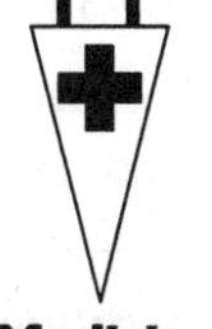
Medicine

Science

Social Sciences

Vocational

Special Criteria

Athletics

Disability

Ethnic

Military

Religion

Women

GPA 2.5+

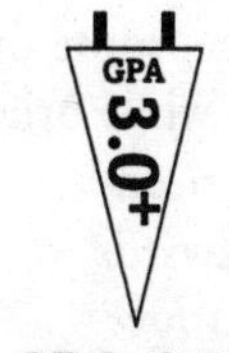

GPA 3.0+

GPA 3.5+

52 Tips for Optimizing Your Money for College

For their help in suggesting and reviewing these tips, Student Services, Inc., wishes to thank: Lee Gordon, Executive Associate Director of Financial Aid at Purdue University; Ellen Frishberg, Director of Student Financial Services at Johns Hopkins University; and Derek Bates, President of Student Aid Research Through Technology.

Tip 1. Prioritize Your Effort According to the Amount of Funding Available from Each Source of College Financial Aid

Each year, between $40 and $50 billion is made available to college students in the form of financial aid.

By far, the greatest source of this funding is the federal government. Federal grant, work-study, and loan programs include:

- Federal Pell Grants
- Federal Supplemental Educational Opportunity Grants
- Federal Work-Study
- Federal Stafford Loans
- Federal Direct Student Loans
- Federal PLUS Loans (Loans for Parents)
- Federal Consolidation Loans
- Federal Perkins Loans
- AmeriCorps
- Veterans Affairs Programs

Graduate students are not eligible for Federal Pell Grants or Federal Supplemental Educational Opportunity Grants; however, other grant programs *are* available to graduate students, such as Javits, GAANN, and Harris.

The next biggest source of scholarships and loans, involving several billion dollars, comes from the colleges themselves. Depending on the college, some of these awards will be financial need-based, while other awards will be merit-based (non-financial need-based). To determine eligibility for these awards, many colleges require students to fill out a *Free Application for Federal Student Aid* (FAFSA) form (or a Renewal FAFSA, if applicable) as well as customized, supplemental forms. Additional forms are also required for the Federal Family Education Loans, including Stafford Loans and PLUS Loans.

As a result, when seeking financial aid for college, three important priorities for most students are to:

1. Submit a FAFSA (or Renewal FAFSA).
2. Submit a PROFILE (if required by your college), or any other financial aid form and supporting documents required by the colleges to which you apply.
3. Submit additional forms, if applicable, for Federal Family Education Loans.

Depending on where you live and where you will attend college, you may also be eligible to receive financial aid from the few billion dollars contributed by state governments. To apply for this aid, additional forms may be necessary. Key programs include:

- The State Student Incentive Grant Program, which goes by different names in different states
- The Robert C. Byrd Honors Scholarship Program
- Various state-specific programs

To find out more, contact the career center or guidance counseling office at your high school, or the financial aid office at the college(s) to which you will apply.

Beyond these traditional opportunities for college financial aid, another important source is philanthropic foundations, religious organizations, employers, clubs, local governments, corporations, and civic organizations who offer millions of dollars in financial aid through tuition and work-study programs. In fact, over 5,000 such opportunities for scholarships, grants, fellowships, internships, and loans are listed in this book.

However, do not rely on the opportunities in this book to be your *only* potential sources of financial aid. It is always wise to pursue several options, including government and college-sponsored programs.

Tip 2. Learn All You Can About the College Financial Aid Process

It took 12 YEARS for you to learn enough to be eligible for a college education. With that in mind, please do not be disconcerted if it takes a few weeks to learn how to best *finance* a college education.

For most parents and students, paying for college is the third largest investment they will ever make.[1] Yet despite the importance, many parents and students stumble confused through the college financial aid process. That is unfortunate for them, but fortunate for you, since you can gain a tremendous advantage by learning thoroughly about college financial aid. Such knowledge can help you to:

[1] The largest investment tends to be retirement. The second largest tends to be a home.

- Not miss deadlines
- Position yourself to get a better financial aid package

Good sources of information include:

- The *Student Guide: Financial Aid from the U.S. Department of Education*[2]
- The career center or guidance counseling office at your high school
- The financial aid office at the college(s) to which you will apply
- *Don't Miss Out: The Ambitious Student's Guide to Financial Aid*
- Financial planners, if they are reputable and specialize in college financing

Several sites on the internet offer information about college financial aid. However, be discerning, since the quality of the information available varies. Links to the plethora of financial aid information available on the internet can be found by accessing: *http://www.fastweb.com*

Tip 3. Understand How a College's Financial Aid Policies Will Affect You

You have the right to receive the following information from the financial aid office at each accredited college:

- The financial assistance that is available, including information on all federal, state, local, private, and institutional financial aid programs
- The procedures and deadlines for submitting applications for each available financial aid program
- How the school selects financial aid recipients
- How the school determines your financial need
- How the school determines each type and amount of assistance in your financial aid package
- How and when you'll receive your aid (if granted)
- How the school determines whether you're making 'satisfactory academic progress,' and what happens if you do not[3]
- The nature, if offered, of a Federal Work-Study job, what the job is, what hours you must work, what your duties will be, what the rate of pay will be, and how and when you will be paid
- The location, hours, and counseling procedures of the school's financial aid office
- The school's refund policy, in the event that you leave the school prior to completing your coursework

[2] To order this free guide from the Federal Student Aid Information Center, call 800-4-FED-AID, or access an electronic version through the internet at *http://www.ed.gov*

[3] Whether you continue to receive federal financial aid depends, in part, on whether you make satisfactory academic progress.

Tip 4. Focus on *Optimizing,* Rather Than *Maximizing,* Your Financial Aid

To ***maximize*** means 'to get the **most**.' To ***optimize*** means 'to get the **best**.' It is critical to focus on optimizing, rather than maximizing, your financial aid.

If you aim to optimize your financial aid, you will stay focused on the right things, including:

- Striking the right balance between the quality of your education versus the amount of debt that becomes your burden when you graduate from school
- Improving the composition of your financial aid awards, i.e., increasing the ratio of grants to loans

On the other hand, it would be easy (though undesirable) to simply maximize your financial aid eligibility. In that case, all you would have to do is apply to the college in the United States in which the Cost of Attendance is highest. According to the federal methodology for determining financial need, that would maximize your financial aid eligibility, since:

Cost of Attendance at College X – Expected Family Contribution = Financial Aid Eligibility for College X

In this formula, 'Expected Family Contribution' is a constant. In other words, the federal government expects you (and your family) to contribute the same amount of cash out of family resources, regardless of the tuition at the college.[4]

As an example, suppose that the federal government determines your Expected Family Contribution to be $6,000. If you decided to attend 'College A' in which the Cost of Attendance is $10,000, then you would be ***eligible*** to receive $4,000 of financial aid:

Cost of Attendance at College A	Expected Family Contribution	Financial Aid Eligibility for College A
$10,000	– $6,000	= $4,000

If you decided to attend 'College B' in which the Cost of Attendance is $25,000, then you would be eligible to receive $19,000 of financial aid:

Cost of Attendance at College B	Expected Family Contribution	Financial Aid Eligibility for College B
$25,000	– $6,000	= $19,000

Therefore, the easiest way to increase your financial aid eligibility is to attend a more expensive college.

[4] You can get a free booklet call called *Expected Family Contribution (EFC) Formulas,* which describes how the EFC formulas are calculated, by writing to the Federal Student Aid Information Center, P.O. Box 84, Washington, DC 20044, or by calling 1-800-4-FED-AID.

HOWEVER, most of this additional eligibility for financial aid may come in the form of loans which need to be repaid. There is no great honor in graduating from college with the most debt. Yet, that is the folly of people who seek to maximize financial aid eligibility without regard to:

- The ratio of grants to loans
- The amount of cumulative debt incurred

Tip 5. Ensure that 'Cost of Attendance' Calculations Include All Reasonable Costs

Since financial aid eligibility is based, in part, on 'Cost of Attendance,' ensure that your financial aid administrator(s) include *all* reasonable costs in your Cost of Attendance calculation. For instance:

- If you are dyslexic, you may be able to include costs for special reading devices in the Cost of Attendance calculation.
- If you have children, you may be able to include child care expenses in the Cost of Attendance calculation.

Within reason, be expansive about the items you try to include in 'Cost of Attendance.'

Tip 6. Apply for Federal Financial Aid as Soon as Possible After January 1

Apply for college financial aid from the federal government as soon as possible **after** January 1 of the year in which you want to receive financial aid. For instance, to receive financial aid for the 1997-98 academic year, apply as soon as possible after January 1, 1997.

It is easier to complete the FAFSA form when you (and your parents and/or spouse) have already calculated your federal income tax return, so you may want to consider finishing these tax returns as early as possible. However, you do NOT have to submit your tax returns prior to submitting your FAFSA form. In fact, you can get an advantage by submitting your FAFSA before most people, even if that means making (reasonably accurate) guesses about the information which is likely to appear on your income tax return. This will increase the chance that all of your financial need will be met.[5]

[5] To avoid having the processor return your FAFSA form to you, do **not** sign, date, or send your application before January 1 of the relevant year.

Tip 7. Apply for Financial Aid from Each College Prior to Its 'Priority Filing' Deadline Date

To increase the possibility of having all of your financial need met, ensure that your financial aid applications are considered among the first batch of requests, by submitting your forms prior to each college's 'priority filing' deadline date.

Tip 8. Submit a FAFSA, Even If You Do Not Think You Will Be Eligible for Federal Financial Aid

To be considered for federal financial aid for college, you *must* submit a FAFSA form.

Even if you think that you will not be eligible for federal financial aid, submit a FAFSA anyway. There are four reasons:

1. You might be pleasantly surprised by the results; many middle class families *are* eligible for federal financial aid (typically, loans with favorable interest rates and payment deferment options).
2. Even if you do not qualify for federal loans with deferred payment options, you might still qualify for loans with favorable interest rates.
3. Submitting a FAFSA is often a prerequisite for many nonfederal financial aid programs.
4. Being rejected for financial aid from the government is sometimes a precondition for private sector awards.

Tip 9. If You Are Classified As a 'Dependent' Student, but Have 'Unusual Circumstances,' Ask Your Financial Aid Administrator to Change Your Status to 'Independent'

Students are classified as either 'dependent' or 'independent' because federal student aid programs are based on the idea that students (and their parents or spouse, if applicable) have the primary responsibility for paying for postsecondary education. According to the federal government, students who have access to parental support (dependent students) should not receive as much need-based federal funds as students who do not have such access to parental support (independent students).

Based on the federal government's methodology for determining Expected Family Contribution, it is generally in your best interest to be considered 'independent' from your parents, rather than 'dependent' on them.

If you are considered dependent, then the income and assets owned by you **and your parents** will be considered in determining your Expected Family Contribution. If you are considered *in*dependent, then only the income and assets owned by you (and your spouse, if married) will be considered.

Declaring yourself to be independent can be advantageous, especially if your parents are wealthy.

You are automatically considered to be an independent student if at least one of the following applies to you:

- You will be at least 24 years of age on or before December 31st of the year in which you receive the financial aid
- You are married
- You are enrolled in a graduate or professional education program
- You are an orphan or a ward of the court (or were a ward of the court until age 18)
- You are a veteran of the United States Armed Forces

Otherwise, you will have to convince the financial aid administrator at your college that 'unusual circumstances' make your situation similar to an independent student. 'Unusual circumstances' include situations which cause your parents to be absolutely unable to help pay for your college education.

If you think that you have unusual circumstances that would make you independent, talk to a financial aid administrator at your college. He or she can change your status if he or she thinks your circumstances warrant it based on the documentation you provide. But remember, the aid administrator will not automatically do this. That decision is based on his or her judgment, and it is final—you cannot appeal to the U.S. Department of Education.

Tip 10. Carefully Calculate the *Pros* and *Cons* before Shifting Assets between You and Your Parents

According to the federal methodology for calculating financial need, a 'dependent' student is expected to contribute approximately 35% of his or her assets towards current-year college costs. On the other hand, parents are only expected to contribute approximately 5.6% of their money. For instance, if a 'dependent' student had $20,000 in a mutual fund, he would be expected to contribute $7,000 of this money toward current-year college costs. However, if the student's parents had the same $20,000 in their mutual fund, the parents would be expected to contribute only $1,120.

So, should dependent students shift their assets to their parents? Not necessarily, since the parents are probably in a higher income tax bracket. Here is a simplified example that shows the trade-offs: Suppose that the $20,000 in the mutual fund earns $3,000 a year. If the parents are in a 33% tax bracket and they own the mutual fund, then they would have to pay $1,000 annually in income taxes for the fund. However, if the dependent student is in a 15% tax bracket and owned the same mutual fund, then the student would have to pay only $450 annually in incomes taxes for the fund.

So, before shifting assets between parents and children, families should carefully calculate the trade-offs between financial aid eligibility and income taxes.

Tip 11. Consider Reducing 'Reportable Assets' by Shifting Assets from Cash to Retirement Savings or to Equity in Your Primary Home

Section G of the FAFSA form asks you to report certain assets. Your financial aid eligibility for federal funds will be based, in part, on the amount of assets you report.

You can increase your financial aid eligibility by reducing reportable assets. To do so legally, you need to find acceptable ways to shift funds from reportable assets to nonreportable assets. *Non*reportable assets include equity in your primary home and retirement savings. Therefore, prior to filling out the FAFSA, if you have disposable cash, considering investing more in your retirement savings account or paying off part of your mortgage.

However, these techniques only work in some cases, since most high-priced colleges use forms, in addition to the FAFSA, to probe for supplemental financial information, including home equity and retirement savings. This supplemental data is used in determining eligibility for institutional aid.

Tip 12. Consider Reducing 'Reportable Assets' by Making Large Purchases Prior to Filling Out the FAFSA

Another acceptable way of reducing reportable assets is to get rid of cash by buying a *non*reportable asset such as a computer or a car. So, if you were going to make large purchases anyway, do so prior to filling out the FAFSA.

Tip 13. Inform Financial Aid Administrators About Recent Declines in Family Income or Assets

Generally, financial aid forms base the calculation of 'Expected Family Contribution' on your family's income and assets from the *prior* year. (The greater your family's income and assets, the more you will be expected to contribute to college costs.)

So, if a calculation based on last year's financial position unfairly overstates your family's *current* income or assets, ask a financial aid administrator at your college to make an adjustment. For instance, if you are a dependent student and your father lost his $45,000-a-year job last week, or if your parents divorced nine months ago and you lived just with your mother ever since, this could make you eligible for additional grants or low-interest loans.

Tip 14. Inform Financial Aid Administrators About Atypical Expenses

To increase your financial aid eligibility, ensure that your financial aid administrator is aware of *all* of your family's relevant costs. For instance, you might be eligible for additional financial aid if:

- One or more of your siblings attends an elementary or secondary school in which your parents pay tuition
- You or your parents have documented medical or dental expenses which are not covered by insurance
- You or your parents support elderly relatives

Tip 15. Try to Establish Residency in the State Where You Will Attend College

Publicly-funded colleges charge in-state students substantially less tuition than out-of-state students for identical educational programs. For instance, at Rutgers, The State University of New Jersey, tuition for New Jersey residents in the 1996-97 academic year was $3,786 while tuition for *non*-New Jersey residents was $7,707.[6] Over four years, that would translate to a difference of almost $16,000.

If you plan to attend a public college, an easy way to save several thousand dollars is to attend a public college that is located in the state where you have already satisfied residency requirements.

[6] For a few special programs, both in-state and out-of-state students at Rutgers paid $843 in additional tuition.

Alternatively, if you have strong reasons to attend an out-of-state public college, you can try to establish new residency in the state where the college you attend is located.

Guidelines for establishing residency vary, so check with each of the public colleges that interest you. Generally, some of the factors considered include:

- Do you and/or your parents own property in the state?
- Have you and/or your parents lived primarily in that state during the previous two years?
- Do you possess a driver's license in the state?
- Did you earn a significant portion of your income in the state in the year prior to attending college? Did you file an income tax return for that state?

Tip 16. Consider Attending a Lower-Priced College, Particularly If Your Expected Family Contribution Is High

In general, a wealthy student will have to pay most or all of the cost of college tuition without the benefit of government grants. Therefore, the easiest way for a wealthy student to reduce his or her college debt burden is to attend a lower-priced college.

On the other hand, if your family's income and assets are more modest, the difference in the cost of attendance between a low-priced and high-priced college may be negated, in whole or in part, by grants and work-study programs, especially if a particular high-priced college is committed to meeting your financial need with an attractive financial aid package.

For instance, even though undergraduate tuition at Johns Hopkins University is over $20,000 a year, students at that university with 'average' family incomes receive over $15,000 in grants and work-study opportunities. As a result, the average total debt incurred by students graduating from Johns Hopkins University is only $16,600, which is close to the average debt owed by graduating students at many publicly-funded state universities.

If you are considering a variety of colleges at which your out-of-pocket costs would be substantially different, your decision can be assisted by comparing graduation rates, job placement rates, graduate school admission rates, and any other factors which you value. At many colleges, career counselors can tell you the percentage of students that find jobs within their chosen fields within six months of graduation. Average salary statistics and graduate school admission rates may also be available. Comparing statistics such as these can help you determine whether or not the extra tuition charged by more expensive colleges is worth it.

Keep in mind, *highly motivated* students can get a great education at almost any accredited college in the United States, no matter how inexpensive; whereas, *un*motivated students will get a lousy education even at the most expensive private colleges.

Tip 17. Do Not Absorb More Debt Than You Can Handle

To put college debt in perspective, suppose that after graduation you could afford to pay a maximum of $600 a month toward a total of $70,000 in loans with an average interest rate of 10%. Paying off that debt would take over 33 years!

Here's another example: It would take over 10 years to pay back $20,000 in loans at 10% interest, if the most you could afford to pay off is $250 a month.

A high debt burden can take a staggering toll on the quality of your life. *During the time that every cent is diverted to paying back college loans, you may have to forgo: buying a car, saving for a house, going on vacation, and perhaps even starting a family.*

Be especially wary of building up too much debt on high-interest credit cards.

Tip 18. Consider Attending a Community College for the First Two Years of Postsecondary Education

If you cannot afford the full cost of a four-year college, consider enrolling in a two-year community college for the first two years of your postsecondary education. Community colleges tend to charge annual tuitions which are substantially less than tuitions charged by four-year colleges.

If you earn good grades at a community college, you may be able to transfer, as a junior, to a four-year college. Upon graduation from the four-year college, you would enjoy the best of both worlds:

- You would have the prestige of a degree from the four-year college
- You would have paid less tuition, in total, than your classmates at the four-year college

Tip 19. Consider Accumulating Credits Faster Than Normal

Suppose you are attending a degree program which takes most students four years to complete. If you finish that degree in three-and-a-half years, you will save $12\frac{1}{2}$% on tuition and be able to work full-time for half a year longer. If you finish in three years, you will save 25% on tuition and be able to work full-time for a full year longer.

To accumulate credits faster than most people, you can:

- Attend credit courses during intersessions and summer
- Enroll in as many classes per semester or quarter as you can handle[7]
- Earn credit for college during high school by scoring well on advanced placement tests

Tip 20. Consider Earning a Three-Year Degree Rather Than a Four-Year Degree

Many fine colleges help students afford post secondary education by offering degrees which are *meant* to be earned in three years rather than four. Perhaps this is a good option for you. However, be mindful of the disadvantages:

- Some people believe that a full four years is required to develop intellectual and occupational skills fully.
- Many people consider their college years to be among the best times of their life. Therefore, why rush?

Tip 21. Combine Degrees

If you are planning to earn multiple degrees anyway, you can save a year's tuition and time by finding a college which will allow you to combine degrees, such as:

- Combining a B.Sc. with an MBA
- Combining a B.A. with an M.A.
- Combining a master's degree with a Ph.D.
- Combining an undergraduate degree with a Master's in Education degree

Tip 22. Consider Attending a College in an Area Where the Cost of Living is Lower

Tuition is only one component of the cost of attendance. Other major costs include food and rent—both

[7] For instance, at The University of Chicago, a full-time undergraduate student can enroll in three *or* four courses per quarter, for the same fixed price of nearly $7,000 per quarter. By taking the full four courses per quarter, a student would be able to graduate early and save several thousand dollars in tuition.

of which are affected by the local cost of living. For instance, a hamburger at a fast food chain in Boston, Massachusetts, might cost $1.79 whereas the same hamburger from the same fast food chain might cost only $1.29 in Little Rock, Arkansas. For similar accommodations, rent can also vary considerably from city to city.

In fact, you can save hundreds or thousands of dollars per year by attending a college in an area where the cost of living is lower.

Tip 23. Improve Your High School Grades and SAT Scores

To enhance their reputations, colleges need to attract outstanding students, especially students who excel academically. As a result, most colleges offer preferential financial aid packages to students with excellent academic records. Generally, the better your grades, the better the financial aid package offered to you by a college.

For instance, suppose that Johnny (who has an 'A' average) and Jimmy (who has a 'B' average) both apply to the same college, in which the cost of attendance is $10,000. Further suppose that, according to the federal methodology for determining financial need, Johnny and Jimmy are both expected to contribute the same amount for college out of cash flow: $4,000. Does this mean that Johnny and Jimmy will both be treated the same when the college makes financial aid offers? The answer is 'Yes' *and* 'No.'

Yes, Johnny and Jimmy will both be eligible to receive the same amount of financial aid: $6,000.

But 'No,' since Johnny may get more grants than loans, while Jimmy gets more loans than grants. For instance, Johnny might receive $4,000 in grants and $2,000 in loans, while Jimmy might receive $1,000 in grants and $5,000 in loans. Johnny may get preferential treatment since his 'A' grade average is more desirable to the college.

Tip 24. Improve Your College Grades

To encourage strong academic performance, many colleges offer scholarships for students who *continue* to earn high grades. Make sure you are aware of the qualification criteria at your college, which might include:

- Making the Dean's List
- Attaining a specific grade point average
- Earning grades which place your academic performance among the top rank of students

Sometimes, the value of academic scholarships will increase with performance. Substantial scholarships may be available to continuing students who attain grades at the very top of their class.

Tip 25. Apply to Colleges in Which Your Academic Performance Ranks Among the Top 25% of Applicants

Colleges offer their best financial aid packages to their best applicants. Therefore, you can often improve the financial aid package offered to you by applying to colleges in which your academic and extracurricular record is better than most of the other applicants.

For instance, suppose that Janice, who has a 3.7 GPA, applies to a highly competitive college (at which the average GPA among applicants is 3.7) and a moderately competitive college (at which the average GPA among applicants is 3.1). Further suppose that the cost of attendance is the same at the highly competitive college and the moderately competitive college. In that instance, it is likely that Janice will be offered a better financial aid package by the moderately competitive college, since her record compares more favorably to the rest of that college's applicants.

Tip 26. Apply to At Least Three Colleges Which Are Likely to Accept You

One of the most direct ways to improve your financial aid choices is to increase the number of colleges to which you apply. By applying to several colleges, you will be offered a variety of different financial aid packages. Based on the schools' particular needs, some of these financial aid offers will be more attractive than others. Even similar schools may make very different offers, for reasons that are difficult to foresee. For instance, you might receive an unexpectedly favorable financial aid offer from a college if they desperately need a harp player for the symphonic orchestra and you are the only harp player that applied.

Applying to a few extra colleges may cost $100 to $150 in extra application fees, but this investment could save thousands of dollars if one of these colleges offers an especially attractive financial aid package.

Some schools use financial aid as a recruiting tool. Others do not.

Tip 27. Encourage Your Professor(s) to Convert Poor Grades into an Assessment Marked 'Incomplete'

A poor grade will lower your GPA. An 'incomplete' grade will not be factored into your GPA, and thus will have the effect of artificially 'raising' your average. Therefore, if your GPA is dangerously close to disqualifying you from a scholarship, then try to encourage your professor to change your worst grade into an assessment marked 'incomplete.'

'Incomplete' means that you will receive a final grade at some point in the future, after you have had an opportunity to submit additional material to your professor(s) for evaluation.

Tip 28. Money from Grandparents Should Be Paid, in Your Name, Directly to the College

If your grandparents want to help pay for your college tuition, ask them to send money, in your name, directly to the college. In that way, you will get the full benefit of their generosity while avoiding:

- Gift tax liability
- Artificially overstating your own assets

Tip 29. Take Advantage of Tuition Pre-Payment Discounts, If Available

Some colleges offer discounts as high as 10% if tuition is paid in full by a specific date. Taking advantage of this early payment discount is often better than keeping the money in the bank and paying tuition in installments. If the discount is high enough, and if you have the money available to you anyway, take the discount option.

Tip 30. Take Advantage of Discounts for Employees and Children of Employees

Many colleges offer **substantial** discounts for employees and children of employees. To qualify for the discount, the college employee does not necessarily need to be a professor; the same discount options will often be made available to secretaries and janitors too. As a result, you may be able to save thousands in tuition if you or a parent are able to get a full-time job at a college.

If you are really tight for cash, perhaps you could work at the college full-time and attend courses part-time.

Tip 31. Take Advantage of Discounts for Children of Alumni

To encourage long-term 'customer loyalty' among families, many colleges offer discounts for children of alumni. These discounts can be significant, so find out how much you might save by attending Mom's or Dad's former college.

Tip 32. Start Saving for College as Soon as Possible

College costs can place a severe financial drain on family resources, especially cash flow. Many families make these problems more extreme by waiting too long to start saving for college. Setting aside a few hundred dollars each month for several years, although difficult, is a lot easier than setting aside twenty thousand dollars a year for four years.

To minimize the monthly financial outlay, parents may want to start saving for college as soon as possible, even when their children are just a few years old.

Tip 33. Plan Ahead

To avoid the confusion and frustration that can occur by waiting until the last moment, your family should start to investigate thoroughly the college financial aid process while you are still a high school **junior**.

In your junior year, it is helpful to:

- Gather and review all of the government and college financial aid forms that need to be submitted
- Request additional information from some of the scholarship providers listed in this book
- Create a milestone chart which indicates the deadlines for each financial aid activity and form
- Seek advice from a financial specialist, if appropriate, to reposition family assets in a way that optimizes financial aid eligibility and income tax payments
- Investigate loan options from commercial lenders

In your high school senior year, you will need to repeat this process to ensure that you have up-to-date forms and information.

Tip 34. Plant 'Seeds' for Scholarships While You Are Still in High School

Many privately-sponsored scholarships are awarded based, in part, on the student's references and extracurricular activities. For instance, a student is more likely to win a scholarship if:

- The people who provide references write spectacular comments rather than merely above average comments
- The references come from people who are leaders in their field, rather than from people who have less established reputations
- The student has engaged in activities which demonstrate extraordinary talent and good citizenship

Therefore, while you are still in high school, it is wise to 'build your resume' and 'build your reference pool' by engaging in extracurricular activities and volunteer activities that will position you to get excellent references or awards for laudable activities.

Other applicants will have awards from the Mayor for helping underprivileged children. What about you?

Tip 35. Leverage Your Athletic Talents

Athletic scholarships are awarded to many students who are capable of competing at an intercollegiate (NCAA Division I) level. You do not have to be a high school superstar to receive an athletic scholarship. Colleges need excellent 'reserve' players in addition to superstars.

High school superstar athletes who compete in popular sports will likely be approached by college recruiters. However, other high school athletes may need to take a more assertive role in attracting the interest of college coaches. This effort can be worth it, since many colleges set aside considerable money for athletic scholarships and preferential financial aid packages.

To learn more about opportunities for student athletes, contact the National Collegiate Athletic Association (NCAA), a Financial Aid Administrator, your high school coach, or the relevant coaches at the colleges which interest you.

Tip 36. Build a 'Portfolio' That Can Be Used to Demonstrate Your Accomplishments

To help support your applications for jobs, college admissions, and private scholarships, it is useful to have various sources from which to demonstrate your accomplishments. Therefore, build a 'portfolio' of sources by doing things such as:

- Videotaping your finest acting performances
- Encouraging former employers to write 'To Whom It May Concern' reference letters
- Photographing your best artworks
- Saving clippings from the newspaper that report on your track and field victories
- Keeping a copy of the certificate you received for winning the science fair

Tip 37. Find Out Whether Your Parents' Employer(s) Offer College Scholarships

Many big corporations offer college scholarships and tuition reimbursement programs to children of employees. Refer questions about availability and eligibility requirements to the human resources department at your parents' employer(s).

Tip 38. Investigate Company-Sponsored Tuition Plans

Some employers will subsidize the cost of college tuition if, in return, you promise to work for the employer for a certain number of years upon graduation. In some cases, the employer will grant a leave of absence so that you can attend college full-time. More often, however, employers prefer participants to attend college part-time while maintaining a full-time schedule at work.

As long as you like the employer and the job opportunity, company-sponsored tuition plans can be a great deal. You get substantial tuition subsidies *and* 'guaranteed' employment upon graduation.

Tip 39. Investigate Cooperative Education Opportunities

Cooperative education opportunities combine traditional classroom teaching with off-campus work experience related to your major. In practice, this could mean that you would:

- Attend classes in the morning and work in the afternoon (or vice versa)

\- or -

- Work during the day and attend classes during the evenings

- or -

- Attend classes for a semester, then work for a semester, then attend classes for a semester, then work for a semester, etc.

The biggest disadvantage of cooperative education is that it lengthens the time required to earn a college degree.

The biggest advantages of cooperative education include:

- Earning money while you're learning
- The opportunity to build a strong relationship with a prospective full-time employer
- Graduating from college with more practical experience than students who did not attend a cooperative education program

Opportunities for cooperative education vary considerably by college. To learn more, contact the colleges which interest you, or refer to *A College Guide to Cooperative Education*, published by Oryx Press.

Tip 40. Consider Joining the Military

Ignore this idea if you dislike hierarchy, rebel against authority, or conscientiously object to the activities of the military. However, if you would consider it an honor to serve your country as a member of the armed services, the military can be a tremendous source of college financial aid.

In return for military service, the U.S. armed forces provides several options that help students defray or eliminate their college costs:

- Military academies
- Reserve Officer Training Corps (ROTC) scholarships
- The regular ROTC program
- ROTC/cooperative education combination
- Graduate education for commissioned officers
- Off-duty course work through the Army's Concurrent Admissions Program
- National Guard duty
- Army Reserve duty
- Payment of federal student loans
- Montgomery GI Bill
- Benefits for military dependents

ROTC programs are especially popular among undergraduate students.

- For more information on Army ROTC programs, contact 800-USA-ROTC.
- For more information on Navy ROTC programs, contact 800-NAV-ROTC.
- For more information on Marine Corps ROTC programs, contact 800-NAV-ROTC.
- For more information on Air Force ROTC programs, contact 800-423-USAF.

Tip 41. If Applicable, Use Your Minority Status to Your Advantage

Have you ever wondered why some financial aid applications ask questions about race and heritage? Do you find this offensive, and therefore refuse to answer? If you leave such questions blank, you might be missing out on significant scholarship and grant opportunities.

To promote cultural diversity and understanding, many colleges offer special financial aid opportunities to ethnic minorities. As well, many college scholarships provided by the private sector are also based, in part, on race or ancestry. Even if just one of your parents or grandparents were a member of a 'minority' group, this might improve your financial aid package.

Tip 42. Establish a Relationship with Your Financial Aid Administrator

Theoretically, establishing a relationship with your financial aid administrator is not supposed to give you an advantage, since financial aid calculations are based on pre-defined rules and mathematical formulas. However, when borderline situations or unusual circumstances occur, a financial aid administrator is allowed to use discretion. In such situations, the financial aid administrator's decision could mean the difference between receiving $2,000 in loans versus $2,000 in grants. Therefore, the financial aid administrator is an important person to know. Be a face, not just a name.

Tip 43. Maintain Your Eligibility for Renewable Awards

If you receive an award which can be renewed, ensure that you understand, and do, whatever it takes to maintain eligibility for future years. For instance, many renewable awards will expect you to maintain a predetermined grade point average.

Sometimes the criteria for renewal will be very creative, such as remaining a nonsmoker or doing a certain number of hours of volunteer work.

Tip 44. Pursue Scholarships from Private Donors, Even If the Awards Will Not Reduce Your Out-of-Pocket Payments

You may have heard that winning a scholarship from a private organization is a mixed blessing. That is true for some students, but not others, depending on their financial need. The following example illustrates the possible scenarios.

Scenario 1

Suppose:

- Sally won a $2,000 scholarship for winning a science competition.
- Sally's Cost of Attendance at College 'X' is $10,000 and her Expected Family Contribution is $10,000.
- Sally will be attending College 'X' at which her federal financial aid eligibility is $0.

In this scenario, Sally would benefit fully from the $2,000 scholarship.

Scenario 2

Suppose:

- Sally won a $2,000 scholarship for winning a science competition.
- Sally's Cost of Attendance at College 'Y' is $10,000 and her Expected Family Contribution is $7,000.
- Sally will be attending College 'Y' at which her federal financial aid eligibility is $3,000.

In this scenario, Sally may not benefit *financially* from the scholarship—because the financial aid administrator at 'College Y' will be legally obligated to reduce Sally's federal financial aid eligibility by the amount of the nongovernment award, from $3,000 to $1,000. So, even though Sally will gain $2,000 from the private donor, she will lose $2,000 in federal financial aid eligibility.

Even if your situation is consistent with Scenario 2 rather than Scenario 1, there are two important reasons to apply for scholarships from private organizations anyway:

1. If a private scholarship reduces your federal financial aid eligibility, many financial aid administrators will reduce the loan portion of your federal financial aid package rather than the grant portion.
2. Even if you do not benefit *financially* from the private sector award, you will benefit from the *prestige.* A scholarship from a private organization will be a great addition to your resume.

Tip 45. Register for Selective Service, If Required by Law

To receive college financial aid from the federal government, you must register, or arrange to register, with the Selective Service, if required by law. The requirement to register applies to males who were born on or after January 1, 1960, are at least 18 years old, are citizens of the United States or eligible noncitizens, and are not currently on active duty in the armed forces. (Citizens of the Federated States of Micronesia, the Marshall Islands, or Palau are exempt from registering.)

Tip 46. Just Say 'No' to Drugs

Being convicted for drug distribution or possession may make you ineligible to receive college financial aid from the federal government.

Tip 47. Double-Check Your Forms for Accuracy...Then Check Them Again

Even small errors or omissions on a financial aid form can cause the form to be rejected and returned to you. By the time you correct the mistake and resubmit the form, the money set aside for the better financial aid programs may have run out. So, read the instructions carefully. Ensure that you answer all questions, use specific numbers rather than ranges (such as $100-$200), write legibly, include correct social security numbers, sign the form, do not write in the margins, etc.

Tip 48. Do Not Rely on Out-of-Date Information or Forms

College financial aid programs, forms, and rules change every year. Relying on old information, or using old forms, can seriously delay the financial aid process or cause ineligibility. Be sure to use forms which are valid for the *upcoming* school year.

Tip 49. Get a Job

In an ideal world, students would be able to attend high school and college without having to get a job. Instead, ample time would be available for homework and extracurricular activities, along with a little time left over for relaxing.

Unfortunately, this ideal is not a luxury that most families can afford anymore. To avoid the burden of an unbearable debt after graduating from college, you may need to:

- Get a full-time job during the summer
- Strike a reasonable balance, during the school-year, between your course load and the hours spent at a part-time job

Tip 50. Get a High-Paying Job

If you have to supplement your income by getting a part-time job while attending school, try to limit the number of hours at that job by maximizing *earnings per hour.*[8] This seems obvious, yet many students sell themselves short by aiming too low. Frying burgers at a fast food chain or washing dishes at a restaurant is an achingly slow way to earn money.

Often, finding a higher paying job is not terribly difficult. The first and most important step is increasing your expectations. For instance, higher expectations will lead you to look for work at restaurants where the tips are big rather than at restaurants where the tips are meager.

As you pursue your job search, be aware that the best jobs are rarely advertised. Discovering excellent jobs often requires 'knocking on doors' and seeking tips from friends. Persistence and a positive attitude are critical.

Remember, in life, you don't always get what you deserve, you get what you settle for.

Tip 51. Check into Residence Hall Counselor Scholarships

Many colleges with on-campus housing need students to serve as counselors for their residence halls, in return for a scholarship which is sometimes worth as much as the value of room and board. Most often, colleges do not announce the availability of these scholarships publicly, so you may have to approach people who are in charge of on-campus residences and dormitories.

Tip 52. Actually Apply

You cannot receive financial aid for awards for which you do not apply. A great number of students 'kick the tires' of the financial aid process without following up. These passive students seem to get overwhelmed by the process, or lose interest, or both. Whatever the reason, their loss can be your gain.

However, you must keep motivated. Optimizing your financial aid can be time consuming and exasperating. But it's worth it.

In Summary...

Be an informed, educated, and assertive consumer of higher education services and resources. Do not leave your financial aid eligibility to chance. Research as many resources as possible. Read and understand your rights, responsibilities, and opportunities. Get acquainted with your financial aid administrator. Be persistent in talking to all of the people on campus who could either help you or direct you to the right resources for help.

[8] There is one exception to this advice: If you get a job opportunity that enriches your education or career opportunities, it may be wise to accept this opportunity, instead of a job that pays more.

Scholarships

1

5th Year Athletic Scholarship Fund

AMOUNT: None Specified **DEADLINE:** Mar 1
FIELDS/MAJORS: All Areas Of Study

Scholarships are available at the University of New Mexico for full-time students who will be participating in the intercollegiate athletics program, who are within thirty hours of completing a degree. Must have a GPA of at least 2.5. Write to the address listed below for information.

University Of New Mexico, Albuquerque
Department Of Student Financial Aid
Mesa Vista Hall North
Albuquerque, NM 87131

2

A & M Gallagher Business Talent Award

AMOUNT: None Specified **DEADLINE:** Mar 1
FIELDS/MAJORS: Management

Scholarships are awarded to returning Purdue University, Calumet students having satisfactory completed fifteen credit hours and are enrolled at least 3/4 time (9-11 credit hours) pursuing a degree in management. Must have a GPA of 2.0 or better. Write to the address below for more information.

Purdue University, Calumet
Office Of Financial Aid
Hammond, IN 46322

3

A. Conner Daily And William C. Fielder Scholarships

AMOUNT: Varies **DEADLINE:** Mar 1
FIELDS/MAJORS: Pharmacy

Awards are available at the University of New Mexico for full-time pharmacy students demonstrating academic excellence and financial need. Write to the address below for more information.

University Of New Mexico, Albuquerque
Office Of Financial Aid
Albuquerque, NM 87131

4

A. Franklin Pilchard Foundation

AMOUNT: Tuition And Fees **DEADLINE:** Apr 15
FIELDS/MAJORS: All Areas Of Study

Applicant must be a high school senior with a GPA of a "B" or above. Must attend a college or university located within Illinois and demonstrate financial need. Write to the address below for more information.

McCarthy, Pacilio, Eiesland & Gibbert
P.C. Certified Public Accountants
1661 Feehanville Drive, Suite 120
Mount Prospect, IL 60056

5

A. Marlyn Moyer, Jr. Scholarship Foundation

AMOUNT: None Specified **DEADLINES:** Apr 21
FIELDS/MAJORS: All Areas Of Study

Scholarships are awarded to candidates may be graduating high school seniors or other persons enrolling full-time in postsecondary schools for the first time. Must be a U.S. citizen who resides in Bucks County. Must be a resident of a qualifying township or borough. Write to the address below for more information.

A. Marlyn Moyer, Jr. Scholarship Foundation
409 Hood Blvd.
Fairless Hills, PA 19030

6

A. Patrick Charnon Memorial Scholarship

AMOUNT: $1,500 **DEADLINE:** Apr 30
FIELDS/MAJORS: All Areas Of Study

Scholarships are for students enrolled in a full-time undergraduate program of study in an accredited four-year college or university. Must maintain good academic standing. Applicants are required to submit a 500-1,000 word essay about what they would to do with their studies and what they would like to accomplish. Contact A. Patrick Charnon Memorial Scholarship, The Center for Education Solutions, Box 192956, San Francisco, CA 94119-2956, for more information.

Indiana University/Purdue University, Indianapolis
Purdue School Of Technology
799 West Michigan St.
Indianapolis, IN 46202

7

A. Verville Fellowship At The National Air And Space Museum

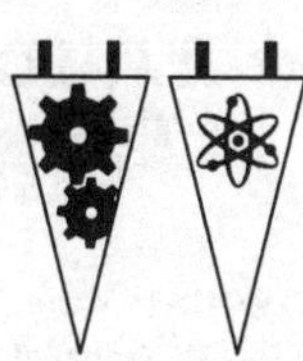

AMOUNT: $30,000 **DEADLINE:** Jan 15
FIELDS/MAJORS: Aeronautics, Astronomy, Astrophysics, Space Research

Residential fellowship for researchers in the above areas. An advanced degree is not a requirement, but applicants are expected to be able to provide a critical analytical approach to major trends, developments, and accomplishments in some aspect of aviation and space studies. Good writing skills are needed as recipient will be required to write articles or a book on his/her project.

Write to the Fellowship Coordinator, Museum Programs, at the address below for details.

National Air And Space Museum
Smithsonian Institution, Aeronautics Department
Fellowship Coordinator
Rm. 3312, MRC 312
Washington, DC 20560

8

A.D. Garten Scholarship Fund

Amount: $200 **Deadline:** Mar 1
Fields/Majors: Physical Education

Award for students who are majoring in physical education and have a GPA of at least 3.0. Recipient must be classified as a junior on the effective date of the award. Financial need is a strong consideration. Write to the address below for more information.

Eastern New Mexico University
College Of Education And Technology
Station 25
Portales, NM 88130

9

A.E. Clark Memorial Graduate Scholarship

Amount: $500 **Deadline:** Fall
Fields/Majors: Education

Scholarships are available at the University of Oklahoma, Norman for full-time Ph.D. candidates in education at the dissertation stage. Write to the address listed below for information.

University Of Oklahoma, Norman
College Of Education
Room 105, ECH
Norman, OK 73019

10

A.F. Nunes Scholarship

Amount: None Specified **Deadline:** Nov 30
Fields/Majors: All Areas Of Study

Scholarships are available at UCSD for undergraduate students who are of Portuguese descent. Write to the address listed below for information.

University Of California, San Diego
Student Financial Services
9500 Gilman Drive
La Jolla, CA 92093

11

A.F.U.D. Research Scholars, Practising Urologist's Research Award

Amount: Varies **Deadline:** Sep 1
Fields/Majors: Urology, Nephrology

Research support for postdoctoral, postresidency, and practicing scientists and medical doctors concentrating in the area of urologic diseases and dysfunctions. Peer review is available, if desired, for research proposals. Write to the A.F.U.D. at the address below for details.

American Foundation For Urologic Disease, Inc.
Research Program Division
300 West Pratt Street, Suite 401
Baltimore, MD 21201

12

A.G.R. Agriculture Scholarship, Wilson W. Carnes Scholarship

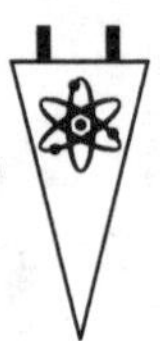

Amount: $400-$1,000 **Deadline:** Feb 15
Fields/Majors: Agricultural Communications

Available to FFA students who are pursuing a degree in agricultural communications at a four-year institution. Information should be available from your local FFA leader. If not, write to the address below for further information.

National FFA Foundation, Scholarship Office
P.O. Box 15160
Alexandria, VA 22309

13

A.H.B. Scholarship Foundation Grants

Amount: $600 **Deadline:** Jun 15-Oct 15
Fields/Majors: All Areas Of Study

Awards for Christian students who are active members of their church and residents of Alabama. Send an SASE with your request for complete information. Contact the address below for further information.

A.H.B. Scholarship Foundation
First Alabama Bank—Trust Department
P.O. Box 2509
Tuscaloosa, AL 35403

14

A.J. Deandrade Scholarships

Amount: $500 **Deadline:** Feb 15
Fields/Majors: All Areas Of Study

Must be graduating high school senior or a recent high school graduate who has not completed more than one semester of college. Must be a dependent of a member of the Graphic Communications International Union. Renewable for four years. Write to the address below for complete details. Applications are not available until after October 1 of the year before you are applying.

Graphic Communications International Union
Attn: Deandrade Scholarship Program
1900 L Street, NW
Washington, DC 20036

15

A.L. Cosgrove Student Service Award

Amount: $300-$500 **Deadline:** Mar 15
Fields/Majors: All Areas Of Study

Scholarships are available at the University of Oklahoma, Norman for students who are active members of St. Thomas More University Parish, with a minimum GPA of at least 3.0, and junior standing or above. Write to the address listed below for information.

University Of Oklahoma, Norman
Father Joe Ross, St. Thomas More Parish
100 East Stinson
Norman, OK 73072

16

A.W. "Winn" Brindle Memorial Scholarship Loan Fund

AMOUNT: Varies **DEADLINE:** None Specified
FIELDS/MAJORS: Fisheries, Food Technology, And Related

Privately funded loans for Alaska residents for studies related to the fishing industry. Renewable for up to 8 years. For full-time study. Interest rate is 5%, and recipients are eligible for 50% forgiveness upon graduation and employment in Alaska in the fishing industry. Write to A.W. "Winn" Brindle Memorial Scholarship Loan Fund at the address below for details.

Alaska Commission On Postsecondary Education
3030 Vintage Blvd.
Juneau, AK 99801

17

A.W. Bodine—Sunkist Memorial Scholarship

AMOUNT: $3,000 (max) **DEADLINE:** Apr 30
FIELDS/MAJORS: All Areas Of Study

Scholarships for undergraduate students from agricultural backgrounds in Arizona or California. Renewable. Based on grades, test scores, essay, and references. Must have a GPA of at least 3.0. Write to the address below for details.

Sunkist Growers, Inc.
Claire H. Peters, Administrator
P.O. Box 7888
Van Nuys, CA 91409

18

AAAA Minority Advertising Intern Program

AMOUNT: $3,000 **DEADLINE:** Jan 1
FIELDS/MAJORS: Advertising, Communications, Liberal Arts, Marketing

Summer internship program for minority students beyond their junior year of undergraduate work or in graduate school. Must be a U.S. citizen or permanent resident and have a GPA of at least 2.5. Write to the address below for more information.

American Association Of Advertising Agencies, Inc.
AAAA Minority Advertising Intern Program
666 Third Ave.
New York, NY 10017

19

AAAS Beller Internship

AMOUNT: $4,000 **DEADLINE:** Jan 25
FIELDS/MAJORS: Science, Math, Or Liberal Education

Two internships are available for junior, senior, and graduate students pursuing a degree in education with emphasis on math and science (two years course credits in these two fields required). Write to the address listed below for additional information.

American Association For The Advancement Of Science
Amie Hubbard
1333 H Street, NW
Washington, DC 20005

20

AABJ Xernona Clayton Scholarship Competition

AMOUNT: $500-$1,000 **DEADLINE:** Mar 1
FIELDS/MAJORS: Journalism, Mass Communications, English, Public Relations

Scholarships (3) for African American college students pursuing a degree in one of the areas listed above. Must be currently enrolled at a college or university in the state of Georgia. Must write an essay on a predetermined topic and have a cumulative GPA of 2.5 or greater. Information should be available from either your department head or your financial aid office. If not, write to the address below in November or December.

Atlanta Association Of Black Journalists
Scholarship Committee
P.O. Box 54128
Atlanta, GA 30308

21

AACC Graduate Fellowship Program

AMOUNT: $1,000-$3,000 **DEADLINE:** Apr 1
FIELDS/MAJORS: Cereal Chemistry And Technology (Including Oilseed Chemistry/Tech)

Scholarships for graduate students who plan to pursue a career in the field of cereal and oilseed science and technology. Seven awards offered per year. Purpose of the awards is to encourage graduate research in cereal- and oilseed-related areas (including genetics, horticulture, nutrition, micro-biology, engineering, chemistry). For study toward M.S. or Ph.D. Write to the address below for information and application forms. Please specify that you are interested in the graduate awards.

American Association Of Cereal Chemists
Scholarship Program
3340 Pilot Knob Road
St Paul, MN 55121

22

AACC Undergraduate Scholarship Program

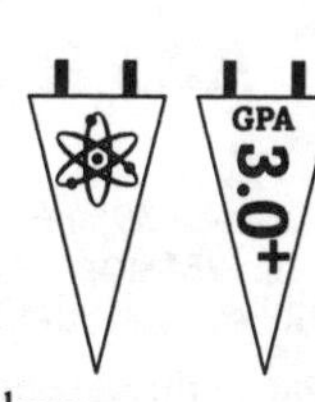

AMOUNT: $1,000-$2,000 **DEADLINE:** Apr 1
FIELDS/MAJORS: Cereal Chemistry And Technology (Including Oilseed Chemistry/Tech)

Scholarships for undergraduate students who have completed at least one term and plan to pursue a career in the field of cereal and oilseed science and technology. Must have a college GPA of at least 3.0. Fifteen awards per year. Write to the address below for information and application forms. Please specify that you are interested in the undergraduate awards.

American Association Of Cereal Chemists
Scholarship Program
3340 Pilot Knob Road
St Paul, MN 55121

23

AACP-AFPE First Year Graduate Scholarship Program

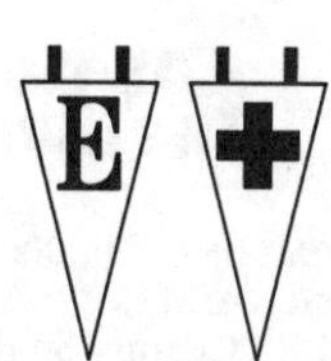

AMOUNT: $5,000 **DEADLINE:** May 1
FIELDS/MAJORS: Pharmacy, Pharmacology

Scholarships for undergraduates in a pharmacy college. Created to encourage students to pursue Ph.D. degrees after undergraduate studies. Must be a participant in the AACP undergraduate research participation program for minorities or the Merck undergraduate research scholar program. For U.S. citizens or permanent residents. Information may be available in your school or department of pharmacy. If not, write to the address below.

American Foundation For Pharmaceutical Education
One Church Street, Suite 202
Rockville, MD 20850

24

AADE Scholarship Awards And Research Grants

AMOUNT: $3,750-$7,500 **DEADLINE:** Varies
FIELDS/MAJORS: Public Health, Medical Research, Etc.

Three scholarships for members (at least one year) of the American Association of Diabetes Educators. For furthering educational or professional goals (including continuing education). The deadline for most awards is Apr 1 or May 1. Write to the address below for details.

American Association Of Diabetes Educators
Scholarship Committee
444 N. Michigan Ave., Suite 1240
Chicago, IL 60611

25

AAPA Veteran's Caucus Scholarships

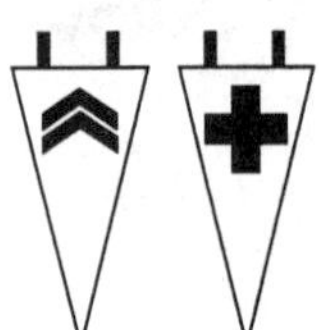

AMOUNT: $1,000 **DEADLINE:** Apr 1
FIELDS/MAJORS: Physician Assisting

Awards for outstanding PA students who are veterans of U.S. military forces and currently enrolled in a CAHEA/CAAHEP-approved program. Write to the address below for more information.

AAPA Veteran's Caucus
P.O. Box 2510
Linden, TX 75563

26

AAS Short-Term Fellowships

AMOUNT: $950 (per month) **DEADLINE:** None Specified
FIELDS/MAJORS: American History, History Of Publishing, 18th Century Studies, Etc.

One to three month fellowships in support of research utilizing the collections of the American Antiquarian Society. The AAS has extensive holdings of published materials (books, pamphlets, almanacs, etc.) from antebellum America. Joint application with the Newberry Library (in Chicago) is encouraged. Write to the society at the address below for further information. Please specify the award name when writing.

American Antiquarian Society
Director Of Research And Publication
185 Salisbury St., Room 100
Worcester, MA 01609

27

AAS-National Endowment For The Humanities Fellowships

AMOUNT: $30,000 (max) **DEADLINE:** Jan 15
FIELDS/MAJORS: American History, History Of Publishing, 18th Century Studies, Etc.

Six to twelve month fellowships in support of research utilizing the collections of the American Antiquarian Society. Must hold Ph.D. and be U.S. citizen or legal resident for more than three years. The AAS has extensive holdings of published materials (books, pamphlets, almanacs, etc.) from antebellum America. Joint application with the Newberry Library (in Chicago) is encouraged. Write to the society at the address below for further information. Please specify the award name when writing.

American Antiquarian Society
Director Of Research And Publication
185 Salisbury St., Room 100
Worcester, MA 01609

28

AASA-Convention Exhibitors Scholarship

AMOUNT: $2,000 **DEADLINE:** Jun 1
FIELDS/MAJORS: School Administration

Scholarships to encourage graduate students to prepare for careers in school administration. For graduate students enrolled in a school administration program at an accredited institution. Five awards per year. To express your interest to be considered as a candidate, check with the office of the dean of education at your school.

American Association Of School Administrators
1801 N. Moore St.
Arlington, VA 22209

29

AAUW Grants

AMOUNT: None Specified **DEADLINE:** May 15
FIELDS/MAJORS: All Areas Of Study

Scholarships for female graduate students from the Norwalk-Westport area or for women (in the same area) who are furthering their education or who are changing careers. Must be a resident of Norwalk, Westport, Wilton, Weston, or Darien. Please enclose a self-addressed stamped legal envelope with 62 cents postage with your request for an application. Write to Willadean Hart, Chair, at the address below.

American Association Of University Women
Norwalk-Westport Branch
Chair, Student Grant Committee
36 Colony Road
Westport, CT 06880

30

AAUW Scholarships

AMOUNT: Varies **DEADLINE:** Mar 1
FIELDS/MAJORS: All Areas Of Study

Award for a female student at Eastern. Preference is given to an older woman. Write to the address below for more information.

Eastern Oregon State College
Financial Aid Office
1041 "I" Avenue
La Grande, OR 97850

31

Abba Schwartz Fellowship

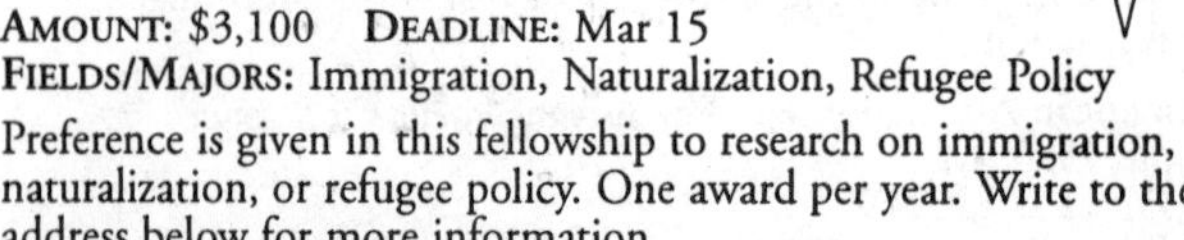

AMOUNT: $3,100 **DEADLINE:** Mar 15
FIELDS/MAJORS: Immigration, Naturalization, Refugee Policy

Preference is given in this fellowship to research on immigration, naturalization, or refugee policy. One award per year. Write to the address below for more information.

John F. Kennedy Library Foundation
William Johnson, Chief Archivist
Columbia Point
Boston, MA 02125

32

Abe And Annie Seibel Foundation Educational Loans

GPA 3.0+

AMOUNT: None Specified **DEADLINE:** Feb 28
FIELDS/MAJORS: All Areas Of Study

Loans available to Texas residents who are enrolled or planning to attend a Texas college or university to obtain a bachelor's degree. All applicants must have graduated from a Texas high school and have a minimum grade point average of 3.0. Write to the address below for details. Information will not be sent to students until the first working day after Christmas.

Abe And Annie Seibel Foundation
c/o United States National Bank—Trust Dept.
P.O. Box 8210
Galveston, TX 77553

33

Abe And Esther Hagiwara Student Aid Award

AMOUNT: Varies **DEADLINE:** Apr 1
FIELDS/MAJORS: All Areas Of Study

Open to students of Japanese ancestry who can demonstrate financial need. Applications and information may be obtained from local JACL chapters district offices and national headquarters at the address below. Please indicate your level of study and be certain to include a legal-sized SASE.

Japanese American Citizens League
National Scholarship And Award Program
1765 Sutter St.
San Francisco, CA 94115

34

Abel Wolman Doctoral Fellowship

AMOUNT: $15,000 (max) **DEADLINE:** Jan 15
FIELDS/MAJORS: Water Supply And Treatment

Fellowships are available to encourage promising students to pursue advanced training and research in the field of water supply and treatment. Applicants must anticipate completing the requirements for a Ph.D. within two years of the award and be a citizen or permanent resident of the U.S., Canada, or Mexico. Write to the address below for more information.

American Water Works Association
Fellowship Coordinator
6666 W. Quincy Avenue
Denver, CO 80235

35

Abigail Associates Research Grants

AMOUNT: $3,000 (max) **DEADLINE:** Apr 17
FIELDS/MAJORS: Womens Studies

Awards are available at from the College of St. Catherine for preparation and presentation of publishable quality research in women's studies. Grants are awarded in two categories—contribution of women from the Catholic tradition to public policy and/or services, and self-esteem among women and girls. For female researchers. Does not require residency at the center. Write to Sharon Doherty at the address listed below for information.

College Of St. Catherine
Abigail Quigley McCarthy Center
2004 Randolph Avenue
St. Paul, MN 55105

36

ABM Alumni Association Scholarship

AMOUNT: Varies **DEADLINE:** Feb 1
FIELDS/MAJORS: Agricultural Business, Management, Agricultural Education

Student must be a sophomore of above majoring in agricultural business management and agricultural education. Must have a GPA of 2.5 or better. Write to the address below for more information.

California State Polytechnic University, Pomona
College Of Agriculture
Building 2, Room 215
Pomona, CA 91768

37

Abraham A. Spack Fellowship

AMOUNT: VARIES **DEADLINE:** APR 30
FIELDS/MAJORS: Jewish Education

Awards are available for undergraduate college students who are interested in serving the Jewish people as a Jewish educator. Write to the address below for more information.

Coalition For The Advancement Of Jewish Education
261 W. 35th St., Floor 12A
New York, NY 10001

38

Abraham Baldwin Alumni Scholarship

AMOUNT: $1,000 **DEADLINE:** Apr 15
FIELDS/MAJORS: All Areas Of Study

Open to full-time students who have completed at least 30 quarter hours of degree credit at ABAC and have a current minimum GPA of 2.5. Priority is given to children of alumni. Write to the address below for additional information.

Abraham Baldwin Agricultural College
Office Of Admissions
2802 Moore Highway
Tifton, GA 31794

39

Abraham Baldwin Opportunity & James Perry Gleaton Scholarships

AMOUNT: None Specified **DEADLINE:** Apr 15
FIELDS/MAJORS: All Areas Of Study

Open to entering freshmen who have a GPA of at least 2.0 from their high school years. Renewable with a GPA of at least 2.5. Preference for Gleaton award will be given to children of employees of the Plant Telephone company. Write to the address below for additional information.

Abraham Baldwin Agricultural College
Office Of Admissions
2802 Moore Highway
Tifton, GA 31794

40

Abraham Franck, Evelyn Franck, And Esther Franck Memorial Scholarships

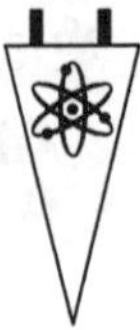

Amount: Varies **Deadline:** Mar 1
Fields/Majors: Mathematics And Statistics

Awards are available at the University of New Mexico for sophomores, juniors, or seniors enrolled in a mathematics program. Must demonstrate academic ability and financial need. Renewable for one year. Write to the address below for more information.

University Of New Mexico, Albuquerque
Office Of Financial Aid
Albuquerque, NM 87131

41

Abraham Lincoln Mitchell Memorial Scholarships

Amount: Varies **Deadline:** Mar 1
Fields/Majors: All Areas Of Study

Awards are available at the University of New Mexico for African American students. Write to the address below for more information.

University Of New Mexico, Albuquerque
Office Of Financial Aid
Albuquerque, NM 87131

42

Academic Achievement Awards

Amount: $1,000 **Deadline:** None Specified
Fields/Majors: All Areas Of Study

Scholarships for students at Peace College with a GPA of at least 3.0. Contact the director of financial aid at the address below for details.

Peace College
Director Of Financial Aid
15 East Peace Street
Raleigh, NC 27604

43

Academic Achievement Awards

Amount: $2,500 **Deadline:** Mar 15
Fields/Majors: All Areas Of Study

Awards open to students who rank in the top 25% of their class. Renewable. Write to the address below for more information.

Teikyo Post University
Office Of Financial Aid
800 Country Club Road
Waterbury, CT 06723

44

Academic Achievement Scholarship

Amount: $1,900 (max) **Deadline:** None Specified
Fields/Majors: All Areas Of Study

Awards for freshmen who have an ACT score of at least 23 and are in the top 25% of their graduating class. Renewable with a GPA of 3.0 or better. Write to the address below for more information.

Northwestern College
Financial Aid Office
101 7th St., SW
Orange City, IA 51041

45

Academic Achievement Scholarship

Amount: $600-$1,400 **Deadline:** None Specified
Fields/Majors: All Areas Of Study

Awards for high school seniors or transfer students with a GPA of at least 3.0. High school seniors must also have an SAT score of 1120-1300 or an ACT score of 25-26. Write to the address below for more information.

Cedarville College
Financial Aid Office
P.O. Box 601
Cedarville, OH 45314

46

Academic Achievement Scholarships

Amount: $4,000-$30,000 **Deadline:** Feb 1
Fields/Majors: All Areas Of Study

Applicants must be in the top 25% of their high school class with at least a GPA of 3.4 and an ACT score of 24 or an SAT score of 1000. For undergraduate study. Contact the financial aid office at the address below for details.

Bellarmine College
Financial Aid Office
2001 Newburg Road
Louisville, KY 40205

47

Academic And Achievement Scholarships

Amount: $500-$750 **Deadline:** Mar 15
Fields/Majors: All Areas Of Study

Scholarships for incoming freshmen who rank in the top 25% of their high school graduating class. Based primarily on a combination of ACT score and high school rank. Write to the address below for more information.

Moorhead State University
Office Of Scholarship And Financial Aid
107 Owens Hall
Moorhead, MN 56563

48

Academic Awards

Amount: $1,000-$1,500 **Deadline:** Mar 31
Fields/Majors: All Areas Of Study

Awards for undergraduate students at Columbia Union who have a GPA of at least 3.0. Renewable. Write to the address below for more information.

Columbia Union College
Financial Aid Office
7600 Flower Ave.
Takoma Park, MD 20912

49

Academic Division Scholarships

Amount: Varies **Deadline:** None Specified
Fields/Majors: All Areas Of Study

Awards given to full-time undergraduates who demonstrate excellence in academic work in a particular department or division. Renewable at the discretion of the division chair and as funds allow. Write to the address below for more information.

Concordia College, Nebraska
Office Of Financial Aid
800 N. Columbia Ave.
Seward, NE 68434

50 Academic Excellence Award

Amount: $2,500 **Deadline:** Jun 1
Fields/Majors: All Areas Of Study

Awards for entering freshmen who have a high school GPA of 3.4 or better and an ACT score of at least 26 or SAT score of 1060. Scholarships can be pro-rated for part-time attendance. Write to the address below for more information.

Long Island University
Financial Aid Office
Southampton, NY 11968

51 Academic Finalist Award

Amount: Varies **Deadline:** Mar 1
Fields/Majors: All Areas Of Study

Scholarships are available at Northern Illinois University for full-time entering freshmen or transfer students who qualified for university scholar awards but were not recipients. Award is $300 plus a tuition waiver. Must have a GPA of at least 3.5 to apply. Write to the address listed below for information.

Northern Illinois University
University Scholarship Committee
DeKalb, IL 60115

52 Academic Honors Scholarship

Amount: $2,500-$5,000 **Deadline:** Mar 1
Fields/Majors: All Areas Of Study

Awards for freshmen and transfer students at UMass. Entering freshmen are required to have a GPA of 3.5 or better, SAT score of at least 1300, and rank in the top 10% of his/her class. Transfer students are expected to have a GPA of 3.0 or better. Students must file a FAFSA as soon as possible after January 1 and before the March 1 financial aid priority consideration date. You will automatically be considered for this scholarship if you are enrolled at the university and apply for financial aid. Separate applications, requests, or inquiries are not required and cannot be honored.

University Of Massachusetts—Amherst
Office Of Financial Aid Services
255 Whitmore Admin. Bldg.
Box 38230
Amherst, MA 01003

53 Academic Scholarship

Amount: $1,000 (max) **Deadline:** Apr 15
Fields/Majors: All Areas Of Study

Awards for students who rank in the top 15% of their high school class with appropriate test scores. Must be enrolled for full-time study. Renewable with a GPA of at least 3.2. Write to the address below for more information.

Bethel College
Office Of Financial Planning
3900 Bethel Dr.
St. Paul, MN 55112

54 Academic Scholarship For Michigan Community College Transfers

Amount: $500 **Deadline:** Mar 1
Fields/Majors: All Areas Of Study

Awards for students at Western Michigan who have transferred from Michigan community colleges. Applicants must have a GPA of at least 3.5. No special application is required; students who qualify are automatically considered.

Western Michigan University
Office Of Admissions And Orientation
2240 Seibert Administration Bldg.
Kalamazoo, MI 49008

55 Academic Scholarship Program For Studies In The Sciences

Amount: Varies **Deadline:** Mar 1
Fields/Majors: Mathematics, Engineering, Science

Scholarships for Jewish men and women living in the Chicago metropolitan area, who are identified as having promise for significant contributions in their chosen careers, and are in need of financial assistance for full-time academic programs in one of the above fields. Must be above the junior level of study. The largest portion of the fund goes to residents of Cook County. Write to the address below after December 1 for details.

Jewish Federation Of Metropolitan Chicago
Attn: Scholarship Secretary
One South Franklin Street
Chicago, IL 60606

56 Academic Scholarships

Amount: $1,000 (min) **Deadline:** May 1
Fields/Majors: Real Estate

Scholarships for residents of Illinois who will be attending schools in Illinois. Based on desire to pursue a career in real estate or a related field, academics, need, and references. Must have completed 30 college credit hours. Write to the address below for details.

Illinois Real Estate Educational Foundation
3180 Adloff Ln.
P.O. Box 19451
Springfield, IL 62794

57 Academic Scholarships

Amount: Varies **Deadline:** Apr 15
Fields/Majors: All Areas Of Study

Awards available at Loras College to full-time students who have demonstrated academic achievement. Renewable with a GPA of

3.2. Write to the address below for details.

Loras College
Office Of Financial Planning
1450 Alta Vista St.
P.O. Box 178
Dubuque, IA 52004

58

Academic Scholarships

Amount: $2,500-$10,000 **Deadline:** Jan 15
Fields/Majors: All Areas Of Study

Scholarships for high school seniors entering Valparaiso University who have demonstrated outstanding academic achievement and substantial leadership in extracurricular activities in school, church, and community. A minimum undergraduate GPA of at least 3.0 is required for renewal. Write to the address below for additional information.

Valparaiso University
Office Of Admissions And Financial Aid
Kretzmann Hall
Valparaiso, IN 46383

59

Academic Scholarships

Amount: $1,000 (max) **Deadline:** Mar 15, Nov 15
Fields/Majors: All Areas Of Study

Awards for full-time students who have demonstrated outstanding academic achievement. Applicants must have earned at least 24 credits at Rampano and have at least a 3.3 GPA.

Rampano College Of New Jersey
Office Of Academic Affairs
505 Rampano Valley Road
Mahwah, NJ 07430

60

Academic Scholarships

Amount: $500-$1,250 **Deadline:** Apr 1
Fields/Majors: All Areas Of Study

Awards available to entering or returning students who have demonstrated academic ability. Must have a GPA of at least 3.0.

Rocky Mountain College
Office Of Financial Assistance
1511 Poly Drive
Billings, MT 59102

61

Academic Scholarships And Leadership Awards

Amount: $1,000-Tuition **Deadline:** Jan 15
Fields/Majors: All Areas Of Study

Scholarships available to entering first-year students at the University of Dayton who demonstrate a special aptitude for their chosen field of study or academic achievement and leadership. Awards are renewable for 8 undergraduate semesters as long as a GPA of at least 3.0 is maintained. Write to the address below for additional information.

University Of Dayton
Office Of Scholarships And Financial Aid
300 College Park
Dayton, OH 45469

62

Academic Scholarships For Incoming Freshmen And Transfer Students

Amount: $350-$1,000 **Deadline:** Mar 1
Fields/Majors: All Areas Of Study

Scholarships for incoming freshmen or transfer students at Black Hills State University with a GPA of 3.0 or better. Write to the address below for more information.

Black Hills State University
Office Of Financial Aid
University Station
Box 9509
Spearfish, SD 57799

63

ACB Of Colorado Scholarships

Amount: $1,500 **Deadline:** Mar 1
Fields/Majors: All Areas Of Study

Scholarships are available to legally blind students who are residents of Colorado. Write to the address below for details.

American Council Of The Blind
Scholarship Coordinator
1155 15th St., NW
Suite 720
Washington, DC 20005

64

Access Loan Program

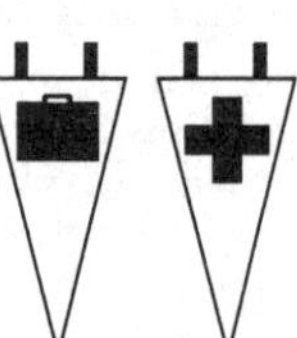

Amount: None Specified
Deadline: None Specified
Fields/Majors: Law, Business, Medical, Dental

Applicants must attend an accredited law, business, medical, or dental school, have satisfactory credit history, and plans to enroll for at least half-time. Must be a U.S. citizen to apply. Call 1-800-282-1550 or write to address below for details.

Access Group
P.O. Box 7430
Wilmington, DE 19803

65

Accountancy Scholarships At Case Western

Amount: $2,000 **Deadline:** Feb 1
Fields/Majors: Accounting

Two scholarships for freshmen who intend to major in accounting at Case Western Reserve University. Scholarships are renewable for a second year if high academic achievement is maintained. Write to the address below for details.

Case Western Reserve University
Office Of Financial Aid
109 Pardee Hall
10900 Euclid Avenue
Cleveland, OH 44106

66

Accounting Club Scholarship

AMOUNT: Varies **DEADLINE:** None Specified
FIELDS/MAJORS: Accounting

Awards for Mesa State accounting students at the undergraduate level. Contact the Mesa State College Accounting Club for more details.

Mesa State College
Office Of Financial Aid
P.O. Box 2647
Grand Junction, CO 81501

67

Accounting Club Scholarship

AMOUNT: $250 **DEADLINE:** None Specified
FIELDS/MAJORS: Accounting

Student must be an accounting major who is an active member of the accounting club. Contact the accounting club for more information.

Southwest Missouri State University
Office Of Financial Aid
901 South National Ave.
Springfield, MO 65804

68

Accounting Department Scholarships

AMOUNT: None Specified **DEADLINE:** Feb 1
FIELDS/MAJORS: Accounting

Awards for students majoring in accounting. Based on academic excellence. Write to the address below for more information.

Murray State University
University Scholarship Office
Ordway Hall
1 Murray St.
Murray, KY 42071

69

Accounting Scholarship

AMOUNT: $500 **DEADLINE:** None Specified
FIELDS/MAJORS: Accounting

Student must be a junior or senior accounting major with a GPA of 3.0 or better. Contact the COBA office for more information.

Southwest Missouri State University
Office Of Financial Aid
901 South National Ave.
Springfield, MO 65804

70

Accounting Scholarship

AMOUNT: $250 **DEADLINE:** Feb 9
FIELDS/MAJORS: Accounting

Award for accounting major who will be a junior at time of application. GPA will be considered. Use Bloomsburg University scholarship application. Contact Dr. Richard Baker, Chairperson, Accounting, for additional information.

Bloomsburg University
19 Ben Franklin Hall
400 E. Second St.
Blomsburg, PA 17815

71

Accounting Scholarships

AMOUNT: $250 **DEADLINE:** Mar 1
FIELDS/MAJORS: Accounting

Awards for accounting undergraduates at North Carolina State University. Write to the address below for more information.

North Carolina State University
Erin O. Dixon, Director Of Admissions
College Of Management
Box 8614
Raleigh, NC 27695

72

Accounting Technology Scholarship

AMOUNT: $1,500 **DEADLINE:** Apr 1
FIELDS/MAJORS: Accounting Technology

Scholarships for new students at Kent State who have a superior academic, record, and are pursuing a degree in accounting technology. Contact the financial aid office at your campus for details.

Kent State University, Tuscarawas Campus
Financial Aid Office
University Drive, NE
New Philadelphia, OH 44663

73

ACE Fellows Program

AMOUNT: Varies **DEADLINE:** Nov 1
FIELDS/MAJORS: Education Administration

Thirty fellowships for persons who have at least 5 years of college-level experience as faculty or administrators. Requires nomination by your institution's chief executive or chief academic officer. Fellows gain experience in university administration in a mentor/intern role. Program is highly competitive. Write to the address below for details. Additional funding sources for fellows and host institutions are listed in the application materials from

A.C.E. American Council On Education Ace Fellows Program
One Dupont Circle, NW, Suite 800
Washington, DC 20036

74

ACE National Merit Scholarships

AMOUNT: $1,000 (max) **DEADLINE:** Dec 1
FIELDS/MAJORS: All Areas Of Study

Scholarships available in amounts from $750 to $2,000 to students who participated in the Advanced College Experience program. Write to the address below for details.

Ripon College
300 Seward Street
P.O. Box 248
Ripon, WI 54971

75

ACFEI Scholarship

AMOUNT: Varies **DEADLINE:** Ongoing
FIELDS/MAJORS: Culinary Arts

Awards are available for current members of the American Culinary Federation who are in good standing. Applicants must have completed at least one full grading period in the program prior to the date of the scholarship. Write to the address below for more information.

American Culinary Federation
P.O. Box 3466
St. Augustine, FL 32085

76

Achievement Awards

AMOUNT: $200-$600 **DEADLINE:** Feb 15
FIELDS/MAJORS: All Areas Of Study

Scholarship is awarded to recognize outstanding potential and performance in students which is determined by Central Missouri State University academic department. Write to the address below for more details.

Southwest Missouri State University
Financial Aid Office
901 South National Ave.
Springfield, MO 65804

77

Acres Scholarships

AMOUNT: $500 **DEADLINE:** Feb 1
FIELDS/MAJORS: Special Education

Scholarships for current teachers who are working with (or changing areas of teaching to) special needs children in a rural school setting. Write to the address below for details.

American Council On Rural Special Education
Department Of Special Education
221 Milton Bennion Hall
University Of Utah
Salt Lake City, UT 84112

78

Active Duty Commissioning Programs (ADCP)

AMOUNT: $2,000 **DEADLINE:** None Specified
FIELDS/MAJORS: All Areas Of Study

Grants for students enrolled in a program leading to a commission in the Navy or Marine Corps. Programs include NROTC, ECP, NESP, MECEP, EEAP, etc. Interest-free loans are also available from the relief society. These programs are for undergraduate study only. Write to the address below for details.

Navy-Marine Corps Relief Society
Education Programs
801 N. Randolph Street, Suite 1228
Arlington, VA 22203

79

Activity And Departmental Awards

AMOUNT: None Specified **DEADLINE:** None Specified
FIELDS/MAJORS: All Areas Of Study

Awards are available to students in various departments and activities who are enrolled in St. Petersburg Junior College. The individual criteria of each department may vary. Contact the office the director of scholarships and student financial assistance at the campus you attend or your departmental chairperson for more information.

St. Petersburg Junior College
Office Of Financial Aid
P.O. Box 13489
St. Petersburg, FL 33733

80

Activity Awards For Athletics, Drama, Music

AMOUNT: Varies **DEADLINE:** Varies
FIELDS/MAJORS: Athletics, Drama, Music

Awards for Concordia students who demonstrate special ability in one of these three areas: athletic, music, or drama. Must be U.S. citizens and have a GPA of at least 2.5. Write to the address below for more information.

Concordia University, Irvine
Financial Aid Office
1530 Concordia West
Irvine, CA 92715

81

ACTR/Accels Summer Language Teacher Exchange Program

AMOUNT: Varies **DEADLINE:** Feb 28
FIELDS/MAJORS: Russian Language And Culture

Program for teachers at any level of Russian language or culture. Recipients spend six weeks in Russia to experience first-hand the latest developments in the discipline. Program will cover the costs of international travel and expense, but participants are responsible for the cost of domestic transportation. Write to the address below for more information.

American Council Of Teachers Of Russian
Office Of The Executive Director
1776 Massachusettes Ave., NW, Suite 700
Washington, DC 20036

82

Actuarial Scholarships For Minority Students

AMOUNT: Varies **DEADLINE:** May 1
FIELDS/MAJORS: Actuarial Science

Scholarships for minority students enrolled or accepted in a program in actuarial science. Applicant must demonstrate financial need and be a U.S. citizen or legal resident. Write to the address below for details.

Society Of Actuaries
475 N. Martingale Road
Schaumburg, IL 60173

83

ACTWU Scholarship

AMOUNT: $1,000 **DEADLINE:** None Specified
FIELDS/MAJORS: All Areas Of Study

Scholarships for incoming freshmen. Parent must be member of the Amalgamated Clothing and Textile Workers Union in good standing for at least two years. Children of employees of the

ACTWU itself are not eligible. Three awards per year. Renewable once. Write to the address below for more information.

Amalgamated Clothing And Textile Workers Union
ACTWU Scholarship Program
15 Union Square
New York, NY 10003

84

Adams State College Alumni Scholarships

AMOUNT: Varies **DEADLINE:** None Specified
FIELDS/MAJORS: All Areas Of Study

Scholarships for students attending Adams State College given by the alumni department. Contact the alumni office at the address below for details.

Adams State College
Alumni Office
Alamosa, CO 81102

85

Adams State College Private Scholarships

AMOUNT: Varies **DEADLINE:** None Specified
FIELDS/MAJORS: All Areas Of Study

Scholarships, administered by the Adams State College financial aid office, are available for students attending ASC. Criteria for each program varies. Contact the financial aid office at the address below for details. Request the publication, "Adams State College Private Scholarship Directory." Also, be certain to inquire at your high school guidance office and, if you have participated in high school athletics, your high school coach.

Adams State College
Financial Aid Office
Alamosa, CO 81102

86

Addison H. Gibson Student Loan Program

AMOUNT: Varies **DEADLINE:** None Specified
FIELDS/MAJORS: All Areas Of Study

Low-cost student loans available to residents of western Pennsylvania who have successfully completed one or more years of their undergraduate or graduate education and can demonstrate financial need. Write to the address listed below for further information.

Addison H. Gibson Foundation
One PPG Place, Suite 2230
Pittsburgh, PA 15222

87

Adele Smith Strong Fund

AMOUNT: Varies **DEADLINE:** None Specified
FIELDS/MAJORS: All Areas Of Study

Awards available to female students at Rockford College. Write to the address below for more information.

Rockford College
Financial Aid Office
5050 East State St.
Rockford, IL 61108

88

Adelle and Erwin Tomash Fellowship In History Of Information Processing

AMOUNT: $12,000 (max) **DEADLINE:** Jan 15
FIELDS/MAJORS: Computer Science, History Of Technology

Fellowships to be carried out at any appropriate research facility, into the history of computers and of information processing. Research may be into the technical, social, legal, or business aspects of information processing. Preference is given for dissertation research, but all doctoral students are invited to apply. Two one-year continuations are permitted. Write to the institute at the address below for details.

Charles Babbage Institute, University Of Minnesota
103 Walter Library
117 Pleasant Street, SE
Minneapolis, MN 55455

89

ADMA Scholarship Endowment Fund

AMOUNT: $1,000 **DEADLINE:** May 1
FIELDS/MAJORS: Aviation, Aviation Management

Scholarships are available for aviation and aviation management majors. Write to the address listed below for information.

Aviation Distributors And Manufacturers Association
ADMA Scholarship Program
1900 Arch Street
Philadelphia, PA 19103

90

Admiral Grace Murray Hopper Scholarship

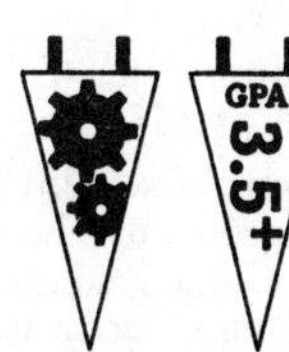

AMOUNT: $1,000 **DEADLINE:** May 15
FIELDS/MAJORS: Engineering, Computer Science

Scholarship is for a female freshman entering the study of engineering or computer science in any form of a our-year program. Two awards per year. Must have a GPA of at least 3.5. Information and applications for the SWE awards are available from the deans of engineering schools or from the address below. Please be certain to enclose an SASE.

Society Of Women Engineers
120 Wall Street, 11th Floor
New York, NY 10005

91

Admissions And Academic Scholarships

AMOUNT: Varies **DEADLINE:** Dec 15
FIELDS/MAJORS: All Areas Of Study

Scholarships awarded to incoming freshmen and transfer students who show outstanding academic ability. Contact the office of admissions for details.

Appalachian State University
Office Of Admissions
Scholarship Section
Boone, NC 28608

92
Adolph Van Pelt, Inc. Scholarship

AMOUNT: $500-$800 **DEADLINE:** Jun 1
FIELDS/MAJORS: All Areas Of Study

Open to American Indian or Alaskan Natives. Must have tribal affiliation and proof of enrollment and be at least 25% native American/Alaskan. Recipients are eligible to reapply in subsequent years. Write to the address below for complete details.

Association On American Indian Affairs, Inc.
Box 268
Sisseton, SD 57262

93
Adult Degree Completion Scholarship Program

AMOUNT: $500-$1,000 **DEADLINE:** Mar 31
FIELDS/MAJORS: All Areas Of Study

Must hold an AAL certificate of membership in his or her own name before application deadline during senior undergraduate year. Must be 25 years old or older and be in the final year of study in a bachelor's or associate degree program. Write to the address below for complete details.

Aid Association For Lutherans
Attn: AAL Scholarships
4321 N. Ballard Rd.
Appleton, WI 54915

94
Adult Learner Scholarship

AMOUNT: $200 **DEADLINE:** None Specified
FIELDS/MAJORS: All Areas Of Study

Awards for SMSU students who are 25 years or older who are returning to school after an absence or are just beginning school. For undergraduate study. Contact the continuing education office for information.

Southwest Missouri State University
Financial Aid Office
901 South National Ave.
Springfield, MO 65804

95
Adult Scholarship/Grant Program

AMOUNT: Varies **DEADLINE:** Apr 15
FIELDS/MAJORS: All Areas Of Study

Awards available at Loras College to full-time undergraduate students who are 24 years of age or older. Write to the address below for details.

Loras College
Office Of Financial Planning
1450 Alta Vista St.
P.O. Box 178
Dubuque, IA 52004

96
Adult Student Center Scholarship

AMOUNT: $275 **DEADLINE:** None Specified
FIELDS/MAJORS: All Areas Of Study

Scholarships are available for UW adult student 25 years or older

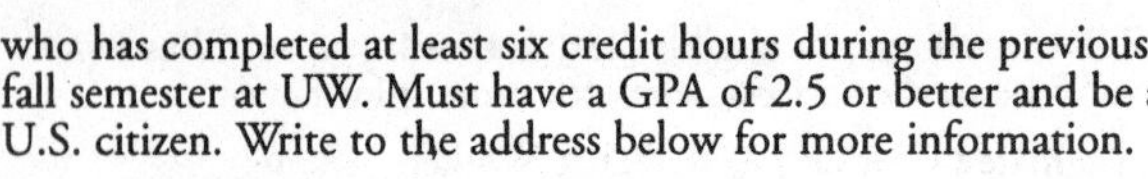
who has completed at least six credit hours during the previous fall semester at UW. Must have a GPA of 2.5 or better and be a U.S. citizen. Write to the address below for more information.

University Of Wyoming
Adult Student Center
P.O. Box 3808
Laramie, WY 82071

97
Adult Student Scholarships

AMOUNT: None Specified **DEADLINE:** Feb 15
FIELDS/MAJORS: All Areas Of Study

Scholarships are available at the University of New Orleans for full-time students, who have been out of high school for at least five years but who have never attended college. This award allows students to register for one course. Write to the address below for details.

University Of New Orleans
Student Financial Aid Office
1005 Administration Building, Lake Front
New Orleans, LA 70148

98
Adult Vocational Grant Program

AMOUNT: Varies **DEADLINE:** Mid Nov
FIELDS/MAJORS: Vocational And Technical Fields

Scholarships for adult students who will be entering a full-time vocational or technical course of study. Applications are taken by local BPO Elks Lodges between September and November. Contact your local BPO Elks Lodge for details. The telephone number may be found in your local telephone directory. Information is also available from many vocational/technical schools' financial aid offices.

Elks National Foundation
2750 N. Lakeview Ave.
Chicago, IL 60614

99
Advanced Graduate Student Member Award

AMOUNT: $1,000 **DEADLINE:** June 1
FIELDS/MAJORS: History

Awards available to graduate student members of Phi Alpha Theta for projects leading to the completion of the doctorate degree. Write to address below for details. Please indicate the name of your chapter. Information may be available from your chapter officers.

Phi Alpha Theta—International Honor Society In History
Headquarters Office
50 College Dr.
Allentown, PA 18104

100
AESF Graduate Scholarships

AMOUNT: $1,000 **DEADLINE:** Apr 15
FIELDS/MAJORS: See Listed Below

Awards for graduate students in the fields of metallurgy, metallurgical engineering, materials science or engineering, chemistry, chemical engineering, or environmental engineering. Based on achievement, scholarship potential, and motivation and interest in the finishing technologies. For full-time study. Write to the address below for more information.

American Electroplaters And Surface Finishers Society
Central Florida Research Park
12644 Research Parkway
Orlando, FL 32826

101

AFCEA Educational Foundation Fellowship

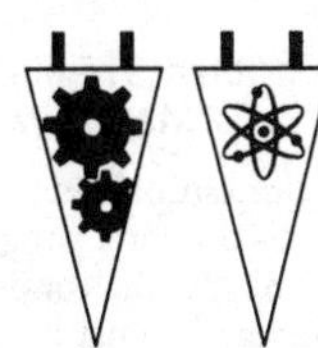

AMOUNT: $25,000 **DEADLINE:** Apr 1
FIELDS/MAJORS: Technology Fields

Awards are available for scholars or Ph.D. students enrolled full-time in an accredited degree granting four-year college or university in the U.S. Must be a U.S. citizen of good moral character and leadership abilities who demonstrates academic excellence and dedication to completing his/her education. Must also demonstrate financial need. Write to the address below for more information.

Armed Forces Communications And Electronics Association
AFCEA Educational Foundation
4400 Fair Lakes Court
Fairfax, VA 22033

102

Affirmative Action Scholarship Program

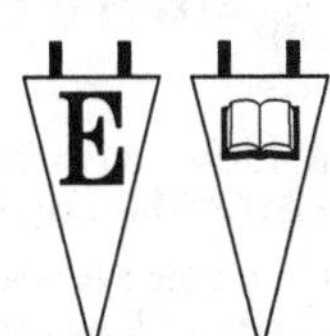

AMOUNT: $6,000 **DEADLINE:** Oct 31
FIELDS/MAJORS: Library/Information Science

Open to minority students who are graduate students with an interest in librarianship. Extra consideration given to members of the SLA and people who have worked in special libraries, but awards are not limited to these persons. One award per year. Write to the address below for complete details. Please specify that you are interested in the Affirmative Action Scholarship Program.

Special Libraries Association
SLA Scholarship Committee
1700 Eighteenth St., NW
Washington, DC 20009

103

AFGM International Union Scholarship Program

AMOUNT: $1,000 **DEADLINE:** Mar 1
FIELDS/MAJORS: All Areas Of Study

Scholarships for members of the American Federation of Grain Millers union or dependent children of AFGM members. For students who will be entering their first year of college or vocational school. Write to the address below for more information.

American Federation Of Grain Millers
International Union Scholarship Program
4949 Olson Memorial Highway
Minneapolis, MN 55422

104

AFL-CIO Council Of Buffalo Scholarship

AMOUNT: $1,000 **DEADLINE:** Mar 22
FIELDS/MAJORS: All Areas Of Study

Scholarship for graduating high school seniors who are sons or daughters of affiliated members of the Buffalo Council, AFL-CIO. Based on academics, extracurricular activities, recommendation, essay, and need. Write to the address below for more information.

Buffalo AFL-CIO Council
532 Ellicott Square Building
295 Main St
Buffalo, NY 14203

105

AFL-CIO Of Pennsylvania Unionism In America Essay Contest

AMOUNT: $50-$1,000 **DEADLINE:** Dec 31
FIELDS/MAJORS: All Areas Of Study

Scholarship contest for graduating high school seniors from Pennsylvania high schools. Awards (8) may be used for full-time study at any postsecondary institution. 1500 word essay required. Recommendation by a labor organization is required. Write to the address below for details. Information may also be found in many high schools or union halls.

Pennsylvania AFL-CIO
William G. Reck, Director Of Education
230 State St.
Harrisburg, PA 17101

106

AFL-CIO Union MasterCard Scholarship Program

AMOUNT: $500-$4,000 **DEADLINE:** Feb 28
FIELDS/MAJORS: All Areas Of Study

Scholarships for members and their children of AFL-CIO unions that participate in the union MasterCard program (offers this MasterCard to its members). Having a MasterCard is not necessary for this scholarship. For undergraduate study only. Contact (or have your parent contact) your local union to get more information on this program. Write to the address below (on a postcard) if necessary.

Union Mastercard Scholarship Program
P.O. Box 9389
Minneapolis, MN 55440

107

AFL-CIO, Texas, Scholarships

AMOUNT: Varies **DEADLINE:** Jan 31
FIELDS/MAJORS: All Areas Of Study

Scholarships for members or children of members of AFL-CIO unions affiliated with the Texas AFL-CIO and the local central labor council. For graduating high school seniors. Interview required. Information should be available from your central labor council or from the address below. If writing, please specify your (your parent's) local union.

Texas AFL-CIO Scholarship Program
Education Department
P.O. Box 12727
Austin, TX 78711

108

AFPE Fellowship Programs

AMOUNT: $6,000-$10,000 **DEADLINE:** Mar 1
FIELDS/MAJORS: Pharmacy

Applicants must provide proof of outstanding scholarship and potential. Must be a U.S. citizen or permanent resident. For students who have at least three years of graduate work remaining toward a Ph.D. degree. AFPE administers about seventy awards per year. Information may be available at your pharmacy school. If not, write to the address below.

American Foundation For Pharmaceutical Education
One Church Street, Suite 202
Rockville, MD 20850

109

AFPE First Year Graduate Scholarship Program

AMOUNT: $7,500 **DEADLINE:** Jan 15
FIELDS/MAJORS: Pharmacy, Pharmacology

Scholarships for members of either Rho Chi or Phi Lambda Sigma who are in their first year of graduate studies toward a Ph.D. in pharmacy studies. Must be a U.S. citizen or permanent resident. Details on how to apply may be obtained at your school of pharmacy, from your chapter of Rho Chi/Phi Lambda Sigma, or from the AFPE at the address below.

American Foundation For Pharmaceutical Education
One Church Street, Suite 202
Rockville, MD 20850

110

AFPE Gateway Scholarship Program

AMOUNT: $4,250 **DEADLINE:** Dec 1
FIELDS/MAJORS: Pharmacy, Pharmacology

Scholarships for undergraduates in a pharmacy college. Purpose is to encourage students to pursue Ph.D. degree after undergraduate studies. Undergraduate award funds research project. An additional $5,000 scholarship is given once the recipient enters graduate school. Must be a U.S. citizen or permanent resident in last three years of B.S. or Pharm.D. program. Information may be available in your school or department of pharmacy. If not, write to the address below (be sure to include your year in school).

American Foundation For Pharmaceutical Education
One Church St., Suite 202
Rockville, MD 20850

AFPE Glaxo Graduate Studies Scholarship Program

AMOUNT: $5,000 **DEADLINE:** May 1
FIELDS/MAJORS: Pharmacy

Awards for students in the final year of a B.S. or Pharm.D program who are planning to pursue a graduate or professional degree that will provide background for a pharmaceutical industry career. Write to the address below for more information.

American Foundation For Pharmaceutical Education
One Church Street, Suite 202
Rockville, MD 20850

AFPE Postdoctoral Research Fellowships For Faculty Members

AMOUNT: $27,500 **DEADLINE:** Mar 1
FIELDS/MAJORS: Pharmacy

Research fellowships, funded by the Gustavus A. Pfeiffer Foundation, for pharmacy faculty members performing research into several diverse areas of pharmacy and pharmacology. Must be a U.S. citizen or permanent resident. Write to the address below for details.

American Foundation For Pharmaceutical Education
One Church Street, Suite 202
Rockville, MD 20850

Africa Doctoral Predissertation Research Fellowships

AMOUNT: $15,000 **DEADLINE:** Nov 1
FIELDS/MAJORS: African Studies, Social Sciences

Fellowships are available for social science students enrolled in a U.S. doctoral program are eligible. Applicants must have completed all the doctoral program requirements except the dissertation. Research must be on topics related to agriculture and health in sub-Sahara Africa. $2,000 travel grants for short-term field studies in Africa area also available. Write to the address listed below for information.

Social Science Research Council
Fellowships And Grants
605 Third Avenue
New York, NY 10158

Africa Grants

AMOUNT: $15,000 (max) **DEADLINE:** Dec 1
FIELDS/MAJORS: African Studies

Grants are available for postdoctoral scholars who are U.S. citizens, whose competence for research on Africa has been demonstrated, and to those who intend to make continuing contributions to the field. Write to the address listed below for information.

Social Science Research Council
Fellowships And Grants
605 Third Avenue
New York, NY 10158

115

African Dissertation Internship Awards

AMOUNT: Varies **DEADLINE:** Varies
FIELDS/MAJORS: All Areas Of Study.

Doctoral dissertation internships are available for African doctoral candidates currently enrolled in U.S. or Canada institutions to travel to Africa for twelve to eighteen months of supervised doctoral research. Please write to the address below for complete information.

Rockefeller Foundation
Fellowship Office
1133 Avenue Of The Americas
New York, NY 10036

116

African-American Scholarships

AMOUNT: $500-$1,500 **DEADLINE:** Dec 15
FIELDS/MAJORS: All Areas Of Study

Scholarships awarded to African American incoming freshmen and transfer students who have a minimum GPA of 3.0. Contact the office of admissions for details.

Appalachian State University
Office Of Admissions
Scholarship Section
Boone, NC 28608

117

Afro-American and African Studies Fellowships

AMOUNT: $12,500-$25,000 **DEADLINE:** Dec 2
FIELDS/MAJORS: African American And African Studies

One-year postdoctoral and two-year predoctoral residential fellowships at the University of Virginia Carter G. Woodson Institute. Supports projects in the disciplines of the humanities concerning themselves with Afro-American and African studies. Predoctoral candidates should have completed all requirements except the dissertation. Current University of Virginia employees are not eligible (until at least one year of separation). Contact William E. Jackson, Associate Director of Research, at the address below, or (804)924-3109 for details.

University Of Virginia, Carter G. Woodson Institute
For Afro-American And African Studies
102 Minor Hall
Charlottesville, VA 22903

118

AFSA Financial Aid Program

AMOUNT: $500-$2,500 **DEADLINE:** Feb 15
FIELDS/MAJORS: All Areas Of Study

Scholarships for undergraduate dependent children of American Foreign Service Personnel (active, retired w/ pension, or deceased) who have served abroad with a foreign service agency (defined in the Foreign Service Act of 1980) for at least one year. Write to the address below for details.

American Foreign Service Association
2101 E St., NW
Washington, DC 20037

119

AFSA/AAFSW Merit Award Program

AMOUNT: $750 **DEADLINE:** Feb 15
FIELDS/MAJORS: Visual Or Musical Arts

Scholarships for graduating high school seniors who are dependents of American foreign service personnel (active, retired w/ pension, or deceased) who have served with a foreign service agency (defined in the Foreign Service Act of 1980) for at least 1 year. Approximately 20 awards annually. Write to the address below for details.

American Foreign Service Association
2101 E Str., NW
Washington, DC 20037

120

Ag Radio Network Scholarships

AMOUNT: $500 **DEADLINE:** Feb 15
FIELDS/MAJORS: Agriculture

Scholarships are available for FFA members pursuing a two-year degree in any area of agriculture. Applicant must reside in Connecticut, Maine, Vermont, Massachusetts, New Hampshire, New York or Rhode Island. Write to the address below for details.

National FFA Foundation
Scholarship Office
P.O. Box 15160
Alexandria, VA 22309

121

Ag. Biology/Edward C. Appel & Kenneth Hobbs Scholarship

AMOUNT: $250 **DEADLINE:** Apr 15
FIELDS/MAJORS: Agricultural Biology

Open to students majoring in agricultural biology and active members of the agricultural biology club. Write to the address below for more information.

California State Polytechnic University, Pomona
College Of Agriculture
Building 7, Room 110
Pomona, CA 91768

122

AGBU Loans, Grants, And Fellowships

AMOUNT: $1,000-$3,000 **DEADLINE:** Apr 30
FIELDS/MAJORS: All Areas Of Study

Programs for graduate students of Armenian descent. Based on a variety of criteria. Write to the address below for more information. Deadline for requesting applications is Mar 15.

Armenian General Benevolent Union
Ms. Anita Anserian
585 Saddle River Rd.
Saddle Brook, NJ 07662

123

AGC Saul Horowitz Jr. Memorial, And Heffner Graduate Scholarships

AMOUNT: $7,500 **DEADLINE:** Nov 1
FIELDS/MAJORS: Civil Engineering/Construction

Applicants must be seniors in or possess an undergraduate degree in a civil engineering or construction program. Must be enrolled or planning to enroll in a graduate program in construction or civil engineering. Awards are paid in two installments of $3,750. For applications and additional information write to the address below.

AGC Education And Research Foundation
Director Of Programs
1957 E Street, NW
Washington, DC 20006

124

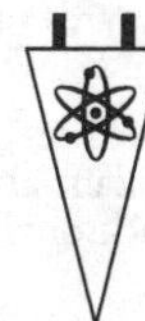

Agco Corporation Scholarships

AMOUNT: $1,000-$2,000 **DEADLINE:** Feb 15
FIELDS/MAJORS: Agricultural Engineering

Scholarships are available for FFA members pursuing a four-year degree in agricultural engineering. Write to the address below for details.

National FFA Foundation
Scholarship Office
P.O. Box 15160
Alexandria, VA 22309

125

Agnes Davis Donaldson Scholarship

AMOUNT: Varies **DEADLINE:** Apr 15
FIELDS/MAJORS: All Areas Of Study

Scholarships available for students at ABAC who have completed at least thirty quarter hours of degree credits and have a minimum GPA of 3.3. Residents of Tift County, GA, will be given priority for this award, when other factors are equal. Write to the address below for additional information.

Abraham Baldwin Agricultural College
Office Of Admissions
2802 Moore Highway
Tifton, GA 31794

126

Agnes Drexler Kujawa Memorial Scholarship

Amount: $1,000 **Deadline:** Feb 16
Fields/Majors: All Areas Of Study

Award for female, single parents at least 30 years old, having physical custody of one or more minor children, enrolled for at least six undergraduate of three graduate credits per semester. Contact the financial aid office, UW Oshkosh for more information.

University Of Wisconsin, Oshkosh
Financial Aid Office, Dempsey 104
800 Algoma Blvd.
Oshkosh, WI 54901

127

Agnes Jones Jackson Scholarship

Amount: $1,500 To $2,500 **Deadline:** Apr 30
Fields/Majors: All Areas Of Study

Applicants must be members of NAACP for at least one year or fully paid life members. Undergraduates must have a GPA of 2.5 and graduates must have a GPA of 3.0. Write to the address below for details and include the scholarship name on the envelope.

NAACP Special Contribution Fund
Education Department
4805 Mount Hope Drive
Baltimore, MD 21215

128

Agnes Manes Memorial Scholarship

Amount: Varies **Deadline:** Mar 15
Fields/Majors: All Areas Of Study

Awards for Jacksonville State University students in any area of study. Write to the address below for more information.

Jacksonville State University
Financial Aid Office
Jacksonville, AL 36265

129

Agnes Ripple Adams Scholarship

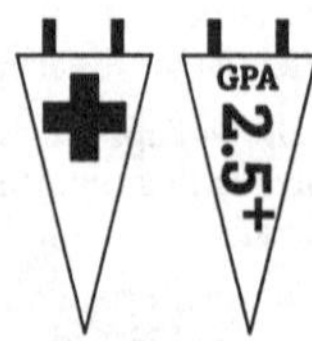

Amount: Varies **Deadline:** Mar 1
Fields/Majors: Nursing

Awards are available at the University of New Mexico for full-time nursing students with a minimum GPA of 2.5 and financial need. Write to the address below or contact the school of nursing for more details.

University Of New Mexico, Albuquerque
Office Of Financial Aid
Albuquerque, NM 87131

130

Agricultural Engineering Departmental Scholarships

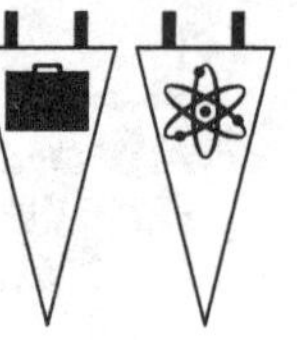

Amount: $500 **Deadline:** Mar 1
Fields/Majors: Agricultural Engineering/Mechanization Or Business

For entering freshmen or sophomores in agricultural engineering, mechanization, or agribusiness. Based on potential for achievement and professional leadership in the field of agriculture. Four nonrenewable awards available. Write to the address below for complete details.

Clemson University
Financial Aid Office
G01 Sikes Hall
Clemson, SC 29634

131

Agricultural Scholarship Program

Amount: $1,500 **Deadline:** Apr 15
Fields/Majors: Agriculture

Scholarships are available for Wisconsin residents who are enrolled in an agriculture program at an accredited college or university, with a commendable academic record, and good moral character. Write to the address listed below for information.

Didion, Inc.
Scholarship Committee
P.O. Box 400
Johnson Creek, WI 53038

132

Agriculture Alumni Scholarship

Amount: $400 **Deadline:** None Specified
Fields/Majors: Agriculture

Students must be agriculture majors who demonstrate scholarship, leadership, and character. Contact the agriculture department for more information.

Southwest Missouri State University
Office Of Financial Aid
901 South National Ave.
Springfield, MO 65804

133

Agriculture Alumni Scholarships

Amount: $250 **Deadline:** Feb 15
Fields/Majors: Agriculture

Awards for UW Platteville continuing students in the area of agriculture who have academic ability, financial need, and campus activity involvement. Write to the address below for more information.

University Of Wisconsin, Platteville
Office Of Admissions And Enrollment
Platteville, WI 53818

134

Agriculture And Life Sciences Scholarships

Amount: $500-$1,200 **Deadline:** Mar 1
Fields/Majors: Agriculture And Life Sciences

Awards for NCSU undergraduates in the fields of agriculture or life science. Forty awards given per year (twenty one-year, twenty renewable). Write to the address below for more information.

North Carolina State University
Associate Dean
Box 7642
College Of Agriculture And Life Sciences
Raleigh, NC 29695

135

Agriculture Council Scholarship

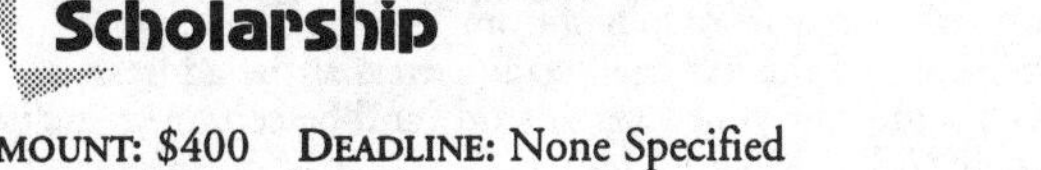

AMOUNT: $400 **DEADLINE:** None Specified
FIELDS/MAJORS: Agriculture

Student must be a sophomore or above agriculture major who demonstrate scholarship, leadership, and character. Contact the agriculture department for more information.

Southwest Missouri State University
Office Of Financial Aid
901 South National Ave.
Springfield, MO 65804

136

Agriculture Education Loan Forgiveness Program

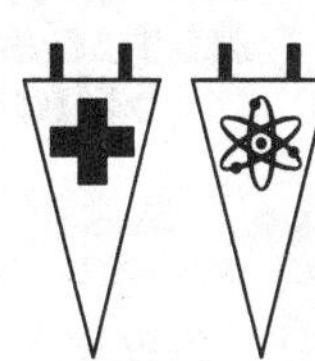

AMOUNT: $10,000 (max) **DEADLINE:** None Specified
FIELDS/MAJORS: Agriculture, Veterinary Medicine

Applicants must hold a degree in a field related to the production of agricultural products or veterinary medicine from a Pennsylvania school or college. Agriculture students must work on the family farm to be eligible. Write to the address below for more information.

Pennsylvania Higher Education Assistance Agency
1200 N. 7th Street
P.O. Box 8114
Harrisburg, PA 17102

137

AGS/Merrell Dow Geriatrics Clinician Of The Year Award

AMOUNT: $2,000 **DEADLINE:** Dec 5
FIELDS/MAJORS: Geriatrics

Awards are available for geriatrics clinicians whose primary focus is the delivery of patient care in the office, hospital, long-term care facility, or community. Must be AGS members. Write to the address below for more information.

American Geriatrics Society
770 Lexington Ave., Suite 300
New York, NY 10021

138

Ahmanson And Getty Postdoctoral Fellowships

AMOUNT: $9,200 per quarter **DEADLINE:** Mar 15
FIELDS/MAJORS: 17th, 18th Century Studies

Residential fellowships for scholars who hold a doctorate and would benefit from the interdisciplinary, cross-cultural programs at the Clark Library Center for 17th and 18th Century Studies at UCLA. Topics of study include Western Americana, British studies, history of science, literature, law, philosophy, and musicology. Write to the fellowship coordinator at the address below for details.

UCLA Center For 17th and 18th-Century Studies
395 Dodd Hall, UCLA
405 Hilgrad Ave.
Los Angeles, CA 90024

139

AIAA Technical Committee Graduate Scholarship Awards

AMOUNT: $1,000 **DEADLINE:** Jan 31
FIELDS/MAJORS: Astronautics, Aeronautical Engineering, Aerospace Engineering

Awards for master's or doctoral students in specific areas of interest to the AIAA. Must have a GPA of at least 3.0, have completed at least one year of graduate studies, and be a U.S. citizen. Write to technical committee graduate scholarships at the address below for details. Deadline to request applications is January 15.

American Institute Of Aeronautics And Astronautics
Scholarship Program
370 L'Enfant Promenade, SW
Washington, DC 20024

140

AIAA Undergraduate Scholarship Program

AMOUNT: $1,000 **DEADLINE:** Jan 31
FIELDS/MAJORS: Aeronautical Engineering, Aerospace Engineering, Astronautics

One or more annual scholarships for sophomore, junior, or senior year of study in areas of interest to AIAA. Must have a GPA of at least 3.0 and be a U.S. citizen. Applicant does not have to be an AIAA member to apply, but must become one before scholarship is awarded. Write to the address below for details. Deadline to request applications is Jan 15.

American Institute Of Aeronautics And Astronautics
Mr. Patrick Gouhin
370 L'Enfant Promenade, SW
Washington, DC 20024

141

AICPA Doctoral Fellowships

AMOUNT: $5,000 **DEADLINE:** Apr 1
FIELDS/MAJORS: Accounting

Doctoral fellowships for students who hold CPA certificates and are applying to or accepted into doctoral programs in accounting. Preference given to students with academic performance or significant professional experience. Must be a U.S. citizen. Renewable for up to three years. Write to the address below for details.

American Institute Of Certified Public Accountants
AICPA Doctoral Fellowships Program
1211 Avenue Of The Americas
New York, NY 10036

142

AICPA Minority Doctoral Fellowships

AMOUNT: $12,000 **DEADLINE:** Apr 1
FIELDS/MAJORS: Accounting

Doctoral fellowships for minority students who have master's degrees or three years of accounting experience and are enrolled full-time in a doctoral accounting program. Renewable. Write to the address below for details.

American Institute Of Certified Public Accountants
AICPA Doctoral Fellowships Program
1211 Avenue Of The Americas
New York, NY 10036

143

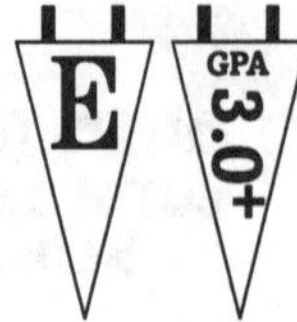

AICPA Scholarships For Minority Accounting Students

AMOUNT: $5,000 (max) **DEADLINE:** Jul 1
FIELDS/MAJORS: Accounting

For U.S. citizens or permanent residents. Must be full-time undergraduate or master level minority students with a GPA of at least 3.0. Must demonstrate financial need and academic achievement. Applicants must have completed thirty semester hours, with at least six in accounting. Write to the address below for details.

American Institute Of Certified Public Accountants
Minority Scholarships Program
1211 Avenue Of The Americas
New York, NY 10036

144

Aid To Blind Students

AMOUNT: $200 **DEADLINE:** Jun 1
FIELDS/MAJORS: All Areas Of Study

Scholarship program for undergraduate students in Washington state who are legally blind, to help offset the cost of equipment required because of their visual impairment. Must attend a Washington postsecondary institution. Write to the address listed below for information.

Washington Higher Education Coordinating Board
917 Lakeridge Way
P.O. Box 43430
Olympia, WA 98504

145

AIDS International Research Collaboration Award

AMOUNT: $20,000 **DEADLINE:** Varies
FIELDS/MAJORS: AIDS Research

Awards for scientists who have some affiliation with public or private institutions in foreign countries and can use these connections in their AIDS research efforts. Renewable. Write to the address below for more information.

National Institutes Of Health, Division Of Research Grants
Building 31, Room B2C39
31 Center Dr., MSC 2220
Bethesda, MD 20892

146

AIFS Minority Scholarships

AMOUNT: $500-$1,000
DEADLINE: Apr 15, Oct 15
FIELDS/MAJORS: Foreign Studies

Awards are available to help currently enrolled undergraduate students participate in an AIFS summer or spring exchange program. Applicants must have a GPA of 3.0 or better and be of Asian, African American, Hispanic, or Native American heritage. Write to the address below for more information.

American Institute For Foreign Study
102 Greenwich Ave.
Greenwich, CT 06830

147

Aiko Susanna Tashiro Hiratsuka Memorial Scholarship

AMOUNT: Varies **DEADLINE:** Apr 1
FIELDS/MAJORS: Performing Arts

Applicants must be undergraduates who are of Japanese ancestry and majoring in the performing arts. Applications and information may be obtained from local JACL chapters, district offices, and the national headquarters at the address below. Please indicate your level of study and be certain to include a legal-sized SASE.

Japanese American Citizens League
National Scholarship And Award Program
1765 Sutter St.
San Francisco, CA 94115

148

Air & Waste Management Association Graduate Study Scholarships

AMOUNT: Varies **DEADLINE:** Dec 6
FIELDS/MAJORS: Waste Management, Air Quality Management

Scholarships are available to assist graduate students working toward and training for careers in areas of air pollution control or waste management. Write to the address listed below for information.

Air & Waste Management Association
Scholarship Program
P.O. Box 2861
Pittsburgh, PA 15230

149

Air Force Association Scholarship

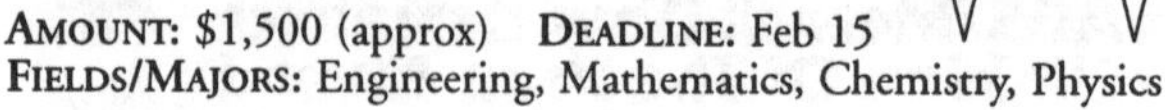

AMOUNT: $1,500 (approx) **DEADLINE:** Feb 15
FIELDS/MAJORS: Engineering, Mathematics, Chemistry, Physics

Scholarships are available at the University of Utah for full-time juniors or seniors majoring in one of the areas listed above. Based on grade point average. Write to the address below for information.

University Of Utah
Financial Aid And Scholarships Office
105 Student Services Building
Salt Lake City, UT 84112

150

Air Traffic Control Association Scholarship

AMOUNT: $600-$2,500 **DEADLINE:** May 1
FIELDS/MAJORS: Aeronautics/Aviation

Applicants must be aviation majors, U.S. citizens, and enrolled in or accepted at an accredited college or university. Essays are required. Must have a minimum of thirty semester hours (forty-five quarter hours) remaining toward bachelor's degree. Write to the address below for details.

Air Traffic Control Association, Inc.
2300 Clarendon Blvd., Suite 711
Arlington, VA 22201

151

Air Traffic Control Association Scholarship

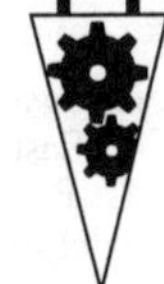

AMOUNT: $600-$2,500 **DEADLINE:** May 1
FIELDS/MAJORS: Aeronautics/Aviation

Scholarships are available to full-time employees in aviation-related fields at the government, military, or private industry level. Applicants must be U.S. citizens and taking courses designed to enhance skills used in an ATC or aviation discipline. Write to the address below for details.

Air Traffic Control Association, Inc.
2300 Clarendon Blvd., Suite 711
Arlington, VA 22201

152

Airline Pilots Association Scholarships

AMOUNT: Varies **DEADLINE:** None Specified
FIELDS/MAJORS: All Areas Of Study

Scholarship is offered to sons or daughters of retired or deceased pilot members of the Airline Pilots Association. Financial need and academics are considered (but no criteria are set). Scholarship is for four years. Graduating high school seniors or current undergraduates may apply. Write to Jan Redden at the address below for details.

Air Line Pilots Association
Scholarship Program
1625 Massachusetts Ave.
Washington, DC 20036

153

Airman Memorial Foundation Scholarship Fund

AMOUNT: $1,000-$4,000 **DEADLINE:** Apr 15
FIELDS/MAJORS: All Areas Of Study

Scholarships are available to single dependent children of retired or currently enlisted members of the Air Force, Air National, or Air Reserve. Contact the AFS/AMF Scholarships, Scholarship Administrator, P.O. Box 50, Suitland, MD 20748-0050 for more information.

Indiana University/Purdue University, Indianapolis
Purdue School Of Technology
799 West Michigan St.
Indianapolis, IN 46202

154

Al Qoyawayma Award

AMOUNT: $2,000 **DEADLINE:** Jun 15
FIELDS/MAJORS: Engineering, Science

Scholarships are available for Native Americans enrolled in a science or engineering program who also show interest or skill in one of the arts (art, music, dance). Must have a GPA of 2.0 or better. Write to the address listed below for information.

George Bird Grinnell American Indian Children's Education Foundation
American Indian Science/Engineering Society
1630 30th St., Suite 301
Boulder, CO 80301

155

Al Thompson Junior Bowler Scholarship

AMOUNT: $1,000-$1,500 **DEADLINE:** Jun 15
FIELDS/MAJORS: All Areas Of Study

Two scholarships for graduating high school seniors who have been active in and contributed to the sport of bowling. Renewable. Must have a GPA of at least 2.5. For members of the ABC/WIBC/YABA bowling leagues. Write to "Al Thompson Junior Bowler Scholarship Fund" at the address below for details.

Professional Bowlers Association Education Fund
Young American Bowling Alliance
5301 S. 76th St.
Greendale, WI 53129

156

Alabama Forensic Council Scholarship

AMOUNT: $1,000 **DEADLINE:** Feb 15
FIELDS/MAJORS: Speech Communication

Renewable $1,000 award given to students at the University of Alabama who have an interest in and an aptitude for the forensics (debate team) program. Freshman through senior year availability. Write to the address listed below for further information and an application.

University Of Alabama
College Of Communications
P.O. Box 870172
Tuscaloosa, AL 35487

157

Alabama Funeral Directors Association Scholarships

AMOUNT: $1,000 **DEADLINE:** None Specified
FIELDS/MAJORS: Mortuary Science

Awards for Alabama residents studying mortuary science. Monies are paid directly to the school. Write to the address below for more information.

Alabama Funeral Directors Association, Inc.
P.O. Box 56
Montgomery, AL 36101

158

Alabama Indian Affairs Commission Scholarship

AMOUNT: Varies **DEADLINE:** Varies
FIELDS/MAJORS: All Areas Of Study

Scholarships are available for American Indian undergraduate students who are members of one of the seven federally recognized Alabama Indian tribes. Write to the address listed below for information.

Alabama Indian Affairs Commission
669 South Lawrence Street
Montgomery, AL 36104

159

Alabama Nursing Scholarship Program

AMOUNT: Varies **DEADLINE:** None Specified
FIELDS/MAJORS: Nursing

Scholarship and loans available to Alabama residents admitted to nursing programs at Alabama institutions participating in this program. Students must agree to practice nursing for at least one year in Alabama following completion of the nursing program. Write to the address below for details.

Alabama Commission On Higher Education
P.O. Box 30200
Montgomery, AL 36130

160 Alabama Power Company Foundation Endowed Scholarship

Amount: $1,000 **Deadline:** Feb 15
Fields/Majors: Communications

Renewable, $1,000 scholarship created to honor 1991 Birmingham News Pulitzer Prize winners. Applicant must be enrolled at the University of Alabama, be a freshman, sophomore, or junior whose current record predicts a successful career as a communicator. Must also be legal resident of Alabama. Please write to the address listed below for additional information and an application.

Alabama Power Company Foundation
College Of Comm., University Of Alabama
P.O. Box 870172
Tuscaloosa, AL 35487

161 Alabama Power Foundation, Inc. Scholarships

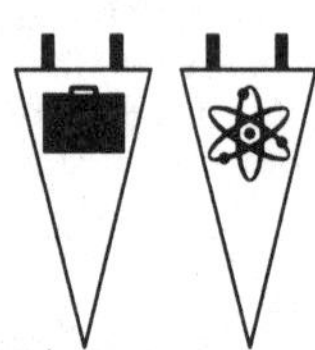

Amount: $1,500 **Deadline:** Feb 15
Fields/Majors: Agriculture, Agribusiness

Scholarships are available for FFA members pursuing a four-year degree in any area of agriculture or agribusiness. Four awards are offered annually. Must be from Alabama. Write to the address below for details.

National FFA Foundation
Scholarship Office
P.O. Box 15160
Alexandria, VA 22309

162 Alabama Power Scholarship

Amount: $1,000 **Deadline:** Mar 15
Fields/Majors: Commerce, Business

Awards for Alabama residents attending Jacksonville State University who are majoring in commerce or business. Write to the address below for more details.

Jacksonville State University
Financial Aid Office
Jacksonville, AL 36265

163 Alabama Scholarship Challenge Program

Amount: $500 **Deadline:** Mar 15
Fields/Majors: Travel And Tourism, Hotel/Motel Management

Awards for Alabama residents in one of the areas listed above who are enrolled in any four-year college. Must have a GPA of 3.0 or better and be in junior or senior year. Write to the address below for more information.

National Tour Foundation
546 East Main St.
P.O. Box 3071
Lexington, KY 40596

164 Alabama Student Assistance Program

Amount: $300-$2,500 **Deadline:** Mar 15
Fields/Majors: All Areas Of Study

Assistance for undergraduate students who are Alabama residents attending eligible Alabama institutions. Based on financial need. Write to the address below for details.

Alabama Commission On Higher Education
P.O. Box 30200
Montgomery, AL 36130

165 Alabama Student Grant Program

Amount: $1,200 **Deadline:** None Specified
Fields/Majors: All Areas Of Study

Grants for undergraduate students—both half-time and full-time—who are Alabama residents attending Birmingham-Southern College, Concordia College, Faulkner University, Huntingdon College, Judson College, Miles College, Spring Hill College, Oakwood College, Samford University, Selma University, Southeastern Bible College, Southern Vocational College, Stillman College, and University of Mobile. Write to the address below for details.

Alabama Commission On Higher Education
P.O. Box 30200
Montgomery, AL 36130

166 Alana Leadership Merit Award

Amount: One-Half Tuition **Deadline:** Mar 2
Fields/Majors: All Areas Of Study

Scholarships are awarded to entering freshmen African American, Hispanic, Asian, and Native American Indian students who demonstrate academic excellence, leadership, and participation in school and community activities. Write to the address below for more information.

Dominican College Of San Rafael
Office Of Admissions
50 Acacia Avenue
San Rafael, CA 94901

167 Alaska Native Brotherhood/ Sisterhood Scholarship

Amount: Varies **Deadline:** None Specified
Fields/Majors: All Areas Of Study

Scholarships are available for Alaska native undergraduate students. Write to the address listed below for information.

Alaska Native Brotherhood/Sisterhood
318 Willoughby Street
Juneau, AK 99801

168

Alaska Pacific University Distinguished Scholars And University Award

GPA 3.0+

AMOUNT: Varies **DEADLINE:** Mar 1
FIELDS/MAJORS: All Areas Of Study

Scholarships for students at or planning to attend Alaska Pacific University. Must have high school GPA of at least 3.0 for university award and 3.5 for distinguished scholar awards. Varying criteria with each of the grants and awards. For both undergrad and graduate students. Contact the financial aid office or the admissions office for further information.

Alaska Pacific University
APU Scholarships
4101 University Drive
Anchorage, AK 99508

169

Alaska Sea Services Scholarship Program

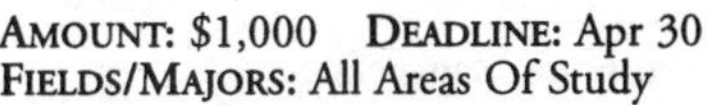

AMOUNT: $1,000 **DEADLINE:** Apr 30
FIELDS/MAJORS: All Areas Of Study

Awards for dependent child of regular/reserve member of the Navy, Marines or Coast Guard on active duty, retired with pay, deceased, or MIA. Must be a legal resident of Alaska, have high academic standards and show character, leadership ability, and financial need. Contact address below for additional information and application.

Navy League Fleet Reserve Association
U.S. Navy League Council 55-151
Box 201510
Anchorage, AK 99520

170

Alaska State Educational Incentive Grant Program

AMOUNT: $100-$1,500 **DEADLINE:** May 31
FIELDS/MAJORS: All Areas Of Study

Need-based grants are available to Alaska residents enrolled in their first undergraduate program at eligible Alaska colleges and universities. Write to the address listed below for information.

Alaska Commission On Postsecondary Education
3030 Vintage Blvd.
Juneau, AK 99801

171

Alaska Student Summer Internship Program

AMOUNT: $4.75-$16.50/hour **DEADLINE:** None Specified
FIELDS/MAJORS: Most Areas Of Study

Internship program for Alaska residents at any level of study who are at least 16 years of age. Applicants must be enrolled as a full time student at any college, university, or technical program. Write to the address below for more information.

Alaska Department Of Natural Resources
Division Of Support Services
3601 C Street, Suite 1222
Anchorage, AK 99503

172

Alaska Teacher Scholarship Loan Program

AMOUNT: $7,500 (max) **DEADLINE:** Jul 1
FIELDS/MAJORS: Education

Special loans are available for Alaska residents who live in rural areas who wish to pursue a secondary or elementary teaching career in a rural area. Applicants must be enrolled in a four-year bachelors degree in elementary or secondary education or a fifth-year teacher certification program. Write to the address listed below for information.

Alaska Commission On Postsecondary Education
3030 Vintage Blvd.
Juneau, AK 99801

173

Alaskan Aviation Safety Foundation Scholarships

AMOUNT: $500 **DEADLINE:** Mar 31
FIELDS/MAJORS: Aviation

Scholarships available to residents of Alaska who are enrolled in an aviation-related program in an accredited college, university, trade school, or approved training center. Applicant must have completed at least two semesters, or 30% of the work toward his/her professional goal, or has at minimum a private pilot certificate. Write to the address below for details.

Alaskan Aviation Safety Foundation
Scholarship Committee
4550 Aircraft Dr., #1A
Anchorage, AK 99502

174

Albert Baker Fund Student Loans

AMOUNT: $3,500 (max) **DEADLINE:** Jul 1
FIELDS/MAJORS: All Areas Of Study

Applicants must be members of the Mother Church, The First Church of Christ, Scientist, Boston, MA, and be currently active as Christian Scientists. Open to undergraduates, graduates, and Christian Science nurses in training. Write to the address below for details.

Albert Baker Fund
5 Third St., Suite 717
San Francisco, CA 94103

175

Albert Bruno Prouvost Memorial Scholarship

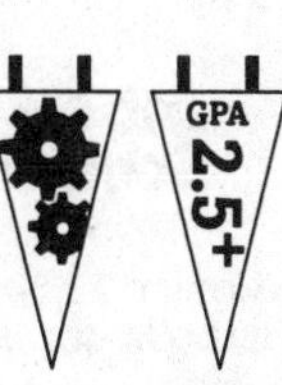

AMOUNT: Varies **DEADLINE:** None Specified
FIELDS/MAJORS: Engineering Technology, Industrial Technology, Health Science

Awards for TTC students pursuing an associate degree in the fields above. Must have a GPA of at least 2.5. Write to the address below for more information.

Trident Technical College
Financial Aid Office
P.O. Box 118067
Charleston, SC 29423

176

Albert E. And Florence W. Newton Fund

AMOUNT: $150-$1,100 **DEADLINE:** Apr 1, Oct 1
FIELDS/MAJORS: Nursing

Scholarships are available for Rhode Island resident RNs who are pursuing a B.S.N. degree at a Rhode Island college or university. Write to the address listed below for information.

Northwest Community Nursing Association
Ms. Beverly McGuire
P.O. Box 234
Harmony, RI 02829

177

Albert L. Wrigley, Jr. Award

AMOUNT: None Specified **DEADLINE:** None Specified
FIELDS/MAJORS: Hotel, Restaurant, and Travel Administration

Scholarships are awarded to students in one of the areas listed above. Based on academic achievement, activities in and contributions to the department, and financial need. For entering sophomores, juniors, or seniors. Contact the Chair, Hotel, Restaurant, and Travel Administration for more information.

University Of Massachusetts, Amherst
Chairperson
Hotel, Restaurant, And Travel Administration
Amherst, MA 01003

178

Albert M. Lappin Scholarship, Hugh A. Smith Scholarship

AMOUNT: $500-$1,000 **DEADLINE:** Feb 15
FIELDS/MAJORS: All Areas Of Study

Scholarships for Kansas residents who are or will be attending a college or University in Kansas. Applicant must be a U.S. citizen and a current high school senior or a freshman or sophomore in college. Smith award is $500, Lappin award is $1,000. For children of legion or auxiliary members. Write to the address listed below for additional information or application.

American Legion, Department Of Kansas
1314 SW Topeka Blvd.
Topeka, KS 66612

179

Albert O. Halse Memorial Scholarship Award

AMOUNT: $1,500 **DEADLINE:** May 24
FIELDS/MAJORS: Architecture

Scholarship awarded to an undergraduate student for excellence in architectiural delineation and/or architectural models. The student must reside in the Architects League membership area (Bergen, Hudson, Passaic, Sussex, Essex, and Morris counties). Write to the address below for more information.

Architects League Of Northern New Jersey
Albert Zaccone, AIA
P.O. Box 152
Paramus, NJ 07653

180

Albert Pierpont Madeira Scholarship

AMOUNT: Varies **DEADLINE:** Mar 1
FIELDS/MAJORS: All Areas Of Study

Awards for sophomores, juniors, or seniors studying at UMass. Based on good scholastic performance and demonstrated service to the university and fellow students. Students must file a FAFSA as soon as possible after January 1 and before the March 1 financial aid priority consideration date. You will automatically be considered for this scholarship if you are enrolled at the university and apply for financial aid. Separate applications, requests, or inquiries are not required and cannot be honored.

University Of Massachusetts, Amherst
255 Whitmore Administration Building
Box 38230
Amherst, MA 01003

181

Albert W. Dent Scholarship

AMOUNT: $3,000 **DEADLINE:** Mar 31
FIELDS/MAJORS: Hospital/Healthcare Management

Varying number of scholarships for students in an accredited graduate program in healthcare management. Must be student associate of the American College of Healthcare Executives. Financial need is considered. Must be U.S. or Canada citizen. Previous scholarship recipients ineligible. Goal of scholarship is to increase enrollment of minority students. Write to address below for details.

Foundation Of The American College Of Healthcare Executives
1 North Franklin Street, Suite 1700
Chicago, IL 60606

182

Albert W. Smith Scholarships And The Alexander Treuhaft Scholarships

AMOUNT: Full Tuition **DEADLINE:** Feb 1
FIELDS/MAJORS: Science And Engineering

Six full-tuition scholarships offered to qualified applicants for admission as freshmen. Awards are renewable for each of the four years of undergraduate study, provided high academic achievement is achieved. Students must already be accepted into a science or engineering program at CWRU. Write to the address below for details.

Case Western Reserve University
Office Of Financial Aid, 109 Pardee Hall
10900 Euclid Avenue
Cleveland, OH 44106

183

Alberta E. Crowe Star Of Tomorrow Scholarship

AMOUNT: $1,000 **DEADLINE:** Jan 15
FIELDS/MAJORS: All Areas Of Study

Awards are available for females age 22 or under who are amateur bowlers. Must be at least a senior in high school or attending college. For bowlers in the ABC/WIBC/YABA leagues. Send SASE to the address below for more information.

Women's International Bowling Congress
Young American Bowling Alliance
5301 S. 76th St.
Greendale, WI 53129

184

Albuquerque Music Club

AMOUNT: Varies **DEADLINE:** Mar 1
FIELDS/MAJORS: Music

Awards are available at the University of New Mexico for music students. Based on talent and an audition. Must have a GPA of 3.0 or better. Write to the address below for more information.

University Of New Mexico, Albuquerque
Office Of Financial Aid
Albuquerque, NM 87131

185

Albuquerque Music Teachers' Association Scholarship

AMOUNT: Varies **DEADLINE:** Mar 1
FIELDS/MAJORS: Performing Or Composition Music

Awards are available at the University of New Mexico for music students seeking a degree in performance or composition. Must be a junior or senior. Performers are invited to perform a recital for the AMTA. Write to the address below for more information.

University Of New Mexico, Albuquerque
Office Of Financial Aid
Albuquerque, NM 87131

186

Albuquerque Press Club Endowment

AMOUNT: Varies **DEADLINE:** Mar 1
FIELDS/MAJORS: Journalism Or Communication

Awards are available at the University of New Mexico for students in the fields of journalism or communication who can demonstrate financial need. Write to the address listed below for information.

University Of New Mexico, Albuquerque
Office Of Financial Aid
Albuquerque, NM 87131

187

Albuquerque Professional Mortgage Women Scholarship

AMOUNT: Varies **DEADLINE:** Mar 1
FIELDS/MAJORS: Business, Finance

Awards are available at the University of New Mexico for students in the fields of business or finance. References are needed to be eligible. Write to the address below for more information.

University Of New Mexico, Albuquerque
Office Of Financial Aid
Albuquerque, NM 87131

188

Albuquerque Veterinary Association Scholarship

AMOUNT: Varies **DEADLINE:** Mar 1
FIELDS/MAJORS: Pre-Veterinary

Awards are available at the University of New Mexico for pre-veterinary students with a GPA of at least 3.0. Must be a resident of New Mexico. Write to the address below for more information.

University Of New Mexico, Albuquerque
Office Of Financial Aid
Albuquerque, NM 87131

189

Alden Undergraduate Fellowships In Systems Engineering

AMOUNT: $3,500 **DEADLINE:** Feb 1
FIELDS/MAJORS: Systems Engineering (Computer Science)

Scholarships for junior or senior undergraduates majoring in systems engineering at Case Western Reserve University. Applicants must have a minimum GPA of 3.2 for the last three semesters preceding the application. Write to the department of systems engineering at the address below for additional information and application procedures.

Case Western Reserve University
Office Of Financial Aid, 109 Pardee Hall
10900 Euclid Avenue
Cleveland, OH 44106

190

Alexander And Geraldine Wanek Graduate Scholarship

AMOUNT: Varies **DEADLINE:** Mar 1
FIELDS/MAJORS: Geological Resources

Awards are available at the University of New Mexico for graduate students studying geological resources with preference given to those concentrating in the area of leasable minerals. Write to the address below for more information.

University Of New Mexico, Albuquerque
Office Of Financial Aid
Albuquerque, NM 87131

191

Alf Van Hoose Endowed Scholarship

AMOUNT: $1,000 **DEADLINE:** Feb 15
FIELDS/MAJORS: Journalism

Renewable $1,000 award given to students at the University of Alabama pursuing a print journalism career. Priority given to freshmen. Full-time students only. Write to the address listed below for further information or an application.

University Of Alabama
College Of Communications
P.O. Box 870172
Tuscaloosa, AL 35487

192

Alfa Laval Agri, Inc. Scholarships

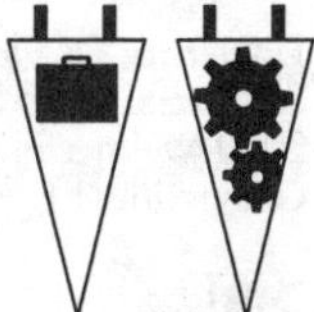

AMOUNT: $500-$1,000 **DEADLINE:** Feb 15
FIELDS/MAJORS: Agricultural Economics, Marketing and Engineering, Dairy Science

Scholarships are available for FFA members pursuing a four-year degree in one of the above areas. Write to the address below for details.

National FFA Foundation
Scholarship Office
P.O. Box 15160
Alexandria, VA 22309

193

Alfred C. Fones Scholarship

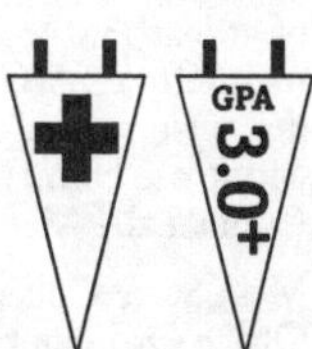

AMOUNT: Varies **DEADLINE:** Jun 1
FIELDS/MAJORS: Dental Hygiene Education

Scholarship for baccalaureate or graduate degree candidate who has completed their first year of study and intends to be a dental hygiene teacher. Must have a GPA of at least 3.0. Based on need. Write to the address below more information.

American Dental Hygienists' Association Institute For Oral Health
444 N. Michigan Ave., Suite 3400
Chicago, IL 60611

194

Alfred Grunsfeld Memorial Scholarship

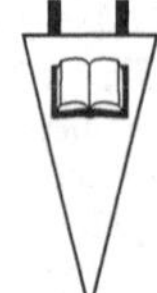

AMOUNT: Varies **DEADLINE:** Mar 1
FIELDS/MAJORS: History

Awards are available at the University of New Mexico for students majoring in history who can demonstrate financial need. Write to the address below for more information.

University Of New Mexico, Albuquerque
Office Of Financial Aid
Albuquerque, NM 87131

195

Alfred Jurzykowski Foundation Awards

AMOUNT: Varies **DEADLINE:** None Specified
FIELDS/MAJORS: All Areas Of Study

Awards for postdoctoral scholars of Polish heritage who have made significant achievements in their area of specialization. Individuals must be nominated by institutions or organizations in order to be considered for the award. Write to the address below for more information.

Cultural Advisory Committee
15 East 65th St.
New York, NY 10021

196

Alfred M. Kohn Memorial Scholarship

AMOUNT: $1,600 **DEADLINE:** Mar 1
FIELDS/MAJORS: Journalism

Must be a junior or senior majoring in journalism at the University of Florida. Must have at least a 2.8 GPA. Write to the address below for details.

University Of Florida
Scholarship and Placement Director
2070 Weimer Hall
Gainesville, FL 32611

197

Alfred Max Shideler, M.D. Scholarship Fund

AMOUNT: Tuition And Fees
DEADLINE: None Specified
FIELDS/MAJORS: Medicine And Engineering

Award for incoming freshman who intends to study medicine or engineering full-time. Must have a GPA of at least 3.0 to apply and to renew, recipient must maintain a 3.5 GPA or higher. Preference is given to students from rural high schools; in particular, those from Montrose county and other locations in west-central Colorado. Contact the Mesa State College Foundation for more details.

Mesa State College
Office Of Financial Aid
P.O. Box 2647
Grand Junction, CO 81501

198

Alice Allen Everett American Indian Scholarship

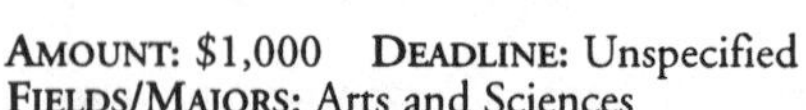

AMOUNT: $1,000 **DEADLINE:** Unspecified
FIELDS/MAJORS: Arts and Sciences

Student must be an incoming American Indian freshman at the University of Oklahoma, Norman. Student must be on the roll of a recognized Indian tribe or be a descendant of a relative who is on the roll. Student must have a GPA of 3.5 or better with preference given to those students entering the medical field. Write to the address listed below for information.

University Of Oklahoma, Norman
College Of Arts And Sciences
601 Elm, Room 429
Norman, OK 73019

199

Alice E. Healy Art Student Scholarship Fund

AMOUNT: Varies **DEADLINE:** Feb 1
FIELDS/MAJORS: Art

Scholarships are available at the University of Hawaii, Hilo for full-time art students. Write to the address listed below for information.

University Of Hawaii At Hilo
Financial Aid Office
200 West Kawili Street
Hilo, HI 96720

200

Alice E. Smith Fellowship

AMOUNT: $2,000 **DEADLINE:** Jul 15
FIELDS/MAJORS: American History

An outright grant for any woman doing research in american history. Preference will be given to graduate research on the history of the Middle West or Wisconsin. Applicants should submit four copies of a two-page, single-spaced letter of application describing her training in historical research and summarize her current project. Write to the address below for details.

State Historical Society Of Wisconsin
State Historian
816 State St.
Madison, WI 53706

201

Alice Fisher Society Historical Scholarship

AMOUNT: $2,500 **DEADLINE:** Dec 31
FIELDS/MAJORS: Nursing

Awards for master's or doctoral level nursing students at the University of Pennsylvania. Recipients will spend four to six weeks using the collections of the Center for the Study of the History of Nursing to benefit their research project. Write to the address below for more information.

University Of Pennsylvania
School Of Nursing
307 Nursing Education Bldg.
Philadelphia, PA 19104

202

Alice Sowers Scholarship

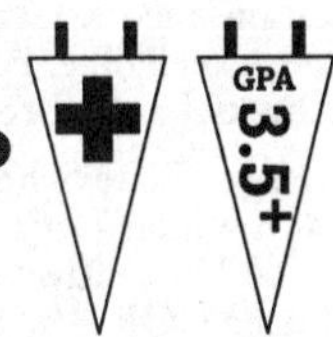

AMOUNT: $250 **DEADLINE:** Fall
FIELDS/MAJORS: Nursing

Scholarships are available at the University of Oklahoma, Norman for full-time nursing students, with a minimum GPA of 3.7. Write to the address listed below for information.

University Of Oklahoma, Norman
College Of Nursing
P.O. Box 26901
Oklahoma City, OK 73190

203

Alice T. Schafer Mathematics Prize

AMOUNT: None Specified **DEADLINE:** Apr 1
FIELDS/MAJORS: Mathematics

Awards are available for undergraduate female mathematics majors who show a high level of academic ability and a real interest in mathematics. Must be nominated by a faculty member. Write to the address listed below for information.

Association For Women In Mathematics
Alice T. Schafer Award Selection Committee
U Of Md., 4114 Computer and Space Science Bldg.
College Park, MD 20742

204

Alice Thomas Motts Trust Scholarships

AMOUNT: Varies **DEADLINE:** Mar 15
FIELDS/MAJORS: All Areas Of Study

Scholarships are available for Chicago residents or students who have completed at least one year of study in an accredited Chicago area college or university. Write to the address below for details.

Alpha Kappa Alpha Educational Advancement Foundation
5656 S. Stony Island Avenue
Chicago, IL 60637

205

All-College Scholarship Program

AMOUNT: $1,000-$2,000 **DEADLINE:** Nov 30
FIELDS/MAJORS: All Areas Of Study

Must hold an AAL certificate of membership in his or her own name before application deadline during senior year. Must submit SAT or ACT score, be in the top 10% of the graduating class, and intend to earn bachelor's degree. 325 scholarships renewable. 500 scholarships not renewable. Write to the address below for complete details.

Aid Association For Lutherans
Attn: AAL Scholarships
4321 N. Ballard Rd.
Appleton, WI 54915

206

All-Teke Academic Team Recognition & John A. Courson Top Scholar Award

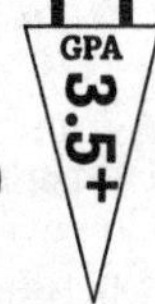

AMOUNT: $100-$1,000 **DEADLINE:** Feb 15
FIELDS/MAJORS: All Areas Of Study

Applicants must have senior year, full-time student status and a GPA of 3.5 or above the all men's average. They must also be an active member, in good standing, with their chapter of TKE. Write to the address below for more information.

TKE Educational Foundation
8645 Founders Rd.
Indianapolis, IN 46268

207

Allen & Hanburys (Glaxo) Scholarship

AMOUNT: $1,000 **DEADLINE:** Feb 1
FIELDS/MAJORS: Pharmacy

Scholarships are available at the University of Utah for full-time second-year pharmacy majors, with demonstrated academic ability, leadership skills, and participation in school/community activities. Write to the address below for details.

University Of Utah
College Of Pharmacy
Office Of Student Affairs
Salt Lake City, UT 84112

208

Allen Harris, Jr., Carl A. Jones Endowments

AMOUNT: None Specified **DEADLINE:** None Specified
FIELDS/MAJORS: All Areas Of Study

Scholarships for students at ETSU in an honors program. Contact the office of financial aid or the honors program office at ETSU.

East Tennessee State University
Office Of Financial Aid
Box 70722
Johnson City, TN 37614

209

Allflex U.S.A., Inc. Scholarships

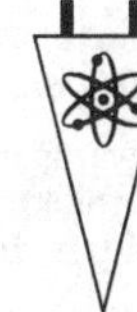

AMOUNT: $1,000 **DEADLINE:** Feb 15
FIELDS/MAJORS: Animal Science

Scholarships are available for FFA members pursuing a four-year degree in animal science. Two awards are offered annually. Write to the address below for details.

National FFA Foundation
Scholarship Office
P.O. Box 15160
Alexandria, VA 22309

210

Allie Raney Hunt Memorial Scholarship Award

AMOUNT: $250-$1,000 **DEADLINE:** Apr 15
FIELDS/MAJORS: All Areas Of Study

Applicants must be born deaf or became deaf before acquiring language. Must use speech/residual hearing or lip-reading as primary communication and be a student entering or attending a college or university program for hearing students. One award per year. Write to the address below for complete details.

Alexander Graham Bell Association For The Deaf
3417 Volta Place, NW
Washington, DC 20007

211

Allied Health Scholarship

AMOUNT: Varies **DEADLINE:** None Specified
FIELDS/MAJORS: Nursing, Lab Or Radiology

Awards for residents of the South Lake tax district who are studying in one of the fields above. Based on academics, interview, and recommendations. Recipients must return to South Lake Memorial Hospital for full-time employment upon graduation. Write to the address below for more information.

South Lake Memorial Hospital
Director Of Personnel
Clermont, FL 34711

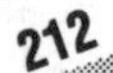

212

Allied Health Student Loan-for-Service

AMOUNT: $12,000 (max) **DEADLINE:** Jul 1
FIELDS/MAJORS: See Below

Loans for students who are studying the following areas of health: physical therapy, occupational therapy, speech-language pathology, audiology, pharmacy, nutrition, respiratory care practice, laboratory technology, radiologic technology, mental health services, or emergency medical services. Applicants must be New Mexico residents doing postgraduate study in New Mexico. Write to the address below for more information. Loans will be forgiven if the student works in a shortage area upon graduation.

New Mexico Commission On Higher Education
1068 Cerrillos Rd.
Santa Fe, NM 87501

213

Allstate Foundation Scholarships

AMOUNT: Varies **DEADLINE:** Open
FIELDS/MAJORS: Nursing

Awards for Native American Indians and Alaska natives who are enrolled in an accredited nursing degree program. Write to the address below for more information.

American Indian/Alaskan Native Nurses Association
Scholarship Coordinator
P.O. Box 1588
Norman, OK 73070

214

Alpha Delta Kappa Scholarship

AMOUNT: $400 **DEADLINE:** Apr 15
FIELDS/MAJORS: Education

Awards are available for female students from Ohio who are planning to enter the field of education. Must have financial need and a GPA of at least 3.0. Write to the address below for more information.

Alpha Delta Kappa Educational Sorority, Beta Gamma Chapter
ADK Scholarship Committee
1917 Yorktown Court
Lancaster, OH 43130

215

Alpha Delta Kappa Scholarships

AMOUNT: None Specified **DEADLINE:** Mar 1
FIELDS/MAJORS: Education (Elementary, Secondary)

Scholarships for senior or fifth-year elementary or secondary education majors. Graduate students leading to a teaching certificate are also eligible. For Oregon residents only. Contact your college financial aid office, or write to the address below for details.

Oregon State Scholarship Commission
Attn: Grant Department
1500 Valley River Dr., #100
Eugene, OR 97401

216

Alpha Mu Gamma Scholarships

AMOUNT: $500 **DEADLINE:** Jan 10
FIELDS/MAJORS: Foreign Languages

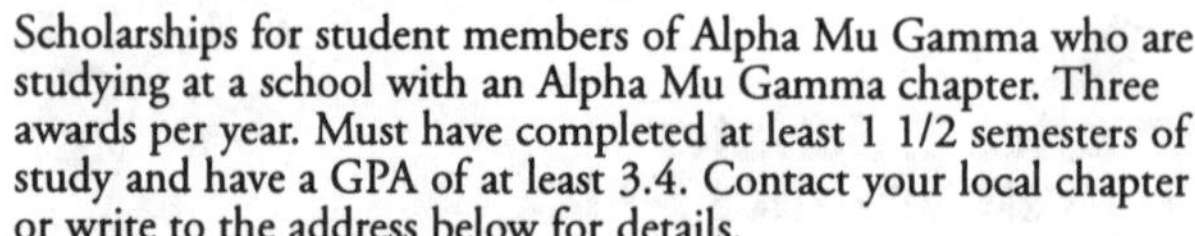

Scholarships for student members of Alpha Mu Gamma who are studying at a school with an Alpha Mu Gamma chapter. Three awards per year. Must have completed at least 1 1/2 semesters of study and have a GPA of at least 3.4. Contact your local chapter or write to the address below for details.

Alpha Mu Gamma National
Los Angeles City College
855 N. Vermont Ave.
Los Angeles, CA 90029

217

Alpha Phi Alpha Fraternity Scholarship

AMOUNT: $150 **DEADLINE:** Mar 2
FIELDS/MAJORS: All Areas Of Study

Essay contest for Cal Poly Pomona students on the topic, "What is the role of the African American student at Cal Poly Pomona." Contact the Alpha Phi Alpha Fraternity, Inc., at 490, Box 784, Pomona, CA 91769 for more details.

California State Polytechnic University, Pomona
Office Of Financial Aid
3801 West Temple Ave.
Pomona, CA 91768

218

Alpha Phi Scholarship

AMOUNT: $7,000 **DEADLINE:** None Specified
FIELDS/MAJORS: All Areas Of Study

Preference of award given to descendants of alumnae of Beta Kappa chapter of Alpha Phi. Open to all admitted freshman who demonstrate financial need. Criteria is based on academic performance and potential. Write to the address below for details.

Denison University
Financial Aid Office
Box M
Granville, OH 43023

219

Alphonso Deal Scholarship Award

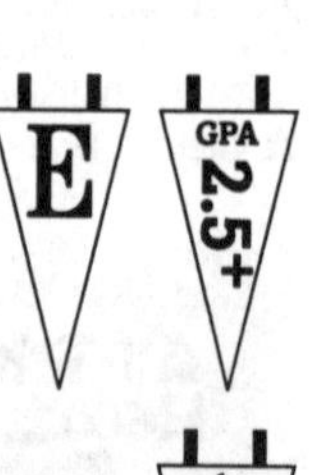

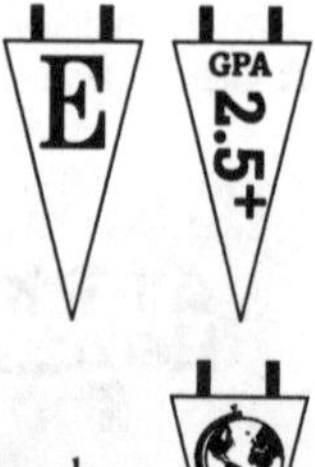

AMOUNT: None Specified **DEADLINE:** Jun 1
FIELDS/MAJORS: Law Enforcement, Criminal Justice

Scholarships for graduating high school seniors who plan to attend a two-year college or a university and study law enforcement or a related field. Must be a U.S. citizen. Based on character, transcripts, and recommendation.

Write to the address below for details.

National Black Police Association
NBPA Scholarship Award
3251 Mt. Pleasant Street, NW
Washington, DC 20010

220 ALTA Endowment Fund Travel Fellowships

AMOUNT: $750 **DEADLINE:** Jun 30
FIELDS/MAJORS: Translation

Awards are available for outstanding students or beginning translators who would interested in attending the ALTA conference in Austin, TX. Write to the address below for more information.

American Literary Translators Association
UTD, MC35
P.O. Box 830688
Richardson, TX 75083

221 Altar (Augie J.) Scholarship

AMOUNT: $500 **DEADLINE:** May 31
FIELDS/MAJORS: Medical, Psychology, Agricultural, and Horticultural Fields

Scholarship for undergraduate students of Lithuanian descent from Illinois. Must have at least a 2.0 GPA. Must be enrolled or accepted to an accredited college or university. Financial need is a major consideration. Write to the address below and include an SASE for details. Requests for applications must be mailed by Apr 8.

Augie J. Altar Scholarship
7115 W. 91st St.
Bridgeview, IL 60455

222 Alumni Association Minority Scholarship

AMOUNT: Varies **DEADLINE:** None Specified
FIELDS/MAJORS: All Areas Of Study

Awards for minority juniors at UMass for use during their senior year of study. Must demonstrate a high level of motivation and potential for leadership. Contact the Alumni Relations Office, not the address below for more information.

University Of Massachusetts–Amherst
Office Of Financial Aid Services
255 Whitmore Administration Bldg.
Box 38230
Amherst, MA 01003

223 Alumni Association Scholarship

AMOUNT: Varies **DEADLINE:** Mar 15
FIELDS/MAJORS: All Areas Of Study

Awards open to Teikyo post juniors enrolled in a bachelor's degree program with a GPA of at least 3.25. Renewable. Write to the address below for more information.

Teikyo Post University
Office Of Financial Aid
800 Country Club Road
Waterbury, CT 06723

224 Alumni Association Scholarships

AMOUNT: $750 **DEADLINE:** Mar 1
FIELDS/MAJORS: All Areas Of Study

Awards are available at Plymouth State for junior or seniors in any area of study. Five awards are offered yearly. Write to the address listed below for information.

Plymouth State College
Director Of Alumni Relations
Plymouth, NH 03264

225 Alumni Chapter-at-Large Grant

AMOUNT: $500 **DEADLINE:** Dec 15
FIELDS/MAJORS: Home Economics/Related Fields

Applicants must be Kappa Omicron Nu members. Awarded annually as a project of the alumni chapter-at-large. Write to the address below for details.

Kappa Omicron Nu Honor Society
4990 Northwind Dr., Suite 140
East Lansing, MI 48823

226 Alumni Fund Scholarship

AMOUNT: $500 **DEADLINE:** Feb 29
FIELDS/MAJORS: Management

Scholarships are awarded to one sophomore and above level and one to a graduate level student on the basis of financial need. Write to the SOM Development Office, Room 206, for more information.

University Of Massachusetts, Amherst
SOM Development Office, Room 206
Amherst, MA 01003

227 Alumni Honor Awards

AMOUNT: 50% Tuition **DEADLINE:** May 1
FIELDS/MAJORS: All Areas Of Study

Awards for freshmen who are from South Carolina who rank in the top 25% of their class and have a minimum SAT score of 1000. Write to the address below for more information.

Winthrop University
Financial Resource Center
119 Tillman Hall
Rock Hill, SC 29733

228 Alumni Journalism Scholarship

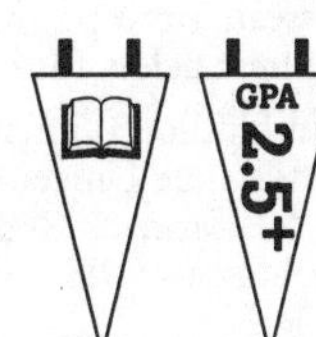

AMOUNT: $500 **DEADLINE:** Mar 1
FIELDS/MAJORS: Journalism

Must be a student majoring in journalism at the University of Florida or planning a career in the newspaper industry. Must have a GPA of at least 2.8. Write to the address below for details.

University Of Florida
Scholarship & Placement Director
2070 Weimer Hall
Gainesville, FL 32611

229

Alumni Leadership Scholarship

AMOUNT: $300 **DEADLINE:** Mar 2
FIELDS/MAJORS: All Areas Of Study

Scholarships are available at the University of California, Berkeley for entering freshmen and transfer students with a GPA of at least 3.3, demonstrated academic ability, and an essay. Must be a U.S. citizen or permanent resident. Write to the address below for complete details.

University Of California, Berkeley
Office Of Financial Aid
Room 211, Sproul Hall
Berkeley, CA 94720

230

GPA 2.5+

Alumni Past Presidents Scholarship

AMOUNT: $3,500 **DEADLINE:** Mar 1
FIELDS/MAJORS: All Areas Of Study

Scholarship for entering freshmen with outstanding academic potential. Renewable for three years. For South Carolina residents. Contact the financial aid office at the address below for details.

Clemson University
Financial Aid Office
G01 Sikes Hall
Clemson, SC 29634

231

Alumni Regional Scholarship

AMOUNT: $500-$1,000 **DEADLINE:** Feb 15
FIELDS/MAJORS: All Areas Of Study

Scholarships are available to Nazareth College for full-time undergraduate students who reside in an area where an alumni committee exists. Applicant must be a U.S. citizen. Write to the address below for details.

Nazareth College
Office Of Financial Aid
4245 East Avenue
Rochester, NY 14618

232

Alumni Research Grant

AMOUNT: $2,000 **DEADLINE:** Mar 1
FIELDS/MAJORS: Home Economics And Related

Grants awarded bi-annually for postgraduate research by members of Phi U. Studies need not lead to an advanced degree. Based on use of funds, research question, and personal qualifications. Research prospectus must accompany application. Write to the address below for details.

Phi Upsilon Omicron National Office
Ohio State University, 171 Mount Hall
1050 Carmack Road
Columbus, OH 43210

233

GPA 3.5+

Alumni Scholars Program, University Scholars Program

AMOUNT: $1,000 **DEADLINE:** May 4
FIELDS/MAJORS: All Areas Of Study

Scholarships are available at the University of Oklahoma, Norman for entering freshmen who are graduating high school seniors with a minimum GPA of 3.75. Forty to fifty awards offered annually. Write to the address listed below for information.

University Of Oklahoma, Norman
Honors Program
347 Cate Center Drive
Norman, OK 73019

234

Alumni Scholarship

AMOUNT: $5,000 **DEADLINE:** Feb 1
FIELDS/MAJORS: All Areas Of Study

Scholarships for students at Denison University. Based on superior academic performance and potential. Open to all incoming freshmen who are deemed to be high achievers. Contact the office of admissions or the financial aid office at the address below for details.

Denison University
Financial Aid Office
Box M
Granville, OH 43023

235

Alumni Scholarship

AMOUNT: $1,500 **DEADLINE:** Mar 31
FIELDS/MAJORS: All Areas Of Study

Awards for entering freshman who rank in the upper 20% of their class, have an ACT composite of 24 or above, and demonstrate involvement in community and school activities. Must demonstrate financial need. Renewable with a GPA of at least 3.25. Write to the address below for more details.

Southwest Missouri State University
Financial Aid Office
901 South National Ave.
Springfield, MO 65804

236

Alumni Scholarships

AMOUNT: $1,000 **DEADLINE:** None Specified
FIELDS/MAJORS: All Areas Of Study

Scholarships for entering freshmen and transfers at East Tennessee State University. Renewable. Contact the financial aid office at the address below for details.

East Tennessee State University
Office Of Financial Aid
Box 70722
Johnson City, TN 37614

237

Alumni Scholarships

AMOUNT: Varies **DEADLINE:** Mar 10
FIELDS/MAJORS: All Areas Of Study

Scholarships for upperclass/graduate and freshmen or transfer students with a GPA of 2.5 or better. Must be in top 25% of high school class and be involved in extracurricular activities. Write to the address below for details.

University Of Missouri, Columbia
MU Alumni Association
123 Reynolds Alumni And Vistor Center
Columbia, MO 65211

238
Alumni Scholarships

GPA 3.0+

Amount: $200-$1,000 **Deadline:** Mar 2
Fields/Majors: All Areas Of Study

Awards for Holy Names students who have demonstrated academic merit. Renewable with a GPA of at least 3.0. Preference is given to relatives of alumni. Write to the address below for more information.

Holy Names College
Financial Aid Office
3500 Mountain Blvd.
Oakland, CA 94619

239
Alumni Scholarships—SUNY At Albany

Amount: $100-$600 **Deadline:** None Specified
Fields/Majors: All Areas Of Study

Awards to SUNY at Albany students who demonstrate both academic achievement and financial need. Write to the address below for more information.

State University Of New York, Albany
Administration Building, Room 152
1400 Washington Ave.
Albany, NY 12222

240
Alumni Society Of Christopher Newport University Scholarship

GPA 3.0+

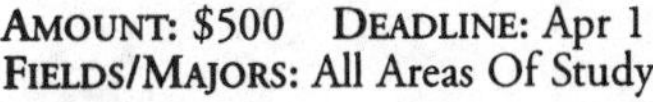

Amount: $500 **Deadline:** Apr 1
Fields/Majors: All Areas Of Study

Awards for students who are full-time juniors or seniors with a GPA of at least 3.0. Financial need is also considered. Write to the address below for more information.

Christopher Newport University
Office Of Financial Aid
50 Shoe Lane
Newport News, VA 23606

241
Alumni, Presidential And Dudley Academic Scholarships

GPA 3.5+

Amount: $2,100 **Deadline:** Mar 1
Fields/Majors: All Areas Of Study

Scholarships for high school seniors who have an ACT score of at least 29 and a GPA of at least 3.5. Non-renewable. Write to the address below for more information.

Auburn University
Office Of Student Financial Aid
203 Martin Hall
Auburn University, AL 36849

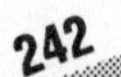

242
Alvan T. & Viola D. Fuller Research Fellowships

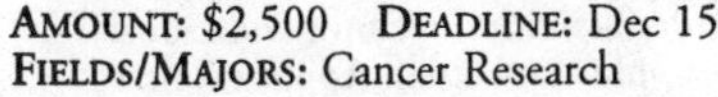

Amount: $2,500 **Deadline:** Dec 15
Fields/Majors: Cancer Research

Summer fellowships for students who are interested in cancer

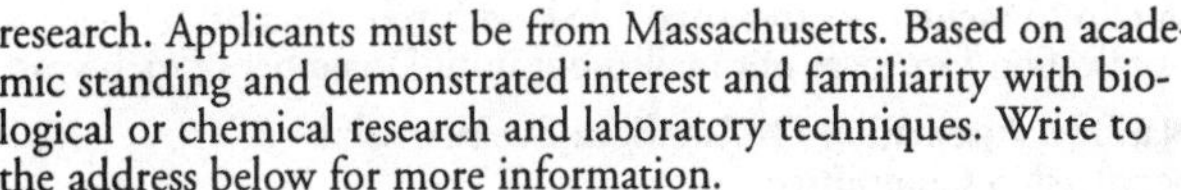

research. Applicants must be from Massachusetts. Based on academic standing and demonstrated interest and familiarity with biological or chemical research and laboratory techniques. Write to the address below for more information.

American Cancer Society, Massachusetts Division
Fuller Committee
247 Commonwealth Ave.
Boston, MA 02116

243
Alvie Reddin Memorial Scholarship

Amount: Varies **Deadline:** None Specified
Fields/Majors: Art

Awards for Mesa State students majoring in art. Contact the school of humanities and social sciences for more information.

Mesa State College
Office Of Financial Aid
P.O. Box 3692
Grand Junction, CO 81501

244
Alvin E. Heaps Memorial Scholarship

Amount: None Specified **Deadline:** Jul 1
Fields/Majors: All Areas Of Study

Scholarship available to all RWDSU members, their spouses, or their children. Write to Stuart Appelbaum, Alvin E. Heaps Memorial Scholarship Committee, at the address below for more information.

Retail, Wholesale and Department Store Union
30 E. 29th St.
New Yor, NY 10016

245
Alvin Terrell Dixon Memorial Scholarship

GPA 3.0+

Amount: $500-$1,000
Deadline: None Specified
Fields/Majors: Arts And Sciences

Scholarships are available at the University of Oklahoma, Norman for students in the college of arts and sciences who are older than the traditional freshman-senior year student. Minimum GPA of 3.25 required. Write to the address listed below for information.

University Of Oklahoma, Norman
College Of Arts And Sciences
601 Elm, Room 429
Norman, OK 73019

246
Ambucs Scholarships For Therapists

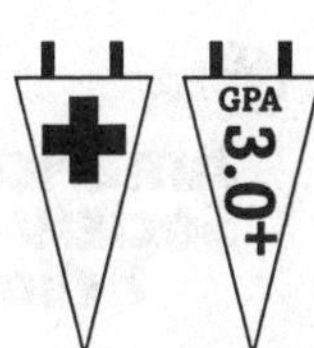

GPA 3.0+

Amount: $300-$1,000 **Deadline:** Apr 15
Fields/Majors: All Types Of Therapy, Audiology, Special Education

Candidates must be U.S. citizens, prove financial need, document good scholastic standing (min GPA: 3.0), and be accepted at the junior or senior undergraduate or graduate level in an accredited therapy program in one of the above areas of study. Assistant programs are not eligible. Write to the address below for details. Be certain to include a letter-sized SASE with your request. Application forms are not mailed out until December of each year.

National Association Of American Business Clubs
Scholarship Committee
P.O. Box 5127
High Point, NC 27262

247

Amelia Earhart Fellowship Awards

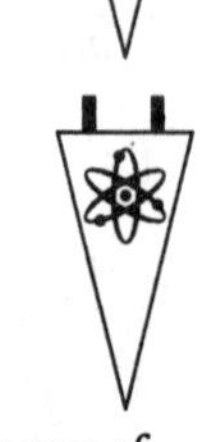
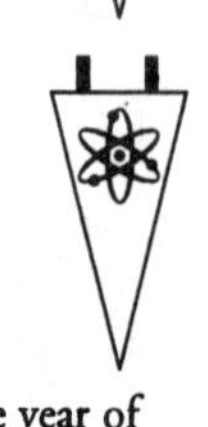
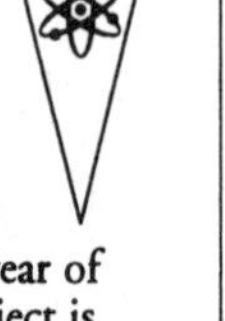

Amount: $6,000 **Deadline:** Nov 1
Fields/Majors: Aerospace Engineering and Related Sciences

Graduate fellowships for women. Must have a bachelor's degree in science as preparation for graduate work in aerospace sciences. Must be women of exceptional ability and character. Approximately forty fellowships per year. Renewable once (or twice in exceptional cases). Completion of one year of graduate school or well-defined research on a specific project is required. Write to the address below for details.

Zonta International Foundation
Amelia Earhart Fellowships
557 W. Randolph Street
Chicago, IL 60661

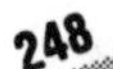

248

America's Junior Miss National Scholarship Awards

Amount: $1,000-$30,000 **Deadline:** None Specified
Fields/Majors: All Areas Of Study

Scholarships are available for the winner, finalists, and other select contestants in the America's Junior Miss competition. Applicants must be high school seniors who demonstrate scholastic excellence and future potential for outstanding contribution to society. Applicants must never have been married and be U.S. citizens. Write to the address listed below for information.

America's Junior Miss Program
P.O. Box 2786
Mobile, AL 36652

249

American Action Fund Scholarship

Amount: $10,000 **Deadline:** Mar 31
Fields/Majors: All Areas Of Study

Award recipient must be legally blind student. Based upon academic ability. Write to the address below for details.

National Federation Of The Blind
Mrs. Peggy Elliott, Chairman
814 Fourth Ave., Suite 200
Grinnell, IA 50112

250

American Antiquarian Society–Newberry Library Fellowships

Amount: $800 Per Month **Deadline:** Jan 20
Fields/Majors: American & European History, Literature, Humanities, Cartography

Fellowships for scholars who could benefit from access to the Newberry's collections or the American Antiquarian Society. Applicants must possess Ph.D. or have completed all requirements except the dissertation. Award amount is paid monthly. Write to the committee at the address below for details.

Newberry Library
Committee On Awards
60 W. Walton St.
Chicago, IL 60610

251

American Association For Geodetic Surveying And Joseph F. Dracup Award

Amount: $2,000 **Deadline:** Dec 15
Fields/Majors: Surveying, Cartography

Awards for undergraduate students committed to a career in cartography. Write to the address below for complete details.

American Congress On Surveying And Mapping
ACSM Awards Director
5410 Grosvenor Lane, Suite 100
Bethesda, MD 20814

252

American Association Of Family And Consumer Sciences

Amount: None Specified **Deadline:** Dec 30
Fields/Majors: Family And Consumer Sciences

Scholarships are awarded to support graduate study in the field of family and consumer sciences. Write to the address below for more information.

American Association Of Family And Consumer Sciences
Fellowships, Awards And Grants Program
1555 King St.
Alexandria, VA 22314

253

American Association Of University Women Scholarships

Amount: $500 **Deadline:** Feb 1
Fields/Majors: All Areas Of Study

Awards for female residents of Livermore, Pleasanton, Dublin, or Sunol who have junior or senior standing at an accredited four-year college or university. Must have financial need and demonstrated academic achievement. Write to the address below for more information.

American Association Of University Women, Pleasanton, CA
Ms. Marilyn Foreman, Scholarship Coordinator
1167 Kottinger Dr.
Pleasanton, CA 94566

254

American Board Of Funeral Service Education National Scholarships

Amount: $250-$500 **Deadline:** Mar 15, Sep 15
Fields/Majors: Funeral Service, Mortuary Science

Applicants must be enrolled in an accredited ABFSE program and a U.S. citizen. Must have completed at least one term of study and have at least one remaining before graduation. Based on need, academics, extracurricular activities, recommendations, and the articulateness of the application itself. Applications are available from each American Board school or write to the address below for details. If writing, please indicate what school you are attending.

American Board Of Funeral Service Education
Scholarship Committee
P.O. Box 1305, #316
Brunswick, ME 04011

255 American Business Women's Assoc. (Santa Fe Trail Chapter) Scholarship

AMOUNT: None Specified **DEADLINE:** Mar 1
FIELDS/MAJORS: Business

Scholarships are available at the University of New Mexico for full-time undergraduate female business majors who reside in the Santa Fe area. Write to the address listed below for information.

University Of New Mexico, Albuquerque
Department Of Student Financial Aid
Mesa Vista Hall North
Albuquerque, NM 87131

256 American Business Women's Association Scholarship

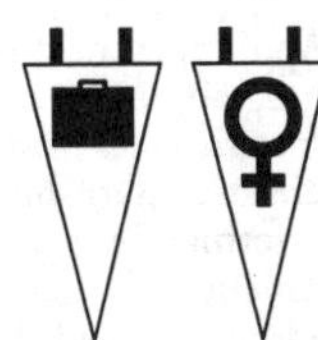

AMOUNT: Varies **DEADLINE:** None Specified
FIELDS/MAJORS: Business

Awards for Mesa State business students at the undergraduate level. Based on financial need, scholastic ability, and character. Write to the address below for more details and an application.

Mesa State College
Office Of Financial Aid
P.O. Box 2647
Grand Junction, CO 81501

257 American Business Women's Association, Nani' O Hilo Scholarship

AMOUNT: Varies **DEADLINE:** Feb 1
FIELDS/MAJORS: All Areas Of Study

Scholarships are available at the University of Hawaii, Hilo for full-time female students at the junior, senior, or graduate level of study. Write to the address listed below for information.

University Of Hawaii At Hilo
Ms. Bernadette V. Baker, ABWA
134 Kimo Place
Hilo, HI 96720

258 American Business Women's Association, Sun & Surf Chapter Scholarship

AMOUNT: $500-$1,500 **DEADLINE:** None Specified
FIELDS/MAJORS: All Areas Of Study

Scholarships are available for Sarasota county women who demonstrate financial need and academic ability. Write to the address listed below for information.

American Business Women's Association—Sun & Surf Chapter
P.O. Box 117
Nokomis, FL 34274

259 American Business Women's Association, Sunset Chapter Scholarship

AMOUNT: $100-$1,000 **DEADLINE:** None Specified
FIELDS/MAJORS: All Areas Of Study

Scholarships are available for Sarasota or Manatee County women who demonstrate financial need and have a GPA of at least 2.5. Must be a U.S. citizen. Write to the address listed below for information.

American Business Women's Association–Sunset Chapter
Nancy Cooke, Education Chairwoman
905 68th Avenue Drive West
Bradenton, FL 34207

260 American Cancer Society Scholarships

AMOUNT: $2,250 **DEADLINE:** Apr 10
FIELDS/MAJORS: All Areas Of Study

Awards for Florida residents who are U.S. citizens and have had a diagnosis of cancer before age 21. Must demonstrate financial need. Write to the address below for more information.

American Cancer Society—Florida Division, Inc.
Scholarship Coordinator
3709 W. Jelton Ave.
Tampa, FL 33629

261 American Cartographic Association Scholarship

AMOUNT: $1,000 **DEADLINE:** Dec 15
FIELDS/MAJORS: Cartography/Surveying

The purpose of the award is to provide financial assistance to persons pursuing a full-time course of graduate study in cartography or a related field. Recipients will be chosen by a fellowship awards committee. Must be a junior or senior undergraduate. For additional information, contact the address below.

American Congress On Surveying And Mapping
ACSM Awards Director
5410 Grosvenor Lane, Suite 100
Bethesda, MD 20814

262 American College Of Healthcare Executives MHA Scholarships

AMOUNT: $3,000 **DEADLINE:** Mar 1
FIELDS/MAJORS: Health

Awards for minority and handicapped students who enroll in a full-time accredited MHA program. Write to the address below for more information.

American College Of Healthcare Executives
840 North Lake Shore Dr.
Chicago, IL 60611

263 American College Of Musicians Scholarships

AMOUNT: $100 **DEADLINE:** None Specified
FIELDS/MAJORS: Music Performance

Must have entered guild auditions, received the Paderewski

Medal, and performed the high school diploma program. Winners are selected by auditions. 150 awards per year. Applications are available from your teacher, or write to the address below for details.

American College Of Musicians
808 Rio Grande
Box 1807
Austin, TX 78767

264

American Concrete Institute–Oregon Chapter

Amount: $500 **Deadline:** May 1
Fields/Majors: Engineering–Concrete Technology

Award for students enrolled at least nine hours with a GPA of 2.5 or better. Based on financial need, GPA, residency/citizenship, enrollment in an applicable program, and contribution in the field of concrete technology. Contact the civil engineering department for more information.

Portland State University
Civil Engineering Department
138 Science Building 2
Portland, OR 97207

265

American Concrete Institute Scholarships

Amount: $3,000 **Deadline:** Jan 15
Fields/Majors: Engineering, Construction, Material Science, Etc.

Graduate fellowships for first- or second-year students in engineering, architectural, and/or material science programs in the area of concrete where design, materials, construction (or combination of these) are studied. Membership in the American Concrete Institute is not required. Write to the address below for details. Awards offered are the Katharine and Bryant Mather Fellowship (one award), ACI-W.R. Grace fellowship (one award), the ACI Fellowships (two awards), and the V. Mohan Malhotra Fellowship (one award) only one application is required to apply for all of the above awards.

American Concrete Institute
Director Of Education
P.O. Box 19150
Detroit, MI 48219

266

American Council Of Independent Laboratories, Inc. Scholarships

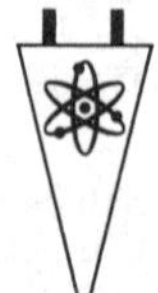

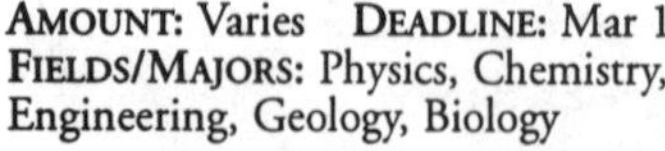

Amount: Varies **Deadline:** Mar 1
Fields/Majors: Physics, Chemistry, Engineering, Geology, Biology

Awards are available at the University of New Mexico for women in their junior year of study in one of the fields listed above. Contact: 11665 Sunset Loop, Bainbridge Island, WA 98110, for more details.

University Of New Mexico, Albuquerque
Office Of Financial Aid
Albuquerque, NM 87131

267

American Cyanamid Scholarships

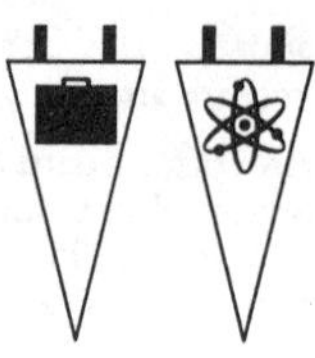

Amount: $1,000 **Deadline:** Feb 15
Fields/Majors: Agriculture, Agribusiness

Scholarships are available for FFA members pursuing a four-year degree in one of the above areas. Write to the address below for details.

National FFA Foundation
Scholarship Office
P.O. Box 15160
Alexandria, VA 22309

268

American Dietetic Association Programs

Amount: $400-$5,000 **Deadline:** Jan 15
Fields/Majors: Dietetics/Nutrition

Applicants must be enrolled in an advanced degree program. Must be a U.S. citizen. Some scholarships require specific areas of study. Includes the graduate scholarships, dietetic internships, and preprofessional practice program. Information is published annually in the Journal of the American Dietetic Association. Alternately, write to the address below for details.

American Dietetic Association Foundation
216 W. Jackson St., Suite 800
Chicago, IL 60606

269

American Drug Stores Minority Scholarship

Amount: $6,500 (max) **Deadline:** Feb 1
Fields/Majors: Pharmacy

Scholarships are available at the University of Utah for full-time minority entering freshmen pharmacy majors. Award is spread over a three-year period. Write to the address below for details.

University Of Utah
College Of Pharmacy
Office Of Student Affairs
Salt Lake City, UT 84112

270

American Electroplater And Surface Refinishers Society Award

Amount: Varies **Deadline:** Mar 1
Fields/Majors: Metallurgy; Metallurgical, Chemical, or Environmental Engineering

Awards are available at the University of New Mexico for undergraduates in one of the fields listed above or in the fields of materials science or engineering chemistry. Based on achievement, scholarship potential, motivation, and interest in the finishing technologies. Write to the address below for more information.

University Of New Mexico, Albuquerque
Office Of Financial Aid
Albuquerque, NM 87131

271 American Family Insurance Company Scholarships

AMOUNT: $1,000 **DEADLINE:** Feb 15
FIELDS/MAJORS: All Areas Of Study

Scholarships are available for FFA members pursuing a four-year degree in any field. Applicant must reside in Wisconsin, Missouri or Minnesota. Three awards will be offered. Write to the address below for details.

National FFA Foundation
Scholarship Office
P.O. Box 15160
Alexandria, VA 22309

272 American Federal Bank Scholarships

AMOUNT: $500 **DEADLINE:** Mar 1
FIELDS/MAJORS: Financial Management

Award for juniors studying financial management. Based on character and potential for contributions to the field of financial management. Award is nonrenewable. Transfer students must have completed one full-time semester at Clemson. Minimum GPA 2.5. Write for complete details.

Clemson University
Financial Aid Office
G01 Sikes Hall
Clemson, SC 29634

273 American Fellowships–Postdoctoral or Dissertation

AMOUNT: $5,000-$25,000 **DEADLINE:** Nov 15
FIELDS/MAJORS: All Areas Of Study

Fellowships for postdoctoral or dissertation research for female scholars. Must be a citizen or permanent resident of the United States. Available for the summer as well as the school year. One-year fellowships and summer programs start June 1. Write to the address below for complete details.

American Association Of University Women
Educational Foundation
2201 N. Dodge Street
Iowa City, IA 52243

274 American Floral Endowment Scholarships

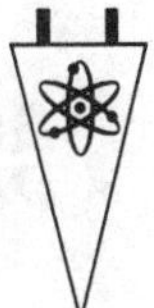

AMOUNT: $1,000 **DEADLINE:** Feb 15
FIELDS/MAJORS: Floriculture, Environmental Horticulture

Scholarships are available for FFA members pursuing a four-year degree in floriculture or environmental horticulture. Write to the address below for details.

National FFA Foundation
Scholarship Office
P.O. Box 15160
Alexandria, VA 22309

275 American Foundation For Vision Awareness Educational Grant

AMOUNT: $1,000 **DEADLINE:** Feb 1
FIELDS/MAJORS: Optometry

Scholarships for students studying optometric education. Must be a U.S. citizen. Write to the address below for more information.

American Foundation For Vision Awareness Research Grant
Huck Roberts, Executive Director
243 North Lindbergh Blvd.
St. Louis, MO 63141

276 American Foundation For Vision Awareness Research Grant

AMOUNT: $6,000 (max) **DEADLINE:** None Specified
FIELDS/MAJORS: Optometry

To assist on projects concerning children's vision and how it relates to the learning process. Must be a U.S. citizen. Write to the address below for more information.

American Foundation For Vision Awareness Research Grant
Huck Roberts, Executive Director
243 North Lindbergh Blvd.
St. Louis, MO 63141

277 American Helicopter Society Awards

AMOUNT: $2,000 **DEADLINE:** None Specified
FIELDS/MAJORS: Engineering

Awards are available for graduate students and Ph.D. candidates pursuing engineering degrees. Write to the address below for more information.

American Helicopter Society
217 N. Washington St.
Alexandria, VA 22314

278 American History Scholarships

AMOUNT: $1,000-$2,000 **DEADLINE:** Feb 1
FIELDS/MAJORS: American History

Scholarships available to graduating high school seniors who will be majoring in American history. Foreign students may apply for this award through an overseas chapter of the DAR. Applicant must obtain a letter of sponsorship from a local DAR chapter. Must be a U.S. citizen to apply. Contact your local chapter or write to the address below for details.

National Society Daughters Of The American Revolution
NSDAR Scholarship Committee
1776 D St., NW
Washington, DC 20006

279 American Humanics, Inc. Loans

AMOUNT: Varies **DEADLINE:** None Specified
FIELDS/MAJORS: Youth or Human Service

Loan funds are available for students studying youth or human services. These funds are only available at the following universities: Cal State-LA, Haskell, High Point, Clemson, LSU, Lindenwood College, College of the Ozarks, Missouri Valley College, Montclair State, Rockhurst, Murray State, Pepperdine, Houston, Northern Iowa, Springfield College, Salem/Teikyo, San Diego, and Arizona State. Write to the address below for more information. The schools above sponsor undergraduate programs, graduate programs are offered at Murray State and the University of Northern Iowa.

American Humanics, Inc.
4601 Madison Ave., Suite B
Kansas City, MO 64112

280

American Indian Endowed Scholarship

Amount: $1,000 **Deadline:** Jun 1
Fields/Majors: All Areas Of Study

Scholarship program for undergraduate American Indian students who reside in Washington state and are enrolled in a Washington state schools. Write to the address listed below for information.

Washington Higher Education Coordinating Board
917 Lakeridge Way
P.O. Box 43430
Olympia, WA 98504

281

American Indian Scholarship

Amount: $500 **Deadline:** Aug 1, Dec 1
Fields/Majors: All Areas Of Study

Awards available for Native American students at the undergraduate or graduate level. Applicants must have a GPA of at least 2.75, have proof of Indian blood as indicated in letters or proof papers, and have financial need. Send a SASE to the address below for additional information.

National Society Daughters Of The American Revolution
American Indians Committee
3738 South Mission Dr.
Lake Havasu City, AZ 86406

282

American Indian Scholarship Fund

Amount: $750 **Deadline:** None Specified
Fields/Majors: All Areas Of Study

Scholarships are available for undergraduate American Indian students at the University of California, Riverside. Write to the address listed below for additional information.

University Of California
Native American Student Program
224 Costo Hall
Riverside, CA 92521

283

American Indian Student Legislative Grant Program

Amount: $500-$4,000 **Deadline:** None Specified
Fields/Majors: All Areas Of Study

Grants offered to students entering or enrolled in a regular degree granting program at one of the sixteen constituent institutions of the University of North Carolina. Applicants must reside in North Carolina and be a member of an Indian tribe recognized by the state of North Carolina or by the federal government. Student must demonstrate financial need. Write to the address below for details.

North Carolina State Education Assistance Authority
P.O. Box 2688
Chapel Hill, NC 27515

284

American Institute Of Aeronautics And Astronautics Scholarships

Amount: Varies **Deadline:** Mar 1
Fields/Majors: Engineering, Computer Science

Awards are available at the University of New Mexico for upperclassmen or graduate students in engineering or computer science with a GPA of at least 2.8. Must be a U.S. citizen or permanent resident. Write to the address below for more information.

University Of New Mexico, Albuquerque
Office Of Financial Aid
Albuquerque, NM 87131

285

American Institute Of Aeronautics And Astronautics Scholarships

Amount: Varies **Deadline:** Mar 1
Fields/Majors: Aeronautics, Astronautics, Or Any Related Field

Awards are available at the University of New Mexico for students in any field of aeronautics or astronautics. Must be a U.S. citizen or permanent resident. Write to the address below for more information.

University Of New Mexico, Albuquerque
Office Of Financial Aid
Albuquerque, NM 87131

286

American Institute Of Baking Scholarships

Amount: $500-$3,000 **Deadline:** Nov 1, May 1
Fields/Majors: Baking Industry

Scholarships are awarded on the basis of work experience, formal education, letters of recommendation, and financial need. Over forty private scholarships administered by the institute are available. Write to the address below for details.

American Institute Of Baking
Ken Embers, Scholarship Chairman
1213 Bakers Way
Manhattan, KS 66502

287

American Institute Of Pakistan Studies Fellowships

Amount: Varies **Deadline:** Feb 1
Fields/Majors: Humanities and Social Sciences

All fields of humanities and social sciences if engaged in research relevant to Pakistan or Pakistani international relations. For pre- or postdoctoral study. Write to the director of the institute at the address below for details.

American Institute Of Pakistan Studies
Wake Forest University
P.O. Box 7568
Winston-Salem, NC 27109

288
American Iris Society Scholarship

AMOUNT: $2,000 **DEADLINE:** Mar 1
FIELDS/MAJORS: Plant Sciences, Horticulture, Floriculture

Scholarships are available to support graduate study in the plant sciences. Applicants must be U.S. citizens enrolled in a plant science program at an accredited U.S. institution. Write to the address listed below for information.

American Iris Society Scholarship Committee
16516 25th, NE
Seattle, WA 98155

289
American Legion "Scout Of The Year" Scholarship

AMOUNT: $2,000-$8,000 **DEADLINE:** None Specified
FIELDS/MAJORS: All Areas Of Study

Scholarships are available for high school seniors who are Eagle Scouts in a troop sponsored by an American Legion post or auxiliary unit, or are sons of American Legion or auxiliary members. Award must be used within four years of high school graduation. Applicant must be a U.S. citizen. For more information write to the address below.

American Legion National Americanism Commission
P.O. Box 1055
Indianapolis, IN 46206

290
American Legion Auxiliary—Department Of Texas

AMOUNT: $500 **DEADLINE:** Apr 1
FIELDS/MAJORS: All Areas Of Study

Scholarships available to Texas residents who are or will be attending a college or university in Texas. Applicant must be a U.S. citizen and the child of a veteran. Write to the address listed below for additional information.

American Legion Auxiliary Department Headquarters
709 East 10th Street
Austin, TX 78701

291
American Legion Auxiliary Health Occupation Scholarships

AMOUNT: $300 **DEADLINE:** May 15
FIELDS/MAJORS: Health Related Fields

Scholarships are available for Arizona residents who are pursuing a degree in a health related field. Applicant must be a U.S. citizen, a child of a WWI, WWII, Korea, Vietnam, Beirut, Granada, Panama, or Desert Storm veteran, and be enrolled at an accredited school in Arizona. Write to the address listed below for information.

American Legion Auxiliary, Department Of Arizona
4701 North 19th Avenue, Suite 100
Phoenix, AZ 85015

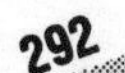

292
American Legion Auxiliary Memorial Scholarships

AMOUNT: $500 **DEADLINE:** Mar 15
FIELDS/MAJORS: All Areas Of Study

Scholarships available for Michigan residents who will be or are attending a college or university in Michigan. Applicants must be citizens of the U.S., and daughters of veterans. Write to the address listed below for additional information.

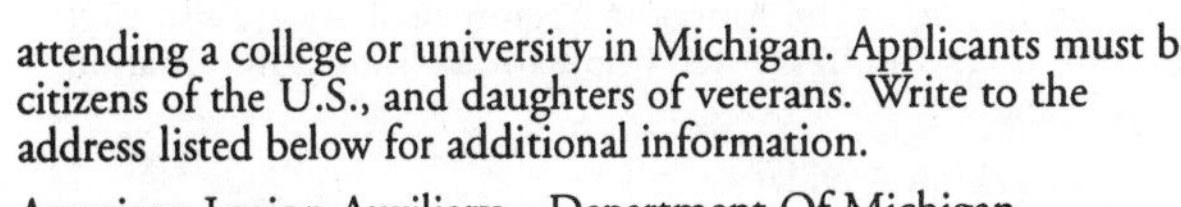

American Legion Auxiliary—Department Of Michigan
212 North Verlinden
Lansing, MI 48915

293
American Legion Auxiliary National President's Scholarships

AMOUNT: $1,500-$2,000 **DEADLINE:** Mar 10
FIELDS/MAJORS: All Fields Of Study

Applicants must be dependents of veterans of WWI, WWII, Korean, Vietnam, Lebanon, Grenada, Panama, or the Persian Gulf. All applicants must be high school seniors. Ten scholarships per year. Write to your local American Legion auxiliary for more information. The address shown below does not administer the program; five regional divisions are responsible for the screening process.

American Legion Auxiliary, National Headquarters
P.O. Box 1055
Indianapolis, IN 46206

294
American Legion Auxiliary Scholarship

AMOUNT: Varies **DEADLINE:** Apr 1
FIELDS/MAJORS: All Areas Of Study

Scholarships are available to Alabama residents enrolled at or planning to enroll at an Alabama public institution. Applicant must be a U.S. citizen and a child of a WWI, WWII, Korea, Vietnam, Beirut, Granada, Panama, or Desert Storm veteran. Forty awards are offered each year. Write to the address listed below for information, and please enclose an SASE (at least 4" x 9 1/2").

American Legion Auxiliary, Department Of Alabama
Department Headquarters
120 North Jackson Street
Montgomery, AL 36104

295
American Legion Auxiliary Scholarship

AMOUNT: $150 **DEADLINE:** None Specified
FIELDS/MAJORS: All Areas Of Study

A scholarship is available for a female Nebraska student currently enrolled at the University of Nebraska as a sophomore. Applicant must be a Nebraska resident, and the daughter of a veteran. Write to the address listed below for additional information.

American Legion Auxiliary—Department Of Nebraska, Univ. Of Nebraska
Office Of Scholarships and Financial Aid
16 Admin. Bldg., P.O. Box 880411
Lincoln, NE 68588

296
American Legion Auxiliary Scholarships

AMOUNT: $200 **DEADLINE:** Jun 1
FIELDS/MAJORS: All Areas Of Study

Scholarships for Iowa residents who are or will be attending a college or university in Iowa. Applicant must be a U.S. citizen, and a descendant of a WWI, WWII, Korea, Vietnam, Grenada, Lebanon, Panama, or Persian Gulf veteran. Members of the

American Legion or the American Legion auxiliary are also eligible. Write to the address listed below for additional information or application.

American Legion Auxiliary
Department Of Iowa
720 Lyon Street
Des Moines, IA 50309

297 American Legion Auxiliary Scholarships

AMOUNT: $350 **DEADLINE:** Jan 10
FIELDS/MAJORS: All Areas Of Study

Four scholarships are available for residents of North Dakota currently enrolled in a North Dakota college or university. Applicants must be citizens of the U.S. who demonstrate academic excellence and financial need. For undergraduate study. Write to the address listed below for additional information.

American Legion Auxiliary, Department Of North Dakota
c/o Maion Devlin
HC 2 Box 61
Hope, ND 58046

298 American Legion Auxiliary Scholarships

AMOUNT: $300 **DEADLINE:** None Specified
FIELDS/MAJORS: All Areas Of Study

Scholarships are available for residents of West Virginia who are or will be attending a college or university in West Virginia. Applicants must be U.S. citizens and children of veterans. Must be under 22 years of age. Write to the address listed below for additional information.

American Legion Auxiliary, Department Of West Virginia
Mrs. Mary Yoho, Dept. Secretary/Treasurer
R.R. 1, Box 144A
Proctor, WV 26055

299 American Legion Auxiliary Spirit Of Youth Scholarship

AMOUNT: $1,000 **DEADLINE:** None Specified
FIELDS/MAJORS: All Areas Of Study

Scholarships for junior members of the American Legion auxiliary who have held membership for at least three years. Applicant must be in her senior year of an accredited high school and have a GPA of at least 3.0. Must continue membership in the American Legion auxiliary during the four-year scholarship period. Contact your local unit president for information.

American Legion Auxiliary
P.O. Box 1055
Indianapolis, IN 46206

300 American Legion Boy Scout Scholarship

AMOUNT: $200-$1,000 **DEADLINE:** Mar 15
FIELDS/MAJORS: All Areas Of Study

Scholarships for Boy Scouts or Explorer Scouts in an Illinois troop or council. Based on 500 word essay. Must be a senior in high school. Information and applications can be obtained from the local scout office or from the Dept. of Illinois American Legion Scout Chairman of the post, county, district, or division or write to the address below for details.

American Legion, Department Of Illinois Legion Scout Chairman
P.O. Box 2910
Bloomington, IL 61701

301 American Legion Music Scholarships

AMOUNT: $1,000 **DEADLINE:** Feb 15
FIELDS/MAJORS: Music

Scholarships for Kansas residents who are or will be attending a college or University in Kansas. Applicant must be a U.S. citizen. For study in music. Write to the address listed below for additional information or application.

American Legion, Department Of Kansas
1314 SW Topeka Blvd.
Topeka, KS 66612

302 American Legion Scholarship

AMOUNT: None Specified **DEADLINE:** None Specified
FIELDS/MAJORS: All Areas Of Study

Eight scholarships are available for Ohio residents who will be enrolling in college as entering freshmen. Applicants must be U.S. citizens and children of American Legion or auxiliary members. Write to the address listed below for additional information.

American Legion, Department Of Ohio
Dept. Scholarship Committee
4060 Indianola Avenue
Columbus, OH 43214

303 American Legion Scholarship Program

AMOUNT: Varies **DEADLINE:** Apr 1
FIELDS/MAJORS: All Areas Of Study

Grants for children or grandchildren of Alabama veterans of World War I, World War II, Korea, or Vietnam. Must be an Alabama resident attending a public institution with on-campus housing, and a U.S. citizen. One hundred thirty awards are offered each year. Write to the address below for details, enclosing a SASE (size at least 4" x 9 1/2").

American Legion, Department Of Alabama
Department Adjutant
P.O. Box 1069
Montgomery, AL 36101

304 American Legion Scholarships

AMOUNT: Varies **DEADLINE:** Apr 1
FIELDS/MAJORS: All Areas Of Study

Scholarship for Maryland residents who are less than 20 years old. Applicants must be U.S. citizens and children of a veteran. For full-time study. For more information, write to the address below.

American Legion, Department Of Maryland War Memorial
Building 101
N. Gay Street, Room E
Baltimore, MD 21202

305

American Legion Scholarships

AMOUNT: $500 **DEADLINE:** Mar 15
FIELDS/MAJORS: All Areas Of Study

Scholarships are available for Minnesota residents who are or will be enrolled at a Minnesota college or university. Applicant must be a U.S. citizen and the child of a legion or auxiliary member. For more information contact the address below.

American Legion, Department Of Minnesota
State Veterans Service Bldg.
St. Paul, MN 55155

306

American Legion Scholarships

AMOUNT: Varies **DEADLINE:** None Specified
FIELDS/MAJORS: All Areas Of Study

Scholarships are available for Pennsylvania residents who are children of deceased Legionnaires or children of members in good standing in an American Legion post in Pennsylvania. Award is made in senior year of high school and renewed based on student's progress. Write to the address listed below for additional information.

American Legion, Department Of Pennsylvania
Attn: Scholarship Secretary
P.O. Box 2324
Harrisburg, PA 17105

307

American Legion/ Chief Ouray Voiture No. 878 Scholarship

AMOUNT: $150 **DEADLINE:** None Specified
FIELDS/MAJORS: Nursing

Awards for a sophomore Mesa State nursing student. Write to the address below for more details and an application.

Mesa State College
Office Of Financial Aid
P.O. Box 2647
Grand Junction, CO 81501

308

American Medical Technologists Scholarship

AMOUNT: None Specified **DEADLINE:** Apr 1
FIELDS/MAJORS: Medical Technology, Dental Assisting, Medical Assisting

Applicant must be a graduate of, or a senior in high school. Also, must be enrolled in, or contemplating enrolling in, a U.S. accredited school to pursue studies in medical laboratory technology, medical assisting, or dental assisting. Students pursuing studies other than those listed above are ineligible. Write to the address below for details. State your educational interest and career goal and include a legal-size SASE with your request.

American Medical Technologists
710 Higgins Rd.
Park Ridge, IL 60068

309

American Mensa Education & Research Foundation Scholarships

AMOUNT: $1,000 (max) **DEADLINE:** Jan 31
FIELDS/MAJORS: All Areas Of Study

Scholarship contest for students who will be enrolled in a degree program at an American institution in the fall. Based on a 550-word essay. Not renewable. Affiliation with Mensa is not required. Must be a U.S. citizen or permanent resident. Applications should be available at your high school guidance office or your college financial aid office. If unavailable there, they may be obtained from your local Mensa group. If that address is unknown, send a SASE to the below address for details and an application.

American Mensa Education & Research Foundation
National Scholarship Co-Chairperson
6019 Celtic Dr.
San Antonio, TX 78240

310

American Morgan Horse Institute, Inc. Scholarships

AMOUNT: $500-$1,000 **DEADLINE:** Feb 15
FIELDS/MAJORS: Animal Science, Equine Studies

Scholarships are available for FFA members pursuing a two- or four-year degree in animal science with an equine concentration. Write to the address below for details.

National FFA Foundation Scholarship Office
P.O. Box 15160
Alexandria, VA 22309

311

American Nuclear Society—John And Muriel Landis Scholarships

AMOUNT: Varies **DEADLINE:** Mar 1
FIELDS/MAJORS: Nuclear Science or Nuclear Engineering

Awards are available at the University of New Mexico for students in the fields of nuclear science or engineering. Must demonstrate financial need. Applications are available at the engineering department on campus in January of each year.

University Of New Mexico, Albuquerque
Office Of Financial Aid
Albuquerque, NM 87131

312

American Numismatic Society Fellowship

AMOUNT: $3,500 **DEADLINE:** Mar 1
FIELDS/MAJORS: Numismatics, Classical Studies, Art and Economic History

Fellowship for graduate students who have completed general examinations for doctorate. Significant utilization of numismatics in dissertation is required. Prior attendance at an N.S. graduate seminar is preferred. Write to the address below for details.

American Numismatic Society
Broadway At 155th Steet
New York, NY 10032

313

American Paralysis Association Research Grants

Amount: $30,000 (max) **Deadline:** Dec 15
Fields/Majors: Paralysis Research

Awards are available for research related to spinal cord injuries and paralysis. Grants are intended for new research projects and are allocated based on scientific merit and adherence to the APA's priorities. Write to the address below for more information.

American Paralysis Association
Ms. Susan P. Howley, Research, Director
500 Morris Ave.
Springfield NJ 07081

314

American Public Works—Oregon Section

Amount: $900 **Deadline:** May 1
Fields/Majors: Civil Engineering

Award for full-time students enrolled in the department of civil engineering who have been Oregon residents of at least four years. Financial need is a consideration. Contact the civil engineering department for more information.

Portland State University
Civil Engineering Department
138 Science Building 2
Portland, OR 97207

315

American Research Institute In Turkey

Amount: $30,000 (max) **Deadline:** Nov 15
Fields/Majors: Humanities, Social Sciences

Scholarships are available for graduate students engaged in research in ancient, medieval, or modern times in Turkey, in any field of the humanities and social sciences. Write to the address below for more information.

University Of Pennsylvania Museum
33rd And Spruce Streets
Philadelphia PA 19104

316

American Saw And Manufacturing Company Scholarship

Amount: Varies **Deadline:** Feb 29
Fields/Majors: Operations Management

Awards for outstanding students in the field of operations management who show great promise and needs financial assistance to complete their education. For students in their sophomore, junior, or senior year. Contact the SOM Development Office, Room 206, for more information and an application.

University Of Massachusetts
Amherst SOM Development Office, Room 206
Amherst MA 01003

317

American Saw And Manufacturing Company Scholarship

Amount: Varies **Deadline:** Feb 29
Fields/Majors: Operations Management

Awards for outstanding students in the field of operations management based on academic performance and financial need. Contact the SOM Development Office, Room 206, for more information and an application.

University Of Massachusetts
Amherst Office Of Financial Aid Services
255 Whitmore Admin. Bldg.
Box 38230
Amherst, MA 01003

318

American Seed Trade Association, Inc. Scholarships

Amount: $1,000 **Deadline:** Feb 15
Fields/Majors: Agriculture

Scholarships are available for former FFA members pursuing a graduate degree in any area of agriculture. Preference may be given to agronomy majors. Write to the address below for details.

National FFA Foundation
Scholarship Office
P.O. Box 15160
Alexandria, VA 22309

319

American Soc. Of Criminology Gene Carte Student Paper Competition

Amount: $100-$300 **Deadline:** Apr 15
Fields/Majors: Criminology

Awards are available to any undergraduate or graduate student currently enrolled in a full-time basis in an academic program. Papers must be typewritten, double-spaced on 8 1/2" x 11" white paper, and no longer than 7,500 words related to criminology. Must also include a manuscript including the title and a 100-word abstract. Write to the address below for more information.

University Of Cincinnati
Division Of Criminal Justice
P.O. Box 210389
Cincinnati, OH 45221

320

American Society For Dermatological Surgery Research Grants

Amount: $10,000 (max) **Deadline:** Oct 2
Fields/Majors: Dermatology Research

Research grants to investigators in the areas of dermatology surgery and oncology. Research must be carried out in the U.S. or Canada. Grants do not support indirect/overhead costs. Three grants per year. Please write to American Society for Dermatologic Surgery in care of the below address for details and grant application procedures.

Dermatology Foundation
Medical And Scientific Committee
1560 Sherman Ave.
Evanston, IL 60201

321

American Society For Eighteenth-Century Studies Fellowships

Amount: $800 per Month **Deadline:** Mar 1, Oct 15
Fields/Majors: 18th Century Studies (1660-1815)

Postdoctoral residential fellowships lasting 1-3 months for

scholars of 18th century studies. All fellowship offers are residential. Write to the committee on awards at the address below.

Newberry Library
Committee On Awards
60 W. Walton St.
Chicago, IL 60610

322 American Society For Enology And Viticulture Scholarship Program

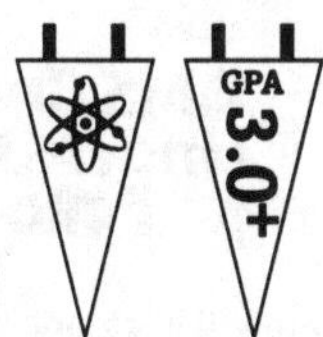

Amount: None Specified **Deadline:** Mar 1
Fields/Majors: Viticulture, Enology

For students accepted as undergraduate or graduate student in an accredited college in North America. Must be enrolled in a curriculum stressing a science basic to the wine and grape industry. Financial need is considered. Must be a junior, senior, or graduate student. Minimum GPA is 3.0 for undergraduates, 3.2 for graduate students. Write to the address below for details.

American Society For Enology And Viticulture
Scholarship Committee
P.O. Box 1855
Davis, CA 95617

323 American Society For Metals Foundation Merit Scholarships

Amount: $500-$2,000 **Deadline:** None Specified
Fields/Majors: All Areas Of Study

Scholarships are available to graduating high school seniors who are National Merit Finalists planning a career in materials engineering. Write to the address listed below for information.

National Merit Scholarship Corporation/ASM Foundation
1560 Sherman Avenue, Suite 200
Evanston, IL 60201

324 American Society Of Agronomy/Outstanding Senior

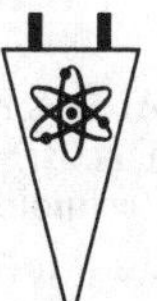

Amount: $100 **Deadline:** None Specified
Fields/Majors: Agronomy, Soil Science

Open to students majoring in agronomy or soil science. Write to the address below for more information.

California State Polytechnic University
Pomona College Of Agriculture
Building 7, Room 110
Pomona, CA 91768

325 American Society Of Clinical Pathologists (ASCP)

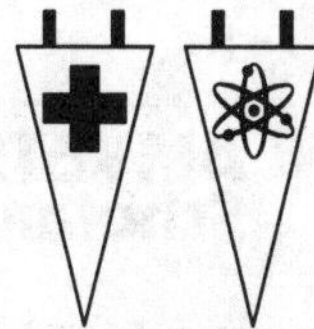

Amount: $1,000 **Deadline:** Oct 27
Fields/Majors: Cytotechnology, Histologic Tech/Technologist, Medical Lab Tech.

Open to outstanding students who are enrolled in cytotechnologists, histologic technician/technologist, medical laboratory technician, or medical technologist programs. Must be enrolled in a NAACLS or CAAHEP accredited program and in your final clinical year of education. Must be a U.S. citizen or permanent resident. Write to the address below for more information.

American Society Of Clinical Pathologists
2100 West Harrison St.
Chicago, IL 60612

326 American Society Of Crime Laboratory Directors Scholarships

Amount: $2,000 **Deadline:** Mar 1
Fields/Majors: Forensic Science

Scholarships for full-time undergraduate or graduate students maintaining a GPA of 3.0 or above, in an ASCLD recognized forensic science program. Applicants must be nominated by an ASCLD member or an academic advisor. Contact the address below for further information.

American Society Of Crime Laboratory Directors, Inc.
Education And Training Committee
P.O. Box 496
Lockport, NY 14094

327 Americo Toffoli Scholarship

Amount: Varies **Deadline:** May 31
Fields/Majors: All Areas Of Study

Scholarships for graduating high school seniors who are sons or daughters of members of a union in good standing with the Colorado AFL-CIO. Six awards are offered per year (3 men/3 women). Based on academic achievement and a 1000-15000 word essay. Contact your parent's local or write to the address below for details.

Colorado AFL-CIO
Americo Toffoli Scholarship Committee
2460 W. 26th Ave., Building C #350
Denver, CO 80211

328 AMHI Scholarships

Amount: $3,000 **Deadline:** Mar 1
Fields/Majors: All Areas Of Study

Scholarships for students who will be high school graduates. Completed or involved in AMHA horsemastership program, or involved in 4H/FFA, or won AHSA and/or AMHA medal for equitation, or placed among top finalists in open competition. Based on ability/aptitude for serious study, financial need, community service, leadership and achievement with horses. Write to the address below for details.

American Morgan Horse Institute, Inc.
Dane Bettes, AMHI Scholarships
7112 County Road 802
Burleson, TX 76028

329 Amity Institute Internships

Amount: None Specified **Deadline:** None Specified
Fields/Majors: Foreign Language

Applicants must be single, between the ages of 20 to 30, students or graduates of a university, professional or technical institution, have ability to communicate effectively in English with interests in the following languages: Spanish, French,

German, Japanese, Chinese, Russian and other languages. Write to the address below for more information.

Amity Institute
10671 Roselle Street, Suite 101
San Diego, CA 92121

330

AMS 75th Anniversary Scholarship

AMOUNT: $2,000 **DEADLINE:** Jun 16
FIELDS/MAJORS: Meteorology, Atmospheric Science

Scholarships for students entering their last year of study toward a degree in one of the fields listed above. Based on academic ability and financial need. Requires a GPA of at least 3.0 and U.S. citizenship or permanent residency. Application forms and further information may be obtained through the AMS headquarters at the address below.

American Meteorological Society
45 Beacon Street
Boston, MA 02108

331

AMS Centennial Research Fellowship

AMOUNT: $36,000 **DEADLINE:** Dec 1
FIELDS/MAJORS: Mathematics

Postdoctoral research fellowships. May be held at any institution the fellow selects or at more than one in succession. Open to citizens or legal residents of a country in North America. Applicants must not hold permanent tenure. Write to the address below for complete details or e-mail: ams@ams.org.

American Mathematical Society
Research Fellowships
P.O. Box 6248
Providence, RI 02940

332

AMS Minority Scholarships

AMOUNT: $3,000 **DEADLINE:** Jan 26
FIELDS/MAJORS: Meteorology, Atmospheric Science, Hydrology, Oceanic Science

Awards for minority students who will be entering their freshman year of college and are planning to study in one of the areas listed above. Write to the address below for more information.

American Meteorological Society
Attn: Fellowship/Scholarship
45 Beacon St.
Boston, MA 02108

333

AMS/Industry Graduate Fellowships

AMOUNT: $15,000 **DEADLINE:** Feb 2
FIELDS/MAJORS: See Listing Of Fields Below

Fellowships for graduate students in their first year of study who wish to pursue advanced degrees in meteorology, hydrology, atmospheric science, ocean science, or those planning a career in one of the above fields who are currently studying chemistry, computer science, engineering, environmental science, mathematics, or physics. Application forms and

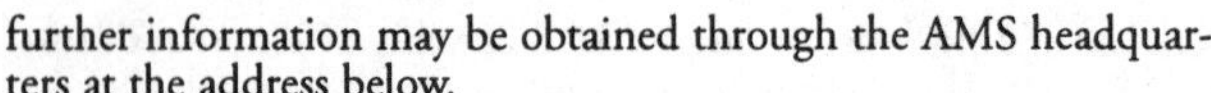

further information may be obtained through the AMS headquarters at the address below.

American Meteorological Society
45 Beacon Street
Boston, MA 02108

334

AMS/Industry Undergraduate Fellowships

AMOUNT: $2,000 **DEADLINE:** Feb 16
FIELDS/MAJORS: See Listing Of Fields Below

Scholarships for undergraduate students in their junior of study who wish to pursue degrees in meteorology, hydrology, atmospheric science, or ocean science, or those planning a career in one of the above fields who are currently studying chemistry, computer science, engineering, environmental science, mathematics, or physics. Application forms and further information may be obtained through the AMS headquarters at the address below.

American Meteorological Society
45 Beacon Street
Boston, MA 02108

335

AMT Two-Year Scholarship Program

AMOUNT: $2,000 **DEADLINE:** May 1
FIELDS/MAJORS: Manufacturing Technology

Awards for students at junior or community colleges who are majoring in manufacturing technology. The award is given directly to the student's institution of study. Write to the address below for more details.

The Association For Manufacturing Technology
7901 Westpark Dr.
Mclean, VA 22102

336

AMTF Undergraduate And Graduate Awards

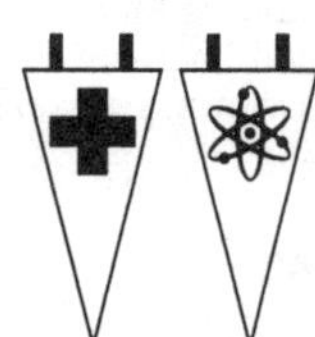

AMOUNT: $1,000-$1,500 **DEADLINE:** Mar 15
FIELDS/MAJORS: Clinical Laboratory Research, Medical Technology

Awards for undergraduate seniors or graduate students studying one of the fields above. Includes the AMTF Graduate and Undergraduate, Ruth M. French, Dorothy Morrison, and ASCLS Education and Research Fund scholarships. Undergraduate awards require that students attend a NAACLS accredited program. Applicants must be U.S. citizens or permanent residents. Write to the address below for more information.

Alpha Mu Tau Fraternity
AMTF Executive Secretary
8666 E. Traverse Highway
Traverse City, MI 49684

337

AMVETS Memorial Scholarships

AMOUNT: $1,000 **DEADLINE:** Apr 15
FIELDS/MAJORS: All Areas Of Study

Son or daughter of an American veteran. Based on academics, need, and extracurricular activities. Must be U.S. citizen and current H.S. graduate. Veterans who have exhausted governmental aid may also apply (as entering freshman or continuing student). Fifteen awards are offered each year and may be renewed for an additional three years. Write for details (information may also be available at many high schools). Requests for applications must be postmarked by Feb 15.

AMVETS National Scholarship Program
Attn: Scholarships
4647 Forbes Blvd.
Lanham, MD 20706

338

AMWA Medical Education Loans

AMOUNT: $1,000, $2,000 **DEADLINE:** Apr 30
FIELDS/MAJORS: Medicine (Medical and Osteopathic)

Loans for women who are members of the American Medical Women's Assn. Must be U.S. citizen or permanent resident enrolled in accredited U.S. medical or osteopathic medicine school. Additional loans may be made to a maximum of $4,000. Payment and interest deferred until graduation. Write to the address below (or call 703-838-0500) for details.

American Medical Women's Association
Student Loan Fund
801 N. Fairfax Street, Suite 400
Alexandria, VA 22314

339

ANA/Allstate Scholarships–Doctoral

AMOUNT: $8,000 **DEADLINE:** Jan 1
FIELDS/MAJORS: Behavioral Sciences Or Psychiatric Nursing

Scholarships are available for minority students in a program leading to a doctoral degree in the behavioral sciences or psychiatric nursing. Applicants must be enrolled in an accredited program. Write to the address below for more information.

American Nurses' Association
Minority Fellowship Programs
600 Maryland Ave. SW, Suite 100 West
Washington, DC 20024

340

ANA/Allstate Scholarships–Undergraduate

AMOUNT: $2,000 **DEADLINE:** Jan 1
FIELDS/MAJORS: Nursing

Scholarships are available for minority students majoring in nursing at the undergraduate level. Write to the address below for more information.

American Nurses' Association
Minority Fellowship Programs
600 Maryland Ave., SW, Suite 100 West
Washington, DC 20024

341

Andrew Curley Memorial Scholarship

AMOUNT: $300 **DEADLINE:** Mar 15
FIELDS/MAJORS: Education

Awards for Jacksonville State University students in the field of education. Based on academics and character. Write to the address below for more information.

Jacksonville State University
Financial Aid Office
Jacksonville, AL 36265

342

Andrew Squire Scholarships And The Adelbert Alumni Scholarships

AMOUNT: Full Tuition **DEADLINE:** Feb 1
FIELDS/MAJORS: All Areas Of Study

Seven full tuition scholarships offered to qualified applicants for admission as freshmen. Awards are renewable for each of the four years of undergraduate study, provided high academic achievement is maintained. Write to the address below for details.

Case Western Reserve University
Office Of Financial Aid
109 Pardee Hall
10900 Euclid Avenue
Cleveland, OH 44106

343

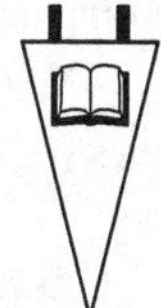

Andrew W. Mellon Fellowship Program

AMOUNT: Varies **DEADLINE:** None Specified
FIELDS/MAJORS: Classical Studies; Middle Ages, Renaissance, and Romance Periods

Grants for doctoral students working on their dissertation or postdoctorates doing research in any of the fields above. The award provides for travel expenses and a reasonable per diem to researchers with well-defined projects who wish to use the facilities of the Pius XII Memorial Library at Saint Louis University. Write to the address below for more information.

Saint Louis University
Vatican Film Library, Pius XII Library
3650 Lindell Boulevard
St. Louis, MO 63108

344

Andrew W. Mellon Fellowships

AMOUNT: Varies **DEADLINE:** Jan 5
FIELDS/MAJORS: Art History, Art Conservation, Museum Studies

Applicants should be at an advanced level of art conservation training and should have a few years of practical experience. Write to "fellowships in conservation" at the address below for details.

Metropolitan Museum Of Art
Office Of Academic Programs
1000 Fifth Avenue
New York, NY 10028

345

Andrew W. Mellon Postdoctoral Fellowship In The Humanities

AMOUNT: $29,000 **DEADLINE:** Jan 15
FIELDS/MAJORS: Humanities

Postdoctoral fellowships at Bryn Mawr are available for scholars in the humanities, with preference given to those specializing in multi-cultural areas. Applicants must have obtained the Ph.D. within the past five years. Write to the address listed below for information.

Bryn Mawr College
Dean James C. Wright
Graduate School Of Arts & Sciences
Bryn Mawr, PA 19010

346

Angel Flight/Silver Wings Society Scholarship

AMOUNT: $1,000 **DEADLINE:** None Specified
FIELDS/MAJORS: All Areas Of Study

Applicants must be an active member of Angel Flight/Silver Wings Society for a minimum of one year. Awards based solely on merit and community service, not on financial needs. Applicant should project positive image of ANF/SWS, AFROTC, and USAF. Applicant must also be recommended by ANF/SWS advisor. For junior or senior undergraduates. Write to the address below for details or call the foundation national headquarters at (703) 247-5839; fax (703) 247-5853.

Aerospace Education Foundation
Financial Information Department
1501 Lee Highway
Arlington, VA 22209

347

Angela Scholarship

AMOUNT: $2,500 **DEADLINE:** May 31
FIELDS/MAJORS: All Areas Of Study

Scholarships are available for entering freshmen of Italian-American heritage. Recipient must be willing to intern at the National Italian American Foundation for one semester. Write to the address below for details.

National Italian American Foundation
Dr. Maria Lombardo, Education Director
1860 19th Street, NW
Washington, DC 20009

348

Angelo Scheno Scholarship

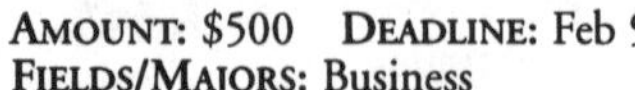

AMOUNT: $500 **DEADLINE:** Feb 9
FIELDS/MAJORS: Business

For students enrolled in college of business. Use Bloomsburg University scholarship application. Contact Mr. Gene Remoff, Dean, College of Business, for further information.

Bloomsburg University
19 Ben Franklin Hall
400 E. Second St.
Bloomsburg, PA 17815

349

Anheuser-Busch Foundation

AMOUNT: $250-$400 **DEADLINE:** None Specified
FIELDS/MAJORS: All Areas Of Study

Available for male or female minority students who are heads of households and currently enrolled in Harold Washington College. Write to the address below for more information.

Chicago Urban League
Gina Blake, Scholarship Specialist
4510 South Michigan Ave.
Chicago, IL 60653

350

Ann August Moser Scholarship

AMOUNT: $1,000 **DEADLINE:** Mar 1
FIELDS/MAJORS: All Areas Of Study

Scholarships are available at the University of Oklahoma, Norman for female students demonstrating financial need. Applicant must have a GPA of at least 3.25 to qualify. Three or four awards are offered annually. Write to the address listed below for information.

University Of Oklahoma, Norman
Office Of Financial Aid Services
731 Elm
Norman, OK 73019

351

Ann Cannon Memorial Scholarship

AMOUNT: $1,000 (max) **DEADLINE:** Feb 15
FIELDS/MAJORS: Art–Painting Or Drawing

Scholarships are available at the University of Utah for full-time students enrolled in an art program, with a GPA of at least 3.0. Preference is given to applicants in a painting or drawing concentration. Write to the address below for details.

University Of Utah
Delores Simons
161 Art And Architecture Center
Salt Lake City, UT 84112

352

Ann Garrison Scholarship

AMOUNT: $500 **DEADLINE:** Spring
FIELDS/MAJORS: Nursing

Scholarships are available at the University of Oklahoma, Norman for full-time junior nursing students, with a minimum GPA of 3.0. Write to the address listed below for information.

University Of Oklahoma, Norman
College Of Nursing
P.O. Box 26901
Oklahoma City, OK 73190

353

Ann J. Jarrett Scholarship

AMOUNT: $300 **DEADLINE:** Feb 9
FIELDS/MAJORS: Elementary Education

Award for elementary education major who can demonstrate financial need, academic achievement, and activities. Use Bloomsburg University scholarship application. Contact Dr. William O'Bruba, Chairperson, Department of Curriculum and Foundations, for further information.

Bloomsburg University
19 Ben Franklin Hall
400 E. Second St.
Bloomsburg, PA 17815

354

Ann Lane Homemaker Scholarship

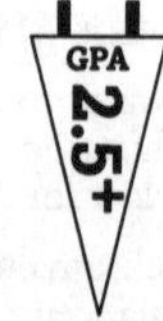

AMOUNT:$1,000 **DEADLINE:** Mar 1
FIELDS/MAJORS: All Areas Of Study

Must be graduating high school senior and active member of a local Texas chapter of the Future Homemakers of America. Award based on scholastic achievement, school/community leadership and involvement, and financial need. Write to the address below for further information.

Ann Lane Homemaker Scholarship Committee
c/o Texas Electric Cooperatives, Inc.
P.O. Box 9589
Austin, TX 78766

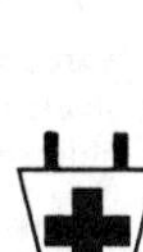

355

Ann Olson Memorial Doctoral Scholarship

AMOUNT: $3,000 **DEADLINE:** Dec 1
FIELDS/MAJORS: Oncology Nursing

Grants available to doctoral students in the field of oncology nursing. All applicants must be registered nurses. Write to the address below for more information.

Oncology Nursing Foundation
501 Holiday Dr.
Pittsburgh, PA 15220

356

Ann Sheldon Memorial, C. Eugene Springer Scholarships

AMOUNT: $200-$500 **DEADLINE:** Feb 14
FIELDS/MAJORS: Mathematics

Scholarships are available at the University of Oklahoma, Norman for students majoring in mathematics. Write to the address listed below for information.

University Of Oklahoma, Norman
Department Of Mathematics
601 Elm Ave.
Norman, OK 73019

357

Anna & Pietro Dapolonia Trust

GPA 3.0+

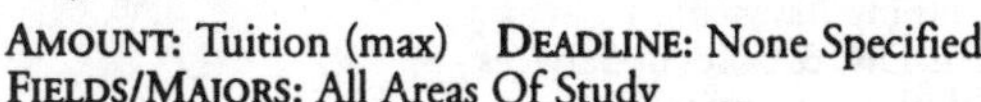

AMOUNT: Tuition (max) **DEADLINE:** None Specified
FIELDS/MAJORS: All Areas Of Study

Scholarships are available at the University of Iowa for undergraduate students who are descendents of Italian emigrants who came to Iowa prior to January 1, 1929. Applicant must have a GPA of at least 3.0. Write to the address listed below for information.

University Of Iowa
Office Of Student Financial Aid
208 Calvin Hall
Iowa City, IA 52242

358

Anna B. Jefferson Memorial Scholarship

AMOUNT: $300 **DEADLINE:** Mar 31
FIELDS/MAJORS: All Areas Of Study

Student must be a junior or senior who demonstrates satisfactory scholarship and financial need. Write to the address below for more information.

Southwest Missouri State University
Office Of Financial Aid
901 South National Ave.
Springfield, MO 65804

359

Anna Bell Karr Scholarship

AMOUNT: None Specified **DEADLINE:** Nov 30
FIELDS/MAJORS: All Areas Of Study

Scholarships are available at UCSD for undergraduate students who reside in Yuba, Sierra, Plumas, Butte, Sutter, Placer, or Nevada counties. Write to the address listed below for information.

University Of California San Diego
Student Financial Services
9500 Gilman Drive
La Jolla, CA 92093

360

Anna Louise Hoffman Award For Achievement In Graduate Research

AMOUNT: $400 **DEADLINE:** Feb 14
FIELDS/MAJORS: Chemistry, Biochemistry, Electrochemistry

Awards for female graduate students studying chemistry and directly related areas. Must be nominated by department. Need not be a member of Iota Sigma Pi. Applicant must be a full-time student. Write to Dr. Barbara A. Sawrey, Ph.D., at the address below for more details.

Iota Sigma Pi National Honor Society For Women
In Chemistry UCSD
Dept. Of Chemistry & Biochemistry
9500 Gilman Dr., Dept. 0303
La Jolla, CA 92093

361

Anna Ruhl Page Scholarship

AMOUNT: Varies **DEADLINE:** None Specified
FIELDS/MAJORS: Science

Award available for students at Rockford College who are studying science. Write to the address below for more information.

Rockford College
Financial Aid Office
5050 East State St.
Rockford, IL 61108

362

Anna-Lowrie Welles Scholarship

AMOUNT: $100 **DEADLINE:** None Specified
FIELDS/MAJORS: All Areas Of Study

Award for student who plans a religious vocation. Must demonstrate financial need, academic achievement, and activities. Contact Mrs. Kishbaugh, Financial Aid Office, for further information.

Bloomsburg University
19 Ben Franklin Hall
400 E. Second St.
Bloomsburg, PA 17815

363

Anne A. Agnew Scholarship Program

AMOUNT: Varies **DEADLINE:** Mar 1
FIELDS/MAJORS: All Areas Of Study

Scholarships for members and children of members of the South

Carolina State Employees Association or for deserving others. Must have completed at least one year at a college, university, or trade/vocational school. Based on character, school/community activities, 200-word essay, personal motivation, and leadership potential. Write to the address below for details.

South Carolina State Employees Association
Anne A. Agnew Scholarship Foundation
P.O. Box 5206
Columbia, SC 29250

364 Anne Maureen Whitney Barrow Memorial Scholarship

Amount: $5,000 (approx) **Deadline:** May 15
Fields/Majors: Engineering, Engineering Technology

Renewable scholarship for entering undergraduate women in engineering or engineering technology. One award per year. Must have a GPA of at least 3.5. Information and applications for the swe awards are available from the deans of engineering schools, or you may write to the address below. Please be certain to enclose an SASE.

Society Of Women Engineers
120 Wall Street, 11th Floor
New York, NY 10005

365 Annis Irene Fowler/ Kaden Scholarship

Amount:$1,000 **Deadline:** None Specified
Fields/Majors: Elementary Education

Scholarships are available for residents of South Dakota, enrolled in an elementary education program at South Dakota public university. Applicants must be entering freshmen, with a minimum GPA of at least 3.0. Write to the address listed below for information.

South Dakota Board Of Regents
207 East Capitol Avenue
Pierre, SD 57501

366 Annual Chemistry Scholarship

Amount: $2,400 **Deadline:** Mar 1
Fields/Majors: Chemistry

Scholarship for entering freshmen with outstanding academic potential. Renewable for three years. Contact the financial aid office at the address below for details.

Clemson University
Financial Aid Office
G01 Sikes Hall
Clemson, SC 29634

367 Annual Giving Awards

Amount: Varies **Deadline:** Mar 15
Fields/Majors: All Areas Of Study

Awards for Jacksonville State University students in any discipline. Write to the address below for more details.

Jacksonville State University
Financial Aid Office
Jacksonville, AL 36265

368 Annual Short Story Competition

Amount: $150-$300 **Deadline:** Feb 5
Fields/Majors: All Areas Of Study

Awards are available to the first and second place winners of a university-wide short story writing competition. Contact the UW Oshkosh foundation for more details.

University Of Wisconsin, Oshkosh
Financial Aid Office, Dempsey 104
800 Algoma Blvd.
Oshkosh, WI 54901

369 Anthropology Departmental Scholarships

Amount: Varies **Deadline:** Feb 15
Fields/Majors: Anthropology

Scholarships are available at the University of Utah for full-time students majoring in anthropology. Write to the address below for information.

University Of Utah
Ms. Ursala Hanley
102 Stewart Building
Salt Lake City, UT 84112

370 APA Fellowships

Amount: $2,000-$4,000 **Deadline:** May 15
Fields/Majors: Urban Planning

Applicants must be minority graduate students enrolled in an accredited planning program. Must be able to document need for financial assistance. Must be a United States citizen. Minority groups eligible for this program are African American, Hispanic, and Native American. Contact your department, or write to "APA Planning Fellowships" at the below address for further information and application forms.

American Planning Association
Attn: Asst. For Div. & Student Services
1776 Massachusetts Avenue, NW
Washington, DC 20036

371 Appalachian College Scholars Program

Amount: $1,000 **Deadline:** Dec 15
Fields/Majors: Arts & Sciences

Scholarships awarded to incoming freshmen and transfer students enrolling in the following. Requires a minimum GPA of 3.3. For students in psychology, anthropology, biology, chemistry, english, foreign language, social work, literature, geography, planning, geology, history, math, philosophy, sociology religious studies, physics, astronomy, political science, and criminology. Contact the office of admissions for details.

Appalachian State University
Office Of Admissions
Scholarship Section
Boone, NC 28608

372

Appalachian Scholarship

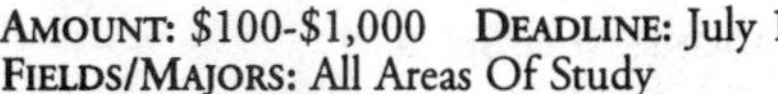

AMOUNT: $100-$1,000 **DEADLINE:** July 1
FIELDS/MAJORS: All Areas Of Study

Scholarships for undergraduate students who are residents of Appalachia, U.S. citizens or permanent residents, and members of the Presbyterian Church (U.S.A.). Write to the address listed below for information and an application.

Presbyterian Church (U.S.A.)
Office Of Financial Aid For Studies
100 Witherspoon Street
Louisville, KY 40202

373

Appalachian Youth Scholarship Program

AMOUNT: None Specified **DEADLINE:** None Specified
FIELDS/MAJORS: All Areas Of Study

Program eligibility is limited to youth from the 35 Appalachian counties in Alabama. Priority will be given to youth who live in the eight Alabama counties designated by the Appalachian Regional Commissions as "distressed." Applicants should be first-time freshmen who graduated high school in the upper third of their class. Write to the address below for details.

Alabama Commission On Higher Education
P.O. Box 30200
Montgomery, AL 36130

374

Applied Social Issues Internship Program

AMOUNT: $1,500-$2,500 **DEADLINE:** Sep 1
FIELDS/MAJORS: Psychology and Applied Social Science

Internships for college seniors, graduate students, and first-year postdoctorates in psychology, applied social science, and related disciplines. Awards are to encourage applied research, intervention projects, non-partisan advocacy projects, and writing and implementing public policy. Write to the address below for a description of the program.

Society For The Psychological Study Of Social Issues
Attn: Applied Social Issues Intern Program
P.O. Box 1248
Ann Arbor, MI 48106

375

Appraisal Institute Education Trust Scholarships

AMOUNT: $2,000-$3,000 **DEADLINE:** Mar 15
FIELDS/MAJORS: Real Estate and Related

Scholarships for undergraduate and graduate students of real estate appraisal, land economics, real estate, or allied fields. Must be a U.S. citizen. Write to the attention of Charlotte Timms, Project Coordinator, at the address listed below for more information.

Appraisal Institute Education Trust
Appraisal Institute
875 N. Michigan Avenue, Suite 2400
Chicago, IL 60611

376

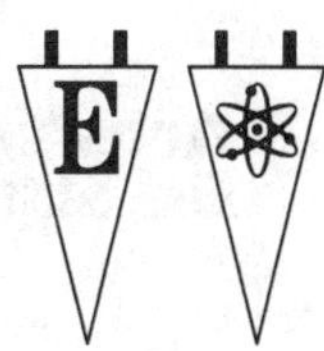
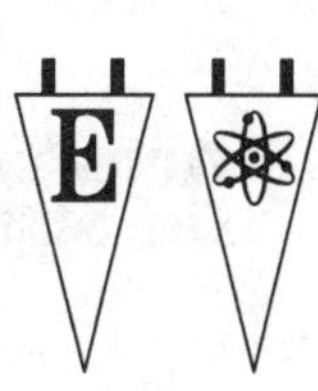
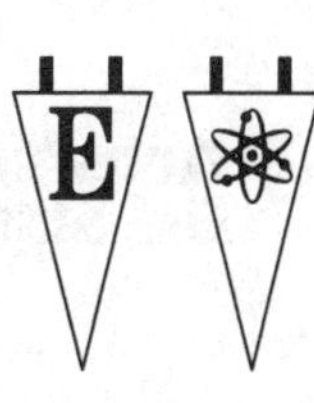
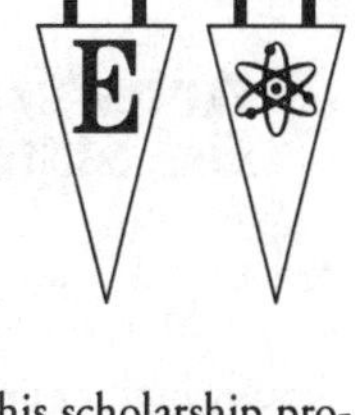

APS Minorities Scholarship Program

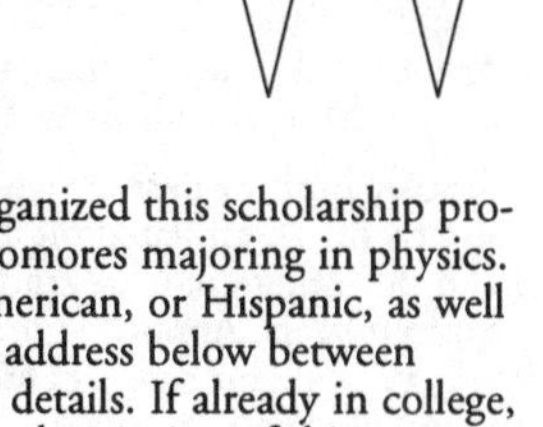

AMOUNT: $2,000 **DEADLINE:** Feb 2
FIELDS/MAJORS: Physics

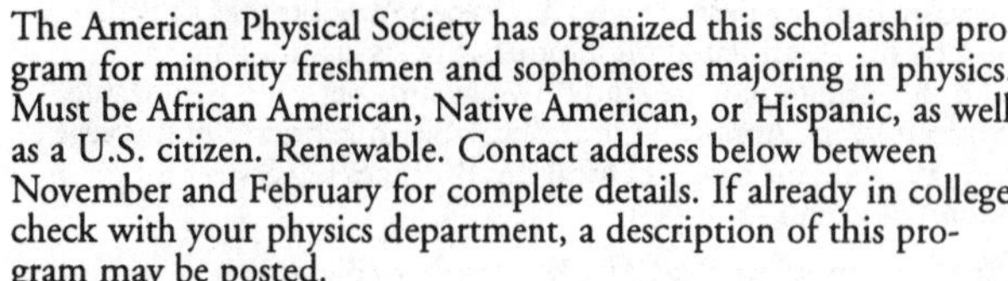

The American Physical Society has organized this scholarship program for minority freshmen and sophomores majoring in physics. Must be African American, Native American, or Hispanic, as well as a U.S. citizen. Renewable. Contact address below between November and February for complete details. If already in college, check with your physics department, a description of this program may be posted.

American Physical Society
One Physics Ellipse
College Park, MD 20740

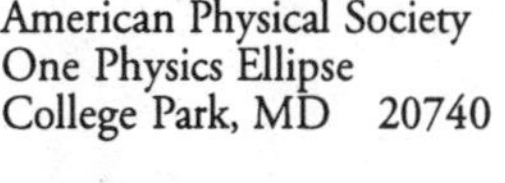

377

APSA Graduate Fellowships For African American Students

AMOUNT: $6,000 **DEADLINE:** Nov 1
FIELDS/MAJORS: Political Science

Graduate fellowships for African American doctoral students. Preference will be given to students just starting their doctoral program. Must be a U.S. citizen. Based on potential for success in graduate studies and financial needs. Fellowships will be awarded on an annual basis. Write to the address below for complete details.

American Political Science Association
1527 New Hampshire Ave., NW
Washington, DC 20036

378

APTRA-Clete Roberts Memorial Journalism Scholarship Awards

AMOUNT: $1,500 **DEADLINE:** Dec 15
FIELDS/MAJORS: Broadcast Journalism

Scholarships are available for broadcast journalism majors enrolled in a college or university in Nevada or California. Applicants must have a career objective of broadcast journalism. Three awards are offered annually. Write to the address listed below for information.

Associated Press Television-Radio Association Of California/Nevada
The Associated Press, c/o Rachel Ambrose
221 South Figueroa Street, #300
Los Angeles, CA 90012

379

Arabian Horse Assoc. Of Cal. Scholarships

AMOUNT: $600 **DEADLINE:** Nov 1
FIELDS/MAJORS: Equine Studies

Open to full-time Cal Poly Pomona students enrolled in a minimum of 12 units/quarter with a GPA of 2.5 or better. Four to eight awards per year. Write to the address below for more information.

California State Polytechnic University, Pomona
College Of Agriculture
Building 29, Room 100
Pomona, CA 91768

380

Arby's/Big Brothers/ Big Sisters Scholarship

Amount: $5,000 **Deadline:** Apr 30
Fields/Majors: All Areas Of Study

Scholarships for persons who are/were a little brother or little sister with an affiliated big brothers/big sisters program in the U.S. for undergraduate study. Two awards per year. Renewable for four years. Applications are available in February of the year you are applying, contact local Big Brothers/Big Sisters for more information.

Arby's Foundation And The Big Brothers/Big Sisters
Foundation Of America
230 North Thirteenth Street
Philadelphia, PA 19107

381

ARCF Scholarship

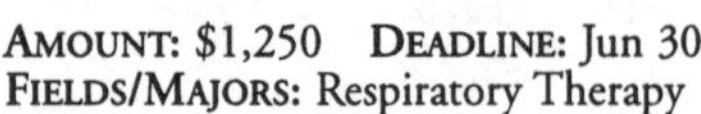

Amount: $1,250 **Deadline:** Jun 30
Fields/Majors: Respiratory Therapy

One scholarship for a second-year student in a respiratory therapy program. Based on academics, potential in the career field, and recommendations. Must have a GPA of at least 3.0. Write to the address below for details.

American Respiratory Care Foundation
11030 Ables Lane
Dallas, TX 75229

382

Archbold Scholarship For L.P.N.s, Medical & Radiology Technicians

Amount: $250 Per Quarter **Deadline:** None Specified
Fields/Majors: Licensed Practical Nursing, Medical Lab and Radiology Technicians

Awards for students in the above fields of study who are within two years of completing their college course work. Applicants must agree to full-time employment at Archbold Memorial Hospital for one to two years following graduation. Write to the address below for more information.

John D. Archbold Memorial Hospital
Gordon Ave. At Mimosa Drive
Thomasville, GA 31792

383

Archbold Scholarship For Physical Or Occupational Therapy

Amount: $2,500-$6,000 **Deadline:** None Specified
Fields/Majors: Occupational Or Physical Therapy

Awards for students in the above fields of study who are within two years of completing their college course work. Applicants must agree to full-time employment at Archbold Memorial Hospital for one to two years following graduation. Occupational and physical therapy assistants are also eligible for this award. Write to the address below for more information.

John D. Archbold Memorial Hospital
Gordon Ave. At Mimosa Drive
Thomasville, GA 31792

384

Archbold Scholarship For Registered Nursing

Amount: $4,000 **Deadline:** None Specified
Fields/Majors: Registered Nursing

Awards for students majoring in registered nursing who are within two years of completing their college course work. Applicants must agree to full-time employment at Archbold Memorial Hospital for one to two years following graduation. Write to the address below for more information.

John D. Archbold Memorial Hospital
Gordon Ave. At Mimosa Drive
Thomasville, GA 31792

385

Archdiocesan Scholarships

Amount: Full Tuition **Deadline:** Feb 15
Fields/Majors: All Areas Of Study

Scholarships are available at the Catholic University of America for entering freshman students who demonstrate academic aptitude and achievement. Write to the address below for details.

Catholic University Of America
Office Of Admissions And Financial Aid
Washington, DC 20064

386

Architectural Study Tour Scholarship

Amount: Varies **Deadline:** Jun 30
Fields/Majors: Architecture, Architectural History, City Planning, Landscape Architecture

Awards are available for graduate students in any of the fields listed above to participate in the SAH tour of the Adirondacks in August. All tour expenses are paid for by the society. Applicants must be members of the SAH to apply. Write to the address below for more information.

Society Of Architectural Historians
1365 North Astor St.
Chicago, IL 60610

387

Archival Internships

Amount: None Specified
Deadline: None Specified
Fields/Majors: History, Journalism, Political Science, Library Science, English

Library internships are available to help graduate and undergraduate students gain career-relevant archival experience in a presidential library while contributing constructively to the work of the library. Write to the address listed below for information.

John F. Kennedy Library
Archival Internships–Intern Registrar
Columbia Point
Boston, MA 02125

388

Arco Aspen Scholarship

Amount: None Specified **Deadline:** Mar 1
Fields/Majors: Accounting

Scholarships are available at the University of New Mexico for full-time minority or female accounting majors. Write to the address listed below for information.

University Of New Mexico, Albuquerque
Department Of Student Financial Aid
Mesa Vista Hall North
Albuquerque, NM 87131

389

Arden Reed Sparks Scholarship Fund

Amount: $1,000 **Deadline:** None Specified
Fields/Majors: Elementary Education

Scholarship available for El Paso County resident student majoring in elementary education at the University of Texas, El Paso. Selection based upon scholastic achievement and financial need. Write to the address listed below for additional information.

El Paso Community Foundation
201 East Main, Suite 1616
El Paso, TX 79901

390

Arizona Chapter Gold Scholarship

Amount: $3,000 **Deadline:** Jul 26
Fields/Majors: Travel and Tourism

Awards for sophomores, juniors, or seniors studying travel and tourism at an accredited college, university, or proprietary travel school in the state of Arizona. Applicants must be U.S. citizens or permanent residents and have a minimum GPA of 2.5. Based on different criteria such as essays, recommendations, or academics. Write to the address below for more information.

American Society Of Travel Agents
Scholarship Committee
1101 King St., Suite 200
Alexandria, VA 22314

391

Arizona Funeral Directors Association Scholarships

Amount: Varies **Deadline:** None Specified
Fields/Majors: Mortuary Science

Awards for Arizona residents studying mortuary science. Monies are paid directly to the school in quarterly/semester installments. Must have a GPA of at least 3.0. Write to the address below for more information.

Arizona Funeral Directors Association, Inc.
6901 First St.
Scottsdale, AZ 85251

392

Arkansas Academic Challenge Scholarship

Amount: $1,500 **Deadline:** Oct 1, Jul 1
Fields/Majors: All Areas Of Study

Scholarships for graduating Arkansas high school seniors. Must have a GPA of at least 2.5 and an ACT composite of at least 19. For use in public or private Arkansas college or university. Financial need is a major factor. Write to the address below for more details.

Arkansas Department Of Higher Education
Financial Aid Division
114 East Capitol
Little Rock, AR 72201

393

Arkansas Alumni Scholarship, Arkansas Scholarship, Chapter Scholarship

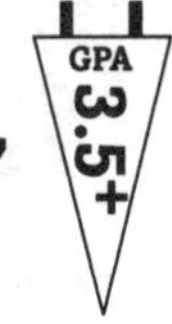

Amount: $1,000 **Deadline:** Mar 1
Fields/Majors: All Areas Of Study

Scholarships are available for Arkansas residents at the University of Arkansas. Applicants must be graduating high school seniors with a minimum GPA of at least 3.5. Renewable. Write to the address listed below for information.

Arkansas Alumni Association
P.O. Box 1070
Fayetteville, AR 72702

394

Arleigh Burke And Colin L. Powell Joint Warfighting Essay Contests

Amount: $1,000-$3,000 **Deadline:** Dec 1
Fields/Majors: Naval Studies

Contest for the most persuasive essay on a topic relating to the objective of the U.S. Naval Institute. Essays may be up to 3500 words in length. The Powell essay must discuss combat readiness in a joint context. Write to the address below for more information.

U.S. Naval Institute
118 Maryland Ave.
Anapolis, MD 21402

395

Armed Forces Essay Contests

Amount: $500-$1,000 **Deadline:** Varies
Fields/Majors: Military Science

Contest for essays on current issues and new directions for the armed services. Includes the Marine Corps, Coast Guard, and International Navies essay contests. Write to the address below for more information.

U.S. Naval Institute
118 Maryland Ave.
Anapolis, MD 21402

396

Armelagos Medical Anthropology Fund

AMOUNT: Varies **DEADLINE:** Mar 1
FIELDS/MAJORS: Anthropology

Awards for students in good academic standing who are committed to work in the field of medical anthropology. For entering sophomores, juniors, or seniors. Contact the Chair, Anthropology Department, for more information.

University Of Massachusetts, Amherst
Chair, Anthropology Department
Amherst, MA 01003

397

Armenian Alumni Association Scholarships

AMOUNT: $500 **DEADLINE:** May 31
FIELDS/MAJORS: All Areas Of Study

Awards for full-time, new, continuing, or graduate students at UC Berkeley with a minimum 3.25 GPA. Financial need not considered. Write to the address below for more details.

University Of California, Berkeley
P.O. Box 10113
Berkeley, CA 94709

398

Armenian American Middle East Club Scholarships

AMOUNT: $500-$750 **DEADLINE:** Feb 28
FIELDS/MAJORS: All Areas Of Study

Awards for full-time juniors, seniors, or graduate students in an accredited college or university in California. Based on academics and extracurricular activities. Write to the address below for more information.

Armenian American Middle East Club
AAMEC Scholarship Committee
P.O. Box 15175
North Hollywood, CA 91615

399

Armenian Professional Society Of The Bay Area Scholarships

AMOUNT: $1,000 **DEADLINE:** Nov 15
FIELDS/MAJORS: All Areas Of Study

Scholarships for students at the sophomore level or higher who are enrolled enrolled full-time at an accredited four-year college or university and are in need of financial assistance. Applicants must maintain a GPA of 3.2 or higher and be California residents. Write to the address below for details.

Armenian Professional Society Of The Bay Area
Dr. John Missirian
839 Marina Boulevard
San Francisco, CA 94123

400

Armenian Professional Society Scholarships

AMOUNT: $1,000 **DEADLINE:** None Specified
FIELDS/MAJORS: All Areas Of Study

Postgraduate (master's, Ph.D., M.D., etc.) scholarships granted annually to full-time candidates enrolled at an accredited college or university who are in need of financial assistance and are maintaining a GPA of 3.2 or higher. Applicants must be California residents. Write to the address below for details.

Armenian Professional Society
Mrs. Seda G. Marootian
215 Mariners View Lane
La Canada Flintridge, CA 91011

401

Armenian Scholarships

AMOUNT: Varies **DEADLINE:** Mar 1, Nov 30
FIELDS/MAJORS: All Areas Of Study

Awards for full-time, new, continuing, or graduate students at UC Berkeley. Includes the Mangasar A. Mangarsarian, Aram Torossian, and Neshan Zovick scholarships. Write to the address below for more details.

University Of California, Berkeley
Scholarship Coordinator
201 Sproul Hall
Berkeley, CA 94720

402

Armenian Scholarships

AMOUNT: Varies **DEADLINE:** Feb 11
FIELDS/MAJORS: All Areas Of Study

Awards for full-time, new, continuing, or graduate students at UCLA. Includes the Mangasar A. Mangarsarian, Kaspar Hovannisian Memorial, and Karekin Deravedisian Memorial Scholarships. Write to the address below for more details.

University Of California, Los Angeles
Fellowship & Assistantship Secretary
1228 Murphy Hall
Los Angeles, CA 90024

403

Armenian Women's Educational Club Undergraduate Scholarship Program

AMOUNT: Varies **DEADLINE:** Apr 30
FIELDS/MAJORS: All Areas Of Study

Awards for students, male or female, of Armenian descent who are entering their freshmen year in a four-year college or university. Based on academic record, references and financial need. Write to the address below for more information.

Armenian Women's Educational Club
Chairperson Of Scholarship Committee
114 Pleasant St.
Arlington, MA 02174

404

Armenian-American Citizens' League Scholarships

Amount: $500-$1,500 **Deadline:** May 1
Fields/Majors: All Areas Of Study

Awards for U.S. citizens or permanent residents of Armenian descent who have been living in California for at least two years and are enrolled full-time at an accredited college or university. Must have a GPA of at least 3.0. For undergraduate study. Write to the address below for more information.

Armenian-American Citizens' League
Mr. Aram H. Darmanian/Chairman
P.O. Box 391835
Mountain View, CA 94039

405

Army Collegiate Program

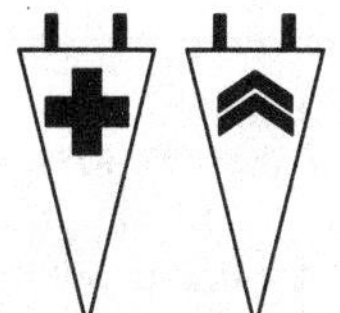

Amount: Varies **Deadline:** None Specified
Fields/Majors: Nursing

Scholarships for B.S. or M.S. nursing students who commit to remain on active duty for two years, if participation in the program is twelve months or less. Three year commitment if participation is 12 to 24 months. Write to the address listed below or contact your local army recruiter.

U.S. Army Recruiting Command
Army Nursing Opportunities
Hampton, VA 23369

406

Army ROTC Scholarship

Amount: $12,000 (max)
Deadline: None Specified
Fields/Majors: Military Science

Student must be full-time with a GPA of 2.5 or better. Students must pass a physical fitness test, a written test, and a free physical exam. Contact the military science department for more information.

Southwest Missouri State University
Office Of Financial Aid
901 South National Ave.
Springfield, MO 65804

407

Army/Air Force ROTC Scholarship

Amount: None Specified **Deadline:** Feb 15
Fields/Majors: All Areas Of Study

Scholarships are available at the University of New Orleans for full-time students who will be participating in the campus ROTC program. Requires a GPA of at least 2.5. Write to the address below for details.

University Of New Orleans
Department Of Military Science
New Orleans, LA 70148

408

Arnold H. Koschmann Memorial Prize In Electrical Engineering

Amount: Varies **Deadline:** Mar 1
Fields/Majors: Electrical Engineering

Awards are available at the University of New Mexico for juniors in the field of electrical engineering. Based on GPA and service, including activities in the institute of electrical and electronics engineers (student branch) or Eta Kappa Nu. Write to the address below for more information.

University Of New Mexico, Albuquerque
Office Of Financial Aid
Albuquerque, NM 87131

409

Arnold Ostwald Memorial Science Scholarship

Amount: $2,000 **Deadline:** Mar 1
Fields/Majors: Science

Scholarships are available to legally blind entering freshmen majoring in science. Based on academic ability. Write to the address below for details.

American Council Of The Blind
Scholarship Coordinator
1155 15th St., NW, Suite 720
Washington, DC 20005

410

Arnold Sadler Memorial Scholarship

Amount: $2,000 **Deadline:** Mar 1
Fields/Majors: Service To The Disabled

Awards for students who are legally blind and are studying in a field of service to the disabled. Write to the address below for more information.

American Council Of The Blind
Attn: Jessica Beach, Scholarship Admins.
1155 15th St., NW, Suite 720
Washington, DC 20005

411

Arnold W. Brunner Grant

Amount: $15,000 **Deadline:** Nov 15
Fields/Majors: Architecture (Research)

Research grants for research at the graduate level or beyond into areas of use and interest to the practice, teaching, or the corpus of knowledge of architecture. Must be a professional architect for at least 5 years and a U.S. citizen. Write to the address below for details.

American Institute Of Architects, New York Chapter
Arnold W. Brunner Grant
200 Lexington Avenue
New York, NY 10016

412

Arrow, Inc. Foundation Scholarships

Amount: $100 **Deadline:** Open
Fields/Majors: All Areas Of Study

Emergency funds are available to American Indian undergraduate students who need a small amount to further their education. Write to the address listed below for additional information.

Arrow, Inc. Foundation
1000 Connecticut Avenue, NW, Suite 1206
Washington, DC 20036

413

Art (Visual) General Scholarship

AMOUNT: $1,200 (max) **DEADLINE:** May 1
FIELDS/MAJORS: Visual Art

Awards for freshmen who demonstrate artistic ability. Based primarily on a portfolio review. Write to the chair of the department of art and design below for more details.

Winthrop University
Department Of Art And Design
119 Tillman Hall
Rock Hill, SC 29733

414

Art Conservation Internship Program

AMOUNT: $19,000 **DEADLINE:** None Specified
FIELDS/MAJORS: Art Conservation

Internship program for advanced students in the field of art conservation. Most interns already have a master's degree, but in some cases students may complete the internship as part of a master's program. Write to the address below for more information.

Harvard University Art Museums
32 Quincy St.
Cambridge, MA 02138

415

Art Department Graphic Design Scholarships

AMOUNT: Varies **DEADLINE:** Apr 1
FIELDS/MAJORS: Graphic Design

Awards are available to students who have completed the lower-division requirements in the graphic design program. Selection is made on the basis of portfolio, financial need, and GPA. Contact the address below for more information.

Portland State University
Art Department
239 Neuberger Hall
Portland, OR 92707

416

Art Department Scholarships

AMOUNT: Varies **DEADLINE:** Apr 1
FIELDS/MAJORS: Art

Awards are available to students who are majoring in art. Based on portfolio and GPA. Undergraduate applicants must have completed at least twenty credits in art. Contact the address below for more information.

Portland State University
Art Department
239 Neuberger Hall
Portland, OR 92707

417

Art Departmental Scholarships

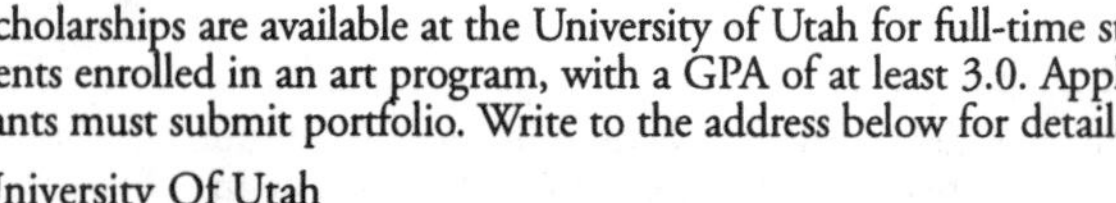

AMOUNT: Varies **DEADLINE:** Feb 15
FIELDS/MAJORS: Art

Scholarships are available at the University of Utah for full-time students enrolled in an art program, with a GPA of at least 3.0. Applicants must submit portfolio. Write to the address below for details.

University Of Utah
Delores Simons
161 Art and Architecture Center
Salt Lake City, UT 84112

418

Art Grants

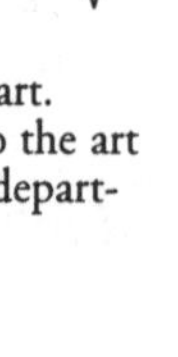

AMOUNT: Varies **DEADLINE:** Apr 1
FIELDS/MAJORS: Art

Awards available for students at RMC who are studying art. Applicants will be asked to submit a portfolio or slides to the art department. For undergraduate studies. Contact the art department for more information.

Rocky Mountain College
Office Of Financial Assistance
1511 Poly Drive
Billings, MT 59102

419

Art Institutes International Merit Scholarship Program

AMOUNT: Varies **DEADLINE:** None Specified
FIELDS/MAJORS: All Areas Of Study

Awards for entering freshman or transfer students at the Colorado Institute of Art who are unable to enter classes or continue in the program without additional financial assistance. Must have a GPA of at least 2.5. Write to the address below for more information.

Colorado Institute Of Art
Financial Aid Office
200 E. 9th Ave.
Denver, CO 80203

420

Art Portfolio Review Scholarship

AMOUNT: $2,500-$3,600 **DEADLINE:** Feb 15
FIELDS/MAJORS: Art and Design

Award given for portfolio review of entering full-time freshmen in the school of art and design in the New York State College of Ceramics. Renewable for four years. Write to the address below for details.

Alfred University
Student Financial Aid Office
26 N. Main St.
Alfred, NY 14802

421

Art Scholarship

AMOUNT: $1,500 **DEADLINE:** Jun 15
FIELDS/MAJORS: Art

Scholarships are available to art students of sophomore standing or higher who reside in Middletown, Monroe, Trenton, Franklin, Carlisle, Springboro, or Germantown. Applicants must have a GPA of at least 2.5. Write to the address listed below for information.

Middletown Fine Arts Center
130 North Verity Parkway
P.O. Box 441
Middletown, OH 45042

422

Art, Drama, And Music Scholarships

AMOUNT: $2,500 (max) **DEADLINE:** Feb 1
FIELDS/MAJORS: Art/Drama/Music

Applicants must show talent and potential in the arts. Portfolios, auditions, and recommendations by teachers and instructors are mandatory. Renewable. Write to the address below for details.

Mount Mercy College
Office Of Admission
1330 Elmhurst Dr., NE
Cedar Rapids, IA 52402

423

Art/Music Scholarships

AMOUNT: $2,000 **DEADLINE:** Feb 1
FIELDS/MAJORS: Art, Music

Scholarships are available at Bellarmine College for full-time students who are majoring in art or music. Art students must submit a portfolio, and music majors must audition. For undergraduate study. Contact the financial aid office at the address below for details.

Bellarmine College
Financial Aid Office
2001 Newburg Road
Louisville, KY 40205

424

Arther And Anna Hall Scholarships

AMOUNT: Varies **DEADLINE:** Mar 1
FIELDS/MAJORS: Pharmacy

Awards are available at the University of New Mexico for full-time pharmacy students with financial need. Write to the address below for more information.

University Of New Mexico, Albuquerque
Office Of Financial Aid
Albuquerque, NM 87131

425

Arthur Anderson And Company Scholarship

AMOUNT: Varies **DEADLINE:** Mar 1
FIELDS/MAJORS: Accounting

Award for sophomore accounting majors at ENMU. Must demonstrate academic excellence. Write to the address below for more information.

Eastern New Mexico University
ENMU College Of Business
Station 49
Portales, NM 88130

426

Arthur F. Gale Memorial Scholarship

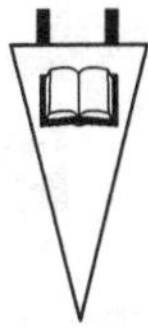

AMOUNT: $1,000 **DEADLINE:** None Specified
FIELDS/MAJORS: History

Award available for University of Texas at El Paso students majoring in history. Applicants must be El Paso County residents. Write to the address listed below for further information.

El Paso Community Foundation
201 East Main
Suite 1616
El Paso, TX 79901

427

Arthur H. Carter Scholarships

AMOUNT: $2,500 **DEADLINE:** Apr 1
FIELDS/MAJORS: Accounting

Open to undergraduate and graduate accounting majors who have completed at least two years of study. School must be an assembly member of the AACSB. Not for doctoral study. Must have at least one year of study remaining before degree. Applicant must be a U.S. citizen. Application must be obtained from the accounting department at your school and must be submitted by the department. Contact your department for details. (Accounting department chairs may obtain applications from Marie Hamilton at the below address.)

American Accounting Association
5717 Bessie Drive
Sarasota, FL 34233

428

Arthur J. Harvey Scholarship

AMOUNT: Varies **DEADLINE:** Varies
FIELDS/MAJORS: All Areas Of Study

Scholarships are available at the University of New Mexico for full-time sophomores with a GPA of at least 3.2 who are involved in campus activities. Write to the address listed below for information.

University Of New Mexico, Albuquerque
Student Financial Aid Office
Mesa Vista Hall North, Room 1044
Albuquerque, NM 87131

429

Arthur M. Schlesinger, Jr. Fellowship

AMOUNT: $5,000 **DEADLINE:** Aug 15
FIELDS/MAJORS: Latin American History, Western Hemisphere History

Preference in this fellowship is given to applicants specializing in Latin American or Western Hemisphere history or policy studies during the Kennedy administration or the period from the Roosevelt through the Kennedy presidencies. One or two awards per year. Write to the address below for more information.

John F. Kennedy Library Foundation
William Johnson, Chief Archvist
Columbia Point
Boston, MA 02125

430

Arthur N. Wilson, M.D. Scholarship

Amount: $3,000 **Deadline:** Mar 8
Fields/Majors: Medicine

Award for medical students who graduated from high schools in southeast Alaska. Award is not renewable, but recipients may reapply. Write to the address below for more information.

American Medical Association
Secretary, AMA
535 North Dearborn Street
Chicago, IL 60610

431

Arthur S. Tuttle Memorial National Scholarship

Amount: $3,000-$5,000 **Deadline:** Mar 1
Fields/Majors: Civil Engineering

Applicant must be a national ASCE member in good standing academically. Financial need and academic performance will be considered in selection. Award is to be used to finance first year of graduate school in a civil engineering program. Write to the address below for complete details.

American Society Of Civil Engineers
Member Scholarships And Awards
345 E. 47th Street
New York, NY 10017

432

Arthur Vining Davis Science Scholarship

Amount: $2,000 **Deadline:** Feb 15, Apr 1
Fields/Majors: Science, Mathematics, Computer Science

Scholarship for entering freshman or transfer student who has demonstrated strong ability and interest in the science, mathematics, or computer science. Award based on merit and is renewable as long as the student stays in the same field of study and maintains a 3.0 GPA. Write to the address below for more complete details.

Mills College
Office Of Financial Aid
5000 Macarthur Blvd.
Oakland, CA 94613

433

Arthur Weinberg Fellowships For Independent Scholars

Amount: $800 **Deadline:** Mar 1
Fields/Majors: History (American and European), Humanities, Literature

Fellowships are available for scholars doing research or working outside the academic setting who need to use the library's collections. Applicants need not have the Ph.D., but must have demonstrated, through their publications, particular expertise in a field appropriate to the Newberry. Write to the address below for more details.

Newberry Library
Committee On Awards
60 W. Walton St.
Chicago, IL 60610

434

Arthur Welker Scholarship Fund

Amount: $2,500 (max) **Deadline:** Mar 1
Fields/Majors: All Areas Of Study

Award for a student at Eastern New Mexico University who is active in the University Symphony Orchestra. Must be at the junior level or above and have an acceptable GPA. Financial need is a determining factor. Write to the address below for more information.

Eastern New Mexico University
College Of Fine Arts
Station 16
Portales, NM 88130

435

Artist Awards Competition For Singers

Amount: $2,500 To $5,000 **Deadline:** Aug 7
Fields/Majors: Singing

Purpose of the program is to select young singers who are ready for professional careers and to encourage them to carry on the tradition of fine singing. Applicants at least 21-35 years old and must have either studied with a teacher for at least one academic year or be a member of NATS. Write to the address below for details.

National Association of Teachers of Singing
Artist Competition
2800 University Blvd., N.
Jacksonville, FL 32211

436

Arts Awards

Amount: $1,000 **Deadline:** Apr 8
Fields/Majors: Fine Arts, Music, Dance, Drama, Theater

Awarded to a Latino student who is attending any postsecondary institution majoring in fine arts, music, dance, drama, or theater with a GPA of 2.5 or better. Must reside in the city of Los Angeles, Montebello, Commerce, Bell Gardens, or Monterey Park. Write to the address below for more information.

Telacu Education Foundation
5400 East Olympic Blvd., Suite 300
Los Angeles, CA 90022

437

Arts Scholarships

Amount: None Specified **Deadline:** Feb 15
Fields/Majors: Jazz/Classical Music, Fine Arts, Drama, Communications, Creative Writing

Scholarships are available at the University of New Orleans for full-time students enrolled in a one of the areas listed above. Requires and audition or submission of a portfolio or manuscript. Write to the address below for details.

University Of New Orleans
Student Financial Aid Office
1005 Administration Building, Lake Front
New Orleans, LA 70148

438

ASA Minority Fellowship Program

Amount: $10,008 **Deadline:** Dec 31
Fields/Majors: Sociology, Mental Health

Applicants must be minority graduate students who have an interest and can express a commitment to the sociological aspects of mental health issues relevant to ethnic and racial minorities. Write to the address below for details.

American Sociological Association
Minority Fellowship Program
1722 N Street, NW
Washington, DC 20036

439

ASBO International Exhibitor Scholarships

Amount: $1,500 **Deadline:** Aug 1
Fields/Majors: Areas Related To School Administration and Business Operations

Scholarships for members of ASBO who are improving their technical skills and competence by pursuing further academic training. Must be both a member of ASBO and employees full-time in school business management for at least 36 months. Recommendation by chief school administrator (employer) required. Three awards per year. Write to the ASBO at the address below for details.

Association Of School Business Officials
Exhibitor Scholarship Coordinator
11401 North Shore Dr.
Reston, VA 22090

440

ASCAP Foundation/ Rudolf Nissim Award

Amount: $5,000 **Deadline:** Nov 15
Fields/Majors: Music Composition

ASCAP foundation awards for composers. Candidates must be from an ASCAP school and submission must be an original work that has not been performed professionally. To encourage performance of the work, supplementary funds for rehearsal preparation may be available to the ensemble performing the premiere. Write to Frances Richard at the address listed below for information.

American Society Of Composers, Authors, And Publishers
One Lincoln Plaza
New York, NY 10023

441

ASCAP Foundation Grants To Young Composers

Amount: None Specified **Deadline:** Mar 15
Fields/Majors: Music Composition

ASCAP foundation grants for young composers. Candidates must be under 30 years of age as of March 15 of the year of application. Applicant must be a U.S. citizen. Awards help young composers continue their studies and develop their skills. Write to Frances Richard at the address below for details.

American Society Of Composers, Authors, And Publishers
One Lincoln Plaza
New York, NY 10023

442

ASCAP Foundation Louis Armstrong Scholarship

Amount: None Specified **Deadline:** None Specified
Fields/Majors: Music (Composition-Jazz)

Annual scholarship for a composition student interested in jazz at Queens College (in the city university of New York). Contact the financial aid office at Queens College. ASCAP does not accept any requests for applications.

American Society Of Composers, Authors, And Publishers
One Lincoln Plaza
New York, NY 10023

443

ASCAP Foundation Max Dreyfus Scholarship

Amount: None Specified **Deadline:** None Specified
Fields/Majors: Music (Theater-Performance)

Annual scholarship for a student at the Eastman School of Music (Univ. Of Rochester). Contact the financial aid office at Eastman. ASCAP does not accept any requests for applications.

American Society Of Composers, Authors, And Publishers
One Lincoln Plaza
New York, NY 10023

444

ASCAP Lieber & Stoller Music Scholarships

Amount: None Specified **Deadline:** None Specified
Fields/Majors: Music

Scholarships available to young songwriters and musicians from the New York and Los Angeles area. Applicant must be a senior in high school. Funds to be used for study at accredited music schools, conservatories, and university music programs. Contact your guidance counselor or university music department chairman for further information.

American Society Of Composers, Authors, And Publishers
One Lincoln Plaza
New York, NY 10023

445

ASCAP Michael Masser Scholarship Honoring Johnny Mercer

Amount: None Specified **Deadline:** None Specified
Fields/Majors: All Areas Of Study

Scholarships for employees of and immediate family members of the American Society of Composers, Authors, and Publishers foundation (ASCAP). Contact (or have your parent contact) your ASCAP office.

American Society Of Composers, Authors, And Publishers
One Lincoln Plaza
New York, NY 10023

446

ASCE Construction Engineering Scholarship and Student Prizes

Amount: $1,000 **Deadline:** Mar 1
Fields/Majors: Construction Engineering

Scholarships are available to freshmen, sophomore, and junior students whose interests are in construction engineering. Write to the address below for more information.

American Society Of Civil Engineers
Member Scholarships and Awards
345 E. 47th St.
New York, NY 10017

447 ASCSA Summer Sessions

AMOUNT: $2,500 **DEADLINE:** Feb 15
FIELDS/MAJORS: Classical Greek Studies

Awards are available for undergraduates and graduate students in the field of classical Greek studies. Write to the address below for more information.

American School Of Classical Studies At Athens
Committee On Admissions And Fellowships
993 Lenox Drive, Suite 101
Lawrenceville, NJ 08648

448 ASGROW Seed Company Scholarships

AMOUNT: $1,000 **DEADLINE:** Feb 15
FIELDS/MAJORS: Agricultural Sales/Marketing, Agribusiness

Scholarships are available for FFA members pursuing a four-year degree in agribusiness or agricultural sales/marketing. Applicant must have competed in the FFA agricultural sales contest above the local level. Write to the address below for details.

National FFA Foundation
Scholarship Office
P.O. Box 15160
Alexandria, VA 22309

449 ASHRAE Scholarship

AMOUNT: $3,000 **DEADLINE:** Dec 1
FIELDS/MAJORS: Air Conditioning/Refrigeration, HVAC Engineering

Scholarship for full-time undergraduate students studying HVAC/refrigeration. Applicant must have a GPA of at least 3.0 and at least one year remaining of undergraduate studies. Character and leadership ability, as well as potential service to the HVAC/refrigeration profession and financial need also considered. Write to the address below for details.

American Society Of Heating, Refrigerating and AC Engineers
Manager Of Research
1791 Tullie Circle, NE
Atlanta, GA 30329

450 ASHRAE Scholarship

AMOUNT: Varies **DEADLINE:** Mar 1
FIELDS/MAJORS: Mechanical Engineering

Awards are available at the University of New Mexico for students in the field of mechanical engineering. Must demonstrate academic ability and financial need and be a resident of New Mexico. Write to the address below for more information.

University Of New Mexico, Albuquerque
Office Of Financial Aid
Albuquerque, NM 87131

451 Asian American Journalists Association Scholarships

AMOUNT: $250-$2,000 **DEADLINE:** Apr 15
FIELDS/MAJORS: Print Journalism, Photojournalism, Broadcast Journalism

Applicants must be Asian Americans who are pursuing careers in journalism (print, photo, or broadcast). Based on academics and financial need. Send an SASE to the address below for details.

Asian American Journalists Association
Scholarship Committee
1765 Sutter St., Suite 1000
San Francisco, CA 94115

452 Asian Pacific American Support Group Scholarships

AMOUNT: Varies **DEADLINE:** Mar 22
FIELDS/MAJORS: All Areas Of Study

Scholarships for Asian Pacific American students at the University of Southern California. Based on academic achievement, personal merit, and financial need. Must be U.S. citizen or permanent resident enrolled in full-time study and have a GPA of 3.0 or better. Write to the address below for details.

Asian Pacific American Support Group
Scholarship Committee University Of Southern California
Student Union 410, University Park
Los Angeles CA 90089

453 ASID Educational Foundation/ Harris Memorial Scholarship

AMOUNT: $1,500 **DEADLINE:** Mar 22
FIELDS/MAJORS: Interior Design

For undergraduates above their sophomore year of study at a degree-granting institution. Based primarily on academic achievements and financial need. Two awards per year. Send a SASE to the address below for details.

American Society Of Interior Designers
Educational Foundation Scholarship And Awards Program
608 Massachusetts Ave., NE
Washington, DC 20002

454 ASIWA Letter Writing Contest

AMOUNT: $100-$1,000 **DEADLINE:** Mar 1
FIELDS/MAJORS: Property Rights

Contest open to high school students who write a letter to their state's national senators or U.S. representatives discussing why property rights are important to your state. Applicants must be U.S. citizens. Write to the address below for more information.

American Sheep Industry Women's Auxiliary
Ms. Doris Haby
P.O. Box 1496
Brackettville, TX 78832

455

ASM Student Travel Awards

AMOUNT: $400 **DEADLINE:** Varies
FIELDS/MAJORS: Microbiological Sciences

Awards to students in the field of microbiological sciences to use to travel and attend ASM and other scientific meetings. Must have an approved abstract to present at the meeting. Write to the address below for more information.

American Society For Microbiology
Office Of Education And Training
1325 Massachussettes Ave., NW
Washington, DC 20005

456

ASM/NCID Postdoctoral Research Associates Program

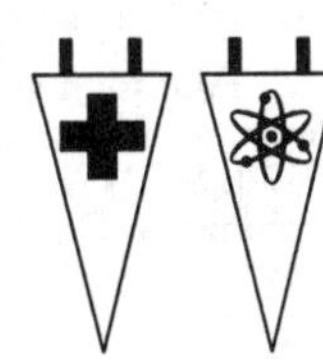

AMOUNT: $35,000 (max) **DEADLINE:** Dec 1
FIELDS/MAJORS: Infectious Diseases and Public Health Microbiology

Two-year fellowship for an individual who holds a doctorate degree or has completed a primary residency within the past three years in the field indicated above. Applicants must be U.S. citizens, permanent residents, or English speaking non-U.S. citizens. Write to the address below for additional information.

American Society For Microbiology
Office Of Education And Training
1325 Massachussettes Ave., NW
Washington, DC 20005

457

ASME Graduate Fellowship Program

AMOUNT: $5,000 **DEADLINE:** Oct 7
FIELDS/MAJORS: Mechanical Engineering (Education)

Program for ASME student members in graduate school and working toward a doctorate. Must have career goal of engineering eduction. Must be U.S. citizen or permanent resident. Must have received an undergraduate degree from an ABET accredited program. Renewable. Contact the ASME faculty advisor or student section chairman, call or write your ASME regional office, or contact the education service at ASME headquarters at the address below for details.

American Society Of Mechanical Engineers
Education Services Department
345 E. 47th Street
New York, NY 10017

458

ASME Student Assistance Loans

AMOUNT: $2,500 (max) **DEADLINE:** Oct 7, Apr 15
FIELDS/MAJORS: Mechanical Engineering

Loans for ASME student members. Based on need. Must be U.S. citizen enrolled in an ME or MET program. Contact the ASME faculty advisor or student section chairman, call or write your ASME regional office, or contact the education service at ASME headquarters at the address below for details.

American Society Of Mechanical Engineers
Education Services Department
345 E. 47th St.
New York, NY 10017

459

ASNE Scholarship Program

AMOUNT: $2,000 **DEADLINE:** Feb 15
FIELDS/MAJORS: Naval Engineering And Related Fields

Undergraduate and graduate scholarships are available. U.S. citizens and candidates for degree in engineering or physical science only. Based on motivation toward career in naval engineering and scholastic aptitude. Majors which apply: naval architecture, marine, civil, mechanical, aeronautical, and electrical engineering. Students holding advanced degrees are not eligible. For 4th year undergraduates and first-year master's study. Special consideration may be given to members of the society and their children. Write to the address below for complete details.

American Society Of Naval Engineers
Scholarship Program
1452 Duke Street
Alexandria, VA 22314

460

Aspinall Foundation Awards

AMOUNT: $1,000-$4,000
DEADLINE: None Specified
FIELDS/MAJORS: Social Science

Awards for a junior or senior Mesa State students in the field of social science. Applicants must have a GPA of at least 3.0. Contact the Mesa State school of humanities and social science.

Mesa State College
Office Of Financial Aid
P.O. Box 2647
Grand Junction, CO 81501

461

ASSE Student Paper Awards

AMOUNT: $500-$1,000 **DEADLINE:** Jan 31
FIELDS/MAJORS: Safety Engineering And Related Fields

Awards are available to undergraduate students majoring in some aspect of safety engineering for submitting a 10-20 page paper on a relevant safety issue. Write to the address listed below for information.

American Society Of Safety Engineers/Marsh & Mclennan, Inc.
ASSE Student Paper Awards
1800 East Oakton
Des Plaines, IL 60018

462

Assistance Fund For Professionals

AMOUNT: $1,000 **DEADLINE:** Any Time
FIELDS/MAJORS: Journalism, Film, Writing, Publishing

Fund available to students to help offset expenses for participation in career-enhancing activities. Write to the address below for details.

Institute For Humane Studies At George Mason University
4084 University Dr., Suite 101
Fairfax, VA 22030

463

Assistant Attorney General's Graduate Research Fellowship Program

AMOUNT: $35,000 (max) **DEADLINE:** Varies
FIELDS/MAJORS: Law Enforcement, Criminal Justice, Criminology

Must be doctoral candidates with all course work completed who have passed all examinations prior to start of grant. The research fellowships will last for up to 18 months. For more information, call the national criminal justice reference service at 800-851-3420, e-mail askncjrs@ncjrs.aspensys.com, or write to the address below.

National Institute Of Justice
Graduate Research Fellowship Program
633 Indiana Avenue, NW
Washington, DC 20531

464

Assoc. Of Pennsylvania State College And University Faculties

AMOUNT: None Specified **DEADLINE:** None Specified
FIELDS/MAJORS: All Areas Of Study

One scholarship is awarded each spring by the Association of Pennsylvania State College and University Faculties at Clarion University. Candidates must have completed sixty credits at Clarion. Selections are also based on academic record, contribution to the university, and participation in extra-curricular activities. Contact the APSCUF office for more information.

Clarion University
104 Egbert Hall
Office Of Financial Aid
Clarion, PA 16214

465

Associated General Contractors Of America Education & Research Foundation

AMOUNT: $6,000 (max) **DEADLINE:** Nov 15
FIELDS/MAJORS: Construction Management And Related Fields

Awards are available for full-time continuing students at UW Platteville who are studying construction management or a related field. Write to the address below for more information.

University Of Wisconsin, Platteville
Professor Stuelke
311 Pioneer Tower
Platteville, WI 53818

466

Associated General Contractors Of America, Wisconsin Scholarships

AMOUNT: $500 **DEADLINE:** Apr
FIELDS/MAJORS: Construction Management and Related Fields

Awards are available for full-time continuing students at UW Platteville who are studying construction management or a related field. Write to the address below for more information.

University Of Wisconsin, Platteville
Professor Stuelke
311 Pioneer Tower
Platteville, WI 53818

467

Associated General Contractors Undergraduate Scholarships

AMOUNT: $1,500 **DEADLINE:** Nov 1
FIELDS/MAJORS: Civil Engineering/Construction

The Associated General Contractors of America offers scholarships for undergraduates who are enrolled in a degree program in construction or civil engineering. Renewable for up to four years. Must be enrolled at the time of application and be a freshman, sophomore or junior. For additional information and applications, write to the address below. Several "special awards" are also given (only one application is needed to compete for all of the undergraduate awards).

AGC Education and Research Foundation
Director Of Programs
1957 E St., NW
Washington, DC 20006

468

Associated Industries Of Massachusetts Award

AMOUNT: None Specified **DEADLINE:** Feb 29
FIELDS/MAJORS: Management

Scholarships are awarded to Massachusetts residents who have done outstanding graduate work in the School of Management and who plan to work in a Massachusetts enterprise upon graduation. Applications for School of Management scholarships will be available in the SOM Development Office, Room 206.

University Of Massachusetts, Amherst
School Of Management
SOM Development Office, Room 206
Amherst, MA 01003

469

Associated Landscape Contractors Of America (ALCA) Scholarships

AMOUNT: Varies **DEADLINE:** Feb 1
FIELDS/MAJORS: Horticulture, Landscape

Open to horticulture students with a demonstrated interest in the landscape industry. Write to the address below for more information.

California State Polytechnic University, Pomona
College Of Agriculture
Building 7, Room 110
Pomona, CA 91768

470

Associated Landscape Contractors Of America Scholarships

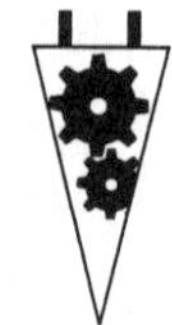

AMOUNT: $500 **DEADLINE:** Feb 15
FIELDS/MAJORS: Landscape Architecture

Scholarships are available for FFA members pursuing a two- or four-year degree in the landscaping industry. Write to the address below for details.

National FFA Foundation
Scholarship Office
P.O. Box 15160
Alexandria, VA 22309

471 Associated Press Minority Summer Internships

Amount: None Specified
Deadline: None Specified
Fields/Majors: Print Editorial, Broadcasting, Photojournalism, Graphic Communications

Minority internship program for full-time upperclass men or graduate students enrolled in a four-year college or university in the U.S. Selection is based on a testing process which takes place in an AP bureau or designated testing site. There is no application form. Check the editor and publisher international yearbook at your local library or contact the address below for the location of the nearest AP bureau.

Associated Press
Director Of Recruiting
50 Rockefeller Plaza
New York, NY 10020

472 Association For The Advancement Of Health Education

Amount: $500 **Deadline:** Jan 15
Fields/Majors: Health Education

Award is open to a graduate student who is currently enrolled in a health education program with a GPA of 3.0 or better. Write to the address below for more information.

Association For The Advancement Of Health Education
AAHE Scholarship Committee
1900 Association Dr.
Reston, VA 22091

473 Association For Women Veterinarians Scholarship

Amount: $1,500 **Deadline:** Feb 20
Fields/Majors: Veterinary Medicine

Awarded to current second- or third-year veterinary medical students who are attending a college or school of veterinary medicine in the U.S. or in Canada. Write to the address below for more information.

Association For Women Veterinarians
Chris Stone Payne, DVM
32205 Allison Dr.
Union City, CA 94587

474 Association Of Connecticut Fairs, Inc. Scholarships

Amount: $750 **Deadline:** May 8
Fields/Majors: Home Economics, Agriculture, and Related Fields

Awards for students who are Connecticut residents and are or have been participants in a member fair. Contact a high school guidance counselor for information and an application or write to: The Waterbury Foundation, 156 W. Main St., Waterbury, CT 06702 (enclose $1.75 for shipping & handling).

Association Of Connecticut Fairs, Inc.
The Waterbury Foundation
156 W. Main
Waterbury, CT 06702

475 Association Of Old Crows Scholarship Fund

Amount: Varies **Deadline:** Mar 1
Fields/Majors: Electrical Engineering

Awards are available at the University of New Mexico for junior or senior electrical engineering majors with a minimum GPA of 3.0 and demonstrated financial need. Must be a New Mexico resident. Write to the address below for more information.

University Of New Mexico, Albuquerque
Office Of Financial Aid
Albuquerque, NM 87131

476 Association Of Retired Teachers Of Connecticut Scholarships

Amount: $4,000 (max) **Deadline:** Mar 30
Fields/Majors: Education

Award for high school seniors who show scholastic achievement, extra-curricular activities and intention to remain in education field. Must demonstrate financial need and be a Connecticut resident. Contact your high school guidance counselor for further information and an application or write to: The Waterbury Foundation, 156 W. Main St., Waterbury, CT 06702 (enclose $1.75 for shipping and handling).

Association Of Retired Teachers Of Connecticut
The Waterbury Foundation
156 W Main
Waterbury, CT 06702

477 Assumption Program Of Loans For Education

Amount: $8,000 (max) **Deadline:** Jun 30
Fields/Majors: Education, Elementary And Secondary

Loan program for California students who have completed at least sixty hours of undergraduate study in the field of education. Recipients must teach full-time in a California public school in a designated subject matter shortage area for loan forgiveness. Write to the address below for more information.

California Student Aid Commission
P.O. Box 51845
Sacramento, CA 94245

478 ASTA Undergraduate Scholarships

Amount: $1,000-$3,000 **Deadline:** Jun 23
Fields/Majors: Travel And Tourism

Awards are available for undergraduate students who are studying travel and tourism at any two- or four-year school or are enrolled in a proprietary travel school. Must be U.S. citizens or legal residents and have a GPA of at least 2.5. There are many different awards available which are based on various criteria such as academics, recommendations, or essays. Write to the address below for more information. This includes the American Express, Air Travel Card, Healy, Holland America Line–Westours, Inc., Princess Cruises & Tours, and George Reinke scholarships.

American Society Of Travel Agents
Scholarship Committee
1101 King St., Suite 200
Alexandria, VA 22314

479

Asthma Athlete Scholarship Program

Amount: $1,000-$3,500 **Deadline:** Mar 24
Fields/Majors: All Areas Of Study

Scholarships for high school senior athletes who have asthma and will graduate in the current school year. Students must be nominated by school faculty or staff. Contact your guidance counselor for further information.

Schering-Key Foundation
Schering Asthma Athlete Scholarship
21 Spielman Road
Fairfield, NJ 07004

480

Astral Career Grant

Amount: $250 **Deadline:** Mar 1, Sep 1
Fields/Majors: Music or Dance

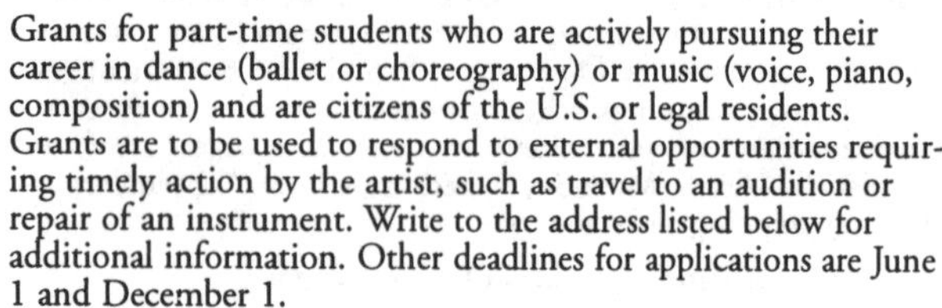

Grants for part-time students who are actively pursuing their career in dance (ballet or choreography) or music (voice, piano, composition) and are citizens of the U.S. or legal residents. Grants are to be used to respond to external opportunities requiring timely action by the artist, such as travel to an audition or repair of an instrument. Write to the address listed below for additional information. Other deadlines for applications are June 1 and December 1.

National Foundation For Advancement In The Arts (NFAA)
NFAA/ASTRAL
800 Brickell Avenue, Suite 500
Miami, FL 33131

481

Astrid G. Cates Scholarship Fund

Amount: $500-$750 **Deadline:** Mar 1
Fields/Majors: All Areas Of Study

Open to undergraduates between the ages of 17 and 22 who are members of Sons of Norway or children or grandchildren of Sons of Norway members. Financial need is required. Renewable one time. Write to the address below for details.

Sons Of Norway Foundation
1455 W. Lake St.
Minneapolis, MN 55408

482

ASWA Scholarships

Amount: $1,500-$2,500 **Deadline:** Mar 1
Fields/Majors: Accounting

Awards are available for accounting students pursuing a bachelor's or a master's degree in a full or part-time program. Must have completed at least sixty semester hours or ninety quarter hours at an accredited college, university, or professional school. Write to the address below for more information.

American Society Of Women Accountants
Educational Foundation
1255 Lynnnfield Rd. Suite 257
Memphis, TN 38119

483

AT&T Achievement Award For Minority Engineering Students

Amount: $2,500 **Deadline:** Mar 1
Fields/Majors: Engineering

Awards for college sophomores enrolled in the college of engineering who demonstrate superior academic achievement, potential for leadership, and an unwavering goal of obtaining a degree in engineering. Contact the director of the minority engineering program for more information.

University Of Massachusetts, Amherst
Director, Minority Engineering Program
Amherst, MA 01003

484

AT&T TQM Scholarship Award

Amount:$5,000 **Deadline:** Feb 29
Fields/Majors: Management

Scholarships are awarded to an outstanding junior to undertake concentrated study of TQM in their senior year. Applications for School of Management scholarships will be available in the SOM Development Office, Room 206.

University Of Massachusetts, Amherst
School Of Management
SOM Development Office, Room 206
Amherst, MA 01003

485

Athlete Scholarship Program

Amount: Varies **Deadline:** None Specified
Fields/Majors: Athletics

Athletic scholarship program for students enrolled at the University of New Mexico, New Mexico State University, Eastern New Mexico University, New Mexico Highlands University, Western New Mexico University, or New Mexico Junior College. For undergraduate study. Write to the address listed below for additional information or contact the athletic department at the school of your choice.

New Mexico Commission On Higher Education
1068 Cerrillos Road
Santa Fe, NM 87501

486

Athletic Awards

Amount: Varies **Deadline:** Mar 1
Fields/Majors: All Areas Of Study

Scholarships available at Sterling for undergraduate full-time students who participate in the intercollegiate athletics program. Awards are available for men in the following sports: baseball, basketball, cross country, track, football, soccer, and tennis. Women sports are the same except softball and volleyball replace men's football and baseball. Write to the address below for details.

Sterling College
Financial Aid Office
Sterling, KS 67579

487

Athletic Grants

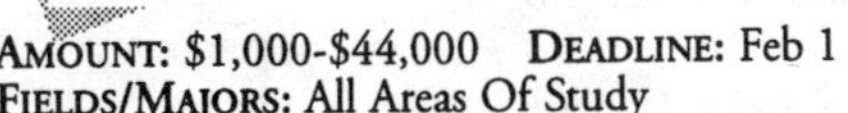

Amount: $1,000-$44,000 **Deadline:** Feb 1
Fields/Majors: All Areas Of Study

Scholarships are available at Bellarmine College for full-time students who plan to participate in the intercollegiate athletics program. Applicable sports include basketball, cross country, golf, soccer, tennis, baseball, field hockey, softball, and volleyball. For undergraduate study. Contact the financial aid office at the address below for details.

Bellarmine College
Financial Aid Office
2001 Newburg Road
Louisville, KY 40205

488

Athletic Grants

Amount: Varies **Deadline:** Jan 15
Fields/Majors: All Areas Of Study

Grants are available for freshman and transfer students entering Valparaiso University in many different collegiate athletics. Renewable. Contact the athletic department for more information.

Valparaiso University
Office Of Admissions And Financial Aid
Kretzmann Hall
Valparaiso, IN 46383

489

Athletic Grants-in-Aid

Amount: Varies **Deadline:** Feb 1
Fields/Majors: All Areas Of Study

Non-need based scholarships for Loyola undergraduates. Based on athletic ability which is determined by the Director of Athletics. Contact the athletic department or write to the address below for additional information.

Loyola College In Maryland
Director Of Financial Aid
4501 North Charles St.
Baltimore, MD 21210

490

Athletic Program Grants-in-Aid

Amount: Varies **Deadline:** None Specified
Fields/Majors: All Areas Of Study

Grants for students at Cal Poly (San Luis Obispo) who are participating in one of 11 sports programs (6 men's and 5 women's). Renewable. Contact the athletic department for further details.

California Polytechnic State University
Financial Aid Office
212 Administration Bldg.
San Luis Obispo, CA 93407

491

Athletic Scholarship

Amount: Varies **Deadline:** None Specified
Fields/Majors: All Areas Of Study

Scholarships are available to John Brown College for full-time undergraduate students who plan to participate in the intercollegiate athletic program. Write to the address below for details.

John Brown University
Office Of Financial Aid
2000 West University Dr.
Siloam Springs, AR 72761

492

Athletic Scholarships

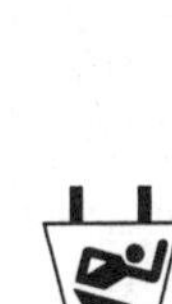

Amount: Varies **Deadline:** None Specified
Fields/Majors: All Areas Of Study

Scholarship offered to students attending or planning to attend Loyola University on a full time basis, with outstanding athletic ability who plan to participate in the intercollegiate athletics program. Scholarships for men are offered in basketball, cross-country, track, golf, soccer, and swimming. Write to the address below for details.

Loyola University
Director Of Athletics
6525 North Sheridan Road
Chicago, IL 60626

493

Athletic Scholarships

Amount: Varies **Deadline:** Apr 1
Fields/Majors: All Areas Of Study

Awards are available to full-time Elon College freshmen who will be participating in the intercollegiate athletics program. Men's and women's athletic events differ. Contact the athletics department at Elon or write to the address below for information.

Elon College
Office Of Financial Planning
2700 Campus Box
Elon College, NC 27244

494

Athletic Scholarships

Amount: None Specified **Deadline:** Apr 1
Fields/Majors: All Areas Of Study

Scholarships are available at Evangel for full-time students who plan to participate in the intercollegiate athletics program. Write to the address listed below for information.

Evangel College
Director Of Athletics
Springfield, MO 65802

495

Athletic Scholarships

Amount: Varies **Deadline:** Feb 15
Fields/Majors: All Areas Of Study

Scholarships are available at the University of New Orleans for full-time students who plan to participate in the intercollegiate athletics program. Write to the address below for details.

University Of New Orleans
Director Of Athletics
Lakefront Arena
New Orleans, LA 70148

496

Athletic Scholarships

AMOUNT: Varied **DEADLINE:** Aug 1, Jan 1
FIELDS/MAJORS: All Areas Of Study

Awards for Liberty University students with athletic talents and ability. Renewable. Contact the coach of the appropriate sport for more details.

Liberty University
Office Of Student Financial Aid
Box 20000
Lynchburg, VA 24506

497

Athletic Scholarships

AMOUNT: Varies **DEADLINE:** Mar 31
FIELDS/MAJORS: All Areas Of Study

Awards for students with talents or abilities in athletics. For men, eligible sports include: basketball, cross country, track and field, and soccer. For women, the eligible sports are: basketball, softball, cross-country, and track and field. Renewable. Must maintain full-time study. Contact the athletic department for more information.

Columbia Union College
Financial Aid Office
7600 Flower Ave.
Takoma Park, MD 20912

498

Athletic Scholarships

AMOUNT: None Specified **DEADLINE:** Varies
FIELDS/MAJORS: All Areas Of Study

Scholarships for incoming freshmen who demonstrate athletic activity. Interested applicants should call the men's athletic department at (218) 236-2622 or the women's athletic department at (218) 299-5824 for more information.

Moorhead State University
Office Of Scholarship And Financial Aid
107 Owens Hall
Moorhead, MN 56563

499

Athletic Scholarships

AMOUNT: Varies **DEADLINE:** Mar 1
FIELDS/MAJORS: All Areas Of Study

Scholarships for students at Black Hills State university who participate in intercollegiate athletics. Individual award requirements may vary. Write to the address below for more information.

Black Hills State University
Office Of Financial Aid
University Station, Box 9509
Spearfish, SD 57799

500

Athletic Scholarships at Flagler College

AMOUNT: Varies **DEADLINE:** None Specified
FIELDS/MAJORS: All Areas Of Study

Scholarships for students at Flagler College who will participate in one of several sports. Men's sports include baseball, basketball, cross country, golf, soccer, and tennis. Womens sports include basketball, cross country, volleyball, and tennis. Awards are made at the discretion of the coach. Contact the coach, the athletic director, or the address below for details.

Flagler College
Director Of Financial Aid
P.O. Box 1027
St. Augistine, FL 32085

501

Athletic Scholarships/Grants

AMOUNT: Varies **DEADLINE:** None Specified
FIELDS/MAJORS: All Areas Of Study

Grants awarded for ability in the sports listed below. Award amount also based on need. Sports: basketball, baseball, tennis, crew, soccer, swimming, cross country, golf, volleyball, and softball. Apply to the coach within the athletic department. Write to the address below for details.

Mercyhurst College
Glenwood Hills
Erie, PA 16546

502

Athletic Work Service Grant

AMOUNT: Varies **DEADLINE:** Apr 1
FIELDS/MAJORS: All Areas Of Study

Scholarships are available at Siena Heights College for full-time students who plan to participate in the intercollegiate sports program. Write to the address listed below for information.

Siena Heights College
Financial Aids Office
1247 East Siena Heights Drive
Adrian, MI 49221

503

Atlantic Rural Exposition Scholarships

AMOUNT: $1,000 **DEADLINE:** May 1
FIELDS/MAJORS: Agriculture, Life Sciences

Five scholarships for entering freshmen at Virginia Tech who have been active in 4-H or FFA for at least two years. Must be VA resident. Based on academics, character, leadership potential, and need. Write to the address below for details.

Virginia Tech College Of Agriculture And Life Sciences
Dr. John M. White, Associate Dean
1060 Litton Reaves Hall
Blacksburg, VA 24061

504

Auburn University Merit Scholarships

AMOUNT: $750-$2,000 **DEADLINE:** Mar 1
FIELDS/MAJORS: All Areas Of Study

Awards for National Merit and National Achievement finalists naming Auburn as their first-choice institution. Renewable with a GPA of 3.0 or better. Write to the address below for more information.

Auburn University
Office Of Student Financial Aid
203 Mary Martin Hall
Auburn University, AL 36849

505

Auburn University Scholarships

Amount: Varies **Deadline:** Mar 1
Fields/Majors: All Areas Of Study

Scholarships are available for students at Auburn University. Application forms are available in the office of student financial aid. Based on a wide variety of criteria. All applicants must be U.S. citizens or permanent residents. A brochure describing all of the scholarships is available from the address below. One application form will serve to apply for all scholarships.

Auburn University
Office Of Student Financial Aid
203 Martin Hall
Auburn University, AL 36849

506

Audio Engineering Society Educational Foundation Grants

Amount: $3,000 **Deadline:** May 15
Fields/Majors: Audio Engineering

Grants for graduate students in audio engineering, based on interest and accomplishments in the field and on faculty recommendations. Renewable for one additional year. Write to the address below for details.

Audio Engineering Society
60 East 42nd Street
New York, NY 10165

507

Audre Lorde Memorial Prose Prize

Amount: $250 **Deadline:** Nov 17
Fields/Majors: Creative Writing

Award available for feminist writers for a submitted work taking up a topic of discourse found in the works of Lorde, or seeking to illustrate a condition, idea, or ideal inherent in her fiction or prose. Two awards, one for fiction and one for non-fiction. Write to the address below for details.

National Women's Studies Association
7100 Baltimore Avenue
Suite 301
University Of Maryland
College Park, MD 20740

508

Audrey Lumsden-Kouvel Fellowship

Amount: $3,000 (max) **Deadline:** Jan 20
Fields/Majors: Late Medieval Or Renaissance Studies

Fellowships are available for postdoctoral scholars wishing to carry on extended research in late medieval or renaissance studies. Write to the address below for more details.

Newberry Library
Committee On Awards
60 W. Walton St.
Chicago, IL 60610

509

Aura E. Severinghaus Award

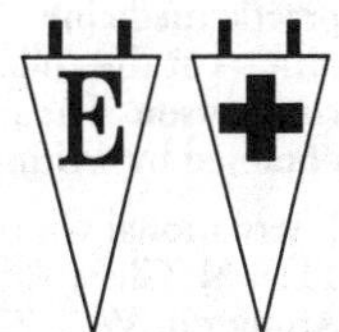

Amount: $2,000 **Deadline:** Aug 31
Fields/Majors: Medicine

Awards for minority medical students attending Columbia University, College of Physicians and Surgeons. Must be U.S. citizen. Minorities are defined as African American, Mexican American, mainland Puerto Rican, and American Indian. Based on academics and leadership. Send a SASE to the address below for additional information.

National Medical Fellowships, Inc.
110 West 32nd Street
New York, NY 10001

510

Austin Roberts Scholarships

Amount: Varies **Deadline:** Mar 1
Fields/Majors: All Areas Of Study

Awards are available at the University of New Mexico for students from San Juan County, New Mexico with financial need and academic ability. Write to the address below for more information.

University Of New Mexico, Albuquerque
Office Of Financial Aid
Albuquerque, NM 87131

511

Austrian Cultural Institute Grants

Amount: $740-$810 **Deadline:** Jan 31
Fields/Majors: Music, Art

Grants are for foreign students for studies at academies of music and dramatic art or at art academies in Austria. Applicants for the program must be advanced students and between 19 and 35 years old. Write to the address below for more information.

Austrian Cultural Institute
950 Third Ave., 20th Floor
New York, NY 10022

512

Auxiliary Nursing Scholarships

Amount: $1,500 **Deadline:** None Specified
Fields/Majors: Nursing

Awards given to students who attend St. Petersburg Junior College who are majoring in the field of nursing. Contact the Nursing Program Director, Health Education Center, or the address below for more details.

St. Petersburg Junior College
Office Of Financial Aid
P.O. Box 13489
St. Petersburg, FL 33733

513

Auxiliary Of ICA Scholarships

Amount: None Specified **Deadline:** None Specified
Fields/Majors: Chiropractic Medicine

Scholarships for students at ICA affiliate colleges studying chiropractic medicine. Applications are available from SICA chapter officers at the colleges or from the ICA auxiliary scholarship chairperson. The name and address of the chairperson may be obtained by writing to the address below.

International Chiropractors Association
1110 N. Glebe Rd., Suite 1000
Arlington, VA 22201

514 Auxiliary To The Lovelace Medical Foundation Scholarship

Amount: Varies **Deadline:** Mar 1
Fields/Majors: Nursing

Awards are available at the University of New Mexico for full-time junior or senior nursing students with a minimum GPA of 3.0. Applicants should exemplify the "best in nursing." Write to the address below or contact the school of nursing for more details.

University Of New Mexico, Albuquerque
Office Of Financial Aid
Albuquerque, NM 87131

515 Avery Brundage Scholarship

Amount: $1,000 (approx) **Deadline:** Jan 19
Fields/Majors: All Areas Of Study

Scholarships are available at the University of Illinois for students who participate in amateur athletics programs. For undergraduate study. Write to the address listed below for information.

University Of Illinois At Champaign Urbana
Office Of Student Financial Aid
610 E. John Street, 4th Floor
Champaign, IL 61820

516 Averyl Elaine Keriakedes Memorial Scholarship

Amount: $500 **Deadline:** Apr 12
Fields/Majors: Elementary/Secondary Education

A scholarship is available for a female Nebraska student who is a U.S. citizen enrolled in at the University of Nebraska, studying for a career in elementary or secondary education. Must be the daughter of a veteran. Write to the address listed below for additional information.

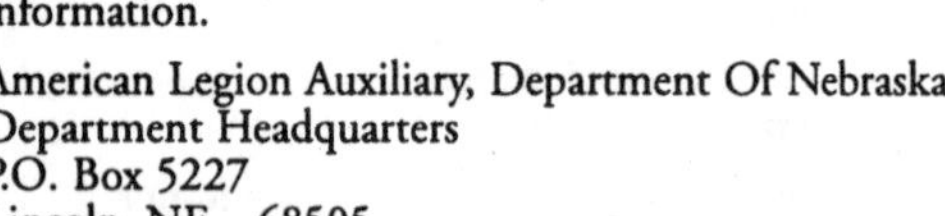

American Legion Auxiliary, Department Of Nebraska
Department Headquarters
P.O. Box 5227
Lincoln, NE 68505

517 Aviation Career Scholarships

Amount: Varies **Deadline:** Apr 1
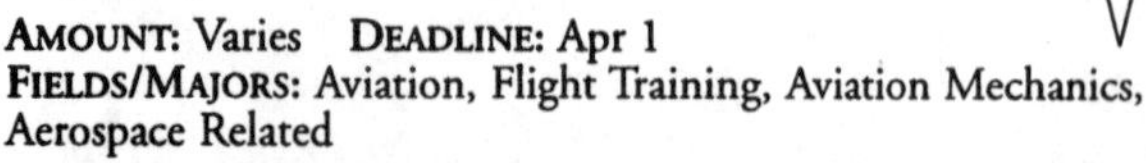
Fields/Majors: Aviation, Flight Training, Aviation Mechanics, Aerospace Related

Scholarships for residents of the greater Los Angeles area who are furthering their education in an aviation-related field of study. Must be a least 18 years old. Financial need is considered. Interview required (at Van Nuys airport). While the sponsor is an organization of women pilots, no restriction is placed on gender. Please be certain to include a SASE when requesting information. Write to the address below for details.

Ninety Nines, Inc., San Fernando Valley Chapter
c/o Sandra L. Bullock
4365 W. 141 St., #107
Hawthorne, CA 90250

518 Avis Rent A Car Scholarship

Amount: $2,000 **Deadline:** Jul 26
Fields/Majors: Travel And Tourism

Awards are available for sophomores, juniors, seniors, or graduate students studying travel and tourism at any institution who have worked part-time in the travel industry. Must be U.S. citizens or legal residents and have a GPA of at least 2.5. Write to the address below for more information.

American Society Of Travel Agents
Scholarship Committee
1101 King St., Suite 200
Alexandria, VA 22314

519 Avon Foundation For Women In Business Studies

Amount: $1,000 **Deadline:** Apr 15
Fields/Majors: Business

Women 25 or older seeking the necessary education for a career in a business-related field. Must be within 24 months of graduation. Must demonstrate need and be a U.S. citizen. The pre-application screening form is only available between October 1 and April 1. Up to 100 scholarships are available. Not for doctoral or correspondence programs, or non-degreed programs. Write to the address listed below for information and enclose a business-size (#10), self-addressed, double stamped envelope.

Business And Professional Women's Foundation
Scholarships
2012 Massachusetts Avenue, NW
Washington, DC 20036

520 Avon Lake Kiwanis Scholarship Loan Fund

Amount: $600-$1,200 **Deadline:** None Specified
Fields/Majors: All Areas Of Study

Low-cost loans are available to residents of Avon and Avon Lake, Sheffield Lake, and Sheffield Village for use at any accredited college or university. Write to the address listed below for information.

Avon Lake Kiwanis
Frank Hoerrle
32180 Hampton Court
Avon Lake, OH 44012

521 Award Design Medals, Inc. Scholarships

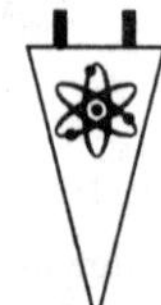

Amount: $1,000 **Deadline:** Feb 15
Fields/Majors: Agriculture

Scholarships are available for FFA members pursuing a four-year degree in any area of agriculture. Write to the address below for details.

National FFA Foundation
Scholarship Office
P.O. Box 15160
Alexandria, VA 22309

522

Award Of Excellence

AMOUNT: $1,500 Fee Waiver **DEADLINE:** Feb 15
FIELDS/MAJORS: All Areas Of Study

Fee waivers are available at the University of Oklahoma, Norman for entering freshmen with academic achievement. Applicants applying early will receive preference. Write to the address listed below for information.

University Of Oklahoma, Norman
Honors Program
347 Cate Center Drive
Norman, OK 73019

523

Awards For Study In Scandinavia

AMOUNT: Varies **DEADLINE:** Nov 1
FIELDS/MAJORS: Scandinavian Studies

Awards for graduate students who have a well-defined research or study project that makes a stay in Scandinavia essential. Applicants must be U.S. citizens or permanent residents and have completed their undergraduate degree by the start of their project in Scandinavia. Write to the address below for more information.

The American-Scandinavian Foundation
725 Park Ave.
New York, NY 10021

524

Awards Programs

AMOUNT: Varies **DEADLINE:** Jun 15
FIELDS/MAJORS: Arc Welding, Engineering-Technology

Awards are given to engineering and technology students in solving design engineering or fabricating problems involving the knowledge or application of arc welding. Must submit paper in either one of two divisions. Write to the address below for complete details.

James F. Lincoln Arc Welding Foundation
Secretary
P.O. Box 17035
Cleveland, OH 44117

525

AWIS Predoctoral Awards

AMOUNT: $500 (max) **DEADLINE:** Jan 15
FIELDS/MAJORS: Engineering, Mathematics, Physical, Life, And Behavioral Sciences

Scholarship aid and incentive awards for women actively toward a Ph.D. degree in the above fields. For U.S. citizens who are studying in the U.S.A. or abroad, or for foreign citizens studying in the U.S. Usually awarded to a student at dissertation level. Four awards per year. (AWIS also publishes a directory of financial aid.) Write to the address below for details.

Association For Women In Science Educational Foundation
Awis National Headquarters
1522 K St., NW, Suite 820
Washington, DC 20005

526

B. Charles Tiney Memorial ASCE Student Chapter Scholarship

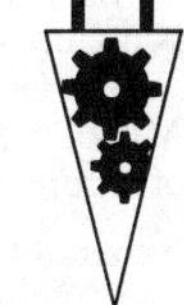

AMOUNT: $2,000-$3,000 **DEADLINE:** Mar 1
FIELDS/MAJORS: Civil Engineering/Hydraulics

Applicant must be a freshman, sophomore, or junior student ASCE member in good standing. Applicant must demonstrate financial need. Write to the address below for complete details.

American Society Of Civil Engineers
Students Services Department
345 E. 47th Street
New York, NY 10017

527

B. Jack White Scholarship

AMOUNT: Varies **DEADLINE:** Feb 1
FIELDS/MAJORS: Psychology

Scholarships are available at the University of Utah for full-time students majoring in psychology, who are entering freshmen. Write to the address below for information.

University Of Utah
Sally Ozonoff
502 Behavioral Science Building
Salt Lake City, UT 84112

528

B.H. Taylor Scholarship

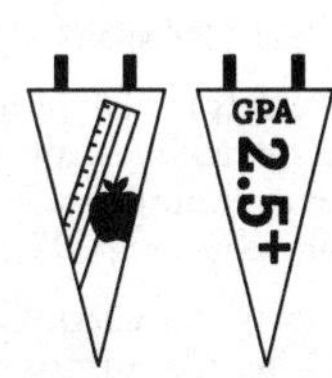

AMOUNT: Varies **DEADLINE:** Feb 17
FIELDS/MAJORS: Early Childhood Education

Scholarships are available at the University of Oklahoma, Norman for full-time early childhood education majors. Applicant must be at least a sophomore, have a GPA of at least 2.5, and be a resident of Oklahoma. Write to the address listed below for information.

University Of Oklahoma, Norman
College Of Education, Student Services
Room 137, ECH
Norman, OK 73019

529

B.I. Barnes Scholarships

AMOUNT: $1,300 **DEADLINE:** Mar 1
FIELDS/MAJORS: Accounting

Scholarships are available at the University of Iowa for full-time undergraduates majoring in accounting. Write to the address listed below for information.

University Of Iowa
College Of Business Admin., Suite W160
108 Pappajohn Business Admin. Bldg.
Iowa City, IA 52245

530

B.M. Woltman Foundations Scholarship Program

AMOUNT: Varies **DEADLINE:** None Specified
FIELDS/MAJORS: Theology, Religious Studies

Scholarship grants are available for Texas resident students who will be attending Concordia Theological Seminary (Fort Wayne, IN), Concordia Seminary (St. Louis), or Concordia Lutheran College (Austin, TX). Must be members of the Lutheran Church (Missouri Synod). Contact the financial aid office at your school for information.

Lutheran Church–Missouri Synod, Texas District
B.M. Woltman Foundation
7900 E. Highway 290
Austin, TX 78724

531 B.R.I.D.G.E. Endowment Fund Scholarships

AMOUNT: $5,000 **DEADLINE:** Feb 15
FIELDS/MAJORS: Agriculture

Scholarships for handicapped FFA members who are pursuing two- or four-year degrees in any area of agriculture. Write to the address below for details.

National FFA Foundation
Scholarship Office
P.O. Box 15160
Alexandria, VA 22309

532 Babara Hirschi Neely And Trustee Scholarships

AMOUNT: Full Tuition **DEADLINE:** Feb 1
FIELDS/MAJORS: All Areas Of Study

Awards for Lewis and Clark students interested in science, natural systems, intercultural issues, or international issues. Must have outstanding academic credentials. Awarded to freshmen students, but renewable. Write to the address below for complete details.

Lewis and Clark College
Office Of Admissions
Portland, OR 97219

533 Baccalaureate Or Coordinated Program

AMOUNT: $400-$5,000 **DEADLINE:** Jan 15
FIELDS/MAJORS: Dietetics/Nutrition

Scholarships for juniors and seniors in an ADA-accredited program. Must be U.S. citizen and show potential in the field of nutrition/dietetics. Information is published annually in the Journal of the American Dietetic Association. Alternately, write to the address below for details.

American Dietetic Association Foundation
216 W. Jackson St., Suite 800
Chicago, IL 60606

534 Baccalaureate Scholarship

AMOUNT: Varies **DEADLINE:** Jun 1
FIELDS/MAJORS: Dental Hygiene

Scholarships for students who have at least been accepted in a four-year accredited program leading toward a B.A. in dental hygiene. Must have a GPA of at least 3.0. Based on need and career goals. Write to the address below for more information.

American Dental Hygienists' Association Institute
For Oral Health
444 N. Michigan Ave., Suite 3400
Chicago, IL 60611

535 Baccalaureate Scholarship

AMOUNT: Full Scholarship **DEADLINE:** Mar 1
FIELDS/MAJORS: All Areas Of Study

Applicant must be a first time entering freshman residing in Oklahoma. Must have an excellent GPA and ACT score of 30. Write to the address below for more information.

Southwestern Oklahoma State University
Student Financial Services Office
100 Campus Dr.
Weatherford, OK 73096

536 Bach Organ Scholarship Fund

AMOUNT:$500 **DEADLINE:** Jul 1
FIELDS/MAJORS: Music-Keyboard

Scholarships are available for music majors (piano or organ) who are either Rhode Island residents or who are attending school in Rhode Island. Up to three awards are offered annually. For undergraduate study. Write to the address listed below for information.

Rhode Island Foundation
70 Elm Street
Providence, RI 02903

537 Bader/Nelson Scholarship

AMOUNT: Varies **DEADLINE:** Mar 1
FIELDS/MAJORS: All Areas Of Study

Awards are available at the University of New Mexico for full-time undergraduates with satisfactory academic progress who are from New Mexico. Write to the address below for more information.

University Of New Mexico, Albuquerque
Office Of Financial Aid
Albuquerque, NM 87131

538 Badger Boy/Girls State Scholarship

AMOUNT: $2,000 (max) **DEADLINE:** Mar 1
FIELDS/MAJORS: All Areas Of Study

Scholarships for students at Ripon who have participated in Badger Boys' State or Badger Girls' State. Write to the admissions office at the address below for details.

Ripon College
300 Seward Street
P.O. Box 248
Ripon, WI 54971

539 Badgley Memorial Scholarship

AMOUNT: Varies **DEADLINE:** Mar 1
FIELDS/MAJORS: Math Or Science

Award for an Eastern student who is completing a program in math or in one of the sciences. Write to the address below for more information.

Eastern Oregon State College
Financial Aid Office
1041 "1" Avenue
La Grande, OR 97850

540

Baird, Kurtz & Dobson Scholarship

Amount: $500 **Deadline:** None Specified
Fields/Majors: Accounting

Student must be a full-time junior or senior accounting major who has completed Intermediate Accounting I with a minimum 3.0 GPA. Contact the COBA office for more information.

Southwest Missouri State University
Office Of Financial Aid
901 South National Ave.
Springfield, MO 65804

541

Baker Awards

Amount: $1,200-$2,250 **Deadline:** Apr 1
Fields/Majors: All Areas Of Study

Awards for entering freshmen and transfers who bring leadership, academic ability, and good citizenship to Baker University. Must have a GPA of at least 2.7 and demonstrate financial need. Renewable with a GPA of 2.5. Write to the address below for more information.

Baker University
Office Of Financial Aid
P.O. Box 65
Baldwin City, KS 66006

542

Baker Scholarship

Amount: Varies **Deadline:** Feb 15
Fields/Majors: Environmental Design, Landscape Architecture

Awards for Stockbridge students in the area the environmental design or landscape architecture. For students in their sophomore, junior, or senior year at UMass. Contact the Director, Stockbridge School, for more information.

University Of Massachusetts, Amherst
Director, Stockbridge School
Amherst, MA 01003

543

Baker Tuition Awards

GPA 3.0+

Amount: $750 **Deadline:** Apr 1
Fields/Majors: All Areas Of Study

Awards for incoming students who are not residents of Kansas are eligible for this award. Must have a GPA of 3.0 or better to receive the award and a 2.5 or higher to renew. Write to the address below for more information.

Baker University
Office Of Financial Aid
P.O. Box 65
Baldwin City, KS 66006

544

Ballet Departmental Scholarships

Amount: Varies **Deadline:** Feb 1
Fields/Majors: Dance-Ballet

Scholarships are available at the University of Utah for full-time ballet students. Includes the Walter E. Cosgriff Memorial, John H. Morgan Memorial, Alice Walton Call Memorial, Herbert I. and Elsa B. Michael Foundation, Mrs. Walter E. Cosgriff, and Etta Keith Eskridge scholarships. Individual award requirements may vary. Write to the address below for details.

University Of Utah
Barbara Hamblin
116 Marriott Center For Dance
Salt Lake City, UT 84112

545

Ballut Abyad Scholarship

Amount: Varies **Deadline:** Mar 1
Fields/Majors: All Areas Of Study

Awards are available at the University of New Mexico for juniors or seniors with financial need and satisfactory academic progress. Write to the address below for more information.

University Of New Mexico, Albuquerque
Office Of Financial Aid
Albuquerque, NM 87131

546

Band Scholarships

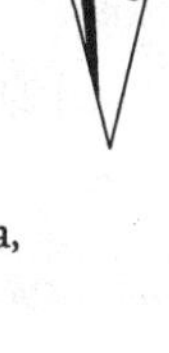

Amount: $800-$1,500 **Deadline:** None Specified
Fields/Majors: Music-Band

Scholarships are available at the University of Oklahoma, Norman for students who are members of the pride marching band or the symphonic band. Includes the Band Service Award, Pride Scholarship, C.E. Springer, Gene A. Braught, Leonard Haug, Lloyd B. Curtis, Oscar J. Lehrer, and William R. Wehrend awards. Up to 17 awards offered annually. Write to the address listed below for information.

University Of Oklahoma, Norman
Director, School Of Music
560 Parrington Oval
Norman OK 73019

547

Band Scholarships

Amount: Varies **Deadline:** None Specified
Fields/Majors: Band

Scholarships are available to students who participate in the marching and symphonic bands. Selections are based on musicianship, instrumentation needs, academic promise, and leadership potential. Contact the conductor of bands for more information.

Clarion University
104 Egbert Hall
Office Of Financial Aid
Clarion, PA 16214

548

Bank Of America—Giannini Foundation Fellowships

AMOUNT: $25,000 (max) **DEADLINE:** Dec 1
FIELDS/MAJORS: Medical Research

Fellowships for California postdoctorate students who are U.S. citizens or permanent residents and sponsored by an accredited California medical school. Applicant must have doctor of medicine or philosophy degree or be assured of one prior to the start of the fellowship. Fellowship is for research work in any field of medical science or basic science. Contact the address below for further information.

Bank Of America-Giannini Foundation
Department 3246
Box 37000
San Francisco, CA 94137

549

Bank One Western Colorado N.A. Scholarship

AMOUNT: $1,000 **DEADLINE:** None Specified
FIELDS/MAJORS: Business

Awards for full-time juniors or seniors studying business who participate in the cooperative education program. Applicants must meet qualifications for employment at any of Bank One's Western Colorado centers. Contact the school of professional studies/business area at Mesa State for more information.

Mesa State College
Financial Aid Office
P.O. Box 2684
Grand Junction, CO 81501

550

Banneker/Key Scholarship

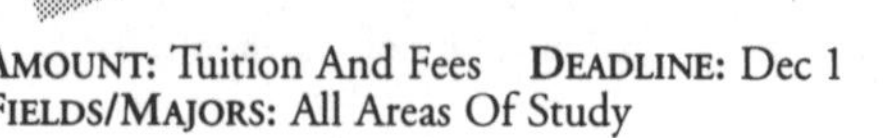

AMOUNT: Tuition And Fees **DEADLINE:** Dec 1
FIELDS/MAJORS: All Areas Of Study

Scholarships at UM College Park for excellent high school seniors. Recipients receive full financial support for four years, admission to the university honors program, and eligibility for honors housing. Based on GPA. SAT scores, and the rigor of their academic program. Write to the address below for details.

University Of Maryland, College Park
Office Of Student Financial Aid
0102 Lee Building
College Park, MD 20742

551

Baptist Employee Family Scholarship

AMOUNT: $500 **DEADLINE:** Jul 15
FIELDS/MAJORS: All Areas Of Study

Scholarships are awarded to college seniors, juniors, sophomores, freshmen, and technical students. Must attend any accredited four-year college or two-year technical school. Preference is given to a child or spouse of a Baptist employee with one or more years of employment. Write to the address below for details.

Baptist Health Care Foundation
P.O. Box 11010
Montgomery, AL 36111

552

Baptist Health Center Auxiliary Nursing Scholarship

AMOUNT: $1,000 **DEADLINE:** Jul 15
FIELDS/MAJORS: Nursing

Scholarships are awarded to nursing students working or residing in the Montgomery area. Must have a GPA of 3.0 or better and demonstrate academic performance, commitment to excellence, and financial need. Preference is given to BMC employees and volunteers. Write to the address below for details.

Baptist Health Care Foundation
P.O. Box 11010
Montgomery, AL 36111

553

Baptist Medical Center Auxiliary Allied Health Scholarship

AMOUNT: $1,000 **DEADLINE:** Jul 15
FIELDS/MAJORS: Allied Health

Scholarships are awarded to allied health students working or residing in the Montgomery area with a GPA of 2.75 or better. Preference is given to BMC employees and volunteers. Based on academic performance, commitment to excellence, and financial need. Write to the address below for details.

Baptist Health Care Foundation
P.O. Box 11010
Montgomery, AL 36111

554

Baptist Medical Center Of Oklahoma Interest-Free Loan Program

AMOUNT: $1,500 **DEADLINE:** Varies
FIELDS/MAJORS: Health Science

Scholarships are available at the University of Oklahoma, Norman for full-time health science majors, with a GPA of at least 2.5. Write to the address listed below for information.

University Of Oklahoma, Norman
College Of Allied Health
P.O. Box 26901
Oklahoma City, OK 73190

555

Barbara Alice Mower Memorial Scholarship

AMOUNT: $1,000-$3,000 **DEADLINE:** May 1
FIELDS/MAJORS: Women's Studies

Scholarships for Hawaii residents who are juniors, seniors, graduate- or post-graduate students, currently enrolled in a women's studies program. Based upon academic excellence, character and personality, and a commitment to help women in the future, especially the women of Hawaii. Write to the address below for details.

Barbara Alice Mower Memorial Scholarship
Mrs. Nancy A. Mower
1536 Kamole St.
Honolulu, HI 96821

556

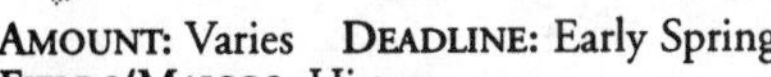

Barbara Donner Monteith Memorial Scholarship

Amount: Varies **Deadline:** Early Spring
Fields/Majors: History

Award for a junior history major who has shown outstanding scholastic activity in history. Contact the Department of History, UW Oshkosh, for more details.

University Of Wisconsin, Oshkosh
Financial Aid Office, Dempsey 104
800 Algoma Blvd.
Oshkosh, WI 54901

557

Barbara Gaynes Scholarships

Amount: $625 **Deadline:** Mar 1
Fields/Majors: Journalism

Awards for juniors and seniors majoring in journalism. Must have a GPA of at least 2.8. Write to the address below for more information.

University Of Florida
Knight Scholarship and Placement Director
2070 Weimer Hall
Gainesville, FL 32611

558

Barbara Goldwin Garland Award

Amount: Varies **Deadline:** Mar 1
Fields/Majors: Psychology

Awards are available at the University of New Mexico for graduate students in psychology involved in treatment with teenagers. Write to the address below for more information.

University Of New Mexico, Albuquerque
Office Of Financial Aid
Albuquerque, NM 87131

559

Barbara H. Lingenfelter Scholarship

Amount: $1,000 **Deadline:** None Specified
Fields/Majors: All Areas Of Study

Scholarships are available for full-time graduate students, student teachers, and teacher prep students. Must have a GPA of 3.0 or better. Must be a U.S. citizen. Write to the address below for more information.

California State Polytechnic University, Pomona
Office Of Financial Aid
3801 West Temple Ave.
Pomona, CA 91768

560

Barbara L. Frye Scholarship

Amount: $2,000 **Deadline:** Jun 15
Fields/Majors: Journalism

Must be a Florida resident or an undergraduate student at a Florida college/university. Must be studying journalism. Write to the address below for details.

Florida Capital Press Club/Barbara L. Frye Scholarship
Florida Press Center
336 E. College Ave.
Tallahassee, FL 32301

561

Barbara MacCaulley Endowment Scholarship Fund For Archaeology

Amount: Varies **Deadline:** Mar 1
Fields/Majors: Archaeology

Scholarships are available at the University of New Mexico for full-time female senior archaeology majors with a GPA of at least 3.0. Write to the address listed below for information.

University Of New Mexico, Albuquerque
Anthropology Department
Albuquerque, NM 87131

562

Barbara Oakley Scholarship

Amount: None Specified **Deadline:** None Specified
Fields/Majors: Nursing

Awards are available for ETSU students in the A.A.S. or B.S.N. nursing program. Contact the Dean's Office, College of Nursing, for more information.

East Tennessee State University
Office Of Financial Aid
Box 70722
Johnson City, TN 37614

563

Barber Dairies Scholarship

Amount: $2,500 **Deadline:** Mar 15
Fields/Majors: Commerce, Business

Awards for Jacksonville State University juniors or seniors who are majoring in commerce or business. Based on leadership, academics, and entrepreneurship. Write to the address below for more details.

Jacksonville State University
Financial Aid Office
Jacksonville, AL 36265

564

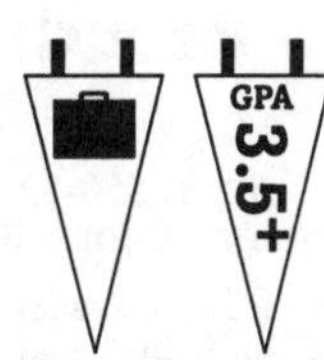

Barnet Bank Of Lake County Co-op Scholarship

Amount: $500 **Deadline:** Apr 30
Fields/Majors: Business Or Finance

Awards for graduating seniors from the following Lake County high schools: Eustis, Leesburg, Mount Dora, Taveres, or Umatilla. Applicants must be in the top 10% of their class, be studying business or finance, and work well with the public. Contact your high school guidance department for more information.

Barnet Bank Of Lake County
Lake County Schools, Student Services Department
509 S. Palm Ave.
Howey In The Hills, FL 34737

565

Barnett Bank Scholarship Fund

Amount: $1,500 **Deadline:** None Specified
Fields/Majors: All Areas Of Study

Awards given to students who will attend St. Petersburg Junior

College who are residents of Pinellas County. Based on academic qualifications. Preference will be given to students in bank related professions. Contact the office of the director of scholarships and student financial assistance at the campus you attend or write to the address below.

St. Petersburg Junior College
Office Of Financial Aid
P.O. Box 13489
St. Petersburg, FL 33733

566

Baron M. Stuart Endowed Scholarship

GPA 3.0+

AMOUNT: $1,000 **DEADLINE:** Mar 1
FIELDS/MAJORS: Business

Award for a full-time undergraduate business student who has a GPA of at least 3.0 and has successfully completed sixty credit hours by the effective date of the award. Write to the address below for more information.

Eastern New Mexico University
ENMU College Of Business
Station 49
Portales, NM 88130

567

Barry M. Goldwater Scholarship

GPA 3.0+

AMOUNT: $7,000 (max) **DEADLINE:** Nov 1
FIELDS/MAJORS: Mathematics, Natural Science, Engineering

Scholarships are available at the University of Oklahoma, Norman for sophomore and junior math, natural science, and engineering majors with outstanding academic credentials. Write to the address listed below for information.

University Of Oklahoma, Norman
Honors Program
347 Cate Center Drive
Norman, OK 73019

568

Baruch Essay Contest

AMOUNT: $50-$200 **DEADLINE:** Mar 1
FIELDS/MAJORS: Rehabilitation

Awards are available for students submitting the best essays in one of the fields listed above. Must not be more than 3,000 words in length. For undergraduate and graduate students. Essay contests for professionals in rehabilitation and the annual Conrad Jobst Foundation Award are also available. Write to the address listed below for information.

American Congress Of Rehabilitation Medicine
Baruch Essay Contest
5700 Old Orchard Road, 1st Floor
Skokie, IL 60077

569

Basil Maltsberger Memorial Scholarships

GPA 2.5+

AMOUNT: None Specified
DEADLINE: None Specified
FIELDS/MAJORS: All Areas Of Study

Scholarships for students at East Tennessee State University who participate in intercollegiate sports. Must be full-time student and have a GPA of at least 2.8. Contact the office of financial aid at the address below for details.

East Tennessee State University
Office Of Financial Aid
Box 70722
Johnson City, TN 37614

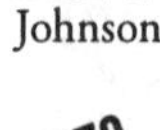

570

Basketball Band Scholarship

AMOUNT: Varies **DEADLINE:** Mar 1
FIELDS/MAJORS: All Areas Of Study

Awards are available at the University of New Mexico for students in the Lobo Marching Band. Recipients are selected by audition. Write to the address below for more information.

University Of New Mexico, Albuquerque
Office Of Financial Aid
Albuquerque, NM 87131

571

Batelle Memorial Institute Foundation Scholarship

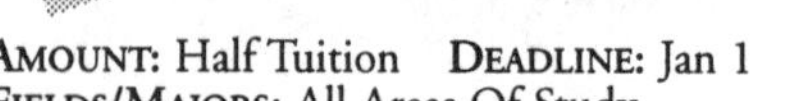

AMOUNT: Half Tuition **DEADLINE:** Jan 1
FIELDS/MAJORS: All Areas Of Study

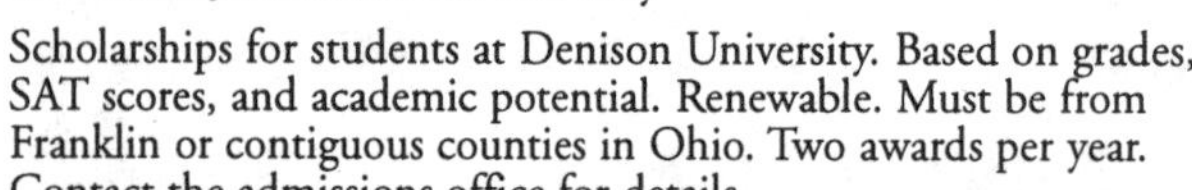

Scholarships for students at Denison University. Based on grades, SAT scores, and academic potential. Renewable. Must be from Franklin or contiguous counties in Ohio. Two awards per year. Contact the admissions office for details.

Denison University
Financial Aid Office
Box M
Granville, OH 43023

572

Bateman Scholarships

GPA 3.5+

AMOUNT: $500 **DEADLINE:** Mar 1
FIELDS/MAJORS: Journalism, Communications, Public Relations, Advertising

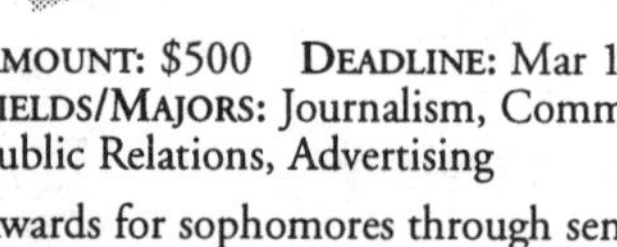

Awards for sophomores through seniors in the college who have a GPA of 3.5 or better. Financial need is not a factor for these awards. Write to the address below for more information.

University Of Florida
Knight Scholarship and Placement Director
2070 Weimer Hall
Gainesville, FL 32611

573

Bates Scholarship

AMOUNT: Varies **DEADLINE:** None Specified
FIELDS/MAJORS: Most Areas Of Study

Awards for female CHC students who have a GPA of 3.5 or greater in the areas of science, liberal arts, education, fine arts, or business. Must be a U.S. citizen. Write to the address below for more information.

Christian Heritage College
Financial Aid Office
2100 Greenfield Dr.
El Cajon, CA 92019

574

Batson Printing, Inc. Scholarship

Amount: $1,000 **Deadline:** None Specified
Fields/Majors: Pulp And Paper Science, Graphic Arts

Scholarships for juniors and seniors in the department of paper and printing science and engineering at WMU. Based on need. Renewable if awarded as a junior. Write to the address below for more information.

Western Michigan University
College Of Engineering & Applied Science
Dept. Of Paper & Printing Science & Engineering
Kalamazoo, MI 49008

575

Baxter Graduate Student Research Award

Amount: $1,000 **Deadline:** Mar 30
Fields/Majors: Clinical Laboratory Science

Awards to directly fund proposed investigation in the field of clinical laboratory science. Applicants must be graduate students or scholars currently working in the field. Write to the address below for more information.

American Society For Clinical Laboratory Science
Director Of Education
7910 Woodmont Ave., Suite 1301
Bethesda, MD 20814

576

Bay State Council Of The Blind Scholarships

Amount: $1,000 **Deadline:** Mar 1
Fields/Majors: All Areas Of Study

Scholarships are available to legally blind students who are residents of Massachusetts. Write to the address below for details.

American Council Of The Blind
Scholarship Coordinator
1155 15th St., NW, Suite 720
Washington, DC 20005

577

Bazard Award

Amount: Varies **Deadline:** Mar 1
Fields/Majors: Architecture

Scholarships are available at the University of New Mexico for full-time architecture students who are of Native American Indian heritage. Write to the address listed below for information.

University Of New Mexico, Albuquerque
School Of Architecture
Office Of The Dean
Albuquerque, NM 87131

578

BC&T Scholarship

Amount: $500-$4,000 **Deadline:** Feb 28
Fields/Majors: All Areas Of Study

Applicants must be BC&T union members in good standing (at any level of study) or children of BC&T union members in good standing who are entering college (or vocational/technical school) for the first time. Application forms and further information are available at the local union or from the international union at the address below.

Bakery, Confectionery, and Tobacco Workers International Union
Scholarship Program
10401 Connecticut Ave.
Kensington, MD 20895

579

BCI Graduate Student Scholarship Awards

Amount: $500-$2,500 **Deadline:** Jan 15
Fields/Majors: Speleology, Bat Research

Awards are available to fund relevant research of graduate students in the study of bats. Some relevant research topics include roosting needs, bat feeding behavior, bat nuisance problems, bat conservation needs, and many others. Write to the address below for more information.

Bat Conservation International
Scholarship Awards Coordinator
P.O. Box 162603
Austin, TX 78716

580

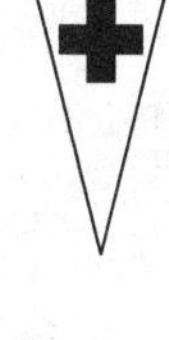

Bea Holmes Nursing Scholarships

Amount: Varies **Deadline:** None Specified
Fields/Majors: Nursing

Awards available for qualified nursing students at Cedarville College. Must have a GPA of at least 2.0. Write to the address below for more information.

Cedarville College
Financial Aid Office
P.O. Box 601
Cedarville, OH 45314

581

BEA Scholarships

Amount: $1,250-$5,000 **Deadline:** Jan 16
Fields/Majors: Radio and TV Broadcasting

Competitive scholarships for juniors, seniors, and graduate students working toward a career in broadcasting. Based primarily on academic accomplishment. Applicants with some broadcast training or experience are preferred. Information may be available from your campus faculty, if not, write to the broadcast education association at the address below.

Broadcast Education Association
1771 N. St., NW
Washington, DC 20036

582

Beacon/Woodstream Corporation Scholarships

Amount: $500-$2,000 **Deadline:** Feb 15
Fields/Majors: Animal Science

Scholarships are available for FFA members pursuing a two- or four-year degree in animal science. Write to the address below for details.

National FFA Foundation
Scholarship Office
P.O. Box 15160
Alexandria, VA 22309

583

Beard & Company Accounting Scholarship

Amount: $350 **Deadline:** Feb 9
Fields/Majors: Accounting

Award for accounting major who will be starting senior year. Outstanding academic achievement, financial need, and a demonstrated interest in pursuing a career in the field of public accounting. Use Bloomsburg University scholarship application. Contact Dr. Richard Baker, Chairperson, Accounting, for additional information.

Bloomsburg University
19 Ben Franklin Hall
400 E. Second St.
Bloomsburg, PA 17815

584

Beard, Flowe, Frazier, Jones And Trustee Scholarships

Amount: $5,000-$7,000 **Deadline:** None Specified
Fields/Majors: All Areas Of Study

Renewable scholarships for students at Peace College. Must be in top 5% of class, have a GPA of at least 3.5, and SAT (combined) of at least 1,180, and be involved in community service projects. Write to the address below for additional information.

Peace College
Director Of Financial Aid
15 East Peace Street
Raleigh, NC 27604

585

Bedding Plant Foundation Scholarships

Amount: Varies **Deadline:** Apr 1
Fields/Majors: Horticulture

Open to horticulture students with demonstrated interests in various area of horticulture. Write to the address below for more information.

California State Polytechnic University, Pomona
College Of Agriculture
Building 7, Room 110
Pomona, CA 91768

586

Beem Foundation Scholarships

Amount: Varies **Deadline:** None Specified
Fields/Majors: Music

Scholarships for music students from Los Angeles County, CA. Write to the address below for more information.

Beem Foundation For The Advancement Of Music
3864 Grayburn Ave.
Los Angeles, CA 90008

587

Behavioral Science And Health Departmental Scholarships

Amount: Varies **Deadline:** Feb 15
Fields/Majors: Behavioral Science, Health Studies

Scholarships are available at the University of Utah for full-time students majoring in health studies or behavioral sciences. Write to the address below for information.

University Of Utah
Ms. Cinda Baldwin
102 Stewart Building
Salt Lake City, UT 84112

588

Behavioral Science Endowed And Private Scholarships

Amount: Varies **Deadline:** Feb 15
Fields/Majors: Behavioral Sciences

Scholarships are available at Evangel for full-time students who will be or are pursuing a degree in the behavioral sciences. Applicant must have a GPA of at least 3.0. Other requirements vary. Includes the Mary Ann McCorcle Memorial Scholarship, the Dr. Billie Davis Sociology Scholarship, the Behavioral Science Alumni Scholarship, and Amy Dawn Marks Memorial Scholarship. Write to the address listed below for information.

Evangel College
Office Of Enrollment
1111 N. Glenstone
Springfield, MO 65802

589

Behavioral Sciences Student Fellowship, Mary Litty Memorial Fellowship

Amount: $2,000 **Deadline:** Mar 1
Fields/Majors: Behavioral and Social Sciences, Nursing

Applicant must be enrolled in a degree program. For work on an epilepsy study project. An investigator/advisor must accept responsibility for the study and its supervision. Litty Fellowship is reserved for vocational rehabilitation. Write to the address below for further information.

Epilepsy Foundation Of America
Fellowship Program
4351 Garden City Drive
Landover, MD 20785

590

Beliasov Family Scholarships

Amount: Varies **Deadline:** Mar 11
Fields/Majors: Food Science

Awards for students at Penn State University who are studying food science. Based on academic ability. Renewable annually. Write to the address below for more information.

Pennsylvania State University
College Of Agriculture, Associate Dean
Penn State University
University Park, PA 16802

591

Bellarmine Scholars Program

Amount: Tuition **Deadline:** Feb 1
Fields/Majors: All Areas Of Study

Scholarships are available at Bellarmine College for undergraduates who were in the top 10% of their high school class, with a minimum 3.8 GPA, and an ACT composite of at least 29 (or

SAT of 1260 or more). An essay and interview are also required. Contact the financial aid office at the address below for details.

Bellarmine College
Financial Aid Office
2001 Newburg Road
Louisville, KY 40205

592

Ben & Patricia Abruzzo Memorial Scholarship

AMOUNT: None Specified **DEADLINE:** Mar 1
FIELDS/MAJORS: Management

Scholarships are available at the University of New Mexico for full-time management majors who are members of the UNM ski team. Write to the address listed below for information.

University Of New Mexico, Albuquerque
Department Of Student Financial Aid
Mesa Vista Hall North
Albuquerque, NM 87131

593

Ben Barnett MBA, Ph.D. Scholars Awards

AMOUNT: $1,000-$5,000 **DEADLINE:** Feb 8
FIELDS/MAJORS: Business Administration

Scholarships are available at the University of Oklahoma, Norman for full-time MBA or Ph.D. Candidates in business administration. Write to the address listed below for information.

University Of Oklahoma, Norman
College Of Business Administration
208 Adams Hall
Norman, OK 73019

594

Ben Barnett, Edgar Burdette & Flora Morin Deloe Memorial Scholarships

AMOUNT: $250-$2,000 **DEADLINE:** Mar 1
FIELDS/MAJORS: Art, Art History

Scholarships are available at the University of Oklahoma, Norman for full-time art or art history majors, who have a minimum GPA of 3.0 Write to the address listed below for information.

University Of Oklahoma, Norman
Director, School Of Art
520 Parrington, Room 202
Norman, OK 73019

595

Ben G. Owen Scholarship

AMOUNT:$1,000 **DEADLINE:** Mar 1
FIELDS/MAJORS: All Areas Of Study

Scholarships are available at the University of Oklahoma, Norman for former high school athletes not participating in the sports program at OU. Requires a GPA of 3.25 to qualify. Two or three awards are offered annually. Write to the address listed below for information.

University Of Oklahoma, Norman
Office Of Financial Aid Services
731 Elm
Norman,OK 73019

596

Benedict Galas Scholarship

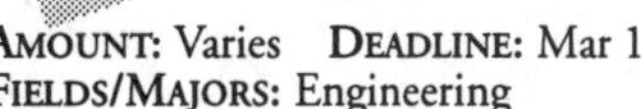

AMOUNT: Varies **DEADLINE:** Mar 1
FIELDS/MAJORS: Engineering

Awards for students entering their sophomore, junior, or senior year studying in the college of engineering. Contact the Director of Recruitment, Marston Hall, for more information.

University Of Massachusetts, Amherst
Director of Recruitment, Marston Hall
Amherst, MA 01003

597

Beneficial-Hodson Scholarship

AMOUNT: $12,000 **DEADLINE:** None Specified
FIELDS/MAJORS: All Areas Of Study

Awards for full-time accepted freshmen. Renewable if 3.0 GPA is maintained. Nominations by high school guidance counselors are required. Write to the address below for more information.

Johns Hopkins University
3400 N. Charles Street
Baltimore, MD 21218

598

Beneficial-Hodson Scholarships For Academic Excellence

AMOUNT: $7,500 (max) **DEADLINE:** Mar 31
FIELDS/MAJORS: All Areas Of Study

Awards for students with outstanding academic records who have been accepted to Hood. Write to the address below for more information.

Hood College
Admissions Office
401 Rosemont Ave.
Frederick, MD 21701

599

Benjamin C. Blackburn & Russell W. Myers Scholarships

AMOUNT: $1,000-$2,000 **DEADLINE:** Nov 22
FIELDS/MAJORS: Horticulture, Botany, Landscape Architecture, or Related Field

Scholarships for New Jersey students who have completed at least 24 hours of study in one of the fields of study listed above. Write to the address below for more information.

Friends Of The Frelinghuysen Arboretum
53 East Hanover Ave.
P.O. Box 1295
Morristown, NJ 07962

600

Benjamin Eaton Scholarship Fund

AMOUNT: None Specified **DEADLINE:** Mar 1
FIELDS/MAJORS: All Areas Of Study

Two scholarships for foster children and one scholarship for natural-born children of foster parents. Parents must be current members of the National Foster Parent Association. Must apply in senior year of high school for use in college or university study, vocational/job training, correspondence/GED, and other educational pursuits. Write to the address below for more information.

National Foster Parent Association
Benjamin Eaton Scholarship Fund
9 Dartmoor Dr.
Crystal Lake, IL 60014

601 Benjamin F. Fairless Scholarship Award

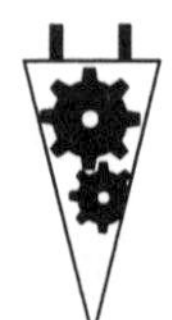

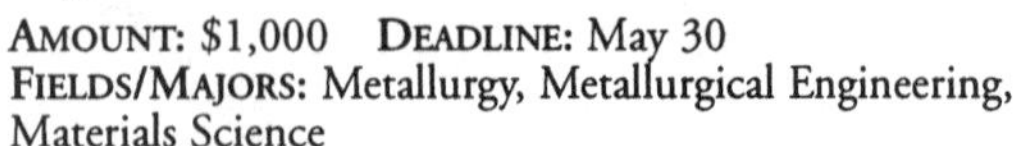

AMOUNT: $1,000 **DEADLINE:** May 30
FIELDS/MAJORS: Metallurgy, Metallurgical Engineering, Materials Science

Awards are available for students entering their final undergraduate year in any of the fields listed above. Only one candidate will be considered per school. Students must apply in their junior year. Write to the address below for more details.

Iron and Steel Society
Kathryn E. Kost
410 Commonwealth Dr.
Warrendale, PA 15086

602 Berenice Barnard Music Specialist Scholarships

AMOUNT: Varies **DEADLINE:** Apr 8
FIELDS/MAJORS: Music—Education Or Performance

Applicants must be from the city of San Buenaventura or the city of Ojai, successful in school, and have demonstrated interest/involvement in music. Based on academic record, letters of recommendation, written essay, and a possible personal interview. Applicants can not be related to the Barnard family. Write to the address below for more information.

Ventura County Community Foundation
1355 Del Norte Road
Camarillo, CA 93010

603 Berger Memorial Scholarship

AMOUNT: $1,000 **DEADLINE:** Mar 1
FIELDS/MAJORS: Engineering, Business

Scholarships are available to Native American Indian students at Montana State University in the fields of engineering or business. One award is given to first-year students, one award is given to transfer students from a tribally controlled community college, and one award is given to a first-year graduate student. Write to the address listed below for information.

Montana State University
Center For Native American Studies
2-152 Wilson Hall
Bozeman, MT 59717

604 Berna Lou Cartwright Scholarship

AMOUNT: $1,500 **DEADLINE:** Feb 15
FIELDS/MAJORS: Mechanical Engineering

Scholarships for mechanical engineering students entering their final year of undergraduate study. Application must be made in junior year (students enrolled in a 5 year program would apply in the 4th year). Must be a student member of ASME and be a U.S. citizen. Information sheets are forwarded to the colleges and universities in the fall of each year. If necessary to write for more details, please be certain to enclose an SASE.

American Society Of Mechanical Engineers Auxiliary, Inc.
ASME Foundation
345 East 47th Street
New York, NY 10017

605 Bernadina Olivares Scholarship

AMOUNT: Varies **DEADLINE:** Mar 1
FIELDS/MAJORS: Vocal Music

Awards at the University of New Mexico for vocal music students with demonstrated talent and academic achievement. Write to the address below for more information.

University Of New Mexico, Albuquerque
Office Of Financial Aid
Albuquerque, NM 87131

606 Bernard "Bunny" Dillon Scholarships

AMOUNT: $200 **DEADLINE:** Feb 15
FIELDS/MAJORS: Music

Awards for students at UW Platteville who participate in two or more music performing organizations. Write to the address below for more information.

University Of Wisconsin, Platteville
Office Of Enrollment and Admissions
Platteville, WI 53818

607 Bernard & Francis Young Scholarship

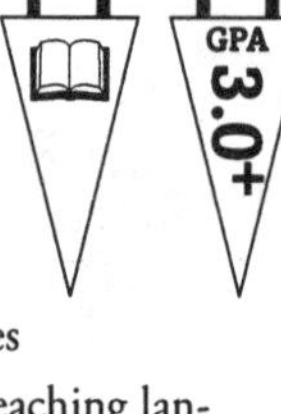

AMOUNT: $1,000 **DEADLINE:** Feb 9
FIELDS/MAJORS: Secondary Education, Languages

Award for junior or senior planning a career in teaching languages. Must have a minimum GPA of 3.0, be accepted into the teaching program and demonstrate financial need. Use Bloomsburg University scholarship application. Contact Dr. William O'Bruba, Chairperson, Department of Curriculum and Foundations, for further information.

Bloomsburg University
19 Ben Franklin Hall
400 E. Second St.
Bloomsburg, PA 17815

608 Bernardine Bess Memorial Trust Fund

AMOUNT: None Specified **DEADLINE:** Mar 15
FIELDS/MAJORS: All Areas Of Study

Scholarships for graduating high school seniors from St. Albans High School (St. Albans, WV). Based on scholarship, character, and need. Two awards per year are anticipated. Write to the address below for details.

Greater Kanawha Valley Foundation
Scholarship Committee
P.O. Box 3041
Charleston, WV 25331

609 Bernice A. Rebord Memorial Scholarship

AMOUNT: Varies **DEADLINE:** Mar 1
FIELDS/MAJORS: History

Awards are available at the University of New Mexico for juniors, seniors, or master's degree students in history. Applicants must have GPA of at least 3.0 and financial need. Write to the address below for more information.

University Of New Mexico, Albuquerque
Office Of Financial Aid
Albuquerque, NM 87131

610 Bernice Pickens Parsons Fund

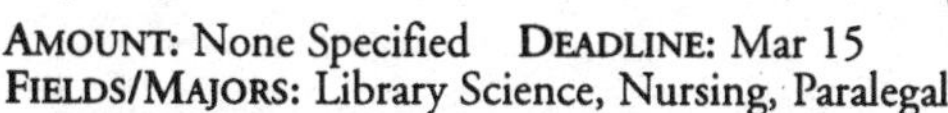

AMOUNT: None Specified **DEADLINE:** Mar 15
FIELDS/MAJORS: Library Science, Nursing, Paralegal

Scholarships for West Virginia residents studying in one of the fields above who are from Jackson County (West Virginia). Ten awards per year. Write to the address below for details.

Greater Kanawha Valley Foundation
Scholarship Committee
P.O. Box 3041
Charleston, WV 25331

611 Berntsen Scholarship, Schonstedt Scholarship, & NSPS Scholarships

AMOUNT: $500-$1,500 **DEADLINE:** Jan 1
FIELDS/MAJORS: Surveying

Any person who is enrolled in a four-year degree program in surveying may apply for these scholarships. Selection will be on the following: (1) justification of award, (2) educational plan, (3) academic performance and standing, (4) potential for development, and (5) financial need. Please contact address below for complete information.

American Congress On Surveying And Mapping
ACSM Awards Director
5410 Grosvenor Lane, Suite 100
Bethesda, MD 20814

612 Berry M. Berish Scholarships

AMOUNT: $800 **DEADLINE:** Mar 1
FIELDS/MAJORS: Advertising

Awards for juniors and seniors majoring in the field of advertising. Must have a GPA of at least 2.8. Write to the address below for more information.

University Of Florida
Knight Scholarship and Placement Director
2070 Weimer Hall
Gainesville, FL 32611

613 Berryman and Henigar Award

AMOUNT: $1,500 **DEADLINE:** Mar 2
FIELDS/MAJORS: Civil Engineering

Award for civil engineering students who are from south central

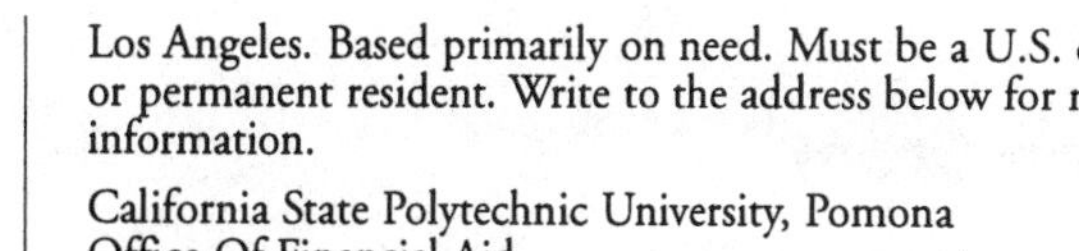

Los Angeles. Based primarily on need. Must be a U.S. citizen or permanent resident. Write to the address below for more information.

California State Polytechnic University, Pomona
Office Of Financial Aid
3801 West Temple Ave.
Pomona, CA 91768

614 Berta Van Stone Awards

AMOUNT: Varies **DEADLINE:** Mar 1
FIELDS/MAJORS: Music

Awards at the University of New Mexico for music students recommended by a faculty member. Write to the address below for more information.

University Of New Mexico, Albuquerque
Office Of Financial Aid
Albuquerque, NM 87131

615 Bertha B. Hollis And Louise E. Johnson Scholarships

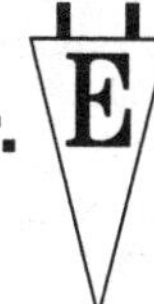

AMOUNT: Varies **DEADLINE:** Mar 1
FIELDS/MAJORS: All Areas Of Study

Awards are available at the University of New Mexico for American Indian students. Write to the address below for more information.

University Of New Mexico, Albuquerque
Office Of Financial Aid
Albuquerque, NM 87131

616 Bertha P. Singer Scholarship

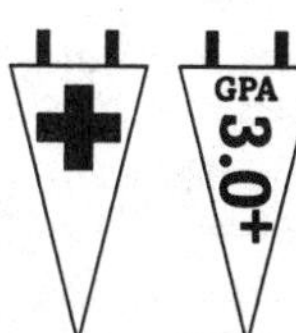

AMOUNT: None Specified **DEADLINE:** Mar 1
FIELDS/MAJORS: Nursing

Scholarships for Oregon residents enrolled in a nursing program in the state of Oregon. Must have a GPA of at least 3.0. For students entering their sophomore year of study or higher. Write to the address below for details.

Oregon State Scholarship Commission
Attn: Grant Department
1500 Valley River Dr., #100
Eugene, OR 97401

617 Beta Sigma Phi-xi Upsilon Chi Chapter

AMOUNT: $200 **DEADLINE:** May 1
FIELDS/MAJORS: All Areas Of Study

Scholarships for female freshman who attend the College of the Siskiyous full-time and are residents of Siskiyou County. Applicants must demonstrate financial need, have a minimum GPA of 3.0 and have graduated from a Siskiyou County high school. Write to the address below for details.

College Of The Siskiyous
Financial Aid Office
800 College Ave.
Weed, CA 96094

618

Bethel Grant

AMOUNT: $100-$4,000 **DEADLINE:** None Specified
FIELDS/MAJORS: All Areas of Study

Awards for students who demonstrate financial need and do not have adequate funding from other grants. Write to the address below for more information.

Bethel College
Office Of Financial Planning
3900 Bethel Dr.
St. Paul, MN 55112

619

Betsy Brogan Scholarship

AMOUNT: None Specified **DEADLINE:** None Specified
FIELDS/MAJORS: Nursing

Awards are available for ETSU students majoring in nursing. Contact the Dean's Office, College of Nursing, for more information.

East Tennessee State University
Office Of Financial Aid
Box 70722
Johnson City, TN 37614

620

Betsy L. Lantz Scholarship In The Liberal Arts

AMOUNT: Varies **DEADLINE:** None Specified
FIELDS/MAJORS: Liberal Arts

Award given to a deserving liberal arts student at Mercyhurst College. Write to the address below for more information.

Mercyhurst College
Financial Aid Office
Glenwood Hills
Erie, PA 16546

621

Bettsy Ross Educational Fund

AMOUNT:$250 (max) **DEADLINE:** Mar 1
FIELDS/MAJORS: All Areas Of Study

Grants for members of the noncommissioned officers association auxiliary division. To be used for preparation for employment or improvement on employable skills. Contact your chapter or the address below for details.

Non-Commissioned Officers Association Auxiliary
NCOA Scholarship & Bettsy Ross Funds
P.O. Box 33610
San Antonio, TX 78233

622

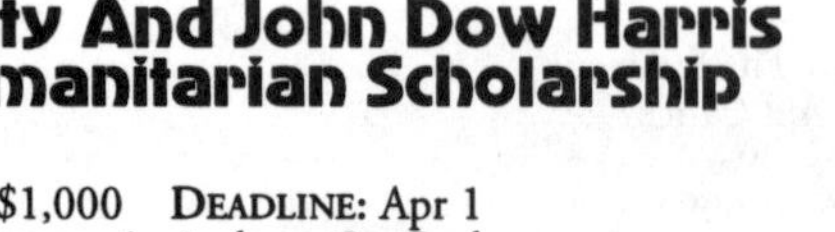

Betty And John Dow Harris Humanitarian Scholarship

AMOUNT: $1,000 **DEADLINE:** Apr 1
FIELDS/MAJORS: Agriculture Or Geology

Awards for undergraduate students at Sul Ross who are U.S. citizens and are majoring in the fields above. Write to the address below for more information.

Sul Ross State University
Financial Aid Office
Box C-113
Alpine, TX 79832

623

Betty Porter-Anderson Scholarship

AMOUNT: None Specified **DEADLINE:** None Specified
FIELDS/MAJORS: Nursing

Scholarships are open to junior and senior BSN students. Write to the address below for more information.

Indiana University/Purdue University, Indianapolis
School Of Nursing
1111 Middle Dr., Nu. 122
Indianapolis, IN 46202

624

Bettye Miller Memorial Scholarships

AMOUNT: Varies **DEADLINE:** Mar 1
FIELDS/MAJORS: All Areas Of Study

Awards are available at the University of New Mexico for full-time sophomores, juniors, or seniors who have a GPA of at least 2.5. Contact: Mrs. Sunny Wilde, Rebekah Assembly Scholarship Trustee, P.O. Box 475, Las Cruces, NM 88004-0475, for more details.

University Of New Mexico, Albuquerque
Office Of Financial Aid
Albuquerque, NM 87131

625

Beulah Clinton Memorial Scholarships

AMOUNT: None Specified **DEADLINE:** Feb 1
FIELDS/MAJORS: Elementary Education

Scholarships are available to Murray State University students majoring or intending to major in elementary education. A minimum GPA of 3.0 or better. Write to the address below for details.

Murray State University
Office Of University Scholarships, Ordway Hall
1 Murray St.
Murray, KY 42071

626

Bev Sellers Memorial Scholarship

AMOUNT: $1,000 **DEADLINE:** Feb 15
FIELDS/MAJORS: Vocal Music

Awards are available for full-time students studying vocal music in an accredited institution. Must have a GPA of at least 3.0. Based on transcripts, activities, and recommendations. Write to the address below for more information.

Young Singers Foundation, c/o Sweet Adelines International
Attn: Corporate Secretary
P.O. Box 470168
Tulsa, OK 74147

627
Beverly M. McCurdy Scholarship Fund

AMOUNT: None Specified **DEADLINE:** None Specified
FIELDS/MAJORS: All Areas Of Study

Awards for graduating seniors from Machias High School in Machias, ME, who plan to attain postsecondary education. Contact the Machias High School guidance office for more information.

Maine Community Fund
P.O. Box 148
Ellsworth, ME 04605

628
Beverly Myers Award

AMOUNT: $200-$500 **DEADLINE:** Apr 12
FIELDS/MAJORS: Optometry

Candidates must be senior students currently enrolled in an opticianry program accredited by the commission on opticianry accreditation. Write to the address below for more information.

National Academy Of Opticianry
10111 M.I. King, Jr. Hwy., Suite 112
Bowie, MD 20720

629
BGC Grant

AMOUNT: $400 **DEADLINE:** Apr 15
FIELDS/MAJORS: All Areas Of Study

Awards for full-time students who are members of Baptist General Conference churches. Contact your local pastor for more information or an application form.

Bethel College
Office Of Financial Planning
3900 Bethel Dr.
St. Paul, MN 55112

630
Bia Higher Education/Hopi Supplemental Grant

AMOUNT: $4,000 **DEADLINE:** Varies
FIELDS/MAJORS: All Areas Of Study

Awards for Hopi tribe members who are pursuing any level degree and can demonstrate financial need. Applicants must have a GPA of at least 2.0 and be enrolled in full-time study. Grants are also available for summer sessions. Write to the address below for more information.

Hopi Tribe Grants And Scholarship Program
Scholarship Committee
P.O. Box 123
Kykotsmovi, AZ 86039

631
Big Island High School Awards

AMOUNT: Varies **DEADLINE:** Feb 1
FIELDS/MAJORS: All Areas Of Study

Scholarships are available at the University of Hawaii, Hilo for full-time students who graduated from a Big Island high school. Includes the Barney S. Fujimoto Memorial, Hilo High School Class of 1940, Constance E. Masutani Memorial, Dr. Frances F.C. Wong Memorial, James S. Yagi Memorial, and Michio Yoshimura Memorial Art Scholarship. Individual award requirements may vary. Write to the address listed below for information.

University Of Hawaii At Hilo
Financial Aid Office
200 West Kawili Street
Hilo, HI 96720

632
Big Island Press Club's Robert Miller Scholarship

AMOUNT: Varies **DEADLINE:** Feb 1
FIELDS/MAJORS: Communications, Journalism

Scholarships are available at the University of Hawaii, Hilo for full-time students who are planning a career in the media. Must be a Big Island resident. Write to the address listed below for information.

University Of Hawaii At Hilo
Big Island Press Club
P.O. Box 1920
Hilo, HI 96720

633
Big R Stores/Watseka Rural King Supply, Inc. Scholarships

AMOUNT: $1,000 **DEADLINE:** Feb 15
FIELDS/MAJORS: Agriculture

Scholarships are available for FFA members pursuing a two- or four-year degree in any area of agriculture who reside in Champaign, Dewitt, Ford, Iroquois, Livingston, McLean, or Vermillion counties in Illinois, or in Benton, Newton, Warren, Fountain, or Vermillion counties in Indiana. Write to the address below for details.

National FFA Foundation
Scholarship Office
P.O. Box 15160
Alexandria, VA 22309

634
Bill And Gean Cherry Scholarship

AMOUNT: None Specified **DEADLINE:** Feb 1
FIELDS/MAJORS: Agricultural Mechanization, Agricultural Education

Scholarship awarded to U.S. citizens who have at least a 2.0 GPA and plan to pursue a career in agricultural education or agricultural mechanization. Financial need must be demonstrated. Write to the address below for details.

Murray State University
Office Of University Scholarships, Ordway Hall
1 Murray St.
Murray, KY 42071

635
Bill And Lynne Stamm Kovach Scholarship

AMOUNT: None Specified **DEADLINE:** None Specified
FIELDS/MAJORS: All Areas Of Study

Scholarships for undergraduate students at East Tennessee State University who demonstrate financial need. Must have a GPA of at least 2.5, and an ACT score of 24 for entering freshmen and current students must have a 3.0 or better. Contact the Office of

Admissions or the Office of Financial Aid for details.

East Tennessee State University
Office Of Financial Aid
Box 70722
Johnson City, TN 37614

636

Bill And Mary Russell, 40 & 8, And Voiture 130 Scholarship Fund

AMOUNT: Varies **DEADLINE:** Jul 1
FIELDS/MAJORS: Healthcare, Nursing

Scholarships for students in healthcare or nursing fields. For residents of Missouri and Kansas that are served by the Heartland Health Foundation (generally, northwest Missouri and northeast Kansas). Write to the address below for further information.

Heartland Health Foundation
801 Faraon St.
St. Joseph, MO 64501

637

Bill Douglas Memorial Scholarship

AMOUNT: None Specified **DEADLINE:** Feb 1
FIELDS/MAJORS: Psychology

Scholarships are awarded to psychology majors and a resident of Kentucky. Must be in the upper half of his or her classes and be U.S. citizens. Write to the address below for details.

Murray State University
Office of University Scholarships, Ordway Hall
1 Murray St.
Murray, KY 42071

638

Billy Lindsey Scholarship

AMOUNT: $250 **DEADLINE:** None Specified
FIELDS/MAJORS: All Areas Of Study

Awards for Jacksonville State University students who are in any field of study. Write to the address below for more information.

Jacksonville State University
Financial Aid Office
Jacksonville, AL 36265

639

Billy Welu Scholarship

AMOUNT: $500 **DEADLINE:** May 31
FIELDS/MAJORS: All Areas Of Study

One scholarship for current college student involved with bowling. Based on academic and bowling achievements. Must have a GPA of 2.5 or better. Males must carry a current average of 190 and females must carry a current average of 170. For members of the ABC/WIBC/YABA bowling leagues. Write to "Billy Welu Scholarship" at the address below for details.

Professional Bowlers Association Education Fund
Young American Bowling Alliance
5301 S. 76th St.
Greendale, WI 53129

640

Biola Departmental Scholarships

AMOUNT: Varies **DEADLINE:** None Specified
FIELDS/MAJORS: All Areas Of Study

Athletic, academic, music, or leadership scholarships are available for students at Biola University through the respective departments. Based mainly on abilities and not need. Write to the address below for more information.

Biola University
Financial Aid Office
13800 Biola Ave.
La Mirada, CA 90639

641

Biola Need Grant

AMOUNT: $4,000 (max) **DEADLINE:** Mar 2, Aug 25
FIELDS/MAJORS: All Areas Of Study

Grant available for Biola undergraduate students. Based solely on need. The amount of this grant is the difference between the cost of school and the resources available to the student. Write to the address below for more information. The August 25 deadline enables students to receive a partial grant, and March 2 is for the full amount.

Biola University
Financial Aid Office
13800 Biola Ave.
La Mirada, CA 90639

642

Biology Alumni Scholarship

AMOUNT: $500 **DEADLINE:** None Specified
FIELDS/MAJORS: Biology

Student must be a full-time sophomore or above biology major with a GPA of 3.0 or better. Contact the biology department for more information.

Southwest Missouri State University
Office Of Financial Aid
901 South National Ave.
Springfield, MO 65804

643

Biology Department Scholarship

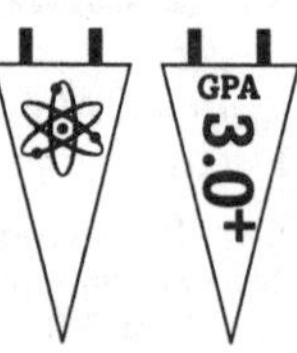

AMOUNT: $200 **DEADLINE:** None Specified
FIELDS/MAJORS: Biology

Awards for all Sul Ross biology students with financial need and a GPA of at least 3.0. Write to the address below for more information.

Sul Ross State University
Financial Aid Office
Box C-113
Alpine, TX 79832

644

Biology Education Scholarship

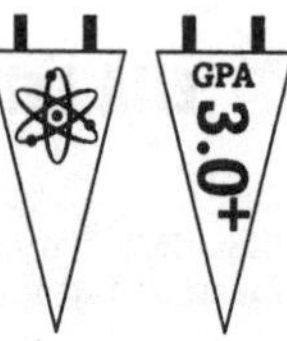

AMOUNT: $500 **DEADLINE:** None Specified
FIELDS/MAJORS: Biology

Student must be a full-time junior or senior biology major with a

GPA of 3.0 or better. Must have completed 15 hours of biology, including Bio 235, with a 3.0 GPA. Contact the biology department for more information.

Southwest Missouri State University
Office Of Financial Aid
901 South National Ave.
Springfield, MO 65804

645

Biology Excellence Fund Scholarship

AMOUNT: $500-$1,000 **DEADLINE:** None Specified
FIELDS/MAJORS: Biology

Awards for all Sul Ross biology undergraduates. Write to the address below for more information.

Sul Ross State University
Financial Aid Office
Box C-113
Alpine, TX 79832

646

Biology Research Program

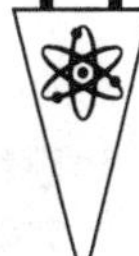

AMOUNT: $1,000 **DEADLINE:** Feb 15
FIELDS/MAJORS: Biology

Scholarships are available at the University of Utah for full-time biology majors who have not yet completed their sixth quarter of study, and are interested in pursuing laboratory research work. Up to twenty awards are offered annually. Write to the address below for details, or call (801) 581-8921 for information.

University of Utah
Dr. Fred Montague
135 Building 44
Salt Lake City, UT 84112

647

Bioquip Products Scholarship And Iselin & Associates Scholarships

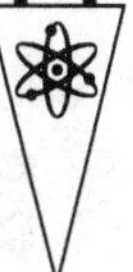

AMOUNT: $500, $1,500 **DEADLINE:** May 31
FIELDS/MAJORS: Entomology, Biology, Zoology

For undergraduate study in the above fields. Must have accumulated at least thirty semester hours at the time award is presented. Criteria: interest and achievement in biology and academic credentials. Must be enrolled at a recognized university or college in the U.S., Canada, or Mexico. Write to the address below for complete details.

Entomological Society Of America
Education Committee
9301 Annapolis Road
Lanham, MD 20706

648

Biotechnology Scholarships In Agriculture

AMOUNT: $1,900 **DEADLINE:** Dec 1
FIELDS/MAJORS: Agriculture

Awards are available to freshmen at Iowa State University who are studying agriculture. Based on scholarship, ACT, and SAT scores, and science interest. Write to the address below for more information.

Iowa State University
Associate Dean Of Academic Programs
Ames, IA 50011

649

Bird Scholarship

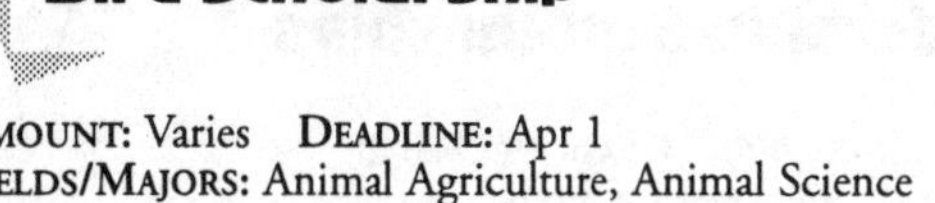

AMOUNT: Varies **DEADLINE:** Apr 1
FIELDS/MAJORS: Animal Agriculture, Animal Science

Awards for UMass students based on academic standing and financial need. Preference given to upperclass students in the pre-veterinary field of study who are residents of Massachusetts. Contact the Chair, Scholarship Committee, Veterinary and Animal Sciences, for more information.

University Of Massachusetts, Amherst
Chair, Scholarship Committee
Veterinary And Animal Sciences
Amherst, MA 01003

650

Birdell Chew Moore Scholarship Award

AMOUNT: None Specified **DEADLINE:** Apr 7
FIELDS/MAJORS: Medicine, Health Services

Awards for graduating high school seniors from Los Angeles who are enrolled in an accredited school and intend to study in the field of medicine or health. Must have a GPA of 2.5 or better and show evidence of financial need. Write to the address below for more information.

Watts Health Foundation, Inc.
Health Education And Promotion
10300 S. Compton Ave
Los Angeles, CA 90002

651

Birmingham Legacy Scholarship

AMOUNT: $500 **DEADLINE:** Mar 15
FIELDS/MAJORS: Travel And Tourism, Hotel/Motel Management

Awards for Alabama juniors or seniors in one of the areas listed above who are enrolled in any four-year college. Must have a GPA of 3.0 or better. Students enrolled in a two-year college are also eligible to apply. Write to the address below for more information.

National Tour Foundation
546 East Main St.
P.O. Box 3071
Lexington, KY 40596

652

Bishop Greco Graduate Fellowship Program

AMOUNT: $2,000 (max) **DEADLINE:** May 1
FIELDS/MAJORS: Special Education

Fellowship for graduate students in a full-time program for the preparation of classroom teachers of mentally retarded children. Applicants also must be a member of the Knights in good standing or the wife, son, or daughter of a member and have a good academic record. Special consideration will be given to students who attend a Catholic graduate school. Write to the Secretary of the Committee on Fellowships at the address below for details.

Knights Of Columbus
Secretary Of The Committee On Fellowships
P.O. Box 1670
New Haven, CT 06507

653

Bishop Maher Catholic Leadership Scholarships

Amount: $200-$3,000 **Deadline:** Feb 20
Fields/Majors: All Areas Of Study

Scholarships are available at the University of San Diego for undergraduate Catholic students who demonstrate academic excellence, parish leadership, and campus and community service. Write to the address listed below for information.

University Of San Diego
Office Of Financial Aid
5998 Alcala Park
San Diego, CA 92110

654

Bishop Meyers Scholarship

Amount: Half Tuition **Deadline:** None
Fields/Majors: All Areas Of Study

Scholarships for "high-achieving" students, recommended by pastor. Renewable. Must demonstrate financial need. Write to the address below for details.

Mercyhurst College
Glenwood Hills
Erie, PA 16546

655

Bishop Quayle Award

Amount: $1,200 (max) **Deadline:** Apr 1
Fields/Majors: All Areas Of Study

Awards for students who are members of participating churches. Baker will match the church's contribution from an established fund. Must have a GPA of at least 2.3. Renewable with a GPA of at least 2.0. Write to the address below for more information.

Baker University
Office Of Financial Aid
P.O. Box 65
Baldwin City, KS 66006

656

Bishop W. Bertrand Stevens Foundation Grants & Loans

Amount: None Specified **Deadline:** May 15
Fields/Majors: All Areas Of Study

Grants of part gift and part loan for residents of the (Episcopal) Diocese of Los Angeles (LA, Orange, Ventura, Santa Barbara, and parts of San Bernardino and Riverside counties). Interview required. Zero percent interest, repay after graduation. Membership in the Episcopal Church is not a requirement. Some preference is given to students planning to attend a seminary. Students in all fields of study are encouraged to apply. Write for details.

Bishop W. Bertrand Stevens Foundation
P.O. Box 80251
San Marino, CA 91118

657

Bishop Watson Christian Service Scholarships

Amount: $1,000 **Deadline:** Jun 1
Fields/Majors: All Areas Of Study

Grants for high school seniors who exemplify Christian leadership.

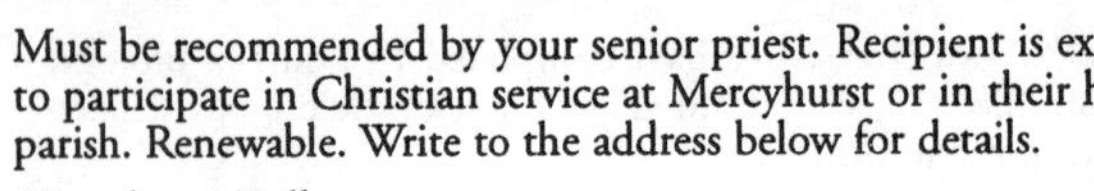

Must be recommended by your senior priest. Recipient is expected to participate in Christian service at Mercyhurst or in their home parish. Renewable. Write to the address below for details.

Mercyhurst College
Glenwood Hills
Erie, PA 16546

658

Black Alumni Association Scholarship

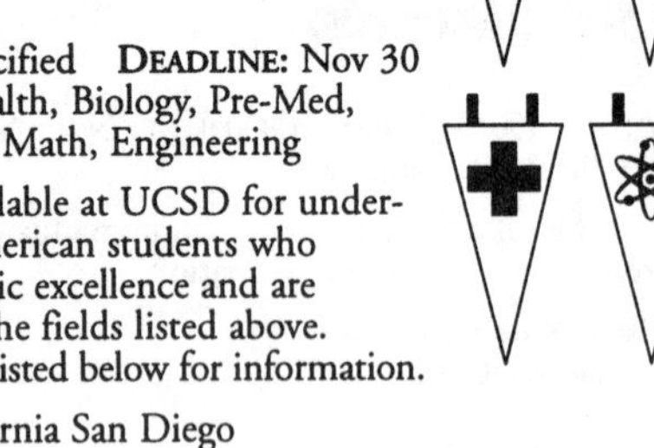

Amount: None Specified **Deadline:** Nov 30
Fields/Majors: Health, Biology, Pre-Med, Pre-Dental, Science, Math, Engineering

Scholarships are available at UCSD for undergraduate African American students who demonstrate academic excellence and are majoring in one of the fields listed above. Write to the address listed below for information.

University Of California San Diego
Student Financial Services
9500 Gilman Drive
La Jolla, CA 92093

659

Black Hills Stock Show Foundation Scholarship

Amount: $1,000 **Deadline:** Dec 31
Fields/Majors: All Areas Of Study

Scholarships are available for residents of South Dakota, North Dakota, Montana, Wyoming, or Nebraska. Based on academic ability, extracurricular activities, work history, community service, financial need, and interview, and a short essay on "how do you plan to perpetuate your western heritage through your education?" Write to the address listed below for information.

Black Hills Stock Show Foundation
P.O. Box 2560
Rapid City, SD 57709

660

Blackfeet Higher Education Program

Amount: None Specified **Deadline:** Mar 1
Fields/Majors: All Areas Of Study

Scholarships are available for members of the Blackfeet tribe who are actively pursuing an undergraduate degree in any area of study. Special awards are also available for adult students. Write to the address below for more information.

Blackfeet Tribe
P.O. Box 850
Browning, MT 59417

661

Blanche Ausley Montgomery Memorial Scholarship

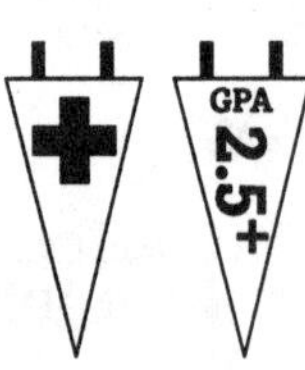

Amount: Varies **Deadline:** Mar 1
Fields/Majors: Nursing

Awards are available at the University of New Mexico for junior, senior, or graduate nursing students with financial need and a GPA of at least 2.5. For residents of New Mexico only. Write to the address below or contact the school of nursing for more details.

University Of New Mexico, Albuquerque
Office Of Financial Aid
Albuquerque, NM 87131

662

Blanche Fischer Foundation

AMOUNT: None Specified **DEADLINE:** Rolling
FIELDS/MAJORS: All Areas Of Study

Open to disabled or physically handicapped persons (excluding mental problems) residing within the state of Oregon. Must demonstrate financial need and medical confirmation is required. Write to the address below for more information.

Blanche Fischer Foundation
7912 SW 35th Avenue, Suite 7
Portland, OR 97219

663

Blanche Honaker Brakebill Scholarship

AMOUNT: $500-$1,000 **DEADLINE:** Feb 17
FIELDS/MAJORS: Elementary Education

Scholarships are available at the University of Oklahoma, Norman for full-time elementary education majors. Applicant must be a female, and plan to work in a public school setting upon graduation. For sophomore level and above. Write to the address listed below for information.

University Of Oklahoma, Norman
College Of Education
Student Services Room 137, ECH
Norman OK 73019

664

Blind and Deaf Students Scholarship

AMOUNT: Tuition **DEADLINE:** None Specified
FIELDS/MAJORS: All Areas Of Study

Exemption of tuition and fees to blind and deaf students at public colleges and universities in Texas. Student must present certification of deafness or blindness from the appropriate state vocational rehabilitation agency and have a high school diploma or its equivalent. Write to the address below for details.

Texas Higher Education Coordinating Board
P.O. Box 12788
Austin, TX 78711

665

Blind Service Association Scholarship Grant Program

AMOUNT: $2,500 (max) **DEADLINE:** Apr 1
FIELDS/MAJORS: All Areas Of Study

Scholarships for legally blind students. For study at college, university, professional, or vocational educational program. Applicants must reside in the six-county Chicago metropolitan area. Applications are available after January 1 by writing to the address below. You must be legally blind to qualify for these awards.

Blind Service Association, Inc.
22 W. Monroe St.
Chicago, IL 60603

666

Bliss Prize Fellowship In Byzantine Studies

AMOUNT: $33,500 (max) **DEADLINE:** Nov 1
FIELDS/MAJORS: Byzantine Studies

Fellowships for students who are (or are soon to be) graduated with a bachelor of arts degree and intend to enter the field of byzantine studies. Must have studied at least one year of Greek. Fellows are usually offered a junior fellowship at Dumbarton Oaks after completing 2 years of the Bliss Fellowship. These are non-residential fellowships. Write to the address below for details.

Dumbarton Oaks
Office Of The Director
1703 32nd St., NW
Washington, DC 20007

667

Bloomsburg Chapter Professional Secretaries Int'l Scholarship

AMOUNT: $150 **DEADLINE:** None Specified
FIELDS/MAJORS: Education (Business)

Award for junior business education teaching majors with a minimum GPA of 2.5. Consideration for those in activities that provide educational instruction and career guidance. Selection is made by the business education and office administration department. Contact a member of the business education department for further information.

Bloomsburg University
19 Ben Franklin Hall
400 E. Second St.
Bloomsburg, PA 17815

668

Bloomsburg University International Faculty Association

AMOUNT: $250 **DEADLINE:** Feb 9
FIELDS/MAJORS: International Affairs

Student must demonstrate strong interest in international affairs, have high academic standards and be serious about pursuing quality education. Use Bloomsburg University scholarship application. Contact Dr. Reza Boubary, Math and Computer Science Department, for further information.

Bloomsburg University
19 Ben Franklin Hall
400 E. Second St.
Bloomsburg, PA 17815

669

Blount Presidential Scholarship

AMOUNT: $5,000 **DEADLINE:** Mar 1
FIELDS/MAJORS: Engineering

One award for Alabama residents planning to major in civil engineering, mechanical engineering, or building science. Award is renewable with the maintenance of a "B" average. Write to the address below for complete details.

Auburn University
Office Of Student Financial Aid
203 Mary Martin Hall
Auburn University, AL 36849

670

Blount/Rush/Meiller/Bragg Scholarships

AMOUNT: None Specified **DEADLINE:** Mar 10
FIELDS/MAJORS: All Areas Of Study

Scholarships for needy and necessitous residents of Virginia who

are enrolled as full-time students in Bluefield College. Write to the address below for more information.

Bluefield College
Financial Aid Office
3000 College Drive
Bluefield, VA 24605

671 Blue Mountain Barbershoppers

Amount: Tuition And Fees **Deadline:** Mar 1
Fields/Majors: Vocal Music

Award for a student at Eastern who has demonstrated excellence in performance as a singer. Write to the address below for more information.

Eastern Oregon State College
Financial Aid Office
1041 "I" Avenue
La Grande, OR 97850

672 Bluebird Society Research Grants–Bluebird Research Grants

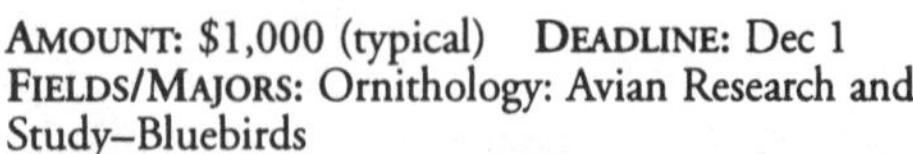

Amount: $1,000 (typical) **Deadline:** Dec 1
Fields/Majors: Ornithology: Avian Research and Study–Bluebirds

Research grants available to student, professional, and individual researchers for a research project focused on any of the three species of bluebird from the genus "sialia." Proposal required. Supported on a one-year basis. Interested persons should write to the address below for further information.

North American Bluebird Society, Inc.
Kevin Berner, Research Comm. Chairman
State University Of New York
Cobleskill, NY 12043

673 Bluebird Society Research Grants–General Research Grant

Amount: $1,000 (typical) **Deadline:** Dec 1
Fields/Majors: Ornithology: Avian Research and Study–Bluebirds

Research grants available to student, professional, and individual researchers for a research project focused on any North American cavity-nesting bird species. Proposal required. Supported on a one-year basis. Interested persons should write to the address below for further information.

North American Bluebird Society, Inc.
Kevin Berner, Research Comm. Chairman
State University Of New York
Cobleskill, NY 12043

674 Bluebird Society Research Grants–Student Research Grant

Amount: $1,000 (typical) **Deadline:** Dec 1
Fields/Majors: Ornithology: Avian Research and Study–Bluebirds

Student research grant (1) available to a full-time college or university student, For a research project focused on any North American avian cavity-nesting species (genus "sialia" and cavity-nesting species native to North America). Proposal required. Supported on a one-year basis. Interested students should write to the address below for further information.

North American Bluebird Society, Inc.
Kevin Berner, Research Comm. Chairman
State University Of New York
Cobleskill, NY 12043

675 Bluefield College Grant

Amount: $1,000 (max) **Deadline:** Mar 10
Fields/Majors: All Areas Of Study

Awards for full-time students with proven need or academic abilities. Write to the address below for more information.

Bluefield College
Financial Aid Office
3000 College Drive
Bluefield, VA 24605

676 BMI Student Composers Awards

Amount: $500-$3,000 **Deadline:** Feb 9
Fields/Majors: Music Composition

Awards are available for citizens of countries in the western hemisphere who are enrolled in accredited public, private, or parochial secondary schools of music. Applicant must not have reached his/her 26th birthday by December 31. Send a stamped, self-addressed business size envelope to the address below for more details.

BMI and BMI Foundation, Inc.
Mr. Ralph N. Jackson, Director
320 West 57th St.
New York, NY 10019

677 Board Of Governors Medical Scholarship Program

Amount: $5,000 **Deadline:** None Specified
Fields/Majors: Medical

Scholarships for students accepted to one of four medical schools in North Carolina: Bowman Gray School of Medicine of Wake Forest Univ., Duke Univ. School of Medicine, East Carolina Univ School of Medicine and the Univ. of North Carolina at Chapel Hill School of Medicine. Applicants must be residents of North Carolina and have financial need. Students must express the intent to practice medicine in North Carolina. The program encourages minorities to pursue a medical education. Write to the address below for details.

North Carolina State Education Assistance Authority
P.O. Box 2688
Chapel Hill, NC 27515

678 Board Of Nursing And General Assembly-Nursing Scholarships

Amount: $100-$4,000 **Deadline:** Varies
Fields/Majors: Nursing

Open to undergraduate and graduate Virginia residents who are enrolled at Virginia nursing schools, have financial need, and are studying full-time. Recipients must practice nursing in Virginia after graduation for one month for every hundred dollars received. Must have GPA of at least 3.0. Write to the address below for details. The financial aid office at your school or department of nursing may also have information on this scholarship program.

Virginia Department Of Health
Office Of Public Health Nursing
P.O. Box 2448
Richmond, VA 23218

679

Board Of Regents Scholarship

AMOUNT: Varies **DEADLINE:** None Specified
FIELDS/MAJORS: All Areas Of Study

Awards for first-time, full-time freshmen. Amount of award depends on GPA (must be over 3.0) and if the applicant was a National Merit Finalist. Renewable if applicant maintains a GPA of at least 3.0. Write to the address below for more information.

Concordia College, Nebraska
Office Of Financial Aid
800 N. Columbia Ave.
Seward, NE 68434

680

Board Of Supervisors Fee Exemption Scholarships

AMOUNT: None Specified **DEADLINE:** Feb 15
FIELDS/MAJORS: All Areas Of Study

Scholarships are available at the University of New Orleans for full-time entering freshman who are Louisiana high school graduating seniors. Write to the address below for details.

University Of New Orleans
Office Of Student Financial Aid
1005 Administration Building, Lake Front
New Orleans, LA 70148

681

Board Of Trustee Scholarships

AMOUNT: None Specified **DEADLINE:** None Specified
FIELDS/MAJORS: All Areas Of Study Except Law

Graduate scholarships are available at the Catholic University of America in any school except law. Contact the financial aid office at the address below for details.

The Catholic University Of America
Office Of Admissions And Financial Aid
Washington, DC 20064

682

Boatmen's Bank Of Oklahoma Scholarships

AMOUNT: $1,000 **DEADLINE:** Feb 3
FIELDS/MAJORS: Marketing

Scholarships are available at the University of Oklahoma, Norman for full-time senior marketing majors. Students must apply in their junior year. Write to the address listed below for information.

University Of Oklahoma, Norman
Director, Division Of Marketing
1 Adams Hall
Norman, OK 73019

683

Boatmen's First National Bank Of Oklahoma Scholarship

AMOUNT:$500-$1,000 **DEADLINE:** Jan 1
FIELDS/MAJORS: Arts And Sciences

Scholarships open to all majors in the college of arts and sciences. For use during senior year of undergraduate study. Minimum GPA of 3.5 required. Write to the address listed below for information.

University Of Oklahoma, Norman
College Of Arts And Sciences
601 Elm, Room 429
Norman, OK 73019

684

Bob And Lou Kennamer Scholarships

AMOUNT: $1,000 **DEADLINE:** Mar 15
FIELDS/MAJORS: Commerce, Business

Awards for Jacksonville State University juniors or seniors who are majoring in commerce or business. Based on leadership, academics, and financial need. Must have a GPA of at least 3.0. Write to the address below for more details.

Jacksonville State University
Financial Aid Office
Jacksonville, AL 36265

685

Bob Comer Memorial Scholarship

AMOUNT: None Specified **DEADLINE:** None Specified
FIELDS/MAJORS: Theatre Management

Awards to students who must be an upperclassman or graduate student interested in theatre management and selected to participate in the summer theatre. Contact the theatre and dance department for more information.

Southwest Missouri State University
Office Of Financial Aid
901 South National Ave.
Springfield, MO 65804

686

Bob East Scholarship

AMOUNT: $1,000 **DEADLINE:** Mar 1
FIELDS/MAJORS: Photojournalism/Photography

Applicants must be undergraduates or be planning to pursue postgraduate work. All applicants must submit a portfolio that includes at least five individual prints and a photo essay. Send an SASE to the address below for information sheet. Information may also be available in many journalism, photography, or photojournalism departments.

National Press Photographers Foundation
3200 Crossdaile Dr., Suite 306
Durham, NC 27705

687

Bob Eddy Scholarship

Amount: $1,000-$2,000 **Deadline:** Apr 15
Fields/Majors: Journalism

Scholarships are available for Connecticut residents or students attending a Connecticut college or university and majoring in journalism. For students who will be entering their junior or senior year. The journalism department at your college may have details on this award. If not, write to the address listed below for details.

Connecticut Society Of Professional Journalists Foundation
c/o Bob Eddy Scholarship Committee
71 Kenwood Avenue
Fairfield, CT 06430

688

Bob Jones Memorial Endowed Scholarship

Amount: $300 **Deadline:** Feb 15
Fields/Majors: Telecommunications

Renewable $300 scholarship given to full-time freshmen, sophomores, and juniors majoring in telecommunications with high academic potential who intend to pursue a career in broadcast journalism. Write to the address listed below for further information.

University Of Alabama
College Of Communications
P.O. Box 870172
Tuscaloosa, AL 35487

689

Bob Leach Broadcasting Scholarship

Amount: $1,000 **Deadline:** Mar 1
Fields/Majors: Telecommunications

Must be a junior or senior majoring in telecommunications at the University of Florida and have at least a 2.8 GPA. Write to the address below for complete details.

University Of Florida
2070 Weimer Hall
Scholarship and Placement Director
Gainesville, FL 32611

690

Bob Quinn Memorial Scholarship

Amount: $500 **Deadline:** Mar 1
Fields/Majors: All Areas Of Study

Award for a returning Eastern student who has lettered in an intercollegiate athletic team and who is eligible to represent Eastern in an intercollegiate athletic event. Must have a GPA of at least 3.0. Write to the address below for more information.

Eastern Oregon State College
Financial Aid Office
1041 "l" Avenue
La Grande, OR 97850

691

Bobby Foster Scholarship

Amount: Varies **Deadline:** Mar 1
Fields/Majors: All Areas Of Study

Awards are available at the University of New Mexico for minority juniors or seniors with financial need and a GPA of at least 2.0. Write to the address below for more information.

University Of New Mexico, Albuquerque
Office Of Financial Aid
Albuquerque, NM 87131

692

Bobette Bibo Gugliotta Memorial Scholarship For Creative Writing

Amount: $2,500 (max) **Deadline:** Mar 29
Fields/Majors: Creative Writing

Scholarships for graduates of high schools located on the San Francisco peninsula who plan to pursue a career in creative writing. For full-time study. Write to the address below for details.

Peninsula Community Foundation
1700 S. El Camino Real, #300
San Mateo, CA 94402

693

Boeing Student Research Award

Amount: $1,000 **Deadline:** Mar 1
Fields/Majors: Travel/Tourism

Students matriculated in a bachelor's or master's degree granting program are eligible to submit a paper on a subject related to the travel and tourism industry. Non-winning papers may still receive a merit award of $250. Write to the address below for details.

Travel And Tourism Research Association
TTRA Awards Committee
10200 W. 44th Ave., Suite 304
Wheat Ridge, CO 80033

694

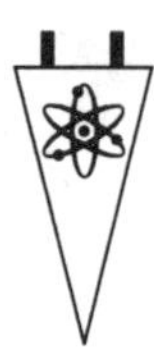

Boge Chemistry Award

Amount: $1,000 **Deadline:** None Specified
Fields/Majors: Chemistry

Awards for outstanding chemistry students at Mesa State College. Write to the address below for more information.

Mesa State College
Financial Aid Office
P.O. Box 2684
Grand Junction, CO 81501

695

Bohannan-Huston Scholarship

Amount: Varies **Deadline:** Mar 1
Fields/Majors: Civil Or Construction Engineering

Awards are available at the University of New Mexico for full-time students demonstrating academic achievement and financial need. Write to the address below for more information.

University Of New Mexico, Albuquerque
Office Of Financial Aid
Albuquerque, NM 87131

696

Bolla Wines Scholarship

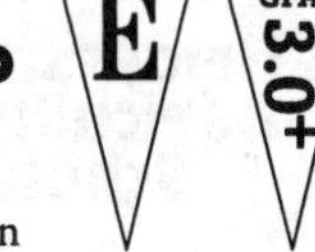

AMOUNT: $1,000 **DEADLINE:** May 31
FIELDS/MAJORS: International Business, Italian Studies, Italian American History

Scholarships are available for Italian American students who are at least 21 years of age with a GPA of at least 3.0, enrolled in one of the program areas listed above. Preference is given to those studying Italian business issues. Write to the address below for details.

National Italian American Foundation
Dr. Maria Lombardo, Education Director
1860 19th Street, NW
Washington, DC 20009

697

Bolt, Isom, Jackson, And Bailey Scholarship

AMOUNT: $1,000 **DEADLINE:** Mar 15
FIELDS/MAJORS: All Areas Of Study

Awards for Jacksonville State University students in any discipline who are residents of Calhoun or Cleburne counties in Alabama. Write to the address below for more details.

Jacksonville State University
Financial Aid Office
Jacksonville, AL 36265

698

Bolton Scholars Program At Case Western

AMOUNT: Half Tuition **DEADLINE:** Apr 30
FIELDS/MAJORS: Nursing

Half tuition scholarships for students in the B.S. program at the Frances Payne Bolton School of Nursing at Case Western. Contact the office of financial aid at the address below for details.

Case Western Reserve University
Office Of Financial Aid
109 Pardee Hall
10900 Euclid Avenue
Cleveland, OH 44106

699

Bonner Scholars

AMOUNT: $1,870 **DEADLINE:** Mar 31
FIELDS/MAJORS: All Areas Of Study

Awards for students with good academic potential and low family income. Write to the address below for more information.

Hood College
Admissions Office
401 Rosemont Ave.
Frederick, MD 21701

700

Boone Newspapers, Inc. Scholarship

AMOUNT: None Specified **DEADLINE:** Feb 15
FIELDS/MAJORS: Print Journalism

Renewable scholarship covering tuition and fees for juniors or seniors with 3.0 GPA pursuing a career in print journalism. Priority is given to students working part time while attending college. University of Alabama students only. Write to the address listed below for further information and an application.

James B. Boone, Jr. College Of Comm., University Of Alabama
P.O. Box 870172
Tuscaloosa, AL 35487

701

Borden Foundation, Inc. Scholarships

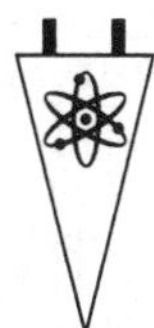

AMOUNT: $1,000 **DEADLINE:** Feb 15
FIELDS/MAJORS: Food Science And Technology, Agricultural Economics

Scholarships are available for FFA members pursuing a four-year degree in food science and technology or agricultural economics at Texas A&M University. Write to the address below for details.

National FFA Foundation
Scholarship Office
P.O. Box 15160
Alexandria, VA 22309

702

Boris Franzus Corporation Scholarship

AMOUNT: None Specified **DEADLINE:** None Specified
FIELDS/MAJORS: Chemistry (Organic)

Scholarships for organic chemistry majors at East Tennessee State University. Contact the chemistry department or the office of financial aid for details.

East Tennessee State University
Office Of Financial Aid
Box 70722
Johnson City, TN 37614

703

Bound-to-Stay-Bound Books Scholarship

AMOUNT: $5,000 **DEADLINE:** Mar 1
FIELDS/MAJORS: Library Science, Children's

Applicants must be entering or enrolled in an ALA-accredited program for the master's or beyond the master's with a concentration in children's library services. Must be U.S. or Canada citizen. Recipients are required to work in a children's library for a minimum of one year after graduation. Write to the address shown below for details.

American Library Association
Assn. For Library Service To Children
50 E. Huron Street
Chicago, IL 60611

704

Bowen Trust Fund Scholarships

AMOUNT: None Specified **DEADLINE:** None Specified
FIELDS/MAJORS: All Areas Of Study

Scholarships for students of the Macon territory (central Georgia), with preference given to students from Bibb County. Students from other states studying in central Georgia are also eligible. Need based. For undergraduate study. Must have a GPA of at least 2.0 to renew scholarship. For full-time study. All applications will be considered. Write to the address below for details.

R.A. Bowen Trust Scholarship Program
P.O. Box 4611
Macon, GA 31208

705

Bowles, McDavid, Graff And Love Scholarship Fund

AMOUNT: None Specified **DEADLINE:** Mar 15
FIELDS/MAJORS: Law

Scholarships for law students at the West Virginia University, School of Law. Based on need and academics. Renewable. Must be a resident of West Virginia. Write to the address below for details.

Greater Kanawha Valley Foundation
Scholarship Committee
P.O. Box 3041
Charleston, WV 25331

706

Brandel Presidential Scholarships

AMOUNT: $8,000 **DEADLINE:** Mar 1
FIELDS/MAJORS: Mechanical Engineering

Awards for entering freshmen with an ACT score of 29 or better and a GPA of at least 3.5. Renewable with a GPA of 3.0 or higher. Applicants must be planning to major in mechanical engineering. Preference is given to residents of Orange County, Florida, and the state of Alabama, in that order. Write to the address below for more information.

Auburn University
Office Of Student Financial Aid
203 Mary Martin Hall
Auburn University, AL 36849

707

Brenda K. Hafner Memorial Music Scholarship

AMOUNT: Varies **DEADLINE:** None Specified
FIELDS/MAJORS: Music, Wind Instrument

Award for performer in one or more of the department's three ensembles. Must have made a significant contribution and will continue participation in the ensemble through the award year. Selection is made by the music department faculty. Contact a member of the music department faculty for further information.

Bloomsburg University
19 Ben Franklin Hall
400 E. Second St.
Bloomsburg, PA 17815

708

Brian F. Scott Mem. Scholarship & Robert C. Gormley Scholarship

AMOUNT: None Specified **DEADLINE:** None Specified
FIELDS/MAJORS: All Areas Of Study

Scholarships are awarded annually to an Eagle Scout registered with the National Capital Council who is a graduating high school senior. Write to the address below for more information.

National Capital Area Council, Boy Scouts Of America
9190 Wisconsin Ave.
Bethesda, MD 20814

709

Bridgestone/Firestone Agricultural Mechanics Scholarships

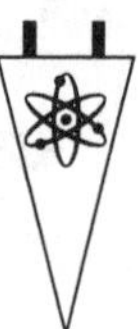

AMOUNT: $500 **DEADLINE:** Feb 15
FIELDS/MAJORS: All Areas Of Study

Scholarships are available for FFA members pursuing a two- or four-year degree in any field. Applicant must have competed in a state FFA agricultural mechanics competition. Write to the address below for details.

National FFA Foundation
Scholarship Office
P.O. Box 15160
Alexandria, VA 22309

710

Bridgestone/Firestone, Inc. Merit Scholarships

AMOUNT: $500-$2,000 **DEADLINE:** None Specified
FIELDS/MAJORS: All Areas Of Study

Scholarships are available to graduating high school seniors who are national merit finalists and children of employees of Bridgestone/Firestone, Inc. Up to 35 awards offered annually. Write to the address listed below for information, or contact the human resources department at Bridgestone/Firestone, Inc.

National Merit Scholarship Corporation/Bridgestone/
Firestone, Inc.
1560 Sherman Avenue, Suite 200
Evanston, IL 60201

711

Bristol Bar Association Scholarships

AMOUNT: Varies **DEADLINE:** Apr 12
FIELDS/MAJORS: Law

Scholarships for students entering law school who are residents of the city of Bristol (CT) or the surrounding towns of Burlington, Plainville, Terryville, and Plymouth. Based also on need, achievement, and extracurricular activities. Number and amount of awards varies. Contact attorney Margaret M. Hayes, Chairperson of the Bristol Bar Association Scholarship Committee, for details.

Bristol Bar Association Anderson
Alden, Hayes & Ziogas, Llc
P.O. Box 1197
Bristol, CT 06011

712

Bristol Children's Home Fund

AMOUNT: $750 **DEADLINE:** May 1
FIELDS/MAJORS: All Areas Of Study

Scholarships are available for residents of Bristol who have lived there for at least four years. Write to the address listed below for information.

Rhode Island Foundation
Mrs. Jessie Huey
26 Acacia Road
Bristol, RI 02809

713

British Marshall Scholarships

AMOUNT: Tuition and Expense **DEADLINE:** Oct 16
FIELDS/MAJORS: All Areas Of Study

Scholarships for American graduate students to study in a university in the United Kingdom. The primary purpose for this program is to allow young americans who will one day become leaders, opinion formers, and decision makers in their own country to study in Great Britain and understand and appreciate British culture. Must be U.S. citizen, under age 26, and have a minimum 3.7 GPA. Write to the address below for complete details.

British Information Services
845 Third Ave.
New York, NY 10022

714

Britt & Muryl Yow Memorial Scholarships

AMOUNT: None Specified **DEADLINE:** Apr 15
FIELDS/MAJORS: All Areas Of Study

Open to entering freshmen or current students at ABAC. Based on financial need and potential academic success in your field of study. Applicants must have a GPA of at least 2.0. Write to the address below for additional information.

Abraham Baldwin Agricultural College
Office Of Admissions
2802 Moore Highway
Tifton, GA 31794

715

Brown Scholar Awards

AMOUNT: Tuition And Fees **DEADLINE:** None Specified
FIELDS/MAJORS: All Areas Of Study

Awards for high school seniors who rank in the top 5% of their high school class or have at least a 3.7 grade point average. Applicants must score at least a 1300 on the SAT and a 31 on the ACT. Finalists will be invited to campus to interview and compete for the award in March. Renewable. Write to the address below for more information.

Southwestern University
Admissions Office
Georgetown, TX 78626

716

Bruce And Marjorie Sundlun Scholarship Fund

AMOUNT: $500-$1,000 **DEADLINE:** Apr 15
FIELDS/MAJORS: All Areas Of Study

Scholarships are available for residents of Rhode Island who are single parents returning to school to upgrade their skills. Write to the address listed below for information.

Rhode Island Foundation
70 Elm Street
Providence, RI 02903

717

Bruce B. Melchert Scholarship

AMOUNT: $300 **DEADLINE:** Jun 1
FIELDS/MAJORS: Political Science, Government

Scholarship is available to any undergraduate member of Tau Kappa Epsilon who is a full-time student of sophomore, junior, or senior standing, pursuing a degree in political science or government with a GPA of 3.0 or higher. Must be able to demonstrate leadership within his chapter. Write to the address below for more information.

TKE Educational Foundation
8645 Founders Rd.
Indianapolis, IN 46268

718

Bruce M. Robertson Scholarships

AMOUNT: $1,300 **DEADLINE:** Mar 1
FIELDS/MAJORS: Business

Scholarships are available at the University of Iowa for full-time junior business majors who are graduates of an Iowa high school. Write to the address listed below for information.

University Of Iowa
College Of Business Admin., Suite W160
108 Pappajohn Business Admin. Bldg.
Iowa City, IA 52245

719

Bruce Wilson Memorial Scholarship

AMOUNT: $500-$1,000 **DEADLINE:** None Specified
FIELDS/MAJORS: Political Science

Scholarships are available to students majoring in political science. Write to the address below for more information.

California State Polytechnic University, Pomona
Office Of Financial Aid
3801 West Temple Ave.
Pomona, CA 91768

720

Brython P. Davis Scholarship

AMOUNT: None Specified **DEADLINE:** Nov 30
FIELDS/MAJORS: All Areas Of Study

Scholarships are available at UCSD for undergraduate students with a parent who was a regular member of the U.S. Navy or Marine Corps. Write to the address listed below for information.

University Of California San Diego
Student Financial Services
9500 Gilman Drive
La Jolla, CA 92093

721

Bucks County Police Association Scholarship

AMOUNT: $1,000 **DEADLINE:** May 1
FIELDS/MAJORS: Law Enforcement

Awards for high school seniors from Bucks County, PA, accepted into a law enforcement program at any college or university. Applicants must have a GPA of at least 2.5 and scored at least 1000 on the SAT. Write to the address below for more information.

Bucks County Police Association Scholarship
Education Committee Chairman
26 Forrester Road
Horsham, PA 19044

722

Buddy Baker Memorial Scholarships

Amount: $1,000 **Deadline:** Mar 1
Fields/Majors: Journalism

Awards for juniors and seniors majoring in journalism who plan to pursue a career in arts and entertainment reporting or editing. Must have a GPA of at least 2.8 and have demonstrated financial need. Write to the address below for more information.

University Of Florida
Knight Scholarship and Placement Director
2070 Weimer Hall
Gainesville, FL 32611

723

Buddy Davis Scholarship

Amount: $2,800 **Deadline:** Mar 1
Fields/Majors: Newspaper Reporting Or Editing

Must be an incoming H.S. senior studying newspaper reporting or editing at the University of Florida. Awarded on basis of character, scholarship and promise to the profession. Financial need is a lesser criterion. Must have a GPA of 2.8 or better. Write to the address below for details.

University Of Florida
2070 Weimer Hall
Scholarship and Placement Director
Gainesville, FL 32611

724

Budweiser-USO Scholarship Program

Amount: $1,000 **Deadline:** Mar 1
Fields/Majors: All Areas Of Study

Scholarships for immediate families of active-duty armed forces personnel. Must be a graduating high school senior or have graduated within the last four years. Based on scholastic record, test scores, and extracurricular activities. Fifteen awards per year. Write to the address below for details.

USO World Headquarters
Budweiser-USO Scholarship Program
601 Indiana Ave., NW
Washington, DC 20004

725

Buffalo Sigma Delta Chi Journalism Scholarships

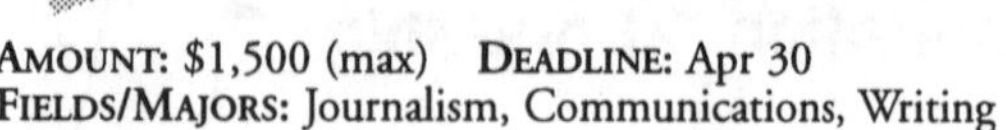

Amount: $1,500 (max) **Deadline:** Apr 30
Fields/Majors: Journalism, Communications, Writing

Scholarships for undergraduate juniors and seniors, graduate students, and journalism professionals living in western New York, northwestern Pennsylvania, and southeastern Ontario. Must be majoring in courses leading to a career in one of the above fields. Renewable once. Students in western NY, northwestern PA, and southeastern ON should write to the address below for details.

Society Of Professional Journalists, Greater Buffalo Chapter
John C. Connolly, Scholarship Secretary
160 Schimwood Ct.
Getzville, NY 14068

726

Buford Boone Memorial Scholarship

Amount:$1,000 **Deadline:** Feb 15
Fields/Majors: Journalism

Renewable $1,000 scholarship given to outstanding juniors and seniors with a 3.0 GPA who intend to pursue a career in journalism at the University of Alabama. Priority is given to students who work part time while attending college. Write to the address listed below for further information and an application.

James B. Boone, Jr. College Of Communications
University Of Alabama
P.O. Box 870172
Tuscaloosa, AL 35487

727

Building Construction Management–Alumni And Friends Scholarships

Amount: $200-$500 **Deadline:** Feb 15
Fields/Majors: Construction Management And Related Fields

Awards are available for full-time continuing students at UW Platteville who are studying construction management or a related field. Must demonstrate scholastic achievement. Write to the address below for more information.

University Of Wisconsin, Platteville
Office Of Enrollment And Admissions
Platteville, WI 53818

728

Bundeskanzler Scholarships For Germany

Amount: Varies **Deadline:** Oct 31
Fields/Majors: Humanities, Social Sciences, Law, And Economics Of Germany

Scholarships for students and postdoctorates to initiate or continue their studies at a university in Germany in order to gain an insight into the political, economic, social, and cultural life of the republic of Germany. Must be U.S. citizens under the age of 30. Write to the address below for more information.

Alexander Von Humboldt Foundation
1055 Thomas Jefferson St., NW, Suite 2020
Washington, DC 20007

729

Bunge Corporation Scholarships

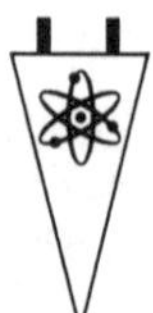

Amount: $1,000 **Deadline:** Feb 15
Fields/Majors: Agriculture

Scholarships are available for FFA members pursuing a four-year degree in any area of agriculture at a four-year institution. Write to the address below for details.

National FFA Foundation
Scholarship Office
P.O. Box 15160
Alexandria, VA 22309

730

Bureau Of Alcohol, Tobacco, & Firearms Special Agents' Scholarships

AMOUNT: $1,000 **DEADLINE:** Apr 1
FIELDS/MAJORS: Law Enforcement

Scholarships are presented every year to law enforcement explorers whose achievements reflect the high degree of motivation, commitment, and community concern that epitomize the law enforcement profession. Write to the address below for more information.

Bureau Of Alcohol, Tobacco, And Firearms
Attn: Liaison Program Manager
650 Massachusetts Ave., Room 7150
Washington, DC 20226

731

Burke County Scholarships

AMOUNT: $300–$600 **DEADLINE:** Mar 31
FIELDS/MAJORS: All Areas Of Study

Awards for high school seniors attending Freedom High School or East Burke High School in Burke County, NC. Financial need is considered when evaluating applicants. Special preference may be given to those interested in a teaching career only when two applicants seem to be equally qualified. Contact your guidance counselor for the address below for more information.

Burke County Retired School Personnel
P.O. Box 235
Glen Alpine, NC 28628

732

Burlington Northern Foundation Scholarships

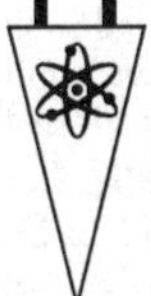

AMOUNT: $1,000 **DEADLINE:** Feb 15
FIELDS/MAJORS: Agriculture

Scholarships are available for FFA members who are pursuing a degree in any area of agriculture and reside in Alabama, Arkansas, Colorado, Idaho, Iowa, Illinois, Kansas, Minnesota, Mississippi, Missouri, Montana, Nebraska, North Dakota, Oklahoma, Oregon, South Dakota, Tennessee, Texas, or Washington. Ten awards offered annually. Write to the address below for details.

National FFA Foundation
Scholarship Office
P.O. Box 15160
Alexandria, VA 22309

733

Burns And Haynes Scholarship Fund

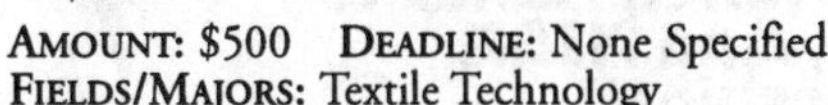

AMOUNT: $500 **DEADLINE:** None Specified
FIELDS/MAJORS: Textile Technology

Scholarships are available for residents of Rhode Island who are studying textile technology. Preference is given to children of members of the National Association of Textile Supervisors. Write to the address listed below for information.

Rhode Island Foundation
70 Elm Street
Providence, RI 02903

734

Burroughs-Wellcome Scholarship

AMOUNT: Varies **DEADLINE:** Mar 1
FIELDS/MAJORS: Pharmacy

Awards are available at the University of New Mexico for full-time pharmacy students demonstrating academic excellence and financial need. Write to the address below for more information.

University Of New Mexico, Albuquerque
Office Of Financial Aid
Albuquerque, NM 87131

735

Burton W. Marsh Fellowship

AMOUNT: $4,000 **DEADLINE:** Mar 15
FIELDS/MAJORS: Transportation/Traffic Management, Civil Engineering

At least one fellowship for graduate study in transportation or civil engineering (relating to transportation). Awarded to the highest ranked candidate(s). Write to the address below for details.

Institute Of Transportation Engineers
525 School St., SW, Suite 410
Washington, DC 20024

736

Business Administration Endowment Scholarship

AMOUNT: $200 **DEADLINE:** Apr 1
FIELDS/MAJORS: Business

Awards for Sul Ross business students with a good academic record. Write to the address below for more information.

Sul Ross State University
Financial Aid Office
Box C-113
Alpine, TX 79832

737

Business And Economics Endowed And Private Scholarships

AMOUNT: Varies **DEADLINE:** Feb 15
FIELDS/MAJORS: Business, Economics

Scholarships are available at Evangel for full-time students who will be or are pursuing a degree in business or economics. Applicants must have a GPA of at least 3.0. Includes the Troy & Marjorie Compton, Charles W. Elmendorf Memorial, Max & Audrey Ephraim, Allen & Udell Lawrence, Phi Beta Lambda Club, the Business and Economics Alumni, and Baird, Kurtz & Dobson scholarships. Write to the address listed below for information.

Evangel College
Office Of Enrollment
1111 N. Glenstone
Springfield, MO 65802

738

Business Educators Awards

AMOUNT: $750 **DEADLINE:** May 1
FIELDS/MAJORS: Business

Awards for Five Towns business students who demonstrate academic potential, service to the college, and economic need. Write to the address below for further details.

Five Towns College
305 N. Service Road/Lie Exit 50
Dix Hills, NY 11746

739 Butch Leitl Memorial Scholarship

Amount: $300 **Deadline:** Feb 15
Fields/Majors: All Areas Of Study

Awards for UW Platteville sophomores, juniors, or seniors who have a GPA of at least 3.3, outstanding character, leadership ability, and participation in extracurricular activities. Write to the address below for more information.

University Of Wisconsin, Platteville
Office Of Admissions And Enrollment
Platteville, WI 53818

740 Butterworth Scholarship

Amount: None Specified **Deadline:** Jun 1
Fields/Majors: Plant/Soil Science

Scholarships are awarded to students in the areas of plant and soil science. Based on scholarship and need. For entering sophomores, juniors, or seniors. Contact the Chair, Scholarship Committee, Plant and Soil Sciences for more information.

University Of Massachusetts, Amherst
Chair, Scholarship Committee
Plant And Soil Sciences
Amherst, MA 01003

741 Buttrick Scholarship

Amount: None Specified **Deadline:** Oct 15
Fields/Majors: Food Science

Scholarships are awarded to food science majors who have demonstrated scholarship and financial need. For entering sophomores, juniors, or seniors. Contact the Undergraduate Program Director, Food Science for more information.

University Of Massachusetts, Amherst
Undergraduate Program Director, Food Science
Amherst, MA 01003

742 Buxton-Shaw Scholarships

GPA 3.0+

Amount: $3,500 **Deadline:** None Specified
Fields/Majors: All Areas Of Study

Awards to recognize strong academic achievement and exemplary leadership qualities. Candidates must have a GPA of at least 3.0, rank in the upper two-fifths of their graduating class, and show leadership ability in student government, school publications, community service, academic activities, or creative and performing arts. Write to the address below for more information.

Hollins College
Financial Aid Office
P.O. Box 9718
Roanoke, VA 24020

743 Byron E. Colby Scholarship

Amount: None Specified **Deadline:** Mid-Oct
Fields/Majors: Animal Science

Scholarships are awarded to students in their sophomore, junior, or senior year majoring in animal science and based on financial need. Contact the Chair, Scholarship Committee, Veterinary and Animal Sciences for more information.

University Of Massachusetts, Amherst
Chair, Scholarship Committee
Veterinary And Animal Sciences
Amherst, MA 01003

744 Byron Good Memorial Scholarship

GPA 2.5+

Amount: $600 **Deadline:** Nov 1
Fields/Majors: Animal Science, Equine Studies

Open to full-time Cal Poly students majoring in animal science, preferably equine industry with a GPA of 2.5 or better. Write to the address below for more information.

California State Polytechnic University, Pomona
College Of Agriculture
Building 29, Room 100
Pomona, CA 91768

745 Byron Hanke Fellowships

Amount: $2,500 **Deadline:** Ongoing
Fields/Majors: Related To Community Associations

Fellowships are available for pre- and postdoctoral candidates researching topics related to community associations. Write to the address listed below for information.

CAI Research Foundation
1630 Duke Street
Alexandria, VA 22314

746 BYU Multicultural Program

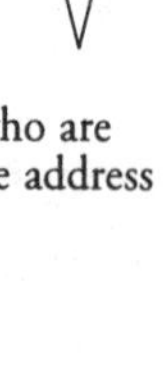

Amount: Varies **Deadline:** None Specified
Fields/Majors: All Areas Of Study

Scholarships are available for American Indian students who are undergraduates at Brigham Young University. Write to the address listed below for information.

Brigham Young University
353 ELWC
P.O. Box 27908
Provo, UT 84602

747 C. Armel Nutter, Nancy F. Reynolds, And NJAR Scholarships

Amount: $1,250–$2,000 **Deadline:** Apr 28
Fields/Majors: Real Estate And Related Fields

Scholarships available to New Jersey residents studying real estate.

Must be a member of NJAR or a relative to a member. Write to the address below for details.

New Jersey Association Of Realtors
Educational Foundation Scholarships
P.O. Box 2098
Edison, NJ 08818

748

C. Jay Starr Research Scholarship

AMOUNT: Tuition **DEADLINE:** Aug 1
FIELDS/MAJORS: Communications

Scholarships are available at the University of Iowa for full-time students who develop a promising research prospectus. Recipient will work on a research project for one year with a faculty member. Write to the address listed below for information.

University of Iowa
Department Of Communication Studies
105 Communication Studies Building
Iowa City, IA 52245

749

C. Vance Shepard Finance Scholarship

AMOUNT: Varies **DEADLINE:** Mar 1
FIELDS/MAJORS: Finance

Scholarships are available at the University of Iowa for full-time undergraduate finance majors. Write to the address listed below for information.

University of Iowa
College Of Business Admin., Suite W160
108 Pappajohn Business Admin. Bldg.
Iowa City, IA 52245

750

C. Wallace Walter Memorial Scholarship

AMOUNT: $1,250 **DEADLINE:** Mar 31
FIELDS/MAJORS: All Areas Of Study

Student must be enrolled in 15 hours each semester with a GPA of 2.5 or above. Write to the address below for more information.

Southwest Missouri State University
Office Of Financial Aid
901 South National Ave.
Springfield, MO 65804

751

C.I. Herrick Scholarship

AMOUNT: Varies **DEADLINE:** Mar 1
FIELDS/MAJORS: All Areas Of Study

Awards are available at the University of New Mexico for students with academic ability and financial need. Write to the address below for more information.

University Of New Mexico, Albuquerque
Office Of Financial Aid
Albuquerque, NM 87131

752

C.M. Lee Distinguished Scholar Award

AMOUNT: $3,500 (max) **DEADLINE:** None Specified
FIELDS/MAJORS: All Areas Of Study

Two scholarships available for incoming freshmen at Geneva College. Based upon grades, test scores, a written essay, an interview, and commitment to the Christian religion. Contact the office of admissions for further information.

Geneva College
Office Of Admissions
Beaver Falls, PA 15010

753

Cabaniss, Johnston Scholarship

AMOUNT: $5,000 (max) **DEADLINE:** Jun 14
FIELDS/MAJORS: Law

Scholarship is awarded annually to a law student who is a resident of Alabama, is attending an accredited law school in the United States, and will be a second year student. Write to the address below for more information.

Alabama Law Foundation, Inc.
P.O. Box 671
Montgomery, AL 36101

754

Caddie Scholarship Foundation (NJ Golf Assn.) Scholarships

AMOUNT: $800–$2,500 **DEADLINE:** May 1
FIELDS/MAJORS: All Areas Of Study

Scholarships for students who have caddied for at least one year at an NJSGA club. For full-time study. Based on academics, need, character, and length of service as a caddie. Renewable for four years. Write to the address below for details.

New Jersey State Golf Association
Golf Cottage, 1000 Broad St.
Bloomfield, NJ 07003

755

CAHPERD Scholarship

AMOUNT: Varies **DEADLINE:** May 15
FIELDS/MAJORS: Health/Physical Education, Recreation, Dance

Awards for high school seniors who are considering majoring in any of the four fields of study indicated above. Must be a Connecticut resident. Contact your high school guidance counselor, or the address below for further information and an application.

Connecticut Assoc. Health, Physical Education,
Recreation & Dance
Mr. Robert N. Laemel
54 Meadow St. Gateway Center
New Haven, CT 06519

756

Cal Grant And Graduate Fellowship Program

AMOUNT: Varies **DEADLINE:** Mar 2
FIELDS/MAJORS: All Areas Of Study

Graduate awards are available to California residents who wish to pursue a doctoral degree at an accredited California college or university, and plan to follow a career as a college or university faculty member. Write to the address listed below for information.

California Student Aid Commission
Customer Service Division
P.O. Box 510845
Sacramento, CA 94245

757 Cal Grants

Amount: $1,410–$6,660 **Deadline:** Feb 20
Fields/Majors: All Areas Of Study

Scholarships are available at the University of San Diego for undergraduate students who are California residents. Based on academic ability and financial need. Write to the address listed below for information.

University Of San Diego
Office Of Financial Aid
5998 Alcala Park
San Diego, CA 92110

758 Cal Poly Black Faculty And Staff Association

Amount: Varies **Deadline:** None Specified
Fields/Majors: All Areas Of Study

Must have completed at least one quarter at Cal Poly by the end of fall quarter with a GPA of 2.0 or better. Must be enrolled in at least 18 units (4 units for graduate students) during the following winter quarter. Contact Ms. Rose Smith, Enrollment Services Office, Cal Poly Pomona, Bldg 98, Room R 2-9 for more information.

California State Polytechnic University, Pomona
College Of Agriculture
Building 45, Room 109B
Pomona, CA 91768

759 Cal Poly Scholarships

Amount: None Specified **Deadline:** Mar 2
Fields/Majors: All Areas Of Study

Scholarships for both undergrad and graduate full-time students at Cal Poly based on academics, need, school activities, and community service. Generally must have a minimum GPA of 2.5. Contact the financial aid office at the address below for details. The financial aid office also administers many scholarships from outside sources.

California Polytechnic State University
Financial Aid Office
212 Administration Bldg.
San Luis Obispo, CA 93407

760 Cal-Diego Paralyzed Veterans Association Scholarship

Amount: None Specified **Deadline:** Nov 30
Fields/Majors: All Areas Of Study

Scholarships are available at UCSD for undergraduate students who are post-Vietnam disabled veterans, or are dependents of disabled Vietnam veterans. Write to the address listed below for information.

University Of California, San Diego
Student Financial Services
9500 Gilman Drive
La Jolla, CA 92093

761 Calcot Seitz Cotton Industry

Amount: $2,500 **Deadline:** Mar 31
Fields/Majors: Agriculture

Open to students majoring in agriculture from a cotton-producing region of California with a GPA of 3.0 or better. Write to the address below for more information.

California State Polytechnic University, Pomona
College Of Agriculture
Building 7, Room 110
Pomona, CA 91768

762 California Agricultural Production Consultants (CAPCA) Scholarship

Amount: $2,000 **Deadline:** May 1
Fields/Majors: Agricultural Biology, Horticulture, Agronomy, Soil Science

Open to students in agricultural biology, horticulture, agronomy, or soil science interested in pursuing careers in the consulting field with a GPA of 2.5 or better. Write to the address below for more information.

California State Polytechnic University, Pomona
College Of Agriculture
Building 7, Room 110
Pomona, CA 91768

763 California Assn. Of Nurserymen Endowment For Research & Scholarship

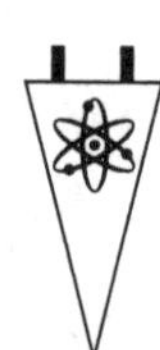

Amount: Varies **Deadline:** Mar 1
Fields/Majors: Horticulture, Fruit Industry

Open to horticulture and fruit industries students interested in pursuing careers in the nursery or pomology industry. Write to the address below for more information.

California State Polytechnic University, Pomona
College Of Agriculture
Building 7, Room 110
Pomona, CA 91768

764 California Crop Improvement Association Scholarship

Amount: $600 **Deadline:** Apr 15
Fields/Majors: Agronomy, Crop Science, Crop Production

Open to sophomores and juniors majoring in agronomy, crop science, or crop production with a GPA of 2.75 or better. Write to the address below for more information.

California State Polytechnic University, Pomona
College Of Agriculture
Building 7, Room 110
Pomona, CA 91768

765

California Faculty Association Scholarship

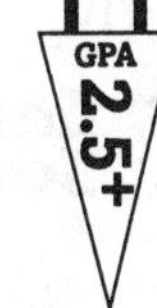

Amount: $100 **Deadline:** Mar 2
Fields/Majors: All Areas Of Study

Awards given from each of Cal Poly Pomona's six colleges to a student who is enrolled full-time and has a minimum GPA of 2.5. Write to the address below for more information.

California State Polytechnic University, Pomona
Office Of Financial Aid
3801 West Temple Ave.
Pomona, CA 91768

766

California Home Economics Association Graduate Fellowship

Amount: $1,000–$2,000 **Deadline:** Feb 1
Fields/Majors: Home Economics

Student must be a home economics major (in nutrition and allied fields) who have been or will be admitted for graduate study at an accredited college or university. Must have a GPA of 3.0 or better and a member of CHEA. The Annie McDonald Lindsay Graduate Fellowship is a $2,000 award. Write to California Home Economics Association, 3040 Dwight Way, Stockton, CA 95204 for more information.

California State Polytechnic University, Pomona
College Of Agriculture
Building 7, Room 110
Pomona, CA 91768

767

California Masonic Foundation Scholarships

Amount: Varies **Deadline:** Feb 29
Fields/Majors: All Areas Of Study

Scholarships are available for graduating high school seniors who reside in California. Acceptance at an accredited college or technical school and financial need is mandatory. Applicant must be a U.S. citizen. Write to the address below for details. Please enclose an SASE with your request.

California Masonic Foundation
Scholarship Committee
1111 California Street
San Francisco, CA 94108

768

California Physicians' Merit Scholarships

Amount: $500–$2,000 **Deadline:** None Specified
Fields/Majors: Medicine Or Health Related Fields

Scholarships are available to graduating high school seniors who are National Merit finalists and residents of California who plan to pursue a career in medicine- or a health-related field. Four awards are offered each year. Write to the address listed below for information.

National Merit Scholarship Corporation
1560 Sherman Avenue, Suite 200
Evanston, IL 60201

769

California Restaurant Writers Association Scholarship

Amount: $600 **Deadline:** Mar 2
Fields/Majors: Animal Science, Veterinary Medicine

Awards for juniors, seniors or graduate students with at least a 3.0 GPA studying in one of the areas above. Must be a graduate of a California high school. Write to the address below for more information.

California State Polytechnic University, Pomona
Office Of Financial Aid
3801 West Temple Ave.
Pomona, CA 91768

770

California Retired Teachers Association Scholarships

Amount: $250 **Deadline:** May 1
Fields/Majors: Education

Scholarships for students who intend to enroll at the College of the Siskiyous and pursue a career in education. Must be a graduate of a Siskiyou County high school and have a GPA of at least 3.0. Write to the address below for details.

College of the Siskiyous
Financial Aid Office
800 College Ave.
Weed, CA 96094

771

California Sea Grant State Fellow Program

Amount: $13,500 (min) **Deadline:** Aug 31
Fields/Majors: Marine Sciences

Awards for graduate students in a marine-related field at a California university. Applicant should demonstrate an interest in marine science and public policy. College seniors are also eligible to apply if they intend to continue school. Write to the address below for more information.

Universities Of California
9500 Gilman Drive
La Jolla, CA 92093

772

California State Retired Association Scholarships

Amount: $500 **Deadline:** Mar 2
Fields/Majors: Education

Awards for students enrolled full-time in a teacher preparation program. Write to the address below for more information.

California State Polytechnic University, Pomona
Office Of Financial Aid
3801 West Temple Ave.
Pomona, CA 91768

773

California State Universities/ Claudia H. Hampton Scholarship

Amount: $3,000 **Deadline:** None Specified
Fields/Majors: All Areas Of Study

Scholarships are available for entering full-time freshmen. Must have a GPA of 2.0 or better. Preference for graduate from a south central Los Angeles high school. Write to the address below for more information.

California State Polytechnic University, Pomona
Office Of Financial Aid
3801 West Temple Ave.
Pomona, CA 91768

774

California State University, Fullerton Endowed Scholarships

AMOUNT: Varies **DEADLINE:** None Specified
FIELDS/MAJORS: All Areas Of Study

Scholarships for students at Cal State-Fullerton. Several different programs available. Criteria for each program depends upon the stipulations of the donors of the awards. Contact the financial aid office at the address below for details.

California State University, Fullerton
University Hall, UH-146
P.O. Box 34080
Fullerton, CA 92634

775

Call To Action Opportunity Scholarship

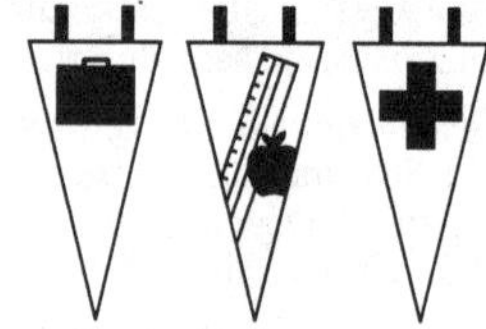

AMOUNT: Varies **DEADLINE:** Sep 1
FIELDS/MAJORS: Business, Education, Law Enforcement, Health Care, Public Services

Awards for California women who wish to pursue careers in one of the areas listed above. Write to the address below for more information.

California Office Of The Governor
Attn: Rosalie Zalis
300 South Spring St., 16th Floor
Los Angeles, CA 90013

776

Cambridge Scholarships

GPA 3.5+

AMOUNT: $11,700 **DEADLINE:** Feb 1
FIELDS/MAJORS: All Areas Of Study

Awards for entering students based on academics. Must have a GPA of at least 3.8 and a minimum SAT score of 1300 or ACT score of 32. Renewable with continued academic achievement. Write to the address below for more information.

Rhodes College
Office Of Admissions
2000 North Parkway
Memphis, TN 38112

777

Cameron Galindo Memorial Scholarship

AMOUNT: None Specified **DEADLINE:** Mar 1
FIELDS/MAJORS: Business

Scholarships are available at the University of New Mexico for full-time business majors with a GPA of at least 3.0. Write to the address below for information.

University Of New Mexico, Albuquerque
Department Of Student Financial Aid
Mesa Vista Hall North
Albuquerque, NM 87131

778

CAMFT - Clinton E. Phillips Scholarship

AMOUNT: $1,000 **DEADLINE:** Feb 26
FIELDS/MAJORS: Marriage/Family Counseling

Scholarship providing assistance for students pursuing an advanced degree in marriage and family therapy. Based on academics, financial need, community activities, and commitment to the profession of marriage and family therapy. Write to the address below for further information.

California Association Of Marriage And Family Therapists
Educational Foundation
7901 Raytheon Road
San Diego, CA 92111

779

CAMFT - Educational Foundation Scholarships

AMOUNT: $1,000 **DEADLINE:** Feb 26
FIELDS/MAJORS: Marriage/Family Therapy

Scholarship or research grant for members of CAMFT who are engaged in any of the following pursuits in the field of marriage and family therapy: pursuing an advanced degree beyond the master's level, conducting research, or participating in advanced training, education, or an internship. Contact the Foundation at the address below for details.

California Association Of Marriage And Family Therapists
Educational Foundation
7901 Raytheon Road
San Diego, CA 92111

780

CAMFT - Ronald D. Lunceford Scholarship

AMOUNT: $1,000 **DEADLINE:** Feb 26
FIELDS/MAJORS: Counseling (Marriage, Family, Child Counseling)

Scholarship for a member of an under-represented minority group studying toward an M.A., M.S., or Ph.D. and qualifying for licensure as a marriage, family, and child counselor. Write to the address below for details.

California Association Of Marriage And Family Therapists
Educational Foundation
7901 Raytheon Road
San Diego, CA 92111

781

Campion Grants

AMOUNT: Varies **DEADLINE:** None Specified
FIELDS/MAJORS: All Areas Of Study

Awards for students in intercollegiate athletics. Varsity sports for men include: basketball, soccer, track, swimming, cross country, and golf. Those for women include: basketball, soccer, track, cross country, volleyball, golf, and swimming. Contact the appropriate coach for further information.

Wheeling Jesuit College
Student Financial Planning
316 Washington Ave.
Wheeling, WV 26003

782

Campus & Program Scholarships

AMOUNT: Varies **DEADLINE:** None Specified
FIELDS/MAJORS: All Areas Of Study

Scholarships are available at Pima for full-time students. Based on academic ability, financial need, or both. Individual award requirements will vary. Write to the address listed below for information.

Pima Community College
Financial Aid Office
Tucson, AZ 85709

783

Campus Activities Council Scholarship

AMOUNT: $250 **DEADLINE:** Mar 15
FIELDS/MAJORS: All Areas Of Study

Scholarships are available at the University of Oklahoma, Norman for juniors, seniors and graduate students. Based on academics, campus involvement, leadership, and participation in community service projects. Requires a GPA of 3.0 or above. Write to the address listed below for information.

University Of Oklahoma, Norman
Campus Activities Council
OMU, Room 215-C
Norman, OK 73019

784

Campus Diversity Awards

AMOUNT: $500–$3,000 **DEADLINE:** Feb 15
FIELDS/MAJORS: All Areas Of Study

Scholarships are available to Nazareth College for full-time undergraduate minority students who demonstrate superior academic potential. Write to the address below for details.

Nazareth College
Office Of Financial Aid
4245 East Avenue
Rochester, NY 14618

785

Campus Lost & Found Scholarship

AMOUNT: $1,000 **DEADLINE:** None Specified
FIELDS/MAJORS: All Areas Of Study

Scholarships are available for full-time undergraduates with a GPA of at least a 3.0. Write to the address below for more information.

California State Polytechnic University, Pomona
Office Of Financial Aid
3801 West Temple Ave.
Pomona, CA 91768

786

Candle Fellowships And Diamond Anniversary Fellowships

AMOUNT: $1,000 **DEADLINE:** Mar 1
FIELDS/MAJORS: Home Economics

Applicants must be member of Phi Upsilon Omicron who are pursuing master's or doctoral study in home economics. Based on academics, participation in Phi U and AHEA, and personal statement. Four awards per year. Write to the address below for details.

Phi Upsilon Omicron National Office
Ohio State University, 171 Mount Hall
1050 Carmack Road
Columbus, OH 43210

787

Canfield And New Nebraskans Scholarships

AMOUNT: $1,000 (min) **DEADLINE:** Varies
FIELDS/MAJORS: All Areas Of Study

Scholarships for UNL entering freshmen. Canfield awards are for Nebraska residents only and New Nebraskans awards are for residents of all other states. Based on superior academic achievement in high school. Write to the address below for more details and to obtain an application for freshman scholarship aid. Deadline for Nebraska residents to apply is January 15.

University Of Nebraska, Lincoln
Office Of Scholarships And Financial Aid
16 Administration Bldg., P.O. Box 880411
Lincoln, NE 68588

788

Canton Student Loan Fund

AMOUNT: $3,000 (max/year) **DEADLINE:** Jun 1
FIELDS/MAJORS: All Areas Of Study

Loans are available for students who graduated from a Stark County high school or any Stark County resident who received a high school diploma through participation in the ABC program. For full-time undergraduate study. Must have a GPA of 2.0 or better. Write to the address below for more information.

Canton Student Loan Foundation
4974 Higbee Ave., NW
Atrium South #204
Canton, OH 44718

789

Cape Canaveral Chapter Retired Officers Association Scholarship

AMOUNT: $1,500 **DEADLINE:** May 31
FIELDS/MAJORS: All Areas Of Study

Candidates must be Brevard County, Florida, residents, at least a junior, at any four-year college in the United States, and must be the son or daughter of an active duty, reserve, retired, or deceased member of the uniformed services (Army, Navy, Air Force, Marines, Coast Guard, NOAA, or USPHS). Write to the address below for details. Please be certain to enclose a 52 cent SASE with your request.

Retired Officers Association, Cape Canaveral Chapter
Troacc Scholarship Committee
P.O. Box 4186
Patrick AFB, FL 32925

790

Cape Cod Landscape Association Scholarship

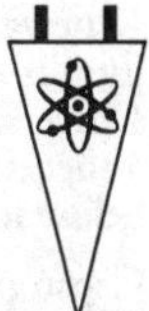

AMOUNT: Varies **DEADLINE:** Apr 30
FIELDS/MAJORS: Green Industries

Awards for College of Food and Natural Resources or Stockbridge students who have a career interest in green industries. For students in their sophomore, junior, or senior year at UMass.

Contact the Director, Stockbridge School, for more information.

University Of Massachusetts, Amherst
Director, Stockbridge School
Amherst, MA 01003

791 Capital Agriculture Property Services, Inc. Scholarships

AMOUNT: $1,000 **DEADLINE:** Feb 15
FIELDS/MAJORS: Agricultural Economics

Scholarships are available for FFA members pursuing an agricultural economics degree in a four-year program. Write to the address below for details.

National FFA Foundation
Scholarship Office
P.O. Box 15160
Alexandria, VA 22309

792 Capital Area Regional Scholarships

AMOUNT: $1,000 **DEADLINE:** May 31
FIELDS/MAJORS: All Areas Of Study

Scholarships for Italian American residents of Maryland, Virginia, West Virginia, or Washington, DC. For undergraduate study. Write to the address listed below for information.

National Italian American Foundation
Dr. Maria Lombardo, Education Director
1860 19th St., NW
Washington, DC 20009

793 Capitol Hill News Internships

AMOUNT: $1,000 Per Month **DEADLINE:** Jan 15, Mar 1
FIELDS/MAJORS: Electronic Journalism

Internship positions available for recent college graduates with degrees in electronic journalism. Internships run in the spring and the summer. Excellent writing skills are essential. Interns will work side by side with the Washington press and congressional staff to cover the political process. Write to the address below for more information.

Radio And News Directors Foundation
1000 Connecticut Ave., NW, Suite 615
Washington, DC 20036

794 Capstone Communications Society Memorial Endowed Scholarship

AMOUNT: $1,000 **DEADLINE:** Feb 15
FIELDS/MAJORS: Communications

Renewable $1,000 scholarship for freshmen, sophomores or juniors enrolled in the college of communications at the University of Alabama, whose current record and potential predict a successful career as a communicator. Write to the address listed below for further information and an application.

Capstone Communications Society
College Of Communications, University Of Alabama
P.O. Box 870172
Tuscaloosa, AL 35487

795 Captain Caliendo College Assistance Fund

AMOUNT: $250–$1,500 **DEADLINE:** May 1
FIELDS/MAJORS: All Areas Of Study

Awards for children of members of the USCG Chief Petty Officers Assn. or sons or daughters of active, reserve, retired, or deceased enlisted USCG personnel (pay grades E-6 and below). Ten awards per year. For full-time study. Essay will be required to apply. Applicants must be under the age of 23, or be a handicapped dependent child. Write to the address below for details.

U.S. Coast Guard Chief Petty Officers Association (CCCAF)
5520-G Hampstead Way
Springfield, VA 22151

796 Captain James J. Regan Memorial Scholarship

AMOUNT: $500 **DEADLINE:** Mar 31
FIELDS/MAJORS: Law Enforcement

Any law enforcement explorer who is in the twelfth grade or in an accredited college program may apply. Candidates will be evaluated based on their academic record, leadership ability, extracurricular activities, and a personal statement on "what significance I place on a technical background in law enforcement." Write to the address below for more information.

Boy Scouts Of America
Exploring Division, S210
1325 West Walnut Hill Ln., P.O. Box 152079
Irving, TX 75015

797 Cardinal Gibbons Scholarships

AMOUNT: None Specified **DEADLINE:** None Specified
FIELDS/MAJORS: All Areas Of Study

Scholarships are available at the Catholic University of America for freshmen students who have demonstrated outstanding academic ability. Students must also have exhibited strong leadership qualities in school, church, and community activities. Write to the address below for more information.

Catholic University Of America
Office Of Admissions And Financial Aid
Washington, DC 20064

798 Cardiovascular Section Lamport Awards

AMOUNT: $200 **DEADLINE:** None Specified
FIELDS/MAJORS: Cardiovascular Research

Awards are available for young investigators, under the age of 36, who show outstanding promise in the field of cardiovascular research. Write to the address below for more information.

American Psychology Society
9650 Rockville Pike
Bethesda, MD 20814

799

Career Advancement Scholarship Program

Amount: $500–$1,000 **Deadline:** Apr 15
Fields/Majors: Computer Science, Education, Paralegal, Engineering Or Science

Up to 100 scholarships for women 30 or older. Criteria: within 24 months of completing an accredited course of study in U.S. should lead to entry or advancement in the workforce. U.S. citizen. The preapplication screening form is only available between October 1 and April 1. Not for doctoral study, correspondence schools, or nondegreed programs. Write to address below for details.

Business And Professional Women's Foundation Scholarships
2012 Massachusetts Avenue, NW
Washington, DC 20036

800

Career Development Award In Skin Research

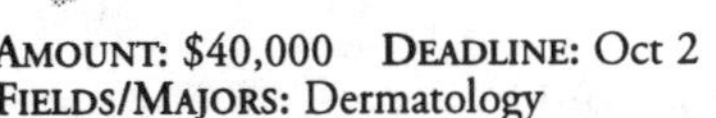

Amount: $40,000 **Deadline:** Oct 2
Fields/Majors: Dermatology

Applicants must be in the early stages of their academic careers with two to three years fellowship or equivalent experience in bio-medical research. Renewable. Write to the address below for details.

Dermatology Foundation
Medical And Scientific Committee
1560 Sherman Ave.
Evanston, IL 60201

801

Career Development Grants

Amount: $1,000–$5,000 **Deadline:** Jan 3
Fields/Majors: All Areas Of Study

Grants to prepare for re-entry into workforce or training for a career change. Special consideration is given to qualified AAUW members, minorities, women pursuing their first terminal degrees, and women pursuing degrees in non-traditional fields. Must be a U.S. citizen or permanent resident and have earned your last degree at least five years previously. Write to the address below for details.

American Association Of University Women Educational Foundation
2201 N. Dodge Street
Iowa City, IA 52243

802

Carey Rose Winski Dance Competition

Amount: $500–$1,000 **Deadline:** Aug 27
Fields/Majors: Dance

Scholarship competition for students who show a talent in dance. Based on performance (in person) in both classical ballet (en pointe for women) and in any eclectic style (jazz, modern, character, etc.). Must be between 13-18 years old. Competition takes place at the Marjorie Ward Marshall Dance Center located on the Northwestern University campus in Evanston, IL. Write to the address below for details.

Carey Rose Winski Memorial Foundation, Inc.
69 Woodley Rd.
Winnetka, IL 60093

803

Cargill Scholarships For Rural America

Amount: $1,000 **Deadline:** Mar 1
Fields/Majors: All Areas Of Study

Two hundred and fifty awards for high school seniors who will be attending a postsecondary school. Must be from a farm family (at least 50% of income from farming). Based on academics, potential, leadership, extracurriculars, and need. FFA membership not required. Information/ applications may be obtained at any Cargill office, high school FFA department, or by sending a request to the address below.

National FFA Foundation
Cargill Scholarship Coordinator
Box 9300
Minneapolis, MN 55440

804

Cargill, Inc. Scholarships

Amount: $1,000 **Deadline:** Mar 1
Fields/Majors: Accounting, Management

Scholarships are available at the University of Iowa for full-time juniors majoring in accounting or management. Write to the address listed below for information.

University of Iowa
College Of Business Admin., Suite W160
108 Pappajohn Business Admin. Bldg.
Iowa City, IA 52245

805

Carl Albert Center Undergraduate Research Fellowship

Amount: $500/Semester **Deadline:** Feb 15
Fields/Majors: Political Science

Research fellowships are available at the University of Oklahoma, Norman, for juniors or seniors majoring in political science. Recipients will be selected during the second semester of their freshman year. Write to the address listed below for information.

University Of Oklahoma, Norman
Director, Carl Albert Research Center
Monnet Hall 101
Norman, OK 73019

806

Carl F. Dietz Memorial, Jerry Wilmot, Harold Bettinger Scholarships

Amount: $1,000–$2,000 **Deadline:** Apr 1
Fields/Majors: Horticulture

Scholarships for students in four-year college or university with a major in horticulture. Need minimum GPA of 3.0. Award requirements vary slightly. Write to the address below for details. The BPFI also sponsors two awards through Future Farmers of America (check with your FFA advisor).

Bedding Plants Foundation, Inc.
Scholarship Program
P.O. Box 27241
Lansing, MI 48909

807

Carl F.H. Henry Scholarship

AMOUNT: $5,000 **DEADLINE:** Jun 1
FIELDS/MAJORS: Christian Studies

Award for full-time undergraduates of Christian colleges which hold membership in the coalition for Christian colleges and universities. Based on an article written to communicate biblical truth to a secular audience. Write to the address below for more information.

Amy Foundation
Coalition For Christian Colleges & Universities
329 Eighth St., NE
Washington, DC 20002

808

Carl Greenberg Prize

AMOUNT: $1,000 **DEADLINE:** Feb 15
FIELDS/MAJORS: News Journalism

For those who intend to work in news journalism. This is open to juniors, seniors, and graduate students who are residents of, or students in, Los Angeles, Ventura, or Orange counties. Based on achievement in political or investigative reporting. Write to the address below for details.

Society Of Professional Journalists, Los Angeles Professional Chapter
SPJ Scholarship Chairman
P.O. Box 4200
Woodland Hills, CA 91365

809

Carl Hiaasen Scholarships

AMOUNT: $250 **DEADLINE:** Mar 1
FIELDS/MAJORS: Journalism

Awards for juniors and seniors majoring in journalism. Must have a GPA of at least 2.8. Write to the address below for more information.

University Of Florida
Knight Scholarship & Placement Director
2070 Weimer Hall
Gainesville, FL 32611

810

Carlton And Katherine Roundtree Christian Scholarships

AMOUNT: Varies **DEADLINE:** Apr 15
FIELDS/MAJORS: All Areas Of Study

Open to ABAC students with demonstrated academic achievement. Applicants must have a GPA of at least a 3.0 and entering freshmen must have a composite SAT score of at least 1000. Write to the address below for additional information.

Abraham Baldwin Agricultural College
Office Of Admissions
2802 Moore Highway
Tifton, GA 31794

811

Carnegie Institute Fellowships

AMOUNT: Varies **DEADLINE:** Jan 15
FIELDS/MAJORS: Earth Science, Geophysics

Fellowship program for predoctoral and postdoctoral research in the fields listed above. Based on recommendations, accomplishments, and course records. Write to the address below for more information.

Carnegie Institute Of Washington
Geophysical Laboratory
2801 Upton St., NW
Washington, DC 20008

812

Carol A. Hochwalt Fellowship

AMOUNT: Tuition
DEADLINE: None Specified
FIELDS/MAJORS: Arts And Sciences

Scholarships are available at the Catholic University of America for graduate arts and sciences majors. Contact the financial aid office at the address below for details.

The Catholic University Of America
Office Of Admissions And Financial Aid
Washington, DC 20064

813

Carol Lawler Scholarship

AMOUNT: Varies **DEADLINE:** Mar 15
FIELDS/MAJORS: Nursing

Awards for Jacksonville State University students who are in the field of nursing. Contact the College of Nursing for more information.

Jacksonville State University
Financial Aid Office
Jacksonville, AL 36265

814

Caroline Holt Nursing Scholarships

AMOUNT: $500 **DEADLINE:** Feb 15, Aug 15
FIELDS/MAJORS: Nursing

Must be undergraduates currently enrolled in an accredited school of nursing and sponsored by a local DAR chapter. Must be a U.S. citizen. Contact your local chapter or write to address below for details.

National Society Daughters Of The American Revolution
NSDAR Scholarship Committee
1776 D St., NW
Washington, DC 20006

815

Caroline M. Hewins Scholarship

AMOUNT: $4,000 **DEADLINE:** Mar 1
FIELDS/MAJORS: Children's Library Science

Scholarship open only to those who specialize in children's library science and who hold, or are about to receive, a bachelor's degree. Also must have applied to a school accredited by the American Library Association for graduate studies. Write to the address below for details.

Hartford Public Library
c/o Chief Librarian
500 Main St.
Hartford, CT 06103

816

Caroline Thornton Carson Fund

AMOUNT: Varies **DEADLINE:** Mar 1
FIELDS/MAJORS: Engineering

Awards are available at the University of New Mexico for freshmen planning to enroll in an engineering program. Based on high academic record, high moral character, and financial need. Write to the address below for more information.

University Of New Mexico, Albuquerque
Office Of Financial Aid
Albuquerque, NM 87131

817

Caroline Tum Suden/Frances Hellenbrandt Professional Opportunity Award

AMOUNT: $500 **DEADLINE:** None Specified
FIELDS/MAJORS: Psychology

Award for junior psychologists or postdoctoral fellows in the field of psychology. Based on abstract submitted to the APS. Write to the address below for more information.

American Psychological Society
Education Office
9650 Rockville Pike
Bethesda, MD 20814

818

Carolyn Elizabeth Spivey Memorial Scholarship

AMOUNT: $3,000 **DEADLINE:** Jun 1
FIELDS/MAJORS: Nursing

Awards for graduating high school seniors or college students with a GPA greater than 2.5 on a 4.0 scale as verified by official transcripts. Applicants must demonstrate economic need, as verified by parent's tax return or other suitable document. Also based on 3 letters of reference, an essay on the challenge to American families today, and school and community involvement. For more information and an application, contact Nylcare Customer Service at (800) 635-3121.

Nylcare/Mid-Atlantic Scholarship Foundation, Inc.
7617 Ora Glen Drive
Greenbelt, MD 20770

819

Carquest Corporation Scholarships

AMOUNT: $1,000 **DEADLINE:** Feb 15
FIELDS/MAJORS: All Areas Of Study

Scholarships are available to FFA members who are full-time students planning to complete a four-year degree in any major. Information should be available from your local FFA leader. If not, write to the address below for further information.

National FFA Foundation
Scholarship Office
P.O. Box 15160
Alexandria, VA 22309

820

Carrie Schaeffer Scholarships

AMOUNT: Varies **DEADLINE:** Mar 1
FIELDS/MAJORS: All Areas Of Study

Awards are available at the University of New Mexico for African American students demonstrating academic merit. Write to the address below for more information.

University Of New Mexico, Albuquerque
Office Of Financial Aid
Albuquerque, NM 87131

821

Carrol C. Hall Memorial Scholarship

AMOUNT: $600 **DEADLINE:** Jun 1
FIELDS/MAJORS: Education, Science

GPA 3.0+

Scholarship is available to any undergraduate member of Tau Kappa Epsilon who is earning a degree in education or science and has plans to become a teacher or pursue a profession in science. Must have a GPA of 3.0 or higher and be a full-time student in good standing. Must be able to demonstrate leadership within his chapter, on campus, and in the community. Write to the address below for more information.

TKE Educational Foundation
8645 Founders Rd.
Indianapolis, IN 46268

822

Carroll L. Birch Award

AMOUNT: $500 **DEADLINE:** Jun 30
FIELDS/MAJORS: Medicine

This award is presented to an AMWA student member for the best original research paper. Write to the address below for details.

American Medical Women's Association
Carroll L. Birch Award
801 N. Fairfax Street, Suite 400
Alexandria, VA 22314

823

Carter Elliot Family Scholarship

AMOUNT: Varies **DEADLINE:** None Specified
FIELDS/MAJORS: All Areas Of Study

Award for full-time Mesa State students who are active in the tennis program and have a GPA of at least 2.5. For undergraduate study. Write to the address below for more information.

Mesa State College
Office Of Financial Aid
P.O. Box 2647
Grand Junction, CO 81501

824

Carter Endowed Scholarship

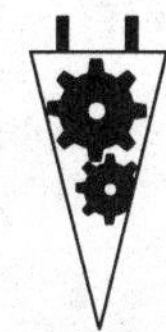

AMOUNT: Varies **DEADLINE:** Mar 1
FIELDS/MAJORS: Engineering

Awards are given to engineering students at the University of New Mexico based on scholastic average and, more importantly, financial need. Write to the address below for more information.

University Of New Mexico, Albuquerque
Office Of Financial Aid
Albuquerque, NM 87131

825

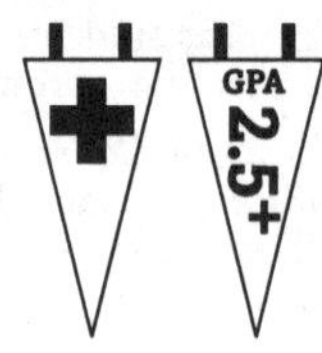

Carter Endowed, Diane Doherty Memorial, And Friends Of Nursing Awards

Amount: Varies **Deadline:** Mar 1
Fields/Majors: Nursing

Awards are available at the University of New Mexico for full-time nursing students with a minimum GPA of 2.5 and financial need. Write to the address below or contact the school of nursing for more details.

University Of New Mexico, Albuquerque
Office Of Financial Aid
Albuquerque, NM 87131

826

Carter Scholarship Grants For New England Scouts

Amount: $1,500/year **Deadline:** Apr 15
Fields/Majors: All Areas Of Study

Scholarships for boys from New England who have been scouts for at least two years. Based on financial need, academics, and leadership potential. Award is renewable for one year. Details are available from any of the New England scout councils or write to the address below.

Marjorie Sells Carter Scholarship Trust
c/o Mrs. B.J. Shaffer, Admin. Secy.
P.O. Box 527
West Chatham, MA 02669

827

Carthage Grant

Amount: $2,000 **Deadline:** None Specified
Fields/Majors: All Areas Of Study

Award available to qualified students on the basis of academic performance. Renewable. Write to the address below for more information.

Carthage College
Financial Aid Office
Kenosha, WI 53140

828

Casaday-Elmore Ministerial Scholarship

Amount: None Specified **Deadline:** Apr 1
Fields/Majors: Religion/Theology

Applicants must be CAP Cadet members with plans to enter the ministry. Write to the address below for details.

Civil Air Patrol
National Headquarters CAP(tt)
Maxwell AFB, AL 36112

829

Case Alumni Association Junior And Senior Scholarships

Amount: Varies **Deadline:** Feb 1
Fields/Majors: All Areas Of Study

A number of scholarships funded by the Case Alumni Association of the Case School of Engineering are awarded to juniors and seniors on the basis of academic achievement, financial need, and participation in extracurricular activities. Write to the address below for details.

Case Western Reserve University
Office Of Financial Aid, 109 Pardee Hall
10900 Euclid Avenue
Cleveland, OH 44106

830

Casey's General Stores, Inc. Scholarships

Amount: $1,000 **Deadline:** Feb 15
Fields/Majors: Agriculture, Agribusiness

Scholarships are available for FFA members pursuing a two-year degree in agriculture or agribusiness, who reside in Illinois, Iowa, Missouri, or Minnesota. Write to the address below for details.

National FFA Foundation
Scholarship Office
P.O. Box 15160
Alexandria, VA 22309

831

CASW-Nate Haseltine Fellowships In Science Writing

Amount: $2,000 (max) **Deadline:** Jun 15
Fields/Majors: Science Writing

Fellowships for students who hold an undergraduate degree in science or journalism. Preference is given to persons with journalism experience in journalism. Based on resume, transcript, recommendations, writing samples, and application. Write to the address below for full details. Not for pursuit of careers in public relations or public information work.

Council For The Advancement Of Science Writing, Inc.
Ben Patrusky, Executive Director
P.O. Box 404
Greenlawn, NY 11740

832

Cataract Fire Company #2 Scholarship Fund

Amount: $1,000 **Deadline:** Apr 8
Fields/Majors: All Areas Of Study

Scholarships are available for residents of Warwick, Rhode Island, who are graduating high school seniors. Write to the address listed below for information.

Warwick Public Schools
Director Of Secondary Education
34 Warwick Lake Avenue
Warwick, RI 02889

833

Caterpillar Scholars Award

Amount: $2,000 Deadline: Mar 1
Fields/Majors: Manufacturing Engineering, Manufacturing Engineering Technology

Scholarships for full-time undergraduate students who have completed at least 30 credit hours. Student must have a minimum GPA of 3.5. The Caterpillar Scholars Award will provide five $2,000 scholarship awards to students as a one-time gift. Write to the address below for details. Information may also be available in your department office.

If writing, please specify what scholarship(s) you are interested in.

SME Manufacturing Engineering Education Foundation
One SME Drive
P.O. Box 930
Dearborn, MI 48121

834

Catherine Beattie Fellowship

Amount: $4,000 (max) **Deadline:** Dec 31
Fields/Majors: Botany Or Related Fields

Fellowships are available for graduate students at a botanical garden jointly serving the center for plant conservation and the student's academic research. Open to students with academic qualifications and an interest in rare plant conservation. Preference given to those with an interest in and whose projects focus on the endangered flora of the Carolinas and southeastern U.S. Write to the address listed below for information.

Garden Club Of America–Center For Plant Conservation
Ms. Peggy Olwell
P.O. Box 299, Missouri Botanical Garden
St. Louis, MO 63166

835

Catherine Cassidy Scholarships

Amount: $400 **Deadline:** Feb 15
Fields/Majors: Middle Level Education

Awards for students at UW Platteville in the area of middle level education. Write to the address below for more information.

University Of Wisconsin, Platteville
Office Of Enrollment And Admissions
Platteville, WI 53818

836

Catherine Martin Henry Scholarship

Amount: $500 **Deadline:** Mar 15, Nov 15
Fields/Majors: Nursing

Awards for students majoring in the field of nursing. Must demonstrate financial need. Write to the address below for more information.

Gwynedd-Mercy College
Student Financial Aid
Sumneytown Pike
Gwynedd Valley, PA 19437

837

Catherine Oplinger Renninger Memorial Scholarship

Amount: $1,000 **Deadline:** Feb 9
Fields/Majors: Secondary Education–English

Award for sophomore or junior secondary education major in English. Must have a minimum GPA of 3.0 in English and demonstrate financial need. Use Bloomsburg University scholarship application. Contact Dr. William Baillie, Chairperson, Department of English for further information.

Bloomsburg University
19 Ben Franklin Hall
400 E. Second St.
Bloomsburg, PA 18715

838

Catholic Foundation Of Oklahoma Scholarships

Amount: $500–$1,000 **Deadline:** Mar 1, Mar 15
Fields/Majors: All Areas Of Study

Scholarships are available at the University of Oklahoma, Norman for Catholic students in the archdiocese of Oklahoma City. Preference is given to students who need financial aid. Write to the address listed below for information.

University Of Oklahoma, Norman
The Catholic Foundation
P.O. Box 32038
Oklahoma City, OK 73123

839

Catholic High School Grant

Amount: $1,000 **Deadline:** Apr 1
Fields/Majors: All Areas Of Study

Scholarships are available at Siena Heights College for full-time students who graduated from a Catholic high school. Catholic high school scholarship recipients are not eligible. Write to the address listed below for information.

Siena Heights College
Financial Aid Office
1247 East Siena Heights Drive
Adrian, MI 49221

840

Cathy S. Hinton Scholarship

Amount: $1,000 **Deadline:** None Specified
Fields/Majors: Engineering

Scholarships are available at the University of Iowa for full-time undergraduates majoring in engineering, who are residents of Iowa, with preference given to graduates of North Linn High School. Write to the address listed below for information.

University of Iowa
Student Services, College Of Engineering
3100 Engineering Building
Iowa City, IA 52242

841

Cay Drachnik Minorities Fund

Amount: None Specified **Deadline:** Jun 15
Fields/Majors: Art Therapy

Scholarships for minority students who are enrolled in an AATA approved art therapy program. Applicants must demonstrate financial need. This award is designed primarily for the purchase of books. Write to the address below for complete details.

The American Art Therapy Association, Inc.
Scholarship Committee
1202 Allanson Road
Mundelein, IL 60060

842

CCAC Scholarships And Creative Achievement Scholarships

AMOUNT: $500–$6,000 **DEADLINE:** Mar 2
FIELDS/MAJORS: All Areas Of Study

Scholarships for students at the California College of Arts and Crafts. Some scholarships are need-based; some, talent-based. Contact the school at the address below for details.

California College Of Arts And Crafts
Office Of Enrollment Services
5212 Broadway At College
Oakland, CA 94618

843

CECNJ Scholarships

AMOUNT: $1,000 **DEADLINE:** Feb 2
FIELDS/MAJORS: Engineering, Land Surveying

Applicants must be enrolled in an ABET-accredited engineering or land surveying program in a New Jersey college or university, seeking a bachelor's degree. Must be in the third or fourth year of study (fifth year of a five-year program). For U.S. citizens. Write to the address below for more information.

Consulting Engineers Council Of New Jersey
66 Morris Ave., Suite 1A
Springfield, NJ 07081

844

Cedarville College Memorial Endowment

AMOUNT: Varies **DEADLINE:** None Specified
FIELDS/MAJORS: All Areas Of Study

Awards are available for full-time students at Cedarville College who have demonstrated financial need. Must have a GPA of at least 2.0. Write to the address below for more information.

Cedarville College
Financial Aid Office
P.O. Box 601
Cedarville, OH 45314

845

CELSOC Scholarship Award

AMOUNT: None Specified **DEADLINE:** Feb 16
FIELDS/MAJORS: Engineering, Surveying

Scholarships for juniors, seniors, or graduate students in engineering programs. Must be U.S. citizen, have a GPA of at least 3.2, and plan a career in either consulting engineering or in land surveying. Write to the address below for details (info may also be available from your department).

Consulting Engineers And Land Surveyors Of California
Scholarship Program
1303 J St., Suite 370
Sacramento, CA 95814

846

Cenex Agriculture Scholarships

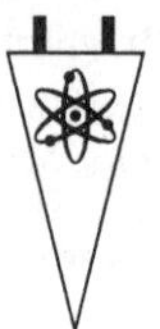

AMOUNT: $600 **DEADLINE:** Feb 15
FIELDS/MAJORS: Agriculture

Scholarships for students in their first or second year of a two-year program in vocational agriculture at institutions in the Cenex trade area (Great Plains and Mountain States). Seventy-seven awards per year. Application is made through individual schools. The foundation also offers awards for students in cooperative courses of studies at four-year schools. Contact the financial aid office at your college for information on either program.

Cenex Foundation Scholarship Program
5500 Cenex Dr.
Inver Grove Heights, MN 55077

847

Cenex Cooperative Studies Scholarships

AMOUNT: $750 **DEADLINE:** Varies
FIELDS/MAJORS: Agriculture

Scholarships for juniors or seniors attending the agriculture college of a participating university in the Cenex trade area enrolled in courses of cooperative principles & business practices. Renewable if awarded as junior. Seventeen schools participate in this scholarship. Universities select their own recipients. Contact the financial aid office at your school for details.

Cenex Foundation Scholarship Program
5500 Cenex Dr.
Inver Grove Heights, MN 55077

848

Center For Advanced Study In The Visual Arts Fellowships

AMOUNT: $13,000 **DEADLINE:** Nov 15
FIELDS/MAJORS: Visual Arts And Related Areas

Fellowships for Ph.D. candidates who have completed all coursework except the dissertation. Requires knowledge of two foreign languages related to topic of dissertation. Applicants must be U.S. citizens or legal residents. Application must be made through graduate departments of art history (or other appropriate departments). Direct inquiries to the address below.

National Gallery Of Art
Center For Advanced Study In Visual Arts
Fellowship Programs
Washington, DC 20565

849

Center For Creative Retirement Scholarships

AMOUNT: $550 **DEADLINE:** Jun 1
FIELDS/MAJORS: All Areas Of Study

Awards for nontraditional students, age 25 or older, based on academic merit. Write to the address below for more information.

Long Island University
Financial Aid Office
Southampton, NY 11968

850

Center For Defense Information Internships

AMOUNT: $700/Month
DEADLINE: Apr 1, Nov 1
FIELDS/MAJORS: See Listing Below

Internships are available at the Center for students enrolled in one of the following programs: political science, communications, journalism, humanities, military science, public policy. This is a full-time position. Recipients are responsible for their own living arrangements. Write to the address listed below for information.

Center For Defense Information
Kathryn Schultz
1500 Massachusetts Avenue, NW
Washington, DC 20005

851

Center For Global Education Scholarships

AMOUNT: $2,500 **DEADLINE:** Oct 1, Apr 1
FIELDS/MAJORS: Foreign Study

Scholarships are available to enable students of color, who otherwise may not have sufficient funding, to participate in semester abroad programs. Priority will be given to U.S. citizens and permanent residents. Write to the address below for more information.

Center For Global Education At Augsburg College
2211 Riverside Ave.
Minneapolis, MN 55454

852

Center For Medieval And Renaissance Studies Research Assistantships

AMOUNT: $500 **DEADLINE:** Feb 9
FIELDS/MAJORS: Renaissance Studies, Medieval Studies

Research assistantships available for research scholars who wish to pursue studies in the medieval or renaissance periods in the Los Angeles area. The recipient receives temporary membership in the center with its attendant campus privileges. Write to the address below for details.

University Of California, Los Angeles
Center For Medieval And Renaissance Studies
212 Royce Hall, Box 951485
Los Angeles, CA 90095

853

Center For Renaissance Studies Fellowships

AMOUNT: Varies **DEADLINE:** None Specified
FIELDS/MAJORS: Renaissance Studies

Fellowships are available for graduate students and faculty members of the center's thirty-two member institutions, to participate in a broad range of archival or interdisciplinary programs. Write to the address below for details.

Newberry Library/Center For Renaissance Studies
Committee On Awards
60 W. Walton St.
Chicago, IL 60610

854

Central College Grants

AMOUNT: $1,000 **DEADLINE:** None Specified
FIELDS/MAJORS: All Areas Of Study

Students must show qualities of leadership, involvement and Christian character. Write to address below for additional information.

Central College
Financial Aid Office
1200 S. Main St.
McPherson, KS 67460

855

Central Colorado Soil Conservation District Scholarships

AMOUNT: Varies **DEADLINE:** None Specified
FIELDS/MAJORS: Agriculture And Related Fields

Scholarships available at CSU for freshmen, sophomores and juniors majoring in any agriculture-related field. Applicants must be U.S. citizens and permanent residents living in Douglas, Elbert, El Paso, Fremont, Lincoln, Pueblo, or Teller Counties. Write to the address below for details.

Colorado State University
College Of Agricultural Sciences
121 Shepardson
Fort Collins, CO 80523

856

Central Florida Jazz Society Scholarships

AMOUNT: $500–$1,000 **DEADLINE:** Mar 31
FIELDS/MAJORS: Music-Jazz

Scholarship competition for students who are graduating high school seniors, college freshmen, sophomores, and juniors. Auditions will be held at the University of Central Florida on May 13th. A prescreening tape must be mailed with the application. Five awards will be offered. For Florida residents or students attending a Florida college or university. Write to the address below for details.

Central Florida Jazz Society
Scholarship Program
881 Silversmith Circle
Lake Mary, FL 32746

857

Central Pennsylvania Communications Scholarship

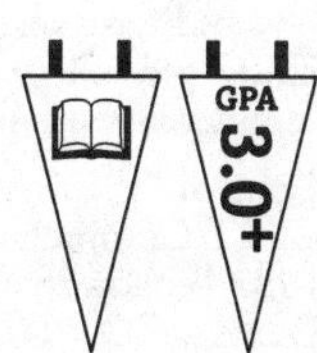

AMOUNT: $500 **DEADLINE:** Mar 25
FIELDS/MAJORS: Any Area Of Communications

Scholarships available to male or female communication majors completing their junior year who either attend a college in the central Pennsylvania area or who are residents of the area. Students must have maintained a 3.0 GPA in communications courses. A portfolio of the student's published or broadcast work must be submitted. Also required is a letter of verification from the student's advisor and a statement from the student explaining why he/she has chosen to major in a field of communications and his/her plans for the future. Write to the address below for details.

Women In Communications, Inc.
Central Pennsylvania Chapter
426 N. Prince St.
Millersville, PA 17551

858

Central Virginia Scholarships

Amount: $5,000 **Deadline:** Mar 1
Fields/Majors: Liberal Arts

Awards for high school seniors in the Richmond metropolitan area. Program is intended to help bridge the gap for worthy students whose preference is to attend the more expensive private institutions. Applicants must have been admitted to an accredited four-year college or university in the continental U.S. and should intend to pursue a major in liberal arts. Students who would like to be considered for this award must contact their high school guidance counselor or principal to be nominated.

Community Foundation Serving Richmond And Central Virginia
1025 Boulders Parkway, Suite 405
Richmond, VA 23225

859

Centre College Scholarships

Amount: $2,500–$9,000 **Deadline:** Mar 1
Fields/Majors: All Areas Of Study

Renewable scholarships for entering freshmen at Centre College (KY). Based primarily on academics. Requires an interview on campus. Includes the Centre Honor, Academic Recognition, President's, Trustee, Dean's, Faculty, Day, and Heritage scholarships. Special application and interview required. Contact the office of admissions or the financial aid office as soon as possible to make sure you have current information about the financial aid programs and the application process.

Centre College
Elaine Larson, Dir. Of Student Financial Planning
600 West Walnut Street
Danville, KY 40422

860

CERT Scholarship Program

Amount: $1,000
Deadline: Jan 30, Jul 15
Fields/Majors: Business, Engineering, Science, Energy Or Environmental-Related Fields

Scholarships are available for American Indian students pursuing degrees in one of the above fields. Applicant must have a GPA of at least 2.5, and have successfully completed either a CERT pre-college summer program tribes, or the CERT ten-week summer internship. Write to the address listed below for information.

Council Of Energy Resource Tribes
CERT Comprehensive Education Program
1999 Broadway, Suite 2600
Denver, CO 80202

861

Certificate/Associate Scholarship Program

Amount: Varies **Deadline:** Jun 1
Fields/Majors: Dental Hygiene

Scholarships for students in their second year of a full-time certificate or associates program of an accredited dental school. Minimum GPA of 3.0. Based on need. Write to the address below for more information.

American Dental Hygienists' Association Institute For Oral Health
444 N. Michigan Ave., Suite 3400
Chicago, IL 60611

862

Certified Public Accountants, Colorado Society, Scholarships

Amount: $750 **Deadline:** Jun 30, Nov 30
Fields/Majors: Accounting

Scholarships for Colorado residents who have completed at least eight semester hours of accounting courses. Must have a GPA of at least 3.0. For study at Colorado colleges and universities. Re-application is allowed. Write to the address below for details.

Colorado Society Of Certified Public Accountants
Educational Foundation
7979 E. Tufts Avenue, #500
Denver, CO 80237

863

CFF/NIH Funding Award

Amount: $75,000 (max) **Deadline:** Ongoing
Fields/Majors: Medical Research-Cystic Fibrosis

This award is to support excellent CF-related research projects that have been submitted to and approved by the NIH, but cannot be supported by available NIH funds. Applications must fall within the upper 40th percentile with a priority score of 200 or better. Maximum award of $75,000 per year for two years. Write to the address below for details.

Cystic Fibrosis Foundation
Office Of Grants Management
6931 Arlington Rd.
Bethesda, MD 20814

864

Chadron State College Scholarships

Amount: Varies **Deadline:** None Specified
Fields/Majors: All Areas Of Study

Awards for students at Chadron State University. Individual criteria for each award such as: academics, field of study, extracurricular activities, or test scores will vary. Write to the address below for more information.

Chadron State University
Financial Aid Office
1000 Main St.
Chadron, NE 69337

865

Chadwick, Steinkirchner, And Davis Scholarship

Amount: $400 **Deadline:** None Specified
Fields/Majors: Accounting

Awards for students at Mesa State College who are majoring in accounting. Contact the professional studies/business area for further details.

Mesa State College
Financial Aid Office
P.O. Box 2684
Grand Junction, CO 81501

866

Challenge Scholarships

AMOUNT: $4,000 (max) **DEADLINE:** Jan 15
FIELDS/MAJORS: All Areas Of Study

Scholarships of $1,000 to $4,000 are available to African American undergraduate students at the University of Pittsburgh with satisfactory academic records. Renewable. Write to the address below for details.

University Of Pittsburgh
Office Of Admissions And Financial Aid
Bruce Hall, Second Floor
Pittsburgh, PA 15260

867

Challenger Scholarship

AMOUNT: $1,000 **DEADLINE:** None Specified
FIELDS/MAJORS: Science, Social Science, Engineering

Scholarships are for full-time undergraduate students pursuing a career in science, social science, and engineering. Must have a GPA of 3.5 or higher and have completed 12 or more hours entering their junior year. Write to the address below for more information.

Indiana University Purdue University, Indianapolis
Office Of The Dean, School Of Education
E/S Building, #3138
Indianapolis, IN 46202

868

Champion Laboratories, Inc. Scholarships

AMOUNT: $1,250 **DEADLINE:** Feb 15
FIELDS/MAJORS: Agriculture

Scholarships are available for FFA members pursuing a four-year degree in any area of agriculture. Financial need will be considered. Write to the address below for details.

National FFA Foundation
Scholarship Office
P.O. Box 15160
Alexandria, VA 22309

869

Champion Seed Company Scholarship

AMOUNT: $600 **DEADLINE:** Apr 15
FIELDS/MAJORS: Vegetable Industry

Open to students with demonstrated interest in the vegetable industry. Write to the address below for more information.

California State Polytechnic University, Pomona
College Of Agriculture
Building 7, Room 110
Pomona, CA 91768

870

Champions Choice/ Akzo Salt Scholarships

AMOUNT: $1,000 **DEADLINE:** Feb 15
FIELDS/MAJORS: Dairy Or Cattle Science

Scholarships are available for FFA members pursuing a two- or four-year degree in dairy or cattle science. Preference will be given to students with outstanding leadership skills and ag-related work experience. Write to the address below for details.

National FFA Foundation
Scholarship Office
P.O. Box 15160
Alexandria, VA 22309

871

Champlin Foundations Scholarship

AMOUNT: None Specified **DEADLINE:** None Specified
FIELDS/MAJORS: All Areas Of Study

Scholarships are available to graduating high school seniors who reside in Rhode Island and will be attending Brown University. Contact the financial aid office at Brown or your high school counselor for information, do not write to the address listed below.

Champlin Foundations
410 South Main Street
Providence, RI 02903

872

Chancellor's Freshman Academic Award

AMOUNT: $1,000 **DEADLINE:** Jan 15
FIELDS/MAJORS: All Areas Of Study

Awards are available to new freshmen admitted to UW Oshkosh who rank in the top quarter of their class. Contact the admissions office at UW Oshkosh for more details.

University Of Wisconsin, Oshkosh
Financial Aid Office, Dempsey 104
800 Algoma Blvd.
Oshkosh, WI 54901

873

Chancellor's Freshman Leadership Award

AMOUNT: $1,000 **DEADLINE:** Jan 15
FIELDS/MAJORS: All Areas Of Study

Awards are available to new freshmen admitted to UW Oshkosh who rank in the top quarter of their class. Applicants must have had significant leadership experience. Contact the admissions office at UW Oshkosh for more details.

University Of Wisconsin, Oshkosh
Financial Aid Office, Dempsey 104
800 Algoma Blvd.
Oshkosh, WI 54901

874

Chancellor's Merit Scholarship Fund

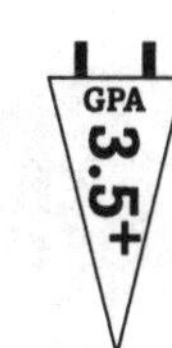

AMOUNT: Varies **DEADLINE:** Mar 1
FIELDS/MAJORS: All Areas Of Study

Awards for students at UMass who are academically gifted. This fund was established by a donation from Big Y Foods. Students must file a FAFSA as soon as possible after January 1 and before the March 1 financial aid priority consideration date. You will automatically be considered for this scholarship if you are enrolled at the university and apply for financial aid. Separate applications, requests, or inquiries are not required and cannot be honored.

University Of Massachusetts–Amherst
Office Of Financial Aid Services
255 Whitmore Admin. Bldg., Box 38230
Amherst, MA 01003

875

Chancellor's Scholarship

GPA 3.0+

AMOUNT: $4,000 **DEADLINE:** Dec 15
FIELDS/MAJORS: All Areas Of Study

Scholarships awarded to incoming freshmen on the basis of high school merit. Scholarship is renewable for an additional three years, provided a 3.4 GPA is maintained. Recipient is required to reside in the honors residence hall and to take at least one honors course each semester during the first two years. Contact the office of admissions at the address below for details.

Appalachian State University
Office Of Admissions
Scholarship Section
Boone, NC 28608

876

Chancellor's Scholarships

GPA 3.0+

AMOUNT: Varies **DEADLINE:** Jan 15
FIELDS/MAJORS: All Areas Of Study

Full tuition and fees scholarship for ten students who show outstanding academic potential. Applicants must be undergraduates who maintain at least a 3.0 GPA. Renewable. Write to the address below for details.

University Of Pittsburgh
Office Of Admissions And Financial Aid
Bruce Hall, Second Floor
Pittsburgh, PA 15260

877

Chancellor's Talent Award For Academics

GPA 3.0+

AMOUNT: $5,000 **DEADLINE:** None Specified
FIELDS/MAJORS: All Areas Of Study

Awards for selected Massachusetts residents who enroll at UMass and are academically talented. Students must have exceptional academic records (typically rank in the top 5% of their class and have combined SAT scores of 1300 or higher). Applicants must be nominated during their junior year by their high school guidance counselor. Contact your high school guidance department for more details.

University Of Massachusetts–Amherst
Office Of Financial Aid Services
255 Whitmore Admin. Bldg., Box 38230
Amherst, MA 01003

878

Chapter VV Of Scholarship

GPA 3.0+

AMOUNT: $600 **DEADLINE:** Varies
FIELDS/MAJORS: All Areas Of Study

Scholarships are available for female students over age 18 from Siskiyou County who currently attend the College of the Siskiyous. For undergraduate study, not intended for freshmen. Must have a GPA of at least 3.0. Write to the address below for additional information.

College Of The Siskiyous
Office Of Financial Aid
800 College Ave
Weed, CA 96094

879

Charis Ann McKelvy Fund

AMOUNT: Varies **DEADLINE:** Mar 1
FIELDS/MAJORS: Music

Awards are made to the Music Department at the University of New Mexico for graduates of an Albuquerque public high school. Recipients must have artistic ability, good academic standing, and be above the sophomore level of study. Write to the address below for more information.

University Of New Mexico, Albuquerque
Office Of Financial Aid
Albuquerque, NM 87131

880

Charitabulls Scholarship Program

AMOUNT: None Specified **DEADLINE:** Feb 5
FIELDS/MAJORS: All Areas Of Study

Open to high school seniors in the city of Chicago as well as the surrounding suburbs. Must complete an essay (500 words or less). Scholarships are available to students living in the following counties only: McHenry, Lake, Cook, DuPage, and Will counties. Write to the address below for more information.

Chicago Bulls
1901 West Madison St.
Chicago, IL 60612

881

Charity Day Scholarship

GPA 3.0+

AMOUNT: None Specified **DEADLINE:** None Specified
FIELDS/MAJORS: All Areas Of Study

Awards given to students who will attend St. Petersburg junior college, are enrolled full-time, and who have a GPA of at least 3.0. Contact the office of the director of scholarships and student financial assistance at the campus you attend or write to the address below.

St. Petersburg Junior College
Office Of Financial Aid
P.O. Box 13489
St. Petersburg, FL 33733

882

Charles A. Dana And Julius Seelye Bixler Scholarships

AMOUNT: Varies **DEADLINE:** None Specified
FIELDS/MAJORS: All Areas Of Study

Scholarships for upperclass students primarily on the basis of academic excellence. Write to the address below for additional information.

Colby College
Office Of Financial Aid
Lunder House
Waterville, ME 04901

883

Charles A. Lauffer Scholarship Fund

AMOUNT: $1,900 **DEADLINE:** Jun 14
FIELDS/MAJORS: Medicine

Scholarships are limited to students in the last two years of studying for a medical degree at a qualified medical school in the U.S. and who plan to practice medicine as a career. Must be in good academic standing at the current or previous. Write to the address below for more information.

Nations Bank
Private Client Group
830 Central Ave., P.O. Box 15507
St. Petersburg, FL 33701

884 Charles Abrams Scholarship Program

AMOUNT: $2,000 **DEADLINE:** Apr 30
FIELDS/MAJORS: Urban Planning

Scholarships for master's students enrolled in a planning program at one of the following schools: Columbia Univ., Harvard Univ., Massachusetts Institute of Technology, New School for Social Research, or Univ. of Pennsylvania. Nomination by department, financial need, and U.S. citizenship required. Contact your department head, or write to "Charles Abrams Scholarship Program" at the address below if further information is required.

American Planning Association
Fellowships And Scholarships In Planning
1776 Massachusetts Avenue, NW
Washington, DC 20036

885 Charles And Ellora Alliss Foundation Grant

AMOUNT: $500–$2,400 **DEADLINE:** Aug 1, Jan 1
FIELDS/MAJORS: All Areas Of Study

Awards for students ranking in the top 40% of their class. Recipients must give permission for their data to be reported to the foundation. Applicants must demonstrate financial need. Write to the address below for more information.

Bethel College
Office Of Financial Planning
3900 Bethel Dr.
St. Paul, MN 55112

886 Charles And Louise Rosenbaum Scholarship Fund

AMOUNT: None Specified **DEADLINE:** Mar 29
FIELDS/MAJORS: All Areas Of Study

Scholarships for Jewish graduating high school seniors from Colorado who will be entering their freshmen year of college. Write to the address below for details.

Endowment Fund Of The Allied Jewish Federation
300 Dahlia St.
Denver, CO 80222

887 Charles And Lucille King Family Foundation Scholarships

AMOUNT: $2,500 **DEADLINE:** Apr 30
FIELDS/MAJORS: Television And Film

Awards for sophomores, juniors, or seniors in the areas of film or television. Scholarship is renewable with a GPA of 3.0 or better. Based on financial need, academic achievement, personal statement, and letters of recommendation. Contact your department chairperson or bursar or write to the address below for more information.

Charles And Lucille King Family Foundation, Inc.
366 Madison Ave., 10th Floor
New York, NY 10017

888 Charles E. Fahrney Education Foundation Scholarship

AMOUNT: $1,500 **DEADLINE:** Feb 15
FIELDS/MAJORS: All Areas Of Study

Scholarships available to residents of Wapello County, Iowa, who are U.S. citizens and need financial aid. Applicants must be enrolled in a full-time course of study in a four-year accredited Iowa college or university leading toward a bachelor degree, or a two-year Iowa college associate arts or science program leading to a four-year course of study and bachelor degree. Write to the address below for details.

Firstar Bank Ottumwa
Trust Department
123 East Third Street
Ottumwa, IA 52501

889 Charles E. Fahrney Foundation

AMOUNT: $1,500 (max) **DEADLINE:** None Specified
FIELDS/MAJORS: All Areas Of Study

Scholarships are available at the University of Iowa for undergraduate students who are residents of Wapello County. Write to the address listed below for information.

University of Iowa
Firstar Bank Ottumwa, Trust Department
123 East 3rd Street
Ottumwa, IA 52501

890 Charles E. Pettijohn Excellence In Sales And Sales Management Award

AMOUNT: $250 **DEADLINE:** None Specified
FIELDS/MAJORS: Marketing, Sales

Student must be a full-time sophomore or above marketing major with an emphasis in sales and sales management. Must have a GPA of 3.0 or higher. Contact the COBA office for more information.

Southwest Missouri State University
Office Of Financial Aid
901 South National Ave.
Springfield, MO 65804

891 Charles F. Coan Memorial Prize

AMOUNT: Varies **DEADLINE:** Mar 1
FIELDS/MAJORS: History

Award is available at the University of New Mexico for the student in the graduating class with the highest GPA. Write to the address below for more information.

University Of New Mexico, Albuquerque
Office Of Financial Aid
Albuquerque, NM 87131

892
Charles G. Wellborn, Jr. Scholarship

Amount: $900 **Deadline:** Mar 1
Fields/Majors: Public Relations, Magazines

Must be a junior or senior at the University of Florida studying public relations or magazines. Must have at least a 2.8 GPA. Should intend to pursue a career in publication design, editing, writing or production. Write to the address below for details.

University Of Florida
2070 Weimer Hall
Scholarship & Placement Director
Gainesville, FL 32611

893
Charles Gregory Forgan, Lottie Conlan Scholarships

Amount: $1,000–$2,000 **Deadline:** Mar 1
Fields/Majors: All Areas Of Study

Scholarships are available at the University of Oklahoma, Norman, for students of American Indian heritage. Requires a GPA of at least 3.25. The Conlan award is for sophomores, juniors and seniors only. Five to six awards are offered annually. Write to the address listed below for information.

University Of Oklahoma, Norman
Office Of Financial Aid Services
731 Elm
Norman, OK 73019

894
Charles H. Feoppel Educational Loan Trust

Amount: None Specified **Deadline:** May 30
Fields/Majors: All Areas Of Study

Recipients must be residents of Harrison County, unmarried, and must have completed high school or possess an equivalent certification. Write to the address below for more information.

Huntington National Bank WV
Attn: Trust Department
230 W. Pike St., P.O. Box 2490
Clarksburg, WV 26302

895
Charles K. Barker Award

Amount: $300 **Deadline:** None Specified
Fields/Majors: Computer Technology

Awards for outstanding minority computer technology students recommended by and voted upon by the faculty. Write to the address below for more information.

Indiana University Purdue University, Indianapolis
Purdue School Of Technology
799 West Michigan St.
Indianapolis, IN 46202

896
Charles M. Goethe Memorial Scholarship

Amount: None Specified **Deadline:** Jun 10
Fields/Majors: All Areas Of Study

Applicants must be members or senior members of the Order of Demolay or who are the sons or daughters of a member (or a deceased member) of a constituent Masonic lodge of the Grand Lodge of Free and Accepted Masons of California. All areas of study are acceptable but preference will be given to students majoring in eugenics, genetics, biology, or life sciences. Write to the address below for details.

Sacramento Bodies Ancient And Accepted Scottish Rite Of Freemasonry
P.O. Box 19497
Sacramento, CA 95819

897
Charles M. Ross Trust

Amount: $500–$1,200 **Deadline:** Aug 1
Fields/Majors: Religion, Sociology, Medicine, Teaching

Candidate should be an active member of a local church and should have earned grades in their undergraduate education, which are within the first 10% of their class. Must have courses in religion, sociology, medicine, and teaching. Scholarships are available at Lexington Theo. Seminary, Marquette Univ., Univ. of Chicago, Texas Christian Univ., Centenary Coll., and Vanderbilt Univ. Write to the address below for more information.

Charles M. Ross Trust
Paul G. Mason, Executive Director
113 W. Walnut
Fairbury, IL 61739

898
Charles Mattox Prize

Amount: Varies **Deadline:** Apr 1
Fields/Majors: Art–Sculpture

Scholarships are available at the University of New Mexico for full-time junior or senior art students, with a concentration in sculpture. Write to the address listed below for information.

University Of New Mexico, Albuquerque
College Of Fine Arts, Office Of The Dean
Albuquerque, NM 87131

899
Charles P. Bell Conservation Scholarship

Amount: $500 **Deadline:** Jan 15
Fields/Majors: Conservation And Related Fields

Scholarships available for undergraduate juniors and seniors who are Missouri residents (preference will be given to students enrolled in Missouri schools) who are pursuing a degree in a field related to conservation. Write to the address below for details.

Conservation Foundation Of Missouri Charitable Trust
728 West Main Street
Jefferson City, MO 65101

900
Charles P. Bell Conservation Scholarship

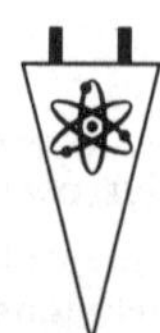

Amount: $600 **Deadline:** Jan 15
Fields/Majors: Conservation And Related Fields

Scholarships available for graduate students who are Missouri residents (preference will be given to students enrolled in Missouri schools) who are pursuing an advanced degree in a field related to conservation. Write to the address below for details.

Conservation Foundation Of Missouri Charitable Trust
728 West Main Street
Jefferson City, MO 65101

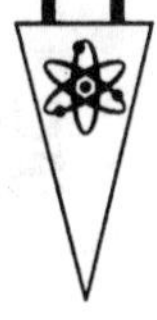

901 Charles P. Lake/Rain For Rent Scholarships

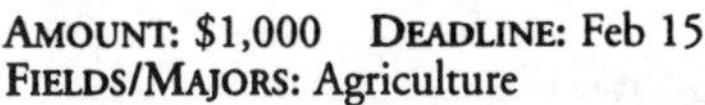

AMOUNT: $1,000 **DEADLINE:** Feb 15
FIELDS/MAJORS: Agriculture

Scholarships are available for FFA members pursuing a four-year degree in any area of agriculture. Preference may be given to agronomy majors. Applicant must be a sophomore or above, and reside in California, Idaho, or Arizona. Write to the address below for details.

National FFA Foundation
Scholarship Office
P.O. Box 15160
Alexandria, VA 22309

902 Charles P. Lake/Rain For Rent Scholarship

AMOUNT: $1,000 **DEADLINE:** May 31
FIELDS/MAJORS: Agriculture

Open to all agriculture majors. Preference is given to students specializing in irrigation and soils technology. Write to the address below for more information.

California State Polytechnic University, Pomona
College Of Agriculture
Building 7, Room 110
Pomona, CA 91768

903 Charles Plumb Scholarship

AMOUNT: Varies **DEADLINE:** Jun 1
FIELDS/MAJORS: Animal Science, Veterinary Medicine

Awards for UMass students in one of the fields listed above. This is to assist students with travel expenses for trips to inspect stock farms. For entering sophomores, juniors, or seniors. Contact the Chair, Scholarship Committee, Veterinary and Animal Sciences for more information.

University Of Massachusetts, Amherst
Chair, Scholarship Committee
Veterinary And Animal Sciences
Amherst, MA 01003

904 Charles R. Spail Memorial Scholarship

AMOUNT: Varies **DEADLINE:** Mar 1
FIELDS/MAJORS: Education

Awards are available at the University of New Mexico for students majoring in education with academic ability and financial need. Write to the address below for more information.

University Of New Mexico, Albuquerque
Office Of Financial Aid
Albuquerque, NM 87131

905 Charles Richard Drew Scholarships

GPA 2.5+

AMOUNT: None Specified **DEADLINE:** None
FIELDS/MAJORS: All Areas Of Study

Up to ten scholarships per year. Must be nominated by your guidance counselor. Based on achievement in leadership role. Applicants must graduate in the top 50% of their high school class and have a GPA of at least 2.5. Renewable with continued achievement. Write to the address below for details.

Mercyhurst College
Glenwood Hills
Erie, PA 16546

906 Charles River District Medical Society Scholarships

AMOUNT: None Specified **DEADLINE:** Apr 1
FIELDS/MAJORS: Medicine

Open to any first year medical student enrolled at an accredited school who is a resident of the following towns in the Charles River district: Needham, Newton, Waltham, Wellesley, or Weston. Write to the society at the address below for details.

Charles River District Medical Society
Attn: Scholarship Program
1440 Main St.
Waltham, MA 02154

907 Charles Scarritt Memorial Endowed Scholarship

AMOUNT: $500 **DEADLINE:** Feb 15
FIELDS/MAJORS: Journalism

Renewable $500 award given to outstanding juniors and seniors who intend to pursue a career in the newspaper business, currently enrolled or planning to enroll in the College of Communication at the University of Alabama. Write to the address listed below for further information and an application.

University Of Alabama
College Of Communications
P.O. Box 870172
Tuscaloosa, AL 35487

908 Charleston Rotary Club Scholarship Fund

AMOUNT: None Specified **DEADLINE:** Mar 15
FIELDS/MAJORS: Business

Scholarships for Charleston (WV) residents who will be in their first year at a WV college or university. Criteria considered include community service and previous business/entrepreneurial experience. Write to the address below for details.

Greater Kanawha Valley Foundation
Scholarship Committee
P.O. Box 3041
Charleston, WV 25331

909

Charlie Carpenter Vocational Scholarship

AMOUNT: $1,000 **DEADLINE:** Mar 1
FIELDS/MAJORS: All Areas Of Study

Awards for Minnesota high school seniors planning to attend a vocational school. Based on academics, financial need, leadership, character, and recommendations. Write to the address below for more information.

Minnesota Federation Of Teachers
168 Aurora Ave.
St. Paul, MN 55103

910

Charlotte Hess Memorial Scholarship

AMOUNT: $250 **DEADLINE:** Feb 9
FIELDS/MAJORS: Elementary Education

Award for junior or senior elementary education major with a minimum GPA of 3.5. Student must be a member of Phi Kappa Phi. Financial need will be considered in case of a tie. Contact Dr. William O'Bruba, Chairperson, Department of Curriculum and Foundations, for further information.

Bloomsburg University
19 Ben Franklin Hall
400 E. Second St.
Bloomsburg, PA 17815

911

Charlotte W. Newcomb Scholarship

AMOUNT: Varies **DEADLINE:** Mar 15, Nov 15
FIELDS/MAJORS: All Areas Of Study

Awards for women who are 25 years or older and are bachelor's degree candidates. Must have financial need and definite career goals. Write to the address below for more information.

Gwynedd-Mercy College
Student Financial Aid
Sumneytown Pike
Gwynedd Valley, PA 19437

912

Charlotte W. Newcombe Doctoral Dissertation Fellowships

AMOUNT: $14,000 **DEADLINE:** Dec 12
FIELDS/MAJORS: Social Sciences/Humanities

For doctoral candidates in the above fields who will soon complete all doctoral requirements except the dissertation. These awards are not designed to finance field work but rather the completion of dissertation research. Write to the address below for complete details.

Woodrow Wilson National Fellowship Foundation
Attn: Charlotte Newcombe Fellowships
CN 5281
Princeton, NJ 08543

913

Chase Manhattan Scholarship

AMOUNT: $1,200 **DEADLINE:** Mar 15
FIELDS/MAJORS: All Areas Of Study

Awards open to Teikyo post full-time minority students with a GPA of 2.5 and who can demonstrate leadership abilities. Renewable. Write to the address below for more information.

Teikyo Post University
Office Of Financial Aid
800 Country Club Road
Waterbury, CT 06723

914

Chemical And Fuels Engineering Departmental Scholarships

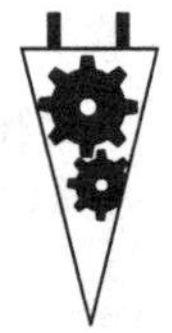

AMOUNT: Varies **DEADLINE:** Feb 1
FIELDS/MAJORS: Chemical Engineering

Scholarships are available at the University of Utah for full-time students enrolled in a chemical or fuels engineering program. Write to the address below for details.

University Of Utah
Christie Perry
3290 Merrill Engineering Building
Salt Lake City, UT 84112

915

Chemical Rubber Company Freshman Achievement Award

AMOUNT: Varies **DEADLINE:** Mar 1
FIELDS/MAJORS: Chemistry

Scholarships are available at the University of New Mexico for freshmen who are studying chemistry. Must exhibit a good GPA and progress in the program. Write to the address listed below for information.

University Of New Mexico, Albuquerque
Office Of Financial Aid
Albuquerque, NM 87131

916

Chemistry Scholarship Award

AMOUNT: $350 **DEADLINE:** None Specified
FIELDS/MAJORS: Chemistry

Award for incoming freshmen with potential for academic excellence. Recipient will be selected by the admissions office and the department of chemistry. Contact the admissions office for additional information.

Bloomsburg University
19 Ben Franklin Hall
400 E. Second St.
Bloomsburg, PA 17815

917

Chemists' Club Scholarships

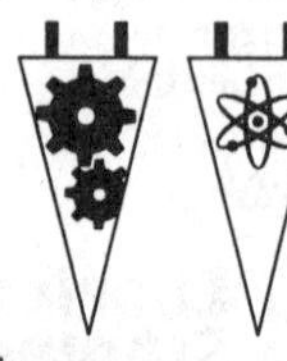

AMOUNT: Varies **DEADLINE:** May 1
FIELDS/MAJORS: Chemistry/Chemical Engineering

Awards for undergraduate, graduate, postgraduates, teachers, and researchers in all branches of chemistry. Literature searches using the chemists' club library computer system are also available. Must be at least a sophomore undergraduate when scholarship begins. For study at a college or university in New York, New Jersey, or Connecticut. Write for complete details. Please specify your year in school.

Chemists' Club Of New York
Scholarship Committee
40 West 45th St.
New York, NY 10036

918

Cheney Foundation Scholarships

AMOUNT: $1,000 **DEADLINE:** Feb 1
FIELDS/MAJORS: All Areas Of Study

Awards for currently enrolled freshmen to use in their sophomore year. Must demonstrate academic excellence and community and college service. Renewable. Write to the address below for complete details.

Lewis And Clark College
Office Of Admissions
Portland, OR 97219

919

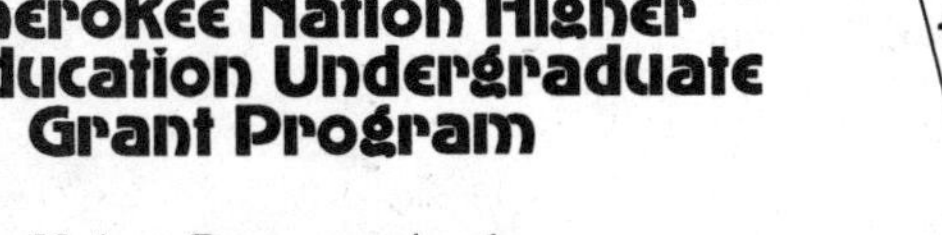

Cherokee Nation Higher Education Undergraduate Grant Program

AMOUNT: Varies **DEADLINE:** Apr 1
FIELDS/MAJORS: All Areas Of Study

Scholarships are available for undergraduate students who are members of the Cherokee Nation. Write to the address listed below for information.

Cherokee Nation
P.O. Box 948
Tahlequah, OK 74465

920

Cheryl Conniff-Carroll Memorial Scholarship

AMOUNT: Varies **DEADLINE:** Apr 1
FIELDS/MAJORS: Art

Scholarships are available at the University of New Mexico for full-time undergraduate art majors with financial need. Must be sophomores or above and have a minimum 3.5 GPA. Write to the address listed below for information.

University Of New Mexico, Albuquerque
College Of Fine Arts
Office Of The Dean
Albuquerque, NM 87131

921

Cheryl Dant Hennesy Scholarship

AMOUNT: $1,000 **DEADLINE:** Feb 15
FIELDS/MAJORS: All Areas Of Study

Scholarships are available for FFA members pursuing a full-time two- or four-year degree. Applicant must be female and reside in Kentucky, Georgia, or Tennessee. Write to the address below for details.

National FFA Foundation
Scholarship Office
P.O. Box 15160
Alexandria, VA 22309

922

Chester A. Phillips Scholarships

AMOUNT: Varies **DEADLINE:** Mar 1
FIELDS/MAJORS: Business

Scholarships are available at the University of Iowa for full-time senior business majors who rank in the top 10% of their class. Write to the address listed below for information.

University of Iowa
College Of Business Admin., Suite W160
108 Pappajohn Business Admin. Bldg.
Iowa City, IA 52245

923

Chester Dale Fellowships

AMOUNT: Varies **DEADLINE:** Nov 9
FIELDS/MAJORS: Fine Arts, Art History, Art Conservation

Research grants for three months to one year are available for those whose fields of study are related to the fine arts of the western world and who are U.S. citizens under the age of forty. Write to the address below for details. Applicant may also apply at the National Gallery of Art, Fellowship Program Center for Advanced Study in the Visual Arts, Washington, DC 20565.

Metropolitan Museum Of Art
Office Of Academic Programs
1000 Fifth Avenue
New York, NY 10028

924

Chester French Scholarship

AMOUNT: Varies **DEADLINE:** Mar 1
FIELDS/MAJORS: Political Science

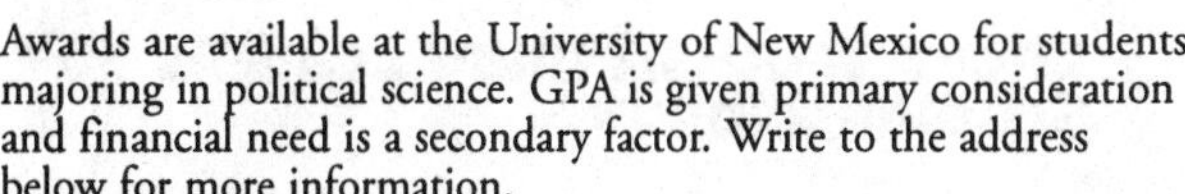

Awards are available at the University of New Mexico for students majoring in political science. GPA is given primary consideration and financial need is a secondary factor. Write to the address below for more information.

University Of New Mexico, Albuquerque
Office Of Financial Aid
Albuquerque, NM 87131

925

Chevrolet Corporation Scholarship

AMOUNT: $300 **DEADLINE:** None Specified
FIELDS/MAJORS: All Areas Of Study

Awards for Jacksonville State University students in any discipline. Based primarily on GPA. Write to the address below for more information.

Jacksonville State University
Financial Aid Office
Jacksonville, AL 36265

926

Chevron Corporation, U.S.A. Scholarships

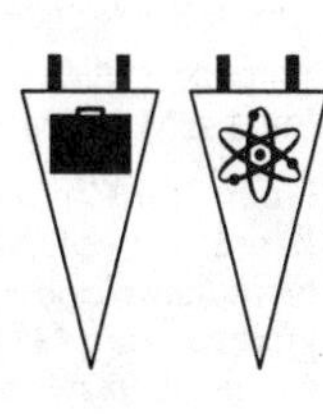

AMOUNT: $2,000 **DEADLINE:** Feb 1
FIELDS/MAJORS: Business, Math, Science

Awards for Lewis and Clark students seeking a future in one of the fields listed above. Awarded to entering freshmen who are from Oregon. Recipients must declare a business, math, or science major by junior year. Renewable. Write to the address below for complete details.

Lewis And Clark College
Office Of Admissions
Portland, OR 97219

927

Chevron Geophysics Award

AMOUNT: $1,500 **DEADLINE:** Mar 1
FIELDS/MAJORS: Geophysics

Scholarships are available at the University of Oklahoma, Norman for full-time undergraduate geophysics majors. Write to the address listed below for information.

University Of Oklahoma, Norman
Director, School Of Geology & Geophysics
100 East Boyd Street, Room 810
Norman, OK 73019

928

Chevron Scholarships

AMOUNT: $2,000 **DEADLINE:** Feb 1
FIELDS/MAJORS: Chemical, Mechanical, Petroleum Engineering

Scholarships for sophomores or juniors majoring in chemical, mechanical, or petroleum engineering. Write to the address below for additional information.

Society Of Women Engineers
120 Wall St., 11th Floor
New York, NY 10005

929

Chevy Trucks/Future Leaders Scholarships

AMOUNT: $2,500 **DEADLINE:** Feb 15
FIELDS/MAJORS: All Areas Of Study

Scholarships for FFA members who are pursuing two- or four-year degrees in any field. Applicant must have demonstrated leadership and recruitment skills which have contributed to the local FFA chapter, and participated in a supervised agricultural experience (SAE). Write to the address below for details.

National FFA Foundation
Scholarship Office
P.O. Box 15160
Alexandria, VA 22309

930

Cheyenne And Arapaho Tribes Of Oklahoma Higher Education Grants

AMOUNT: Varies **DEADLINE:** Jun 1, Nov 1
FIELDS/MAJORS: All Areas Of Study

Grants for Cheyenne or Arapaho tribal members of Oklahoma. Based on need. Must be 1/4 or more Indian blood (certificate of Indian blood required). Applicant must be a high school graduate or a GED recipient and approved for admission by a college, in need of financial aid, and give assurance that they will be successful in completing a four-year college degree program. Contact the C & A tribal offices at the address below for details. Deadlines are June 1 for first semester, November 1 for second semester, and April 1 for summer semester.

Cheyenne And Arapaho Tribes Of Oklahoma
Education Department
P.O. Box 38
Concho, OH 73022

931

Chicago Mercantile Exchange Beef And Pork Industry Scholarships

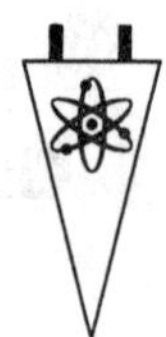

AMOUNT: $2,500 **DEADLINE:** Nov 1 , Dec 1
FIELDS/MAJORS: Agriculture

Student must be enrolled in a college of agriculture at a four-year institution. Chicago Mercantile Exchange Beef Industry gives four awards yearly and Chicago Mercantile Exchange Pork Industry gives ten awards yearly. Deadlines for the beef industry is November 1 and for the pork industry is December 1. Write to the address below for more information.

California State Polytechnic University, Pomona
College Of Agriculture
Building 2, Room 215
Pomona, CA 91768

932

Chicano Scholarship Fund

AMOUNT: $500 (min) **DEADLINE:** Feb 10
FIELDS/MAJORS: All Areas Of Study

Scholarships are available at the University of Utah for full-time students of Hispanic descent. Write to the address below for information.

University Of Utah
Scholarship Chairperson
112 Carlson Hall
Salt Lake City, UT 84112

933

Chicanos For Creative Medicine Scholarships

AMOUNT: Varies **DEADLINE:** Apr 1
FIELDS/MAJORS: Medicine

Awards for students of Chicano/Latino/Hispanic ancestry who are high school students at a school in East Los Angeles or for students at East Los Angeles college who have completed at least 24 units. Based on academics, financial need, recommendations, and personal statements. Write to the address below for more information.

Chicanos For Creative Medicine
1301 Avenida Cesar Chavez
Monterey Park, CA 91754

934

Chickasaw Nation Education Foundation Program

AMOUNT: $200–$350 **DEADLINE:** May 1
FIELDS/MAJORS: All Areas Of Study

Scholarships are available for undergraduate or graduate students who are members of the Chickasaw Nation. Write to the address listed below for information.

Chickasaw Nation Education Foundation
P.O. Box 1548
Ada, OK 74820

935

Chief Industries, Inc. Scholarships

AMOUNT: $500–$1,000 **DEADLINE:** Feb 15
FIELDS/MAJORS: Agriculture

Scholarships are available for FFA members pursuing a two- or four-year degree in any area of agriculture. Must be residents of Nebraska. Write to the address below for details.

National FFA Foundation
Scholarship Office
P.O. Box 15160
Alexandria, VA 22309

936

Child Care Grants

AMOUNT: Varies **DEADLINE:** None Specified
FIELDS/MAJORS: All Areas Of Study

Funds are available to assist undergraduate and graduate student-parents. Applicants must be enrolled at least in part-time study in a New Mexico institution of higher learning. Priority is given to residents of New Mexico, but it is not required. Contact the financial aid office at any New Mexico public postsecondary institution.

New Mexico Commission On Higher Education
1068 Cerrillos Rd.
Santa Fe, NM 87501

937

Child Care Provider Grant

AMOUNT: $2,000 (max) **DEADLINE:** Apr 15
FIELDS/MAJORS: All Areas Of Study

Applicants must be Maryland residents attending a college in Maryland on a full-time basis, who are single parents or the head of the household. For undergraduate study. Write to the address below for details.

Maryland State Higher Education Commission
16 Francis Street
Annapolis, MD 21401

938

Children And Youth Scholarships

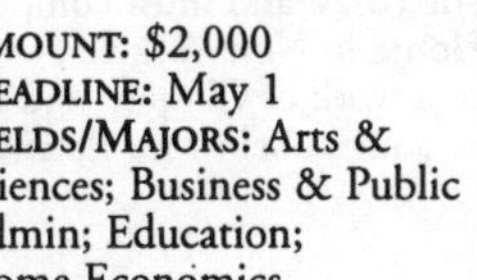

AMOUNT: $2,000
DEADLINE: May 1
FIELDS/MAJORS: Arts & Sciences; Business & Public Admin; Education; Home Economics

Scholarships are available to female students from Maryland whose parents were/are veterans, with preference going to children of members of the American Legion or the American Legion Auxiliary. Must attend college in Maryland and be a U.S. citizen. Renewable. Write to the address below for more details.

American Legion Auxiliary, Maryland
Department Of Maryland, Inc.
5205 East Drive
Baltimore, MD 21227

939

Children Of Deceased, Active Duty, And Retired Programs

AMOUNT: Varies **DEADLINE:** None Specified
FIELDS/MAJORS: All Areas Of Study

Must be dependent child of active duty Navy or Marine Corps personnel who are deceased, or who died in retired status. CDAD combines grants and loans. CDR is a grant program. Special program exists for children of personnel assigned to the USS Tennessee, families of servicemen killed on the USS Iowa (on April 19, 1989) or on the USS Stark (May 17, 1987). Applications available only from NMCRS headquarters. Write for complete details. Children of personnel of the USS Tennessee (past or present) are limited to schools in Tennessee.

Navy-Marine Corps Relief Society
Education Programs
801 N. Randolph Street, Suite 1228
Arlington, VA 22203

940

Children Of Prisoners Of War Or Persons Missing In Action

AMOUNT: Tuition **DEADLINE:** None Specified
FIELDS/MAJORS: All Areas Of Study

Exemption from tuition and fees to students at public colleges or universities in Texas who are children of prisoners of war or persons missing in action. Applicant must provide proof of parent's status from the department of defense and be under 21 years of age, or a person under 25 years of age who received the majority of his support from his parent(s). Write to the address below for details.

Texas Higher Education Coordinating Board
P.O. Box 12788
Austin, TX 78711

941

Children Of Texas Disabled Firemen And Peace Officers

AMOUNT: Tuition **DEADLINE:** None Specified
FIELDS/MAJORS: All Areas Of Study

Exemption from tuition and fees to children of firemen, peace officers, custodial employees of the department of corrections, or game wardens whose death or disability was sustained in the line of duty while serving in Texas. Students must apply prior to their 21st birthday. Write to the address below for details.

Texas Higher Education Coordinating Board
P.O. Box 12788
Austin, TX 78711

942

Children Of Unitarian Universalist Ministers

AMOUNT: Varies **DEADLINE:** None Specified
FIELDS/MAJORS: All Areas Of Studies

Awards for children of Unitarian Universalist ministers. Limited funding is available. Write to the address below for more information.

Unitarian Universalist Association Of Congregations
Office Of Church Staff Finances
25 Beacon St.
Boston, MA 02108

943
Children Of Veterans Scholarship

AMOUNT: Tuition **DEADLINE:** Mar 13
FIELDS/MAJORS: All Areas Of Study

Scholarships available at the University of Illinois for undergraduates who are the children of World War II, Korean, Vietnam, or Southwest Asian veterans. Applicants must be Illinois residents. Contact your high school principal or the address listed below for information.

University Of Illinois At Champaign Urbana
Office Of Student Financial Aid
610 E. John Street, 4th Floor
Champaign, IL 61820

944
Chilean Nitrate Corporation Scholarships

AMOUNT: $2,000 **DEADLINE:** Feb 15
FIELDS/MAJORS: Agriculture, Agribusiness

Scholarships are available for FFA members pursuing a four-year degree in any area of agriculture or agribusiness and reside in Virginia or North Carolina. Applicant must have produced tobacco as part of their SAE program. Preference may be given to agronomy majors. Write to the address below for details.

National FFA Foundation
Scholarship Office
P.O. Box 15160
Alexandria, VA 22309

945
China Area Studies Fellowships

AMOUNT: $25,000 (max) **DEADLINE:** Dec 1
FIELDS/MAJORS: Foreign Studies: China

Fellowship for Ph.D candidates requiring dissertation research abroad (except the Peoples Republic of China). While there are no citizenship restrictions, foreign nationals must have resided in the U.S. for at least two consecutive years at the time of application. Master's level and postdoctoral fellowships are also available. Write to the address below for details.

American Council Of Learned Societies
Office Of Fellowships And Grants
228 E. 45th St.
New York, NY 10017

946
Chinese American Medical Society Scholarships

AMOUNT: $1,500 **DEADLINE:** Mar 31
FIELDS/MAJORS: Medicine, Dentistry

Awards for medical and dental students of Chinese heritage for completion of their studies. Must be able to demonstrate financial need. Contact the address below for further information.

Chinese American Medical Society
Dr. H.H. Wang, Executive Director
281 Edgewood Ave.
Teaneck, NJ 07666

947
Chinese Fellowships For Scholarly Development

AMOUNT: None Specified **DEADLINE:** Nov 3
FIELDS/MAJORS: Social Science, Humanities

This program supports Chinese scholars with the M.A., Ph.D. or equivalent who are doing research in humanities or social science at a U.S. institution. Requires nomination by American host and residence at host's institution for research and collaborative academic programs. Write to the address listed below for information.

Committee On Scholarly Communication With China
1055 Thomas Jefferson Street, NW, Suite 2013
Washington, DC 20007

948
Chinese Professional Club Scholarship

AMOUNT: $500–$1,500 **DEADLINE:** Nov 15
FIELDS/MAJORS: All Areas Of Study

Scholarships are available to graduating high school seniors who are residents of Houston, and of Chinese descent. Applicant must be planning to enroll on a full-time basis in any accredited college or university in the U.S. Write to the address listed below for information. Applications will not be available until June.

Chinese Professional Club
Dr. Beng T. Ho, Chairman, Schlrshp. Cmt.
2615 South Glen Haven
Houston, TX 77025

949
Chloe Annette Cook Scholarship

AMOUNT: Varies **DEADLINE:** None Specified
FIELDS/MAJORS: Nursing

Scholarships are available at the University of Oklahoma, Norman for full-time nursing students. Write to the address listed below for information.

University Of Oklahoma, Norman
College Of Nursing
P.O. Box 26901
Oklahoma City, OK 73190

950
Chopin Piano Competition

AMOUNT: $1,000–$2,500 **DEADLINE:** Apr 15
FIELDS/MAJORS: Piano

Applicants must be between the ages of 16-22 and must compete during mid-May at the Foundation House in New York. Competition based on performance of a work of Chopin, and two or three other composers. Write to the address below for details.

Kosciuszko Foundation
Grants Office
15 E. 65th St.
New York, NY 10021

951
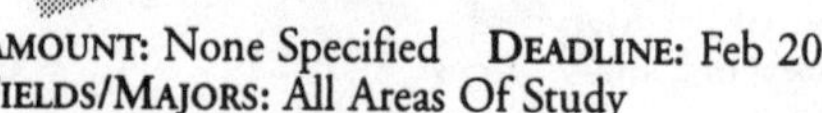

Choral Scholars

AMOUNT: None Specified **DEADLINE:** Feb 20
FIELDS/MAJORS: All Areas Of Study

Scholarships are available at the University of San Diego for students who plan to participate in the choral scholars singing group. Requires a GPA of at least 3.0. Write to the address listed below for information.

University Of San Diego
Office Of Financial Aid
5998 Alcala Park
San Diego, CA 92110

952

Christa McAuliffe Award For Excellence

AMOUNT: $2,500 **DEADLINE:** Jan 1
FIELDS/MAJORS: Education

Scholarship program for current teachers, principals, or administrators who wish to continue their education in a Washington state college or university. Write to the address listed below for information.

Washington Higher Education Coordinating Board
917 Lakeridge Way
P.O. Box 43430
Olympia, WA 98504

953

Christa McAuliffe Teacher Scholarship Loan

AMOUNT: $1,000 (min) **DEADLINE:** Mar 31
FIELDS/MAJORS: Education

Scholarship for students who meet academic requirements and enroll in a program at a Delaware college leading to a teacher qualification. Renewable. Write to the address below for more information.

Delaware Higher Education Commission
Carvel State Office Building
820 North French St.
Wilmington, DE 19801

954

Christian Ministry Scholarship Fund

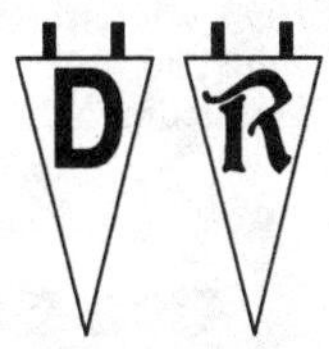

AMOUNT: Varies **DEADLINE:** None Specified
FIELDS/MAJORS: Bible Studies

Awards are available for full-time students at Cedarville College majoring in Bible studies. Priority given to a student with cystic fibrosis or a learning disability. Must have a GPA of at least 2.0. Write to the address below for more information.

Cedarville College
Financial Aid Office
P.O. Box 601
Cedarville, OH 45314

955

Christian Record Services Scholarships

AMOUNT: $500 (max) **DEADLINE:** Apr 1
FIELDS/MAJORS: All Areas Of Study

Scholarships for legally blind, undergraduate students. Awards are to assist students in becoming more independent and self-supportive. Write to the address shown for details.

Christian Record Services
4444 S. 52nd St.
Box 6097
Lincoln, NE 68506

956

Christopher E. Evangel Memorial Scholarship

AMOUNT: Varies **DEADLINE:** Mar 1
FIELDS/MAJORS: Computer Or Electrical Engineering

Awards are available at the University of New Mexico for junior, senior, or graduate level computer or electrical engineering majors with a minimum GPA of 2.8 and financial need. Write to the address below for more information.

University Of New Mexico, Albuquerque
Office Of Financial Aid
Albuquerque, NM 87131

957

Christopher Hughes Memorial Scholarship

AMOUNT: Varies **DEADLINE:** Feb 1
FIELDS/MAJORS: Agricultural Business Mgmt., Agricultural Ed., International Agriculture

Student must be a junior or senior majoring in agricultural business management and agricultural education or international agriculture. Must have a GPA of 2.5 or better. Write to the address below for more information.

California State Polytechnic University, Pomona
College Of Agriculture
Building 2, Room 215
Pomona, CA 91768

958

Christopher Love Scholarship

AMOUNT: Varies **DEADLINE:** Mar 15
FIELDS/MAJORS: All Areas Of Study

Awards open to Teikyo Post students who have made significant community service contributions involving minority youth within an urban setting, and have a strong commitment toward pursuing academic excellence on the graduate and undergraduate levels. For continuing students only. Write to the address below for more information.

Teikyo Post University
Office Of Financial Aid
800 Country Club Road
Waterbury, CT 06723

959

Christopher McGee Award

AMOUNT: Varies **DEADLINE:** Mar 1
FIELDS/MAJORS: Sociology, Criminology, Criminal Justice

Awards are available at the University of New Mexico for juniors and seniors studying sociology, criminology, or criminal justice. Awards are offered each spring. Contact the department of sociology for more information.

University Of New Mexico, Albuquerque
Office Of Financial Aid
Albuquerque, NM 87131

960

Christopher Newport Single Parent Scholarship

AMOUNT: Varies **DEADLINE:** Apr 1
FIELDS/MAJORS: All Areas Of Study

Awards for students who are full-time juniors or seniors with at least thirty credit hours earned at CNU and a GPA of 2.0. Recipients must be working single parents, male or female, with a dependent child or children. Write to the address below for more information.

Christopher Newport University
Office Of Financial Aid
50 Shoe Lane
Newport News, VA 23606

961

Chrysalis Scholarship

AMOUNT: $750 **DEADLINE:** Feb 28
FIELDS/MAJORS: Geoscience Fields

Scholarships available to women who are candidates for an advanced degree in a geoscience field. Applicants must have had their education interrupted for at least one year. Scholarship is to be used for typing, drafting, childcare, or whatever it takes to complete the thesis. Write to the address below for further details.

Association For Women Geoscientists Foundation
G & H Production
518 17th St. #930
Denver, CO 80202

962

Chrysler Corporation Fund Scholarship Program

AMOUNT: $1,000–$5,000 **DEADLINE:** Feb 15
FIELDS/MAJORS: All Areas Of Study

Scholarship are available to children age 21 or under of regular full-time employees, retirees or deceased employees of Chrysler corporation and its U.S. based subsidiaries. Approximately 125 awards per year. Write to the address below for more information.

Citizens' Scholarship Foundation Of America, Inc.
P.O. Box 297
St. Peter, MN 56082

963

Chrysler Junior Golf Scholarship Program

AMOUNT: $1,000 **DEADLINE:** Oct 1
FIELDS/MAJORS: All Areas Of Study

Awards for junior high or high school students with academic ability and extracurricular activities (including golf). Based on academics, recommendations, and a personal statement. Write to the address below for more information.

Chrysler Junior Golf Program Headquarters
Golf Scholarship
75 Rockefeller Plaza, 6th Floor
New York, NY 10019

964

Chuck Hall Star Of Tomorrow Scholarship

AMOUNT: $1,000 **DEADLINE:** Jan 15
FIELDS/MAJORS: All Areas Of Study

Awards are available for males age 21 or under who are amateur bowlers. Must be at least a senior in high school or attending college. For members of the ABC/WIBC/YABA bowling leagues. Send a SASE to the address below for more information.

American Bowling Congress
Young American Bowling Alliance
5301 S. 76th St.
Greendale, WI 53129

965

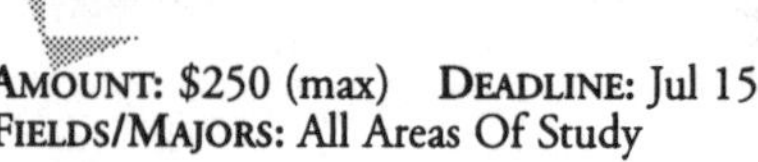

Church Matching Grant

AMOUNT: $250 (max) **DEADLINE:** Jul 15
FIELDS/MAJORS: All Areas Of Study

Matching scholarships available at Sterling for undergraduate full-time students who receive a scholarship from their church. Write to the address below for details.

Sterling College
Financial Aid Office
Sterling, KS 67579

966

Church Matching Scholarship

AMOUNT: $200 **DEADLINE:** Mar 10
FIELDS/MAJORS: Ministerial Studies

Awards for full-time ministerial students at Bluefield College. Write to the address below for more information.

Bluefield College
Financial Aid Office
3000 College Drive
Bluefield, VA 24605

967

CIAR Postdoctoral Fellowship

AMOUNT: $30,000 (max) **DEADLINE:** Oct 31
FIELDS/MAJORS: Indoor Air Research

Fellowship grants are awarded to individuals for the purpose of providing stipends in support of postdoctoral candidates engaged in research of indoor air. Applicants must hold the Ph.D. or the M.D. at the time of the award. Write to the address below for more information.

Center For Indoor Air Research
1099 Winterson Road
Suite 280
Linthicum, MD 21090

968

Ciba-Geigy Annual Prestige Chemistry Scholarship

AMOUNT: $6,000 **DEADLINE:** Mar 1
FIELDS/MAJORS: Chemistry

Scholarship for entering freshmen with outstanding academic potential. Renewable for three years. Contact the financial aid office at the address below for details.

Clemson University
Financial Aid Office
G01 Sikes Hall
Clemson, SC 29634

969

CIC Minorities Fellowships Program

AMOUNT: $11,000 + Tuition **DEADLINE:** Dec 1
FIELDS/MAJORS: Social Sciences, Humanities, Sciences, Mathematics, Engineering

Doctoral fellowships for U.S. citizens who are African American, American Indians, Mexican Americans, or Puerto Ricans, who are accepted into a Ph.D. program at one of the eligible universities.

Write for complete details or call toll-free between 9 am and 4 pm EST at (800) 457-4420.

Committee On Institutional Cooperation
CIC Predoctoral Fellowship Program
Indiana University, 803 East Eighth St.
Bloomington, IN 47408

970

Cindy Esther Moncarz Scholarship

AMOUNT: Varies **DEADLINE:** None Specified
FIELDS/MAJORS: Accounting

Awards for students in their sophomore, junior, or senior year in the Department of Accounting. Contact the Department of Accounting and Information Services for more details and an application.

University Of Massachusetts, Amherst
Department Of Accounting
Information Services
Amherst, MA 01003

971

CIRES Visiting Fellowship

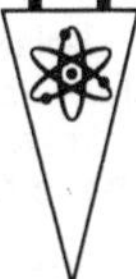

AMOUNT: $27,000 (average) **DEADLINE:** Jan 15
FIELDS/MAJORS: Environmental Sciences, Atmospheric Chemistry, Remote Sensing

One-year visiting fellowship for senior scientists and recent Ph.D. recipients in the fields of study above. Preference is given to candidates with research experience at institutions outside the Boulder scientific community. Write to Dr. Howard P. Hanson at the address below for more details.

Cooperative Institute For Research In Environmental Sciences
CIRES Visiting Fellows Program
University Of Colorado
Boulder, CO 80309

972

Citizenship Scholarship

AMOUNT: $1,000 **DEADLINE:** Apr 1
FIELDS/MAJORS: All Areas Of Study

Scholarships for students at Kent State who display excellent citizenship through community activities or social awareness activities, and have a superior academic record. Contact the financial aid office at your campus for details.

Kent State University, Tuscarawas Campus
Financial Aid Office
University Drive, NE
New Philadelphia, OH 44663

973

Civil And Environmental Engineering Scholarships

AMOUNT: Varies **DEADLINE:** Mar 1
FIELDS/MAJORS: Civil And Environmental Engineering

Awards for students studying civil or environmental engineering at UMass. Includes the William W. Boyer, Stanley F. Gizienski, and Merit P. White scholarships. Contact the Department Head, Civil and Environmental Engineering, for more information.

University Of Massachusetts, Amherst
255 Whitmore Administration Bldg.
Box 38230
Amherst, MA 01003

974

Civil Engineering Departmental Scholarships

AMOUNT: Varies **DEADLINE:** Feb 1
FIELDS/MAJORS: Civil Engineering

Scholarships are available at the University of Utah for full-time students enrolled in a civil engineering program. Write to the address below for details.

University Of Utah
Janice Sherwood
3220 Merrill Engineering Building
Salt Lake City, UT 84112

975

Civil Engineering Honors Scholarships

AMOUNT: $500–$1,000 **DEADLINE:** Feb 15
FIELDS/MAJORS: Civil Engineering

Scholarships are available at the University of Iowa for full-time entering freshmen majoring in civil engineering. Based upon test scores, GPA and high school activities. Write to the address listed below for information.

University of Iowa
Dept. Of Civil & Environmental Engineering
1134 Engineering Building
Iowa City, IA 52245

976

Clara Carter Higgins Conservation Scholarship

AMOUNT: $1,000–$1,500 **DEADLINE:** Feb 15
FIELDS/MAJORS: Environmental Studies/Ecology

Award is open to students who wish to attend a summer course in environmental studies. Send an SASE to the address below for details.

Garden Club Of America
Clara Carter Higgins Scholarship
598 Madison Ave.
New York, NY 10022

977

Clarence A. And Eugenie B. Smith Scholarship Fund

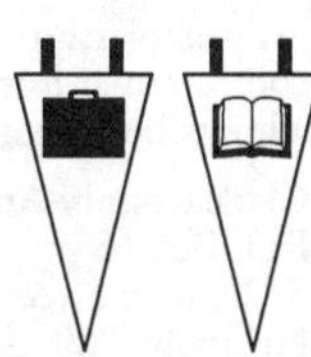

AMOUNT: Varies **DEADLINE:** None Specified
FIELDS/MAJORS: Marketing, Poetry, Creative Writing

Award for academically qualified students at Mercyhurst who are studying marketing, poetry, or creative writing. Write to the address below for more information.

Mercyhurst College
Financial Aid Office
Glenwood Hills
Erie, PA 16546

978

Clarence Botts Scholarship

AMOUNT: Varies **DEADLINE:** Mar 1
FIELDS/MAJORS: Pre-Med

Awards are available at the University of New Mexico for pre-med juniors or seniors with financial need and satisfactory academic progress. Write to the address below for more information.

University Of New Mexico, Albuquerque
Office Of Financial Aid
Albuquerque, NM 87131

979

Clarence Tabor Memorial Scholarship Award

AMOUNT: $1,500 **DEADLINE:** May 24
FIELDS/MAJORS: Architecture

Scholarship awarded to a student entering the last year of undergraduate studies in architecture. The student must reside in the Architects League membership area (Bergen, Hudson, Passaic, Sussex, Essex, and Morris counties). Write to the address below for more information.

Architects League Of Northern New Jersey
Albert Zaccone, AIA
P.O. Box 152
Paramus, NJ 07653

980

Clarion University Alumni Association Scholarships

AMOUNT: None Specified **DEADLINE:** None Specified
FIELDS/MAJORS: All Areas Of Study

Scholarships are available to candidates who have completed at least sixteen credits. Two scholarships are awarded to children of university graduates. Contact the director of alumni relations for more information.

Clarion University
104 Egbert Hall
Office Of Financial Aid
Clarion, PA 16214

981

Clark County Association For Home & Community Scholarship

AMOUNT: $250 **DEADLINE:** May 31
FIELDS/MAJORS: All Areas Of Study

Two scholarships for residents of Clark County, WI who have completed at least one year of college. Contact the office at the address below for details.

Clark County Association For Home & Community
P.O. Box 68
517 Court Street, Room 104
Neillsville, WI 54456

982

Clark E. Dehaven Scholarship Trust

AMOUNT: $1,500 **DEADLINE:** Mar 15
FIELDS/MAJORS: Food Service

Award for sophomores, juniors, or seniors who are majoring in a food service field or who plan to enter a food service career. Applicants must be enrolled in a college or university that is a member of the NACUFS and have a GPA of 2.75 or better. For U.S. or Canadian citizens only. Write to the address below for more information.

National Associaiton Of College And University Food Services
1405 S. Harrison Road, Suite 303
Manly Miles Building, Michigan State Univ.
East Lansing, MI 48824

983

Clark Fellowships

AMOUNT: Up To $4,500/month **DEADLINE:** Mar 15
FIELDS/MAJORS: English Culture, Classical Studies

Pre- and postdoctoral residential fellowships for advanced study and research at the Clark Library. ASECS/Clark Fellowships are restricted to members of the American Society for eighteenth-century studies. Includes the Clark Predoctoral Fellowship and the ASECS/Clark Fellowship. Write to the address below for details.

UCLA William Andrews Clark Memorial Library
Fellowship Coordinator
2520 Cimarron St.
Los Angeles, CA 90018

984

Class Of '42 Memorial Scholarships

AMOUNT: Varies **DEADLINE:** Varies
FIELDS/MAJORS: All Areas Of Study

Scholarships are available at the University of New Mexico for full-time juniors and seniors with a GPA of at least 3.20 who are involved in campus activities and who demonstrate financial need. Write to the address listed below for information.

University Of New Mexico, Albuquerque
Student Financial Aid Office
Mesa Vista Hall North, Room 1044
Albuquerque, NM 87131

985

Class Of 1936/Lanphear Scholarship

AMOUNT: Varies **DEADLINE:** Mar 1
FIELDS/MAJORS: All Areas Of Study

Awards for undergraduate students at UMass with a GPA of 3.0 or higher and financial need of greater than $4,000. Students must file a FAFSA as soon as possible after January 1 and before the March 1 financial aid priority consideration date. You will automatically be considered for this scholarship if you are enrolled at the university and apply for financial aid. Separate applications, requests, or inquiries are not required and cannot be honored.

University Of Massachusetts–Amherst
Office Of Financial Aid Services
255 Whitmore Admin. Bldg., Box 38230
Amherst, MA 01003

986

Class Of 1937 Scholarship

AMOUNT: Varies **DEADLINE:** None Specified
FIELDS/MAJORS: All Areas Of Study

Award given to an academically qualified junior or senior who needs financial assistance. Write to the address below for more information.

Mercyhurst College
Financial Aid Office
Glenwood Hills Erie, PA 16546

987

Class Of 1938 Scholarship

AMOUNT: Varies **DEADLINE:** Mar 1
FIELDS/MAJORS: All Areas Of Study

Awards for juniors or seniors at UMass with a GPA of 3.0 or better. Recipient must demonstrate financial need for at least 30% of the cost of attending UMass. Students must file a FAFSA as soon as possible after January 1 and before the March 1 financial aid priority consideration date. You will automatically be considered for this scholarship if you are enrolled at the University and apply for financial aid. Separate applications, requests, or inquiries are not required and cannot be honored.

University Of Massachusetts–Amherst
Office Of Financial Aid Services
255 Whitmore Admin. Bldg., Box 38230
Amherst, MA 01003

988

Class Of 1956 Merit Scholarship

AMOUNT: Varies **DEADLINE:** Mar 1
FIELDS/MAJORS: All Areas Of Study

Awards for incoming freshmen at UMass based on academic merit. Preference is given to descendants of the Class of 1956. Students must file a FAFSA as soon as possible after January 1 and before the March 1 financial aid priority consideration date. You will automatically be considered for this scholarship if you are enrolled at the University and apply for financial aid. Separate applications, requests, and inquiries are not required and cannot be honored.

University Of Massachusetts–Amherst
Office Of Financial Aid Services
255 Whitmore Admin. Bldg., Box 38230
Amherst, MA 01003

989

Class Of 1968 Scholarship

AMOUNT: Varies **DEADLINE:** Mar 1
FIELDS/MAJORS: All Areas Of Study

Awards for Massachusetts residents at UMass. Applicants must be children affected by the Vietnam war or children of Southeast Asian descent. Must have financial need. Students must file a FAFSA as soon as possible after January 1 and before the March 1 financial aid priority consideration date. You will automatically be considered for this scholarship if you are enrolled at the university and apply for financial aid. Separate applications, requests, or inquiries are not required and cannot be honored.

University Of Massachusetts–Amherst
Office Of Financial Aid Services
255 Whitmore Admin. Bldg., Box 38230
Amherst, MA 01003

990

Class Of 1968 Scholarship

AMOUNT: $125 **DEADLINE:** Feb 1
FIELDS/MAJORS: All Areas Of Study

Applicants must demonstrate financial need, academic achievement and activities. Use Bloomsburg University scholarship application. Contact Mrs. Kishbaugh, Financial Aid Office, for further information.

Bloomsburg University
19 Ben Franklin Hall
400 E. Second St.
Bloomsburg, PA 17815

991

Claude Goodrich Scholarship

AMOUNT: None Specified **DEADLINE:** None Specified
FIELDS/MAJORS: Aviation, Flight Training

Award for a nongraduating flight training student who has demonstrated maturity, responsibility, and an avid interest in aviation. Write to the address below for more details.

Daniel Webster College
Financial Assistance Office
20 University Dr.
Nashua, NH 03063

992

Claudius G. And Katherine Earnest Clemmer Scholarship

AMOUNT: None Specified **DEADLINE:** None Specified
FIELDS/MAJORS: Teaching/Education

Scholarships for full-time juniors, seniors or graduate students at East Tennessee State who show great promise as a teacher. Contact the Dean of the College of Education or the Office of Financial Aid for details.

East Tennessee State University
Office Of Financial Aid
Box 70722
Johnson City, TN 37614

993

Claver Scholarships And Grants

AMOUNT: Varies **DEADLINE:** Jan 15
FIELDS/MAJORS: All Areas Of Study

Awards for full-time African American Loyola undergraduate students. Based on academic potential, community service, or financial need. Write to the address below for additional information.

Loyola College In Maryland
Director Of Financial Aid
4501 North Charles St.
Baltimore, MD 21210

994

Clayton Carpenter Scholarship

AMOUNT: None Specified **DEADLINE:** None Specified
FIELDS/MAJORS: Psychology

Scholarships for psychology majors at East Tennessee State University. Contact the Department of Human Development and Learning or the Office of Financial Aid for details.

East Tennessee State University
Office Of Financial Aid
Box 70722
Johnson City, TN 37614

995

Clayton H. Brace Scholarship

AMOUNT: None Specified **DEADLINE:** Nov 30
FIELDS/MAJORS: Communications

Scholarships are available at UCSD for entering freshmen students who plan to major in communications. Write to the address listed below for information.

University Of California San Diego
Student Financial Services
9500 Gilman Drive
La Jolla, CA 92093

996

Clear Creek Valley Medical Society Scholarships

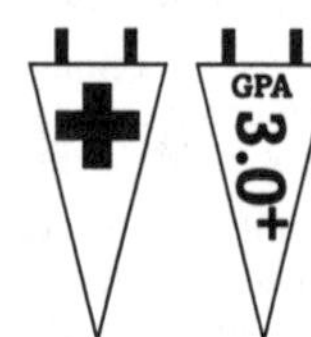

AMOUNT: Varies **DEADLINE:** Apr 15
FIELDS/MAJORS: Health-Related Fields

Scholarships for students in health-related fields of study who reside in one of Jefferson, Clear Creek, Gilpin, or southwestern Adams counties in Colorado. Based on need, a GPA of at least 3.0, and recommendations. Write to the address below for details.

Clear Creek Valley Medical Society
1420 Vance Street, Suite 100
Lakewood, CO 80215

997

Clemson-Palmetto Fellows Scholarships

AMOUNT: $2,500 **DEADLINE:** Mar 1
FIELDS/MAJORS: All Areas Of Study

Scholarships offered competitively to outstanding entering freshmen who are South Carolina residents. Selection based on academic credentials. Renewable. Contact the financial aid office at the address below for details.

Clemson University
Financial Aid Office
G01 Sikes Hall
Clemson, SC 29634

998

Clergy And Synod Grants

AMOUNT: 15% Of Tuition **DEADLINE:** None Specified
FIELDS/MAJORS: All Areas Of Study

Renewable scholarships for dependent, unmarried children of ordained ministers or missionaries. For full-time study. Contact the office of admissions for details.

Geneva College
Office Of Admissions
Beaver Falls, PA 15010

999

Cleve Hamm Scholarship

AMOUNT: $900 **DEADLINE:** Mar 1
FIELDS/MAJORS: Journalism, Communications, Advertising, Public Relations

Must be a junior or senior attending the University of Florida. Must have at least a 2.8 GPA and be studying in one of the areas above. Write to the address below for details.

University Of Florida
Scholarship & Placement Director
2070 Weimer Hall
Gainesville, FL 32611

1000

Cleveland Forestry Scholarship

AMOUNT: None Specified **DEADLINE:** Mar 1
FIELDS/MAJORS: Forestry

Scholarship for entering freshmen with outstanding academic potential. Renewable for three years. Contact the financial aid office at the address below for details.

Clemson University
Financial Aid Office
G01 Sikes Hall
Clemson, SC 29634

1001

Cleveland Legacy Scholarships

AMOUNT: $500–$1,000 **DEADLINE:** Mar 15
FIELDS/MAJORS: Travel And Tourism, Hotel/Motel Management

Awards for Ohio juniors or seniors in one of the areas listed above who are enrolled in a four-year college. Must have a GPA of 3.0 or better. For study anywhere in North America. Students enrolled in a two-year college are also eligible. Write to the address below for more information.

National Tour Foundation
546 East Main St.
P.O. Box 3071
Lexington, KY 40596

1002

Clinical Fellowships

AMOUNT: $30,000–$45,000 **DEADLINE:** Oct 1, Sep 1
FIELDS/MAJORS: Medical Research-Cystic Fibrosis

Fellowships for early-career M.D.s and Ph.D.s interested in preparing for a career in academic medicine. Applicants must be eligible for board certification in pediatrics or internal medicine by the time the fellowship begins. Awards are $30,000 (first year), $31,000 (second year) and up to $45,000 (optional third year with $10,000 being applied to research costs). Applicants must be U.S. citizens or permanent residents. Write to the address below for more information.

Cystic Fibrosis Foundation
Office Of Grants Management
6931 Arlington Rd.
Bethesda, MD 20814

1003

Clinical Research Grants

AMOUNT: $50,000 (max) **DEADLINE:** Oct 1
FIELDS/MAJORS: Medical Research-Cystic Fibrosis

These awards offer support of small or pilot/feasibility clinical research projects directly related to CF treatment and care. Projects may address diagnostic or therapeutic methods. Applicants must demonstrate access to a sufficient number of CF patients and appropriate controls. Up to $50,000 per year for up to three years may be requested. Write to the address below for details.

Cystic Fibrosis Foundation
Office Of Grants Management
6931 Arlington Rd.
Bethesda, MD 20814

1004 Clinical Training Fellowship

AMOUNT: $834/month (max) **DEADLINE:** Jan 15
FIELDS/MAJORS: Psychology, Clinical

Fellowships for minority doctoral students of psychology who are specializing in clinical training. Must be a U.S. citizen or permanent resident enrolled in a full-time academic program. Write to the address below for more information.

American Psychological Association
750 First Street, NE
Washington, DC 20002

1005 Clinton And Leta Reed Scholarship

AMOUNT: $450 **DEADLINE:** Mar 31
FIELDS/MAJORS: All Areas Of Study

Student must be a full-time junior or senior with a GPA of 3.0 or better. Write to the address below for more information.

Southwest Missouri State University
Office Of Financial Aid
901 South National Ave.
Springfield, MO 65804

1006 Clyde R. Johnson Award

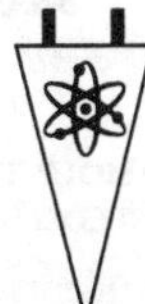

AMOUNT: Varies **DEADLINE:** None Specified
FIELDS/MAJORS: Chemistry

Awards are available at Portland State University for top-ranked chemistry majors. Academic excellence is a primary consideration. Contact the chemistry department at the address below for more information.

Portland State University
Chemistry Department
262 Science Building 2
Portland, OR 97207

1007 Clyde Russell Scholarship Fund

AMOUNT: $10,000 (max) **DEADLINE:** Feb 1
FIELDS/MAJORS: Nature

Three different awards are awarded to high school seniors, full or part-time students, and for citizens of Maine pursuing further educational/cultural opportunities majoring in nature. All awardees must be citizens of Maine. Write to the address below for more information.

Maine Education Association
P.O. Box 2457
Augusta, ME 04338

1008 Coast Guard Mutual Assistance Education Grants

AMOUNT: Varies **DEADLINE:** Mar 10
FIELDS/MAJORS: All Areas Of Study

Grants for dependents of Coast Guard members in one of the following categories: active duty, retired, or deceased while on active duty or retired. For undergraduate study in a school accredited by the department of education. Must have a GPA of at least 2.0. Write to the address below for more details.

U.S. Coast Guard
Commandant (G-ZMA)
2100 2nd St., NW
Washington, DC 20593

1009 Coca Cola Athletic Scholarship

AMOUNT: Tuition And Fees **DEADLINE:** None Specified
FIELDS/MAJORS: All Areas Of Study

Awards for students at Mesa State College who are active in the volleyball program. Contact the athletic department for further details.

Mesa State College
Financial Aid Office
P.O. Box 2684
Grand Junction, CO 81501

1010 Coca Cola Clemson Scholars Program

AMOUNT: $2,500 **DEADLINE:** Mar 1
FIELDS/MAJORS: All Areas Of Study

Scholarship offered to each top-ranked minority and non-minority South Carolina high school senior. Renewable for three years if recipient maintains a minimum GPA of 2.5. Contact the Financial Aid Office at the address below for details.

Clemson University
Financial Aid Office
G01 Sikes Hall
Clemson, SC 29634

1011 Coca Cola Clemson-Independent School Scholars Program

AMOUNT: $2,500 **DEADLINE:** Mar 1
FIELDS/MAJORS: All Areas Of Study

Scholarships offered competitively to students attending South Carolina high schools. Selection based on academic credentials and nominations from high school principals. Renewable for three years. Contact the financial aid office at the address below for details.

Clemson University
Financial Aid Office
G01 Sikes Hall
Clemson, SC 29634

1012 Coffee, Sugar & Cocoa Exchange, Inc. Scholarships

AMOUNT: $1,000 **DEADLINE:** Feb 15
FIELDS/MAJORS: Agricultural Economics, Dairy Industry

Scholarships are available for FFA members pursuing a four-year degree in agricultural economics or dairy studies. Write to the address below for details.

National FFA Foundation
Scholarship Office
P.O. Box 15160
Alexandria, VA 22309

1013

Cole/Stewart Scholarship

Amount: $3,000 (max) **Deadline:** Mar 1
Fields/Majors: All Areas Of Study

Scholarships are available for undergraduate students who were raised by gay/lesbian parents who wish to pursue their education at an accredited college, university, or vocational school. Must be under the age of 25. Write to the address listed below for information.

GSBA/Pride Scholarships
2033 Sixth Avenue, Suite 804
Seattle, WA 98121

1014

Coles-Moultrie Electric Cooperative Scholarships

Amount: $500 **Deadline:** May 28
Fields/Majors: All Areas Of Study

Scholarships for members or dependent child of member of the co-op. Four scholarships are awarded. Applicants who are children of subscribers of the co-op must be under 21 years old. Write to the attention of Sandra Fisher at the address below for details. Applications are also sent to area colleges.

Coles-Moultrie Electric Cooperative
P.O. Box 709
Mattoon, IL 61938

1015

Colgate "Bright Smiles, Bright Futures" Minority Scholarships

Amount: None Specified **Deadline:** Apr 1
Fields/Majors: Dental Hygiene

Awarded to members of a minority group(s) currently under represented in dental hygiene programs. Two awards per year. Write to the address below for more information.

American Dental Hygienists' Association Institute For Oral Health
444 North Michigan Ave., Suite 3400
Chicago, IL 60611

1016

Colgate Scholarships For Academic Excellence

Amount: None Specified **Deadline:** Apr 1
Fields/Majors: Dental Hygiene

Awarded to certificate/associate and baccalaureate degree candidates with a minimum dental hygiene GPA of 3.5 or better. Six awards per year. Write to the address below for more information.

American Dental Hygienists' Association Institute For Oral Health
444 North Michigan Ave., Suite 3400
Chicago, IL 60611

1017

Collaborative Projects & Fellowships At The National Humanities Center

Amount: Varies **Deadline:** Oct 15
Fields/Majors: Humanities

Two or three qualified scholars commit themselves to working with the center on a proposal to the NEH or other funding sources and will spend 50% of their time on the collaborative project during their residency at the center. This project will not displace fellowships that might be funded under a regular fellowship program. Must hold Ph.D. or have equivalent accomplishments. Write to the address below for more information.

National Humanities Center
Fellowship Program
P.O. Box 12256
Research Triangle Pk, NC 27709

1018

College Of Aeronautics Scholarship

Amount: $3,000 **Deadline:** Mar 12
Fields/Majors: Aircraft Repair, Avionics

Scholarships for students in a two-year avionics program. Write to the AEA for information on these and other awards (fourteen total) offered by the AEA.

Aircraft Electronics Association Educational Foundation
P.O. Box 1981
Independence, MO 64055

1019

College Of Applied Science And Technology Scholarships

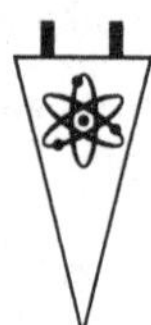

Amount: Varies **Deadline:** Mar 1
Fields/Majors: Applied Sciences And Technology

Scholarships for students at Black Hills State University who are enrolled in the College of Applied Sciences and Technology. Individual award requirements may vary. Write to the address below for more information.

Black Hills State University
Office Of Financial Aid
University Station, Box 9509
Spearfish, SD 57799

1020

College Of Business Administration Lower-Division Scholarship

Amount: $500 **Deadline:** None Specified
Fields/Majors: Business

Students must be freshmen or sophomore COBA majors with outstanding academic records and financial need. Contact the COBA office for more information.

Southwest Missouri State University
Office Of Financial Aid
901 South National Ave.
Springfield, MO 65804

1021

College Of Business Administration Scholarships

Amount: $600–$2,000 **Deadline:** Mar 1
Fields/Majors: Business

Scholarships are available at the University of Iowa for full-time undergraduate business majors. Award requirements will vary. Includes the John F. Murray, H.R. & Alberta Ponder, John A. Schneider Memorial, Richard C. Sheehan, Margaret Shriner, Earl

A. Wimmer, and Robert A. Young Memorial Scholarships. Write to the address listed below for information.

University of Iowa
College Of Business Admin., Suite W160
108 Pappajohn Business Admin. Bldg.
Iowa City, IA 52245

1022

College Of Business Administration Transfer Scholarship

AMOUNT: None Specified **DEADLINE:** None Specified
FIELDS/MAJORS: Business

Student must be a full-time COBA major who has completed at least sixty credit hours from an accredited community college with a GPA of 3.2 or better. Recipient must be a U.S. citizen, with preference give to native Missourians. Contact the COBA office for more information.

Southwest Missouri State University
Office Of Financial Aid
901 South National Ave.
Springfield, MO 65804

1023

College Of Business Scholarship

AMOUNT: $250 **DEADLINE:** Feb 9
FIELDS/MAJORS: Business

Award for business majors who show academic achievement, financial need, and participation in student activities. Use Bloomsburg University scholarship application. Contact Mr. Eugene Remoff, Dean, College of Business, for further information.

Bloomsburg University
19 Ben Franklin Hall
400 E. Second St.
Bloomsburg, PA 17815

1024

College Of Business Scholarships

AMOUNT: $500–$1,000 **DEADLINE:** Dec 15
FIELDS/MAJORS: All Areas Of Study In The College Of Business

Scholarships for students entering or enrolled in the College of Business at Appalachian State University. Contact the Office of Admissions at the address below for details.

Appalachian State University
Office Of Admissions
Scholarship Section
Boone, NC 28608

1025

College Of Business Scholarships

AMOUNT: Varies **DEADLINE:** None Specified
FIELDS/MAJORS: Business

Scholarships at ETSU for student business majors. Write to the address below for details.

East Tennessee State University
Office Of Financial Aid
Box 70722
Johnson City, TN 37614

1026

College Of Education Awards

AMOUNT: None Specified
DEADLINE: None Specified
FIELDS/MAJORS: Education

Scholarships for graduate students enrolled in the college of education who have a minimum cumulative GPA of 3.0. Write to the address below for further details.

Wayne State University
Dean's Office
Room 441, Education Building
Detroit, MI 48202

1027

College Of Education Graduate Scholarship

AMOUNT: $500 **DEADLINE:** Fall
FIELDS/MAJORS: Education

Scholarships are available at the University of Oklahoma, Norman for full-time doctoral level graduate students, with preference given to those at the dissertation stage. Write to the address listed below for information.

University Of Oklahoma, Norman
College Of Education
Room 105, ECH
Norman, OK 73019

1028

College Of Education Scholarships

AMOUNT: Varies **DEADLINE:** None Specified
FIELDS/MAJORS: Education

Scholarship at ETSU for students pursuing a career in education. Includes the Dr. Scott Honaker, Jr. Memorial Scholarship, Carolyn G. Palmer Scholarship. Requirements vary. Write to the address below for details.

East Tennessee State University
Office Of Financial Aid
Box 70722
Johnson City, TN 37614

1029

College Of Education Undergraduate Scholarship Award

AMOUNT: Varies **DEADLINE:** Feb 17
FIELDS/MAJORS: Education

Scholarships are available at the University of Oklahoma, Norman for full-time education majors, sophomore level or higher, with a GPA of at least 3.0. Write to the address listed below for information.

University Of Oklahoma, Norman
College Of Education, Student Services
Room 137, ECH
Norman, OK 73019

1030

College Of Engineering And Applied Science Endowed

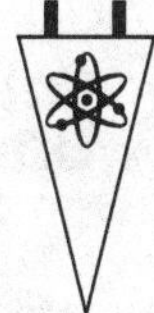

AMOUNT: Varies **DEADLINE:** None Specified
FIELDS/MAJORS: Pulp and Paper Science, Graphic Arts

Scholarships for freshmen through seniors in the Department of

Paper Science and Engineering at WMU. Awarded on either academics or on need. Includes the Lawrence J. Brink Scholarship, Flexographic Technical Association Scholarship, and the Quimby Walstrom Paper Company Scholarship. Write to the address below for more information.

Western Michigan University
College Of Engineering & Applied Science
Dept. Of Paper and Printing Science & Engineering
Kalamazoo, MI 49008

1031

College Of Fine And Applied Arts Scholarships

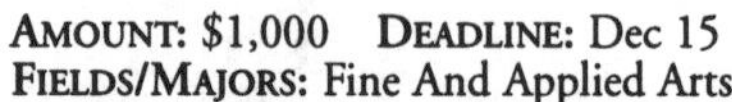

AMOUNT: $1,000 **DEADLINE:** Dec 15
FIELDS/MAJORS: Fine And Applied Arts

Scholarships awarded to incoming freshmen and transfer students enrolling in the College of Fine and Applied Arts. Requires a minimum GPA of 3.25. For students in art, communications, health, leisure, exercise science, home economics, military science, theater, and dance. Entering freshmen must be in the top 25% of their class with an SAT score of 1100 or better. Contact the office of admissions for details.

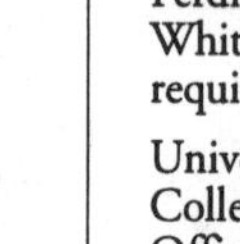

Appalachian State University
Office Of Admissions
Scholarship Section
Boone, NC 28608

1032

College Of Nursing Departmental Scholarships

AMOUNT: Varies **DEADLINE:** Feb 1
FIELDS/MAJORS: Nursing

Scholarships are available at the University of Utah for full-time nursing students. Includes the Jane Dooly Porter Scholarship, and the Arch and Peggy Madsen Scholarship. Individual award requirements may vary. Write to the address below for details.

University Of Utah
Joyce Rathbun
430 Nursing Building
Salt Lake City, UT 84112

1033

College Of Nursing Graduate Departmental Scholarships

AMOUNT: Varies **DEADLINE:** Feb 1
FIELDS/MAJORS: Nursing

Scholarships are available at the University of Utah for full-time graduate nursing students. Includes the Cynthia Shauna Anderson Oncology, Dr. Robert E. & Evelyn M. Long, John Christopher & Mary Catherine Clark Oncology, Joseph & Evelyn Rosenblatt, Linda Derrick Wood, and Nurse Practitioner Scholarships. Individual award requirements may vary. Write to the address below for details.

University Of Utah
Joyce Rathbun
430 Nursing Building
Salt Lake City, UT 84112

1034

College Of Nursing Undergraduate Departmental Scholarships

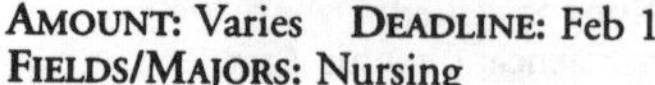

AMOUNT: Varies **DEADLINE:** Feb 1
FIELDS/MAJORS: Nursing

Scholarships are available for full-time undergraduate nursing students. Includes the Allen-Perkins, David & Kathy Anderson, Rosanna Frances Anderson, Bamberger Foundation, Disabled American Veterans, Delores Dore & Eloise Eccles Clara Hansen Jensen, Deanne H. Harmon Memorial, Elva Jex, Alumni, and Herbert I. & Elsa B. Michael Foundation Scholarships. Award requirements may vary. Write to the address below for details.

University Of Utah
Joyce Rathbun
430 Nursing Building
Salt Lake City, UT 84112

1035

College Of Pharmacy Departmental Scholarships

AMOUNT: Varies **DEADLINE:** Feb 1
FIELDS/MAJORS: Pharmacy

Scholarships are available at the University of Utah for full-time sophomore, junior or senior pharmacy majors. Includes the Alumni Association, Burroughs Wellcome Company, Leota Craner, Ferdinand A. & Ruth Anderson Peterson, Ewart A. Swinyard, and Whitmire Distribution Corporation scholarships. Individual award requirements may vary. Write to the address below for details.

University Of Utah
College Of Pharmacy
Office Of Student Affairs
Salt Lake City, UT 84112

1036

College Of Pharmacy Upperclass Departmental Scholarships

AMOUNT: Varies **DEADLINE:** Feb 1
FIELDS/MAJORS: Pharmacy

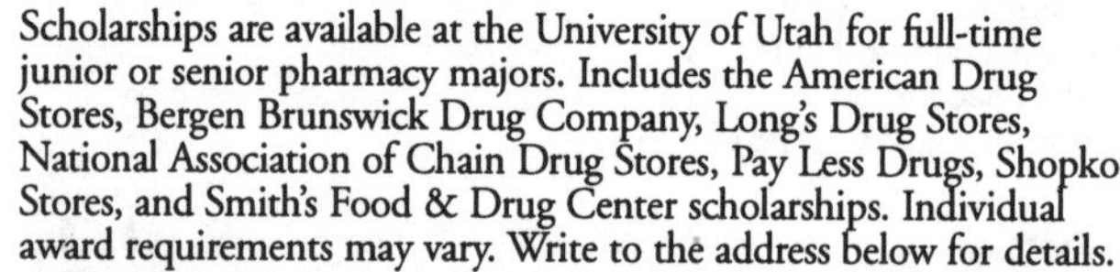

Scholarships are available at the University of Utah for full-time junior or senior pharmacy majors. Includes the American Drug Stores, Bergen Brunswick Drug Company, Long's Drug Stores, National Association of Chain Drug Stores, Pay Less Drugs, Shopko Stores, and Smith's Food & Drug Center scholarships. Individual award requirements may vary. Write to the address below for details.

University of Utah
College Of Pharmacy
Office Of Student Affairs
Salt Lake City, UT 84112

1037

College Of The Siskiyous Resident Scholarships

AMOUNT: Varies **DEADLINE:** Varies
FIELDS/MAJORS: All Areas Of Study

Scholarships are available for residents of Siskiyou County who attend school at the College of the Siskiyous. Individual criteria may differ. Includes the James G. Edwards and Bill Lefevre scholarships. Write to the address below for additional information.

College Of The Siskiyous
Office Of Financial Aid
800 College Ave.
Weed, CA 96094

1038

College Photographer Of The Year Competition

AMOUNT: $100–$1,000 **DEADLINE:** Mar 30
FIELDS/MAJORS: Photojournalism

This is a competition that recognizes outstanding work of students currently working toward a degree. "Dozens" of prizes. Fourteen different categories. Write to Lisa Barnes, Coordinator, or David Rees, CPOY Director, at the University of Missouri, at the address below for further information. Information may also be found at many college newspapers across the country.

National Press Photographers Foundation
Missouri School Of Journalism
105 Lee Hills Hall
Columbia, MO 65211

1039

College Scholarship Assistance Program

AMOUNT: $400–$5,000 **DEADLINE:** None Specified
FIELDS/MAJORS: All Areas Of Study

Scholarships are available for Virginia students in undergraduate study at eligible Virginia colleges or universities. Must demonstrate financial need and be a U.S. citizen or legal resident. Renewable. Write to the address below for complete details.

Virginia Council Of Higher Education
James Monroe Building
101 N. 14th Street
Richmond, VA 23219

1040

Collegiate License Plate Scholarship

AMOUNT: $500 **DEADLINE:** Mar 31
FIELDS/MAJORS: All Areas Of Study

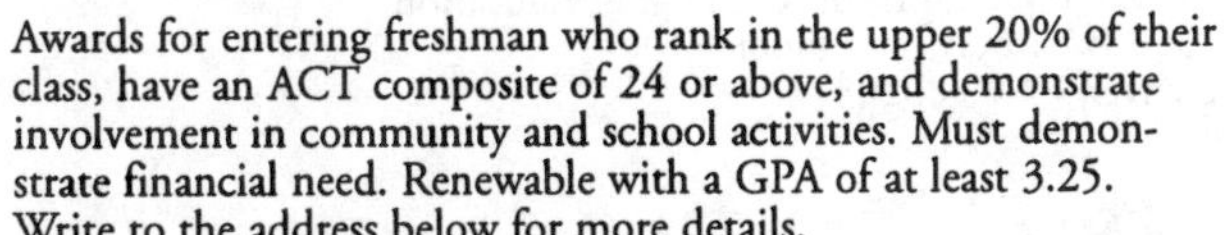

Awards for entering freshman who rank in the upper 20% of their class, have an ACT composite of 24 or above, and demonstrate involvement in community and school activities. Must demonstrate financial need. Renewable with a GPA of at least 3.25. Write to the address below for more details.

Southwest Missouri State University
Financial Aid Office
901 South National Ave.
Springfield, MO 65804

1041

Collegiate Scholarship

AMOUNT: $1,650 **DEADLINE:** Mar 1
FIELDS/MAJORS: All Areas Of Study

Scholarships available at Sterling for undergraduate full-time students who demonstrate a record of leadership in school, church and community. Must have a minimum GPA of at least 3.25 and an ACT score of 22 or SAT score of at least 920. Write to the address below for details.

Sterling College
Financial Aid Office
Sterling, KS 67579

1042

Collegiate Scholarship

AMOUNT: $2,000-$3,850 **DEADLINE:** None Specified
FIELDS/MAJORS: All Areas Of Study

Awards for freshmen who have an ACT score of at least 26 and are in the top 10% of their graduating class. Renewable with a GPA of 3.0 or better. Write to the address below for more information.

Northwestern College
Financial Aid Office
101 7th St., SW
Orange City, IA 51041

1043

Colonel Hayden W. Wagner Memorial Scholarship

AMOUNT: $1,000 **DEADLINE:** Mar 31
FIELDS/MAJORS: All Areas Of Study

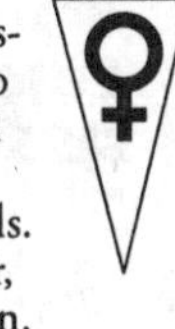

Scholarships for daughters or granddaughters of commissioned officers or warrant officers in the U.S. Army who are on active duty, died while on active duty, or retired after at least 20 years of service. For undergraduate study. Renewable. Write to the address below for details. Specify the officer's name, rank, social security number, and dates of active duty when requesting an application.

Society Of Daughters Of The U.S. Army
Janet B. Otto, Scholarship Chairman
7717 Rockledge Court
West Springfield, VA 22152

1044

Colonel Louisa Spruance Morse CAP Scholarships

AMOUNT: None Specified **DEADLINE:** Apr 1
FIELDS/MAJORS: Aeronautics/Aviation

Applicants must be CAP members or former CAP members currently enrolled in Air Force ROTC at Embry-Riddle University. Write to the address below for details.

Civil Air Patrol
National Headquarters CAP(tt)
Maxwell AFB, AL 36112

1045

Colorado Diversity Grants

AMOUNT: None Specified **DEADLINE:** None Specified
FIELDS/MAJORS: All Areas Of Study

Grants available as part of a statewide effort to increase participation of underrepresented minorities in the Colorado public higher education system. Applicants must be Colorado residents enrolled or intending to enroll in a Colorado institution. Contact your institution for specific eligibility requirements and applications.

Colorado Commission On Higher Education
Colorado History Museum
1300 Broadway, 2nd Floor
Denver, CO 80203

1046

Colorado Funeral Directors Association Scholarships

AMOUNT: $500 **DEADLINE:** None Specified
FIELDS/MAJORS: Mortuary Science

Awards for Colorado residents studying mortuary science. Monies are paid directly to the mortuary science school. Write to the address below for more information.

Colorado Funeral Directors Association
7853 E. Arapahoe Ct., #2100
Englewood, CO 80112

1047

Colorado Graduate Grants

AMOUNT: None Specified **DEADLINE:** None Specified
FIELDS/MAJORS: All Areas Of Study

Grants available for Colorado graduate students who attend a

Colorado institution. Based primarily on financial need. Contact your institution for specific eligibility requirements and applications.

Colorado Commission On Higher Education
Colorado History Museum
1300 Broadway, 2nd Floor
Denver, CO 80203

1048

Colorado Grain & Feed Association Scholarships

Amount: $500 **Deadline:** Apr 1
Fields/Majors: Agriculture

Scholarships for high school seniors who are children of Colorado Grain and Feed Association member employees. Write to the address below for details. Information is sent to high schools throughout the area each year.

Colorado Grain and Feed Association
6210 Brighton Blvd.
Commerce City, CO 80022

1049

Colorado Institute Of Art Scholarships For High School Seniors

Amount: Varies **Deadline:** None Specified
Fields/Majors: All Areas Of Study

Awards for graduating high school seniors planning to attend the Colorado Institute of Art who submit the best slides or original work that follows the requirements of the scholarship bulletin sent to high school guidance counselors each year. Write to the address below for more information.

Colorado Institute Of Art
Financial Aid Office
200 E. 9th Ave.
Denver, CO 80203

1050

Colorado Masons Scholarships

Amount: $5,000 (max) **Deadline:** Varies
Fields/Majors: All Areas Of Study

Scholarships for graduates of Colorado high schools who are planning to attend college in Colorado. Selection is made without regard to masonic affiliation. Applications are available from all Colorado public high schools and all masonic lodges in Colorado. Write to address below for application only if necessary.

Colorado Masons Benevolent Fund Scholarships
Scholarship Correspondent
1130 Panorama Dr.
Colorado Springs, CO 80904

1051

Colorado Nursing Scholarships

Amount: None Specified **Deadline:** None Specified
Fields/Majors: Nursing

Scholarships available to residents of Colorado who wish to pursue nursing education and who agree to practice in Colorado. Applicant must not be in default on an educational loan or owe a repayment of an educational grant. For study at a Colorado institution. Contact the institution you plan to attend for complete information and details about application procedures and deadlines.

Colorado Commission On Higher Education
1300 Broadway, 2nd Floor
Denver, CO 80203

1052

Colorado River Indian Tribes Grants & Scholarships

Amount: Varies **Deadline:** Jun 30, Oct 30
Fields/Majors: All Areas Of Study

For students pursuing degrees from AA through doctorate. Applicants for grants will need to demonstrate financial need. All applicants must be an enrolled member of the Colorado River Indian tribes, be admitted/enrolled at an accredited school, have a minimum GPA of 2.0 ,and have a certificate of Indian blood. Contact the address below for further information/ requirements/applications.

Colorado River Indian Tribes
Career Development Office
Route 1 Box 23-B
Parker, AZ 85344

1053

Colorado Student Grant

Amount: Varies **Deadline:** None Specified
Fields/Majors: All Areas Of Study

Scholarships are available to residents of Colorado who are undergraduate students at a Colorado school with financial need and good academic standing. Contact the institution you plan to attend for complete information and details about application procedures and deadlines.

Colorado Commission On Higher Education
1300 Broadway, 2nd Floor
Denver, CO 80203

1054

Colorado Student Incentive Grant

Amount: $2,500 (max) **Deadline:** None Specified
Fields/Majors: All Areas Of Study

Scholarships are available to residents of Colorado who demonstrate extreme financial need. Must be in good academic standing. For undergraduate study at a Colorado institution. Contact the institution you plan to attend for complete information and details about application procedures and deadlines.

Colorado Commission On Higher Education
1300 Broadway, 2nd Floor
Denver, CO 80203

1055

Colorado Undergraduate Merit And Graduate Fellowships

Amount: None Specified **Deadline:** None Specified
Fields/Majors: All Areas Of Study

Awards available for Colorado students who attend a Colorado institution. Based primarily on academic achievement. Contact your institution for specific eligibility requirements and applications.

Colorado Commission On Higher Education
Colorado History Museum
1300 Broadway, 2nd Floor
Denver, CO 80203

1056

Columbia County Medical Auxiliary Memorial Scholarship

AMOUNT: $250 **DEADLINE:** Feb 9
FIELDS/MAJORS: Nursing

Applicant must have finished first year of nursing program and be a resident of Columbia County. Must have graduated from one of the following high schools: Berwick, Bloomsburg, Benton, Central, Millville, Southern Columbia, Columbia, Montour AVTS, Berwick Heritage Christian, or Bloomsburg Christian School. Must also demonstrate financial need. Use Bloomsburg University scholarship application. Contact Dr. Christine Ali Chnie, Chairperson, Department of Nursing, for further information.

Bloomsburg University
19 Ben Franklin Hall
400 E. Second St.
Bloomsburg, PA 17815

1057

Columbia National Bank Of Chicago College Scholarship Award

AMOUNT: $1,000 **DEADLINE:** Feb 28
FIELDS/MAJORS: All Areas Of Study

Applicant must be a high school senior and reside within one of the boundaries served by Columbia National Bank (north to Devon, south to North Ave., west to Cumberland, and east to Pulaski or north to Golf Rd., south to Oakton St., east to Harlem Ave., and west to the Tri-State Tollway) or be a bank customer. Must be in the upper 1/4 of your class. Ten awards per year. Write to the address below for more information. All applicants must be pursuing a baccalaureate degree.

Columbia National Bank Of Chicago
Community & Public Relations
5250 North Harlem Ave.
Chicago, IL 60656

1058

Columbian Squire Scholarships

AMOUNT: $1,000 **DEADLINE:** None Specified
FIELDS/MAJORS: All Areas Of Study

Scholarships are available at the Catholic University of America for entering freshmen who were Columbian Squires (Knights of Columbus). Write to the address listed below or your local KOC chapter for information.

Catholic University Of America
Office Of Admissions And Financial Aid
Washington, DC 20064

1059

Columbus College Of Art And Design Scholarships

AMOUNT: None Specified **DEADLINE:** None Specified
FIELDS/MAJORS: Art

Awards for undergraduate students at CCAD based on artistic ability. Write to the address below for complete details.

Columbus College Of Art And Design
Financial Aid Office
107 North Ninth St.
Columbus, OH 43215

1060

Combined Health Appeal Of Greater St. Louis Scholarships

AMOUNT: $1,000-$2,000 **DEADLINE:** Apr 10
FIELDS/MAJORS: Medicine, Healthcare, And Related

Scholarships for students in the St. Louis area studying toward a career in healthcare. Geographic area: St. Louis, Jefferson, Warren, Lincoln, Franklin, and St. Charles counties in Missouri and St.Clair, Monroe, Madison, Clinton, and Randolph counties in Illinois. The foundation does not mail out applications. Information is available at your school.

Combined Health Appeal Of Greater St. Louis
Ms. Judy Deutsch, Scholarship Chair
9440 Manchester, Suite 106
St. Louis, MO 63119

1061

Communication Departmental Scholarships

AMOUNT: Varies **DEADLINE:** Feb 1
FIELDS/MAJORS: Communications

Scholarships are available at the University of Utah for full-time students enrolled in a communications program. Write to the address below for details.

University Of Utah
Scholarship Chairperson
301 Leroy Cowles Building
Salt Lake City, UT 84112

1062

Communication Disorder Scholarship

AMOUNT: $500 **DEADLINE:** Mar 1
FIELDS/MAJORS: Communication Disorders

Applicants must be maintaining legal residence in Massachusetts and present a letter of endorsement from sponsoring women's club in your community. For graduate study in communication disorders. Men or women may apply for this scholarship. Write to the address below for details.

General Federation Of Women's Clubs Of Massachusetts
Scholarship Chariman, 245 Dutton Road
P.O. Box 679
Sudbury, MA 01776

1063

Communication Disorders Departmental Scholarships

AMOUNT: Varies **DEADLINE:** Feb 15
FIELDS/MAJORS: Communication Disorders

Scholarships are available at the University of Utah for full-time students enrolled in a communication disorders program. Write to the address below for details.

University Of Utah
Dr. Geary McCandless
1201 Behavior Science Building
Salt Lake City, UT 84112

1064

Communication For Agriculture Scholarships

AMOUNT: $250 **DEADLINE:** Ongoing
FIELDS/MAJORS: Agricultural Communications

Awards are available for rural young people who plan to major in an agricultural communications field which will return them to the rural community. Financial need is not necessary. For undergraduate study. Write to the address below for more information.

Communication For Agriculture
101 E. Lincoln
Fergus Falls, MN 56357

1065

Communication Scholarship For Continuing Students

AMOUNT: $400 **DEADLINE:** None Specified
FIELDS/MAJORS: Communications

Awards for Jacksonville State University continuing students in the field of communications. Contact the head of the communication department for more information.

Jacksonville State University
Financial Aid Office
Jacksonville, AL 36265

1066

Communications Endowed And Private Scholarships

AMOUNT: Varies **DEADLINE:** Feb 15
FIELDS/MAJORS: Communications

Scholarships are available at Evangel for full-time students who will be or are pursuing a degree in communications. Applicants must have a GPA of at least 3.0. Includes the Dr. Nonna D. Dalan Memorial Speech Scholarship, the Society for Collegiate Journalists Scholarship, the Inez H. Spence Memorial Scholarship, and the Communications Alumni Scholarship. Write to the address listed below for information.

Evangel College
Office Of Enrollment
1111 N. Glenstone
Springfield, MO 65802

1067

Communications Intern

AMOUNT: None Specified
DEADLINE: None Specified
FIELDS/MAJORS: Communications, Public Relations, Marketing

Educational background in communications, public relations, or marketing. Strong writing/organizing skills. Ability to communicate with a wide variety of people. Familiarity with IBM computers and on-line networks. For minority students only. Write to the address below for more information.

Nature Conservancy
Post Offfice Square Building
79 Milk St., Suite 300
Boston, MA 02109

1068

Communications Scholarships

AMOUNT: $5,000 **DEADLINE:** May 31
FIELDS/MAJORS: Communications, Journalism

Scholarships for Italian American journalism and communications majors. Based on an essay describing strategies and techniques for "preserving the Italian language and culture in the U.S." 1000 words or less. For undergraduate study. Write to the address below for details.

National Italian American Foundation
Dr. Maria Lombardo, Education Director
1860 Nineteenth Street, NW
Washington, DC 20009

1069

Communications Scholarships

AMOUNT: Varied **DEADLINE:** Varies
FIELDS/MAJORS: All Areas Of Study

Awards for Liberty University students with experience in the fields of debate, yearbook staff, or school newspaper. Renewable. Contact the Liberty University activity advisor for more information.

Liberty University
Office Of Student Financial Aid
Box 20000
Lynchburg, VA 24506

1070

Community College Presidential Scholarship

AMOUNT: $3,000 **DEADLINE:** Varies
FIELDS/MAJORS: All Areas Of Study

Scholarships are available at WMU for transfer students with a GPA of at least 3.5. Contact your graduate college for further information about these programs.

Western Michigan University
Student Financial Aid
3306 Faunce Student Services Building
Kalamazoo, MI 49008

1071

Community College Scholarship

AMOUNT: Tuition And Fees **DEADLINE:** None Specified
FIELDS/MAJORS: All Areas Of Study

Awards for students transferring into SMSU from Missouri public community colleges. Renewable with a GPA of at least 3.25. Write to the address below for more details.

Southwest Missouri State University
Financial Aid Office
901 South National Ave.
Springfield, MO 65804

1072

Community College Scholarships

AMOUNT: $400 **DEADLINE:** Mar 15
FIELDS/MAJORS: All Areas Of Study

Awards for students who transfer to Pittsburg State University who have a GPA of at least 3.5 and forty-five hours of academic work. Write to the address below for more information.

Pittsburg State University
Office Of Academic Affairs
203 Russ Hall
Pittsburg, KS 66762

1073

Comparative Physiology Section Scholander Award

Amount: $100 **Deadline:** None Specified
Fields/Majors: Comparative Physiology Research

Awards are available to students interested in comparative physiology. The recipient must be the first author on the abstract and not more than five years past their highest degree. Write to the address below for more information.

American Psychology Society
9650 Rockville Pike
Bethesda, MD 20814

1074

Competition Scholarships

GPA 3.0+

Amount: $1,000 **Deadline:** None Specified
Fields/Majors: All Areas Of Study

Competition among freshmen in their respective areas of study through exams, auditions, or essays. A schedule of all contests is available from the office of admissions or the provost's office. Renewable upon maintaining a GPA of at least 3.0. Contact the admissions office at the address below during autumn of the senior year of high school for more information.

Alfred University
Student Financial Aid Office
26 N. Main St.
Alfred, NY 14802

1075

Competitive Scholarship

Amount: $100 (min) **Deadline:** None Specified
Fields/Majors: All Areas Of Study

Grants to encourage out of state students who have demonstrated high academic achievement in high school to enroll in public institutions of higher learning in New Mexico. Students must meet certain high school GPA and ACT score requirements. Awarded to high school seniors. Write to the financial aid office at any New Mexico public postsecondary institution.

New Mexico Commission On Higher Education
1068 Cerrillos Rd.
Santa Fe, NM 87501

1076

Competitive Scholarship

GPA 3.0+

Amount: $700 **Deadline:** None Specified
Fields/Majors: All Areas Of Study

Scholarships for entering freshmen who have a high school GPA of at least 3.0 and ACT scores of 27 or SAT scores of 1110. Transfer students are also eligible for this award given they have a GPA of at least 3.25 and a past high school GPA of at least 3.0. For non-residents of New Mexico. Write to the address below for more information.

New Mexico Tech
Admission Office
Socorro, NM 87801

1077

Composers' Symposium Composition Prize

Amount: Varies **Deadline:** Mar 1
Fields/Majors: Composition Music

Awards are available at the University of New Mexico for the winner of an annual competition for best chamber music work composed during the year. Write to the address below for more information.

University Of New Mexico, Albuquerque
Office Of Financial Aid
Albuquerque, NM 87131

1078

Computational Science Fellowship Program

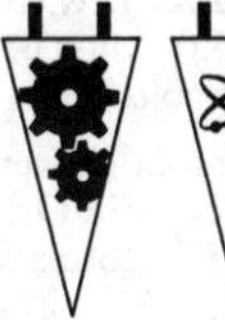

Amount: $18,000–$21,600 **Deadline:** Jan 24
Fields/Majors: Life Or Physical Science, Engineering, Mathematics

Fellowships are available at Iowa State for graduate students who are in their second year of graduate studies (or above) for science or engineering students with career objectives in computational science. Must be a U.S. citizen or permanent resident. Write to the address listed below for information.

Iowa State University
Ames Laboratory
125 S. Third Street, Sherman Place
Ames, IA 50010

1079

Computer Science Departmental Scholarships

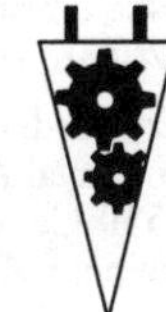

Amount: Varies **Deadline:** Feb 1
Fields/Majors: Computer Science

Scholarships are available at the University of Utah for full-time students enrolled in a computer science program. Write to the address below for details.

University Of Utah
Mary Rawlinson
3190 Merrill Engineering Building
Salt Lake City, UT 84112

1080

Conagra, Inc. Scholarships

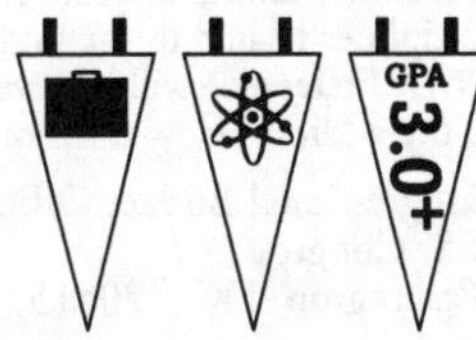

Amount: $1,750 **Deadline:** Feb 15
Fields/Majors: Agribusiness

Scholarships for graduating high school seniors who intend to major in agribusiness at the University of Nebraska-Lincoln. Must be a current, active member of FFA and be in the top 15% of graduating class. Renewable. Write to the address below for details.

National FFA Foundation
Scholarship Office
P.O. Box 15160
Alexandria, VA 22309

1081

Concordia Private Donor Aid

Amount: Varies **Deadline:** None Specified
Fields/Majors: All Areas Of Study

Awards given to full-time undergraduates which are based on

unmet financial eligibility as determined by the FAFSA which you must file. Write to the address below for more information.

Concordia College, Nebraska
Office Of Financial Aid
800 N. Columbia Ave.
Seward, NE 68434

1082

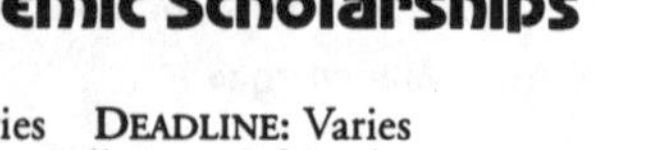

Concordia University Academic Scholarships

AMOUNT: Varies **DEADLINE:** Varies
FIELDS/MAJORS: All Areas Of Study

Award for new students who achieved a high school GPA of at least 3.0. Must be a full-time student and a U.S. citizen. Renewable. Write to the address below for more information.

Concordia University, Irvine
Financial Aid Office
1530 Concordia West
Irvine, CA 92715

1083

Concordia University Lutheran Awards

AMOUNT: Varies **DEADLINE:** Varies
FIELDS/MAJORS: All Areas Of Study

Awards for Concordia students who graduated from a Lutheran high school or who are members of the Aid Association for Lutherans or the Lutheran Brotherhood. Must have a GPA of at least 2.5 and be enrolled in full-time study. For U.S. citizens. Write to the address below for more information.

Concordia University, Irvine
Financial Aid Office
1530 Concordia West
Irvine, CA 92715

1084

Congressional Budget Summer Intern Program

AMOUNT: None Specified **DEADLINE:** Mar 20
FIELDS/MAJORS: Economics, Public Policy

Open to candidates who have quantitative skills and academic training in economics, public policy, and other disciplines related to the budget activities carried out by the CBO. Preference will be given to minority students. Write to the address below for more information.

Congressional Budget Office
U.S. Congress
Washington, DC 20515

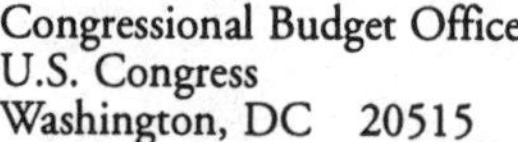

1085

Congressional Fellows Program Science And Engineering Fellowships

AMOUNT: $40,000 **DEADLINE:** Jan 15
FIELDS/MAJORS: Engineering/Science

Two fellowships are offered in the White House Office of Science & Technology: one a senior industrial scientist or engineer with at least fifteen years professional experience; the other, for those with at least five years. Fellows will be expected to apply technical knowledge to formulating public policy. Write to "Science and Technology Programs" at the address below for details.

American Association For The Advancement Of Science
1333 H Street, NW
Washington, DC 20005

1086

Connecticut Association Of Educational Secretaries

AMOUNT: $750 **DEADLINE:** Feb 1
FIELDS/MAJORS: Business, Secretarial

Student must be sponsored by the Connecticut Association of Educational Secretaries and have scholastic achievement and community service activities. Must also be a Connecticut resident. Contact the address below if applicant is already in college, or if a high school senior, see your guidance counselor.

Connecticut Association Of Boards Of Education
Ms. Norma Berry
309 Franklin Ave.
Hartford, CT 06114

1087

Connecticut Broadcasters Association Grant

AMOUNT: $2,000 **DEADLINE:** Varies
FIELDS/MAJORS: Communications, Marketing

Awards for college juniors or seniors who can demonstrate scholastic achievement, and extracurricular activities in electronic media. Must also demonstrate financial need and be a Connecticut resident. Contact your local radio station for further information and an application or write to: The Waterbury Foundation, 156 W. Main St., Waterbury, CT 06702 (enclose $1.75 for postage & handling).

Connecticut Broadcasters Association
The Waterbury Foundation
156 W. Main St.
Waterbury, CT 06702

1088

Connecticut Building Congress Scholarships

AMOUNT: Varies **DEADLINE:** Jul 1
FIELDS/MAJORS: Architecture, Engineering, Construction, Drafting

Awards for high school seniors who can demonstrate financial need, scholastic achievement and extracurricular activities. Must be a Connecticut resident. Contact your high school guidance counselor or the address below for further information and an application.

Connecticut Building Congress
2600 Dixwell Ave.
Hamden, CT 06514

1089

Connecticut Funeral Directors Association Scholarships

AMOUNT: $500 **DEADLINE:** None Specified
FIELDS/MAJORS: Mortuary Science

Awards for Connecticut residents enrolled in a mortuary science school. Write to the address below for more information.

Connecticut Funeral Directors Association
350 Silas Deane Highway, Suite 202
Weathersfield, CT 06109

1090 Connecticut Home Economics Association Scholarships

AMOUNT: $500 **DEADLINE:** Apr 27
FIELDS/MAJORS: Home Economics Related Field

Award for high school senior who can demonstrate scholastic achievement, extracurricular activities, leadership and character. Must be a Connecticut resident. Contact your high school guidance counselor for further information and an application or write to: The Waterbury Foundation, 156 W. Main, Waterbury, CT 06702 (enclose $1.75 for postage & handling).

Connecticut Home Economics Association
The Waterbury Foundation
156 W. Main
Waterbury, CT 06702

1091 Connecticut League For Nursing

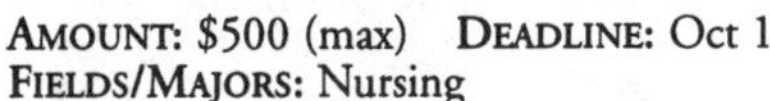

AMOUNT: $500 (max) **DEADLINE:** Oct 1
FIELDS/MAJORS: Nursing

Applicants must be Connecticut residents who are entering their last year of study (2nd year of two-year program, 4th year of four-year program, etc.). Graduate students must have completed 20 credits in an accredited nursing program. Write to the address below for details.

Connecticut League For Nursing
P.O. Box 365
Wallingford, CT 06492

1092 Connecticut Nurserymen's Association, Inc. Scholarships

AMOUNT: $4,000 (max) **DEADLINE:** Mar 15
FIELDS/MAJORS: Agriculture, Landscaping, Nursery Industry

Awards for high school seniors who can demonstrate financial need, extra-curricular activities, scholastic achievement and community service. Must be a Connecticut resident. Contact your high school guidance counselor or Connecticut Nurserymen's Association, Inc., at the address below for further information.

Connecticut Nurserymen's Association, Inc.
P.O. Box 117
Vernon, CT 06066

1093 Connecticut Scholarship Challenge Program

AMOUNT: $500 **DEADLINE:** Mar 15
FIELDS/MAJORS: Travel And Tourism, Hotel/Motel Management

Awards for Connecticut residents in one of the areas listed above who are enrolled in any four-year college. Must have a GPA of 3.0 or better and be in junior or senior year. Write to the address below for more information.

National Tour Foundation
546 East Main St.
P.O. Box 3071
Lexington, KY 40596

1094 Conservation Biology Intern

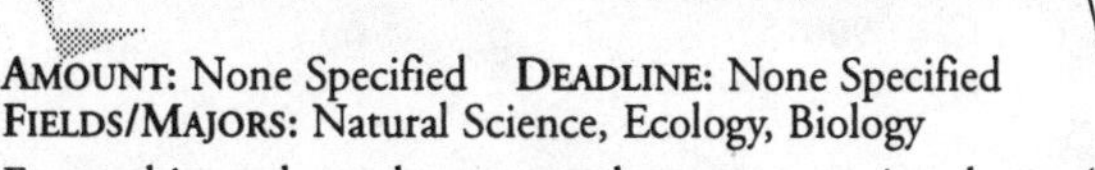

AMOUNT: None Specified **DEADLINE:** None Specified
FIELDS/MAJORS: Natural Science, Ecology, Biology

Engaged in undergraduate or graduate conservation degree (nat-

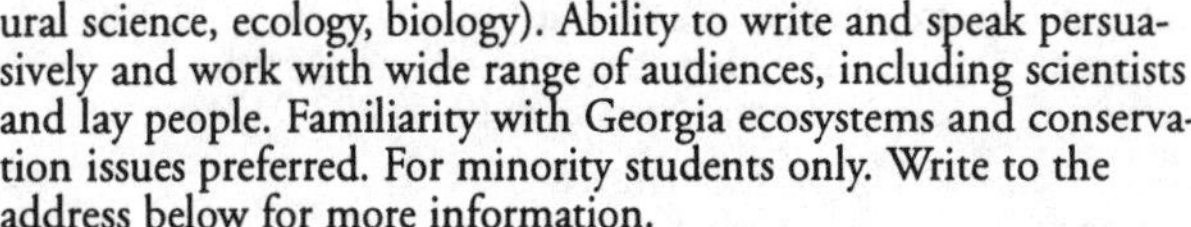

ural science, ecology, biology). Ability to write and speak persuasively and work with wide range of audiences, including scientists and lay people. Familiarity with Georgia ecosystems and conservation issues preferred. For minority students only. Write to the address below for more information.

Nature Conservancy
Jonathan P. Streich, Dir. Of Sci/Steward
1401 Peachtree St., Suite 236
Atlanta, GA 30309

1095 Conservation Management Intern

AMOUNT: None Specified
DEADLINE: None Specified
FIELDS/MAJORS: Conservation, Natural Resources, Environmental Law

Graduate degree in conservation, natural resources or environmental law. Minimum one year prior experience in conservation. Basic understanding of research, monitoring techniques and budgeting. For minority students only. Write to the address below for more information.

Nature Conservancy
Career Development Prog., Human Resources
201 Mission St.
San Francisco, CA 94105

1096 Consortium For Graduate Study In Management

AMOUNT: None Specified **DEADLINE:** Feb 1
FIELDS/MAJORS: Business, Economics

Graduate fellowships for minorities. U.S. citizenship required. Must have received B.A. degree from accredited institution and must submit GMAT scores. Each fellow undertakes the regular MBA curriculum at one of the eleven consortium graduate schools of business. Must be a member of one of the following minority groups: Native American, African American, or Hispanic. Write to the address below for details.

Consortium For Graduate Study In Management
200 S. Hanley Rd., Suite 1102
St. Louis, MO 63105

1097 Constance L. Lloyd, Facmpe Scholarship

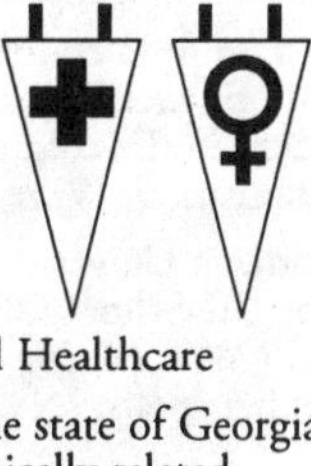

AMOUNT: $1,000 (max) **DEADLINE:** Jun 1
FIELDS/MAJORS: Health Administration, Clinical Healthcare

Award for female students attending school in the state of Georgia who are pursuing either an administrative or clinically related degree in the health care field. Write to the address below for more information.

American College Of Medical Practice Executives
Attn: Ms. Laurie J. Draizen
104 Inverness Terrace East
Englewood, CO 80112

1098 Constance Welsh Memorial Scholarship

AMOUNT: $2,000 **DEADLINE:** Sep 15
FIELDS/MAJORS: Drama/Theater, Children's

Scholarships are available for graduate students who are studying children's theatre, drama, or arts. Must be a resident of North Carolina. Write to the address below or call Ms. Martha Keravuori, NCTC Admin. Director, at (919) 832-9171.

North Carolina Theater Conference
Constance Welsh Scholarship Committee
P.O. Box 33343
Raleigh, NC 27636

1099 Constantinople Armenian Relief Society (C.A.R.S.) Scholarship

AMOUNT: $400–$600 **DEADLINE:** Jul 15
FIELDS/MAJORS: All Areas Of Study

Awards for Armenian students enrolled in an accredited college or university at the sophomore level or above. Based mainly on merit and financial need. Write to the address below for more information.

Constantinople Armenian Relief Society
Mr. Berc Araz
66 Stephenville Parkway
Edison, NJ 08820

1100 Construction Financial Manager's Association Scholarship

AMOUNT: Varies **DEADLINE:** Mar 1
FIELDS/MAJORS: Construction Management

Awards are available at the University of New Mexico for construction management majors from New Mexico with financial need. Write to the address below for more information.

University Of New Mexico, Albuquerque
Office Of Financial Aid
Albuquerque, NM 87131

1101 Construction League Of Indianapolis Construction Advancement Program

AMOUNT: Varies **DEADLINE:** None Specified
FIELDS/MAJORS: Construction

Award for a construction student based on academic achievement and financial need. Preference is given to those pursuing employment in the commercial industry in the Indianapolis region upon graduation. Write to the address below for more information.

Indiana University/Purdue University, Indianapolis
Purdue School Of Technology
799 West Michigan St.
Indianapolis, IN 46202

1102 Consulting Engineers Council Of New Mexico Scholarships

AMOUNT: Varies **DEADLINE:** Mar 1
FIELDS/MAJORS: Engineering

Awards are available at the University of New Mexico for junior or senior students in engineering who have an interest in the consulting engineering profession. Must be a U.S. citizen or permanent resident. Write to the address below for more information.

University Of New Mexico, Albuquerque
Office Of Financial Aid
Albuquerque, NM 87131

1103 Contests Open To PSA Members

AMOUNT: Varies **DEADLINE:** Dec 22
FIELDS/MAJORS: Poetry

Various awards are open to members. Only one submission may be sent per award. All submissions must be unpublished on date of entry and not scheduled for publication by the date of the PSA awards ceremony held in spring. Contact address below for complete information. Be certain to enclose a self-addressed, stamped envelope with your request.

Poetry Society Of America
15 Gramercy Park
New York, NY 10003

1104 Continental Society Daughters Of Indian Wars Scholarship

AMOUNT: $500 **DEADLINE:** Jun 15
FIELDS/MAJORS: Education, Social Service

Scholarships are available to certified tribal members enrolled in one the the areas of study listed above, who plan to work on a reservation upon graduation. Preference will be given to juniors. Must have a GPA of at least 3.0. Write to the address listed below for information.

Continental Society Daughters Of Indian Wars
Miss Eunice T. Connally
206 Springdale Drive
La Grange, GA 30240

1105 Continuing Departmental Scholarship

AMOUNT: Full Tuition **DEADLINE:** Apr 15
FIELDS/MAJORS: Elementary Education

Scholarships are available to resident sophomore, junior and senior students pursuing elementary education with a GPA of 3.5 or better. Must be admitted to the University of Utah. Write to the address below for details.

University Of Utah
Financial Aid And Scholarship Office
105 Student Services Building
Salt Lake City, UT 84112

1106 Continuing Education Scholarships

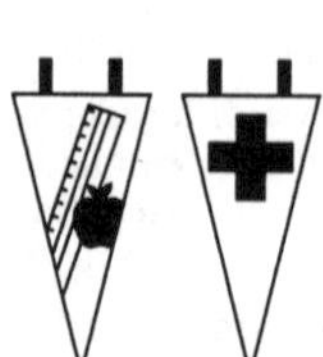

AMOUNT: None Specified **DEADLINE:** Nov 30
FIELDS/MAJORS: Teaching, Nursing

Open to credentialed classroom teachers and school nurses. Send an SASE (legal size) envelope to the address below for an application.

California Congress Of Parents, Teachers, And Students, Inc.
930 Georgia St., P.O. Box 15015
Los Angeles, CA 90015

1107

Contra Costa Central Labor Council Scholarships

Amount: $500 **Deadline:** Feb 12
Fields/Majors: All Areas Of Study

Scholarships for students who are members, or family of members, of an AFL-CIO union affiliated with the Contra Costa CLC. For students currently enrolled at Contra Costa Community College, Diablo Valley, or Los Medanos College (may be used at a four-year school if graduating). Full-time. Ten awards per year. GPA and need considered. Contact your parent's local CLC or write to the address below for details.

Central Labor Council Of Contra Costa County, AFL-CIO
Scholarship Coordinator
P.O. Box 389
Martinez, CA 94553

1108

Cooperative Research Fellowship Program For Minorities

Amount: Tuition & Fees **Deadline:** Jan 15
Fields/Majors: Chemical Engineering, Chemistry, Mathematics, Physics, Also See Below

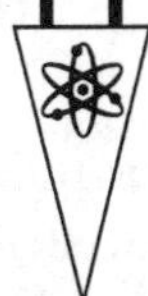

Fellowships are awarded to minority students who are accepted into an accredited doctoral program for the following fall. Eligible fields of study are those listed above as well as communications, materials, or information sciences; computer, electrical, or mechanical engineering; operations research and statistics. Applicants must be U.S. citizens or permanent residents. Write to the address below for complete details.

AT&T Bell Laboratories
600 Mountain Ave., Room 3D-304
Murray Hill, NJ 07974

1109

Coors Pure Water 2000 Fund

Amount: Varies **Deadline:** None Specified
Fields/Majors: Biology, Chemistry, Geosciences

Student must be pursuing a graduate degree in biology, chemistry, or geo-sciences, with water-related emphasis. Contact the college of natural and applied sciences for more information.

Southwest Missouri State University
Office Of Financial Aid
901 South National Ave.
Springfield, MO 65804

1110

Corbut Scholarship

Amount: None Specified **Deadline:** Dec 15
Fields/Majors: Forestry

Scholarships are awarded to forestry majors at any level at UMass. Both scholarship and financial need may be considered in granting this award. Contact the Department Head, Forestry and Wildlife Management, for more information.

University Of Massachusetts, Amherst
Department Head
Forestry And Wildlife Management
Amherst, MA 01003

1111

Corcoran Scholarships

Amount: $2,000 (max) **Deadline:** None Specified
Fields/Majors: All Areas Of Study

Scholarships and grants for students at Corcoran School of Art. Based on talent, academics, and or need. Contact the address below for details.

Corcoran School Of Art
Financial Aid Office
500 17th St., NW
Washington, DC 20006

1112

Cornaro Scholarships

Amount: $1,000 **Deadline:** May 31
Fields/Majors: All Areas Of Study

Scholarship for Italian American women entering or continuing college. Two programs: Agnes E. Vaghi Cornaro Scholarship & NIAF-Cornaro Scholarship. Write to the address below for details.

National Italian American Foundation
Dr. Maria Lombardo, Education Director
1860 19th Street, NW
Washington, DC 20009

1113

Corning Scholarship

Amount: $2,000–$3,000 **Deadline:** Mid-may
Fields/Majors: Optometry

Two awards are available for fourth-year optometry students who submit the best papers of 600-1200 words on any one of a given list of topics decided each year by Corning. Write to the address listed below or contact your department of optometry for information.

American Optometric Foundation
4330 East West Highway, Suite 1117
Bethesda, MD 20814

1114

Corps Scholarships

Amount: $2,000 (total) **Deadline:** None
Fields/Majors: All Areas Of Study

Awards available to Eagle Scouts planning to join the TAMU Corps of Cadets. Funds are awarded at the rate of $500 each year for four years. Selection selection based upon academic performance and demonstrated leadership potential. Applicant must be a U.S. citizen. Twenty awards given per year. Write to the Office of the Commandant, Division of Student Services, at the address below for details. Information may also be obtained by calling Lt. Col. Mark Satterwhite at (800)-TAMU-AGS.

Texas A & M University
Office Of The Commandant
College Station, TX 77843

1115

Correspondents Fund Scholarships In Journalism

Amount: $2,000 **Deadline:** April 28
Fields/Majors: Journalism/Mass Communications

Applicants must be children of print or broadcast media foreign correspondents and pursuing a journalism career. Write to Jennifer H. McGill, Executive Director, at the address below for details.

Association For Education In Journalism And Mass Communication
University Of South Carolina
1621 College St.
Columbia, SC 29208

1116

Cortez A.M. Ewing Public Service Fellowship

AMOUNT: $2,000 **DEADLINE:** Varies
FIELDS/MAJORS: Political Science

Research fellowships are available at the University of Oklahoma, Norman, for sophomores, juniors, or seniors majoring in political science. Preference is given to students returning to OU after their summer congressional intern experience. Write to the address listed below for information.

University Of Oklahoma, Norman
Political Science Department
455 West Lindsey
Norman, OK 73019

1117

COS–Faculty Scholarships

GPA 3.0+

AMOUNT: Varies **DEADLINE:** May 1
FIELDS/MAJORS: All Areas Of Study

Scholarships for academically promising freshman entering the College of the Siskiyous. Must have a GPA of at least 3.4 and be enrolling for full-time study. Renewable with a GPA of 3.0. Write to the address below for details.

College Of The Siskiyous
Financial Aid Office
800 College Ave.
Weed, CA 96094

1118

COS Vocational Nursing Scholarship

GPA 3.0+

AMOUNT: Varies **DEADLINE:** May 1
FIELDS/MAJORS: Nursing

Scholarships for students at the College of the Siskiyous who are majoring in nursing. Must have a GPA of 3.0 in classroom theory and clinical performance. Must be enrolled in the third semester of the vocational nursing program. Two awards per year. Write to the address below for details.

College Of The Siskiyous
Financial Aid Office
800 College Ave.
Weed, CA 96094

1119

Cotton Franklin V-12 Scholarship

AMOUNT: $200 **DEADLINE:** Feb 9
FIELDS/MAJORS: All Areas Of Study

Awards for full-time sophomores who are direct descendants of U.S. Navy veterans. Use Bloomsburg University scholarship application. Contact Mrs. Kishbaugh, Financial Aid Office for more information.

Bloomsburg University
19 Ben Franklin Hall
400 E. Second St.
Bloomsburg, PA 17815

1120

Counselor's Choice Scholarship

AMOUNT: $1,500 **DEADLINE:** None Specified
FIELDS/MAJORS: All Areas Of Study

Scholarships for entering freshmen from New Mexico who are nominated by their high school counselor. Must have a GPA of at least 2.5 and an ACT score of 21 or an SAT score of 860 or better. For U.S. citizens enrolled in full-time study. Renewable. Write to the address below for more information.

New Mexico Tech
Admission Office
Socorro, NM 87801

1121

Countrymark Cooperative, Inc. Scholarships

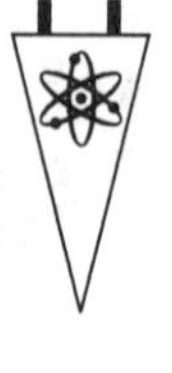

AMOUNT: $1,000 **DEADLINE:** Feb 15
FIELDS/MAJORS: Agriculture

Scholarships are available for FFA members pursuing a four-year degree in any area of agriculture. Applicant must be from Indiana, Michigan, or Ohio. Preference will be given to applicants with outstanding leadership skills and work-related experience. Write to the address below for details.

National FFA Foundation
Scholarship Office
P.O. Box 15160
Alexandria, VA 22309

1122

County Of Colorado Sheriffs Scholarship

AMOUNT: $500 **DEADLINE:** None Specified
FIELDS/MAJORS: All Areas Of Study

Awards for Mesa State students who are residents of Colorado. Write to the address below for more information.

Mesa State College
Office Of Financial Aid
P.O. Box 3692
Grand Junction, CO 81501

1123

Cox Minority Scholarship Program

E

GPA 3.0+

AMOUNT: Tuition & Fees **DEADLINE:** Apr 30
FIELDS/MAJORS: Newspaper Journalism

Scholarship offered to minority high school seniors planning to pursue a career in the newspaper industry. Applicants must have a GPA of 3.0 and plan to attend college at Georgia State, Clark, Spelman, or Morehouse. Awards are renewable. Must be a U.S. citizen. Students that are chosen are required to intern at a local Atlanta newspaper during summer and holiday breaks. Write to the address below for details.

Atlanta Journal And Constitution
Cox Enterprises
P.O. Box 4689
Atlanta, GA 30302

1124

Cozad Scholarships

AMOUNT: $2,000 **DEADLINE:** Mar 1
FIELDS/MAJORS: Business

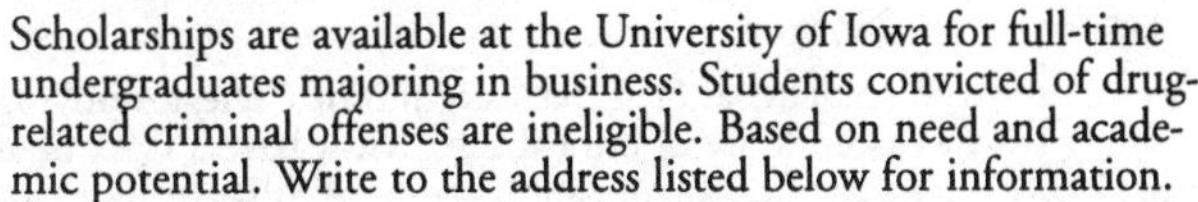

Scholarships are available at the University of Iowa for full-time undergraduates majoring in business. Students convicted of drug-related criminal offenses are ineligible. Based on need and academic potential. Write to the address listed below for information.

University of Iowa
College Of Business Admin., Suite W160
108 Pappajohn Business Admin. Bldg.
Iowa City, IA 52245

1125

Crain Educational Grants

AMOUNT: $5,000 (max) **DEADLINE:** Mar 29
FIELDS/MAJORS: All Areas Of Study

Scholarships for graduates of San Mateo or Santa Clara County high schools. For assistance with full-time undergraduate studies. Must be a U.S. citizen. Write to the address below for details.

Peninsula Community Foundation
1700 S. El Camino Real, #300
San Mateo, CA 94402

1126

Crane-Rogers Foundation Fellowship

AMOUNT: Varies **DEADLINE:** Apr 1, Sep 1
FIELDS/MAJORS: Foreign Studies—Mexico, Asia, Japan, Caribbean, Banking, Water Use

Fellowships are available to postdoctoral scholars to support research in an area of interest to the foundation, including those areas mentioned above. Tenure is two years. Applicants must be age 36 or less. Write to the address listed below for information.

Institute Of Current World Affairs
Gary L. Hansen, Program Administrator
4 West Wheelock Street
Hanover, NH 03755

1127

Cray Research Foundation Award

AMOUNT: $1,000 **DEADLINE:** Mar 15
FIELDS/MAJORS: Science, Computer Science, Mathematics

Applicants must be full-time Edgewood undergraduate students majoring in science, mathematics, or computer science. Minorities and women are encouraged to apply. Write to the address below for details.

Edgewood College
Office Of Admissions
855 Woodrow Street
Madison, WI 53711

1128

Creative Achievement Award At Case Western

AMOUNT: $8,000 **DEADLINE:** Feb 1
FIELDS/MAJORS: Art, Drama/Theatre, Music

Scholarships offered to entering freshmen at Case Western Reserve University. Must demonstrate outstanding creative ability and achievement. Awards are renewable for four years, provided there is continued evidence of outstanding creative achievement and satisfactory academic achievement. Write to the address below for additional information.

Case Western Reserve University
Office Of Financial Aid, 109 Pardee Hall
10900 Euclid Avenue
Cleveland, OH 44106

1129

Creative And Performing Arts & Theater Patrons Assoc. Scholarships

AMOUNT: $1,000 **DEADLINE:** Feb 1
FIELDS/MAJORS: Theater

Scholarships for undergraduate students studying in or contributing to the department of theater at the University of Maryland, College Park. Write to the address below for more information.

University Of Maryland, College Park
Department Of Theater
0202 Tawes
College Park, MD 20742

1130

Creative And Performing Arts Scholarships

AMOUNT: None Specified **DEADLINE:** Varies
FIELDS/MAJORS: Art, Music, Dance, Drama, Theatr

Competitive scholarships for talented students in the above areas. Preference is given to freshmen or transfer students. Renewable. Fifteen awards per year. Contact your department or write to the address below for complete details.

University Of Maryland, College Park
Office Of Student Financial Aid
0110 Lee Building
College Park, MD 20742

1131

Creative Arts Scholarships

AMOUNT: Varies **DEADLINE:** None Specified
FIELDS/MAJORS: Music, Art, Or Dance

Tuition grants available for talented students. Ability is judged by the appropriate department. Renewable with a GPA of at least 2.5. Apply to the appropriate department director. Write to the address below for details.

Mercyhurst College
Glenwood Hills
Erie, PA 16546

1132

Creative Writing And Art Scholarships

AMOUNT: $500–$1,000 **DEADLINE:** Dec 15
FIELDS/MAJORS: Creative Writing, Poetry, Art

Scholarships for students majoring in one of the fields above. Based on talent and ability in the area of study. Must have a GPA of at least a 2.5 for renewal.

University Of Redlands
Office Of Financial Aid
1200 East Colton Ave, P.O. Box 3080
Redlands, CA 92373

1133

Creswell, Munsell, Fultz & Zirbel Ag Communications Scholarships

Amount: $1,000 **Deadline:** Feb 15
Fields/Majors: Agricultural Communications, Journalism, Or Marketing

Awards for junior or senior undergraduates in one of the fields listed above who were former FFA members and attend one of the following schools: Cal-Poly (San Luis Obispo), Iowa State, Kansas State, North Carolina State, The Ohio State, Purdue, Univ. of Illinois, Univ. of Nebraska-Lincoln, Univ. of Minnesota, Univ. of Missouri, or Univ. of Wisconsin-Madison. Write to the address below for complete information.

Creswell, Munsell, Fultz, & Zirbel
Scholarship Office, National FFA Center
P.O. Box 15160
Alexandria, VA 22309

1134

Creswell, Munsell, Fultz & Zirbel Scholarships

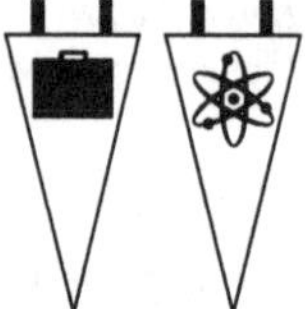

Amount: $500 **Deadline:** Feb 15
Fields/Majors: Agriculture, Agribusiness

Scholarships are available for FFA members pursuing a two-year degree in any area of agriculture. Applicant must be from Iowa. Based on grades, extracurricular activities, and community involvement. Write to the address below for details.

National FFA Foundation
Scholarship Office
P.O. Box 15160
Alexandria, VA 22309

1135

Criminal Justice Scholarship

Amount: Varies **Deadline:** None Specified
Fields/Majors: Criminal Justice

Awards available to students pursuing a career in the field of criminal justice. Based on merit, need, and an essay. Write to the address below for more information.

Rockford College
Financial Aid Office
5050 East State St.
Rockford, IL 61108

1136

Criterion Scholarship Award

Amount: Varies **Deadline:** Apr 15
Fields/Majors: All Areas Of Study

Awards for graduating seniors from the following Lake County high schools: Eustis, Leesburg, Mount Dora, Taveres, or Umatilla. Applicants must have a GPA of at least 3.0 and demonstrate financial need. Not renewable. Contact your high school guidance department for more information.

Lake County Schools
Student Services Department
509 S. Palm Ave.
Howey In The Hills, FL 34737

1137

Critical Care Nursing Scholarship

Amount: $200 **Deadline:** None Specified
Fields/Majors: Nursing

Awards given to students at St. Petersburg Junior College studying nursing with a career desire of critical care. Must have a GPA of at least 2.5. Contact the health education center at SPJC or write to the address below for more information.

St. Petersburg Junior College
Office Of Financial Aid
P.O. Box 13489
St. Petersburg, FL 33733

1138

Critical Teacher Shortage Student Loan Forgiveness Program

Amount: $5,000 (max) **Deadline:** Jul 15
Fields/Majors: Education

Open to certified Florida public school teachers. Program provides repayment of educational loans in return for teaching in a critical teacher shortage area. Up to $2,500 per year for four years for teachers with undergraduate loans or $5,000 per year for up to two years for teachers with graduate loans. Write to the address below for details.

Florida Department Of Education
Office Of Student Financial Assistance
1344 Florida Education Center
Tallahassee, FL 32399

1139

Critical Teacher Shortage Tuition Reimbursement Program

Amount: Varies **Deadline:** Varies
Fields/Majors: Education

Education incentive program to encourage Florida public school teachers to become certified to teach or to gain a graduate degree in a department of education critical teacher shortage area and then teach in that area in Florida. Must maintain 3.0 or better GPA. Write to the address below for details.

Florida Department Of Education
Office Of Student Financial Assistance
1344 Florida Education Center
Tallahassee, FL 32399

1140

Crow's Hybrid Corn Agricultural Scholarship

Amount: $600 **Deadline:** Nov 17
Fields/Majors: Agriculture

Scholarships are available for full-time students majoring in agriculture. First consideration is given to a regular employee or a descendent of a regular employee or dealer of Crow's Hybird Company or it's successor. Based on academic excellence and financial need. Write to the address below for more information.

Illinois State University, Dept. Of Agriculture
Turner Hall 150
Campus Box 5020
Normal, IL 61761

1141

CSA Scholarship

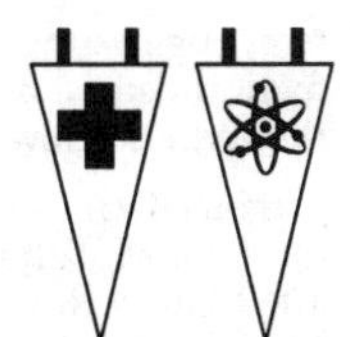

Amount: $500 **Deadline:** Apr 1
Fields/Majors: Occupational Safety, Environmental Health

Awards for students in academic programs leading to a degree in occupational safety, environmental health, or a related field. Candidates must be in good academic standing and recommended by their college or university. Contact the financial aid office at your school for more information. The financial aid administrator must collect the application forms and return them to the National Safety Council.

Campus Safety, Health And Environmental Management Association
c/o Eve Brouwer, National Safety Council
1121 Spring Lake Dr.
Itasca, IL 60143

1142

CSB Sister Joyce Williams/SJU Morton Katz Scholarships

Amount: $1,500–$5,000 **Deadline:** Feb 1
Fields/Majors: All Areas Of Study

Scholarships for students of color at CSB or SJU. Applicants must be U.S. citizens or permanent residents and demonstrate financial eligibility and academic promise. Renewed automatically with satisfactory academic progress and continued financial eligibility. Write to the address below for more information.

College Of Saint Benedict And Saint John's University
Office Of Financial Aid
37 South College Ave.
St. Joseph, MN 56374

1143

CSU Trustees' Award For Outstanding Achievement

Amount: $2,500 **Deadline:** None Specified
Fields/Majors: All Areas Of Study

Open to all majors; continuing Cal Poly students only with full-time enrollment. Write to the address below for more information.

California State Polytechnic University, Pomona
College Of Agriculture
Building 45, Room 109B
Pomona, CA 91768

1144

CTA Scholarships

Amount: $2,000 **Deadline:** Feb 15
Fields/Majors: All Areas Of Study

Open to active members of CTA or their dependent children. Award can be used at any accredited institution of higher learning for a degree or credential or vocational program. Write to the address below for complete details.

California Teachers Association
c/o CTA Human Rights Department
1705 Murchison Drive, P.O. Box 921
Burlingame, CA 94011

1145

Culinary Careers Scholarship

Amount: Tuition **Deadline:** Feb 16
Fields/Majors: Culinary Arts

High school seniors interested in culinary careers can win a four-year tuition scholarship worth $37,000 to Johnson & Wales University in Rhode Island during the National High School Recipe Contest. Applicants should submit original recipes for a healthy family dinner which follows the American Cancer Society nutrition guidelines, which are included with the official entry blank. Write to the address below for official entry blank and details.

Johnson & Wales University
c/o Culinary School, Recipe Contest
8 Abbott Park Place
Providence, RI 02903

1146

Cultural Collaborations

Amount: $1,000–$6,000
Deadline: Feb 1, Jun 15
Fields/Majors: Visual, Performing, Theater, And Literary Arts

Awards for professional artists of color who are legal residents of the state of Minnesota. Must be over 18 years of age to apply. Based primarily on the quality of work and merit of the artist's career plans. Not intended for use in gaining a degree. Write to the address below for more information.

Minnesota State Arts Board
Percent For Art Program Institute
432 Summit Ave.
St. Paul, MN 55102

1147

Curry Awards For Girls And Young Women

Amount: $500 **Deadline:** Apr 15
Fields/Majors: All Areas Of Study

Scholarships are available for young women, age 16 to 26, who are residents of San Mateo County, and have experienced undue hardship in attempting to complete their education. Three awards are offered annually. Write to the address listed below for additional information.

Peninsula Community Foundation
1700 South El Camino Real, Suite 300
San Mateo, CA 94402

1148

Curt And Linda Hanson Scholarships

Amount: $250 **Deadline:** Feb 15
Fields/Majors: Agriculture

Awards for UW Platteville students who are agriculture majors active in agricultural organizations. Must have a GPA of at least 2.5 and have completed at least thirty credits at the time of application. Write to the address below for more information.

University Of Wisconsin, Platteville
Office Of Admissions & Enrollment Mgt.
Platteville, WI 53818

1149 Curtis J. Riendeau, Helen Nixon, & Gerald Hardy Memorial Amount:

Amount: None Specified **Deadline:** None Specified
Fields/Majors: All Areas Of Study

Awards for sophomores in the baccalaureate program. Based on contribution to student life on campus, financial need, or academic standing. Write to the address below for more details.

Daniel Webster College
Financial Assistance Office
20 University Dr.
Nashua, NH 03063

1150 Curtis Lee Smith Scholarship And The Elizabeth Walker Scholarship

Amount: $12,000 (max) **Deadline:** Feb 1
Fields/Majors: All Areas Of Study

Two scholarships awarded once every four years to a qualified applicants for admission as a freshmen. This award is renewable for each of the four years of undergraduate study, provided high academic achievement is maintained. Write to the address below for details.

Case Western Reserve University
Office Of Financial Aid, 109 Pardee Hall
10900 Euclid Avenue
Cleveland, OH 44106

1151 Cushman Scholarship Fund

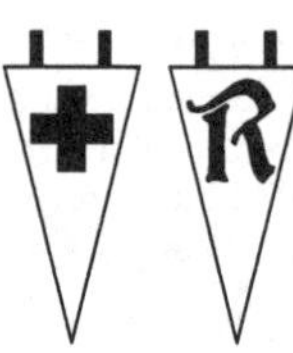

Amount: None Specified **Deadline:** May 1
Fields/Majors: Medical Or Christian Education Fields

Scholarship fund provides scholarship assistance to Hancock County residents pursuing education in the medical or christian education fields. Write to Patti D'Angelo at the address below for details.

Maine Community Foundation Scholarship Funds
P.O. Box 148
Ellsworth, ME 04605

1152 Cynthia Foster Burke Scholarship

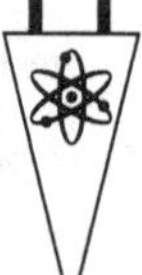

Amount: Varies **Deadline:** Mar 1
Fields/Majors: Marine Biology, Oceanography, Environmental Science

Awards for students in one of the areas of study listed above at the sophomore, junior, or senior level of study. Contact the Dean, Natural Sciences and Mathematics, for more information.

University Of Massachusetts, Amherst
Dean of Natural Sciences And Mathematics
Amherst, MA 01003

1153 Cyrus H. McCormick Undergraduate Scholarships

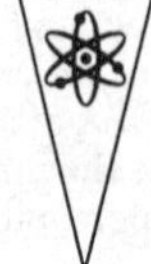

Amount: $1,000 **Deadline:** May 1
Fields/Majors: Agriculture, Life Sciences

Scholarships for incoming freshmen and returning or transfer students in the fields of agriculture and life sciences, biological systems engineering, and agricultural education. Based on academic merit, financial need, and extracurricular achievements. Write to the address below for more information.

Virginia Tech College Of Agriculture And Life Sciences
Dr. John M. White, Associate Dean
1060 Litton Reaves Hall
Blacksburg, VA 24061

1154 D.C. Jackling Loan

Amount: Varies **Deadline:** Feb 1
Fields/Majors: Mining Engineering

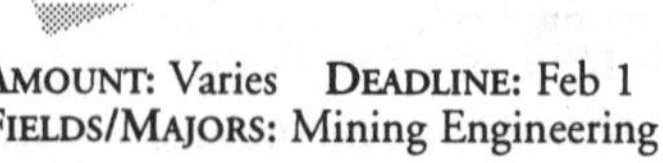

Low-cost loans are available at the University of Utah for full-time students who are mining engineering majors. Write to the address below for details.

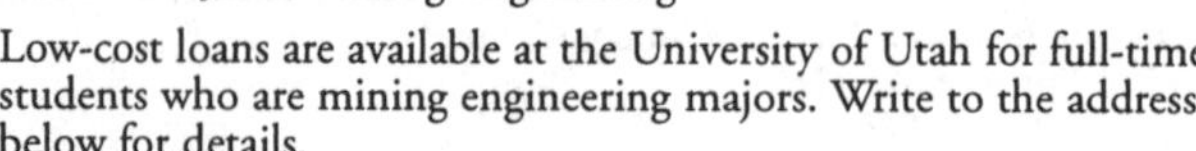

University Of Utah
Dr. M.K. McCarter
313 William C. Browning Building
Salt Lake City, UT 84112

1155 D.H. Lawrence Fiction Contest

Amount: Varies **Deadline:** Mar 1
Fields/Majors: Fiction Writing

Awards are available at the University of New Mexico for students interested in fiction writing. Contact the English department for details.

University Of New Mexico, Albuquerque
Office Of Financial Aid
Albuquerque, NM 87131

1156 D.J. Angus-Scientech Educational Foundation Award

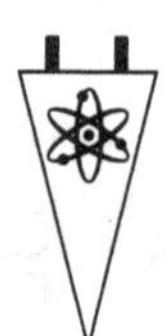

Amount: None Specified **Deadline:** None Specified
Fields/Majors: Science

Scholarships are awarded to students in his/her sophomore or junior year when presented the award as it is intended to serve as both an award and as impetus for continuing excellence. Write to the address below for more information.

Indiana University/Purdue University, Indianapolis
Purdue School Of Technology
799 West Michigan St.
Indianapolis, IN 46202

1157 D.I. Scurry Scholarship

Amount: Varies **Deadline:** None Specified
Fields/Majors: All Areas Of Study

Awards for full-time TTC students who are enrolled in an associate degree program and have a GPA of at least 3.0. Must have completed a semester of college work at the time of application. Write to the address below for more information.

Trident Technical College
Financial Aid Office
P.O. Box 118067
Charleston, SC 29423

1158

DAAD Fulbright Grants

Amount: Varies **Deadline:** Oct 31
Fields/Majors: German Studies

Grants for graduate study/research in Germany for one academic year. Applicants must be U.S. citizens between 18 and 32 years of age and be fluent in German. Contact your campus Fulbright program advisor or write to the address below for further details.

Daad German Academic Exchange Service
Institute Of International Education
809 United Nations Plaza
New York, NY 10017

1159

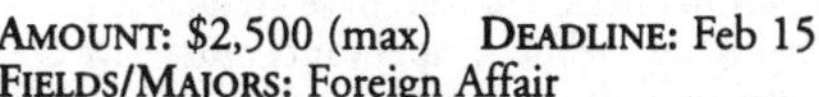

Dacor Bacon House Heyward G. Hill Scholarship Program

Amount: $2,500 (max) **Deadline:** Feb 15
Fields/Majors: Foreign Affair

Scholarships for undergraduate junior and seniors who are dependents of American foreign service personnel (active, retired w/pension, or deceased) who have served with a foreign service agency (defined in the Foreign Service Act of 1980) for at least one year. Approximately twenty awards annually. For study toward a career in the foreign service or international affairs. Write to the address below for details.

American Foreign Service Association
2101 E St., NW
Washington, DC 20037

1160

Dade County Youth Fair & Exposition, Dade County Agri Council Grants

Amount: $1,000-$2,000 **Deadline:** Jul 1
Fields/Majors: All Areas Of Study

Scholarships for Dade County, Florida, high school graduates. Based on academics, references, extracurricular activities, essay, and need. For use at college, universities, or a vocational/trade school. Applicants must be U.S. citizens or resident aliens. Contact your counselor or C.A.P. advisor, or write to the address below for details.

Dade County Youth Fair And Exposition
Scholarship Screening Committee
10901 Coral Way
Miami, FL 33165

1161

Dairy Cattle Judging Scholarships

Amount: $1,000 **Deadline:** Feb 15
Fields/Majors: Dairy Science

Scholarships are available for FFA members pursuing a four-year degree in dairy science, who have competed in the dairy contest above the local level. Five awards are offered annually. Write to the address below for details.

National FFA Foundation
Scholarship Office
P.O. Box 15160
Alexandria, VA 22309

1162

Dairy Foods Scholarships

Amount: $1,000 **Deadline:** Feb 15
Fields/Majors: Agriculture, Agribusiness

Scholarships are available for FFA members pursuing a four-year degree in agriculture or agribusiness. Applicant must have competed in the dairy foods contest above the local level. Write to the address below for details.

National FFA Foundation
Scholarship Office
P.O. Box 15160
Alexandria, VA 22309

1163

Dairy Industry Scholarships

Amount: $500-$1,250 **Deadline:** None Specified
Fields/Majors: Dairy Science

Twenty seven scholarships for dairy science students at VPI and SU. Some awards are limited to residence or activities. Generally, must have a GPA of at least 2.0 to be eligible. Write to the address below for details.

Virginia Tech College Of Agriculture And Life Sciences
Department Of Dairy Science
2435 Litton-Reaves Hall
Blacksburg, VA 24061

1164

Dale & Coral Courtney Scholarship

Amount: $2,000 **Deadline:** Mar-Apr
Fields/Majors: Geography

Awards are available at Portland State University for graduate students studying geography. Application consists of an essay and recommendations. Contact the geography department office for more details.

Portland State University
Geography Department Office
424 Cramer Hall
Portland, OR 97207

1165

Dan A. Brant, Jr. Memorial Scholarship

Amount: $1,000 **Deadline:** None Specified
Fields/Majors: All Areas Of Study

Awards for students at Mesa State College with a GPA of at least 3.0. Applicants must be a walk-on athlete in any varsity sport. For undergraduate study. Contact the athletic department for further details.

Mesa State College
Financial Aid Office
P.O. Box 2684
Grand Junction, CO 81501

1166

Dan Blocker/Freda Powell Scholarships

Amount: $50-$400 **Deadline:** Varies
Fields/Majors: Theater

Awards for Sul Ross students in theater who are active in campus theater productions. Write to the address below for more information.

Sul Ross State University
Financial Aid Office
Box C-113
Alpine, TX 79832

1167

Dana S. Still Scholarships

AMOUNT: None Specified **DEADLINE:** Mar 30
FIELDS/MAJORS: All Areas Of Study

Scholarships are available to incoming students in honor of the former provost. Based on financial need. Nonrenewable. Contact the dean of enrollment management and academic records for further information.

Clarion University
104 Egbert Hall
Office Of Financial Aid
Clarion, PA 16214

1168

Dance Department Scholarships, Extracurricular Study Awards

AMOUNT: $50-$200 **DEADLINE:** None Specified
FIELDS/MAJORS: Dance

Scholarships are available at the University of Iowa for full-time students majoring in dance who show exceptional talent and potential. Write to the address listed below for information.

University of Iowa
Department Of Dance
E114 Halsey Hall
Iowa City, IA 52245

1169

Dance General Scholarship

AMOUNT: $500 (max) **DEADLINE:** May 1
FIELDS/MAJORS: Dance

Awards for freshmen who demonstrate ability or talent in the field of dance. Based primarily on an audition. Write to the chair of the department of theater and dance at the address below for more information.

Winthrop University
Department Of Theater And Dance
119 Tillman Hall
Rock Hill, SC 29733

1170

Dance Performing Stipends

AMOUNT: $250-$500 **DEADLINE:** None Specified
FIELDS/MAJORS: Dance

Stipends for students participating in the touring companies of the department of dance at the University of Alabama at Birmingham. Write to the address below for more information.

University Of Alabama, Birmingham
Department Of Theatre And Dance
101 Bell Bldg., UAB Station
Birmingham, AL 35294

1171

Dance: The Next Generation Scholarships

AMOUNT: Varies **DEADLINE:** None Specified
FIELDS/MAJORS: Dance

Award for students to participate in a program sponsored by the Sarasota Ballet. Must be able to demonstrate financial need. Write to the address below for further information.

Sarasota Ballet
P.O. Box 49094
Sarasota, FL 49094

1172

Dane County High School Award

AMOUNT: $250-$1,000 **DEADLINE:** Mar 15
FIELDS/MAJORS: All Areas Of Study

Applicants must be first-time freshmen who have graduated from Dane County, Wisconsin, high schools. Applicants must have at least a 2.5 GPA. Renewable. Write to the address below for details.

Edgewood College
Office Of Admissions
855 Woodrow Street
Madison, WI 53711

1173

Daniel B. Goldberg Scholarship

AMOUNT: $3,500 **DEADLINE:** Feb 18
FIELDS/MAJORS: Business and Finance

Scholarship for graduate students preparing for a career in state and local government finance. For full-time study. Must have superior academic record. One award per year. Must be a legal resident of the U.S. or Canada. Information may be available from the head of your accounting department. If not, write to the address below. Applications are available in November for awards in the following spring.

Government Finance Officers Association
Scholarship Committee
180 N. Michigan Avenue, Suite 800
Chicago, IL 60601

1174

Daniel E. Lambert Memorial Scholarship

AMOUNT: None Specified **DEADLINE:** May 1
FIELDS/MAJORS: All Areas Of Study

Open to residents of Maine entering their first year or higher of post-high school education or training. Must be a U.S. citizen and a dependent of a veteran. Write to the address below for more information.

American Legion, Department Of Maine
P.O. Box 900
Waterville, ME 04903

1175

Daniel G. Fox Prize For Excellence In Computer Science

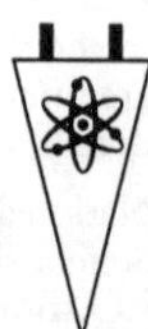

AMOUNT: $500 **DEADLINE:** Feb 1
FIELDS/MAJORS: Computer Science

Scholarships are available at the University of Hawaii, Hilo for full-time senior computer science majors who demonstrate great academic achievement. Award is $500 plus a tuition waiver. Write to the address listed below for information.

University Of Hawaii At Hilo
Financial Aid Office
200 West Kawili Street
Hilo, HI 96720

1176

Daniel J. Carrison Americanism & Andrew Watson Scholarship

AMOUNT: $350-$750 **DEADLINE:** Feb 1
FIELDS/MAJORS: All Areas Of Study

Applicants must demonstrate financial need and submit an essay on Americanism or government. Write to the address below for details.

Bob Jones University
Attn: Director Of Student Financial Aid
Greenville, SC 29614

1177

Danielson Memorial Scholarship

AMOUNT: Varies **DEADLINE:** None Specified
FIELDS/MAJORS: Counseling/Psychology

Awards for CHC students majoring in counseling or psychology who can demonstrate financial need. Write to the address below for more information.

Christian Heritage College
Financial Aid Office
2100 Greenfield Dr.
El Cajon, CA 92019

1178

Dann Gann Scholarship

AMOUNT: Varies **DEADLINE:** None Specified
FIELDS/MAJORS: Music

Awards for CHC students majoring in music and showing exceptional overall academic potential. Write to the address below for more information.

Christian Heritage College
Financial Aid Office
2100 Greenfield Dr.
El Cajon, CA 92019

1179

Danny Lee Wing Scholarship

AMOUNT: $1,000 **DEADLINE:** Feb 29
FIELDS/MAJORS: Management

Awards for Asian American school of management students in their sophomore, junior, or senior year from an urban area who have good academic standing and are in financial need. Applications for school of management scholarships will be available in the SOM Development Office, Room 206.

University Of Massachusetts, Amherst
School Of Management
SOM Development Office, Room 206
Amherst, MA 01003

1180

Dante B. Fascell Fellowship Program

AMOUNT: $50,000 (max) **DEADLINE:** May 1
FIELDS/MAJORS: Physical Or Social Sciences

Fellowships are available for Latin American and Caribbean emerging leaders who have been instrumental in developing successful approaches to grassroots development for reflection upon, analysis, and dissemination of their experiences to audiences across the hemisphere. For postdoctoral research. Write to the address below for details.

Inter-American Foundation
IAF Fellowship Programs
901 N. Stuart St., 10th Floor, Dept. 555
Arlington, VA 22203

1181

Dartmouth Grants

AMOUNT: $19,000 (max) **DEADLINE:** Feb 1
FIELDS/MAJORS: All Areas Of Study

Grant funds are available for Dartmouth students who demonstrate financial need. The amount of the grant is based upon the difference between the cost of attending Dartmouth and the estimated family contribution. Write to the address below for more complete details.

Dartmouth College
Financial Aid Office
6024 McNutt Hall
Hanover, NH 03755

1182

Datatel Scholars Foundation

AMOUNT: $700-$2,000 **DEADLINE:** Feb 28
FIELDS/MAJORS: All Areas Of Study

Open to full-time and part-time undergraduate or graduate students attending a secondary, undergraduate, or graduate program at a Datatel client site. Must remain employed at the organization during the scholarship award period. Write to the address below for more information.

Datatel Scholars Foundation
4375 Fair Lakes Ct.
Fairfax, VA 22033

1183

Daughters Of Minos Scholarship, Emorphia T. Diamant Scholarship

AMOUNT: Varies **DEADLINE:** Feb 15
FIELDS/MAJORS: All Areas Of Study

Scholarships are available at the University of Utah for full-time students of Cretan-Greek descent (Minos), or of Greek descent (Diamant). Write to the address below for information.

University Of Utah
Financial Aid And Scholarships Office
105 Student Services Building
Salt Lake City, UT 84112

1184

Daughters Of Penelope National Scholarship Awards (Graduate)

AMOUNT: $1,500 **DEADLINE:** Jun 20
FIELDS/MAJORS: All Areas Of Study

Scholarships for women who are currently enrolled in a postgraduate degree program (M.A., Ph.D., M.D., etc.) who are immediate family members (or members themselves) of Daughters of Penelope, Order of Ahepa, or Maids of Athena. Must be enrolled for nine credits/year minimum. Not renewable. Five award programs are offered each year. Write to the address below for details.

Daughters Of Penelope National Headquarters
National Scholarship Awards
1909 Q St., NW, Suite 500
Washington, DC 20009

1185

Daughters Of Penelope National Scholarship Awards (Undergraduate)

AMOUNT: $500 **DEADLINE:** Jun 20
FIELDS/MAJORS: All Areas Of Study

Scholarships for women who are or will be attending college or university as an undergraduate and who are immediate family members (or members themselves) of Daughters of Penelope, Order of Ahepa, or Maids of Athena. Five award programs are offered each year. Renewable at $500 per year for not more than two years. Write to the address below for details.

Daughters Of Penelope National Headquarters
National Scholarship Awards
1909 Q St., NW, Suite 500
Washington, DC 20009

1186

Daughters Of Penelope Scholarship

AMOUNT: $500 **DEADLINE:** Apr 1
FIELDS/MAJORS: All Areas Of Study

Awards for full-time, degree-seeking students with a GPA of 3.0 or higher and financial need. Preference is given to females. Write to the address below for more information.

Christopher Newport University
Office Of Financial Aid
50 Shoe Lane
Newport News, VA 23606

1187

Daughters Of The Cincinnati Scholarships

AMOUNT: Varies **DEADLINE:** Mar 15
FIELDS/MAJORS: All Areas Of Study

Open to high school senior daughters of commissioned regular active or retired officers in U.S. Army, Navy, Air Force, Marine Corps, or Coast Guard. Based on need and merit. Renewable. The sponsor has requested that we stress that the award is only for daughters of commissioned officers. Also, please be certain to put your name, address, parent's rank, and parent's branch of service on your letter (not just on the outside of the envelope).

Daughters Of The Cincinnati
Attn: Scholarship Administrator
122 East 58th Street
New York, NY 10022

1188

Davey Arboriculture Grant

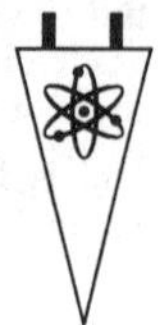

AMOUNT: Varies **DEADLINE:** Feb 15
FIELDS/MAJORS: Urban Forestry, Arboriculture, Park Management

Awards for UMass students in the fields listed above who have commercial arboriculture experience and financial need. For entering sophomores, juniors, or seniors. Contact the Director, Stockbridge School, for additional information.

University Of Massachusetts, Amherst
Director, Stockbridge School
Amherst, MA 01003

1189

David Arver Memorial Scholarship

AMOUNT: $1,000 **DEADLINE:** Mar 12
FIELDS/MAJORS: Aircraft Repair, Avionics

Scholarship for a student planning to study avionics or aircraft repair at a school in AEA region III (includes the states of IL, IN, IA, KS, MI, MN, MO, NE, ND, SD, WI). Write to the AEA for information on these and other awards (fourteen total) offered by the AEA.

Aircraft Electronics Association Educational Foundation
P.O. Box 1981
Independence, MO 64055

1190

David Boozer Scholarship

AMOUNT: $1,000 **DEADLINE:** Mar 15
FIELDS/MAJORS: All Areas Of Study

Awards for Jacksonville State University students in any discipline. Based on criteria determined by the JSU scholarship committee. Write to the address below for more details.

Jacksonville State University
Financial Aid Office
Jacksonville, AL 36265

1191

David C. Knapp Political Science Scholarship

AMOUNT: Varies **DEADLINE:** Mar 1
FIELDS/MAJORS: Political Science

Awards for students majoring in political science. Based on scholarship and merit. For entering sophomores, juniors, or seniors. Contact the Head, Political Science Department, for more information.

University Of Massachusetts, Amherst
Head, Political Science Department
Box 38230
Amherst, MA 01003

1192

David E. Finley Fellowship, Paul Mellon Fellowship

AMOUNT: $13,000 **DEADLINE:** Nov 15
FIELDS/MAJORS: Western Art, Visual Arts, And Related Areas

Three-year fellowships are available for doctoral scholars researching for the dissertation. Two years will be spent in Europe in research, and one year will be spent at the National Gallery of

Art. Applicants must be U.S. citizens or legal residents. Write to the address listed below for information.

National Gallery Of Art
Center For Advanced Study In Visual Arts
Predoctoral Fellowship Program
Washington, DC 20565

1193

David Eccles School Of Business Departmental Scholarships

AMOUNT: Varies **DEADLINE:** Varies
FIELDS/MAJORS: Accounting, Finance, Management, Marketing

Scholarships are available at the University of Utah for full-time students from Utah majoring in one of the areas listed above. Deadline varies for entering freshmen, transfers, and continuing students. Write to the address below for details.

University Of Utah
Undergraduate Studies Office
108 Business Classroom Building
Salt Lake City, UT 84112

1194

David Eugene And Adeline Morehouse Holmes Scholarship

AMOUNT: Varies **DEADLINE:** None Specified
FIELDS/MAJORS: All Areas Of Study

Awards available to female students in their sophomore year of study. Write to the address below for more information.

Rockford College
Financial Aid Office
5050 East State St.
Rockford, IL 61108

1195

David F. Stanke Memorial Scholarship

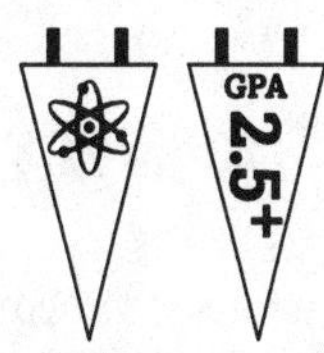

AMOUNT: $500 **DEADLINE:** None Specified
FIELDS/MAJORS: Agriculture, Dairy Science

Student must be a full-time sophomore or above agriculture major with an interest in dairy science. Contact the agriculture department for more information.

Southwest Missouri State University
Office Of Financial Aid
901 South National Ave.
Springfield, MO 65804

1196

David H. And Edith W. Clark Scholarship Fund

AMOUNT: Varies **DEADLINE:** None Specified
FIELDS/MAJORS: All Areas Of Study

Awards are available for full-time students at Cedarville College who have demonstrated financial need and have completed one year of study. Must have a GPA of at least 2.5. Write to the address below for more information.

Cedarville College
Financial Aid Office
P.O. Box 601
Cedarville, OH 45314

1197

David H. Clift Scholarship

AMOUNT: $3,000 **DEADLINE:** Dec 22
FIELDS/MAJORS: Library Science

Applicants must be graduate students who are entering or enrolled in an ALA-accredited master's program and be U.S. or Canada citizen. Based on academic accomplishment, leadership potential, and desire to pursue a career in librarianship. For students who have completed fewer than 12 semester hours toward master's (by June of preceding year). Write to the address below for details.

American Library Association
Staff Liaison, ALA Scholarship Juries
50 E. Huron Street
Chicago, IL 60611

1198

David Jay Gambee Memorial Fellowship

AMOUNT: None Specified **DEADLINE:** Nov 30
FIELDS/MAJORS: All Areas Of Study

Fellowships are available at UCSD for undergraduate students involved in special studies and projects under faculty supervision. Applicants must demonstrate involvement in community service. Write to the address listed below for information.

University Of California, San Diego
Student Financial Services
9500 Gilman Drive
La Jolla, CA 92093

1199

David L. Owens Scholarship

AMOUNT: $15,000 **DEADLINE:** Apr 1
FIELDS/MAJORS: Water Utility Industry

Scholarship for graduating seniors or graduate students pursuing a degree in the water utility industry. Must be a U.S. citizen. Write to the address below for more information.

National Association Of Water Companies
Scholarship Committee
1725 K St., NW, Suite 1212
Washington, DC 20006

1200

David Lawrence, Sr. Scholarship

AMOUNT: $1,000 **DEADLINE:** Mar 1
FIELDS/MAJORS: Journalism

Must be a junior or senior enrolled at the University of Florida. Must show interest in political reporting for the print media. Must have at least a 2.8 GPA. Write to the address below for details.

University Of Florida
Scholarship and Placement Director
2070 Weimer Hall
Gainesville, FL 32611

1201

David Lloyd Scholarships And Ruby Lloyd Apsey Scholarships

AMOUNT: Tuition And Fees **DEADLINE:** None Specified
FIELDS/MAJORS: Drama And Theatre/Dance

Applicants must be incoming freshmen who have a minimum

ACT score of 25. Write to the address below for more information.

University Of Alabama, Birmingham
Department Of Theatre And Dance
700 13th Street South, UAB Station
Birmingham, AL 35294

1202

David M. Webb Computer Science Scholarship

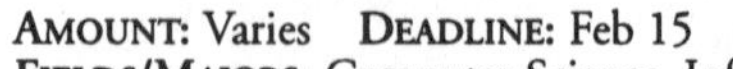

AMOUNT: Varies **DEADLINE:** Feb 15
FIELDS/MAJORS: Computer Science, Information Technology

Scholarships are available at Evangel for full-time students who will be or are pursuing a career in computer science. Applicants must have a GPA of at least 3.0. Write to the address listed below for information.

Evangel College
Office Of Enrollment
1111 N. Glenstone
Springfield, MO 65802

1203

David Marc Belkin Fellowship

AMOUNT: None Specified **DEADLINE:** Nov 30
FIELDS/MAJORS: Environmental Studies

Fellowships are available at UCSD for undergraduate students involved in special studies and projects under faculty supervision. Write to the address listed below for information.

University Of California, San Diego
Student Financial Services
9500 Gilman Drive
La Jolla, CA 92093

1204

David Memorial Scholarship & Distinguished Scholar Award

AMOUNT: $1,000 **DEADLINE:** Jan 15
FIELDS/MAJORS: All Areas Of Study

Awards for UNL freshmen who have displayed academic accomplishments in high school. Renewable for four years with a GPA of at least 3.5 and continued full-time study. Write to the address below for additional information and to obtain an application for freshman scholarships.

University Of Nebraska, Lincoln
Office Of Scholarships And Financial Aid
16 Administration Bldg., P.O. Box 880411
Lincoln, NE 68588

1205

David Murphy Memorial Scholarship

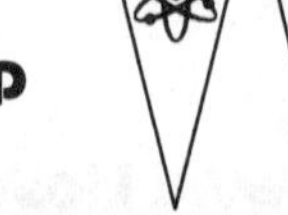

AMOUNT: Varies **DEADLINE:** Feb 9
FIELDS/MAJORS: Chemistry

Award for junior or senior chemistry majors with a minimum GPA of 2.5. Must demonstrate financial need. Use Bloomsburg University scholarship application. Award is used to pay the community activities fee for the appropriate semesters. Contact Dr. David Hill, Comptroller of Community Activities/Kehr Union for further information.

Bloomsburg University
19 Ben Franklin Hall
400 E. Second St.
Bloomsburg, PA 17815

1206

David Rozkuszka Scholarship

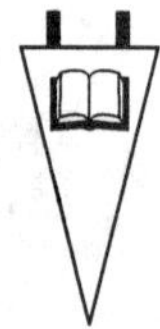

AMOUNT: $3,000 **DEADLINE:** Dec 1
FIELDS/MAJORS: Library Science

Awards for ALA-accredited master's degree candidate currently working in a library with government documents, with a commitment to government documents librarianship. Write to the address listed below for additional information.

American Library Association
Susan Tulis, L Library
University Of Virginia, 580 Massie Rd.
Charlottesville, VA 22901

1207

David T. Cole Scholarship For Continuing Education

AMOUNT: Varies **DEADLINE:** Mar 1
FIELDS/MAJORS: All Areas Of Study

Awards for upper-class students at UMass in the continuing education program who are making career changes and have financial need. Contact the Continuing Education Office, not at the address below for more information.

University Of Massachusetts, Amherst
Office Of Financial Aid Services
255 Whitmore Admin. Bldg., Box 38230
Amherst, MA 01003

1208

David T. Woolsey Scholarship

AMOUNT: $1,000 **DEADLINE:** Apr 2
FIELDS/MAJORS: Landscape Architecture/Design

Applicants must submit a 500-word autobiography, two letters of recommendation, and a sample of design work. Must be a resident of Hawaii. For junior or senior undergraduates or graduate students. Write to the address below for details.

Landscape Architecture Foundation
4401 Connecticut Ave., NW, Suite 500
Washington, DC 20008

1209

David Tamotsu Kagiwada Memorial Scholarship

AMOUNT: Varies **DEADLINE:** Mar 15
FIELDS/MAJORS: Theology

Applicants must be Asian American members of the Christian Church (Disciples of Christ) who are preparing for the ordained ministry. For full-time study. Financial need is considered. Must have at least a C+ grade average. Write to the address below for details.

Christian Church (Disciples Of Christ)
Attn: Scholarships
P.O. Box 1986
Indianapolis, IN 46206

1210

David W. Stahl Endowed Memorial Scholarship

AMOUNT: Varies **DEADLINE:** None Specified
FIELDS/MAJORS: Music

Awards are available for full-time music students at Cedarville College who are in the sophomore year of study. Must have a GPA of at least 3.0. Write to the address below for more information.

Cedarville College
Financial Aid Office
P.O. Box 601
Cedarville, OH 45314

1211

Davis Scholarship

AMOUNT: $1,500-Tuition **DEADLINE:** Jan 15
FIELDS/MAJORS: All Areas Of Study

Scholarship for African American, Native American, or Hispanic freshman entering UNL. Must have excellent academic performance, demonstrate leadership, and be from Nebraska. Write to the address below for further details and for an application for freshman scholarship aid.

University Of Nebraska, Lincoln
Office Of Scholarships And Financial Aid
16 Administration Bldg., P.O. Box 880411
Lincoln, NE 68588

1212

Davis-Roberts Scholarship Fund

AMOUNT: None Specified **DEADLINE:** Jun 15
FIELDS/MAJORS: All Areas Of Study

Open to full-time students who are Wyoming residents and a Demolay Chapter or Jobs Daughter Bethel member. Based on character and worthiness. Must have at least average grades. Write to the address below for details.

Davis-Roberts Scholarship Fund, Inc.
Secretary/Treasurer
P.O. Box 1974
Cheyenne, WY 82003

1213

Dawn M. Glitsch Memorial Scholarship Fund

AMOUNT: Varies **DEADLINE:** Feb 17
FIELDS/MAJORS: Education

Scholarships are available at the University of Oklahoma, Norman for full-time education majors, sophomore level or higher, with a GPA of at least 3.0. Must be a U.S. citizen. Write to the address listed below for information.

University Of Oklahoma, Norman
College Of Education, Student Services
Room 137, ECH
Norman, OK 73019

1214

Dayco Products Inc. Scholarship

AMOUNT: $1,000 **DEADLINE:** None Specified
FIELDS/MAJORS: All Areas Of Study

Awards for TTC students enrolled in at least twelve credit hours who have a GPA of at least 3.0. Write to the address below for more information.

Trident Technical College
Financial Aid Office
P.O. Box 118067
Charleston, SC 29423

1215

DCE Nontraditional Student Scholarships

AMOUNT: Varies **DEADLINE:** Varies
FIELDS/MAJORS: All Areas Of Study

Scholarships are available at the University of Utah for full-time nontraditional students who are from Utah. Applicants must meet any two of the following criteria: financially self-supporting, at least two-year interruption in his/her education, graduated from high school more than seven years ago, or are managing multiple roles. Write to the address below for more information.

University Of Utah
Center For Adult Development
1195 Annex Building
Salt Lake City, UT 84112

1216

Dean E. Uhl Merit Scholarship In Chemistry

AMOUNT: Varies **DEADLINE:** Mar 1
FIELDS/MAJORS: Chemistry, Chemical Engineering

Awards are available at the University of New Mexico for juniors or seniors studying chemistry or chemical engineering. Must exhibit a good GPA and progress in the program. Write to the address listed below for information.

University Of New Mexico, Albuquerque
Office Of Financial Aid
Albuquerque, NM 87131

1217

Dean James R. Nichols Scholarships

AMOUNT: $1,500 **DEADLINE:** May 1
FIELDS/MAJORS: Agriculture, Life Sciences

Scholarships for incoming freshmen and returning undergraduates in the fields of agriculture and life sciences. Based on scholarship, leadership, and financial need. Write to the address below for more information.

Virginia Tech College Of Agriculture And Life Sciences
Dr. John M. White, Associate Dean
1060 Litton Reaves Hall
Blacksburg, VA 24061

1218

Dean's Merit Scholarship

AMOUNT: $1,000 (max) **DEADLINE:** May 1
FIELDS/MAJORS: Theater, Music, Art, Dance

Awards for freshmen who demonstrate artistic ability and academic achievement. Nonrenewable. Write to the address below for more information.

Winthrop University
Department Of Art And Design
119 Tillman Hall
Rock Hill, SC 29733

1219 Dean's Scholarship

Amount: $4,000 **Deadline:** None Specified
Fields/Majors: All Areas Of Study

Award available to qualified students on the basis of academic performance. Write to the address below for more information.

Carthage College
Financial Aid Office
Kenosha, WI 53140

1220 Dean's Scholarship For Continuing Majors

Amount: None Specified
Deadline: None Specified
Fields/Majors: Science

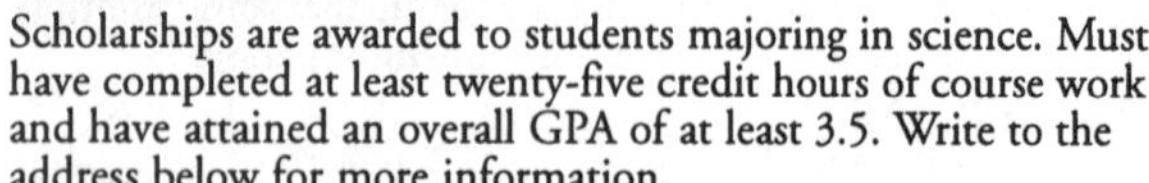

Scholarships are awarded to students majoring in science. Must have completed at least twenty-five credit hours of course work and have attained an overall GPA of at least 3.5. Write to the address below for more information.

Indiana University/Purdue University, Indianapolis
Purdue School Of Technology
799 West Michigan St.
Indianapolis, IN 46202

1221 Dean's Scholarship Fund

Amount: Varies **Deadline:** None Specified
Fields/Majors: Architecture

Scholarships are available at the University of Oklahoma, Norman for students who demonstrate academic ability and financial need. Write to the address listed below for information.

University Of Oklahoma, Norman
Dean, College Of Architecture
OMS, Room 252
Norman, OK 73019

1222 Dean's Scholarships

Amount: Varies **Deadline:** Mar 1
Fields/Majors: All Areas Of Study

Awards for African American or Native American freshman who have demonstrated academic performance and leadership potential. Up to 60 awards given per year. Write to the address below for more details.

North Carolina State University
Financial Aid Office
Box 7302
Raleigh, NC 27695

1223 Dean's Scholarships

Amount: $3,000 (min) **Deadline:** Mar 1
Fields/Majors: All Areas Of Study

Awards for entering freshmen who rank in the top 10% of their class and have a combined SAT score of at least 1240 or an ACT of 28. Write to the address below for more information.

Bradley University
Office Of Financial Assistance
Peoria, IL 61625

1224 Dean's Scholarships

Amount: $1,000-$3,000 **Deadline:** Feb 1
Fields/Majors: All Areas Of Study

Scholarships for first-year students who have demonstrated academic excellence in high school and who have the ability to become excellent students at CBU or SJU. Applicants must have a GPA of at least 3.35 or be in the top 10% of their high school class and have demonstrated leadership skills. Renewed automatically with satisfactory academic progress. Write to the address below for more information.

College Of Saint Benedict And Saint John's University
Office Of Financial Aid
37 South College Ave.
St. Joseph, MN 56374

1225 Dean's Scholarship

Amount: $2,200 **Deadline:** Mar 1
Fields/Majors: All Areas Of Study

Scholarships available at Sterling for undergraduate full-time students who demonstrate a record of leadership in school, church, and community. Must have a minimum GPA of at least 3.5 and an ACT score of 26 or SAT score of at least 1090. Renewable. Write to the address below for details.

Sterling College
Financial Aid Office
Sterling, KS 67579

1226 Dean's Scholarship

Amount: $2,000 (max) **Deadline:** Apr 15
Fields/Majors: All Areas Of Study

Awards for students who rank in the top 5% of their high school class with appropriate test scores. Must be enrolled for full-time study. Renewable with a GPA of at least 3.2. Write to the address below for more information.

Bethel College
Office Of Financial Planning
3900 Bethel Dr.
St. Paul, MN 55112

1227 Dean's Scholarships

Amount: $400 **Deadline:** Mar 1
Fields/Majors: All Areas Of Study

Awards for incoming freshmen at Pittsburg State University who graduated in the top 15% of their class. Write to the address below for more information.

Pittsburg State University
Office Of Academic Affairs
203 Russ Hall
Pittsburg, KS 66762

1228

Deans' Scholars

AMOUNT: None Specified **DEADLINE:** Feb 20
FIELDS/MAJORS: All Areas Of Study

Scholarships are available at the University of San Diego for freshmen with a GPA of at least 3.4 and high SAT scores. Write to the address listed below for information.

University Of San Diego
Office Of Financial Aid
5998 Alcala Park
San Diego, CA 92110

1229

Debate Scholarship

AMOUNT: $500-$1,000 **DEADLINE:** Dec 15
FIELDS/MAJORS: All Areas Of Study

Scholarships for students with talent and experience in debate. Renewable upon continued involvement in debate. For undergraduate study. Write to the address below for more details.

University Of Redlands
Office Of Financial Aid
1200 East Colfax Ave., P.O. Box 3080
Redlands, CA 92373

1230

Deborah Fennessey Scholarship

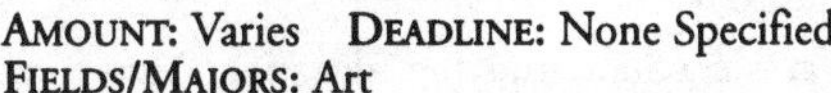

AMOUNT: Varies **DEADLINE:** None Specified
FIELDS/MAJORS: Art

Awards for full-time students entering their sophomore, junior, or senior year in the field of art. Contact the Art Department, not the address below for more information.

University Of Massachusetts-Amherst
Office Of Financial Aid Services
255 Whitmore Admin. Bldg., Box 38230
Amherst, MA 01003

1231

Deborah Partridge Wolfe International Fellowship

AMOUNT: $500-$1,000 **DEADLINE:** Feb 1
FIELDS/MAJORS: All Areas Of Study

Fellowship for international students studying in the U.S. or U.S. citizens studying abroad. For full-time study for one year. No affiliation with Zeta Phi Beta is required. For graduate or undergraduate study. Send an SASE to the national headquarters at the address below for further information. Proof of enrollment will be required of recipient.

Zeta Phi Beta Sorority
National Educational Foundation
1734 New Hampshire Ave., NW
Washington, DC 20009

1232

Debra Anne Wiltgen Memorial Scholarship

AMOUNT: $100 **DEADLINE:** None Specified
FIELDS/MAJORS: Music

Awards for Mesa State student majoring in the field of music who can demonstrate financial need. Contact the music department for more information.

Mesa State College
Financial Aid Office
P.O. Box 2647
Grand Junction, CO 81501

1233

Debra Lynn Baker Mauney Memorial Scholarship

AMOUNT: Varies **DEADLINE:** Mar 1
FIELDS/MAJORS: Nursing

Awards are available at the University of New Mexico for full-time junior nursing students with a minimum GPA of 2.5 and financial need. Write to the address below or contact the school of nursing for more details.

University Of New Mexico, Albuquerque
Office Of Financial Aid
Albuquerque, NM 87131

1234

DEED (Demonstration Of Energy-Efficient Developments) Scholarships

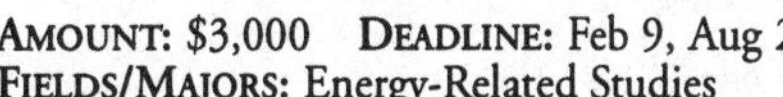

AMOUNT: $3,000 **DEADLINE:** Feb 9, Aug 2
FIELDS/MAJORS: Energy-Related Studies

Graduate or undergraduate students in energy-related disciplines from accredited four-year colleges or universities are eligible. Write to the address below for additional information.

American Public Power Association
Deed Administrator
2301 M St., NW
Washington, DC 20037

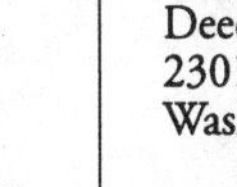

1235

Defense Acquisition Scholarship Program-NCEE

AMOUNT: $13,000-$15,000 **DEADLINE:** Mar 20
FIELDS/MAJORS: Business, Engineering, Mathematics, Physical Sciences

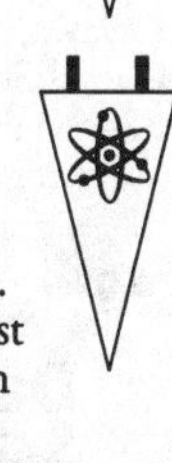

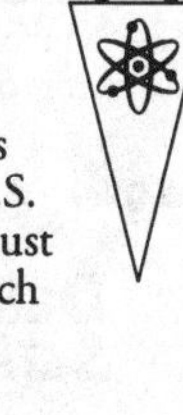

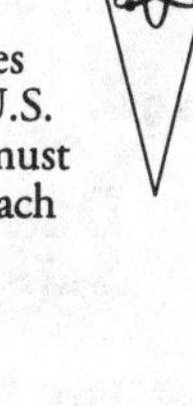

Awards for graduate students pursuing master's degrees in one of the areas listed above. Applicants must be U.S. citizens and have a GPA of 3.0 or better. Recipients must agree to serve the government one calendar year for each year they were provided a scholarship. Write to the address below for more information.

U.S. Department Of Defense
1101 Massachusetts Ave.
St. Cloud, FL 34769

1236

DeKalb Genetics Corporation Scholarships

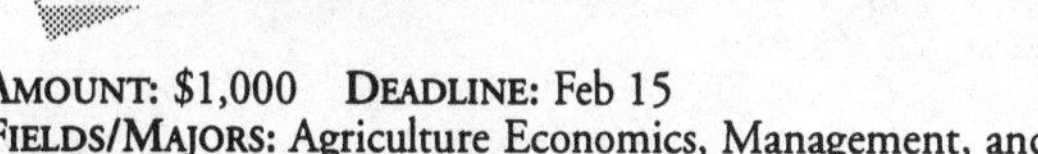

AMOUNT: $1,000 **DEADLINE:** Feb 15
FIELDS/MAJORS: Agriculture Economics, Management, and Marketing; Agronomy; Agribusiness

Scholarships are available for FFA members pursuing a four-year degree in one of the above areas. Write to the address below for details.

National FFA Foundation
Scholarship Office
P.O. Box 15160
Alexandria, VA 22309

1237

Del Amo Endowment

Amount: $8,000 (max) **Deadline:** Jan 26
Fields/Majors: Spain, Spanish Culture

Fellowships and grants for students and faculty at UCLA to support study of Spain and Spanish culture. Eighteen awards are available. Contact your department or write to the address below for details.

University Of California, Los Angeles, College Of Letters And Science
Committee On The Del Amo Endowment
1312 Murphy Hall, Campus 143801
Los Angeles, CA 90024

1238

Delaware Nursing Incentive Scholarship Loan

Amount: $3,000 (max) **Deadline:** Mar 31
Fields/Majors: Nursing

Scholarship for students who meet academic requirements and enroll in a nursing program. Write to the address below for more information.

Delaware Higher Education Commission
Carvel State Office Building
820 North French St.
Wilmington, DE 19801

1239

Delaware Scholarship Incentive Program

Amount: $1,000 (max) **Deadline:** Apr 15
Fields/Majors: All Areas Of Study

Program for Delaware residents enrolled full-time in a degree program at a Delaware college. In certain instances, Delaware residents attending out-of-state colleges may apply. All recipients must have a GPA of 2.5 or better. Write to the address below for more information.

Delaware Higher Education Commission
Carvel State Office Building
820 North French St.
Wilmington, DE 19801

1240

Delmar Publishers, Inc. Scholarships

Amount: $500-$1,000 **Deadline:** Feb 15
Fields/Majors: Agriculture Education, Environmental Science

Scholarships are available for FFA members pursuing a four-year degree in agricultural education, or a two-year degree in environmental science. Write to the address below for details.

National FFA Foundation
Scholarship Office
P.O. Box 15160
Alexandria, VA 22309

1241

Delta And Pine Land Company Scholarships

Amount: $1,000 **Deadline:** Feb 15
Fields/Majors: Agriculture

Scholarships are available for FFA members pursuing a four-year degree in any area of agriculture, who reside in Alabama, Arizona, Arkansas, California, Florida, Georgia, Kansas, Louisiana, Mississippi, Missouri, New Mexico, North Carolina, Oklahoma, South Carolina, Tennessee, Texas, or Virginia. Write to the address below for details.

National FFA Foundation
Scholarship Office
P.O. Box 15160
Alexandria, VA 22309

1242

Delta Gamma Foundation Florence Margaret Harvey Memorial Scholarship

Amount: $1,000 **Deadline:** Apr 1
Fields/Majors: Rehabilitation: Education Of Visually Impaired and Blind Persons

Legally blind junior, senior, or graduate students studying in the field of rehabilitation and/or education of visually impaired and blind persons. Applicant must be a U.S. citizen and show outstanding scholarship. Write to the address below for complete details.

American Foundation For The Blind
Scholarship Committee
11 Penn Plaza, Suite 300
New York, NY 10001

1243

Delta Kappa Gamma Chapter Scholarships

Amount: Varies **Deadline:** None Specified
Fields/Majors: Education

Awards for students at Mesa State studying education. Must be residents of Mesa County, Colorado, and have a GPA of at least 3.0. Contact the financial aid office for further details.

Mesa State College
Financial Aid Office
P.O. Box 2684
Grand Junction, CO 81501

1244

Delta Kappa Gamma Society International Beta Beta State Scholarship

Amount: Varies **Deadline:** Feb 1
Fields/Majors: Education

Scholarships are available at the University of Hawaii, Hilo for full-time students committed to a career in education. Write to the address listed below for information.

University Of Hawaii At Hilo
Financial Aid Office
200 West Kawili Street
Hilo, HI 96720

1245

Delta Sigma Theta Sorority-New Haven Alumnae Scholarship

Amount: Varies **Deadline:** Feb 1
Fields/Majors: Mathematics, Science

Awards for high school minority seniors. Must demonstrate scholastic achievement, extra-curricular activities, community service, financial need, and be in the upper 25% of their class. Must also be a Connecticut resident. Contact your high school guidance counselor for further information or write to the address below.

Delta Sigma Theta Sorority-New Haven Alumnae
Juanita P. Kent
90 Union City Rd.
Prospect, CT 06712

1246

Delta Tau Alpha Scholarship

AMOUNT: $400 **DEADLINE:** None Specified
FIELDS/MAJORS: Agriculture

Student must be an agriculture major and preferably a Delta Tau Alpha member. Contact the agriculture department for more information.

Southwest Missouri State University
Office Of Financial Aid
901 South National Ave.
Springfield, MO 65804

1247

Delta Waterfowl And Wetlands Research

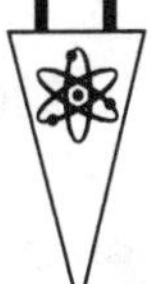

AMOUNT: $1,000 Per Month **DEADLINE:** Oct 27
FIELDS/MAJORS: Waterfowl, Wetland Ecology

Funds are available for graduate students to do research on waterfowl. Based on personal letter, GRE scores, a resume, and letters of reference. Write to the address below for more details.

Louisiana State University
School Of Forestry, Wildlife, Fisheries
Baton Rouge, LA 70803

1248

Dension Scholarship

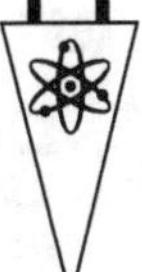

AMOUNT: None Specified **DEADLINE:** None Specified
FIELDS/MAJORS: Food, Resources, Agriculture, Crop Science, Nutrition, Horticulture/Floriculture

Scholarships are awarded to Stockbridge seniors who are chosen based on academic standing, leadership, and nominations of advisors. Contact the Director, Stockbridge School, for more information.

University Of Massachusetts, Amherst
Office Of Financial Aid Services
255 Whitmore Admin. Bldg, Box 38230
Amherst, MA 01003

1249

Dental Assisting Scholarship Program

AMOUNT: Varies **DEADLINE:** Varies
FIELDS/MAJORS: Dental Assisting

Scholarships for Florida residents (for at least 2 years) who have completed at least one semester or quarter in a Florida Board of Dentistry approved program with a GPA of at least 2.0. Program is designed to alleviate shortage of dental assistants in certain parts of Florida. Renewable. Requests for scholarships should be made at least 45 days before the date the funds are needed. Write to the Florida Dental Health Foundation at the address below for details.

Florida Dental Association
Florida Dental Health Foundation
1111 E. Tennessee Street, #102
Tallahassee, FL 32308

1250

Dental Assisting Scholarship Program

AMOUNT: $1,000 **DEADLINE:** Sep 1
FIELDS/MAJORS: Dental Assisting

Applicant must be a U.S. citizen and must be enrolled full time as an entering student in a dental assisting program accredited by the commission on dental accreditation of the American Dental Association. Students must have a GPA of 2.8 or above and demonstrate financial need. Students receiving a full scholarship from any other source are ineligible for this scholarship. Recipients may apply to renew the scholarship for a second year provided the student has completed the previous year's academic requirements in good standing. Write to the address below for details.

ADA Endowment And Assistance Fund, Inc.
211 East Chicago Avenue
Chicago, IL 60611

1251

Dental Hygiene Scholarship Program

AMOUNT: $1,000 **DEADLINE:** Aug 15
FIELDS/MAJORS: Dental Hygiene

Applicant must be a U.S. citizen and enrolled full time as an entering or first year student at a dental hygiene school accredited by the Commission on Dental Accreditation of the American Dental Association. Students must have a GPA of 2.8 or above and show financial need. Students receiving a full scholarship from any other source are ineligible for this scholarship. Recipients may apply to renew the scholarship for a second year provided the student has completed the previous year's academic requirements in good standing. Contact the financial aid office at your school for details.

ADA Endowment And Assistance Fund, Inc.
211 East Chicago Avenue
Chicago, IL 60611

1252

Dental Student Scholarship

AMOUNT: $2,500 **DEADLINE:** Jun 15
FIELDS/MAJORS: Dentistry

Applicant must be a U.S. citizen enrolled full time as an entering, first, or second-year student in a dentistry program accredited by the Commission on Accreditation of the American Dental Association. Students must have a GPA of 3.0 or above and demonstrate financial need. Students receiving a full scholarship from any other source are ineligible for this scholarship. Recipients may apply to renew the scholarship for a second year provided the student has completed the previous year's academic requirements in good standing. Write to the address below for details.

ADA Endowment And Assistance Fund, Inc.
211 East Chicago Avenue
Chicago, IL 60611

1253

Department Of Accounting Scholarship

AMOUNT: $300 **DEADLINE:** None Specified
FIELDS/MAJORS: Accounting

Professional accounting firms that recruit on campus have provided the department of accounting with the funds to finance two scholarships for accounting students. Contact the College of Business Administration, UW Oshkosh, for more details.

University Of Wisconsin, Oshkosh
Financial Aid Office, Dempsey 104
800 Algoma Blvd.
Oshkosh, WI 54901

1254

Department Of Clinical Dietetics Scholarships

AMOUNT: $100-$1,500 **DEADLINE:** Feb 1
FIELDS/MAJORS: Dietetics

Scholarships are available at the University of Oklahoma, Norman for full-time dietetics majors. Includes the American Dietetic Association scholarships, the Oklahoma Dietetic Association scholarships, and the Shirley Enders Smith Memorial Scholarship. Individual award requirements may vary. Write to the address listed below for information.

University Of Oklahoma, Norman
College Of Allied Health
P.O. Box 26901
Oklahoma City, OK 73190

1255

Department Of Crop And Soil Environmental Sciences Scholarships

AMOUNT: $500-Tuition **DEADLINE:** None Specified
FIELDS/MAJORS: Environmental Sciences, Agronomy-Turf Management

Scholarships are administered through the Department of Crop and Soil Environmental Sciences. Fifteen to twenty awards are given per year. Write to Dr. Dave Chalmers at the address below for details.

Virginia Tech College Of Agriculture And Life Sciences
Crop And Soil Environmental Sciences
421 Smyth Hall
Blacksburg, VA 24061

1256

Department Of Minnesota Scholarships

AMOUNT: $500 **DEADLINE:** Mar 15
FIELDS/MAJORS: All Areas Of Study

Scholarships for Minnesota residents who are children of veterans of one of WWI, WWII, Korea, Vietnam, Grenada, Lebanon (82-84), or Panama. For study in Minnesota. Must be high school senior or graduate with a good scholastic record and at least a "C" average. For tuition, books, etc. Based on character and need. Seven awards per year. Information for this award and the National Presidents Scholarship are available from the address below.

American Legion Auxiliary, Department Of Minnesota
State Veterans Service Bldg.
St. Paul, MN 55155

1257

Department Of Music Service Scholarships

AMOUNT: Varies **DEADLINE:** None Specified
FIELDS/MAJORS: Music, Vocals, Instrumentalists

Awards for students who will be enrolled for a minimum of two semesters in one or more department ensembles or serve as accompanists or piano soloist. Must have made a significant musical contribution, show academic achievement, and financial need. Selection is made by the music department faculty. Contact a member of the music department faculty for further information.

Bloomsburg University
19 Ben Franklin Hall
400 E. Second St.
Bloomsburg, PA 17815

1258

Departmental And Enrichment Scholarships

AMOUNT: Varies **DEADLINE:** Mar 15
FIELDS/MAJORS: All Areas Of Study

Awards for students who are qualified for admission to or currently enrolled in Middle Tennessee State University. Individual criteria for awards may differ. Write to the address below for more details.

Middle Tennessee State University
Office Of Student Financial Aid
Murfreesboro, TN 37132

1259

Departmental And Other Awards

AMOUNT: Varies **DEADLINE:** None Specified
FIELDS/MAJORS: All Areas Of Study

Numerous awards for Mesa State students are available based on a variety of criteria such as: academics, extracurricular activities, seriousness of purpose of endeavor, or major field of study. Contact the office of financial aid at the address below for more details.

Mesa State College
Office Of Financial Aid
P.O. Box 2647
Grand Junction, CO 81501

1260

Departmental And Other Scholarships

AMOUNT: Varies **DEADLINE:** None Specified
FIELDS/MAJORS: All Areas Of Study

Scholarships are available for undergraduates at the University of Dayton from academic or athletic departments, and from the Army ROTC. Individual criteria for each department varies. Write to the director of student scholarships at the address below for complete details.

University Of Dayton
Office Of Scholarships And Financial Aid
300 College Park
Dayton, OH 45469

1261

Departmental Awards

AMOUNT: None Specified **DEADLINE:** None Specified
FIELDS/MAJORS: All Areas Of Study

Many departments in the graduate school award teaching and research assistantships to graduate students. The awards provide a stipend, 6-10 credits of graduate tuition per term, and subsidized health insurance. Write to the chairperson of your department for further details.

Wayne State University
Graduate School
Office Of The Dean
Detroit, MI 48202

1262

Departmental Awards

GPA 3.0+

AMOUNT: $4,000 **DEADLINE:** Apr 1
FIELDS/MAJORS: All Areas Of Study

Awards for entering freshmen and transfers who are selected by the faculty of Baker University based on academics or abilities. Music and theater majors must audition and art majors must submit a portfolio or their work for consideration. Renewable with a GPA of 3.0. Write to the address below for more information.

Baker University
Office Of Financial Aid
P.O. Box 65
Baldwin City, KS 66006

1263

Departmental Awards And Scholarships

AMOUNT: Varies **DEADLINE:** None Specified
FIELDS/MAJORS: All Areas Of Study

Awards for students at Tennessee Technological University who are enrolled in any area of study. Individual criteria for each department and for specific awards will vary based on academic credentials, activities, leadership, financial need, etc. Write to the address below or contact the head of the appropriate department for more details.

Tennessee Technological University
Financial Aid Office
Box 5076
Cookeville, TN 38505

1264

Departmental Scholarship

AMOUNT: $100-$3,000 **DEADLINE:** Jun 1
FIELDS/MAJORS: All Areas Of Study

Award for Harding University students based on talent or academics. Contact the head of the appropriate department for more details on eligibility.

Harding University
Director Of Student Financial Services
Box 2282
Searcy, AR 72149

1265

Departmental Scholarship And University Scholarships At Virginia Tech

AMOUNT: Varies **DEADLINE:** Varies
FIELDS/MAJORS: All Areas Of Study

Many different scholarship programs are available for students at Virginia Tech. Most scholarships are awarded and administered by individual departments. University scholarships require no application forms (all students are considered for these based on admission and FAF forms). Contact your department to find out what scholarships you are eligible for. Graduate students should contact 112 Burruss Hall as well as their departments.

Virginia Polytechnic Institute And State University
Office Of Scholarships And Financial Aid
112 Burruss Hall
Blacksburg, VA 24061

1266

Departmental Scholarships

AMOUNT: Varies **DEADLINE:** Feb 1
FIELDS/MAJORS: Film Studies

Various scholarships are available at the University of Utah for full-time film studies majors. Write to the address below for details.

University Of Utah
Theatre Department
206 Performing Arts Building
Salt Lake City, UT 84112

1267

Departmental Scholarships

AMOUNT: Varies **DEADLINE:** Feb 1
FIELDS/MAJORS: Dance—Modern

Scholarships are available at the University of Utah for full-time modern dance majors. Includes the Etta Keith Eskridge Scholarship, the Cordelia Quick Memorial Scholarship, and the Tim Wengard Scholarship. Individual award requirements may vary. Write to the address below for details.

University Of Utah
Sally Fitt
110 Marriott Center For Dance
Salt Lake City, UT 84112

1268

Departmental Scholarships

AMOUNT: Varies **DEADLINE:** Feb 15
FIELDS/MAJORS: All Areas Of Study

Scholarships are offered for entering freshmen from various departments on the Meredith College campus based on academic achievement or special abilities in a subject. Renewable with a minimum 3.0 GPA. For full-time study. Write to the address below for more information.

Meredith College
Office Of Admissions
3800 Hillborough St.
Raleigh, NC 27607

1269

Departmental Scholarships

AMOUNT: Varies **DEADLINE:** None Specified
FIELDS/MAJORS: Most Areas Of Study

Awards for Northwestern students based on their academic interests and achievements. Most awards are renewable. Individual criteria may vary. Write to the address below for more information.

Northwestern College
Financial Aid Office
101 7th St., SW
Orange City, IA 51041

1270

Departmental Scholarships

AMOUNT: Varies **DEADLINE:** Mar 1
FIELDS/MAJORS: All Areas Of Study

Scholarships for New Mexico Tech students based on academic

interests and academic achievements. Must be a U.S. citizen enrolled in full-time study. Renewable. Write to the address below for more information.

New Mexico Tech
Admission Office
Soccorro, NM 87801

1271

Departmental Scholarships

Amount: $1,000 **Deadline:** Mar 31
Fields/Majors: All Areas Of Study

Departmental awards for freshmen in each academic department. Renewable if a GPA of 3.0 is maintained. Contact the appropriate department for more information.

Columbia Union College
Financial Aid Office
7600 Flower Ave.
Takoma Park, MD 20912

1272

Departmental Scholarships For Armenian Students

Amount: Varies **Deadline:** None Specified
Fields/Majors: Most Areas Of Study

Awards for undergraduate or graduate students at USC who are of Armenian descent. The criteria for awards in each department that offers these awards will differ. Write to the address below or contact the chairperson of your department for more details.

University Of Southern California
Financial Aid Office
Los Angeles, CA 90089

1273

Dependent Scholarships

Amount: $1,000 (max) **Deadline:** Mar 1
Fields/Majors: All Areas Of Study

Award for undergraduate dependent students whose parents are involved in full-time Christian service. The applicant's family income must come from a church, mission board, Christian school, or Christian organization. Write to the address below for additional information.

Biola University
Financial Aid Office
13800 Biola Ave.
La Mirada, CA 90639

1274

Dependents Educational Assistance Program

Amount: Varies **Deadline:** Varies
Fields/Majors: All Areas Of Study

Open to children age 16-25, widows of deceased war veterans or of veterans who are 100 percent permanently disabled who were Louisiana residents for at least one year prior to service. Awards are for use at state-supported Louisiana schools only. Student must attend on full-time basis. Write to the address below for details.

Louisiana Department Of Veterans Affairs
P.O. Box 94095, Capitol Station
Baton Rouge, LA 70804

1275

Dependents Tuition Assistance Program

Amount: Tuition **Deadline:** None Specified
Fields/Majors: All Areas Of Study

This program pays tuition for dependents of Colorado law enforcement officers, fire, or national guard personnel killed or disabled in the line of duty, and for dependents of prisoners of war or service personnel listed as missing in action. Dependents of disabled personnel must have demonstrated financial need for the assistance. For study at a Colorado institution. Applicant must not be in default on an educational loan or owe a repayment of an educational grant. Write to the address below for applications and details.

Colorado Commission On Higher Education
1300 Broadway, 2nd Floor
Denver, CO 80203

1276

Descendents Of The Signers

Amount: None Specified **Deadline:** None Specified
Fields/Majors: All Areas Of Study

Scholarships for as many as nine students enrolled in a four-year college who can prove a direct family line to a Declaration of Independence signer. Send a #10 SASE ($.62) to the address below for details.

Mrs. Phillip F. Kennedy
P.O. Box 224
Suncook, NH 03275

1277

Detroit Free Press Internships

Amount: $465 Per Week **Deadline:** Dec 1
Fields/Majors: Editing, Graphics, Design, Photography

Internship program for students in the fields of study listed above. Based on resume, work samples, personal essay, references, and an explanation why the internship would be beneficial. Write to the address below for more information.

Detroit Free Press
Joe Grimm, Recruiter
321 W. Lafayette Blvd.
Detroit, MI 48226

1278

Diamond State Scholarship

Amount: $1,000 **Deadline:** Mar 31
Fields/Majors: All Areas Of Study

Scholarship for high school seniors who rank in the upper quarter of the class, have an 1100 or better on the SAT or 27 or better on the ACT, and enroll full-time at an accredited college. Write to the address below for more information.

Delaware Higher Education Commission
Carvel State Office Building
820 North French St.
Wilmington, DE 19801

1279

Diamond V. Mills, Inc. Scholarships

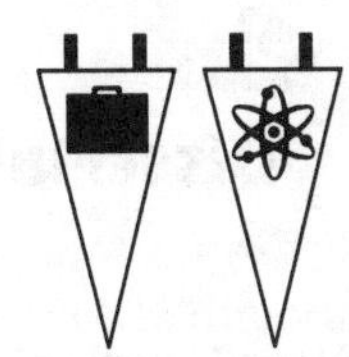

AMOUNT: $500-$1,000 **DEADLINE:** Feb 15
FIELDS/MAJORS: Agriculture, Agribusiness

Scholarships are available for FFA members pursuing a two- or four-year degree in agriculture or agribusiness who reside in Iowa. Applicant must be enrolled at Iowa State University or at Kirkwood Community College. Write to the address below for details.

National FFA Foundation
Scholarship Office
P.O. Box 15160
Alexandria, VA 22309

1280

Diane D. Tempest Memorial Scholarship

AMOUNT: $1,000 **DEADLINE:** Feb 15
FIELDS/MAJORS: All Areas Of Study

Scholarships are available at the University of Utah for full-time female nontraditional students, over the age of 34, and raising a family. Write to the address below for information.

University Of Utah
Financial Aid And Scholarships Office
105 Student Services Building
Salt Lake City, UT 84112

1281

Diane Lynn Adamo Memorial Scholarship In Nursing

AMOUNT: Varies **DEADLINE:** Mar 1
FIELDS/MAJORS: Pediatric Nursing

Awards are available at the University of New Mexico for full-time students with and intent to pursue pediatric nursing and a minimum GPA of 2.5. Must demonstrate financial need. Write to the address below or contact the school of nursing for more details.

University Of New Mexico, Albuquerque
Office Of Financial Aid
Albuquerque, NM 87131

1282

Diane Ren'ee Jones Memorial Scholarship Fund

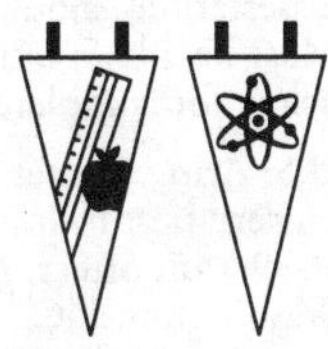

AMOUNT: Varies **DEADLINE:** None Specified
FIELDS/MAJORS: Biological Science, Science Education

Awards are available for students at Cedarville College who are studying in one of the fields above. Must have a GPA of at least 2.0. Write to the address below for more information.

Cedarville College
Financial Aid Office
P.O. Box 601
Cedarville, OH 45314

1283

Dick Bergman Baseball Scholarships

AMOUNT: Tuition And Fees **DEADLINE:** None Specified
FIELDS/MAJORS: All Areas Of Study

Award is available to a baseball player recommended by the baseball coach. The award covers tuition for one term or up to one full year, and can be renewed annually. Write to the address below for more information.

Portland State University
Department Of Athletics
159 Mill St. Building
Portland, OR 97207

1284

Dick Van Santen/American Chemistry Society Award

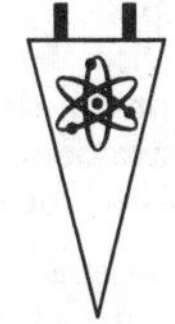

AMOUNT: $1,000 **DEADLINE:** None Specified
FIELDS/MAJORS: Chemistry

Awards are available at Portland State University for students who intend to pursue a career in chemistry. Academic excellence is a primary consideration. Contact the chemistry department at the address below for more information.

Portland State University
Chemistry Department
262 Science Building 2
Portland, OR 97207

1285

Dietetic Technician Scholarships

AMOUNT: $400-$5,000 **DEADLINE:** Jan 15
FIELDS/MAJORS: Dietetics/Nutrition

Scholarships for students in their second year of an ADA Accredited program. Must be a U.S. citizen and show potential in the field of nutrition/dietetics. Information is published annually in the Journal of the American Dietetic Association. Alternately, write to the address below for details.

American Dietetic Association Foundation
216 W. Jackson St., Suite 800
Chicago, IL 60606

1286

Director's Award

AMOUNT: $500 **DEADLINE:** Mar 1
FIELDS/MAJORS: Music

Award for juniors or seniors at Eastern New Mexico University who are majoring in music and participating in ensembles. GPA may be considered. Write to the address below for more information.

Eastern New Mexico University
College Of Fine Arts
Station 16
Portales, NM 88130

1287

Disadvantaged Health Professions Students Financial Assistance Program

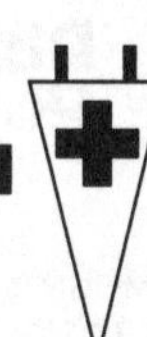

AMOUNT: Varies **DEADLINE:** Open
FIELDS/MAJORS: Health

Program that provides funds to cover reasonable education expenses and tuition. Financial need must be proven. Must be enrolled in a participating school, and studying in the field of health. Write to the address below for more information.

Bureau Of Health Professions
Student Assistance Division
5600 Fishers Lane
Rockville, MD 20857

1288

Disciple Chaplains' Scholarship

AMOUNT: Varies **DEADLINE:** Mar 15
FIELDS/MAJORS: Theology

Applicants must be members of the Christian Church (Disciples of Christ) who are entering first year in seminary. For full-time study. Financial need is considered. Must have better than a C+ grade average. Write to the address below for details.

Christian Church (Disciples Of Christ)
Attn: Scholarships
P.O. Box 1986
Indianapolis, IN 46206

1289

Discover Card Tribute Award Scholarship Program

AMOUNT: $1,000-$20,000 **DEADLINE:** None Specified
FIELDS/MAJORS: All Areas Of Study

Scholarships are available for current high school juniors who demonstrate academic excellence, participation in extra-curricular and community activities, and have a GPA of at least 2.75. Write to the address listed below for information.

American Association Of School Administrators/Discover Card Services
Discover Card Tribute Award Program
P.O. Box 9338
Arlington, VA 22219

1290

Displaced Homemaker Scholarships

AMOUNT: None Specified **DEADLINE:** Sep 1
FIELDS/MAJORS: All Areas Of Study

Open to American Indian or Alaskan Natives. Program aimed at students with child care, transportation, and basic living expenses. Must be at least 25% Native Indian/Alaskan. Recipients are eligible to reapply in subsequent years. Write to the address below for complete details.

Association On American Indian Affairs, Inc.
Box 268
Sisseton, SD 57262

1291

Dissertation & Postdoctoral Research Fellowships

AMOUNT: $1,000-$2,000 **DEADLINE:** Apr 1
FIELDS/MAJORS: Jewish Studies

Eight fellowships are available for postdoctoral candidates or persons at the doctoral dissertation stage for up to three months of active research or writing at the American Jewish Archives during the stipend year. Contact address below for complete information.

American Jewish Archives
Administrative Director
3101 Clifton Ave.
Cincinnati, OH 45220

1292

Dissertation Awards

AMOUNT: $1,000 **DEADLINE:** None Specified
FIELDS/MAJORS: All Areas Of Study

Cash awards are available at the University of Oklahoma, Norman for the four best dissertations by graduate students in the preceding year. Write to the address listed below for information.

University Of Oklahoma, Norman
Graduate College
1000 Asp Avenue, Room 313
Norman, OK 73019

1293

Dissertation Fellowship

AMOUNT: $7,500 **DEADLINE:** May 1
FIELDS/MAJORS: U.S. Military And Naval History

A fellowship is available for doctoral candidates performing dissertation research in an area of history relevant to the Marine Corps. Applicant must be a U.S. citizen and have all requirements for the doctoral degree completed by the time of application, except the dissertation. Some portion of the work is expected to be done at the Marine Corps Historical Center in Washington, DC. Write to the address listed below for information

Marine Corps Historical Center
Building 58
Washington Navy Yard
Washington, DC 20374

1294

Dissertation Fellowships

AMOUNT: $8,000 Stipend **DEADLINE:** Feb 1
FIELDS/MAJORS: American Military History

Doctoral dissertation fellowships for civilian Ph.D candidates at recognized graduate schools. All requirements for Ph.D (except dissertation) should be completed by september of award year. Must be a U.S. citizen or legal resident. Write to the address below for complete details.

U.S. Army Center Of Military History
Dissertation Fellowship Committee
1099 14th Street, NW
Washington, DC 20005

1295

Dissertation Fellowships

AMOUNT: Varies **DEADLINE:** Nov 1
FIELDS/MAJORS: Music, Drama, Playwriting

Fellowships are available to Ph.D. candidates for dissertation research that is directly related to the musical works of Kurt Weill and to the perpetuation of his artistic legacy. Write to the address listed below for information.

Kurt Weill Foundation For Music, Inc.
Joanna C. Lee, Associate Director
7 East 20th Street
New York, NY 10003

1296

Dissertation Fellowships In Urban, Labor, And Metropolitan Affairs

AMOUNT: None Specified **DEADLINE:** Apr 15
FIELDS/MAJORS: Urban Studies, Labor Studies, Workplace Issues

Dissertation fellowships for doctoral candidates at Wayne State University whose thesis topics relate to areas of interest to the College of Urban, Labor, and Metropolitan Affairs. Write to the address below for details.

Wayne State University, College Of Urban, Labor, and Metropolitan Affairs
Office Of The Dean, Donna Walker
3198 Faculty Administration Bldg.
Detroit, MI 58202

1297

Dissertation Grants Program

AMOUNT: $1,500 **DEADLINE:** Feb 15
FIELDS/MAJORS: Women's Studies

Doctoral dissertation grants to support use of Schlesinger Library materials. Two or more grants each year. Must be matriculated in doctoral program and have completed all coursework before application. Write to "Dissertation Grants Program" at the address below for details

Radcliffe College
Arthur And Elizabeth Schlesinger Library
10 Garden St.
Cambridge, MA 02138

1298

Dissertation Year Fellowships In U.S. Military Aerospace History

AMOUNT: $10,000 **DEADLINE:** Mar 15
FIELDS/MAJORS: U.S. Military Aerospace History

Doctoral dissertation fellowships for applicants who are U.S. citizens enrolled in a recognized graduate school, who have completed all work for a Ph.D. except the dissertation and who have an approved topic. Not compatible with other Department of Defense grants. Write to the address below for complete details.

U.S. Air Force
Office Of The Air Force Historian
170 Luke Ave, Suite 400
Bolling AFB, DC 20332

1299

Distinguished Community College Scholars Award

AMOUNT: $3,000 (max) **DEADLINE:** Mar 1
FIELDS/MAJORS: All Areas Of Study

Annual scholarships for transfer students entering their first year at Western Michigan University. Minimum GPA: 3.75. Transfers must have completed the associate degree by the time of enrollment at WMU. Contact the office of student financial aid at the address below for details.

Western Michigan University
Student Financial Aid
3306 Faunce Student Services Building
Kalamazoo, MI 49008

1300

Distinguished Freshman

AMOUNT: $1,200 **DEADLINE:** Mar 1
FIELDS/MAJORS: All Areas Of Study

Applicant must be a first time entering freshman residing in Oklahoma. Write to the address below for more information.

Southwestern Oklahoma State University
Student Financial Services Office
100 Campus Dr.
Weatherford, OK 73096

1301

Distinguished Honor Scholarships

AMOUNT: $3,500 (max) **DEADLINE:** Dec 1
FIELDS/MAJORS: All Areas Of Study

The honor scholarships are designed to recognize and encourage academic potential and accomplishment of students at Ripon. Based on a combination of academics and recommendations. Approximately twenty awards per year. Write to the admissions office at the address below for details.

Ripon College
300 Seward Street
P.O. Box 248
Ripon, WI 54971

1302

Distinguished Honor Scholarships

AMOUNT: $3,500 (max) **DEADLINE:** Feb 1
FIELDS/MAJORS: All Areas Of Study

Applicants must be incoming students who have a minimum GPA of at least 3.75 and have scored at least 26 on the ACT or 1000 on the SAT. Write to the address below for details.

Mount Mercy College
Office Of Admission
1330 Elmhurst Dr., NE
Cedar Rapids, IA 52402

1303

Distinguished Scholarship

AMOUNT: $1,500-$3,750 **DEADLINE:** Jan 15
FIELDS/MAJORS: All Areas Of Study

Awards for high school seniors with a ACT composite score of 26 or higher and ranked in the top 10% of their graduating class. Based on an exam in which the top seven scores determine the recipient. Renewable with a GPA of 3.5 or better. Write to the address below for more information.

University Of Nebraska, Omaha
Office Of Financial Aid, EAB 103
60th And Dodge Streets
Omaha, NE 68182

1304

Distributive Education Clubs Of America Scholarships

AMOUNT: Varies **DEADLINE:** Dec 1
FIELDS/MAJORS: Business, Marketing

Scholarships are available at the University of New Mexico for high school seniors who have completed one semester of marketing education and are interested in a career in marketing, business, or a related field. Write to the address listed below or contact your high school office for information.

University Of New Mexico, Albuquerque
Student Financial Aid Office
Mesa Vista Hall North, Student Services
Albuquerque, NM 87131

1305

Diversity Grant

Amount: Varies **Deadline:** Apr 15
Fields/Majors: All Areas Of Study

Awards available at Loras College to full-time students who are Asian, Hispanic, African American, or Native American. Write to the address below for details.

Loras College
Office Of Financial Planning
1450 Alta Vista St., P.O. Box 178
Dubuque, IA 52004

1306

Diversity Grants

Amount: $2,000 **Deadline:** Feb 20
Fields/Majors: All Areas Of Study

Scholarships are available at the University of San Diego for undergraduate minority students. Write to the address listed below for information.

University Of San Diego
Office Of Financial Aid
5998 Alcala Park
San Diego, CA 92110

1307

Divinity Hall Burses

Amount: Varies **Deadline:** None Specified
Fields/Majors: Theology

Scholarships are available at the Catholic University of America for graduate theology majors planning to enter the priesthood. Contact the financial aid office at the address below for details.

The Catholic University Of America
Office Of Admissions And Financial Aid
Washington, DC 20064

1308

Divisional Scholarship, Academic Scholarship

Amount: Varies **Deadline:** Feb 10, May 1
Fields/Majors: All Areas Of Study

Scholarships are available to John Brown College for full-time undergraduate students who demonstrate superior academic and leadership potential with a GPA of at least 3.5, who were in the top 10% of their graduating class. Write to the address below for details.

John Brown University
Office Of Financial Aid
2000 West University Dr.
Siloam Springs, AR 72761

1309

Doctoral Dissertation Fellowships In Jewish Studies

Amount: $6,000-$8,500 **Deadline:** Jan 3
Fields/Majors: Jewish Studies

Awards are available for students who have completed all academic requirements for the doctoral degree except the dissertation in the field of Jewish studies. Must be a U.S. citizen or permanent resident and give evidence of a proficiency in a Jewish language. Write to the address below for more information.

National Foundation For Jewish Culture
330 Seventh Ave., 21st Floor
New York, NY 10001

1310

Doctoral Dissertation Fellowships In Law And Social Science

Amount: $14,000 **Deadline:** Feb 1
Fields/Majors: Law, Social Science

Fellowships are available for Ph.D. candidates who have completed all doctoral requirements except the dissertation. Proposed research must be in the areas of sociolegal studies, or in the social scientific approaches to law, the legal profession, or legal institutions. Fellowships are held in residence at the AFB. Write to the address listed below for information.

American Bar Foundation
Ann Tatalovich, Assistant Director
750 N. Lake Shore Drive
Chicago, IL 60611

1311

Doctoral Dissertation Grant Program

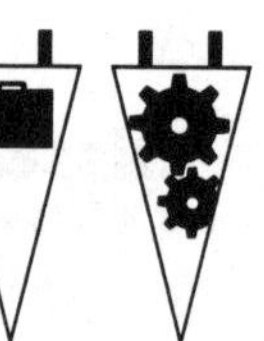

Amount: $10,000 **Deadline:** Jan 31
Fields/Majors: Purchasing, Business, Management, Logistics, Economics, Industrial Engineering

Doctoral dissertation research grants are available for research that can be applied to the management of the purchasing and materials management functions and to help develop high-potential academicians who will teach and conduct research in the field. For doctoral candidates in an accredited U.S. college or university. Write to the address listed below for information.

National Association Of Purchasing Management
Doctoral Research Grant Committee
P.O. Box 22160
Tempe, AZ 85285

1312

Doctoral Dissertation Research In Chinese Studies Scholarships

Amount: $8,000 **Deadline:** Aug 15
Fields/Majors: Humanities, Social Science

Applicants must be doctoral candidates in humanities or social sciences, with an approved dissertation prospectus. Enrollment in a university in the U.S. or Canada required. Write to the address below for more information.

China Times Cultural Foundation
43-27 36th Street
Long Island City, NY 11101

1313

Doctoral Fellowship

AMOUNT: Varies **DEADLINE:** Nov 1
FIELDS/MAJORS: Japanese Studies

Fellowships available to doctoral students in field of Japanese studies who have completed all the academic requirements except the dissertation. Applicants must be able to speak Japanese in order to successfully continue their research in Japan. Write to the address below for additional information.

The Japan Foundation
New York Office
152 West 57th St.
New York, NY 10019

1314

Doctoral Fellowship Program In Biomedical Engineering

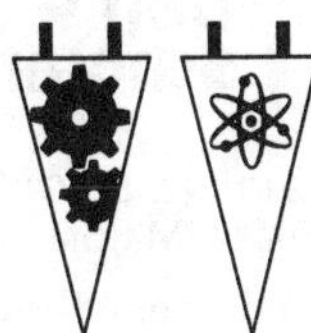

AMOUNT: Tuition and Stipend **DEADLINE:** Dec 11
FIELDS/MAJORS: Biomedical Engineering

Doctoral fellowships are available to support graduate students of outstanding scholarship, ability, and aptitude for future achievements in biomedical engineering research. Write to the address listed below for information.

Whitaker Foundation
Fellowship Programs
1700 North Moore St., Suite 2200
Rosslyn, VA 22209

1315

Doctoral Scholarships

AMOUNT: None Specified **DEADLINE:** None Specified
FIELDS/MAJORS: All Areas Of Study

Doctoral scholarships are available at the Catholic University of America in selected programs. Mainly based on undergraduate academics and GRE scores. Contact the financial aid office at the address below for details.

The Catholic University Of America
Office Of Admissions And Financial Aid
Washington, DC 20064

1316

Doctoral Scholarships

AMOUNT: $3,000 **DEADLINE:** Dec 1
FIELDS/MAJORS: Oncology Nursing

Grants available to doctoral students in the field of oncology nursing. All applicants must be registered nurses. Write to the address below for more information.

Oncology Nursing Foundation
501 Holiday Dr.
Pittsburgh, PA 15220

1317

Doctoral/Law/Veterinary Medicine Program

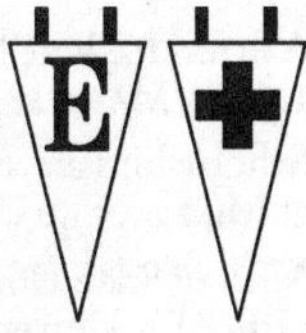

AMOUNT: $4,000 **DEADLINE:** None Specified
FIELDS/MAJORS: Doctoral/Law/Veterinary Medicine

Grants available to African American North Carolinians who are enrolled in a full time doctoral degree program at East Carolina Univ., North Carolina State Univ., the Univ. of North Carolina at Chapel Hill and the Univ. of North Carolina at Greensboro. Priority is given to students pursuing degrees in fields of study where African American participation has been low historically. Students must demonstrate financial need. Write to the address below for details.

North Carolina State Education Assistance Authority
P.O. Box 2688
Chapel Hill, NC 27515

1318

Documentation Intern

AMOUNT: None Specified
DEADLINE: None Specified
FIELDS/MAJORS: Writing

Available for minority students who have strong technical writing experience and skills. Write to the address below for more information.

Nature Conservancy
Cristina Garcia, Recruiting Director
1815 N. Lynn St.
Arlington, VA 22209

1319

Dodd And Dorothy L. Bryan Foundation Student Loans

AMOUNT: $4,000 **DEADLINE:** Varies
FIELDS/MAJORS: All Areas Of Study

Loans for Wyoming residents who live in Sheridan, Campbell, or Johnson counties. Montana residents may also apply if you live in Powder River, Rosebud, or Big Horn counties. Applicant must live in the above areas at least one year prior to applying. For academic loans, the student must be under the age of 25 and have (or had) a minimum GPA of 2.2 and carry 12 credit hours. Contact the address below for further information.

Dodd And Dorothy L. Bryan Foundation
P.O. Box 6287
First Plaza-2 N. Main #401
Sheridan, WY 82801

1320

Dodge Trucks Scholarships

AMOUNT: $1,000 **DEADLINE:** Feb 15
FIELDS/MAJORS: Agricultural Mechanics

Scholarships are available for FFA members pursuing a two- or four-year degree in agricultural mechanics. Write to the address below for details.

National FFA Foundation
Scholarship Office
P. O. Box 15160
Alexandria, VA 22309

1321

Dofflemyer Honors Scholarships For Eagle Scouts

AMOUNT: Varies **DEADLINE:** Mar 31
FIELDS/MAJORS: All Areas Of Study

For Eagle Scouts residing in Arizona, California, Hawaii, Nevada, Utah, or Rock Springs, Wyoming, who are seeking a bachelor's degree from Stanford University. Based primarily on financial need. Write to the address below for complete details.

Stanford University
Financial Aid Office
Room 214, Old Union
Stanford, CA 94025

1322

Dolphin Scholarship Foundation

AMOUNT: $1,750 **DEADLINE:** Apr 15
FIELDS/MAJORS: All Areas Of Study

These scholarships are intended for sons/daughters of members or former members of the submarine force. These members must have served in the submarine force for at least five years of active duty. Applies to undergraduate study only. Write to the address below for details. Include a list of commands in which your parent served and the dates of service at those commands. If retired or discharged, specify the last command served under. Also include an SASE with your request.

Dolphin Scholarship Foundation
Norfolk Naval Station
405 Dillingham Blvd.
Norfolk, VA 23511

1323

Dominican Honor Scholarship

GPA 3.0+

AMOUNT: $3,500 (max) **DEADLINE:** Mar 15
FIELDS/MAJORS: All Areas Of Study

Applicants must be incoming freshmen who meet two of the three requirements for eligibility: minimum 3.0 GPA, ACT score of 20 (SAT-1000), or rank in the top 25% of their graduating class. Renewable. Write to the address below for details.

Edgewood College
Office Of Admissions
855 Woodrow Street
Madison, WI 53711

1324

Don & Rose Kutchera Scholarship

AMOUNT: $350 **DEADLINE:** Apr 1
FIELDS/MAJORS: All Areas Of Study

Award for entering freshmen who were graduates of Oshkosh North, West, or Lourdes Academy. Must have a good academic record and involvement in community activities. Contact the Admissions Office, UW Oshkosh, for more information.

University Of Wisconsin, Oshkosh
Financial Aid Office, Dempsey 104
800 Algoma Blvd.
Oshkosh, WI 54901

1325

Don L. Calame Scholarship

AMOUNT: $500 **DEADLINE:** None Specified
FIELDS/MAJORS: Business

Students must be full-time COBA majors with leadership potential and financial need. Contact the COBA office for more information.

Southwest Missouri State University
Office Of Financial Aid
901 South National Ave.
Springfield, MO 65804

1326

Don Lugo Sports Booster Club Scholarship

AMOUNT: None Specified **DEADLINE:** None Specified
FIELDS/MAJORS: All Areas Of Study

Scholarship offered to graduating seniors at Don Lugo high school who have participated in one or more varsity athletic programs. Write to the address below for details.

Don Lugo Sports Booster Club Scholarship Fund
P.O. Box 3000-353
Chino, CA 91710

1327

Don Wessel Management Scholarship

AMOUNT: $250 **DEADLINE:** None Specified
FIELDS/MAJORS: Management

Student must be a management major or a member of the Society for the Advancement of Management. Contact the COBA office for more information.

Southwest Missouri State University
Office Of Financial Aid
901 South National Ave.
Springfield, MO 65804

1328

Donald A. Norton Memorial Scholarship

AMOUNT: $500 **DEADLINE:** Apr 1
FIELDS/MAJORS: All Areas Of Study

Awards for full-time students with a GPA of 2.0 or higher and demonstrated financial need. Write to the address below for more information.

Christopher Newport University
Office Of Financial Aid
50 Shoe Lane
Newport News, VA 23606

1329

Donald Groves Fund Awards In Numismatics

AMOUNT: None Specified **DEADLINE:** None Specified
FIELDS/MAJORS: Numismatics

Grants to support the study and publishing of works involving early American coinage and currency (pre-1800). Funds support travel, research, and publication. Write to the address below for details.

American Numismatic Society
Broadway At 155th Street
New York, NY 10032

1330

Donald J. Leitch Memorial Scholarships

AMOUNT: None Specified **DEADLINE:** Feb 1
FIELDS/MAJORS: Accounting

Scholarships are awarded to students who are majoring in accounting at Murray State University. Write to the address below for details.

Murray State University
Office Of University Scholarships
Ordway Hall, 1 Murray St.
Murray, KY 42071

1331

Donald Leo Netzer Memorial Scholarship

Amount: $600 **Deadline:** Mar 1
Fields/Majors: Secondary Education

Awards for secondary education majors in natural science, social science, geography, geology, or biology. Elementary education majors with a minor in elementary science or social science are also eligible. Four-year or five-year prep program students with 3.0 GPA, and courses in conservation, environmental education, and/or ecology are also eligible. Contact the College of Education and Human Services, UW Oshkosh for more details.

University Of Wisconsin, Oshkosh
Financial Aid Office, Dempsey 104
800 Algoma Blvd.
Oshkosh, WI 54901

1332

Donald Malcolm MacArthur Scholarship

Amount: $2,500 **Deadline:** Mar 15
Fields/Majors: All Areas Of Study

Scholarships for students of Scottish descent in their third or forth year of undergraduate studies or in graduate school. Based on need, academics, and goals. Preference to students attending schools or from within 200 miles of Washington. Further preference is given to students who will contribute to the knowledge of Scottish history and culture. Write to the address listed below for additional information.

St. Andrew's Society Of Washington, DC
Charity And Education Committee
7012 Arandale Rd.
Bethesda, MD 20817

1333

Donald N. McDowell Honorary Scholarships

Amount: $750 **Deadline:** Feb 15
Fields/Majors: Agriculture

Scholarships are available for FFA members pursuing a four-year degree in any area of agriculture who reside in Wisconsin. Write to the address below for details.

National FFA Foundation
Scholarship Office
P.O. Box 15160
Alexandria, VA 22309

1334

Dorchester Woman's Club Scholarship

Amount: $500 **Deadline:** Feb 15
Fields/Majors: Music-Voice

Applicant must be a senior in a Massachusetts high school who will enroll in a four-year accredited college or university and present a letter of endorsement from sponsoring women's club in your community. Write to the address below for details.

General Federation Of Women's Clubs Of Massachusetts
Chairman, Music Division
245 Dutton Rd., P.O. Box 679
Sudbury, MA 01776

1335

Doreen Pollack Scholarship Fund

Amount: Varies **Deadline:** Mar 1
Fields/Majors: Communication Disorders

Scholarships for graduates or postgraduates of a program in communication disorders, who are members of AVI, Inc. Write to AVI at the address below for details. This program is in honor of Ms. Doreen Pollack.

Auditory-Verbal International, Inc.
Executive Director
2121 Eisenhower Ave., Suite 402
Alexandria, VA 22314

1336

Doris And Thornton Seligman Memorial Scholarships

Amount: Varies **Deadline:** Mar 1
Fields/Majors: All Areas Of Study

Awards are available at the University of New Mexico for undergraduates from New Mexico who have academic ability. Write to the address below for more information.

University Of New Mexico, Albuquerque
Office Of Financial Aid
Albuquerque, NM 87131

1337

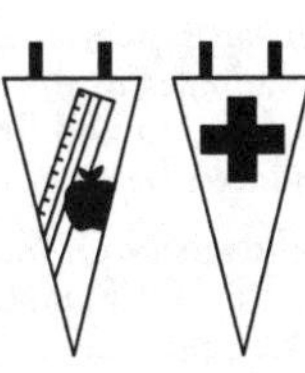

Doris Ledbetter Memorial Scholarship

Amount: $1,000 **Deadline:** Mar 15
Fields/Majors: Education Or Nursing

Awards for Jacksonville State University students in the field of education or nursing. Financial need considered. Write to the address below for more information.

Jacksonville State University
Financial Aid Office
Jacksonville, AL 36265

1338

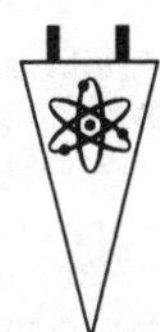

Doris-Glenn Hextell Agriculture Scholarship

Amount: $500 **Deadline:** Nov 17
Fields/Majors: Agriculture

Scholarships are available for students majoring in agriculture. Based on academic excellence and financial need. Write to the address below for more information.

Illinois State University, Dept. Of Agriculture
Turner Hall 150
Campus Box 5020
Normal, IL 61761

1339

Dorothy Armstrong Community Service Scholarship Fund

Amount: $1,500 **Deadline:** Mar 1
Fields/Majors: All Areas Of Study

Award for qualified seniors at Thomas Dale High School in Chesterfield County, Virginia. Selection is based on scholarship, financial need, and participation in school and community service activities. Must have been admitted to an accredited two- or four-year college or university in the continental U.S. Renewable. Students who would like to be considered for this award must contact their high school guidance counselor or principal to be nominated.

Community Foundation Serving Richmond And Central Virginia
1025 Boulders Parkway, Suite 405
Richmond, VA 23225

1340

Dorothy Hatch Scholarship

AMOUNT: Varies **DEADLINE:** Mar 1
FIELDS/MAJORS: All Areas Of Study

Awards are available at the University of New Mexico for American Indian students. Write to the address below for more information.

University Of New Mexico, Albuquerque
Office Of Financial Aid
Albuquerque, NM 87131

1341

Dorothy I. Cline Scholarship

AMOUNT: Varies **DEADLINE:** Mar 1
FIELDS/MAJORS: American Politics And Government, Public Policy, Political Theory

Awards are available at the University of New Mexico for undergraduates in the areas of study above. GPA is given primary consideration and financial need is a secondary factor. Write to the address below for more information.

University Of New Mexico, Albuquerque
Office Of Financial Aid
Albuquerque, NM 87131

1342

Dorothy I. Mitstifer Fellowship

AMOUNT: $2,000 **DEADLINE:** Jan 15
FIELDS/MAJORS: Home Economics/Related Fields

Applicants must be chapter advisers of Kappa Omicron Nu and wish to pursue graduate or postgraduate study. Write to the address below for details.

Kappa Omicron Nu Honor Society
4990 Northwind Dr., Suite 140
East Lansing, MI 48823

1343

Dorothy Lemke Howarth Scholarship

AMOUNT: $1,000 To $2,000 **DEADLINE:** Feb 1
FIELDS/MAJORS: Engineering

Two scholarships for female students who will be sophomores and majoring in engineering. Must be a U.S. citizen and have a GPA of at least 3.5. Information and applications for the SWE awards are available from the deans of engineering schools, or write to the address below for complete details. Please be certain to enclose an SASE.

Society Of Women Engineers
120 Wall Street, 11th Floor
New York, NY 10005

1344

Dorothy Ornest Award

AMOUNT: Varies **DEADLINE:** Mar 1
FIELDS/MAJORS: Music

Award for a sophomore, junior, or senior for outstanding vocal and academic accomplishment and commitment to making music in as many ways as possible. Contact the Director of Scholarships, Department of Music, not the address below, for more information.

University Of Massachusetts, Amherst
255 Whitmore Administration Building
Box 38230
Amherst, MA 01003

1345

Dorothy Sterne Scholarship

AMOUNT: Varies **DEADLINE:** Mar 15
FIELDS/MAJORS: Nursing

Awards for Jacksonville State University students who are in the field of nursing. Contact the dean of the college of nursing for more information.

Jacksonville State University
Financial Aid Office
Jacksonville, AL 36265

1346

Dorothy Vandercook Peace Scholarship

AMOUNT: $250 **DEADLINE:** Mar 1
FIELDS/MAJORS: All Areas Of Study

Scholarships for graduating high school seniors or college freshmen who are devoted to the cause of world peace and the reduction of nuclear weapons. Write to the address below for details.

Grandmothers For Peace
Dorothy Vandercook Peace Scholarship
9444 Medstead Way
Elk Grove, CA 95758

1347

Douglas E. Flaherty Sr. Memorial Poetry Award

AMOUNT: $50-$200 **DEADLINE:** Mar 15
FIELDS/MAJORS: Poetry

Awards for students at UW Oshkosh who write poetry. There is no restriction on form, content, or style of poems; maximum of six poems per entrant. Contact the English Department, UW Oshkosh, for more details.

University Of Wisconsin, Oshkosh
Financial Aid Office, Dempsey 104
800 Algoma Blvd.
Oshkosh, WI 54901

1348

Douglas Products And Packaging Scholarships

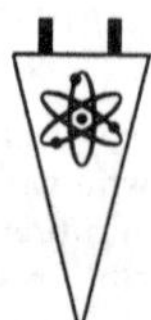

AMOUNT: $1,000 **DEADLINE:** Feb 15
FIELDS/MAJORS: Agriculture

Scholarships are available for FFA members pursuing a two- or four-year degree in any area of agriculture who reside in Missouri.

Write to the address below for details.

National FFA Foundation
Scholarship Office
P.O. Box 15160
Alexandria, VA 22309

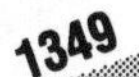

1349 Dow Chemical Scholarships

Amount: Varies **Deadline:** Mar 1
Fields/Majors: Engineering

Awards are available at the University of New Mexico for minority undergraduates who have demonstrated high proficiency in math and science. Selection based on scholastic performance and extracurricular activities. Write to the address below for more information.

University Of New Mexico, Albuquerque
Office Of Financial Aid
Albuquerque, NM 87131

1350 Dr. Kiyoshi Sonoda Memorial Scholarship

Amount: Varies **Deadline:** Apr 1
Fields/Majors: Dentistry

Applicants must be of Japanese ancestry and majoring in dentistry. Applications and information may be obtained from local JACL chapters, district offices, and the national headquarters at the address below. Please indicate your level of study and be certain to include a legal-sized SASE.

Japanese American Citizens League
National Scholarship And Award Program
1765 Sutter St.
San Francisco, CA 94115

1351 Dr. A.F. Zimmerman Award

Amount: $1,250 **Deadline:** Mar 15
Fields/Majors: History

Applicants must be a student member of Phi Alpha Theta entering a graduate program leading to a master's degree in history. Write to address below for details. Please indicate the name of your chapter. Information may be available from your chapter officers.

Phi Alpha Theta—International Honor Society In History
Headquarters Office
50 College Dr.
Allentown, PA 18104

1352 Dr. Agnes Logan Braganza Scholarship

Amount: $500 **Deadline:** Apr 1
Fields/Majors: All Areas Of Study

Awards for students who are sophomores or higher with a GPA of at least 2.0 and 30 or more credit hours earned. Applicants must be females who are age 30 or above. Write to the address below for more information.

Christopher Newport University
Office Of Financial Aid
50 Shoe Lane
Newport News, VA 23606

1353 Dr. And Mrs. Emil Amberg Memorial Scholarship

Amount: Varies **Deadline:** Mar 1
Fields/Majors: Medicine

Awards are available at the University of New Mexico for medical students who demonstrate academic ability and financial need. Write to the address below for more information.

University Of New Mexico, Albuquerque
Office Of Financial Aid
Albuquerque, NM 87131

1354 Dr. And Mrs. R.G. Kennedy Endowed Scholarship Fund

Amount: Varies **Deadline:** None Specified
Fields/Majors: Christian Service

Awards are available for students at Cedarville College who are preparing for full-time Christian service careers. Must have a GPA of at least 2.0. Write to the address below for more information.

Cedarville College
Financial Aid Office
P.O. Box 601
Cedarville, OH 45314

1355 Dr. And Mrs. Robert Moersch Scholarship

Amount: $500 **Deadline:** Mar 15
Fields/Majors: Commerce, Business

Awards for Jacksonville State University juniors and seniors who are majoring in commerce or business. Must have a major GPA of 3.0 and a cumulative GPA of at least 2.5. Contact the college of commerce and business for more details.

Jacksonville State University
Financial Aid Office
Jacksonville, AL 36265

1356 Dr. Barrett Walker Loan Program

Amount: $1,500 (max) **Deadline:** None Specified
Fields/Majors: All Areas Of Study

A student loan program for Mercyhurst upperclassmen. Preference will be given to juniors and seniors who have acceptable academic records. Write to the address below for details.

Mercyhurst College
Glenwood Hills
Erie, PA 16546

1357 Dr. D.H. & Catherine Dean Christiansen Scholarship

Amount: $1,500 **Deadline:** Apr 15
Fields/Majors: Education

Scholarships are available at the University of Utah for full-time students enrolled in a teacher education program. Preference is given to single parent heads of households. Write to the address below for details.

University Of Utah
Education Advising Center
226 Milton Bennion Hall
Salt Lake City, UT 84112

1358 Dr. Dan Trigg Scholarships

AMOUNT: Varies **DEADLINE:** Mar 1
FIELDS/MAJORS: All Areas Of Study

Awards are available at the University of New Mexico for New Mexico residents who have academic ability and financial need. Write to the address below for more information.

University Of New Mexico, Albuquerque
Office Of Financial Aid
Albuquerque, NM 87131

1359 Dr. Ernest Stone Memorial Scholarship

AMOUNT: $1,000 **DEADLINE:** Mar 15
FIELDS/MAJORS: All Areas Of Study

Awards for Jacksonville State University upperclassmen. Write to the address below for more details.

Jacksonville State University
Financial Aid Office
Jacksonville, AL 36265

1360 Dr. Florence L. Burger Scholarship

AMOUNT: Varies **DEADLINE:** None Specified
FIELDS/MAJORS: All Areas Of Study

Award given to an academically qualified undergraduate student who needs financial assistance. Write to the address below for more information.

Mercyhurst College
Financial Aid Office
Glenwood Hills
Erie, PA 16546

1361 Dr. George Alterman Award

AMOUNT: $2,000 **DEADLINE:** May 1
FIELDS/MAJORS: All Areas Of Study

Award established in the name of the first chairperson of the Five Towns College Board of Trustees. It is awarded annually to a Five Towns student based on academic achievement. Write to the address below for more information.

Five Towns College
305 N. Service Road/Lie Exit 50
Dix Hills, NY 11746

1362 Dr. George Gibbons Memorial Scholarships

AMOUNT: Varies **DEADLINE:** Mar 15
FIELDS/MAJORS: Nursing

Awards for Jacksonville State University students who are in the field of nursing. Contact the college of nursing for more information.

Jacksonville State University
Financial Aid Office
Jacksonville, AL 36265

1363 Dr. Glenn R. McElhattan Scholarship

AMOUNT: None Specified **DEADLINE:** None Specified
FIELDS/MAJORS: All Areas Of Study

Scholarships are for high school seniors enrolled at the Venango campus for their freshman year. Contact the Venango campus scholarship committee for more information.

Clarion University
104 Egbert Hall
Office Of Financial Aid
Clarion, PA 16214

1364 Dr. Gombojab Hangin Scholarship

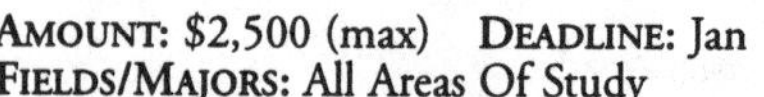

AMOUNT: $2,500 (max) **DEADLINE:** Jan 1
FIELDS/MAJORS: All Areas Of Study

Scholarships are available for students of Mongolian heritage. Write to the address listed below for information.

Mongolia Society, Inc.
Hangin Scholarship Committee
322 Goodbody Hall, Indiana University
Bloomington, IN 47405

1365 Dr. Hannah K. Vuolo Memorial Scholarship

AMOUNT: $250 **DEADLINE:**May 1
FIELDS/MAJORS: Secondary Education

One scholarship is available for residents of New York who will be enrolled in college as an entering freshman. Applicant must be under age 21, a descendant of an American Legion or auxiliary member, and pursuing a degree in secondary education. Based upon academic ability and financial need. Write to the address listed below for additional information.

American Legion, Department Of New York
Department Adjutant
112 State Street, Suite 400
Albany, NY 12207

1366 Dr. Harold Hillenbrand Scholarship

GPA 3.5+

AMOUNT: Varies **DEADLINE:** Jun 1
FIELDS/MAJORS: Dental Hygiene

Scholarships for students who have completed at least one year in a full-time accredited program in dental hygiene. Must have a GPA of at least 3.5. Based on academics, need, and clinical performance. Write to the address below for more information.

American Dental Hygienists' Association Institute For Oral Health
444 N. Michigan Ave., Suite 3400
Chicago, IL 60611

Dr. Harold McGee Scholarship

Amount: $1,000 **Deadline:** Mar 15
Fields/Majors: All Areas Of Study

Awards for JSU freshmen in any area of study. Academics and leadership record considered. Write to the address below for more information.

Jacksonville State University
Financial Aid Office
Jacksonville, AL 36265

Dr. Harry Britenstool Scholarship Fund

Amount: Varies **Deadline:** Jun 1
Fields/Majors: All Areas Of Study

Award for NY students who have been boy, explorer, or star scouts for at least two years and demonstrate academic excellence, financial need, service scouting, and a strong scouting history. Must be accepted in an undergraduate program at an accredited college or university. Write to the address below for complete details.

Boy Scouts Of America, Greater New York Councils
Britenstool Scholarship Committee
345 Hudson St.
New York, NY 10014

Dr. Henry H. And Margaret Zeigel

Amount: $1,000 **Deadline:** None Specified
Fields/Majors: Nursing

Awards for Mesa State sophomores, juniors, or seniors majoring in the field of pre-med or nursing. Must have a GPA of 3.0 or higher. Contact the school of professional studies/nursing area or the school of natural sciences and mathematics.

Mesa State College
Financial Aid Office
P.O. Box 2647
Grand Junction, CO 81501

Dr. Herman Arnold Memorial Scholarship

Amount: $500 **Deadline:** None Specified
Fields/Majors: All Areas Of Study

Awards for Jacksonville State University students in any discipline. Contact the Director, Baptist Campus Ministry.

Jacksonville State University
Financial Aid Office
Jacksonville, AL 36265

Dr. J.R. Van Atta Memorial Scholarship

Amount: Varies **Deadline:** Mar 1
Fields/Majors: Medicine

Awards are available at the University of New Mexico for third-year medical students. Write to the address below for more information.

University Of New Mexico, Albuquerque
Office Of Financial Aid
Albuquerque, NM 87131

Dr. James J. Gorman Memorial Scholarship

Amount: $500 **Deadline:** None Specified
Fields/Majors: Medicine

Scholarship for El Paso resident graduate student who is pursuing a career in medicine. Write to the address listed below for further information.

El Paso Community Foundation
201 East Main, Suite 1616
El Paso, TX 79901

1373

Dr. James Reaves Memorial Scholarship

Amount: Varies **Deadline:** Mar 15
Fields/Majors: All Areas Of Study

Awards for Jacksonville State University upperclassmen. Write to the address below for more details.

Jacksonville State University
Financial Aid Office
Jacksonville, AL 36265

1374

Dr. Lauranne Sams Scholarship

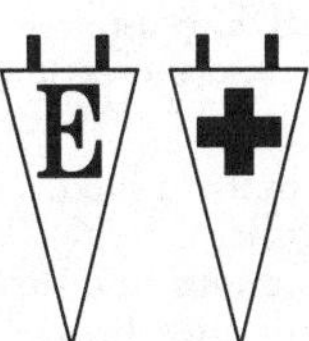

Amount: $1,000-$4,000 **Deadline:** Apr 15
Fields/Majors: Nursing

Scholarships are available for undergraduate African American nursing students. Based on academic record, nursing commitment, involvement in African American community, integrity, and financial need. Preference is given to NBNA members. Write to the address listed below for information.

National Black Nurses Association
NBNA Scholarship Program
P.O. Box 1823
Washington, DC 20013

1375

Dr. Loy Allison Memorial Scholarship

Amount: Varies **Deadline:** Mar 15
Fields/Majors: All Areas Of Study

Awards for Jacksonville State University students. Based on various criteria determined by the JSU scholarship committee. Write to the address below for more details.

Jacksonville State University
Financial Aid Office
Jacksonville, AL 36265

1376

Dr. Mae Davidow Memorial Scholarship

Amount: $1,000 **Deadline:** Mar 1
Fields/Majors: All Areas Of Study

Applicants must be legally blind graduate students who

demonstrate outstanding academic achievement. Write to the address below for details.

American Council Of The Blind
Scholarship Coordinator
1155 15th St., NW, Suite 720
Washington, DC 20005

Dr. Malcolm J. Norwood Memorial Award

Amount: $2,000 **Deadline:** Apr 1
Fields/Majors: Media Communication, Media Technology

Award for students who are deaf or hard-of-hearing and enrolled in a program of media communication or technology. Applicants must be U.S. citizens. Write to the address below for more information.

National Captioning Institute, Inc.
1900 Gallows Road, Suite 3000
Vienna, VA 22182

Dr. Martin Luther King, Jr. Scholarship & Humanitarian Award

Amount: Tuition + $100 **Deadline:** Oct 28
Fields/Majors: All Areas Of Study

E

Award for a full-time African American undergraduate at SIUE. Must have a GPA of at least a 3.0. Applicant must have demonstrated the characteristics and ideals of Dr. King. Write to the address below for more information.

Southern Illinois University At Edwardsville
Office Of The VP For Student Affairs
Campus Box 1058
Edwardsville, IL 62026

Dr. Natividad Macaranas Psi Chi Scholarship Endowment

Amount: $200 **Deadline:** Mar 1
Fields/Majors: Psychology

Award for juniors, seniors, or master's students in their final year of study who are majoring in psychology. Must have a GPA of at least 3.5 and be an active member of the Psi Chi honor society. Write to the address below for more information.

Eastern New Mexico University
College Of Education And Technology
Station 25
Portales, NM 88130

Dr. Pedro Grau Undergraduate Scholarship

Amount: $2,500 **Deadline:** Jun 14
Fields/Majors: Metrology, Atmospheric Science, Ocean Science, Hydrology

Scholarships for students entering their last year of study toward a degree in one of the fields listed above. Based on academic ability and financial need. Requires a GPA of at least 3.0 and U.S. citizenship or permanent residency. Application forms and further information may be obtained through the AMS headquarters at the address below.

American Meteorological Society
45 Beacon Street
Boston, MA 02108

1381

Dr. Robert B. Pamplin, Jr. Society Of Fellows

Amount: Tuition and Fees **Deadline:** Feb 1
Fields/Majors: All Areas Of Study

Awards for entering freshmen who have demonstrated academic achievement. Students named to the society of fellows are guaranteed full tuition and fees without the use of loan programs as well as a $500 stipend each year for books, computers, travel expenses, etc. Renewable. Write to the address below for complete details.

Lewis And Clark College
Office Of Admissions
Portland, OR 97219

1382

Dr. Robert H. Goddard Scholarship

Amount: $10,000 **Deadline:** Jan 9
Fields/Majors: Space Related Science and Engineering, Aerospace Sciences and Technology

Scholarships for students who are U.S. citizens and in at least their junior year of an accredited university. Applicants must have the intention of pursuing undergraduate or graduate studies in aerospace sciences and technology or space-related science and engineering during the interval of the scholarship. Personal need is considered, but is not controlling. Upon final completion of his/her work, the winner may be asked to prepare a brief report on a topic of his/her selection to be presented to the National Science Club. Write to the address below for details.

National Space Club
655 15th Street, NW, Suite 300
Washington, DC 20005

1383

Dr. Roy Morgan Memorial Award

Amount: $150 **Deadline:** Mar 1
Fields/Majors: Psychology

Award for outstanding juniors who are majoring in psychology. Write to the address below for more information.

Eastern New Mexico University
College Of Education And Technology
Station 25
Portales, NM 88130

1384

Dr. Sherman A. Wengerd And Florence Mather Wengerd Fellowship

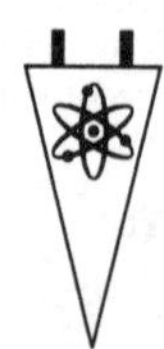

Amount: Varies **Deadline:** Mar 1
Fields/Majors: Earth And Planetary Sciences

Awards are available at the University of New Mexico for doctoral students in the areas above to support field work and other travel related to dissertation work. Write to the address below for more information.

University Of New Mexico, Albuquerque
Office Of Financial Aid
Albuquerque, NM 87131

1385 Dr. Theodore Von Karman Graduate Scholarship Program

AMOUNT: $5,000 **DEADLINE:** None Specified
FIELDS/MAJORS: Engineering, Mathematics, Sciences

Scholarships for graduating ROTC cadets who plan to pursue a graduate degree in engineering, mathematics, or science. Write to the address below for details.

Aerospace Education Foundation
Financial Information Department
1501 Lee Highway
Arlington, VA 22209

1386 Dr. Theron Montgomery Scholarship

AMOUNT: $1,000 **DEADLINE:** Mar 15
FIELDS/MAJORS: All Areas Of Study

Awards for JSU juniors in any area of study. Preference is given to a sensory impaired student. Write to the address below for more information.

Jacksonville State University
Financial Aid Office
Jacksonville, AL 36265

1387 Dr. Theron Montgomery Scholarship

AMOUNT: $1,500 **DEADLINE:** Mar 15
FIELDS/MAJORS: All Areas Of Study

Awards for JSU upperclassmen in any area of study. Write to the address below for more information.

Jacksonville State University
Financial Aid Office
Jacksonville, AL 36265

1388 Dr. Tom Anderson Memorial Scholarship

AMOUNT: $2,000 **DEADLINE:** Mar 15
FIELDS/MAJORS: Travel And Tourism, Hotel/Motel Management

Awards for juniors or seniors in one of the areas listed above who are enrolled in a four-year college. Must have a GPA of 3.0 or better. For study anywhere in North America. Students enrolled in a two-year college are also eligible. Write to the address below for more information.

National Tour Foundation
546 East Main St.
P.O. Box 3071
Lexington, KY 40596

1389 Dr. William Calvert Memorial Scholarship

AMOUNT: Tuition **DEADLINE:** None Specified
FIELDS/MAJORS: English

Awards for Jacksonville State University juniors or seniors in the field of English. Contact the head of the English department for more information.

Jacksonville State University
Financial Aid Office
Jacksonville, AL 36265

1390 Dr. William L. Ullom Memorial Scholarship

AMOUNT: Varies **DEADLINE:** Mar 1
FIELDS/MAJORS: All Areas Of Study

Awards are available at the University of New Mexico for physically handicapped students with financial need who are enrolled for full-time study. Write to the address below for more complete details.

University Of New Mexico, Albuquerque
Office Of Financial Aid
Albuquerque, NM 87131

1391 Dragoco Scholarships

AMOUNT: $500-$2,500 **DEADLINE:** Feb 15
FIELDS/MAJORS: Food Science

Scholarships are available for FFA members pursuing a degree in food science or a related field. Write to the address below for details.

National FFA Foundation
Scholarship Office
P.O. Box 15160
Alexandria, VA 22309

1392 Drake Scholarship

AMOUNT: Varies **DEADLINE:** Apr 15
FIELDS/MAJORS: All Areas Of Study

Awards for graduating seniors of Brewer High School who plan to pursue a postsecondary degree in any discipline. Contact the Brewer High School guidance office for more information.

Maine Community Fund
P.O. Box 148
Ellsworth, ME 04605

1393 Drake University Scholarship Programs

AMOUNT: Varies **DEADLINE:** None Specified
FIELDS/MAJORS: All Areas Of Study

Scholarships, administered by the office of student financial planning, are available to students at Drake University. Criteria for these awards varies. Visit the office of student financial planning to learn more about these scholarship programs.

Drake University
Office Of Admission
2507 University Ave.
Des Moines, IA 50311

1394

Drama Scholarships

AMOUNT: Varies **DEADLINE:** None Specified
FIELDS/MAJORS: Drama

Award for Mesa State drama students. Recipient is selected by the drama department at the school. Write to the address below for more information.

Mesa State College
Office Of Financial Aid
P.O. Box 2647
Grand Junction, CO 81501

1395

Drama Scholarships

AMOUNT: Varies **DEADLINE:** None Specified
FIELDS/MAJORS: Drama

Awards for Jacksonville State University students who are studying in the field of drama. Contact the head of the drama department for more information.

Jacksonville State University
Financial Aid Office
Jacksonville, AL 36265

1396

Drysdales Scholarships

AMOUNT: $1,000 **DEADLINE:** Feb 15
FIELDS/MAJORS: Agriculture

Scholarships are available for FFA members pursuing a two- or four-year degree in any area of agriculture who attend school in Oklahoma. Write to the address below for details.

National FFA Foundation
Scholarship Office
P.O. Box 15160
Alexandria, VA 22309

1397

DuPont Challenge-Science Essay Awards Program

AMOUNT: $50-$1,500 **DEADLINE:** Jan 31
FIELDS/MAJORS: Science

Scholarships in the form of cash awards are available to graduating high school seniors who enter a winning science-related essay in the DuPont Challenge. Entries must be 700-1000 words in length, and can be on any subject within the realm of science. Write to the address listed below for information and an entry blank.

General Learning Corporation
60 Revere Drive
Northbrook, IL 60062

1398

Duracell/National Urban League Scholarship

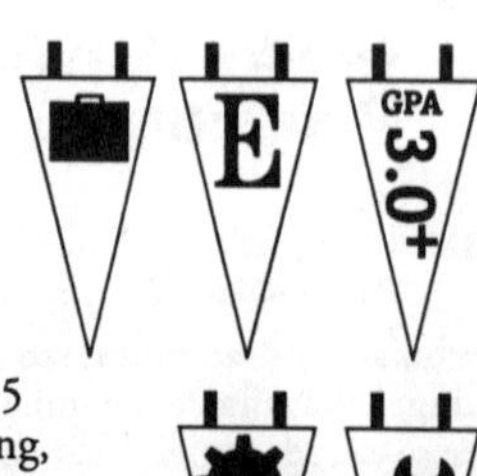

AMOUNT: $10,000 **DEADLINE:** Apr 15
FIELDS/MAJORS: Engineering, Marketing, Finance, Sales, Manufacturing Operations

Scholarships for minority students in their sophomore year of college. Must be in top 1/4 of class in one of the fields above. Renewable for senior year. Contact your local Urban League or write to the address below for details.

National Urban League
500 E. 62nd St.
New York, NY 10021

1399

Duracell/NSTA Scholarships

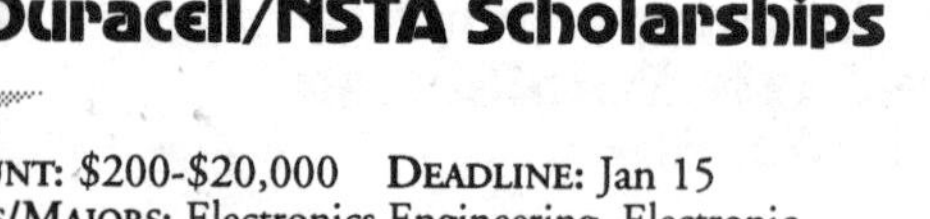

AMOUNT: $200-$20,000 **DEADLINE:** Jan 15
FIELDS/MAJORS: Electronics Engineering, Electronic Technology, Etc.

Contest for high school students who are U.S. citizens and reside in the U.S. or U.S. territories. Students design and build working devices powered by Duracell batteries. Write to the address below for more information.

National Science Teachers Association
Duracell/NSTA Scholarships
1840 Wilson Blvd.
Arlington, VA 22201

1400

Dwayne A. Rohweder Forage Extension Scholarships

AMOUNT: $200 **DEADLINE:** Feb 15
FIELDS/MAJORS: Agriculture

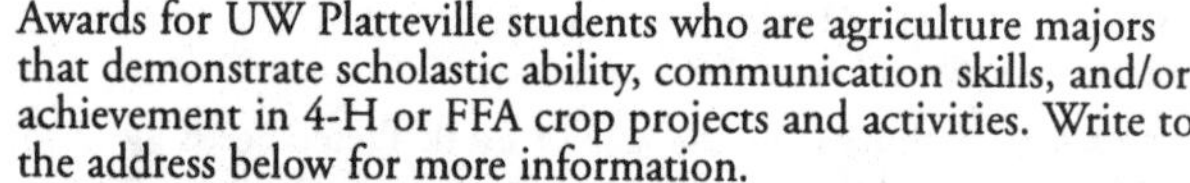

Awards for UW Platteville students who are agriculture majors that demonstrate scholastic ability, communication skills, and/or achievement in 4-H or FFA crop projects and activities. Write to the address below for more information.

University Of Wisconsin, Platteville
Office Of Admissions and Enrollment Mgt.
Platteville, WI 53818

1401

Dwight David Eisenhower Transportation Fellowship Program

AMOUNT: $16,800-$19,200 **DEADLINE:** Feb 15
FIELDS/MAJORS: Any Fields Related To Transportation

Graduate awards are available to assist in upgrading the total transportation community in the U.S. Applicants must be U.S. citizens who wish to obtain research-based graduate degrees and who plan to enter the transportation profession after the completion of their education. Write to the address listed below for information.

Federal Highway Administration
901 North Stuart St., Suite 300
National Highway Institute, HHI-20
Arlington, VA 22203

1402

Dwight L. Smith Prize

AMOUNT: $500 **DEADLINE:** Jun 30
FIELDS/MAJORS: Western History

A biennial award (given in even numbered years) of $300 to the author and $200 to the publisher given to the creator of a bibliographic or research work serving historians and other persons engaged in research on western history. Write to the address listed below for information.

Western History Association
University Of New Mexico
1080 Mesa Vista Hall
Albuquerque, NM 87131

1403

E. Ray Love Memorial Scholarship

AMOUNT: $1,000 **DEADLINE:** None Specified
FIELDS/MAJORS: Business

Student must be a full-time COBA major. Preference is given to an upper division student with financial need. Contact the COBA office for more information.

Southwest Missouri State University
Office Of Financial Aid
901 South National Ave.
Springfield, MO 65804

1404

E. Winthrop Taylor Memorial Scholarships

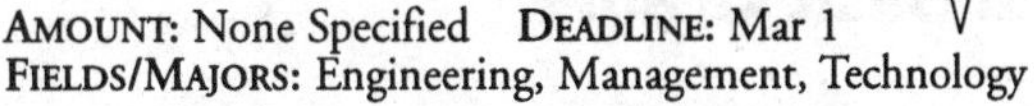

AMOUNT: None Specified **DEADLINE:** Mar 1
FIELDS/MAJORS: Engineering, Management, Technology

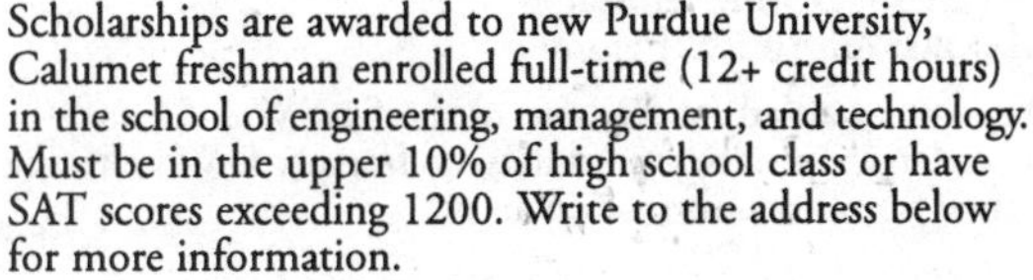

Scholarships are awarded to new Purdue University, Calumet freshman enrolled full-time (12+ credit hours) in the school of engineering, management, and technology. Must be in the upper 10% of high school class or have SAT scores exceeding 1200. Write to the address below for more information.

Purdue University, Calumet
Office Of Financial Aid
Hammond, IN 46322

1405

E.J. Kelly Endowment Award

AMOUNT: $500 **DEADLINE:** None Specified
FIELDS/MAJORS: Pulp and Paper Science, Graphic Arts

Grant for sophomores and juniors in the Department of Paper and Printing Science and Engineering at WMU. Based on need. Renewable. Write to the address below for more information.

Western Michigan University
College Of Engineering and Applied Science
Dept. Of Paper and Printing Science and Eng.
Kalamazoo, MI 49008

1406

E.P. Kuhl Shakespeare Essay Prize

AMOUNT: $100 **DEADLINE:** Mar 15
FIELDS/MAJORS: English, Literature, Creative Writing

A scholarship is available at the University of Iowa for a full-time junior or senior who submits the best essay on Shakespeare. Write to the address listed below for information.

University of Iowa
Department Of English
308 English—Philosophy Building
Iowa City, IA 52242

1407

E.W. Eldridge, Jr. Scholarship

AMOUNT: Varies **DEADLINE:** Mar 1
FIELDS/MAJORS: Economics

Awards for students enrolled in economics who have financial need and strong academic achievement. For entering sophomores, juniors, or seniors. Contact the Chair, Economics Department, for more information.

University Of Massachusetts, Amherst
Chair, Economics Department
Amherst, MA 01003

1408

Eagle Scout Award

AMOUNT: $1,000 **DEADLINE:** None Specified
FIELDS/MAJORS: All Areas Of Study

Award for deserving Eagle Scout who will be entering Birmingham-Southern College as a freshman. Applicants must participate in the National Eagle Scout Scholarship Competition. Automatically renewable for three years. Based on academics, test scores, and recommendations. Write to the address below for further details.

Birmingham-Southern College
Office Of Admissions
900 Arkadelphia Rd.
Birmingham, AL 35254

1409

Eagle Scout Award

AMOUNT: $500 **DEADLINE:** None Specified
FIELDS/MAJORS: All Areas Of Study

Awards for Eagle Scouts or explorer post members admitted to Columbia College. Write to the address below for more information.

Columbia College
Office Of Financial Aid
1001 And Rogers
Columbia, MO 65216

1410

Eagle Scout Leadership Award

AMOUNT: $500 **DEADLINE:** Mar 15
FIELDS/MAJORS: All Areas Of Study

Awards for Eagle Scouts attending Drury College. Must submit a list of leadership activities during high school. Scholarship is for undergraduate or graduate study and is renewable with a GPA of at least 2.5. Write to the address below for more information.

Drury College
Office Of Admissions
900 North Benton Ave.
Springfield, MO 65802

1411

Eagle Scout Scholarship

AMOUNT: Varies **DEADLINE:** Varies
FIELDS/MAJORS: All Areas Of Study

Scholarship is available to the current class of Eagle Scouts who have passed their board of review within the last year. Please contact your local Boy Scout chairman for complete information, or write to the address below. Application is made through each state society.

National Society Of The Sons Of The American Revolution
Scholarship Office
1000 South Fourth Street
Louisville, KY 40203

1412 Eagle Scout/John S. Bell Scholarships

AMOUNT: Varies **DEADLINE:** None Specified
FIELDS/MAJORS: All Areas Of Study

Scholarship is available to new or old cadets who are active in scouting and plan to remain so, and are Eagle Scouts. Must be under 23 years old. Renewal is contingent on the recipient maintaining satisfactory academic record and remain active in scouting. Write to the address below for complete details.

New Mexico Military Institute
Director Of Admissions
101 W. College Blvd.
Roswell, NM 88201

1413 Earl J. Small Growers, Inc. Scholarships

AMOUNT: $2,000 **DEADLINE:** Apr 1
FIELDS/MAJORS: Horticulture

Two scholarships for students in four-year college or university programs in horticulture, with emphasis on greenhouse production. Applicants must be undergraduates and citizens of the U.S. or Canada. Write to the address below for details. The BPFI also sponsors two awards through Future Farmers of America (check with your FFA advisor).

Bedding Plants Foundation, Inc.
Scholarship Program
P.O. Box 27241
Lansing, MI 48909

1414 Earle Graham Scholarship

AMOUNT: $2,000 **DEADLINE:** None Specified
FIELDS/MAJORS: All Areas Of Study

Scholarships available for male undergraduate students at Texas A & M university who are not participants in intercollegiate athletics. Write to the address listed below for further information.

El Paso Community Foundation
201 East Main, Suite 1616
El Paso, TX 79901

1415 Early Childhood Education Professional Loan Forgiveness Program

AMOUNT: $10,000 (max) **DEADLINE:** Dec 1
FIELDS/MAJORS: Early Childhood Education, Childhood Development

Applicants must have a bachelor's degree and Pennsylvania early childhood certification, or an associate's degree in early childhood education or child development. Must be a resident of Pennsylvania. For each year that you work in a Pennsylvania DPW approved day care center or group child care home, and are selected as a participant, PHEAA will pay up to 25% of indebtedness. Write to the address below for more information.

Pennsylvania Higher Education Assistance Agency
1200 N. 7th Street
Harrisburg, PA 17102

1416 East European Area Studies Fellowships And Grants

AMOUNT: $30,000 (max) **DEADLINE:** Dec 1, Feb 1
FIELDS/MAJORS: East European Studies

Fellowships for advanced graduate training and dissertation work, and grants for language training and travel (for fieldwork). For U.S. citizens or permanent residents. Write to address below for details.

American Council Of Learned Societies
Office Of Fellowships And Grants
228 E. 45th St.
New York, NY 10017

1417 East-West Center Scholarships And Basic Grants

AMOUNT: Varies **DEADLINE:** Mar 1
FIELDS/MAJORS: All Areas Of Study

Scholarships are awarded for students at the East-West Center. Based on academics, abilities, potential, and/or need. Write to the address below for more information.

East-West Center
Office Of Student Affairs and Open Grants
1777 East-West Rd.
Honolulu, HI 96848

1418 Easter Seal Society Of Iowa Scholarships

AMOUNT: $400-$600 **DEADLINE:** Apr 15
FIELDS/MAJORS: Rehabilitation/Related Fields

Scholarships for Iowa residents majoring in physical or psychological rehabilitation. For full-time study. Must have a GPA of at least 2.8 and show financial need. Open to college sophomores through graduate students. six awards per year. Renewable. Write to the address below for details. Application forms are available after January 1 of each year.

Easter Seal Society Of Iowa, Inc.
P.O. Box 4002
Des Moines, IA 50333

1419 Eastern Apiculture Society Of North America Scholarships

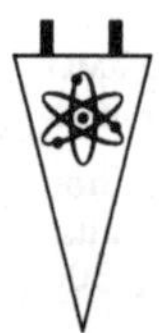

AMOUNT: $500 **DEADLINE:** Feb 15
FIELDS/MAJORS: Agriculture, Agribusiness

Scholarships are available for FFA members pursuing a two-year degree in any area of agriculture or agribusiness who attend school in Connecticut, Delaware, Maine, Maryland, Massachusetts, New Hampshire, New Jersey, New York, North Carolina, Ohio, Pennsylvania, Rhode Island, Tennessee, Vermont, Virginia, or West Virginia. Preference given to those with an apiculture background. Write to the address below for details.

National FFA Foundation
Scholarship Office
P.O. Box 15160
Alexandria, VA 22309

1420

Eastern Equipment Dealers Association Scholarships

Amount: $500 **Deadline:** May 1
Fields/Majors: Agriculture, Life Sciences

Scholarships for students who have completed at least thirty credits while enrolled in the college of agriculture and life sciences and a GPA of at least 2.75. Preference is given to Virginia residents. Write to the address below for more information.

Virginia Tech College Of Agriculture And Life Sciences
Dr. John M. White, Associate Dean
1060 Litton Reaves Hall
Blacksburg, VA 24061

1421

Eastern Theater Scholarship

Amount: Varies **Deadline:**Mar 1
Fields/Majors: All Areas Of Study

Award for an Eastern student active in theater production. Write to the address below for more information.

Eastern Oregon State College
Financial Aid Office
1041 "l" Avenue
La Grande, OR 97850

1422

Eastman Cartwright Lumber, Inc. Scholarships

Amount: $250 **Deadline:** Feb 15
Fields/Majors: Construction Management And Related Fields

Awards are available for full-time continuing students at UW Platteville who are studying construction management or a related field. Write to the address below for more information.

University Of Wisconsin, Platteville
Office Of Enrollment And Admissions
Platteville, WI 53818

1423

Eastman Kodak/U.S. Naval Institute Maritime Photography Contest

Amount: $100-$500 **Deadline:** Dec 31
Fields/Majors: All Areas Of Study

Photo contest for amateur and professional photographers. Photos must pertain to a naval or maritime subject. Three prizes ($500, $300, and $250) and fifteen honorable mention prizes ($100). Write to the address below for further information.

U.S. Naval Institute
Naval And Maritime Photo Contest
118 Maryland Ave.
Annapolis, MD 21402

1424

Ebba Alm Scholarship

Amount: Varies **Deadline:** None Specified
Fields/Majors: All Areas Of Study

Awards for male students at St. Petersburg Junior College. Must have a GPA of at least 3.0 and demonstrated financial need. Preference is given to upper-Pinellas County residents studying natural science. Contact the office of the director of scholarships and student financial assistance or write to the address below for additional information.

St. Petersburg Junior College
Office Of Financial Aid
P.O. Box 13489
St. Petersburg, FL 33733

1425

Ebben Family Scholarship

Amount: $500-$3,000 **Deadline:** Mar 15
Fields/Majors: All Areas Of Study

Applicants must be incoming freshmen who have been involved in co-curricular activities and have displayed academic promise. Preference will be given to Wisconsin residents from the Fox River Valley area. Write to the address below for details.

Edgewood College
Office Of Admissions
855 Woodrow Street
Madison, WI 53711

1426

Ebsco/NMRT Scholarship

Amount: $1,000 **Deadline:** Dec 1
Fields/Majors: Library And Information Science

Applicants must be ALA/NMRT members who are entering an ALA-accredited master's program or beyond. Must be U.S. or Canadian citizens. Write to NMRT scholarship committee chair at the address below for details.

American Library Association/NMRT Scholarship Committee
University Of The Pacific Libraries
3601 Pacific Avenue
Stockton, CA 95211

1427

Economic Assistance Loan, Education Grants, Part-Time Study Grants

Amount: $4,500 (max) **Deadline:** None Specified
Fields/Majors: All Areas Of Study

Scholarships for residents of Wisconsin who are veterans or unremarried surviving spouses and minor dependent children of deceased eligible veterans who are living in Wisconsin at time of application. Unspecified number of loans and grants per year. Contact your county veterans service office, listed in your telephone directory under "Government."

Wisconsin Department Of Veterans Affairs
P.O. Box 7843
30 West Mifflin Street
Madison, WI 53707

1428

Economics Alumni Scholarship

Amount: $350 **Deadline:** None Specified
Fields/Majors: Economics

Student must be a sophomore or above economics major. Must be full-time with a GPA of 3.0 or better. Contact the economics department for more information.

Southwest Missouri State University
Office Of Financial Aid
901 South National Ave.
Springfield, MO 65804

Economics Departmental Scholarships

AMOUNT: Varies **DEADLINE:** Feb 15
FIELDS/MAJORS: Economics

Scholarships are available at the University of Utah for full-time students majoring in economics. Write to the address below for information.

University Of Utah
Dr. E.K. Hunt
308 Business Classroom Building
Salt Lake City, UT 4112

Ed Bradley And Carole Simpson Scholarships

AMOUNT: $2,000-$5,000 **DEADLINE:** Mar 1
FIELDS/MAJORS: Broadcast Or Electronic Journalism

Must be a minority undergraduate seeking a career in broadcast journalism. Based on examples of reporting and/or photographic skills. Thirteen awards are offered per year. Write to the address below for details.

Radio And Television News Directors Foundation, Inc.
RTNDF Scholarships
1000 Connecticut Ave., NW, Suite 615
Washington, DC 20036

Edgar J. Boschult Memorial Scholarship

AMOUNT: $200 **DEADLINE:** None Specified
FIELDS/MAJORS: All Areas Of Study

Four scholarships are available for Nebraska students currently enrolled at the University of Nebraska. Applicant must be enrolled in the ROTC program, be able to demonstrate financial need, and be a U.S. citizen. Veterans attending the University of Nebraska are also encouraged to apply. Write to the address listed below for additional information.

American Legion, Department Of Nebraska
Department Adjutant
P.O. Box 5205
Lincoln, NE 68505

Edgewood Employment Work Program

AMOUNT: $200-$1,600 **DEADLINE:** None Specified
FIELDS/MAJORS: All Areas Of Study

Students in this program work an average of ten hours per week on campus. A limited number of positions are available for those without financial need. Write to the address below for details.

Edgewood College
Office Of Admissions
855 Woodrow Street
Madison, WI 53711

Edgewood Grant

AMOUNT: $200-$2,000 **DEADLINE:** Mar 15
FIELDS/MAJORS: All Areas Of Study

Grants for Edgewood College students, with preference given to students with financial need. For undergraduate study. Write to the address below for details.

Edgewood College
Office Of Admissions
855 Woodrow Street
Madison, WI 53711

1434

Edith H. Henderson Scholarship

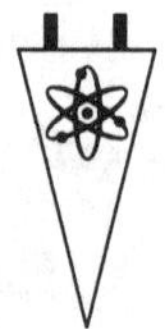

AMOUNT: $1,000 **DEADLINE:** Apr 2
FIELDS/MAJORS: Landscape Architecture/Design

Applicants must be freshman or senior undergraduates, or any level graduate student enrolled in a landscape architect or design program. Must demonstrate an interest in creative writing or public speaking. Write to the address below for additional information.

Landscape Architecture Foundation
4401 Connecticut Ave., NW, Suite 500
Washington, DC 20008

1435

Edmund F. Maxwell Scholarships

AMOUNT: $3,500 **DEADLINE:** None Specified
FIELDS/MAJORS: All Areas Of Study

Scholarships for entering freshmen from Washington, particularly the Seattle area, who have a combined SAT scores of over 1200. Write to the address below for more information.

Edmund F. Maxwell Foundation
P.O. Box 22537
Seattle, WA 98122

1436

Edmund Kieltyka Scholarship

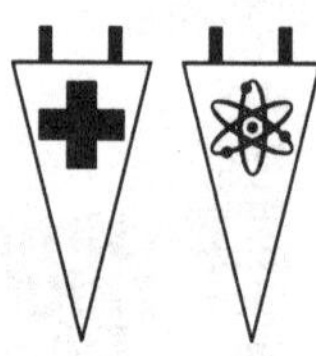

AMOUNT: None Specified
DEADLINE: None Specified
FIELDS/MAJORS: Food, Resources, Agriculture, Crop Science, Nutrition, Horticulture/Floriculture

Scholarships are awarded to Stockbridge students, with preference given to Berkshire students. Contact the director of the Stockbridge School for more information.

University Of Massachusetts, Amherst
Office Of Financial Aid Services
255 Whitmore Admin. Bldg, Box 38230
Amherst, MA 01003

1437

Edna Buchanan Memorial Scholarship

AMOUNT: $500 **DEADLINE:** Apr 1
FIELDS/MAJORS: All Areas Of Study

Scholarship available to students planning to attend any college or vocational school conforming to the GI Bill qualifications, who are currently regular or associate members of the Rocky Mountain

Farmers Union. One award given per year. Write to the address listed below for further information and an application.

Rocky Mountain Farmers Union Scholarship Program
10800 E. Bethany Drive, 4th Floor
Aurora, CO 80014

1438

Edna Meudt Memorial Scholarship Fund

AMOUNT: $500 **DEADLINE:** Feb 1
FIELDS/MAJORS: Poetry

Awards are available for juniors or seniors at any accredited college or university. Students are selected on the basis ten original poems which are submitted. Write to the address below for more information.

National Federation Of State Poetry Societies (NFSPS)
P.J. Doyle
4242 Stevens
Minneapolis, MN 55409

1439

Edna Yelland Memorial Scholarship

AMOUNT: $2,000 **DEADLINE:** May 31
FIELDS/MAJORS: Library Science

Applicants must be a member of ethnic minority group who is pursuing a graduate library degree in library or information sciences. Must be U.S. citizen or permanent resident and California resident. For study in a master's program at a California library school. Number and amount of awards varies. Request an application form and further information from the address below.

California Library Association
Scholarship Committee
717 K St., Suite 300
Sacremento, CA 95814

1440

EDS Scholarship

AMOUNT: Varies **DEADLINE:** Feb 29
FIELDS/MAJORS: Operations Management

Awards for outstanding students in the field of operations management who are U.S. citizens or permanent residents and have a minimum GPA of 3.0. For entering sophomore, junior, or senior students. Contact the SOM Development Office, Room 206, for more information and an application.

University Of Massachusetts, Amherst
SOM Development Office, Room 206
Amherst, MA 01003

1441

Edsel H. Lester Scholarship, Street Family Scholarship

AMOUNT: None Specified **DEADLINE:** None Specified
FIELDS/MAJORS: All Areas Of Study

Scholarships for students from southwestern Virginia attending East Tennessee State University and enrolled in the school of business or participating in varsity sports. Eligible counties are Buchanan, Dickenson, Lee, Russell, Scott, Washington, and Wise. Contact the office of financial aid at the address below for details.

East Tennessee State University
Office Of Financial Aid
Box 70722
Johnson City, TN 37614

1442

Education And Psychology Scholarships

AMOUNT: $600-$2,200 **DEADLINE:** Mar 1
FIELDS/MAJORS: Education And Psychology

Awards for undergraduates in the fields of education or psychology at North Carolina State University. Twenty-five awards given per year. Write to the address below for more information.

North Carolina State University
Anona Smith, Director Student Services
College Of Education and Psychology, Box 7801
Raleigh, NC 27695

1443

Education And Research Trust Award

AMOUNT: $90,000 **DEADLINE:** Dec 20
FIELDS/MAJORS: Allergy/Immunology Medical Research

Grants for M.D. members of the American Academy of Allergy and Immunology (or persons who are awaiting acceptance into the academy) who are junior faculty members (either instructors, assistant professors or equivalent). Applicant must be a U.S. or Canadian citizen or permanent resident. Award amount is spread over three years. Write to the address below for details.

American Academy Of Allergy And Immunology
Jerome Schultz
611 E. Wells Street
Milwaukee, WI 53202

1444

Education Endowed And Private Scholarships

AMOUNT: Varies **DEADLINE:** Feb 15
FIELDS/MAJORS: Education

Scholarships are available at Evangel for full-time students who will be or are pursuing a degree in education. Applicants must have a GPA of at least 3.0. Includes the Thomas and Laura Ardovino Memorial, John Dickinson Memorial, Bessye Hillin Memorial, Rev. and Mrs. T.H. Spence, Jan Sylvester Memorial, and the Education Alumni scholarships. Write to the address listed below for information.

Evangel College
Office Of Enrollment
1111 N. Glenstone
Springfield, MO 65802

1445

Education Incentive Loan Forgiveness Program

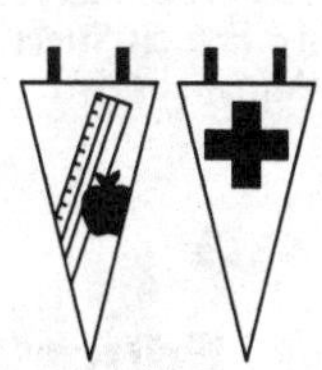

AMOUNT: None Specified **DEADLINE:** Jan 31
FIELDS/MAJORS: Nursing, Education

Forgivable loan program for current or recent (within two years) high school graduates who wish to pursue a career in either nursing or teaching. Must be an Idaho resident, enroll in an Idaho school, and agree to work in Idaho for at least two years after graduation. Write to the address listed below for information.

Idaho State Board Of Education
P.O. Box 83720
Boise, ID 83720

1446

Educational Advancement Foundation Scholarships

AMOUNT: $1,000-$1,500 **DEADLINE:** Feb 15
FIELDS/MAJORS: All Areas Of Study

Scholarships are available to college students with sophomore status or higher, who demonstrate exceptional academic achievement. Applicant must be a full-time student planning on completing degree requirements. Includes the Merit Scholarship ($1,000), based upon academic ability, and the Financial Assistance Scholarship ($1,500), based upon demonstrated financial need. Write to the address below for details.

Alpha Kappa Alpha
5656 S. Stony Island Ave.
Chicago, IL 60637

1447

Educational Advancement Scholarships And Grants

AMOUNT: Varies **DEADLINE:** Varies
FIELDS/MAJORS: Nursing

Applicant must be a registered nurse and a current AACN member who has junior status in an NLN-accredited program. GPA of 3.0 and current employment or employment in last three years as a critical care nurse is required. Write to address below for more information. American Association of Critical Care Nurses has several other scholarships and grants available.

American Association Of Critical-Care Nurses
Educational Advancement Scholarships
101 Columbia
Aliso Viejo, CA 92656

1448

Educational Assistance Grant

AMOUNT: $200-$3,000 **DEADLINE:** Apr 15
FIELDS/MAJORS: All Areas Of Study

Need-based awards for Maryland residents attending a school in Maryland on a full-time basis. Applicant must be an undergraduate with a GPA of 2.5 or above and be able to demonstrate financial need in order for renewal. Write to address below for details.

Maryland State Higher Education Commission
16 Francis Street
Annapolis, MD 21401

1449

Educational Foundation Trust Fund

AMOUNT: $500-$3,000 **DEADLINE:** None
FIELDS/MAJORS: Pharmacy

Applicants must be United States citizens and a member of the academy of students of pharmacy chapter at their school. Write to the address below for more details.

California Pharmacists Association
CPHA Educational Foundation
1112 I St., Suite 300
Sacramento, CA 95814

1450

Educational Grants

AMOUNT: None Specified **DEADLINE:** None Specified
FIELDS/MAJORS: All Areas Of Study

Applicants must be residents of either Auglaize or Allen County, Ohio, who graduated in the top 50% of their high school class, and can demonstrate financial need. Write to the address below for details.

Hauss-Helms Foundation, Inc.
P.O. Box 25
Wapakoneta, OH 45895

1451

Educational Grants For Specialized Training In Guidance & Counseling

AMOUNT: Varies **DEADLINE:** Dec 10
FIELDS/MAJORS: Guidance And Counseling

Grants are available to graduate students enrolled in a master's or Ph.D. level guidance or counseling program. Based on scholastic achievement, financial need, and personal qualifications. Write to the address listed below for information.

Delta Theta Tau Sorority, Inc.
Chariman, Philanthropy Committee
R.R. 4, Box 812
Bloomfield, IN 47424

1452

Educational Opportunity Fund Grants

AMOUNT: $200-$4,000 **DEADLINE:** Oct 1, Mar 1
FIELDS/MAJORS: All Areas Of Study

Economically and educationally disadvantaged high school graduates who need financial assistance for undergraduate and graduate levels of study are eligible. Applicants must demonstrate financial need and who have resided in the state of New Jersey for a minimum of one year. Contact the financial aid officer at your college or your high school guidance counselor to determine what forms are required.

New Jersey Department Of Higher Education
Office Of Student Assistance
CN 540
Trenton, NJ 08625

1453

Educational Opportunity Grant

AMOUNT: $2,500 **DEADLINE:** None Specified
FIELDS/MAJORS: All Areas Of Study

Scholarship program for undergraduate students who have completed their associate degree, who wish to pursue their education in a Washington state college or university. Must demonstrate financial need. Write to the address listed below for information.

Washington Higher Education Coordinating Board
917 Lakeridge Way
P.O. Box 43430
Olympia, WA 98504

1454

Educational Resources Foundation Scholarship

AMOUNT: $1,000 **DEADLINE:** None Specified
FIELDS/MAJORS: All Areas Of Study

Awards for second-year, full-time TTC students who are within two semesters of completing graduation requirements and have a GPA of at least 3.0. Write to the address below for more information.

Trident Technical College
Financial Aid Office
P.O. Box 118067
Charleston, SC 29423

1455

Educational Trust Program

AMOUNT: Varies **DEADLINE:** None
FIELDS/MAJORS: All Areas Of Study

Applicants must be children of members of the order who either a) were in the military and killed or disabled in a war or conflict, or b) were policemen or firemen killed or disabled in the line of duty. Must attend a Catholic school. For undergraduate study. Unspecified number of awards per year. Write to the address below for details.

Knights Of Columbus
Director Of Scholarship Aid
P.O. Box 1670
New Haven, CT 06507

1456

Educator Of Tomorrow Award

AMOUNT: $3,000 **DEADLINE:** Mar 31
FIELDS/MAJORS: Education

Award recipient must be legally blind, and studying toward a career in education at the primary, secondary, or postsecondary level. Write to the address below for details.

National Federation Of The Blind
Mrs. Peggy Elliott, Chairman
814 Fourth Ave., Suite 200
Grinnell, IA 50112

1457

Edward & Marie Plucinski Memorial Scholarship

AMOUNT: None Specified **DEADLINE:** Mar 1
FIELDS/MAJORS: All Areas Of Study

Scholarships are awarded to full-time (12+ credit hours) Purdue University, Calumet junior or senior undergraduate students. Must have a GPA of 3.0 or better. Write to the address below for more information.

Purdue University, Calumet
Office Of Financial Aid
Hammond, IN 46322

1458

Edward B. Holmes Engineering Scholarships

AMOUNT: Varies **DEADLINE:** None Specified
FIELDS/MAJORS: Engineering

Awards available for qualified engineering students at Cedarville College. Must have a GPA of at least 2.0. Write to the address below for more information.

Cedarville College
Financial Aid Office
P.O. Box 601
Cedarville, OH 45314

1459

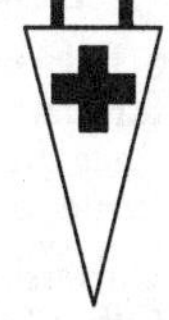

Edward Bangs Kelley And Elza Kelley Foundation Scholarships

AMOUNT: Varies **DEADLINE:** None Specified
FIELDS/MAJORS: Healthcare, Medicine

Applicants must be residents of Barnstable County, Massachusetts, whose education will benefit the health and welfare of the communities of the cape and islands. Write to the address below for details.

Edward Bangs Kelley And Elza Kelley Foundation
Lock Drawer M
243 South St.
Hyannis, MA 02601

1460

Edward D. Stone Jr. And Associates Minority Scholarship

AMOUNT: $1,000 **DEADLINE:** Apr 2
FIELDS/MAJORS: Landscape Architecture/Design

Applicants must be minority students in the last two years of undergraduate study. Must submit a 500-word essay and photo or slide examples of design work. Two awards per year. Financial need is considered. Write to the address below for details.

Landscape Architecture Foundation
4401 Connecticut Ave., NW, Suite 500
Washington, DC 20008

1461

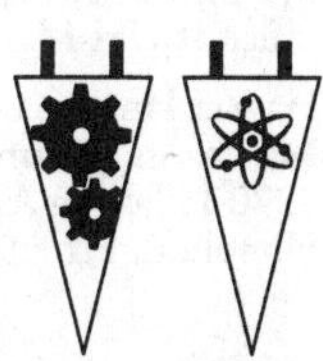

Edward E. Hood Scholarships

AMOUNT: $3,500 **DEADLINE:** Mar 1
FIELDS/MAJORS: Science And Engineering

Awards for African American or Native American freshman who have demonstrated academic performance and leadership potential. Applicants must be from North Carolina and be majoring in science or engineering. Four awards offered per year. Write to the address below for more details.

North Carolina State University
Financial Aid Office
Box 7302
Raleigh, NC 27695

1462

Edward Elliot Scholarship

AMOUNT: Varies **DEADLINE:** Mar 1
FIELDS/MAJORS: Education

Award for a student majoring in education. Preference is given to dyslexic students or those who plan on teaching in a dyslexic program. Write to the address below for more information.

Eastern Oregon State College
Financial Aid Office
1041 "I" Avenue
La Grande, OR 97850

1463

Edward Grisso Memorial Scholarship

AMOUNT: $1,000 **DEADLINE:** Mar 1
FIELDS/MAJORS: All Areas Of Study

Scholarships are available at the University of Oklahoma, Norman for male junior students from Oklahoma, whose GPA has risen since their freshman year. Six or seven awards are offered annually. Write to the address listed below for information.

University Of Oklahoma, Norman
Office Of Financial Aid Services
731 Elm
Norman, OK 73019

1464

Edward Grisso Scholarship

AMOUNT: Varies **DEADLINE:** Mar 1
FIELDS/MAJORS: All Areas Of Study

Awards are available at the University of New Mexico for male juniors who showed improvement in their grades during the sophomore year. Write to the address below for more information.

University Of New Mexico, Albuquerque
Office Of Financial Aid
Albuquerque, NM 87131

1465

Edward Hastings Scholarship

AMOUNT: $500 **DEADLINE:** None Specified
FIELDS/MAJORS: Hotel Management

Scholarships for Hawaii residents studying hotel management at the University of Hawaii at Manoa. Contact the financial aid office at UH Manoa for details.

Hawaii Hotel Association
Ms. Susan Haramoto
2270 Kalakaua Ave, Suite 1103
Honolulu, HI 96815

1466

Edward Henderson Student Award

AMOUNT: None Specified **DEADLINE:** Dec 5
FIELDS/MAJORS: Geriatrics

Award available for a student who has demonstrated a commitment to the field of geriatrics through leadership in areas pertinent to geriatrics, initiation of new information or programs in geriatrics, or scholarship in geriatrics through original research or reviews. Write to the address below for more information.

American Geriatrics Society
770 Lexington Ave., Suite 300
New York, NY 10021

1467

Edward J. & Sadie A. Dempsey Memorial Teaching Scholarship

AMOUNT: $1,350 **DEADLINE:** Mar 1
FIELDS/MAJORS: Education

Awards are available to full-time, second semester junior education majors. Applicant must be from a family of four or more children or have at least one child of their own. Financial need considered. Contact Curriculum and Instruction, UW Oshkosh for more details.

University Of Wisconsin, Oshkosh
Financial Aid Office, Dempsey 104
800 Algoma Blvd.
Oshkosh, WI 54901

1468

Edward J. Schwartz Perpetual Educational Trust Fund

AMOUNT: $1,500 (max) **DEADLINE:** Mar 1
FIELDS/MAJORS: All Areas Of Study

Scholarships are available at the University of Iowa for students who are residents of Wapello County, Iowa. Write to the address listed below for information.

University of Iowa
Office Of Student Financial Aid
208 Calvin Hall
Iowa City, IA 52242

1469

Edward J. Thompson Memorial Scholarship

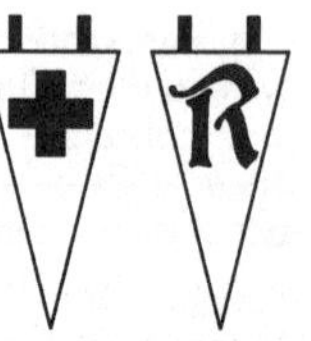

AMOUNT: Varies **DEADLINE:** None Specified
FIELDS/MAJORS: Most Areas Of Study

Awards are available for full-time students at Cedarville College who have a GPA of at least 2.0 and financial need. Preference is given to seminary and nursing students in choosing recipients. Write to the address below for more information.

Cedarville College
Financial Aid Office
P.O. Box 601
Cedarville, OH 45314

1470

Edward L. Murphy Trust Scholarship

AMOUNT: $1,000 **DEADLINE:** Mar 1
FIELDS/MAJORS: All Areas Of Study

Scholarships are available at the University of Oklahoma, Norman for students with "average" grades, who show future potential. Three awards are offered annually. Write to the address listed below for information.

University Of Oklahoma, Norman
Office Of Financial Aid Services
731 Elm
Norman, OK 73019

1471

Edward L. Stanley Scholarship

AMOUNT: None Specified
DEADLINE: None Specified
FIELDS/MAJORS: Mathematics

Scholarships for freshmen at East Tennessee State University majoring in mathematics. Applicants must have a GPA of at least 3.2 and an ACT composite of at least 25. Renewable with a GPA of at least 3.2. Contact the department of mathematics or the office of financial aid for details.

East Tennessee State University
Office Of Financial Aid
Box 70722
Johnson City, TN 37614

1472

Edward Leon Duhamel Scholarship Fund

AMOUNT: $500 **DEADLINE:** Mar 1
FIELDS/MAJORS: All Areas Of Study

Scholarships are available for children of freemasons who are residents of Westerly, Rhode Island. Write to the address listed below for information.

Franklin Lodge
Secretary
20 Elm Street
Westerly, RI 02891

1473

Edward Rosenbaum Scholarship

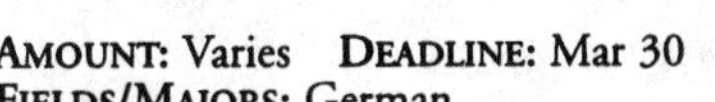

AMOUNT: Varies **DEADLINE:** Mar 30
FIELDS/MAJORS: German

Scholarships are available at the University of Utah for full-time students majoring in German. For juniors, seniors, or graduate students. Write to the address below for details.

University Of Utah
Dr. Randall Stewart
152F Orson Spencer Hall
Salt Lake City, UT 84112

1474

Edward S. Moore Foundation Scholarship

AMOUNT: $2,500 **DEADLINE:** Mar 1
FIELDS/MAJORS: Forestry

Scholarship offered to entering freshmen who are South Carolina residents, and plan to major in forestry. Renewable with a minimum GPA of 2.5. Contact the financial aid office at the address below for details.

Clemson University
Financial Aid Office
G01 Sikes Hall
Clemson, SC 29634

1475

Edward T. Conroy Memorial Grants

AMOUNT: $3,480 (max) **DEADLINE:** Jul 15
FIELDS/MAJORS: All Areas Of Study

Scholarships for disabled public safety employees, children of POWs, and dependents of military/public safety personnel deceased or disabled in the line of duty. Must be Maryland residents attending Maryland schools. Write to the state scholarship administration at the address below for more details.

Maryland State Higher Education Commission
16 Francis Street
Annapolis, MD 21401

1476

Edwin A. Pruchnik Scholarship

AMOUNT: None Specified **DEADLINE:** Dec 15
FIELDS/MAJORS: Forestry

Scholarships are awarded to juniors or seniors who are majoring in forestry. Contact the Department Head, Forestry and Wildlife Management, for more information.

University Of Massachusetts, Amherst
Department Of Forestry And Wildlife Management
Amherst, MA 01003

1477

Edwin G. & Lauretta M. Michael Scholarship

AMOUNT: Varies **DEADLINE:** Mar 15
FIELDS/MAJORS: All Areas Of Study

Open to minister's wives who are members of the Christian Church (Disciples of Christ). Must have at least a 2.3 GPA. For full-time study. Write to the address below for details.

Christian Church (Disciples Of Christ)
Attn: Scholarships
P.O. Box 1986
Indianapolis, IN 46206

1478

Edwin G. Nourse Award, E.A. Stokdyk Award, Kenneth D. Naden Award

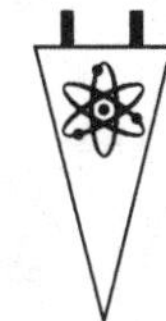

AMOUNT: $600-$1,500 **DEADLINE:** Apr 15
FIELDS/MAJORS: Agriculture

Nourse award is for best doctoral dissertation. Other awards are for top two master theses on topics concerned with agricultural cooperatives. Graduate students in economics, business, communications, or sociology who intend a career in agriculture are eligible. Each entry must be accompanied by a registration form which is available from NCFC. Write to "Graduate Scholarships" at the address below for details and registration.

National Council Of Farmer Cooperatives Education Foundation
50 F Street, NW, Suite 900
Washington, DC 20001

1479

Edwin H. Angevine Fund

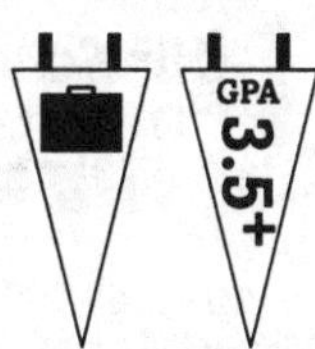

AMOUNT: Varies **DEADLINE:** Mar 15
FIELDS/MAJORS: Business

Awards open to Teikyo Post seniors who are in the school of business administration with a GPA of at least 3.5. Write to the address below for more information.

Teikyo Post University
Office Of Financial Aid
800 Country Club Road
Waterbury, CT 06723

1480

Edwin J. Forand Memorial Scholarship

AMOUNT: None Specified **DEADLINE:** Apr 28
FIELDS/MAJORS: Theater Arts

Scholarship offered to students pursuing or planning to pursue studies in the theater arts. Must live in a 25-mile radius of Enfield, CT/Springfield, MA and be enrolled in undergraduate study. College seniors are eligible only if continuing on to graduate work majoring in theatre. To apply, provide two letters of recommendation, one from a dramatic or musical reference and one from an academic source; a current resume; and a signed letter explaining your involvement in the performing arts and goals for your future. Write to the address below for more details.

St. Martha's Players
c/o Lorry Potvin
27 Green Valley Drive
Enfield, CT 06082

1481

Edwin O. Stene Scholarship Program

Amount: $1,000 **Deadline:** Apr 26
Fields/Majors: Public Administration

Scholarships are available for public administration graduate students specializing in local government. Write to the address below for more information.

International City/county Management Association (ICMA)
Monica Bowman
777 North Capitol St, NE, Suite 500
Washington, DC 20002

1482

Egan Honors Scholarships

Amount: $500-50% Tuition **Deadline:** None Specified
Fields/Majors: All Areas Of Study

Scholarships for students who scored over 500 on each section of the SAT (over 24 composite ACT) and ranked in the top 20% of their high school class. Renewable. Write to the address below for details.

Mercyhurst College
Glenwood Hills
Erie, PA 16546

1483

EIF Scholarship Program For Students With Disabilities

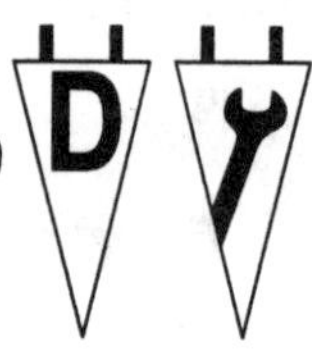

Amount: $5,000 **Deadline:** Feb 1
Fields/Majors: Technical And Electronic Related Studies

Scholarships for students with disabilities, as defined by the 1990 Americans with Disabilities Act, pursuing technical and electronics degrees. Must be accepted or enrolled. For undergraduate or graduate study. Must be a U.S. citizen. Write to the address below for details.

Electronic Industries Foundation
Scholarship Program Coordinator
919 18th Street, NW, Suite 900
Washington, DC 20006

1484

Eileen C. Maddex Fellowship

Amount: $2,000 **Deadline:** Apr 1
Fields/Majors: Home Economics/Related Fields

Applicants must be members of Kappa Omicron Nu and a master's candidate. Write to the address below for details.

Kappa Omicron Nu Honor Society
4990 Northwind Dr., Suite 140
East Lansing, MI 48823

1485

Eileen Marie Mahan Nursing Scholarship

Amount: $1,500 (max) **Deadline:** None Specified
Fields/Majors: Nursing

Awards for second year females at St. Petersburg Junior College studying nursing. Based on academic and personal qualities that are likely to enable them to give leadership in the field of nursing in the future. Write to the address below or contact the nursing program director at your campus location.

St. Petersburg Junior College
Financial Aid Office
P.O. Box 13489
St. Petersburg, FL 33733

1486

Eileen Townsend Nagatomo Memorial Scholarship

Amount: $1,000 **Deadline:** None Specified
Fields/Majors: Theater

Awards for Mesa State sophomores, juniors, or seniors majoring in theater. Must have a GPA of at least 2.5. Contact the theater department for more information.

Mesa State College
Financial Aid Office
P.O. Box 2647
Grand Junction, CO 81501

1487

ELCA-Women Of The ELCA Scholarships

Amount: $500-$2,000 **Deadline:** Mar 1
Fields/Majors: All Areas Of Study (except church-certified professions)

Scholarships for laywomen, 21 years old or older, who are members of an ELCA congregation and have experienced an interruption in their schooling of at least 2 years since high school. Cannot be studying for ordination, the diaconate, or church-certified professions. Based on academics, need, educational goals, and Christian commitment. Must be a U.S. citizen. Write to the address below for details.

Women Of The Evangelical Lutheran Church In America
8765 W. Higgins Road
Chicago, IL 60631

1488

ELCA Grant

Amount: $500 **Deadline:** None Specified
Fields/Majors: All Areas Of Study

Award available to students at Carthage who are members of parishes affiliated with the Evangelical Lutheran Church in America. Renewable. Write to the address below for more information.

Carthage College
Financial Aid Office
Kenosha, WI 53140

1489

Eleanor H. Lowry Scholarship

Amount: None Specified **Deadline:** None Specified
Fields/Majors: Nursing

Awards are available for ETSU students in the A.A.S. nursing program. Contact the Dean's Office, College of Nursing, for more information.

East Tennessee State University
Office Of Financial Aid
Box 70722
Johnson City, TN 37614

1490

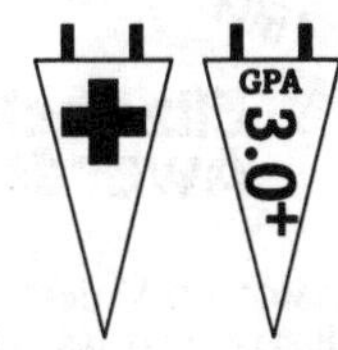

Eleanor Hansen Memorial Fund Scholarship

Amount: $200 **Deadline:** None Specified
Fields/Majors: Nursing

Award for full-time Mesa State students who are studying nursing. Must have a GPA of at least 3.0. Preference is given to student nurses whose goal is to work in the area of cancer research and care of cancer patients. Contact the School of Professional Studies/Nursing Area for more details.

Mesa State College
Office Of Financial Aid
P.O. Box 2647
Grand Junction, CO 81501

1491

Eleanor Roosevelt Teacher Fellowships

Amount: $10,000 (max) **Deadline:** Jan 9
Fields/Majors: Elementary And Secondary School Teaching

The teacher fellowships are designed for elementary and secondary school teachers who are seeking to advance gender equity in the classroom, increase their effectiveness at teaching math and science to girls, and/or tailor their teaching to the needs of minority students and girls at the risk of dropping out. Fellowships available only to female teachers. Applicants must be U.S. citizens or permanent residents; teach full time at U.S. public schools in grades K-12; have at least five consecutive years full-time teaching experience; and plan to continue teaching for the next five years. Write to the address below for details.

American Association Of University Women
Educational Foundation
2201 N. Dodge Street
Iowa City, IA 52243

1492

Electrical And Computer Engineering Scholarships

Amount: Varies **Deadline:** Mar 1
Fields/Majors: Electrical And Computer Engineering

Awards for students studying electrical or computer engineering at UMass. Includes the Keith R. Carver and the Richard V. Monopoli scholarships. Contact the Department Head, Electrical and Computer Engineering, for more information.

University Of Massachusetts, Amherst
255 Whitmore Administration Bldg.
Box 38230
Amherst, MA 01003

1493

Electrical Engineering Departmental Scholarships

Amount: Varies **Deadline:** Feb 1
Fields/Majors: Electrical Engineering

Scholarships are available at the University of Utah for full-time students enrolled in an electrical engineering program. Write to the address below for details.

University Of Utah
Marian Swenson
3276 Merrill Engineering Building
Salt Lake City, UT 84112

1494

Electronic Data Systems Vision Of Success Scholarship

Amount: Varies **Deadline:** Mar 1
Fields/Majors: Engineering

Awards for juniors enrolled full-time in the college of engineering. Must have a GPA of 3.0 or better and an interest in software development. Contact the director of the minority engineering program for more information.

University Of Massachusetts, Amherst
Director, Minority Engineering Program
Amherst, MA 01003

1495

Elie Wiesel Prize In Ethics

Amount: $500-$5,000 **Deadline:** Jan 13
Fields/Majors: All Areas Of Study

Awards are available to five winners of this annual essay contest. Students are challenged to examine and analyze urgent ethical issues confronting them in today's complex world in a 3000-4000 word essay. Theme-creating an ethical society: personal responsibility and the common good. All college juniors and seniors are encouraged to submit an essay. Write to the address listed below for information.

Elie Wiesel Foundation For Humanity
1177 Avenue Of The Americas
New York, NY 10036

1496

Elinor Fierman Fund

Amount: Varies **Deadline:** Mar 1
Fields/Majors: Geoscience

Awards for sophomore students or above in the department of geoscience. Contact the Head, Geoscience, for more information.

University Of Massachusetts, Amherst
Head, Geoscience
Amherst, MA 01003

1497

Elisabeth M. & Winchell M. Parsons Scholarship

Amount: $1,500 **Deadline:** Feb 15
Fields/Majors: Mechanical Engineering

Applicants must be studying toward a doctorate in mechanical engineering and ASME members if there is a chapter at your university. Must be a U.S. citizen. Application may be made any time during graduate studies. Write to the address below for details. Please be certain to enclose an SASE with your request.

American Society Of Mechanical Engineers Auxiliary, Inc.
345 East 47th Street
New York, NY 10017

1498

Eliza M. Claybrooke Memorial Scholarship

Amount: None Specified **Deadline:** None Specified
Fields/Majors: All Areas Of Study

Scholarships for students at Vanderbilt University who are lineal descendents of confederate soldiers or sailors. Write to the address below for details.

Vanderbilt University
Admissions And Financial Assistance
Box 327, Peabody College
Nashville, TN 37203

1499

Elizabeth Hubler Award

Amount: $275 **Deadline:** None Specified
Fields/Majors: Elementary Education

Award for elementary education major who must demonstrate financial need, academic achievement, and activities. Recipient is selected by the faculty of the curriculum and foundations department. Contact a faculty member of the curriculum and foundations department for further information.

Bloomsburg University
19 Ben Franklin Hall
400 E. Second St.
Bloomsburg, PA 17815

1500

Elizabeth Little Scofield Scholarship

Amount: Varies **Deadline:** Fall
Fields/Majors: Nursing

Scholarships are available at the University of Oklahoma, Norman, for full-time junior or senior nursing students, who demonstrate financial need. Write to the address listed below for information.

University Of Oklahoma, Norman
College Of Nursing
P.O. Box 26901
Oklahoma City, OK 73190

1501

Elizabeth Monroe Drews Scholarships

Amount: $500 **Deadline:** None Specified
Fields/Majors: Education

Award for outstanding graduate students in education who meet admission requirements. Based on letters of recommendation, an essay, and possibly an interview. Contact the Dean's Office in the School of Education.

Portland State University
Student Services
412 School Of Education Building
Portland, OR 97207

1502

Elizabeth S. Johnston Memorial Fund

Amount: $500 **Deadline:** Mar 15
Fields/Majors: All Areas Of Study

Scholarships for West Virginia residents who attend the University of Charleston (WV). Write to the address below for details.

Greater Kanawha Valley Foundation
Scholarship Committee
P.O. Box 3041
Charleston, WV 25331

1503

Elizabeth Waters Dance Awards

Amount: Varies **Deadline:** Mar 1
Fields/Majors: Theater Arts

Awards are available at the University of New Mexico for incoming freshmen who enroll as theater arts majors. Must have an overall GPA of at least 2.0 in high school. Write to the address below for more information. An audition by the applicant is required.

University Of New Mexico, Albuquerque
Office Of Financial Aid
Albuquerque, NM 87131

1504

Elks Foundation Scholarship

Amount: $1,000 **Deadline:** None Specified
Fields/Majors: All Areas Of Study

Awards for full-time TTC students enrolled in an associate degree or diploma or certificate program. Based on motivation, need, skills, grades, and application preparation. For South Carolina residents only. Write to the address below for more information.

Trident Technical College
Financial Aid Office
P.O. Box 118067
Charleston, SC 29423

1505

Elks Lodge #575 Scholarship

Amount: Varies **Deadline:** None Specified
Fields/Majors: All Areas Of Study

Award for Mesa State incoming freshmen who are also residents of Mesa County and graduated high school from District #51. Applicants must have a GPA of at least 3.0 and have financial need. Athletes are not eligible for this award. Write to the address below for more information.

Mesa State College
Office Of Financial Aid
P.O. Box 2647
Grand Junction, CO 81501

1506

Ella Schulz Lynn Scholarship

Amount: $3,000 **Deadline:** Mar 1
Fields/Majors: Liberal Arts

Awards for freshmen females at Lake Erie College who plan to major in a discipline within the liberal arts. Applicant must be a citizen of the united states and demonstrate financial need. Write to the address below for more information.

Lake Erie College
Financial Aid Office
391 W. Washington St.
Painesville, OH 44077

1507

Ella V. Ross Scholarship

Amount: None Specified **Deadline:** None Specified
Fields/Majors: Music

Awards are available for ETSU juniors or seniors majoring in music. Contact the department of music for more information.

East Tennessee State University
Office Of Financial Aid
Box 70722
Johnson City, TN 37614

1508

Ellen Barker Memorial Scholarship

Amount: $275 **Deadline:** Feb 9
Fields/Majors: Psychology

Award for junior or senior psychology major with a high GPA. Preference may be given to a returning adult student. Use Bloomsburg University scholarship application. Contact Dr. Michael Gaynor, Chairperson, Psychology Department, for further information.

Bloomsburg University
19 Ben Franklin Hall
400 E. Second St.
Bloomsburg, PA 17815

1509

Ellert-Brauner Scholarship

Amount: Varies **Deadline:** None Specified
Fields/Majors: Germanic Languages And Literature

Awards for students entering their sophomore, junior, or senior year at UMass enrolled in a germanic languages and literature department. Based on academic achievement and financial need. Contact the head of the germanic languages and literature department, not the address below for additional information.

University Of Massachusetts-Amherst
Office Of Financial Aid Services
255 Whitmore Admin. Bldg., Box 38230
Amherst, MA 01003

1510

Ellice T. Johnston Scholarship

Amount: $1,000 **Deadline:** Jul 1
Fields/Majors: Ceramic Art

Renewable scholarship, awarded twice annually, for Oregon or northern California residents or students. Need is considered but not necessary. Clayfolk members are not eligible. Based on portfolio review. Applicants must have two years of art classes or the equivalent. Write to the address below for details.

Clayfolk
P.O. Box 274
Talent, OR 97540

1511

Elliot Scholarship

Amount: None Specified **Deadline:** Dec 15
Fields/Majors: Forestry

Scholarships are awarded to Massachusetts residents who are majoring in forestry and have demonstrated good character. Scholarship and need will be considered. For entering sophomores, juniors, or seniors. Contact the Department Head, Forestry and Wildlife Management, for more information.

University Of Massachusetts, Amherst
Department Of Forestry And Wildlife Mgmt.
Amherst, MA 01003

1512

Elmer E. Johnson Memorial Scholarships

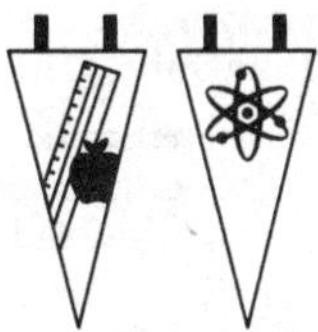

Amount: $1,000 **Deadline:** Feb 15
Fields/Majors: Agricultural Education

Scholarships are available for FFA members pursuing a four-year degree in agricultural education. Write to the address below for details.

National FFA Foundation
Scholarship Office
P.O. Box 15160
Alexandria, VA 22309

1513

Elmer Leach Foundation Scholarship

Amount: $500 **Deadline:** May 1, Dec 1
Fields/Majors: Nursing

Award for full-time student on admission to professional nursing component of program. Financial need is considered. Contact the College of Nursing, UW Oshkosh, for more information.

University Of Wisconsin, Oshkosh
Financial Aid Office, Dempsey 104
800 Algoma Blvd.
Oshkosh, WI 54901

1514

Eloise And Charles Poellnitz Johnston Endowed Scholarship

Amount: $600 **Deadline:** Feb 15
Fields/Majors: Telecommunications

Renewable $600 award given to freshmen, sophomores, and juniors majoring in telecommunications with financial need, high academic ability, and the desire to become successful broadcasters. Priority is given to Alabama residents. Write to the address listed below for additional information.

University Of Alabama
College Of Communications
P.O. Box 870172
Tuscaloosa, AL 35487

1515

Eloise Gerry Fellowships

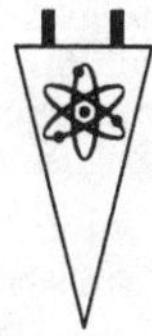

Amount: $1,500-$3,000 **Deadline:** Dec 1
Fields/Majors: Biological And Chemical Research

Awards to support women in biological and chemical research.

Open to graduate and postdoctoral students only. Send an SASE (.55) to the address below for more information.

Graduate Women In Science, Inc.
Sigma Delta Epsilon
P.O. Box 19947
San Diego, CA 92159

1516

Elsa Everette Memorial Scholarship Fund

AMOUNT: $1500 (max) **DEADLINE:** Jun 1
FIELDS/MAJORS: Christian Ministry Or Education

Awards for students from the First Presbyterian Church who are studying for the ministry or Christian education work. Must be from Tulsa, OK.

First Presbyterian Church
709 South Boston Ave."
Tulsa, OK 74119

1517

Elsa Jorgenson Awards

AMOUNT: $6,000 **DEADLINE:** Apr 15
FIELDS/MAJORS: Foreign Language, English, Science

Awards are available at Portland State University for full-time graduate students in the areas of study above. Selection is based on merit and need. Every applicant must also receive a full tuition remission from another source for the award year. Applications are not available until Mar 1.

Portland State University
Office Of Graduate Studies & Research
105 Neuberger Hall
Portland, OR 97207

1518

Elsie Bell Grosvenor Scholarship Awards

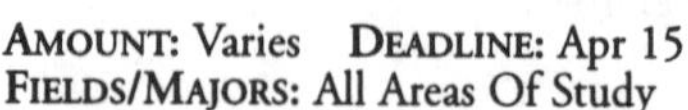

AMOUNT: Varies **DEADLINE:** Apr 15
FIELDS/MAJORS: All Areas Of Study

Applicants must be born deaf or became deaf before acquiring language, and must use speech/residual hearing or lip-reading as primary communication. Also, must be a student from the metropolitan Washington D.C. area—or a student accepted by or attending a metropolitan Washington school—in a college or university program for hearing students. Two scholarships are awarded each year.

Alexander Graham Bell Association For The Deaf
3417 Volta Place, NW
Washington, DC 20007

1519

Elsie Rohrbough English Teaching Major Scholarship

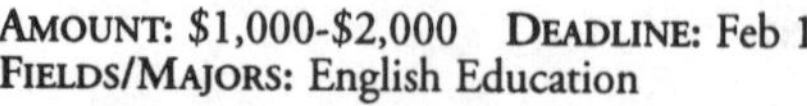

AMOUNT: $1,000-$2,000 **DEADLINE:** Feb 1
FIELDS/MAJORS: English Education

Scholarships are available at the University of Utah for full-time students enrolled in the teacher certification program in secondary education with a concentration in English education. Must be Utah residents.

University Of Utah
Scholarship Chairperson
3500 Lnco
Salt Lake City, UT 84112

1520

Elton Hunsinger Scholarship

AMOUNT: $225 **DEADLINE:** Feb 9
FIELDS/MAJORS: All Areas Of Study

Award for resident advisor with outstanding performance. Must demonstrate financial need, academic achievement, and be considering graduate school. Use Bloomsburg University scholarship application. Contact Mrs. Linda Sowash, Director of Residence Life, for further information.

Bloomsburg University
19 Ben Franklin Hall
400 E. Second St.
Bloomsburg, PA 17815

1521

Elvin S. Douglas, Jr. Scholarship

AMOUNT: Varies **DEADLINE:** Apr 20
FIELDS/MAJORS: Healthcare, Medicine

Scholarships for Cass County, MO, residents who are studying in a health-related field. Based on ability, motivation, continuing good progress, and need.

Elvin S. Douglas, Jr. Scholarship Committee
Linda Wheeler, Chair
1202 East South Street
Harrisonville, MO 64701

1522

Emblem Club Scholarship Grants

AMOUNT: Varies **DEADLINE:** None Specified
FIELDS/MAJORS: Special Education, Particularly Of Deaf And Hearing Impaired

For students enrolled in/accepted to a participating master's degree program which provides training for teachers of deaf and hearing impaired persons. Applicants must be full-time students under the age of fifty with the intention of teaching in the U.S. Students studying special education in other areas will also be considered.

Emblem Club Scholarship Foundation
P.O. Box 712
San Luis Rey, CA 92068

1523

Emergency Aid And Health Professions Scholarships

AMOUNT: $50-$300 **DEADLINE:** None Specified
FIELDS/MAJORS: All Areas Of Study

Scholarships are available for undergraduate American Indian or Alaskan Indian students who require funds for emergency needs. Write to the address below for details. Application allowed only after classes begin.

Association On American Indian Affairs, Inc.
Box 268
Sisseton, SD 57262

1524

Emergency Secondary Education Loan

Amount: $2,500 **Deadline:** Apr 1
Fields/Majors: Education

Scholarships open to full-time undergraduates or graduate students pursuing a secondary education teaching certification at an approved Arkansas school. Applicant must be an Arkansas resident. Repayment of loan is forgiven at 20% for each year taught in approved subject shortage areas in Arkansas secondary schools after graduation. Write to the address below for details.

Arkansas Department Of Higher Education
Financial Aid Division
114 East Capitol
Little Rock, AR 72201

1525

Emerson Grants

Amount: None Specified **Deadline:** None Specified
Fields/Majors: All Areas Of Study

Awarded to enrolled, full-time students who demonstrate financial need. Students must apply for aid each year. Write to the address below for complete details.

Emerson College
Office Of Financial Aid
100 Beacon St.
Boston, MA 02116

1526

Emilio Pucci Scholarship

Amount: $1,800 **Deadline:** Mar 15
Fields/Majors: Design

Scholarships for graduating high school seniors who will be entering the American College for the Applied Arts (Los Angeles, Atlanta, or London). Based on interest and ability in the areas relating to design. Write to the address below for more information.

American College For The Applied Arts
Scholarship Admissions Committee
3330 Peachtree Road, NE
Atlanta, GA 30326

1527

Emily Nelson Moseley Memorial Scholarship

Amount: $1,500 **Deadline:** None Specified
Fields/Majors: Special Education

Student must be a sophomore or above special education major. Contact the curriculum and instruction department for more information.

Southwest Missouri State University
Office Of Financial Aid
901 South National Ave.
Springfield, MO 65804

1528

Emily Reuwsaat Scholarship

Amount: $500 **Deadline:** Feb 9
Fields/Majors: Special Education-Communication Disorders

Awards for students enrolled in special education or the teaching of the deaf, blind, handicapped, or gifted. Must demonstrate financial need, academic achievement and activities. Use Bloomsburg University scholarship application. Contact Dr. Carroll Redfern, Chairperson, Department of Communication Disorders and Special Education, for further information.

Bloomsburg University
19 Ben Franklin Hall
400 E. Second St.
Bloomsburg, PA 17815

1529

Emma May Olson Memorial Scholarship In Education

Amount: Varies **Deadline:** Mar 1
Fields/Majors: Education

Awards are available at the University of New Mexico for students enrolled full-time in the College of Education with demonstrated academic performance. First preference given to American Indians. Write to the address below for more information.

University Of New Mexico, Albuquerque
Office Of Financial Aid
Albuquerque, NM 87131

1530

Emma May Olson Memorial Scholarship In Library Science

Amount: Varies **Deadline:** Mar 1
Fields/Majors: Nutrition Or Family Studies

Awards are available at the University of New Mexico for female students in a nutrition or family studies program. Must be in the top 1/3 of the class. Write to the address below for more information.

University Of New Mexico, Albuquerque
Office Of Financial Aid
Albuquerque, NM 87131

1531

Employee Dependents' Scholarship Program

Amount: None Specified **Deadline:** Mar 15
Fields/Majors: All Areas Of Study

Scholarship program and loan program for children of Fluor Corporation employees. Have your parent contact the Fluor Corporation in Irvine to learn more about these two programs.

Fluor Corporation / Fluor Foundation
Employee Dependents Scholarship Program
3333 Michelson Dr.
Irvine, CA 92730

1532

ENA Foundation Doctoral Scholarship

Amount: $5,000 (max) **Deadline:** Apr 1
Fields/Majors: Nursing

Scholarship is for a nurse pursuing a doctoral degree. Write to the address below for more information.

Emergency Nurses Association (ENA) Foundation
Funding Program
216 Higgins Rd.
Park Ridge, IL 60068

1533

ENA Foundation Undergraduate Scholarship

AMOUNT: $1,500 (max) **DEADLINE:** Aug 15
FIELDS/MAJORS: Nursing

Scholarship is for a nurse pursuing an undergraduate degree in nursing. Write to the address below for more information.

Emergency Nurses Association (ENA) Foundation
Funding Program
216 Higgins Rd.
Park Ridge, IL 60068

1534

ENA Foundation/Sigma Theta Tau Joint Research Grant

AMOUNT: $6,000 (max) **DEADLINE:** Mar 1
FIELDS/MAJORS: Nursing

Scholarship is for emergency nurses advancing their specialized practice. Write to the address below for more information.

Emergency Nurses Association (ENA) Foundation
Funding Program
216 Higgins Rd.
Park Ridge, IL 60068

1535

Endowed And Institutional Scholarships And Awards At Salem College

AMOUNT: Varies **DEADLINE:** None Specified
FIELDS/MAJORS: All Areas Of Study

Merit and need-based financial aid programs are available to students at Salem College. To be considered, one must request an application form at the time of application to the college. Contact the office of admissions of the office of financial aid for further information.

Salem College
Director Of Financial Aid
P.O. Box 10548
Winston-Salem, NC 27108

1536

Endowed Scholarship

AMOUNT: Varies **DEADLINE:** Mar 15
FIELDS/MAJORS: All Areas Of Study

Awards for students with a GPA of 2.0 or better and full-time enrollment. Individual award restrictions may apply. Check with the financial aid office for more information.

McMurry University
Box 908 Mc M Station
Abilene, TX 79697

1537

Endowed Scholarships

AMOUNT: $100-$1,000 **DEADLINE:**None Specified
FIELDS/MAJORS: Pulp & Paper Science, Graphic Arts

Between 6 and 10 scholarships for freshmen in the department of paper and printing science and engineering at WMU. Includes the Ann Arbor Graphic Arts Memorial Foundation and Kalamazoo Valley Printing House Craftsmen Club. Awards are renewable. Write to the address below for more information.

Western Michigan University
College Of Engineering & Applied Science
Dept. Of Paper & Printing Science & Engineering
Kalamazoo, MI 49008

1538

Endowment Grants

AMOUNT: Varies **DEADLINE:** Varies
FIELDS/MAJORS: Theology, Religion

Awards for Concordia students preparing for full-time church careers in the LCMS and/or as specified by the donor. Must have a GPA of at least 2.5 and be enrolled in full-time study. For U.S. citizens. Write to the address below for more information.

Concordia University, Irvine
Financial Aid Office
1530 Concordia West
Irvine, CA 92715

1539

Endowment Scholarships

AMOUNT: $500 **DEADLINE:** Jul 1, Dec 1
FIELDS/MAJORS: All Areas Of Study

Awards for Liberty University students with financial need and satisfactory academic progress. Renewable. Write to the address below for more information.

Liberty University
Office Of Student Financial Aid
Box 20000
Lynchburg, VA 24506

1540

Energy Exchange Of Greater Los Angeles Scholarship

AMOUNT: Varies **DEADLINE:** None Specified
FIELDS/MAJORS: Business, Engineering

Scholarships are available for full-time sophomore students majoring in business and engineering. Preference given to students in the energy field. Must have a GPA of 3.0 or better. Renewable. Write to the address below for more information.

California State Polytechnic University, Pomona
Office Of Financial Aid
3801 West Temple Ave.
Pomona, CA 91768

1541

Energy Fellowship Program

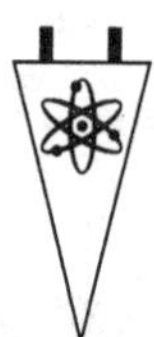

AMOUNT: $18,000 **DEADLINE:** Dec 1
FIELDS/MAJORS: Energy Research

Open to Ph.D. candidates with proposals for energy research. For theoretical or applied research. This is a nonresidential fellowship. Write to the Office of the Provost, at the address below for details.

Link Foundation Fellowship
University Of Rochester
200 Administration Bldg.
Rochester, NY 14627

1542

Energy Research Summer Fellowships

Amount: $15,000 **Deadline:** Jan 1
Fields/Majors: Electrochemistry And Related Fields

Awards are available for graduate students enrolled in a college or university in the U.S. or Canada. Applicants must be studying a field related to the objectives of the electrochemical society. Renewable. This program is supported by the U.S. Department of Energy. Write to the address below for more information.

Electrochemical Society, Inc.
10 South Main St.
Pennington, NJ 08534

1543

Energy, Exploration, Education Fund

Amount: Varies **Deadline:** Mar 1
Fields/Majors: Petroleum Geology

Awards are available at the University of New Mexico to enhance the education of geology students in petroleum geology, basin studies, and related fields. Write to the address listed below for information.

University Of New Mexico, Albuquerque
Office Of Financial Aid
Albuquerque, NM 87131

1544

Engineering Alumni Association Scholarship Fund

Amount: Varies **Deadline:** Mar 1
Fields/Majors: Engineering

Awards for sophomores, juniors or seniors enrolled full-time. Applicants must have a GPA of 2.5 or better, demonstrate financial need, and have involvement in engineering professional society activities. Contact the Director of Recruitment, Marston Hall, for more information.

University Of Massachusetts, Amherst
Director, Recruitment
Marston Hall
Amherst, MA 01003

1545

Engineering Merit And Honors Scholarships

Amount: $9,000 (max) **Deadline:** Jan 15
Fields/Majors: Engineering

Scholarships of $500 to $9,000 are available to undergraduate students at the University of Pittsburgh who maintain at least a 3.0 GPA, and are pursuing a degree in engineering. Write to the address below for details.

University Of Pittsburgh
Office Of Admissions And Financial Aid
Bruce Hall, Second Floor
Pittsburgh, PA 15260

1546

Engineering Scholarships

Amount: $2,000 **Deadline:** Mar 1
Fields/Majors: Engineering

Renewable awards for engineering undergraduates at North Carolina State University. Approximately seven awards given per year. Write to the address below for more information.

North Carolina State University
College Of Engineering, Robert Turner, Assistant Dean
Box 7904
Raleigh, NC 27695

1547

Enid Hall Griswold Memorial Scholarship

Amount: $1,000 **Deadline:** Feb 20
Fields/Majors: Political Science, Government, History, Economics

Applicants must be undergraduate juniors or seniors majoring in political science, history, government, or economics. U.S. citizenship is required. Not renewable. Applicant must obtain a letter of sponsorship from a local DAR chapter. Contact your local chapter or write to the address below for details.

National Society Daughters Of The American Revolution
NSDAR Scholarship Committee
1776 D St., NW
Washington, DC 20006

1548

ENMU Accounting Society, Jeanne Stephens Memorial Scholarship

Amount: $150 **Deadline:** Mar 1
Fields/Majors: Accounting

Award for an undergraduate accounting major who has a GPA of at least 3.0 and has successfully completed or is currently enrolled in Acct 202. Write to the address below for more information.

Eastern New Mexico University
ENMU College Of Business
Station 49
Portales, NM 88130

1549

Enos Spencer Reid Memorial Award

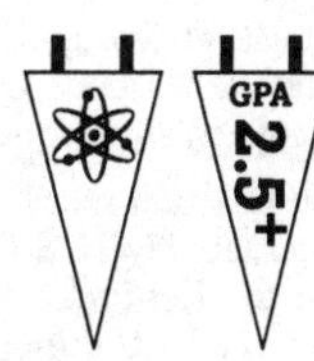

Amount: $650 **Deadline:** Feb 1
Fields/Majors: Agricultural Business Management

Student must be a sophomore or above majoring in agricultural business management with a GPA of 2.5 or better. Must complete a minimum of twelve units per quarter. Write to the address below for more information.

California State Polytechnic University, Pomona
College Of Agriculture
Building 2, Room 215
Pomona, CA 91768

1550

Environmental & Exercise Physiology Section Young Investigator Award

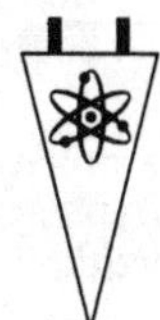

Amount: $150 **Deadline:** None Specified
Fields/Majors: Environmental Physiology

Awards are available to students interested in environmental physiology. The recipient must be the first author on the abstract presented at the APS annual meeting. Write to the address below for more information.

American Psychology Society
Membership Services Office
9560 Rockville Pike
Bethesda, MD 20814

Environmental Education Preserve Assistant

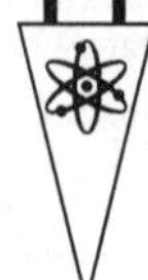

Amount: None Specified **Deadline:** None Specified
Fields/Majors: Environmental Education, Environmental Conservation

Current enrollment in a degree program for environmental education or environmental conservation at the associate, undergraduate or graduate level. Three- to four-year seasonal internship. For New York minority students only. Write to the address below for more information.

Nature Conservancy
Chris, Preserve Manager
41 S. Moger Ave.
Mt. Kisco, NY 10549

Environmental Industries

Amount: $1,000 **Deadline:** Apr 15
Fields/Majors: Horticulture

Open to full-time students majoring in horticulture with work experience in contracting or landscape management. Must have a GPA of 3.0 or better. Write to the address below for more information.

California State Polytechnic University, Pomona
College Of Agriculture
Building 7, Room 110
Pomona, CA 91768

Environmental Protection Scholarships

Amount: None Specified **Deadline:** Feb 15
Fields/Majors: Chemistry, Civil/Mining/Chemical Eng., Geology, Agronomy, Soil Science

Contractual scholarships for students from junior through graduate levels. Students must agree to work full time for the Kentucky National Resources & Environmental Protection Cabinet after graduation. Must have good academic standing and a letter of recommendation from a faculty advisor. An essay will also be required. Write to the address below for details.

Kentucky Water Resources Research Institute
233 Mining/Mineral Resources Building
Lexington, KY 40506

Environmental Protection Scholarships

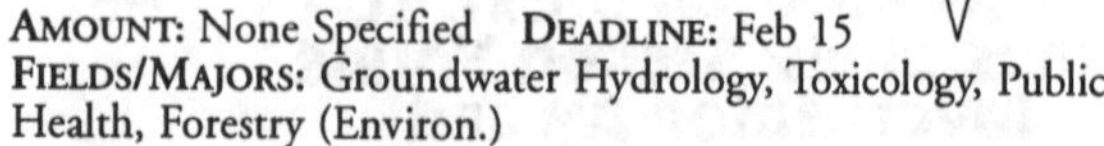

Amount: None Specified **Deadline:** Feb 15
Fields/Majors: Groundwater Hydrology, Toxicology, Public Health, Forestry (Environ.)

Contractual scholarships available for students in graduate levels of study. Students must agree to work full time for the Kentucky National Resources & Environmental Protection Cabinet after graduation. Must have good academic standing and a letter of recommendation from a faculty advisor. An essay will also be required. Write to the address below for details.

Kentucky Water Resources Research Institute
233 Mining/Mineral Resources Building
Lexington, KY 40506

1555

Environmental Science Scholarship Program

Amount: $4,000 **Deadline:** Jun 15
Fields/Majors: Env. Science, Hydrology, Chemistry, Biology, Toxicology, Entomology

Scholarships are available for American Indian juniors, seniors, or graduate students pursuing a degree in one of the above fields.

EPA Environmental Science Program
1630 30th Street. Suite 301
Boulder, CO 80301

1556

Environmental Toxicology And Chemistry (SETAC) Fellowship

Amount: $15,000 **Deadline:** Sep 1
Fields/Majors: Environmental Chemistry And Toxicology

Awards are available for predoctoral students pursuing dissertation research in the areas of environmental chemistry or toxicology.

Society Of Environmental Toxicology And Chemistry
Mr. Rodney Parrish, Executive Director
1010 North 12th Avenue
Pensacola, FL 32501

1557

Eoin Gray Memorial Scholarship

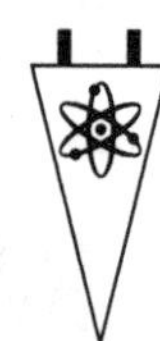

Amount: Varies **Deadline:** Mar 1
Fields/Majors: Physics

Awards are available at the University of New Mexico for full-time students pursuing a degree in physics. Write to the address below for more information.

University Of New Mexico, Albuquerque
Office Of Financial Aid
Albuquerque, NM 87131

1558

Eppley Foundation Support For Advanced Scientific Research

Amount: $15,000 (aver.) **Deadline:** Ongoing
Fields/Majors: Physical Sciences, Biological Sciences

Postdoctoral grants supporting research and publication in the physical and biological sciences. Applicants must be associated with a recognized educational or research institution. Indirect costs may be supported up to 15%. The foundation is able to support approximately twelve scientists per year.

Eppley Foundation For Research, Inc.
245 Park Ave.
New York, NY 10167

1559

Equestrian Grants

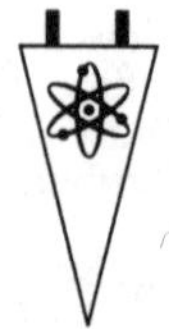

Amount: Varies **Deadline:** Apr 1
Fields/Majors: Equine Studies

Awards available for students at RMC who are active in equestrian and equine studies. For undergraduate studies. Contact the Equestrian Department for more information.

Rocky Mountain College
Office Of Financial Assistance
1511 Poly Drive
Billings, MT 59102

1560

Equestrian Scholarships

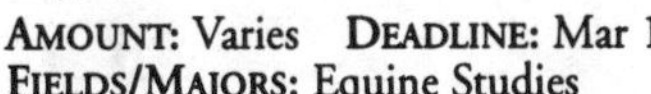

AMOUNT: Varies **DEADLINE:** Mar 1
FIELDS/MAJORS: Equine Studies

Awards for students at Lake Erie College who are majoring in equine studies. Applicants must be in good academic standing. For some awards, preference is given to members of the Pony Club, Inc., USTCA, 4-H, USDF, USPC, Inc., or the ASHA. Write to the address below for more information.

Lake Erie College
Financial Aid Office
391 W. Washington St.
Painesville, OH 44077

1561

Ercel D. Bidleman Scholarship

AMOUNT: $400 **DEADLINE:** Feb 9
FIELDS/MAJORS: All Areas Of Study

Award for minority student based on financial need, academic achievement, and activities. Use Bloomsburg University scholarship application. Contact Mrs. Kishbaugh, Financial Aid Office, for further information.

Bloomsburg University
19 Ben Franklin Hall
400 E. Second St.
Bloomsburg, PA 17815

1562

Eric & Bette Friedheim, H. Neil Mecaskey, And Treadway Scholarships

AMOUNT: $500 **DEADLINE:** Mar 15
FIELDS/MAJORS: Travel And Tourism, Hotel/Motel Management

Awards for juniors or seniors in one of the areas listed above who are enrolled in a four-year college. Must have a GPA of 3.0 or better. For study anywhere in North America. Write to the address below for more information.

National Tour Foundation
546 East Main St.
P.O. Box 3071
Lexington, KY 40596

1563

Eric Clem Memorial Scholarship

AMOUNT: $100-$300 **DEADLINE:** May 1
FIELDS/MAJORS: Drama

Scholarships for freshmen at the College of the Siskiyous who are majoring in drama. $100 award is for beginning students; $300 award is for returning students. Contact the drama department or write to the address below for details.

College Of The Siskiyous
Financial Aid Office
800 College Ave.
Weed, CA 96094

1564

Erma M. Hefferan Study Abroad Scholarship

AMOUNT: $100 **DEADLINE:** Feb 1
FIELDS/MAJORS: History-Social Studies-Education

Two awards for full time undergraduates majoring in history or social studies. Must have GPA of 3.3 in history or social studies, a cumulative GPA of 3.0, and demonstrate financial need. Applicants must also have a career goal of teaching. Student must be enrolled in an organized foreign study program for credit. Use Bloomsburg University scholarship application. Contact Dr. James Sperry, Chairperson, Department of History, for further information.

Bloomsburg University
19 Ben Franklin Hall
400 E. Second St.
Bloomsburg, PA 17815

1565

Ernest I. & Eurice Miller Bass Scholarship

AMOUNT: Varies **DEADLINE:** Jun 1
FIELDS/MAJORS: Theology, Religious Studies

Scholarships are available for Methodist students planning to enter the ministry or another full-time religious vocation. Applicants should have above average grades and be U.S. citizens.

General Board Of Higher Education And Ministry
Office Of Loans And Scholarships
P.O. Box 871
Nashville, TN 37202

1566

Ernest W. Johnson Memorial Baseball Scholarship

AMOUNT: None Specified **DEADLINE:** None Specified
FIELDS/MAJORS: Athletics, Baseball

Scholarship awarded to a member of the Clarion University baseball team who is a resident of Pennsylvania. Must have completed at least three academic semesters.

Clarion University
104 Egbert Hall
Office Of Financial Aid
Clarion, PA 16214

1567

Ertl Company Scholarships

AMOUNT: $1,000 **DEADLINE:** Feb 15
FIELDS/MAJORS: Agriculture, Agribusiness

Scholarships are available for FFA members pursuing a two- or four-year degree in any area of agriculture. Applicant must be a graduating high school senior and a resident of Illinois, Indiana, Iowa, Kansas, Kentucky, Michigan, North Dakota, Minnesota, Missouri, Nebraska, Ohio, South Dakota, or Wisconsin. Write to the address below for details.

National FFA Foundation
Scholarship Office
P.O. Box 15160
Alexandria, VA 22309

1568

Espenscheid Fellowships And Teaching Fellowships

AMOUNT: $15,360 **DEADLINE:** None Specified
FIELDS/MAJORS: Chemistry

University fellowships to students who have their B.A. or B.S. or equivalent to earn a Ph.D. degree in chemistry.

Georgetown University
Department Of Chemistry
Box 571227
Washington, DC 20057

1569

Established Investigator Grant

AMOUNT: $75,000 **DEADLINE:** None Specified
FIELDS/MAJORS: Medical Research (Cardiovascular And Other Related Areas)

Grants for investigators beyond four to nine years of their first faculty appointment in the fields of cardiovascular research. Based on demonstrated outstanding progress in leading an independent research program and the scientific merit and originality of the proposed project.

American Heart Association
National Center
7272 Greenville Ave.
Dallas, TX 75231

1570

Estelle H. Rosenblum Thesis/Dissertation Award

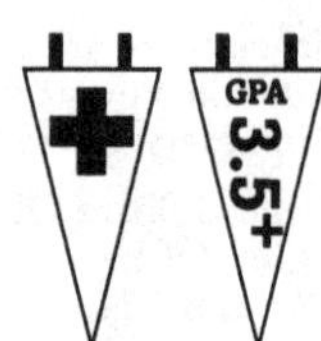

AMOUNT: Varies **DEADLINE:** Mar 1
FIELDS/MAJORS: Nursing

Awards are available at the University of New Mexico for nursing students pursuing a master's degree a GPA of at least 3.5.

University Of New Mexico, Albuquerque
Office Of Financial Aid
Albuquerque, NM 87131

1571

Esther Fulk-Ross Scholarship

AMOUNT: None Specified
DEADLINE: None Specified
FIELDS/MAJORS: Nursing

Scholarships are open to full-time B.S.N. students who have financial need. Must be at least a sophomore and have a GPA of 2.5 or higher.

Indiana University/ Purdue University, Indianapolis
School Of Nursing
1111 Middle Dr., No. 122
Indianapolis, IN 46202

1572

Esther Herr Memorial Scholarship

AMOUNT: $1,000 **DEADLINE:** None Specified
FIELDS/MAJORS: Language And Literature

Award for students enrolled in the school of humanities and social sciences and are studying language and literature. Must have a GPA of at least 2.75. Contact the School of Humanities and Social Sciences for more information.

Mesa State College
Office Of Financial Aid
P.O. Box 2647
Grand Junction, CO 1501

1573

Esther Spain-bey Memorial Scholarship

AMOUNT: $200 **DEADLINE:** Apr 15
FIELDS/MAJORS: Agricultural Biology

Open to students majoring in agricultural biology. Write to the address below for more information.

California State Polytechnic University, Pomona
College Of Agriculture
Building 7, Room 110
Pomona, CA 91768

1574

Esther Stone Endowed Trust Fund

AMOUNT: Varies **DEADLINE:** None Specified
FIELDS/MAJORS: Preministerial

Awards are available for students at Cedarville College who are studying to be a minister. Must have a GPA of at least 2.0. Based on moral character, academic potential, and demonstrated financial need. Write to the address below for more information.

Cedarville College
Financial Aid Office
P.O. Box 601
Cedarville, OH 45314

1575

Eta Sigma Phi Summer Scholarships

AMOUNT: $2,600-$3,150 **DEADLINE:** Dec 15
FIELDS/MAJORS: Classical Studies, Greek And Latin

Awards for Eta Sigma Phi members and alumni who have a bachelor's degree and are seeking a graduate degree in the fields of study above. Recipients are awarded the amount above to study at the American Academy in Rome or the American School of Classical Studies in Athens during the summer. Write to the address below for further details.

Trustees Of Eta Sigma Phi Fraternity
Professor David Kubiak, Dept. Of Classics
Wabash College
Crawfordsville, IN 47933

1576

Ethel J. Viles Scholarship Fund

AMOUNT: Varies **DEADLINE:** None Specified
FIELDS/MAJORS: All Areas Of Study

Awards for female graduating seniors from CONY High School who plan to attend a college or university in Maine. Based on character and academic achievement. Contact the CONY High School guidance office for more information.

Maine Community Fund
P.O. Box 148
Ellsworth, ME 04605

1577

Ethel Long Nipkow Memorial Scholarship

AMOUNT: $50-$200 **DEADLINE:** Apr 1
FIELDS/MAJORS: All Areas Of Study

Awards for all Sul Ross students. Renewable with a GPA of at least 2.5. Based primarily on need. Write to the address below for more information.

Sul Ross State University
Financial Aid Office
Box C-113
Alpine, TX 79832

1578

Ethel Mae Moor Applied Music Fund

AMOUNT: $500 **DEADLINE:** None Specified
FIELDS/MAJORS: Music

Awards for Mesa State sophomores, juniors, or seniors majoring in the field of music with a GPA of at least 2.5. Contact the music department for more information.

Mesa State College
Financial Aid Office
P.O. Box 2647
Grand Junction, CO 81501

1579

Ethicon, Inc. Scholarship In Nursing

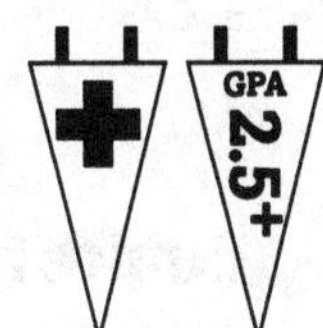

AMOUNT: Varies **DEADLINE:** Mar 1
FIELDS/MAJORS: Nursing

Awards are available at the University of New Mexico for full-time junior nursing students with a minimum GPA of 2.5 and financial need. Write to the address below or contact the School of Nursing for more details.

University Of New Mexico, Albuquerque
Office Of Financial Aid
Albuquerque, NM 87131

1580

Ethnic Minority And Women's Enhancement Programs

AMOUNT: $1,400 Per Month **DEADLINE:** Feb 15
FIELDS/MAJORS: Intercollegiate Athletics Administration

Postgraduate scholarships, internships, and curricula vitae bank for ethnic minorities and women who intend to pursue careers in intercollegiate athletics. Twenty non-renewable scholarships per year. Contact the athletic director of the financial aid office at an NCAA member institution for details or write to the director of personal development at the address below for details.

National Collegiate Athletic Association
6201 College Blvd.
Overland Park, KS 66211

1581

Ethnic Minority Fellowship Program

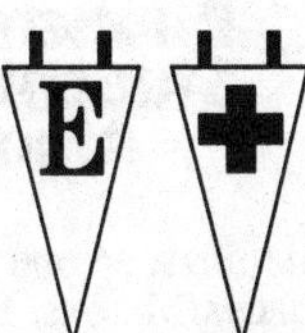

AMOUNT: $8,800 **DEADLINE:** Jan 15
FIELDS/MAJORS: Nursing, Behavioral Sciences, Clinical Research, Biomedical Research

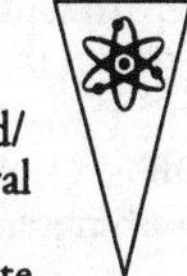

Fellowships for minorities with a commitment to a career in nursing related to minority mental health; and/or the research training program for careers in behavioral science or the clinical training program for careers in psychiatric nursing. For pre- or postdoctoral study. Write to the address below for more information.

American Nurse's Association, Inc.
Minority Fellowships Office
600 Maryland Ave., SW, Suite 100 West
Washington, DC 20024

1582

Ethnic Minority Scholarship, Hana Scholarship

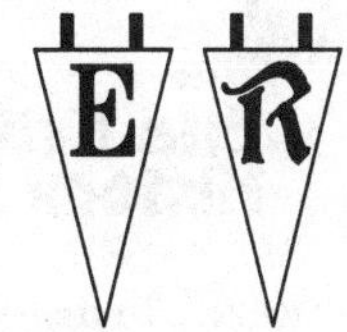

AMOUNT: Varies **DEADLINE:** May 1
FIELDS/MAJORS: All Areas Of Study

Scholarships are available for minority Methodist students, who have been members of the Methodist Church for at least one year, and are U.S. citizens. For students of African American, Asian, Hispanic, or Native American heritage with a GPA of at least 2.3. Write to the address listed below for information.

General Board Of Higher Education & Ministry
Office Of Loans And Scholarships
P.O. Box 871
Nashville, TN 37202

1583

ETSU Art Scholarships

AMOUNT: Varies **DEADLINE:** None Specified
FIELDS/MAJORS: Art

Scholarships for students at ETSU majoring in and exhibiting a talent in art. Several different art scholarships are available. Contact the Department of Art or the Financial Aid Office for details.

East Tennessee State University
Office Of Financial Aid
Box 70722
Johnson City, TN 37614

1584

ETSU Family Scholarship

AMOUNT: None Specified **DEADLINE:** None Specified
FIELDS/MAJORS: All Areas Of Study

Scholarships for dependents of ETSU employees. Financial need considered.

East Tennessee State University
Office Of Financial Aid
Box 70722
Johnson City, TN 37614

1585

ETSU Retirees Association Scholarship

AMOUNT: None Specified **DEADLINE:** None Specified
FIELDS/MAJORS: All Areas Of Study

Scholarships for entering freshmen or transfer students at ETSU with a good academic record. Freshmen must have a GPA of at least 3.2 and transfers must have a 3.0 or better. Contact the office of financial aid at the address below.

East Tennessee State University
Office Of Financial Aid
Box 70722
Johnson City, TN 37614

1586 Etta Keith Eskridge Art History Scholarship

AMOUNT: Tuition **DEADLINE:** Feb 1
FIELDS/MAJORS: Art History

Scholarships are available at the University of Utah for full-time students enrolled in an art history program. Write to the address below for details.

University Of Utah
Mary Francey
156 Art And Architecture Center
Salt Lake City, UT 84112

1587 Eugene Isenburg Award

AMOUNT: Varies **DEADLINE:** Mar 1
FIELDS/MAJORS: Engineering And Science

Awards for UMass students who demonstrate academic merit and a commitment to the integration of sciences and engineering or management. Applicants must be entering their sophomore, junior, or senior year of study. Contact the Dean, College of Natural Sciences and Mathematics, for more details.

University Of Massachusetts, Amherst
Dean, Natural Sciences And Mathematics
Amherst, MA 01003

1588 Eugene Shorb Scholarship

AMOUNT: None Specified **DEADLINE:** Mar 1
FIELDS/MAJORS: Engineering

Scholarships are awarded to a Purdue University, Calumet undergraduate student enrolled in an engineering program who is the son, daughter, niece, or nephew of a Northern Indiana Public Service Company (NIPSCO) employee. Incoming students must have a minimum SAT score of 925 and at least a (B) average and continuing students must have a GPA 3.0 or better. Based on financial need. Write to the address below for more information.

Purdue University, Calumet
Office Of Financial Aid
Purdue University, Calumet
Hammond, IN 46322

1589 Eugenia Bradford Roberts Memorial Scholarship

AMOUNT: $1,000 **DEADLINE:** Mar 31
FIELDS/MAJORS: All Areas Of Study

Scholarships for worthy daughters or granddaughters of career commissioned officer (including warrant) in the U.S. Army who retired after twenty years active duty, died while on duty, or is currently on duty. Preference given to student best qualified academically and most deserving of financial assistance. Eight renewable scholarships per year. Write to the address below for details. Please include name, rank, and social security number of qualifying parent when requesting application. Be certain to include a self-addressed, stamped envelope.

Society Of Daughters Of The U.S. Army
Janet B. Otto, Scholarship Chairman
7717 Rockledge Court
West Springfield, VA 22152

1590 Eula Mae Jett Scholarship

AMOUNT: $1,000 **DEADLINE:** Apr 1
FIELDS/MAJORS: Legal Secretary, Paralegal, Court Reporting

Scholarships are available for graduating high school seniors, undergraduates, and individuals who wish to re-enter the work force. Applicant must have career goal of working in the legal field. Write to the address listed below for information.

Legal Secretaries, Incorporated
Claudell Leverich
13406 Heritage Way, #304
Tustin, CA 92680

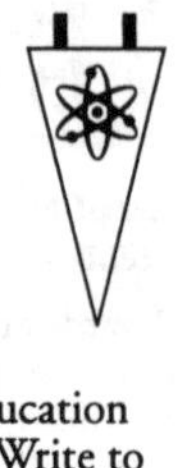

1591 Eunice Miles Scholarship

AMOUNT: $500 **DEADLINE:** Nov 1
FIELDS/MAJORS: Gemology

Awards are available for students enrolled in any GIA education program. Must be a U.S. citizen or permanent resident. Write to the address below for more information.

Gemological Institute Of America
Office Of Student Financial Assistance
1660 Stewart St.
Santa Monica, CA 90404

1592 Euola Cox Scholarship For Minorities

AMOUNT: $125 **DEADLINE:** Mar 1
FIELDS/MAJORS: Education

Award for minority students who are pursuing a teaching career. Financial need is a major consideration factor. Write to the address below for more information.

Eastern New Mexico University
College Of Education And Technology
Station 25
Portales, NM 88130

1593 Euphemia Lofton Haynes Student Loan Fund, Nursing Alumni Fund

AMOUNT: $5,000 (max) **DEADLINE:** None Specified
FIELDS/MAJORS: Education

Low-interest loans are available for graduate students in the department of education at the Catholic University of America. Contact the financial aid office at the address below for details.

The Catholic University Of America
Office Of Admissions And Financial Aid
Washington, DC 20064

1594 Eva A. Josephi Scholarship

AMOUNT: None Specified **DEADLINE:** Nov 30
FIELDS/MAJORS: All Areas Of Study

Scholarships are available at UCSD for undergraduate students who have a hearing disability. Write to the address listed below for information.

University Of California San Diego
Student Financial Services
9500 Gilman Drive
La Jolla, CA 92093

1595

Eva Benson Memorial Scholarship

AMOUNT: Varies **DEADLINE:** Mar 1
FIELDS/MAJORS: All Areas Of Study

Awards are available at the University of New Mexico for Native American students. Write to the address below for more information.

University Of New Mexico, Albuquerque
Office Of Financial Aid
Albuquerque, NM 87131

1596

Evans And Aleene McReynolds Memorial Scholarship

AMOUNT: $600 **DEADLINE:** Mar 31
FIELDS/MAJORS: All Areas Of Study

Student must be enrolled full-time with a GPA of 3.0 or better. Write to the address below for more information.

Southwest Missouri State University
Office Of Financial Aid
901 South National Ave.
Springfield, MO 65804

1597

Evans Scholars Foundation

AMOUNT: Tuition **DEADLINE:** None Specified
FIELDS/MAJORS: All Areas Of Study

Candidates must have completed their junior year in high school, rank in the upper 25% of their class, demonstrate financial need, and have a superior caddie record for a minimum of two years and be recommended by club officials. Approximately 200 scholarships awarded annually. Application forms are available from your local club or sponsoring association. Write to the address below for further information and more specific limitations on where you may attend school.

Evans Scholars Foundation
Western Golf Association
Golf, IL 60029

1598

Evelyn A. Porter Scholarship

AMOUNT: $650 **DEADLINE:** Mar 31
FIELDS/MAJORS: All Areas Of Study

Student must be enrolled full-time with a GPA of 3.0 or better. Write to the address below for more information.

Southwest Missouri State University
Office Of Financial Aid
901 South National Ave.
Springfield, MO 65804

1599

Exceptional Financial Need Scholarship Program

AMOUNT: Varies **DEADLINE:** Feb 1
FIELDS/MAJORS: Health

Awards for full-time students in a health professions program who display exceptional financial need. Write to the address below for more information.

Bureau Of Health Professions
Student Assistance Division
5600 Fishers Lane
Rockville, MD 20857

1600

Exceptional Student Fellowship Awards

AMOUNT: $3,000 **DEADLINE:** Feb 15
FIELDS/MAJORS: Business And Related

Applicant must be a college junior or senior at time of application, have a 3.4 or higher GPA, and be in a business-related major: accounting, business administration, actuarial science, computer science, economics, finance, insurance, investments, management, marketing, statistics, and mathematics. Must be U.S. citizen. Contact your major department at your university or write to the address below for more information. Applications are available from Nov 1 to Feb 1.

State Farm Companies Foundation
One State Farm Plaza, SC-3
Bloomington, IL 61710

1601

Exchange Club Scholarship

AMOUNT: Tuition & Books **DEADLINE:** None Specified
FIELDS/MAJORS: All Areas Of Study

Awards for TTC students who are Trident area residents and have been involved in community organizations or projects that emphasize service. Must have a a GPA of at least 3.0. Write to the address below for more information.

Trident Technical College
Financial Aid Office
P.O. Box 118067
Charleston, SC 29423

1602

Exercise And Sports Science Departmental Scholarships

AMOUNT: Varies **DEADLINE:** Feb 15
FIELDS/MAJORS: Exercise And Sports Science

Scholarships are available at the University of Utah for full-time students enrolled in an exercise or sports science program. Write to the address below for details.

University Of Utah
Dr. Hester Anderson
255 HPEM
Salt Lake City, UT 84112

1603

Explosive Ordnance Disposal Memorial Scholarship

AMOUNT: None Specified **DEADLINE:** May 1
FIELDS/MAJORS: All Areas Of Study

Scholarships for sons and daughters of Explosive Ordinance Disposal personnel who are active duty, reserve (incl Natl. Guard), retired, or deceased. Widowed spouses are also eligible for this program. Students at the service academies (Annapolis, etc.) are not eligible. For undergraduate study. Children of EOD officers and technicians must be age 23 or under and never married. Write to EOD Memorial Scholarship Committee at the address below to request the application form and a detailed description of the scholarship.

EOD Memorial Scholarship Committee
Attn: Patricia Moore
14803 Wharf Road
Accokeek, MD 20607

1604

F.D. Stella Scholarship

AMOUNT: $1,000 **DEADLINE:** May 31
FIELDS/MAJORS: Business

Scholarships for undergraduate and graduate business majors who are of the Italian American heritage. Write to the address below for details.

National Italian American Foundation
Dr. Maria Lombardo, Education Director
1860 19th Street, NW
Washington, DC 20009

1605

Faculty Advisor Award

AMOUNT: $1,000 **DEADLINE:** June 1
FIELDS/MAJORS: History

Awards available to graduate student members of Phi Alpha Theta who have served as an advisor for at least five years. Write to address below for details. Please indicate the name of your chapter. Information may be available from your chapter officers.

Phi Alpha Theta—International Honor Society In History
Headquarters Office
50 College Drive
Allentown, PA 18104

1606

Faculty Disadvantaged Student Fund

AMOUNT: Varies **DEADLINE:** Mar 1
FIELDS/MAJORS: Medicine

Awards are available at the University of New Mexico for medical students with emergency financial need. Write to the address below for more information.

University Of New Mexico, Albuquerque
Office Of Financial Aid
Albuquerque, NM 87131

1607

Faculty Scholars

AMOUNT: $6,400 (max) **DEADLINE:** Feb 15
FIELDS/MAJORS: All Areas Of Study

Awards for high school seniors with a minimum GPA of 3.5 and combined SAT of 1270 or ACT of 28. Award is renewable by maintaining a minimum GPA of 3.0. Write to address below for information and application.

Florida International University
Office Of Admissions
PF 140 University Park
Miami, FL 33199

1608

Faculty Scholars Awards

AMOUNT: $5,500 **DEADLINE:** Mar 15
FIELDS/MAJORS: All Areas Of Study

Awards open to full-time freshman students with a GPA of 3.3 and score 970 and above on their SAT. Write to the address below for more information.

Teikyo Post University
Office Of Financial Aid
800 Country Club Road
Waterbury, CT 06723

1609

Faculty Scholarship

AMOUNT: $3,000 **DEADLINE:** None Specified
FIELDS/MAJORS: All Areas Of Study

Award available to qualified students on the basis of academic performance. Renewable. Write to the address below for more information.

Carthage College
Financial Aid Office
Kenosha, WI 53140

1610

Faculty Scholarship For Achievement

AMOUNT: Full Tuition **DEADLINE:** Jan 1
FIELDS/MAJORS: All Areas Of Study

Scholarships for students who were valedictorian or salutatorian of their high school class. Must meet criteria of the honors program; must have interview or attend a campus visitation program. Renewable for four years. Write to the address below for details.

Denison University
Financial Aid Office
Box M
Granville, OH 43023

1611

Faculty Scholarships

AMOUNT: Tuition **DEADLINE:** Mar 15
FIELDS/MAJORS: All Areas Of Study

Awards for Jacksonville State University freshmen who are from Alabama and scored at least a 28 on the ACT or a 1230 on the

SAT. Renewable. Write to the address below for more information.

Jacksonville State University
Financial Aid Office
Jacksonville, AL 36265

1612 Faculty Scholarships

Amount: $500 **Deadline:** Mar 1
Fields/Majors: All Areas Of Study

Academic awards for Muskingum freshmen. Based on high school academic record and ACT/SAT scores. Eligibility may be enhanced by performance in an on-campus competition. Write to the address below for more information.

Muskingum College
Office Of Admission
New Concord, OH 43762

1613 Faculty/Administrators Development

Amount: None Specified **Deadline:** Jun 1
Fields/Majors: Education

Minority American teachers or administrators at, or alumni of, sponsoring Arkansas public colleges or universities who have been admitted as full-time, in-residence doctoral program students. Write to the address below for more information.

Arkansas Department Of Higher Education
Financial Aid Division
114 East Capitol
Little Rock, AR 72201

1614 Falcon Foundation Scholarships

Amount: Varies **Deadline:** Varies
Fields/Majors: Air Force Military Career

Scholarships for students entering the USAF Academy. Applicant must be between the ages of 17 and 21 on July 1 of the year they are admitted to prep school. Must be a U.S. citizen and plan to follow a lifetime career as an officer in the U.S. Air Force after graduation. Contact address below for further information.

Falcon Foundation
3116 Academy Dr. #200
USAF Academy, CO 80840

1615 Falmouth Institute Scholarships

Amount: $1,000 **Deadline:** May 1
Fields/Majors: All Areas Of Study

Scholarships are available for American Indian graduating high school seniors. Write to the address listed below for information.

Falmouth Institute
3918 Prosperity, Suite 302
Fairfax, VA 22031

1616 Family And Consumer Studies Departmental Scholarships

Amount: Varies **Deadline:** Feb 15
Fields/Majors: Family And Consumer Studies

Scholarships are available at the University of Utah for full-time students majoring in family and consumer studies. Write to the address below for information.

University Of Utah
Dr. Robert N. Mayer
228 Alfred Emery Building
Salt Lake City, UT 84112

1617 Family Plan Scholarships

Amount: Varies **Deadline:** None Specified
Fields/Majors: All Areas Of Study

Special family tuition rates are available to students who have a brother/sister/parent attending Mercyhurst as a full-time undergraduate student and who can demonstrate financial need. The eldest family member pays full tuition: all others pay a reduced tuition, as long as more than one family member is attending Mercyhurst and all are residing in the same home. Write to the address below for details.

Mercyhurst College
Glenwood Hills
Erie, PA 16546

1618 Family Practice Medical Scholarship

Amount: $7,500 **Deadline:** Apr 15
Fields/Majors: Medicine

Applicants must be Maryland residents attending the University of Maryland at Baltimore Medical School. Based primarily on financial need. Write to the address below for details.

Maryland State Higher Education Commission
16 Francis Street
Annapolis, MD 21401

1619 Family Scholarships

Amount: $3,000 & $12,000 **Deadline:** Dec 1
Fields/Majors: All Areas Of Study

Scholarships are for sons and daughters of current Westinghouse employees or employees of wholly-owned subsidiaries of Westinghouse. Only sons and daughters of employees from business units are eligible. Applicant's parents must be employed by Westinghouse for a period of one year. Contact the human resources department where your parent is (or was, if deceased, retired, or disabled) employed. Request information and a family scholarship application.

Westinghouse Foundation
Six Gateway Center
11 Stanwix St.
Pittsburgh, PA 15222

1620

Fannie And John Hertz Foundation Graduate Fellowship Program

AMOUNT: $17,000 And Fees **DEADLINE:** Feb 25
FIELDS/MAJORS: Applied Physical Sciences

Applicants must have at least a B.A. degree to be eligible for these fellowships for doctoral studies in the physical sciences. Tenable at thirty-four different graduate schools. Must have a GPA of at least 3.8 and be a U.S. citizen (or in process of naturalization). Renewable. Write to the address below for complete details.

Fannie And John Hertz Foundation
P.O. Box 5032
Livermore, CA 94551

1621

Farley Scholarship

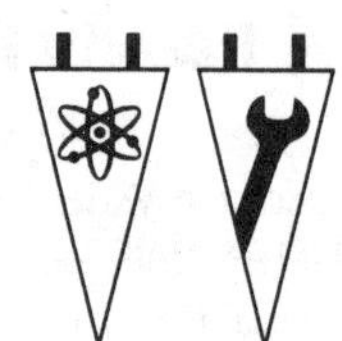

AMOUNT: Varies **DEADLINE:** Jan 1
FIELDS/MAJORS: Most Areas Of Study

Awards for UMass students in the College of Food and Natural Resources or Stockbridge School. Must have previous involvement with 4-H. For entering sophomores, juniors, or seniors. Contact the director, MA 4-H Program, Stockbridge Hall, for additional information.

University Of Massachusetts, Amherst
Director, MA 4-H Program
Stockbridge Hall
Amherst, MA 01003

1622

Farm Aid Scholarships

AMOUNT: $3,000 Over 3 Years **DEADLINE:** Feb 15
FIELDS/MAJORS: Agriculture

Scholarships for FFA members who are pursuing four-year degrees in any area of agriculture. Applicant must be a graduating high school senior and be from a farm family. Ten awards are offered annually. Write to the address below for details.

National FFA Foundation
Scholarship Office
P.O. Box 15160
Alexandria, VA 22309

1623

Farm Safety 4 Just Kids Scholarships

AMOUNT: $2,000 **DEADLINE:** Feb 15
FIELDS/MAJORS: All Areas Of Study

Scholarships are available for FFA members pursuing a four-year degree in any area of study. Applicant must have served as the coordinator of the local FFA chapter safety program and be a member of the Farm Safety 4 Just Kids. Write to the address below for details.

National FFA Foundation
Scholarship Office
P.O. Box 15160
Alexandria, VA 22309

1624

Farmer Fund Internship Award

AMOUNT: $2,000 **DEADLINE:** Apr 5
FIELDS/MAJORS: All Areas Of Study

Ten-week internship in position of recipient's choice. Must be Massachusetts resident, be between 18 and 25 years old, have a GPA of at least 3.0, and have political campaign experience. Preference given to registered democrats, but not essential. Two awards per year (one to a man, one to a woman). Write to the address below for further information.

Massachusetts Democratic State Committee
Scholarship Committee
45 Bromfield St., 7th Floor
Boston, MA 02108

1625

Farmer's Daughter Scholarship Pageant

AMOUNT: $75-$300 **DEADLINE:** None Specified
FIELDS/MAJORS: Agriculture

Awards are available for students studying agriculture at Western Illinois University. Write to the address below for more details.

Western Illinois University Agricultural Mechanization Club At Macomb
Western Illinois University
Department Of Agriculture
Macomb, IL 61455

1626

Farmers And Merchants Bank Of Piedmont Scholarships

AMOUNT: $1,000 **DEADLINE:** Mar 15
FIELDS/MAJORS: All Areas Of Study

Awards for Jacksonville State University students who are graduates of the Piedmont city school system. Write to the address below for more information.

Jacksonville State University
Financial Aid Office
Jacksonville, AL 36265

1627

Farmers Group Insurance Scholarship

AMOUNT: Varies **DEADLINE:** None Specified
FIELDS/MAJORS: Business

Awards for business majors at California Baptist College. Must have a GPA of at least 2.5. Contact the division of business administration for more information.

California Baptist College
8432 Magnolia Ave.
Riverside, CA 92504

1628

Farmers Insurance Group Of Companies Scholarship

AMOUNT: Varies **DEADLINE:** None Specified
FIELDS/MAJORS: Insurance, Mathematics, Business Administration

Scholarships are available to students majoring in insurance, mathematics, and business administration courses. Must have at least a C+ average. Write to the address below for more information.

California State Polytechnic University, Pomona
Office Of Financial Aid
3801 West Temple Ave.
Pomona, CA 91768

Farmers Insurance Group Of Companies Scholarships

Amount: $825 **Deadline:** Mar 1
Fields/Majors: Business

Scholarships are available at the University of Iowa for full-time undergraduates majoring in business. Based on need and merit. Write to the address listed below for information.

University Of Iowa
College Of Business Admin., Suite W160
108 Pappajohn Business Admin. Bldg.
Iowa City, IA 52245

Farmers Insurance Group Scholarship

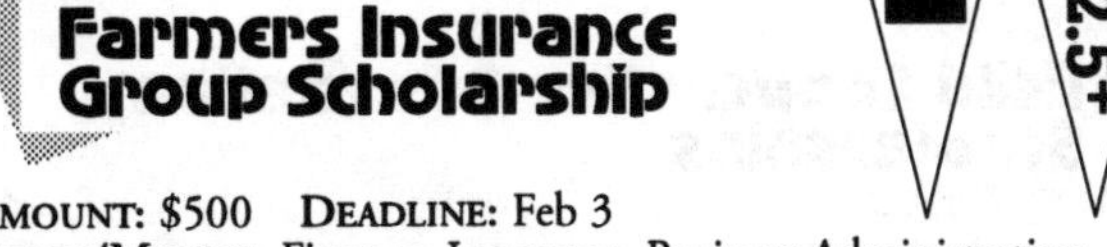

Amount: $500 **Deadline:** Feb 3
Fields/Majors: Finance, Insurance, Business Administration

Scholarships are available at the University of Oklahoma, Norman for full-time sophomores, juniors or seniors majoring in one of the areas listed above. Requires a minimum GPA of 2.5. Write to the address listed below for information.

University Of Oklahoma, Norman
Director, Division Of Finance
205-A Adams Hall
Norman, OK 73019

Farmers Mutual Hail Insurance Company Of Iowa Scholarships

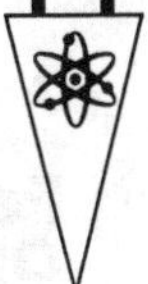

Amount: $1,000 **Deadline:** Feb 15
Fields/Majors: Agriculture

Scholarships for FFA members who are pursuing four-year degrees in any area of agriculture. Applicants must reside in Iowa, Illinois, Wisconsin, Indiana, Ohio, Michigan, Minnesota, North Dakota, Nebraska, or Missouri. Fourteen awards offered annually. Write to the address below for details.

National FFA Foundation
Scholarship Office
P.O. Box 15160
Alexandria, VA 22309

Farris Engineering Memorial Scholarship

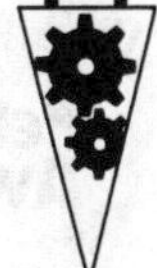

Amount: Varies **Deadline:** Mar 1
Fields/Majors: Engineering

Awards are available at the University of New Mexico for students enrolled in the school of engineering. Must demonstrate academic ability, character, and motivation. Write to the address below for more information.

University Of New Mexico, Albuquerque
Office Of Financial Aid
Albuquerque, NM 87131

1633

Fastline Publications Scholarships

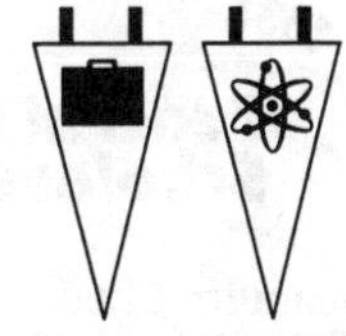

Amount: $1,000 **Deadline:** Feb 15
Fields/Majors: Agricultural Business Management

Scholarships are available for FFA members pursuing a four-year degree in agricultural business management. Ten awards are offered annually to residents of the states of Illinois, Indiana, Kansas, Kentucky, Missouri, Nebraska, North Carolina, South Carolina, Ohio, Tennessee, and Texas. Write to the address below for details.

National FFA Foundation
Scholarship Office
P.O. Box 15160
Alexandria, VA 22309

Father Anthony J. O'Driscoll Memorial Scholarship Award

Amount: $500 **Deadline:** Jul 1
Fields/Majors: All Areas Of Study

Scholarship available to New Jersey students entering his or her freshmen year in an accredited four-year college. Applicants must be a member of the American Legion or Auxiliary, or a descendant of a member. Boy's/Girl's State students are also eligible. Write to the address listed above for additional information.

American Legion Press Club Of New Jersey
Jack W. Kuepfer, ALPC Education Chairman
68 Merrill Road
Clifton, NJ 07012

Father James B. Macelwane Annual Awards

Amount: $100-$300 **Deadline:** Jun 14
Fields/Majors: Meteorology, Atmospheric Sciences

Awards are available from the American Meteorological Society for the top three papers submitted by undergraduate students on the subject of atmospheric science or meteorology. Write to address shown for details. A bulletin listing more information about this award may be posted in your department.

American Meteorological Society
45 Beacon Street
Boston, MA 02108

FCRV Scholarships

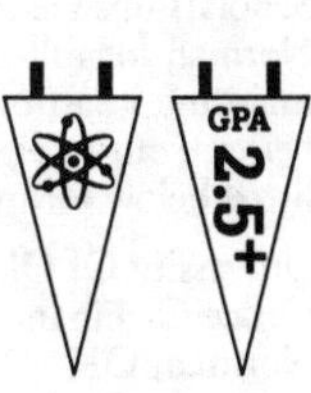

Amount: $500-$2,000 **Deadline:** Apr 15
Fields/Majors: Conservation, Forestry, Wildlife Management, Geology

Awards for undergraduates attending a two- or four-year institution majoring in one of the fields above. Applicants must have a GPA of at least 2.7 and be dependents of or members of the Family Campers and Rvers Association. Write to the address below prior to Apr 1 for more information.

National Campers And Hikers Association, Inc.
Scholarship Director
74 West Genessee St.
Skaneateles, NY 13152

1637

Federal Cartridge Company Scholarships

AMOUNT: $1,000 **DEADLINE:** Feb 15
FIELDS/MAJORS: Natural Resources

Scholarships are available for FFA members pursuing a degree in natural resources. Write to the address below for details.

National FFA Foundation
Scholarship Office
P.O. Box 15160
Alexandria, VA 22309

1638

Federated Garden Clubs Scholarship

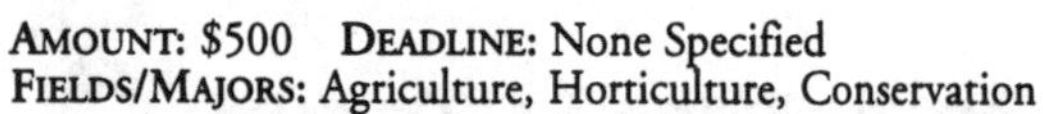

AMOUNT: $500 **DEADLINE:** None Specified
FIELDS/MAJORS: Agriculture, Horticulture, Conservation

Student must be an agriculture major interested in a career in horticulture or conservation. Contact the agriculture department for more information.

Southwest Missouri State University
Office Of Financial Aid
901 South National Ave.
Springfield, MO 65804

1639

Federated Genetics Scholarships

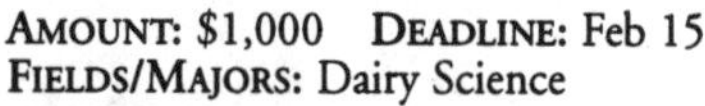

AMOUNT: $1,000 **DEADLINE:** Feb 15
FIELDS/MAJORS: Dairy Science

Scholarships are available for FFA members pursuing a degree in dairy science at a four-year institution. Write to the address below for details.

National FFA Foundation
Scholarship Office
P.O. Box 15160
Alexandria, VA 22309

1640

Fee Waiver Scholarship

AMOUNT: $1,200 **DEADLINE:** Apr 15
FIELDS/MAJORS: Art, Art History

Scholarships are available at the University of Oklahoma, Norman for full-time students who are residents of Oklahoma majoring in art or art history. Must have a GPA of 3.0 or better. Four to eight awards per year. Write to the address listed below for information.

University Of Oklahoma, Norman
Office Of Financial Aid
Norman, OK 73019

1641

FEEA Scholarships

AMOUNT: None Specified **DEADLINE:** May 31
FIELDS/MAJORS: All Areas Of Study

Scholarships for employees, or dependents of employees, of either the federal government or the U.S. Postal Service. Based on academic merit. Must have a GPA of 3.0 or better. Write to the address below for details. Please include an SASE (#10 business-size).

Federal Employee Education And Assistance Fund
Educational Programs
8441 W. Bowles Ave., Suite 200
Littleton, CO 80123

1642

EA Student Loans

AMOUNT: None Specified **DEADLINE:** None Specified
FIELDS/MAJORS: All Areas Of Study

Educational loans for employees, or children of employees, of either the federal government or the U.S. Postal Service. Employee must have been employed for at least three years. For undergraduate study. Write to the address below for details. Please enclose SASE.

Federal Employee Education And Assistance Fund
Educational Programs
8441 W. Bowles Ave., Suite 200
Littleton, CO 80123

1643

Feild Cooperative Association Scholarships

AMOUNT: $2,000 **DEADLINE:** None Specified
FIELDS/MAJORS: All Areas Of Study

Loans for Mississippi residents in at least their junior undergraduate year. Academic record, financial need, and financial responsibility are used to evaluate loan requests. Interest is 6% per year and repayment starts three months after graduation. Renewable four times. Write to the address below for details.

Feild Cooperative Association, Inc.
2506 Lakeland Drive, Suite 607
P.O. Box 5054
Jackson, MS 39296

1644

Fellowship And Career Opportunity Grants

AMOUNT: $100-$6,000 **DEADLINE:** Feb 1, Jun 15
FIELDS/MAJORS: Visual, Performing, Theater, And Literary Arts

Awards for professional artists who are legal residents of the state of Minnesota. Must be over 18 years of age to apply. Based primarily on the quality of work and merit of the artist's career plans. Not intended for use in seeking a degree or for tuition or fees. Write to the address below for more information.

Minnesota State Arts Board
Percent For Art Program Institute
432 Summit Ave.
Saint Paul, MN 55102

1645

Fellowship And Worksites Awards

AMOUNT: $5,000 **DEADLINE:** Jan 18
FIELDS/MAJORS: Art, Dance, Music

Awards for artists from Idaho who are in need of project funds or who a significant portion of their livelihood comes from artistic activity. Must be over age 18 and a U.S. citizen. Write to the address below for additional details.

Idaho Commission On The Arts
P.O. Box 83720
Boise, ID 83720

1646

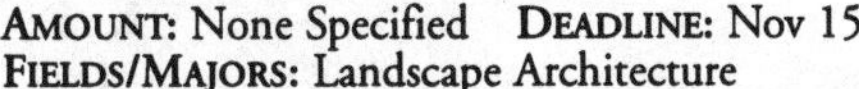

Fellowship In Landscape Architecture

Amount: None Specified **Deadline:** Nov 15
Fields/Majors: Landscape Architecture

One year fellowship at the American Academy in Rome. Open to certified landscape architects. Funds one student annually. Write to the address below for more information.

American Academy In Rome
Ms. Buff Kavelman
7 East 60th St.
New York, NY 10022

1647

Fellowship In Roman Studies

Amount: $5,000 (max) **Deadline:** Mar 1
Fields/Majors: Numismatics, Byzantine Studies, Classical Studies

Fellowship for research in residence at the society to study the ancient Roman world using the facilities and collections of the society. Applicants must be U.S. citizens associated with a North American institute of higher learning. Write to the address below for details.

American Numismatic Society
Broadway At 155th Street
New York, NY 10032

1648

Fellowship Of United Methodists In Music & Worship Arts

Amount: Varies **Deadline:** Mar 1
Fields/Majors: Church Music, Worship Arts

Open to a full-time music degree candidate either entering as a freshman or already in an accredited university, college, school of theology, or doing special education in worship or the arts related to worship. Write to the address below for more information.

Fellowship Of United Methodists In Music & Worship Arts
P.O. Box 24787
Nashville, TN 37202

1649

Fellowship On Women And Public Policy

Amount: $9,000 **Deadline:** May 31
Fields/Majors: All Areas Of Study

Fellowships are available to encourage greater participation of women in the public policy process, develop public policy leaders, and encourage the formulation of state policy which recognizes and responds to the need of women and families. Applicants must be female graduate students with at least twelve credit hours completed in an accredited New York university. Write to the address listed below for information.

University At Albany, Center For Women In Government
Joeanna Hurston Brown, Director
135 Western Ave, Draper Hall, Room 302
Albany, NY 12222

1650

Fellowship Program In Academic Medicine

Amount: Varies **Deadline:** Aug 31
Fields/Majors: Biomedical Research And Academic Medicine

Scholarships, fellowships and awards for minority medical students. Minorities are defined here as African American, Mexican American, mainland Puerto Rican, and American Indian. Must be a U.S. citizen. Send an SASE (55 cent) to the address below for additional information.

National Medical Fellowships, Inc.
110 West 32nd Street
New York, NY 10001

1651

Fellowship Programs In International Peace And Security Studies

Amount: Varies **Deadline:** None Specified
Fields/Majors: International Security And Peace

Fellowships are available for dissertation and postdoctoral research in international peace and security issues. Write to the address listed below for information.

MacArthur Foundation
Social Science Research Council
605 3rd Avenue
New York, NY 10158

1652

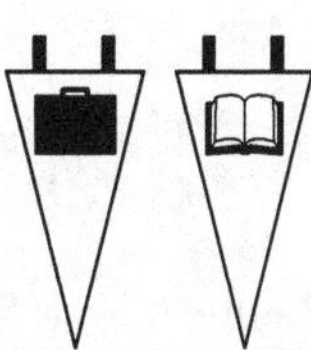

Fellowship Research Grants

Amount: $20,200 (max)
Deadline: None Specified
Fields/Majors: Government, International Affairs, Philosophy, Economics

Research grants are available to individuals for postdoctoral research. The applicant must be associated with educational or research institutions and the effort supported should lead to the advancement of knowledge through teaching, lecturing, or publication. Write to the address listed below for information.

Earhart Foundation
2200 Green Road, Suite H
Ann Arbor, MI 48105

1653

Fellowships And Junior Fellowships

Amount: Varies **Deadline:** Nov 1
Fields/Majors: Byzantine Studies, Pre-Columbian Studies, Landscape Architecture

Applicants must hold a doctorate or have established themselves in their field and wish to pursue their own research at the Harvard University Dumbarton Oaks research facilities (residential fellowships). Scholars who have fulfilled all preliminary requirements for the Ph.D. (or other terminal degree) are eligible for the junior fellowships. Write to the address below for details.

Dumbarton Oaks
Office Of The Director
1703 32nd Street, NW
Washington, DC 20007

1654

Fellowships At The Smithsonian Astrophysical Observatory

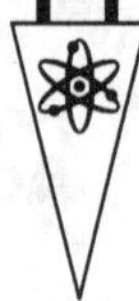

AMOUNT: None Specified **DEADLINE:** Varies
FIELDS/MAJORS: Astronomy, Astrophysics And Related Fields

Fellowships are available to graduate and postgraduate students at the Smithsonian Astrophysical Observatory. Write to address below for details. Request the publication Smithsonian Opportunities for Research and Study.

Smithsonian Astrophysical Observatory
Office Of The Director
60 Garden Street
Cambridge, MA 02138

1655

Fellowships For Advanced Training In Fine Arts Conservation

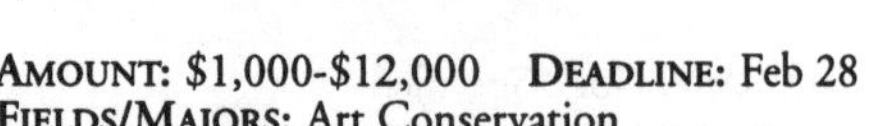

AMOUNT: $1,000-$12,000 **DEADLINE:** Feb 28
FIELDS/MAJORS: Art Conservation

Award for art conservation students at the doctoral level of study at any institution in the U.S. Write to the address below for more information.

Samuel H. Kress Foundation
Fellowship Administrator
174 East 80th St.
New York, NY 10021

1656

Fellowships For Senior Scholarly Development

AMOUNT: None Specified **DEADLINE:** Jul 1
FIELDS/MAJORS: Humanities, Philosophy, Archaeology, History, Language, Linguistics

Fellowships are available for postdoctoral scholars who wish to do research in India. Write to the address listed below for an application.

American Institute Of Indian Studies
1130 East 59th Street
Chicago, IL 60637

1657

Fenton Hopi Scholarship Fund

AMOUNT: Varies **DEADLINE:** None Specified
FIELDS/MAJORS: All Areas Of Study

Scholarships are available at NAU for full-time students who are at least 50% Hopi indian. Write to the address listed below for information.

Northern Arizona University
NAU Scholarship Office
P.O. Box 4199
Flagstaff, AZ 86011

1658

Ferdinand Torres AFB Scholarship

AMOUNT: $1,000 **DEADLINE:** None Specified
FIELDS/MAJORS: All Areas Of Study

Awards are available for students in the New York metropolitan area or new immigrants to the U.S. who are legally blind. Applicants must demonstrate financial need. Write to the address below for more information.

American Foundation For The Blind
11 Penn Plaza, Suite 300
New York, NY 10001

1659

Fermenta Animal Health Company Scholarships

AMOUNT: $1,000 **DEADLINE:** Feb 15
FIELDS/MAJORS: Agriculture

Scholarships are available for FFA members pursuing a four-year degree in any area of agriculture. Two are awarded nationally, two are awarded to members or either Indiana's North Knox or South Knox chapter, and one is awarded to a graduate of Kansas City East Environmental Science/Agribusiness Magnet High School. Write to the address below for details.

National FFA Foundation
Scholarship Office
P.O. Box 15160
Alexandria, VA 22309

1660

Fieri National Matching Scholarships

AMOUNT: $1,000 **DEADLINE:** May 31
FIELDS/MAJORS: All Areas Of Study

Scholarships for Italian American undergraduate students who are members of Fieri. Write to the address below for details.

National Italian American Foundation
Dr. Maria Lombardo, Education Director
1860 19th Street, NW
Washington, DC 20009

1661

Film And Fiction Scholarship

AMOUNT: $10,000 (max) **DEADLINE:** Jan 15
FIELDS/MAJORS: Film, Fiction Writing, And Playwriting

Scholarships for graduate MFA students in the areas of film, fiction, or playwriting with an interest in the classical liberal or libertarian principles. Write to the address below or visit the website http://osf1.gmu.edu/~ihs/ for more information. Application requests will only be taken in the fall preceding the January deadline.

Institute For Humane Studies At George Washington University
4084 University Drive, Suite 101
Fairfax, VA 22030

1662

Fina/Dallas Morning Star All-State Scholar-Athlete Team

AMOUNT: $500-$4,000 **DEADLINE:** Dec 13
FIELDS/MAJORS: All Areas Of Study

Scholarships for Texas high school seniors who have received a varsity letter in a U.I.L. sport, have a GPA of at least 3.6, and are in top 10% of high school class. Based on academics and extra- and co-curricular activities. U.I.L. sports are baseball, basketball, football, golf, soccer, softball, swimming, tennis, track and field, and volleyball. Write to the address below for details.

Fina Oil And Chemical Company, Public Affairs
All-State Scholar-Athlete Team
P.O. Box 2159
Dallas, TX 75221

1663

Financial Aid For Florida Residents

Amount: $1,200-$4,000 **Deadline:** None Specified
Fields/Majors: All Areas Of Study

Scholarships for Florida residents attending Eckerd College. Several programs are available. Some are need-based, some are not. Contact the director of financial aid at Eckerd College at the address below for details.

Eckerd College
Director Of Financial Aid
P.O. Box 12560
St. Petersburg, FL 33733

1664

Financial Assistance For Disadvantaged Students

Amount: Varies **Deadline:** Mar 1
Fields/Majors: Medicine

Awards are available at the University of New Mexico for full-time medical students with exceptional financial need. Includes the program of financial assistance for disadvantaged health profession students, exceptional financial need scholarship and scholarships for disadvantaged students. Applicants must be U.S. citizens or permanent residents. Write to the address below for more information.

University Of New Mexico, Albuquerque
Office Of Financial Aid
Albuquerque, NM 87131

1665

Financial Management Association Scholarship

Amount: $100 **Deadline:** None Specified
Fields/Majors: Financial Management

Student must be full-time and an active member of the financial management. Contact the COBA office for more information.

Southwest Missouri State University
Office Of Financial Aid
901 South National Ave.
Springfield, MO 65804

1666

Fine Art Scholarships

Amount: $2,500 **Deadline:** Mar 1
Fields/Majors: All Areas Of Study

Award for applicants with particular talent in the fine and performing arts, including art, music, theater, and forensics. Selection is competitive and, with the exception of forensics, requires applicants to declare a major in the specialty area. Auditions and/or portfolio submissions are required. Write to the address below for more information.

Bradley University
Office Of Financial Assistance
Peoria, IL 61625

1667

Fine Arts Grants In Art, Music, And Drama

Amount: $250-$1,500 **Deadline:** Mar 1
Fields/Majors: All Areas Of Study

Open to incoming freshmen who are interested, but not necessarily majoring in music, art, or drama, and plan to continue their participation in the arts at Edgewood. Transfer students are also eligible. Financial need must be demonstrated. Renewable. Write to the address below for details.

Edgewood College
Office Of Admissions
855 Woodrow Street
Madison, WI 53711

1668

Fine Arts Scholarship

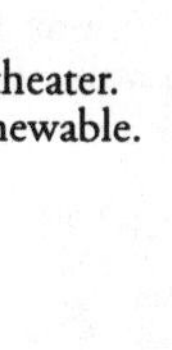

Amount: $500-$5,000 **Deadline:** None Specified
Fields/Majors: Art, Music, Theater

Award available to students who excel in art, music, or theater. Based on auditions held in October and November. Renewable. Write to the address below for more information.

Carthage College
Financial Aid Office
Kenosha, WI 53140

1669

Fine Arts Scholarships

Amount: Varies **Deadline:** Apr 1
Fields/Majors: Music, Theater

Awards are available to freshman full-time Elon College students who will be pursuing a major in theater or music. Based upon high school record of academic excellence and an audition. Awards start at $200, and range up to the Fletcher Music Scholarship of $7,500. Write to the address below for details.

Elon College
Office Of Financial Planning
2700 Campus Box
Elon College, NC 27244

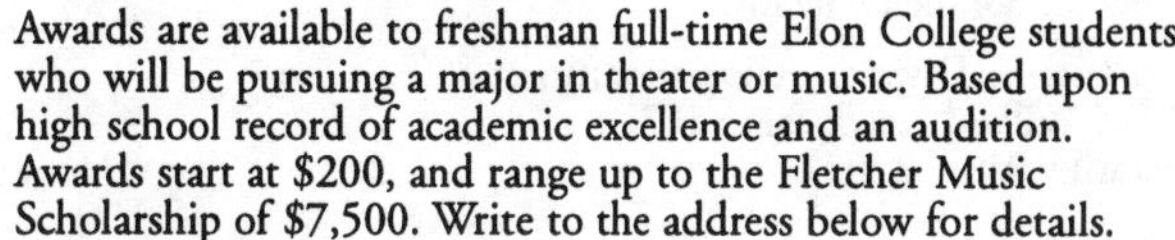

1670

First Catholic Slovak Ladies Association Member Scholarships

Amount: $750 **Deadline:** Mar 1
Fields/Majors: All Areas Of Study

Scholarships for members in good standing of the First Catholic Slovak Ladies Association, and be or soon to be enrolled in an accredited university or college in the U.S. or Canada. Write to the address below for details.

First Catholic Slovak Ladies Association
Director Of Fraternal Scholarship Aid
24950 Chagrin Blvd.
Beachwood, OH 44122

1671

First Interstate Bank Of California

Amount: $1,000 **Deadline:** None Specified
Fields/Majors: Business, Liberal Arts

Scholarships are awarded to a minority undergraduate students from the college of arts, and from the college of business majoring in business and liberal arts. Must be full-time junior or senior students with a GPA of at least a 2.0. Write to the address below for more information.

California State Polytechnic University, Pomona
Office Of Financial Aid
3801 West Temple Ave.
Pomona, CA 91768

1672

First Interstate Bank Scholarship Program

Amount: $1,500 **Deadline:** None Specified
Fields/Majors: Business, Finance, Economics

Scholarships are available for entering freshmen students who are residents of Washington, who will be enrolling in one of the fields of study listed above. For study at any of sixteen Washington colleges and universities. Contact the financial aid office of the school of your choice for details.

First Interstate Bank Of Washington, N.A.
Administration
P.O. Box 160
Seattle, WA 98111

1673

First Marine Division Association Scholarships

Amount: None Specified **Deadline:** None Specified
Fields/Majors: All Areas Of Study

For dependent of person who served in the First Marine Division or in a unit attached to the division and is deceased from any cause or is totally disabled due to wounds received in action. For undergraduate study. Write to the address below for complete details.

First Marine Division Association, Inc.
14325 Willard Road, Suite 107
Chantilly, VA 22021

1674

First National Bank In Alpine Scholarship

Amount: $1,000 **Deadline:** Apr 1
Fields/Majors: Business

Awards for Sul Ross undergraduate students who have a GPA of at least 3.0 prior to each semester. Write to the address below for more information.

Sul Ross State University
Financial Aid Office
Box C-113
Alpine, TX 79832

1675

First Presbyterian Church Scholarship Fund

Amount: Varies **Deadline:** Jun 1
Fields/Majors: All Areas Of Study

Scholarships for undergraduate or graduate students from Tulsa, Oklahoma who are members of the Presbyterian Church. Based primarily on need, academic performance, and individual potential. Also includes the Clarence Warren, Harry Allen, and Ethel Francis Crate scholarships. Crate scholarships are for junior or senior undergraduates only. Write to the address below for more specific details.

First Presbyterian Church
709 South Boston Ave.
Tulsa, OK 74119

1676

First Year Graduate Scholarship Programs

Amount: $5,000 **Deadline:** May 1
Fields/Majors: Pharmacy

Awards to encourage undergraduates or college graduates in pharmacy to pursue an advanced degree providing a valuable background for a career in the pharmaceutical industry. Must be in the final year of an undergraduate degree program or a recent graduate. For U.S. citizens or permanent residents. Write to the address below for more information.

American Foundation For Pharmaceutical Education
One Church Street, Suite 202
Rockville, MD 20850

1677

First Year Pharmacy Awards

Amount: $500-$2,500 **Deadline:** Feb 1
Fields/Majors: Pharmacy

Scholarships are available at the University of Oklahoma, Norman, for full-time freshmen pharmacy majors. Based on academic excellence. Includes the Henry D. & Ida Mosier Scholar Program, the Burroughs-Wellcome Scholarship, the Roy Sanford Scholarship, and the Pharmacists Mutual Scholarship. Individual awards requirements may vary. Write to the address listed below for information.

University Of Oklahoma, Norman
College Of Pharmacy
P.O. Box 26901
Oklahoma City, OK 73190

1678

Fisco Farm And Home Stores Scholarships

Amount: $1,000 **Deadline:** Feb 15
Fields/Majors: Agriculture, Agribusiness, Animal Science

Scholarships are available for FFA members pursuing a four-year degree in any area of agriculture, agribusiness or animal science, residing within a 25-mile radius of a Fisco location, and enrolled at an institution in California. Write to the address below for details.

National FFA Foundation
Scholarship Office
P.O. Box 15160
Alexandria, VA 22309

1679

Fisher College Scholarship

Amount: $600 **Deadline:** Mar 1
Fields/Majors: All Areas Of Study

Applicants must be young women high school graduates with credits acceptable to admittance committee of school as well as indication of financial need. For study at Fisher College. Not renewable. Write to the address below for details.

General Federation Of Women's Clubs Of Massachusetts
118 Beacon St.
Boston, MA 02116

1680

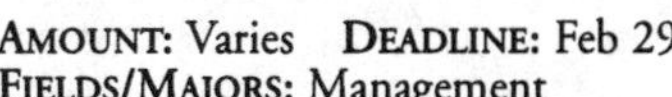

Flavin Fellowships

Amount: Varies **Deadline:** Feb 29
Fields/Majors: Management

Awards for MBA/M.S. degree candidates. Based on academic merit, financial need, and volunteer services. Applications for school of management scholarships will be available in the SOM Development Office, Room 206.

University Of Massachusetts, Amherst
School Of Management
Som Development Office, Room 206
Amherst, MA 01003

1681

Fleet Reserve Association Scholarships

Amount: None Specified **Deadline:** Apr 15
Fields/Majors: All Areas Of Study

Sons or daughters of the Fleet Reserve Association (in good standing as of April 1 of year award is made). Selection is based on financial need, academic standing, character, and leadership. Open to high school seniors, college, and graduate students. Also available is the Fleet Reserve Association Award for children of active, retired w/ pay, or deceased USN, USMC, or USCG personnel. Write to the address below for complete details.

Fleet Reserve Association
FRA Scholarship Administrator
125 N. West Street
Alexandria, VA 22314

1682

Fleet Scholars

Amount: $1,000 **Deadline:** None Specified
Fields/Majors: All Areas Of Study

Applicants must be a member of a minority group as established by federal guidelines and must have demonstrated financial need and scholastic achievement. Preference is given to students that have a desire to enter a career in business. Write to the address below for more information.

Fleet Charitable Trust
111 Westminster St.
Providence, RI 02903

1683

Fleischman Awards

Amount: Varies **Deadline:** Dec 1
Fields/Majors: All Areas Of Study

Awards for female graduating high school seniors who are attending a secondary school in Santa Barbara County and who have a GPA of at least 3.8. Write to the address below or contact your high school guidance counselor for more information.

Santa Barbara Foundation
Student Aid Programs
15 East Carrillo St.
Santa Barbara, CA 93101

1684

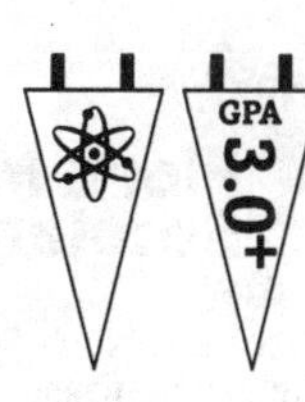

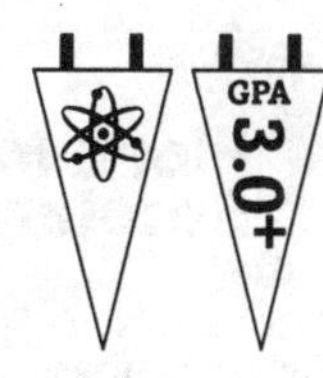

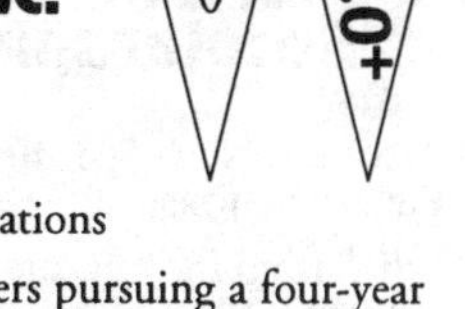

Fleishman-Hillard, Inc. Scholarships

Amount: $1,000 **Deadline:** Feb 15
Fields/Majors: Agricultural Communications

Scholarships are available for FFA members pursuing a four-year degree in agricultural communications. Applicant must be a junior or senior with a GPA of at least 3.0. Write to the address below for details.

National FFA Foundation
Scholarship Office
P.O. Box 15160
Alexandria, VA 22309

1685

Flemish Community Fellowship

Amount: None Specified **Deadline:** Mar 1
Fields/Majors: Art, Music, Humanities, Social/Political Science, Law, Economics

Fellowships are available to American College students who wish to study at a Flemish university in Flanders, Belgium. Awards are given to candidates doing research in one of the fields listed above or in the science/medical fields, and their affiliation with the Flemish community. Applicant must hold at least a bachelor's degree, be under age 35, and be a U.S. citizen. Write to the address listed below for information.

Embassy Of Belgium
Flemish Community Fellowship
3330 Garfield Street, NW
Washington, DC 20008

1686

Flemmie P. Kittrell Memorial Foundation

Amount: $3,000 **Deadline:** Jan 15
Fields/Majors: Home Economics

Scholarships for minority students enrolled in graduate home economics programs. Write to the address below for more information.

American Home Economics Association
1555 King St.
Alexandria, VA 22314

1687

Flora L. Daugherty Scholarship

Amount: $2,000 **Deadline:** None Specified
Fields/Majors: All Areas Of Study

$2,000 scholarship available for full-time female students who attend Sul Ross State University in Alpine, Texas, and who graduated from Alpine High School. Write to the address listed below for additional information.

El Paso Community Foundation
201 East Main, Suite 1616
El Paso, TX 79901

1688

Flora M. Von Der Ahe Scholarship

AMOUNT: None Specified **DEADLINE:** Mar 1
FIELDS/MAJORS: All Areas Of Study

Scholarship for students who were graduates from Umatilla County (OR) high schools with a GPA of at least 2.5 (HS GPA). For study at Oregon colleges. Contact your financial aid office or write to the address below for details.

Oregon State Scholarship Commission
Attn: Grant Department
1500 Valley River Drive #100
Eugene, OR 97401

1689

Flora Rogge College Scholarship

AMOUNT: $1,000 **DEADLINE:** Mar 1
FIELDS/MAJORS: Education

Awards for Minnesota high school seniors planning to pursue a career in teaching. Based on academics, financial need, leadership, character, and recommendations. Write to the address below for more information.

Minnesota Federation Of Teachers
168 Aurora Ave.
St. Paul, MN 55103

1690

Floren And Mary Thompson Instrumental Scholarship

AMOUNT: $300 **DEADLINE:** Mar 1
FIELDS/MAJORS: Instrumental Music

Award for a student at Eastern New Mexico University who is majoring in instrumental music and is a participant in marching or symphonic band for at least one year. Must be a junior with a GPA of 3.0 or better or a graduate student with at least a 3.2 GPA. Write to the address below for more information.

Eastern New Mexico University
College Of Fine Arts
Station 16
Portales, NM 88130

1691

Florence Frydenlund Memorial Scholarships

AMOUNT: $150 **DEADLINE:** Feb 15
FIELDS/MAJORS: Elementary Education

Awards for students at UW Platteville in the area of elementary education with a GPA of 2.55 or higher. Extracurricular activities and financial need also considered. Write to the address below for more information.

University Of Wisconsin, Platteville
Office Of Enrollment And Admissions
Platteville, WI 53818

1692

Florence Nightingale, Diane Groff, Ruth Orum-Organ Scholarship

AMOUNT: None Specified **DEADLINE:** None Specified
FIELDS/MAJORS: Nursing

Scholarships are open to nursing students in financial need who have demonstrated good academic achievement. Write to the address below for more information.

Indiana University/Purdue University, Indianapolis
School Of Nursing
1111 Middle Drive, No. 122
Indianapolis, IN 46202

1693

Florence Saltzman-Heidel Art Scholarships

AMOUNT: Varies **DEADLINE:** Apr 1
FIELDS/MAJORS: Art

Awards are available to art majors on the basis of portfolio and GPA. Nonrenewable, but students may apply again during the next school year. Write to the address below for more information.

Portland State University
Art Department
239 Neuberger Hall
Portland, OR 97207

1694

Florence Urban Murray Memorial Scholarship

AMOUNT: Varies **DEADLINE:** None Specified
FIELDS/MAJORS: All Areas Of Study

Award given to Erie students demonstrating a high potential for service to humanity and excellent scholarship ability. Write to the address below for more information.

Mercyhurst College
Financial Aid Office
Glenwood Hills
Erie, PA 16546

1695

Florence Ware Endowment Scholarship

AMOUNT: Tuitio **DEADLINE:** Feb 1
FIELDS/MAJORS: Art

Scholarships are available at the University of Utah for full-time continuing students enrolled in an art program. Must be of sophomore standing or above. Based on a presentation of portfolio and judged on merit. Write to the address below for details.

University Of Utah
Mary Francey
156 Art And Architecture Center
Salt Lake City, UT 84112

1696

Florence Warnock Scholarship

AMOUNT: $1,250 **DEADLINE:** Mar 15
FIELDS/MAJORS: All Areas Of Study

Scholarship offered to a Black Hawk County High School graduate. Must be an active member in a church or synagogue. Renewable for four years. Must have a GPA of 3.0 or better. Write to the address below for details.

Florence Warnock Scholarship Committee
First Presbyterian Church
505 Franklin Street
Waterloo, IA 50703

1697

Florida College Student Of The Year Award

Amount: $30,000 (max) **Deadline:** Feb 1
Fields/Majors: All Areas Of Study

Scholarships are available for Florida students enrolled on at least a halftime basis at any accredited Florida school. Applicant must have completed at least 30 credit hours, have a GPA of at least 3.2, and demonstrate financial self-reliance by working or and/or receiving scholarships. Must be involved in college/community activities. Write to the address listed below for information.

Florida Leader Magazine
P.O. Box 14081
Gainesville, FL 32604

1698

Florida Funeral Directors Association Scholarships

Amount: $500-$1,000
Deadline: None Specified
Fields/Majors: Mortuary Science

Awards for Florida residents enrolled in a mortuary science school. Must be a student member of the Florida Funeral Directors Association and have completed 30 credit hours in an accredited mortuary science school with no "D" grade in any mortuary science required class and an overall GPA of at least 2.5. Write to the address below for more information.

Florida Funeral Directors Association
P.O. Box 6009
Tallahassee, FL 32314

1699

Florida Library Association Graduate Grants

Amount: $2,000 (varies) **Deadline:** Mar 31
Fields/Majors: Library Science

Grants for master's level library science students in Florida. Foreign students may apply. two awards per year. Based on professional promise and GPA. Write to the address listed below for additional information.

Florida Library Association
Chair, FLA Scholarship Committee
1133 W. Morse Blvd., Suite 201
Winter Park, FL 32789

1700

Florida Peanut Producers Association Scholarships

Amount: $750 **Deadline:** Jul 1
Fields/Majors: All Areas Of Study

Scholarships for sons and daughters of active peanut farmers in Florida. Award is intended for use at a Florida college. Two awards per year. Membership in the FPPA is not necessary. Write to the address below for details.

Florida Peanut Producers Association
Scholarship Award Committee
P.O. Box 447
Graceville, FL 32440

1701

Florida Public Relations Association Scholarship

Amount: $1,000 **Deadline:** Mar 1
Fields/Majors: Public Relations

Must be a junior public relations major attending the University of Florida, and have at least a 3.0 GPA. This scholarship is provided by the Gainesville chapter of FPRA. Write to the address below for complete details.

University Of Florida
Scholarship & Placement Director
2070 Weimer Hall
Gainesville, FL 32611

1702

Florida Rural Rehabilitation Scholarships

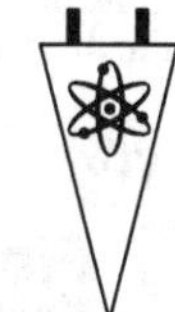

Amount: $1,200 **Deadline:** Mar 1
Fields/Majors: Agriculture

Scholarships for upper division students at the University of Florida who intend to pursue a degree in an agricultural field. Must be a resident of Florida to apply. Contact the office of the dean at the address below for details.

University Of Florida, Institute Of Food & Agricultural Sciences
Office Of The Dean
1001 McCarty Hall
Gainesville, FL 32611

1703

Florida Scholarship Challenge Program

Amount: $500 **Deadline:** Mar 15
Fields/Majors: Travel And Tourism, Hotel/Motel Management

Awards for Florida residents in one of the areas listed above who are enrolled in any four-year college. Must have a GPA of 3.0 or better and be in junior or senior year. Write to the address below for more information.

National Tour Foundation
546 East Main St.
P.O. Box 3071
Lexington, KY 40596

1704

Florida Student Assistance Grants

Amount: $200-$1,500 **Deadline:** May 15
Fields/Majors: All Areas Of Study

Florida resident for at least one year. Proven need of required financial help. Must be full-time undergraduate student at an eligible Florida institution. Open to U.S. citizens or eligible non-citizen. For more details, contact the address below or your high school guidance counselor.

Florida Department Of Education
Office Of Student Financial Assistance
1344 Florida Education Center
Tallahassee, FL 32399

1705

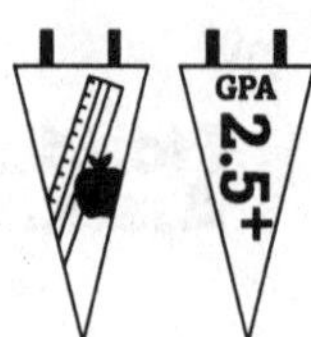

Florida Teacher Scholarship And Forgivable Loan Program

AMOUNT: $1,500-$8,000 **DEADLINE:** Mar 1
FIELDS/MAJORS: Education

For full-time undergraduate junior, senior, or graduate student enrolled in a state-approved teacher education program which leads to certification in a state-designated critical teacher shortage area. Can be repaid by teaching in Florida. Write to the address below for details.

Florida Department Of Education
Office Of Student Financial Assistance
1344 Florida Education Center
Tallahassee, FL 32399

1706

Florida Times-Union Scholarships

AMOUNT: $3,000 **DEADLINE:** Mar 1
FIELDS/MAJORS: Print Journalism

Must be a minority student (junior or senior) from Florida or Georgia. Must intend to pursue a career in print journalism or newspaper advertising at the University of Florida. Must have at least a 2.8 GPA. Write to the address below for complete details.

University Of Florida
Director, Minority Scholarship Program
2070 Weimer Hall
Gainesville, FL 32611

1707

Florida Undergraduate Scholars Fund

AMOUNT: $2,500 **DEADLINE:** Apr 1
FIELDS/MAJORS: Liberal Arts, Education

Florida resident for at least one year. Florida public high school seniors enrolling as first-time-in-college students at a state university or community college in Florida. Must be pursuing a liberal arts or teaching degree. Renewable for up to four years. Top-ranked high school graduates from each county may also receive a Challenger Astronauts Memorial Award of an additional $1,500. Applications are available from your guidance counselor or high school principal. Write to the address below for complete details.

Florida Department Of Education
Office Of Student Financial Assistance
1344 Florida Education Center
Tallahassee, FL 32399

1708

Florida Work Experience Program

AMOUNT: Varies **DEADLINE:** Varies
FIELDS/MAJORS: All Areas Of Study

Must have been Florida resident for at least one year. Undergraduate students who completed at least fifteen hours of coursework for academic credit and are enrolled at an eligible Florida institution. Provides student with employment as teacher aide or science laboratory assistant in a public elementary or secondary school in Florida. Contact the financial aid office at the school you plan to attend or write to the address below for details.

Florida Department Of Education
Office Of Student Financial Assistance
1344 Florida Education Center
Tallahassee, FL 32399

1709

Floyd Cargill Scholarship

AMOUNT: $750 **DEADLINE:** Jun 15
FIELDS/MAJORS: All Areas Of Study

Award for an outstanding blind student enrolled in an academic, vocational, technical, or professional training program in Illinois beyond the high school level. Applicants must be legally blind U.S. citizens from the state of Illinois. Write to the address below for more information.

Illinois Council Of The Blind
P.O. Box 1336
Springfield, IL 62705

1710

Floyd M. And Bertha E. Holt Scholarship

AMOUNT: $200 **DEADLINE:** Mar 31
FIELDS/MAJORS: All Areas Of Study

Student must be a senior with a GPA of 2.5 or better. Write to the address below for more information.

Southwest Missouri State University
Office Of Financial Aid
901 South National Ave.
Springfield, MO 65804

1711

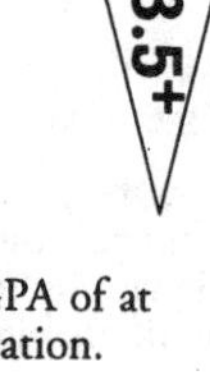

Floyd Neill Scholarship

AMOUNT: $1,000-$2,000 **DEADLINE:** Apr 1
FIELDS/MAJORS: All Areas Of Study

Awards for all Sul Ross undergraduates who have a GPA of at least 3.5. Write to the address below for more information.

Sul Ross State University
Financial Aid Office
Box C-113
Alpine, TX 79832

1712

Floyd Qualls Memorial Scholarships

AMOUNT: $2,500 **DEADLINE:** Mar 1
FIELDS/MAJORS: All Areas Of Study

Scholarships are for legally blind applicants who have been admitted for vocational/technical, professional, or academic studies at postsecondary levels. Eight awards per year. Write to the address below for details.

American Council Of The Blind
Scholarship Coordinator
1155 15th St., NW, Suite 720
Washington, DC 20005

1713

FLSSAR Essay Contest

AMOUNT: Varies **DEADLINE:** Jan 1
FIELDS/MAJORS: Writing

Essay contest open to high school seniors and college freshman and sophomores. The topic of writing will vary annually. Write to the address below for more information.

Florida Society Of The Sons Of The American Revolution, Inc.
3790 Helicon Dr.
Jacksonville, FL 32223

1714

FLSSAR Oration Contest

AMOUNT: Varies **DEADLINE:** None Specified
FIELDS/MAJORS: Oration

Oration contest open to high school seniors in the state of Florida. To participate, students must give a five to six minute oration to their local chapter of the FLSSAR. Write to the address below for more information.

Florida Society Of The Sons Of The American Revolution, Inc.
2441 North Atlantic Blvd.
Fort Lauderdale, FL 33305

1715

Fluor Daniel Engineering Scholarship Program

AMOUNT: None Specified **DEADLINE:** Mid-Mar
FIELDS/MAJORS: Chemical, Civil, Electrical, Environmental Or Mechanical Engineering;

Scholarships are available for sophomore undergraduate students pursuing a degree in one of the above fields or in the area of construction. For full-time study. Contact the dean of engineering at your school for information.

Fluor Corporation / Fluor Foundation
Scholarhsip Program
3333 Michelson Dr.
Irvine, CA 92730

1716

FMA Scholarship Program

AMOUNT: $1,250 (max) **DEADLINE:** Mar 15
FIELDS/MAJORS: Engineering, Manufacturing Technology

Awards for high school seniors and college sophomores and juniors in the fields of engineering or manufacturing technology. Must have a GPA of 3.0 or better and be children of members of FMA or its affiliates to apply. Write to the address below for more information.

Fabricators And Manufacturers Association, Intl.
Scholarship Committee
833 Featherstone Road
Rockford, IL 61107

1717

FMC Corporation Scholarships

AMOUNT: $500 **DEADLINE:** Feb 15
FIELDS/MAJORS: Agricultural Communications

Scholarships are available for FFA members pursuing a four-year degree in agricultural communications. Preference will be given to students with demonstrated leadership ability and academic achievement. Write to the address below for details.

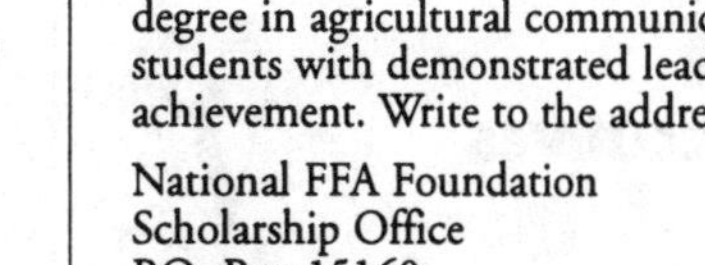

National FFA Foundation
Scholarship Office
P.O. Box 15160
Alexandria, VA 22309

1718

Focus Scholarship

AMOUNT: Varies **DEADLINE:** May 1
FIELDS/MAJORS: Education

Scholarships available for minority students for their junior year. Renewable for senior year. Write to the address below for information and application.

Florida International University
College Of Education-ACI 140
3000 NE 145th St.
North Miami, FL 33181

1719

Fogerty International Research Collaboration Award: HIV/AIDS Studies

AMOUNT: $20,000 **DEADLINE:** Varies
FIELDS/MAJORS: AIDS Research

Awards for scientists who propose a research project related to the study of HIV/AIDS. Renewable. For study at U.S. or foreign institutions. Write to the address below for more information.

National Institutes Of Health, Division Of Research Grants
Office Of Grant Inquiries
Westwood Building, Room 449
Bethesda, MD 20892

1720

Foley Scholarship

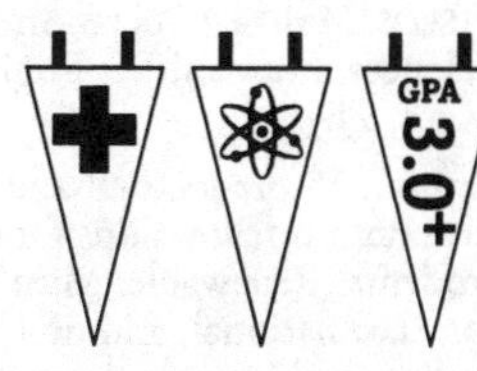

AMOUNT: None Specified
DEADLINE: Mid-Oct
FIELDS/MAJORS: Animal Science

Scholarships are awarded to students majoring in animal science who rank in the top 20% of their class after three years at UMass and show character and leadership. For students in their sophomore, junior, or senior year. Contact the Chair, Scholarship Committee, Veterinary and Animal Sciences, for more information.

University Of Massachusetts, Amherst
Chair, Scholarship Committee
Veterinary And Animal Sciences
Amherst, MA 01003

1721

Fontanelle Hybrids Scholarships

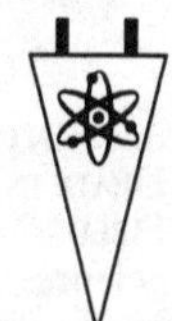

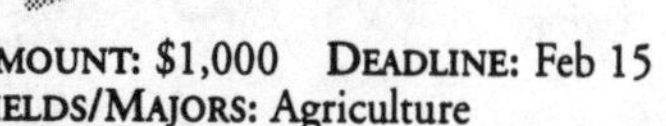

AMOUNT: $1,000 **DEADLINE:** Feb 15
FIELDS/MAJORS: Agriculture

Scholarships are available for FFA members pursuing a four-year degree in any area of agriculture, who reside in Illinois, Iowa, Kansas, Minnesota, Missouri, Nebraska, South Dakota, or Wisconsin. Write to the address below for details.

National FFA Foundation
Scholarship Office
P.O. Box 15160
Alexandria, VA 22309

1722

Food Service Executives Association

AMOUNT: $500-$1,500 **DEADLINE:** Mar 8
FIELDS/MAJORS: Food, Nutrition

Students must be undergraduates majoring in foods and nutrition. Write to the address below for more information.

California State Polytechnic University, Pomona
College Of Agriculture
Building 7, Room 110
Pomona, CA 91768

1723

Foods & Nutrition/Plant & Crop Science Scholarship

AMOUNT: $1,900 **DEADLINE:** Nov 1
FIELDS/MAJORS: All Areas Of Study

Scholarships for members of Minnesota 4-H or FFA clubs who have been active in production or nutrition areas of plant and soil science projects or food science and nutrition projects. To be used for educational expenses at a post secondary school. Money will be held in trust if the winner does not attend school immediately. Write to the address below for details.

Minnesota Soybean Research And Promotion Council
360 Pierce Avenue, Suite 110
North Mankato, MN 56003

1724

Ford Foundation Doctoral Fellowships For Minorities

AMOUNT: $6,000-$18,000
DEADLINE: Nov 3
FIELDS/MAJORS: Social And Life Sciences, Humanities, Engineering, Math, Physics

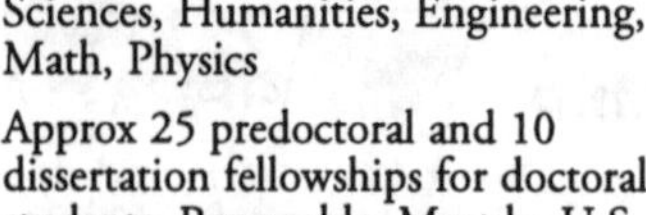

Approx 25 predoctoral and 10 dissertation fellowships for doctoral students. Renewable. Must be U.S. or U.S. national, and of African American, Native American Indian, or Hispanic descent. Contact your fellowship office or write to the address below for details.

National Research Council
The Fellowship Office/FFPD
2101 Constitution Avenue, NW
Washington, DC 20418

1725

Ford Foundation Postdoctoral Fellowships For Minorities

AMOUNT: $25,000 + Fees
DEADLINE: Jan 5
FIELDS/MAJORS: Social And Life Sciences, Humanities, Engineering, Math, Physics

Postdoctoral fellowships are available for scholars in the fields above. Renewable. Must be U.S. citizen or U.S. national, and of African American, Native American Indian, or Hispanic descent. Contact your fellowship office or write to the address below for details.

National Research Council
The Fellowship Office/FFPD
2101 Constitution Avenue, NW
Washington, DC 20418

1726

Ford Motor Company Fund Scholarships

AMOUNT: $1,200 **DEADLINE:** Feb 15
FIELDS/MAJORS: All Areas Of Study

Scholarships are available for FFA members pursuing a four-year degree in any area of study. Two awards are offered annually. Write to the address below for details.

National FFA Foundation
Scholarship Office
P.O. Box 15160
Alexandria, VA 22309

1727

Ford Pele Soccer Scholarship Program

AMOUNT: $1,000 **DEADLINE:** Apr 5
FIELDS/MAJORS: Soccer

Open to Georgia graduating high school seniors and continuing college students who are participating in a bonafide soccer program. Write to the address below for more information.

Georgia Soccer
3684 B-1 Stewart Rd.
Atlanta, GA 30340

1728

Ford Scholarships-Seniors To Be Returning To Farm

AMOUNT: $1,000 **DEADLINE:** Mar 15
FIELDS/MAJORS: Agriculture

Ten scholarships for seniors in college who are from farming families (parents or guardians derive majority of income from farming) and plan to return to farming after graduation. Must have a GPA of at least 3.0, be enrolled in an approved agricultural curriculum in a four-year college, and demonstrate leadership potential through extracurricular activities and work. Write to the address below for details.

Successful Farming-Ford Scholarships
1716 Locust Street
Des Moines, IA 50309

1729

Ford/EEOC Endowed Scholarship

AMOUNT: $1,000 **DEADLINE:** None Specified
FIELDS/MAJORS: All Areas Of Study

Scholarships are available for full-time undergraduate students. Must be a minority or woman. Preference given to Ford employees and their spouses and children. Must have a GPA of 2.5 or better. Write to the address below for more information.

California State Polytechnic University, Pomona
Office Of Financial Aid
3801 West Temple Ave.
Pomona, CA 91768

1730

Foreign Languages Department Scholarships

AMOUNT: $1,850 **DEADLINE:** Mar 31
FIELDS/MAJORS: Foreign Language

Awards for full-time students with a GPA of 3.0 or better who have taken at least 12 hours of one language in the foreign languages department, with a grade of "A" in each course. Students must agree to take two more upper-division language courses. Contact the foreign languages department for more information.

Southwest Missouri State University
Office Of Financial Aid
901 South National Ave.
Springfield, MO 65804

1731 

Forensics Talent Awards

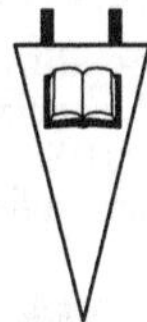

AMOUNT: None Specified **DEADLINE:** Mar 15
FIELDS/MAJORS: Forensics

Scholarships are available to students at Appalachian State University who plan to participate in the forensics program. Write to the address listed below for information.

Appalachian State University
Department Of Communications
Boone, NC 28608

1732 

Forest Resources Scholarships

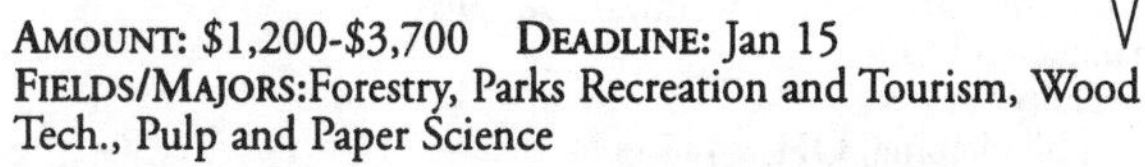

AMOUNT: $1,200-$3,700 **DEADLINE:** Jan 15
FIELDS/MAJORS: Forestry, Parks Recreation and Tourism, Wood Tech., Pulp and Paper Science

Renewable awards for undergraduates studying in one of the fields listed above at North Carolina State University. Write to the address below for more information, except for pulp and paper science students, who need to contact Ben Chilton, Development Officer, Pulp and Paper Foundation, Box 8005, Raleigh, NC 27695, for more information.

North Carolina State University
Dr. Douglas Wellman, Associate Dean
College Of Forest Resources, Box 8001
Raleigh, NC 27695

1733 

Forest Scholarship

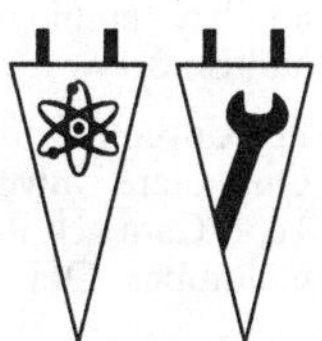

AMOUNT: Varies **DEADLINE:** Mar 31
FIELDS/MAJORS: Resource Economics, Animal Science, Food Science

Awards for UMass students in the fields listed above. Must have good academic standing and demonstrate interest in public service to agriculture and/or dairy industries. For juniors or seniors only. Contact the department of resource economics for more information.

University Of Massachusetts, Amherst
Department Of Resource Economics
Amherst, MA 01003

1734 

Fort Lewis College Tuition Waiver

AMOUNT: Tuition **DEADLINE:** Jun 30, Dec 1
FIELDS/MAJORS: All Areas Of Study

Scholarships are available for American Indian students attending Fort Lewis College. For undergraduate study. Write to the address listed below for information.

Fort Lewis College
Native American Center
Durango, CO 81301

1735

Fort Peck Tribal Higher Education Program

AMOUNT: None Specified **DEADLINE:** Varies
FIELDS/MAJORS: All Areas Of Study

Applicants must be members of the Fort Peck Assiniboine and Sioux tribes of the Fort Peck reservation. Must be a high school graduate or possess a GED certificate and enrolled, or accepted for enrollment, in an accredited college or university. Must have a GPA of 2.0 or higher. Deadlines for applications are for fall quarter July 15, winter quarter December 1, spring quarter March 1, and summer quarter May 1 (college seniors). Write to the address below for more information.

Fort Peck Tribal Education Department
P.O. Box 1027
Poplar, MT 59255

1736

Foster G. McGaw Student Scholarship

AMOUNT: $3,000 **DEADLINE:** Mar 31
FIELDS/MAJORS: Hospital And Health Services Administration

Scholarships are available to graduate students in hospital administration. Student must show good character/potential for success and academic promise. Must be student associate of American College of Healthcare Executives and be a U.S. or Canadian citizen. To apply, obtain an application from your program director. For further details, inquire to address below.

Foundation Of The American College Of Healthcare Executives
1 North Franklin Street, Suite 1700
Chicago, IL 60606

1737

Foster-Harris Scholarship

AMOUNT: $700 **DEADLINE:** Feb 15
FIELDS/MAJORS: Creative Writing

Scholarships are available at the University of Oklahoma, Norman, for students majoring in creative writing. Application must include writing samples. Write to the address listed below for information.

University Of Oklahoma, Norman
School Of Journalism and Mass Communication
860 Van Vleet Oval
Norman, OK 73019

1738

Foundation Honors Scholarships

AMOUNT: None Specified **DEADLINE:** None Specified
FIELDS/MAJORS: All Areas Of Study

Scholarships are available to academically talented students at Clarion University who participate in the honors program. Based on academic achievement and evidence of leadership and motivation. Scholarships are available for four years. Contact the director of the honors program for more information.

Clarion University
104 Egbert Hall
Office Of Financial Aid
Clarion, PA 16214

1739

Foundation Leadership Scholarships

AMOUNT: $1,500 **DEADLINE:** None Specified
FIELDS/MAJORS: All Areas Of Study

Scholarships are available to freshmen on a one-time basis. Applicants must have a minimum SAT score of 1,100 and be in the upper 2/5 of his or her high school graduating class. Contact the office of enrollment management and academic records for more information.

Clarion University
104 Egbert Hall
Office Of Financial Aid
Clarion, PA 16214

1740

Foundation Non-Instructional Staff Scholarship

AMOUNT: $500 **DEADLINE:** None Specified
FIELDS/MAJORS: All Areas Of Study

Scholarships are available for university staff members and their dependents. Six $500 scholarships are awarded. Contact the foundation office for more information.

Clarion University
104 Egbert Hall
Office Of Financial Aid
Clarion, PA 16214

1741

Foundation Of Flexographic Technical Association Scholarship

GPA 3.0+

AMOUNT: $500-$1,200 **DEADLINE:** Jan 26
FIELDS/MAJORS: Flexography, Graphic Art

Scholarships are awarded to students who demonstrate interest in a career in flexography, enrolled as a sophomore or junior at a college offering a course of study in flexography, exhibit exemplary performance in his/her studies, particularly in the area of graphic arts, and have at least 3.0 (B average or better). Write to the address below for more information.

Foundation Of Flexographic Technical Association, Inc.
John Dimarco, Marketing Manager
900 Marconi Ave.
Ronkonkoma, NY 11779

1742

Foundation Scholarship

GPA 3.0+

AMOUNT: $1,000 **DEADLINE:** None Specified
FIELDS/MAJORS: Aviation Related

Awards are available for students with a junior class standing or higher, who are enrolled in an aviation program and have a GPA of 3.0 or higher. Based on academics, financial need, participation in school, community activities, work experience, and a personal statement. Contact the financial aid office or the scholarship department at your school for more details.

American Association Of Airport Executives
4212 King Street
Alexandria, VA 22302

1743

Foundation Scholarships

AMOUNT: Varies **DEADLINE:** Varies
FIELDS/MAJORS: All Areas Of Study

Awards are given to children of Central alumni. Write to the address below for more details.

Southwest Missouri State University
Financial Aid Office
901 South National Ave.
Springfield, MO 65804

1744

Foundation Scholarships And General Scholarships

AMOUNT: $1,500 **DEADLINE:** Apr 1
FIELDS/MAJORS: All Areas Of Study

Scholarships for new students at Kent State University. Awards are based on superior academic record. Includes Preston Memorial Scholarship, William Mellor scholarship, Richard Demuth Scholarship, Mary Hanhart Scholarship, and General Foundation Scholarship. Contact the financial aid office at your campus for details.

Kent State University, Tuscarawas Campus
Financial Aid Office
University Dr., NE
New Philadelphia, OH 44663

1745

Founders Fellowship

AMOUNT: $1,500 **DEADLINE:** Mar 1
FIELDS/MAJORS: Home Economics

Applicants must be Phi U members who have completed at least half of the requirements toward the doctorate in home economics and have employment experience within the field. Write to the address below for details.

Phi Upsilon Omicron National Office
Ohio State University, 171 Mount Hall
1050 Carmack Road
Columbus, OH 43210

1746

Founders Fund Scholarship

AMOUNT: None Specified **DEADLINE:** None Specified
FIELDS/MAJORS: All Areas Of Study

Applicants must be members or dependents of members of Beta Theta Pi in good standing. Previous winners are not eligible. sixty awards per year. Write to the address below for details.

Beta Theta Pi Foundation
Scholarship Coordinator
5134 Bonham Rd, P.O. Box 6277
Oxford, OH 45056

1747

Founders Heritage Grant

AMOUNT: $4,000 **DEADLINE:** Mar 15
FIELDS/MAJORS: All Areas Of Study

Grants are available to St. Andrews College students who are residents of the local seven-county area. For undergraduate study. Contact the admissions office or write to the address below for more information.

St. Andrews College
Office Of Financial Aid
1700 Dogwood Mile
Laurinburg, NC 28352

1748

Founders Scholars Program

Amount: One Third Tuition **Deadline:** Feb 15
Fields/Majors: All Areas Of Study

Scholarships are available to Nazareth College for full-time undergraduate students who demonstrate outstanding academic performance. Must be a U.S. citizen. Write to the address below for details.

Nazareth College
Office Of Financial Aid
4245 East Avenue
Rochester, NY 14618

1749

Four Shra Nish Foundation Student Loan

Amount: $3,000 (max)
Deadline: None Specified
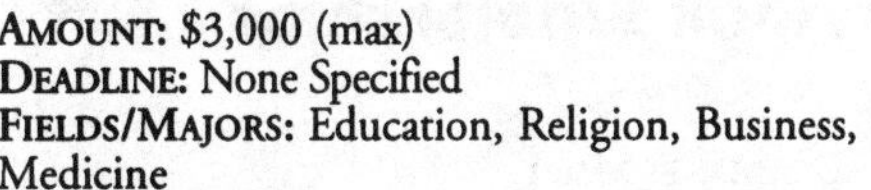
Fields/Majors: Education, Religion, Business, Medicine

Loans are available for residents of Darke County, Ohio (with residence there of at least 18 months) who are of sophomore standing or above, with a GPA of at least 2.0. Applicant must be enrolled in one of the fields listed above. Write to the address listed below for information.

Four Shra Nish Foundation
P.O. Box 126
Arcanum, OH 45304

1750

Fran Johnson Scholarship For Non-Traditional Students

Amount: $500-$1,000 **Deadline:** Apr 1
Fields/Majors: Floriculture

Scholarship for undergrad or graduate student who is re-entering school after an absence of at least five years. Must be enrolled in an accredited four-year school in the U.S. or Canada. Open to U.S. and Canadian citizens. Write to the address below for details.

Bedding Plants Foundation, Inc.
Scholarship Program
P.O. Box 27241
Lansing, MI 48909

1751

Frances Aust Silbereisen Scholarship

Amount: None Specified **Deadline:** None Specified
Fields/Majors: All Areas Of Study

Awards are available for students at SUNY, Potsdam, based on financial need. Write to the address below for more information.

SUNY, Potsdam
Office Of Admissions
44 Pierrepont Ave
Potsdam, NY 13676

1752

Frances C. Allen Fellowships

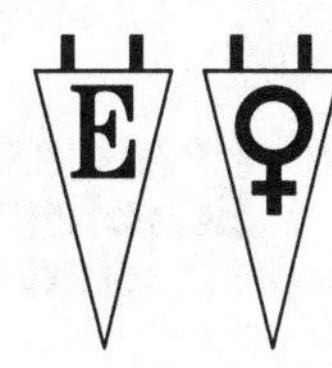

Amount: Varies **Deadline:** Feb 1
Fields/Majors: All Areas Of Study

You must be a tribal American Indian in any academic program beyond the undergraduate level. Candidates may be working in any field of study, but they must use the resources of the Newberry Library. The award is limited to females. Write to the address below for complete details.

Newberry Library
Frances C. Allen Fellowships
60 W. Walton St.
Chicago, IL 60610

1753

Frances Fay Derose Memorial Scholarship

Amount: $400 **Deadline:** Feb 9
Fields/Majors: Speech Therapy-Communication Disorders

Award for incoming junior majoring in speech therapy. Must have strong academic record and demonstrate financial need. Use Bloomsburg University scholarship application. Contact Dr. Carroll Redfern, Chairperson, department of Communication Disorders and Special Education.

Bloomsburg University
19 Ben Franklin Hall
400 E. Second St.
Bloomsburg, PA 17815

1754

Frances Hamilton Buchholz Memorial Scholarship

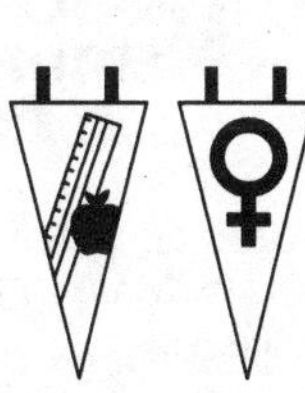

Amount: $375 **Deadline:** None Specified
Fields/Majors: Elementary Education

Student must be a female elementary education major. Contact the curriculum and instruction department for more information.

Southwest Missouri State University
Office Of Financial Aid
901 South National Ave.
Springfield, MO 65804

1755

Frances M. Lee Memorial Scholarship

Amount: Varies **Deadline:** Mar 1
Fields/Majors: Political Science

Awards are available at the University of New Mexico for students majoring in political science with a GPA of at least 3.0. Recipient is chosen at the end of sophomore year and renewed for four semesters given a GPA of 3.0 is maintained. Write to the address below for more information.

University Of New Mexico, Albuquerque
Office Of Financial Aid
Albuquerque, NM 87131

1756

Frances M. Peacock Scholarship For Native Bird Habitat

AMOUNT: $4,000 (max) **DEADLINE:** Jan 15
FIELDS/MAJORS: Ornithology

Scholarships are available for seniors and graduate students in ornithology, to study areas in the U.S. that provide winter or summer habitat for threatened and endangered native birds. Write to the address listed below for information.

Garden Club Of America
Cornell Lab Of Ornithology
Sapsucker Woods Road
Ithaca, NY 14850

1757

Frances M. Schwartz Fellowship

AMOUNT: $2,000 (max) **DEADLINE:** Mar 1
FIELDS/MAJORS: Numismatics, Museum Studies, Art and Economic History, Classical Studies

Applicants must have a B.A. degree or equivalent. The fellowship supports the work and study of numismatic and museum methodology at the society. Write to the address below for details.

American Numismatic Society
Broadway At 155th Street
New York, NY 10032

1758

Frances Weitzenhoffer Memorial Fellowship In Art History

AMOUNT: $4,000 **DEADLINE:** Mar 1
FIELDS/MAJORS: Art History

Fellowships are available at the University of Oklahoma, Norman for full-time graduate art history majors. Write to the address listed below for information.

University Of Oklahoma, Norman
Director, School Of Art
520 Parrington, Room 202
Norman, OK 73019

1759

Francine Shoenfeld Award

AMOUNT: Varies **DEADLINE:** Mar 1
FIELDS/MAJORS: Chemistry

Awards for sophomore, junior or senior students in the chemistry program. Contact the chemistry department for more information.

University Of Massachusetts, Amherst
Chemistry Department
Amherst, MA 01003

1760

Francis C. Allen Fellowship

AMOUNT: None Specified
DEADLINE: None Specified
FIELDS/MAJORS: History

Fellowships are available for American Indian women graduate history students who wish to use the facilities at the Newberry Library for research into American Indian history. Write to the address listed below for additional information.

The Newberry Library
Center Of History Of The American Indian
60 West Walton
Chicago, IL 60610

1761

Francis Doc Sell Scholarship (Football)

AMOUNT: $500 **DEADLINE:** Unspecified
FIELDS/MAJORS: All Areas Of Study

Award for currently enrolled or incoming freshmen male athletes. Recipient determined by the coaches of men's athletics from members of football teams. Contact a member of the coaching staff for additional information.

Bloomsburg University
19 Ben Franklin Hall
400 E. Second St.
Bloomsburg, PA 17815

1762

Francis Hook Scholarships

AMOUNT: Varies **DEADLINE:** Mar 1
FIELDS/MAJORS: Art

Awards for college undergraduates under the age of 24 in the field of art. Applicants must be sponsored by professors or deans who must request a brochure and guidelines. Based on the submission of three slides of original art work. Write to the address below for more information.

Francis Hook Scholarship Fund
Executive Director
P.O. Box 597346
Chicago, IL 60659

1763

Francis Ouimet Scholarship

AMOUNT: $2,500 (max) **DEADLINE:** Dec 1
FIELDS/MAJORS: All Areas Of Study

Awards granted to high school and college students who were caddies or worked in a golf environment for three or more years at any Massachusetts golf club. This is available for undergraduate study at a community college or four-year college or university. Over 200 awards per year. Write to the address below for complete details.

Francis Ouimet Caddie Scholarship Fund
Golf House
190 Park Rd.
Weston, MA 02193

1764

Frank And Helen Clarke Memorial Fund Award

AMOUNT: Varies **DEADLINE:** None Specified
FIELDS/MAJORS: Writing

Awards are available at Portland State University for students who submit a work of excellence as a regular assignment in an English course. Faculty may nominate more than one noteworthy student paper or students may submit essays directly to the English department. Contact the English department at the address below for more information.

Portland State University
English Department
405 Neuburger Hall
Portland, OR 97207

1765

Frank And Louise Groff Foundation

Amount: $100-$2,000 **Deadline:** Apr 1
Fields/Majors: Registered Nurse, Medical Doctor

Open to women and men who have graduated from a public school in Monmouth, New Jersey, with an interest in becoming a registered nurse or medical doctor. Write to the address below for more information.

Frank And Louise Groff Foundation
15 Floyd Wycoff Rd.
Morganville, NJ 07751

1766

Frank B. Sessa Scholarship For Continuing Education

Amount: $750 **Deadline:** Mar 1
Fields/Majors: Library And Information Science

Applicants must be members of Beta Phi Mu. An explanation of proposed study or research must accompany application form. For junior, senior, or graduate study. Write to the executive secretary at the address below for details.

Beta Phi Mu International Library Science Honor Society
School Of Library and Information Science
University Of Pittsburgh
Pittsburgh, PA 15260

1767

Frank D. Visceglia Memorial Scholarship

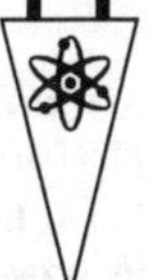

Amount: $1,000 **Deadline:** Sep 30
Fields/Majors: Environmental Studies

Preference will be given to those scouts whose Eagle Service Projects are related to the environment and/or the economy. Must plan to attend an accredited four-year college. Write to the address below for more information.

Frank D. Visceglia Memorial Scholarship Program
Dennis Kohl, Scout Executive
12 Mount Pleasant Turnpike
Denville, NJ 07834

1768

Frank F. Thompson Memorial Scholarship

Amount: $700 **Deadline:** None Specified
Fields/Majors: Teacher Education

Student must demonstrate special promise in the teaching profession with a GPA of 3.0 or better. Contact the curriculum and instruction department for more information.

Southwest Missouri State University
Office Of Financial Aid
901 South National Ave.
Springfield, MO 65804

1769

Frank G. Lambertus Memorial Scholarship

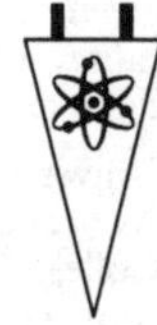

Amount: None Specified **Deadline:** None Specified
Fields/Majors: Science

Scholarships are awarded to students who have shown the greatest improvement in academic performance since the previous year. Write to the address below for more information.

Indiana University/Purdue University, Indianapolis
Purdue School Of Technology
799 West Michigan St.
Indianapolis, IN 46202

1770

Frank J. Jervey Alumni & Samuel C. Mayne Memorial Scholarships

Amount: $2,000 **Deadline:** Mar 1
Fields/Majors: All Areas Of Study

Several scholarships available to entering freshmen with outstanding academic potential. Renewable for three years. Contact the financial aid office at the address below for details.

Clemson University
Financial Aid Office
G01 Sikes Hall
Clemson, SC 29634

1771

Frank L. Weil Memorial Scholarship

Amount: Varies **Deadline:** Jan 1
Fields/Majors: All Areas Of Study

Awards for Boy Scouts or Eagle Scouts who are Jewish and have earned their Ner Tamid emblem. Awarded freshman year. Nonrenewable. Write to the address below for more information.

National Jewish Committee On Scouting, S226
Boy Scouts Of America
1325 West Walnut Hill Lane
Irving, TX 75015

1772

Frank M. Chapman Memorial Grants

Amount: $200-$1,000 **Deadline:** Jan 15
Fields/Majors: Ornithology

Open to young scientists and graduate students to encourage research in ornithology. Funds are to be used for modest support of museum/field/laboratory research projects (i.e., not for tuition, etc.). Collection study grants are also available. Write to the address below for complete details.

American Museum Of Natural History
Central Park West At 79th Street
New York, NY 10024

1773

Frank Plumb Scholarship

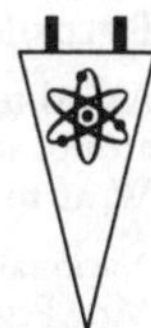

Amount: Varies **Deadline:** Jun 1
Fields/Majors: Agriculture

Awards for UMass students in the field of agriculture. Preference given to residents of Middlesex County, MA. For entering sophomores, juniors, or seniors. Contact the Associate Dean, College of Food and Natural Resources for more information.

University Of Massachusetts, Amherst
Associate Dean
College Of Food And Natural Resources
Amherst, MA 01003

1774

Frank Prentise Rand Scholarship

AMOUNT: Varies **DEADLINE:** Mar 1
FIELDS/MAJORS: Fine Arts, Drama

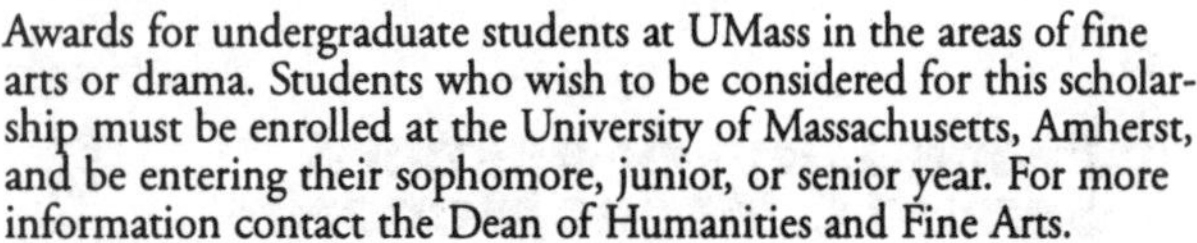

Awards for undergraduate students at UMass in the areas of fine arts or drama. Students who wish to be considered for this scholarship must be enrolled at the University of Massachusetts, Amherst, and be entering their sophomore, junior, or senior year. For more information contact the Dean of Humanities and Fine Arts.

University Of Massachusetts, Amherst
255 Whitmore Administration Building
Box 38230
Amherst, MA 01003

1775

Frank Roberts Community Service Scholarship

AMOUNT: Varies **DEADLINE:** Varies
FIELDS/MAJORS: All Areas Of Study

Awards are available at Portland State University for graduate students who are involved in community service related to the graduate student's academic program. Contact the office of graduate studies and research for more information.

Portland State University
Office Of Graduate Studies and Research
105 Neuberger Hall
Portland, OR 97207

1776

Frank W. Radford Award

AMOUNT: $250 **DEADLINE:** Mar 3
FIELDS/MAJORS: All Areas Of Study

Awards are available to students who graduated from a Winnebago County high school and are full-time sophomores or juniors. Based upon scholastic achievement, good character, and financial need. Contact the financial aid office, UW Oshkosh for more information.

University Of Wisconsin, Oshkosh
Financial Aid Office, Dempsey 104
800 Algoma Blvd.
Oshkosh, WI 54901

1777

Frank Walton Horn Memorial Scholarship

AMOUNT: $3,000 **DEADLINE:** Mar 31
FIELDS/MAJORS: Architecture, Engineering

Award recipient must be legally blind. Students may be in any area of study, but architecture or engineering majors are preferred. Write to the address below for complete details.

National Federation Of The Blind
Mrs. Peggy Elliott, Chairman
814 Fourth Ave., Suite 200
Grinnell, IA 50112

1778

Frank Warner Memorial Scholarship

AMOUNT: Varies **DEADLINE:** Mar 1
FIELDS/MAJORS: Finance, Banking

Scholarships are available at the University of Iowa for full-time undergraduates majoring in finance or banking. Write to the address listed below for information.

University Of Iowa
College Of Business Admin., Suite W160
108 Pappajohn Business Admin. Bldg.
Iowa City, IA 52245

1779

Frank William & Dorothy Given Miller Asme Auxiliary Scholarship

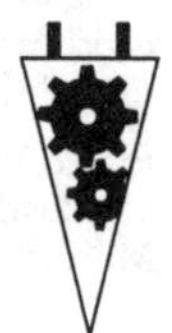

AMOUNT: $1,500 **DEADLINE:** Apr 15
FIELDS/MAJORS: Mechanical Engineering

Two scholarships for ASME junior and senior student members who are majoring in mechanical engineering. Applicants must be U.S. citizens and reside in North America. For additional information, call or write the ASME foundation.

American Society Of Mechanical Engineers
Education Services Department
345 E. 47th Street
New York, NY 10017

1780

Franklin Lindsey Student Aid Fund

AMOUNT: $12,000 (max) **DEADLINE:** None Specified
FIELDS/MAJORS: All Areas Of Study

Loans for students who attending college or a university in Texas. Must have a GPA of at least 2.0. Must have completed at least one year or 24 hours of study. Must be a U.S. citizen. Interview required. Write to the address below for details. Recipients must have a co-signer for their loans.

Texas Commerce Bank-Austin, Franklin Lindsey
Student Aid Fund
Trust Department, Attn: Polly Randell
P.O. Box 550
Austin, TX 78789

1781

Franklin Mosher Baldwin Memorial Fellowships

AMOUNT: $8,500 Per Year **DEADLINE:** Jan 2
FIELDS/MAJORS: Anthropology

Fellowships for African American students who seek an advanced degree at a major institution. Priority is given to students involved in disciplines related to human evolution. Write to the address below for more information.

L.S.B. Leaky Foundation
Grants Administration
77 Jack London Square
Oakland, CA 94607

1782

Fraser Scholarships

AMOUNT: Tuition **DEADLINE:** Apr 30
FIELDS/MAJORS: All Areas Of Study

Awards for children of Chrysler workers who are attending Wayne State University in Detroit. For undergraduate study. Write to the address below for more information.

Wayne State University
Office Of Scholarships And Financial Aid
HNJ Student Services Center, #3 West
Detroit, MI 48202

1783

Fraternal College Scholarship Program

AMOUNT: $500-$2,000 **DEADLINE:** Jan 1
FIELDS/MAJORS: All Areas Of Study

Scholarships for members of Modern Woodmen of America who are high school seniors enrolling in a four-year college. Must be in top 1/2 of high school class. Write to the address below for details.

Modern Woodmen Of America
Fraternal Scholarship Administrator
1701 1st Avenue
Rock Island, IL 61201

1784

Fraternal Non-Traditional Scholarship Program

AMOUNT: None Specified **DEADLINE:** Apr 1
FIELDS/MAJORS: All Areas Of Study

Applicants must have attained age 25 or older by the date of the application deadline. Must be a beneficial member of Royal Neighbors of America for at least two years. Write to the address below for more information.

Royal Neighbors Of America
Fraternal Scholarship Program
230 16th St.
Rock Island, IL 61201

1785

Fred A. Bryan Collegiate Students Fund Grants

AMOUNT: $2,500/year **DEADLINE:** None Specified
FIELDS/MAJORS: All Areas Of Study

Open to graduating seniors from South Bend, Indiana who are/were Boy Scouts. Grant renewable up to four years. Write to the address below for complete details.

Fred A. Bryan Collegiate Students Fund
Norwest Bank Indiana, NA, Trust Dept.
112 W. Jefferson Blvd.
South Bend, IN 46601

1786

Fred M. Chreist, Sr. Scholarship

AMOUNT: Varies **DEADLINE:** Mar 1
FIELDS/MAJORS: Communicative Disorders

Awards are available at the University of New Mexico for full-time juniors or seniors majoring in the fields of communicative disorders. Write to the address listed below for information.

University Of New Mexico, Albuquerque
Office Of Financial Aid
Albuquerque, NM 87131

1787

Fred S. Bailey Scholarships

AMOUNT: $500-$1,500 **DEADLINE:** Feb 15
FIELDS/MAJORS: All Areas Of Study

Scholarships are available at the University of Illinois for students who demonstrate academic ability, financial need, and concern for the needs of others and the betterment of society. More than 100 awards offered annually. For undergraduates only. Write to the address below for more information.

University Of Illinois At Champaign Urbana
University Of Illinois YMCA
1001 South Wright St.
Champaign, IL 61820

1788

Freddie Palmisano Memorial Scholarship

AMOUNT: None Specified **DEADLINE:** Feb 15
FIELDS/MAJORS: Drama And Communications

Scholarships are available at the University of New Orleans for full-time entering freshmen students, enrolled in a one of the areas listed above. Write to the address below for details.

University Of New Orleans
Student Financial Aid Office
1005 Administration Building, Lake Front
New Orleans, LA 70148

1789

Frederic G. Melcher Scholarships

AMOUNT: $5,000 **DEADLINE:** Mar 1
FIELDS/MAJORS: Library Science, Children's

Applicants must be graduate students entering an ALA-accredited master's program and specializing in children's libraries. Must be U.S. or Canadian citizen. Recipients are expected to work in the children's library field for a minimum of two years. Write to the address shown for details.

American Library Association
Assn. For Library Service To Children
50 E. Huron Street
Chicago, IL 60611

1790

Frederick A Downes Scholarship-American Foundation Of The Blind

AMOUNT: $2,500 **DEADLINE:** Apr 1
FIELDS/MAJORS: Vocational/Technical

Scholarships are available to legally blind undergraduate students who are 22 years of age or less, enrolled in a course of study leading to a degree or vocational credentials. Applicant must be a U.S. citizen. Write to the foundation at the address below to receive information on this award and other programs they administer.

American Foundation For The Blind
Scholarship Coordinator
11 Penn Plaza, Suite 300
New York, NY 10001

1791

Frederick J. Benson Scholarship Fund

AMOUNT: $1,000 - $4,000 **DEADLINE:** None Specified
FIELDS/MAJORS: All Areas Of Study

Scholarships are available for residents of Block Island who are of sophomore standing or above. Applicant must have lived on Block Island for eight years or more, or attended high school there for at least three years. Write to the address listed below for information.

Rhode Island Foundation
Ms. Michelle Phelan
P.O. Box B-2
Block Island, RI 02807

1792

Frederick W. And Grace P. Brecht Scholarship

AMOUNT: None Specified **DEADLINE:** Apr 15
FIELDS/MAJORS: All Areas Of Study

Scholarships are available for students that reside in Brevard County and have a GPA of 2.0 or better. Write to the address below for more information.

University Of Florida
P.O. Box 114025
S-107 Criser Hall
Gainesville, FL 32611

1793

Frederick/Christine Kent Scholarships

AMOUNT: Varies **DEADLINE:** Mar 1
FIELDS/MAJORS: All Areas Of Study

Awards are available at the University of New Mexico for freshmen students from New Mexico with financial need. Based on high school grades and recommendations from the high school principal or counselor. Awards are given in the spring only. Write to the address below for more information.

University Of New Mexico, Albuquerque
Office Of Financial Aid
Albuquerque, NM 87131

1794

Freeman Fellowship

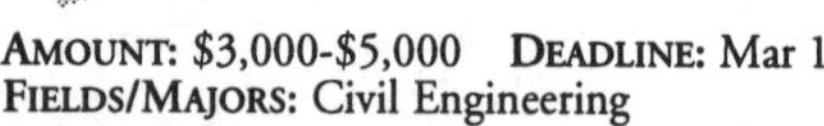

AMOUNT: $3,000-$5,000 **DEADLINE:** Mar 1
FIELDS/MAJORS: Civil Engineering

Applicant must be a national ASCE member in any year of graduate study. Award is used for experiments, observations and compilations to discover new and accurate data that will be useful in engineering, particularly hydraulics. Write to the address below for complete details.

American Society Of Civil Engineers
Member Scholarships And Awards
345 E. 47th Street
New York, NY 10017

1795

French Scholarship

AMOUNT: Varies **DEADLINE:** Jun 1
FIELDS/MAJORS: Animal Science, Dairy, Forestry

Awards for UMass students in the fields listed above. Must have 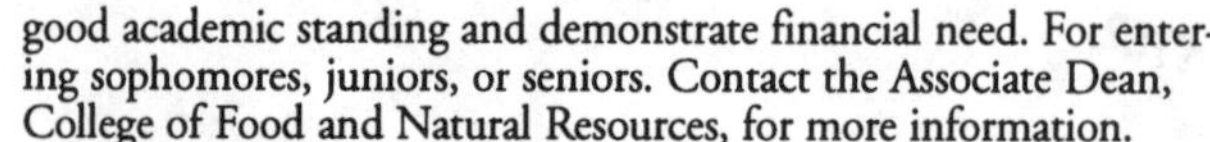 good academic standing and demonstrate financial need. For entering sophomores, juniors, or seniors. Contact the Associate Dean, College of Food and Natural Resources, for more information.

University Of Massachusetts, Amherst
Associate Dean
College Of Food And Natural Resources
Amherst, MA 01003

1796

Freshman Academic Scholarship

AMOUNT: $1,200 **DEADLINE:** Mar 31
FIELDS/MAJORS: All Areas Of Study

Awards for entering freshman who have demonstrated academic achievement as shown by grades and ACT scores. Applicants must have a GPA of at least 2.4. Write to the address below for more details.

Southwest Missouri State University
Financial Aid Office
901 South National Ave.
Springfield, MO 65804

1797

Freshman Academic Scholarships

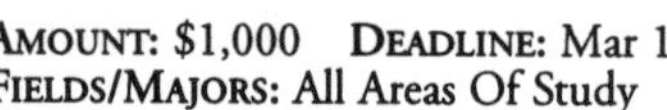

AMOUNT: $1,000 **DEADLINE:** Mar 1
FIELDS/MAJORS: All Areas Of Study

Scholarships are awarded to incoming full-time freshmen graduating in the top 15% of their high school classes as long as candidates have been enrolled in college preparatory classes. These scholarships may be renewed each year that the student maintains a cumulative GPA of 3.25 or better and makes a positive contribution to the college. Write to address below for details.

College Of St. Joseph
71 Clement Road
Office Of Admissions
Rutland, VT 05701

1798

Freshman Academic Scholarships

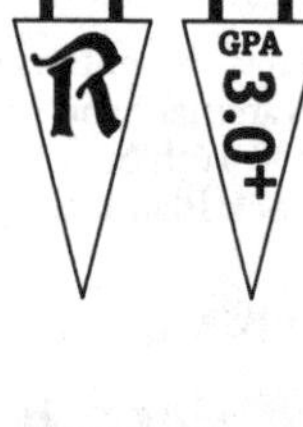

AMOUNT: $1,000-$2,000
DEADLINE: None Specified
FIELDS/MAJORS: All Areas Of Study

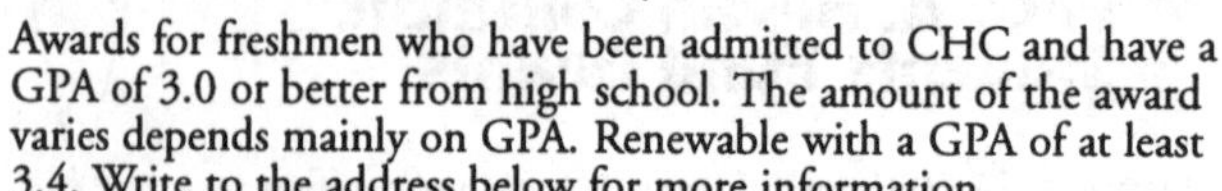

Awards for freshmen who have been admitted to CHC and have a GPA of 3.0 or better from high school. The amount of the award varies depends mainly on GPA. Renewable with a GPA of at least 3.4. Write to the address below for more information.

Christian Heritage College
Financial Aid Office
2100 Greenfield Dr.
El Cajon, CA 92019

1799

Freshman Awards

AMOUNT: Varies **DEADLINE:** Mar 1
FIELDS/MAJORS: All Areas Of Study

Open to incoming freshmen of Japanese ancestry. Several award programs are available. Applications and information may be obtained from local JACL chapters, district offices, and national headquarters at the address below. Please be certain to include a legal-sized SASE.

Japanese American Citizens League
National Scholarship And Award Program
1765 Sutter St.
San Francisco, CA 94115

1800

Freshman Communication Scholarship

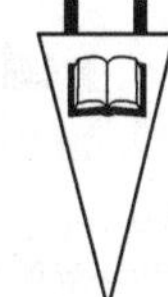

AMOUNT: $1,000 **DEADLINE:** Mar 15
FIELDS/MAJORS: Communications

Awards for Jacksonville State University freshmen in the field of communications. Renewable. Contact the head of the communication department for more information.

Jacksonville State University
Financial Aid Office
Jacksonville, AL 36265

1801

Freshman New Mexico Native Americans Scholarship Fund

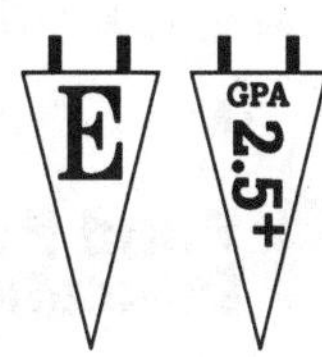

AMOUNT: None Specified **DEADLINE:** Mar 1
FIELDS/MAJORS: All Areas Of Study

Applicant must be a freshman Native American from New Mexico and must have a minimum GPA of 2.86. Write to the address below for details.

New Mexico State University
American Indian Program
Box 30001, Dept 5100
Las Cruces, NM 88003

1802

Freshman Regents Scholarship

AMOUNT: Tuition And Fees **DEADLINE:** Mar 31
FIELDS/MAJORS: All Areas Of Study

Awards for entering freshman who rank in the upper 10% of their class and have an ACT composite score of 27 or above. Renewable with a GPA of at least 3.5. Write to the address below for more details.

Southwest Missouri State University
Financial Aid Office
901 South National Ave.
Springfield, MO 65804

1803

Freshman Research Associateships

AMOUNT: $1,500 (max) Deadline: None Specified
FIELDS/MAJORS: All Areas Of Study

Ten awards for entering freshmen at Eckerd College to work closely on a research project with a faculty member. Based on high school record. Write to the address below for details.

Eckerd College
Director Of Financial Aid
P.O. Box 12560
St. Petersburg, FL 33733

1804

Freshman Scholarships In Teacher Education

AMOUNT: $1,000 **DEADLINE:** Dec 15
FIELDS/MAJORS: Education

Applicants must be incoming freshmen majoring in education. GPA of 3.4 is required. Renewable. Write to the address below for details.

Appalachian State University
Reich College Of Education
Boone, NC 28608

1805

Frieda D. Butler Scholarship Fund

AMOUNT: Varies **DEADLINE:** Mar 1
FIELDS/MAJORS: Ethnology

Scholarships are available at the University of New Mexico for full-time undergraduate of graduate students enrolled in an ethnology program. Write to the address listed below for information.

University Of New Mexico, Albuquerque
Anthropology Department
Albuquerque, NM 87131

1806

Frieda's Scholarship For Women In Agriculture

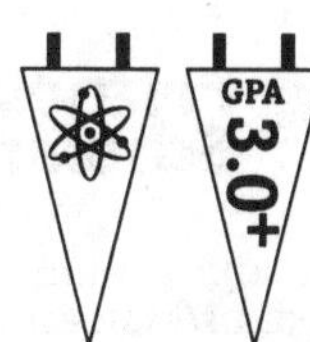

AMOUNT: $1,000 **DEADLINE:** Mar 10
FIELDS/MAJORS: Agriculture

Open to sophomore, junior, or senior female students with a declared agricultural major and plans to pursue a career in a related field. Must have a GPA of 3.4 or better. Write to the address below for more information.

California State Polytechnic University, Pomona
College Of Agriculture
Building 7, Room 110
Pomona, CA 91768

1807

Friedrich Ebert Doctoral Research Fellowships

AMOUNT: Varies **DEADLINE:** Feb 29
FIELDS/MAJORS: German Studies (Political Science, Sociology, History, Economics)

Fellowships for students in the above area of study who have an approved dissertation proposal. Applicants must be U.S. citizens and provide evidence that they have knowledge of German that is adequate for research purposes. Write to the address below for more information.

Friedrich Ebert Foundation
New York Office
950 Third Ave., 28th Floor
New York, NY 10022

1808

Friedrich Ebert Pre-Dissertation/Advanced Graduate Fellowships

AMOUNT: Varies **DEADLINE:** Feb 29
FIELDS/MAJORS: German Studies (Political Science, Sociology, History, Economics)

Fellowships for students in the above area of studies who intend to pursue a doctoral degree. Applicants must be U.S. citizens, must have completed two years of graduate study, and provide proof that they have sufficient knowledge of German. The expected outcome of this program is the development of a dissertation proposal or completion of a specific research topic. Write to the address below for more information.

Friedrich Ebert Foundation
New York Office
950 Third Ave., 28th Floor
New York, NY 10022

1809

Friends Of The Library Of Hawaii Scholarships

AMOUNT: $1,000-$3,000 **DEADLINE:** Jun 1
FIELDS/MAJORS: Library Science, Information Science

Open to graduate students enrolled in library science at the University of Hawaii. For master's level study. Fifteen awards are anticipated in the coming years. Write to the address below for further information.

University Of Hawaii
School Of Library and Information Studies
2550 The Mall
Manoa, HI 96822

1810

Friends Of Theater Scholarship

AMOUNT: Varies **DEADLINE:** None Specified
FIELDS/MAJORS: Theater

Scholarship at ETSU for students pursuing a career in the performing arts, with emphasis on theater. Write to the address below for details.

East Tennessee State University
Office Of Financial Aid
Box 70722
Johnson City, TN 37614

1811

Fukunaga Scholarships In Business Administration

GPA 3.0+

AMOUNT: $1,500-$2,000 **DEADLINE:** Apr 15
FIELDS/MAJORS: Business Administration

Scholarships for Hawaii residents pursuing a four-year degree in business. Program is designed to encourage graduating high school seniors, but students who are already attending college will also be considered. Must have a GPA of at least 3.0. Write to the address below for more details.

Fukunaga Scholarship Foundation
Scholarship Selection Committee
P.O. Box 2788
Honolulu, HI 96803

1812

Fulbright Awards

AMOUNT: Varies **DEADLINE:** None Specified
FIELDS/MAJORS: International Studies

Awards are available to master's degree candidates to foster mutual understanding among nations through educational and cultural exchanges. The program enables U.S. students to benefit from unique resources and gain international competence in an increasingly interdependent world. Must be a U.S. citizen at the time of application. Write to the address listed below for information.

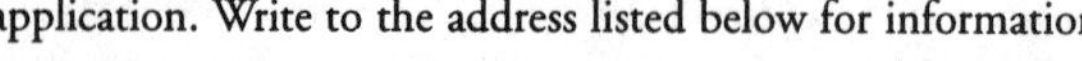

Institute Of International Education
Fulbright Awards
809 United Nations Plaza
New York, NY 10017

1813

Full University Scholarship

AMOUNT: Tuition & Fees **DEADLINE:** Feb 15
FIELDS/MAJORS: All Areas Of Study

Scholarships at UM College Park for excellent high school seniors from Maryland. Recipients receive full financial support for four years (includes tuition and fees, room and board). To be considered, students must submit their undergraduate admissions packets by December 1. Write to the address below for details.

University Of Maryland, College Park
Office Of Student Financial Aid
0102 Lee Building
College Park, MD 20742

1814

Fund For Podiatric Medical Education

AMOUNT: None Specified **DEADLINE:** May 1
FIELDS/MAJORS: Podiatric Medicine

Open to third and fourth year students studying podiatric medicine. Write to the address below for more information.

Fund For Podiatric Medical Education
9312 Old Georgetown Rd.
Bethesda, MD 20814

1815

Furman Teacher Education Scholarships

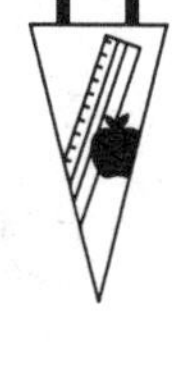

AMOUNT: $2,000 **DEADLINE:** Feb 1
FIELDS/MAJORS: Education

Awards for entering freshmen who have indicated teaching as their career goal. Write to the address below for more information.

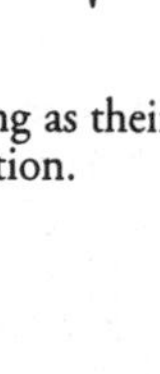

Furman University
Director Of Financial Aid
3300 Poinsett Highway
Greenville, SC 29613

1816

Futurama Interim Scholarship

AMOUNT: $500 **DEADLINE:** Apr 20
FIELDS/MAJORS: All Areas Of Study

Applicant must be a female Maine resident who has or will have completed (at end of spring semester) at least one year of college. Must demonstrate financial need and be in good academic standing. Student will need to send two letters of recommendation (from teachers, employers, ministers, etc). Contact the address below for further information.

Business & Professional Women's Clubs—Maine
Myra Chaloult
P.O. Box 585
Waterville, ME 04903

1817

Futurama Youth Scholarships In Memory Of Rachel E. Lemieux

Amount: $500 **Deadline:** Apr 20
Fields/Majors: All Areas Of Study

Award for entering female freshman, current high school senior, or recent graduate. Must be a Maine resident and able to demonstrate financial need. Student will need to furnish a school transcript, acceptance from college and a letter from a high school teacher, principal, employer, or minister, etc. Contact the address below for further information and an application.

Business & Professional Women's Clubs-Maine
Myra Chaloult
P.O. Box 585
Waterville, ME 04903

1818

Future Farmers Of America Minority Scholarships

Amount: $5,000-$10,000 **Deadline:** Feb 15
Fields/Majors: Agriculture

Four renewable scholarships for FFA members from any state who are members of an ethnic minority group (specifically American Indian, Alaskan Native, Asian or Pacific Islander, Black, or Hispanic), and pursuing a degree in agriculture. For undergraduate study. Write to the address below for details.

National FFA Foundation
Scholarship Office
P.O. Box 15160
Alexandria, VA 22309

1819

Future Teachers Scholarship

Amount: $1,000 **Deadline:** Apr 30
Fields/Majors: Education

Open to undergraduate students pursuing degrees in education. Contact Future Teacher Scholarship, c/o Concerned Educators Against Forced Unionism, 8001 Braddock Rd., Suite 500, Springfiled, VA 22160, or call (703) 321-8519 for more information.

California State Polytechnic University, Pomona
College Of Agriculture
Building 45, Room 109b
Pomona, CA 91768

1820

Future Teachers Scholarship Program

Amount: $500-$1,500 **Deadline:** Aug 1
Fields/Majors: Education

Scholarships are available for full-time education majors at Oklahoma colleges and universities. Applicants must be sophomores or above, who graduated in the top 15% of their high school class. Recipient must commit to teaching for three years in a teacher-shortage designated area in Oklahoma. Must be an Oklahoma resident. Write to the address listed below for information.

Oklahoma State Regents For Higher Education
State Capitol Complex
500 Education Building
Oklahoma City, OK 73105

1821

G. Layton Grier Scholarship Fund

Amount: $1,000 (avg.) **Deadline:** Mar 1
Fields/Majors: Dentistry

Open to full-time dental students entering their second year of study at an accredited dental school, who are residents of Delaware. Three awards per year. Based on grades, test scores, recommendations, and interview. Write to the address below for details.

Delaware State Dental Society
Academy Of Medicine Bldg.
Lovering Ave. & Union St.
Wilmington, DE 19806

1822

G. Marvin Wright Memorial Scholarship

Amount: Varies **Deadline:** None Specified
Fields/Majors: Ministry

Awards are available for full-time students at Cedarville College who have a GPA of at least 3.0 and are involved in student ministry. Write to the address below for more information.

Cedarville College
Financial Aid Office
P.O. Box 601
Cedarville, OH 45314

1823

G.I. Dependents Scholarship Program

Amount: Varies **Deadline:** None
Fields/Majors: All Areas Of Study

Applicants must be dependents of Alabama residents who were residents of Alabama before entry into the service and as a result of service died, was MIA/POW, or over 20% service-connected disabled. Must be attending an Alabama state-supported school. Write to the address below for details.

Alabama Department Of Veterans Affairs
P.O. Box 1509
Montgomery, AL 36102

1824

Gabriel A. "Gabe" Nava Memorial Scholarship

Amount: None Specified **Deadline:** Mar 1
Fields/Majors: All Areas Of Study

Scholarships are available at the University of New Mexico for full-time students who will be participating in the intercollegiate athletics program. Applicants must be graduates of a New Mexico high school and U.S. citizens. Write to the address listed below for information.

University Of New Mexico, Albuquerque
Department Of Student Financial Aid
Mesa Vista Hall North
Albuquerque, NM 87131

1825

Gabriel J. Brown Trust Loan

Amount: None Specified **Deadline:** None Specified
Fields/Majors: All Areas Of Study

Loans available to students who are residents of North Dakota with interest repaid at 6%. Must have completed two years of college and have a GPA of 2.5 average or better. Applications are available at Bismarck State College, any four-year college or university in North Dakota, or from the address below.

Gabriel J. Brown Trust Loan Fund
112 Ave. E West
Bismarck, ND 58501

1826

Gainesville Advertising Federation Scholarship

Amount: $400 **Deadline:** Mar 1
Fields/Majors: Advertising

Must be a junior studying advertising at the University of Florida who has at least a 3.0 GPA. Write to the address below for details.

University Of Florida
2070 Weimer Hall
Scholarship & Placement Director
Gainesville, FL 32611

1827

Gale Scholarship

Amount: Varies **Deadline:** Apr 1
Fields/Majors: Art History

Scholarships are available at the University of New Mexico for full-time undergraduate art history majors. Must be sophomores or above with a GPA of 3.5 or higher. Write to the address listed below for information.

University Of New Mexico, Albuquerque
College Of Fine Arts
Office Of The Dean
Albuquerque, NM 87131

1828

Gamewardens Of Vietnam Association Scholarship Fund

Amount: $500 **Deadline:** Apr 15
Fields/Majors: All Areas Of Study

Scholarships for descendants of living or deceased U.S. Navy River Patrol Force, who served in or supported Operation Gamewarden (1966-1971/Task Force 116). Must be unmarried high school senior under age 21 or college freshman under the age of 23. Three awards given per year. Write to the address below for details. List those units to which your parent was attached (including dates of service). Also enclose a 55 cent stamped, self-addressed, business size #10 envelope.

Gamewardens Of Vietnam Association, Inc.
P.O. Box 1866
Georgetown, TX 78627

1829

GAR Foundation Scholarship

Amount: Varies **Deadline:** None Specified
Fields/Majors: All Areas Of Study

Awards are available for students at Cedarville College who have financial need. Must have a GPA of at least 2.0. Write to the address below for more information.

Cedarville College
Financial Aid Office
P.O. Box 601
Cedarville, OH 45314

1830

Garden Club Federation Of Massachusetts, Inc. Scholarship

Amount: Varies **Deadline:** Apr 1
Fields/Majors: Environmental Science, Floriculture, Horticulture, Land Architecture

Awards for UMass sophomores, juniors, or seniors in the fields listed above. Contact the Director, Stockbridge School, for additional information.

University Of Massachusetts, Amherst
Director, Stockbridge School
Amherst, MA 01003

1831

Garden Club Federation Of Pennsylvania Scholarships

Amount: $400-$1,000 **Deadline:** Feb 15
Fields/Majors: See Below

Scholarships for Pennsylvania residents studying in a field of interest to the Garden Club Federation. Based on academics, goals, background, and need. Must have a GPA of at least 3.0. Fields include horticulture, floriculture, landscape architecture, conservation, forestry, botany, agronomy, plant science, environmental studies, ecology, wildlife resources management, and related. Write to the address below for details.

Garden Club Federation Of Pennsylvania
Mrs. Robert R. Leto, Scholarship Chair
710 Rosedale Road
Kennett Square, PA 19348

1832

Garden Club Of America-WWF Scholarships In Tropical Botany

Amount: $5,000 **Deadline:** Dec 31
Fields/Majors: Tropical Botany And Related Fields

Scholarships to support field work of students enrolled in doctoral programs at U.S. institutions. Projects supported in the past include taxonomic studies, reproductive biology, plant/animal interactions, applied research, and plant ecology of tropical ecosystems. Two awards per year. Write to Lori Michaelson at the address below. Information may also be found posted in your department (or the department may be interested in posting an announcement of these awards). Application is made with vitae, transcripts, necessary language skills, two-page outline of research, letter stating career goals, and letter of recommendation/evaluation by your advisor.

World Wildlife Fund-Garden Club Of America
Scholarships In Tropical Botany
1250 Twenty-Fourth St., NW
Washington, DC 20037

1833

Garden Club Of Harwich Scholarship

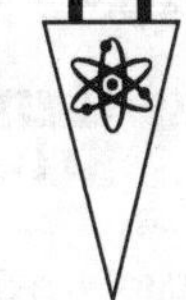

Amount: Varies **Deadline:** Apr 10
Fields/Majors: Environmental Science, Horticulture, Or Related Fields

Awards for UMass sophomores, juniors, or seniors in the fields listed above. Contact the Director, Stockbridge School, for additional information.

University Of Massachusetts, Amherst
Director, Stockbridge School
Amherst, MA 01003

1834

Garden Clubs Advanced Scholarships

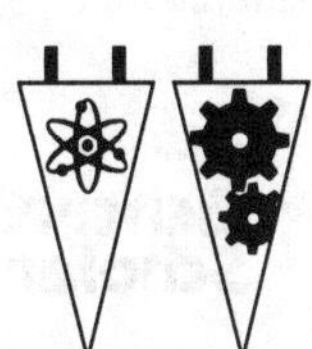

Amount: $3,500 **Deadline:** Mar 1
Fields/Majors: Horti/Floriculture, Landscape Design, City Planning, Land Management

Scholarships for juniors, seniors, and graduate students in the above areas of study. Application is made through your state of legal residence. Must be a U.S. citizen or permanent resident. Contact your state garden club. If the address is unknown, write to the address below to request the scholarship chairperson for your state.

National Council Of State Garden Clubs, Inc.
Mrs. Kathleen Romine
4401 Magnolia Ave.
St. Louis, MO 63110

1835

Garden State Scholars Program

Amount: $500 **Deadline:** May 1
Fields/Majors: All Areas Of Study

Resident of New Jersey for at least twelve months prior to receiving award. Must be a H.S. senior. Must demonstrate high academic achievement (based on high school records and SAT scores). For undergraduate study in New Jersey only. Renewable. See your guidance counselor for more information.

New Jersey Department Of Higher Education
Office Of Student Assistance
CN 540
Trenton, NJ 08625

1836

Gardenswartz Family Endowed Scholarship

Amount: Varies **Deadline:** Mar 1
Fields/Majors: Vocal Music

Awards are available at the University of New Mexico for juniors, seniors, or graduate students majoring in vocal music. Must have a GPA of at least 3.0 and demonstrated artistic ability. Write to the address below for more information.

University Of New Mexico, Albuquerque
Office Of Financial Aid
Albuquerque, NM 87131

1837

Garland Duncan Scholarship

Amount: $2,500 **Deadline:** Apr 15
Fields/Majors: Mechanical Engineering

Two scholarships for ASME student members. For additional information, call or write the ASME Foundation.

American Society Of Mechanical Engineers
Education Services Department
345 E. 47th Street
New York, NY 10017

1838

Garland Tillery Memorial Scholarship In Business

Amount: $200 **Deadline:** Mar 1
Fields/Majors: Business

Award for a full-time undergraduate business student who has a GPA of at least 3.0 and will be a sophomore by the effective date of the award. Must be a New Mexico resident with a family history of New Mexico residency. Write to the address below for more information.

Eastern New Mexico University
ENMU College Of Business
Station 49
Portales, NM 88130

1839

Garnet Keck Benzel

Amount: None Specified **Deadline:** None Specified
Fields/Majors: Nursing

Scholarships are open to nursing students residing in Indiana and have completed ar least one full academic year of study at IU School of Nursing. Write to the address below for more information.

Indiana University/Purdue University, Indianapolis
School Of Nursing
1111 Middle Drive, No. 122
Indianapolis, IN 46202

1840

Gary Merrill Memorial Fund

Amount: None Specified **Deadline:** Apr 1
Fields/Majors: Political Science Or Government Studies

Scholarship support for a Maine resident who will be a second-, third-or fourth-year student enrolled in a Maine college or university and majoring in political science or government studies. Write to Patti d'Angelo at the address below for details.

Maine Community Foundation Scholarship Funds
P.O. Box 148
Ellsworth, ME 04605

1841

Gastrointestinal Physiology Section Student Prize

Amount: $300 **Deadline:** None Specified
Fields/Majors: Gastrointestinal Physiology

Awards are available to students interested in gastrointestinal physiology. The recipient must be the first author on the abstract presented at the APS annual meeting. Write to the address below for more information.

American Psychology Society
Membership Services Office
9560 Rockville Pike
Bethesda, MD 20814

1842 Gay Ann Pitts Memorial Scholarships

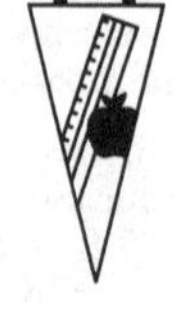

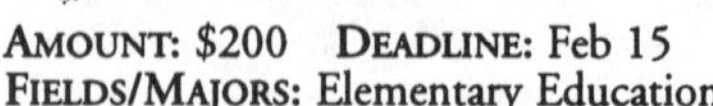

Amount: $200 **Deadline:** Feb 15
Fields/Majors: Elementary Education

Awards for students at UW Platteville who are in the area of elementary education and demonstrate scholastic achievement, moral character, and leadership. Write to the address below for more information.

University Of Wisconsin, Platteville
Office Of Enrollment And Admissions
Platteville, WI 53818

1843 GCA Awards For Summer Environmental Studies

Amount: $1,500 **Deadline:** Feb 15
Fields/Majors: Environmental Studies

Financial aid toward a summer course in environmental studies to encourage studies and careers in the field. Annually funds two or more students. Write to the address below for more details.

Garden Club Of America
Mrs. Monica Freeman
598 Madison Ave.
New York, NY 10022

1844 GEM Fellowships

Amount: Varies **Deadline:** Dec 1
Fields/Majors: Engineering, Sciences, Mathematics

Applicants must be engineering or science majors in their senior year or beyond. Must be U.S. citizen and one of the following minorities: African American, Native American, Hispanic, or Puerto Rican. Award is for graduate use only. Must have a GPA of at least 2.7. Write to the address below for details. Please note if you are seeking a master's or doctoral degree.

Consortium For Graduate Degrees For Minorities
GEM Central Office
P.O. Box 537
Notre Dame, IN 46556

1845 Gene L. Mills Engineering Scholarship

Amount: Varies **Deadline:** Feb 15
Fields/Majors: Engineering

Scholarships are available at Evangel for full-time students who will be or are pursuing a career in engineering. Applicants must have a GPA of at least 3.0. Write to the address listed below for information.

Evangel College
Office Of Enrollment
1111 N. Glenstone
Springfield, MO 65802

1846 General Agricultural Scholarships

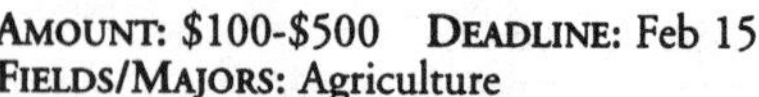

Amount: $100-$500 **Deadline:** Feb 15
Fields/Majors: Agriculture

Awards for UW Platteville continuing students studying agriculture. Based on financial need, academics, activities, etc. Includes the Alpha Zeta, Atkinson Memorial, Jerry Cooper, Charles Denure Memorial and V.E. Nylin Scholarships. Write to the address below for more information.

University Of Wisconsin, Platteville
Office Of Admissions And Enrollment
Platteville, WI 53818

1847 General Assembly Scholarship

Amount: Tuition **Deadline:** Feb 15
Fields/Majors: All Areas Of Study

Scholarships are available at the University of Illinois for Illinois residents based on nomination by local legislators. Write to your local state senator or representative for information.

University Of Illinois At Urbana-Champaign
Office Of Student Financial Aid
610 East John Street, 4th Floor
Champaign, IL 61820

1848 General Awards And Scholarships

Amount: Varies **Deadline:** Varies
Fields/Majors: All Areas Of Study

Awards are available for Sul Ross students based on various criteria such as: GPA, academic interest, extracurricular activities, etc. Write to the address below for more information.

Sul Ross State University
Financial Aid Office
Box C-113
Alpine, TX 79832

1849 General Awards And Scholarships

Amount: Varies **Deadline:** None Specified
Fields/Majors: All Areas Of Study

Awards for students at Liberty University in all levels of study. Based on various criteria such as: financial need, academic interests, grades, activities, etc. Write to the address below for more information.

Liberty University
Office Of Student Financial Aid
Box 20000
Lynchburg, VA 24506

1850 General Awards And Scholarships

Amount: Varies **Deadline:** Mar 31
Fields/Majors: All Areas Of Study

Awards for students at Columbia Union. Individual criteria for each award will vary, but most are based on academic interests, grades, work experience, activities, etc. Write to the address below for more information.

Columbia Union College
Financial Aid Office
7600 Flower Ave.
Takoma Park, MD 20912

1851

General Awards And Scholarships

AMOUNT: Varies **DEADLINE:** None Specified
FIELDS/MAJORS: All Areas Of Study

Awards are available to students at Rockford College of all levels of study. Based on academics, potential, motivation, field of study, activities, financial need, etc. Individual criteria for each award will vary. Write to the address below for more information.

Rockford College
Financial Aid Office
5050 East State St.
Rockford, IL 61108

1852

General Dillingham Produce Scholarship

AMOUNT: $1,000 **DEADLINE:** Feb 1
FIELDS/MAJORS: Agricultural Business Mgmt., Agricultural Ed., International Agriculture

Student must be a junior or senior majoring in agricultural business management and agricultural education or international agriculture with an interest in food distribution. Must have a GPA of 2.5 or better. Two awards are given yearly. Write to the address below for more information.

California State Polytechnic University, Pomona
College Of Agriculture
Building 2, Room 215
Pomona, CA 91768

1853

General Education Scholarships

AMOUNT: $300-$500 **DEADLINE:** Feb 15
FIELDS/MAJORS: Education

Awards for students at UW Platteville in the area of education. Individual award requirements may vary. Includes the Lois Goldman Memorial, Harold and Dolores Hutcheson, John William Livingston, Iota Rho Chapter-Kappa Delta Pi, and Elisa Ann Neal Memorial Scholarships. Write to the address below for more information.

University Of Wisconsin, Platteville
Office Of Enrollment And Admissions
Platteville, WI 53818

1854

General Electric Foundation Scholarships

AMOUNT: $1,000 **DEADLINE:** May 15
FIELDS/MAJORS: Engineering

Three scholarships for freshman women majoring in engineering in an accredited engineering program. Must be a U.S. citizen and have a GPA of at least 3.5. Recipients also receive a $500 grant to defray costs of attending the annual SWE convention. Write to address below for details. Information is also available from the deans of accredited engineering schools. If writing to SWE, please be certain to enclose an SASE.

Society Of Women Engineers
120 Wall Street, 11th Floor
New York, NY 10005

1855

General Electric Fund Scholarship

AMOUNT: Varies **DEADLINE:** Mar 1
FIELDS/MAJORS: Engineering

Awards for minority students entering their sophomore, junior, or senior year studying full-time in the College of Engineering. Must demonstrate academic excellence. Contact the Director of the Minority Engineering Program for more information.

University Of Massachusetts, Amherst
Director, Minority Engineering Program
Amherst, MA 01003

1856

General Electric Scholarship Program

AMOUNT: None Specified **DEADLINE:** Jan 15
FIELDS/MAJORS: All Areas Of Study

Scholarships for dependent children of General Electric Company employees. Must be a graduating high school senior. Write to the address below or call (800) 537-4180 for more information.

General Electric Scholarship Program
Citizens Scholarship Foundation
P.O. Box 297
St. Peter, MN 56082

1857

General Emmett Paige Scholarships

AMOUNT: $1,500 **DEADLINE:** May 1
FIELDS/MAJORS: Technology Fields

Awards are available for undergraduates who were on active duty or veterans of the military services or to their dependents. Must be enrolled in accredited institution in the U.S. Must be a U.S. citizen of good moral character who demonstrates academic excellence and dedication to completing his/her education. Must also demonstrate financial need. Write to the address below for more information.

Armed Forces Communications And Electronics Association
AFCEA Educational Foundation
4400 Fair Lakes Court
Fairfax, VA 22033

1858

General Engineering Scholarships

AMOUNT: $100-$2,000 **DEADLINE:** Feb 15
FIELDS/MAJORS: Engineering

Awards are available for at UW Platteville for engineering students. Includes the Ward Beetham Memorial, Corporate/Alumni, Engineering Alumni, Paul Faherty, Robert P. Hlavac Memorial, Heinie Miller, Larry Ottensman, and Carl Viet Memorial Scholarships. Write to the address below for more information.

University Of Wisconsin, Platteville
Office Of Enrollment And Admissions
Platteville, WI 53818

1859

General Ernest C. Hardin, Jr. Scholarship

AMOUNT: Varies **DEADLINE:** Mar 1
FIELDS/MAJORS: Nuclear Engineering

Awards are available at the University of New Mexico for students in the nuclear engineering program. Based on scholastic and future nuclear industry career goals. Write to the address below for more information.

University Of New Mexico, Albuquerque
Office Of Financial Aid
Albuquerque, NM 87131

1860

General Graduate Fellowships (Zeta Phi Beta)

AMOUNT: $2,500 **DEADLINE:** Feb 1
FIELDS/MAJORS: All Areas Of Study

Fellowships for graduate women working on a professional, master's, or doctoral degree or engaged in postdoctoral study. For full-time study for one academic year. No affiliation with Zeta Phi Beta is required. Send an SASE to the national headquarters at the address below for further information.

Zeta Phi Beta Sorority
National Educational Foundation
1734 New Hampshire Ave., NW
Washington, DC 20009

1861

General Henry H. Arnold Education Grant Program

AMOUNT: $1,000 **DEADLINE:** None Specified
FIELDS/MAJORS: All Areas Of Study

Scholarships are available for children of active duty, retired and deceased Air Force personnel with a GPA of at least 2.0. Must be a U.S. citizen and under age 24. For undergraduate study. Write to the address below for details.

Air Force Aid Society
Education Assistance Department
1745 Jeff Davis Highway, Suite 202
Arlington, VA 22202

1862

General John A. Wickham Scholarships

AMOUNT: $1,500 **DEADLINE:** May 1
FIELDS/MAJORS: Technology Fields

Awards are available for sophomores, juniors, or seniors enrolled full-time in an accredited degree granting four-year college or university in the U.S. Must be a U.S. citizen of good moral character and leadership abilities who demonstrates academic excellence and dedication to completing his/her education. Must also demonstrate financial need. Write to the address below for more information.

Armed Forces Communications And Electronics Association
AFCEA Educational Foundation
4400 Fair Lakes Court
Fairfax, VA 22033

1863

General Motors Foundation Graduate Scholarships

AMOUNT: $1,000 **DEADLINE:** Feb 1
FIELDS/MAJORS: Engineering: Mech., Elec., Industrial, Materials, Auto, Manufacturing

One scholarship for a woman entering her first year of master's level study. Must have a GPA of at least 3.5, have demonstrated leadership qualities, and show a career interest in the automotive industry or the manufacturing sector. One award per year. Information and applications for the SWE awards are available from the deans of engineering schools, or you may write to the address below. Please be certain to enclose an SASE.

Society Of Women Engineers
120 Wall Street
New York, NY 10005

1864

General Motors Foundation Scholarships

AMOUNT: $1,000 **DEADLINE:** Feb 1
FIELDS/MAJORS: Engineering

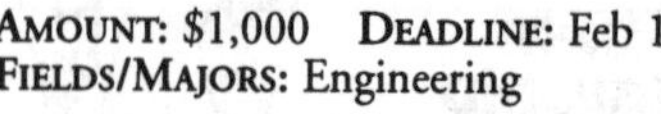

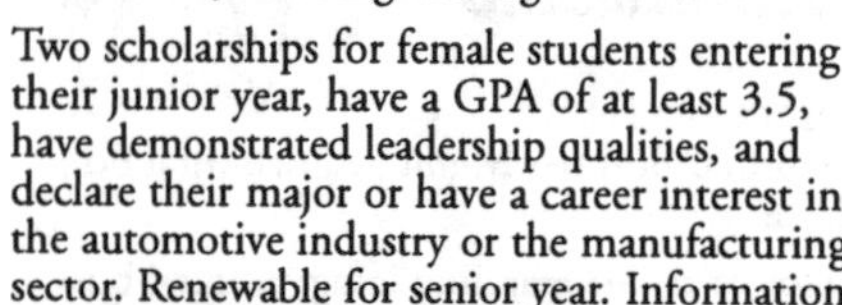

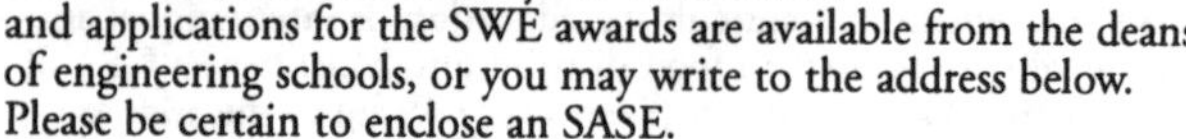

Two scholarships for female students entering their junior year, have a GPA of at least 3.5, have demonstrated leadership qualities, and declare their major or have a career interest in the automotive industry or the manufacturing sector. Renewable for senior year. Information and applications for the SWE awards are available from the deans of engineering schools, or you may write to the address below. Please be certain to enclose an SASE.

Society Of Women Engineers
120 Wall Street, 11th Floor
New York, NY 10005

1865

General Motors Scholarship

AMOUNT: None Specified **DEADLINE:** Mar 1
FIELDS/MAJORS: Business

Scholarships are available at the University of New Mexico for full-time business majors with a GPA of at least 3.2. Applicants must be U.S. citizens. Write to the address listed below for information.

University Of New Mexico, Albuquerque
Department Of Student Financial Aid
Mesa Vista Hall North
Albuquerque, NM 87131

1866

General Petroleum/ Geological Engineering Awards

AMOUNT: $500-$2,000 **DEADLINE:** Mar 1
FIELDS/MAJORS: Petroleum And Geological Engineering

Scholarships are available at the University of Oklahoma, Norman for full-time petroleum and geological engineering majors. Two to four awards offered each year. Includes the Lester Wilkonson Scholar-ship, and the Petroleum and Geological Engineering Distinguished Scholarship. Write to the address listed below for information.

University Of Oklahoma, Norman
Scholarship Coord., Petroleum & Geological Engineering
T301 Energy Center
Norman, OK 73019

1867

General Scholarship

AMOUNT: $1,000 **DEADLINE:** Apr 1
FIELDS/MAJORS: All Areas Of Study

Scholarships for students at Kent State who have a superior academic record and are at least in their sophomore year. Contact the financial aid office at your campus for details.

Kent State University, Tuscarawas Campus
Financial Aid Office
University Drive, NE
New Philadelphia, OH 44663

1868

General Scholarships

AMOUNT: $300-$1,000 **DEADLINE:** Jun 1
FIELDS/MAJORS: All Areas Of Study

Scholarships are available to undergraduates who are members of Tau Kappa Epsilon. Must have demonstrated leadership capability, within his chapter, on campus or the community, should have a GPA of 2.5 or higher, and be a full-time student in good standing. Include such scholarships: Donald A. Fisher, Eugene C. Beach, Miles Gray, J. Russel Salsbury, and T.J. Schmitz. Write to the address below for more information.

TKE Educational Foundation
Director Of Development
8645 Founders Road
Indianapolis, IN 46268

1869

General Scholarships And Awards

AMOUNT: Varies **DEADLINE:** May 1
FIELDS/MAJORS: All Areas Of Study

Awards open to Winthrop students at all levels of study. Based on various criteria, such as: academic interests, grades, activities, etc. Write to the address below for more information.

Winthrop University
Office Of Student Services
119 Tillman Hall
Rock Hill, SC 29733

1870

General Scholarships And Awards At Mercyhurst College

AMOUNT: Varies **DEADLINE:** None Specified
FIELDS/MAJORS: All Areas Of Study

Award for students of all levels at Mercyhurst College. Individual criteria for each award will vary based on academics, activities, field of study, area of permanent residence, etc. Write to the address below for more information.

Mercyhurst College
Financial Aid Office
Glenwood Hills
Erie, PA 16546

1871

General Scholarships And Grants

AMOUNT: Varies **DEADLINE:** None Specified
FIELDS/MAJORS: All Areas Of Study

Awards for students at WJC that are based on many different criteria such as academic interest, grades, extracurricular activities, etc. Write to the address below for more information.

Wheeling Jesuit College
Student Financial Planning
316 Washington Ave.
Wheeling, WV 26003

1872

General Scholarships At Eastern Oregon State College

AMOUNT: Varies **DEADLINE:** None Specified
FIELDS/MAJORS: All Fields Of Study

Awards for undergraduates at Eastern Oregon State College. Individual criteria for each award may vary. Write to the address below for details.

Eastern Oregon State College
Financial Aid Office
1410 "I" Avenue
La Grande, OR 97850

1873

General Student Loan Program, Schwalenberg Medical School Loan Program

AMOUNT: Varies **DEADLINE:** Feb 1
FIELDS/MAJORS: All Areas Of Study

Loans for undergraduate or med students. Must be a graduate of a Santa Barbara county high school and have lived in the county for at least six years. Loans are interest free. When 50% of the total has been repaid, the loan is considered paid in full. Repayment deferred until graduation. Must be U.S. citizen or permanent resident. Write to the address below for details. Applicants who do not meet the residency guidelines but have demonstrated strong ties to Santa Barbara County will be considered.

Santa Barbara Foundation
Student Aid Director
15 East Carrillo Street
Santa Barbara, CA 93101

1874

General Thomas D. Campbell Memorial Scholarship

AMOUNT: Varies **DEADLINE:** Mar 1
FIELDS/MAJORS: Earth and Planetary Sciences

Awards are available at the University of New Mexico for juniors or seniors pursuing a degree in earth or planetary sciences. Applicants must have a GPA of at least 2.7 in their major and a cumulative GPA of 2.2 or better and financial need. Write to the address listed below for information.

University Of New Mexico, Albuquerque
Office Of Financial Aid
Albuquerque, NM 87131

1875

General Undergraduate Scholarships (Zeta Phi Beta)

AMOUNT: $500-$1,000 **DEADLINE:** Feb 1
FIELDS/MAJORS: All Areas Of Study

Scholarships for current high school seniors and undergraduate freshmen, sophomores, and juniors studying full-time. No affiliation with Zeta Phi Beta is required. Award length is one year.

Send an SASE to the national headquarters at the address below for further information.

Zeta Phi Beta Sorority
National Educational Foundation
1734 New Hampshire Ave., NW
Washington, DC 20009

1876

General UNM Scholarships

Amount: Varies **Deadline:** Varies
Fields/Majors: All Areas Of Study

Scholarships are available at the University of New Mexico. Includes the UNM Presidential Scholarship for Branch Transfer Students, ASUNM Freedom Scholarship Fund, Residence Hall Community Acholars Award, and the Omega Scholarship. Individual award requirements will vary. Write to the address listed below for information.

University Of New Mexico, Albuquerque
Student Financial Aid Office
Mesa Vista Hall North, Room 1044
Albuquerque, NM 87131

1877

Geneva Athletic Grants

Amount: Varies **Deadline:** None Specified
Fields/Majors: All Areas Of Study

Grants for undergraduate students at Geneva College who will be participating in intercollegiate athletics. Contact the coach of your sport or the office of admissions for further information.

Geneva College
Office Of Admissions
Beaver Falls, PA 15010

1878

Geneva Grants

Amount: Varies **Deadline:** None Specified
Fields/Majors: All Areas Of Study

Grants for students at Geneva College. Based on need and academics. Renewable as necessary. Must be a full-time student. Contact the financial aid office or the office of admissions for details.

Geneva College
Office Of Admissions
Beaver Falls, PA 15010

1879

Geneva Scholar Award

GPA 3.0+

Amount: $3,000 **Deadline:** None Specified
Fields/Majors: All Areas Of Study

Scholarships available for full-time freshmen at Geneva College who have a GPA of at least 3.0 from high school and a minimum score of 1000 on the SAT or a 24 on the ACT. Scholarships are renewable if 3.0 GPA is maintained. Transfer students are also eligible for this award. Contact the Office of Admissions for further information.

Geneva College
Office Of Admissions
Beaver Falls, PA 15010

1880

Geography Departmental Scholarships

Amount: Varies **Deadline:** Feb 15
Fields/Majors: Geography

Scholarships are available at the University of Utah for full-time students majoring in geography. Write to the address below for information.

University Of Utah
Dr. Roger M. McCoy
270 Orson Spencer Hall
Salt Lake City, UT 84112

1881

Geology Alumni Scholarship

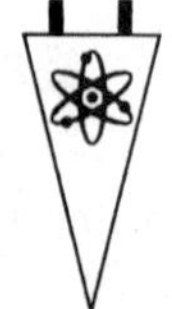

Amount: Varies **Deadline:** Mar 1
Fields/Majors: Geology

Awards are available at the University of New Mexico for students in the field of geology who have merit and have provided service to the department. Must demonstrate financial need. Recipient is chosen by the geology department. Write to the address listed below for information.

University Of New Mexico, Albuquerque
Office Of Financial Aid
Albuquerque, NM 87131

1882

Geology Scholarships

Amount: None Specified **Deadline:** Mar 15
Fields/Majors: Geology

Scholarships awarded to students at Appalachian State University who are geology majors. Contact the office of admissions for details.

Appalachian State University
Department Of Geology
Boone, NC 28608

1883

George & Masuo Nagatomo Memorial Scholarship

Amount: Varies **Deadline:** None Specified
Fields/Majors: All Areas Of Study, Except Theater

Awards for Mesa State sophomores, juniors, or seniors majoring in any field except theater. Must have a GPA of at least 3.0 and be of Asian descent. Must be U.S. citizen. Contact the School of Natural Sciences and Mathematics for more information.

Mesa State College
Financial Aid Office
P.O. Box 2647
Grand Junction, CO 81501

1884

George A. Dickerman Scholarship

Amount: $6,500 **Deadline:** Feb 29
Fields/Majors: Management

Scholarships are awarded to a school of management students on the basis of academics and financial need. For students in their sophomore, junior, or senior year. Applications for School of Management Scholarships will be available in the SOM Development Office, Room 206.

University Of Massachusetts, Amherst
School Of Management
SOM Development Office, Room 206
Amherst, MA 01003

1885

George A. Strait Minority Stipend

Amount: $3,500 **Deadline:** Mar 1
Fields/Majors: Library Science, Law

Open to minorities with bachelor degrees and library experience who are working toward an advanced library degree or a law degree. Write to the address below for details.

American Association Of Law Libraries Scholarships
53 W. Jackson Blvd., Suite 940
Chicago, IL 60604

1886

George Baumann Memorial Scholarship

Amount: Varies **Deadline:** None Specified
Fields/Majors: All Areas Of Study

Award given in memory of George Baumann by Baumann Brothers Carpetowne, Inc., and awarded to a deserving Erie County student. Write to the address below for more information.

Mercyhurst College
Financial Aid Office
Glenwood Hills
Erie, PA 16546

1887

George Bullis Scholarships

Amount: Resident Tuition **Deadline:** Feb 15
Fields/Majors: Mathematics And Related Fields

Awards are available for at UW Platteville for students pursuing a career requiring high mathematical aptitude. Preference given to National Merit Scholars. Renewable. Write to the address below for more information.

University Of Wisconsin, Platteville
Office Of Enrollment And Admissions
Platteville, WI 53818

1888

George Chancellor Rawlings, III & Christopher Rawlings Scholarships

Amount: $5,000 **Deadline:** Mar 1
Fields/Majors: All Areas Of Study

Awards for qualified graduates of James Monroe High School in Fredericksburg, Virginia. Selection is based on scholarship, financial need, and participation in school and community service activities. Must have been admitted to an accredited two- or four-year college or university in the continental United States. Renewable. Students who would like to be considered for this award must contact their high school guidance counselor or principal to be nominated.

Community Foundation Serving Richmond And Central Virginia
1025 Boulders Parkway, Suite 405
Richmond, VA 23225

1889

George D. And Marion K. Roberts Scholarship Award

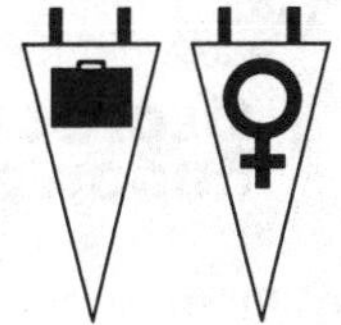

Amount: $1,250 **Deadline:** Feb 29
Fields/Majors: Management

Awards for female school of management students who have demonstrated financial need, outstanding academic achievement, and community involvement. The recipient must agree to make a donation of $1,500 to the school of management within 15 years of graduation. For females in their sophomore, junior, or senior year. Applications for School of Management scholarships will be available in the SOM Development Office, Room 206.

University Of Massachusetts, Amherst
School Of Management
SOM Development Office, Room 206
Amherst, MA 01003

1890

George David Weiss Award

Amount: $2,000 **Deadline:** May 1
Fields/Majors: Music

Award for a student at Five Towns College pursuing a bachelor's degree in music. Given to the student that best exemplifies the virtues of the gifted composer and songwriter, George David Weiss. Write to the address below for additional information.

Five Towns College
305 N. Service Road/Lie Exit 50
Dix Hills, NY 11746

1891

George E. Breece Prize

Amount: Varies **Deadline:** Mar 1
Fields/Majors: Engineering

An award is given to the graduating senior in the University of New Mexico engineering program with the highest scholastic average in his or her last two years. Write to the address below for more information.

University Of New Mexico, Albuquerque
Office Of Financial Aid
Albuquerque, NM 87131

1892

George Goodwin, Jr. Scholarship

Amount: Varies **Deadline:** Mar 1
Fields/Majors: Public Service

Awards for students interested in a career in public service. Preference given to students studying political science. For entering sophomores, juniors, or seniors. Contact the Head, Political Science Department, for more information.

University Of Massachusetts, Amherst
Head, Political Science Department
Amherst, MA 01003

1893
George H. And Dena F. Louys Endowed Grant Fund

Amount: Varies **Deadline:** None Specified
Fields/Majors: Pastors, Missionary

Awards are available for full-time students at Cedarville College who are training to become pastors or missionaries. Must have a GPA of at least 2.0. Write to the address below for more information.

Cedarville College
Financial Aid Office
P.O. Box 601
Cedarville, OH 45314

1894
George Hill Memorial Scholarship

Amount: $4,000 **Deadline:** Aug 31
Fields/Majors: Medicine

Scholarship for African American medical students from Westchester County, NY. Must be a U.S. citizen. Based on demonstrated financial need. Write to "Special Programs" at the address below for details.

National Medical Fellowships, Inc.
110 West 32nd Street
New York, NY 10001

1895
George J. Maloof Award In Management

Amount: None Specified **Deadline:** Mar 1
Fields/Majors: Management

Scholarships are available at the University of New Mexico for full-time senior management majors with the highest improvement in GPA during the junior year. Write to the address listed below for information.

University Of New Mexico, Albuquerque
Department Of Student Financial Aid
Mesa Vista Hall North
Albuquerque, NM 87131

1896
George J. Record School Foundation Scholarships

Amount: $3,000 (max) **Deadline:** May 20, Jun 20
Fields/Majors: All Areas Of Study

Awards for legal residents of Ashtabula County, Ohio. Deadline date for high school seniors is May 20. Deadline date for undergraduates is June 20. Students will be (or are) attending a private, Protestant-based school full-time. Financial need must be demonstrated. Contact the address below for further information.

George J. Record Foundation
Charles N. Lafferty, Executive Director
P.O. Box 581, 365 Main St.
Conneaut, OH 44030

1897
George M. Booker Scholarship

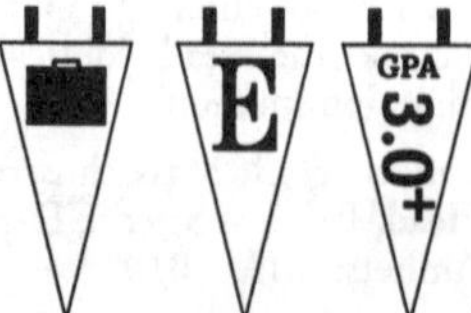

Amount: $1,000-$2,500
Deadline: Mar 15
Fields/Majors: Real Estate

Scholarships for minority students studying real estate. Must have a GPA of at least a 3.0 and be a U.S. citizen. Students should have completed at least two courses in real estate at the time of application. Write to the address below for more information.

Institute Of Real Estate Management Foundation
Attn: Booker Scholarship
430 North Michigan Ave.
Chicago, IL 60611

1898
George M. Cruise Charitable Foundation

Amount: None Specified **Deadline:** Mar 10
Fields/Majors: All Areas Of Study

Scholarships for students at Bluefield College with financial need and academic achievement. Write to the address below for more information.

Bluefield College
Financial Aid Office
3000 College Drive
Bluefield, VA 24605

1899
George M. Helberg Memorial Scholarships

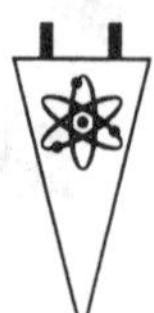

Amount: $5,000 **Deadline:** Feb 15
Fields/Majors: Agronomy, Water Conservation

Scholarships for FFA members who are pursuing four-year undergraduate degrees in agronomy or water conservation. Eight awards are offered annually. Write to the address below for details.

National FFA Foundation
Scholarship Office
P.O. Box 15160
Alexandria, VA 22309

1900
George M. Wardlaw Art Department Scholarship

Amount: Varies **Deadline:** None Specified
Fields/Majors: Visual Art

Awards for full-time students at UMass entering their sophomore, junior, or senior year in the field of visual art. Contact the art department, not the address below for more information.

University Of Massachusetts-Amherst
Office Of Financial Aid Services
255 Whitmore Admin. Bldg., Box 38230
Amherst, MA 01003

1901
George Petrol Memorial Scholarship

Amount: None Specified **Deadline:** Mar 1
Fields/Majors: All Areas Of Study

Scholarships are available at the University of New Mexico for full-time students who will be participating in the intercollegiate baseball program. Write to the address listed below for information.

University Of New Mexico, Albuquerque
Department Of Student Financial Aid
Mesa Vista Hall North
Albuquerque, NM 87131

1902

George St. Clair Memorial Award

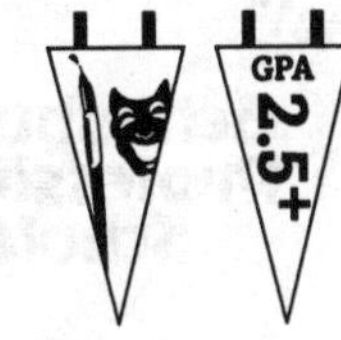

AMOUNT: Varies **DEADLINE:** Mar 1
FIELDS/MAJORS: Theater And Dance

Awards are available at the University of New Mexico for students with a GPA of at least 2.5 and financial need. Students must have past involvement in department/production activities and demonstrate talent. Write to the address below for more information.

University Of New Mexico, Albuquerque
Office Of Financial Aid
Albuquerque, NM 87131

1903

George W. Frye Scholarship Fund

AMOUNT: None Specified **DEADLINE:** None Specified
FIELDS/MAJORS: All Areas Of Study

Awards for graduating seniors from Narraguagus High School in Harrington, ME, who plan to attend a two- or four-year college or university. Based on financial need and academic standing. First priority will be given to a student from the town of Harrington. Contact the Narraguagus High School guidance office for more information.

Maine Community Fund
P.O. Box 148
Ellsworth, ME 04605

1904

George Washington University Assistantships And Fellowships

AMOUNT: Varies **DEADLINE:** Feb 15, Nov 1
FIELDS/MAJORS: All Areas Of Study

Scholarships and fellowships for students in one of the graduate schools at George Washington University. Contact the Columbian College and Graduate School of Arts and Sciences at the address below for details.

George Washington University
801 22nd St NW, Suite 106
Washington, DC 20052

1905

Georgia Boot, Inc. Scholarships

AMOUNT: $1,250 **DEADLINE:** Feb 15
FIELDS/MAJORS: Agriculture

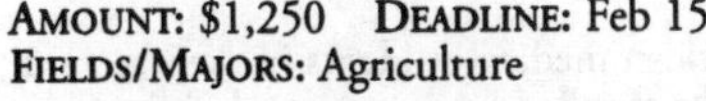

Scholarships are available for FFA members pursuing a four-year degree in any area of agriculture. Two awards are offered annually. Write to the address below for details.

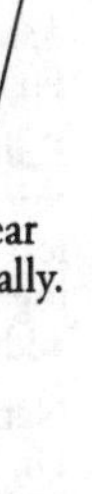

National FFA Foundation
Scholarship Office
P.O. Box 15160
Alexandria, VA 22309

1906

Georgia Engineering Scholarships

AMOUNT: $500-$2,000 **DEADLINE:** Aug 25
FIELDS/MAJORS: Engineering

Awards for high school seniors who are residents of Georgia and intend to study engineering. Applicants must be U.S. citizens. Contact your high school guidance counselor, math/science teacher, or the address below for an application and further details.

Georgia Engineering Foundation, Inc.
Oak Park Place, Suite 226
1900 Emery St., NW
Atlanta, GA 30318

1907

Geoscience Scholarships For Ethnic Minorities

AMOUNT: Varies **DEADLINE:** Feb 1
FIELDS/MAJORS: Earth, Space, Or Marine Sciences

Scholarships are available at the undergraduate and graduate level in the geosciences listed above. Applicants must be U.S. citizens and underrepresented minorities. For full time study. Based upon academic record and financial need. Write to the address below for details.

American Geological Institute
AGI Minority Geoscience Scholarships
4220 King Street
Alexandria, VA 22302

1908

Gerald T. Wilkerson Scholarships

AMOUNT: Varies **DEADLINE:** Mar 1
FIELDS/MAJORS: All Areas Of Study

Awards are available at the University of New Mexico for full-time Native American students with academic achievement and financial need. Write to the address below for more information.

University Of New Mexico, Albuquerque
Office Of Financial Aid
Albuquerque, NM 87131

1909

Gerber Prize For Excellence In Pediatrics

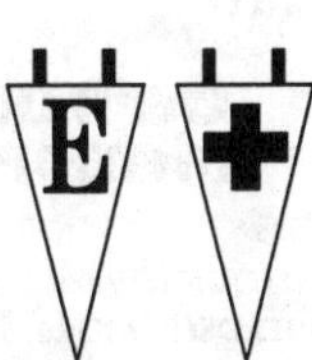

AMOUNT: Varies **DEADLINE:** Aug 31
FIELDS/MAJORS: Pediatric Medicine

Scholarships, fellowships and awards for minority medical students in pediatrics. Minorities are defined here as African American, Mexican-American, mainland Puerto Rican, and American Indian. For study at Michigan medical schools. Academics is primary consideration; need is considered. Must be a U.S. citizen. Write to "Special Programs" at the address below for details.

National Medical Fellowships, Inc.
110 West 32nd Street
New York, NY 10001

1910

Gerlach Music Scholarship

AMOUNT: $1,000 **DEADLINE:** None Specified
FIELDS/MAJORS: Music

Award for full-time Mesa State students studying music and enrolled in the School of Humanities and Social Science. Must have a GPA of at least 3.0. Preference will be given to a keyboard player. Contact the music department at Mesa State for more information.

Mesa State College
Office Of Financial Aid
P.O. Box 2647
Grand Junction, CO 81501

1911

German Marshall Fund Postdoctoral Fellowship Program

AMOUNT: $32,000 (max) **DEADLINE:** Nov 15
FIELDS/MAJORS: International Relations

Grants are offered to U.S. scholars for postdoctoral research that seeks to improve the understanding of significant contemporary economic, political, and social developments involving the United States and Europe. Write for complete details on this and other fellowship programs of the German Marshall Fund.

German Marshall Fund Of The United States
Fellowships For American Scholars
11 Dupont Circle NW, Suite 750
Washington, DC 20036

1912

Gertrude Botts-Saucier Scholarship

AMOUNT: None Specified **DEADLINE:** None Specified
FIELDS/MAJORS: All Areas Of Study

Scholarships for lineal descendents of worthy confederates or collateral descendents who are members of the Children of the Confederacy or the United Daughters of the Confederacy. This award is for students from Texas, Louisiana, or Mississippi. Write to the UDC chapter nearest you. If address is not known, write to the address below for further information and the address.

United Daughters Of The Confederacy
Scholarship Coordinator
328 N. Boulevard
Richmond, VA 23220

1913

Gertrude Horn Condrey Memorial Scholarship

AMOUNT: Varies **DEADLINE:** Varies
FIELDS/MAJORS: Nursing

Scholarships are available for nursing students from Siskiyou County who are enrolled in the LVN program at the College of the Siskiyous. Based primarily on financial need. Write to the address below for additional information.

College Of The Siskiyous
Office Of Financial Aid
800 College Ave
Weed, CA 96094

1914

Gertrude Parker Memorial Scholarship

AMOUNT: Varies **DEADLINE:** Mar 15
FIELDS/MAJORS: Education

Awards for Jacksonville State University students in the field of education. Write to the address below for more information.

Jacksonville State University
Financial Aid Office
Jacksonville, AL 36265

1915

Gettysburg Business And Professional Women's Club Scholarship

AMOUNT: $500 **DEADLINE:** Jan 15
FIELDS/MAJORS: All Areas Of Study

Scholarships to women residing in Adams County who are pursuing further education or training in order to re-enter the labor market. Write to the address below for details.

Business And Professional Women's Club Of Gettysburg
YWCA
909 Fairfield Road
Gettysburg, PA 17325

1916

GFWC Of Massachusetts "Pennies For Art" Scholarship

AMOUNT: $400 **DEADLINE:**Feb 15
FIELDS/MAJORS: Art

Applicant must be a senior in a Massachusetts high school and present a letter of endorsement from sponsoring women's club in your community. Write to the address below for details.

General Federation Of Women's Clubs Of Massachusetts
Chariman, Art Division
245 Dutton Rd., P.O. Box 679
Sudbury, MA 01776

1917

GHI Dissertation Scholarships

AMOUNT: None Specified **DEADLINE:** May 31
FIELDS/MAJORS: German Studies

Awards for doctoral students working on topics related to the Institute's general scope of interest. Write to the address below for more information.

German Historical Institute
1607 Hew Hampshire Ave., NW
Washington, DC 20009

1918

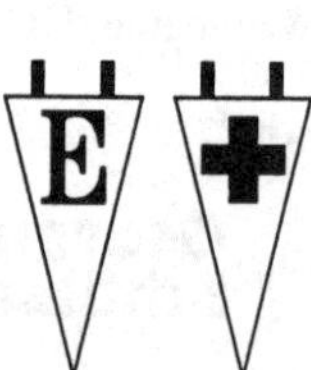

Giargiari Fellowship

AMOUNT: $5,000 **DEADLINE:** May 31
FIELDS/MAJORS: Medicine

Fellowships for Italian American medical students in their second, third, or fourth year. Must be enrolled in an approved U.S. medical school. Applicants must write a 750-word essay on "maintaining Italian culture in the U.S. in the medical field." Write to the address below for details.

National Italian American Foundation
Dr. Maria Lombardo, Education Director
1860 Nineteenth Street, NW
Washington, DC 20009

1919

Gibran Kahlil Gibran Educational Fund

AMOUNT: None Specified **DEADLINE:**Jun 1
FIELDS/MAJORS: All Areas Of Study

Scholarships for Syrian and Lebanese peoples. Preference given to persons whose ancestors are from the town of Becherre or to other towns in Lebanon. Write to the address below for details.

Gibran Kahlil Gibran Educational Fund, Inc.
4 Longfellow Place, Suite 3802
Boston, MA 02114

1920

Gilbert Chinard Scholarships

Amount: $1,000 **Deadline:** Jan 15
Fields/Majors: French History, Literature, Art And Music

Awards for research in France for Ph.D dissertation or Ph.D held no longer than six years before time of application. A two page description of research project and trip as well as a recommendation from the dissertation director will be required. Write to the address below for additional information. Contact: Catherine A. Maley, President, Institut Francais de Washington.

University Of North Carolina-Institut Francais de Washington
Department Of Romance Languages
Cb 3170
Chapel Hill, NC 27599

1921

Gilbert F. White Postdoctoral Fellowship Program

Amount: $27,000 **Deadline:** Mar 1
Fields/Majors: Natural Resources, Energy, Environmental Sciences

Fellowship is for researchers in social science or public policy programs in he areas of natural resources, energy, or the environment. Applicants must have completed doctoral requirements and preference will be given to those with teaching and/or research experience. This is a residential fellowship. Write to the address below for details.

Resources For The Future
1616 P Street, NW
Washington, DC 20036

1922

Gilbert Grant & Tuition Waiver

Amount: Varies **Deadline:** Varies
Fields/Majors: All Areas Of Study

For permanent residents of Massachusetts. Must be enrolled in a Massachusetts undergraduate public institution. Be certain to file for a needs analysis (FAFSA, FAF, etc.) and contact your college financial aid office for further information.

Massachusetts Board Of Regents Of Higher Education
State Scholarship Office
330 Stuart Street
Boston, MA 02116

1923

Gilbert May Endowed Scholarship

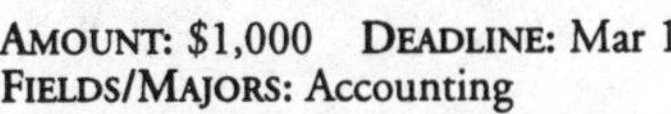

Amount: $1,000 **Deadline:** Mar 1
Fields/Majors: Accounting

Award for a full-time undergraduate accounting student who has a cumulative GPA of at least 3.0 and has successfully completed twelve credit hours by the effective date of the award. Write to the address below for more information.

Eastern New Mexico University
ENMU College Of Business
Station 49
Portales, NM 88130

1924

Gilbert Neiman Scholarships

Amount: None Specified
Deadline: None Specified
Fields/Majors: Secondary Education, Liberal Arts, English

Scholarships are for second semester sophomores, second semester juniors, and an incoming freshman majoring in English, liberal arts, and secondary education-English. Write to the address below for more information.

Clarion University
104 Egbert Hall
Office Of Financial Aid
Clarion, PA 16214

1925

Gina Finzi Memorial Student Summer Fellowships

Amount: $2,000 **Deadline:** Feb 1
Fields/Majors: Medical Research

Awards for undergraduate, graduate, or medical students to foster an interest among young researchers in Lupus Erythematosus through the conduct of basic, clinical, or psychosocial research under the supervision of an established investigator. Preference is given to students with a college degree. Write to the address below for more information.

Lupus Foundation Of America, Inc.
4 Research Place, Suite 180
Rockville, MD 20850

1926

Gladys Agell Award For Excellence In Research

Amount: None Specified **Deadline:** Jun 15
Fields/Majors: Art Therapy

Designed to encourage student research, this award will go to the most outstanding project, completed within the past year, by an art therapist using statistical measure in the area of applied art therapy. Must be a graduate student in an AATA approved program and be a student member of AATA. Write to the address below for complete details.

The American Art Therapy Association, Inc.
Scholarship Committee
1202 Allanson Road
Mundelein, IL 60060

1927

Gladys Anderson Emerson Scholarship

Amount: $1,000 **Deadline:** Feb 16
Fields/Majors: Chemistry, Biochemistry

Scholarships for members of Iota Sigma Pi, National Society for Women in Chemistry. Must be in at least junior year of study at an accredited school. Nominations for the scholarship must be made by a member of Iota Sigma Pi and supported by members of the faculty of the nominee's institution. Write to Dr. Barbara A. Sawrey, Ph.D., at the address below.

Iota Sigma Pi
UCSD, Dept. Of Chemistry & Biochemistry
9500 Gilman Drive, Dept 0303
La Jolla, CA 92093

1928

Gladys C. Anderson Memorial Scholarship

Amount: $1,000 **Deadline:** Apr 1
Fields/Majors: Religious Music, Classical Music

Must be legally blind woman studying religious or classical music at the undergraduate level. Applicant must be a U.S. citizen. One annual award. Student must submit a sample performance tape of voice or instrumental selection (not to exceed 30 minutes). Write to the address below for complete details.

American Foundation For The Blind
Scholarship Committee
11 Penn Plaza, Suite 300
New York, NY 10001

1929

Gladys J. Larson Scholarship

Amount: Varies **Deadline:** Feb 23
Fields/Majors: All Areas Of Study

Award for full-time second semester freshmen with a GPA of 2.9 or above. Financial need is considered. Contact the Dean of Student's Office, UW Oshkosh, for more information.

University Of Wisconsin, Oshkosh
Financial Aid Office, Dempsey 104
800 Algoma Blvd.
Oshkosh, WI 54901

1930

Gladys York Memorial Scholarship

Amount: Varies **Deadline:** None Specified
Fields/Majors: All Areas Of Study

Awards are available for full-time students at Cedarville College who attend the Calvary Baptist Church of Parkertown, New Jersey. Must have a GPA of at at least 2.0. Write to the address below for more information.

Cedarville College
Financial Aid Office
P.O. Box 601
Cedarville, OH 45314

1931

Gladys Zuelke Memorial Scholarship

Amount: $250 **Deadline:** Apr 30
Fields/Majors: All Areas Of Study

Awards for Jacksonville State University students who are in any field of study. Contact the Covenant Lutheran Church in Jacksonville, AL, for more information.

Jacksonville State University
Financial Aid Office
Jacksonville, AL 36265

1932

Glaxo Scholarship, Walmart Scholarship

Amount: $1,000 **Deadline:** Feb 1
Fields/Majors: Pharmacy

Scholarships are available at the University of Oklahoma, Norman for full-time sophomore pharmacy majors. Based on academic excellence. Write to the address listed below for information.

University Of Oklahoma, Norman
College Of Pharmacy
P.O. Box 26901
Oklahoma City, OK 73190

1933

Glaxo Wellcome Opportunity Scholarship Program

Amount: $5,000 **Deadline:** Apr 1
Fields/Majors: All Areas Of Study

Any person who is a U.S. citizen and who has lived in Durham, Orange, or Wake Counties for the past six months and can demonstrate the potential to succeed despite adversity as well as an exceptional desire to improve himself or herself through further education or training. Write to the address below for more information.

Triangle Community Foundation
P.O. Box 12834
Research Triangle Pk, NC 27709

1934

Glen C. Nelson Ceramic Scholarship

Amount: $200-$500 **Deadline:** May 1
Fields/Majors: Art-Ceramics

Scholarships are available at the University of Iowa for full-time under-graduate students majoring in ceramics. Write to the address listed below for information.

University Of Iowa
School Of Art And Art History
E100 Art Building
Iowa City, IA 52245

1935

Glen T. Simpson Scholarships

Amount: Varies **Deadline:** Mar 1
Fields/Majors: All Areas Of Study

Awards are available at the University of New Mexico for American Indian seniors who have academic achievement and financial need. Write to the address below for more information.

University Of New Mexico, Albuquerque
Office Of Financial Aid
Albuquerque, NM 87131

1936

Glenn E. And Ruth Z. Karls Agriculture Scholarship

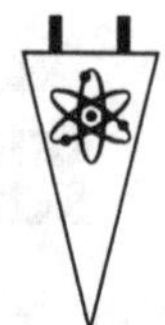

Amount: $400 **Deadline:** None Specified
Fields/Majors: Agriculture

Students must be outstanding agriculture majors. Contact the agriculture department for more information.

Southwest Missouri State University
Office Of Financial Aid
901 South National Ave.
Springfield, MO 65804

1937 Gloria Fecht Memorial Scholarship

AMOUNT: $1,000-$3,000
DEADLINE: None Specified
FIELDS/MAJORS: All Areas Of Study

Scholarships are available for female southern California residents enrolled at a four-year college or university, with a GPA of at least 3.0, and a demonstrated interest in golf. Financial need is considered. Fifteen to twenty awards are offered annually, renewable for up to four years. Write to the address listed below for information.

Gloria Fecht Memorial Scholarships Fund
402 West Arrow Highway, Suite 10
San Dimas, CA 91773

1938 Gloria J. Gonzalez Endowed Scholarship

AMOUNT: Tuition & Fees **DEADLINE:** Dec 1
FIELDS/MAJORS: All Areas Of Study

Scholarship for full-time undergraduate students at UT Austin who are of Hispanic background and from tarrant county. Preference given to residents of Ft. Worth and to students in the natural sciences. Write to the address below for details.

University Of Texas, Austin
Office Of Student Financial Services
P.O. Box 7758
Austin, TX 78713

1939 Gloria McQuillen Williams Student Athlete Fund

AMOUNT: Varies **DEADLINE:** None Specified
FIELDS/MAJORS: All Areas Of Study

Awards for female athletes at Mercyhurst College. Write to the address below for more information.

Mercyhurst College
Financial Aid Office
Glenwood Hills
Erie, PA 16546

1940 Goddard Historical Essay Award Competition

AMOUNT: $1,000 **DEADLINE:** Dec 5
FIELDS/MAJORS: History Aeronautics/Aviation, Writing Aviation/Space

Essays will be judged on originality and scholarship by the Committee for the History of Rocketry and Astronautics of the NSC, and its decision will be final. Previously published essays are not eligible. Essays must be legible, typewritten, double-spaced, on paper approximately 8-1/2 x 11, not exceeding 5,000 words, and be submitted in duplicate, each copy complete in itself. Essays remain the property of the authors, although the National Space Club retains the right to publish and distribute winning essays. Write to the address below for details.

National Space Club
655 15th Street, NW, Suite 300
Washington, DC 20005

1941 Golden Anniversary Scholarships: Classes Of 1936, 1938, And 1940

AMOUNT: $1,000-$3,500 **DEADLINE:** Mar 1
FIELDS/MAJORS: All Areas Of Study

Scholarship for entering freshmen with outstanding academic potential. Established by the classes of 1936, 1938, and 1940. Renewable for three years. Contact the financial aid office at the address below for details.

Clemson University
Financial Aid Office
G01 Sikes Hall
Clemson, SC 29634

1942 Golden Drum Scholarship

AMOUNT: Varies **DEADLINE:** Dec 20
FIELDS/MAJORS: All Areas Of Study

For African American high school seniors. Must be recommended by Achievers of Greater Miami (Dade County only) and FIU Golden Drum Committee. Scholarship is renewable. Write to address below for additional information.

Florida International University
Office Of Minority Student Services
University Park
Miami, FL 33199

1943 Golden Drum/Ronald A. Hammond Scholarships

AMOUNT: Tuition **DEADLINE:** None Specified
FIELDS/MAJORS: All Areas Of Study

Scholarships for well-qualified high school seniors of African descent. Renewable. Write to the address below for more information.

University Of Miami
Office Of Financial Assistance Services
P.O. Box 248187
Coral Gables, FL 33124

1944 Golden Gate Scholarships

AMOUNT: Varies **DEADLINE:** Mar 31
FIELDS/MAJORS: Food Service, Restaurant/Hotel Management

Awards for students from the San Francisco Bay Area who have taken a food education and service training or other commercial food course approved by the GGRASF trustees. Preference is given to students enrolling full-time at the City College of San Francisco or Diablo Valley College. Must have a GPA of at least 2.75 or higher in hotel and restaurant courses. Write to the address below for more information.

Golden Gate Restaurant Association Scholarship Foundation
720 Market St., Suite 200
San Francisco, CA 94102

1945

Golden Harvest Seeds, Inc. Scholarships

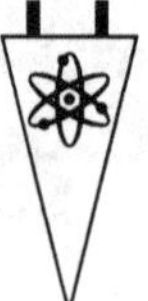

Amount: $1,000 **Deadline:** Feb 15
Fields/Majors: Agronomy

Scholarships are available for FFA members pursuing a four-year degree in agronomy. Applicant must be a U.S. citizen. Other state and school restrictions apply. Write to the address below for details.

National FFA Foundation
Scholarship Office
P.O. Box 15160
Alexandria, VA 22309

1946

Golf Foundation Undergraduate Scholarships

Amount: $2,000 **Deadline:** Apr 5
Fields/Majors: All Areas Of Study

Scholarships for graduating high school senior women who have been involved with the sport of golfing (skill or excellence in golf is not a criterion). Must be a U.S. citizen. Selection is made on the basis of academics, financial need, character, and an involvement with the sport of golf. Applications may be obtained by sending a request and a business-size SASE to the address below.

Women's Western Golf Foundation
Mrs. Richard W. Willis
393 Ramsay Road
Deerfield, IL 60015

1947

Goodrich Scholarship

Amount: Tuition & Fees **Deadline:** Mar 1
Fields/Majors: All Areas Of Study

Awards for undergraduate students enrolled full-time with a GPA of 2.0 or better, demonstrate financial need through the FAFSA, and are Nebraska residents. Must have less than 31 college credits accumulated before applying. Renewable. Write to the address below for more information.

University Of Nebraska, Omaha
Office Of Financial Aid, EAB 103
60th And Dodge Streets
Omaha, NE 68182

1948

Goodwin Foundation Scholarship

Amount: Tuition And Fees
Deadline: None Specified
Fields/Majors: Natural Science And Math

Award for Mesa State juniors and seniors who are studying natural science or math. Applicant must have and maintain a GPA of at least 3.5 and demonstrate financial need. Contact the School of Natural Sciences and Mathematics for more information.

Mesa State College
Office Of Financial Aid
P.O. Box 2647
Grand Junction, CO 81501

1949

Gordon Allport Intergroup Relations Prize

Amount: $1,000 **Deadline:** Dec 31
Fields/Majors: Psychology, Social-Intergroup Relations

Award for unpublished or recently published paper relating to intergroup relations. Papers may be theoretical or empirical. Membership in SPSSI not required. Research area may include age, sex, race, and socioeconomic status. Graduate students as well as postdoctorates are welcome to apply. Write to the address below for a description of this competition.

Society For The Psychological Study Of Social Issues
P.O. Box 1248
Ann Arbor, MI 48106

1950

Gordon Scheer Scholarship

Amount: $1,000 **Deadline:** Jun 30
Fields/Majors: Accounting

Scholarships for Colorado residents who will be in at least their second year of college studying accounting. Must have a GPA of at least 3.5. For study at Colorado colleges and universities. Write to the address below for details.

Colorado Society Of Certified Public Accountants
Educational Foundation
7979 East Tufts Avenue, #500
Denver, CO 80237

1951

Gore Family Memorial Foundation Trust Scholarships

Amount: None Specified **Deadline:** Apr 15
Fields/Majors: All Areas Of Study

Undergraduate and graduate scholarships for severely handicapped students and/or financially needy students from Broward County, FL. Write to the address below for complete details.

Gore Family Memorial Foundation Trust
4747 N. Ocean Drive, Suite 204
Fort Lauderdale, FL 33308

1952

Government Accounting Scholarship

Amount: $2,000 **Deadline:** None Specified
Fields/Majors: Accounting

One or more scholarships for senior undergraduate accounting majors who plan to pursue a career in governmental accounting or public administration. For full-time study. Must have superior academic record. Information may be available from the head of your accounting department. If not, write to the address below. Applications are available in November for awards in the following spring.

Government Finance Officers Association
Scholarship Committee
180 N. Michigan Avenue, Suite 800
Chicago, IL 60601

1953

Governor Frank Dixon Memorial Scholarship

Amount: $1,000 **Deadline:** Mar 15
Fields/Majors: All Areas Of Study

Awards for Jacksonville State University students who are from the state of Alabama. Write to the address below for more information.

Jacksonville State University
Financial Aid Office
Jacksonville, AL 36265

1954

Governor James G. Martin Scholarship

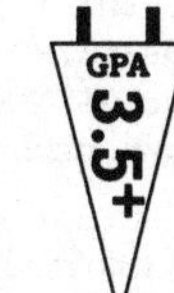

AMOUNT: None Specified **DEADLINE:** Dec 15
FIELDS/MAJORS: All Areas Of Study

Scholarships awarded to students at Appalachian State University who display outstanding academic ability, leadership qualities, and participation in community activities. Must be a resident of North Carolina to apply. Contact the Office of Admissions for details.

Appalachian State University
Office Of Admissions
Scholarship Section
Boone, NC 28608

1955

Governor R.H. Gore Scholarships

AMOUNT: $500-$1,500 **DEADLINE:** Mar 1
FIELDS/MAJORS: Journalism, Advertising

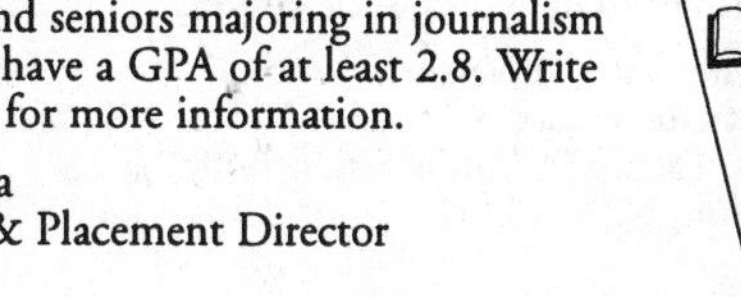

Awards for juniors and seniors majoring in journalism or advertising. Must have a GPA of at least 2.8. Write to the address below for more information.

University Of Florida
Knight Scholarship & Placement Director
2070 Weimer Hall
Gainesville, FL 32611

1956

Governor's Conference For Women

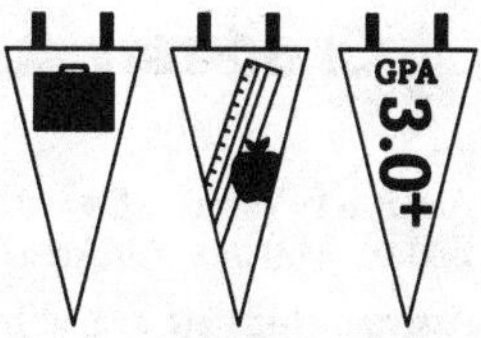

AMOUNT: $5,000
DEADLINE: Aug 31
FIELDS/MAJORS: Business, Education, Health Care, Law Enforcement/Public Service

Scholarships will be awarded to five California women who to pursue careers in business, education, health care, law enforcement/public service, and mathematics/science. Must have a GPA of at least 3.3. Essays will be required. Write to the address below for more information.

A Call To Action
Office Of The Governor, Rosalie Zalis
300 South Spring St., 16th Floor
Los Angeles, CA 90013

1957

Governor's Fellowship Program

AMOUNT: $20,000 **DEADLINE:** Feb 9
FIELDS/MAJORS: Government Work

Fellowship for graduating college seniors from Indiana who majored in any field of study, but who are interested in working in government service. Applicants must have a GPA of at least 2.7, have demonstrated leadership skills and good references. Write to the address below for more information.

Governor's Office, State Of Indiana
c/o Kim Tarnacki
Statehouse, Room 206
Indianapolis, IN 46204

1958

Governor's Scholars Program

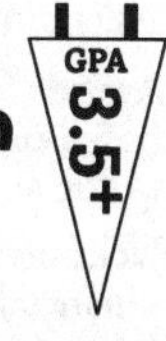

AMOUNT: $4,000 **DEADLINE:** Mar 1
FIELDS/MAJORS: All Areas Of Study

Arkansas high school student planning to attend an approved public or private school in Arkansas. Based on academic achievement and leadership qualities. 100 awards per year. A minimum GPA of 3.6 or better. An ACT score of at least 27 or an SAT score of 1100 is required. Write to the address below for further information.

Arkansas Department Of Higher Education
Financial Aid Division
114 East Capitol
Little Rock, AR 72201

1959

Governor's Teaching Scholarship Program And Teacher Loan Program

AMOUNT: $5,000 (max) **DEADLINE:** None Specified
FIELDS/MAJORS: Education

Loans for South Carolina students intending to pursue a career in teaching. High school seniors must be in the top 10% of their high school class or have an 1100 or better on the SAT. Current undergraduates must have passed the EEE exam and maintain a GPA of at least 3.5. Contact your school's financial aid office or the address below for more information.

South Carolina Student Loan Corporation
Suite 210
Interstate Center
Columbia, SC 29221

1960

Governors Scholarships

AMOUNT: Varies **DEADLINE:** None Specified
FIELDS/MAJORS: All Areas Of Study

Scholarships are available at Pima for full-time students. Based on academic ability, financial need, or both. Individual award requirements will vary. Applicants must be Native Americans. Write to the address listed below for information.

Pima Community College
Financial Aid Office
Tucson, AZ 85709

1961

GPA Scholarships

AMOUNT: Varied **DEADLINE:** Open
FIELDS/MAJORS: All Areas Of Study

Awards for Liberty University transfer or continuing students who have established a collegiate GPA of at least 3.0 and are enrolled full-time. For undergraduate study. Write to the address below for more information.

Liberty University
Office Of Student Financial Aid
Box 20000
Lynchburg, VA 24506

1962

Grace Barnard Memorial Scholarship

AMOUNT: $1,000 **DEADLINE:** Mar 15
FIELDS/MAJORS: All Areas Of Study

Awards for Jacksonville State University students in any discipline. Based on high moral character and academic achievement. Write to the address below for more details.

Jacksonville State University
Financial Aid Office
Jacksonville, AL 36265

1963

Grace Foundation Scholarship Fund

AMOUNT: $2,500 (max)
DEADLINE: Jan 31
FIELDS/MAJORS: Christian Service, Health Care, Teaching, Theology, Welfare

Scholarships for students studying at a college or university with the intent of providing service in one of the above areas to the poor and uneducated in their own country. Must be able to express himself/herself in English and have financial need. Renewable with reapplication. Intended primarily for students from developing countries (including China). Minimum GPA: 3.0. If interested, write to the address below between Sep. 1 & Oct. 31 to request an application. Must indicate (in English) name/address of applicant, name and address of college (include beginning date), intended course of study, statement of financial need, and a brief background of Christian testimony.

Grace Foundation Scholarship Fund
P.O. Box 924
Menlo Park, CA 94026

1964

Grace P. Swinyard Memorial Scholarship

AMOUNT: $1,000 **DEADLINE:** Feb 1
FIELDS/MAJORS: Pharmacy

Scholarships are available at the University of Utah for full-time sophomore, junior or senior female pharmacy majors. Write to the address below for details.

University Of Utah
College Of Pharmacy
Office Of Student Affairs
Salt Lake City, UT 84112

1965

Graco Children's Products, Inc., Scholarship

AMOUNT: $1,500 **DEADLINE:** Apr 1
FIELDS/MAJORS: Business Administration, Management, Marketing, Finance, Accounting

Applicant must be majors in the School of Business Administration who demonstrate financial need, academic achievement, and spiritual leadership. Three awards per year. Write to the address below for details.

Bob Jones University
Attn: Director Of Student Financial Aid
Greenville, SC 29614

1966

Graduate & Postdoctoral Grants For Research

AMOUNT: $5,000-$10,000
DEADLINE: Ongoing
FIELDS/MAJORS: Business, Finance, Human Resources, Law, Economics, Labor Relations

Grants to support original research on an aspect of employee benefit issues such as health care, retirement, fringe benefits, and others. For graduate and post-graduate research. Social and health science majors are also encouraged to apply. Must be a U.S. or Canadian citizen. Write to the director of research at the address below for details. This program is for research purposes only.

International Foundation Of Employee Benefit Plans
18700 West Bluemound Road
P.O. Box 69
Brookfield, WI 53008

1967

Graduate And Research Support Funds

AMOUNT: $200-$1,000 **DEADLINE:** Varies
FIELDS/MAJORS: All Areas Of Study

Programs for Wayne State University graduate students to help defray unusual expenses or pay for any travel necessary to the students research. Write to the address below for further details.

Wayne State University
Graduate School
4300 Faculty/Administration Building
Detroit, MI 48202

1968

Graduate Assistantships

AMOUNT: Varies **DEADLINE:** None Specified
FIELDS/MAJORS: All Areas Of Study

Assistantships are available at the University of Oklahoma, Norman for full-time graduate students. Contact your department or write to the address listed below for information.

University Of Oklahoma, Norman
Graduate College
1000 Asp Avenue, Room 313
Norman, OK 73019

1969

Graduate Assistantships And Fellowships

AMOUNT: None Specified **DEADLINE:** None Specified
FIELDS/MAJORS: All Areas Of Study

Assistantships are available for graduate students to receive a stipend plus tuition remission in exchange for part time work in the college or school in which they are enrolled. Fellowships for research during the third term of the academic year or the summer term in the student's field of study are also available. Write to the chairperson or director of the desired graduate program, or to the address below for details.

University Of Dayton
Office Of Scholarships And Financial Aid
300 College Park
Dayton, OH 45469

1970

Graduate Awards

AMOUNT: Varies **DEADLINE:** Apr 1
FIELDS/MAJORS: All Areas Of Study

Applicants must be graduate students of Japanese ancestry. Several award programs are available. Applications and information may be obtained from local JACL chapters, district offices and national headquarters at the address below. Please indicate your level of study and be certain to include a legal-sized SASE (offices are in San Francisco, Seattle, LA, Chicago, & Fresno).

Japanese American Citizens League
National Scholarship And Award Program
1765 Sutter St.
San Francisco, CA 94115

1971

Graduate Dean's Multicultural Award

AMOUNT: $6,600 **DEADLINE:** Jun 10
FIELDS/MAJORS: All Areas Of Study

Awards for graduate students at UW Oshkosh who are members of an under-represented minority group. Contact the Graduate School & Research, UW Oshkosh for more details.

University Of Wisconsin, Oshkosh
Financial Aid Office, Dempsey 104
800 Algoma Blvd.
Oshkosh, WI 54901

1972

Graduate Fellowship Fund (GFF)

AMOUNT: Varies **DEADLINE:** Apr 20
FIELDS/MAJORS: All Areas Of Study

Fellowships for graduate students who are deaf or hard of hearing. Must undergo an audiological assessment comparable to that required for admission to Gallaudet University in order to qualify. Preference is given to doctoral students, but master's students are also eligible. For full-time study at any college or university. Write to the address below for more information.

Gallaudet University Alumni Association (GUAA)
Peikoff Alumni House
800 Florida Ave., NE
Washington, DC 20002

1973

Graduate Fellowship Program

AMOUNT: Varies **DEADLINE:** Nov 1
FIELDS/MAJORS: Theology, Education

Aid for students in the Episcopal Seminary is offered by the Episcopal Church Foundation for students who are interested in pursuing a Ph.D in order to teach at an Episcopal Seminary in the U.S. Contact the Dean's Office for more information.

Episcopal Church Foundation
815 Second Avenue
New York, NY 10017

1974

Graduate Fellowships

AMOUNT: None Specified **DEADLINE:** Jan 10
FIELDS/MAJORS: Graphic Communications

Open to graduate student in graphic communications with more than one year of study to complete and graduating college seniors who wish to pursue advanced training. Write to the address below for details. Please specify that you are interested in support for graduate studies.

National Scholarship Trust Fund Of The Graphic Arts
4615 Forbes Avenue
Pittsburgh, PA 15213

1975

Graduate Fellowships

AMOUNT: $7,000 **DEADLINE:** Mar 1
FIELDS/MAJORS: All Fields Of Study

Fellowships are open to active members of Phi Kappa Phi who will be enrolling as a first-year graduate student. Nomination by current chapter or the chapter in which you were initiated is required. Fifty awards per year. 25-30 honorable mention awards of $1,000 are also available. Application forms are available through the chapter secretaries. Contact your chapter's secretary to indicate your interest in becoming the chapter's nominee.

Phi Kappa Phi Honor Society
Louisiana State University
P.O. Box 16000
Baton Rouge, LA 70893

1976

Graduate Fellowships

AMOUNT: Tuition **DEADLINE:** None Specified
FIELDS/MAJORS: All Areas Of Study

Applicants must be graduate students who have been accepted to the Catholic University of America. Knights of Columbus members as well as their dependents are eligible. Write to address below for details.

Knights Of Columbus
Catholic University Of America
Attn: Director Of Financial Aid
Washington, DC 20064

1977

Graduate Fellowships And Scholarships

AMOUNT: Full Tuition **DEADLINE:** Mar 1
FIELDS/MAJORS: All Areas Of Study

Scholarships and fellowships available to students at Wayne State who are pursuing advanced or professional degrees. Many departmental awards also available. Contact the University at the address below for details. For departmental awards, contact your department.

Wayne State University
Graduate Scholarship/fellowship Office
4302 Faculty Administration Bldg.
Detroit, MI 48202

1978

Graduate Fellowships At National Laboratories & Cooperating Facilities

AMOUNT: $1,300/month (min) **DEADLINE:** Feb 15
FIELDS/MAJORS: Science, Engineering

Program to support thesis or dissertation research for students in the fields of science or engineering at a member AWU campus or research facility. Contact the dean of your department or use the on-line internet URL address: http://online.awu.org/homepage.html to obtain further information.

Associated Western Universities, Inc.
4190 So. Highland Dr., Suite 211
Salt Lake City, UT 84124

1979

Graduate Fellowships For Chicano And Latino Students

AMOUNT: $6,000 **DEADLINE:** Nov 1
FIELDS/MAJORS: Political Science

Graduate fellowships for Hispanic students. APSA fellows must enroll in doctoral programs. Priority will be given to those about to enter graduate school. Must be a U.S. citizen. Based on potential for success in graduate studies and financial needs. Fellowships will be awarded on an annual basis. Write to the address below for details.

American Political Science Association
1527 New Hampshire Ave., NW
Washington, DC 20036

1980

Graduate Fellowships For Minorities And Women In The Physical Sciences

AMOUNT: $15,000/yr. (max)
DEADLINE: Nov 15
FIELDS/MAJORS: Physical Science Or Related Fields

Six year fellowship program for current college seniors or recent graduates not enrolled in a postgraduate program, who want to obtain a Ph.D. and are an underrepresented minority and/or female. Must be a U.S. citizen, and have at least a GPA of 3.0. For study at a participating NPSC member university. Recipients must agree to work two summers at a consortium member employer. Write to L. Nan Snow, Executive Director, at the address below for more information.

National Physical Science Consortium
New Mexico State University
Box 30001, Dept 3 NPS
Las Cruces, NM 88003

1981

Graduate Fellowships For Study In Belgium

AMOUNT: $12,000 **DEADLINE:** Jan 31
FIELDS/MAJORS: Belgian Studies

Grant for students working toward a Ph.D. in areas of Belgian studies. Must be a U.S. citizen, preferably under the age of 30, with speaking and reading knowledge of Dutch, Flemish, or German. The grant is for travel and expenses to Belgium for a period of ten months. Write to the address below for more information.

Belgian American Educational Foundation, Inc.
195 Church St.
New Haven, CT 06510

1982

Graduate Fellowships, Assistantships, And Tuition Scholarships

AMOUNT: Varies **DEADLINE:** Feb 1
FIELDS/MAJORS: All Areas Of Study

Grant and fellowship aid available to graduate students in any field of study at UMCP. For fellowships and assistantships, contact the department you are in or will be applying to. For scholarships, contact the graduate school. Write to the address below for further information.

University Of Maryland, College Park
Graduate Studies And Research Dept.
College Park, MD 20742

1983

Graduate Grants

AMOUNT: $750 **DEADLINE:** Mar 15
FIELDS/MAJORS: History

Grants are available to student members of Phi Alpha Theta who are entering graduate school or are enrolled in a master's program and pursuing an advanced degree. Write to address below for details. Please indicate the name of your chapter. Information may be available from your chapter officers.

Phi Alpha Theta-International Honor Society In History
Headquarters Office
50 College Dr.
Allentown, PA 18104

1984

Graduate Journalism & Mass Communications Awards

AMOUNT: Varies **DEADLINE:** Mar 15
FIELDS/MAJORS: Journalism and Mass Communications

Scholarships are available at the University of Oklahoma, Norman, for graduate students in journalism. Includes the Chester H. Westfall, Fayette Copeland Memorial, John Scott Graduate Fellowship, Julie Blakley, Mrs. Walter B. Ferguson Memorial, and O.H. Lachenmeyer scholarships. Individual award requirements may vary. Write to the address listed below for information.

University Of Oklahoma, Norman
School Of Journalism & Mass Communications
860 Van Vleet Oval
Norman, OK 73019

1985

Graduate Research Assistant Program

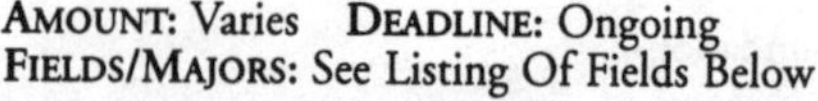

AMOUNT: Varies **DEADLINE:** Ongoing
FIELDS/MAJORS: See Listing Of Fields Below

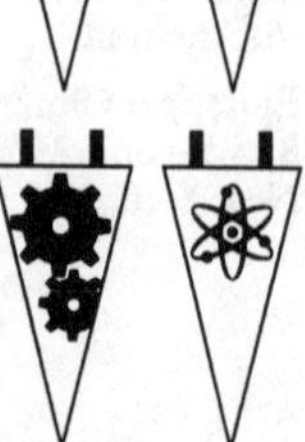

Resident graduate assistantships are available at Los Alamos for students with a GPA of at least 2.50 who are looking to get paid relevant work experience while pursuing an advanced degree. Fields of study are chemistry, computer science, economics, chemical, electrical, mechanical and nuclear engineering, health, environmental, life, earth and space science. Other applicable fields include materials science, metallurgy, mathematics, physics and optical engineering. Write to the address listed below for information.

Los Alamos National Laboratory
Personnel Services Division
Mail Stop P282
Los Alamos, NM 87545

1986

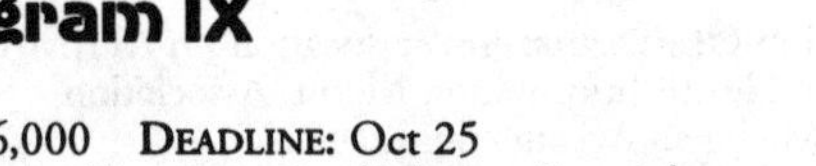

Graduate Research Award Program IX

Amount: $6,000 **Deadline:** Oct 25
Fields/Majors: Transportation/Aviation Research

Award for development of research paper on public-sector aviation issues will be made to up to seven graduate (master's or doctoral) students. Must be U.S. citizen and currently enrolled in an accredited graduate program. Write to the address below for details.

National Research Council, Transportation Research Board
Graduate Research Award Program
2101 Constitution Ave., NW, Room GR-326E
Washington, DC 20418

1987

Graduate Research Fellowships (Viets Fellowship)

Amount: $3,000 **Deadline:** Mar 15
Fields/Majors: Neuromuscular Medicine

Fellowships are available for medical or graduate students involved in basic or clinical research related to Myasthenia Gravis (MG). Write to the address listed below for information.

Myasthenia Gravis Foundation Of America
Fellowship Program
222 S. Riverside Plaza, Suite 1540
Chicago, IL 60606

1988

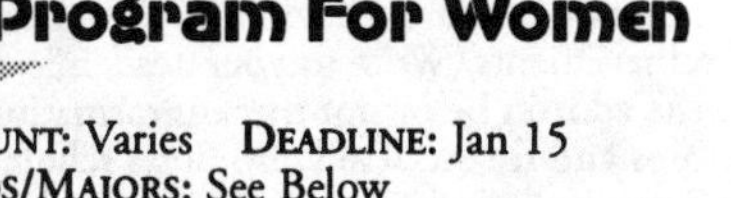

Graduate Research Program For Women

Amount: Varies **Deadline:** Jan 15
Fields/Majors: See Below

For women students who have been accepted into an accredited doctoral program for the following fall, in the field of: chemistry and chemical engineering, communication computer science, computer engineering, physics, electrical and electronic engineering, information sciences, materials science, mathematics, mechanical engineering, operations research, or statistics. Applicants must also be U.S. citizens or permanent residents. Write to the address below for complete details.

AT&T Bell Laboratories
600 Mountain Ave.
Room 3D-304
Murray Hill, NJ 07974

1989

Graduate Research Scholarship

Amount: $500 (max) **Deadline:** None Specified
Fields/Majors: All Areas Of Study

Award given to New Mexico resident graduate students for the purpose of paying costs of research projects. Students in full or part-time study are eligible. Applicants must be enrolled in a New Mexico institution. Contact the department head at the New Mexico four-year public postsecondary institution where enrolled.

New Mexico Commission On Higher Education
1068 Cerrillos Road
Santa Fe, NM 87501

1990

Graduate Scholarship Award

Amount: $5,000 **Deadline:** Feb 29
Fields/Majors: Civil Engineering, Architecture, Construction Management

Awards are available for graduate students currently enrolled in a program in one of the areas listed above. Based on an essay submitted on a subject which varies annually. Must be a U.S. citizen or permanent resident. College seniors are also eligible. Write to the address listed below for information.

Wilson Management Associates, Inc.
80 Glen Head Road
Glen Head, NY 11545

1991

Graduate Scholarship In Agricultural Engineering

Amount: $5,000 **Deadline:** Apr 15
Fields/Majors: Agricultural And Biological Engineering

Awards available for graduate students in the areas of agricultural engineering. Applicants must have a desire to pursue a graduate degree in a field related to the development of poultry equipment. Write to the address below for more information.

Midwest Poultry Consortium, Inc.
Box 191, 13033 Ridgedale Drive
Minneapolis, MN 55343

1992

Graduate Scholarship Program

Amount: Varies **Deadline:** Jun 15
Fields/Majors: Medicine, Dentistry

Applicants must be Georgia residents who are pursuing a degree in one of the above majors. Write to the address below for details.

Ty Cobb Educational Foundation
P.O. Box 725
Forest Park, GA 30051

1993

Graduate Scholarship Program

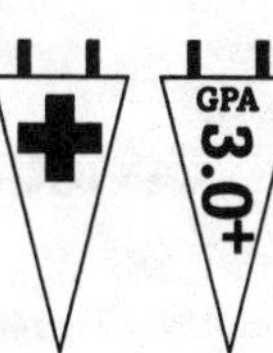

Amount: Varies **Deadline:** Jun 1
Fields/Majors: Dental Hygiene, Dental Research

Scholarships for students who have at least been accepted to a full-time master's or doctoral program. Minimum GPA of 3.0. Licensure as a dental hygienist is required. Write to the address below for more information.

American Dental Hygienists' Association Institute
For Oral Health
444 N. Michigan Ave., Suite 3400
Chicago, IL 60611

1994

Graduate Scholarship Program

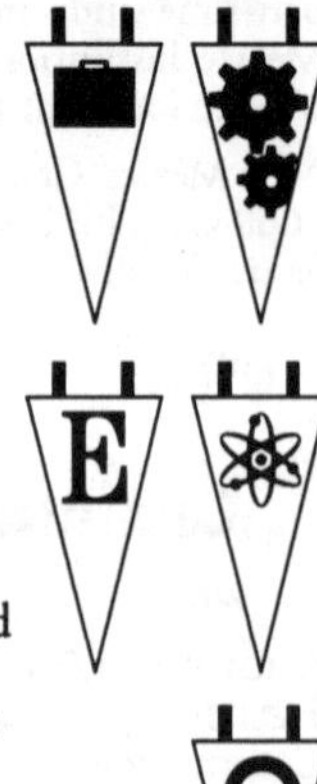

Amount: $7,200 (max)
Deadline: None Specified
Fields/Majors: All Areas Of Study

Renewable award given to New Mexico resident graduate students, with preference given to women and minorities in the fields of business, engineering, computer science, mathematics, and agriculture. Applicants must continue education in a New Mexico public university and serve ten hours per week in an unpaid internship or assistantship. Contact the dean of graduate studies at a New Mexico four-year public postsecondary institution.

New Mexico Commission On Higher Education
1068 Cerrillos Road
Santa Fe, NM 87501

1995

Graduate Scholarships

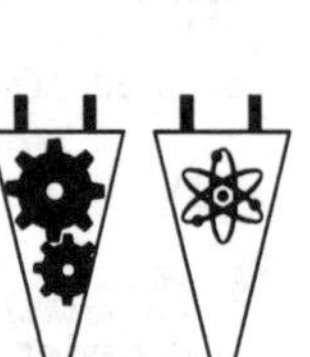

Amount: None Specified **Deadline:** Apr 1
Fields/Majors: Aerospace Education, Science

Applicants must be CAP members and majoring in aerospace education or science. Write to the address below for details.

Civil Air Patrol
National Headquarters CAP(TT)
Maxwell AFB, AL 36112

1996

Graduate Scholarships

Amount: $2,000 (max) **Deadline:** Mar 1
Fields/Majors: Library Science, Law

The Association offers several types of scholarships for law school graduates, library school graduates who are attending law school, college graduates with law library experience who are studying library science, and J.D.s studying library science. Write to the address below for details.

American Association Of Law Libraries
Scholarships
53 W. Jackson Blvd., Suite 940
Chicago, IL 60604

1997

Graduate Scholarships

Amount: $6,340 (max) **Deadline:** None Specified
Fields/Majors: All Areas Of Study

The Graduate Division offers scholarships which are reserved for graduate students at the California College of Arts and Crafts. Four scholarship programs are available with an unspecified number of awards. Contact the school at the address below for details.

California College Of Arts And Crafts
Office Of Enrollment Services
5212 Broadway At College
Oakland, CA 94618

1998

Graduate Scholarships

Amount: $1,000-$5,000 **Deadline:** Aug 1
Fields/Majors: Health Or Information Sciences

Scholarships are available to graduate students furthering their education in a health related information management or technology field. Applicant must be a credentialed health information management professional holding a bachelors degree, and a member of AHIMA. Write to the address listed below for information.

Foundation Of Research And Education Of AHIMA
American Health Information Mgmt. Association
919 N. Michigan Avenue, Suite 1400
Chicago, IL 60611

1999

Graduate Scholarships And Fellowships

Amount: $1,000-$5,000 **Deadline:** Feb 1
Fields/Majors: Food Science & Technology

Graduate fellowships to encourage and support research in food science and technology at accredited institution in the USA or Canada. In addition Arthur T. Schramm Fellowship will provide tuition assistance for needy Ph.D candidates. Twenty-four awards per year. Write to the address below for details. Please specify your year in school or what degree you are pursuing.

Institute Of Food Technologists
Scholarship Department
221 North Lasalle Street
Chicago, IL 60601

2000

Graduate Scholarships And Grants

Amount: None Specified **Deadline:** None Specified
Fields/Majors: All Areas Of Study

Several scholarships and grants are available to Dayton graduate students through the various academic departments on campus, and from some local companies and organizations. Based on academic or professional achievements. Write to your academic chairperson/director or to the address below for more information. The office of scholarships and financial aid also posts scholarship opportunities on the lobby bulletin board, St. Mary's Hall, 202.

University Of Dayton
Office Of Scholarships And Financial Aid
300 College Park
Dayton, OH 45469

2001

Graduate Scholarships In Chemistry

Amount: Varies **Deadline:** Mar 1
Fields/Majors: Chemistry

Awards are available at the University of New Mexico for graduate students studying chemistry who have an outstanding record in the chemistry department. Write to the address listed below for information.

University Of New Mexico, Albuquerque
Office Of Financial Aid
Albuquerque, NM 87131

2002

Graduate Scholarships In The Marine Sciences

Amount: $3,000 (max) **Deadline:** Mar 1
Fields/Majors: Marine Sciences

Scholarships are available to qualified graduate students of marine science. Write to the address below for more information.

International Women's Fishing Association Scholarship Trust
P.O. Drawer 3125
Palm Beach, FL 33480

2003

Graduate Student Researchers Program (Minority & Disabled Focus)

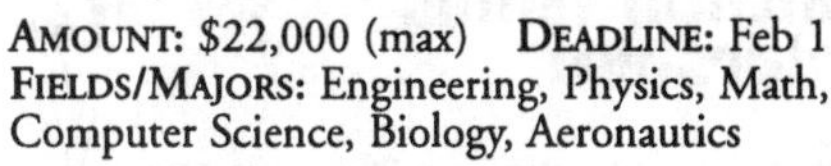

Amount: $22,000 (max) **Deadline:** Feb 1
Fields/Majors: Engineering, Physics, Math, Computer Science, Biology, Aeronautics

Applicants must be sponsored by their graduate department chair or faculty advisor; enrolled in a full-time graduate program at an accredited U.S. college or university; studying in one of the fields listed above. Student must be highly motivated to pursue their plans of study in NASA related research. Applicant must be a U.S. citizen. Write to the program manager at the address listed below for information. The focus of this program is to bring underrepresented racial minorities and students with disabilities into these fields of study.

NASA Graduate Student Researchers Program
NASA Headquarters
Scholarships & Fellowships
Washington, DC 20546

2004

Graduate Student Scholarships

Amount: $2,000-$4,000
Deadline: Jun 14
Fields/Majors: Speech-Language Pathology, Communications Disorders

Awards for master's level studies in communication sciences and disorders programs. Four general awards per year. Also available are one award for a foreign or minority student, and one award giving preference to a disabled student pursuing graduate studies in the field. Up to six awards total. Write to the address below for complete details.

American Speech-Language-Hearing Foundation
10801 Rockville Pike
Rockville, MD 20852

2005

Graduate Student Travel Awards

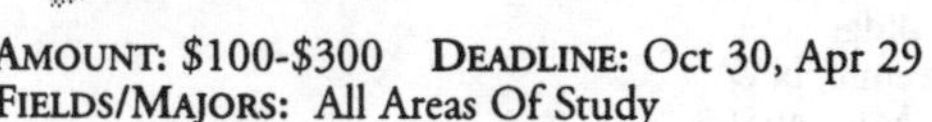

Amount: $100-$300 **Deadline:** Oct 30, Apr 29
Fields/Majors: All Areas Of Study

Grants for graduate students at the University of Oregon to use to travel to presentations, panel discussions, national organizations, or other research libraries. Applications must be submitted for travel occurring six months before or after each deadline. Write to the address below for more information.

University Of Oregon
Center For The Study Of Women In Society
340 Hendricks Hall
Eugene, OR 97403

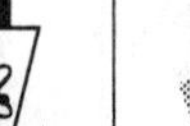
2006

Graduate Study/ Dissertation Research

Amount: None Specified **Deadline:** Oct 13
Fields/Majors: Social Science, Humanities

This program supports scholars with the M.A. who are doing dissertation research in the humanities or social science to work at a Chinese university. Requires proficiency in the Chinese language and a tenure of one academic year. Applicant must be a U.S. citizen or permanent resident. Write to the address listed below for information.

Committee On Scholarly Communication With China
1055 Thomas Jefferson Street, NW, Suite 2013
Washington, DC 20007

2007

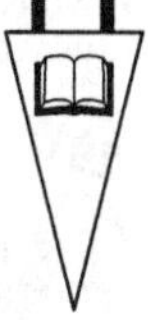

Graduate Study-Library Science Scholarship

Amount: Varies **Deadline:** May 15
Fields/Majors: Library Science, Information Science

Tuition and fee assistance for Pennsylvania residents enrolled in an ALA approved program of graduate work in an institution located in Pennsylvania. Write to Ms. Margaret Bauer, Executive Director, at the address below for complete details.

Pennsylvania Library Association
1919 N. Front St.
Harrisburg, PA 17102

2008

Graduate Teaching Fellowship

Amount: Full Tuition **Deadline:** Feb 1
Fields/Majors: Sociology

Scholarships available to sociology students enrolled in graduate studies at the University of Oregon. Based on academics and financial need. Write to the address below for details.

University Of Oregon
Department Of Sociology
College Of Arts And Sciences
Eugene, OR 97403

2009

Graduate Tuition Waiver

Amount: Resident Tuition **Deadline:** Varies
Fields/Majors: All Areas Of Study

Awards for graduate students who demonstrate financial need as well as high GPA. Must enroll full-time. Write to the address below for more information.

University Of Nebraska, Omaha
Office Of Financial Aid, EAB 103
60th And Dodge Streets
Omaha, NE 68182

2010

Graduating High School Senior Scholarships

Amount: None Specified **Deadline:** Mar 15
Fields/Majors: All Areas Of Study

Open to graduating high school seniors who have volunteered in the school and community. Send a legal-size SASE to the address below for an application.

California Congress Of Parents, Teachers, And Students, Inc.
930 Georgia St., P.O. Box 15015
Los Angeles, CA 90015

Graham Foundation Grants

Amount: $10,000 (max) **Deadline:** Jan 15, Jul 15
Fields/Majors: Architecture

Grants are offered to individuals and institutions in support of activities focused on architecture and the built environment. Write to the address below for more information.

Graham Foundation
4 West Burton Pl.
Chicago, IL 60610

Gramley Leadership And Service Scholarship

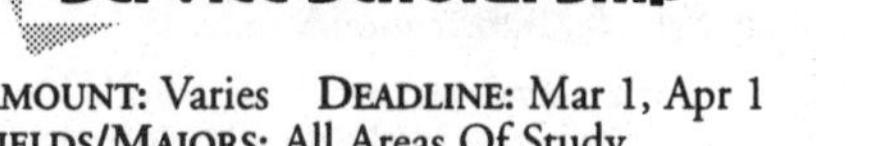

GPA 2.5+

Amount: Varies **Deadline:** Mar 1, Apr 1
Fields/Majors: All Areas Of Study

Award given to incoming freshmen in recognition of outstanding achievement in leadership and service. Recipients must maintain full-time status and a GPA of 2.5 or better. Write to the address below for more information.

Salem College
Financial Aid Office
P.O. Box 10548
Winston-Salem, NC 27108

Grand Army Of The Republic Living Memorial Scholarship

Amount: $200 **Deadline:** Feb 1
Fields/Majors: All Areas Of Study

For lineal descendants of a Union veteran of Civil War. Must be junior or senior in college in good scholastic standing, of good moral character, and have a firm belief in our form of government. Applicant must send a self-addressed, stamped envelope when writing for an application. Write to the address below for details. Information on your Civil War ancestor can be found through the State Historical Soc.-Dept of Civil War Records, the State Adjutant Generals Office-Dept of Civil War Records (state where the veteran enlisted), or (for $5) from: Military Service Branch (NNMS), National Archives and Record Service, 8th and Penn. Ave, NW, Washington, DC 20408.

Daughters Of Union Veterans Of The Civil War Headquarters
503 S. Walnut Street
Springfield, IL 62704

Grand Junction Lion's Club Non-traditional Student Award

Amount: Tuition And Fees **Deadline:** None Specified
Fields/Majors: All Areas Of Study

Awards for non-traditional students (age 25 and over) who are entering Mesa State for full-time study. Must have a GPA of at least 2.5 and demonstrate financial need. Recipients must be Mesa County residents for at least five years. For undergraduate study. Write to the address below for more details.

Mesa State College
Office Of Financial Aid
P.O. Box 2647
Grand Junction, CO 81501

Grand Junction Lion's Club Scholarship

Amount: Tuition And Fees
Deadline: None Specified
Fields/Majors: All Areas Of Study

Awards for high school graduates from Mesa County who intend to enter Mesa State. Must have a GPA of at least 3.0 and demonstrate financial need. Recipients must not have additional scholarship money exceeding $1,000 per academic year. Renewable. Write to the address below for more details.

Mesa State College
Office Of Financial Aid
P.O. Box 2647
Grand Junction, CO 81501

2016

Grand Junction Tennis Club Scholarship

Amount: Varies **Deadline:** None Specified
Fields/Majors: All Areas Of Study

Award for Mesa State students enrolled in any area of study, but who are active participants in the tennis program. Must have a GPA of at least 2.5. Contact the tennis coaches for more information.

Mesa State College
Office Of Financial Aid
P.O. Box 2647
Grand Junction, CO 81501

2017

Grand Lodge Of Iowa Masonic Student Loans

Amount: $4,000 (max) **Deadline:** Varies
Fields/Majors: All Areas Of Study

Loans to residents of Iowa going to Iowa schools. If approved, may be used for study outside of Iowa. All applicants must have a Masonic sponsor, leadership abilities, and financial need. Contact the address below for further information.

Grand Lodge Of Iowa AF & AM
P.O. Box 896
Sioux City, IA 51102

2018

Grand Rapids Foundation Scholarships

Amount: $500-$2,500 **Deadline:** Apr 14
Fields/Majors: All Areas Of Study

Scholarships for residents of Kent County who are full-time undergraduate students with a GPA of at least 3.0 who can demonstrate financial need. Write to the address below for details.

Grand Rapids Foundation
209-C Waters Bldg.
161 Ottawa Avenue, NW
Grand Rapids, MI 49503

2019

Grant And Programs For Theological Studies

Amount: $500-$1,500 **Deadline:** None Specified
Fields/Majors: Theology, Religion

Grants for theology students at the graduate level of study who are members of the Presbyterian Church, U.S.A. Applicants must be U.S. citizens, demonstrate financial need, and be recommended by an academic advisor or church pastor. Write to the address below for more information.

Presbyterian Church, (U.S.A.)
Office Of Financial Aid
100 Witherspoon St.
Louisville, KY 40202

2020

Grant County Farmers Union Milk Marketing Co-op Scholarships

AMOUNT: $150 **DEADLINE:** Feb 15
FIELDS/MAJORS: Agriculture

Awards for UW Platteville students who are agriculture majors and whose family is a member of either sponsoring organization. Must have a GPA of at least 2.0 and have completed at least fifteen credits at the time of application. Write to the address below for more information.

University Of Wisconsin, Platteville
Office Of Admissions & Enrollment Mgt.
Platteville, WI 53818

2021

Grant M. Mack Memorial Scholarships

AMOUNT: $2,000 **DEADLINE:** Mar 1
FIELDS/MAJORS: Business

Two scholarships for graduate and undergraduate students. Must be legally blind and majoring in business. Write to the address below for details.

American Council Of The Blind
Scholarship Coordinator
1155 15th St., NW, Suite 720
Washington, DC 20005

2022

Grant Program For Dependents Of Correctional Officers

AMOUNT: $3,500 **DEADLINE:** Sep 1
FIELDS/MAJORS: All Areas Of Study

The Correctional Officer's Grant provides payment of tuition and mandatory fees for the spouse and children of Illinois correctional officers killed or at least 90% disabled in the line of duty. Recipients must be enrolled on at least half-time basis. Applicants must be U.S. citizens residing in Illinois and attending Illinois postsecondary institutions. Write to the address below for complete details.

Illinois Student Assistance Commission
1755 Lake Cook Road
Deerfield, IL 60015

2023

Grant Program For Medical Studies

AMOUNT: $500-$1,500
DEADLINE: None Specified
FIELDS/MAJORS: Medicine

Grants for medical students at the graduate level of study who are members of the Presbyterian Church, U.S.A. Applicants must be U.S. citizens, demonstrate financial need, and be recommended by an academic advisor or church pastor. Write to the address below for more information.

Presbyterian Church, (U.S.A.)
Office Of Financial Aid
100 Witherspoon St.
Louisville, KY 40202

2024

Grant Program For New Investigators

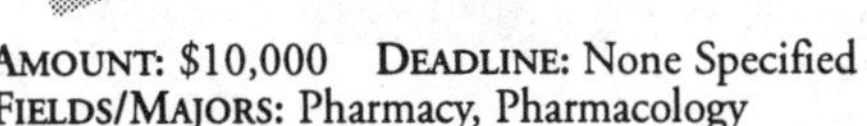

AMOUNT: $10,000 **DEADLINE:** None Specified
FIELDS/MAJORS: Pharmacy, Pharmacology

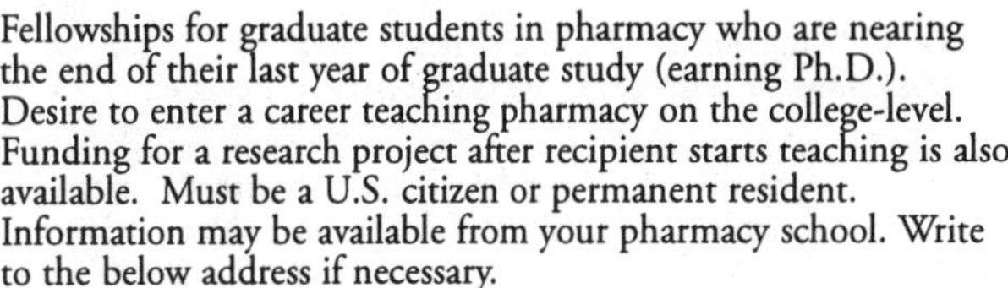

Fellowships for graduate students in pharmacy who are nearing the end of their last year of graduate study (earning Ph.D.). Desire to enter a career teaching pharmacy on the college-level. Funding for a research project after recipient starts teaching is also available. Must be a U.S. citizen or permanent resident. Information may be available from your pharmacy school. Write to the below address if necessary.

American Foundation For Pharmaceutical Education
One Church Street, Suite 202
Rockville, MD 20850

2025

Grant-In-Aid And National University Higher Education Program (NUHELP)

AMOUNT: $50-$400 **DEADLINE:** None Specified
FIELDS/MAJORS: All Areas Of Study

Grant is institutionally funded and assists students with partial tuition assistance. Eligible applicants must receive less than 85% of the tuition cost from a tuition reimbursement program and receive less than full tuition from other financial aid programs. NUHELP is a low interest loan for students with financial need and good credit history. Write to the address below for more information.

National University
Office Of Financial Aid
4025 Camino Del Rio S
San Diego, CA 92108

2026

Grant-In-Aid For Graduate Students

AMOUNT: $7,500 (max) **DEADLINE:** Dec 15
FIELDS/MAJORS: Air Conditioning/Refrigeration, HVAC Engineering

Grant for full-time, graduate students in ASHRAE related fields. Program is designed "to encourage the student to continue his/her preparation for service in the HVAC&R industry." relevance of proposed research is considered. Not renewable. Applications are made by your advisor on your behalf. Consult with your advisor and write to the address below for further details and application forms. Please specify that your interest is in the graduate student Grant-In-Aid Program.

American Society Of Heating, Refrigerating And AC Engineers
Manager Of Research
1791 Tullie Circle, NE
Atlanta, GA 30329

2027

Grant-In-Aid For Undergraduate Students

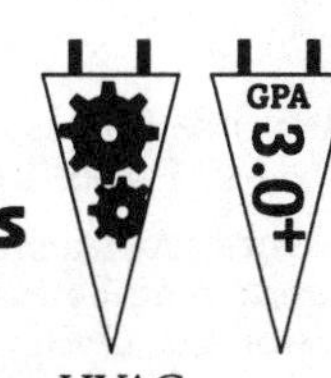

AMOUNT: $2,500 (max) **DEADLINE:** Dec 15
FIELDS/MAJORS: Air Conditioning/Refrigeration, HVAC Engineering

Grant for full-time, undergraduate students in ASHRAE related fields. Program designed "to encourage the student to continue his/her preparation for service in the HVAC&R industry." applicant must have at least a 3.25 GPA in order to apply. Write to the address below for details.

American Society Of Heating, Refrigerating And AC Engineers
Manager Of Research
1791 Tullie Circle, NE
Atlanta, GA 30329

2028

Grant-In-Aid For Wildlife Research

AMOUNT: None Specified **DEADLINE:** Nov 1
FIELDS/MAJORS: Wildlife, Large Game Animal Research

Awards for graduate students and more advanced investigators to support research on wildlife, and particularly North American big game animals and/or their habitat. Write to the address below for more information.

Boone And Crockett Club
Old Milwaukee Depot
250 Station Drive
Missoula, MT 59801

2029

Grant-In-Aid Of Research

AMOUNT: $500-$2,000 **DEADLINE:** Jan 31, Jul 31
FIELDS/MAJORS: American History, Political History

Grants for researchers of subjects that are addressed by the holdings of the LBJ Library. Research is done at the library. Interested applicants must contact the library at the address below (or call 512-482-5137) to obtain info about materials available in the library on the proposed research topic.

Lyndon Baines Johnson Foundation Archives
Lyndon B. Johnson Library
2313 Red River Street
Austin, TX 78705

2030

Grant-In-Aid Program

AMOUNT: $55,000 Deadline: None Specified
FIELDS/MAJORS: Medical Research (Cardiovascular And Other Related Areas)

Grants for investigators in the fields of cardiovascular research with no restriction on seniority and academic rank. Based on innovation, originality, and potential impact of new research directions. Write to the address below for more information.

American Heart Association
National Center
7272 Greenville Ave.
Dallas, TX 75231

2031

Grants & Awards

AMOUNT: $500-$5,000 **DEADLINE:** Varies
FIELDS/MAJORS: Reading Research and Disabilities

Grant & Award programs designed to support research in & recognize contributions to the field of reading research and reading disabilities. Open to recent and current Ph.D candidates (for dissertations) and to teachers, reporters, writers, and researchers. Some awards limited to IRA members. Write for complete details on membership and award programs. Information can also be

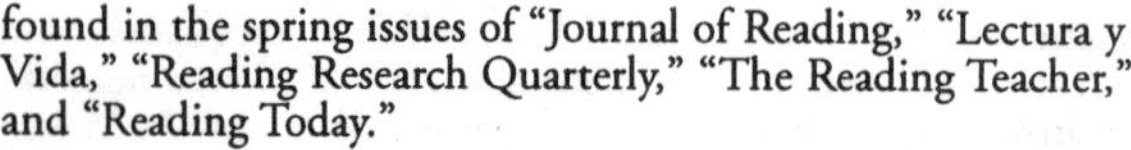

found in the spring issues of "Journal of Reading," "Lectura y Vida," "Reading Research Quarterly," "The Reading Teacher," and "Reading Today."

International Reading Association
800 Barksdale Rd.
P.O. Box 8139
Newark, DE 19714

2032

Grants & Fellowships In Arthritis Research

AMOUNT: $10,000-$75,000 **DEADLINE:**Sep 1
FIELDS/MAJORS: Arthritis Research

Various fellowship and grant programs open to doctors and scientists to further their training in patient care and research into arthritis. Doctoral dissertation awards are also available. Write to the address below for complete details.

Arthritis Foundation
Research Department
1314 Spring Street, NW
Atlanta, GA 30309

2033

Grants & Loans

AMOUNT: Varies **DEADLINE:** Nov 15
FIELDS/MAJORS: All Areas Of Study

Must be female resident of the greater New York City area or live within a 50 mile radius beyond New York. Must be financially needy. For any area of undergraduate study or 2nd year graduate study in a MD, veterinarian, or clinical psychology program. No religious affiliation required. Write to the address below for details.

Jewish Foundation For The Education Of Women
330 West 58th Street
New York, NY 10019

2034

Grants And Loans

AMOUNT: None Specified **DEADLINE:** None Specified
FIELDS/MAJORS: All Areas Of Study

Need-based grants for students at the French Culinary Institute. Must be a U.S. citizen or legal resident. Contact a financial aid counselor at school or write to the address below for details.

French Culinary Institute
Elizabeth Johansen, Dir. Of Admissions
462 Broadway
New York, NY 10013

2035

Grants For Courses In German Studies And Language In Germany

AMOUNT: Varies **DEADLINE:** Jan 31
FIELDS/MAJORS: German Language And Studies

Grants to strengthen German language skills or knowledge of german culture by studying in Germany. Open to students of junior level and above who are U.S. or Canadian citizens. Different programs are available, with various individual criteria for each. Write to the address below for more details.

DAAD German Academic Exchange Service
New York Office
950 Third Ave., 19th Floor
New York, NY 10022

2036

Grants For Field Research

AMOUNT: $1,200 **DEADLINE:** Jan 31
FIELDS/MAJORS: Science

Grants for graduate students in support of exploration and field research. Expeditions aided will be for specific scientific purposes, in accordance with the club's stated objective, "to broaden our knowledge of the universe." Write to the address below for more information.

Explorers Club Exploration Fund
Exploration Fund Committee
46 East 70th Street
New York, NY 10021

2037

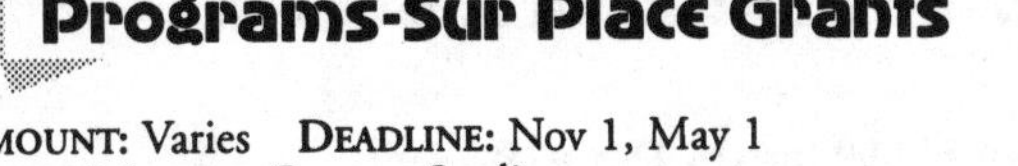

Grants For German Studies Programs-Sur Place Grants

AMOUNT: Varies **DEADLINE:** Nov 1, May 1
FIELDS/MAJORS: German Studies

Grants to promote the study of German affairs from an inter- and multi-disciplinary perspective. Open to undergraduate juniors and seniors pursuing a German studies track or minor and to master's and Ph.D. candidates working on a certificate in German studies. Ph.D. candidates doing dissertation work are ineligible. Must be U.S. or Canadian citizens. Write to the address below for additional information.

DAAD German Academic Exchange Service
New York Office
950 Third Ave., 19th Floor
New York, NY 10022

2038

Grants For Graduate Study And Advanced Research In French

AMOUNT: Varies **DEADLINE:** Varies
FIELDS/MAJORS: French Studies

Grants for graduate students or postdoctorates in the field of French language or culture. Applicants must be U.S. citizens. Some programs are for travel to France. Write to the address below for more information.

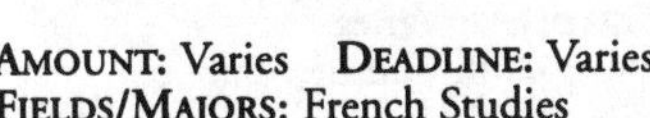

Cultural Services Of The French Embassy
972 Fifth Ave.
New York, NY 10021

2039

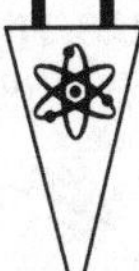

Grants For Orchid Research

AMOUNT: $12,000 (max) **DEADLINE:** Jan 1, Aug 1
FIELDS/MAJORS: Floriculture, Horticulture

Grants for experimental projects and fundamental and applied research on orchids. Qualified graduate students with appropriate interests may apply for grants in support of their research if it involves or applies to orchids. Postgraduates may only apply on behalf of the accredited institution or appropriate research institute they are associated with. Contact address below for complete details.

American Orchid Society
Research Grants
6000 South Olive Ave.
West Palm Beach, FL 33405

2040

Grants For Public Policy Research On Contemporary Hispanic Issues

AMOUNT: $20,000 (max) **DEADLINE:** Sep 15
FIELDS/MAJORS: Public Policy, Social Science

Fellowships are available to encourage research that will both have value to the Hispanic community as well as to demonstrate the use of social science research in public policy formation and to benefit the field of Hispanic studies by increasing the number and quality of trained researchers. Applicants must hold a Ph.D. and be citizens of the U.S. Write to the address listed below for information.

Social Science Research Council
Fellowships And Grants
605 Third Avenue
New York, NY 10158

2041

Grants For Research Projects

AMOUNT: $10,580 (max)
DEADLINE: Jun 11
FIELDS/MAJORS: Conservation, Health Research, Waste Mgt, Aviation, Education, Agriculture

Postgraduate level research grants will be annually awarded to individuals whose proposed projects represent a significant contribution toward the achievement of a balance between technological progress and the preservation of our natural environment. Grants are for research not for tuition or scholarships. Write to the address below for complete information.

Charles A. And Anne Morrow Lindbergh Foundation Inc.
708 S. 3rd St., Suite 110
Minneapolis, MN 55415

2042

Grants For Study, Research, And Information Visits To Germany

AMOUNT: Varies **DEADLINE:** Varies
FIELDS/MAJORS: German Language And Studies

Grants to strengthen German language skills or knowledge of German culture by traveling to Germany. Open to doctoral students or postdoctoral scholars who are U.S. or Canadian citizens. Different programs are available, with varying lengths and areas of research. Write to the address below for more details.

DAAD German Academic Exchange Service
New York Office
950 Third Ave., 19th Floor
New York, NY 10022

2043

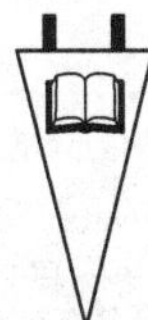

Grants In Aid For Graduate Seminar

AMOUNT: $2,000 **DEADLINE:** Mar 1
FIELDS/MAJORS: Numismatics

Applicants must have completed one year of graduate study at a North American university in one of the above fields. The seminar is held from June 13 through August 12 at the Museum of the American Numismatic Society. For graduate students with an interest in numismatics, the seminar will explore the contributions made by numismatics to other fields of study. Write to the address below for details.

American Numismatic Society
Broadway At 155th Street
New York, NY 10032

2044 Grants-In-Aid

AMOUNT: $2,000 (max) **DEADLINE:** Jan 15
FIELDS/MAJORS: Petroleum Geology, Geology, Geophysics, Paleontology

Grants are available to graduate students in studies relating to the earth science aspects of the petroleum industry. Several grant programs are offered by the AAPG. Write to the address below for details.

American Association Of Petroleum Geologists
W.A. Morgan, Chairman/AAPG Grants Cmte.
P.O. Box 979
Tulsa, OK 74101

2045 Grants-In-Aid

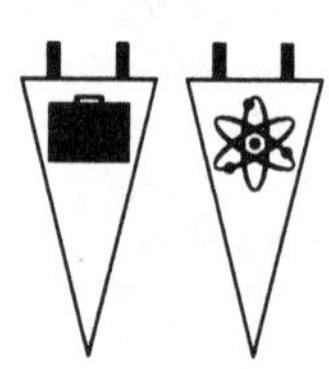

AMOUNT: $1,000/Month **DEADLINE:** Varies
FIELDS/MAJORS: History: Business, Technology, Industry, Economics, Science

Grants-In-Aid are available to scholars at all levels who are working within the Hagley's Research Collection topics. Stipends are for a minimum of two weeks and a maximum of two months. Write to the address shown below for details.

Hagley Museum And Library
P.O. Box 3630
Wilmington, DE 19807

2046 Grants-In-Aid

AMOUNT: Varies **DEADLINE:** Varies
FIELDS/MAJORS: All Areas Of Study

Awards for Concordia students who are in good standing and can demonstrate financial need. Must be a U.S. citizen and have a GPA of at least 2.5. Write to the address below for more information.

Concordia University, Irvine
Financial Aid Office
1530 Concordia West
Irvine, CA 92715

2047 Grants-In-Aid At Flagler College

AMOUNT: $200-$6,000 **DEADLINE:** Apr 1
FIELDS/MAJORS: All Areas Of Study

Awards for students at Flagler College based on any one of academics, need, athletic ability, community service, or character. Write to the address below for details.

Flagler College
Director Of Financial Aid
P.O. Box 1027
St. Augustine, FL 32085

2048 Grants-In-Aid For Affiliated Faculty And Students

AMOUNT: Varies **DEADLINE:** Nov 1, Mar 1
FIELDS/MAJORS: Renaissance And Eighteenth-Century Studies

Faculty members, postdoctoral, and graduate students from institutions affiliated with the Shakespeare Library are eligible for grants for study at the Library. Contact your campus representative or write to the committee on research fellowships at the address below for details.

Folger Institute
Folger Shakespeare Library
201 E. Capitol St., SE
Washington, DC 20003

2049 Grants-In-Aid Of Research

AMOUNT: $1,000 (max) **DEADLINE:** Varies
FIELDS/MAJORS: Scientific Research And Investigation

Grants to support scientific investigation in any field. All funds must be expended directly in support of the proposed investigation. Priority is given to research scientists in early stage of career. Applicant should ask two specialists in proposed research field to send statements confirming importance of research and qualifications to headquarters. Write to the address below for complete details.

Sigma Xi, The Scientific Research Society
Committee On Grants-In-Aid Of Research
99 Alexander Drive-Box 13975
Research Triangle Park, NC 27709

2050 Grants-In-Aid Program

AMOUNT: $1,000-$16,000 **DEADLINE:** Varies
FIELDS/MAJORS: American History-20th Century, Public Policy, Political Science

These awards are for scholars investigating some aspect of the political, economic, and social development of the U.S., principally between April 12, 1945 and January 20, 1953 or the public career of Harry S. Truman. Institute grant is for $1,000. Research grant is for $12,000. Dissertation fellowship is $20,000 and is offered every other year. Application forms may be obtained from the address below. Write for complete details.

Harry S. Truman Library Institute
Committee Of Research And Education
U.S. Highway 24 And Delaware Street
Independence, MO 64050

2051 Grants-In-Aid Program

AMOUNT: $1,000-$2,000 **DEADLINE:** Nov 13, Apr 1
FIELDS/MAJORS: Social Psychology

Grants for scientific research in a social problem area related to the basic interests and goals of SPSSI. Funding up to $1,000 is also available for doctoral dissertation research. Proposals for event-related research and for time-sensitive research are encouraged and welcomed year-round. Contact the address below for complete information on this and other programs offered by the SPSSI. Time-sensitive or event-oriented research may be proposed at any time during the year. Information may also be available in the psychology departments of many universities.

Society For The Psychological Study Of Social Issues
P.O. Box 1248
Ann Arbor, MI 48106

2052 Grants-In-Aid Program In Support Of Anthropological Research

Amount: $15,000 (max) **Deadline:** May 1, Nov 1
Fields/Majors: Anthropology

Open to qualified scholars affiliated with accredited institutions and organizations. Awards are for individual postdoctoral research or for dissertation thesis research. Write to the address below for details.

Wenner-Gren Foundation For Anthropological Research
Grants Programs
220 Fifth Ave.
New York, NY 10001

2053 Grape Workers Scholarship

Amount: Varies **Deadline:** Mar 15
Fields/Majors: All Areas Of Study

Scholarships for persons who worked in the California Table Grape fields at the last harvest or whose parents worked on the harvest. $3,000 university scholarship, and $2,500 vocational scholarships. Write to the address below for details.

California Table Grape Commission
2975 N. Maroa
P.O. Box 5498
Fresno, CA 93755

2054 Graphic Arts Scholarship

Amount: None Specified **Deadline:** Mar 15
Fields/Majors: Graphic Art

Open to high school seniors who are studying graphic art. Send a SASE to the address below for an application.

California Congress Of Parents, Teachers, And Students, Inc.
930 Georgia St., P.O. Box 15015
Los Angeles, CA 90015

2055 Grass Fellowships In Neurophysiology

Amount: Varies **Deadline:** Dec 1
Fields/Majors: Neurophysiology

Summer fellowships for late predoctoral or early postdoctoral researchers who are academically prepared for independent research in neurophysiology. This is a resident fellowship at the marine biological laboratory at Woods Hole, Massachusetts. Requires research proposal, budget, and recommendation. Interested persons should write to the address below for further information. Request bulletin FA-296.

Grass Foundation
77 Reservoir Road
Quincy, MA 02170

2056 Gravure Education Foundation

Amount: $1,500 **Deadline:** None Specified
Fields/Majors: Pulp & Paper Science, Graphic Arts

Two scholarships are awarded, one to a minority freshmen and one to a junior in the department of paper and printing science and engineering at WMU. Write to the address below for more information.

Western Michigan University
College Of Engineering & Applied Science
Dept. Of Paper & Printing Science & Eng.
Kalamazoo, MI 49008

2057 Greater Bridgeport Area Foundation Scholarships

Amount: Varies **Deadline:** May 3
Fields/Majors: All Areas Of Study

Over fifty different scholarships are available for students who are residents of the Greater Bridgeport Area Foundation service area, which does include Bridgeport, Easton, Fairfield, Milford, Monroe, Shelton, Stratford, Trumbull and Westport. Individual requirements will vary. Write to the address listed below for information.

Greater Bridgeport Area Foundation
280 State Street
Bridgeport, CT 06604

2058 Gretchen Von Loewe Kreuter Scholarship

Amount: Varies **Deadline:** None Specified
Fields/Majors: All Areas Of Study

Award available to outstanding female students at Rockford College. Write to the address below for more information.

Rockford College
Financial Aid Office
5050 East State St.
Rockford, IL 61108

2059 Grey Forest Utilities Scholarships

Amount: $1,000 **Deadline:** Mar 19
Fields/Majors: All Areas Of Study

Scholarships are available for students residing in the Grey Forest Utilities service area in Texas. Four awards are offered annually, with one award given to residents of Grey Forest, Texas. Write to the address listed below for information.

Grey Forest Utilities
14570 Bandera Road
P.O. Box 258
Helotes, TX 78023

2060 Growmark, Inc. Scholarship

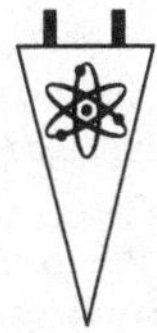

Amount: $500 **Deadline:** Feb 15
Fields/Majors: Agriculture

Scholarships are available for FFA members pursuing a two-year degree in any area of agriculture who reside in Illinois, Iowa or Wisconsin, and attend a school in their state of residence. Must be graduating high school seniors. Write to the address below for details.

National FFA Foundation
Scholarship Office
P.O. Box 15160
Alexandria, VA 22309

2061 GTE Corporation Merit Scholarships

Amount: $500-$2,000 **Deadline:** None Specified
Fields/Majors: All Areas Of Study

Scholarships are available to graduating high school seniors who are National Merit finalists and children of employees of the GTE Corporation and its subsidiaries. Write to the address listed below for information, or contact the Human Resources Department at GTE.

National Merit Scholarship Corporation/GTE Corporation
1560 Sherman Avenue, Suite 200
Evanston, IL 60201

2062 Guaranteed Access Grant

Amount: $6,000 (max) **Deadline:** Apr 15
Fields/Majors: All Areas Of Study

Applicants must be Maryland residents attending a college in Maryland on a full-time basis. Applicant must have entered college immediately after high school, have a GPA of at least 2.5, and be under the age of 22. Applicant must demonstrate great financial need. Write to the address below for details.

Maryland State Higher Education Commission
16 Francis Street
Annapolis, MD 21401

2063 Guggenheim Fellowship At The National Air And Space Museum

Amount: $14,000-$25,000 **Deadline:** Jan 15
Fields/Majors: Aeronautics, Astronomy, Astrophysics, Space Research

Residential fellowship for researchers in the above areas. Persons holding Ph.D. must have received doctorate within 7 years of award. Doctoral candidates must have completed preliminary coursework. Write to the fellowship coordinator, museum programs, at the address below for details.

National Air And Space Museum, Smithsonian Institution
Aeronautics Department
Fellowship Coordinator, Rm. 3312, MRC 312
Washington, DC 20560

2064 Guggenheim Fellowships

Amount: $28,105 (avg) **Deadline:** Oct 1
Fields/Majors: Research And Art

Grants and fellowships to support research in any field of study and to support creation/creative efforts in the arts. For advanced study or professional artistic work. Write to the address below or

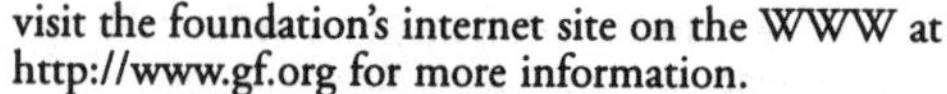

visit the foundation's internet site on the WWW at http://www.gf.org for more information.

John Simon Guggenheim Memorial Foundation
90 Park Ave.
New York, NY 10016

2065 Guggenheim Foundation Dissertation Awards & Research Grants

Amount: $15,000-$35,000 **Deadline:** Feb 1
Fields/Majors: Subspecialties Directly Related To Violence, Aggression, & Dominance

Fellowships supporting the writing (i.e., not the preliminary work) of Ph.D. dissertations and grants supporting advanced research in areas of concern to the foundation. Priority given to research that can increase understanding and amelioration of urgent problems in the modern world related to these topics. Research area must be directly related to these topics. Write for details. Dissertation applicants are asked to take particular care in deciding to apply and in organizing and completing application.

Harry Frank Guggenheim Foundation
Research Grants and Dissertation Awards
527 Madison Ave.
New York, NY 10022

2066 Guido Zerilli-Marimo Fellowships

Amount: $1,000 **Deadline:** May 31
Fields/Majors: All Areas Of Study

Fellowships are available for Italian American students enrolled at New York University. Write to the address below for details.

National Italian American Foundation
Dr. Maria Lombardo, Education Director
1860 19th Street, NW
Washington, DC 20009

2067 Guild Hall Summer Intern Program

Amount: $100 Per Week **Deadline:** None Specified
Fields/Majors: Performing Arts, Theater

Internship for college students interested in working in theater. Possible housing is available, but transportation expenses are not provided. Write to the address below for more information.

Guild Hall
Ms. Brigitte Blachere, General Manager
158 Main Street
East Hampton, NY 11937

2068 Guild School Scholarship Program

Amount: $900 **Deadline:** Aug 1
Fields/Majors: Art, Painting And Miniatures

Awards are available for students who have an enthusiasm for and involvement in miniature art. Must exhibit a serious commitment to fine miniatures as a form of art. Must be at least 14 years of age. Write to the address below for more information.

International Guild Of Miniature Artisans
88 Carrollton Ave.
Elmira, NY 14905

Gus Archie Memorial Scholarship And Section Scholarships

AMOUNT: $3,000 **DEADLINE:** Apr 30
FIELDS/MAJORS: Petroleum Engineering

Scholarships for promising students in the field of petroleum engineering. Renewable for up to four years. For undergraduate study. Write to the address below for details on the Archie Scholarship and the SPE Section Scholarships.

Society Of Petroleum Engineers
Professional Development/Sections Mgr.
P.O. Box 833836
Richardson, TX 75083

Gustafson, Inc. Scholarship

AMOUNT: $2,500 **DEADLINE:** Feb 15
FIELDS/MAJORS: Agronomy, Seed Technology

Scholarships are available for FFA members pursuing a degree in agronomy or seed technology at Colorado State, Mississippi State, or Iowa State University preference is given to those with demonstrated leadership skills and academic ability. For undergraduate study. Write to the address below for details.

National FFA Foundation
Scholarship Office
P.O. Box 15160
Alexandria, VA 22309

Gustave Adam Efroymson Memorial Endowment Fund

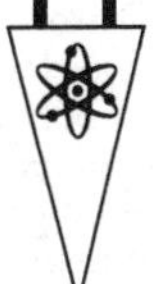

AMOUNT: Varies **DEADLINE:** Mar 1
FIELDS/MAJORS: Mathematics And Statistics

Awards are available at the University of New Mexico for graduate students who demonstrate academic ability. Write to the address below for more information.

University Of New Mexico, Albuquerque
Office Of Financial Aid
Albuquerque, NM 87131

Gustavus B. Capito Fund For Nursing Education

AMOUNT: None Specified **DEADLINE:** Mar 15
FIELDS/MAJORS: Nursing

Scholarships for West Virginia residents who will be majoring in nursing at a college in the greater Kanawha Valley (Kanawha/Putnam Counties). Financial need is considered. Write to the address below for details.

Greater Kanawha Valley Foundation
Scholarship Committee
P.O. Box 3041
Charleston, WV 25331

Guy D. And Mary Edith Halladay Scholarships

AMOUNT: $500-$2,500 **DEADLINE:** Apr 14
FIELDS/MAJORS: All Areas Of Study

Scholarships for residents of Kent County who are postgraduate students who are studying at a school in western Michigan. Based upon academic ability and demonstrated financial need. Requires a minimum GPA of at least 3.0. Write to the address below for details.

Grand Rapids Foundation
209-C Waters Bldg.
161 Ottawa Avenue, NW
Grand Rapids, MI 49503

Guy M. Wilson, William D. Brewer, Jewell W. Brewer Scholarships

AMOUNT: $500 **DEADLINE:** Feb 1
FIELDS/MAJORS: All Areas Of Study

Scholarships available for Michigan residents who will be or are attending a college or university in Michigan. Applicants must be citizens of the U.S., and children of veterans. 28 awards offered annually. Write to the address listed below for additional information.

American Legion/Auxiliary-Department Of Michigan
212 North Verlinden
Lansing, MI 48915

2075

Guyton Music Theater Scholarship

AMOUNT: $600 **DEADLINE:** None Specified
FIELDS/MAJORS: Music Theater

Award for Mesa State sophomores, juniors, or seniors majoring in music theater and who have a GPA of at least 3.0. Recipients must have tried out for and participated in two theatrical productions. Contact the theater department for more information.

Mesa State College
Office Of Financial Aid
P.O. Box 2647
Grand Junction, CO 81501

2076

Gwinn "Bub" Henry Scholarships

AMOUNT: Varies **DEADLINE:** Varies
FIELDS/MAJORS: All Areas Of Study

Scholarships are available at the University of New Mexico for full-time juniors with a GPA of at least 3.20 who are involved in community activities. Write to the address listed below for information.

University Of New Mexico, Albuquerque
Student Financial Aid Office
Mesa Vista Hall North, Room 1044
Albuquerque, NM 87131

2077

Gwynedd-Mercy Grant

AMOUNT: Varies **DEADLINE:** Mar 15, Nov 15
FIELDS/MAJORS: All Areas Of Study

Awards for students based on financial need. The recipient is required to provide ninety hours of assistance on campus for each year a grant is received. Renewable. Write to the address below for more information.

Gwynedd-Mercy College
Student Financial Aid
Sumneytown Pike
Gwynedd Valley, PA 19437

2078

Gwynedd-Mercy Scholarship

Amount: Varies **Deadline:** Mar 15, Nov 15
Fields/Majors: All Areas Of Study

Awards for students based on achievement and financial need. The recipient of this award must provide 70 service hours for each year he/she holds the scholarship. Renewable with a GPA of at least 2.5. Write to the address below for more information.

Gwynedd-Mercy College
Student Financial Aid
Sumneytown Pike
Gwynedd Valley, PA 19437

2079

H. Bowman Hawkes Scholarship

Amount: Varies **Deadline:** Feb 15
Fields/Majors: Geography

Scholarships are available at the University of Utah for full-time entering freshmen geography majors. Write to the address below for information.

University Of Utah
Dr. Roger M. Mccoy
270 Orson Spencer Hall
Salt Lake City, UT 84112

2080

H. Thomas Austern Memorial Writing Competition

Amount: $1,000-$3,000 **Deadline:** May 17
Fields/Majors: Law

Writing competition open to law students interested in the areas of law that affect foods, drugs, devices, and biologics. Submitted papers are judged by a committee of practicing attorneys with relevant expertise on a variety of factors. Write to the address below for more information.

Food And Drug Law Institute
Director Of Academic Programs
1000 Vermont Ave., NW, Suite 1200
Washington, DC 20005

2081

H.E.M. Erzurumlu Scholarship

Amount: Varies **Deadline:** Spring
Fields/Majors: Engineering, Computer Science

Awards are available to students majoring in engineering or computer science with upper division standing. Write to the address below for more information.

Portland State University
Engineering And Applied Sciences
118 Science Building 2
Portland, OR 92707

2082

H.F. Jones Scholarship

Amount: Varies **Deadline:** Mar 1
Fields/Majors: All Areas Of Study

Award for students at UMass preparing for careers in social services professions. Students must file a FAFSA as soon as possible after January 1 and before the March 1 financial aid priority consideration date. You will automatically be considered for this scholarship if you are enrolled at the university and apply for financial aid. Separate applications, requests, or inquiries are not required and cannot be honored.

University Of Massachusetts, Amherst
255 Whitmore Administration Building
Box 38230
Amherst, MA 01003

2083

H.J. Holden Medical Scholarship Fund

Amount: Varies **Deadline:** Mar 1
Fields/Majors: Medicine

Awards are available at the University of New Mexico for students accepted for attendance at UNM medical school. Based on merit and financial need. Write to the address below for more information.

University Of New Mexico, Albuquerque
Office Of Financial Aid
Albuquerque, NM 87131

2084

H.T. Ewald Foundation Scholarships

Amount: $500-$3,000 **Deadline:** Apr 1
Fields/Majors: All Areas Of Study

Scholarships available to graduating high school seniors in Detroit, Michigan (Wayne County). Applicants must submit three letters of recommendation, a complete transcript of high school grades and ACT or SAT scores, an autobiography (typed) of at least 500 words concerning future aspirations, and a small photograph. Must be in the top 50% of your graduating class. Write to the address below for details.

H.T. Ewald Foundation
15175 East Jefferson Ave.
Grosse Pointe, MI 48230

2085

Hach Scientific Foundation Scholarship

Amount: $20,000 (max) **Deadline:** Mar 1
Fields/Majors: Chemistry Or Chemical Engineering

Entering freshmen must have ranked in the upper 10% through their senior year of high school. Selection is based on scholarship, character, industry, and aspiration to make a contribution to his/her chosen discipline. Renewable with maintaining a GPA of 3.0 on a 4.0 scale. Write to the address below for information and application.

Hach Scientific Foundation
P.O. Box 389
Loveland, CO 80539

2086

Hackerman Loan

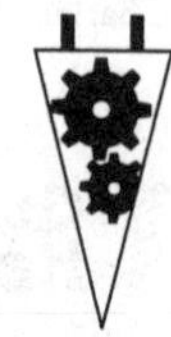

Amount: $4,000 (max) **Deadline:** Feb 1
Fields/Majors: Engineering

Interest-free loans offered to undergraduate Johns Hopkins students enrolled in the G.W.C. Whiting School of Engineering.

Students are given up to eight years to repay. Write to the address below for details.

Johns Hopkins University
3400 N. Charles Street
Baltimore, MD 21218

2087 Hagley Winterthur Fellowships In Arts And Industries

Amount: $1,000/Month **Deadline:** None Specified
Fields/Majors: History: Art, Industry, Economics

Open to all scholars who are researching in the fields above and interested in relationships between economic life and the arts. Stipends are for period of one to six months. Write to address shown below for details.

Hagley Museum And Library
P.O. Box 3630
Wilmington, DE 19807

2088 Hai Guin Scholarship

Amount: $500 **Deadline:** Dec 15
Fields/Majors: All Areas Of Study

Award for an Armenian residing and attending college in Massachusetts. Based on scholastic and financial need. Write to the address below for more information.

Hai Guin Scholarship Association
Scholarship Chairwomen
P.O. Box 509
Belmont, MA 02178

2089 Haines Memorial Scholarship

Amount: $1,750 **Deadline:** Feb 18
Fields/Majors: Education: Elementary, Secondary

Must be full-time sophomore, junior or senior in one of the public colleges or universities in South Dakota planning a career in elementary or secondary education. Applicant must have a cumulative GPA of at least 2.5. Apply through your college financial aid office.

South Dakota Board Of Regents
Scholarship Committee
207 East Capitol Avenue
Pierre, SD 57501

2090 Hal Connolly Scholar-Athlete Award

Amount: $1,000 **Deadline:**Mar 1
Fields/Majors: All Areas Of Study

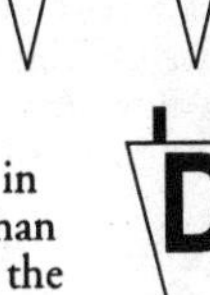

Applicant must be a California resident, competed in high school varsity athletics, be an incoming freshman under the age of 20, and have a disability. Write to the address below for details.

California Governor's Committee For Employment
Of Disabled Persons
Scholar-Athlete Awards Program
P.O. Box 826880, MIC 41
Sacramento, CA 94280

2091 Hal Reed Tunnell Scholarship In Education

Amount: $400 **Deadline:** Mar 1
Fields/Majors: Education

Award for students at Eastern New Mexico University who are pursuing a teaching career. Write to the address below for more information.

Eastern New Mexico University
College Of Education And Technology
Station 25
Portales, NM 88130

2092 Hal W. Hunt Scholarship

Amount: $1,000 **Deadline:** None Specified
Fields/Majors: Industrial Engineering

Scholarships are available at the University of Iowa for full-time undergraduates majoring in industrial engineering. Write to the address listed below for information.

University Of Iowa
Student Services, College Of Engineering
3100 Engineering Building
Iowa City, IA 52242

2093 Hall-Carper Award Fund In Nursing

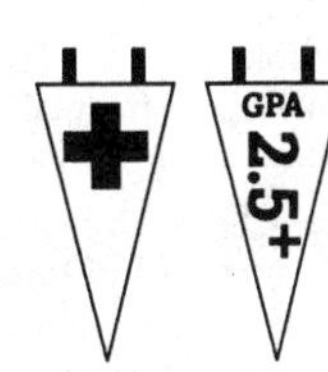

Amount: Varies **Deadline:** Mar 1
Fields/Majors: Nursing

Awards are available at the University of New Mexico for full-time nursing students with a minimum GPA of 2.6 and financial need. Must demonstrate excellence in medical-surgical nursing. Write to the address below or contact the school of nursing for more details.

University Of New Mexico, Albuquerque
Office Of Financial Aid
Albuquerque, NM 87131

2094 Hampden Academy Fund

Amount: Varies **Deadline:** None Specified
Fields/Majors: All Areas Of Study

Awards for graduating seniors from Hampden Academy in Bangor, Maine. Contact the Hampden Academy Guidance Office for more information.

Maine Community Fund
P.O. Box 148
Ellsworth, ME 04605

2095 Handicapped Student Scholarship

Amount: $1,000 **Deadline:** None Specified
Fields/Majors: All Areas Of Study

Award for full-time Mesa State students who are handicapped. Must have been a full-time student the prior academic year as well. Contact the Physical and Learning Disadvantaged TDD office for more information.

Mesa State College
Office Of Financial Aid
P.O. Box 2647
Grand Junction, CO 81501

2096 Hank Finger Ras Exes Scholarship

AMOUNT: $200-$600 **DEADLINE:** Varies
FIELDS/MAJORS: Range Animal Science

Awards for Sul Ross undergraduates who are studying range animal science, have a GPA of at least 2.0, and are NIRA eligible. Write to the address below for more information.

Sul Ross State University
Division Of Range Animal Science
Box C-110
Alpine, TX 79832

2097 Hannah Pittis Schoenbrunn Grange Scholarship

AMOUNT: $200 **DEADLINE:** Apr 1
FIELDS/MAJORS: Nursing, Agriculture

Scholarships for female students at KSU pursuing a degree in nursing or for male students studying agriculture. Contact the financial aid office for details.

Kent State University, Tuscarawas Campus
Financial Aid Office
University Dr., NE
New Philadelphia, OH 44663

2098 Hanrahan Family Award

AMOUNT: $200 **DEADLINE:** Mar 1
FIELDS/MAJORS: Accounting, Marketing

Award for a full-time undergraduate accounting or marketing major who has a GPA of at least 3.0 and has successfully completed 60 credit hours by the effective date of the award. Must demonstrate financial need. Preference is given to Phi Kappa Psi members. Write to the address below for more information.

Eastern New Mexico University
ENMU College Of Business
Station 49
Portales, NM 88130

2099 Harcourt General Insurance Companies Scholarship

AMOUNT: $1,250 **DEADLINE:** Feb 15
FIELDS/MAJORS: Agriculture

Scholarships are available for FFA members pursuing a four-year degree in any area of agriculture who reside in California, Colorado, Illinois, Indiana, Iowa, Kentucky, Michigan, Minnesota, Missouri, Nebraska, North Dakota, Ohio, Oklahoma, Pennsylvania, South Dakota, Texas or Wisconsin. Write to the address below for details.

National FFA Foundation
Scholarship Office
P.O. Box 15160
Alexandria, VA 22309

2100 Harding Academic Scholarship

AMOUNT: $500-$4,000 **DEADLINE:** None Specified
FIELDS/MAJORS: All Areas Of Study

Award for entering freshmen who scored 910 or better on the SAT or 22 or better on the ACT. Write to the address below for more information.

Harding University
Director Of Student Financial Services
Box 2282
Searcy, AR 72149

2101 Hariri Scholars Loan Program

AMOUNT: Varies **DEADLINE:** None Specified
FIELDS/MAJORS: All Areas Of Study

Interest-free loans are available to Lebanese students pursuing a graduate degree in a U.S. or Canadian school. Applicants must be Lebanese citizens with a bachelor's degree or equivalent. The foundation goal is to build the human resources of Lebanon through education. Write to the address listed below for information.

Hariri Foundation
Public Affaris Department
1020 19th Street, NW, Suite 320
Washington, DC 20036

2102 Harlien Perino Hispanic Scholarship

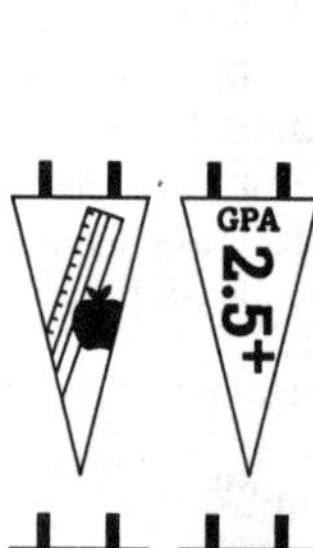

AMOUNT: Varies **DEADLINE:** None Specified
FIELDS/MAJORS: Nursing, Education

Awards for sophomore, junior, or senior nursing or education students of Hispanic origin who have a GPA of at least 2.5. Contact the Teacher Education Office or the School of Professional Studies/ Nursing Area for more details.

Mesa State College
Office Of Financial Aid
P.O. Box 3692
Grand Junction, CO 81501

2103 Harlien Perino Scholarship

AMOUNT: Varies **DEADLINE:** None Specified
FIELDS/MAJORS: Education

Awards for sophomore, junior, or senior education students who have a GPA of at least 2.5. Contact the teacher education office for more details.

Mesa State College
Office Of Financial Aid
P.O. Box 3692
Grand Junction, CO 81501

2104 Harman And Frances Deen Pugsley Scholarship Fund

AMOUNT: None Specified **DEADLINE:** None Specified
FIELDS/MAJORS: Nursing

Scholarships are open to junior and senior BSN students pursuing a degree in nursing. Write to the address below for more information.

Indiana University/Purdue University, Indianapolis
School Of Nursing
1111 Middle Drive, No. 122
Indianapolis, IN 46202

2105

Harness Tracks Of America Scholarships

Amount: $3,000 **Deadline:** May 31
Fields/Majors: All Areas Of Study

Awards for children of licensed harness racing drivers, trainers, breeders, or caretakers. Applicants may also be young people actively engaged in harness racing. For any level of study. Write to the address below for more information.

Harness Tracks Of America
4640 East Sunrise, Suite 200
Tucson, AZ 85718

2106

Harold Davis Memorial Endowment Scholarships

Amount: $1,000 **Deadline:** Feb 15
Fields/Majors: Animal Science, Agricultural Education, Agribusiness, Dairy Science

Scholarships are available for FFA members pursuing a two or four-year degree in one of the above areas. Must have a livestock background in swine, beef, dairy, or any combination of the three. Write to the address below for details.

National FFA Foundation
Scholarship Office
P.O. Box 15160
Alexandria, VA 22309

2107

Harold E. Ennes Scholarship, Ennes Broadcast Technology Scholarship

Amount: $1,000 **Deadline:** Jul 1
Fields/Majors: Broadcast Technology And Engineering

Applicant must be an undergraduate student pursuing a career in the technical aspects of broadcasting. Harold Ennes Fund requires recommendation by two members of SBE and preference is given to members of SBE. Write to the address below for details.

Society Of Broadcast Engineers
Harold E. Ennes Scholarship Committee
8445 Keystone Crossing, Suite 140
Indianapolis, IN 46240

2108

Harold E. Hardy Scholarship

Amount: Varies **Deadline:** Feb 29
Fields/Majors: Marketing

Awards for graduate students in the field of marketing with financial need. Contact the SOM Development Office, Room 206, for more information and an application.

University Of Massachusetts, Amherst
SOM Development Office, Room 206
Amherst, MA 01003

2109

Harold Lancour Scholarship For Foreign Study

Amount: Varies **Deadline:** Mar 15
Fields/Majors: Library And Information Science

Applicants must be library students who plan to study abroad. For graduate study. Write to the executive secretary at the address below for details.

Beta Phi Mu International Library Science Honor Society
Executive Secretary, Beta Phi Mu
SLIS-Florida State University
Tallahassee, FL 32306

2110

Harold P. Howdy Endowed Memorial Scholarship

Amount: Varies **Deadline:** None Specified
Fields/Majors: All Areas Of Study

Awards are available for full-time students at Cedarville College who have financial need. Must have a GPA of at least 2.0. Write to the address below for more information.

Cedarville College
Financial Aid Office
P.O. Box 601
Cedarville, OH 45314

2111

Harold R. Belknap Journalism Scholarship

Amount: $1,000 **Deadline:** Feb 15
Fields/Majors: News Communications

Scholarships are available at the University of Oklahoma, Norman for students majoring in news communications. Applicants must be sophomores, Oklahoma residents, with a GPA of at least 3.0. Write to the address listed below for information.

University Of Oklahoma, Norman
School Of Journalism And Mass Communication
860 Van Vleet Oval
Norman, OK 73019

2112

Harold Zeh/American Chemistry Society Award

Amount: $1,000 **Deadline:** None Specified
Fields/Majors: Chemistry

Awards are available at Portland State University for students who intend to pursue a career in chemistry. Academic excellence is a primary consideration. Contact the Chemistry Department at the address below for more information.

Portland State University
Chemistry Department
262 Science Building 2
Portland, OR 97207

2113

Harrell Education Fund

Amount: $1,000 (max) **Deadline:** None Specified
Fields/Majors: All Areas Of Study

Scholarships for graduates of Volunteer High School (Hawkins Co.,

TN). Must have a GPA of at least 2.0. Renewable. Based on need. Contact the Volunteer High School, The First American Bank Trust Dept. (Kingsport, TN), or the Office of Financial Aid for details.

East Tennessee State University
Office Of Financial Aid
Box 70722
Johnson City, TN 37614

2114

Harriet And Leon Pomerance Fellowship

AMOUNT: $3,000 **DEADLINE:** Nov 1
FIELDS/MAJORS: Aegean Bronze Age Archaeology

Applicants must be working on a project of a scholarly nature relating to Aegean Bronze Age archaeology. Preference will be given to candidates whose project requires travel to the mediterranean for purposes stated above. Must be U.S. or Canadian citizen. Write to the address below for details.

Archaeological Institute Of America
Boston University
656 Beacon Street, 4th Floor
Boston, MA 02215

2115

Harriet Becker Scholarship

AMOUNT: None Specified **DEADLINE:** None Specified
FIELDS/MAJORS: Nursing

Scholarships are open to BSN students who have incurred or are incuring major financial problems. Write to the address below for more information.

Indiana University/Purdue University, Indianapolis
School Of Nursing
1111 Middle Drive, No. 122
Indianapolis, IN 46202

2116

Harriet Engstrom Nelson Fund

AMOUNT: None Specified **DEADLINE:** Apr 15
FIELDS/MAJORS: All Areas Of Study

Scholarships for West Virginia residents attending Salem-Teikyo University. Preference is given to upperclassmen studying education. Based primarily on academic ability. Write to the address below for details.

Greater Kanawha Valley Foundation
Scholarship Committee
P.O. Box 3041
Charleston, WV 25331

2117

Harriet Hoffman Memorial, Teacher Training Scholarships

AMOUNT: $100-$200 **DEADLINE:** Jun 1
FIELDS/MAJORS: Education

Scholarships for Iowa residents who are pursuing a teaching career in an Iowa school. Applicant must be a U.S. citizen and a descendant of a veteran, with preference given to children of deceased or disabled veterans. Write to the address listed below for additional information or application.

American Legion Auxiliary, Department Of Iowa
720 Lyon St.
Des Moines, IA 50309

2118

Harriett Barnhart Wimmer Scholarship

AMOUNT: $1,000 **DEADLINE:** Apr 2
FIELDS/MAJORS: Landscape Architecture/Design

Applicants must be female undergraduates in their last year of studying landscape architecture or design. Write to the address listed below for additional information.

Landscape Architecture Foundation
4401 Connecticut Ave., NW, Suite 500
Washington, DC 20008

2119

Harris Foundation Scholarships

AMOUNT: None Specified
DEADLINE: None Specified
FIELDS/MAJORS: Business And Finance

Scholarships for sophomores, juniors, and seniors in the college of business at ETSU. Must be a Tennessee resident with at least a 3.0 GPA. Contact the Dean of the College of Business or the Office of Financial Aid for details.

East Tennessee State University
Office Of Financial Aid
Box 70722
Johnson City, TN 37614

2120

Harrison Schmitt Scholarships

AMOUNT: Varies **DEADLINE:** Mar 1
FIELDS/MAJORS: All Areas Of Study

Awards are available at the University of New Mexico for freshmen who graduated from a New Mexico high school and have academic ability and financial need. Write to the address below for more information.

University Of New Mexico, Albuquerque
Office Of Financial Aid
Albuquerque, NM 87131

2121

Harry A. Applegate Scholarship Award

AMOUNT: Varies **DEADLINE:** None Specified
FIELDS/MAJORS: Marketing, Merchandising, Management, Marketing Education

Scholarships for active members of deca who are furthering their education in marketing. For full-time study in a two- or four-year program. Obtain an application through the school guidance counselor, chapter advisor, state DECA advisor, or from the national DECA at the address listed below.

Distributive Education Clubs Of America, Inc.
1908 Association Drive
Reston, VA 22091

2122

Harry A. Larsh Scholarship Fund

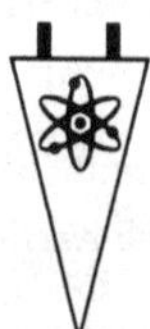

AMOUNT: $1,000 (max) **DEADLINE:** Mar 1
FIELDS/MAJORS: Geology

Scholarships are available at the University of Oklahoma, Norman for full-time geology majors, making satisfactory progress toward a degree. Write to the address listed below for information.

University Of Oklahoma, Norman
Director, School Of Geology And Geophysics
100 East Boyd Street, Room 810
Norman, OK 73019

2123

Harry And Mabel F. Leonard Award

AMOUNT: Varies **DEADLINE:** Mar 1
FIELDS/MAJORS: Computer Or Electrical Engineering

Awards are available at the University of New Mexico for undergraduates in the fields of computer or electrical engineering. Based on academic ability and financial need. Must be a resident of New Mexico. Write to the address below for more information.

University Of New Mexico, Albuquerque
Office Of Financial Aid
Albuquerque, NM 87131

2124

Harry And Mabel F. Leonard Scholarship

AMOUNT: Varies **DEADLINE:** Mar 1
FIELDS/MAJORS: Engineering

Awards are available at the University of New Mexico for freshmen planning to enroll in an engineering program. Based on scholastic ability and financial need. Must be a New Mexico resident. Write to the address below for more information.

University Of New Mexico, Albuquerque
Office Of Financial Aid
Albuquerque, NM 87131

2125

Harry And Mabel F. Leonard Scholarship Fund

AMOUNT: Varies **DEADLINE:** Mar 1
FIELDS/MAJORS: Engineering

Awards are available at the University of New Mexico for students with academic ability and financial need who are residents of New Mexico. Write to the address below for more information.

University Of New Mexico, Albuquerque
Office Of Financial Aid
Albuquerque, NM 87131

2126

Harry B. McLachlin Scholarship

AMOUNT: $500 **DEADLINE:** None Specified
FIELDS/MAJORS: Animal Science

Student must be a sophomore or junior majoring in animal science with a GPA of 2.5 or better. Must have completed at least one year of course work at Cal Poly Pomona. Write to the address below for more information.

California State Polytechnic University, Pomona
College Of Agriculture
Building 2, Room 215
Pomona, CA 91768

2127

Harry C. Bates Merit Scholarship Award

AMOUNT: $500-$2,000 **DEADLINE:** None Specified
FIELDS/MAJORS: All Areas Of Study

Open to natural or legally adopted child of current, retired, or deceased member of the Int'l Union of Bricklayers and Allied Craftsmen. Student must submit PSAT/NMSQT scores. Criteria: academics, test scores, extracurricular activities, and leadership. Renewable for up to four years of study. Write to the address below for complete details. Program is administered by the National Merit Scholarship Corporation.

International Union Of Bricklayers And Allied Craftsmen
Education Department
815 15th Street, NW
Washington, DC 20005

2128

Harry Cohen Endowed Scholarship

AMOUNT: Varies **DEADLINE:** Dec 1
FIELDS/MAJORS: All Areas Of Study

Scholarships for students at UT Austin with preference given to students from Gainesville, Texas, high schools. Write to the address below for details.

University Of Texas, Austin
Office Of Student Financial Services
P.O. Box 7758
Austin, TX 78713

2129

Harry Crebbin Memorial Scholarship

AMOUNT: $1,000 **DEADLINE:** May 1
FIELDS/MAJORS: Business And Related

Scholarships for students at the College of the Siskiyous who graduated from Siskiyou County high schools, are enrolled (or planning to enroll) at the College of the Siskiyous for full-time study, and intend to transfer to a four-year college in a business-related major. Write to the address below for details.

College Of The Siskiyous
Financial Aid Office
800 College Ave.
Weed, CA 96094

2130

Harry J. And Rhoda White Scholarship

AMOUNT: Resident Tuition **DEADLINE:** Spring
FIELDS/MAJORS: Engineering, Computer Science

Awards are available to students majoring in engineering or computer science with upper-division standing. Write to the address below for more information.

Portland State University
Engineering And Applied Sciences
118 Science Building 2
Portland, OR 92707

2131 Harry J. Brown Scholarship Fund

AMOUNT: $2,000 (max) **DEADLINE:** Mar 1
FIELDS/MAJORS: Geology, Mineralogy And Related Fields

Scholarships are available at the University of Oklahoma, Norman for full-time junior, senior, or graduate students, majoring in one of the above areas. Write to the address listed below for information.

University Of Oklahoma, Norman
Director, School Of Geology & Geophysics
100 East Boyd Street, Room 810
Norman, OK 73019

2132 Harry J. Donnelly Memorial Scholarship

AMOUNT: $300 **DEADLINE:** Jun 1
FIELDS/MAJORS: Accounting, Law

Awards for undergraduates who are initiated members of Tau Kappa Epsilon and studying in the field of accounting. Graduate students in the field of law are also eligible. Applicants must be full-time students and have a GPA of at least 3.0. Write to the address below for more information.

TKE Educational Foundation
Director Of Development
8645 Founders Road
Indianapolis, IN 46268

2133 Harry R. Horvitz Scholarship

AMOUNT: $7,500 **DEADLINE:** Mar 10
Fields/Majors: All Areas Of Study

Award for graduating high school seniors who are legal residents of any of the following counties: in Ohio; Lake, Lorain, Richland or Tuscarawas and in New York; Renesselaer. Students must demonstrate financial need. Contact address below for additional information.

HRH Family Foundation
1001 Lakeside Ave. #900
Cleveland, OH 44114

2134 Harry S. Truman Scholarship

AMOUNT: Varies **DEADLINE:** Dec 1
FIELDS/MAJORS: Public Service/Government

Must be U.S. citizen or U.S. national from American Samoa or the Commonwealth of the Northern Marina Islands. Must be enrolled in an accredited four-year institution. Must be a college junior in the upper quarter of class planning to attend graduate school and committed to a career of public or government service. Must be nominated by your department. The foundation does not accept applications directly from students. Information should be available from your school's financial aid office.

Harry S. Truman Scholarship Foundation
712 Jackson Place, NW
Washington, DC 20006

2135 Harry S. Truman Scholarship

AMOUNT: $3,000-$27,000 **DEADLINE:** Oct 29
FIELDS/MAJORS: All Areas Of Study

Scholarships are available at the University of Oklahoma, Norman for students in the upper 25% of their class. Applicants must be juniors, and award is given in the senior year. Write to the address listed below for information.

University Of Oklahoma, Norman
Honors Program
347 Cate Center Drive
Norman, OK 73019

2136 Harry S. Truman Scholarship

AMOUNT: Varies **DEADLINE:** Mar 1
FIELDS/MAJORS: Public Service

Awards are available at the University of New Mexico for students pursuing a career in public service. Selected by nominations. Contact the Department of Political Science for more information.

University Of New Mexico, Albuquerque
Office Of Financial Aid
Albuquerque, NM 87131

2137 Harry Shwachman Clinical Investigator Award

AMOUNT: $60,000 (max) **DEADLINE:** Aug 1
FIELDS/MAJORS: Medical Research-Cystic Fibrosis

This three-year award provides the opportunity for clinically-trained physicians to develop into independent biomedical research investigators who are actively involved in CF-related areas. It is also intended to facilitate the transition from postdoctoral training to a career in academic medicine. Support is available for up to $60,000 per year ($45,000 maximum for salary). Write to the address below for details.

Cystic Fibrosis Foundation
Office Of Grants Management
6931 Arlington Rd.
Bethesda, MD 20814

2138 Harry Welch Memorial Scholarship

AMOUNT: $500 **DEADLINE:** Apr 15
FIELDS/MAJORS: Soil Science

Open to students majoring in soil science. Write to the address below for more information.

California State Polytechnic University, Pomona
College Of Agriculture
Building 7, Room 110
Pomona, CA 91768

2139 Hartley B. Dean Scholarship

AMOUNT: Varies **DEADLINE:** Mar 1
FIELDS/MAJORS: All Areas Of Study

Awards are available at the University of New Mexico for

American Indian students who have financial need and satisfactory academic progress. Preference is given to students who would not be able to continue without support. Write to the address below for more information.

University Of New Mexico, Albuquerque
Office Of Financial Aid
Albuquerque, NM 87131

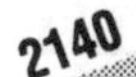

2140
Harvey A. Andruss Scholarship

Amount: $400 **Deadline:** Feb 9
Fields/Majors: Business

Award for students enrolled in the College of Business. Must show financial need, academic achievement, and participation in student activities. Use Bloomsburg University Scholarship application. Contact Mr. Gene Remoff, Dean, College of Business, for further information.

Bloomsburg University
19 Ben Franklin Hall
400 E. Second St.
Bloomsburg, PA 17815

2141
Harvey C. Jackson Memorial Scholarship

Amount: $3,000 **Deadline:** None Specified
Fields/Majors: All Areas Of Study

Awards for graduating high school seniors from Highland Park Community High School in Highland Park, Michigan. Applicants must have a GPA of at least 3.0, show evidence of satisfactory behavior and citizenship, participate in extracurricular activities, and be accepted into a college or university. Write to the address below for more information.

Mothers Club Of Highland Park
School District Of Highland Park
20 Bartlett
Highland Park, MI 48203

2142
Harvey Fellows Program

Amount: $12,000 **Deadline:** Nov 30
Fields/Majors: See Fields Listed Below

Awards for graduate students in certain disciplines at top schools, whose career goals include leadership positions in fields where Christians have little influence. Fields of study include: high-tech research, science, news media, international economics or finance, business, journalism, visual and performing arts, telecommunications, gov't, public policy, teaching and law. Write to the address below or e-mail to harvey@cccu.org for more information. Applications available through Nov 15.

Harvey Fellows Program
329 Eighth St. Ne
Washington, DC 20002

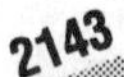

2143
Harvey L. Friedman Scholarship

Amount: Varies **Deadline:** Mar 1
Fields/Majors: Labor Relations

Awards for sophomores, juniors, or seniors studying labor relations. Contact the head, Labor Relations Department for more information.

University Of Massachusetts, Amherst
Head, Labor Relations Department
Amherst, MA 01003

2144
Harwood Memorial Real Estate Scholarships

Amount: $500 **Deadline:** Dec 4
Fields/Majors: Real Estate And Related

Ten scholarships awarded to full-time undergraduate and graduate students who plan to pursue a career in real estate. Must have completed two semesters of college coursework and have an overall GPA of at least 3.2. Contact your school's real estate department, or write to the address below.

Real Estate Educators Association
Scholarship Coordinator
11 S. Lasalle, Suite 1400
Chicago, IL 60603

2145
Haskell Awards

Amount: $1,000 (min) **Deadline:** Nov 1
Fields/Majors: Architectural Writing

Awards given for fine writing on architectural subjects at an advanced level of study. Applicants may only submit unpublished works for consideration. Write to the address below for details.

American Institute Of Architects, New York Chapter
Arnold W. Brunner Grant
200 Lexington Avenue
New York, NY 10016

2146
Hatterschiedt Foundation, Inc. Educational Scholarships

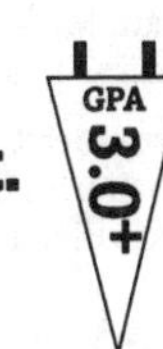

Amount: $1,000 **Deadline:** Feb 15
Fields/Majors: All Areas Of Study

Scholarships for incoming freshmen at Black Hills State University who are South Dakota residents, have a GPA of 3.0 or better and demonstrate financial need. Write to the address below for more information.

Black Hills State University
Office Of Financial Aid
University Station, Box 9509
Spearfish, SD 57799

2147
Hattie M. Strong Foundation Student Loans

Amount: $2,500 (max) **Deadline:** Mar 31
Fields/Majors: All Areas Of Study

Interest free loans for students entering their final year of study at an accredited four-year college or graduate school. Must be a U.S. citizen or permanent resident. Applications are mailed out only Jan 1 to Mar 31. Write to the address below for details.

Hattie M. Strong Foundation
1620 Eye Street, NW, Suite 700
Washington, DC 20006

2148

Hatton Lovejoy Scholarship

Amount: $13,200 (max) **Deadline:** None Specified
Fields/Majors: All Areas Of Study

Applicants must be residents of Troup County, Georgia, for a minimum of two years and high school seniors, in the upper 25% of class, or recent graduates. Seniors may get further information from their high schools. Write to address below for details.

Fuller E. Callaway Foundation
Attn: Hatton Lovejoy Scholarship
P.O. Box 790
La Grange, GA 30241

2149

Hatton W. Sumners Scholarship

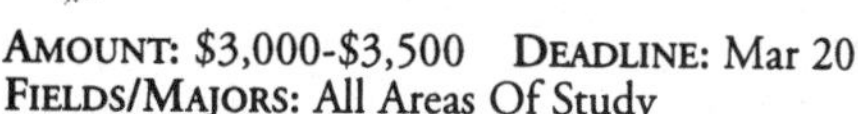

Amount: $3,000-$3,500 **Deadline:** Mar 20
Fields/Majors: All Areas Of Study

Scholarships for juniors or seniors with a minimum GPA of 3.0 who demonstrate talent for leadership and service. Must be a U.S. citizen. Write to the address below for more information.

Schreiner College
Financial Aid Office
Kerrville, TX 78028

2150

Hatton W. Sumners Sophomore Grant

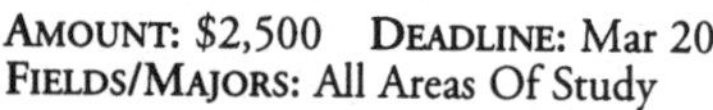

Amount: $2,500 **Deadline:** Mar 20
Fields/Majors: All Areas Of Study

Grant for sophomores with a minimum GPA of 3.0 who demonstrate leadership quality. Must be a U.S. citizen. Write to the address below for more information.

Schreiner College
Financial Aid Office
Kerrville, TX 78028

2151

Hawaii Island Chamber Of Commerce Scholarship

Amount: Tuition **Deadline:** Feb 1
Fields/Majors: Business, Economics

Scholarships are available at the University of Hawaii, Hilo, for full-time sophomores and juniors with a declared major in either business or economics. Write to the address listed below for information.

University Of Hawaii At Hilo
Financial Aid Office
200 West Kawili Street
Hilo, HI 96720

2152

Hawk Mountain Internship Program

Amount: $375 Per Month
Deadline: Jan 15, Jun 15
Fields/Majors: Ornithology, Environmental Studies, Natural History

Internship for students who have completed at least two years of college coursework in the fields listed above and exhibit a willingness and ability to relate to the public. Award also includes housing and travel allowance. Write to the address below for more information.

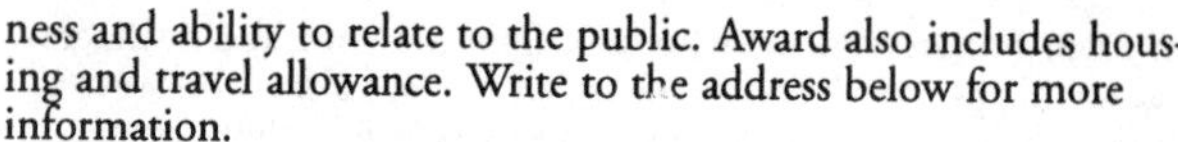

Hawk Mountain Sanctuary
Ms. Annette Edwards, Intern Coordinator
Howk Mountain Sanctuary, Rd 2, Box 191
Kempton, PA 19529

2153

Hawkeye Steel Products, Inc. Scholarship

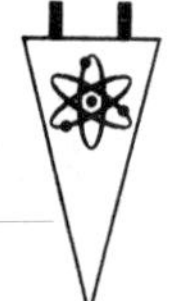

Amount: $1,000 **Deadline:** Feb 15
Fields/Majors: Animal Science, Agribusiness

Scholarships are available for FFA members pursuing a degree in agribusiness or animal science. Applicant must be a resident of Iowa, attending Iowa State University. Write to the address below for details.

National FFA Foundation
Scholarship Office
P.O. Box 15160
Alexandria, VA 22309

2154

Hayek Fund For Scholars

Amount: $1,000 **Deadline:** Any Time
Fields/Majors: All Areas Of Study

Fund to help offset expenses for participating in professional meetings. For graduate students and untenured faculty members. Write to attn: Hayek Scholars Program at the address below for details.

Institute For Humane Studies At George Mason University
Hayek Fund For Scholars
4084 University Drive, Suite 101
Fairfax, VA 22030

2155

Hays Art Scholarship

Amount: None Specified **Deadline:** None Specified
Fields/Majors: Art

Scholarships available at ETSU for art majors from east Tennessee, southwest Virginia, and western North Carolina. Financial need and academic excellence considered. Contact the office of financial aid at the address below.

East Tennessee State University
Office Of Financial Aid
Box 70722
Johnson City, TN 37614

2156

Hazel Corbin Assistance Fund Grants

Amount: Varies **Deadline:** Varies
Fields/Majors: Nurse-Midwifery

Grants are available to registered nurses who are seeking nurse-midwifery certification and have been accepted into a nurse-midwifery program in the United States. Write to address below for details.

Maternity Center Association Foundation
Hazel Corbin Assistance Fund
48 E. 92nd Street
New York, NY 10128

2157 Hazel Hemphill Memorial Scholarship

AMOUNT: $500 **DEADLINE:** Apr 1
FIELDS/MAJORS: All Areas Of Study

Scholarship for Rocky Mountain Farmers Union regular or associate members who plan on attending any college or vocational school conforming to GI bill qualifications. One award given out per year. Write to the address listed below for further information or an application.

Rocky Mountain Farmers Union/Morgan County Farmers Union
10800 E. Bethany Drive, 4th Floor
Aurora, CO 80014

2158 Hazel M. Kuehn Graduate Fellowship

AMOUNT: $1,000 **DEADLINE:** Feb 1
FIELDS/MAJORS: Home Economics

Student must be a home economics major (in business or education) who have been or will be admitted for graduate study. Must have a GPA of 3.0 or better and be a member of CHEA. Write to California Home Economics Association, 3040 Dwight Way, Stockton, CA 95204 for more information.

California State Polytechnic University, Pomona
College Of Agriculture
Building 7, Room 110
Pomona, CA 91768

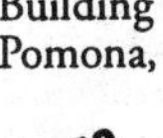

2159 Hazelle Lockhard Rhoads Scholarship

AMOUNT: Varies
DEADLINE: None Specified
FIELDS/MAJORS: Business Admin., Law, Dentistry, Medicine, Religion, Music, Math

Scholarships are available at the University of Iowa to undergraduate students majoring in one of the above fields. Five awards are offered on a rotating basis. Award requires departmental nomination. Check with your academic department for information.

University Of Iowa
Office Of Student Financial Aid
208 Calvin Hall
Iowa City, IA 52242

2160 Hazen H. Bedke Meritorious Award, Shih-Kung Kao Memorial Award

AMOUNT: $100-$500 **DEADLINE:** Feb 1
FIELDS/MAJORS: Meteorology

Scholarships are available at the University of Utah for full-time undergraduate meteorology majors. Based on GPA. Four awards are offered annually. Write to the address below for details.

University Of Utah
J.E. Geisler
819 William C. Browning Building
Salt Lake City, UT 84112

2161 Hazleton General Clinical Careers Scholarships

AMOUNT: $3,224 **DEADLINE:** Feb 9
FIELDS/MAJORS: Nursing

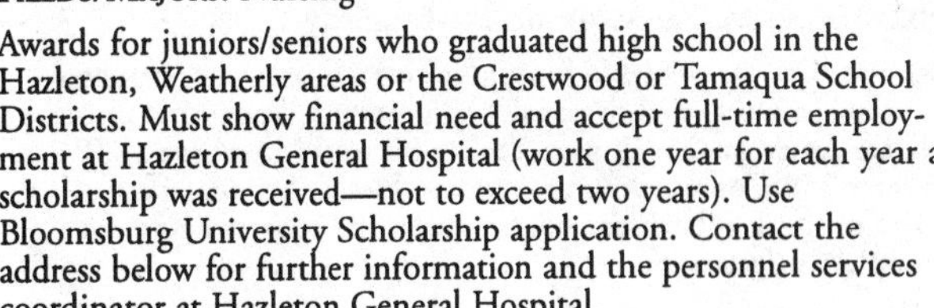

Awards for juniors/seniors who graduated high school in the Hazleton, Weatherly areas or the Crestwood or Tamaqua School Districts. Must show financial need and accept full-time employment at Hazleton General Hospital (work one year for each year a scholarship was received—not to exceed two years). Use Bloomsburg University Scholarship application. Contact the address below for further information and the personnel services coordinator at Hazleton General Hospital.

Bloomsburg University
19 Ben Franklin Hall
400 E. Second St.
Bloomsburg, PA 17815

2162 Heafey Grant

AMOUNT: Varies **DEADLINE:** Mar 2
FIELDS/MAJORS: Most Areas Of Study

Grants for full-time students. Based on financial need and academic achievement. Write to the address below for more information.

Holy Names College
Financial Aid Office
3500 Mountain Blvd.
Oakland, CA 94619

2163 Health Professional Scholarship

AMOUNT: Varies **DEADLINE:** None Specified
FIELDS/MAJORS: Health

Scholarships for Washington state residents who are studying a health profession. Recipients must agree to provide primary care in a state-defined shortage area for a period not less than three years or repay the scholarship with penalty. The scholarships are renewable for up to five years while the student is enrolled in an eligible health profession training program. Applications are available the January prior to the academic year for which the applicant wishes to be considered. Write to the address below for details.

Washington Higher Education Coordinating Board
917 Lakeridge Way
P.O. Box 43430
Olympia, WA 98504

2164 Health Professionals Loan Repayment Program

AMOUNT: Varies **DEADLINE:** None Specified
FIELDS/MAJORS: See Below

Loans for students who are studying the following areas of health: osteopathic and allopathic physician and physician assistants, advanced practice nursing, allied health care providers, podiatrists, optometrists, and dentists. Applicants must be New Mexico residents. For postgraduate level study in New Mexico. Write to the address below for more information. Past student loans will be repaid if he/she agrees to work in shortage areas in New Mexico.

New Mexico Commission On Higher Education
1068 Cerrillos Rd.
Santa Fe, NM 87501

2165
Health Professions Pregraduate Scholarship Program

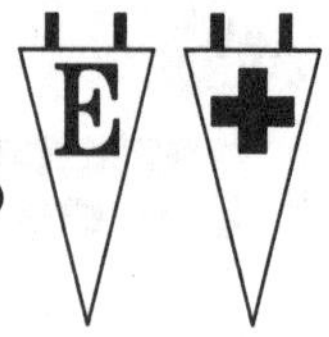

AMOUNT: Varies **DEADLINE:** None Specified
FIELDS/MAJORS: Pre-Medicine, Pre-Dentistry

Scholarships are available for junior and senior undergraduates enrolled in a pre-med or pre-dental program. Applicants must be Native American Indians or Alaskan natives. Must have a GPA of at least 2.0. Contact your area Indian Health Service office or write to the scholarships coordinator at the address below for complete information.

Indian Health Services, U.S. Department Of Health And Human Services
Twinbrook Metro Plaza-Suite 100
12300 Twinbrook Parkway
Rockville, MD 20852

2166
Health Professions Preparatory Scholarship Program

AMOUNT: Varies **DEADLINE:** None Specified
FIELDS/MAJORS: See Listing Of Fields Below

Scholarships are available for freshman and sophomore undergraduates enrolled in a pre-nursing, pre-medical technology, pre-pharmacy, pre-dietetics, pre-social work, or pre-physical therapy program. Applicants must be Native American Indians or Alaskan Natives and have a GPA of at least 2.0. Contact your area Indian Health Service office or write to the scholarships coordinator at the address below for complete information.

Indian Health Services, U.S. Department Of Health And Human Services
Twinbrook Metro Plaza-Suite 100
12300 Twinbrook Parkway
Rockville, MD 20852

2167
Health Professions Scholarship Program

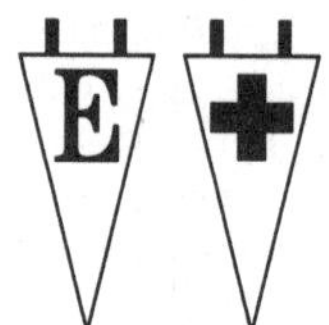

AMOUNT: Varies **DEADLINE:** None Specified
FIELDS/MAJORS: Healthcare And Related

Scholarships are available for junior, senior, and graduate American Indian and Alaskan Native students pursuing a degree in a health related field. For this program, there are payback and service obligation requirements. Must have a GPA of at least 2.0. Contact your area Indian Health Service office or write to the scholarships coordinator at the address below for complete information.

Indian Health Services, U.S. Department Of Health And Human Services
Twinbrook Metro Plaza-Suite 100
12300 Twinbrook Parkway
Rockville, MD 20852

2168
Health Sciences Scholarship Program

AMOUNT: $10,000 (appx.) **DEADLINE:** Nov 3
FIELDS/MAJORS: Allopathic, Osteopathic, Or Family Medicine; Nursing; Physician Asst.

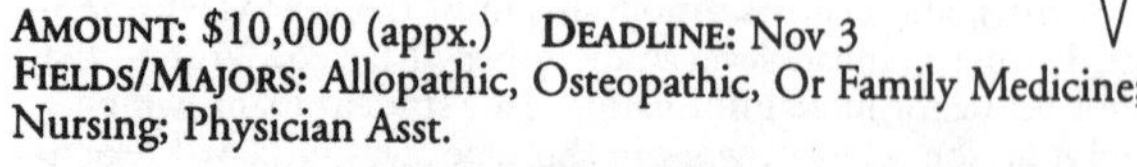

Awards are available for fourth-year medical students in the areas above or students in the final year of a primary care education program for nurse practitioners, physician assistants, or nurse-midwives. Must have an interest in primary care in West Virginia. Recipients are obligated to sign a contract to practice in an underserved rural area for two years upon graduation. Write to the address below for more information. Applicants must attend Marshall University, West Virginia Univ., or Alderson-Broaddus College.

University System Of West Virginia
1018 Kanawha Blvd. E., Suite 901
Charleston, WV 25301

2169
Health Services Dissertation Research

AMOUNT: Varies **DEADLINE:** Varies
FIELDS/MAJORS: Health Care Services Related Areas

Doctoral dissertation grants for research on any aspect of health care services (organization, delivery, financing, quality, etc.). Call (800) 358-9295 (or write to the address below) for details.

Agency For Health Care Policy And Research
Publications Clearinghouse/Dissertations
Silver Spring, MD 20907

2170
Health, Phys. Ed. And Recreation Endowed And Private Scholarships

AMOUNT: Varies **DEADLINE:** Feb 15
FIELDS/MAJORS: Health, Physical Education, Recreation

Scholarships are available at Evangel for full-time students who will be or are pursuing a degree in the above fields. Applicants must have a GPA of at least 3.0. Includes the Holsinger Athletic Academic Excellence Scholarship, the Stair Family Athletic Scholarship, and the HPER Alumni Scholarship. Write to the address listed below for information.

Evangel College
Office Of Enrollment
1111 N. Glenstone
Springfield, MO 65802

2171
Hearst Minority Fellowship

AMOUNT: $15,000 **DEADLINE:** Apr 1
FIELDS/MAJORS: Philanthropic Research

Fellowship for minority students admitted to a master's level program in philanthropic studies at Indiana University. Nonrenewable. Write to the address below for more information.

Indiana University Center On Philanthropy
550 West North Street, Suite 301
Indianapolis, IN 46202

2172
Heartland Employee Trust Fund Scholarship

AMOUNT: None Specified **DEADLINE:** Jul 1
FIELDS/MAJORS: All Areas Of Study

Scholarships for children of employees of the Heartland Health System (in northwest Missouri). Write to the address below for details.

Heartland Health Foundation
801 Faraon St.
St. Joseph, MO 64501

2173

Heavenly Cause Foundation Loan Fund

AMOUNT: $1,500 (max) **DEADLINE:** None Specified
FIELDS/MAJORS: All Areas Of Study

Loans for Irish students at Mercyhurst College. Interest rates are available at 5% and loans must be repaid within six years of graduation. Write to the address below for more information.

Mercyhurst College
Financial Aid Office
Glenwood Hills
Erie, PA 16546

2174

Heed Ophthalmic Foundation Fellowships

AMOUNT: $4,800 (max) **DEADLINE:** Jan 15
FIELDS/MAJORS: Ophthalmology

Fellowship to provide assistance to persons who wish to further their education or conduct research or investigation in ophthalmology. Must be a U.S. citizen and a graduate of an accredited medical school. Write to the address below for details.

Cleveland Clinic Foundation/Heed Ophthamalic Fellowships
F.A. Gutman, M.D.
9500 Euclid Ave., Desk A-31
Cleveland, OH 44195

2175

Helen Esterly Memorial Scholarships

AMOUNT: Varies **DEADLINE:** Mar 1
FIELDS/MAJORS: Secondary Education

Awards are available at the University of New Mexico for students enrolled in a secondary education program in the College of Education. Applicants must have completed sixty hours of course work with a GPA of 3.0 or better. Preference is given to those whose teaching field is social studies. Write to the address below for more information.

University Of New Mexico, Albuquerque
Office Of Financial Aid
Albuquerque, NM 87131

2176

Helen Faison Scholarships

AMOUNT: Varies **DEADLINE:** None Specified
FIELDS/MAJORS: All Areas Of Study

Full tuition and fees scholarship for African American students who show outstanding academic potential. Applicants must be undergraduate full-time students who maintain at least a 3.0 GPA. Renewable. Write to the address below for details.

University Of Pittsburgh
Office Of Admissions And Financial Aid
Bruce Hall, Second Floor
Pittsburgh, PA 15260

2177

Helen Harms Anderson Scholarships

AMOUNT: $250 **DEADLINE:** None Specified
FIELDS/MAJORS: All Areas Of Study

Awards for undergraduate women at UW Platteville who demonstrate financial need. Write to the address below or contact the office at (608) 342-1125 for more information.

University Of Wisconsin, Platteville
Office Of Admissions & Enrollment Mgt.
Platteville, WI 53818

2178

Helen Johnson Scholarship

AMOUNT: $1,000 **DEADLINE:** Feb 15
FIELDS/MAJORS: Radio Or Television News Broadcasting

Scholarship for those who intend to work in news journalism. This is open to juniors, seniors, and graduate students who are residents of, or students in, Los Angeles, Ventura, or Orange counties. Based on achievement and potential in broadcasting. Write to the address below for details.

Society Of Professional Journalists, Los Angeles
Professional Chapter
SPJ Scholarship Chairman
P.O. Box 4200
Woodland Hills, CA 91365

2179

Helen Kray Scholarship

AMOUNT: $1,000 **DEADLINE:**None Specified
FIELDS/MAJORS: Music

Award for Mesa State sophomores, juniors, or seniors in the music program. Must have a GPA of at least 2.5 and demonstrate financial need. Contact the music department at Mesa State for more information.

Mesa State College
Office Of Financial Aid
P.O. Box 2647
Grand Junction, CO 81501

2180

Helen L. Henderson Scholarship Fund

AMOUNT: $8,000 (max) **DEADLINE:** Apr 1
FIELDS/MAJORS: All Areas Of Study

Open to all Benton County residents and to all Benton Central graduates regardless of county of residence. Write to the address below for more information.

Fowler State Bank Trustee
Trust Department
P.O. Box 511
Fowler, IN 47944

2181

Helen M. Malloch And NFPW Junior/Senior Scholarships

AMOUNT: $500-$1,000 **DEADLINE:** May 1
FIELDS/MAJORS: Journalism

Scholarships for undergraduate women junior/senior or graduate student majoring in journalism at an accredited institution. Applicants do not have to be NFPW members. Write for complete details.

National Federation Of Press Women
Box 99
Blue Springs, MO 64013

2182

Helen Mitchell Scholarship

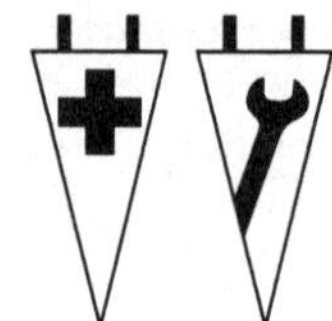

AMOUNT: Varies **DEADLINE:** None Specified
FIELDS/MAJORS: Nutrition

Awards for UMass students studying nutrition based on academic performance, financial need, and professional plans. For entering sophomore, junior, or senior students. Contact the Head, Department of Nutrition, for more information.

University Of Massachusetts, Amherst
Department Head, Nutrition Department
Amherst, MA 01003

2183

Helen S. Pearce Art Award

AMOUNT: Varies **DEADLINE:** Feb 1
FIELDS/MAJORS: Art-Painting

Scholarships are available at the University of New Mexico for full-time undergraduate art students, with a concentration in painting, who have at least 24 hours of coursework in studio activity, and a GPA of at least 3.5. Write to the address listed below for information.

University Of New Mexico, Albuquerque
College Of Fine Arts
Office Of The Dean
Albuquerque, NM 87131

2184

Helen Verba Award

AMOUNT: $500 **DEADLINE:** Apr 6
FIELDS/MAJORS: Print Journalism

Awards for sophomore or junior undergraduates studying print journalism at any state college or university. Write to the address below for more details.

Society Of Professional Journalists
Rose Beetem & Bob Boczkiewicz, Co-Chairs
3225 W. 29th Ave.
Denver, CO 80211

2185

Helena Chemical Company Scholarship

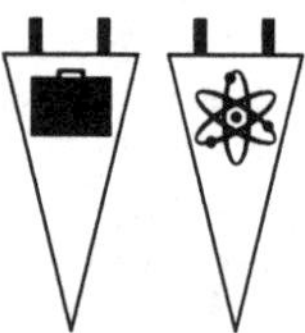

AMOUNT: $1,000 **DEADLINE:** Feb 15
FIELDS/MAJORS: Agricultural Economics, Agribusiness

Scholarships are available for FFA members pursuing a degree in agribusiness or agricultural economics. Not applicable for students from Alaska, Hawaii, or Rhode Island. Must be a graduating high school senior to apply. Write to the address below for details.

National FFA Foundation
Scholarship Office
P.O. Box 15160
Alexandria, VA 22309

2186

Helene Overly Scholarship

AMOUNT: $3,000 **DEADLINE:** Feb 27
FIELDS/MAJORS: Transportation Related

Scholarship for a graduate student who has shown a commitment to the transportation field through her activities and studies. Must be female, have a GPA of at least 3.0, and study/have career goals in transportation-related areas. Write to Ms. Karen M. George at the address below for more details.

Women's Transportation Seminar
c/o Barton-Aschman Associates, Inc.
820 Davis St., Suite 300
Evanston, IL 60201

2187

Helene Robertson Nursing Scholarships

AMOUNT: $700 **DEADLINE:** Feb 9
FIELDS/MAJORS: Nursing

Awards for full-time junior and senior nursing students. Must have a minimum GPA of 3.0 and demonstrate financial need. Use Bloomsburg University Scholarship application. Contact Dr. Christine Alichnie, Chairperson, Department of Nursing, for further information.

Bloomsburg University
19 Ben Franklin Hall
400 E. Second St.
Bloomsburg, PA 17815

2188

Helene W. Simson Memorial Opera Scholarships

AMOUNT: Varies **DEADLINE:** Mar 1
FIELDS/MAJORS: Fine Arts

Awards are available at the University of New Mexico for fine arts majors. Write to the address below or contact the fine arts department for more information.

University Of New Mexico, Albuquerque
Office Of Financial Aid
Albuquerque, NM 87131

2189

Helene Wurlitzer Foundation Of New Mexico

AMOUNT: Rent & Utilities **DEADLINE:** None Specified
FIELDS/MAJORS: Media Or Related Fields

Awards are for individuals involved in the creative, not interpretive, fields in all media. The residences are individual, furnished combined studio-residences located in Taos, New Mexico, which is offered rent-free and utilities-free for these individuals. Must submit examples of their work, references, outline of project, and requested time and length of stay. Write to the address below for more information.

Helene Wurlitzer Foundation Of New Mexico
P.O. Box 545
Taos, NM 87571

2190

Helping-Hand Endowed Fund

AMOUNT: Varies **DEADLINE:** None Specified
FIELDS/MAJORS: All Areas Of Study

Awards are available for students at Cedarville College who have financial need. Must have a GPA of at least 2.0. Write to the address below for more information.

Cedarville College
Financial Aid Office
P.O. Box 601
Cedarville, OH 45314

2191 Hemingway Days Young Writers' Scholarship

Amount: $1,000 **Deadline:** May 1
Fields/Majors: Creative Writing, Poetry

Scholarships are available for high school juniors and seniors who exhibit special talent in the craft of writing. Applicants must submit three copies of up to six pages of original fiction, non-fiction, or poetry. Write to the address listed below for information.

Hemingway Days Festival
Hemingway Days Young Writers Scholarship
P.O. Box 4045
Key West, FL 33041

2192 Henry A. Murray Dissertation Award Program

Amount: $2,500 (max) **Deadline:** Apr 1
Fields/Majors: Social And Behavioral Sciences

Three grants supporting doctoral candidates performing research in the social or behavioral sciences studying individuals in context, in-depth, and across time. Write to the address below for details.

Radcliffe College
The Henry A. Murray Research Center
10 Garden Street
Cambridge, MA 02138

2193 Henry And Chiyo Kuwahara Creative Arts Scholarship

Amount: Varies **Deadline:** Apr 1
Fields/Majors: Creative Arts

Open to students of Japanese ancestry to encourage creative projects, especially those that reflect Japanese American culture and experience. Professional artists should not apply. Applications and information may be obtained from local JACL chapters, district offices, and the national headquarters at the address below. Please indicate your level of study and be certain to include a legal-sized SASE.

Japanese American Citizens League
National Scholarship And Award Program
1765 Sutter St.
San Francisco, CA 94115

2194 Henry B. Tippie University Of Iowa Accounting Scholarships

Amount: $1,500 **Deadline:** Mar 1
Fields/Majors: Accounting

Scholarships are available at the University of Iowa for full-time juniors majoring in accounting. Write to the address listed below for information.

University Of Iowa
College Of Business Admin., Suite W160
108 Pappajohn Business Admin. Bldg.
Iowa City, IA 52245

2195 Henry Belin Du Pont Fellowship

Amount: $1,500/Month **Deadline:** Varies
Fields/Majors: History: Art, Industry, Economics, Museum Studies

Open to postdoctoral scholars who are researching in the areas of study listed above. Stipends are for period of two to six months. Preference is given to students from out of state institutions. Write to address shown below for details.

Hagley Museum And Library
P.O. Box 3630
Wilmington, DE 19807

2196 Henry G. Halladay Awards

Amount: Varies **Deadline:** Aug 31
Fields/Majors: Medicine

Five supplemental scholarships are presented annually to African American men enrolled in the first year of medical school who have overcome significant obstacles to obtain a medical education. Must be a U.S. citizen. Write to "Special Programs" at the address below for details.

National Medical Fellowships, Inc.
110 West 32nd Street, 8th Floor
New York, NY 10001

2197 Henry Hoyns Fellowship

Amount: Varies **Deadline:** Feb 1
Fields/Majors: Creative Writing

Open to anyone who is accepted into the master's of fine arts in creative writing program at the University of Virginia. An original 30-40 page fiction manuscript or ten pages of poetry will be required. There are three fiction and three poetry fellowships awarded each year. Write to the address below for complete details.

University Of Virginia, Department Of English
Creative Writing Office
219 Bryan Hall
Charlottesville, VA 22903

2198 Henry J. Reilly Memorial Scholarship

Amount: $500 **Deadline:** Apr 15
Fields/Majors: All Areas Of Study

Scholarships for children (or grandchildren) of members or associate members of the Reserve Officers Association. Must be accepted for full-time study at a four-year college or university and have a high school GPA of at least 3.3, an SAT score of 1250, or a combined ACT score of 26. Awards are also available for undergraduates and graduate students with a college GPA of at least 3.0. Write to the address below for details. Children, under the age of 26, of deceased members (active and paid up in the roa or roal at the time of their death) are also eligible. When requesting information, please specify your year in school.

Reserve Officers Association Of The United States
Henry J. Reilly Scholarship Program
One Constitution Avenue, NE
Washington, DC 20002

2199

Henry J. Reilly Memorial Scholarship

AMOUNT: $500 **DEADLINE:** None Specified
FIELDS/MAJORS: All Areas Of Study

Scholarships for active or associate members or children (or grandchildren) of active or associate members of the Reserve Officers Association. Must be enrolled in full-time study at a four-year college or university and have a college GPA of at least 3.0. Also based on character and leadership. (first-year students should show a high school GPA of at least 3.3. Write to the address below for details. Children, under the age of 21, of deceased members (active and paid up in the ROA or ROAL at the time of their death) are also eligible. When requesting information, please specify your year in school.

Reserve Officers Association
Henry J. Reilly Scholarship Program
One Constitution Avenue, NE
Washington, DC 20002

2200

Henry J. Reilly Memorial Scholarship

AMOUNT: $500 **DEADLINE:** None Specified
FIELDS/MAJORS: All Areas Of Study

Scholarships for active or associate members of the Reserve Officers Association. Must be accepted for graduate study at a regionally accredited us college or university. Must provide evidence of a GPA of at least 3.3. Also based on character and leadership. Write to the address below for details. When requesting information, please specify your year in school.

Reserve Officers Association
Henry J. Reilly Scholarship Program
One Constitution Avenue, NE
Washington, DC 20002

2201

Henry King Stanford; Jay F.W. Pearson; And Alumni Scholarships

AMOUNT: Varies **DEADLINE:** None Specified
FIELDS/MAJORS: All Areas Of Study

Scholarships for freshmen and transfer students with excellent academic credentials. Renewable. Write to the address below for more information.

University Of Miami
Office Of Financial Assistance Services
P.O. Box 248187
Coral Gables, FL 33124

2202

Henry Luce Foundation/ACLS Fellowship For Scholarship In American Art

AMOUNT: $15,000 **DEADLINE:** Nov 15
FIELDS/MAJORS: American Art

Fellowships for dissertation research in visual art in America. Must be a U.S. citizen or permanent resident. Fellowships are for a one-year nonrenewable term beginning in the summer. Write to the address below for details.

American Council Of Learned Societies
Office Of Fellowships And Grants
228 E. 45th St.
New York, NY 10017

2203

Herbert Hoover Presidential Fellowships And Grants

AMOUNT: $1,200 (max) **DEADLINE:** Mar 1
FIELDS/MAJORS: American History, Political Science, Public Policy

Scholarships are awarded to current graduate students, postdoctoral scholars, qualified nonacademic researchers. Write to the address below for details.

Hoover Presidential Library Association
P.O. Box 696
West Branch, IA 52358

2204

Herbert Kinney Scholarships

AMOUNT: $200 **DEADLINE:** Feb 15
FIELDS/MAJORS: Agriculture, Natural Resources

Awards for UW Platteville students who are agriculture or natural resources majors with a GPA of at least 2.5. Must show economic need and willingness to spend time working in rural Wisconsin after graduation. Write to the address below for more information.

University Of Wisconsin, Platteville
Office Of Admissions & Enrollment Mgt.
Platteville, WI 53818

2205

Herbert Lehman Education Fund Scholarships

AMOUNT: Varies **DEADLINE:** Apr 15
FIELDS/MAJORS: All Areas Of Study

Scholarships for African American high school seniors who will be entering a college in the South or a college which has a student population in which African Americans are substantially underrepresented. Based on financial need and academics. 50-100 awards per year. Renewable. All requests for application forms must be in writing and requested by the applicant. Write to the address below for details.

Herbert Lehman Education Fund
99 Hudson St., Suite 1600
New York, NY 10013

2206

Herbert P. Feibelman Jr (PS)

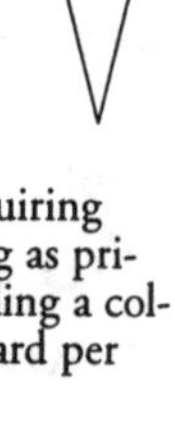

AMOUNT: $250-$1,000 **DEADLINE:** Apr 15
FIELDS/MAJORS: All Areas Of Study

Applicants must be born deaf or became deaf before acquiring language. Must use speech/residual hearing or lip-reading as primary communication and be students entering or attending a college or university program for hearing students. One award per year. Write the address below for complete information.

Alexander Graham Bell Association For The Deaf
3417 Volta Place, NW
Washington, DC 20007

2207

Hercules, Inc. Scholarship

AMOUNT: Varies **DEADLINE:** Mar 1
FIELDS/MAJORS: All Areas Of Study

Awards are available at the University of New Mexico for minority students. Write to the address below for more information.

University Of New Mexico, Albuquerque
Office Of Financial Aid
Albuquerque, NM 87131

2208
Heritage Scholarship

AMOUNT: Half Tuition **DEADLINE:** Jan 1
FIELDS/MAJORS: All Areas Of Study

Applicant must show outstanding academic performance and potential. Must apply for both admission and scholarship; must meet the criteria for honors program; must have interview or attend campus visitation program. Renewable for four years. For entering freshman only. Write to the address below for details.

Denison University
Financial Aid Office
Box M
Granville, OH 43023

2209
Heritage Scholarships

AMOUNT: Varies **DEADLINE:** Mar 1, Apr 1
FIELDS/MAJORS: All Areas Of Study

Award given to minority students in recognition of outstanding achievement in academics and extracurricular activities. Recipients must maintain a GPA of 2.5 or better. Write to the address below for more information.

Salem College
Financial Aid Office
P.O. Box 10548
Winston-Salem, NC 27108

2210
Herman Bernikol Scholarship Fund

AMOUNT: Varies **DEADLINE:** None Specified
FIELDS/MAJORS: All Areas Of Study

Scholarships are available at ASU for full-time American-Indian students. Based on academic ability. Write to the address listed below for information.

Arizona State University
Indian Education Department
Tempe, AZ 85281

2211
Herman H. Holloway, Sr. Memorial Scholarship

AMOUNT: Tuition And Fees **DEADLINE:** Mar 15
FIELDS/MAJORS: All Areas Of Study

Scholarship for high school seniors who rank have a GPA of at least 3.25, has an 850 or better on the SAT or 20 or better on the ACT, and enrolls full-time at a Delaware state university. Write to the address below for more information.

Delaware Higher Education Commission
Carvel State Office Building
820 North French St.
Wilmington, DE 19801

2212
Herman Kahn Resident Fellowships

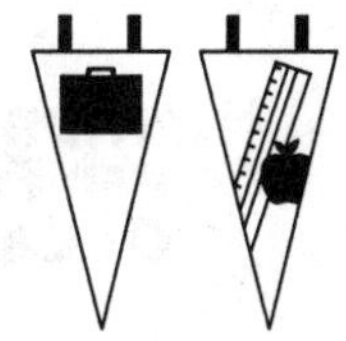

AMOUNT: $18,000 **DEADLINE:** Apr 1
FIELDS/MAJORS: Political Science, Economics, International Relations, Education

Residential fellowships for candidates who have completed all requirements for Ph.D. except dissertation. Fellows are expected to spend 50% of their time on projects the institute assigns in their general area. Areas of fellowship are in education, domestic political economy, international political econ., political theory, and in national security studies. Postdoctoral fellowships also available. Application is made with vitae, 3 letters of recommendation (2 academic, 1 non-academic), recent publications and theses proposal, and graduate school transcripts. Contact the Institute at the below address for details.

Hudson Institute
Herman Kahn Center
P.O. Box 26-919
Indianapolis, IN 46226

2213
Herman O. West Foundation Scholarship Program

AMOUNT: $2,000 **DEADLINE:** Feb 28
FIELDS/MAJORS: All Areas Of Study

Awards for high school seniors or other dependents of a full-time employee of the West Company. For two- or four-year colleges or universities. Extra-curricular activities, motivation and academic achievement will be considered. Information and applications are available in the Human Resource Departments at all West locations. Contact resource department at the location where employed.

Herman O. West Foundation
Human Resource Departments
P.O. Box 645
Lionville, PA 19341

2214
Herman Oscar Schumacher Scholarship Fund

AMOUNT: $500 **DEADLINE:** Oct 1
FIELDS/MAJORS: All Areas Of Study

Awards for male residents of Spokane County, Washington, who have completed at least one year at an accredited college and demonstrate financial need. Applicants must be Christian and loyal to principles of democracy, and support the constitution of the United States. Write to the address below for information. Applications will be accepted no earlier than the first day of class instruction and no later than Oct 1.

Washington Trust Bank
Trust Department
P.O. Box 2127
Spokane, WA 99210

2215
Hermione Grant Calhoun Scholarships

AMOUNT: $3,000 **DEADLINE:** Mar 31
FIELDS/MAJORS: All Areas Of Study

Award recipients must be legally blind women. Contact the address below for complete details.

National Federation Of The Blind
Mrs. Peggy Elliott, Chairman
814 Fourth Ave., Suite 200
Grinnell, IA 50113

2216

Hermon Dunlap Smith Center For The History Of Cartography

AMOUNT: $800 Per Month **DEADLINE:** Mar 1, Oct 15
FIELDS/MAJORS: History Of Cartography

Fellowships for scholars in the study of cartography history are available through the Hermon Dunlap Smith Center for the History of Cartography. Fellowships usually last three months. Write to the address below for details.

Newberry Library
The Smith Center Scholarship Committee
60 W. Walton St.
Chicago, IL 60610

2217

Herschel C. Price Foundation Scholarships

AMOUNT: $100-$1,500 **DEADLINE:** None Specified
Fields/Majors: All Areas Of Study

Scholarships for West Virginia Students who are or will be attending West Virginia institutions. For undergraduate and graduate study. Renewable. Grades are considered for these awards. Write to the address below for details. A self-addressed, stamped envelope is required.

Herschel C. Price Educational Foundation
P.O. Box 412
Huntington, WV 25708

2218

Hess & Clark, Inc. Scholarship

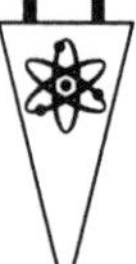

AMOUNT: $1,000 **DEADLINE:** Feb 15
FIELDS/MAJORS: Dairy Science

Scholarships are available for FFA members pursuing a four-year degree in dairy science. Three awards are offered annually. Write to the address below for details.

National FFA Foundation
Scholarship Office
P.O. Box 15160
Alexandria, VA 22309

2219

Heutwell Scholarship

AMOUNT: Tuition **DEADLINE:** None Specified
FIELDS/MAJORS: All Areas Of Study

One scholarship for a student at the University of Michigan who has a disability. This scholarship lasts for four years and covers tuition. Must be a Michigan resident. For undergraduate study. Contact the SSD office at the address below for details.

University Of Michigan
Services For Students With Disabilities
G625 Haven Hall
Ann Arbor, MI 48109

2220

Hewlett-Packard Scholarships

AMOUNT: $1,000 **DEADLINE:** Feb 1
FIELDS/MAJORS: Electrical Engineering, Computer Science

Scholarships for female juniors and seniors studying one of the fields above at an accredited engineering school. Must have a GPA of at least 3.5 and be active supporters and contributors to the Society of Women Engineers. Information and applications for the swe awards are available from the deans of engineering schools, or write to the address below. Please be certain to enclose an SASE.

Society Of Women Engineers
120 Wall Street, 11th Floor
New York, NY 10005

2221

HHMI-NIH Research Scholars Program

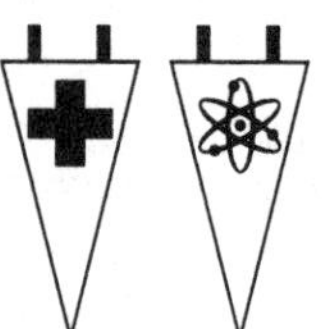

AMOUNT: $16,800 **DEADLINE:** Jan 1
FIELDS/MAJORS: Medicine

This program is available at NIH in Bethesda, Maryland, for medical students to spend a year doing intensive research in the following fields: cell biology and regulation, epidemiology and biostatistics, genetics, immunology, neuroscience and structural biology. Write to the address listed below for additional information.

Howard Hughes Medical Institute
HHMI-NIH Research Scholars Program
1 Cloister Court, Dept. G
Bethesda, MD 20814

2222

HIAS Scholarships

AMOUNT: $1,000 **DEADLINE:** Apr 19
FIELDS/MAJORS: All Areas Of Study

Scholarships for students who were, or whose parents were assisted in immigrating to the United States (after 1985) by the Hebrew Immigrant Aid Society. Only scholarship winners will be notified. Write to the address below for details, and include a self-addressed, stamped envelope.

Hebrew Immigrant Aid Society
Scholarship Awards
333 Seventh Avenue
New York, NY 10001

2223

Hickman Student Loan Fund

AMOUNT: $2,000-$3,000 **DEADLINE:** None Specified
FIELDS/MAJORS: All Areas Of Study

Loans available to residents of King County, Washington, who are full-time undergraduate students with sophomore status or above. Applicant must be 30 years of age or less. Undergraduate students may borrow up to $2,000 per year and graduate students can borrow up to $3,000. Write to the address listed below for information.

Hickman Student Loan Fund
U.S. Bank Of Washington
1420 Fifth Avenue, P.O. Box 720
Seattle, WA 98111

2224

Higgins-Quarles Award

AMOUNT: $1,000 **DEADLINE:** Jan 8
FIELDS/MAJORS: American History

Awards are available for minority graduate students at the dissertation stage of their Ph.D. programs. To apply, students should submit a brief two-page abstract of the dissertation project, along with a one-page budget explaining the travel and research plans for the funds requested. Write to the address below for more information. Each application must also be accompanied by a letter from the dissertation advisor attesting to the student's status.

Organization Of American Historians
112 N. Bryan St.
Bloomington, IN 47408

2225

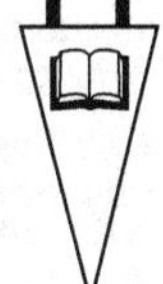

High School Public Speaking Scholarship

AMOUNT: $600-$1,600 **DEADLINE:** None Specified
FIELDS/MAJORS: Speech

Speech contest for California high school students. Speech should be between seven and nine minutes in length on any subject related to past or present history, geography, or cultural development of California. Write to the address below for more information or contact your local area chairmen.

Native Sons Of The Golden West
Grand Parlor Office
414 Mason St., Suite 300
San Franscisco, CA 94102

2226

High School Research Award

AMOUNT: $300 **DEADLINE:** Feb 15
FIELDS/MAJORS: Chemistry

Scholarships are available at the University of Utah for full-time entering freshmen chemistry majors who are graduating high school seniors, who seek the opportunity to join a professor in collaborative laboratory research. Write to the address below for information.

University Of Utah
Dr. Fred Montague
135 Building 44
Salt Lake City, UT 84112

2227

High School Research Program

AMOUNT: $3,200 (max) **DEADLINE:** Nov 3
FIELDS/MAJORS: Health-Related Fields

Scholarships are available for submitting health-related research projects while in the senior year of high school. Typical subjects are: diseases of the elderly, cardiovascular exercise, air pollution attitudes, the effects of smoking on health, diseases of the lungs. For Indiana residents only. Write to the address listed below for information.

American Lung Association Of Indiana
Communications Director
9410 Priority Way West Drive
Indianapolis, IN 46240

2228

Higher Education Loan Program (HELP)

AMOUNT: $6,000 (max) **DEADLINE:** Mar 1, Oct 1
FIELDS/MAJORS: Obstetrics & Gynecology

Must be citizen of a country represented by the ACOG. Must be resident who has completed one year in approved training program in obstetrics or gynecology. Must be junior fellow of the college (ACOG). Write to the address below for more information.

American College Of Obstetricians And Gynecologists
Attn: Higher Education Loan Program
409 12th St., SW
Washington, DC 20024

2229

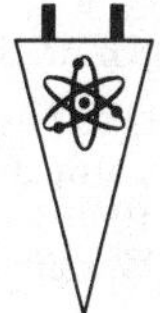

Hillshire Farm & Kahn's Scholarship

AMOUNT: $1,000 **DEADLINE:** Feb 15
FIELDS/MAJORS: Agriculture Or Food Technology

Scholarships are available for FFA members pursuing a four-year degree in agriculture or food technology. Must be a Wisconsin resident attending a college or university in Wisconsin. Write to the address below for details.

National FFA Foundation
Scholarship Office
P.O. Box 15160
Alexandria, VA 22309

2230

Hilmer G. Olson Memorial Scholarship

AMOUNT: Varies **DEADLINE:** Feb 1
FIELDS/MAJORS: Art-Painting

Scholarships are available at the University of New Mexico for full-time art students at the sophomore level and above, with a concentration in painting. Must have a minimum GPA of 3.5. Write to the address listed below for information.

University Of New Mexico, Albuquerque
College Of Fine Arts
Office Of The Dean
Albuquerque, NM 87131

2231

Hilo Women's Club Scholarship

AMOUNT: $550 **DEADLINE:** Feb 1
FIELDS/MAJORS: All Areas Of Study

Scholarships are available at the University of Hawaii, Hilo for full-time female students who are graduating high school seniors at a Big Island High School. Must have a GPA of at least 3.5 or higher. Write to the address listed below for information.

University Of Hawaii At Hilo
Financial Aid Office
200 West Kawili Street
Hilo, HI 96720

2232

Hilton A. Smith Graduate Fellowship

AMOUNT: $500/month **DEADLINE:** Feb 15
FIELDS/MAJORS: All Areas Of Study

Open to any full-time graduate student who is enrolled or pursuing enrollment at the Univ. Of Tennessee (Knoxville). Student must have a GPA of 3.7. Write to the address below for more information.

University Of Tennessee, Knoxville
Graduate Admissions And Records
218 Student Services Bldg.
Knoxville, TN 37996

2233

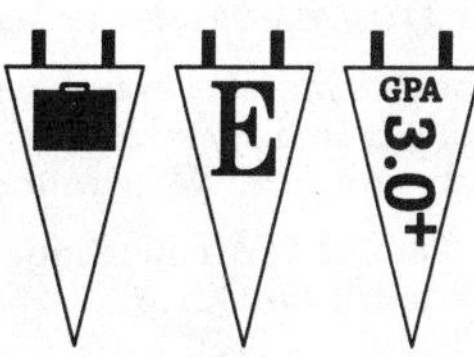

Hispanic Business College Fund

AMOUNT: Varies **DEADLINE:** Jan 31
FIELDS/MAJORS: Business

Awards for Hispanic students in the field of business. Must have a

GPA of at least 3.0, be a U.S. citizen, and show evidence of financial need. Write to the address below for more information.

U.S. Hispanic Chamber Of Commerce
Carmen Ortiz
1030 15th St. NW, Suite 206
Washington, DC 20005

2234

Hispanic Chamber Of Commerce Of Wisconsin Education Fund

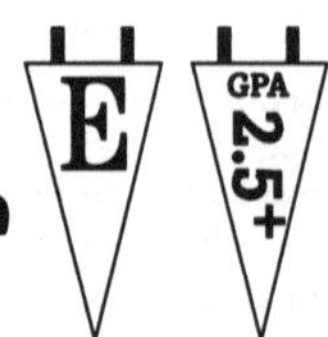

AMOUNT: $1,000 **DEADLINE:** Apr 22
FIELDS/MAJORS: All Areas Of Study

Applicants must be Milwaukee County residents who will attend a four-year Wisconsin college in fall 1996. Must demonstrate an awareness of issues facing Hispanic community. Must have a GPA of 2.5 or better. Includes the Philip Arreola Scholarship. Write to the address below for more information.

University Of Wisconsin, Oshkosh
Financial Aid Office, Dempsey 104
800 Algoma Blvd.
Oshkosh, WI 54901

2235

History Graduate Travel

AMOUNT: Varies **DEADLINE:** None Specified
FIELDS/MAJORS: History

Awards for graduate students at UMass to support academic travel. Contact the chairperson of the department of history, not the address below for more information.

University Of Massachusetts-Amherst
Office Of Financial Aid Services
255 Whitmore Admin. Bldg., Box 38230
Amherst, MA 01003

2236

History Scholarship

AMOUNT: Varies **DEADLINE:** None Specified
FIELDS/MAJORS: History

Awards for students entering their sophomore, junior, or senior year at UMass in the field of history. Based on academics and financial need. Contact the chairperson of the department of history, not the address below for more information.

University Of Massachusetts-Amherst
Office Of Financial Aid Services
255 Whitmore Admin. Bldg., Box 38230
Amherst, MA 01003

2237

Hoard's Dairyman Scholarship

AMOUNT: $1,000 **DEADLINE:** Feb 15
FIELDS/MAJORS: Dairy Science, Agricultural Journalism

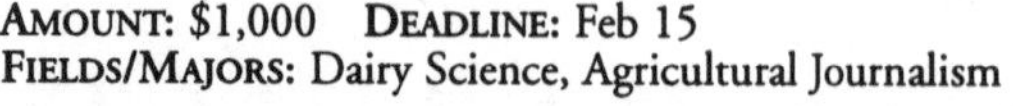

Scholarships are available for FFA members pursuing a four-year degree in dairy science, preferably with an emphasis in agricultural journalism. Write to the address below for details.

National FFA Foundation
Scholarship Office
P.O. Box 15160
Alexandria, VA 22309

2238

Hodges Scholarship

AMOUNT: Varies **DEADLINE:** None Specified
FIELDS/MAJORS: All Areas Of Study

Awards for WJC students based on need and academics. Write to the address below for more information.

Wheeling Jesuit College
Student Financial Planning
316 Washington Ave.
Wheeling, WV 26003

2239

Hodson Achievement Scholarship

AMOUNT: Varies **DEADLINE:** Jan 1
FIELDS/MAJORS: All Areas Of Study

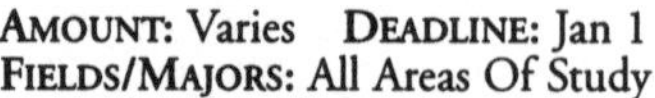

Scholarship available to full-time freshmen who are members of underrepresented minority groups. This is a full grant to meet the student's need (minus work obligation in upperclass years). Write to the address below for details.

Johns Hopkins University
3400 N Charles Street
Baltimore, MD 21218

2240

Hollaender Distinguished Postdoctoral Fellowship Program

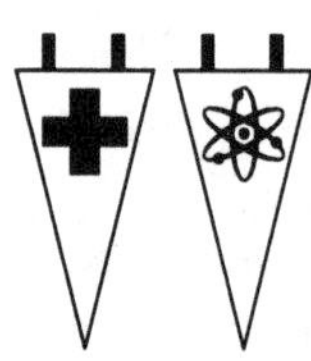

AMOUNT: $41,000 (avg) **DEADLINE:** Jan 15
FIELDS/MAJORS: Biomedical, Life And Environmental Sciences

These fellowships are for positions at the U.S. Department of energy and the office of health and environmental research, to assist in understanding the health and environmental effects associated with energy technologies. Applicant must have received a Ph.D. within the past two years and be a citizen of the United States. Fellowship is for two years. Write to the address listed below for information.

Oak Ridge Associated Universities
Hollaender Postdoctoral Fellowships
P.O. Box 117, Science/Engineering Ed. Div.
Oak Ridge, TN 37831

2241

Hollings Endowment Fund Scholarships

AMOUNT: $1,000 (max) **DEADLINE:** None Specified
FIELDS/MAJORS: All Areas Of Study

Awards for graduating high school seniors from Berkeley, Charleston, or Dorchester counties in South Carolina. Must be in the top 25% of your high school class and have a GPA of at least 3.0. Also based on recommendations from high school faculty. Must maintain at least twelve credit hours per semester and a GPA of 3.0 or better. Write to the address below for more information.

Trident Technical College
Financial Aid Office
P.O. Box 118067
Charleston, SC 29423

2242

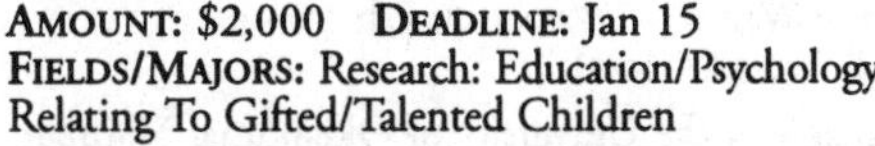

Hollingworth Award

Amount: $2,000 **Deadline:** Jan 15
Fields/Majors: Research: Education/Psychology Relating To Gifted/Talented Children

Research grants for graduate students, teachers, professors, educational administrator, psychologists, etc. Supports educational or psychological research of potential benefit to the gifted and talented. Research must be of publishable quality. Based on abstract and research proposal. Write for details.

Intertel Foundation, Hollingworth Award Committee
Dr. Roxanne Herrick Cramer, Chairman
4300 Sideburn Rd.
Fairfax, VA 22030

2243

Holly A. Cornell Scholarship

Amount: $5,000 **Deadline:** Dec 15
Fields/Majors: Science Or Engineering Relating To Water Supply And Treatment

Fellowships are available to encourage and support outstanding female and/or minority students wishing to pursue advanced training in the field of water supply and treatment. For master's degree candidates. Write to the address listed below for information.

American Water Works Association
Scholarship Coordinator
6666 W. Quincy Avenue
Denver, CO 80235

2244

Holly Donaldson Scholarship

Amount: Varies **Deadline:** Apr 15
Fields/Majors: Art, English, Foreign Language, Journalism, Liberal Arts, Music, Drama

Scholarships available for students at ABAC in one of the fields above with a GPA of at least 2.5. Based on academics, extracurricular activities, and moral character. Write to the address below for additional information.

Abraham Baldwin Agricultural College
Office Of Admissions
2802 Moore Highway
Tifton, GA 31794

2245

Holmes And Narver Scholarship

Amount: Varies **Deadline:** Mar 1
Fields/Majors: Computer, Civil, Electrical Or Mechanical Engineering

Awards are available at the University of New Mexico for juniors or seniors in one of the fields listed above. Write to the address below for more information.

University Of New Mexico, Albuquerque
Office Of Financial Aid
Albuquerque, NM 87131

2246

Holmes Fund

Amount: None Specified **Deadline:** May 1
Fields/Majors: All Areas Of Study

Awards for residents of Calais, ME, wishing to pursue higher education. Contact the Calais High School Guidance Office for more information.

Maine Community Fund
P.O. Box 148
Ellsworth, ME 04605

2247

Holt V. Spicer Communications Scholarships

Amount: $600 (appx) **Deadline:** Mar 31
Fields/Majors: Communications

Awards for juniors or seniors majoring or minoring in communications with a GPA of 3.0 or better. Contact the Communications Department for more information.

Southwest Missouri State University
Office Of Financial Aid
901 South National Ave.
Springfield, MO 65804

2248

Holy Names College Grant

Amount: $200-$5,000 **Deadline:** Mar 2
Fields/Majors: Most Areas Of Study

Grants for full-time undergraduates who have demonstrated need and a GPA of at least 2.4. Write to the address below for more information.

Holy Names College
Financial Aid Office
3500 Mountain Blvd.
Oakland, CA 94619

2249

Home Congregation Grants And Matching Grants

Amount: $100-$1,000 **Deadline:** Varies
Fields/Majors: Religion, Theology

Awards for Concordia students who intend to enter full-time church careers in the Lutheran Church-Missouri Synod. Must have a GPA of at least 2.5 and be a U.S. citizen. These awards are funded by the student's home congregation. Write to the address below for more information.

Concordia University, Irvine
Financial Aid Office
1530 Concordia West
Irvine, CA 92715

2250

Home Economics Scholarships

Amount: None Specified **Deadline:** Mar 15
Fields/Majors: Home Economics

Scholarships are available to students at Appalachian State

University who are home economics majors. Write to the address listed below for information.

Appalachian State University
Department Of Home Economics
Boone, NC 28608

2251

Honda Scholarship

AMOUNT: $1,000 **DEADLINE:** None Specified
FIELDS/MAJORS: All Areas Of Study

Scholarships for freshman at Denison University. Must be graduate of Ohio high schools. Applicants must have a GPA of at least 3.0 and be able to demonstrate financial need. Contact the admissions office or the financial aid office at the address below for details.

Denison University
Financial Aid Office, Box M
Granville, OH 43023

2252

Honda Scholarship

AMOUNT: Varies **DEADLINE:** Mar 1
FIELDS/MAJORS: All Areas Of Study

Award for graduates of Ohio high schools who are in good academic standing and in need of financial aid to attend Lake Erie College. Write to the address below for more information.

Lake Erie College
Financial Aid Office
391 W. Washington St.
Painesville, OH 44077

2253

Honeywell Engineering Scholarship

AMOUNT: Varies **DEADLINE:** Mar 1
FIELDS/MAJORS: Engineering

Awards are available at the University of New Mexico for students admitted to the School of Engineering. Must demonstrate financial need, extracurricular activities, and a GPA of at least 3.0. Write to the address below for more information.

University Of New Mexico, Albuquerque
Office Of Financial Aid
Albuquerque, NM 87131

2254

Honor Grant

AMOUNT: Varies **DEADLINE:** Apr 1
FIELDS/MAJORS: All Areas Of Study

Scholarships are available at Siena Heights College for full-time students who have completed at least 24 credit hours at Siena Heights with a minimum GPA of at least 3.2. Applicant must not have received any prior scholarship at Siena. Write to the address listed below for information.

Siena Heights College
Financial Aid Office
1247 East Siena Heights Drive
Adrian, MI 49221

2255

Honor Scholarship

AMOUNT: $1,000 Fee Waiver **DEADLINE:** Feb 15
FIELDS/MAJORS: All Areas Of Study

Fee waivers are available at the University of Oklahoma, Norman for entering freshmen who demonstrate exceptional academic ability. Write to the address listed below for information.

University Of Oklahoma, Norman
Honors Program
347 Cate Center Drive
Norman, OK 73019

2256

Honor Scholarships

AMOUNT: $2,500 (max) **DEADLINE:** Feb 1
FIELDS/MAJORS: All Areas Of Study

Applicants must be incoming students who have a minimum GPA of at least 3.75 and have scored at least 26 on the ACT or 1000 on the SAT. Write to the address below for details.

Mount Mercy College
Office Of Admission
1330 Elmhurst Dr., NE
Cedar Rapids, IA 52402

2257

Honored Student And Frank C. Naughton Awards

AMOUNT: $500 **DEADLINE:** Oct 15
FIELDS/MAJORS: Chemical Engineering

Awards for graduate students in the field of chemical engineering and focusing on the areas of fats and lipids. Preference will be given to a student working on a project involving castor oil. Applicants must have a good academic record and be nominated by their department to be eligible. Write to the address below for more information.

American Oil Chemists' Society
P.O. Box 3489
Champaign, IL 61826

2258

Honors At Entrance Scholarship

AMOUNT: Tuition **DEADLINE:** Feb 1
FIELDS/MAJORS: All Areas Of Study

Scholarships are available at the University of Utah for full-time students who will be entering freshmen with a minimum GPA of 3.9, or who are National Merit Finalists with an ACT score of 28 or higher. Up to 250 awards are offered annually. Write to the address below for details. Information is also available from your high school guidance counselor.

University Of Utah
Financial Aid And Scholarship Office
105 Student Services Building
Salt Lake City, UT 84112

2259

Honors College Community College Scholarships

AMOUNT: Varies **DEADLINE:** Mar 15
FIELDS/MAJORS: All Areas Of Study

Awards for students who transfer to Pittsburg State University who have a GPA of at least 3.7 and forty hours of academic work. Write to the address below for more information.

Pittsburg State University
Office Of Academic Affairs
203 Russ Hall
Pittsburg, KS 66762

2260 Honors College Presidential Scholarship

Amount: Tuition And Fees **Deadline:** Mar 1
Fields/Majors: All Areas Of Study

Awards for incoming freshmen at Pittsburg State University who have demonstrated academic ability. Applicants must have an ACT score of at least 28. Renewable for three years. Write to the address below for more information.

Pittsburg State University
Office Of Academic Affairs
203 Russ Hall
Pittsburg, KS 66762

2261 Honors Fellowships, Leadership Fellowships, Presidential Scholarships

Amount: Varies **Deadline:** Apr 1
Fields/Majors: All Areas Of Study

Awards are available to full-time Elon College students who demonstrate a high school record of leadership, academic excellence, and high test scores. Honors fellowship awards range from $1,500-$10,000. Leadership fellowship awards range from $1,000-$1,500. Presidential scholarships are usually $1,000 annually. Write to the address below for details.

Elon College
Office Of Financial Planning
2700 Campus Box
Elon College, NC 27244

2262 Honors Program

GPA 3.5+

Amount: $1,800-$5,400 **Deadline:** Apr 1
Fields/Majors: All Areas Of Study

Awards for Liberty University freshmen with a GPA of at least 3.5 who rank in the top 10% of their graduating class. Must have an SAT score of 1200 or better or an ACT score of at least 28. Write to the address below for more information.

Liberty University
Office Of Student Financial Aid
Box 20000
Lynchburg, VA 24506

2263 Honors Program And Tuition Grant

Amount: $200-$1,700 **Deadline:** Apr 1
Fields/Majors: All Areas Of Study

Programs available to residents of Kansas who attend a Kansas independent or private institutions. Applicant must demonstrate financial need and maintain a 2.0 cumulative college GPA to renew grant. Grant is limited to four years unless recipient is enrolled in a designated five-year program. The tuition grant is limited to study at private institutions. Write to the address below for details.

Kansas Assn. Of Student Financial Aid Administrators
c/o Kansas Board Of Regents
700 SW Harrison, Suite 1410
Topeka, KS 66603

2264 Honors Scholarships

Amount: $5,000 (max) **Deadline:** None Specified
Fields/Majors: All Areas Of Study

Fifty renewable scholarships for academically accomplished freshmen and transfer students at Eckerd College. Amount of award is determined in part by financial need. Write to the address below for details.

Eckerd College
Director Of Financial Aid
P.O. Box 12560
St. Petersburg, FL 33733

2265 Honors Scholarships

Amount: $1,000-$5,000 **Deadline:** Jun 1
Fields/Majors: All Areas Of Study

Awards for entering freshmen based on SAT's and high school and/or college GPAs. Write to the address below for more information.

Long Island University
Financial Aid Office
Southampton, NY 11968

2266 Honors Scholarships

GPA 3.5+

Amount: Tuition **Deadline:** None
Fields/Majors: All Areas Of Study

Awards for the top male and female students in each class-sophomore through senior of each college. Must be enrolled full-time with a GPA of 3.5 or higher. Write to the address below for more information.

University Of Nebraska, Omaha
Office Of Financial Aid, EAB 103
60th And Dodge Streets
Omaha, NE 68182

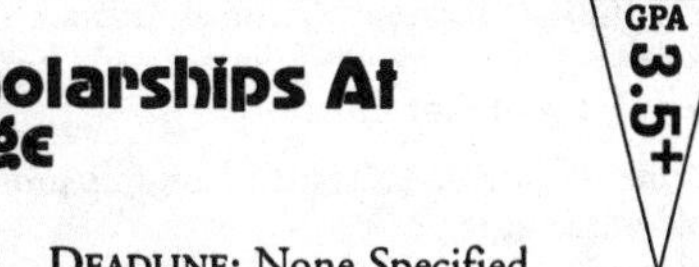

2267 Honors Scholarships At Peace College

Amount: $3,500-$4,500 **Deadline:** None Specified
Fields/Majors: All Areas Of Study

Renewable scholarships for women at Peace College who have a GPA of at least 3.5, SAT scores (combined) of at least 1100, and class rank in top 10% of high school class. Applicant must also be involved in community or on-campus activities. Contact the director of financial aid at the address below for details.

Peace College
Director Of Financial Aid
15 East Peace Street
Raleigh, NC 27604

2268
Hood College Presidential Leadership Scholarship

Amount: $3,000 **Deadline:** Mar 31
Fields/Majors: All Areas Of Study

Awards for transfer students who have above average academic credentials and have been involved in extracurricular or community service efforts which demonstrate special talent, leadership, or social responsibility. Write to the address below for more information.

Hood College Admissions Office
401 Rosemont Ave.
Frederick, MD 21701

2269
Hood Grants And Scholarships

Amount: $100-$1000 **Deadline:** Mar 31
Fields/Majors: All Areas Of Study

Awards for undergraduate students with financial need who are enrolled at least half time and are working toward a Hood degree. Write to the address below for more information.

Hood College Admissions Office
401 Rosemont Ave.
Frederick, MD 21701

2270
Hoosier Award

GPA 3.0+

Amount: $500 **Deadline:** Jan 15
Fields/Majors: All Areas Of Study

Awards for new students (freshmen or transfers) entering Valparaiso University who are residents of the state of Indiana. Must have a GPA of at least 3.0. Award is renewed by Valparaiso University. Write to the address below for additional information.

Valparaiso University
Office of Admissions And Financial Aid
Kretzmann Hall
Valparaiso, IN 46383

2271
Hoosier Scholarships And Higher Education Awards

Amount: Varies **Deadline:** Mar 1
Fields/Majors: All Areas Of Study

For undergraduates at eligible Indiana institutions. Must be a legal Indiana resident. Some awards are merit-based and some awards are need-based. Contact your high school guidance department for more information.

Indiana Student Assistance Commission
150 W. Market St.
Suite 500
Indianapolis, IN 46204

2272
Hopi Scholarship

E | GPA 3.0+

Amount: $1000/semester **Deadline:** Varies
Fields/Majors: All Areas Of Study

Awards for Hopi Tribe members who are pursuing any level degree and can demonstrate academic merit. Undergraduate applicants must have a GPA of at least 3.0, and graduate students must have a GPA of at least 3.2. Write to the address below for more information.

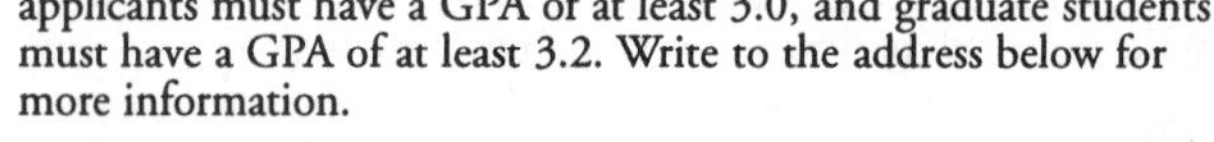

Hopi Tribe Grants And Scholarship Program
Scholarship Committee
P.O. Box 123
Kykotsmovi, AZ 86039

2273
Horace Mann Scholarship

GPA 3.0+

Amount: $1000-$20,000 **Deadline:** Feb 28
Fields/Majors: All Areas Of Study

Scholarships are available for graduating high school seniors who are children of public school employees. Applicants must have GPA of 3.0, or B average, a test score of at least 23 on the ACT, or 1100 on the SAT. Write to the address listed below for information.

Horace Mann Companies Scholarship Program
P.O. Box 20490
Springfield, IL 62708

2274
Horticultural Career Internship Program

Amount: $6.50 Per Hour **Deadline:** None Specified
Fields/Majors: Horticulture

Internship position for students studying horticulture. Most internships are located in the Washington, D.C. metropolitan area. Housing is the responsibility of the intern. Write to the address below for more information.

American Horticultural Society
7931 East Boulevard St.
Alexandria, VA 22308

2275
Hoss's Steak And Sea House Scholarship

Amount: Varies **Deadline:** None Specified
Fields/Majors: Hotel, Restaurant, And Institutional Management

Award given to students studying in the fields listed above who demonstrate financial need. Write to the address below for more information.

Mercyhurst College
Financial Aid Office
Glenwood Hills
Erie, PA 16546

2276
House Of Delegates Scholarships

Amount: Varies **Deadline:** Varies
Fields/Majors: All Areas Of Study

Candidates must be undergraduate, graduate, or vocational Maryland students. Awards are made by state delegates to students in their districts. For study in any Maryland school. Contact your local delegate for details. The address/telephone number can be found in your telephone directory. The SSA also administers the Senatorial Scholarships (application for those is made through your state senator and also filing an FAF).

Maryland State Higher Education Commission
16 Francis Street
Annapolis, MD 21401

2277 Housing Authority Of The County Of Contra Costa

AMOUNT: $400 - $850 **DEADLINE:** May 8
FIELDS/MAJORS: All Areas Of Study

Awards for graduating high school seniors who are currently residents of housing authority of the County of Contra Costa Public Housing Developments or who have received a Section 8 rental housing voucher or certificate. Must be accepted by an accredited four-year college/university, community college, or technical/vocational school, or be currently enrolled in a school or college. Write to the address below for more information.

Housing Authority Of The County Of Contra Costa
Central Administration
3133 Estudillo St., P.O. Box 2759
Martinez, CA 94553

2278 Houston Advertising Federation Scholarship

AMOUNT: $2,500 **DEADLINE:** May 31
FIELDS/MAJORS: Advertising, Marketing, Journalism, Communications

Scholarships for students studying in the fields above who are residents of or attending school in Houston, Texas. Applicants must have a GPA of at least 3.0 and be in their sophomore or junior year of undergraduate study. Write to the address below for more information.

Houston Advertising Federation
P.O. Box 27592
Houston, TX 77227

2279 Houston Livestock Show And Rodeo Scholarship

AMOUNT: $1000 **DEADLINE:** Varies
FIELDS/MAJORS: Range Animal Science

Awards for Sul Ross undergraduates who are studying range animal science and are U.S. citizens. Write to the address below for more information.

Sul Ross State University
Division of Range Animal Science
Box C-110
Alpine, TX 79832

2280 Houston Oil And Minerals Scholarship

AMOUNT: $2,000 **DEADLINE:** Mar 1
FIELDS/MAJORS: Geology, Geophysics

Scholarships are available at the University of Oklahoma, Norman, for full-time geology or geophysics majors. Given to an outstanding junior in each field, for support in the senior year. Write to the address listed below for information.

University of Oklahoma, Norman
Director, School Of Geology And Geophysics
100 East Boyd Street, Room 810
Norman, OK 73019

2281 Howard & Ruth Schumacher Awards, Lucinda Mendenhalle Wilde Scholarship

AMOUNT: $400 - $500 **DEADLINE:** None Specified
FIELDS/MAJORS: Art, Art History

Scholarships are available at the University of Iowa for full-time under graduate students majoring in art or art history, who have a GPA of at least 2.75 and who demonstrate exceptional talent. Write to the address listed below for information.

University Of Iowa
School Of Art And Art History
E100 Art Building
Iowa City, IA 52245

2282 Howard Brown Rickard Scholarship

AMOUNT: $3,000 **DEADLINE:** Mar 31
FIELDS/MAJORS: Architecture, Law, Medicine, Engineering, Natural Sciences

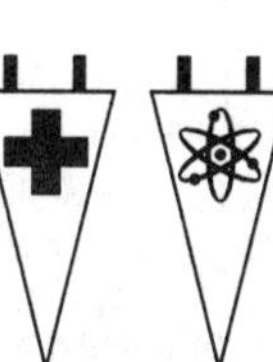

Award recipient must be legally blind, studying toward a career in one of the listed areas of study. Write to the address below for complete details.

National Federation of The Blind
Mrs. Peggy Elliott, Chairman
814 Fourth Ave., Suite 200
Grinnell, IA 50112

2283 Howard F. Denise Scholarship Fund

AMOUNT: None Specified **DEADLINE:** Apr 15
FIELDS/MAJORS: Agriculture Related

Scholarships for New York residents who are/will be undergraduates; have interest/membership in Grange, 4-H, FFA, or FHA; and are committed to a career in agriculture. Contact your local Grange, 4-H, FFA, or FHA, or write to the address below for details.

New York State Grange
Scholarship Coordinator
100 Grange Place
Cortland, NY 13045

2284 Howard F. Fenstemaker Scholarship (Band)

AMOUNT: $400 **DEADLINE:** Feb 9
FIELDS/MAJORS: All Areas Of Study

Award for current marching band member with intention of band participation next year. Must show financial need, academic achievement, and contribution to the Huskies Marching Band. Use Bloomsburg University scholarship application. Contact Mr. Terry Oxley, Director of Bands, for additional information.

Bloomsburg University
19 Ben Franklin Hall
400 E. Second St.
Bloomsburg, PA 17815

2285

Howard H. Hanks Jr. Scholarship In Meteorology

AMOUNT: $700 **DEADLINE:** Jun 16
FIELDS/MAJORS: Meteorology, Atmospheric Sciences, Ocean Science, Hydrology

Applicants must be undergraduates entering their final year in a meteorology program or other program actively engaged in work on some aspect of atmospheric science and must intend to make an atmospheric science their career. Student must be a U.S. citizen or permanent resident and have a grade point average of 3.0 or greater. Write to the address below for details.

American Meteorological Society
45 Beacon Street
Boston, MA 02108

2286

Howard Hughes Predoctoral Fellowships In Biological Sciences

AMOUNT: $14,000 **DEADLINE:** Nov 3
FIELDS/MAJORS: See Listing Of Fields Below

Fellowships for doctoral students in their first year of graduate study in one of these fields: biochemistry, biophysics, biostatistics, cell biology, developmental biology, epidemiology, mathematical biology, microbiology, neuroscience, molecular biology, pharmacology, physiology, structural biology, genetics, and virology. Sixty-six awards offered annually. Write to the address below for further information.

Howard Hughes Medical Institute
Office of Grants And Special Programs
2101 Constitution Ave.
Washington, DC 20418

2287

Howard M. Lebow Memorial Scholarship

AMOUNT: Varies **DEADLINE:** Mar 1
FIELDS/MAJORS: Music

Award for a music student entering their sophomore, junior, or senior year who demonstrates the highest standards of artistic achievement and participation in the life of the department. Contact the Director of Scholarships, Department of Music, at the address below for more information.

University of Massachusetts, Amherst
255 Whitmore Administration Building Box 38230
Amherst, MA 01003

2288

Howard M. Soule Graduate Fellowships In Educational Leadership

AMOUNT: $500-$1,500 **DEADLINE:** May 1
FIELDS/MAJORS: Educational Administration

Open to Phi Delta Kappa members who are full-time students enrolled in a doctoral, master's, or specialist program. Write to the address below for complete details.

Phi Delta Kappa
International Headquarters
P.O. Box 789
Bloomington, IN 47402

2289

Howard Rock Foundation Scholarship Program

AMOUNT: $2,500-$5,000 **DEADLINE:** Mar 15
FIELDS/MAJORS: Economics, Education, Business, Public Administration

Scholarships are available for American Indian students majoring in one of the above fields. Applicants must be residents of Alaska. Write to the address listed below for information.

Howard Rock Foundation
1577 C Street, Suite 304
Anchorage, AK 99501

2290

Howard S. Brembeck Scholarship

AMOUNT: $5,000 **DEADLINE:** Apr 1
FIELDS/MAJORS: Agricultural Engineering

Scholarships are available for graduates of an accredited college or university with a degree in agricultural engineering. Write to the address below for more information.

Midwest Poultry Consortium, Inc.
13033 Ridgedale Drive, Box 191
Minneapolis, MN 55343

2291

Howard Scholarship

AMOUNT: $1,000 **DEADLINE:** May 31
FIELDS/MAJORS: All Areas Of Study

Scholarships for Italian-American residents of New Jersey. For undergraduate study. Write to the address below for details.

National Italian American Foundation
Dr. Maria Lombardo, Education Director
1860 Nineteenth Street, NW
Washington, DC 20009

2292

Howard T. Orville Scholarship In Meteorology

AMOUNT: $2,000 **DEADLINE:** Jun 14
FIELDS/MAJORS: Meteorology, Atmospheric Sciences, Ocean Sciences, Hydrology

Applicants must be undergraduates entering their final year in a meteorology program or other program actively engaged in work on some aspect of atmospheric science and must intend to make atmospheric science their career. Student must have a GPA of 3.0 or above and be U.S. citizens or permanent residents. Write to the address below for details.

American Meteorological Society
45 Beacon Street
Boston, MA 02108

2293

Hualapai Tribal Council Scholarships

AMOUNT: $5,000 (max) **DEADLINE:** None Specified
FIELDS/MAJORS: All Areas Of Study

Scholarships for members of the Hualapai tribe. For full-time study. Contact the Council Office at the address below for details.

Hualapai Tribal Council
Sheri Yellowhawk, Education Program Dir.
P.O. Box 179
Peach Springs, AZ 86434

2294

Hubbard Scholarship

AMOUNT: $3,000 **DEADLINE:** May 1
FIELDS/MAJORS: Library Science

The scholarship's purpose is to recruit excellent librarians for Georgia and will be used to provide financial assistance to qualified candidates for a year's study in completing a master's degree in library science. Must be completing senior year in an accredited college or university or be a graduate of such an institution. Write to the address below for complete details.

Georgia Library Association
Ms. Kathy Adams, Scholarship Committee
100 College Station Dr.
Macon, GA 31297

2295

Hubert H. Humphrey Doctoral Fellowships In Arms Control & Disarmament

AMOUNT: $14,000 (max) **DEADLINE:** Mar 15
FIELDS/MAJORS: Arms Control And Disarmament, International Security

Doctoral dissertation research fellowships for applicants who have completed all Ph.D. course work except for the dissertation at an accredited U.S. institution. Must be a U.S. citizen or legal resident. Up to three fellows per year. Fellowship usually runs twelve months. J.D. candidates in their final year of school are eligible if the project can be published in a law journal. Write to the address below for details.

U.S. Arms Control And Disarmament Agency,
Humphrey Fellowships
Office Of Oper. Analysis & Inf. Mgmt.
320 21st Street, NW
Washington, DC 20451

2296

Huff Scholarships & CHHA/Rambling Willie Memorial Scholarships

AMOUNT: Varies **DEADLINE:** Apr 30
FIELDS/MAJORS: Equine Studies (Horse-Related Fields)

Scholarships for students who have been accepted into post high school study, and are pursuing a horse-related career. Students with harness racing experience will be given preference. For undergraduate study. Write to the address below for more information.

Harness Horse Youth Foundation
14950 Greyhound Court, Suite 210
Carmel, IN 46032

2297

Hugh Cunningham Award

AMOUNT: $200 **DEADLINE:** Mar 1
FIELDS/MAJORS: Newspaper Journalism

Awards for juniors and seniors who are majoring in journalism. Must have completed applied newspaper journalism and have demonstrated the greatest potential for success in a weekly or daily newspaper. Must have a GPA of at least 2.8. Write to the address below for more information.

University of Florida
Knight Scholarship & Placement Director
2070 Weimer Hall
Gainesville, FL 32611

2298

Hugh Sparrow Memorial Endowed Scholarship

AMOUNT: $500 **DEADLINE:** Feb 15
FIELDS/MAJORS: Print Journalism

Renewable $500 award given to University of Alabama sophomores and juniors pursuing a career in print journalism who show high academic performance and professional promise. Write to the address listed below for further information and an application.

University of Alabama
College Of Communications
P.O. Box 870172
Tuscaloosa, AL 35487

2299

Hulda Devaughn Scholarship

AMOUNT: $1,000 **DEADLINE:** May 15
FIELDS/MAJORS: Spanish

Awards are available for female Spanish majors with a GPA of at least 3.25. Write to the address below for more information.

Portland State University
Department Of Foreign Languages
393 Neuberger Hall
Portland, OR 97207

2300

Humane Studies Fellowships

AMOUNT: $17,500 (max) **DEADLINE:** Dec 30
FIELDS/MAJORS: Social Sciences, Law, Humanities, Journalism

Fellowships at the IHS for junior, senior, and graduate students in the social sciences, law, journalism, and the humanities with a demonstrated interest in the classical liberal tradition and intent on pursuing a scholarly or intellectual career. Write to attn: Humane Studies Fellowship Secretary at the address below for details. Applications are available in the fall preceding the Dec deadline.

Institute For Humane Studies At George Mason University
4084 University Drive
Suite 101
Fairfax, VA 22030

2301

Hunsley/Florence Scholarship Fund

AMOUNT: Varies **DEADLINE:** Mar 1
FIELDS/MAJORS: Journalism Or Communication

Awards are available at the University of New Mexico for juniors and senior students who can demonstrate commitment and promise to the fields of journalism or communications. Write to the address listed below for information.

University Of New Mexico, Albuquerque
Office Of Financial Aid
Albuquerque, NM 87131

2302

Huntingdon College Scholarships

AMOUNT: Varies **DEADLINE:** May 1, Dec 1
FIELDS/MAJORS: All Areas Of Study

Huntingdon College scholarships are normally awarded on an annual basis, with one-half of the annual amount of the scholarship being credited to the student's account during the first semester and the other half during the second semester. Scholarships only available to Huntingdon students. Applicant must be an Alabama resident. Write to the address below for details.

Huntingdon College
Student Financial Aid
1500 E. Fairview Ave.
Montgomery, AL 36106

2303

Hydro Agri North America, Inc. Scholarships

AMOUNT: $1,000 **DEADLINE:** Feb 15
FIELDS/MAJORS: Agriculture

Scholarships are available for FFA members pursuing a four-year degree in any area of agriculture. Write to the address below for details.

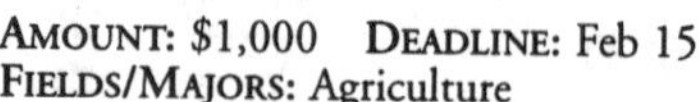

National FFA Foundation
Scholarship Office
P.O. Box 15160
Alexandria, VA 22309

2304

Hyland R. Johns Grant Program

AMOUNT: $5,000-$20,000 **DEADLINE:** May 1
FIELDS/MAJORS: Arboriculture

Awards are available for research in the field of arboriculture. Recipients must be qualified researchers for projects of interest and benefit to the arboriculture industry. Write to the address below for more information.

International Society Of Arboriculture
ISA Research Trust
P.O. Box GG
Savoy, IL 61874

2305

IBD Foundation Graduate Fellowship

AMOUNT: $3,000-$5,000 **DEADLINE:** Apr 8
FIELDS/MAJORS: Interior Design

Awards are available for individuals who have completed their undergraduate study and are practicing commercial interior design full- or part-time or are enrolled in or intending to continue graduate studies in interior design. Write to the address below for more information.

International Interior Design Association Headquarters
341 Merchandise Mart
Chicago, IL 60654

2306

Ichiji Motoki Scholarship

AMOUNT: Varies **DEADLINE:** Feb 15
FIELDS/MAJORS: All Areas Of Study

Scholarships are available at the University of Utah for full-time students of Japanese descent. Write to the address below for information.

University of Utah
Financial Aid And Scholarships Office
105 Student Services Building
Salt Lake City, UT 84112

2307

Ida & Benjamin Cohen And Leo & Alice Kleinman Memorial Scholarships

AMOUNT: None Specified **DEADLINE:** May 1
FIELDS/MAJORS: All Areas Of Study

Open to Five Towns students in a bachelor's or an associate's degree program. Applicants must demonstrate academic potential and/or economic need. Recipients are required to perform a minimum of ten hours community service per semester with an organization approved by the dean of their college. Write to the address below for more information.

Five Towns College
305 N. Service Road/Lie Exit 50
Dix Hills, NY 11746

2308

Ida Belle Ledbetter & William Hubbard Memorial Scholarships

AMOUNT: None Specified **DEADLINE:** Feb 24
FIELDS/MAJORS: Biology

Scholarships awarded to students at Appalachian State University who are biology majors. Write to the address listed below for information.

Appalachian State University
Department Of Biology
Boone, NC 28608

2309

Ida E. Hood And Susan L. Heron Scholarship

AMOUNT: None Specified **DEADLINE:** None Specified
FIELDS/MAJORS: All Areas Of Study

Scholarships for female descendents of Ward Belmont alumnae or a worthy woman in need. For graduate study at Peabody College in Vanderbilt University. Write to the address below for details.

Vanderbilt University
Admissions And Financial Assistance
Box 327 Peabody College
Nashville, TN 37203

2310

Idaho Minority And "At-Risk" Student Scholarship

AMOUNT: $2,700 **DEADLINE:** Jan 31
FIELDS/MAJORS: All Areas Of Study

Scholarships are available for the following types of students:

migrant farm workers or children of migrant farm workers, first-generation college student, handicapped, or minority. For use at Boise State University, Idaho State University, Lewis-Clark State College, University of Idaho, North Idaho College, College of Southern Idaho, or Albertson College of Idaho. Applicant must be an Idaho resident and a U.S. citizen. Write to the address listed below for information.

Idaho State Board Of Education
P.O. Box 83720
Boise, ID 83720

2311 Idamae Cox Otis, Mildred Louise Brackney, Longman Harris Scholarships

AMOUNT: $1,000-$2,000 **DEADLINE:** Feb 15
FIELDS/MAJORS: All Areas Of Study

Scholarships available to graduates of Kate Duncan Smith or Tamassee DAR schools. Must be U.S. citizen. Contact your local or state DAR chapter, or write to the address below for details.

National Society Daughters Of The American Revolution
NSDAR Scholarship Committee
1776 D St., NW
Washington, DC 20006

2312 Iddings Foundation Grants

AMOUNT: Varies **DEADLINE:** None Specified
FIELDS/MAJORS: All Areas Of Study

Scholarships funded by the Iddings Foundation are available at the University of Dayton, Wright State University, Central State University, Wilburforce University, and Wittenberg University. Applicants must be juniors or seniors residing in the greater Dayton area. Students at Sinclair Community College are also eligible to apply. Contact the financial aid office at the schools listed above. Do not write to the foundation.

Iddings Foundation
1620 Kettering Tower
Dayton, OH 45423

2313 Ideas In Science Scholarships

AMOUNT: Varies **DEADLINE:** Mar 1
FIELDS/MAJORS: Engineering

Awards are available at the University of New Mexico for juniors majoring in engineering. Must demonstrate financial need, academic ability (minimum 3.0 GPA), and be a resident of New Mexico. Special consideration is given to students whose program of studies is closely linked to electronic design and applications. Write to the address below for more information.

University Of New Mexico, Albuquerque
Office Of Financial Aid
Albuquerque, NM 87131

2314 Ignatian Honors Program Scholarships

AMOUNT: Tuition **DEADLINE:** Mar 1
FIELDS/MAJORS: All Areas Of Study

Three awards offered to freshman students attending or planning to attend Loyola University on a full time basis. Based upon demonstrated outstanding academic ability in high school. Renewable for three years as long as the student remains in the honors program. Write to the address below for details.

Loyola University
Dr. Joyce Wexler, Director Honors Prog.
6525 N. Sheridan Road
Chicago, IL 60626

2315 Ignatian Scholarships For Academic Excellence

AMOUNT: Tuition **DEADLINE:** Jan 15
FIELDS/MAJORS: All Areas Of Study

To be eligible for this undergraduate award you must have a GPA of 3.5, min., 29 ACT composite, or 1150 SAT composite, community involvement, demonstrated leadership abilities, and an interview with a designated Loyola representative. To renew scholarship you must maintain full-time status of at least twelve semester hours fall and spring, and achieve a GPA of 3.3. Write to the address below for details.

Loyola University-New Orleans
Attn:Coordinator of Scholarship Programs
6363 St. Charles Ave-Campus Box 18
New Orleans, LA 70118

2316 Illinois Amvets Post #204 Scholarship

AMOUNT: $500 **DEADLINE:** Mar 1
FIELDS/MAJORS: All Areas Of Study

Scholarships for children of veterans who served after September 15, 1940. All applicants must be high school seniors from Illinois, unmarried, and have taken the ACT. Write to the address below for more information.

Illinois Amvets Scholarship Program
Illinois Amvets State Headquarters
2200 South Sixth St.
Springfield, IL 62703

2317 Illinois Amvets Sad Sacks Scholarships

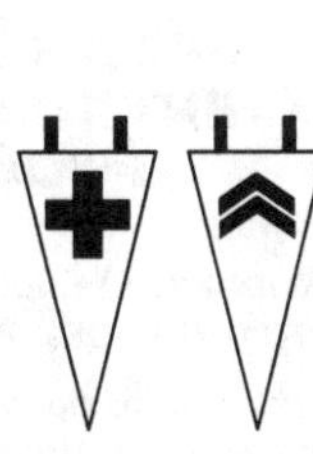
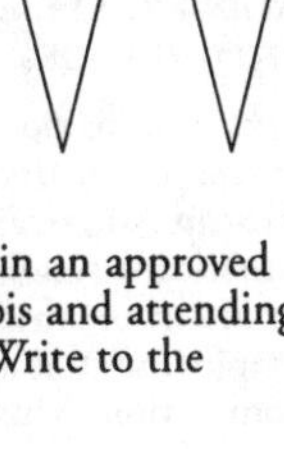

AMOUNT: $500 **DEADLINE:** Mar 1
FIELDS/MAJORS: Nursing

Awards for children of veterans who are enrolled in an approved school of nursing. Applicants must be from Illinois and attending an Illinois institution. For undergraduate study. Write to the address below for more information.

Illinois Amvets Scholarship Program
Illinois Amvets State Headquarters
2200 South Sixth St.
Springfield, IL 62703

2318 Illinois Amvets Service Foundation

AMOUNT: $500 **DEADLINE:** Mar 1
FIELDS/MAJORS: All Areas Of Study

Scholarships for children of veterans who served after September 15, 1940. All applicants must be high school seniors from Illinois, unmarried, and have taken the ACT. Also includes the Albert C. Reichter memorial, Amvets Post #100, Post #235, Post #94, Post

#51, Clarence E. Newlun Memorial, and Frank Tuman Scholarships. Write to the address below for more information.

Illinois Amvets Scholarship Program
Illinois Amvets State Headquarters
2200 South Sixth St.
Springfield, IL 62703

2319 Illinois Funeral Directors Association Scholarships

AMOUNT: $500-$750 **DEADLINE:** None Specified
FIELDS/MAJORS: Mortuary Science

Awards for Illinois residents studying mortuary science at any of the three accredited Illinois schools. Write to the address below for more information.

Illinois Funeral Directors Association
215 South Grand Ave. West
Springfield, IL 62704

2320 Illinois Future, Inc. Scholarships

AMOUNT: None Specified **DEADLINE:** None Specified
FIELDS/MAJORS: All Areas Of Study

Scholarships available to children whose parent has suffered from a serious catastrophic injury and/or permanent and total disability, or has died from an employment-related accident that has resulted in the decrease in family earnings or assets, preventing the continuation of the child's education. Applicants must be a resident of Illinois and under the age of twenty-two. Write to the address below for details.

Illinois Future, Inc.
821 W. Galena Blvd.
Aurora, IL 60506

2321 Illinois Minority Graduate Incentive Program (State Program)

AMOUNT: $14,000 **DEADLINE:** None Specified
FIELDS/MAJORS: All Areas Of Study

Scholarships open to master's or doctoral students in fields where minorities are underrepresented. Applicants must be African American, Hispanic, Asian American, or Native Americans residing in Illinois. Each fellow must sign a letter of intent in which they agree to seek and accept appropriate employment at an Illinois college or university upon degree completion. Must be U.S. citizen. Write to the address below for details.

Rush-Presbyterian—St. Luke's Medical School
Office Of Student Financial Aid
1743 West Harrison Street
Chicago, IL 60612

2322 Illinois National Guard Grant Program

AMOUNT: Tuition & Fees **DEADLINE:** Mar 1, Jun 15
FIELDS/MAJORS: All Areas Of Study

Must be current member of Illinois National Guard having served at least one year. For study at a state-supported college on the undergraduate or graduate level. For enlisted personnel or officers up to the rank of captain. Write to the address below for more details. Information is also available from National Guard units and Naval Militia units in Illinois or from your college.

Illinois Student Assistance Commission
1755 Lake Cook Road
Deerfield, IL 60015

2323 Illinois NWSA Manuscript Award

AMOUNT: $1,000 **DEADLINE:** Jan 31
FIELDS/MAJORS: Women's Studies

Annual award for best book-length manuscript in women's studies. Along with the $1,000 prize, the University of Illinois Press will publish the manuscript. Manuscripts can be on any subject in women's studies that expands our understanding of women's lives and gender systems. Interdisciplinary studies and discipline-specific studies are equally welcome. Write to the NWSA for details.

National Women's Studies Association
University Of Maryland
7100 Baltimore Avenue, Suite 301
College Park, MD 20740

2324 Illinois Odd Fellow-Rebekah Scholarship Program

AMOUNT: Varies **DEADLINE:** Mar 1
FIELDS/MAJORS: All Areas Of Study.

Applicants must be a U.S. citizen, Illinois resident, and maintain a 2.0 GPA. Financial need must also be demonstrated. Odd Fellow and/or Rebekah membership is not required. Must attend school in Illinois. Award is intended for use in the following school year. More than twenty scholarships are available. Dec 1 deadline for application requests. Write to the address listed below for further information.

Independent Order Of Odd Fellows, Grand Lodge Of Illinois
Scholarship Committee
P.O. Box 248
Lincoln, IL 62656

2325 Illinois Scottish Rite Scholarship Fund

AMOUNT: Varies **DEADLINE:** None Specified
FIELDS/MAJORS: Nursing

Awards available to needy nursing students who are in at least their second year of the program. Write to the address below for more information.

Rockford College
Financial Aid Office
5050 East State St.
Rockford, IL 61108

2326 Illinois Sheriffs Association Scholarship

AMOUNT: $500 **DEADLINE:** Feb 15
FIELDS/MAJORS: All Areas Of Study

Scholarships are available at the University of Illinois for Illinois residents who demonstrate academic ability. For undergraduate study. Contact your local sheriff's office for information.

University Of Illinois At Urbana-Champaign
Office of Student Financial Aid
610 East John Street, 4th Floor
Champaign, IL 61820

2327

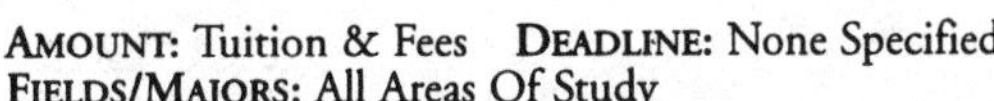

Illinois Veteran Grant Program

Amount: Tuition & Fees **Deadline:** None Specified
Fields/Majors: All Areas Of Study

Must be veteran who served honorably in the U.S. Armed Forces for at least one year. Applicants must have been residents of Illinois upon entering the service, and must have returned to Illinois to reside within six months of leaving the service. Recipients are not required to enroll for a minimum number of credit hours each term. Contact the department of veteran's affairs or write to the address below for details.

Illinois Student Assistance Commission
1755 Lake Cook Road
Deerfield, IL 60015

2328

Independent Colleges Of Texas Valedictorian And Salutatorian Award

Amount: $500-$1,000 **Deadline:** Jul 15
Fields/Majors: All Areas Of Study

Grant for freshmen accepted for full-time admission who were ranked first or second in their high school class. Write to the address below for more information.

Schreiner College
Financial Aid Office
Kerrville, TX 78028

2329

Indian Health Service Scholarships

Amount: Varies **Deadline:** None Specified
Fields/Majors: Health-Related Fields

Scholarships are available for American Indian students studying in health-related fields. Contact your school's financial aid office or write to the address listed below for information.

Department Of Health And Human Services
PHS/IHS/Scholarship Program
12300 Twinbrook Parkway, #100
Rockville, MD 20852

2330

Indiana Chapter Of Electrical Women's Round Table Scholarship

Amount: $300 **Deadline:** May 26
Fields/Majors: Electrical Energy Or Related Field

Scholarships are for a full-time sophomore or junior undergraduate student enrolled in a college or university in Indiana. Must be pursuing studies in electrical energy, architecture, engineering, home economics, environmental science, and construction technology. Contact Mary Thurman, Indiana Power and Light Co., P.O. Box 1595, Indianapolis, IN 46206-1595 for more information.

Indiana University/Purdue University, Indianapolis
Purdue School Of Technology
799 West Michigan St.
Indianapolis, IN 46202

2331

Indiana Farmers Mutual Insurance Group Scholarships

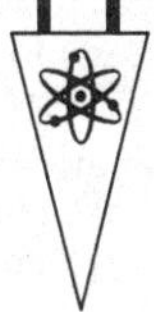

Amount: $1,000 **Deadline:** Feb 15
Fields/Majors: Agriculture

Scholarships are available for FFA members pursuing a four-year degree in any area of agriculture at Purdue University, who are residents of Indiana. Write to the address below for details.

National FFA Foundation
Scholarship Office
P.O. Box 15160
Alexandria, VA 22309

2332

Indiana Funeral Directors Association Scholarships

Amount: $500-$1,000 **Deadline:** None Specified
Fields/Majors: Mortuary Science

Awards for Indiana residents studying mortuary science. Applicants must intend to serve their internship in Indiana, and they must be admitted or enrolled in an accredited program of mortuary science. Write to the address below for more information.

Indiana Funeral Directors Association
1311 West 96th St.
Suite 120
Indianapolis, IN 46260

2333

Indianapolis Indiana Chapter 34 Association of Women In Cnstrt. Award

Amount: Varies **Deadline:** None Specified
Fields/Majors: Construction

Award for a construction student that is a resident of Indiana outside a five-mile radius of sister chapters in South Bend, Ft. Wayne, and Evansville. For full- or part-time study. Write to the address below for more information.

Indiana University Purdue University, Indianapolis
Purdue School Of Technology
799 West Michigan St.
Indianapolis, IN 46202

2334

Inez McDavid Memorial Scholarship

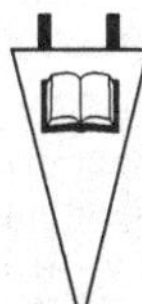

Amount: Varies **Deadline:** Mar 1
Fields/Majors: Communicative Disorders

Awards are available at the University of New Mexico for undergraduate or graduate students majoring in the fields of communicative disorders. Write to the address listed below for information.

University Of New Mexico, Albuquerque
Office Of Financial Aid
Albuquerque, NM 87131

2335

Inmon Memorial Scholarship

Amount: None Specified
Deadline: None Specified
Fields/Majors: Business

Students must be full-time junior or senior COBA majors with a

GPA of 3.2 or better. Must be a U.S. citizen, with preference given to native Missourians. Contact the COBA office for more information.

Southwest Missouri State University
Office Of Financial Aid
901 South National Ave.
Springfield, MO 65804

2336 Institute For International Public Policy

AMOUNT: Varies **DEADLINE:** Mar 1
FIELDS/MAJORS: International Policy

Program which prepares minorities for careers in international affairs through sophomore and junior year summer institutes, a junior year abroad, internships, a senior language institute, and graduate studies leading to a master's degree. Students must apply during their sophomore year of study. Write to the address below for more information.

Woodrow Wilson National Fellowship Foundation
Attn: IIPP
CN 5281
Princeton, NJ 08543

2337 Institute Of American Indian Arts Scholarships

AMOUNT: $300-$10,000
DEADLINE: Apr 15, Nov 15
FIELDS/MAJORS: Art, Museum Studies

Scholarships are available for undergraduate American Indian students at the Institute of American Indian Art. Write to the address listed below for information.

Institute Of American Indian Art
P.O. Box 20007
Santa Fe, NM 87504

2338 Institute Of Water Research Graduate Fellowships

AMOUNT: $17,000 **DEADLINE:** Dec 31
FIELDS/MAJORS: Water Sciences

Graduate fellowships are available for doctoral students to initiate innovative research emphasizing systems sciences/computer modeling simulation as it relates to all aspects of the water sciences. Fields of study include agricultural economics/engineering, agronomy, environmental and civil engineering, crop science, entomology, and related fields. Write to the address listed below for information.

Michigan State University
Institute Of Water Research
115 Manly Miles Bldg.
East Lansing, MI 48823

2339 Instructional Materials Fund For Ethnic Students

AMOUNT: $200 (max) **DEADLINE:** Varies
FIELDS/MAJORS: All Areas Of Study

Awards are available at Portland State University for minority students who have an unusually high book, lab, or other costs for a particular term. Must be enrolled in full-time study and in good academic standing. For undergraduate study. Write to the address below for more information.

Portland State University
Educational Equity Programs And Services
120 Smith Memorial Center
Portland, OR 97207

2340 Integrated Manufacturing Predoctoral Fellowships

AMOUNT: $20,000 **DEADLINE:** Dec 1
FIELDS/MAJORS: Manufacturing Engineering Or A Related Field

Fellowships are available for doctoral candidates who wish to further their education in a field directly relating to integrated manufacturing. A cost-of-education allowance of up to $15,000 is also available. Applicants must be U.S. citizens or nationals. Write to the address listed below for additional information.

National Research Council, U.S. Department Of Energy
Fellowship Office
2101 Constitution Avenue
Washington, DC 20418

2341 Integrated Manufacturing Predoctoral Fellowships

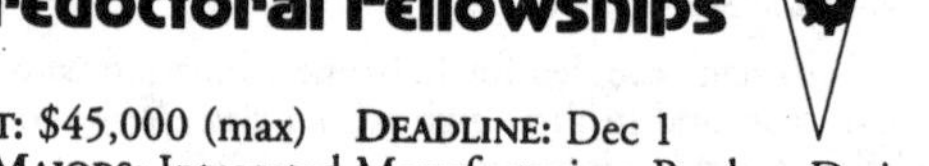

AMOUNT: $45,000 (max) **DEADLINE:** Dec 1
FIELDS/MAJORS: Integrated Manufacturing, Product Design

Awards are available for students who possess a master's degree and are pursuing a Ph.D. in one of the areas of study listed above. Must be a U.S. citizen or permanent resident. Write to the address below for more information.

U.S. Department Of Energy, Fellowship Office
National Research Council
2101 Constitution Ave.
Washington, DC 20418

2342 Interchange Fellowship And Martin McLaren Scholarship

AMOUNT: None Specified **DEADLINE:** Nov 15
FIELDS/MAJORS: Horticulture, Landscape Architecture, And Related Fields

Program for U.S. graduate students to spend a year in Great Britain studying horticulture or landscape architecture as well as working at American universities and botanical gardens in the U.K. Funds two graduate students annually. Send a stamped, self-addressed envelope to the address below for more information.

Garden Club Of America
Mrs. Monica Freeman
598 Madison Ave.
New York, NY 10022

2343 International Affairs Scholarship

AMOUNT: $500 **DEADLINE:** Mar 1
FIELDS/MAJORS: International Affairs/International Relations

Students must be maintaining legal residence in Massachusetts and present a letter of endorsement from sponsoring Women's Club in your community. For study in international affairs. Men or women may apply for this award. Write to the address below for details.

General Federation of Women's Clubs Of Massachusetts
Scholarship Chairman, 245 Dutton Road
P.O. Box 679
Sudbury, MA 01776

2344

International Brotherhood of Boilermakers Scholarship

AMOUNT: $1,000-$5,000 **DEADLINE:** Mar 31
FIELDS/MAJORS: All Areas Of Study

Scholarships for children (sons, daughters, adopted children, dependents) of members in good standing (current, deceased, retired, or totally disabled) of the International Brotherhood of Boilermakers, Iron Ship Builders, Blacksmiths, Forgers & Helpers (AFL-CIO, CLC). Awarded to high school seniors only. Applications may be obtained by writing to the address below or by contacting your parent's local organization.

International Brotherhood Of Boilermakers
New Brotherhood Building
753 State Avenue, Suite 570
Kansas City, KS 66101

2345

International Brotherhood of Electrical Workers Scholarship Fund

AMOUNT: $5,000 (max) **DEADLINE:** None Specified
FIELDS/MAJORS: All Areas Of Study

Scholarships for sons and daughters of members of Local Union #3 of the International Brotherhood of Electrical Workers (IBEW). For graduating high school seniors. Qualifying parent must have been employed (or available for employment), for at least five years, by employer(s) who contribute to the educational and cultural fund. Twenty scholarships per year. Contact your parents' Local Union #3 or write to the address below for details.

Educational And Cultural Fund Of The Electrical Industry
158-11 Harry Van Arsdale Jr. Ave.
Flushing, NY 11365

2346

International Cultural Service Program

AMOUNT: Varies **DEADLINE:** None Specified
FIELDS/MAJORS: All Areas Of Study

Awards are available for international students to help in meeting the costs to attend U.S. Schools. Recipients will receive a partial waiver of their tuition. In return, participating students must provide a minimum of 80 hours of cultural service each year they are in the program. Write to the address below for more information.

Portland State University
International Student & Faculty Services
Sixth Ave. Building
Portland, OR 97207

2347

International Fellows Program

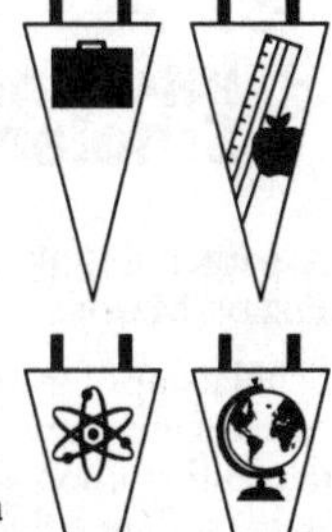

AMOUNT: Varies **DEADLINE:** Apr 5
FIELDS/MAJORS: Social And Physical Sciences, Health, English Educ., Computer, Mrkting

Tuskegee University offers a nine-month fellowship program to support the participation of graduate students in technical and educational transfer of expertise to areas of need in Africa and other Third World countries. Write to the address below for details.

Tuskegee University
International Fellows Program
Office Of International Programs
Tuskegee, AL 36088

2348

International Fellowships

AMOUNT: $15,065 **DEADLINE:** Dec 1
FIELDS/MAJORS: All Areas Of Study

Fellowships for one year of graduate study or advanced research in the U.S. to women of outstanding ability who are citizens of countries other than the U.S.A. Applicants must hold the equivalent of a U.S. bachelor's degree. Write to the address below for details. Previous and current recipients of AAUW fellowships are ineligible. Also six fellowships for members of International Federation of University Women to study in any country except their home country.

American Association Of University Women
Educational Foundation
2201 N. Dodge Street
Iowa City, IA 52243

2349

International Fellowships

AMOUNT: $22,000-$32,300
DEADLINE: Jul 1, Oct 15
FIELDS/MAJORS: Biomedical And Behavioral Science Research

Awards for foreign scientists to pursue research in any area of the biomedical and behavioral sciences in the U.S. Applicants must have an invitation to study at a U.S. nonprofit institution by a scientist from the institution. Write to the address below for more information. The NIH also offers a visiting program for foreign researchers that lasts from two to seven years. Details on this can also be obtained from the address below.

National Institutes Of Health, Fogarty International Center
Building 31, Room B2C39
31 Center DR MSC 2220
Bethesda, MD 20892

2350

International Fellowships in Jewish Studies

AMOUNT: $5,000 **DEADLINE:** Oct 31
FIELDS/MAJORS: Jewish Studies

Applicants must be qualified scholars, researchers, or artists who process the knowledge and experience to formulate and implement a project in a field of Jewish specialization. Write to the address below for details.

Memorial Foundation For Jewish Culture
15 East 26th Street, Room 1901
New York, NY 10010

2351

International Gas Turbine Institute Scholarship Program

AMOUNT: $1,000 **DEADLINE:** Feb 1
FIELDS/MAJORS: Mechanical Engineering

Scholarships for ASME student members who are majoring in mechanical engineer ing with an interest in gas turbine technology. For additional information, call or write the ASME foundation.

American Society Of Mechanical Engineers
Asme International Gas Turbine Institute
5801 Peachtree Dunwoody Road
Atlanta, GA 30342

2352

International Order Of The Golden Rule Awards

Amount: Varies **Deadline:** None Specified
Fields/Majors: Mortuary Science

Awards for mortuary science majors in his/her final semester of study who have maintained a GPA of at least 3.0 and are involved in school and community service activities. Write to the address below for more information.

International Order Of The Golden Rule
1000 Churchill Rd.
P.O. Box 3586
Springfield, IL 62708

2353

International Predissertation Fellowship Program

Amount: Varies **Deadline:** Varies
Fields/Majors: Economics, Political Science, Sociology, Social Sciences

Program is open to Ph.D candidates in the above majors and enrolled at selected universities. Primary purpose is to provide funding for overseas study. Applicants must be in the early phases of their training. Applications must be submitted by the participating university. Write to Int'l Predissertation Fellowship Program at the address below for details.

Social Science Research Council
605 Third Ave.
New York, NY 10158

2354

International Scholars Awards

Amount: $5,000-$7,500 **Deadline:** Mar 15
Fields/Majors: All Areas Of Study

Awards open to full-time freshman students in the top 25% of their graduating class. Must have a B-average or better and a TOFEL score of 550. Write to the address below for more information.

Teikyo Post University
Office Of Financial Aid
800 Country Club Road
Waterbury, CT 06723

2355

International Scholarships

Amount: Varies **Deadline:** Jun 1
Fields/Majors: All Areas Of Study

Awards for incoming international students who demonstrate academic merit and financial need. Write to the address below for more information.

University Of Nebraska, Omaha
Office Of Financial Aid, EAB 103
60th And Dodge Streets
Omaha, NE 68182

2356

International Society Of Arbor (New England Chapter) Scholarship

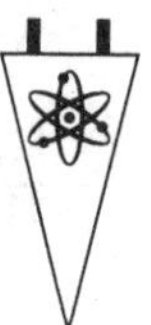

Amount: Varies **Deadline:** Oct 1
Fields/Majors: Plant-Related Studies

Awards for freshmen, sophomores, and juniors in the College of Food and Natural Resources and for seniors in the Stockbridge School. Financial need is the primary basis for this scholarship. Contact Dr. Dennis Ryan or Mr. Tom Houston, Holdsworth Natural Resources Center, for more information.

University Of Massachusetts, Amherst
Holdsworth Natural Resources Center
Amherst, MA 01003

2357

International Student Fee Remission Scholarships

Amount: Varies **Deadline:** Varies
Fields/Majors: All Areas Of Study

Awards are available for international students who meet all the admissions standards, including the TOEFL requirement, and have a GPA of at least 3.0 on all previous academic work. Students must maintain legal non-immigrant status. Write to the address below for more information.

Portland State University
International Student And Faculty Services
Sixth Ave. Building
Portland, OR 97207

2358

International Student Paper Competition

Amount: $50-$500 **Deadline:** May 15
Fields/Majors: Business Administration, Management, and Resource Management

Prize for best paper dealing with operations management; production management; industrial management or business administration. Open to full- or part-time undergraduate or graduate students currently enrolled in an accredited educational institution. Write to the address below or contact your local APICS chapter for details.

American Production And Inventory Control Society Inc.
500 West Annadale Rd.
Falls Church, VA 22046

2359

International Student Scholarships

Amount: $1,000-$10,000 **Deadline:** None Specified
Fields/Majors: All Areas Of Study

Scholarships for non-U.S. citizens who are full-time freshman at Alfred University (under a student visa). Award amounts vary depending upon academic credentials and individual circumstances. Renewable. Contact the international student admissions coordinator at the Alfred University Office of Admissions: (607) 871-2115 or write to the address below.

Alfred University
Student Financial Aid Office
26 N. Main St.
Alfred, NY 14802

2360

International Test And Evaluation Association Awards

AMOUNT: Varies **DEADLINE:** Mar 1
FIELDS/MAJORS: Engineering, Computer Science

Awards are available at the University of New Mexico for upperclassmen or graduate students majoring in engineering or computer science. Applicants must be interested in testing and evaluation of hardware or software. Write to the address below for more information.

University Of New Mexico, Albuquerque
Office Of Financial Aid
Albuquerque, NM 87131

2361

Internships At The Cooper-Hewitt Museum

AMOUNT: None Specified **DEADLINE:** Mar 31
FIELDS/MAJORS: Design, Decorative Arts, Exhibition Development, Museum Science

Summer internships at the Cooper-Hewitt Museum are offered to students who have completed at least two years of college in the areas above. Write to the internship coordinator at the address below for details.

Smithsonian Institution
National Museum Of Design
2 E. 91st St.
New York, NY 10128

2362

Iowa Center For The Arts Scholarships

AMOUNT: $2,500 **DEADLINE:** None Specified
FIELDS/MAJORS: Art, Art History, Drama, Dance, Music

Scholarships are available at the University of Iowa for full-time incoming freshman students majoring in one of the above fields. Write to the address listed below for information.

University Of Iowa
School Of Art And Art History
E100 Art Building
Iowa City, IA 52245

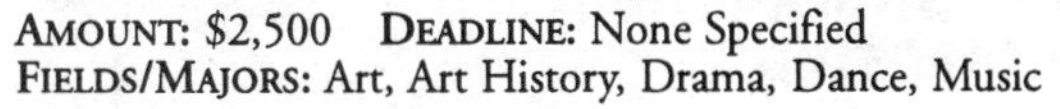

2363

Iowa Center For The Arts Scholarships, Marcia Thayer Scholarship

AMOUNT: Varies **DEADLINE:** Apr 15
FIELDS/MAJORS: Dance, Drama, Music, Art, Art History

Scholarships are available at the University of Iowa for full-time students majoring in one of the above fields who show exceptional talent and potential. Thayer award is aimed at students who excel in a second performing art. Write to the address listed below for information.

University Of Iowa
Department Of Dance
E114 Halsey Hall
Iowa City, IA 52245

2364

Iowa Community College Transfer Scholarship

AMOUNT: $200-Tuition **DEADLINE:** None Specified
FIELDS/MAJORS: All Areas Of Study

Scholarships are available at the University of Iowa for students who are graduates of an Iowa community college, who demonstrates academic excellence and financial need. Write to the address listed below for information.

University Of Iowa
Office Of Student Financial Aid
208 Calvin Hall
Iowa City, IA 52242

2365

Iowa Farm Scholarship

AMOUNT: Tuition **DEADLINE:** Apr 1
FIELDS/MAJORS: All Areas Of Study

Scholarships for freshmen who live on Iowa farms operated by their parents. Must rank in top 25% of high school class. Nonrenewable. Must be enrolled for at least twelve hours per semester. Four awards offered each year. Contact the office of student financial aid for details.

University Of Iowa
Office Of Student Financial Aid
208 Calvin Hall
Iowa City, IA 52242

2366

Iowa Grant Program

AMOUNT: $1,000 **DEADLINE:** None Specified
FIELDS/MAJORS: All Areas Of Study

Grants for Iowa residents enrolled or planing to enroll as undergraduate at eligible postsecondary schools in Iowa. Based on need. Also available is a program to allow students the resources to attend private colleges in Iowa. Contact your college or write to the address below for details.

Iowa College Student Aid Commission
914 Grand Avenue
Suite 201
Des Moines, IA 50309

2367

Iowa Vocational-Technical Tuition Grants

AMOUNT: $600 (max) **DEADLINE:** Apr 22
FIELDS/MAJORS: Vocational/Technical Areas Of Study

Open to Iowa residents enrolled/accepted for enrollment in a program of vocational-technical study at an area school in Iowa. Program must be at least twelve weeks in length. Applicant must be a U.S. citizen, legal resident, or refugee. Contact your college or write to the address below for details.

Iowa College Student Aid Commission
914 Grand Avenue, Suite 201
Des Moines, IA 50309

2368

Iptay Academic Scholarship Fund

AMOUNT: $2,500 **DEADLINE:** Mar 1
FIELDS/MAJORS: All Areas Of Study

Scholarships for entering freshmen who do not participate in intercollegiate athletics. Renewable for three years. Several scholarships awarded. Contact the financial aid office at the address below for details.

Clemson University
Financial Aid Office
G01 Sikes Hall
Clemson, SC 29634

2369

Ira Cobe College Scholarship Program

AMOUNT: None Specified **DEADLINE:** None Specified
FIELDS/MAJORS: All Areas Of Study

Awards for young men who are residents of Waldo County and are in need of financial assistance in meeting the expenses of post-secondary education. Must be under age 23. Write to Ann Tartre at the address below for more information.

Maine Community Foundation
P.O. Box 148
Ellsworth, ME 04605

2370

Irene "Renie" Diplacido Memorial Scholarship

AMOUNT: Varies **DEADLINE:** None Specified
FIELDS/MAJORS: All Areas Of Study

Award for Mercyhurst students from Erie, PA, who have academic achievements. Write to the address below for more information.

Mercyhurst College
Financial Aid Office
Glenwood Hills
Erie, PA 16546

2371

Irene And Daisy MacGregor Memorial & Alice W. Rooke Scholarship

AMOUNT: $5,000 **DEADLINE:** Apr 15
FIELDS/MAJORS: Medicine, Psychiatric Nursing

Scholarship available to students who have been accepted into an accredited school of medicine to pursue an M.D. or are studying in the field of psychiatric nursing. All applicants must be sponsored by a local DAR chapter, and be U.S. citizens. Contact your local DAR chapter or write to the address below for details.

National Society Daughters Of The American Revolution
NSDAR Scholarship Committee
1776 D St., NW
Washington, DC 20006

2372

Irene E. Newman Scholarship

GPA 3.0+

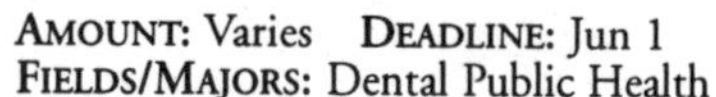

AMOUNT: Varies **DEADLINE:** Jun 1
FIELDS/MAJORS: Dental Public Health

Scholarships for baccalaureate or graduate degree candidate in a full-time accredited program in dental public health. Must have completed at least one year of program and have a GPA of at least 3.0. Write to the address below for more information.

American Dental Hygienists' Association
Institute For Oral Health
444 N. Michigan Ave., Suite 3400
Chicago, IL 60611

2373

Irene Navarre Dental Hygiene Student Award

AMOUNT: Varies **DEADLINE:** Mar 1
FIELDS/MAJORS: Dental Hygiene

Awards are available at the University of New Mexico for second year students in the dental hygiene program. Based on clinical and patient management skills, leadership potential, professionalism, integrity, and participation in student organizations and community involvement. Write to the address listed below for information.

University Of New Mexico, Albuquerque
Office Of Financial Aid
Albuquerque, NM 87131

2374

Irene Parks Student Loan Fund

AMOUNT: $500 (max) **DEADLINE:** Oct 22
FIELDS/MAJORS: Pharmacy

Awards for students in their final two-years of a pharmacy program. Maximum of two recipients per school. Write to the address below for more information.

APHA Auxiliary, Ms. Nann Towers
7327 Danbury Way
Clearwater, FL 33546

2375

Irene Sodborough Scholarship

AMOUNT: $500 **DEADLINE:** Mar 1
FIELDS/MAJORS: All Areas Of Study

Award for Native American students at Eastern who show financial need. Preference is given to students interested in arts, especially visual arts. Write to the address below for more information.

Eastern Oregon State College
Financial Aid Office
1041 "I" Avenue
La Grande, OR 97850

2376

Irex Developmental Fellowships

AMOUNT: Varies **DEADLINE:** Nov 1
FIELDS/MAJORS: All Areas Of Study, Foreign Study

Fellowships are available for pre and postdoctoral scholars to prepare for eventual research in Central and Eastern Europe and the states of the former Soviet region. Training will be in the U.S. Applicants should be interested in developing competence for this research. Funding is not given for routine graduate coursework or dissertation research. Must be a U.S. citizen. Write to the address listed below for information.

International Research And Exchange Board
Fellowship Program
1616 H Street, NW
Washington, DC 20006

2377

Irish American Cultural Institute Grants

AMOUNT: Varies **DEADLINE:** None Specified
FIELDS/MAJORS: Irish Studies

Grants and fellowships are available for scholars and students who are majoring in Irish studies. Certain awards are for study in the U.S. and others are for study in Ireland. Write to the address below for additional information.

The Irish American Cultural Institute
Ms. Kristen A. Gill, Development Coor.
3 Elm St., Suite 204
Morristown, NJ 07960

2378

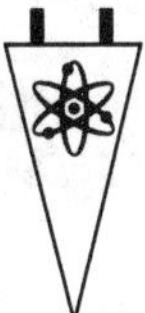

Irrigation Association Scholarships

AMOUNT: $1,000 **DEADLINE:** Feb 15
FIELDS/MAJORS: Agriculture, Horticulture, Landscaping

Scholarships are available for FFA members pursuing a four-year degree in any area of agriculture, horticulture, or landscaping with an interest in irrigation. Write to the address below for details.

National FFA Foundation
Scholarship Office
P.O. Box 15160
Alexandria, VA 22309

2379

Irvine Ranch Water District

AMOUNT: $3,000 (max) **DEADLINE:** Apr 1
FIELDS/MAJORS: All Areas Of Study

Open to students planning to enroll in a graduate program full-time with preference given to residents of Irvine or who plan to make their professional career in Irvine. Contact Irvine Ranch Water District, 15600 San Canyon Ave, P.O. Box 57000, Irvine, CA 92619-7000, or call (714) 453-5500 for more information.

California State Polytechnic University, Pomona
College Of Agriculture
Building 45, Room 109b
Pomona, CA 91768

2380

Irvington Women's Club Scholarships

AMOUNT: $500 **DEADLINE:** None Specified
FIELDS/MAJORS: All Areas Of Study

Award for junior- or senior-level woman with demonstrated professional goals and financial need. Must be full-time student with minimum cumulative GPA of at least 3.0. Contact the Office of Women's Studies for more information.

Portland State University
Department Of Women's Studies
401 Cramer Hall
Portland, OR 97207

2381

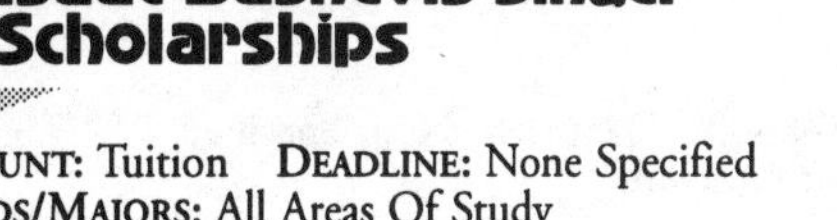

Isaac Bashevis Singer Scholarships

GPA 3.5+

AMOUNT: Tuition **DEADLINE:** None Specified
FIELDS/MAJORS: All Areas Of Study

Scholarships for the top 1% of enrolled freshmen at the University of Miami. Renewable. Write to the address below for more information.

University Of Miami
Office Of Financial Assistance Services
P.O. Box 248187
Coral Gables, FL 33124

2382

Isaacson Incentive Scholarships

GPA 3.0+

AMOUNT: $1,000 **DEADLINE:** Jan 15
FIELDS/MAJORS: All Areas Of Study

Awards for students who have potential for academic success based on previous performance and who are enrolled full-time and maintain a 3.0 GPA. Must be legal residents of the Omaha metro area, graduates of one of the metro area high schools, and maintain that residency for the duration of the scholarship. Renewable. Write to the address below for more information.

University Of Nebraska, Omaha
Office Of Multicultural Affairs, EAB 115
60th And Dodge Streets
Omaha, NE 68182

2383

Isabel M. Herson Scholarship In Education

AMOUNT: $500-$1,000 **DEADLINE:** Feb 1
FIELDS/MAJORS: Education, Elementary And Secondary

Scholarships for undergraduate or graduate students in degree-granting programs in elementary or secondary education. For one full-time academic year. No affiliation with Zeta Phi Beta is required. Send a stamped, self-addressed envelope to the national headquarters at the address below prior to Feb. 1 for further information.

Zeta Phi Beta Sorority
National Educational Foundation
1734 New Hampshire Ave., NW
Washington, DC 20009

2384

ISCLT Scholarships

AMOUNT: None Specified **DEADLINE:** None Specified
FIELDS/MAJORS: All Areas Of Study

Scholarships for ISCLT registrant or regular class members or for children of ISCLT registrant or regular class members. Student class members are not eligible to apply. Write to the address below for details.

International Society for Clinical Laboratory Technology
818 Olive Street, Suite 918
St. Louis, MO 63101

2385

ISU Agricultural Scholarships

AMOUNT: $400-$500 **DEADLINE:** None Specified
FIELDS/MAJORS: Agriculture

Scholarship awarded to incoming freshmen or transfer students enrolling in an agricultural curriculum at Illinois State University. Applicant must have participated in FFA as an officer or section president. Includes the Clarence & Mabel Ropp, Reg & Edith Henry Leadership, and the Agriculture Faculty Scholarships. (4-H participants can also apply for the Ropp Scholarship.) For more information contact your high school guidance counselor or write to the address below.

Illinois State University, Dept. Of Agriculture
Turner Hall 150
Campus Box 5020
Normal, IL 61761

2386

Italian American Chamber Of Commerce Scholarships

AMOUNT: $1,000 **DEADLINE:** May 31
FIELDS/MAJORS: All Areas Of Study

Scholarships available to Illinois residents of Italian ancestry. Selection based on financial need. Write to the address below for details.

Italian American Chamber of Commerce
30 S. Michigan Ave.
Chicago, IL 60603

2387

Italian Catholic Federation Scholarships

AMOUNT: $350 **DEADLINE:** Mar 21
FIELDS/MAJORS: All Areas Of Study

Open to graduating high school seniors of Italian ancestry and of the Catholic faith. Applicants must also be a resident of California, Nevada, or Illinois and have a minimum 3.0 GPA. Approximately two-hundred awards per year. Contact your high school guidance counselor, or write to the address below for details.

Italian Catholic Federation, Inc.
1801 Van Ness Ave., Suite 330
San Francisco, CA 94109

2388

Italian-American Cultural Society Scholarships

AMOUNT: $750-$1,250 **DEADLINE:** Feb 1
FIELDS/MAJORS: All Fields Of Study

Scholarships offered to Ocean County Senior High students of Italian descent. Applicants must submit an essay on Italian culture. Five awards given. Amount of the award depends upon the parents standing in the society. Write to the address below for details.

Italian-American Cultural Society Of Ocean County, Inc.
P.O. Box 1602
Toms River, NJ 08754

2389

ITF Undergraduate Student Scholarship

AMOUNT: Varies **DEADLINE:** Jun 1
FIELDS/MAJORS: Ground Transportation (Taxicab And Paratransit Industry)

Awards for undergraduate students enrolled in a program studying ground transportation. Applicants must have a GPA of at least 3.5. Preference given to dependents of people associated with the taxicab and paratransit industry. Write to the address below for more information.

International Taxicab Foundation
3849 Farragut Ave.
Kengsington, MD 20895

2390

Itleson And Andrew W. Mellon Fellowship

AMOUNT: $13,000 **DEADLINE:** Nov 15
FIELDS/MAJORS: Visual Art, Art History And Theory, Architecture, And Related Areas

Two-year fellowship for doctoral student doing dissertation research in the fields of study above. Scholars are expected to spend half a year at the National Gallery of Art, half a year doing research anywhere in the U.S. or abroad, and the second year at the Center to complete the dissertation. Applicants must know two languages related to the topic of their dissertation. Fellowship is only available to U.S. citizens or legal residents. Contact the chairperson of the graduate department of art history at your school (or other appropriate department) or write to the address below for more information.

National Gallery Of Art
Center For Study In The Visual Arts
Predoctoral Fellowship Program
Washington, DC 20565

2391

Iva W. And Roy Henry Scholarship

AMOUNT: Varies **DEADLINE:** May 15
FIELDS/MAJORS: All Areas Of Study

Awards for students from Edgar County, IL. Applications are only accepted from May 1 through May 15. Contact the Trust Department at the address below for more information.

Citizens National Bank Of Paris
110-114 West Court St.
P.O. Box 790
Paris, IL 61944

2392

Ives Memorial Scholarship

AMOUNT: Varies **DEADLINE:** Mar 1
FIELDS/MAJORS: Teacher Education

Awards are available at the University of New Mexico for female students enrolled in a teacher education program in the college of education. Must demonstrate financial need and scholastic merit. Write to the address below for more information.

University Of New Mexico, Albuquerque
Office Of Financial Aid
Albuquerque, NM 87131

2393

Ivy Parker Memorial Scholarship

Amount: $2,000 **Deadline:** Feb 1
Fields/Majors: Engineering

Scholarship for junior or senior woman majoring in engineering in an accredited program. Must have a GPA of at least 3.5. Based on financial need. Write to address below for details. Please be certain to enclose an SASE. Information and applications for the SWE Awards are also available from the deans of engineering schools.

Society Of Women Engineers
120 Wall Street, 11th Floor
New York, NY 10005

2394

J. Clifford Dietrich, Julie Y. Cross, John Hays Hanly Scholarships

Amount: None Specified **Deadline:** May 1
Fields/Majors: Law Enforcement, Police Administration

Three scholarships for students of law enforcement or police administration at an accredited college or university. Must have completed at least one year of study. No more than one scholarship is awarded to any one family. Students who are working toward an advanced degree are also eligible. Must be a U.S. citizen. Write to the address below for details. Include an SASE for an application.

Association Of Former Agents Of The U.S. Secret Service
P.O. Box 11681
Alexandria, VA 22312

2395

J. Desmond Slattery Marketing Awards

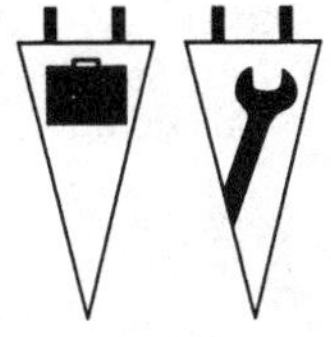

Amount: Varies **Deadline:** Mar 1
Fields/Majors: Marketing-Travel/Tourism

Awards for papers or projects relating to the travel and tourism industry. Only two submissions per school or institution are permitted. Application is made through your school (except entries from current travel marketing professionals). Write to the address below for further information.

Travel And Tourism Research Association
TTRA Awards Committee
10200 W. 44th Ave., Suite 304
Wheat Ridge, CO 80033

2396

J. Edward Kerlin Scholarship

Amount: $250 **Deadline:** Feb 9
Fields/Majors: Mathematics, Computer Science

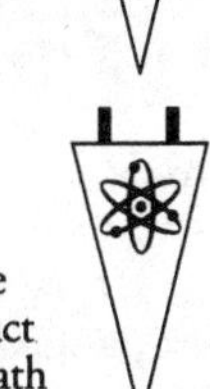

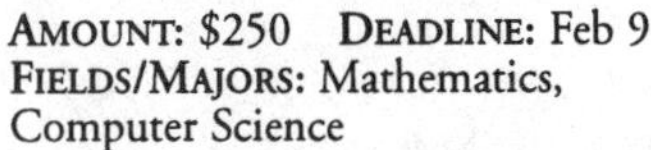

Award for sophomore with a minimum GPA of 3.0. Must have made contributions to the department. Use Bloomsburg University scholarship application. Contact Dr. Charles Brennan, Chairperson, Department of Math and Computer Sciences, for further information.

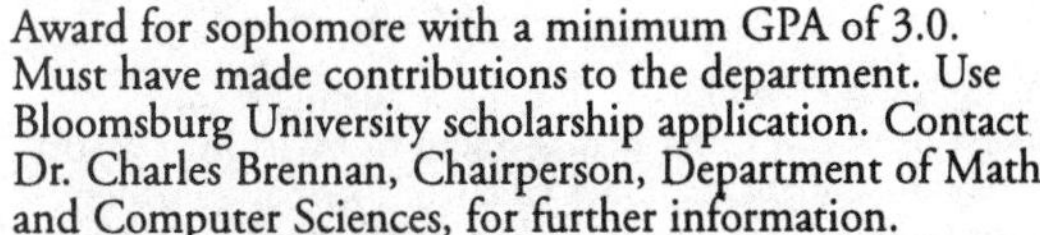

Bloomsburg University
19 Ben Franklin Hall
400 E. Second St.
Bloomsburg, PA 17815

2397

J. Henry Young Endowed Scholarship

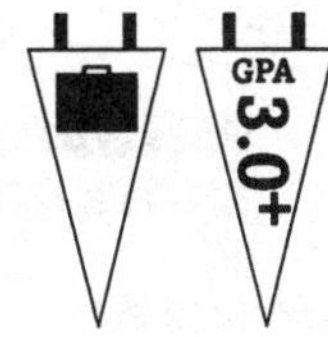

Amount: $2,000 **Deadline:** Mar 1
Fields/Majors: Accounting

Award for a full-time ENMU accounting student who has a GPA of at least 3.0, and has completed ACCT 301 by the effective date of the award. Write to the address below for more information.

Eastern New Mexico University
ENMU College Of Business Station 49
Portales, NM 88130

2398

J. Hugh And Earle W. Fellows Memorial Fund Loans

Amount: Varies **Deadline:** None Specified
Fields/Majors: Medicine, Nursing, Medical Technology, Theology

Low interest loans for residents of Escambia, Santa Rosa, Okaloosa, or Walton Counties in Florida, who are studying in one of the above fields. Renewable. Write to the address below for details.

J. Hugh And Earle W. Fellows Memorial Fund
Pensacola Junior Coll, Exec. Vice Pres.
1000 College Blvd.
Pensacola, FL 32504

2399

J. Kelly Sisk Memorial Endowed Scholarship

Amount: $1,000 **Deadline:** Feb 15
Fields/Majors: Communications

Renewable $1,000 scholarship given to freshmen, sophomores and juniors (with preference given to freshmen) in the College of Communication at the University of Alabama, whose current record and potential suggest a successful career as a communicator. Write to the address listed below for further information and an application.

Multimedia, Inc. Stockholders College Of Comm.
University Of Alabama
P.O. Box 870172
Tuscaloosa, AL 35487

2400

J. L. Bedsole Scholars Program

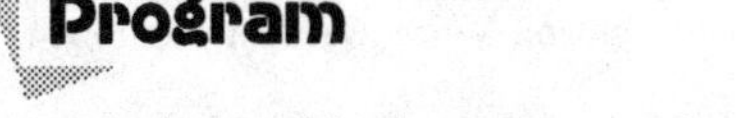

Amount: $2,000-$6,000 **Deadline:** Apr 1
Fields/Majors: All Areas Of Study

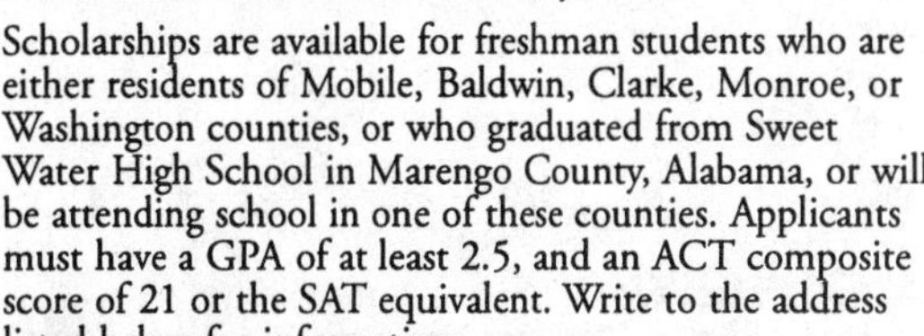

Scholarships are available for freshman students who are either residents of Mobile, Baldwin, Clarke, Monroe, or Washington counties, or who graduated from Sweet Water High School in Marengo County, Alabama, or will be attending school in one of these counties. Applicants must have a GPA of at least 2.5, and an ACT composite score of 21 or the SAT equivalent. Write to the address listed below for information.

J. L. Bedsole Foundation
P.O. Box 1137
Mobile, AL 36633

2401 J. Raymond Stuart Prize In Economics

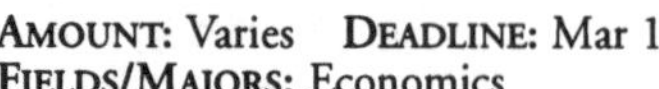

Amount: Varies **Deadline:** Mar 1
Fields/Majors: Economics

Awards are available at the University of New Mexico for undergraduates or graduate students enrolled in the Department of Economics. Must demonstrate financial need. Write to the address listed below for information.

University Of New Mexico
Albuquerque Office Of Financial Aid
Albuquerque, NM 87131

2402 J. Thomas Davis Memorial Scholarship

Amount: None Specified **Deadline:** None Specified
Fields/Majors: Business, Marketing, Advertising

Scholarships for students at East Tennessee State University majoring on one of the above areas. Contact the College of Business or the office of financial aid for details.

East Tennessee State University
Office Of Financial Aid
Box 70722
Johnson City, TN 37614

2403 J. Walter Thompson Scholarships

Amount: $1,000 **Deadline:** Feb 15
Fields/Majors: Agronomy, Food Science

Scholarships are available for FFA members pursuing a four-year degree in any area of agronomy or food science. Applicant must have participated in the cereal grains proficiency program above the local level. Write to the address below for details.

National FFA Foundation
Scholarship Office
P.O. Box 1516
Alexandria, VA 22309

2404 J.A. Knowles Memorial Scholarship

Amount: Varies **Deadline:** Varies
Fields/Majors: All Areas Of Study

Awards are available for active members of the Methodist Church who are enrolled in a United Methodist-related school in Texas. Applicant must be a full-time degree candidate and a U.S. citizen or permanent resident. Write to the address below for more information.

United Methodist Church
Office Of Loans And Scholarships
1001 Nineteenth Ave., South
P.O. Box 871
Nashville, TN 37202

2405 J.B. Cornelius Foundation/Grants

Amount: $1,000 **Deadline:** May 15
Fields/Majors: All Areas Of Study

Open to female students entering or attending Bennett College (Greensboro, NC), Brevard College (Brevard, NC), Greensboro College (Greensboro, NC), High Point University (High Point, NC), or Pfieffer College (Misenheimer, NC). Must demonstrate financial need. Write to the address below for more information.

J.B. Cornelius Foundation
181 Rutledge Rd.
Greenwood, SC 29649

2406 J.F. Edsal And Norman R. McKittrick Memorial Scholarship Funds

Amount: $75 **Deadline:** Mar 31
Fields/Majors: Filmmaking, Advertising

Scholarships are available for Rhode Island residents enrolled in a filmmaking or advertising program with career goals of in one of these fields. For undergraduate study beyond first semester freshman year. Write to the address listed below for information.

Rhode Island Advertising Club
18 Imperial Place
Providence, RI 02886

2407 J.E. Caldwell Centennial Scholarships

Amount: $2,000 **Deadline:** Feb 15
Fields/Majors: Historical Preservation

Scholarships for graduate students in the area of historical preservation. Must be sponsored by a DAR chapter. Must be a U.S. citizen. Contact your local or state DAR chapter, or write to the address below for details.

National Society Daughters Of The American Revolution
NSDAR Scholarship Committee
1776 D St., NW
Washington, DC 20006

2408 J.J. Barr Scholarship

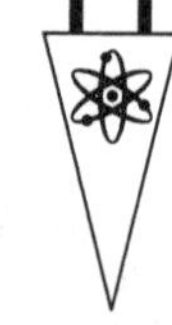

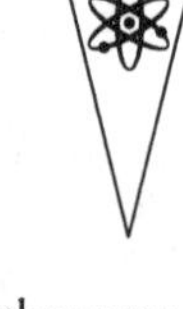

Amount: $5,000 **Deadline:** Apr 1
Fields/Majors: Water Utility Industry

Scholarship for graduate students pursuing a degree in the water utility industry. Must be a U.S. citizen. Write to the address below for more information.

National Association Of Water Companies
Scholarship Committee
1725 K St., NW, Suite 1212
Washington, DC 20006

2409 J.L. Goodwin Memorial Scholarship

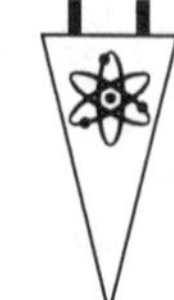

Amount: $1,000-$3,000 **Deadline:** May 18
Fields/Majors: Forest Management, Silviculture

Awards for high school seniors with good academic records who are pursuing a degree in forest management or silviculture. Must be a Connecticut resident. Contact your high school guidance counselor for further information and an application.

Connecticut Forest And Park Association
The Waterbury Foundation
156 W. Main
Waterbury, CT 06702

2410 J.M. Long Foundation Scholarships

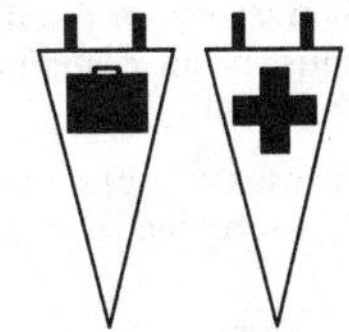

Amount: $500 **Deadline:** Feb 1
Fields/Majors: Health Related, Business

Scholarships are available at the University of Hawaii, Hilo, for full-time students enrolled in either a health-related or business program, who are residents of Hawaii. Write to the address listed below for information.

University Of Hawaii at Hilo
Financial Aid Office
200 West Kawili Street
Hilo, HI 96720

2411 J.W. Coombs Scholarship

Amount: $200 **Deadline:** Spring
Fields/Majors: Engineering

Awards are available to students majoring in engineering who are chosen by the scholarship committee of engineering and applied science. Contact the dean's office at the address below for more information.

Portland State University
Engineering And Applied Sciences
118 Science Building 2
Portland, OR 92707

2412 Jack & June Biggart Scholarships

Amount: None Specified **Deadline:** Feb 1
Fields/Majors: Industrial Education, Industrial Technology

Scholarship for a high school graduate majoring in industrial education and technology at Murray State University. A minimum 3.0 GPA is required. Write to the address below for details.

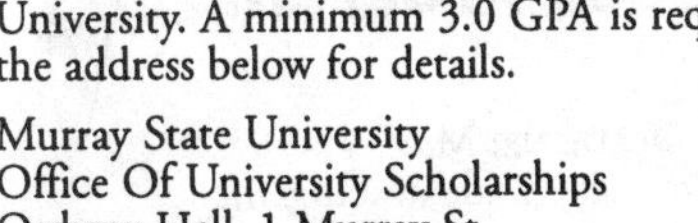

Murray State University
Office Of University Scholarships
Ordway Hall, 1 Murray St.
Murray, KY 42071

2413 Jack And Calvin Gower Scholarship

Amount: Varies **Deadline:** None Specified
Fields/Majors: History

Award for Mesa State students enrolled full-time in history who have a GPA of at least 3.3. Contact the chair of the department of social and behavioral sciences or faculty members teaching history.

Mesa State College
Office Of Financial Aid
P.O. Box 2647
Grand Junction, CO 81501

2414 Jack C. Nisbet Memorial Scholarship

Amount: Varies **Deadline:** July 1
Fields/Majors: All Areas Of Study

Scholarships available to members of the American Jersey Cattle Association who were participants in the last National Youth Achievement Contest. Write to the address below for details.

American Jersey Cattle Association
Scholarship Committee
6486 East Main Street
Reynoldsburg, OH 43068

2415 Jack Gordon Memorial Scholarship

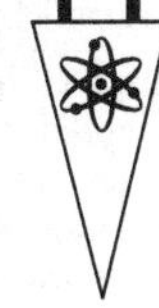

Amount: $300 **Deadline:** None Specified
Fields/Majors: Agriculture

Student must graduate in the top half of their class at Galena High School and have an interest in agriculture. Write to the address below for more information.

Southwest Missouri State University
Office Of Financial Aid
901 South National Ave.
Springfield, MO 65804

2416 Jack In The Box Essay And Photo Scholarship Competition

Amount: $1,000 **Deadline:** Mar 1
Fields/Majors: Writing, Photography

Essay or photo contest on the theme "If I Ruled the World" for high school seniors. Applicants must be from Arizona, California, Hawaii, Washington, or Texas. Winners are selected solely on the quality of their entry, academic transcripts are not required. Write to the address below for more information. Texas residents must live in an area with one of the following zip code prefixes: 750, 751, 752, 754, 760, 761, 762, 765, 767, 794, or 799.

Jack In The Box Restaurants
c/o Anderson Communications Co., Inc.
3 Corporate Plaza, Suite 20
Newport Beach, CA 92660

2417 Jack Millar Scholarship

Amount: $500 **Deadline:** Varies
Fields/Majors: Hotel Management

Scholarships for Hawaii residents studying hotel management at Maui Community College. Contact the financial aid office at Maui Community College for information.

Hawaii Hotel Association
Ms. Susan Haramoto
2270 Kalakaua Ave, Suite 1103
Honolulu, HI 96815

2418 Jack W. Keuffel Scholarship, Thomas J. Parmley Scholarship

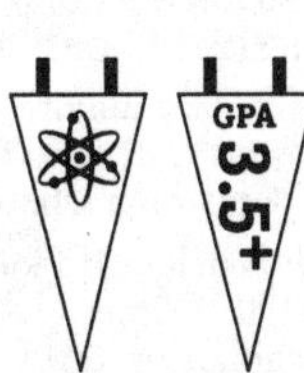

Amount: Varies **Deadline:** Feb 15
Fields/Majors: Physics

Scholarships are available at the University of Utah for full-time physics majors, who have a GPA of at least 3.5 in math and science coursework. Write to the address below for information.

University Of Utah
Dr. Leslie Glaser
239 John A. Widtsoe Building
Salt Lake City, UT 84112

2419
Jackie Robinson Foundation Scholarship

AMOUNT: $5,000 (max) **DEADLINE:** Apr 1
FIELDS/MAJORS: All Areas Of Study

Scholarships for minority high school seniors who have been accepted into a four-year college or university. Based on academic achievement, leadership, and financial need. Must be a U.S. citizen. Check with your high school guidance counselor to see if he or she has details on this program. Otherwise, write to the address below for details.

Jackie Robinson Foundation Scholarship Fund
Attn: Scholarship Program
3 West 35th St.
New York, NY 10011

2420
Jackson Scholarship Fund

AMOUNT: None Specified **DEADLINE:** None Specified
FIELDS/MAJORS: All Areas Of Study

Loans for Lake County, CA, residents who graduated from a Lake County high school and need assistance to pursue or continue advanced schooling. Must be accepted for enrollment in an accredited university, college or trade school. Repayment begins after completion of schooling. Write to the address below for details.

Jackson Scholarship Fund
Crawford, Major & Kranz, Attys At Law
160 5th St.
Lakeport, CA 95453

2421
Jackson SWCD Scholarship

AMOUNT: $500 **DEADLINE:** Mar 15
FIELDS/MAJORS: All Areas Of Study

Scholarships are available for graduating high school seniors who reside in Jackson County. Applicant must have a GPA of at least 3.0. Participation in civic and co-curricular activities will be considered. Write to the address listed below for information.

Jackson Soil And Water Conservation District
34 Portsmouth Street
Jackson, OH 45640

2422
Jacksonville Advertising Federation Scholarship

AMOUNT: $1,000 **DEADLINE:** Mar 1
FIELDS/MAJORS: Advertising

Must be a junior or senior attending the University of Florida. Must have at least a 3.0 GPA and have graduated from a Duval or Nassau County high school. Write to the address below for complete details.

University Of Florida
2070 Weimer Hall
Scholarship & Placement Director
Gainesville, FL 32611

2423
Jacksonville State University Scholarships

AMOUNT: Varies **DEADLINE:** Mar 15
FIELDS/MAJORS: All Areas Of Study

Many awards and scholarships offered by Jacksonville State University for qualified entering or attending students. Applicant must be an Alabama resident. Write to the address below for more information.

Jacksonville State University
Jacksonville, AL 36265

2424
Jacobs Research Funds Small Grants Program

AMOUNT: $1,200 (max) **DEADLINE:** Feb 15
FIELDS/MAJORS: Anthropology

Grants for students with any level of academic credentials who are doing research which supports the sociocultural or linguistic aspects of anthropology. The primary focus of study will be on indigenous peoples of Canada, the mainland U.S. (especially the Pacific Northwest), and Mexico. Write to the address below for more information.

Whatcom Museum
Attn: Museum Representative
121 Prospect St.
Bellingham, WA 98225

2425
Jacqueline Dwyer Gowan Nursing Excellence

AMOUNT: None Specified **DEADLINE:** None Specified
FIELDS/MAJORS: Nursing

Scholarships are open to junior B.S.N. students who are in good standing academically and demonstrate dedication, compassion, and resourcefulness. Write to the address below for more information.

Indiana University/Purdue University, Indianapolis
School Of Nursing
1111 Middle Dr., NU 122
Indianapolis, IN 46202

2426
Jake Gimbel Loan Program

AMOUNT: None Specified **DEADLINE:** Mar 31
FIELDS/MAJORS: Education or Any Graduate Program

Special loans are available for residents of Santa Barbara County, who have attended grades 7-12 in Santa Barbara County, that are either pursuing a teaching career, or are in any graduate program in the state of California. Write to the address below for further information

Santa Barbara Foundation
Student Aid Director
15 East Carrillo Street
Santa Barbara, CA 93101

2427
James A. Finnegan Fellowship Contest

AMOUNT: $1,500 (min) **DEADLINE:** Feb 9
FIELDS/MAJORS: Political Science, Government

Summer fellowships for undergraduates attending accredited Pennsylvania colleges/universities or students from Pennsylvania attending any institution who have completed at least one semester of study. Interns are assigned positions in executive or legislative offices, and they will attend seminars with leading public officials and media figures. Write to the address below for more information.

James A. Finnegan Fellowship Foundation
Contest Coordinator
417 Walnut St., Suite A
Harrisburg, PA 17101

2428
James And Lorna Spencer Endowed Scholarship

Amount: Varies **Deadline:** None Specified
Fields/Majors: All Areas Of Study

Awards are available for full-time students at Cedarville College who have demonstrated financial need. Must have a GPA of at least 2.0. Write to the address below for more information.

Cedarville College Financial Aid Office
P.O. Box 601
Cedarville, OH 45314

2429
James And Mary Dawson Scholarship

Amount: $5,000 **Deadline:**Mar 15
Fields/Majors: All Areas Of Study

Scholarship available to a student of Scottish heritage coming to America for graduate studies. Based on need, academics, and goals. Consideration is made for students contributing to Scottish history or culture. Write to James S. McLeod, Chairman of the Charity and Education Committee, at the address below for details.

St. Andrew's Society Of Washington, DC
Charity And Education Fund Committee
7012 Arandale Rd.
Bethesda, MD 20817

2430
James B. Black Scholarship

Amount: $1,000 **Deadline:** Jan 16
Fields/Majors: Engineering, Computer Science, MIS, Finance, Economics,

Applicants must be high school seniors living in an area serviced by PG&E and enrolled at a four-year accredited college or university in the U.S. The students must not be children of PG&E employees. Write to the address below for details.

Pacific Gas And Electric Company
Mail Code P15C P.O. Box 77000
San Francisco, CA 94177

2431
James B. Carey Scholarship, J. Fitzmaurice Scholarship

Amount: $1,000-$3,000 **Deadline:** Apr 15
Fields/Majors: All Areas Of Study

Must be a child of an IUE (or former UFWA) member or a deceased IUE member. Must be accepted for admission or already enrolled as a full-time student at a college or university, nursing or technical school. Undergraduates only. Information about the David J. Fitzmaurice Scholarship and the William H. Bywater Scholarship (for children of local union officials) is also available. Write to the address below for details or see February or March issue of IUE. Applications should be requested starting in February of the year you are applying.

IUE International
1126 Sixteenth Street, NW
Washington, DC 20036

2432
James Bryden Scholarship

Amount: $500 **Deadline:** Feb 9
Fields/Majors: Special Education-Communication Disorders

Award for students enrolled in communication disorders, teaching of the deaf, blind or general special education. Must demonstrate financial need, academic achievement and activities. Use Bloomsburg University scholarship application. Contact Dr. Carroll Redfern, Chairperson, Department of Communication Disorders and Special Education, for additional information.

Bloomsburg University
19 Ben Franklin Hall
400 E. Second St.
Bloomsburg, PA 17815

2433
James Butler Memorial And Nylcare Health Plans Mid-Atlantic Schlrshps

Amount: $3,000 **Deadline:** Jun 1
Fields/Majors: All Areas Of Study

Awards for students who demonstrate financial need, as verified by parent's tax return for prior year or other suitable documents. Must be graduating high school senior or college student with a GPA of 2.5 or better. Also based upon 3 letters of reference, an essay on the challenge to American families today, and great involvement in school & community activities. Contact Nylcare customer service at (800) 635-3121 for more information.

Nylcare/Mid-Atlantic Scholarship Foundation, Inc.
7617 Ora Glen Drive
Greenbelt, MD 20770

2434
James C. Snapp Memorial

Amount: $900 **Deadline:** None Specified
Fields/Majors: Business

Student must be a full-time COBA major with leadership potential and financial need. Contact the COBA office for more information.

Southwest Missouri State University
Office Of Financial Aid
901 South National Ave.
Springfield, MO 65804

2435
James D. Durante Nurse Scholarships

Amount:$500 **Deadline:** Jun 3
Fields/Majors: Nursing

Awards for continuing or initial training in an R.N.or L.P.N. program for people who intend to work in long-term care facilities associated with the American Health Care Association. 20 awards per year. Write to the James Durante Nurse Scholarship Program, AHCA, at the below address for details. Enclose a legal-size (54 cent) SASE envelope.

National Foundation For Long Term Care
James D. Durante Nurse Scholarships
1201 L St., NW
Washington, DC 20005

2436 James Doolittle Scholarship

Amount: Varies **Deadline:** Mar 1
Fields/Majors: All Areas Of Study

Awards are available at the University of New Mexico for incoming freshmen with financial need and a high scholastic average. Write to the address below for more information.

University Of New Mexico, Albuquerque
Office Of Financial Aid
Albuquerque, NM 87131

2437 James Drew Pfieffer Memorial Award

Amount: Varies **Deadline:** Mar 1
Fields/Majors: Earth And Planetary Sciences

Awards are available at the University of New Mexico for students in the fields of earth and planetary sciences. Applicants must demonstrate financial need and scholastic ability. Write to the address listed below for information.

University Of New Mexico, Albuquerque
Office Of Financial Aid
Albuquerque, NM 87131

2438 James E. Burr Scholarship

Amount: $800-$1,500 **Deadline:** Mar 15
Fields/Majors: All Areas Of Study

Scholarships are available at Wheaton College for freshman minority students who have a minimum GPA of at least 3.5, with an ACT composite score of at least 25 or SAT score of 1050 or more. Transfer students are also eligible with a GPA of at least 3.3. Write to the address below for details.

Wheaton College
Financial Aid Office
Wheaton, IL 60187

2439 James F. And Mary White McIntosh Scholarship

Amount: Varies **Deadline:** None Specified
Fields/Majors: All Areas Of Study

Award available to students at Rockford College who are of Celtic origin and have attended at least eight years of their schooling in the Rockford school system. Write to the address below for more information.

Rockford College
Financial Aid Office
5050 East State St.
Rockford, IL 61108

2440 James F. Lincoln Memorial Scholarships

Amount: Varies **Deadline:** Mar 1
Fields/Majors: All Areas Of Study

Award for female students at Lake Erie who are involved in extracurricular activities and demonstrate financial need. Write to the address below for more information.

Lake Erie College
Financial Aid Office
391 W. Washington St.
Painesville, OH 44077

2441 James F. Mulholland American Legion Scholarships

Amount: $500 **Deadline:** May 1
Fields/Majors: All Areas Of Study

Two scholarships are available for residents of New York who will be enrolling in college as an entering freshman, immediately continuing from high school graduation (New York State H.S.). Applicant must be the child of a legion or auxiliary member. Write to the address listed below for additional information.

American Legion, Department Of New York
Department Adjutant
112 State Street, Suite 40
Albany, NY 12207

2442 James G. Oxnard Memorial Scholarship

Amount: Varies **Deadline:** Mar 1
Fields/Majors: Medicine

Awards are available at the University of New Mexico for first-year students in the medical school with academic ability and financial need. Write to the address below for more information.

University Of New Mexico, Albuquerque
Office Of Financial Aid
Albuquerque, NM 87131

2443 James K. Rathmell, Jr. Memorial Scholarship

Amount: $2,000 **Deadline:** Apr 1
Fields/Majors: Horticulture

Scholarships for juniors, seniors or graduate students pursuing a career in horticulture or floriculture, who wish to study abroad for six months or longer. Write to the address below for details. The BPFI also sponsors two awards through Future Farmers of America (check with your FFA advisor).

Bedding Plants Foundation, Inc.
Scholarship Program
P.O. Box 27241
Lansing, MI 48909

2444 James L. Allhands Essay Competition

Amount: Varies **Deadline:** Nov 1
Fields/Majors: Construction

Competition open to college seniors in the areas of construction or civil engineering. Must be enrolled in an ABET accredited four- or five-year program. Write to the address below for more information.

Associated General Contractors
Education And Research Fund
Director Of Programs
1957 E. Street, NW
Washington, DC 20006

2445 James L. Shive Scholarship

AMOUNT: $500 **DEADLINE:** None Specified
FIELDS/MAJORS: Civil Engineering

Scholarships are available at the University of Iowa for full-time undergraduate civil engineering students who have completed a mechanics of fluid course with an "A" grade. Write to the address listed below for information.

University Of Iowa Student Services
College Of Engineering
3100 Engineering Building
Iowa City, IA 2242

2446 James Lipari/Speedy Enterprises Scholarship

AMOUNT: $500 **DEADLINE:** Apr 15
FIELDS/MAJORS: Turf Grass Management, Seed Industry

Open to students interested in either the turf grass management or seed industry. Write to the address below for more information.

California State Polytechnic University
Pomona College Of Agriculture
Building 7, Room 11
Pomona, CA 91768

2447 James M. Philputt Memorial Scholarship/Loan

AMOUNT: Varies **DEADLINE:** Mar 15
FIELDS/MAJORS: Theology

Applicants must be members of the Christian church who are preparing for the ordained ministry at one of the following schools: University of Chicago Divinity School, Union Theological Seminary, Vanderbilt Divinity School, or Yale Divinity School. Full-time study and financial need is mandatory. Write to the address below for details.

Christian Church (Disciples Of Christ)
Attn: Scholarships
P.O. Box 1986
Indianapolis, IN 46206

2448 James M. Wight Scholar Award

AMOUNT: Varies **DEADLINE:** None Specified
FIELDS/MAJORS: English

Awards available to junior English majors at Rockford College. Preference is given to students with distinguished ability in literary criticism and analysis. Write to the address below for more information.

Rockford College
Financial Aid Office
5050 East State St.
Rockford, IL 61108

2449 James Marshall Public Policy Fellowship

AMOUNT: $37,000 **DEADLINE:** Jan 15
FIELDS/MAJORS: Psychology

Fellowship providing supervised experience in public policy analysis relying on psychological research and policy advocacy. Fellowship is with the public interest directorate and the public policy office of the APA. Must hold Ph.D. or Psy.D. and be eligible for membership in the APA or SPSSI. Persons on sabbatical are encouraged to apply. One year fellowship with possibility for a one year extension. Write to the address below for information about this and other SPSSI programs. Information may also be available in the psychology departments of many universities.

Society For The Psychological Study Of Social Issues
P.O. Box 1248
Ann Arbor, MI 48106

2450 James S. Fish Scholarship

GPA 2.5+

AMOUNT: $250 **DEADLINE:** Mar 1
FIELDS/MAJORS: Advertising

Awards for juniors and seniors who are majoring in advertising. Must have a GPA of at least 2.8. Write to the address below for more information.

University Of Florida
Knight Scholarship & Placement Director
2070 Weimer Hall
Gainesville, FL 32611

2451 Jane Addams Fellowship in Philanthropy

AMOUNT: $15,000 **DEADLINE:** Feb 17
FIELDS/MAJORS: Research, Philanthropy

Fellowships for students at the Center on Philanthropy at Indiana University. Program is to encourage recent college graduates in their pursuit of the study of philanthropy. Residential fellowship program. Not for students already enrolled in a master's program. Write to the address below for details.

Indiana University
Center on Philanthropy
Jane Addams Fellowships
550 W. North St., Suite 301
Indianapolis, IN 46202

2452 Jane Coffin Childs Fund Postdoctoral Fellowships

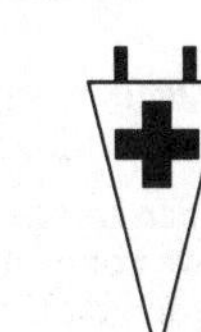

AMOUNT: $25,000 **DEADLINE:** Feb 1
FIELDS/MAJORS: Cancer Research, Oncology

Fellowship is for a three-year period with stipend increases each year. Applicants must hold the M.D. or Ph.D and submit a research proposal. For study into the causes, origins, and treatment of cancer. No restrictions on citizenship or institution. For study in the first few years of postdoctoral career. Write to the address below for details.

Jane Coffin Childs Memorial Fund For Medical Research
Office Of The Director
333 Cedar Street, P.O. Box 3333
New Haven, CT 06510

2453 Jane Grant Dissertation Fellowship

AMOUNT: $6,000 **DEADLINE:** May 6
FIELDS/MAJORS: Women's Studies

Fellowship for candidates for Ph.D. who are working on the topic of women in society. Other small grants are available for research, travel, and curriculum development. Must be working at the University of Oregon. Write to the address below for details.

University Of Oregon
Center For The Study Of Women In Society
340 Hendricks Hall
Eugene, OR 97403

2454

Jane Ives Albee Scholarship

Amount: $750 **Deadline:** Mar 1
Fields/Majors: Elementary Education

Awards are available for first semester juniors or seniors majoring in elementary education with a minimum GPA of 2.5 and a personal interest in teaching grades 4-6. Contact Curriculum and Instruction, UW Oshkosh, for more details.

University Of Wisconsin, Oshkosh
Financial Aid Office
Dempsey 104
800 Algoma Blvd.
Oshkosh, WI 54901

2455

Janet M. Glasgow Essay Award

Amount: $1,500 **Deadline:** May 31
Fields/Majors: Medicine

This award is presented to an AMWA student member for the best essay of approximately 1,000 words identifying a woman physician who has been a significant role model. Write to the address below for details.

American Medical Women's Association
Glasgow Essay Award
801 N. Fairfax Street, Suite 40
Alexandria, VA 22314

2456

Janice Cory Bullock Scholarship

Amount: $650 **Deadline:** Mar 1
Fields/Majors: Home Economics

Open to Phi Upsilon Omicron homemakers who may or may not have completed their degree and desire to continue education in undergraduate or graduate study in home economics. Write to the address below for details.

Phi Upsilon Omicron National Office
Ohio State University
171 Mount Hall, 1050 Carmack Road
Columbus, OH 43210

2457

Janice M. Keesler Scholarship

Amount: None Specified **Deadline:** Nov 1
Fields/Majors: Wildlife Management and Related Fields

Scholarships are available for New York residents enrolled or planning to enroll in a program directly relating to wildlife management. Write to the address listed below for an application.

Janice M. Keesler Scholarship Fund
P.O. Box A
Prospect, NY 13435

2458

Japan Fellowships

Amount: None Specified **Deadline:** Nov 15
Fields/Majors: Japan Related Studies

Fellowships are available for Japanese studies students enrolled in a U.S. doctoral program. Applicants must have completed all the requirements of the doctoral program except the dissertation. Write to the address listed below for information.

Social Science Research Council
Fellowships And Grants
605 Third Avenue
New York, NY 10158

2459

Japan-America Society Of Washington Scholarships For Study In Japan

Amount: $1,500-$8,000 **Deadline:** Mar 1
Fields/Majors: Japanese Study

Scholarships are open to graduate and undergraduate students currently enrolled full-time at an accredited college/university in the District of Columbia, Maryland, Virginia, or West Virginia. Applicants must have completed at least one year of college-level study in the U.S. before beginning study in Japan. Write to the address below for more information.

Japan-America Society Of Washington
Chairman Of The Scholarship Committee
1020 19th St., NW
Washington, DC 20036

2460

Jay A. Pirog Scholarship

Amount: Varies **Deadline:** Mar 1
Fields/Majors: Animal Science, Chemistry

Awards for students in the departments of animal science and chemistry. Recipients will demonstrate financial need and have a GPA of 3.2. or higher. For students entering their sophomore, junior, or senior year of study. Contact the Dean of Natural Sciences and Mathematics, for more information.

University Of Massachusetts, Amherst
Dean Natural Sciences And Mathematics
Amherst, MA 01003

2461

Jay A. Pirog Scholarship

Amount: None Specified
Deadline: Mid-Oct
Fields/Majors: Animal Science

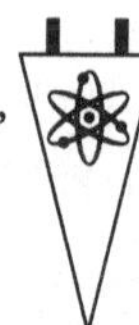

Scholarships are awarded to students in their sophomore, junior, or senior year majoring in animal science with a GPA of 3.2 or better. Contact the Chair, Scholarship Committee, Veterinary and Animal Sciences, for more information.

University Of Massachusetts, Amherst
Chair, Scholarship Committee
Veterinary And Animal Sciences
Amherst, MA 01003

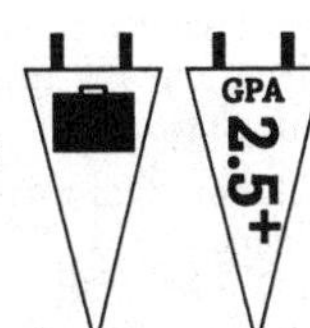
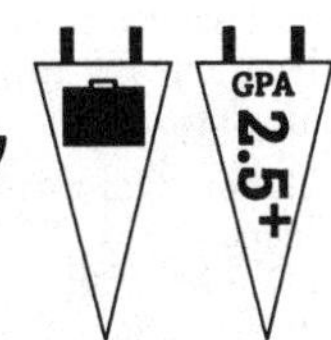

2462

Jay Howland '68 Family Scholarship

Amount: $2,500 **Deadline:** Feb 29
Fields/Majors: Management

Awards to students in their sophomore, junior, or senior year in the school of management. Preference is given to a student who shows interest in being an entrepreneur. Selection is made on the basis of leadership ability, academic strength (minimum 2.8 GPA) and financial need. Applications for school of management scholarships will be available in the S.O.M. Development Office, Room 206.

University Of Massachusetts, Amherst
School Of Management, Development Office
Room 206
Amherst, MA 01003

2463

Jean Boyer Hamlin Scholarship In Ornithology

Amount: Varies **Deadline:** None Specified
Fields/Majors: Ornithology

Awards are available for Maine students in the field of ornithology who are age 18 or over. Preference is given to residents of the Mid-Coast area. Write to the address below for more information.

Mid-Coast Audubon Society Scholarship Chairman
P.O. Box 862
Rockland, ME 04841

2464

Jean Mullins Macey Scholarship

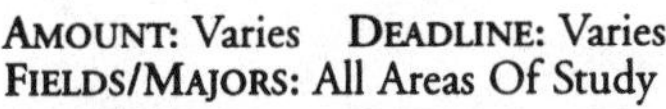

Amount: Varies **Deadline:** Varies
Fields/Majors: All Areas Of Study

Scholarships are available at the University of New Mexico for full-time junior and senior females with academic achievement who are involved in campus service. Write to the address listed below for information.

University Of New Mexico
Albuquerque Alumni Office
Mesa Vista Hall North, Room 1044
Albuquerque, NM 87131

2465

Jean Mullins Macey Scholarship

Amount: None Specified **Deadline:** Mar 1
Fields/Majors: Business

Scholarships are available at the University of New Mexico for full-time female business majors. Write to the address listed below for information.

University Of New Mexico
Albuquerque Department Of Student Financial Aid
Mesa Vista Hall North
Albuquerque, NM 87131

2466

Jean-Luc Miossec Memorial Scholarship

Amount: Varies **Deadline:** Mar 1
Fields/Majors: Earth And Planetary Sciences

Awards are available at the University of New Mexico for students in the fields of earth and planetary sciences. Contact the Rarth and Planetary Sciences Department or the address below for more information.

University Of New Mexico, Albuquerque
Office Of Financial Aid
Albuquerque, NM 87131

2467

Jeanne Bray Scholarship Fund

Amount: $2,000 **Deadline:** None Specified
Fields/Majors: All Areas Of Study

Scholarships for children of law enforcement professionals who either were killed in the line of duty or are members of the NRA. For undergraduate sophomores, juniors, and seniors. Based on character, leadership, academics, transcripts, and references. Must have a GPA of at least 2.5. Write to the address below for more information.

National Rifle Association
Attn: Jeanne E. Bray Scholarship
11250 Waples Mill Road
Fairfax, VA 22030

2468

Jeanne Humphrey Block Dissertation Award

Amount: $2,500 **Deadline:** Apr 1
Fields/Majors: Psychology, Sociology, Behavioral Science

Dissertation grant for women doctoral students researching psychological development of women/girls. Must have completed coursework and be current doctoral candidate. Write to the address below for details.

Radcliffe College
The Henry A. Murray Research Center
10 Garden Street
Cambridge, MA 02138

2469

Jeannette Rankin Foundation Awards

Amount: $1,000 **Deadline:** Jan 15
Fields/Majors: All Areas Of Study

Applicants must be women 35 years or older, U.S. citizens, and accepted or enrolled at a school to pursue an undergraduate degree or technical/vocational training course. 7-10 awards given per year. Financial need is a primary factor. Send a business-sized (9" x 4") SASE to the address below. In the lower, left-hand corner of the envelope, write "JRF 1997." Also, when applying, indicate your gender, age, and level of study or training.

Jeannette Rankin Foundation
P.O. Box 6653
Athens, GA 30604

2470

Jeannine B. Cowles Music Scholarships

Amount: Varies **Deadline:** Mar 15
Fields/Majors: Music

Awards are available to music students who demonstrate academic ability and leadership potential as well as performance ability. Must have and maintain a GPA of at least 2.8. Applicants should be involved in departmental activities. Write to the address below for more information.

Portland State University Music Department
231 Lincoln Hall
Portland, OR 97207

2471 Jeffrey Morgan Scholarship

AMOUNT: Varies **DEADLINE:** Mar 1
FIELDS/MAJORS: Wind Music

Award for a first-year music student who demonstrates excellence in wind performance. Contact the Director of Scholarships, Department of Music, at the address below, for more information.

University Of Massachusetts, Amherst
255 Whitmore Administration Building
Box 3823
Amherst, MA 01003

2472 Jeffrey Parker Scholarship

AMOUNT: Varies **DEADLINE:** None Specified
FIELDS/MAJORS: Business

Awards for Jacksonville State University students in the field of business. Contact the College of Commerce and Business for more details.

Jacksonville State University
Financial Aid Office
Jacksonville, AL 36265

2473 Jennings Randolph Distinguished Fellows

AMOUNT: $83,000 (max) **DEADLINE:** Oct 16

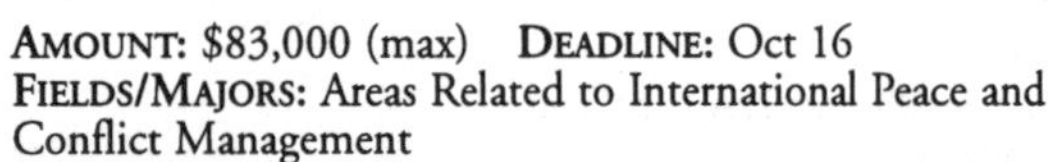

FIELDS/MAJORS: Areas Related to International Peace and Conflict Management

Fellowships are available for scholars to increase understanding about international peace and conflict management, using their wealth of knowledge and experience to produce and important, influential contribution to the peace process. Write to the address listed below for information.

U.S. Institute Of Peace
Jennings Randolph Fellowship Program
1550 M Street, NW, Suite 70
Washington, DC 0005

2474 Jerome B. Steinbach Scholarship

AMOUNT: None Specified **DEADLINE:** Mar 1
FIELDS/MAJORS: All Areas Of Study

Scholarship for Oregon residents who will be entering their sophomore (or above) year in the fall. Must have a GPA of at least 3.25 (college GPA). Contact your college financial aid office, or write to the address below for details.

Oregon State Scholarship Commission
Attn: Grant Department
1500 Valley River Dr., #10
Eugene, OR 97401

2475 Jerry B. Addy Memorial Scholarship

AMOUNT: $600 **DEADLINE:** Mar 1
FIELDS/MAJORS: Mathematics, Physics, Chemistry

For juniors in college. Selection is based on academic proficiency and financial need. Renewable. Transfer students must have completed one full-time semester at Clemson University. Write for complete details.

Clemson University
Financial Aid Office
G01 Sikes Hall
Clemson, SC 29634

2476 Jerry Baker College Freshman Scholarship Program

AMOUNT: $1,000 **DEADLINE:** Apr 1
FIELDS/MAJORS: Horticulture

Scholarships open to entering freshmen interested in careers in horticulture who will be attending a four-year college or university. Students must submit a letter of recommendation from a high school teacher or counselor; a letter of recommendation from a community leader; copy of high school transcripts; and a copy of SAT and ACT scores. Students are also required to submit a copy of acceptance letter from an accredited college. Write to the address below for more details.

Bedding Plants Foundation, Inc.
P.O. Box 27241
Lansing, MI 48909

2477 Jerry Fortner Memorial Scholarship

AMOUNT: $1,750 **DEADLINE:** Mar 31
FIELDS/MAJORS: All Areas Of Study

Student must be in good standing and have financial need. Write to the address below for more information.

Southwest Missouri State University
Office Of Financial Aid
901 South National Ave.
Springfield, MO 65804

2478 Jerry L. Dove Memorial Fund

AMOUNT: $750 **DEADLINE:** Mar 15
FIELDS/MAJORS: All Areas Of Study

Scholarships for graduating seniors from South Charleston, WV, who live within the former service area of Dunbar High School. Based on academics, need, and character. One award per year. Write to the address below for details.

Greater Kanawha Valley Foundation
Scholarship Committee
P.O. Box 3041
Charleston, WV 25331

2479 Jerry L. Pettis Memorial Scholarship

AMOUNT: $2,500 **DEADLINE:** Feb
FIELDS/MAJORS: Medicine

Awards for junior or senior medical students with demonstrated interest in communication of science. Write to the address below for more information.

American Medical Association
Secretary, AMA
535 North Dearborn Street
Chicago, IL 60610

2480

Jerry Voorhis Memorial Scholarship

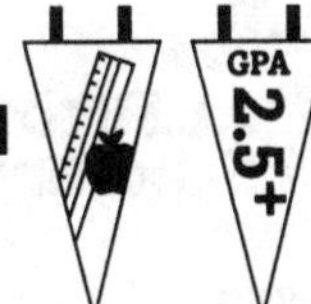

AMOUNT: $2,000 **DEADLINE:** None Specified
FIELDS/MAJORS: Humanities and Liberal Arts

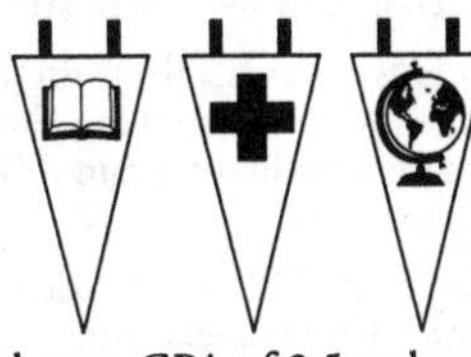

Scholarships are available for full-time sophomore, junior, senior, and graduate students with interests in human services, behavioral science, social services, social work, humanities, teaching, nursing, or counseling. Must have a GPA of 2.5 or better. Applicants must be seeking a credential in teaching. Write to the address below for more information.

California State Polytechnic University, Pomona
Office Of Financial Aid
3801 West Temple Ave.
Pomona, CA 91768

2481

Jess Evans Scholarship

AMOUNT: $200-$500 **DEADLINE:** Varies
FIELDS/MAJORS: Range Animal Science

Awards for Sul Ross undergraduates who are studying range animal science, have a GPA of at least 2.0, and are NIRA eligible. Write to the address below for more information.

Sul Ross State University
Division Of Range Animal Science
Box C-11
Alpine, TX 79832

2482

Jesse And Dorothy Rutherford Scholarship

AMOUNT: $1,000 (max) **DEADLINE:** Feb 1
FIELDS/MAJORS: All Areas Of Study

Awards for students attending Wilberforce who have a GPA of at least 2.5. Renewable. Write to the address below for more information.

Wilberforce University
Financial Aid Office
Wilberforce, OH 45384

2483

Jessup/McHenry Awards

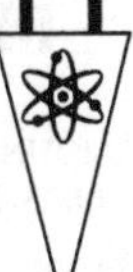

AMOUNT: $500-$1,000 **DEADLINE:** Mar 1, Oct 1
FIELDS/MAJORS: All Areas Of Study

Grants for pre- and postdoctoral students who require the resources of the Academy of Natural Sciences of Philadelphia. Studies are performed under the supervision of a member of the curatorial staff of the Academy. The McHenry Fund is limited to the study of botany. Students from the Philadelphia area are not eligible. Write to Dr. Schuyler, chairman of the Jessup-McHenry Fund Committee at the address below for details.

Academy Of Natural Sciences Of Philadelphia
Dr. A.E. Schuyler, Jessup-McHenry Fund
1900 Benjamin Franklin Parkway
Philadelphia, PA 19103

2484

Jewel/Taylor C. Cotton Scholarship

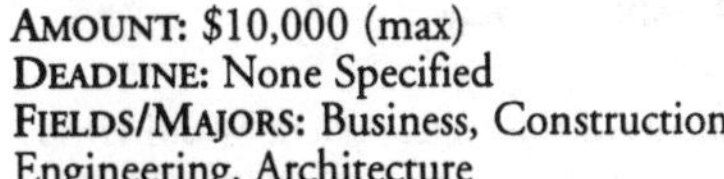

AMOUNT: $10,000 (max)
DEADLINE: None Specified
FIELDS/MAJORS: Business, Construction, Engineering, Architecture

Available for male or female high school graduate must be accepted in a four-year college or university with the intention of majoring in business or a field related to the business or construction industry. Must have a GPA of 2.5 or better and demonstrate financial need. For residents of the Chicago metropolitan area. Write to the address below for more information.

Chicago Urban League
Gina Blake, Scholarship Specialist
4510 South Michigan Ave.
Chicago, IL 60653

2485

Jewelry Foundation Scholarship Fund Group

AMOUNT: $500-$1,000 **DEADLINE:** May 1
FIELDS/MAJORS: Jewelry-Related Studies

Scholarships are available for residents of Rhode Island, who are studying in a jewelry-related curriculum. Write to the address listed below for information.

Rhode Island Foundation
70 Elm Street
Providence, RI 02903

2486

Jewish Community Scholarship Fund

AMOUNT: Varies **DEADLINE:** Apr 15
FIELDS/MAJORS: All Areas Of Study

Scholarships for needy Jewish residents of Los Angeles County, CA pursuing postsecondary education on a full-time basis. Must be above the freshman level of study with a GPA of at least 2.5. Write to the address below for details, applications are available after Dec. 15.

Jewish Vocational Service (L.A.)
6505 Wilshire Blvd., Suite 303
Los Angeles, CA 0048

2487

Jewish Educational Loan Fund

AMOUNT: $2,000 (max) **DEADLINE:** Ongoing
FIELDS/MAJORS: All Areas Of Study

Interest-free loans for residents of the metropolitan Washington area who are within eighteen months of graduation (undergrad or graduate). Repayment begins after graduation. Must be U.S. citizen (or perm. resident intending to apply for citizenship). For Jewish students. Write to the address below or call (301) 881-3700 for details.

Jewish Social Service Agency Of Metropolitan Washington
6123 Montrose Road
Rockville, MD 20852

2488

Jewish Undergraduate Scholarship Fund

AMOUNT: $3,500 (max) **DEADLINE:** May 30
FIELDS/MAJORS: All Areas Of Study

Scholarships for Jewish residents of the metropolitan Washington area who are currently enrolled as undergraduates. Must be less than 30 years old. Special consideration given to refugees. Based primarily on need. Write to the address below or call (301) 881-3700 for details.

Jewish Social Service Agency Of Metropolitan Washington
6123 Montrose Road
Rockville, MD 20852

2489

JFCS Scholarships

AMOUNT: $5,000 **DEADLINE:** None Specified
FIELDS/MAJORS: All Areas Of Study

JFCS provides hundreds of grants and scholarships annually to help Jewish students with financial needs achieve their educational goals. Special scholarships are available for study in Israel. Eligibility requirements: acceptance to a college, vocational school or university; residence in San Francisco, the Peninsula, Marin, or Sonoma Counties; and 3.0 GPA. Write to the address below for details.

Jewish Family And Children's Services
1600 Scott Street
San Francisco, CA 94115

2490

Jim McKee Scholarship

AMOUNT: $200 **DEADLINE:** Nov 17
FIELDS/MAJORS: Agriculture, Agribusiness

Scholarships are available to full-time students majoring in agriculture or agribusiness. Must have completed thirty or more semester hours. Based on academic excellence and dedication to agriculture as exhibited by research, special problems, etc. Write to the address below for more information.

Illinois State University
Dept. Of Agriculture
Turner Hall 15
Campus Box 502
Normal, IL 61761

2491

Jimmy A. Young Memorial Scholarship

AMOUNT: $1,000 **DEADLINE:** Jun 3
FIELDS/MAJORS: Respiratory Therapy

One scholarship for a minority student in an AMA-accepted respiratory care program. The foundation prefers that students be nominated by their schools, but "any student may initiate a request of sponsorship by the school." Must have a GPA of at least 3.0. Write to the address below for additional information.

American Respiratory Care Foundation
11030 Ables Lane
Dallas, TX 75229

2492

J.L.Riebsomer Memorial Scholarship

AMOUNT: Varies **DEADLINE:** Mar 1
FIELDS/MAJORS: Chemistry

Awards are available at the University of New Mexico for sophomores who are studying chemistry. Must exhibit a good GPA and progress in the program. Write to the address listed below for information.

University Of New Mexico, Albuquerque
Office Of Financial Aid
Albuquerque, NM 87131

2493

Jo Anne Smith Scholarship

AMOUNT: $500 **DEADLINE:** Mar 1
FIELDS/MAJORS: Journalism, Communications, Advertising, Public Relations

Must be a junior or senior at the University of Florida and have at least a 2.8 GPA in one of the areas above. Applicants should have a proven interest in reporting on freedom of information issues or practicing the law of mass communication. Write to the address below for complete details.

University Of Florida
Scholarship & Placement Director
2070 Weimer Hall
Gainesville, FL 32611

2494

Jo Gregory Knox RAS Exes Scholarship

AMOUNT: $200-$600 **DEADLINE:** Varies
FIELDS/MAJORS: Range Animal Science

Awards for Sul Ross undergraduates who are studying range animal science, have a GPA of at least 2.0, and are NIRA eligible. Write to the address below for more information.

Sul Ross State University
Division Of Range Animal Science
Box C-11
Alpine, TX 79832

2495

Joanne And Charles Mirabella Scholarship

AMOUNT: $200 **DEADLINE:** Mar 1
FIELDS/MAJORS: Advertising

Awards for juniors and seniors who are majoring in advertising. Must have a GPA of at least 2.8. Write to the address below for more information.

University Of Florida
Knight Scholarship & Placement Director
2070 Weimer Hall
Gainesville, FL 32611

2496

Joanne Grossnickle Scholarships

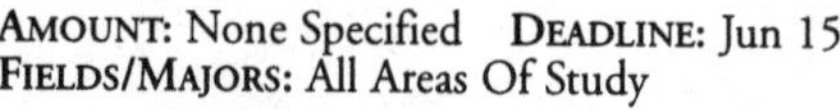

AMOUNT: None Specified **DEADLINE:** Jun 15
FIELDS/MAJORS: All Areas Of Study

Scholarships for graduates of Linganore, Francis Scott Key, or

Walkersville High Schools; members of the Union Bridge Church of the Brethren; or other persons whose heritage ties them to the Union Bridge Church. Based on need, ability, potential, and character. Preference given to first-time applicants and nonwinners from previous years. Applicant must also have completed at least one successful year of postsecondary education. Write to the address below for more information.

Joanne Grossnickle Scholarship Fund Committee
c/o Union Bridge Church Of The Brethren
P.O. Box 518
Union Bridge, MD 21791

2497 Joanne Thomas Memorial Scholarship

Amount: $250 **Deadline:** Feb 9
Fields/Majors: All Areas Of Study

Awards for residence hall students with a minimum GPA of 2.5. Participant in hall, campus, and community activities and organizations. Must show a demonstrated interest in art. Use Bloomsburg University scholarship application. Contact Mrs. Linda Sowash, Director of Residence Life, for further information.

Bloomsburg University
19 Ben Franklin Hall
400 E. Second St.
Bloomsburg, PA 17815

2498 Jody Connell Memorial Scholarship

Amount: Varies **Deadline:** None Specified
Fields/Majors: Music

Awards for Jacksonville State University students in the field of music. Contact the Dean of the Music and Fine Art Department for more information.

Jacksonville State University
Financial Aid Office
Jacksonville, AL 36265

2499 Joe Pat And Frances Knight Industrial Education Scholarships

Amount: None Specified **Deadline:** Feb 1
Fields/Majors: Industry And Technology

Scholarships are awarded annually to students majoring in a technical degree program offered within the College of Industry and Technology. Write to the address below for details.

Murray State University
Office Of University Scholarships
Ordway Hall, 1 Murray St.
Murray, KY 42071

2500 Joel Garcia Memorial Scholarship

Amount: $2,000 (max) **Deadline:** Apr 1
Fields/Majors: Journalism, Mass Communication

This scholarship competition is open to Latino high school seniors and undergraduate students interested in pursuing journalism or mass communications careers. Must be a resident of California. Must include samples of journalism-related work (such as news articles, news scripts, audio or videotapes, or photographs) with application. For complete details, write to the address below.

California Chicano News Media Association
USC School Of Journalism
727 West 27th Street
Los Angeles, CA 90007

2501 Joel Polsky—Fixtures Furniture Prizes And Academic Achievement Awards

Amount: $1,000 **Deadline:** Jan 19
Fields/Majors: Interior Design

Awards for undergraduate and graduate students to aid research, thesis, or other academic projects. The Furniture Prize will be given based on the presentation of topic to a committee. Most other awards are given based on the content and importance of the proposed subject matter. Send a legal-size SASE to the address below for more information.

ASID Educational Foundation, Inc.
Scholarship And Awards Program
608 Massachusettes Ave., NE
Washington, DC 20002

2502 Johanna Fiske Scholarship

Amount: Varies **Deadline:** Mar 1
Fields/Majors: Music

Awards are available at the University of New Mexico for a student in the field of music with demonstrated musical ability. Write to the address below for more information.

University Of New Mexico, Albuquerque
Office Of Financial Aid
Albuquerque, NM 87131

2503 John & Geraldine Hobble L.P.N. Nursing Scholarship

Amount: $250 **Deadline:** Feb 15
Fields/Majors: Nursing

Scholarships for Kansas residents who are or will be attending a college or university in Kansas. Applicant must be a U.S. citizen and be enrolled in or plan to enroll in an LPN program. Write to the address listed below for additional information or application.

American Legion
Department Of Kansas
1314 SW Topeka Blvd.
Topeka, KS 66612

2504 John & Pat Wimberg Scholarship

Amount: None Specified **Deadline:** Mar 1
Fields/Majors: Accounting

Scholarships are available at the University of New Mexico for full-time accounting majors. Based on financial need and academic ability. Write to the address listed below for information.

University Of New Mexico, Albuquerque
Department Of Student Financial Aid
Mesa Vista Hall
North Albuquerque, NM 87131

2505

John A. Howard Rockford Downtown Rotary Club Scholarship

AMOUNT: Varies **DEADLINE:** None Specified
FIELDS/MAJORS: All Areas Of Study

Awards available to outstanding entering freshmen who are from Rockford. Write to the address below for more information.

Rockford College
Financial Aid Office
5050 East State St.
Rockford, IL 61108

2506

John A. Knauss Sea Grant Fellowship

AMOUNT: $32,000 **DEADLINE:** Aug 31
FIELDS/MAJORS: Marine Sciences

This fellowship provides support for independent graduate student thesis or dissertation research in the marine sciences. Write to the address listed below for more information.

National Oceanic And Atmospheric Administration
National Sea Grant College Program
1315 East-West Highway
Silver Spring, MD 20910

2507

John A. Marik Scholarship

AMOUNT: $500 **DEADLINE:** Feb 1
FIELDS/MAJORS: Pharmacy

Scholarships are available at the University of Oklahoma, Norman for full-time third- or fourth-year pharmacy majors. Based on academic excellence. Write to the address listed below for information.

University Of Oklahoma, Norman
College Of Pharmacy
P.O. Box 26901
Oklahoma City, OK 73190

2508

John A. Volpe Scholarship

AMOUNT: $1,000 **DEADLINE:** May 31
FIELDS/MAJORS: All Areas Of Study

Scholarships are available for entering undergraduates from the New England area who are Italian American. Write to the address below for details.

National Italian American Foundation
Dr. Maria Lombardo, Education Director
1860 19th Street, NW
Washington, DC 20009

2509

John A. Walker College Of Business Scholarships

AMOUNT: $2,500 **DEADLINE:** Dec 15
FIELDS/MAJORS: Business

Competitive scholarships offered to students who plan to major in business at the John A. Walker School of Business. Scholarships are renewable for an additional three years provided the student maintains a 3.25 grade point average. Contact the Office of the Dean at the address below for details.

Appalachian State University
Office Of The Dean
Walker College Of Business
Boone, NC 28608

2510

John And Anne Parente Scholarship

AMOUNT: $2,000 **DEADLINE:** May 31
FIELDS/MAJORS: All Areas Of Study

Scholarships for Italian American undergraduates who are planning to attend or are enrolled in King's College (must meet entrance requirements of the college). Preference given to non-residents of Pennsylvania. Write to the address below for details.

National Italian American Foundation
Dr. Maria Lombardo, Education Director
1860 19th Street, NW
Washington, DC 20009

2511

John And Catherine Early Scholarship

AMOUNT: None Specified **DEADLINE:** Dec 1
FIELDS/MAJORS: All Areas Of Study

Scholarship for spouse or descendent of a service-connected disabled U.S. Veteran. Must be UT Austin undergraduate, have a GPA of at least 2.8, and have applied for financial aid through the office of student financial services. Write to the address below for details.

University Of Texas, Austin
Office Of Student Financial Services
P.O. Box 7758
Austin, TX 78713

2512

John And Elsa Gracik Scholarship

AMOUNT: $1,500 **DEADLINE:** Apr 15
FIELDS/MAJORS: Mechanical Engineering

Four scholarships for ASME student members majoring in mechanical engineering, and for entering freshmen who plan to pursue an ME or MET career. Must be a U.S. citizen to apply. For additional information, call or write the ASME Foundation.

American Society Of Mechanical Engineers
Education Services Department
345 E. 47th Street
New York, NY 10017

2513

John And Mabel Livingston Memorial Fund

AMOUNT: $500-$3,000 **DEADLINE:** Mar 31
FIELDS/MAJORS: Religion, Theology

Awards for students majoring in religion or theology who have a GPA of at least 2.0. Must demonstrate financial need. Write to the address below for more information.

Columbia Union College
Financial Aid Office
7600 Flower Ave.
Takoma Park, MD 20912

2514 John Bayliss Broadcast Foundation Scholarship

AMOUNT: $2,000 **DEADLINE:** None Specified
FIELDS/MAJORS: Radio Broadcasting

Scholarships are available for junior, senior, or graduate students planning a career in radio broadcasting. Applicant must have a GPA of at least 3.0. Write to the address listed below for information. Please enclosed a self-addressed, stamped envelope.

John Bayliss Broadcast Foundation
P.O. Box 221070
Carmel, CA 93922

2515 John Burkey Memorial Scholarship

AMOUNT: $500 **DEADLINE:** None Specified
FIELDS/MAJORS: All Areas Of Study

Awards for outstanding seniors at Mesa State College with a GPA of at least 3.0. Contact your appropriate school of study for further details.

Mesa State College
Financial Aid Office
P.O. Box 2684
Grand Junction, CO 81501

2516 John C. Chaffin Educational Fund Scholarship And Loan Programs

AMOUNT: $500-$4,000 **DEADLINE:** None Specified
FIELDS/MAJORS: All Areas Of Study

Open to graduates of Newton North and Newton South High Schools. Eligible applicants will be high school seniors and students who have completed at least 1 year of higher education or successful work experience. For undergraduate study only. Contact your scholarship and loan advisor at your school. Graduates who have been out of school for 1 year or more may write the address below.

John C. Chaffin Educational Fund Secretary
100 Walnut St.
Newtonville, MA 02160

2517 John C. Clendenin Scholarships

AMOUNT: $1,300 **DEADLINE:** Mar 1
FIELDS/MAJORS: Business

Scholarships are available at the University of Iowa for full-time undergraduates majoring in business. Must be a resident of Iowa to apply. Write to the address listed below for information.

University Of Iowa
College Of Business Admin.
108 Pappajohn Business Admin. Bldg., Suite W16
Iowa City, IA 52245

2518 John C. McGalliard Medieval Essay Prize

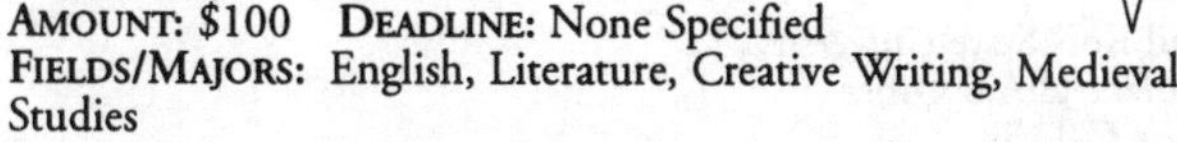

AMOUNT: $100 **DEADLINE:** None Specified
FIELDS/MAJORS: English, Literature, Creative Writing, Medieval Studies

A scholarship is available at the University of Iowa for a full-time junior or senior who submits the most outstanding essay on a medieval subject. Write to the address listed below for information.

University Of Iowa
Department Of English
308 English-Philosophy Building
Iowa City, IA 52242

2519 John Cathcart Melby Scholarship

AMOUNT: $500 **DEADLINE:** None Specified
FIELDS/MAJORS: All Areas Of Study

Scholarship for students who graduated from El Paso High School and were in attendence there for at least three years, to the school of their choice. Applicants must also have demonstrated involvement in school activities and have a GPA of at least 3.3. Write to the address listed below for information.

El Paso Community Foundation
201 East Main, Suite 1616
El Paso, TX 79901

2520 John Cornelius Memorial Scholarship

AMOUNT: $1,500 (min) **DEADLINE:** Mar 15
FIELDS/MAJORS: All Areas Of Study

Scholarships are available for dependents of members of the Marine Corps Tankers Association (or eligible for it—served or serving in Marine Tank Unit). For undergraduate study. Renewable. Active, discharged, and retired marine tankers are also eligible to apply. Write to the address below for details.

Marine Corps Tankers Association, Inc.
Phil Morell, Scholarship Chairman
1112 Alpine Heights Rd.
Alpine, CA 91901

2521 John D. Barnwell Memorial Scholarship

AMOUNT: None Specified
DEADLINE: None Specified
FIELDS/MAJORS: Science

Liberal arts scholarships are awarded to a student in the school of science or school of liberal arts who has effectively integrated the sciences and the arts in his or her undergraduate career. Write to the address below for more information.

Indiana University/Purdue University, Indianapolis
Purdue School Of Technology
799 West Michigan St.
Indianapolis, IN 46202

2522 John D. Clark And Marian Clark Person Memorial Award In Chemistry

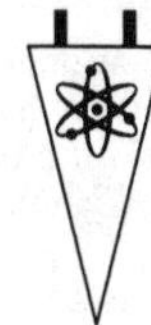

AMOUNT: Varies **DEADLINE:** Mar 1
FIELDS/MAJORS: Chemistry

Awards are available at the University of New Mexico for graduate students studying chemistry and working in the department as a teaching assistant. Write to the address listed below for information.

University Of New Mexico, Albuquerque
Office Of Financial Aid
Albuquerque, NM 87131

2523 John Deere & Co. Minority Accounting Scholarships

AMOUNT: $2,000 **DEADLINE:** Mar 1
FIELDS/MAJORS: Accounting

Scholarships are available at the University of Iowa for full-time minority students majoring in accounting. Write to the address listed below for information.

University Of Iowa
College Of Business Admin., Suite W16
108 Pappajohn Business Admin. Bldg.
Iowa City, IA 52245

2524 John Deere Insurance Group Scholarships

AMOUNT: $3,000 **DEADLINE:** Mar 1
FIELDS/MAJORS: Business

Scholarships are available at the University of Iowa for full-time senior minority business majors. Write to the address listed below for information.

University Of Iowa
College Of Business Admin., Suite W16
108 Pappajohn Business Admin. Bldg.
Iowa City, IA 52245

2525 John Donald Robb Scholarship

AMOUNT: Varies **DEADLINE:** Mar 1
FIELDS/MAJORS: Performance Or Composition Music

Awards at the University of New Mexico for performance or composition music students with music ability and talent. Must be enrolled for full-time study. Write to the address below for more information.

University Of New Mexico, Albuquerque
Office Of Financial Aid
Albuquerque, NM 87131

2526 John F. And Anna Lee Stacey Scholarship Fund

AMOUNT: $5,000 (max) **DEADLINE:** Feb 1
FIELDS/MAJORS: Drawing And Painting

Grants for individuals who are devoted to a career in the classical or conservation tradition of western art. Must be a U.S. citizen and between the age of 18 and 35 years. Applicants must submit a 35mm slide of their work to the judging committee. Write to the address below for details.

National Cowboy Hall Of Fame
Stacey Scholarship Fund
1700 Northeast 63rd Street
Oklahoma City, OK 73111

2527 John F. Kennedy Scholars Award

AMOUNT: $1,500 **DEADLINE:** Apr 5
FIELDS/MAJORS: Political Science (American Politics)

Scholarship for Massachusetts residents who are entering their junior or senior year of undergraduate study majoring in a field related to the study of American politics. Two awards per year (one to a man, one to a woman). Registered Democratic preferred, but not essential. Must have a 3.0 GPA. Write to the address below for details.

Massachusetts Democratic State Committee
Scholarship Committee
45 Bromfield St., 7th Floor
Boston, MA 02108

2528 John F. Leonardi Memorial Scholarship

AMOUNT: $500 **DEADLINE:** Early Spring
FIELDS/MAJORS: Special Education

Award for a student who has at least sixty credits and exhibits strong academic performance and experience in working with handicapped persons. Contact the Special Education Department Office, UW Oshkosh for more information.

University Of Wisconsin, Oshkosh
Financial Aid Office
Dempsey 104
800 Algoma Blvd.
Oshkosh, WI 54901

2529 John Frederick Steinman Fellowships

AMOUNT: $6,000 (max) **DEADLINE:** Feb 1
FIELDS/MAJORS: Psychiatry, Psychology, Social Work

Fellowship is for applicants that have received an M.D. or D.O. degree and wish to continue study for two additional years and become a trained adult psychiatrist, or a trained adult psychiatrist who would like to engage in advanced study for two more years and become a trained child psychiatrist or other comparable psychiatric subspecialies. Applicants who have already received an advanced degree in psychology, who wish to become clinical or public school psychologists, or advanced degree holders who wish to engage in advanced study for the purpose of becoming social case workers, are also encouraged to apply. Write to the address listed below for further information.

John Frederick Steinman Foundation
Jay H. Wenrich, Secretary
8 W. King Street, P.O. Box 1328
Lancaster, PA 17608

2530 John Frisella Scholarship

AMOUNT: $1,000 **DEADLINE:** May 31
FIELDS/MAJORS: All Areas Of Study

Scholarships for Italian American students who are residents of the St. Louis area. Write to the address below for details.

National Italian American Foundation
Dr. Maria Lombardo, Education Director
1860 19th Street, NW
Washington, DC 20009

2531 John G. And Evelyn G. Prude Scholarship

AMOUNT: $2,000 **DEADLINE:** Apr 1
FIELDS/MAJORS: All Areas Of Study

Awards for all Sul Ross students who have financial need and a GPA of at least 3.0. Write to the address below for more information.

Sul Ross State University
Financial Aid Office
Box C-113
Alpine, TX 79832

2532

John Gassner Memorial Playwriting Award

Amount: $250-$500 **Deadline:** Apr 15
Fields/Majors: Playwriting

Plays must be unpublished and unproduced. Purpose is to encourage writing of new plays both one-act and full-length. U.S. or Canadian citizen. This is a writing competition offering cash prizes for those already skilled and immersed in theatrical writing. Write to the address below for details. Be certain to enclose a self-addressed, stamped envelope with your request.

New England Theatre Conference
Northeastern Univ., Dept. Of Theatre
360 Huntington Avenue
Boston, MA 02115

2533

John Glenn And Presidential Scholarships

Amount: Varies **Deadline:** Mar 1
Fields/Majors: All Areas Of Study

Prestigious academic awards for Muskingum freshmen. Based on high school academic record, ACT/SAT scores and results from an on-campus competition. Write to the address below for more information.

Muskingum College
Office Of Admission
New Concord, OH 43762

2534

John H. Lyons, Sr. Scholarship

Amount: $2,500 (max) **Deadline:** Jan 22
Fields/Majors: All Areas Of Study

For graduating high school seniors who are sons or daughters of members (or deceased members) in good standing of the international association of bridge, structural and ornamental iron workers. Must rank in the upper half of class. Study in USA or Canada. Renewable. Based on academics, character, and extracurricular activities. Contact your parent's local or write to the address below for details.

International Association Of Bridge
Structural & Ornamental Iron Workers
John H. Lyons, Sr. Scholarship
1750 New York Ave., NW, Suite 40
Washington, DC 20006

2535

John Halvor Leek Memorial Scholarship

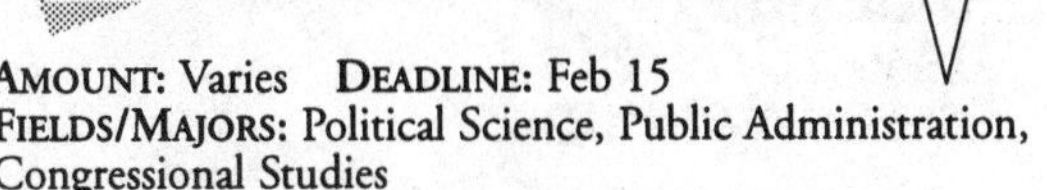

Amount: Varies **Deadline:** Feb 15
Fields/Majors: Political Science, Public Administration, Congressional Studies

Scholarships are available at the University of Oklahoma, Norman, for full-time graduate students majoring in one of the above areas. Requires a minimum GPA of 3.5. Write to the address listed below for information.

University Of Oklahoma, Norman
Political Science Department
455 West Lindsey
Norman, OK 73019

2536

John Henry Dorminy Scholarships

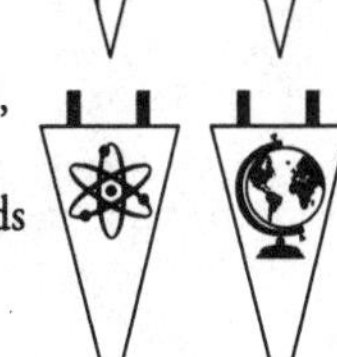

Amount: Varies **Deadline:** Apr 15
Fields/Majors: Pre-Med, Pre-Vet, Pre-Dental, Prelaw, Nursing, Acct., Forestry, Piano

Scholarships for freshmen at ABAC in the fields listed above. Based on academic ability and extracurricular activities. Write to the address below for additional information.

Abraham Baldwin Agricultural College
Office Of Admissions
2802 Moore Highway
Tifton, GA 31794

2537

John L. Dales Scholarship Fund

Amount: Varies **Deadline:** Apr 30
Fields/Majors: All Areas Of Study

Awards for students who are members or dependents of members of the Screen Actors Guild and enrolled in full-time study. Based on academics, essay, and recommendations. Write to the address below for more information.

Screen Actors Guild
5757 Wilshire Blvd.
Los Angeles, CA 90036

2538

John L. Knight Memorial Scholarship

Amount: Varies **Deadline:** Apr 1
Fields/Majors: Art-Ceramics, Photography, Wood Sculpture

Scholarships are available at the University of New Mexico for full-time junior or senior art students, with a concentration in ceramics, photography, or wood sculpture. Write to the address listed below for information.

University Of New Mexico, Albuquerque
College Of Fine Arts
Office Of The Dean
Albuquerque, NM 87131

2539

John M. Olin Pre/Postdoctoral Fellowship In National Security

Amount: $16,500-$28,000 **Deadline:** Jan 15
Fields/Majors: National Security, Economics

Residential fellowships at the Center for International Affairs of Harvard for Ph.D. candidates (course work completed before beginning of fellowship) and postdoctoral scholars. Supports investigation of causes and conduct of war, military strategy and history, defense policy and institutions, economic security, defense economics, and the defense industrial base. Contact Seth Woods at the address below for program details and application guidelines.

Harvard University, Center For International Affairs
CFIA Student Programs And Fellowships
1737 Cambridge St.
Cambridge, MA 02138

2540

John M. Wolper Scholarship

AMOUNT: Varies **DEADLINE:** None Specified
FIELDS/MAJORS: Hotel, Restaurant, Institutional Management

Award for Mercyhurst students studying hotel, restaurant, and institutional management. Write to the address below for more information.

Mercyhurst College
Financial Aid Office
Glenwood Hills
Erie, PA 16546

2541

John Meredith Endowment Fund

AMOUNT: Varies **DEADLINE:** Mar 1
FIELDS/MAJORS: Nursing

Awards are available at the University of New Mexico for nursing students with financial need who graduated from a New Mexico high school. Must take fifteen hours per semester and demonstrate academic ability. Write to the address below or contact the school of nursing for more details.

University Of New Mexico, Albuquerque
Office Of Financial Aid
Albuquerque, NM 87131

2542

John Miller Musser Memorial Forest & Society Fellowship

AMOUNT: Varies **DEADLINE:** Apr 1, Sep 1
FIELDS/MAJORS: Forestry, Environmental Science

Fellowships are available to postdoctoral scholars to support research in an area of interest to the foundation, including those areas mentioned above. Tenure is two years. Applicants must be age 36 or less. Write to the address listed below for information.

Institute Of Current World Affairs
Gary L. Hansen, Program Administrator
4 West Wheelock Street
Hanover, NH 03755

2543

John Milner Memorial Scholarship

AMOUNT: Varies **DEADLINE:** Mar 1
FIELDS/MAJORS: Education

Awards are available at the University of New Mexico for juniors or seniors who plan to teach in public schools. Must demonstrate ability, character, and financial need. Write to the address below for more information.

University Of New Mexico, Albuquerque
Office Of Financial Aid
Albuquerque, NM 87131

2544

John O. Butler Graduate Scholarships

AMOUNT: None Specified **DEADLINE:** Apr 1
FIELDS/MAJORS: Dental Hygiene

Awarded to a candidate enrolled in a master's degree program in dental hygiene or dental hygiene educations. Seven awards per year. Write to the address below for more information.

American Dental Hygienists' Association
Institute For Oral Health
444 North Michigan Ave., Suite 3400
Chicago, IL 60611

2545

John P. Burke Memorial Scholarship

AMOUNT: None Specified **DEADLINE:** May 15
FIELDS/MAJORS: All Areas Of Study

Scholarships for Rhode Island residents who have at least three years successful experience as a caddie for a club belonging to the Rhode Island Golf Association. For undergraduate study. Applications can be obtained in many local golf shops, or write to the address below for further information.

Rhode Island Golf Associaiton, Burke Memorial Fund
Charles Orms Building
10 Orms St., Suite 326
Providence, RI 02904

2546

John P. Foster Memorial Scholarship Fund

AMOUNT: $300 **DEADLINE:** None Specified
FIELDS/MAJORS: Engineering

Scholarship available to students enrolled in an engineering program at the University of Texas, El Paso, who are in their sophomore year or above, and are residents of El Paso County. Write to the address listed below for further information.

El Paso Community Foundation
201 East Main Suite 1616
El Paso, TX 79901

2547

John P. Lamb Memorial Scholarship

AMOUNT: None Specified
DEADLINE: None Specified
FIELDS/MAJORS: Health Education

Scholarships for students at East Tennessee State University majoring in health education or public health. Contact the Department of Health Education or the Office of Financial Aid for details.

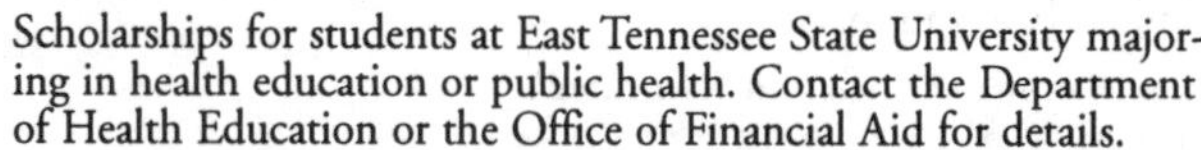

East Tennessee State University
Office Of Financial Aid
Box 70722
Johnson City, TN 37614

2548

John R. Cunningham Scholarship, David Scruggs Memorial Fund

AMOUNT: None Specified **DEADLINE:** None Specified
FIELDS/MAJORS: Law Enforcement/Criminal Justice, Criminology

Scholarships for students at East Tennessee State University who are studying toward a career in law enforcement. Freshmen must have a GPA of at least 2.5, continuing students must have at least 3.0. Contact the Department of Criminal Justice and Criminology or the Office of Financial Aid for details.

East Tennessee State University
Office Of Financial Aid
Box 70722
Johnson City, TN 37614

2549

John T. Caldwell Alumni Scholars Program

Amount: Varies **Deadline:** Nov 1
Fields/Majors: All Areas Of Study

Awards for freshman who meet two of the three following criteria: SAT score of at least 1200, high school GPA of 3.75 or higher, or ranked in the top 10% of your class. Applicants must be U.S. citizens or permanent residents. Write to the address below for more details.

North Carolina State University
Program Coordinator/Merit Awards
Box 7342
Raleigh, NC 27695

John T. Vucurevich Scholarships

Amount: $1,000 **Deadline:** Mar 1
Fields/Majors: All Areas Of Study

Scholarships for third or fourth year students at Black Hills State University who are in good standing and have financial need. Write to the address below for more information.

Black Hills State University
Office Of Financial Aid
University Station, Box 9509
Spearfish, SD 57799

John Taylor/Dean Witter Reynolds Scholarship

Amount: None Specified **Deadline:** Mar 1
Fields/Majors: Finance

Scholarships are available at the University of New Mexico for full-time finance majors who are residents of New Mexico and demonstrate participation in community service activities. Write to the address listed below for information.

University Of New Mexico, Albuquerque
Department Of Student Financial Aid
Mesa Vista Hall North
Albuquerque, NM 87131

John W. And Ruth Brainard Knorr Scholarship & Jupe Means Scholarship

Amount: $500 (may vary) **Deadline:** Mar 1
Fields/Majors: Agriculture

Varying amount offered to students majoring in agriculture at NMSU. Student must demonstrate financial need. Write to the address below for details.

New Mexico State University
College Of Agriculture And Home Economics
Box 30001, Box 3AG
Las Cruces, NM 88003

John W. And Ruth E. Powell Fund

Amount: Tuition & Fees **Deadline:** Mar 15
Fields/Majors: All Areas Of Study

Scholarships are available for residents of West Virginia who plan to or who are attending West Virginia State College. Applicant must reside in Kanawha County. Write to the address listed below for information and an application.

Greater Kanawha Valley Foundation
Scholarship Committee
P.O. Box 3041
Charleston, WV 25331

John W. Anderson Scholarship

Amount: Varies **Deadline:** None Specified
Fields/Majors: Accounting

Awards for students their sophomore, junior, or senior year in the Department of Accounting. Contact the Department of Accounting and Information Services for more details and an application.

University Of Massachusetts, Amherst
Department Of Accounting Information Service
Amherst, MA 01003

John W. Baker Track Scholarship

Amount: None Specified **Deadline:** Mar 1
Fields/Majors: All Areas Of Study

Scholarships are available at the University of New Mexico for full-time students who are members of the UNM track and field team. Write to the address listed below for information.

University Of New Mexico, Albuquerque
Department Of Student Financial Aid
Mesa Vista Hall North
Albuquerque, NM 87131

John W. Strickland And Larry W. (Buck) Wheeler Mem. Scholarships

Amount: Varies **Deadline:** Apr 15
Fields/Majors: All Areas Of Study

Scholarships available for a sophomore at ABAC who has a cumulative GPA of at least 3.2. Preference for Strickland Award will be given to students with an agricultural background and demonstrated achievement in a 4-H club when all other factors are equal. Write to the address below for additional information.

Abraham Baldwin Agricultural College
Office Of Admissions
2802 Moore Highway
Tifton, GA 31794

2557

John Z. Duling Grant Program

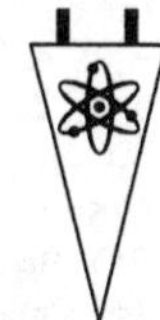

Amount: $5,000 (max) **Deadline:** Nov 1
Fields/Majors: Arboriculture

Awards are available for research in the field of arboriculture. Award amount will depend upon the adjudged value of the project to the needs of the arboriculture industry. Write to the address below for more information.

International Society Of Arboriculture
ISA Research Trust
P.O. Box GG
Savoy, IL 61874

2558

Johnnie Ruth Clarke Scholarships

AMOUNT: None Specified **DEADLINE:** None Specified
FIELDS/MAJORS: All Areas Of Study

Awards given to African American students who will attend St. Petersburg Junior College and are graduates of pinellas county high schools. Based on academic qualifications. Contact the Office of the Director of Scholarships and Student Financial Assistance at the campus you attend or write to the address below.

St. Petersburg Junior College
Office Of Financial Aid
P.O. Box 13489
St. Petersburg, FL 33733

2559

Johns Hopkins Grants

AMOUNT: Varies **DEADLINE:** Feb 1
FIELDS/MAJORS: All Areas Of Study

The Johns Hopkins Grant is available each year to undergraduate students who are able to demonstrate financial need. Renewable each year. Write to the address below for details.

Johns Hopkins University
3400 N. Charles Street
Baltimore, MD 21218

2560

Johnson & Wales University Scholarships

AMOUNT: Tuition **DEADLINE:** Feb 15
FIELDS/MAJORS: Business, Equine Science, Hospitality, Food Service Management

Scholarships are available for FFA members pursuing a four-year degree in one of the above fields at Johnson & Wales University. Write to the address below for details.

National FFA Foundation
Scholarship Office
P.O. Box 1516
Alexandria, VA 22309

2561

Johnson Controls Foundation Scholarship Program

AMOUNT: $1,750 **DEADLINE:** Feb 15
FIELDS/MAJORS: All Areas Of Study

Eligibility for scholarships limited to children of employees of Johnson Controls, Inc. Must be high school senior graduating in the current academic year and be in the upper 1/3rd of class. Applications must be received by Corporate Human Resources, 5757 N. Green Bay Ave., X-34, Milwaukee,WI 53201.

Johnson Controls Foundation
5757 N. Green Bay Ave.
P.O. Box 591
Milwaukee, WI 53201

2562

Johnson Hill Press Scholarships

AMOUNT: $500 **DEADLINE:** Feb 15
FIELDS/MAJORS: All Areas Of Study

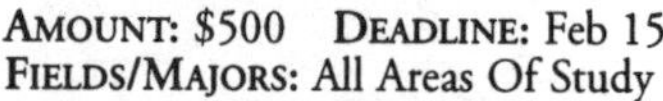

Scholarships are available for FFA members pursuing a two-year degree in any field of study, who reside in Illinois, Indiana, Iowa, Michigan, Minnesota, or Wisconsin. Write to the address below for details.

National FFA Foundation
Scholarship Office
P.O. Box 1516
Alexandria, VA 22309

2563

Johnston Lions Armand Muto Scholarship Fund

AMOUNT: Varies **DEADLINE:** Apr 15
FIELDS/MAJORS: All Areas Of Study

Scholarships are available for residents of Johnston, Rhode Island. Write to the address listed below for information.

Lions Club Of Johnston
c/o William O'Brien
P.O. Box 19131
Johnston, RI 02919

2564

Jonathan Baldwin Turner Agricultural Merit Scholarship Program

AMOUNT: $2,500 **DEADLINE:** None Specified
FIELDS/MAJORS: Agriculture

Awards are available for incoming freshmen at the University of Illinois. Based on high school rank, ACT or SAT score, leadership, and communication ability. Write to the address below for more details.

University Of Illinois, College Of Agriculture
Office Of The Dean
101 Mumford Hall
1301 West Gregory Drive
Urbana, IL 61801

2565

Jonathan Everett Dunbar Scholarship In The Humanities

AMOUNT: Full Tuition **DEADLINE:** Jan 1
FIELDS/MAJORS: Humanities

Freshman intending a humanities major showing outstanding academic performance and potential. Must apply for both admission and scholarship; must meet the criteria for the honors program; must have interview or attend campus visitation program. Scholarship renewable by achieving a GPA of 3.3 (freshman), 3.4 (sophomore), and 3.5 (junior). Write to the address below for details.

Denison University
Financial Aid Office
Box M
Granville, OH 43023

2566

Jones, Ruter And Mood Scholars Awards

AMOUNT: $2,000-$6,000 **DEADLINE:** None Specified
FIELDS/MAJORS: All Areas Of Study

Awards for H.S. seniors who are rank in the top 5% of their high school class or have at least a 3.7 GPA. Applicants must score at least a 1200 on the SAT or a 29 on the ACT. Renewable. Write to the address below for more information.

Southwestern University
Admissions Office
Georgetown, TX 78626

2567 Jose Marti Scholarship Challenge Grant Fund

AMOUNT: $2,000 **DEADLINE:** Apr 1
FIELDS/MAJORS: All Areas Of Study

Applicant must ba a U.S. citizen or legal resident, Hispanic American, and a Florida resident, enrolled as full-time undergraduate or graduate student at an eligible Florida institution. Renewable. A minimum 3.0 GPA is required. Contact the financial aid office at your college or write to the address below for details.

Florida Department Of Education
Office Of Student Financial Assistance
1344 Florida Education Center
Tallahassee, FL 32399

2568 Joseph & Savannah Obutelewicz Memorial Scholarship

AMOUNT: $700 **DEADLINE:** None Specified
FIELDS/MAJORS: Economics

Awards for senior economics majors with highest overall GPA as of September 1 each year. Must have completed or be enrolled in minimum of 21 credit hours of economics courses including intermediate macro and intermediate micro. Selection is made by the faculty of the economics department. Contact a member of the economics department for further information.

Bloomsburg University
19 Ben Franklin Hall
400 E. Second St.
Bloomsburg, PA 17815

2569 Joseph A. Butt, Business Scholarships

AMOUNT: Partial Tuition **DEADLINE:** Jan 15
FIELDS/MAJORS: Business

Scholarships for freshman who will be majoring in a business degree program. To qualify, a minimum 3.2 GPA is required. Applicant should also have significant community involvement and demonstrated leadership abilities. Scholarship is renewable for four years if student remains a business major and achieves a GPA of 3.0. Write to the address below for details.

Loyola University, New Orleans
Attn:Coordinator Of Scholarship Programs
6363 St. Charles Ave, Campus Box 18
New Orleans, LA 70118

2570 Joseph And Christine Alix Scholarship

AMOUNT: Varies **DEADLINE:** Mar 15
FIELDS/MAJORS: Business

Awards open to Teikyo Post continuing students who are majoring in business with a GPA of at least 3.25. Must be from Waterbury, CT. Write to the address below for more information.

Teikyo Post University
Office Of Financial Aid
800 Country Club Road
Waterbury, CT 06723

2571 Joseph C. Basile, II, Memorial Scholarship Fund

AMOUNT: None Specified **DEADLINE:** Mar 15
FIELDS/MAJORS: Education

Scholarship for West Virginia resident majoring in education at a WV school. Based on need, rather than academics. For undergraduate study. Write to the address below for details.

Greater Kanawha Valley Foundation Scholarship Committee
P.O. Box 3041
Charleston, WV 25331

2572 Joseph C. Gordon, Jr. Memorial Scholarship

AMOUNT: Varies **DEADLINE:** Mar 1
FIELDS/MAJORS: Engineering

Awards are available at the University of New Mexico for seniors enrolled in the school of engineering. Must demonstrate academic merit, financial need, and campus/community activities. Write to the address below for more information.

University Of New Mexico, Albuquerque
Office Of Financial Aid
Albuquerque, NM 87131

2573 Joseph Collins Foundation Grants

AMOUNT: $3,000 (max) **DEADLINE:** Mar 1
FIELDS/MAJORS: Medicine, Neurology, Psychiatry

Grants to needy graduate students in the above fields with broad cultural interests and who are enrolled in medical schools east of the Mississippi. Must be in the upper 1/2 of graduating class. The foundation requests that inquiries be made by your medical school. Application forms are mailed to the schools and application is made through the school.

Joseph Collins Foundation
153 East 53rd Street
New York, NY 10022

2574 Joseph Henry Jackson Award

AMOUNT: $2,000 **DEADLINE:** Jan 31
FIELDS/MAJORS: Creative Writing, Poetry

These awards are for authors of an unpublished work-in-progress-fiction, nonfictional prose, or poetry. Applicants must be residents of northern California or Nevada for three years prior to the award year, and be between the ages of 20 and 35. Write to the address listed below for information.

San Francisco Foundation
Intersection For The Arts
446 Valencia Street
San Francisco, CA 94103

2575 Joseph J. Knowles Memorial Scholarship

AMOUNT: None Specified **DEADLINE:** None Specified
FIELDS/MAJORS: Athletics

Scholarships are awarded to a man and a woman each year based on financial need. Contact the athletic director for more information.

Clarion University
104 Egbert Hall
Office Of Financial Aid
Clarion, PA 16214

2576 Joseph L. Boscov Scholarship

Amount: Varies **Deadline:** Mar 1
Fields/Majors: All Areas Of Study

Awards for students accepted for admission to the graduate school at UMass. Preference given to women over the age of 35 whose studies will equip them for increased service to the needs of people and/or the environment. Students must file an FAFSA as soon as possible after January 1 and before the March 1 financial aid priority consideration date. You will automatically be be considered for this scholarship if you are enrolled at the university and apply for financial aid. Separate applications, requests, or inquiries are not required and cannot be honored.

University Of Massachusetts, Amherst
Office Of Financial Aid Services
255 Whitmore Admin. Bldg., Box 3823
Amherst, MA 01003

2577 Joseph L. Fisher Dissertation Award

Amount: $12,000 **Deadline:** Mar 1
Fields/Majors: Natural Resources, Energy, Environmental Sciences

Fellowship is for doctoral candidate dissertation research in economics on issues relating to natural resources, energy, or the environment. Write to the address below for details.

Resources For The Future
1616 P Street, NW
Washington, DC 20036

2578 Joseph P. Riley Sr. Scholarship

Amount: $1,000 **Deadline:** None Specified
Fields/Majors: All Areas Of Study

Awards for needy and worthy residents of South Carolina. Write to the address below for more information.

Trident Technical College
Financial Aid Office
P.O. Box 118067
Charleston, SC 29423

2579 Joseph St. Martin Scholarship

Amount: $700 **Deadline:** Feb 29
Fields/Majors: Management

Awards for School of Management students who have demonstrated financial need, academic achievement and leadership skills. For juniors or seniors only. Applications for School of Management scholarships will be available in the SOM Fevelopment Office, Room 206.

University Of Massachusetts, Amherst
School Of Management
Development Office, Room 206
Amherst, MA 01003

2580 Joseph W. Matlavage Award

Amount: $350 **Deadline:** Feb 9
Fields/Majors: Finance

Award for sophomore and junior finance majors with a minimum GPA of 3.0. Must be residents of Columbia, Lycoming or Schuylkill Counties. Use Bloomsburg University scholarship application. Contact Dr. David Heskel, Chairperson, Finance and Business Law, for information.

Bloomsburg University
19 Ben Franklin Hall
400 E. Second St.
Bloomsburg, PA 17815

2581 Joseph Walker Elliot Scholarship

Amount: Tuition **Deadline:** Mar 15
Fields/Majors: All Areas Of Study

Awards for Jacksonville State University students who are from one of the following Alabama counties: Calhoun, Cherokee, Cleburne, or Etowah. Write to the address below for more information.

Jacksonville State University
Financial Aid Office
Jacksonville, AL 36265

2582 Josephine Beam Scholarship

Amount: $2,000 (max) **Deadline:** Feb 15
Fields/Majors: Engineering

Scholarships are available at the University of Utah for full-time students enrolled in an engineering program. For sophomore standing or above. Write to the address below for details.

University Of Utah
Dean's Office, College Of Engineering
2202 Merrill Engineering Building
Salt Lake City, UT 84112

2583 Josephine Beam Scholarships

Amount: Varies **Deadline:** Feb 1
Fields/Majors: Geology, Geophysics, Metallurgy, Meteorology And Related Fields

Scholarships are available at the University of Utah for full-time students majoring in one of the areas listed above. Write to the address below for details.

University Of Utah
College Of Mines And Earth Sciences
Office Of The Dean
Salt Lake City, UT 84112

2584 Josephine C. Connelly Scholarship

Amount: Varies **Deadline:** Mar 15, Nov 15
Fields/Majors: All Areas Of Study

Awards for new entering highly motivated students pursuing a degree. Must demonstrate academic achievement and participation in campus life. Write to the address below for more information.

Gwynedd-Mercy College
Student Financial Aid
Sumneytown Pike
Gwynedd Valley, PA 19437

2585

Josephine L. Cloudman Scholarship

AMOUNT: Varies **DEADLINE:** Apr 15
FIELDS/MAJORS: All Areas Of Study

The Cloudman Award is open to ABAC students with predicted academic success and financial need. Write to the address below for additional information.

Abraham Baldwin Agricultural College
Office Of Admissions
2802 Moore Highway
Tifton, GA 31794

2586

Josephine Roessler Prinster Award

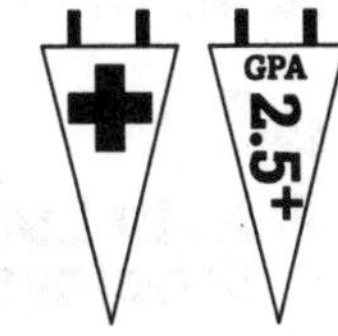

AMOUNT: Tuition And Fees
DEADLINE: None Specified
FIELDS/MAJORS: Registered Nursing

Awards for full-time Mesa State students enrolled in a registered nursing program and who have a GPA of at least 2.75. Contact the School of Professional Studies/Nursing Area for more details.

Mesa State College
Financial Aid Office
P.O. Box 2647
Grand Junction, CO 81501

2587

Journalism And Mass Communications Scholarships

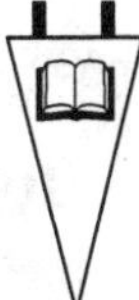

AMOUNT: $500-$1,000 **DEADLINE:** Feb 15
FIELDS/MAJORS: Journalism And Mass Communications

Scholarships are available at the University of Oklahoma, Norman, for students majoring in journalism. Includes the C. Joe Holland, Davie Belle Eaton Mercer Memorial, Elmer J. and Juanita S. Thrower Memorial, H. Merle Woods, Ralph Sewell Jim Biggerstaff, Robert E. and Allie Malvina Stephenson, and Wheeler Mayo Scholarships. Individual award requirements may vary. 18 awards offered. Write to the address listed below for information.

University Of Oklahoma, Norman
School Of Journalism And Mass Communications
860 Van Vleet Oval
Norman, OK 73019

2588

Journalism Awards Program

AMOUNT: $500-$2,000 **DEADLINE:** Varies
FIELDS/MAJORS: Journalism, Photojournalism, Broadcast News

Open to all undergraduate journalism majors who attend an Association of Schools of Journalism and Mass Communication accredited school (95 schools). Contests are held monthly during the school year. Entry forms and information are available only through the journalism department offices of the participating schools. See your department for details. Do not write to address shown for more information; they will only refer you to your department office.

William Randolph Hearst Foundation Journalism Awards
Jan Watten, Director
90 New Montgomery St., Suite 1212
San Francisco, CA 94105

2589

Journalism Merit Scholarship

AMOUNT: $500 **DEADLINE:** Feb 15
FIELDS/MAJORS: Journalism And Mass Communications

Scholarships are available at the University of Oklahoma, Norman for freshmen majoring in journalism, who show exceptional merit and potential. Write to the address listed below for information.

University Of Oklahoma, Norman
School Of Journalism And Mass Communications
860 Van Vleet Oval
Norman, OK 73019

2590

Journalism Scholarships

AMOUNT: Varies **DEADLINE:** None Specified
FIELDS/MAJORS: Journalism

Scholarships available for ETSU students pursuing a career in journalism. Includes the Bristol, Virginia-Tennessee Scholarship, the Greenville Sun Journalism Scholarship, the Johnson City Press Journalism Scholarship, the Kingsport Times-News Journalism Scholarship, and the Richard Cobb Miller Memorial Scholarship in Journalism. Requirements vary. Contact the office of financial aid at the address below.

East Tennessee State University
Office Of Financial Aid
Box 70722
Johnson City, TN 37614

2591

JTB Cultural Exchange Corp Grants

AMOUNT: $3,500-$4,000 **DEADLINE:** Jun 3
FIELDS/MAJORS: Japanese Studies

Applicant must have or be hosting in their own home or teaching Japanese American students (and likely to continue to do so) or must be teaching at a school that has a sister school relationship with a Japanese school. Must have a considerable interest in Japan but must have never has the opportunity to visit Japan. Write to the address below for more information.

JTB Cultural Exchange Corp.
One Rockefeller Plaza, Suite 1250
New York, NY 10020

2592

Juanita West Proffitt Scholarship

AMOUNT: None Specified **DEADLINE:** None Specified
FIELDS/MAJORS: Applied Human Sciences

Scholarship available at ETSU for students majoring in applied human sciences. Contact the applied human sciences department at ETSU for information.

East Tennessee State University
Office Of Financial Aid
Box 70722
Johnson City, TN 37614

2593

Judge Edward Scott Scholarship Fund

Amount: None Specified **Deadline:** None Specified
Fields/Majors: All Areas Of Study

Scholarships for graduate students in Peabody College at Vanderbilt University from Mississippi. Preference given to students from Bolivar County, MS, or other cities in Mississippi. Write to the address below for more information.

Vanderbilt University
Admissions And Financial Assistance
Box 327 Peabody College
Nashville, TN 37203

2594

Judge William M. Beard Scholarship

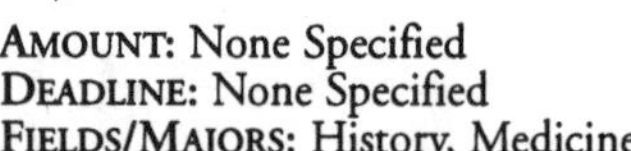

Amount: None Specified
Deadline: None Specified
Fields/Majors: History, Medicine

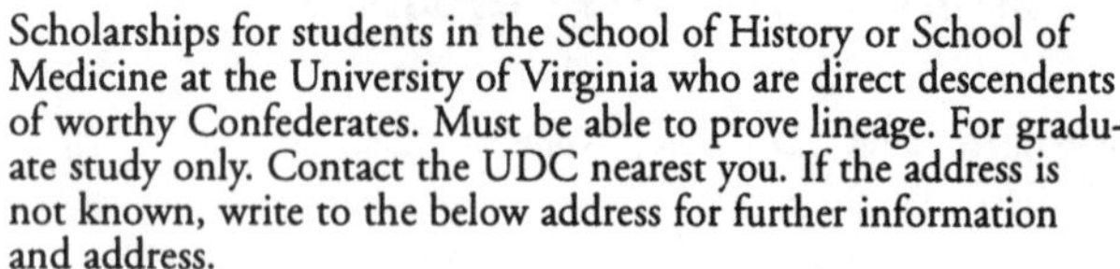

Scholarships for students in the School of History or School of Medicine at the University of Virginia who are direct descendents of worthy Confederates. Must be able to prove lineage. For graduate study only. Contact the UDC nearest you. If the address is not known, write to the below address for further information and address.

United Daughters Of The Confederacy
Education Committee
328 North Boulevard
Richmond, VA 23220

2595

Judicial Fellows Program

Amount: Varies **Deadline:** Nov 17
Fields/Majors: Law And Forensic Research

Highly competitive fellowship program in which selected individuals are placed in various national institutions of the federal judiciary. Must hold at least one advanced degree, have at least two years professional experience, and have multi-disciplinary training and familiarity with the judicial process. Application will be made with curriculum vitae, essay (<700 words) on interest in and qualifications for judicial fellows program, and copies of no more than two publications or writing samples. Write to the address below for more information.

Supreme Court Of The U.S.
Judicial Fellows Program
Administrative Director, Room 5
Washington, DC 20543

2596

Judith Graham Poole Postdoctoral Research Fellowship

Amount: $35,000 (max) **Deadline:** Dec 1
Fields/Majors: Hemophilia Research Postdoctorate (M.D. or Ph.D)

Fellowships for hemophilia-related research. Number of awards per year dependent on available funding. Topics that the NHF has expressed an interest in clinical or basic research on biochemical, genetic, hematologic, orthopedic, psychiatric, or dental aspects of the hemophilias or Von Willebrand disease. Contact the address below for complete details. The NHF has

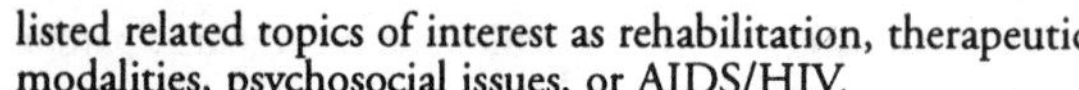

listed related topics of interest as rehabilitation, therapeutic modalities, psychosocial issues, or AIDS/HIV.

National Hemophilia Foundation
Karen O'Hagen
110 Greene Street, Suite 303
New York, NY 10012

2597

Judith Resnik Memorial Scholarship

Amount: $2,000 **Deadline:** Feb 1
Fields/Majors: Engineering (Space Related)

Scholarship for female, senior-year SWE member studying engineering with a space-related major, toward a career in the space industry. Must have a GPA of at least 3.5. Write to address below for details. Please be certain to enclose a self-addressed, stamped envelope. Information and applications for the SWE. Awards are also available from the deans of engineering schools.

Society Of Women Engineers
120 Wall Street, 11th Floor
New York, NY 10005

2598

Judy Lynn Price Scholarships

Amount: $1,000 **Deadline:** Mar 1
Fields/Majors: Telecommunications

Awards for juniors and seniors studying telecommunication. Must have a GPA of 2.8 or better. Write to the address below for more information.

University Of Florida
Knight Scholarship & Placement Director
2070 Weimer Hall
Gainesville, FL 32611

2599

Julia Buchanan Tappan Fund

Amount: Varies **Deadline:** Mar 1
Fields/Majors: Medicine

Awards are available at the University of New Mexico for medical students with financial need. Write to the address below for more information.

University Of New Mexico, Albuquerque
Office Of Financial Aid
Albuquerque, NM 87131

2600

Julian A. Hudgens Trust Fund

Amount: Varies **Deadline:** Aug 1, Jan 1
Fields/Majors: Baptist Ministry

Must be a graduate student from Virginia attending a Southern Baptist Convention School and a member of a church associated with Baptist General Association of Virginia. Loan is forgiven if recipient works for the ministry for two years following graduation. Write to the address below for more information.

Virginia Baptist General Board
Division Of Church And Minister Support
P.O. Box 8568
Richmond, VA 23226

2601

Julian A. McPhee Award

Amount: $300 **Deadline:** None Specified
Fields/Majors: All Areas Of Study

Scholarships are awarded to full-time juniors and seniors. Must have a GPA of 2.8 or better. Write to the address below for more information.

California State Polytechnic University, Pomona
Office Of Financial Aid
3801 West Temple Ave.
Pomona, CA 91768

2602

Julian Jenkins Scholarship

Amount: $1,000 **Deadline:** Mar 15
Fields/Majors: All Areas Of Study

Awards for Jacksonville State University students who are from Calhoun County in Alabama. Write to the address below for more information.

Jacksonville State University
Financial Aid Office
Jacksonville, AL 36265

2603

Julie Silver Memorial Scholarship

Amount: $700 **Deadline:** Mar 1
Fields/Majors: Telecommunications

Must be a junior or senior majoring in telecommunications at the University of Florida. Must have at least a 2.8 GPA. Internship at WTLV-TV in Jacksonville is available for scholarship winner. Write to the address below for complete details.

University Of Florida
Scholarship And Placement Director
2070 Weimer Hall
Gainesville, FL 32611

2604

Juliette A. Southard Scholarship Trust Fund

Amount: $100-$1,000 Deadline: Jan 31
Fields/Majors: Dental Assisting

Scholarships available to students who have been accepted into an accredited dental assisting program at any level of study and are ADAA members or students. Must be a U.S. citizen to apply. Write to the address below for more information.

American Dental Assistants Association
203 N. Lasalle, Suite 132
Chicago, IL 60601

2605

Julius F. Neumueller Awards In Optics

Amount: $500 **Deadline:** Jun 1
Fields/Majors: Optometry

Award for students pursuing a doctor of optometry degree. Based on paper (not to exceed 3000 words) on one of the following topics: geometrical optics, physical optics, ophthalmic optics, or optics of the eye. Cash award. Write to the address below for more information.

American Academy Of Optometry
College Of Optometry
University Of Houston
Houston, TX 7204

2606

June Ebright Textbook Scholarship

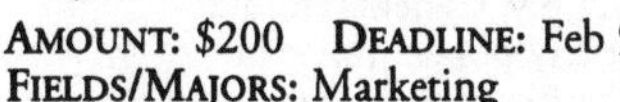

Amount: $200 **Deadline:** Feb 9
Fields/Majors: Marketing

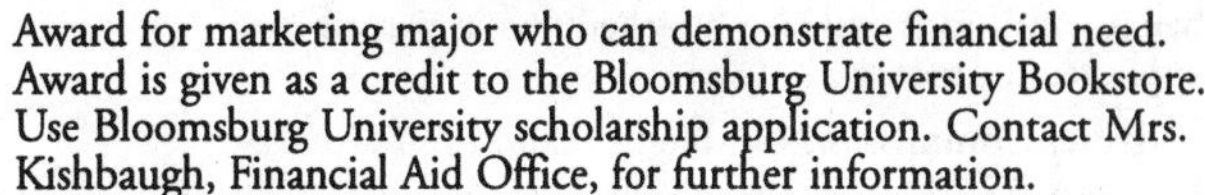

Award for marketing major who can demonstrate financial need. Award is given as a credit to the Bloomsburg University Bookstore. Use Bloomsburg University scholarship application. Contact Mrs. Kishbaugh, Financial Aid Office, for further information.

Bloomsburg University
19 Ben Fraklin Hall
400 E. Second St.
Bloomburg, PA 17815

2607

Junior Academy Of Science Scholarship

Amount: $1,850 **Deadline:** None Specified
Fields/Majors: Science

Student must receive a number one rating in the District Junior Academy of Science competition. Contact the College of Natural and Applied Sciences for more information.

Southwest Missouri State University
Office Of Financial Aid
901 South National Ave.
Springfield, MO 65804

2608

Junior Achievement Scholarship

Amount: $4,000 **Deadline:** May 1
Fields/Majors: Business Administration

Renewable scholarships available for full-time freshmen who were active in Junior Achievement in high school. Must be enrolled in the College of Business Administration. Contact your local Junior Achievement representative, or write to the below address for details.

Alfred University
Student Financial Aid Office
26 N. Main St.
Alfred, NY 14802

2609

Junior And Community College Athletic Scholarship Program

Amount: Tuition **Deadline:** None Specified
Fields/Majors: All Areas Of Study

Awards available to students who participate in a sport. Must be full-time students enrolled in public junior and community colleges in Alabama. Awards may be renewed on the basis of continued participation in the designated sport or activity. Not based on financial need. Applicants should apply through the coach, athletic director, or financial aid officer at any public junior or community college in Alabama, rather than address listed below.

Alabama Commission On Higher Education
P.O. Box 30200
Montgomery, AL 36130

2610

Junior And Community College Performing Arts Scholarship Program

AMOUNT: Tuition **DEADLINE:** None Specified
FIELDS/MAJORS: Performing Arts

Applicants must demonstrate talent through competitive auditions. Awards are restricted to full-time students attending public junior and community colleges in Alabama. Not based on financial need. To apply, students should contact the financial aid office at any public junior or community college in Alabama, rather than address listed below. Auditions will also be scheduled as part of the application process.

Alabama Commission On Higher Education
P.O. Box 30200
Montgomery, AL 36130

2611

Junior And Senior Scholarships In Teacher Education

AMOUNT: $500-$1,000 **DEADLINE:** Mar 15
FIELDS/MAJORS: Education

Applicants must be juniors or seniors majoring in education at Appalachian State University. Must have a GPA of at least 3.0. Contact the Office of the Dean at the address below for details.

Appalachian State University
Reich College Of Education
Boone, NC 28608

2612

Junior Chemistry Achievement Award

AMOUNT: $250 **DEADLINE:** None Specified
FIELDS/MAJORS: Chemistry

Awards for outstanding junior chemistry major. Recipient will be selected by the chemistry department. Contact a chemistry department staff member for further information.

Bloomsburg University
19 Ben Franklin Hall
400 E. Second St.
Bloomsburg, PA 17815

2613

Junior College Transfer Scholarships Amount

AMOUNT: Tuition **DEADLINE:** May 15
FIELDS/MAJORS: All Areas Of Study

Awards for Jacksonville State University transfer students who are from Alabama junior colleges. Write to the address below for more information.

Jacksonville State University
Financial Aid Office
Jacksonville, AL 36265

2614

Junior Fellows Program

AMOUNT: $300 Per Week **DEADLINE:** Mar 1
FIELDS/MAJORS: See Fields Listed Below

Program for juniors, seniors, recent graduates, or graduate students in the areas of American history, literature, geography, cartography, graphic arts, architecture, history of photography, film, television, radio, music, rare books & arts, American popular culture, librarianship, preservation, and Asian, African, Middle Eastern, European, or Hispanic studies. Write to the address below for more information.

Library Of Congress Program Coordinator, Collection Services
Library Of Congress, LM-642
Washington, DC 20540

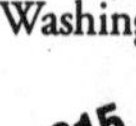

2615

Junior Fellowships

AMOUNT: None Specified **DEADLINE:** Jul 1
FIELDS/MAJORS: Humanities, Philosophy, Archaeology, History, Language, Linguistics

Fellowships are available for dissertation research in India. Write to the address listed below for and application.

American Institute Of Indian Studies
1130 East 59th Street
Chicago, IL 60637

2616

Justinian Society Of Lawyers/DuPage County Chapter

AMOUNT: $1,000 **DEADLINE:** Apr 1
FIELDS/MAJORS: Law

Applicant must have completed one semester of law school and be of Italian heritage. Will also need to include a statement indicating his/her professional objectives and any special factors that should be considered. Must be U.S. citizen. Write to below address for information and application.

Marsha H. Cellucci, Chairwoman-Scholarship
Cellucci, Yacobellis & Holman
1155 S. Washington St. #10
Naperville, IL 60540

2617

Juvenile Diabetes Foundation Awards

AMOUNT: Varies **DEADLINE:** Varies
FIELDS/MAJORS: Medical Research (Juvenile Diabetes)

Postdoctoral grants and fellowships supporting basic and applied research on diabetes and related disorders. Includes research grants, career development awards, postdoctoral fellowships, and new training for established scientist awards. Write to the address below for more information.

Juvenile Diabetes Foundation International
Ruth Marsch, Grant Administrator
120 Wall Street
New York, NY 10005

2618
K & W Cafeteria Corporation Scholarship

AMOUNT: Tuition & Books
DEADLINE: None Specified
FIELDS/MAJORS: Culinary Arts

Awards for TTC students enrolled in the culinary arts program. Must provide written career goals in the food service field and have a GPA of at least 3.0. Write to the address below for more information.

Trident Technical College
Financial Aid Office
P.O. Box 118067
Charleston, SC 29423

2619
Kahabi Scholarship

AMOUNT: None Specified **DEADLINE:** Mar 1
FIELDS/MAJORS: All Areas Of Study

Scholarships are available to graduating seniors from a high school in North Platte with a GPA of at least 3.0. Preference is given to students active in the Camp Fire Youth Program. Write to the address listed below for information.

Mid-Nebraska Community Foundation
410 Rodeo Road
P.O. Box 1321
North Platte, NE 69103

2620
Kamm Family Fund

AMOUNT: Tuition & Fees **DEADLINE:** Mar 15
FIELDS/MAJORS: All Areas Of Study

Scholarships for students who were graduates of Nicholas County High School in Summersville, West Virginia. For study at any state-operated school in West Virginia. Renewable. Write to the address below for details.

Greater Kanawha Valley Foundation
Scholarship Committee
P.O. Box 3041
Charleston, WV 25331

2621
Kankakee County Community Services Scholarships

AMOUNT: $1,100 **DEADLINE:** Apr 1
FIELDS/MAJORS: All Areas Of Study

Scholarships for students from income-qualifying families in Kankakee County, Illinois. For those who are or will be studying in a vocational/technical school or in a two- or four-year college/university in the state of Illinois. Based on need, academic potential and commitment to civic affairs. For undergraduate study. Applications are available from your high school guidance office or from KCCSI at the address below.

Kankakee County Community Services
341 N. St. Joseph Ave.
P.O. Box 2216
Kankakee, IL 60901

2622
Kansas City Southern Industries, Inc. Scholarships

AMOUNT: $1,000 **DEADLINE:** Feb 15
FIELDS/MAJORS: Agriculture

Scholarships are available for FFA members pursuing a two- or four-year degree in any area of agriculture, who reside in Arkansas, Louisiana, Mississippi, Missouri, Oklahoma, or Texas. Write to the address below for details.

National FFA Foundation
Scholarship Office
P.O. Box 1516
Alexandria, VA 22309

2623
Kansas Educational Assistance Program

AMOUNT: Tuition **DEADLINE:** None Specified
FIELDS/MAJORS: All Areas Of Study

Open to children of parents who entered military service as a resident of Kansas and whose status became POW, MIA, or killed in action in Vietnam. Applicants do not have to be residents of Kansas but award must be used at a Kansas school. Renewable. Write to the address below for details.

Kansas Commission On Veterans' Affairs
Jayhawk Tower
700 SW Jackson, Suite 701
Topeka, KS 6603

2624
Kansas Funeral Directors Association Scholarships

AMOUNT: $250-$1,000 **DEADLINE:** Mar 15
FIELDS/MAJORS: Mortuary Science

Awards for Kansas residents studying mortuary science who have at least one but not more than two semesters of mortuary science school remaining. Write to the address below for more information.

Kansas Funeral Directors Association
1200 Kansas Ave.
Topeka, KS 66612

2625
Kansas Library Association Scholarship

AMOUNT: $1,650 **DEADLINE:** Apr 1
FIELDS/MAJORS: Library Sciences

Scholarships for members of the Kansas Library Association. For master's level study. Write to the address below for details.

Kansas Library Association
Mr. Leroy M. Gattlin, Executive Director
901 N. Main St.
Hutchinson, KS 67501

2626
Kansas Wesleyan University Awards

AMOUNT: $4,000 (max) **DEADLINE:** None Specified
FIELDS/MAJORS: All Areas Of Study

Need-based awards for KWU students with outstanding ability in academics or athletics. Write to the address below for more details.

Kansas Wesleyan University
Office Of Financial Assistance
100 E. Claflin
Salina, KS 67401

2627

Kappa Kappa Gamma Member Scholarships And Fellowships

AMOUNT: None Specified **DEADLINE:** Feb 1
FIELDS/MAJORS: All Areas Of Study

Graduate and undergraduate scholarships, and grants for part-time study, are available to members of Kappa Kappa Gamma. Send an SASE to the address below or contact your chapter for more information.

Kappa Kappa Gamma Foundation
Member Scholarships/Fellowships
530 E. Town Street, P.O. Box 38
Columbus, OH 43216

2628

Karen A. Justice Scholarship

AMOUNT: Varies **DEADLINE:** None Specified
FIELDS/MAJORS: Nursing

Awards for Jacksonville State University students who are in the field of nursing. Contact the College of Nursing for more information.

Jacksonville State University
Financial Aid Office
Jacksonville, AL 36265

2629

Karen D. Carsel Memorial Scholarship

AMOUNT: $500 **DEADLINE:** Apr 1
FIELDS/MAJORS: All Areas Of Study

Scholarship open to full-time graduate student who presents evidence of economic need. Student must submit evidence of legal blindness, three letters of recommendation, and transcripts of grades from the college he/she is attending. Write to the address below for complete details.

American Foundation For The Blind
Scholarship Committee
11 Penn Plaza, Suite 30
New York, NY 10001

2630

Karl "Pete" Furhmann IV Memorial Scholarship

AMOUNT: None Specified **DEADLINE:** Apr 15
FIELDS/MAJORS: Horticulture

Scholarships for Ohio high school graduates studying horticulture at the associate's or bachelor's level. Must be an Ohio resident. Renewable. Write to the address below for details.

Fuhrmann Orchards
Karl "Pete" Fuhrmann IV Scholarship Fund
510 Hansgen-Morgan Rd.
Wheelersburg, OH 45694

2631

Karla Scherer Foundation Scholarship

AMOUNT: Varies **DEADLINE:** Ongoing
FIELDS/MAJORS: Manufacturing-Related Fields

Scholarships for women wishing to pursue business careers, especially in the areas of manufacturing economics and finance. Not restricted solely to academic achievers or those with financial need. Drive, desire, and determination to succeed are important criteria as well. Write to the address listed below for information.

Karla Scherer Foundation
100 Renaissance Center, Suite 1680
Detroit, MI 48243

2632

Kate B. & Hall J. Peterson, Albert Boni Fellowships

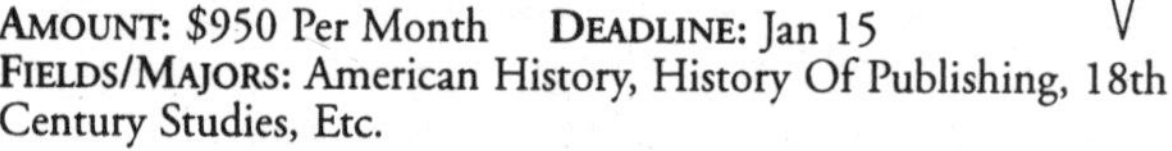

AMOUNT: $950 Per Month **DEADLINE:** Jan 15
FIELDS/MAJORS: American History, History Of Publishing, 18th Century Studies, Etc.

Six- to twelve-month fellowships in support of research utilizing the collections of the American Antiquarian Society. Must hold Ph.D. or be involved in dissertation research. Write to the address listed below for information.

American Antiquarian Society
Director Of Research And Publication
185 Salisbury St., Room 10
Worcester, MA 01609

2633

Kate Neal Kinley Memorial Fellowship

AMOUNT: $7,000 (max) **DEADLINE:** Feb 15
FIELDS/MAJORS: Art, Music, Architecture

Fellowships for graduate students in the College of Fine and Applied Arts at the University of Illinois, Urbana-Champaign. Contact the Office of the Dean of the College of Fine and Applied Arts at the address below for details.

University Of Illinois, Urbana-Champaign
College Of Fine And Applied Arts
608 E Lorado Taft, 110 Architecture Bldg.
Champaign, IL 61820

2634

Katharine M. Grosscup Horticultural Scholarship

AMOUNT: $2,000 (max) **DEADLINE:** Feb 15
FIELDS/MAJORS: Horticulture, Floriculture, Botany, Arboriculture, Landscape Design

Scholarships for juniors, seniors, or graduate students who are pursuing a degree in one of the fields listed above, or any related field. Preference is given to students from Ohio, Pennsylvania, West Virginia, Michigan, and Indiana. Write to the address listed below for information.

Garden Club Of America
Grosscup Scholarship Committee
11030 East Boulevard
Cleveland, OH 44106

2635
Katherine J. Schutze Memorial Scholarship

Amount: Varies **Deadline:** Mar 15
Fields/Majors: Theology

Applicants must be women members of the Christian Church (Disciples of Christ) who are preparing for the ministry. For full-time study. Financial need is considered. Write to the address below for details.

Christian Church (Disciples Of Christ)
Attn: Scholarships
P.O. Box 1986
Indianapolis, IN 46206

2636
Katherine M. Simms Prize

Amount: Varies **Deadline:** Mar 1
Fields/Majors: All Areas Of Study

Prize awarded to the undergraduate student at the University of New Mexico who submits the best essay on a New Mexico topic. Applicants must be from New Mexico. Write to the address below for more information.

University Of New Mexico, Albuquerque
Office Of Financial Aid
Albuquerque, NM 87131

2637
Katherine Wills Coleman And National Foundation Fellowships

Amount: $1,500 **Deadline:** Feb 1
Fields/Majors: All Areas Of Study

Fellowships are available to current or former Mortar Board members for graduate or professional study. Previous Fellows are not eligible. Write to the address below for details.

Mortar Board National Foundation
1250 Chambers Rd., #170
Columbus, OH 43212

2638
Kathern F. Gruber Scholarship Program

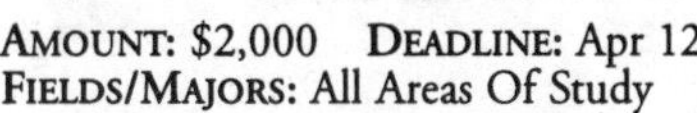

Amount: $2,000 **Deadline:** Apr 12
Fields/Majors: All Areas Of Study

Scholarships for children and spouses of blinded veterans. Veteran must be legally blind (from either service-connected or nonservice connected cause). Must be accepted or enrolled as a full-time student in an undergraduate or graduate program at an accredited institution. 12 awards per year. Write to the address below for details.

Blinded Veterans Association
Kathern F. Gruber Scholarship
477 H Street, NW
Washington, DC 20001

2639
Kathleen Rogers And Lionel Rosenbaum Scholarships

Amount: Varies **Deadline:** Mar 1
Fields/Majors: All Areas Of Study

Awards are available at the University of New Mexico for students making satisfactory academic progress. Rosenbaum Awards are only available for undergraduate students. Write to the address below for more information.

University Of New Mexico, Albuquerque
Office Of Financial Aid
Albuquerque, NM 87131

2640
Kathleen S. Anderson Award

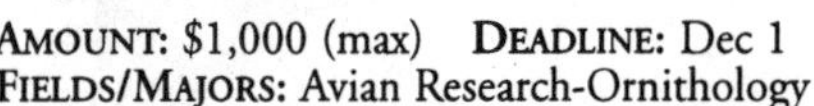

Amount: $1,000 (max) **Deadline:** Dec 1
Fields/Majors: Avian Research-Ornithology

Grants in support of projects in avian research in the following areas: migration, feeding ecology, habitat fragmentation, populations, competition, shorebirds, and endangered species. Projects must take place in the Americas. Work based at the Manomet Observatory is encouraged. Intended to support persons beginning a career in biology. Enrollment in academic program is desirable, but not essential. Write to the address below to request further information and proposal guidelines.

Manomet Observatory
Kathleeen S. Anderson Award
Box 177
Manomet, MA 02345

2641
Kathryn Walker-Clayton Williams, Sr., Memorial Scholarship

Amount: $1,000 **Deadline:** Apr 1
Fields/Majors: English

Awards for Sul Ross students who are studying English and have good academic standing. Write to the address below for more information.

Sul Ross State University
Financial Aid Office
Box C-113
Alpine, TX 79832

2642
Katu Thomas R. Dargan Minority Scholarship

Amount: $3,500 **Deadline:** May 31
Fields/Majors: Any Broadcast Curriculum

Scholarships available to minority students residing in or attending a school in Oregon or Washington. Applicant must be enrolled in the first, second or third year of a broadcast curriculum at a four-year college, university, or an accredited community college. Applicant must have a minimum grade point average of 3.0 and maintain this GPA to renew scholarship. Write to the address below for more information.

Katu Thomas R. Dargan Minority Scholarship
c/o Human Resources
P.O. Box 2
Portland, OR 97207

2643
KCAI Competitive Scholarships

Amount: $8,000-$10,000
Deadline: None Specified
Fields/Majors: All Areas Of Study

For students admitted to the Kansas City Art Institute who demonstrate exceptional artistic and academic ability. Accepted students to

the KCAI must be nominated by their regional coordinator of admissions. Write to the address below for more information.

Kansas City Art Institute
Financial Aid Office
4415 Warwick Blvd.
Kansas City, MO 64111

2644

KCAI Scholarships And Merit Awards

Amount: Varies **Deadline:** Varies
Fields/Majors: All Areas Of Study

For students admitted to the Kansas City Art Institute. Based on academic excellence, portfolio evaluation, and financial need. Write to the address below for more information.

Kansas City Art Institute
Financial Aid Office
4415 Warwick Blvd.
Kansas City, MO 64111

2645

Keepers Preservation Education Fund Fellowship

Amount: $500 **Deadline:** Dec 15
Fields/Majors: Historical Preservation

Awards are available for graduate students in the field of historical preservation to attend the annual meeting of the Society of Architectural Historians. Write to the address below for more information.

Society Of Architectural Historians
1365 North Astor St.
Chicago, IL 60610

2646

Keith And Helen Dunn Scholarships

Amount: $1,000 **Deadline:** Mar 1
Fields/Majors: Accounting

Scholarships are available at the University of Iowa for full-time undergraduates majoring in accounting. Write to the address listed below for information.

University Of Iowa
College Of Business Admin., Suite W16
108 Pappajohn Business Admin. Bldg.
Iowa City, IA 52245

2647

Kelcher Memorial Scholarship

Amount: Varies **Deadline:** Mar 1
Fields/Majors: Journalism Or Communication

Awards are available at the University of New Mexico for juniors and senior students who can demonstrate commitment and promise to the fields of journalism or communications. Must demonstrate financial need. Write to the address listed below for information.

University Of New Mexico, Albuquerque
Office Of Financial Aid
Albuquerque, NM 87131

2648

Kellie Cannon Memorial Scholarship

Amount: $1,000 **Deadline:** Mar 1
Fields/Majors: Computer Science, Information Science, Data Processing

Scholarships are available to legally blind students majoring in computer science or a related field. Based on academic ability. Write to the address below for details.

American Council Of The Blind
Scholarship Coordinator
1155 15th St., NW, Suite 72
Washington, DC 20005

2649

Kellogg Supply Scholarship

Amount: $500 **Deadline:** Apr 15
Fields/Majors: Ornamental Horticulture

Open to ornamental horticulture majors interested in landscape, turf, or nursery careers. Write to the address below for more information.

California State Polytechnic University, Pomona
College Of Agriculture
Building 7, Room 11
Pomona, CA 91768

2650

Kemper Scholars Grant Program

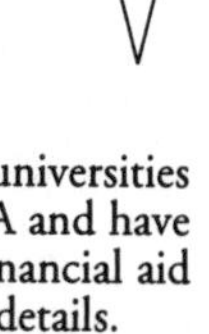

Amount: $1,500-$6,000 **Deadline:** Varies
Fields/Majors: Business

Scholarships for enrolled freshmen at 16 colleges and universities in the U.S. Must have potential to maintain a 3.0 GPA and have a career interest in the field of business. Contact the financial aid office at your school or write to the address below for details.

James S. Kemper Foundation
Kemper Scholars Grant Program
One Kemper Drive
Long Grove, IL 60049

2651

Kempf-Whiting Scholarship

Amount: $350 **Deadline:** Early Spring
Fields/Majors: Special Education

Award for a student who has earned an outstanding record in both their university studies and in the special education sophomore practicum. Based on financial need. Contact the Special Education Department Office, UW Oshkosh, for more information.

University Of Wisconsin, Oshkosh
Financial Aid Office, Dempsey 104
800 Algoma Blvd.
Oshkosh, WI 54901

2652

Ken Dawson Award

Amount: $5,000 **Deadline:** Mar 15
Fields/Majors: Gay And Lesbian History

Award for study in gay and lesbian history. Applicants must submit a vita and a ten-page narrative proposal that includes a summary of work already done in gay and lesbian history. No university affiliation is required. Write to the address below for more information.

Center For Lesbian And Gay Studies
City University Of New York
33 West 42nd St., Room 404N
New York, NY 10036

Ken Gross Scholarship

AMOUNT: $1,000 **DEADLINE:** Feb 9
FIELDS/MAJORS: All Areas Of Study

Award for full time student who is a single parent. Financial need in addition to academic record will be considered. Use Bloomsburg University scholarship application. Contact Dr. Susan Hicks, Social Equity Office for further information.

Bloomsburg University
19 Ben Franklin Hall
400 E. Second St.
Bloomsburg, PA 17815

Ken Inouye Scholarship For Minority Students

AMOUNT: $1,000 **DEADLINE:** Feb 15
FIELDS/MAJORS: News Journalism

Scholarship for minority students who intend to work in news journalism. This is open to juniors, seniors, and graduate students who are residents of or students in Los Angeles, Ventura or Orange Counties. Based on achievements and financial need. Write to the address below for details Society Of Professional Journalists, Los Angeles Professional Chapter

SPJ Scholarship Chairman
P.O. Box 420
Woodland Hills, CA 91365

Kenan T. Erim Award

AMOUNT: $4,000 **DEADLINE:** Nov 1
FIELDS/MAJORS: Archaeology/Classical Studies

This award will be given to an American or international research and/or excavating scholar working on Aphrodisias material. If the project involves work at Aphrodisias, candidates must submit written approval from the field director with their applications. Write to the address below for details.

Archaeological Institute Of America-American Friends Of Aphrodisias
Boston University
656 Beacon Street, 4th Floor
Boston, MA 02215

Kennecott Scholarship

AMOUNT: $2,500 **DEADLINE:** Feb 1
FIELDS/MAJORS: Elementary And Secondary Education

Scholarships are available to undergraduate students, juniors and seniors admitted to teacher education programs who rank in the top 10% of education students. Two awards, one for elementary education and one for secondary education. Write to the address below for details.

University Of Utah
Financial Aid And Scholarship Office
105 Student Services Building
Salt Lake City, UT 84112

Kennedy Center Internship Programs

AMOUNT: $650 **DEADLINE:** Varies
FIELDS/MAJORS: Arts Administration

Various internships for upper level underclassmen, graduate students, and recent college graduates. The internships are held at the JFK center. Award amount is paid monthly. Write to the address below for details.

John F. Kennedy Center For The Performing Arts
Education Dept., Internship Coordinator
The Kennedy Center
Washington, DC 20566

2658

Kennedy Research Grants

AMOUNT: $500-$1,500 **DEADLINE:** Mar 15, Aug 15
FIELDS/MAJORS: Research, Kennedy Period Studies

Preference is given to Ph.D. dissertation research, in recently opened or relatively unused collections and the preparation of recent dissertations for publication, but all proposals are welcomed. Fifteen to twenty awards per year. Write to the address below for more information.

John F. Kennedy Library Foundation
William Johnson, Chief Archivist
Columbia Point
Boston, MA 02125

2659

Kenneth & Ellen Nielsen Cooperative Scholarships

AMOUNT: $1,000 **DEADLINE:** Feb 15
FIELDS/MAJORS: Agriculture

Scholarships are available for FFA members pursuing a four-year degree in any area of agriculture, who reside in & plan to attend school in Colorado, Iowa, Illinois, Kansas, Minnesota, Missouri, Nebraska, North or South Dakota, Texas, Oklahoma, Wisconsin, or Wyoming. Write to the address below for details.

National FFA Foundation
Scholarship Office
P.O. Box 1516
Alexandria, VA 22309

2660

Kenneth & Nedra Bullock Keller Scholarship

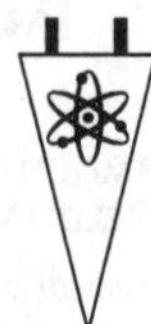

AMOUNT: Tuition **DEADLINE:** Feb 1
FIELDS/MAJORS: Geology

Scholarships are available at the University of Utah for full-time undergraduate geology majors. Write to the address below for details.

University Of Utah
Kim Atwater
714 William C. Browning Building
Salt Lake City, UT 84112

2661

Kenneth A. Christiansen Telecommunication Scholarship

Amount: $1,000 **Deadline:** Mar 1
Fields/Majors: Telecommunications

Must be a senior telecommunications major attending the University of Florida. Must have at least a 2.8 GPA. Granted on the basis of scholarship, concern for ethics and responsibility, and involvement in radio or TV. Write to the address below for details.

University Of Florida
Scholarship & Placement Director
2070 Weimer Hall
Gainesville, FL 32611

2662

Kenneth Andrew Roe Scholarship

Amount: $5,000 **Deadline:** Apr 15
Fields/Majors: Mechanical Engineering

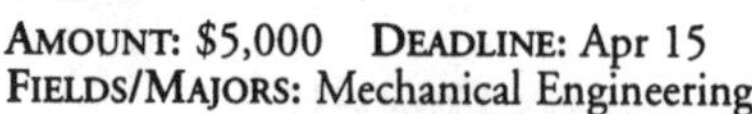

Two scholarships for ASME junior and senior student members who are majoring in mechanical engineering. Applicants must be U.S. citizens and reside in North America. For additional information, call or write the ASME foundation.

American Society Of Mechanical Engineers
Education Services Department
345 E. 47th Street
New York, NY 10017

2663

Kenneth E. Nadel Memorial Scholarship

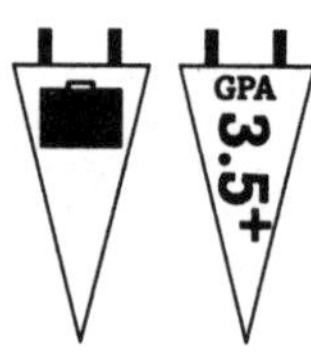

Amount: $300 **Deadline:** Feb 9
Fields/Majors: Accounting

Award for accounting major who is a junior at time of award. Minimum GPA of 3.5 required. Also considered: community service, moral character, and love of mathematics. Use Bloomsburg University scholarship application. Contact Dr. Richard Baker, Chairperson, Accounting Department, for additional information.

Bloomsburg University
19 Ben Franklin Hall
400 E. Second St.
Bloomsburg, PA 17815

2664

Kenneth P. Gifford Scholarship

Amount: $1,000 **Deadline:** None Specified
Fields/Majors: All Areas Of Study

Awards available to a graduate of each public high school in the following districts: El Paso YSD, Ysleta ISD, Socorro ISD, Clint ISD, San Elizario ISD, Canutillo ISD, and Anthony ISD. Scholarship is to the University of Texas at El Paso. Write to the address listed below for further information.

El Paso Community Foundation
201 East Main, Suite 1616
El Paso, TX 79901

2665

Kenneth Peters Memorial Scholarship

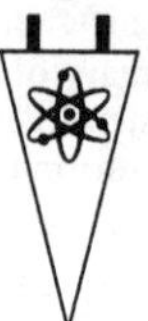

Amount: $200-$500 **Deadline:** Varies
Fields/Majors: Range Animal Science

Awards for Sul Ross undergraduates who are studying range animal science, have a GPA of at least 2.0, and are NIRA eligible. Write to the address below for more information.

Sul Ross State University
Division Of Range Animal Science
Box C-11
Alpine, TX 79832

2666

Kentucky Tuition Waiver Program For Veterans & Their Dependents

Amount: Varies **Deadline:** None Specified
Fields/Majors: All Areas Of Study

Kentucky residents. For veterans/nat'l guardsmen/and children (under age of 23 yrs)/spouse/or non-remarried widow of a permanently and totally disabled war veteran who served during periods of federally recognized hostilities or was POW or MIA. For study at a community college, vocational-technical school or four-year college. Please contact address below for complete information.

Kentucky Division Of Veterans Affairs
545 S. Third St.
Louisville, KY 40202

2667

Kerr-McGee Scholarships

Amount: $4,000 **Deadline:** May 4
Fields/Majors: All Areas Of Study

Scholarships are available at the University of Oklahoma, Norman for juniors or seniors with a GPA of 3.75 or higher. Write to the address listed below for information.

University Of Oklahoma, Norman
Office Of Development
730 College
Norman, OK 73019

2668

Kevin Child Scholarship

Amount: $1,000 **Deadline:** Jul 10
Fields/Majors: All Areas Of Study

Awards for students with a bleeding disorder pursuing a higher education. Applicants must be affiliated with or recommended by the NHF. Write to the address below for more information.

National Hemophilia Foundation
110 Greene St., Suite 303
New York, NY 10012

2669

Kevin R. Sullivan Memorial Scholarship

Amount: $750 **Deadline:** Feb 29
Fields/Majors: Management

Awards for school of management sophomores, juniors, or seniors with at least a 3.0 GPA who come from middle-income families. Applications for School of Management scholarships will be available in the SOM Development Office, Toom 206.

University of Massachusetts, Amherst
School Of Management Development Office, Room 206
Amherst, MA 01003

2670

Kevin Ryan Memorial Scholarship

Amount: Varies **Deadline:** Mar 1
Fields/Majors: Architecture

Scholarships are available at the University of New Mexico for full-time architecture students in their third year of study who have graduated from a New Mexico high school. First preference given to Silver City High School graduates. For full-time study. Write to the address listed below for information.

University Of New Mexico, Albuquerque
School Of Architecture
Office Of The Dean
Albuquerque, NM 87131

2671

KFMB Scholarship

Amount: None Specified **Deadline:** Nov 3
Fields/Majors: Communications (With Emphasis On Media)

Scholarships are available at UCSD for undergraduate students who plan to or who are majoring in communications. Applicant must be a resident of either San Diego or Imperial County. Write to the address listed below for information.

University Of California, San Diego
Student Financial Services
9500 Gilman Drive
La Jolla, CA 92093

2672

Kikkoman Foods, Inc. Scholarships

Amount: $1,000 **Deadline:** Feb 15
Fields/Majors: All Areas Of Study

Scholarships are available for FFA members pursuing a two- or four-year degree at a Wisconsin university. Must be a Wisconsin resident. Write to the address below for details.

National FFA Foundation
Scholarship Office
P.O. Box 1516
Alexandria, VA 22309

2673

Kimber Kuster Scholarship

Amount: $400 **Deadline:** Feb 9
Fields/Majors: All Areas Of Study

Award for students who can demonstrate financial need, academic achievement and activities. Use Bloomsburg University scholarship application. Contact Mrs. Kishbaugh, Financial Aid Office, for further information.

Bloomsburg University
19 Ben Franklin Hall
400 E. Second St.
Bloomsburg, PA 17815

2674

Kimberly A. Soucy Scholarship

Amount: Varies **Deadline:** None Specified
Fields/Majors: Communication Disorders

Awards for seniors in the Department of Communication Disorders who intend to continue as a graduate student in audiology at UMass. Recipients should excel academically, and demonstrate qualities of inner strength, high spirit, perseverance, and dignity. Contact the Chair, Department of Communication Disorders, for more information.

University Of Massachusetts, Amherst
Chair Department Of Communication Disorders
Amherst, MA 01003

2675

Kimmel And Porris Family Scholarship

Amount: Varies **Deadline:** None Specified
Fields/Majors: All Areas Of Study

Award for students at Mercyhurst who are from Erie County, PA, and are in financial need. Write to the address below for more information.

Mercyhurst College
Financial Aid Office
Glenwood Hills
Erie, PA 16546

2676

King Koil Sleep Products Scholarships

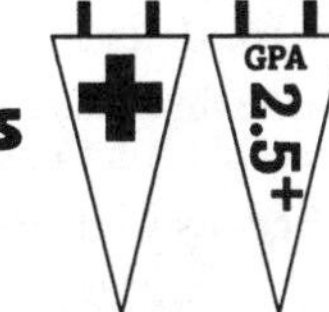

Amount: Varies **Deadline:** Varies
Fields/Majors: Chiropractic Medicine

Open to student members of ICA. Awards based on academic achievement and service. The size and number of scholarships are determined annually. A GPA of at least 2.5 is required. Must be enrolled in an ICA member college. Individual criteria for each chapter may vary. Contact a SICA chapter officer or representative for applications and further information.

International Chiropractors Association
1110 N. Glebe Rd., Suite 1000
Arlington, VA 22201

2677

King Olav V Norwegian American Heritage Fund

Amount: $250-$3,000 **Deadline:** Mar 1
Fields/Majors: Norwegian Studies/American Studies

Open to American or Norwegian student who is interested in the study of Norwegian heritage and/or American heritage at a recognized institution. Write to the address below for details.

Sons Of Norway Foundation
1455 W. Lake St.
Minneapolis, MN 55408

2678

King-Alderson Family Fund

Amount: None Specified **Deadline:** Mar 15
Fields/Majors: All Areas Of Study

Scholarships for West Virginia residents who plan to or are

attending either Alderson-Broaddus College or West Virginia University. Based upon academic ability and demonstrated financial need. Write to the address below for details.

Greater Kanawha Valley Foundation
Scholarship Committee
P.O. Box 3041
Charleston, WV 25331

2679

King-Chavez-Parks Fellowship Program

Amount: $6,250 **Deadline:** Jun 1
Fields/Majors: All Areas Of Study

Scholarships for African American, Native American, or Hispanic students studying at the doctoral level at Wayne State University. Must be U.S. citizen or permanent resident. Recipients should have the intention of teaching in a Michigan postsecondary institution within one year of receiving their degree. Information and application may be obtained through the scholarship and fellowship office at the address below.

Wayne State University
Graduate Scholarship/Fellowship Office
4302 Faculty Administration Bldg.
Detroit, MI 48202

2680

Kingsbury Fund Scholarships

Amount: Varies **Deadline:** None Specified
Fields/Majors: All Areas Of Study

Awards for children of Kingsbury employees who can demonstrate financial need. Contact the address below for further information.

Kingsbury Corporation
80 Laurel St.
Keene, NH 03431

2681

Kirtland Kiwanis Memorial Scholarship

Amount: Varies **Deadline:** None Specified
Fields/Majors: All Areas Of Study

Scholarships for residents of the Kirtland (OH) school district. Not renewable. Must have a GPA of at least 2.5. Write to the address below for details.

Kiwanis Club Of Kirtland
Memorial Scholarship Fund
c/o M.G. Winchell, M.D.
9179 Chillicothe Rd.
Kirtland, OH 44094

2682

Klara D. Eckart Scholarship

Amount: None Specified **Deadline:** Nov 3
Fields/Majors: Computer Science, Physics, Mathematics

Scholarships are available at UCSD for undergraduate students who plan to or who are majoring in computer science, mathematics, or physics. Write to the address listed below for information.

University Of California, San Diego
Student Financial Services
9500 Gilman Drive
La Jolla, CA 92093

2683

Knight Minority Scholarships

Amount: $1,000-$3,000 **Deadline:** Mar 1
Fields/Majors: Print Journalism, Advertising

Must be minority student majoring in print journalism or advertising at the University of Florida. For juniors or seniors. Must have at least a 2.8 GPA. Write to the address below for details.

University Of Florida
Director, Minority Scholarship Program
2070 Weimer Hall
Gainesville, FL 32611

2684

Koch Industries Accounting Scholarship

Amount: $750 **Deadline:** None Specified
Fields/Majors: Accounting

Student must be a full-time accounting major who will complete at least seven hours, including Intermediate Accounting I, by the end of the spring semester with a GPA of 3.25 or better. Contact the COBA office for more information.

Southwest Missouri State University
Office Of Financial Aid
901 South National Ave.
Springfield, MO 65804

2685

Kodak Scholarship

Amount: $10,000 **Deadline:** Apr 8
Fields/Majors: Engineering, Computer Science, Chemistry, Quantitative Business

Open to Latino students seeking engineering degrees with a GPA of 3.0 or better. Must be a U.S. citizen majoring in computer science, quantitative business, chemistry, or engineering (chemical, electrical, industrial, or mechanical). Must be a resident of Los Angeles City, Montebello, Commerce, Bell Gardens, or Monterey Park. Write to the address below for more information.

Telacu Education Foundation
5400 East Olympic Blvd., Suite 300
Los Angeles, CA 90022

2686

KPMG Peat Marwick Scholarship

Amount: Varies **Deadline:** None Specified
Fields/Majors: Accounting

Awards available to promising accounting students with financial need. Write to the address below for more information.

Rockford College
Financial Aid Office
5050 East State St.
Rockford, IL 61108

2687

KRAEF Foodservice Scholarships

AMOUNT: Varies **DEADLINE:** Jul 1, Jan 1
FIELDS/MAJORS: Food Service

Scholarships for Kentucky residents (or persons residing within twenty-five miles of Kentucky's borders) enrolled in or accepted into a full-time college foodservice program. Renewable. Write to the address below for details.

Kentucky Restaurant Association Educational Foundation
Scholarship Committee
422 Executive Park
Louisville, KY 40207

2688

Krapfl/Barnes Scholarships

AMOUNT: $1,700 **DEADLINE:** Mar 1
FIELDS/MAJORS: Business

Scholarships are available at the University of Iowa for full-time senior business majors. Write to the address listed below for information.

University Of Iowa
College Of Business Admin., Suite W16
108 Pappajohn Business Admin. Bldg.
Iowa City, IA 52245

2689

Kress Dissertation Fellowships

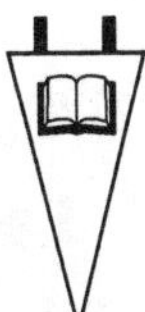

AMOUNT: $1,000-$15,000 **DEADLINE:** Varies
FIELDS/MAJORS: Art History

Applicants must be predoctoral candidates and nominated by their art history department. Award is for the final preparation of doctoral dissertation. Ten awards per year. Applicants must be U.S. citizens. Consult your art history department advisor for further information. If necessary, write to the foundation at the address below.

Samuel H. Kress Foundation
174 East 80th Street
New York, NY 10021

2690

Kuchler-Killian Memorial Scholarship

AMOUNT: $3,000 **DEADLINE:** Mar 31
FIELDS/MAJORS: All Areas Of Study

Award recipient must be legally blind students from Connecticut or attending school in Connecticut. No additional restrictions. Write to the address below for details.

National Federation Of The Blind
Mrs. Peggy Elliott, Chairman
814 Fourth Ave., Suite 20
Grinnell, IA 50112

2691

KWC Grant, Leadership Grant, KWC Scholarship

AMOUNT: Varies **DEADLINE:** Mar 1
FIELDS/MAJORS: All Areas Of Study

Various awards are available at Kentucky Wesleyan College for undergraduate students who demonstrate financial need, academic excellence, or both. Write to the address below for details.

Kentucky Wesleyan College
Financial Aid Office
3000 Frederica Street
Owensboro, KY 43202

2692

Kyutaro And Yasuo Abiko Memorial Scholarships

AMOUNT: Varies **DEADLINE:** Apr 1
FIELDS/MAJORS: Journalism, Agriculture

Applicants must be undergraduates of Japanese ancestry who are majoring in journalism or agriculture. Applications and information may be obtained from local JACL chapters, district offices, and the national headquarters at the address below. Please indicate your level of study and be certain to include a legal-sized SASE.

Japanese American Citizens League
National Scholarship and Award Program
1765 Sutter St.
San Francisco, CA 94115

2693

L. Dudley Phillips Memorial Fellowship

AMOUNT: Varies **DEADLINE:** Mar 1
FIELDS/MAJORS: History

Awards are available at the University of New Mexico for graduate students in history to support the completion of the dissertation project. Applicant must have completed all parts of the Ph.D. program except the dissertation. Write to the address below for more information.

University Of New Mexico, Albuquerque
Office Of Financial Aid
Albuquerque, NM 87131

2694

L.T. Wilson Memorial Scholarships

AMOUNT: $1,000 **DEADLINE:** None Specified
FIELDS/MAJORS: Math Or Physics

Awards for Jacksonville State University students who are in the field of math or physics. Must have a score of at least 28 on the ACT. Contact the head of the physics department for more information.

Jacksonville State University
Financial Aid Office
Jacksonville, AL 36265

2695

LACD Communications Intern

AMOUNT: None Specified
DEADLINE: None Specified
FIELDS/MAJORS: Journalism, English Writing

Engaged in bachelor's degree, experience in journalism or writing (English major). Possess excellent oral/written communication skills with fluency in English/Spanish. Ability to make high quality translation of documents and work independently. Requires strong organizational ability with attention to details. For minority students only. Write to the address below for more information.

Nature Conservancy
Cristina Garcia, Recruiting Director
1815 N. Lynn St.
Arlington, VA 22209

2696

Ladies Auxiliary of The Fleet Reserve Association Scholarships

AMOUNT: None Specified **DEADLINE:** Apr 15
FIELDS/MAJORS: All Areas Of Study

Scholarships for sons and daughters of members of the Fleet Reserve Association (or deceased members) or active duty and retired Navy, Marine Corps, and Coast Guard [active duty, retired with pay (living or deceased)]. Write to the address below for details. If parent is a member, include his or her FRA membership number.

Fleet Reserve Association, Ladies Auxiliary
LA FRA Scholarship Administrator
c/o FRA 125 N. West Street
Alexandria, VA 22314

2697

LAF Student Research Grants

AMOUNT: $500-$1,500 **DEADLINE:** Apr 2
FIELDS/MAJORS: Landscape Architecture/Design

Undergraduate and graduate grants available for research projects that encourage efforts in the expansion of the knowledge base of the profession of landscape architecture. A full proposal is required of all applicants. Applicants must attend UCLA, Cal Poly San Luis Obispo, University of Cal-Davis, or University of Cal-Irvine. Write to the address below for complete details.

Landscape Architecture Foundation
4401 Connecticut Ave., NW, Suite 500
Washington, DC 20008

2698

Lake County Scholarships

AMOUNT: Varies **DEADLINE:** Varies
FIELDS/MAJORS: All Areas Of Study

Scholarships are available for students from Lake County in Florida. Includes the Delta Sigma Theta, Edwin Budge Mead, Business and Professional Women's Club, Eustis Elks Club Scholarships, and many others. Individual award requirements will vary. Write to the address below for more information.

Lake County Schools
Student Services Department
509 S. Palm Ave.
Howey In The Hills, FL 34737

2699

Lakehead Pipeline Scholarship

AMOUNT: None Specified **DEADLINE:** Mar 1
FIELDS/MAJORS: All Areas Of Study

Scholarships are awarded to sophomore, junior, or senior students enrolled full-time (12+ credit hours). Must have a GPA of 3.0 or better and must demonstrate financial need. Must be resident of U.S. or Canada. Write to the address below for more information.

Purdue University, Calumet
Office Of Financial Aid
Purdue University Calumet
Hammond, IN 46322

2700

Lamar Blass Memorial Scholarship

AMOUNT: $200 **DEADLINE:** Feb 9
FIELDS/MAJORS: All Areas Of Study

Athletic award for member of the track, football, and/or basketball teams. Award determined by the coaches of men's athletics. Use Bloomsburg University scholarship application. Contact: Ms. Mary Gardner, Athletic Director Nelson Fieldhouse, for additional information.

Bloomsburg University
19 Ben Franklin Hall
400 E. Second St.
Bloomsburg, PA 17815

2701

Landcadd, Inc. Scholarship

AMOUNT: $500 **DEADLINE:** Apr 2
FIELDS/MAJORS: Landscape Architecture/Design

Undergraduate or graduate prize to be awarded to a student who wishes to utilize such technological advances as computer-aided design, video imaging, or telecommunications in their landscape architecture career. Write to the address below for details.

Landscape Architecture Foundation
4401 Connecticut Ave., NW, Suite 500
Washington, DC 20008

2702

Langford Scholarship-Traditional

AMOUNT: None Specified **DEADLINE:** Mar 1
FIELDS/MAJORS: All Areas Of Study

Scholarships are available to graduating seniors from Lincoln County, Nebraska, with a GPA of at least 2.0 and financial need. Write to the address listed below for information.

Mid-Nebraska Community Foundation
410 Rodeo Road, P.O. Box 1321
North Platte, NE 69103

2703

Languages And Literature Departmental Scholarships

AMOUNT: Varies **DEADLINE:** Feb 15
FIELDS/MAJORS: Languages, Literature

Scholarships are available at the University of Utah for full-time students majoring in languages or literature. Write to the address below for details.

University Of Utah
Dr. Randall Stewart
152F Orson Spencer Hall
Salt Lake City, UT 84112

2704

Lanore Netzer Scholarship

AMOUNT: $500 **DEADLINE:** Mar 1
FIELDS/MAJORS: Education

Awards are available to upper class undergraduate or graduate students in teacher education. Academic performance and financial need will be considered. Contact the College of Education and Human Services, UW Oshkosh for more details.

University Of Wisconsin, Oshkosh
Financial Aid Office, Dempsey 104
800 Algoma Blvd.
Oshkosh, WI 54901

2705

Larry Bird Scholarship Fund

AMOUNT: None Specified **DEADLINE:** None Specified
FIELDS/MAJORS: All Areas Of Study

Awards for Indiana residents planning to enroll in a full-time course of study at a postsecondary school in Indiana. The school must be accredited by the North Central Association of Colleges and Schools. Must be disadvantaged, demonstrate financial need, and be nominated by a member of the clergy, youth worker, counselor, coach, social worker, or director of IBEC or ISC. Write to the address below for more information.

Indiana Sports Corporation And Indiana Black Expo, Inc.
Citizens Scholarship Foundation of America
P.O. Box 633
Franklin, IN 46131

2706

Larry J. Gorden Achievement/ NM Environmental Health Scholarships

AMOUNT: Varies **DEADLINE:** Mar 1
FIELDS/MAJORS: All Areas Of Study

Awards are available at the University of New Mexico for full-time juniors, or seniors who have a GPA of at least 2.7. Write to the address below for more information.

University Of New Mexico, Albuquerque
Office Of Financial Aid
Albuquerque, NM 87131

2707

Larry Lyda Scholarship

AMOUNT: $1,200 **DEADLINE:** Mar 15
FIELDS/MAJORS: All Areas Of Study

Awards for Jacksonville State University students in any area of study. Write to the address below for more information.

Jacksonville State University
Financial Aid Office
Jacksonville, AL 36265

2708

Larson Aquatic Research Support Scholarship

AMOUNT: $3,000-$5,000 **DEADLINE:** Nov 15, Jan 15
FIELDS/MAJORS: Water Industry, Aquatic, Analytical, And Environmental Chemistry

Fellowships are available to encourage outstanding graduate students in science or engineering dedicated to research to improve water quality. Also for master's and Ph.D. level scholars conducting research in corrosion control, and treatment and distribution of domestic and industrial water supplies. Write to the address listed below for information. The deadline for doctoral scholars is Jan. 15 and for master's students, the deadline is Nov. 15.

American Water Works Association
Fellowship Coordinator
6666 W. Quincy Avenue
Denver, CO 80235

2709

Las Mujeres De Lulac Scholarships

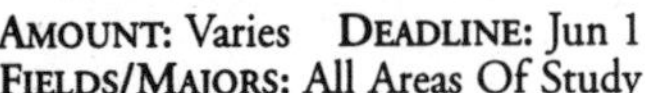

AMOUNT: Varies **DEADLINE:** Jun 1
FIELDS/MAJORS: All Areas Of Study

Awards for Hispanics continuing education after interruption or single parents who can demonstrate financial need. Must submit most current transcript, proof of enrollment, letter of recommendation, and current financial verification. For undergraduate or graduate study. Write to the address below for more details.

Las Mujeres De Lulac
Las Mujeres P.O. Box 2203
Albuquerque, NM 87103

2710

Las Mujeres De Lulac Scholarships

AMOUNT: Varies **DEADLINE:** Mar 1
FIELDS/MAJORS: All Areas Of Study

Awards are available at the University of New Mexico for Hispanic women at any level of study. Write to the address below for more information.

University Of New Mexico, Albuquerque
Office Of Financial Aid
Albuquerque, NM 87131

2711

LASER (Lincoln Advanced Science and Engineering Reinforcement) Program

AMOUNT: Varies **DEADLINE:** Mar 15
FIELDS/MAJORS: Science, Engineering

Awards are available to undergraduate students at Lincoln University who are pursuing a science or engineering degree. Write to the address below for details.

Lincoln University
Financial Aid Office Lincoln Hall, Room 101
Lincoln University, PA 19352

2712

Last Dollar Program

AMOUNT: Varies **DEADLINE:** None Specified
FIELDS/MAJORS: All Areas Of Study

Awards are available for minority Virginia residents who can be classified as first-time freshmen students and are enrolled at least half-time in an eligible baccalaureate program at a state-supported institution. Must demonstrate financial need as determined by the institution. Write to the address below for more information.

Virginia Council of Higher Education
James Monroe Building
101 North 14th St.
Richmond, VA 23219

2713

Latin America & The Caribbean Grants

AMOUNT: $15,000 (max) **DEADLINE:** Dec 1
FIELDS/MAJORS: Latin American/Caribbean Studies

Grants are available for postdoctoral scholars who are U.S. citizens, for research on all aspects of the societies and cultures of Latin America or the Caribbean area. Collaborative grants are also available to two scholars of approximately the same scholarly level who wish to collaborate on a research project. Write to the address listed below after Aug. 1 for information.

Social Science Research Council
Fellowships and Grants
605 Third Avenue
New York, NY 10158

2714 Latin American & Caribbean Fellowship Program

AMOUNT: $30,000 (max) **DEADLINE:** Mar 1
FIELDS/MAJORS: Social Sciences/Humanities

Fellowships for Latin American and Caribbean practitioners and researchers whose work in grassroots development would benefit from advanced academic experience in the U.S.A. Fellowships are awarded to master's candidates and higher. Must demonstrate interest in the problems of poverty and development and be nominated by home institution. Up to forty fellowships are offered per year. Write to the address below for details.

Inter-American Foundation
IAF Fellowship Programs, Dept. 555
901 N. Stuart St., 10th Floor
Arlington, VA 22203

2715 Latin American & Caribbean Fellowships

AMOUNT: None Specified **DEADLINE:** Nov 1
FIELDS/MAJORS: Social Science, Humanities, Latin American Studies

Fellowships are available for scholars enrolled in a U.S. doctoral program. Applicants must have completed all the program requirements except for the dissertation. Research must be in an area of interest or focus on Latin America or the Caribbean. Write to the address listed below after Aug. 1 for information.

Social Science Research Council
Fellowships and Grants
605 Third Avenue
New York, NY 10158

2716 Laura E. Settle (California Retired Teachers Assoc.) Scholarship

AMOUNT: None Specified **DEADLINE:** Nov 3
FIELDS/MAJORS: Education

Scholarships are available at UCSD for junior or senior students who are majoring in education. Write to the address listed below for information.

University Of California San Diego
Student Financial Services
9500 Gilman Drive
La Jolla, CA 92093

2717 Laura E. Settle Scholarship

AMOUNT: $750 **DEADLINE:** Mar 2
FIELDS/MAJORS: All Areas Of Study

Awards for senior or graduate students with at least a 2.5 GPA in any major. Based primarily on need. Applicant must be pursuing teaching credential and be a U.S. citizen or permanent resident. Write to the address below for more information.

California Retired Teacher's Association
Cal Polytech University, Pomona
Office Of Financial Aid
3801 West Temple Ave.
Pomona, CA 91768

2718 Laura Roman Dodd Memorial Scholarship

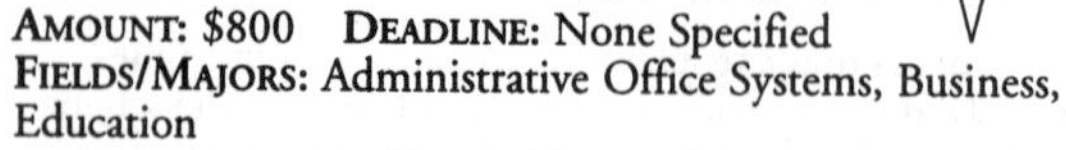

AMOUNT: $800 **DEADLINE:** None Specified
FIELDS/MAJORS: Administrative Office Systems, Business, Education

Student must be an administrative office systems or business education major with a minimum 2.5 GPA. Must have completed at least fifteen hours in business courses with a minimum 3.0 GPA. Contact the COBA office for more information.

Southwest Missouri State University
Office Of Financial Aid
901 South National Ave.
Springfield, MO 65804

2719 Laura Schula Scholarship In Music

AMOUNT: $500-$700 **DEADLINE:** Mar 1
FIELDS/MAJORS: Music

Award for a student at Eastern New Mexico University who is majoring in music and is a participant in ensemble. Applicants must be at the sophomore level or above and have a GPA of 3.0 or better. Financial need is a consideration. Write to the address below for more information.

Eastern New Mexico University
College of Fine Arts, Station 16
Portales, NM 88130

2720 Laurie Ann Richardson Endowed Memorial Scholarship

AMOUNT: $4,000 (max) **DEADLINE:** Mar 1
FIELDS/MAJORS: Special Education

Scholarships for seniors at the University of South Florida. Must have plans to continue on into the graduate program in special education at USF or to do so after working in the field. Must have a GPA of at least 3.0. Contact the chairperson of the Department of Special Education at the below address for details.

University Of South Florida
College of Education Chairperson
Dept. Of Special Education HMS 48
Tampa, FL 33620

2721 Laverne Noyes Foundation Scholarship

AMOUNT: None Specified **DEADLINE:** Nov 30
FIELDS/MAJORS: All Areas Of Study

Scholarships are available at UCSD for undergraduate students who are descendants of World War I veterans. Write to the address listed below for information.

University Of California, San Diego
Student Financial Services
9500 Gilman Drive
La Jolla, CA 92093

2722

Laverne Noyes Scholarship

AMOUNT: $1,000 **DEADLINE:** Mar 1
FIELDS/MAJORS: All Areas Of Study

Scholarships are available at the University of Oklahoma, Norman for students who are direct descendents of World War I veterans. Requires a minimum GPA of 3.25. Three to five awards offered annually. Applicant must be a U.S. citizen. Write to the address listed below for information.

University Of Oklahoma, Norman
Office Of Financial Aid Services
731 Elm
Norman, OK 73019

2723

Lavinia Laible Scholarship

AMOUNT: $500-$2,500 **DEADLINE:** Apr 14
FIELDS/MAJORS: All Areas Of Study

Scholarships for female residents of Kent County who are transferring from Grand Rapids Community College to the University of Michigan for their junior year. Applicants must have a GPA of at least 3.0. Contact the financial aid office at Grand Rapids Community College for information.

Grand Rapids Foundation
209-C Waters Bldg.
161 Ottawa Avenue, NW
Grand Rapids, MI 49503

2724

Law Enforcement Assistance Award

AMOUNT: $1,000 **DEADLINE:** Mar 31
FIELDS/MAJORS: Law Enforcement

Award is available to explorers who assist law enforcement agencies with meaningful and exceptional service. Candidates must have performed "an act which assisted in the prevention or solution of a serious crime or an act which assisted in leading to the apprehension of a felony suspect wanted by a law enforcement agency." Write to the address below for more information.

Boy Scouts of America Exploring Division, S21
1325 West Walnut Hill Ln., P.O. Box 152079
Irving, TX 75015

2725

Law Enforcement Personnel Dependents Scholarships

AMOUNT: Varies **DEADLINE:** None Specified
FIELDS/MAJORS: All Areas Of Study

Program provides educational grants to needy dependents and spouses of California peace officers (highway patrol, marshals, sheriffs, police officers); officers and employees of the department of corrections or youth authority; and permanent and full-time firefighters employed by California who have been killed or totally disabled in the line of duty. Applicants must demonstrate financial need. Write to the address below for more information.

California Student Aid Commission
P.O. Box 510624
Sacramento, CA 94245

2726

Law Fellowship

AMOUNT: $1,000 **DEADLINE:** May 31
FIELDS/MAJORS: Law

Fellowships for Italian-American law students (on the graduate level). Based on essay on "the maintenance of Italian culture in the U.S. In the law field or at the political level." 750-words or less. Write to the address below for details.

National Italian American Foundation
Dr. Maria Lombardo, Education Director
1860 Nineteenth Street, NW
Washington, DC 20009

2727

Law Scholarships

AMOUNT: Varies **DEADLINE:** Apr 1
FIELDS/MAJORS: Law

Applicants must be of Japanese ancestry and entering or enrolled at an accredited law school. Applications and information may be obtained from local JACL chapters, district offices, and the national headquarters at the address below. Please indicate your level of study and be certain to include a legal-sized SASE.

Japanese American Citizens League
National Scholarship And Award Program
1765 Sutter St.
San Francisco, CA 94115

2728

Lawrence County Conservation District Scholarship Program

AMOUNT: $500 **DEADLINE:** Jan 31
FIELDS/MAJORS: Environmental Science, Conservation, Agriculture

Scholarships are available to residents of Lawrence County, PA, who are majoring in one of the above fields. Applicant must at least be in their first semester of schooling. Nonrenewable. Write to the address listed below for information.

Lawrence County Conservation District
Attn: Scholarship Committee
430 Court Street
New Castle, PA 6101

2729

Lawrence White Scholarships

AMOUNT: Varies **DEADLINE:** Mar 1
FIELDS/MAJORS: All Areas Of Study

Awards are available at the University of New Mexico for New Mexico residents making satisfactory academic progress who have financial need. Write to the address below for more information.

University Of New Mexico, Albuquerque
Office Of Financial Aid
Albuquerque, NM 87131

2730

Lawyers Title of El Paso Scholarship

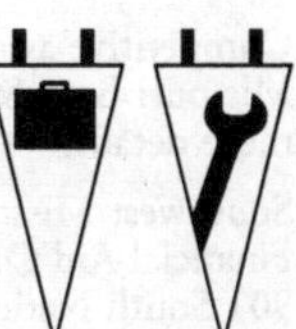

AMOUNT: $1,500 **DEADLINE:** None Specified
FIELDS/MAJORS: Finance, Real Estate Or Related

Scholarship available to University of Texas at El Paso students majoring in finance, real estate or a related field. Applicant must be an El Paso County resident. Write to the address listed below for additional information.

El Paso Community Foundation
201 East Main, Suite 1616
El Paso, TX 79901

2731

Lawyers Title Of El Paso Scholarship

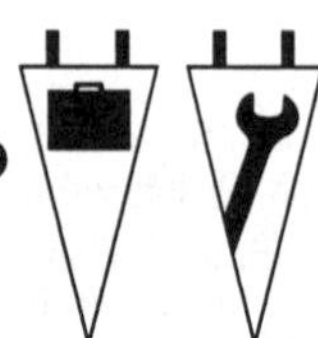

Amount: $1,000 **Deadline:** None Specified
Fields/Majors: Finance, Real Estate Or Related

Scholarship available to El Paso Community College students majoring in finance, real estate, or a related field. Applicant must be an El Paso County resident. Write to the address listed below for additional information.

El Paso Community Foundation
201 East Main, Suite 1616
El Paso, TX 79901

2732

Leadership And Service Scholarship

Amount: $2,000 (max) **Deadline:** Mar 15
Fields/Majors: All Areas Of Study

Open to St. Andrews students who have demonstrated outstanding leadership or community service. Write to the address below for more information and for an application.

St. Andrews College
Office Of Financial Aid
1700 Dogwood Mile
Laurinburg, NC 28352

2733

Leadership Award

Amount: $4,000 (max) **Deadline:** Feb 15
Fields/Majors: All Areas Of Study

Awards for incoming freshmen who have a combined SAT score between 940-1120 or an ACT composite between 20-24. Applicants must be active members in a local Church of Christ. Write to the address below for more information.

Abilene Christian University
Leadership Scholarship Committee
Box 6000
Abilene, TX 79699

2734

Leadership Award For Missouri Boys/Girls State Citizens

Amount: $500 **Deadline:** Dec 1
Fields/Majors: All Areas Of Study

Competitive award for freshmen who participated in 1995 Missouri Boys State or Girls State. Write to the address below for more details.

Southwest Missouri State University
Financial Aid Office
901 South National Ave.
Springfield, MO 65804

2735

Leadership Awards

Amount: $500-$1,000 **Deadline:** Mar 1
Fields/Majors: All Areas Of Study

Awards for Muskingum students demonstrating involvement and leadership in a variety of activities. Write to the address below for more information.

Muskingum College
Office Of Admission
New Concord, OH 43762

2736

Leadership Awards, Achievement Awards

Amount: Varies **Deadline:** Apr 1
Fields/Majors: All Areas Of Study

Applicants must be high school seniors with an SAT score of 1100 or higher or rank in the top twenty percent of high school graduating class and leadership achievement in school, civic, or community organizations. Sixteen awards per year. Achievement awards are for students in the top 30% of high school class. Write to the address below for details.

Lebanon Valley College Of Pennsylvania
Office Of Admissions
101 N. College Ave.
Annville, PA 7003

2737

Leadership Coalition Endowment Scholarship

Amount: $500 **Deadline:** None Specified
Fields/Majors: All Areas Of Study

Scholarships are available for full-time juniors, seniors, and graduate students. Must have a GPA of 3.0 or better. Financial must be demonstrated. Write to the address below for more information.

California State Polytechnic University, Pomona
Office Of Financial Aid
3801 West Temple Ave.
Pomona, CA 91768

2738

Leadership Incentive Award

Amount: $250 + Free Room **Deadline:** Mar 15
Fields/Majors: All Areas Of Study

Open to first-time freshmen who have shown leadership in high school and who will make a commitment to continue involvement in co-curricular activities at Edgewood. Award is designed to meet the cost of a room on campus. Renewable. Write to the address below for details.

Edgewood College
Office Of Admissions
855 Woodrow Street
Madison, WI 53711

2739

Leadership Scholarship Tuition

Amount: **Deadline:** Feb 1
Fields/Majors: All Areas Of Study

Scholarships are available at the University of Utah for full-time students who will be entering freshmen or transfer students with a minimum GPA of 3.0, and demonstrated leadership abilities and participation in school/community activities. At least fifty awards are offered annually. Write to the address below for details. Information is also available from your high school guidance counselor.

University Of Utah Financial Aid And Scholarship Office
105 Student Services Building
Salt Lake City, UT 84112

2740

Leadership Scholarships

AMOUNT: Tuition **DEADLINE:** Mar 15
FIELDS/MAJORS: All Areas Of Study

Awards for Jacksonville State University students who are in any field of study and are active in many extracurricular activities. Academics are also considered by the JSU scholarship committee. Write to the address below for more information.

Jacksonville State University
Financial Aid Office
Jacksonville, AL 36265

2741

Leadership Scholarships

AMOUNT: $1,000 **DEADLINE:** Apr 1
FIELDS/MAJORS: All Areas Of Study

Awards for CHC students based on essays answering three questions posed by a committee. An incoming GPA of 3.0 is required, as well as maintaining a cumulative GPA at CHC of at least 3.25. Write to the address below for more information.

Christian Heritage College
Financial Aid Office
2100 Greenfield Dr.
El Cajon, CA 92019

2742

Leadership Scholarships

AMOUNT: $500-$1,500 **DEADLINE:** Mar 15
FIELDS/MAJORS: All Areas Of Study

Awards for high school seniors or transfer students with a GPA of at least 3.2 and an ACT score of at least 24 or an SAT of 1090 or better. Applicants must have demonstrated leadership skills throughout their high school career. Write to the address below for more information.

Cedarville College
Financial Aid Office P.O. Box 601
Cedarville, OH 45314

2743

Leather Art Scholarship Program

AMOUNT: $500-$2,000 **DEADLINE:** Apr 1
FIELDS/MAJORS: Leather Art

Scholarships are available to graduating high school seniors who create art projects using leather. Write to the address listed below for information.

Tandy Leather Company
Art Scholarship Program
1400 Everman Parkway
Fort Worth, TX 76140

2744

Lee-Jackson Foundation Scholarship Program

AMOUNT: $1,000 **DEADLINE:** None Specified
FIELDS/MAJORS: All Areas Of Study

Awards are available for juniors or seniors in Virginia secondary schools who plan to attend a U.S. institution of higher education. The applicants writing the best essay on the announced topic are eligible for the cash awards. Contact your principal or guidance department for more information.

Virginia Council of Higher Education
James Monroe Building, 101 North 14th St.
Richmond, VA 23219

2745

Legislative Fellows Program

AMOUNT: $22,575 **DEADLINE:** None Specified
FIELDS/MAJORS: Political Science, Government, Public Affairs

Fellows must be full-time graduate students, a New York state citizen or a student enrolled on an accredited campus in New York state, and intending to pursue a career in public service. Fellowship term is usually about 1 year. Up to 14 fellows per year. Write to Dr. Russell J. Williams, Director, at the address below for details.

New York State Senate
Senate Student Programs
90 South Swan Street, Room 401
Albany, NY 12247

2746

Leica Surveying Scholarships

AMOUNT: $1,000 **DEADLINE:** Jan 1
FIELDS/MAJORS: Surveying, Cartography

Undergraduate scholarship for study at an accredited institution in the United States. Based on academics, need, and potential. Either 1) membership in American Congress on Surveying and Mapping or American Society for Remote Sensing, or 2)recommendation of a member of one of those organizations is required. Must be a U.S. citizen. Write to the address below for complete details.

American Congress On Surveying and Mapping
ACSM Awards Director
5410 Grosvenor Lane, Suite 100
Bethesda, MD 20814

2747

Lemelson Fellowships

AMOUNT: None Specified **DEADLINE:** Nov 15, Mar 1
FIELDS/MAJORS: All Areas Of Study

Fellowships are available at Hampshire College for undergraduate students who are sophomores or above, who wish to be part of a team that will strive to create or refine specific programs, devices and concepts that address contemporary problems. Write to the address below for details.

Lemelson National Program In Invention, Innovation, and Creativity
Hampshire College
Amherst, MA 01002

2748

Lemon Men's Club Ted Canham Award Of Merit

AMOUNT: $1,000 **DEADLINE:** Apr 15
FIELDS/MAJORS: Fruit Industry

Open to sophomores, juniors, and seniors majoring in fruit industries with a GPA of 2.0 or better. Write to the address below for more information.

California State Polytechnic University, Pomona
College of Agriculture Building 7, Room 110
Pomona, CA 91768

2749

Lena Heath Scholarship

AMOUNT: Varies **DEADLINE:** Mar 1
FIELDS/MAJORS: All Areas Of Study

Awards are available at the University of New Mexico for juniors or seniors making satisfactory academic progress. Write to the address below for more information.

University Of New Mexico, Albuquerque
Office Of Financial Aid
Albuquerque, NM 87131

2750

Lenna M. Todd Memorial Prize For English Composition

AMOUNT: Varies **DEADLINE:** Mar 1
FIELDS/MAJORS: Creative Writing, Poetry Or Fiction

Awards are available at the University of New Mexico for undergraduate students currently enrolled in a creative writing workshop. Contact the English department for more information.

University Of New Mexico, Albuquerque
Office Of Financial Aid
Albuquerque, NM 87131

2751

Leo Burnett Company, Inc. Scholarships

AMOUNT: $1,000-$2,000 **DEADLINE:** Feb 15
FIELDS/MAJORS: Agriculture

Scholarships are available for FFA members pursuing a two or four-year degree in any area of agriculture. Applicant must be a member of a minority ethnic group. Write to the address below for details.

National FFA Foundation
Scholarship Office, P.O. Box 15160
Alexandria, VA 22309

2752

Leo L. Kubiet Advertising Scholarship

AMOUNT: $500 **DEADLINE:** Mar 1
FIELDS/MAJORS: Advertising

Must be a student enrolled at the University of Florida planning a career in advertising. Must have at least a 2.8 GPA and be in the junior or senior year of study. Write to the address below for details.

University Of Florida
Scholarship & Placement Director
2070 Weimer Hall
Gainesville, FL 32611

2753

Leo S. Rowe Pan American Fund

AMOUNT: $5,000 **DEADLINE:** None Specified
FIELDS/MAJORS: All Areas Of Study

Loan for students who are citizens of member countries of the organization of American states and are enrolled in or wish to study in a college or university in the U.S. Write to the address below for more information.

Organization of American States
General Secretariat
Washington, DC 20006

2754

Leola W. And Charles Hugg Scholarship

AMOUNT: None Specified **DEADLINE:** May 1
FIELDS/MAJORS: All Areas Of Study

Scholarships from this trust are available to students who have resided and attended high school in Williamson County, TX for at least two-years, or have been under the care of the Texas Baptist Children's Home in Round Rock, TX. For undergraduate study. Applications are available at high schools in Williamson County, from the Director of the Texas Baptist Children's Home or at the office of financial aid at Southwestern University in Georgetown.

Leola W. and Charles Hugg Trust
Texas Commerce Bank
P.O. Box 6033, SW Station
Georgetown, TX 78626

2755

Leon Harris/Les Nichols Memorial Scholarship

AMOUNT: $16,000 **DEADLINE:** Mar 12
FIELDS/MAJORS: Aircraft Repair, Avionics

Scholarships for students planning to attend the National Education Center Spartan School of Aeronautics campus in Tulsa, OK. For students who will be working toward an associate's degree. Min. GPA: 2.5. Write to the AEA for information on these and other awards (fourteen total) offered by the AEA.

Aircraft Electronics Association
Educational Foundation
P.O. Box 1981
Independence, MO 64055

2756

Leon J. Rhodes Student Development Award

AMOUNT: $1,200 **DEADLINE:** Feb 1
FIELDS/MAJORS: All Areas Of Study

Scholarships are available at the University of Hawaii, Hilo, for full-time sophomores who have become good citizens, self-determined, and developed successful human relations as a result of their experiences at UHH. Write to the address listed below for information.

University Of Hawaii At Hilo
Financial Aid Office
200 West Kawili Street
Hilo, HI 96720

2757

Leon S. Heseman Scholarship

Amount: $1,000 **Deadline:** None Specified
Fields/Majors: All Areas Of Study

Scholarships are available for full-time undergraduate students. Must have a GPA of 3.0 or better. Preferences are given to residents of Riverside County and San Bernardino. Write to the address below for more information.

California State Polytechnic University, Pomona
Office Of Financial Aid
3801 West Temple Ave.
Pomona, CA 91768

2758

Leona Meyer-Shedd Scholarship

Amount: None Specified **Deadline:** None Specified
Fields/Majors: Nursing

Scholarships are open to full-time undergraduate nursing students who rank scholastically in the upper half of their class. Write to the address below for more information.

Indiana University/Purdue University, Indianapolis
School of Nursing
1111 Middle Dr., No 122
Indianapolis, IN 46202

2759

Leonard A. Haft Memorial and Linda Rosenbaum Scholarship

Amount: None Specified **Deadline:** May 1
Fields/Majors: Fine Arts

Scholarships and grants for students at Corcoran School of Art who are studying fine arts. Rosenbaum Scholarship is reserved for senior students. Contact the address below for details.

Corcoran School Of Art
Financial Aid Office
500 17th St., NW
Washington, DC 20006

2760

Leonard H. Bulkeley Scholarship Fund

Amount: None Specified **Deadline:** None Specified
Fields/Majors: All Areas Of Study

The scholarship fund is available to students under the age of 25 who reside in the city of New London, CT, and are studying at the undergraduate level. Awards are granted on the basis of financial need, academic qualifications, the possibility of success, and a one-time interview. Applicants may receive as many as four grants in as many years. Write to the address below for details.

Leonard H. Bulkeley Scholarship Fund
P.O. Box 1426
New London, CT 06320

2761

Leonard M. Perryman Communications Scholarship For Minority Students

Amount: $2,500 **Deadline:** Feb 15
Fields/Majors: Religious Communications/Journalism

Applicants must be a junior or senior communications student that intends to pursue a career in religious communications. Write to the scholarship committee at the address below for details.

United Methodist Communications Scholarship Committee
Public Media Division
P.O. Box 320
Nashville, TN 37202

2762

Leone Cole Memorial Scholarship

Amount: $300 **Deadline:** None Specified
Fields/Majors: All Areas Of Study

Awards for Jacksonville State University freshmen in any discipline. Based primarily on academics and leadership. Write to the address below for more information.

Jacksonville State University
Financial Aid Office
Jacksonville, AL 36265

2763

Lerner-Scott Prize

Amount: $1,000 **Deadline:** Nov 1
Fields/Majors: American And Women's History

Awards are available for the best doctoral dissertation submitted in U.S. women's history. To apply, students must submit a complete copy of the dissertation. Write to the address below for more information.

Organization of American Historians
112 N. Bryan St.
Bloomington, IN 47408

2764

Lerner-Gray Fund For Marine Research

Amount: $200-$1,000 **Deadline:** Mar 15
Fields/Majors: Marine Research, Marine Zoology

For postdoctoral scholars and marine scientists. Submit details of educational and scientific backgrounds and a description of project to be undertaken. For study of systematics, evolution, ecology, and field-related research of marine animal behavior. Not for botany or biochemistry. Information on collection study grants is also available from the sponsor. Write to the address below for details.

American Museum Of Natural History
Central Park West At 79th St.
New York, NY 10024

2765

Leroy Collins Memorial Scholarships

Amount: $1,000 **Deadline:** Mar 1
Fields/Majors: Telecommunication

Awards for juniors and seniors who are Florida residents and majoring in telecommunication. Preference is given to women and/or minority students. Must have a GPA of at least 2.8. Write to the address below for more information.

University Of Florida
Knight Scholarship & Placement Director
2070 Weimer Hall
Gainesville, FL 32611

2766

Leroy Matthews Physician/ Scientist Award

Amount: $80,000 (max) **Deadline:** Sep 1
Fields/Majors: Medical Research-Cystic Fibrosis

Grants are available to newly trained pediatricians and internists (M.D.'s and M.D./Ph.D.s) to complete subspecialty training, develop into independent investigators, and initiate a research program. Awards range from $32,000 (stipend) plus $10,000 (R&D) for one year to $55,000 (stipend) plus $25,000 (R&D) for year six. Write to the address below for details.

Cystic Fibrosis Foundation
Office Of Grants Management
6931 Arlington Rd.
Bethesda, MD 20814

2767

Leslie Allen Fellowship

Amount: $500 **Deadline:** Mar 15
Fields/Majors: Biology, Microbiology

Awards are available for biology or microbiology majors with demonstrated interest in ecology or field biology. Based on academics, achievements, commitment, and financial need. Contact the Department of Biology and Microbiology, UW Oshkosh, for more details.

University Of Wisconsin, Oshkosh
Financial Aid Office, Dempsey 104
800 Algoma Blvd.
Oshkosh, WI 54901

2768

Leslie Rice Scholarship

Amount: $500 **Deadline:** Feb 15
Fields/Majors: Advertising

Scholarships are available at the University of Oklahoma, Norman, for students majoring in advertising who show exceptional merit and potential. Write to the address listed below for information.

University Of Oklahoma, Norman
School of Journalism and Mass Communications
860 Van Vleet Oval
Norman, OK 73019

2769

Leslie T. Posey And Frances U. Posey Scholarships

Amount: Varies **Deadline:** Mar 1
Fields/Majors: Art, Painting, Sculpture

Applicants must be graduate art majors in traditional painting or sculpture and full-time students. Write to Robert E. Perkins, Administrator at the address below for details.

Leslie T. Posey and Frances U. Posey Foundation
1800 Second St., Suite 905
Sarasota, FL 34236

2770

Lester Walls III Endowment Scholarship

Amount: $500 **Deadline:** Apr 2
Fields/Majors: Landscape Architecture/Design

Award is for disabled landscape architecture students or for research on barrier-free design projects. Write to the address below for details.

Landscape Architecture Foundation
4401 Connecticut Ave., NW, Suite 500
Washington, DC 20008

2771

Lever Brothers Scholarship

Amount: None Specified
Deadline: Mar 1
Fields/Majors: Most Areas of Study

Scholarships are awarded to freshman or transfer students at Purdue University, Calumet admittec to the school of professional studies majoring in education, engineering, or nursing, or the school of liberal arts and sciences majoring in the social sciences. Freshman must be in the top 10% of their high school class and transfer students must a GPA of 3.6 or better. Write to the address below for more information.

Purdue University, Calumet
Office Of Financial Aid
Hammond, IN 46322

2772

Levi Strauss And Company Scholarship Program

Amount: $750-$2,000 **Deadline:** Feb 15
Fields/Majors: All Areas Of Study

For dependents of Levi Strauss & Company employees. For full-time undergraduate study at two- or four-year college/university or vocational/trade school. (students who are already in school may apply). Must have a GPA of 2.5 or better. Write to the address below for more information.

Levi Strauss And Company Scholarship Program
P.O. Box 297
St. Peter, MN 56082

2773

Li Foundation Fellowships

Amount: $18,200 (max) **Deadline:** None Specified
Fields/Majors: All Areas Of Study

Fellowships are awarded to deserving Chinese students and scholars sponsored by selected institutions for one to two years of study and training in the U.S. Write to the address below for more information.

Li Foundation, Inc.
513 Parnassus Ave., S., 1210
San Francisco, CA 94143

2774

Liberty Scholarships

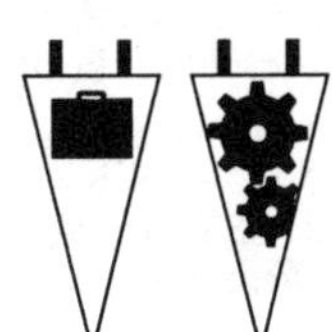

Amount: Varies **Deadline:** Feb 1
Fields/Majors: Business, Economics, Computer Science

Awards for entering freshmen who intend to major in business, economics, or computer science. Write to the address below for more information.

Furman University
Director of Financial Aid
3300 Poinsett Highway
Greenville, SC 29613

2775

Library And Information Studies Awards

Amount: Varies: **Deadline:** None Specified
Fields/Majors: Library and Information Studies

Scholarships are available at the University of Oklahoma, Norman for students in library and information studies. Includes the Carroll-Osla, Floy Elliot Cobb, H.W. Wilson, Irma Rayne Tomberlin, Jesse Lee Rader, and Oxford Seminar Fee Waiver Scholarships. Individual award requirements may vary. Write to the address listed below for information.

University Of Oklahoma, Norman
School of Library & Information Studies
420 W. Brooks, Room 120
Norman, OK 73019

2776

Library Education And Human Resource Development Program

Amount: Varies **Deadline:** Varies
Fields/Majors: Library and Information Science, Information Technology

Awards are available for graduate study in the fields of study listed above at various colleges and universities across the country. Write to the address below for more information or contact the appropriate department office at your school for more information.

U.S. Department Of Education
Office Of Educational Research & Improv.
Library Programs
Washington, DC 20208

2777

Library Education Scholarship, Continuing Education Scholarship

Amount: Varies **Deadline:** Oct 1, Jun 1
Fields/Majors: Library/Information Sciences

Scholarship for Wisconsin resident who plans to continue their education in Wisconsin and study library or information science. Based on academic and professional accomplishments, as well as on financial need. Write to the address below for complete details.

Wisconsin Library Association
Chair, Library Careers Committee
4785 Hayes Rd.
Madison, WI 53704

2778

Library Science Scholarships

Amount: Varies **Deadline:** Aug 1
Fields/Majors: All Areas Of Study

Scholarships for members of the Idaho Library Association in any area of study. Write to the address below for details.

Idaho Library Association
Mr. Randy Simmons, Riley Library
Northwest Nazarene College
Nampa, ID 83686

2779

License To Learn Scholarships

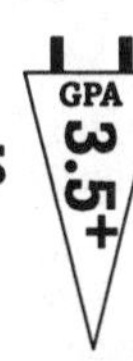

Amount: $2,100 **Deadline:** Mar 1
Fields/Majors: All Areas Of Study

Awards for high school seniors with an ACT score of 29 or better and a GPA of at least 3.5. Renewable with a GPA of 3.0 or higher. Applicants must be Alabama residents. Write to the address below for more information.

Auburn University
Office Of Student Financial Aid
203 Mary Martin Hall
Auburn University, AL 36849

2780

Lieutenant General Eugene F. Tighe, Jr., USAF Memorial Scholarship

Amount: $1,000 **Deadline:** Jan 5
Fields/Majors: Criminal Justice and Related Areas

Open to full-time college under- or postgraduate students in the U.S., or attending U.S. Institutions overseas. Must have a GPA of 3.0 or better. Based primarily on an essay written by the applicant. Write to the address below for more information.

Association of Former Intelligence Officers (AFIO)
San Diego Chapter
J.T. Strong, Scholarship Administrator
13785 Quinton Rd.
San Diego, CA 92129

2781 LIFE Scholarship Program

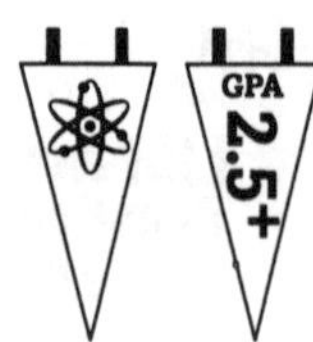

Amount: $1,000 **Deadline:** Mar 15
Fields/Majors: Conservation, Natural Resources

Scholarships for students pursuing a career in natural resources and/or conservation construction. Based on short essay (300 words or less) and recommendations. Up to 3 awards per year. Write to the address below to request a scholarship application.

Land Improvement Foundation For Education
Ms. Mary Ellen Bushnell
1300 Maybrook Dr., P.O. Box 9
Maywood, IL 60153

2782 Liff Business Scholarship

Amount: $300 **Deadline:** None Specified
Fields/Majors: Business

Awards for Mesa State students majoring in a business field. Contact the school of professional studies for more information.

Mesa State College
Office Of Financial Aid
P.O. Box 2647
Grand Junction, CO 81501

2783 Liff Nursing Scholarship

Amount: $100 **Deadline:** None Specified
Fields/Majors: Nursing

Award for full-time Mesa State students who are studying nursing. Contact the school of professional studies/nursing area for more details.

Mesa State College
Office Of Financial Aid
P.O. Box 2647
Grand Junction, CO 81501

2784 Lighthouse Scholarship

Amount: $15,000 **Deadline:** Feb 25
Fields/Majors: Journalism And Communications

Award for an outstanding junior in the field of journalism or communications. The scholarship is divided between junior and senior year for the recipient. Applicants must demonstrate financial need and be U.S. citizens. For full-time study. Write to the address below for more information. When requesting an application, students must state college major, career goals, and year of study. Deadline to request an application is Dec. 20.

Scripps Howard Foundation
312 Walnut St., 28th Floor
P.O. Box 5380
Cincinnati, OH 45201

2785 Lights Of The Jewish Special Needs Scholarships

Amount: $1,000 (max) **Deadline:** May 31
Fields/Majors: All Areas Of Study

Grants for Jewish students in the St. Louis community. For study at a two- or four-year publicly supported college or university in Missouri. Write to the address below for details.

Lights of The Jewish Special Needs Society
6 Sleepy Hollow Lane
St. Louis, MO 63132

2786 Lillian And Arthur Dunn Scholarships

Amount: $1,000 **Deadline:** Feb 15
Fields/Majors: All Areas Of Study

Applicant must be a graduating high school senior whose mother is a current member of the DAR. Applicant must also be a U.S. citizen. Renewable. Contact your local DAR chapter or write to the address below for details.

National Society Daughters Of The American Revolution
NSDAR Scholarship Committee
1776 D St., NW
Washington, DC 20006

2787 Lillian Moller Gilbreth Scholarship

Amount: $5,000 **Deadline:** Feb 1
Fields/Majors: Engineering

Scholarship for junior or senior woman engineering major in an accredited program. Based on superior academic achievement and potential. Must have a GPA of at least 3.5. Write to address below for details. Please be certain to enclose an SASE. Information and applications for the SWE. Awards are also available from the deans of engineering schools.

Society of Women Engineers
120 Wall Street, 11th Floor
New York, NY 10005

2788 Lillian P. Schoephoerster Scholarship, Jean Dickerscheid Scholarship

Amount: $650-$1,000 **Deadline:** Mar 1
Fields/Majors: Home Economics and Related

Scholarships for Phi Upsilon Omicron undergraduate members who have a GPA of at least 3.5. Schoephoerster Scholarship is reserved for nontraditional students (returning to school after several years, older student, etc.). Write to the address below for further information.

Phi Upsilon Omicron National Office
Ohio State University
171 Mount Hall
1050 Carmack Road
Columbus, OH 43210

2789 Lillian Stollar Memorial And Gertrude Kederly Memorial Scholarships

Amount: $1,000 **Deadline:** Apr 1
Fields/Majors: All Areas Of Study

Scholarships for students at Kent State University, Tuscarawas campus who are residents of Tuscarawas County (OH) and graduated from a public school in the county. Must demonstrate financial need. Contact the financial aid office for details.

Tuscarawas Antique Club
Kent State University
Financial Aid Office
330 University Drive, NE
New Philadelphia, OH 44663

2790

Lima Kokua Nursing Scholarship

AMOUNT: $1,000 **DEADLINE:** Apr 25
FIELDS/MAJORS: Nursing, Medical Technology

Scholarships are available to qualified candidates seeking a career in nursing or medical technology. Must be a U.S. citizen and a resident from north Hawaii who has been accepted to an accredited R.N. or medical technology program in the U.S. with a GPA of 2.5 or better. Five awards per year. Write to the address below for more information.

Lima Kokua Nursing Scholarship
Candace Peterson
P.O. Box 111333, Suite 255
Kamuela, HI 96743

2791

Lincoln University Scholarships

AMOUNT: Varies **DEADLINE:** Mar 15
FIELDS/MAJORS: All Areas Of Study

Awards are available to undergraduate students at Lincoln University who demonstrate academic excellence (3.0 GPA or above) and high SAT scores (900+). Award size ranges from $900 (Alumni Merit, Honors Merit), $1,000 (Presidential), $2,000 (W.W. Smith), to full tuition (Founders). Write to the address below for details.

Lincoln University
Financial Aid Office
Lincoln Hall, Room 101
Lincoln University, PA 19352

2792

Linda S. Pettijohn Excellence In Retailing Award

AMOUNT: $250 **DEADLINE:** None Specified
FIELDS/MAJORS: Marketing, Retailing

Student must be a full-time sophomore or above marketing major with an emphasis in retailing. Must have a GPA of 3.0 or higher. Contact the COBA office for more information.

Southwest Missouri State University
Office Of Financial Aid
901 South National Ave.
Springfield, MO 65804

2793

Lions Club of Johnson City Scholarships

AMOUNT: None Specified **DEADLINE:** None Specified
FIELDS/MAJORS: All Areas Of Study

Scholarships for students at East Tennessee State University who have a visual or hearing handicap or who are juniors, seniors, or graduate students majoring in special education. Contact the Office of Financial Aid at the address below for details.

East Tennessee State University
Office Of Financial Aid
Box 70722
Johnson City, TN 37614

2794

LITA/GEAC-CLSI Scholarship

AMOUNT: $2,500 **DEADLINE:** Apr 1
FIELDS/MAJORS: Information Science

Applicants must be entering an ALA-accredited master's program with an emphasis on library automation. Previous experience will be considered. Write to the address shown for details.

American Library Association
Library & Information Technology Assn.
50 E. Huron Street
Chicago, IL 60611

2795

LITA/OCLC & LITA/LSSI Minority Scholarships

AMOUNT: $2,500 **DEADLINE:** Apr 1
FIELDS/MAJORS: Information Science

Applicants must be Native American, Asian American, African American, or Hispanic graduate students who are entering or enrolled in an ALA-accredited master's program with an emphasis on library automation. Previous experience is considered and U.S. or Canadian citizenship is required. Write to the address shown for details.

American Library Association
Library & Information Technology Assn.
50 E. Huron Street
Chicago, IL 60611

2796

Lizzie Lee Bloomstein Fellowship Fund

AMOUNT: None Specified **DEADLINE:** None Specified
FIELDS/MAJORS: History And Social Studies

Fellowships for graduate students in the Peabody College at Vanderbilt whose studies include history and social studies. Write to the address below for more information.

Vanderbilt University
Admissions And Financial Assistance
Box 327 Peabody College
Nashville, TN 37203

2797

Lloyd E. Malm Memorial Award

AMOUNT: $125 **DEADLINE:** Feb 15
FIELDS/MAJORS: Chemistry

Scholarships are available at the University of Utah for full-time entering freshmen chemistry majors who show academic ability and potential. Write to the address below for information.

University Of Utah
Dr. Fred Montague
135 Building 44
Salt Lake City, UT 84112

2798

Lloyd Lewis Fellowships In American History

AMOUNT: $40,000 (max) **DEADLINE:** Jan 20
FIELDS/MAJORS: American History

Fellowships for established scholars in any field of American history which is appropriate to the collections of the library. Must hold Ph.D. Must be U.S. citizen or permanent resident. Write to the address below for details.

Newberry Library Committee On Awards
60 W. Walton St.
Chicago, IL 60610

2799

Lloyd T. Roberts Scholarship

Amount: None Specified **Deadline:** None Specified
Fields/Majors: Physical Education

Scholarship available at ETSU for students majoring in physical education. Write to the address below for details.

East Tennessee State University
Office Of Financial Aid
Box 70722
Johnson City, TN 37614

2800

Lloyd Warren Fellowship—Paris Prize

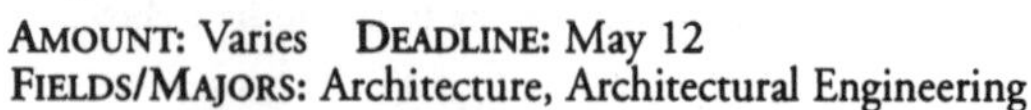

Amount: Varies **Deadline:** May 12
Fields/Majors: Architecture, Architectural Engineering

Open to architecture students who have received or are anticipating their first professional degree from a U.S. school of architecture by Dec. Write to the address below for information on this and other Van Alen Award programs.

Van Alen Institute Design Competitions
30 W. 22nd St.
New York, NY 10010

2801

Lois Borland Fulmer Endowed Scholarship

Amount: None Specified **Deadline:** None Specified
Fields/Majors: All Areas Of Study

Scholarships are available to any entering full-time or continuing part-time adult student of any major. Contact the Dean of Enrollment Management and Academic Records for more information.

Clarion University
104 Egbert Hall
Office Of Financial Aid
Clarion, PA 16214

2802

Lorain County Home Economics Scholarship

Amount: $500 **Deadline:** Mar 25
Fields/Majors: Home Economics

Given to a undergraduate college student or a graduating high school senior who is pursuing the field of home economics at a college or two-year technical school. Must be a resident of Lorain County (OH). Write to the address below for more information.

Lorain County Home Economics Association
Nancy Curci
4670 Washington Avenue
Lorain, OH 44052

2803

Lorain Youth Center Scholarships

Amount: $1,000 **Deadline:** Feb 15
Fields/Majors: All Areas Of Study

Awards for high school seniors from Lorain County, Ohio with financial need and academic achievement. Non-renewable. Write to the address below for more information.

Community Foundation of Greater Lorain County
1865 N. Ridge Road, East Suite A
Lorain, OH 44055

2804

Loras Grants

Amount: Varies **Deadline:** Apr 15
Fields/Majors: All Areas Of Study

Awards available at Loras College to full-time students who demonstrate financial need. Write to the address below for details.

Loras College
Office Of Financial Planning
1450 Alta Vista St., P.O. Box 178
Dubuque, IA 52004

2805

Lorraine Elizabeth Cella Memorial Scholarship

Amount: Varies **Deadline:** None Specified
Fields/Majors: Medieval Studies

Scholarships are available at the Catholic University of America for graduate students in Byzantine and medieval studies. Contact the financial aid office at the address below for details.

The Catholic University Of America
Director of Department Of Medieval And Byzantine Studies
Washington, DC 20064

2806

Los Angeles County Pomona Grange #37 Scholarship

Amount: $600 **Deadline:** Apr 15
Fields/Majors: Agronomy, Soil Science

Open to students majoring in agronomy and soil science with an interest in an agriculturally-related career. Write to the address below for more information.

California State Polytechnic University, Pomona
College of Agriculture
Building 7, Room 110
Pomona, CA 91768

2807

Los Angeles County San Dimas Grange Scholarship

Amount: $600 **Deadline:** Apr 15
Fields/Majors: Agronomy, Soil Science

Open to students majoring in agronomy and soil science with an interest in an agriculturally related career. Write to the address below for more information.

California State Polytechnic University, Pomona
College of Agriculture
Building 7, Room 110
Pomona, CA 91768

2808

Louis Dreyfus Corporation Scholarships

AMOUNT: $1,000 **DEADLINE:** Feb 15
FIELDS/MAJORS: Agriculture

Scholarships are available for FFA members pursuing a four-year degree in any area of agriculture. Write to the address below for details.

National FFA Foundation
Scholarship Office
P.O. Box 15160
Alexandria, VA 22309

2809

Louis Glick Trust

AMOUNT: Varies **DEADLINE:** None Specified
FIELDS/MAJORS: All Areas Of Study

Loans for high school graduates from Jackson County, MI, who are planning to attend or are enrolled in a college within the state of Michigan. Write to the address below for more information.

Louis Glick Memorial and Charitable Trust
903 Belden Road, P.O. Box 1166
Jackson, MI 49204

2810

Louis McRae Scholarships

AMOUNT: Varies **DEADLINE:** Mar 1
FIELDS/MAJORS: All Areas Of Study

Awards are available at the University of New Mexico for freshmen students from New Mexico. Write to the address below for more information.

University Of New Mexico, Albuquerque
Office Of Financial Aid
Albuquerque, NM 87131

2811

Louis Pelzer Memorial Award

AMOUNT: $500 **DEADLINE:** Nov 30
FIELDS/MAJORS: American History

Award for the graduate student who submits the best essay about any topic or period in the history of the U.S. Entries can not exceed 7,000 words. Write to the address below for more information.

Organization Of American History Journal Of American History
1125 E. Atwater, Indiana University
Bloomington, IN 47401

2812

Louise and Henry Poellnitz Johnston Endowed Scholarship

AMOUNT: $350 **DEADLINE:** Feb 15
FIELDS/MAJORS: Telecommunications

Renewable $350 scholarship awarded to full-time freshmen, sophomores and juniors majoring in telecommunications with financial need, high academic ability, and the potential to become successful broadcasters. Priority is given to Alabama residents. Write to the address listed below for additional information.

University Of Alabama
College of Communications
P.O. Box 870172
Tuscallosa, AL 35487

2813

Louise Giles Minority Scholarships

AMOUNT: $3,000 **DEADLINE:** Dec 22
FIELDS/MAJORS: Library Science

Applicants must be Native American, Asian American, African American, or Hispanic graduate students entering or enrolled in an ALA-accredited master's program. U.S. or Canadian citizenship is required. Must not have completed more than twelve semester hours toward master's degree. Write to the address shown for details.

American Library Association
Staff Liaison, ALA Scholarship Juries
50 E. Huron Street
Chicago, IL 60611

2814

Louise J. Snow Scholarship

AMOUNT: Varies **DEADLINE:** Mar 1
FIELDS/MAJORS: All Areas Of Study

Scholarships are available at the University of Utah for full-time students who have an identified physical or learning disability and demonstrate financial need. Applicants must have a GPA of at least 2.5. Write to the address below for information.

University Of Utah
Ms. Olga Nadeau
160 Olpin Union
Salt Lake City, UT 84112

2815

Louisiana Funeral Directors Association Scholarships

AMOUNT: $750 **DEADLINE:** None Specified
FIELDS/MAJORS: Mortuary Science

Awards for Louisiana residents studying mortuary science. Write to the address below for more information.

Louisiana Funeral Directors Association
P.O. Box 8209
Clinton, LA 0722

2816

Louisiana Honors Scholarship Program

AMOUNT: Full Tuition **DEADLINE:** None Specified
FIELDS/MAJORS: All Areas Of Study

Scholarships offered to Louisiana's top students. Must be in top 5% of class and attend college in Louisiana. Full-time undergraduate students only. Write to the address below for details.

Louisiana Office Of Financial Assistance
P.O. Box 91202
Baton Rouge, LA 70821

2817

Louisiana Presbyterian Foundation Scholarship

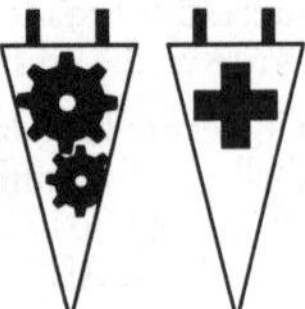

Amount: $300-$1,200 **Deadline:** Mar 15
Fields/Majors: Engineering, Medicine

Scholarships are available at the University of Oklahoma, Norman for full-time engineering students in at least their third year of study, and students accepted into medical school. Write to the address listed below for information.

University Of Oklahoma, Norman
Rev. Thad Holcombe, United Ministry Center
1017 Elm
Norman, OK 3072

2818

Louisiana Tuition Assistance Plan

Amount: Varies **Deadline:** None Specified
Fields/Majors: All Areas Of Study

Scholarships offered to Louisiana residents who will be enrolling as full-time freshman students at a public university in Louisiana. Applicants must be U.S. citizens with a GPA of at least 2.5. Write to the address below for details.

Louisiana Office Of Financial Assistance
P.O. Box 91202
Baton Rouge, LA 70821

2819

Lovell Family Scholarships

Amount: $500 **Deadline:** None Specified
Fields/Majors: Education

Awards for CHC juniors who are majoring in education. Based primarily on GPA and academic achievement. Write to the address below for more information.

Christian Heritage College
Financial Aid Office
2100 Greenfield Dr.
El Cajon, CA 92019

2820

Lowell & Frances Dunham Scholarship

Amount: $500 **Deadline:** Feb 15
Fields/Majors: Foreign Languages, Linguistics

Scholarships are available at the University of Oklahoma, Norman for full-time foreign language or linguistics majors with at least sophomore standing. Must have a 3.0 GPA overall, with a 3.5 GPA in major coursework. Write to the address listed below for information.

University Of Oklahoma, Norman
Modern Languages Department
780 Van Vleet Oval
Norman, OK 73019

2821

Lower Mid-Atlantic Regional Scholarship

Amount: $1,000 **Deadline:** May 31
Fields/Majors: All Areas Of Study

Scholarships for Italian American residents of Pennsylvania, southern New Jersey (up to Trenton), or Delaware. Write to the address below for details.

National Italian American Foundation
Dr. Maria Lombardo, Education Director
1860 19th Street, NW
Washington, DC 20001

2822

Loyola College Grants

Amount: Varies **Deadline:** Feb 1
Fields/Majors: All Areas Of Study

Open to full-time undergraduate students with exceptional financial aid eligibility. Write to the address below for additional information.

Loyola College In Maryland
Director Of Financial Aid
4501 North Charles St.
Baltimore, MD 21210

2823

LS3P Architects, Ltd. Scholarship

Amount: Varies **Deadline:** None Specified
Fields/Majors: All Areas Of Study

Awards for TTC students pursuing an associate degree who are Trident area residents and are enrolled in at least twelve credit hours. Must have a GPA of at least 2.5. Write to the address below for more information.

Trident Technical College
Financial Aid Office
P.O. Box 118067
Charleston, SC 29423

2824

Lubrizol Scholarships

Amount: $500 **Deadline:** Mar 1
Fields/Majors: All Areas Of Study

Award for upperclassmen at Lake Erie that are based on scholastic achievement, good citizenship, and leadership qualities. Write to the address below for more information.

Lake Erie College
Financial Aid Office
391 W. Washington St.
Painesville, OH 44077

2825

Lucas V. Beau (Major General), Order of Daedalians, Flight Scholarship

Amount: None Specified **Deadline:** Apr 1
Fields/Majors: Aviation

Applicants must be CAP cadet members. Award is used for air and ground training toward a FAA private pilots license. Write to the address below for details.

Civil Air Patrol National Headquarters CAP(tt)
Maxwell AFB, AL 36112

2826

Lucile A. Abt Scholarship

AMOUNT: $250-$1,000 **DEADLINE:** Apr 1
FIELDS/MAJORS: All Areas Of Study

Applicants must be born deaf or became deaf before acquiring language. Must also use speech/residual hearing or lip-reading as primary communication and be a student entering or attending a college or university program for hearing students. Five scholarships are awarded each year. Write to the address below for complete details.

Alexander Graham Bell Association For The Deaf
3417 Volta Place, NW
Washington, DC 20007

2827

Lucille Keller Foundation Student Loan Program

AMOUNT: $1,000 (max) **DEADLINE:** May 31
FIELDS/MAJORS: All Areas Of Study

Interest-free loans are available for residents of Bartholomew County, Indiana. Applicants must be enrolled on a full-time basis and have a GPA of at least 2.0. Write to the address listed below for information.

Lucille Keller Foundation Irwin Union Bank & Trust Company
Attn: Trust Department, P.O. Box 929
Columbus, IN 47202

2828

Lucille Morton-Grams Scholarship

AMOUNT: $750 **DEADLINE:** March
FIELDS/MAJORS: All Areas Of Study

Award for a second semester freshman with a minimum GPA of 2.5. Must show no financial need according to federal standards. Contact the Financial Aid Office, UW Oshkosh, for more details.

University Of Wisconsin, Oshkosh
Financial Aid Office, Dempsey 104
800 Algoma Blvd.
Oshkosh, WI 54901

2829

Lucille S. Welch Art Scholarships

AMOUNT: Varies **DEADLINE:** Apr 1
FIELDS/MAJORS: Art

Awards are available to art majors on the basis of portfolio, financial need, and GPA. Write to the address below for more information.

Portland State University Art Department
39 Neuberger Hall
Portland, OR 97207

2830

Lucy Hanes Chatham Scholarship

AMOUNT: $8,000 **DEADLINE:** Feb 28
FIELDS/MAJORS: All Areas Of Study

Two renewable scholarships awarded to freshmen students attending Salem College. Based on academic achievement, leadership, service, and physical vigor. Renewable with full-time study and a GPA of at least 3.0. Write to the address below for more information.

Salem College
Director of Financial Aid
P.O. Box 10548
Winston-Salem, NC 27108

2831

Lugenbeel Scholarships

AMOUNT: Varies **DEADLINE:** None Specified
FIELDS/MAJORS: Health Science

Awards for TTC students pursuing an associate degree in the field of health science and are enrolled in at least twelve credit hours. Must have a GPA of at least 2.5 and have financial need. Write to the address below for more information.

Trident Technical College
Financial Aid Office
P.O. Box 118067
Charleston, SC 29423

2832

Luise Meyer-Schutzmeister Award

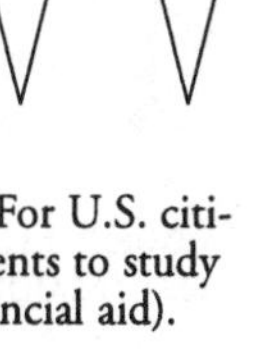

AMOUNT: $500 **DEADLINE:** Jan 15
FIELDS/MAJORS: Physics

Scholarship for female doctoral student in physics. For U.S. citizens to study in U.S. or abroad, or for foreign students to study in U.S. (the AWIS also publishes a directory of financial aid). Write to the address below for details.

Association For Women In Science Educational Foundation
National Headquarters
1522 K St., NW, Suite 820
Washington, DC 20005

2833

Lulac Scholarship Programs

AMOUNT: Varies **DEADLINE:** Varies
FIELDS/MAJORS: All Areas Of Study

The Lulac National Scholarship Fund is a community-based scholarship program that awards over a half a million dollars each year to outstanding Hispanic students in communities served by participating councils of Lulac. To qualify, an applicant must be a U.S. citizen or legal resident and enrolled or planning to enroll in a two- or four-year college or university. Applicants must apply directly to a participating Lulac Council in his/her community. A list of participating lulac councils can be obtained by sending an SASE to the Lulac National Education Service Centers at the address below.

Lulac National Educational Service Centers, Inc.
Department Of Scholarship Inquiries
2100 M Street, NW, Suite 602
Washington, DC 20037

2834

Lullelia W. Harrison Scholarship In Counseling

AMOUNT: $500-$1,000 **DEADLINE:** Feb 1
FIELDS/MAJORS: Counseling, Counseling Psychology

Scholarship for full-time graduate or undergraduate students in degree programs leading to a degree in counseling. Award length is one year. No affiliation with Zeta Phi Beta is required. Send an SASE to the national headquarters at the address below for further information.

Zeta Phi Beta Sorority
National Educational Foundation
1734 New Hampshire Ave., NW
Washington, DC 20009

2835 Lutheran Brotherhood Member Scholarship Program

AMOUNT: Varies **DEADLINE:** Jan 31
FIELDS/MAJORS: All Areas Of Study

For members of Lutheran Brotherhood insured under a LB insurance policy, have a mutual fund account, or are named as eligible riders on a parent's contract. Applicant must have a GPA of at least 3.25 (for entering freshman) or 3.5 (for in-college students). For undergraduate study. Application forms may be obtained by writing to "Member Scholarships" at the address below.

Lutheran Brotherhood Member Scholarships
P.O. Box 59335
Minneapolis, MN 55459

2836 Lutheran Church-Missouri Synod District Grants

AMOUNT: $100-$1,000 **DEADLINE:** Varies
FIELDS/MAJORS: Religion, Theology

Awards for Concordia students who intend to enter full-time church careers in the Lutheran Church-Missouri Synod. Must have a GPA of at least 2.5 and be a U.S. citizen. Renewable. Write to the address below for more information.

Concordia University, Irvine
Financial Aid Office
1530 Concordia
West Irvine, CA 92715

2837 Lutheran Church Career Grant

AMOUNT: $500-$2,000 **DEADLINE:** Varies
FIELDS/MAJORS: Religion, Theology

Awards for Concordia students who intend to enter full-time church careers in the Lutheran Church-Missouri Synod. Must have a GPA of at least 2.5 and be a U.S. citizen. Renewable. Write to the address below for more information

Concordia University, Irvine
Financial Aid Office
1530 Concordia
West Irvine, CA 92715

2838 Lutheran College Scholarships

AMOUNT: $800-$1,500 **DEADLINE:** Varies
FIELDS/MAJORS: All Areas Of Study

Scholarships for Lutheran students attending Lutheran colleges. Based upon academic achievement, financial need and religious leadership. Recipients who are not Lutheran Brotherhood members will receive $800. Members who are insured under a LB contract will receive an additional $700. Contact the financial aid office at your Lutheran college for information.

Lutheran Brotherhood
Fraternal Division, Box 857
625 Fourth Avenue
South Minneapolis, MN 55415

2839 Lutheran Seminary Awards, Seminary Sabbatical Fellowships

AMOUNT: $100-$6,000 **DEADLINE:** None Specified
FIELDS/MAJORS: Religion, Theology

Awards for students who are attending Lutheran seminaries. Based on need. Sabbatical fellowships are available to administrators and faculty of Lutheran seminaries who are on approved sabbatical leave. Based on sabbatical activities and length of leave. No specification is made to what division of Lutheranism the seminary must be (ELCA, LCA, etc.). Information is available from your seminary. Write to the address below if necessary.

Lutheran Brotherhood
Fraternal Division, Box 857
625 Fourth Avenue
South Minneapolis, MN 55415

2840 Lyle Mamer, Julia Kiene Fellowship In Electrical Energy

AMOUNT: $1,000-$2,000 **DEADLINE:** Mar 1
FIELDS/MAJORS: Electrical-Related Fields

Open to women who are graduating seniors or those who have a degree from an accredited institution. The applications are judged on the basis of scholarship, character, financial need, and professional interest in electrical energy. The college or university selected by the recipient for advanced study must be accredited and approved by the EWRT fellowship committee. Write to the address below for further information.

Electrical Women's Round Table, Inc.
Executive Director
P.O. Box 292793
Nashville, TN 37229

2841 Lynch Memorial Scholarship

AMOUNT: Varies **DEADLINE:** Mar 1
FIELDS/MAJORS: Business

Award for a student majoring in business or a related field with a minimum GPA of 3.0. Preference is given to Union or Wallowa County residents. Write to the address below for more information.

Eastern Oregon State College
Financial Aid Office
1041 "I" Avenue
La Grande, OR 97850

2842 Lynch-Reed-Wakefield Scholarship

AMOUNT: None Specified **DEADLINE:** None Specified
FIELDS/MAJORS: All Areas Of Study

Awards for students at St. Petersburg Junior College with academic achievement and financial need. Write to the address below for more information.

St. Petersburg Junior College
Financial Aid Office
P.O. Box 13489
St. Petersburg, FL 33733

2843

Lynn Saxton Memorial Fund

AMOUNT: Varies **DEADLINE:** Mar 1
FIELDS/MAJORS: Medical Technology

Awards are available at the University of New Mexico for students enrolled in the medical laboratory science program. Applicants must have scholastic and leadership ability and exhibit professionalism as a student. Write to the address below for more information.

University Of New Mexico, Albuquerque
Office Of Financial Aid
Albuquerque, NM 87131

2844

Lynnford L. Peterson Scholarship

AMOUNT: Varies **DEADLINE:** Mar 1
FIELDS/MAJORS: Medicine

Awards are available at the University of New Mexico for medical students with financial need and demonstrated merit. Write to the address below for more information.

University Of New Mexico, Albuquerque
Office Of Financial Aid
Albuquerque, NM 87131

2845

M. Geneva Gray Scholarship

AMOUNT: Varies **DEADLINE:** Mar 1
FIELDS/MAJORS: All Areas Of Study

Scholarships are available for Massachusetts residents who are undergraduates, come from families with several children to educate, with a family income in the $25,000 to $50,000 range. In September, write to the address listed below for information. Include a stamped, self-addressed envelope with your request.

M. Geneva Gray Scholarship Fund
PNC Bank, New England, Trust Department
125 High Street
Boston, MA 02110

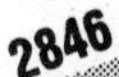
2846

M.A. Cartland Shackford Medical Fellowship

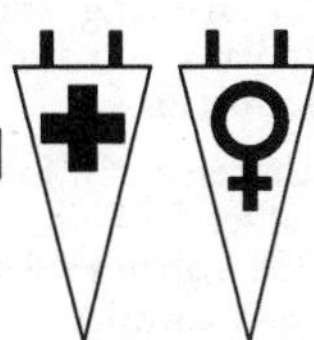

AMOUNT: $3,500 (max)
DEADLINE: None Specified
FIELDS/MAJORS: Medicine

Scholarship for women studying medicine (on the graduate level). Fellowships are intended to support women with a career objective in general practice, not psychiatry. Write to the address listed below for information.

Wellesley College Committee On Graduate Fellowships
106 Central Street, Career Center
Wellesley, MA 02181

2847

M.C. And Hazel McCuiston Scholarship

AMOUNT: None Specified **DEADLINE:** Feb 15
FIELDS/MAJORS: Business Education, Computer Studies, Economics, Office Systems

Scholarship for a high school graduate who plans a bachelor of science degree in one of the areas of business study offered at MSU—accounting, finance, computer studies, economics, management, marketing, office systems, or business education. Write to the address below for details.

Murray State University
Office Of University Scholarships
Ordway Hall, 1 Murray St.
Murray, KY 42071

2848

Mabel C. Jury Music Scholarship

AMOUNT: Varies **DEADLINE:** None Specified
FIELDS/MAJORS: Music, Vocal

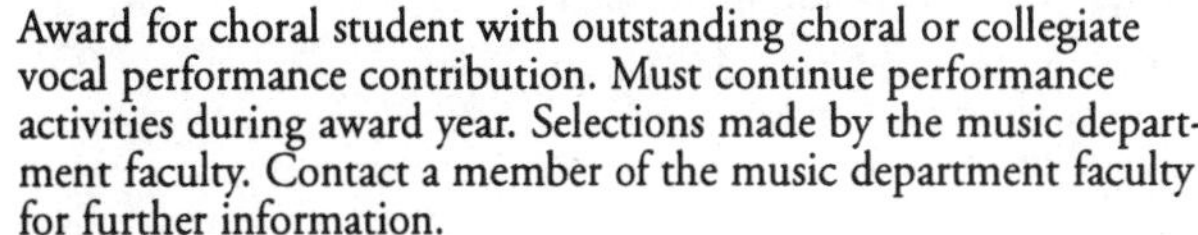

Award for choral student with outstanding choral or collegiate vocal performance contribution. Must continue performance activities during award year. Selections made by the music department faculty. Contact a member of the music department faculty for further information.

Bloomsburg University
19 Ben Franklin Hall
400 E. Second St.
Bloomsburg, PA 17815

2849

Mabel Clair Ligon Memorial Scholarship

AMOUNT: None Specified
DEADLINE: None Specified
FIELDS/MAJORS: Education (Undergraduate Students), Counseling (Graduate Students)

Scholarships for students at East Tennessee State University majoring in education. Must be junior, senior, or graduate student and have a GPA of at least 3.0 (3.5 for graduate students). Must demonstrate financial need. Contact the office of financial aid at the address below for details.

East Tennessee State University
Office Of Financial Aid
Box 70722
Johnson City, TN 37614

2850

Mabel E. Rasmussen Award

AMOUNT: $445 **DEADLINE:** Mar 3
FIELDS/MAJORS: All Areas Of Study

Awards are available to female students who graduated from a Winnebago County high school and are full-time sophomores, juniors, or seniors. Based upon scholastic achievement, leadership qualities, and financial need. Contact the Financial Aid Office, UW Oshkosh for more information.

University Of Wisconsin, Oshkosh
Financial Aid Office, Dempsey 104
800 Algoma Blvd.
Oshkosh, WI 54901

2851

Mabel Hammersley Nursing Scholarships

AMOUNT: $1,500 **DEADLINE:** Apr 1
FIELDS/MAJORS: Nursing

Two scholarships for entering students in nursing at Kent State. Must have a solid academic background (GPA of at least 3.0).

Contact the financial aid office for details.

Kent State University, Tuscarawas Campus
Financial Aid Office
University Drive, NE
New Philadelphia, OH 44663

2852 Mabel Wilson Richards Scholarship

Amount: None Specified **Deadline:** Nov 30
Fields/Majors: All Areas Of Study

Scholarships are available at UCSD for undergraduate female students who are residents of Los Angeles, U.S. citizens, with a GPA of at least 3.0. Must also demonstrate financial need. Write to the address listed below for information.

University Of California, San Diego
Student Financial Services
9500 Gilman Drive
LaJolla, CA 2093

2853 Mabelle Wilhelmina Boldt Memorial Scholarship

Amount: $1,800 **Deadline:** Apr 12
Fields/Majors: Interior Design

Scholarship for graduate-level students who have worked in the field for at least five years and are returning to school for further studies. Based on academic/creative accomplishment. Preference given to students with a focus on design research. Send an SASE to the address below for details.

American Society of Interior Designers
Educational Foundation Scholarship And Awards Program
608 Massachusetts Ave., NE
Washington, DC 20002

2854 Machine Shed Agriculture Scholarship

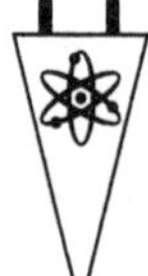

Amount: $1,000 **Deadline:** Feb 1
Fields/Majors: Agriculture

Scholarships are available for freshmen entering Iowa State University; students enrolled in Ft. Hays State University or Kansas State; any students enrolled in an ag program in Iowa, Illinois, Michigan, Kansas, or Wisconsin or students who live in those states and attend school elsewhere. Write to the address listed below for information.

Heart Of America Restaurants And Inns
The Machine Shed Scholarships
111 West 76th Street
Davenport, IA 52806

2855 Mack H. Kennington Mem. Scholarship & O.H. Kruse Grain & Milling Inc.

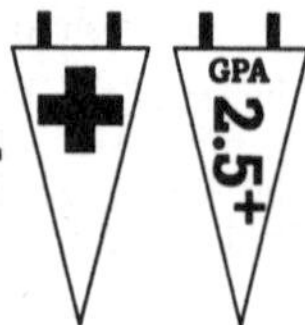

Amount: $500 **Deadline:** None Specified
Fields/Majors: Animal and Veterinary Science

Student must be a full-time sophomore or junior majoring in animal and veterinary science with a GPA of 2.5 or better. Must have completed a minimum of two quarters at Cal Poly Pomona. Two awards are given yearly. Write to the address below for more information.

California State Polytechnic University, Pomona
College Of Agriculture
Building 2, Room 215
Pomona, CA 91768

2856 Mack Thomas Rozelle Scholarship. Leon L. Watters Scholarship

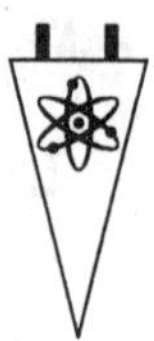

Amount: Varies **Deadline:** Feb 15
Fields/Majors: Chemistry

Scholarships are available at the University of Utah for full-time chemistry majors who show academic ability and potential for success in chemistry. Write to the address below for information.

University Of Utah
Dr. Fred Montague
135 Building 44
Salt Lake City, UT 84112

2857 Madeira Shaner Scholarship

Amount: Varies **Deadline:** None Specified
Fields/Majors: Theater and Related Fields

Scholarships for college-bound students who are majoring in any of the theater disciplines or who are planning to make theater a career. Write to the address below for more information.

Midland Community Theater
Business Office, Scholarship Committee
2000 W. Wadley
Midland, TX 79705

2858 Madeline P. Peterson Scholarship For American Indian Women

Amount: $3,500 + Tuition **Deadline:** None Specified
Fields/Majors: All Areas Of Study

Scholarships are available at the University of Iowa for incoming female freshman students who are American Indians with a tribal affiliation. Write to address below for details.

University Of Iowa
Office Of Student Financial Aid
208 Calvin Hall
Iowa City, IA 52242

2859 Madeline Pickett Cogswell Nursing Scholarships

Amount: $500 **Deadline:** Feb 15, Aug 15
Fields/Majors: Nursing

Applicants must be currently enrolled in an accredited school of nursing. Must also be a U.S. citizen, and a member or related to a member of NSDAR, C.A.R., or SR. For undergraduate study. Contact your local DAR chapter or write to the address below for details.

National Society Daughters Of The American Revolution
NSDAR Scholarship Committee
1776 D St., NW
Washington, DC 20006

2860

Madelyn S. Silver Scholarship

Amount: Varies **Deadline:** Feb 15
Fields/Majors: Literature

Scholarships are available at the University of Utah for full-time students demonstrating a substantial interest in literature, especially biblical literature. Write to the address below for information.

University Of Utah
Financial Aid and Scholarships Office
105 Student Services Building
Salt Lake City, UT 84112

2861

Mader Scholarship

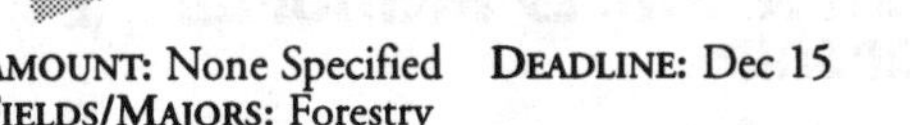

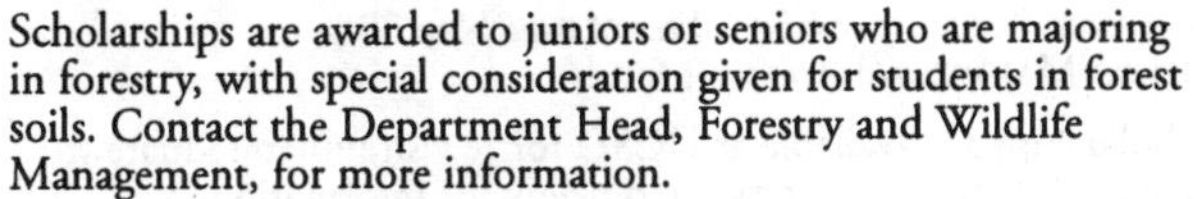

Amount: None Specified **Deadline:** Dec 15
Fields/Majors: Forestry

Scholarships are awarded to juniors or seniors who are majoring in forestry, with special consideration given for students in forest soils. Contact the Department Head, Forestry and Wildlife Management, for more information.

University Of Massachusetts, Amherst
Department Of Forestry and Wildlife Mgmt.
Amherst, MA 01003

2862

Madge Huffer Scholarship

Amount: $1,000 **Deadline:** None Specified
Fields/Majors: Speech and Theater

Award for full-time Mesa State speech and theater students in the school of humanities and social sciences. Must have a GPA of at least 2.5 and be an active participant in speech or theater activities. Contact the school of humanities and social sciences for more details.

Mesa State College
Office Of Financial Aid
P.O. Box 2647
Grand Junction, CO 81501

2863

Madrigal Dinner Scholarship

Amount: Varies **Deadline:** Mar 31
Fields/Majors: Choir

Awards for students who demonstrate outstanding ability in university choral organizations. Contact the music department for more information.

Southwest Missouri State University
Office Of Financial Aid
901 South National Ave.
Springfield, MO 65804

2864

Mae Lasley Osage Scholarship Fund

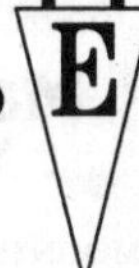

Amount: $250-$1,000 **Deadline:** Jun 15
Fields/Majors: All Areas Of Study

Scholarships are available for Osage Indians who are undergraduate students at any accredited university. Write to the address listed below for information.

Mae Lasley Osage Scholarship Fund
P.O. Box 2009
Tulsa, OK 74101

2865

Magazine Circle Scholarship

Amount: None Specified **Deadline:** None Specified
Fields/Majors: All Areas Of Study

Scholarships for graduate students in Peabody College at Vanderbilt University who are of the Hebrew faith. Write to the address below for further details.

Vanderbilt University Admissions And Financial Assistance
Box 327, Peabody College
Nashville, TN 37203

2866

Magazine Internship Program

Amount: $300/Week **Deadline:** Dec 15
Fields/Majors: Journalism

Summer internships are available with any of 42 different magazines for journalism majors who will be entering their senior year and who plan to pursue a career in editorial journalism. Internships are available in New York and Washington, DC. Write to the address listed below for information.

American Society Of Magazine Editors
Marlene Kahan, Executive Director
919 Third Avenue, 22nd Floor
New York, NY 0022

2867

Magi Scholarships

Amount: Half Tuition **Deadline:** None Specified
Fields/Majors: Church-Related Studies

Scholarships are available at the Catholic University of America for graduate students who plan to serve the church in some capacity (teaching, organist, choral director, or craftsman). Contact the financial aid office at the address below for details.

The Catholic University Of America
Office Of Admissions And Financial Aid
Washington, DC 20064

2868

Magoichi and Shizuko Kato Memorial Scholarship

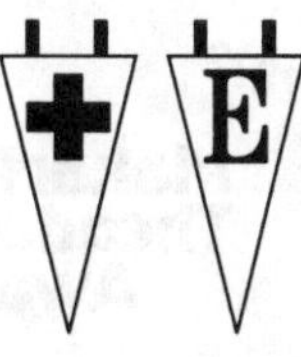

Amount: Varies **Deadline:** Apr 1
Fields/Majors: Medicine, Theology/Religion

Open to graduate students of Japanese ancestry majoring in medicine or the ministry. Applications and information may be obtained from local JACL chapters, district offices, and the national headquarters at the address below. Please indicate your level of study and be certain to include a legal sized SASE.

Japanese American Citizens League
National Scholarship And Award Program
1765 Sutter St.
San Francisco, CA 94115

2869

Mai and William S. Robinson Humanities And Fine Arts Scholarships

Amount: Tuition and Fees **Deadline:** None Specified
Fields/Majors: All Areas Of Study

Awards for full-time Mesa State juniors and seniors who are active in drama or history. Must have a GPA of at least 3.0. Contact the school of humanities for more information.

Mesa State College
Financial Aid Office
P.O. Box 2647
Grand Junction, CO 81501

2870

Maine Campground Owners Association Scholarship

Amount: Varies **Deadline:** Apr 1
Fields/Majors: Outdoor Recreation

Awards are available for Maine residents who have completed at least one year of study in a program leading to a career in outdoor recreation. Must have a GPA of at least 2.5. Write to the address below for more information.

Maine Campground Owners Association
655 Main St.
Lewiston, ME 04240

2871

Maine State Music Theater Summer Internship Program

Amount: Varies **Deadline:** None Specified
Fields/Majors: Performing Arts, Theater Production

Summer internship program for students in the performance and production areas of theater. Interns are provided with housing, food, and a weekly stipend. Write to the address below for more information.

Maine State Music Theater
14 Maine Street, Suite 109
Brunswick, ME 04011

2872

Makarios Scholarship/ Theodore And Wally Lappas Award

Amount: Varies **Deadline:** May 31
Fields/Majors: All Areas Of Study

Scholarships for Greek Cypriots born in Cyprus and having permanent residence and citizenship there. For study in the U.S. Must have financial need and high scholastic ability. Write to the address below for details.

Cyprus Relief Fund of America, Inc.
Makarios Scholarship Fund, Inc.
13 E. 40th St.
New York, NY 10016

2873

Malcolm Baldrige Scholarship Fund

Amount: $2,000 **Deadline:** Apr 1
Fields/Majors: International Trade, Manufacturing

Awards for college juniors or seniors, who must be matriculated in either international trade or manufacturing. Must be fluent in, (or have studied), a foreign language. Must also be able to demonstrate excellent academic achievement and be a Connecticut resident. Contact the address below for further information and an application.

Brian V. Beaudin, President
Malcolm Baldrige Scholarship Fund
370 Asylum St.
Hartford, CT 06103

2874

Malcolm R. Stacey Memorial Scholarship

Amount: None Specified **Deadline:** Nov 30
Fields/Majors: All Areas Of Study

Scholarships are available at UCSD for Jewish undergraduate students. Write to the address listed below for information.

University Of California, San Diego
Student Financial Services
9500 Gilman Drive
La Jolla, CA 92093

2875

Maldef Communications Scholarship Program

Amount: $3,000-$4,000 **Deadline:** Jul 1
Fields/Majors: Communications

Awards are available for Latino students pursuing a graduate or professional degree in the communications and media fields. Write to the address below for more information.

Mexican American Legal Defense And Education Fund
634 South Spring Street, 11th Floor
Los Angeles, CA 90014

2876

Maldef Law School Scholarship Program

Amount: $1,000-$2,000 **Deadline:** May 30
Fields/Majors: Law

Open to full-time law students of Hispanic descent accepted to/enrolled in an accredited law school. Varying number of awards per year, at least nineteen $1,000 awards and one $2,000 award. Write to the address below for details.

Mexican American Legal Defense And Educational Fund
Maldef Law School Scholarship Program
634 S. Spring St., 11th Floor
Los Angeles, CA 90014

2877

Malott Music Scholarship

Amount: $500 **Deadline:** Mar 1
Fields/Majors: Vocal Music

Award for choral education or vocal performance majors at Eastern

New Mexico University who have actively participated in choral ensembles. Write to the address below for more information.

Eastern New Mexico University
College of Fine Arts, Station 16
Portales, NM 88130

2878
Mana Scholarships

AMOUNT: $200-$500 **DEADLINE:** Jun 1
FIELDS/MAJORS: All Areas Of Study

Award for female Hispanic student who has received or will receive their GED in the same year of application. Write to the address below for information.

Mexican American Women's Association Scholarships
Mana De Albuquerque P.O. Box 40580
Albuquerque, NM 87196

2879
Management Of The Industrial Assoc. Minority Engineering Scholarships

AMOUNT: None Specified **DEADLINE:** Mar 1
FIELDS/MAJORS: Engineering

Several scholarships for students planning to study engineering. Renewable if recipients maintain a minimum cumulative GPA of 2.6. Contact the financial aid office at the address below for details.

Clemson University
Financial Aid Office
G01 Sikes Hall
Clemson, SC 29634

2880
Management Scholarship

AMOUNT: $500 **DEADLINE:** None Specified
FIELDS/MAJORS: Management

Student must be a management major with a satisfactory academic record and financial need. Contact the COBA office more information.

Southwest Missouri State University
Office Of Financial Aid
901 South National Ave.
Springfield, MO 65804

2881
Management Scholarships

AMOUNT: $1,200 **DEADLINE:** Mar 1
FIELDS/MAJORS: Management

Awards for management undergraduates at North Carolina State University. Write to the address below for more information.

North Carolina State University
Erin O. Dixon, Director Of Admissions
College of Management, Box 8614
Raleigh, NC 27695

2882
Manuel Pino Scholarships

AMOUNT: Varies **DEADLINE:** Mar 1
FIELDS/MAJORS: All Areas Of Study

Awards are available at the University of New Mexico for Hispanic students. Write to the address below for more information.

University Of New Mexico, Albuquerque
Office Of Financial Aid
Albuquerque, NM 87131

2883
Manufacturing Scholarships

AMOUNT: Varies **DEADLINE:** None Specified
FIELDS/MAJORS: Manufacturing Engineering Technology, Manufacturing Engineering

Awards are available for students at BYU studying in the areas above. Must be accepted in the university in a full-time program of study. Write to the address below for more information.

Brigham Young University
Department Of Manufacturing Engineering & Eng. Tech.
Brigham Young University, 435 CTB
Provo, UT 84602

2884
MAPA Safety Foundation Scholarship

AMOUNT: $1,000 **DEADLINE:** Aug 1
FIELDS/MAJORS: Aviation Safety

Awards for juniors and seniors enrolled in a course of study that would promote general aviation safety. Must have a GPA of 3.0 or better and be a member of MAPA or sponsored by a MAPA member. Contact a local MAPA member or write to the address below for more details.

Mooney Aircraft Pilot Association
Safety Foundation
P.O. 460607
San Antonio, TX 78246

2885
Marathon Geology/ Geophysics Scholarship, James C. Campbell Award

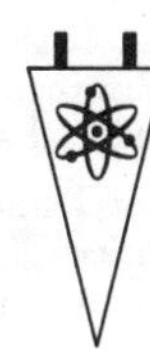

AMOUNT: Varies **DEADLINE:** Mar 1
FIELDS/MAJORS: Geology, Geophysics

Scholarships are available at the University of Oklahoma, Norman for full-time geology or geophysics majors. Write to the address listed below for information.

University Of Oklahoma, Norman
Director, School Of Geology & Geophysics
100 East Boyd Street, Room 810
Norman, OK 73019

2886
Marching Band Scholarship

AMOUNT: Varies **DEADLINE:** Mar 1
FIELDS/MAJORS: All Areas Of Study

Awards are available at the University of New Mexico for students who participate in the Lobo Marching Band. Write to the address below for more information.

University Of New Mexico, Albuquerque
Office Of Financial Aid
Albuquerque, NM 87131

2887

Margaret and Sidney Jaffe Scholarship

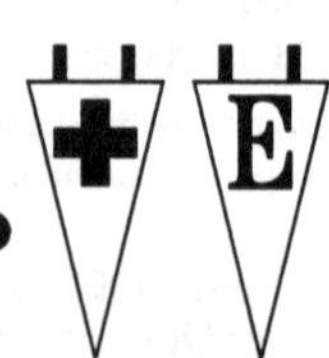

Amount: Varies **Deadline:** Mar 1
Fields/Majors: Medicine

Awards are available at the University of New Mexico for medical students or juniors or seniors in a pre-med curriculum who are of American Indian descent. Applicants must have been New Mexico high school graduates. Contact the medical school for more details.

University Of New Mexico, Albuquerque
Office Of Financial Aid
Albuquerque, NM 87131

2888

Margaret Bittner Parke Scholarship

Amount: $450 **Deadline:** Feb 9
Fields/Majors: English-Secondary Education

Applicant will have completed a minimum of four English courses, including composition. Academic excellence is required. Use Bloomsburg University scholarship application. Contact Dr. William Baillie, Chairperson, Department of English, for further information.

Bloomsburg University
19 Ben Franklin Hall
400 E. Second St.
Bloomsburg, PA 17815

2889

Margaret Campbell Flanary Scholarship

Amount: None Specified **Deadline:** None Specified
Fields/Majors: All Areas Of Study

Scholarships for students at East Tennessee State University from Washington or Sullivan County (TN). Contact the office of financial aid at the address below for details.

East Tennessee State University
Office Of Financial Aid, Box 70722
Johnson City, TN 37614

2890

Margaret E. Swanson Scholarship

Amount: Varies **Deadline:** Jun 1
Fields/Majors: Dental Hygiene

Scholarships for students who have completed at least one year in a full-time accredited program in dental hygiene. Based on need and organization and leadership potential. Must have a GPA of at least 3.0. Write to the address below for more information.

American Dental Hygienists' Association
Institute For Oral Health
444 N. Michigan Ave., Suite 3400
Chicago, IL 60611

2891

Margaret F. Barnes Scholarship

Amount: Varies **Deadline:** Feb 15
Fields/Majors: Environmental Design, Landscape Architecture, Floriculture

Awards for Stockbridge students in the areas of environmental design, landscape architecture, or floriculture. For students in their sophomore, junior, or senior year at UMass. Contact the Director, Stockbridge School, for more information.

University Of Massachusetts, Amherst
Director, Stockbridge School
Amherst, MA 01003

2892

Margaret Freeman Bowers Fellowship

Amount: $1,500 (max)
Deadline: None Specified
Fields/Majors: Social Work, Law, Public Policy, Public Administration

Fellowships for graduates of Wellesley College studying any in any of the above fields or studying for a MBA with career goals in the field of social services. Preference given to candidates with financial need. No applications will be mailed after Nov 25 (but you may be eligible next year). Write to the Secretary of the Committee on Graduate Fellowships for further information.

Wellesley College
Fellowships For Wellesley Alumnae Sec'y
Committee On Graduate Fellowships
106 Central St., Career Center
Wellesley, MA 02181

2893

Margaret Gallagher Scholarships

Amount: Varies **Deadline:** None Specified
Fields/Majors: Nursing

Awards available for qualified nursing students at Cedarville College. Must have a GPA of at least 2.0. Write to the address below for more information.

Cedarville College
Financial Aid Office, P.O. Box 601
Cedarville, OH 45314

2894

Margaret Howard Hamilton Scholarships

Amount: $1,000 **Deadline:** Feb 15
Fields/Majors: All Areas Of Study

Applicants must be graduating high school seniors entering the Jones Learning Center at the University of the Ozarks. U.S. citizenship is required. Renewable. Applications must be requested directly from the learning center.

National Society Daughters Of The American Revolution
NSDAR Scholarship Committee
1776 D St., NW
Washington, DC 20006

2895 Margaret Leuz Einspahr Scholarship

AMOUNT: Varies **DEADLINE:** Mar 1
FIELDS/MAJORS: English

Scholarships are available at the University of Iowa for full-time junior or senior English majors who are residents of Iowa, with preference given to students interested in the teaching profession. Write to the address listed below for information.

University Of Iowa Department Of English
308 English-Philosophy Building
Iowa City, IA 52242

2896 Margaret M. Prickett Scholarship

AMOUNT: $1,000 **DEADLINE:** Mar 31
FIELDS/MAJORS: All Areas Of Study

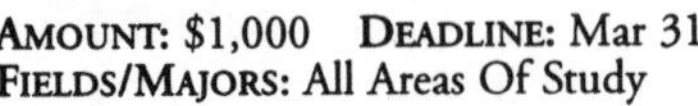

Scholarships for daughters or granddaughters of commissioned officers or warrant officers in the U.S. Army who are on active duty, died on active duty, or retired after at least 20 years of service. For undergraduate study. Renewable. Write to the address below for details. Specify the officer's name, rank, social security number, and dates of active duty when requesting an application.

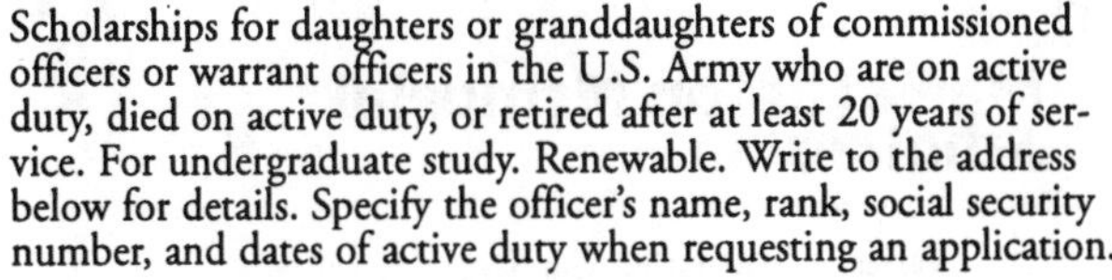

Society of Daughters Of The U.S. Army
Janet B. Otto, Scholarship Chairman
7717 Rockledge Court
West Springfield, VA 22152

2897 Margaret Mary Reese Eustace Scholarship

AMOUNT: Varies **DEADLINE:** None Specified
FIELDS/MAJORS: Education

Award for academically qualified Mercyhurst students who are studying education. Write to the address below for more information.

Mercyhurst College
Financial Aid Office
Glenwood Hills
Erie, PA 16546

2898 Margaret McNamara Memorial Fund Fellowships

AMOUNT: $6,000 (max) **DEADLINE:** Feb 1
FIELDS/MAJORS: All Areas Of Study

Fellowship are available to women from developing countries, with a record of service to women/children. Applicants must be 25 years of age or older, and be planning to return to their country of origin within two years of the grant date. Write to the address listed below for information.

Margaret McNamara Memorial Fund
1818 H Street, NW, Room G-1000
Washington, DC 20433

2899 Margaret Miller Memorial Undergraduate Scholarship

AMOUNT: $1,500 (max) **DEADLINE:** Apr 1
FIELDS/MAJORS: Nursing

Scholarship is for a registered nurse pursuing a bachelors's degree in nursing. Write to the address below for more information.

Emergency Nurses Association (ENA)
Foundation Funding Program
216 Higgins Rd.
Park Ridge, IL 60068

2900 Margaret Minner Memorial Scholarship

AMOUNT: $300 **DEADLINE:** Feb 9
FIELDS/MAJORS: All Areas Of Study

Award for seniors with a minimum GPA of 3.0 and are permanent residents of: Bucks, Chester, Delaware, Montgomery or Philadelphia Counties. Must demonstrate financial need. Use Bloomsburg University scholarship application. Contact Mr. Doug Hippenstiel, Director, Alumni Affairs Office, for further information.

Bloomsburg University
19 Ben Franklin Hall
400 E. Second St.
Bloomsburg, PA 17815

2901 Margaret T. Barnes Scholarship

AMOUNT: Tuition **DEADLINE:** Feb 15
FIELDS/MAJORS: Biology, Geology, Mathematics, Physics, Psychology

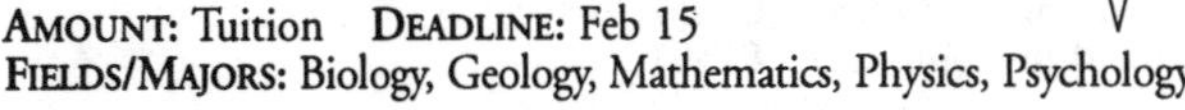

Scholarships are available at Colorado College for new students majoring in one of the areas listed above. Renewable for three additional years. Contact the Barnes Selection Committee at the address listed below for information.

Colorado College
Office Of Financial Aid
14 East Cache La Poudre
Colorado Springs, CO 80903

2902 Marguerite Mansfield Bilby Scholarship

AMOUNT: Varies **DEADLINE:** Apr 15
FIELDS/MAJORS: English

Scholarships are available at the University of Utah for full-time female students enrolled in an English program, who have completed at least five majors courses. Write to the address below for details.

University Of Utah
Scholarship Chairperson
3500 Lnco
Salt Lake City, UT 84112

2903 Maria Jackson/General George A. White Scholarship

AMOUNT: None Specified **DEADLINE:** Mar 1
FIELDS/MAJORS: All Areas Of Study

Scholarship for students who served in the armed forces, or whose parents served in the Armed Forces (U.S.). Must be able to provide documentation (DD93, DD214, discharge papers, etc.). Must have a GPA of at least 3.75. Contact your college financial aid office, contact your high school guidance department, or write to the address below for details.

Oregon State Scholarship Commission
Attn: Grant Department
1500 Valley River Dr., #100
Eugene, OR 97401

2904 Marian Meaker Apteckar Assistance Fund

Amount: $750 **Deadline:** None Specified
Fields/Majors: Music / Piano

Scholarship available for juniors and seniors studying the piano at the University of Texas, El Paso. Applicants must be El Paso County residents and have a GPA of at least 3.5. Write to the address listed below for additional information.

El Paso Community Foundation
201 East Main, Suite 1616
El Paso, TX 9901

2905 Marian Stephens Wethington Memorial Nursing Scholarship

Amount: $2,000 **Deadline:** None Specified
Fields/Majors: Nursing

Awards for Mesa State juniors majoring in the field of nursing. Contact the school of professional studies/nursing area for more details.

Mesa State College
Financial Aid Office, P.O. Box 2647
Grand Junction, CO 81501

2906 Mariana Talentship Awards

Amount: $250-$300 **Deadline:** Mar 1
Fields/Majors: Art

Scholarships are available at UNC for full-time art majors, based on a review of portfolio of studio work (usually three pieces.) Write to the address listed below for information.

University Of Northern Colorado
Frederic L. Myers, Chairman, Visual Arts Department
Greeley, CO 80639

2907 Marianas Naval Officers' Spouses' Club Scholarship

Amount: None Specified **Deadline:** Mar 31
Fields/Majors: All Areas Of Study

Scholarships for dependent sons/daughters of regular or reserve Navy, Marine Corps, or Coast Guard member on active duty, retired with pay, deceased, or missing in action. Must be graduating high school senior. The sponsor must have served on Guam for at least six continuous months or be a current or past member of the MNOSC. Write to the address below for details.

Marianas Naval Officers' Wives' Club
Scholarship Chairperson
PSC 489, Box 49
Comnavmar FPO AP 96540

2908 Mariani Award

Amount: Varies **Deadline:** Mar 1
Fields/Majors: Psychology

Awards are available at the University of New Mexico for graduate

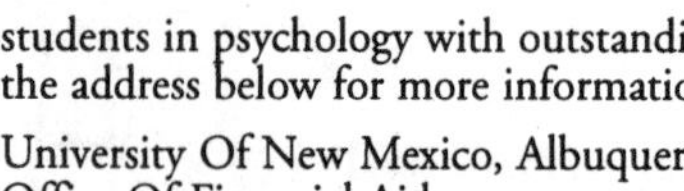

students in psychology with outstanding graduate work. Write to the address below for more information.

University Of New Mexico, Albuquerque
Office Of Financial Aid
Albuquerque, NM 87131

2909 Marie H. Hoch Endowment Scholarship

Amount: Varies **Deadline:** Mar 1
Fields/Majors: Nursing

Awards are available at the University of New Mexico for full-time senior nursing students who are outstanding academically and clinically. Must demonstrate financial need. Write to the address below or contact the school of nursing for more details.

University Of New Mexico, Albuquerque
Office Of Financial Aid
Albuquerque, NM 87131

2910 Marie Hutton Memorial Scholarship

Amount: Varies **Deadline:** Mar 1
Fields/Majors: Medicine

Awards are available at the University of New Mexico for medical students with financial need. Write to the address below for more information.

University Of New Mexico, Albuquerque
Office Of Financial Aid
Albuquerque, NM 87131

2911 Marie Mahoney Egan, Anna Jones Scholarships

Amount: None Specified **Deadline:** Mar 1
Fields/Majors: All Areas Of Study

Scholarships for students who were graduated from a Lake County (OR) High School. Jones Scholarship is for Paisley H.S. graduates and must be used at Oregon public colleges. Egan Scholarship requires Lake County residency during high school for both student and his or her parents. For undergraduate study. Contact your college financial aid office, contact your high school guidance department, or write to the address below for details.

Oregon State Scholarship Commission
Attn: Grant Department
1500 Valley River Dr., #100
Eugene, OR 97401

2912 Marie Mink Scholarship

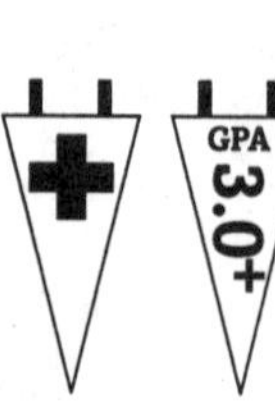

Amount: $500 **Deadline:** Spring
Fields/Majors: Nursing

Scholarships are available at the University of Oklahoma, Norman for full-time junior nursing students, with a minimum GPA of 3.0 in nursing courses and in the clinical portion of N3095. Write to the address listed below for information.

University Of Oklahoma, Norman
College of Nursing
P.O. Box 26901
Oklahoma City, OK 73190

2913

Marie-Louise Vermeiren Jackson Scholarship

Amount: $1,000-$2,000
Deadline: Mar 15, Nov 15
Fields/Majors: Education

Awards for students majoring in the field of education. Renewable with a GPA of at least 3.3. Write to the address below for more information.

Gwynedd-Mercy College
Student Financial Aid
Sumneytown Pike
Gwynedd Valley, PA 19437

2914

Marimac Scholarship

Amount: $500-$2,000 **Deadline:** Mar 1
Fields/Majors: Performing Or Visual Art

Applicants required to submit art portfolio or audition (prefer auditions on-campus). Available for freshman only. Selection based on special aptitudes in this field. Application is made to the fine arts department. Write to the address below for more details.

Denison University
Financial Aid Office
Box M
Granville, OH 43023

2915

Marin County American Revolution Bicentennial Scholarships

Amount: $500-$2,000 **Deadline:** Mar 31
Fields/Majors: All Areas Of Study

Awards for high school seniors who have been residents of Marin County since September 1st of the year prior to submitting an application. Must be planning to attend an approved institution of higher education. Contact your high school counselor or address below for complete information.

Marin County American Revolution Bicentennial Committee
Beryl Buck Institute For Education
18 Commercial Blvd.
Novato, CA 94949

2916

Marine Corps Scholarship Foundation Scholarships

Amount: None Specified **Deadline:** Apr 1
Fields/Majors: All Areas Of Study

Candidates must be the son/daughter of an active duty or reserve Marine in good standing, or the son/daughter of a Marine honorably and/or medically discharged or deceased. Must be a high school senior, high school graduate, or college undergraduate. Gross family income must not exceed $40,000 per year. Write to the address below for complete details.

Marine Corps Scholarship Foundation, Inc.
Scholarship Office
P.O. Box 3008
Princeton, NJ 08543

2917

Marinelli Scholarships

Amount: $2,000 **Deadline:** May 31
Fields/Majors: All Areas Of Study

Scholarships for Italian-American undergraduates who are enrolled at Nova University in Florida or the American Academy in Rome. Write to the address below for details.

National Italian American Foundation
Dr. Maria Lombardo, Education Director
1860 Nineteenth Street, NW
Washington, DC 20009

2918

Marion & Eva Peeples Scholarship Foundation

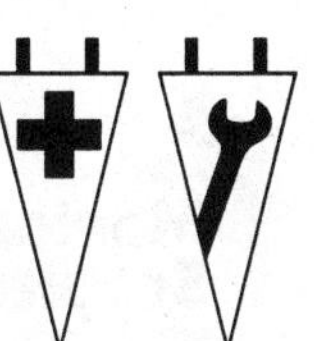

Amount: None Specified **Deadline:** Mar 15
Fields/Majors: Nursing, Dietetics, Industrial Arts Education

Scholarships are awarded to an Indiana high school graduate who is enrolled in an Indiana college or university. Must be pursuing studies in nursing, dietetics, or industrial arts education. Write to the address below for more information.

Peeples Foundation Trust,
Attn: Stacey Gahimer
Bank One Indianapolis, N.
111 Monument Circle, Suite 1501, Box 7700
Indianapolis, IN 46277

2919

Marion Barr Stanfield Art Scholarship

Amount: Varies **Deadline:** Feb 15
Fields/Majors: Art-Painting, Drawing, Sculpturing

Applicants must be active Unitarian Universalist members who are majoring in the following art majors only: painting, drawing, and sculpturing. Financial need must be demonstrated. Write to the address below for details.

Unitarian Universalist Association
Publications Department
25 Beacon St.
Boston, MA 02108

2920

Marion Eugene & John B. Robert Memorial Scholarship

Amount: None Specified **Deadline:** Mar 1
Fields/Majors: Engineering

Scholarships are available at the University of New Mexico for full-time engineering majors who will be participating in the intercollegiate football or basketball programs. Write to the address listed below for information.

University Of New Mexico, Albuquerque
Department Of Student Financial Aid
Mesa Vista Hall North
Albuquerque, NM 87131

2921

Marion Fletcher Scholarship

AMOUNT: Tuition And Fees
DEADLINE: None Specified
FIELDS/MAJORS: Speech and Theater

Award for full-time Mesa State speech and theater students. Must have a GPA of at least 3.0. Write to the address below for more information.

Mesa State College
Office Of Financial Aid
P.O. Box 2647
Grand Junction, CO 81501

2922

Marion T. Wood Scholarship

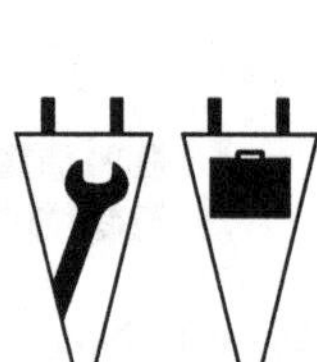

AMOUNT: $1,000 **DEADLINE:** Mar 1
FIELDS/MAJORS: Secretarial/Clerical, Education or Business Administration

Scholarships for business education students who wish to continue education, working toward an office-related career, preferably in the education field. Number of awards per year varies. Awarded to first-year students. Sponsorship by local/area NAEOP will be necessary. The address of the nearest affiliate, if unknown, may be obtained by writing to the address below.

National Association of Educational Office Professionals
PSP Registrar
P.O. Box 12619
Wichita, KS 67277

2923

Marjean Larson Ballard Scholarship

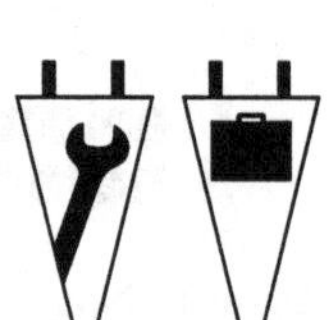
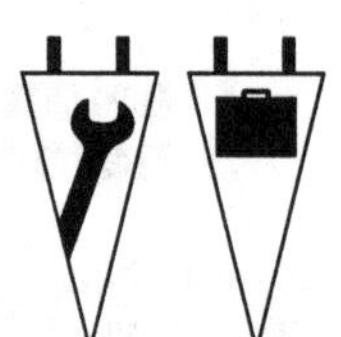

AMOUNT: $600 (approx) **DEADLINE:** Apr 15
FIELDS/MAJORS: Education

Scholarships are available at the University of Utah for full-time juniors, seniors and graduate students in the teacher education program, who have a GPA of at least 3.0. Write to the address below for details.

University Of Utah
Education Advising Center
226 Milton Bennion Hall
Salt Lake City, UT 84112

2924

Marjorie Garland Kuhlmeier Scholarship

AMOUNT: Varies **DEADLINE:** None Specified
FIELDS/MAJORS: All Areas Of Study

Award available to juniors or seniors at Rockford College on the basis of character, academic standing, and financial need. Write to the address below for more information.

Rockford College
Financial Aid Office
5050 East State St.
Rockford,IL 61108

2925

Marjorie Kovler Fellowship

AMOUNT: $2,500 **DEADLINE:** Mar 15
FIELDS/MAJORS: Foreign Studies

Preference is given in this fellowship to research in the area of foreign intelligence and the presidency or a related topic. One award per year. Write to the address below for more information.

John F. Kennedy Library Foundation
William Johnson, Chief Archivist
Columbia Point
Boston, MA 02125

2926

Marjorie Roy Rothermel Scholarship

AMOUNT: $1,500 **DEADLINE:** Feb 15
FIELDS/MAJORS: Mechanical Engineering

Applicants must be master's students in mechanical engineering and ASME members. Write to the address below for details. Please be certain to enclose an SASE with your request.

American Society of Mechanical Engineers Auxiliary, Inc.
ASME Auxiliary
345 East 47th Street
New York, NY 10017

2927

Mark and Catherine Winkler Foundation Grants

AMOUNT: Varies **DEADLINE:** None Specified
FIELDS/MAJORS: All Areas Of Study

Awards available to single parents in any area of study who plan to attend or are enrolled in participating schools. These include Colorado College, George Mason University, Harvard University, and the University of Washington. Write to the address listed below for additional information.

Mark and Catherine Winkler Foundation
4900 Seminary Road
Alexandria, VA 22311

2928

Mark Lindsey Memorial Scholarship

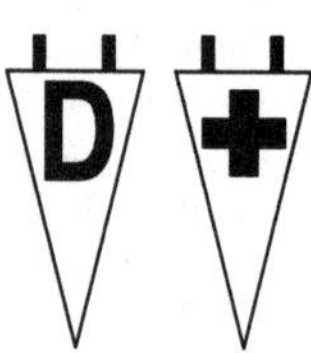

AMOUNT: Varies **DEADLINE:** Mar 1
FIELDS/MAJORS: Medicine

Awards are available at the University of New Mexico for students in need of assistance due to medical conditions or other restrictions. If this criteria cannot be met, then the scholarship shall be awarded to any deserving student. Write to the address below for more information.

University Of New Mexico, Albuquerque
Office Of Financial Aid
Albuquerque, NM 87131

2929

Mark O. Hatfield Scholarship

AMOUNT: $2,000 **DEADLINE:** None Specified
FIELDS/MAJORS: Public Policy

Award for a scholar to do research in the fields above and produce a paper of publishable quality which will reflect the spirit and interests of Senator Mark Hatfield. Write to the address below for more information.

Ripon Educational Fund
Executive Director
227 Massachusetts Ave., NE, Suite 201
Washington, DC 20002

2930

Mark Ulmer Scholarship

AMOUNT: $500 **DEADLINE:** Jun 1
FIELDS/MAJORS: All Areas Of Study

Scholarship available for Native American sophomores, juniors, or seniors who attend one of the schools in the University of North Carolina system. Applicants must have a GPA of at least 2.0, and be U.S. citizens and North Carolina residents. Write to the address below for more information.

Triangle Native American Society
P.O. Box 26841
Raleigh, NC 27611

2931

Mark Zambrano Scholarship

AMOUNT: $1,000 **DEADLINE:** Jan 31
FIELDS/MAJORS: Journalism

Scholarship (1) for junior, senior, or graduate student. Based on academics, need, and a desire to pursue journalism as a career. Applications may be in English or Spanish. Write to the address below for details.

National Association of Hispanic Journalists
529 14th Street, NW
1193 National Press Bldg.
Washington, DC 20045

2932

Mark Zoppel Scholarship

AMOUNT: Varies **DEADLINE:** None Specified
FIELDS/MAJORS: All Areas Of Study

Scholarships for full-time Mesa State international students who have a GPA of at least 3.0. Preference is given to a student formerly enrolled in the intensive English program at the Colorado International Education and Training Institute, Inc. (CIETI). Contact the CIETI for more information.

Mesa State College
Office Of Financial Aid
P.O. Box 2647
Grand Junction, CO 81501

2933

Marketing Scholarship

AMOUNT: $300 **DEADLINE:** None Specified
FIELDS/MAJORS: Marketing

Student must be a junior marketing major with a GPA of 3.25 or higher. Must participate in professional business student organizations. Contact the COBA office for more information.

Southwest Missouri State University
Office Of Financial Aid
901 South National Ave.
Springfield, MO 65804

2934

Marketing/Advertising Scholarship Awards

AMOUNT: $1,000-$2,000 **DEADLINE:** Apr 17
FIELDS/MAJORS: Marketing, Advertising, Communications, Commercial Art

Scholarships for students from Long Island who are in one of the fields of study listed above. Based on transcripts, recommendations, personal statement, and samples of work. Write to the address below for more information.

Long Island Advertising Club, Inc.
Scholarship Committee
34 Richards Road, Suite 100
Port Washington, NY 11050

2935

Martha Fitzpatrick Memorial Scholarships

AMOUNT: $3,000 **DEADLINE:** Mar 15
FIELDS/MAJORS: All Areas Of Study

Awards for Jacksonville State University students who are in any field of study. Write to the address below for more information.

Jacksonville State University
Financial Aid Office
Jacksonville, AL 36265

2936

Martin Agency Scholarships

AMOUNT: $1,500 **DEADLINE:** Feb 15
FIELDS/MAJORS: Agricultural Communications, Agricultural Journalism

Scholarships are available for FFA members pursuing a four-year degree in agricultural journalism or communications. Write to the address below for details.

National FFA Foundation
Scholarship Office
P.O. Box 15160
Alexandria, VA 22309

2937

Martin Luther Award

AMOUNT: $4,000 **DEADLINE:** Jan 15
FIELDS/MAJORS: All Areas Of Study

Awards for new students (freshmen or transfers) who are dependents of full-time professional Lutheran church workers. Must have a GPA of at least 2.0. Renewable. Write to the address below for additional information.

Valparaiso University
Office Of Admissions And Financial Aid
Kretzmann Hall
Valparaiso, IN 46383

2938

Martin Luther King Jr. Memorial Scholarship Fund

AMOUNT: $2,000 **DEADLINE:** Mar 15
FIELDS/MAJORS: Education

Must be a minority active or student member of the CTA, or the dependent child of an active, retired or deceased CTA member. For study in the fields of education or teaching. Write to the address below for details.

California Teachers Association
c/o CTA Human Rights Department
1705 Murchison Drive, P.O. Box 921
Burlingame, CA 94011

2939

Martin Luther King, Jr. Scholarship

Amount: Varies **Deadline:** Feb 1
Fields/Majors: All Areas Of Study

Awards for African American high school seniors who are residents of North Carolina. Priority will be given to children of NCAE members, but other selection criteria include: character, personality, and scholastic achievement. Write to the address below for more details.

North Carolina Association Of Educators
NCAE Minority Affairs Commission
P.O. Box 27347
Raleigh, NC 27611

2940

Martin Luther King, Jr. Scholarship Fund

Amount: Varies **Deadline:** Jan 15
Fields/Majors: All Areas Of Study

Scholarships for Iowa minority students accepted or enrolled in a private or public postsecondary institution listed in Lovejoy's Guide to North Central Accredited Schools. Write to the address below for more information.

Martin Luther King, Jr. Scholarship Fund
1173 25th St.
Des Moines, IA 50311

2941

Mary A. Gardner Scholarship

Amount: $300 **Deadline:** Apr 1
Fields/Majors: Journalism (News-Editorial and News Reporting)

Scholarship for junior or senior journalism student. Must be enrolled in a news-editorial sequence. Based on minimum GPA of 3.0 and career goal in editing or reporting. Application will include statements of qualifications, biography, recommendation, and clippings. Write to the address listed below for information.

Association For Education In Journalism & Mass Communication
Jennifer H. McGill
Univ. Of South Carolina
1621 College St.
Columbia, SC 29208

2942

Mary A. Moore Taubel Scholarship

Amount: $650-$1,000 **Deadline:** Feb 9
Fields/Majors: History

Three awards for juniors with 40 credits at time of application and 12 hours of history. Three awards for seniors with 75 credits at time of application and 24 hours of history. Both levels require an overall GPA of 3.0 and a 3.2 GPA in history courses. Use Bloomsburg University scholarship application. Contact Dr. James Sperry, Chairperson, History Department, for further information.

Bloomsburg University
19 Ben Franklin Hall
400 E. Second St.
Bloomsburg, PA 17815

2943

Mary Ann Reinert Nursing Scholarship

Amount: None Specified **Deadline:** Jul 1
Fields/Majors: Surgical Nursing

Scholarships for nursing students with a primary emphasis on the field of surgical nursing. For residents of Missouri and Kansas in areas served by Heartland Health Foundation (NW Missouri and NE Kansas). Write to the address below for further information.

Heartland Health Foundation
801 Faraon St.
St. Joseph, MO 64501

2944

Mary B. Herrin Scholarships

Amount: None Specified **Deadline:** None Specified
Fields/Majors: English, Speech

Scholarships for English or speech majors at East Tennessee State University. Contact the Department of English, Department of Speech, or the Office of Financial Aid for details.

East Tennessee State University
Office Of Financial Aid
Box 70722
Johnson City, TN 37614

2945

Mary C. Crossman Memorial Scholarship

Amount: Varies **Deadline:** Mar 1
Fields/Majors: Communicative Disorders

Awards are available at the University of New Mexico for full-time juniors or seniors majoring in the fields of communicative disorders. Must demonstrate financial need. Write to the address listed below for information.

University Of New Mexico, Albuquerque
Office Of Financial Aid
Albuquerque, NM 87131

2946

Mary Cassatt Scholarship

Amount: None Specified **Deadline:** May 1
Fields/Majors: All Areas Of Study

Scholarships and grants for women students at Corcoran School of Art. Based on potential. Contact the address below for details.

Corcoran School Of Art
Financial Aid Office
500 17th St., NW
Washington, DC 20006

2947

Mary Clarke Miley Scholarships

AMOUNT: $500-$1,000 **DEADLINE:** Mar 1
FIELDS/MAJORS: Art, Dance, Drama, Music

Scholarships are available at the University of Oklahoma, Norman for fine arts majors, who are of African American or Native American heritage. Write to the address listed below for information.

University Of Oklahoma, Norman
Dean, College of Fine Arts
540 Parrington, Room 122
Norman, OK 73019

2948

Mary Davis Fellowship

AMOUNT: $13,000 **DEADLINE:** Nov 15
FIELDS/MAJORS: Western Art, Visual Art, and Related Areas

Two-year fellowship is available for doctoral scholars researching for the dissertation. One year will be spent in on research, and one year will be spent at the National Gallery of Art. Applicants must know two foreign languages related to the topic of their dissertation and be U.S. citizens or legal residents. Write to the address listed below for information.

National Gallery of Art
Center For Advanced Study In Visual Arts
Predoctoral Fellowship Program
Washington, DC 20565

2949

Mary E. Beyerle Merit Scholarships

AMOUNT: $500-$2,000 **DEADLINE:** None Specified
FIELDS/MAJORS: All Areas Of Study

Scholarships are available to graduating high school seniors who are National Merit Finalists and residents of Maryland, New Jersey, or Pennsylvania. Write to the address listed below for information.

National Merit Scholarship Corporation
1560 Sherman Avenue, Suite 200
Evanston, IL 60201

2950

Mary Helen T. Craig Terrett Nursing Scholarship

AMOUNT: Varies **DEADLINE:** Mar 1
FIELDS/MAJORS: Nursing

Awards are available at the University of New Mexico for nursing students with financial need. Write to the address below or contact the school of nursing for more details.

University Of New Mexico, Albuquerque
Office Of Financial Aid
Albuquerque, NM 87131

2951

Mary Isabel Sibley Fellowship

AMOUNT: $10,000 **DEADLINE:** Jan 15
FIELDS/MAJORS: French Studies, Greek Studies

Fellowship is available to unmarried women between the ages of 23-35 who have completed or are at the dissertation stage of their Ph.D in Greek studies (odd numbered years), or French studies (even numbered years). Write to the Mary Isabel Sibley Fellowship Committee at the address below for details.

Phi Beta Kappa
Mary Isabel Sibley Fellowship Committee
1811 Q Street, NW
Washington, DC 20009

2952

Mary Katona Scholarship

AMOUNT: $500-$1,000 **DEADLINE:** Nov 30
FIELDS/MAJORS: All Areas Of Study

Scholarships are available for Connecticut resident students, enrolled in or planning to enroll in an accredited college or university, who are of Hungarian descent. Based on academic ability, financial need, participation in community activities, and affiliation with Hungarian-American organizations. Must be age 30 or younger. Write to the address listed below for information.

American Hungarian Heritage Association
Ms. Bette S. Johnson
245 Unquowa Road, #107
Fairfield, CT 06430

2953

Mary L. Frymire Kirk Scholarship

AMOUNT: $200 **DEADLINE:** Feb 9
FIELDS/MAJORS: All Areas Of Study

Award for female student. Must demonstrate financial need, academic achievement and activities. Use Bloomsburg University scholarship application. Contact Mrs. Kishbaugh, Financial Aid Office, for further information.

Bloomsburg University
19 Ben Franklin Hall
400 E. Second St.
Bloomsburg, PA 17815

2954

Mary L. Peed Scholarship

AMOUNT: $1,500-$3,000 **DEADLINE:** Mar 1
FIELDS/MAJORS: Music

Award for full-time students at Eastern New Mexico University who are majoring in music and can demonstrate financial need. Applicants must be New Mexico residents and have a GPA of at least 3.0. Write to the address below for more information.

Eastern New Mexico University
College of Fine Arts, Station 16
Portales, NM 88130

2955

Mary Maher Education Grant

AMOUNT: $750 **DEADLINE:** May 1
FIELDS/MAJORS: Early Childhood, Child Development

Student acquires membership in the SCAEYC. The award must be used for courses in early childhood, child development, or for general education. Write to the address below for more information.

California State Polytechnic University, Pomona
College of Agriculture
Building 7, Room 110
Pomona, CA 91768

2956

Mary McClory Scholarship

AMOUNT: $1,500 **DEADLINE:** None Specified
FIELDS/MAJORS: Social Work

Scholarship offered to junior or senior students attending or planning to attend Loyola University, who are pursuing a social work major, with an emphasis on child welfare. The award is renewable if recipient maintains a GPA of at least 3.0 and completes at least two required social work courses or better each year. Write to the address below for details.

Loyola University
Chairperson, Social Work Department
820 North Michigan Avenue
Chicago, IL 60611

2957

Mary McDonald Scholarship

AMOUNT: Varies **DEADLINE:** Mar 1
FIELDS/MAJORS: English

Awards are available at the University of New Mexico for students majoring in English. Applicants must nominated by faculty. Contact the English Department for details.

University Of New Mexico, Albuquerque
Office Of Financial Aid
Albuquerque, NM 87131

2958

Mary McLeod Bethune Scholarship Challenge Grant Fund

AMOUNT: $3,000 **DEADLINE:** None Specified
FIELDS/MAJORS: All Areas Of Study

Applicants must be outstanding high school seniors who will attend the following schools full-time: Florida A & M, Bethune-Cookman College, Edward Waters College, or Florida Memorial College. Applicant must have a minimum 3.0 GPA. Write to the address below for details.

Florida Department Of Education
Office Of Student Financial Assistance
1344 Florida Education Center
Tallahassee, FL 32399

2959

Mary McMillan Scholarship

AMOUNT: Varies **DEADLINE:** None Specified
FIELDS/MAJORS: Physical Therapy

Scholarships are available for physical therapy majors at in their final year of study. Based on academic excellence. Recipients must be nominated by the faculty in an accredited physical therapy or physical therapy assistant program. Contact the program director at your school for more information.

American Physical Therapy Association
1111 North Fairfax Street
Alexander, VA 22314

2960

Mary Meehan Memorial Art Scholarship

AMOUNT: Varies **DEADLINE:** None Specified
FIELDS/MAJORS: Art

Award given to art students demonstrating unusual ability in their field. Write to the address below for more information.

Mercyhurst College
Financial Aid Office
Glenwood Hills
Erie, PA 16546

2961

Mary Moll Jennings Scholarship

AMOUNT: $1,200 **DEADLINE:** Apr 1
FIELDS/MAJORS: All Areas Of Study

Awards for all Sul Ross undergraduates. Freshmen must have a GPA of at least 2.0 to receive the award and continuing students must have a 3.0 GPA or better. Write to the address below for more information.

Sul Ross State University
Financial Aid Office
Box C-113
Alpine, TX 79832

2962

Mary Morrow-Edna Richards Scholarship

AMOUNT: $1,000 (min) **DEADLINE:** Jan 12
FIELDS/MAJORS: Education

Awards for senior year of study at an accredited undergraduate institution in North Carolina. In return for funding recipients agree to teach in N. Carolina for at least two years after graduation. Must be resident of North Carolina. Based on character, scholastic achievement, promise as a teacher and financial need. Application is made through your college or university. Contact the head of the Education Department for more information or write to the address below.

North Carolina Association of Educators
Mary Morrow—Edna Richards Scholarship
P.O. Box 27347
Raleigh, NC 27611

2963

Mary R. Hardwick Scholarship

AMOUNT: None Specified **DEADLINE:** None Specified
FIELDS/MAJORS: All Areas Of Study

Applicants are required to submit an essay describing a relationship possessing the values of nurturance, compassion, collaboration, and respect for all living things. Selection based upon academic record, financial need, and demonstration of the values described in the essay. Contact the director of women's studies program for more information.

Clarion University
104 Egbert Hall
Office Of Financial Aid
Clarion, PA 16214

2964

Mary Rait American Association of University Women Grant (AAUW)

AMOUNT: $600 **DEADLINE:** None Specified
FIELDS/MAJORS: All Areas Of Study

Awards for mature individuals at Mesa State College. Must be returning to earn a bachelor's degree after some years of absence from the academic scene. Contact the American Association of University Women for more details.

Mesa State College
Office Of Financial Aid
P.O. Box 3692
Grand Junction, CO 81501

2965

Mary S. Stotler Scholarship

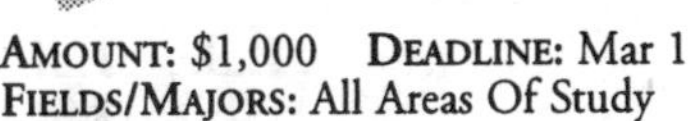

AMOUNT: $1,000 **DEADLINE:** Mar 1
FIELDS/MAJORS: All Areas Of Study

Scholarships are available at the University of Oklahoma, Norman for female students of sophomore status or above. Requires a minimum GPA of at least 3.25. Two or three awards offered annually. Write to the address listed below for information.

University Of Oklahoma, Norman
Office Of Financial Aid Services
731 Elm
Norman, OK 73019

2966

Mary Susan Sieber Memorial Award In History

AMOUNT: Varies **DEADLINE:** Early Spring
FIELDS/MAJORS: History

Awards for sophomore or junior history majors to encourage the further education of underclass majors and minors in history. Contact the Department of History, UW Oshkosh, for more details.

University Of Wisconsin, Oshkosh
Financial Aid Office, Dempsey 104
800 Algoma Blvd.
Oshkosh, WI 54901

2967

Mary Tyler Moore Women In Business Scholarship

AMOUNT: Tuition and Fees **DEADLINE:** Mar 1
FIELDS/MAJORS: Business

Award for a full-time female undergraduate business student who has a GPA of at least 3.0 and has successfully completed 27-40 credit hours by their sophomore year of study. Write to the address below for more information.

Eastern New Mexico University
(Noble Foundation)
ENMU College of Business, Station 49
Portales, NM 88130

2968

Mary Virginia MacRae Nurses Scholarship, Nursing Training Scholarship

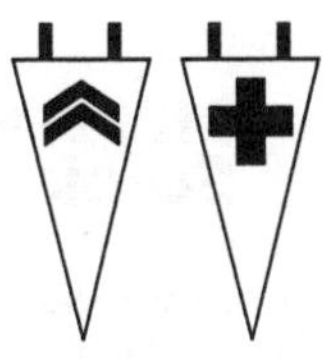

AMOUNT: $400 **DEADLINE:** Jun 1
FIELDS/MAJORS: Nursing

Scholarships for Iowa residents who are or will be attending a school in Iowa and studying nursing. Applicant must be a U.S. citizen, and a descendant of a veteran of WWI, WWII, Korea, Vietnam, Grenada, Lebanon, Panama, or the Persian Gulf. Write to the address listed below for additional information or application.

American Legion Auxiliary
Department Of Iowa
720 Lyon Street
Des Moines, IA 50309

2969

Mary Weaver Evans Scholarship

AMOUNT: $250 **DEADLINE:** None Specified
FIELDS/MAJORS: Elementary-Early Childhood Education

Award for full-time employee of a school district teaching kindergarten through grade 6. B.U. candidacy standing as graduate student in M.Ed. program in elementary education or M.S. in early childhood education. Must have a 4.0 GPA after completion of 9-12 graduate credits. Contact the chairperson of the Curriculum and Foundations Department for further information.

Bloomsburg University
19 Ben Franklin Hall
400 E. Second St.
Bloomsburg, PA 17815

2970

Mary Weiking Franken Scholarship

AMOUNT: $650 **DEADLINE:** Mar 1
FIELDS/MAJORS: Home Economics

Open to Phi Upsilon Omicron member undergraduates pursuing a home economics degree with a major in child/family or home economics education. Write to the address below for details.

Phi Upsilon Omicron National Office
Ohio State University, 171 Mount Hall
1050 Carmack Road
Columbus, OH 43210

2971

Maryland District 5 Scholarships

AMOUNT: Varies **DEADLINE:** Mar 24
FIELDS/MAJORS: All Areas Of Study

Awards are available for graduating high school seniors from Maryland District 5 who are planning to attend a school in Maryland. Awards are based primarily on academic achievement and total school participation. To request further information, submit a letter of application indicating the plans for the scholarship, which school the applicant plans to attend and why, an official high school transcript, a copy of SAT scores, and a letter of recommendation to the address below.

Delegate Richard N. Dixon, District 5
Maryland House of Delegates District 5 Scholarship Committee
156 West Main St.
Westminster, MD 21157

2972 Maryland Farm Bureau Scholarship

AMOUNT: $500 **DEADLINE:** Sep 1
FIELDS/MAJORS: All Areas Of Study

Three scholarships for members or children of members of the Maryland Farm Bureau. One award is not restricted by major, two awards are given to students studying agriculture. For study at any community college or four-year institution. For undergraduate study only. Write to the address below for details.

Maryland Farm Bureau
8930 Liberty Rd
Randallstown, MD 21133

2973 Maryland State Nursing Scholarships

AMOUNT: $2,400 (max) **DEADLINE:** Jun 30
FIELDS/MAJORS: Nursing

Candidates must be Maryland residents attending a Maryland nursing school. Must agree to serve in a Maryland nurse shortage area for one year of each year of the award. Available to undergraduates and graduates, full or part-time students. Renewable. Requires 3.0 GPA. Write to address below for details. The SSA also administers the professional scholarships for nursing students (application for that award is made by filing an FAF).

Maryland State Higher Education Commission
16 Francis Street
Annapolis, MD 21401

2974 MAS Jesse Wrench Scholarship

AMOUNT: $500 **DEADLINE:** None Specified
FIELDS/MAJORS: Archaeology, Anthropology, Paleontology

Awards for students studying in one of the areas listed above at University of Missouri-Columbia. Write to the Society at the address below for details.

Missouri Archaeological Society
P.O. Box 958
Columbia, MO 65205

2975 Mason C. Gilpin Memorial Scholarship

AMOUNT: Varies **DEADLINE:** Mar 11
FIELDS/MAJORS: Agriculture

Awards for freshmen students at Penn State University who are studying agriculture. Based on merit. Write to the address below for more information.

Pennsylvania Master Farmers Association
College of Agriculture, Associate Dean
Penn State University
University Park, PA 16802

2976 Mason Crickard Fund

AMOUNT: None Specified **DEADLINE:** Mar 15
FIELDS/MAJORS: All Areas Of Study

Scholarships for residents of West Virginia, specifically in Randolph, Upshur, Kanawha, or Putnam Counties. For any level of study. Preference is given to students who will be attending West Virginia Wesleyan College. Write to the address below for details.

Greater Kanawha Valley Foundation
Scholarship Committee
P.O. Box 3041
Charleston, WV 25331

2977 Masonic-Range Science Scholarship

AMOUNT: Varies **DEADLINE:** Jan 15
FIELDS/MAJORS: Range Science

Scholarships are available for graduating high school seniors and current freshmen who are majoring in range science. For more information write to the address below.

Society For Range Management
Office Of The Exexcutive Vice President
1839 York Street
Denver, CO 80206

2978 Mass Media Science And Engineering Fellows Program

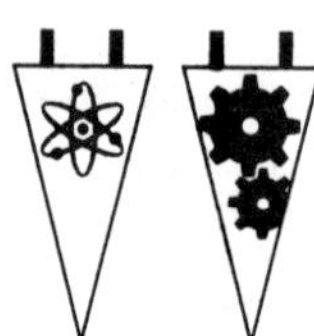

AMOUNT: None Specified **DEADLINE:** Jan 15
FIELDS/MAJORS: Engineering/Science

The Mass Media Science and Engineering Fellows Program offers an opportunity for advanced students in the natural and social sciences and engineering to spend ten weeks during the summer working as reporters, researchers, or production assistants with media organizations nationwide. A modest stipend is included to help cover living expenses for the duration of the fellowship. Write to "Mass Media Science and Engineering Fellows Program" at the below address for details.

American Association For The Advancement Of Science
Amie E. King, Coordinator
1333 H Street, NW
Washington, DC 20005

2979 Massachusetts Arborist Association Scholarship

AMOUNT: Varies **DEADLINE:** Oct 1
FIELDS/MAJORS: Arboriculture, Urban Forestry, Park Management

Awards for students in the fields of study listed above who have good academic standing and financial need. For entering sophomores, juniors, or seniors. Contact Dr. Dennis Ryan or Mr. Tom Houston, Holdsworth Natural Resources Center, for more information.

University Of Massachusetts, Amherst
Holdsworth Natural Resources Center
Amherst, MA 01003

2980 Massachusetts Tree Wardens And Foresters Association Scholarship

AMOUNT: Varies **DEADLINE:** Dec 15
FIELDS/MAJORS: Arboriculture, Urban Forestry, Park Management

Awards for students in the fields of study listed above who have good academic standing and financial need. For entering sophomores, juniors, or seniors. Contact Dr. Dennis Ryan or Mr. Tom Houston,

Holdsworth Natural Resources Center, for more information.

University Of Massachusetts, Amherst
Holdsworth Natural Resources Center
Amherst, MA 01003

2981

Master Printers Of America-Donald E. Summer/A.J. Viehman Awards

Amount: Varies **Deadline:** Mar 1
Fields/Majors: Industrial Relations, Human Resource Management

Awards are available at the University of New Mexico for graduate students in the areas of study above. Contact: Education Trust Fund, 1730 North Lynn St., Arlington, VA 22209, for more details.

University Of New Mexico, Albuquerque
Office Of Financial Aid
Albuquerque, NM 87131

2982

Master's Thesis Fellowships

Amount: $2,500 **Deadline:** May 1
Fields/Majors: U.S. Military And Naval History

Awards are available for master's degree candidates for thesis research in any area of history relevant to the Marine Corps (military and naval history, etc.). Applicants must be U.S. citizens or nationals. It is expected that part of the research will be undertaken at the Marine Corps Historical Archives in Washington D.C. Write to the address listed below for information

Marine Corps Historical Center
Building 58
Washington Navy Yard
Washington, DC 20374

2983

Mastin Scholarship

Amount: Tuition **Deadline:** Mar 1
Fields/Majors: Science, Mathematics

Awards for freshmen at Lake Erie College who scored a 27 or better on their ACT or are National Merit Finalists. They must be pursuing a degree in the natural sciences or mathematics. Renewable with a GPA of 3.0. Write to the address below for more information.

Lake Erie College
Financial Aid Office
391 W. Washington St.
Painesville, OH 44077

2984

MASWE Memorial Scholarship

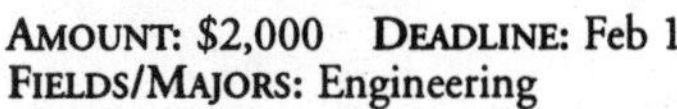

Amount: $2,000 **Deadline:** Feb 1
Fields/Majors: Engineering

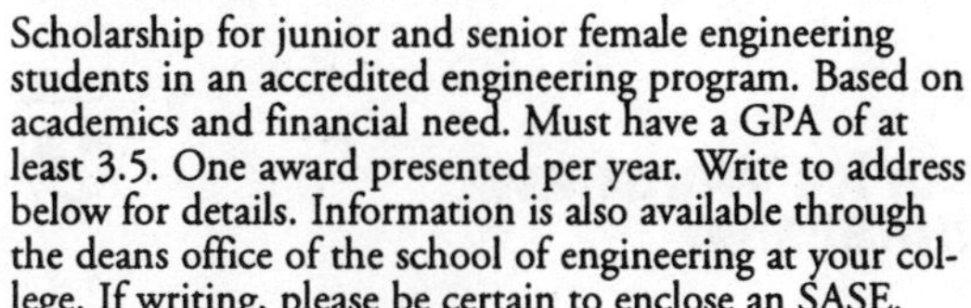

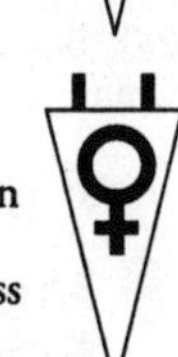

Scholarship for junior and senior female engineering students in an accredited engineering program. Based on academics and financial need. Must have a GPA of at least 3.5. One award presented per year. Write to address below for details. Information is also available through the deans office of the school of engineering at your college. If writing, please be certain to enclose an SASE.

Society Of Women Engineers
120 Wall Street, 11th Floor
New York, NY 10005

2985

Matching Fund Scholarship

Amount: $500 (max) **Deadline:** Jun 1
Fields/Majors: All Areas Of Study

RMC will match dollar for dollar the amount that your church commits to fund you. A letter from the church stating their commitment to fund you must be submitted to the financial aid office. Write to the address below for more information.

Rocky Mountain College
Office Of Financial Assistance
1511 Poly Drive
Billings, MT 59102

2986

Materials Engineering Departmental Scholarships

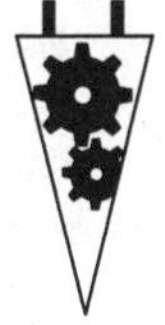

Amount: Varies **Deadline:** Feb 1
Fields/Majors: Materials Engineering

Scholarships are available at the University of Utah for full-time students enrolled in a materials engineering program. Write to the address below for details.

University Of Utah
Dr. Bill Callister
304 Emro
Salt Lake City, UT 84112

2987

Materials Science And Engineering Scholarships At Case Western

Amount: $3,000 **Deadline:** Feb 1
Fields/Majors: Materials Science and Engineering

Five scholarships offered to entering freshmen at Case Western Reserve University who intend to major in materials science and engineering. Scholarships are renewable for each of the four years of undergraduate study if high academic achievement is maintained. Write to the address below for details.

Case Western Reserve University
Office Of Financial Aid, 109 Pardee Hall
10900 Euclid Avenue
Cleveland, OH 44106

2988

Math/Science/Foreign Language Scholarship

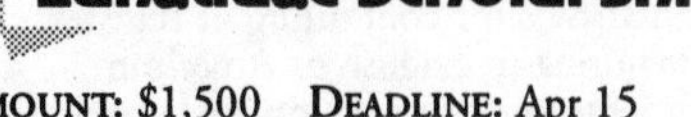

Amount: $1,500 **Deadline:** Apr 15
Fields/Majors: Secondary Education

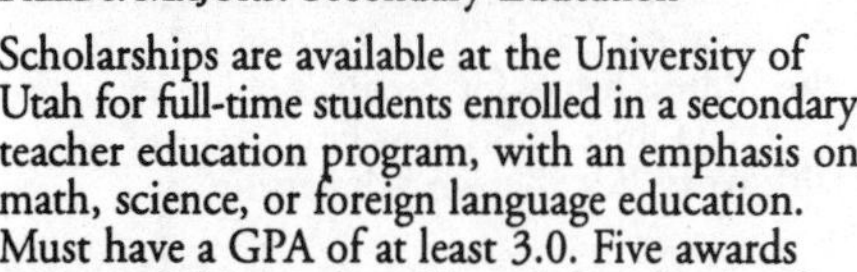

Scholarships are available at the University of Utah for full-time students enrolled in a secondary teacher education program, with an emphasis on math, science, or foreign language education. Must have a GPA of at least 3.0. Five awards per year. Write to the address below for details.

University Of Utah
Education Advising Center
226 Milton Bennion Hall
Salt Lake City, UT 84112

2989
Mathematics Departmental Scholarships

AMOUNT: Varies **DEADLINE:** Feb 15
FIELDS/MAJORS: Mathematics

Scholarships are available at the University of Utah for full-time students majoring in mathematics. Four scholarships are offered annually. Write to the address below for information.

University Of Utah
Dr. Leslie Glaser
239 John A. Widtsoe Building
Salt Lake City, UT 84112

2990
Mathilda Gallmeyer Scholarship

AMOUNT: $500-$2,500 **DEADLINE:** Apr 14
FIELDS/MAJORS: Fine Arts, Painting

Scholarships for residents of Kent County who are undergraduate art majors with an emphasis on painting. Applicant must have a GPA of at least 2.75 and demonstrate artistic talent. Write to the address below for details.

Grand Rapids Foundation
209-C Waters Bldg., 161 Ottawa Avenue, NW
Grand Rapids, MI 49503

2991
Matthew Gadziala Scholarship, Class Of 1941

AMOUNT: Tuition (max) **DEADLINE:** None Specified
FIELDS/MAJORS: All Areas Of Study

Awards to SUNY at Albany undergraduates who demonstrate both academic achievement and financial need. Write to the address below for more information.

State University Of New York, Albany
Administration Building, Room 152
1400 Washington Ave.
Albany, NY 12222

2992
Maud E. McPherson Scholarship In English and American Literature

AMOUNT: Varies **DEADLINE:** Apr 30
FIELDS/MAJORS: English & American Literature

These are need-based scholarships for continuing or transfer undergraduate students majoring in English or American literature. Continuing students must have completed at least fifteen semester hours; transfer students, thirty semester hours. Must demonstrate financial need and have a GPA of 2.7 or better. Write to the address below for details. Application packets are available at the Office of Student Financial Aid (third floor Rice Hall); write "McPherson Scholarship" at the top of the form.

George Washington University
Office Of Student Financial Assistance
Rice Hall, Suite 310
Washington, DC 20052

2993
Maud May Babcock Scholarship, Wilson Special Departmental Scholarship

AMOUNT: Varies **DEADLINE:** Feb 1
FIELDS/MAJORS: Speech Communication, Journalism, Mass Communications

Scholarships are available at the University of Utah for full-time students enrolled in one of the areas listed above. For entering freshmen. Write to the address below for details.

University Of Utah
Scholarship Chairperson
301 Leroy Cowles Building
Salt Lake City, UT 84112

2994
Maude Stewart Smyre Scholarship

AMOUNT: None Specified **DEADLINE:** None Specified
FIELDS/MAJORS: All Areas Of Study

Scholarships at ETSU Kingsport University Center who are residents of Scott County (VA), or Hawkins and Sullivan Counties (TN). Contact the Office of Financial Aid at the address below.

East Tennessee State University
Office Of Financial Aid
Box 70722
Johnson City, TN 37614

2995
Maude Winkler Scholarship Awards

AMOUNT: $250-$1,000 **DEADLINE:** Apr 15
FIELDS/MAJORS: All Areas Of Study

Applicants must be born deaf or became deaf before acquiring language. Must use speech/residual hearing or lip-reading as primary communication and be a student entering or attending a college or university program for hearing students. Five scholarships are awarded each year. Write to the address below for details.

Alexander Graham Bell Association For The Deaf
3417 Volta Place, NW
Washington, DC 20007

2996
Maureen H. Wilson Scholarship

AMOUNT: Varies **DEADLINE:** None Specified
FIELDS/MAJORS: Theater

Awards for full-time Mesa State students enrolled in theater. Must have a GPA of at least 2.5. Contact the fine arts department for more information.

Mesa State College
Financial Aid Office
P.O. Box 2647
Grand Junction, CO 81501

2997
Maurice Warshaw Scholarship

AMOUNT: Varies **DEADLINE:** Feb 15
FIELDS/MAJORS: Political Science

Scholarships are available at the University of Utah for full-time students majoring in political science, who are entering freshmen. Write to the address below for information.

University Of Utah
Dr. Howard Lehman
252 Orson Spencer Hall
Salt Lake City, UT 84112

2998 Maury A. Hubbard Scholarships

Amount: $1,000 **Deadline:** May 1
Fields/Majors: Agriculture, Life Sciences

Scholarships for incoming freshmen and returning or transfer students based on academic merit, financial need, and extracurricular activities. Write to the address below for more information.

Virginia Tech College Of Agriculture And Life Sciences
Dr. John M. White, Associate Dean
1060 Litton Reaves Hall
Blacksburg, VA 4061

2999 Maxie Carroll Memorial Scholarship

Amount: $250 **Deadline:** None Specified
Fields/Majors: All Areas Of Study

Awards for freshmen or sophomores at Mesa State College who are full-time students and active in the varsity baseball program. Must have a GPA of at least 2.5. Contact the baseball coach for further details.

Mesa State College
Financial Aid Office, P.O. Box 2684
Grand Junction, CO 81501

3000 Maxine Williams Scholarship Fund

Amount: $500 **Deadline:** Feb 1, Jun 1
Fields/Majors: Medical Assisting

Applicants must be committed to a medical assisting career, hold a high school diploma or the equivalent, and be enrolled in a postsecondary medical assisting program. Scholarships awarded on the basis of interest, need, and aptitude.

American Association Of Medical Assistants Endowment
20 N. Wacker Dr., Suite 1575
Chicago, IL 60606

3001 May Company Scholarship

Amount: Varies **Deadline:** Feb 29
Fields/Majors: Marketing

Awards for students of color in their sophomore, junior, or senior year who have financial need and strong academic performance. Applications for school of management scholarships will be available in the SOM. Development Office, Room 206.

University Of Massachusetts, Amherst
School of Management Development Office, Room 206
Amherst, MA 01003

3002 Mayme and Herbert Frank Educational Fund

Amount: Varies **Deadline:** Apr 1, Oct 1
Fields/Majors: International Federalism

Awards for students interested in international federalism to do research and complete a project on a proposed topic in that area. For graduate study. Write to the address below for more information.

Association To Unite The Democracies
1506 Pennsylvania Ave., SE
Washington, DC 20003

3003 Mayme Frazier Scholarship

Amount: None Specified **Deadline:** None Specified
Fields/Majors: Nursing

Awards are available for ETSU students majoring in nursing. Contact the Dean's Office, College of Nursing, for more information.

East Tennessee State University
Office Of Financial Aid, Box 70722
Johnson City, TN 37614

3004 Mayport Naval Officers' Wives' Club Scholarship

Amount: Varies **Deadline:** Mar 15
Fields/Majors: All Areas Of Study

Scholarships for children of regular/reserve USN, USMC, or USCG members who are stationed/have served at Naval Station Mayport (FL). Must have graduated or expect to graduate from an accredited high school or equivalent institution and must intend to enter a college or university to earn an undergraduate or graduate degree. Renewable. Write to the address below for details (please be certain to enclose a self-addressed stamped envelope and indicate that your parent(s) is(are) currently stationed or has completed one PCS tour of duty at MAS Mayport.

Mayport Naval Officers' Wives' Club, Attn: Scholarship
P.O. Box 280004
Mayport, FL 32228

3005 Maytag Scholarships In Business Administration

Amount: $500 **Deadline:** Mar 1
Fields/Majors: Accounting, Marketing

Scholarships are available at the University of Iowa for full-time undergraduate business majors pursuing a degree in either accounting or marketing. Write to the address listed below for information.

University Of Iowa
College of Business Admin., Suite W160,
108 Pappajohn Business Admin. Bldg.
Iowa City, IA 52245

3006 Mazzuchelli Catholic High School Enrichment Award

Amount: Half Tuition **Deadline:** Mar 15
Fields/Majors: All Areas Of Study

Applicants must be incoming freshmen who graduated from a Catholic-sponsored high school. Students who have been involved in community service projects are encouraged to apply.

Edgewood College, Office Of Admissions
855 Woodrow Street
Madison, WI 53711

3007

MBA Scholarships

Amount: $3,000-$10,000 **Deadline:** Apr 6
Fields/Majors: All Areas Of Business

Awards for minority students who are enrolled in full-time graduate or doctoral business programs. Based on financial need, activities, and GPA. Write to the address below for more information.

National Black MBA Association, Inc.
180 N. Michigan Ave., Suite 1515
Chicago, IL 60601

3008

MBNA Scholarship Program

Amount: $1,000 **Deadline:** None Specified
Fields/Majors: Automotive Technology

Awards for minority high school graduates who have successfully completed at least two years in the high school auto mechanic program, or have aspirations to pursue a career in the automotive industry. For students in the Chicago metropolitan area with a GPA of 2.5 or greater.

Mercedes-Benz Of North America
Ms. Gina Blake, Chicago Urban League
4510 South Michigan Ave.
Chicago, IL 60653

3009

M.C. Roberts Memorial Law Scholarship

Amount: Varies **Deadline:** Jun 1
Fields/Majors: Law

Applicants must be five-year residents of the County of Peoria, IL. Must have completed all studies that would allow for student to enroll in an accredited L.L.B. or J.D. degree program. Scholarship is open to unmarried male applicants only. Based on need.

First Of America Trust Company
Trustee Of The MC Roberts Fund
301 Southwest Adams Street, P.O. Box 749
Peoria, IL 61652

3010

McAllister Memorial And Burnside Memorial Scholarships

Amount: $1,000 **Deadline:** Mar 31
Fields/Majors: Aviation

Scholarships open to junior and senior undergraduates studying in a non-engineering aviation program. Must have a GPA of at least 3.25. Write to the address below for details.

AOPA Air Safety Foundation, University Aviation Association
McAllister & Burnside Scholarships
21 Aviation Way
Frederick, MD 21701

3011

McAuley Alumni Scholarships

Amount: $1,000 **Deadline:** Mar 15, Nov 15
Fields/Majors: All Areas Of Study

Awards for entering students with outstanding academic credentials and involvement in community and extracurricular activities. Preference is given to children of alumni. Renewable with a GPA of at least 3.0.

Gwynedd-Mercy College
Student Financial Aid
Sumneytown Pike
Gwynedd Valley, PA 19437

3012

McGraw Foundation Merit Scholarships

Amount: $500-$2,000 **Deadline:** None Specified
Fields/Majors: All Areas Of Study

Scholarships are available to graduating high school seniors who are National Merit Finalists and residents of the Chicago area. Two awards are offered annually. Write to the address listed below for information.

National Merit Scholarship Corporation
1560 Sherman Avenue, Suite 200
Evanston, IL 60201

3013

MCI Telecommunications "Strategy & Technology" Award

Amount: $5,000 **Deadline:** Oct 15
Fields/Majors: Computer Science

Scholarships are available at the University of Iowa for full-time female or minority freshman or first semester sophomore students who are in the top 25% of their graduating class. Applicant must be enrolled in the college of engineering or department of computer science. Potential for a summer job at an MCI strategy and technology location as well. Renewable for up to five years.

University Of Iowa
Office Of Student Financial Aid
208 Calvin Hall
Iowa City, IA 2245

3014

McKesson Corporation Scholarship

Amount: $500 **Deadline:** Feb 1
Fields/Majors: Pharmacy

Scholarships are available at the University of Utah for full-time senior pharmacy majors.

University Of Utah
College Of Pharmacy
Office Of Student Affairs
Salt Lake City, UT 84112

3015

McKnight Awards In Neuroscience

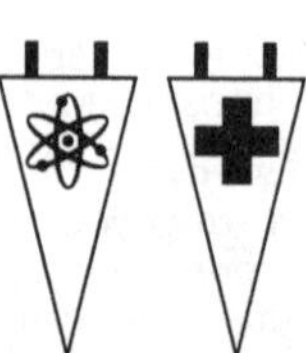

Amount: Varies **Deadline:** Varies
Fields/Majors: Neuroscience

Awards for students at the doctoral or postdoctoral level who are doing research in the area of neuroscience.

McKnight Endowment Fund For Neuroscience
600 TCF Tower
121 South Eighth St.
Minneapolis, MN 55402

3016
McKnight Doctoral Fellowship Program

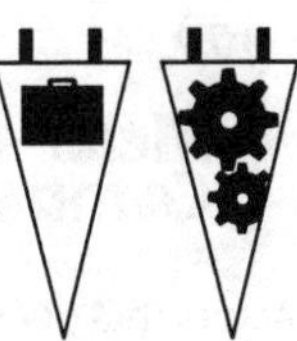

AMOUNT: $16,000 (max) **DEADLINE:** Jan 15
FIELDS/MAJORS: See Below

Up to 25 fellowships for African American doctoral students at participating Florida universities. Not for study toward M.D., D.B.A., D.D.S., J.D., or D.V.M. The applicant must be a U.S. citizen. For study in agriculture, biology, business administration, chemistry, computer science, engineering, marine biology, mathematics, physics, or psychology

Florida Endowment Fund For Higher Education
201 E. Kennedy Blvd.
Suite 1525
Tampa, FL 33602

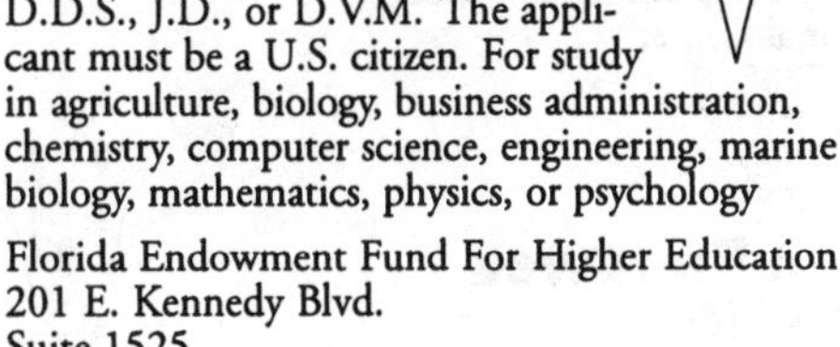

3017
McMahon Memorial Scholarships

AMOUNT: $5,000 **DEADLINE:** Feb 15
FIELDS/MAJORS: News Journalism, Broadcasting

Scholarships are available at the University of Oklahoma, Norman for freshmen majoring in one of the above areas. Based on high school grades, test scores, and personal interviews.

University Of Oklahoma, Norman
School Of Journalism And Mass Communications
860 Van Vleet Oval
Norman, OK 73019

3018
McWane Foundation Scholarships

AMOUNT: $6,000 **DEADLINE:** Mar 1
FIELDS/MAJORS: All Areas Of Study

Awards for high school seniors with an ACT score of 29 or better and a GPA of at least 3.5. Renewable with a GPA of 3.0 or higher.

Auburn University
Office Of Student Financial Aid
203 Mary Martin Hall
Auburn University, AL 36849

3019
Mead C. Armstrong Endowed Memorial Scholarships

AMOUNT: Varies **DEADLINE:** None Specified
FIELDS/MAJORS: Biblical Education

Awards are available for students at Cedarville College majoring in biblical education. Must have a GPA of at least 2.0. Write to the address below for more information.

Cedarville College
Financial Aid Office
P.O. Box 601
Cedarville, OH 45314

3020
Meats Evaluation Scholarships

AMOUNT: $1,000 **DEADLINE:** Feb 15
FIELDS/MAJORS: Animal Science, Food Science (Meat Emphasis), Meat Science

Scholarships are available for FFA members pursuing a four-year degree in animal, meat, or food science.

National FFA Foundation
Scholarship Office
P.O. Box 15160
Alexandria, VA 22309

3021
Mechanical Engineering Department Alumni Fund Scholarships

AMOUNT: Varies **DEADLINE:** Mar 1
FIELDS/MAJORS: Mechanical Engineering

Awards are available at the University of New Mexico for undergraduates enrolled in the mechanical engineering department. Must demonstrate financial need and academic ability.

University Of New Mexico, Albuquerque
Office Of Financial Aid
Albuquerque, NM 87131

3022
Mechanical Engineering Departmental Scholarships

AMOUNT: Varies **DEADLINE:** Feb 1
FIELDS/MAJORS: Mechanical Engineering

Scholarships are available at the University of Utah for full-time students enrolled in a mechanical engineering program.

University Of Utah
Dr. James Strozier
2140 Merrill Engineering Building
Salt Lake City, UT 84112

3023
Mechanical Engineering Scholarships

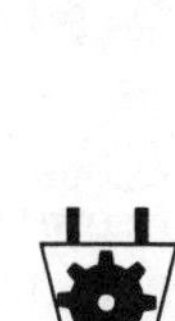

AMOUNT: Varies **DEADLINE:** Mar 1
FIELDS/MAJORS: Mechanical Engineering

Awards for graduates of UMass who are enrolled in a graduate program in the department of mechanical engineering. Based on academic excellence. The applicants thesis or dissertation should be in the area of design. Contact the Department Head, Mechanical Engineering, for more information.

University Of Massachusetts, Amherst
255 Whitmore Administration Bldg.
Box 38230
Amherst, MA 01003

3024
Media Relations Intern

AMOUNT: None Specified
DEADLINE: None Specified
FIELDS/MAJORS: English Education, English Communications, Journalism Education and/or experience in English communications or journalism.

Excellent written, verbal, and organizational skills. Ability to work independently and with IBM PC. For Florida minority students only.

Nature Conservancy Communications Manager,
Florida Chapter 222
South Westmonte Dr., Suite 300
Altamonte Springs, FL 32714

3025

Medical Auxiliary Loan Foundation Loans

Amount: $2,000 **Deadline:** Varies
Fields/Majors: Healthcare

Low interest (6%) loans for upper division healthcare students from El Paso County, Co (exception: pre-medical programs do not apply. Applicant must already be accepted into medical school). Based on academics and need. Repayment starts six months after graduation. Write to the address below for details.

Medical Auxiliary Loan Foundation
P.O. Box 7694
Colorado Springs, CO 80933

3026

Medical Society Of Broome County

Amount: $2,000 **Deadline:** May 1
Fields/Majors: Medicine

Awards are given to students attending medical school in Broome County, or to Broome County residents attending medical school out of the area. Assistance is given primarily to upperclassmen and students who have received funding in past years. Loans are to be repaid within five years of completion of residency training.

Medical Society Of Broome County
4513 Old Vesta Rd.
Vestal, NY 13850

3027

Medical Student Fellowships

Amount: $2,000 **Deadline:** Mar 1
Fields/Majors: Medicine-Epilepsy Research

Research grants for medical students to perform research project related to epilepsy. A faculty advisor/investigator must accept responsibility for the study and its supervision. Write to the address below for details.

Epilepsy Foundation Of America
Fellowship Programs
4351 Garden City Drive
Landover, MD 20785

3028

Medical Student Loan Program

Amount: $5,000 Per Year **Deadline:** None Specified
Fields/Majors: Medicine

Loan for full-time medical students at an approved West Virginia school of medicine. Applicants must not be in default on any previous student loans and they must meet any designated academic standards that have been set. Loans will be forgiven at a rate of $5,000 for each period of twelve consecutive months of full-time practice in a medically underserved area in West Virginia. Write to the address below for more information.

West Virginia Student And Educational Services
Loan Administrator
P.O. Box 4007
Charleston, WV 25364

3029

Meier & Frank, May Company Scholarship

Amount: $1,000 **Deadline:** None Specified
Fields/Majors: Business, Liberal Arts

Awards are available at Portland State University for minority students who are majoring in business or the liberal arts. Must be a U.S. citizen or resident alien to apply.

Portland State University
Educational Equity Programs And Services
120 Smith Memorial Center
Portland, OR 97207

3030

Mel Allen Endowed Scholarship

Award: Tuition & Fees **Deadline:** Feb 15
Fields/Majors: Communications

Scholarship available for full time freshmen entering the College of Communications at the University of Alabama. Set up to honor hall of fame broadcaster Mel Allen.

Kappa Nu Fraternity
College Of Communication, University Of Alabama
P.O. Box 870172
Tuscaloosa, AL 35487

3031

Melba Schumacher Scholarship

Award: None Specified
Deadline: None Specified
Fields/Majors: Nursing

Scholarships are open to female undergraduate nursing students who are graduates of Indianapolis or Marion County public high schools and demonstrate financial need.

Indiana University/Purdue University, Indianapolis
School Of Nursing
1111 Middle Dr., Nu 122
Indianapolis, IN 46202

3032

Melinda Bealmear Endowed Memorial Scholarship

Amount: None Specified **Deadline:** Mar 1
Fields/Majors: Biology

Scholarships are available at the University of New Mexico for full-time graduate biology majors. Write to the address listed below for information.

University Of New Mexico, Albuquerque
Department Of Student Financial Aid
Mesa Vista Hall North
Albuquerque, NM 87131

3033

Mellinger Foundation Awards

Amount: Varies **Deadline:** May 1
Fields/Majors: All Areas Of Study

Scholarships are available at the University of Illinois for Illinois or Iowa residents who demonstrate academic ability.

Mellinger Education Foundation
1025 East Broadway
Monmouth, IL 61462

3034

Mellon Fellowships In Humanistic Studies

AMOUNT: Tuition + $13,750 **DEADLINE:** Dec 31
FIELDS/MAJORS: Humanities

Beginning graduate students only. Program is designed to attract and support fresh talent of outstanding ability enrolled in a program leading to a Ph.D. in one of the humanistic disciplines. Must be a U.S. citizen or permanent resident. These fellowships do not support the more quantifiable social sciences (law, library science, social work, education). The deadline to request an application is Dec 9.

Woodrow Wilson National Fellowship Foundation
CN 5329
Princeton, NJ 08543

3035

Mellon Post-Doctoral Fellowship Program

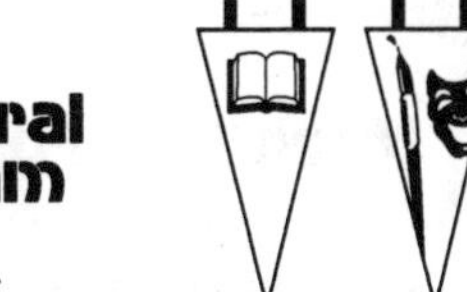

AMOUNT: $28,000 **DEADLINE:** Jan 4
FIELDS/MAJORS: Anthropology, History, Music, Russian Lit., German And Romance Studies

Fellowships for scholars and non-tenured teachers in the above fields who completed their Ph.D. requirements in the last five years. U.S. citizenship, Canadian citizenship, or permanent residency required. These are residential fellowships at Cornell. three or four fellows per year. Must have Ph.D. in hand at time of application.

Cornell University
Agnes Sirrine, Program Administrator
27 East Ave., A.D. White Center
Ithaca, NY 14853

3036

Melva T. Owen Memorial Scholarship

AMOUNT: $2,500 **DEADLINE:** Mar 1
FIELDS/MAJORS: All Areas Of Study

Scholarship for an outstanding entering freshman. Must be legally blind.

American Council Of The Blind
Scholarship Coordinator
1155 15th St., NW, Suite 720
Washington, DC 20005

3037

Melva T. Owen Memorial, Mozelle & Willard Gold Memorial Scholarships

AMOUNT: $3,000-$4,000 **DEADLINE:** Mar 31
FIELDS/MAJORS: All Areas Of Study

Award recipient must be legally blind. This award program is designed to aid blind students achieve financial and physical independence.

National Federation Of The Blind
Mrs. Peggy Elliott, Chairman
814 Fourth Ave., Suite 200
Grinnell, IA 50112

3038

Melvin Howard '57 Honors Research Fellowship In Management

AMOUNT: Varies **DEADLINE:** Feb 29
FIELDS/MAJORS: Management

Graduate research fellowships to support students performing senior-year research in connection with an honors thesis. Applications for School of Management scholarships will be available in the SOM Development Office, Room 206.

University Of Massachusetts, Amherst
SOM Development Office, Room 206
Amherst, MA 01003

3039

Member's And Director's Scholarships

AMOUNT: $350 **DEADLINE:** Jun 1
FIELDS/MAJORS: All Areas Of Study

Awards for undergraduates who are initiated members of Tau Kappa Epsilon and at the junior or senior level of study. Applicants should have demonstrated exceptional understanding of the importance of good alumni relations and have excelled in the promotion of alumni relations. Write to the address below for more information.

TKE Educational Foundation
Director Of Development
8645 Founders Road
Indianapolis, IN 46268

3040

Memorial Conservation Scholarships

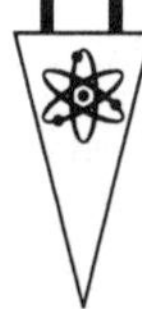

AMOUNT: $1,000 **DEADLINE:** Oct 28
FIELDS/MAJORS: Conservation And Related Fields

Scholarship offered to New Jersey residents in their junior or senior year in college majoring in a field related to the conservation of natural resources. Based upon financial need, academic ability and involvement in extracurricular activities related to conservation. Write to the address below for details.

New Jersey Department Of Agriculture
New Jersey Assoc. Of Conservation Dists.
CN 330, Room 204
Trenton, NJ 08625

3041

Memorial Education Fellowship

AMOUNT: $2,000 **DEADLINE:** Mar 1
FIELDS/MAJORS: Varies

Applicants must be women maintaining legal residence in Massachusetts for at least five years and present a letter of endorsement from the sponsoring women's club in your community. The field of study varies each year. Write to the address below for details.

General Federation Of Women's Clubs Of Massachusetts
Chairman Of Trustees, 245 Dutton Road
P.O. Box 679
Sudbury, MA 01776

3042

Memorial Nurses Training Foundation Scholarship

AMOUNT: Varies **DEADLINE:** None Specified
FIELDS/MAJORS: Nursing

Awards for nursing students at St. Petersburg Junior College at any level of study. Write to the address below or contact the Nursing Program, Health Education Center for more details.

St. Petersburg Junior College, Financial Aid Office
P.O. Box 13489
St. Petersburg, FL 33733

3043

Mental Health Minority Research Fellowship Program

AMOUNT: Varies **DEADLINE:** Feb 28
FIELDS/MAJORS: Social Work

Awards for minorities who have a master's degree in social work and will begin a full-time program leading to a doctoral degree in social work. Applicants must be U.S. citizens or permanent residents and demonstrate a potential for success in their studies. Write to the address below for more information.

National Institute Of Mental Health
1600 Duke St.
Suite 300
Alexandria, VA 22314

3044

Mental Retardation Scholastic Achievement Scholarship

AMOUNT: $1,000 **DEADLINE:** Mar 15
FIELDS/MAJORS: Mental Retardation (Special Education, Mental Health)

Scholarships for sophomores and above who are communicant members of a Lutheran congregation and working toward a career in the field of mental retardation. Must have a GPA of at least 3.0. Write to the address below (or call 1-800-369-INFO, ext. 525) for details.

Bethesda Lutheran Home
National Christian Resource Center
700 Hoffmann Drive
Watertown, WI 53094

3045

Mercyhurst College-Valedictorian/Salutatorian Scholarships

AMOUNT: Tuition **DEADLINE:** None
FIELDS/MAJORS: All Areas Of Study

Scholarships for students who were valedictorian or salutatorian of their high school class. Renewable. Write to address below for details.

Mercyhurst College
Glenwood Hills
Erie, PA 16546

3046

Meredith Teaching Fellows Awards

AMOUNT: Varies **DEADLINE:** Feb 15
FIELDS/MAJORS: Education

Grants available to education majors at Meredith who have received a North Carolina Teaching Fellows Award. The grant will cover the portions of tuition and room board in excess of the $5,000 North Carolina Teaching Fellows Award. Renewable with a minimum 2.5 GPA. Must be a North Carolina resident. Write to the address below for additional information on the Meredith Award or the North Carolina Teaching Fellows Award.

Meredith College
Office of Admissions
3800 Hillsborough St.
Raleigh, NC 27607

3047

Merit Award

AMOUNT: $1,400 (max) **DEADLINE:** Mar 1
FIELDS/MAJORS: All Areas Of Study

Scholarships available at Sterling for undergraduate full-time students who demonstrate a record of leadership in school, church and community. Must have a minimum GPA of at least 2.8 and an ACT score of 19 or SAT score of at least 790. Write to the address below for details.

Sterling College
Financial Aid Office
Sterling, KS 67579

3048

Merit Awards

AMOUNT: $3,500 **DEADLINE:** Mar 15
FIELDS/MAJORS: All Areas Of Study

Awards open to students who rank in the top 20% of their class. Renewable. Write to the address below for more information.

Teikyo Post University
Office of Financial Aid
800 Country Club Road
Waterbury, CT 06723

3049

Merit Plus Scholarships

AMOUNT: $2,000 **DEADLINE:** None Specified
FIELDS/MAJORS: All Areas Of Study

All incoming freshmen who were semifinalists in the National Merit Scholarship competition or National Achievement Scholarship competition who enroll at Texas A&M are eligible for this scholarship. Write to the address below for details.

Texas A&M University
University Honors Program
101 Academic Building
College Station, TX 77843

3050

Merit Recognition Scholarship (MRS) Program

AMOUNT: $1,000 **AMOUNT:** Varies
FIELDS/MAJORS: All Areas Of Study

Scholarship open to qualified students who rank in the top 5% of an accredited Illinois high school at the end of the seventh semester. Recipients must use the award within one year of high school graduation, and must be enrolled at least half-time. MRS Awards are not need-based. Availability of MRS Awards is subject to state funding. Non-renewable. Eligible institutions are approved Illinois public and private, two- and four-year colleges, universities, and hospital schools. Contact your high school guidance counselor or principal for additional information.

Illinois Student Assistance Commission
1755 Lake Cook Road
Deerfield, IL 60015

3051

Merit Scholarships

GPA 3.0+

AMOUNT: Varies **DEADLINE:** None Specified
FIELDS/MAJORS: All Areas Of Study

Merit-based scholarships are available for entering freshman students at Spelman College. Applicant must have a GPA of at least 3.0. Write to the address listed below for additional information.

Spelman College
Office of Admissions And Orientation
350 Spelman Lane, SW, Box 277
Atlanta, GA 30314

3052

Meritorious & Minority Achievement Award John A. Moran Scholarship

AMOUNT: Varies **DEADLINE:** Feb 1
FIELDS/MAJORS: All Areas Of Study

Scholarships are available at the University of Utah for full-time minority students with a GPA of at least 3.5. Write to the address below for information.

University Of Utah
Suzanne Espinoza
80 Olpin Union
Salt Lake City, UT 84112

3053

Mervin Bovaird Foundation Scholarships

AMOUNT: $6,000 **DEADLINE:** Nov 15
FIELDS/MAJORS: All Areas Of Study

Scholarships for students enrolled in or applying to the University of Tulsa. High school seniors in Oklahoma are eligible and should contact their high school principals for information. Tulsa Junior College students should contact the president of TJC for information. Use the two methods listed above to receive further information. Do not contact the organization directly.

Mervin Bovaird Foundation
100 W. 5th St., #800
Tulsa, OK 74103

3054

Mesa County Assoc. Of Realtors Scholarship

AMOUNT: $500 **DEADLINE:** None Specified
FIELDS/MAJORS: Business

Awards for full-time Mesa State juniors or seniors majoring in a business field. Contact the School of Professional Studies/Business Department for more information.

Mesa State College
Office of Financial Aid
P.O. Box 2647
Grand Junction, CO 81501

3055

Mesa County Medical Society Nursing Scholarships

AMOUNT: $1,000 **DEADLINE:** None Specified
FIELDS/MAJORS: Nursing

Awards for full-time Mesa State nursing students who agree to work in Mesa County for at least 2 years following graduation. Must have and maintain a GPA of at least 3.0. Contact the School of Professional Studies/Nursing Area for more details.

Mesa State College
Financial Aid Office
P.O. Box 2647
Grand Junction, CO 81501

3056

Mesa State College Academic Scholarship For Continuing Students

AMOUNT: $700 **DEADLINE:** Mar 15
FIELDS/MAJORS: All Areas Of Study

Awards for current Mesa State College students who are from Colorado. Applicants must have a GPA of 3.0 and be enrolled in at least 12 hours of study. Write to the address below for more information.

Mesa State College
Office of Financial Aid
P.O. Box 2647
Grand Junction, CO 81501

3057

Mesa State College Academic Scholarship For Transfer Students

AMOUNT: $700 **DEADLINE:** Mar 15
FIELDS/MAJORS: All Areas Of Study

Awards for new or transfer students to Mesa State who are from Colorado. Applicants must have a GPA of 3.0 and be enrolled in at least 12 hours of study. Write to the address below for more information.

Mesa State College
Office of Financial Aid
P.O. Box 2647
Grand Junction, CO 81501

3058

Mesbec And Nale Programs

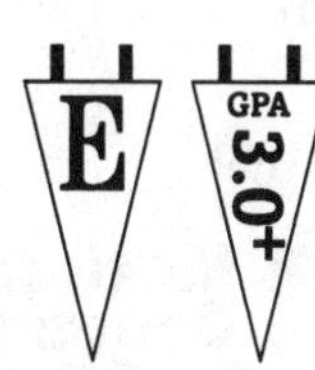

AMOUNT: Varies **DEADLINE:**
FIELDS/MAJORS: All Areas Of Study

Grants, loans, or combination awards awarded competitively to students who are at least 1/4 degree Native American. GPA of at least 3.0 required. Based on goals and potential for improving the lives of Indian peoples. For undergraduate or graduate study at any accredited college/university in the United States. Must have financial need. Write to the address below for details.

Native American Scholarship Fund
Scholarship Programs
8200 Mountain Rd. NE, Suite 203
Albuquerque, NM 87110

3059

Meserve Scholarship

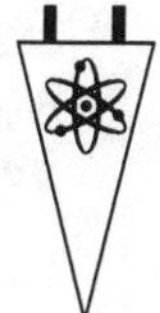

AMOUNT: Varies **DEADLINE:** Jun 1
FIELDS/MAJORS: Arboriculture, Horticulture, Forestry

Awards for students in the fields of study listed above who have demonstrated scholarship and financial need. For entering sophomores, juniors, or seniors. Contact the Associate Dean, College of Food and Natural Resources for more information.

University Of Massachusetts, Amherst
Associate Dean
College Of Food And Natural Resources
Amherst, MA 01003

3060

Metropolitan Life Foundation Program For Excellence In Medicine

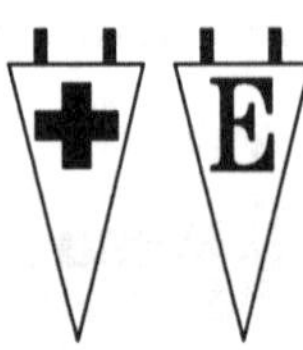

Amount: $2,500 **Deadline:** None Specified
Fields/Majors: Medicine

Awards for minority students from Los Angeles, San Francisco, CA; Denver, CO; Tampa, FL; Atlanta, GA; Chicago/Aurora, IL; Wichita, KS; New York, NY; Tulsa, OK; Pittsburgh, Scranton, PA; Warwick/Providence, RI; Greenville, SC; or Houston, TX in their second or third year of medicine. Based on academics, leadership, and potential for contributions in medicine. Send an SASE (.55) to the address below for more information.

National Medical Fellowships, Inc.
110 West 32nd, 8th Floor
New York, NY 10001

3061

Metropolitan Life Foundation Scholarships

Amount: $2,000 **Deadline:** Feb 15
Fields/Majors: Agriculture

Scholarships are available for FFA members pursuing a four-year degree in any area of agriculture, at Iowa State University (Ames), Kansas State University (Manhattan), University of Missouri (Columbia), University of Nebraska (Lincoln), or Purdue University (West Lafayette). One award is offered for each university. Write to the address below for details.

National FFA Foundation
Scholarship Office
P.O. Box 15160
Alexandria, VA 22309

3062

Mexican American Grocers Assoc. Scholarships

Amount: Varies **Deadline:** Jul 31
Fields/Majors: Business

Open to sophomore or above Hispanic college student studying a business-related field. Must show financial need. Renewable. Must have a GPA of at least 2.5. Write to the address below for more details.

Mexican American Grocers Assoc.
Ms. Rosemarie Vega
405 N. San Fernando Rd.
Los Angeles, CA 90031

3063

Mexican American Women's National Assoc. Scholarships

Amount: Varies **Deadline:** Mar 1
Fields/Majors: All Areas Of Study

Awards are available at the University of New Mexico for Hispanic women at any level of study. Contact Mana de Albuquerque, 1923 Maderia NE, Albuquerque, NM 87110.

University Of New Mexico, Albuquerque
Office of Financial Aid
Albuquerque, NM 87131

3064

MGMA/CRAHCA/ACMPE Scholarship

Amount: $1,000 **Deadline:** Jun 1
Fields/Majors: Health Administration

Award for graduate students enrolled in the M.S. in health administration program at the University of Colorado at Denver. Write to the address below for more information.

American College Of Medical Practice Executives
Attn: Ms. Laurie J. Draizen
104 Inverness Terrace East
Englewood, CO 80112

3065

MHCERF Student Awards Program

Amount: $3,000 **Deadline:** Apr 30
Fields/Majors: Medicine (M.D./Ph.D.)

Stipends for doctoral (M.D. & Ph.D.) students interested in the improvement of health and medical care in the state of Michigan. Supports a wide range of activities including research, pilot projects, intervention/demonstration projects, feasibility studies, proposal development, and critical lit. reviews. Projects must address quality of care, cost containment, healthcare access or a major public health/medical issue. Must focus (geographically) on the state of Michigan. Proposal required. Program announcement may be found in your department office or financial aid office. If not there, write to the below address.

Michigan Health Care Education And Research Foundation
Ms. Nora Maloy, Program Officer
600 Lafayette East, B243
Detroit, MI 48226

3066

MIA/KIA Dependents' Scholarship

Amount: Tuition And Fees **Deadline:** Dec 1, May 1
Fields/Majors: All Areas Of Study

Scholarship open to all full-time undergraduate/graduate students and highschool seniors who are dependent children or spouses of persons who were declared KIA, MIA or POW in 1960 or after. Must attend an Arkansas school and be a state resident. Write to the address below for details.

Arkansas Department of Higher Education
Financial Aid Division
114 East Capitol
Little Rock, AR 72201

3067

MIA/POW Scholarships

Amount: Varies **Amount:** Varies
Fields/Majors: All Areas Of Study

Must be child of Illinois serviceperson who has been declared to be POW, MIA, KIA, or 100% disabled in military action. Student must begin school before 26th birthday. For undergraduate study at any Illinois state-controlled college, university or community college. Scholarships are renewable. Contact the financial aid office at institution of choice or write to the address below.

Illinois Department of Veterans' Affairs
Attn: MIA/POW Scholarship Program
P.O. Box 5054
Springfield, IL 62705

3068

Miami Herald Minority Scholarship

Amount: $1,500-$3,000 **Deadline:** Mar 1
Fields/Majors: Newspaper Journalism, Newspaper Advertising

Open to minority juniors or seniors at the University of Florida who are planning a career in newspaper journalism or newspaper advertising. Must have at least a 2.8 GPA. Renewable. Write to the address below for details.

University Of Florida
2070 Weimer Hall
Director., Minority Scholarship Program
Gainesville, FL 32611

3069

Micah Systems, Inc. Scholarship Fund

Amount: Varies **Deadline:** None Specified
Fields/Majors: Computer Information Systems

Awards are available for full-time students at Cedarville College who are studying computer information systems. Must have a GPA of at least 2.5. Preference given to students from West Virginia. Write to the address below for more information.

Cedarville College
Financial Aid Office
P.O. Box 601
Cedarville, OH 45314

3070

Michael Blake Aspiring Writers Scholarship For Tuition

Amount: Varies **Deadline:** May 27
Fields/Majors: Creative Writing, Poetry, Playwriting

Scholarships are available at the University of New Mexico for entering freshmen who show outstanding talent as writers. Write to the address listed below for information.

University Of New Mexico, Albuquerque
Student Financial Aid Office
Mesa Vista Hall North, Room 1044
Albuquerque, NM 87131

3071

Michael Brian Lopez & Brandon Matthew Sneed Memorial Scholarship

Amount: None Specified **Deadline:** Mar 15
Fields/Majors: All Areas Of Study

Scholarship available to graduating high school seniors of Nitro High School (Nitro, WV). For each program, one award is anticipated. Write to the address below for details.

Greater Kanawha Valley Foundation
Scholarship Committee
P.O. Box 3041
Charleston, WV 25331

3072

Michael D. Coffey-Northeast Utilities Scholarship

Amount: Varies **Deadline:** Mar 1
Fields/Majors: Engineering

Awards for female sophomores, juniors, or seniors enrolled full-time. Must have a GPA of 2.5 or better (2.0 in major) and demonstrate financial need. Contact the Director., of Recruitment, Marston Hall for more information.

University Of Massachusetts, Amherst
Director., Recruitment
Marston Hall
Amherst, MA 01003

3073

Michael J. Turchan Scholarship

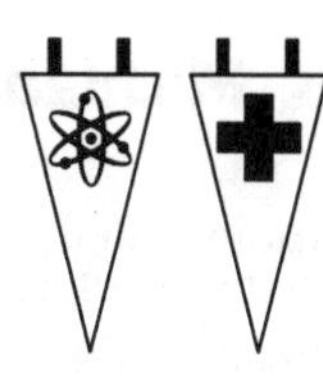

Amount: None Specified
Deadline: None Specified
Fields/Majors: Animal Science, Floriculture, Fruit And Vegetable Crops

Scholarships are awarded to Stockbridge students whose studies include animal science, floriculture, and fruit and vegetable crops. For students in their sophomore, junior, or senior year at UMass. Contact the Director., Stockbridge School, for more information.

University Of Massachusetts, Amherst
Director, Stockbridge School
Amherst, MA 01003

3074

Michael Metcalf Memorial Fund

Amount: $2,000-$5,000 **Deadline:** Jan 31
Fields/Majors: All Areas Of Study

Scholarships are available for sophomore and junior Rhode Island residents. Write to the address listed below for information.

Rhode Island Foundation
70 Elm St.
Providence, RI 02903

3075

Michael Murphy Memorial Scholarship Loan

Amount: $1,000 (max) **Deadline:** Apr 1
Fields/Majors: Law Enforcement, Criminology, Or Other Related Fields

No-interest loans for Alaska residents for studies related to law enforcement or criminology. Recipients shall receive forgiveness of 20% of the loan amount for every year he/she is employed full-time in Alaska in a law enforcement or related field. Write to the address listed below for information.

Alaska Commission On Postsecondary Education
Alaska State Troopers
5700 East Tudor Road
Anchorage, AK 99507

3076 Michaels Jewelers Foundation Scholarship

AMOUNT: $5,000 (max) **DEADLINE:** Mar 15
FIELDS/MAJORS: Business

For high school seniors who will be entering the University of Connecticut. Must be a Connecticut resident and demonstrate financial need. Award based on scholastic achievement and athletics. See your guidance counselor or write to the address below.

Michaels Jewelers Foundation
John Michaels
150 Mattatuck Heights
Waterbury, CT 06705

3077 Michigan Competitive Scholarship

AMOUNT: Varies **DEADLINE:** None Specified
FIELDS/MAJORS: All Areas Of Study

Awards for high school seniors who have achieved high scores on the ACT exam, and can demonstrate financial need. Write to the address below for details.

Michigan Department of Education
Office of Student Financial Assistance
P.O. Box 30462
Lansing, MI 48909

3078 Michigan Funeral Directors Assoc. Scholarships

AMOUNT: $500-$2,000 **DEADLINE:** None Specified
FIELDS/MAJORS: Mortuary Science

Awards for Michigan residents studying mortuary science. Must write an essay. Financial need is not necessary. Write to the address below for more information.

Michigan Funeral Director's Assoc.
c/o Michigan Mortuary Science Foundation
P.O. Box 27158
Lansing, MI 48909

3079 Michigan Scholarship Challenge Program

AMOUNT: $1,000 **DEADLINE:** Mar 15
FIELDS/MAJORS: Travel And Tourism, Hotel/Motel Management

Awards for Michigan residents in one of the areas listed above who are enrolled in a Michigan college. Must have a GPA of 3.0 or better and be in junior or senior year. Write to the address below for more information.

National Tour Foundation
546 East Main St.
P.O. Box 3071
Lexington, KY 40596

3080 Michigan Tuition Grant Program

AMOUNT: $1,900 (max) **DEADLINE:** Feb 15
FIELDS/MAJORS: All Areas Of Study

The Michigan Tuition Grant Program is based on financial need for use at independent (private) nonprofit degree-granting colleges and universities in Michigan. Applicants must be residents of Michigan for at least one year and have a minimum GPA of 2.0. Students enrolling less than full-time will have their awards reduced. Students enrolling for 9-11 credits will receive 3/4 of the award. Students enrolling for 6-8 credits will receive 1/2 the award. Students majoring in theology, divinity or any other religious education programs are ineligible. Write to the address below for details.

Michigan Department of Education
Office of Student Financial Assistance
P.O. Box 30462
Lansing, MI 48909

3081 Microsoft Corporation Scholarships

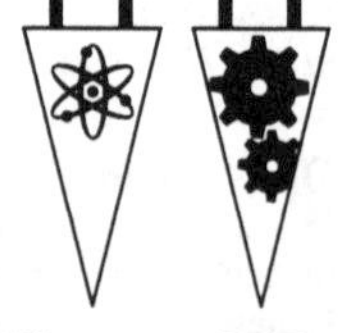

AMOUNT: $1,000 **DEADLINE:** Feb 1
FIELDS/MAJORS: Computer Science Or Computer Engineering

Scholarships for sophomores, juniors, or seniors majoring in or interested in computer science or engineering. First year master's level students are also eligible. Ten awards are given annually. For female students. Write to the address below for more information.

Society Of Women Engineers
120 Wall St., 11th Floor
New York, NY 10005

3082 Mid-America Regional Scholarships

AMOUNT: $1,000 **DEADLINE:** May 31
FIELDS/MAJORS: All Areas Of Study

Scholarships for Italian American residents of Iowa, Missouri, Arkansas, Oklahoma, Kansas, Nebraska, and Colorado. For undergraduate study. Write to the address listed below for information.

National Italian American Foundation
Dr. Maria Lombardo, Education Director.
1860 19th St., NW
Washington, DC 20009

3083 Mid-Career Scholarship Program

AMOUNT: Varies **DEADLINE:** None Specified
FIELDS/MAJORS: Transportation

Awards for employees of a state or local highway department. Applicant must must be a U.S. citizen and wish to pursue continuing education in the traffic or transportation fields. Past scholastic and career performances will be considered. Contact the address below for further information.

American Traffic Safety Services Foundation
5440 Jefferson Davis Highway
Fredericksburg, VA 22407

3084 Mid-Nebraska Community Foundation Scholarships

AMOUNT: None Specified **DEADLINE:** Mar 1
FIELDS/MAJORS: All Areas Of Study

Scholarships are available to graduating high school seniors residing within the mid-Nebraska community foundation boundaries, who have a GPA of at least 2.0. Write to the address listed below for information.

Mid-Nebraska Community Foundation
410 Rodeo Road
P.O. Box 1321
North Platte, NE 69103

3085 Mid-Ohio Chemical Company, Inc. Scholarships

AMOUNT: $1,000 **DEADLINE:** Feb 15
FIELDS/MAJORS: Agriculture

Scholarships are available for FFA members pursuing a four-year degree in any area of agriculture who reside in Ohio, Indiana or West Virginia. Three awards are offered annually. Write to the address below for details.

National FFA Foundation
Scholarship Office
P.O. Box 15160
Alexandria, VA 22309

3086 Mid-Pacific Regional Scholarships

AMOUNT: $1,000 **DEADLINE:** May 31
FIELDS/MAJORS: All Areas Of Study

Scholarships for Italian American residents of California, Nevada, Utah, Guam, and Hawaii. For undergraduate study. Write to the address listed below for information.

National Italian American Foundation
Dr. Maria Lombardo, Education Director.
1860 19th St., NW
Washington, DC 20009

3087 Midas Scholarships For Sons And Daughters

AMOUNT: None Specified **DEADLINE:** None Specified
FIELDS/MAJORS: All Areas Of Study

Scholarships for students whose parents are employed by Midas International Corporation. Have your parent contact the human resources office at his or her workplace.

Midas International Corporation
Midas Scholarship Program
225 N. Michigan Ave.
Chicago, IL 60601

3088 Migratory Bird Intern Central America

AMOUNT: None Specified
DEADLINE: None Specified
FIELDS/MAJORS: Conservation Biology, Animal Ecology, Zoology, Wildlife Management

Engaged in bachelor's or master's degree with experience in conservation biology, animal ecology, zoology or wildlife management. Excellent English/Spanish verbal and written skills, database management and IBM-PC word processing. Desktop publishing a plus. For minority students only. Write to the address below for more information.

Nature Conservancy
Cristina Garcia, Recruiting Director.
1815 N. Lynn St.
Arlington, VA 22209

3089 Mike Foley Scholarships

AMOUNT: $500 **DEADLINE:** Mar 1
FIELDS/MAJORS: Journalism

Awards for juniors and seniors majoring in journalism. Must have a GPA of at least 2.8. Preference is given to married students. Write to the address below for more information.

University Of Florida
Knight Scholarship & Placement Director.
2070 Weimer Hall
Gainesville, FL 32611

3090 Mike Roberts/Oklahoma Independent Petroleum Assoc. Scholarship

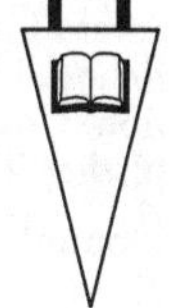

AMOUNT: $1,000 **DEADLINE:** Feb 15
FIELDS/MAJORS: News Journalism, Public Relations

Scholarships are available at the University of Oklahoma, Norman, for junior or senior students majoring in one of the above areas. Write to the address listed below for information.

University Of Oklahoma, Norman
School Of Journalism & Mass Comm.
860 Van Vleet Oval
Norman, OK 73019

3091 Mildred Bailey Evans Memorial Scholarship

AMOUNT: $150 **DEADLINE:** None Specified
FIELDS/MAJORS: Elementary Physical Education

Student must be an elementary physical education major who demonstrates superior grades, involvement in extracurricular activities and financial need. Contact the Health, Physical Education, and Recreation Department for more information.

Southwest Missouri State University
Office of Financial Aid
901 South National Ave.
Springfield, MO 65804

3092 Mildred Cater Bradham Social Work Fellowship

AMOUNT: $500-$1,000 **DEADLINE:** Feb 1
FIELDS/MAJORS: Social Work

Fellowships for members of Zeta Phi Beta studying toward a graduate or professional degree in social work. For one academic year of full-time study. Contact your Zeta Phi Beta chapter or send an SASE to the national headquarters at the address below before February 1 for further information.

Zeta Phi Beta Sorority
National Educational Foundation
1734 New Hampshire Ave., NW
Washington, DC 20009

3093 Mildred E. Troske Music Scholarship

AMOUNT: $500-$2,500 **DEADLINE:** Apr 14
FIELDS/MAJORS: Music

Scholarships for residents of Kent County who are pursuing a music degree. Applicants must have a GPA of at least 3.0 and demonstrate financial need. For full-time undergraduate study. Write to the address below for more information.

Grand Rapids Foundation
209-C Waters Bldg.
161 Ottawa Ave., NW
Grand Rapids, MI 49503

3094 Mildred Eaton Levitt Scholarship

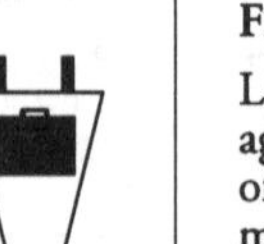

Amount: $400 **Deadline:** Feb 9
Fields/Majors: Business

Award for sophomore and junior business majors. Must show financial need. Use Bloomsburg University scholarship application. Contact Mr. Gene Remoff, Dean, College of Business for further information.

Bloomsburg University
19 Ben Franklin Hall
400 E. Second St.
Bloomsburg, PA 17815

3095 Military Science Departmental Scholarships

Amount: Varies **Deadline:** Jan 31
Fields/Majors: Military Science

Scholarships are available at the University of Utah for full-time students who are military science majors. Write to the address below for information.

University Of Utah
Professor Of Military Science
Military Science Building 23
Salt Lake City, UT 84112

3096 Millender Fellowship Program

Amount: $20,000 **Deadline:** Mar 31
Fields/Majors: Public Serv., Law, Political Science, Business, Public Administration

Applicants must demonstrate a record of successful accomplishment in some graduate educational program and/or through equivalent experience, broadly related to public service careers (as listed above) which would demonstrate a capacity for high-level accomplishment. Applicants must have completed a master's degree or equivalent professional degree. Write to the address below for more information.

Wayne State University
Academic Programs
4116 Faculty/Administration Building
Detroit, MI 48202

3097 Miller Meester Advertising Scholarships

Amount: $2,000 **Deadline:** Feb 15
Fields/Majors: Agricultural Communications

Scholarships are available for FFA members pursuing a four-year degree in agricultural communications. Applicant must be a junior or senior. Write to the address below for details.

National FFA Foundation
Scholarship Office
P.O. Box 15160
Alexandria, VA 22309

3098 Millhollon Educational Trust Estate Loans

Amount: $3,000 (max/year) **Deadline:** Jul 1, Jan 2
Fields/Majors: All Areas Of Study

Loans available to residents of Texas who are under the age of 25, planning to enroll in an accredited institution of higher education for the following term with a minimum of 12 semester hours. A minimum GPA of 2.5 is required. The loan has a current interest rate of 8%. The payments and interest will begin 90 days after graduation or termination of school. Write to the address below for details.

Millhollon Educational Trust Estate
309 West St. Anna
P.O. Box 643
Stanton, TX 79782

3099 Mills Fleet Farm Scholarships

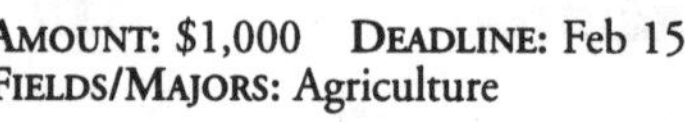

Amount: $1,000 **Deadline:** Feb 15
Fields/Majors: Agriculture

Scholarships are available for FFA members pursuing a two- or four-year degree in any area of agriculture, who reside in Wisconsin or Minnesota. Write to the address below for details.

National FFA Foundation
Scholarship Office
P.O. Box 15160
Alexandria, VA 22309

3100 Milo D. Leavitt, Jr. Memorial Lecture Award

Amount: Expenses & Fees **Deadline:** Dec 5
Fields/Majors: Geriatrics

Recipient may be an individual who has contributed to the field through outstanding teaching and mentorship, the development of innovative educational programs, or the advancement of policy issues related to geriatrics education. Write to the address below for more information.

American Geriatrics Society
770 Lexington Ave., Suite 300
New York, NY 10021

3101 Milton McKevett Teague Scholarships

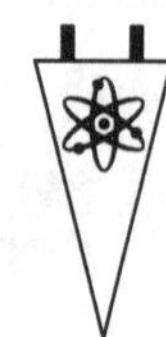

Amount: $2,000 **Deadline:** Apr 8
Fields/Majors: Agriculture

Awards for graduating high school seniors, high school graduates, or holders of GED who are enrolled, or intending to enroll, as a candidate for a degree at a fully accredited college, vocation, trade or business school. Applicants must have resided in Ventura County continuously for at least 3 years at the time of application. Write to the address below or contact your high school counselor for more information.

Ventura County Community Fund
1355 Del Norte Road
Camarillo, CA 93010

3102

Milwaukee Music Scholarships

Amount: $500-$1,500 **Deadline:** Feb 1
Fields/Majors: Music

Scholarships are available for Wisconsin residents who are music majors. All applicants must audition. Must be between the ages of 16 and 26. Write to the address listed below for information

Milwaukee Music Scholarship Foundation
Mrs. Jewel A. Graff
Firstar Trust Co., P.O. Box 2054
Milwaukee, WI 53201

3103

Minerva Scholarship

Amount: None Specified **Deadline:** None Specified
Fields/Majors: All Areas Of Study

Awards are available for incoming freshmen at SUNY, Potsdam, based on academic achievement, special abilities, and demonstrated talents. Renewable for 4 years. Write to the address below for more information.

SUNY, Potsdam
Office of Admissions
44 Pierrepont Ave.
Potsdam, NY 13676

3104

Mining Engineering Departmental Scholarships

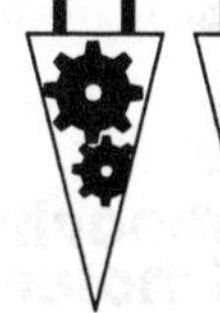

Amount: $750-$1,000 **Deadline:** Feb 1
Fields/Majors: Mining Engineering

Scholarships are available at the University of Utah for full-time mining engineering majors. The AIME/SME Phleider Scholarship is for general majors. The AIME/SME Coal Division Scholarship and the Rocky Mountain Coal Mining Institute Award are for students in a coal mining specialization. Minimum GPA of 3.0 or better required. Write to the address below for details.

University Of Utah
Dr. M.K. McCarter
313 William C. Browning Building
Salt Lake City, UT 84112

3105

Ministerial Grant

Amount: $200-$500 **Deadline:** Apr 15
Fields/Majors: All Areas Of Study

Awards for full-time students who are children of full-time ordained ministers or missionaries of any religious denomination. Must maintain a GPA of at least 2.0. Write to the address below for more information.

Bethel College
Office of Financial Planning
3900 Bethel Drive
St. Paul, MN 55112

3106

Ministerial Student Aid

Amount: Varies **Deadline:** Aug 1, Jan 1
Fields/Majors: Ministry, Christian Service

For members of a Baptist church associated with the Baptist General Assoc. of Virginia. Must have plans to enter Baptist seminary or graduate school for religious training. Awarded in undergraduate years. Loan is forgiven if recipient works for Christian-related service for two years. Write to the address below for more information.

Virginia Baptist General Board
Division Of Church And Minister Support
P.O. Box 8568
Richmond, VA 23226

3107

Minnesota Academic Excellence Scholarship

Amount: Tuition **Deadline:** None Specified
Fields/Majors: English, Writing, Fine Arts, Language, Math, Science, Social Science

Scholarships for students who have demonstrated outstanding ability, achievement, and potential in one of the fields listed above. Scholarship is renewable for up to three additional academic years if the student continues to meet the program's academic standards. Applicants must be residents of Minnesota attending a Minnesota institution. Write to the address below for details.

Minnesota Higher Education Coordinating Board
Capitol Square, Suite 400
550 Cedar St.
Saint Paul, MN 55101

3108

Minnesota Chippewa Tribe Scholarships

Amount: $3,000 **Deadline:** June 1
Fields/Majors: All Areas Of Study

Applicants must be enrolled members of the Minnesota Chippewa Tribe. It is required that you apply for campus-based aid before applying for this scholarship. Write to the address below for details.

Minnesota Chippewa Tribe
P.O. Box 217
Cass Lake, MN 56633

3109

Minnesota Indian Scholarship Program

Amount: Varies **Deadline:** None Specified
Fields/Majors: All Areas Of Study

Scholarship for Minnesota residents who are one-fourth or more Indian ancestry. Applicants must be a member of a federally recognized Indian tribe or eligible for enrollment in a tribe. For full-time study. Write to the address below for details.

Minnesota Higher Education Coordinating Board
c/o Joe Aitken, Indian Education
1819 Bemidji Ave.
Bemidji, MN 56601

3110

Minnesota Legionnaire Insurance Trust Scholarships

AMOUNT: $500 **DEADLINE:** Apr 1
FIELDS/MAJORS: All Areas Of Study

Scholarships are available for Minnesota residents who are or will be enrolled at a Minnesota college or university. Applicant must be a U.S. citizen and the child of a veteran. For more information contact the address below.

American Legion, Department of Minnesota
State Veterans Service Bldg.
St. Paul, MN 55155

3111

Minnie Pearl Scholarship Program

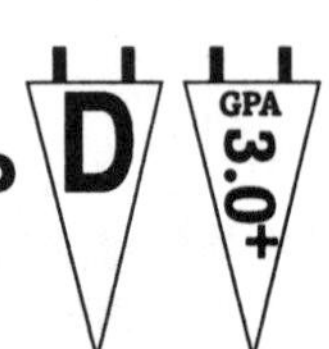

AMOUNT: $2,000 (max) **DEADLINE:** Feb 15
FIELDS/MAJORS: All Areas Of Study

Scholarships for current high school seniors with significant bilateral hearing loss (must be mainstreamed) who have been accepted, but not yet in attendance, at a junior college, college, university, or technical school. Must be a U.S. citizen and have a GPA of at least 3.0. Renewable with GPA of 3.0 ($500 renewal bonus with 3.5 GPA). Write to the address below for further information.

Ear Foundation At Baptist Hospital
Minnie Pearl Scholarship Program
1817 Patterson St.
Nashville, TN 37203

3112

Minor And Bernice Cross Endowed Scholarship

AMOUNT: Varies **DEADLINE:** None Specified
FIELDS/MAJORS: All Areas Of Study

Awards are available for full-time students at Cedarville College who have demonstrated financial need. Must have a GPA of at least 2.0. Write to the address below for more information.

Cedarville College
Financial Aid Office
P.O. Box 601
Cedarville, OH 45314

3113

Minorities In Government Finance Scholarship

AMOUNT: $3,500 **DEADLINE:** Feb 18
FIELDS/MAJORS: Business Or Political Science

Scholarship for minority undergrad or graduate students in the above areas planning to pursue a career in state or local government finance. For full- or part-time study. Must be a U.S. or Canadian citizen or permanent resident. Information may be available from the head of your accounting department. If not, write to the address below.

Government Finance Officers Assoc.
Scholarship Committee
180 N. Michigan Ave., Suite 800
Chicago, IL 60601

3114

Minority Dental Laboratory Technician Scholarship

AMOUNT: $1,000 **DEADLINE:** Aug 15
FIELDS/MAJORS: Dental Laboratory Technology

Applicants must be a U.S. citizen and must be enrolled or planning to enroll in a dental lab technology program accredited by the commission on accreditation of the American Dental Assoc. Students must have a GPA of 2.8 and demonstrate financial need. These awards are for minority students. Write to the address below for details.

ADA Endowment And Assistance Fund, Inc.
211 East Chicago Ave.
Chicago, IL 60611

3115

Minority Dental Student Scholarship Program

AMOUNT: $2,000 **DEADLINE:** Jul 1
FIELDS/MAJORS: Dentistry

Awards for African American, Hispanic, or Native American students entering their first or second year of a dental school accredited by the commission on dental accreditation. Must demonstrate financial need and have a GPA of at least 2.5. Contact your school's financial aid office for more information.

ADA Endowment And Assistance Fund, Inc.
211 East Chicago Ave.
Chicago, IL 60611

3116

Minority Dental Student Scholarships

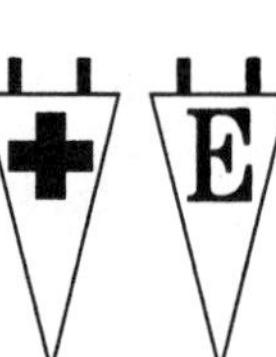

AMOUNT: $1,000 **DEADLINE:** May 1
FIELDS/MAJORS: Dentistry

Open to students from one of the following minority groups: African American, American Indian, Mexican American, and Puerto Rican. Must be first- or second-year students accepted by an accredited U.S. dental school. Must be U.S. citizens or permanent residents. 20-30 awards per year. Applications are available from accredited dental schools or from the AFDH office at the address below.

American Fund For Dental Health
211 E. Chicago Ave., Suite 820
Chicago, IL 60611

3117

Minority Doctoral Assistance Loan-For-Service Program

AMOUNT: $25,000 (max) **DEADLINE:** Varies
FIELDS/MAJORS: Most Areas Of Study

Awards for minority doctoral students who attend a New Mexico institution and who are also New Mexico residents. Must be U.S. citizens or permanent residents and enrolled in full-time study. Women are considered a minority for this award. Contact the graduate dean of your four-year public institution in New Mexico.

New Mexico Commission On Higher Education
1068 Cerrillos Rd.
Santa Fe, NM 87501

3118

Minority Doctoral Study Grant Program

AMOUNT: $6,000 **DEADLINE:** May 1
FIELDS/MAJORS: All Areas Of Study

Grants are available for minority doctoral candidates studying at Oklahoma institutions. This program was created as an incentive to increase the number of minority faculty and staff in the Oklahoma state system of higher education. Recipients must agree to teach in a state system institution two years for each year of aid. Write to the address listed below for information.

Oklahoma State Regents For Higher Education
State Capitol Complex
500 Education Building
Oklahoma City, OK 73105

3119

Minority Engineering Program Scholarship

AMOUNT: $500-$1,500 **DEADLINE:** Feb 1
FIELDS/MAJORS: Engineering

Scholarships are available at the University of Utah for full-time minority students enrolled in an engineering program. For sophomore standing or above. Four to six awards offered annually. Must be a U.S. citizen. In this program minority applies to ethnicity as well as gender. Write to the address below for details.

University Of Utah
Kate Rhodes, MEP Director.
2141 Merrill Engineering Building
Salt Lake City, UT 84112

3120

Minority Fellowship Program

AMOUNT: Varies **DEADLINE:** Jan 15
FIELDS/MAJORS: Psychology

Fellowships for ethnic minority students pursuing doctoral degrees in APA accredited doctoral programs in psychology. Must be a U.S. citizen or a permanent resident. Applicants must be in at least their second year of training. Write to the address below for more information.

American Psychological Assoc.
Minority Fellowship Program
750 First St., NE
Washington, DC 0002

3121

Minority Fellowship Program

AMOUNT: Varies **DEADLINE:** None Specified
FIELDS/MAJORS: Psychiatry

Fellowships for psychiatric minority residents in their PGY-II year or residency. Must be a U.S. citizen. Write to the address below for more information.

American Psychiatric Assoc.
Office of Minority/National Affairs
1400 K. St., NW
Washington, DC 20005

3122

Minority Foundation Scholarship

AMOUNT: Varies **DEADLINE:** None Specified
FIELDS/MAJORS: Business Administration, Economics, And Related

For minority students who are full-time juniors, seniors or graduate students at four-year colleges or universities. Must attend school in or be a resident of California as well as a U.S. citizen or permanent resident. Must not be employed more than 28 hours/week and must maintain GPA of at least 3.0. Contact your financial aid office or write to address below for details. If writing, please be certain to enclose an SASE with your request for information. Applications for students from northern CA are available from Aug 1-Oct 1 and from Feb 1-Apr 1 for southern CA residents.

Golden State Minority Foundation
1055 Wilshire Blvd., Suite 1115
Los Angeles, CA 90017

3123

Minority Grant

AMOUNT: $2,000 (max) **DEADLINE:** Apr 15
FIELDS/MAJORS: All Areas Of Study

Awards for minority students who can demonstrate financial need. Must be a U.S. citizen. Write to the address below for more information.

Bethel College
Office of Financial Planning
3900 Bethel Dr.
St. Paul, MN 55112

3124

Minority Internship Program

AMOUNT: $250-$300/Wk
DEADLINE: Feb 15
FIELDS/MAJORS: Humanities, Art Studies, Anthropology, Astrophysics, Biology, History

Internships are available to minority undergraduate and graduate students at the Smithsonian, for research or museum-related activities. Programs range from 9 to 12 weeks. Write to address below for details. Request the publication "Smithsonian Opportunities for Research and Study."

Smithsonian Institution
Office of Fellowships And Grants
955 L'enfant Plaza, Suite 7,000
Washington, DC 20560

3125

Minority Leadership Scholarship

AMOUNT: Tuition And Fees **DEADLINE:** None Specified
FIELDS/MAJORS: All Areas Of Study

Awards for entering minority SMSU students who are graduating in the upper 50% of their class and have demonstrated leadership in the minority community through involvement in various school and civic organizations. Write to the address below for more details.

Southwest Missouri State University
Financial Aid Office
901 South National Ave.
Springfield, MO 65804

3126

Minority Management Education Program Scholarships

AMOUNT: Varies **DEADLINE:** Feb 29
FIELDS/MAJORS: Management

Awards for students of color for improvement, academic excellence, and leadership in the field of management. For students in their sophomore, junior, or senior year. Applications for School of Management Scholarships will be available in the SOM Development Office, Room 206.

University Of Massachusetts, Amherst
School Of Management
SOM Development Office, Room 206
Amherst, MA 01003

3127

Minority Master's Fellows Program

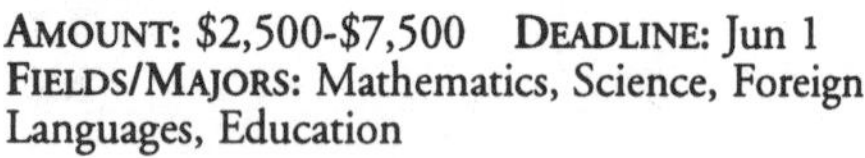

AMOUNT: $2,500-$7,500 **DEADLINE:** Jun 1
FIELDS/MAJORS: Mathematics, Science, Foreign Languages, Education

African American students who are admitted to a master's program in mathematics, the sciences or foreign languages or to African American students in the fifth year of a teacher education program who were recipients of the minority teacher scholarship. Students must be full-time during fall/spring; can go part-time for 3 summers. Write to the address below for more information.

Arkansas Department of Higher Education
Financial Aid Division
114 East Capitol
Little Rock, AR 72201

3128

Minority Medical Faculty Development Program

AMOUNT: $75,000 **DEADLINE:** Apr 1
FIELDS/MAJORS: Medicine/Education

Applicants must be minority physicians who are U.S. citizens, have excelled in their education, are now completing or will have completed formal clinical training and are committed to academic careers. Minorities here are African and Mexican Americans, Native Americans, and mainland Puerto Ricans who have completed college on the mainland. Fellowships aid research and last 4 years. Write to the address listed below for additional information.

Robert Wood Johnson Foundation
James R. Gavin III, M.D., Ph.D., Program Director
4733 Bethesda Ave., Suite 350
Bethesda, MD 20814

3129

Minority Presence Grant

AMOUNT: Varies **DEADLINE:** None Specified
FIELDS/MAJORS: All Areas Of Study

Scholarships are available to minority North Carolina undergraduates who demonstrate financial need. For use at one of the 16 North Carolina constituent institutions. Write to the address below for details.

North Carolina State Education Assistance Authority
P.O. Box 2688
Chapel Hill, NC 27515

3130

Minority Professional Study Grant Program

AMOUNT: $4,000 **DEADLINE:** Jun 1
FIELDS/MAJORS: Medicine, Dentistry, Law, Veterinary Medicine, Optometry

Grants are available for minority students studying at Oklahoma institutions. This program was created as an incentive to increase the number of minority groups in the programs listed above. Must be a U.S. citizen. Write to the address listed below for information.

Oklahoma State Regents For Higher Education
State Capitol Complex
500 Education Building
Oklahoma City, OK 73105

3131

Minority Scholars Program

AMOUNT: None Specified **DEADLINE:** Feb 1
FIELDS/MAJORS: All Areas Of Study

The minority scholars program is a program of career counseling, academic preparation, internships, and mentoring for selected minority students from underrepresented groups. Students must be entering as a freshmen at case Western Reserve University. Write to the address below for details.

Case Western Reserve University
Office of Financial Aid, 109 Pardee Hall
10900 Euclid Ave.
Cleveland, OH 44106

3132

Minority Scholarship

AMOUNT: Varies **DEADLINE:** Jun 1
FIELDS/MAJORS: Dental Hygiene

Scholarships for students of underrepresented groups who have completed at lease one year of a full-time accredited program in dental hygiene. Must have a GPA of at least 3.0. Based on need and career goals. Males are also considered minorities for this award. Write to the address below for more information.

American Dental Hygienists' Assoc. Institute For Oral Health
444 N. Michigan Ave., Suite 3400
Chicago, IL 60611

3133

Minority Scholarship Program

AMOUNT: None Specified **DEADLINE:** None Specified
FIELDS/MAJORS: All Areas Of Study

Scholarships for new undergraduate African American students at ETSU who demonstrate (the potential for) academic excellence. Write to the address below for details.

East Tennessee State University
Office of Financial Aid
Box 70722
Johnson City, TN 37614

3134

Minority Scholarship Program

AMOUNT: $2,500 **DEADLINE:** Oct 15
FIELDS/MAJORS: Psychology

Award for ethnic minority students accepted into a graduate level psychology program in the state of California. Based on community involvement, leadership, knowledge of ethnic minority/cultural issues, career plans, and financial need. Scholarships are given to students in their first year of study. Write to the address below for more information.

California Psychological Assoc. Foundation
1010 Eleventh St. Suite 202
Sacremento, CA 95814

3135

Minority Scholarships

AMOUNT: $1,000-$1,500 **DEADLINE:** Apr 1
FIELDS/MAJORS: All Areas Of Study

Scholarships for minority students at Kent State who have a superior academic record. Contact the financial aid office at your campus for details.

Kent State University, Tuscarawas Campus
Financial Aid Office
University Drive, NE
New Philadelphia, OH 4663

3136

Minority Scholarships

AMOUNT: Varies **DEADLINE:** Dec 1
FIELDS/MAJORS: All Areas Of Study

Scholarships are available at UT Austin for minority undergraduate students. Requirements for the awards will vary. Write to the address below for details.

University Of Texas, Austin
Office of Student Financial Services
P.O. Box 7758
Austin, TX 78713

3137

Minority Scholarships

AMOUNT: Varies **DEADLINE:** Jan 15
FIELDS/MAJORS: Architecture

Scholarships for minority high school seniors and college juniors who are entering degree programs at schools of architecture. Write to the address below for more details.

The American Architectural Foundation
AIA/AAF Scholarship Program Director.
1735 New York Ave. NW
Washington, DC 20006

3138

Minority Scholarships

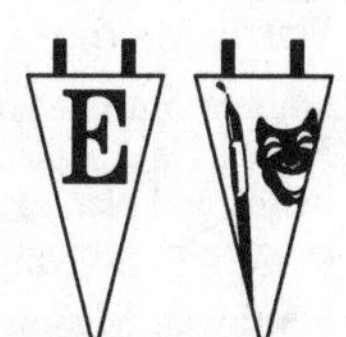

AMOUNT: $250-$1,000 **DEADLINE:** Jul 1
FIELDS/MAJORS: Instrumental And Vocal Music

Awards for minority students between the ages of 18 and 30 who are studying instrumental or vocal music. Must compete in local, regional, and national competition to be considered for an award. Non-renewable. Write to the address below or contact your local branch for more information.

National Assoc. Of Negro Musicians, Inc.
P.O. Box S-011
Chicago, IL 60628

3139

Minority Scholarships, Minority Affairs Graduate Program

AMOUNT: Varies **DEADLINE:** Varies
FIELDS/MAJORS: All Areas Of Study

Scholarships for minority students at the University of Wyoming. For full-time study. Academic accomplishments are considered. Includes the Hearst Minority Scholarship. Graduate students: contact the MAGP director at the address below for more details. Undergraduates: contact the division of student educational opportunity at the address below for details.

University Of Wyoming
Div. Of Student Educational Opportunity
P.O. Box 3808
Laramie, WY 72071

3140

Minority Teacher Scholarship

AMOUNT: $4,000 (max)
DEADLINE: None Specified
FIELDS/MAJORS: Teaching Or Special Education

The minority teacher scholarship program is open to African American and Hispanic students in Indiana planning to pursue a career in teaching or special education. Recipient must demonstrate financial need, pursue a teacher certification program on a full-time basis and teach 3 out of 5 years in an accredited Indiana elementary or secondary school. Write to the address below for details.

Indiana Student Assistance Commission
ISTA Center Building
150 West Market St., Suite 500
Indianapolis, IN 46204

3141

Minority Teachers Of Illinois Scholarship

AMOUNT: $5,000 **DEADLINE:** None Specified
FIELDS/MAJORS: Teaching

Scholarship open to students of African American, Hispanic, Native American, or Asian American origin who plan to become teachers at the preschool, elementary, or secondary level. Recipients must be enrolled as full-time undergraduates, at the sophomore level or above, and must sign a teaching commitment to teach one year for each year assistance is received. Must be a U.S. citizen. MTI recipients must teach at an Illinois preschool, elementary or secondary school where no less than 30% of those enrolled are African American, Hispanic, Asian American or Native American minority students. If the teaching commitment is not fulfilled, the scholarship becomes a loan and must be repaid. Write to the address below for details.

Illinois Student Assistance Commission
1755 Lake Cook Road
Deerfield, IL 60015

3142

Minority Teachers Scholarship

AMOUNT: $5,000 **DEADLINE:** Jun 1
FIELDS/MAJORS: Education

African American college students enrolled full-time, admitted to an approved program resulting in teacher certification, and have at least a 2.5 cumulative GPA. New awards are made to juniors only; continuing awards are made to seniors only. For Arkansas residents. Write to the address below for more information.

Arkansas Department of Higher Education
Financial Aid Division
114 East Capitol
Little Rock, AR 72201

3143

Minority Teaching Fellows Program

AMOUNT: $5,000 **DEADLINE:** None Specified
FIELDS/MAJORS: Education

Financial aid for freshmen entering teaching education program in Tennessee. Must have a GPA of 2.5 or better and agree to teach at a K-12 level in a Tennessee public school for one year. Write to the address listed below for information or an application.

Tennessee Student Assistance Corporation
Suite 1950 Parkway Towers
404 James Robertson Parkway
Nashville, TN 37243

3144

Miriam Grunsfeld Scholarship

AMOUNT: Varies **DEADLINE:** Mar 1
FIELDS/MAJORS: Political Science

Awards are available at the University of New Mexico for students majoring in political science. GPA is given primary consideration and financial need is a secondary factor. Write to the address below for more information.

University Of New Mexico, Albuquerque
Office of Financial Aid
Albuquerque, NM 87131

3145

Miriam Higginbotham Scholarship

AMOUNT: $1,320 **DEADLINE:** Mar 15
FIELDS/MAJORS: All Areas Of Study

Awards for Jacksonville State University students who are in any field of study. Based on grades, moral character, etc. Write to the address below for more information.

Jacksonville State University
Financial Aid Office
Jacksonville, AL 36265

3146

Miriam Paula Romo Fund

AMOUNT: Varies **DEADLINE:** None Specified
FIELDS/MAJORS: Communication Disorders

Awards for students entering their sophomore, junior, or senior year in the Department of Communication Disorders. Contact the chair, Department of Communication Disorders for more information.

University Of Massachusetts, Amherst
Chair, Department of Communication Disorders
Amherst, MA 01003

3147

Miss Outstanding Teenager Of Montana Scholarship Program

AMOUNT: $1,500 (max) **DEADLINE:** Jan 4
FIELDS/MAJORS: All Areas Of Study

Awards for females from Montana who are under age 19. Must be U.S. citizens, have a GPA of at least 3.0., and be unmarried. There is no entry fee, but contestants must have a sponsor that pays a sponsorship fee of $375. Based on teen image, academics, citizenship, personal projection, and an essay. Write to the address below for more information.

Central Montana Jaycees
P.O. Box 9267
Helena, MT 59604

3148

Miss Teenage America Contest

AMOUNT: $15,000 (max) **DEADLINE:** Jul 31
FIELDS/MAJORS: All Areas Of Study

Scholarships are available for young women under the age of 19 with academic ability who are involved in school and community activities. The winner receives a $15,000 scholarship, a monthly column in "Teen," and a year of travel and public appearances. Information and applications are available in the June and July issues of "Teen."

Teen Magazine
Peterson Publishing Company
6420 Wilshire Blvd.
Los Angeles, CA 90048

3149

Missionary Children's Scholarship

AMOUNT: Varies **DEADLINE:** None Specified
FIELDS/MAJORS: All Areas Of Study

Scholarships are available to John Brown College for full-time undergraduate students with at least one parent who is a full-time minister or missionary. Write to the address below for details.

John Brown University
Office of Financial Aid
2000 West University Dr.
Siloam Springs, AR 72761

3150

Missouri Assoc. Of Registered Land Surveyors Scholarship

AMOUNT: $250 **DEADLINE:** None Specified
FIELDS/MAJORS: Land Surveying

Student must be employed full-time in the land surveying profession. Must have completed GRY 275 and GRY 375 with a GPA of 3.0 or better, and plan to enroll in GRY 377 or GRY 379. Contact the geography, geology, and planning department for more information.

Southwest Missouri State University
Office of Financial Aid
901 South National Ave.
Springfield, MO 65804

3151

Missouri Funeral Directors Assoc. Scholarships

AMOUNT: $750 **DEADLINE:** None Specified
FIELDS/MAJORS: Mortuary Science

Awards for residents of Missouri who plan to work in Missouri following graduation. Write to the address below for more information.

Missouri Funeral Director's Assoc.
600 Ellis Blvd., P.O. Box 104688
Jefferson City, MO 65110

3152

Missouri Teacher Education Scholarship

AMOUNT: $2,000 **DEADLINE:** Feb 15
FIELDS/MAJORS: Education

Awards for Missouri freshmen or sophomores attending a college or university in Missouri. Applicants must rank in the top 15% of their high school class or score in the top 15% on a college entry exam (ACT or SAT). Write to the address below for more information.

Missouri Department of Elementary And Secondary Education
P.O. Box 480
Jefferson City, MO 65102

3153

Missouri Teacher Education Scholarship

AMOUNT: $2,000 **DEADLINE:** Feb 15
FIELDS/MAJORS: Education

Student must be a high school senior, a freshman or sophomore at a four-year college or university in Missouri, a community college student in Missouri, or a non-traditional student. Recipient must rank in the top 15 percent in their high school class, or score in the top 15 percent on the ACT or SAT exam, and enter the teacher education program. Must be a Missouri resident. Contact the DESE for more information.

Southwest Missouri State University
Office of Financial Aid
901 South National Ave.
Springfield, MO 65804

3154

Missouri Teacher Education Scholarships

AMOUNT: $2,000 **DEADLINE:** None Specified
FIELDS/MAJORS: Elementary & Secondary Education

Recipients are selected by the Missouri Dept. of Elementary & Secondary Education. Contact Missouri DESE, P.O. Box 480, Jefferson City, MO 65102 for more details.

Southwest Missouri State University
Financial Aid Office
901 South National Ave.
Springfield, MO 65804

3155

Mitchell-Beall Scholarships

AMOUNT: $1,000-$5,000 **DEADLINE:** Feb 15
FIELDS/MAJORS: All Areas Of Study

Scholarships offered to high school seniors under the age of 21, who are members of the NASA credit union. Applicants must submit an essay of 1000 words or less. Write to the address below for details.

NASA Federal Credit Union
Mitchell-Beall Scholarship
P.O. Box 1588
Bowie, MD 20717

3156

MLA Doctoral Fellowship

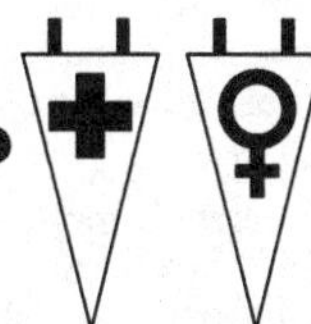

AMOUNT: $1,000 **DEADLINE:** Dec 1
FIELDS/MAJORS: Medical Librarianship

Fellowship for doctoral candidates in medical librarianship. Supports research or travel. Write to the address below for details.

Medical Library Assoc./Institute For Scientific Information
Professional Development Department
Six N. Michigan Ave., Suite 300
Chicago, IL 60602

3157

MLA Scholarship

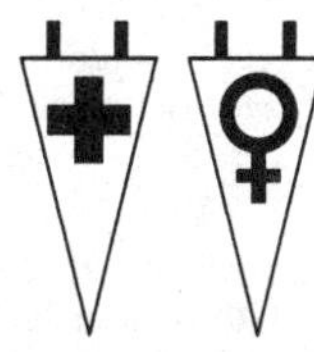

AMOUNT: Varies **DEADLINE:** Dec 1
FIELDS/MAJORS: Medical Library Science

Graduate scholarship for students entering graduate school in medical librarianship or have at least 1/2 of requirements to complete during the year following the granting of the scholarship. Must be studying in an ALA accredited school. Grants support research, etc., into projects which will enhance the field of health science librarianship. Write to the address below for details.

Medical Library Assoc.
Program Services
Six N. Michigan Ave., Suite 300
Chicago, IL 60602

3158

MLA Scholarship For Minority Students

AMOUNT: $2,000 **DEADLINE:** Feb 1
FIELDS/MAJORS: Medical Librarianship

Scholarship for minority students entering or continuing graduate school in health science librarianship. Must be studying in an ALA accredited school. Write to the address below for details.

Medical Library Assoc.
Program Services
Six N. Michigan Ave., Suite 300
Chicago, IL 60602

3159

Modesto Bee Minority Internship

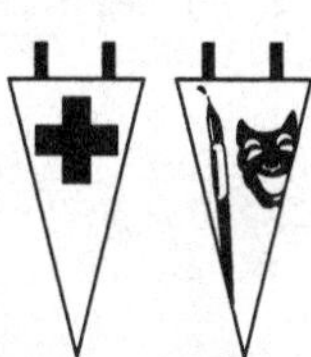

AMOUNT: $350 Per Week **DEADLINE:** Dec 31
FIELDS/MAJORS: Journalism, Photography, Graphics

Open to minority college students focusing on journalism, photography, and graphics. Write to the address below for more information.

Modesto Bee
Sanders Lamont, Executive Editor
P.O. Box 5256
Modesto, CA 95352

3160
Modesto Bee Summer Internship

Amount: $350 Per Week **Deadline:** Dec 31
Fields/Majors: Journalism, Photography, Graphics

Open to college students focusing on journalism, reporting, editing, photography, and graphics. Write to the address below for more information.

Modesto Bee
Sanders Lamont, Executive Editor
P.O. Box 5256
Modesto, CA 95352

3161
Moe And Laura Schwartz Scholarship

Amount: $500-$750 **Deadline:** Mar 1
Fields/Majors: Advertising, Magazines

Must be a junior or senior majoring in advertising or magazines at the University of Florida. Must have at least a 2.8 GPA. Write to the address below for complete details.

University Of Florida
2070 Weimer Hall
Scholarship & Placement Director
Gainesville, FL 32611

3162
Monsignor Joseph M. Luddy Scholarship

Amount: $3,000 **Deadline:** Jun 2
Fields/Majors: Social Work, Roman Catholic Priesthood

Awards for current or former residents of Blair County, PA, who are enrolled in graduate programs in social work or the Roman Catholic priesthood. Write to the address below for more information.

Monsignor Joseph M. Luddy Scholarship Fund, Inc.
P.O. Box 265
Altoona, PA 16603

3163
Montana Scholarship Challenge Program

Amount: $500 **Deadline:** Mar 15
Fields/Majors: Travel And Tourism, Hotel/Motel Management

Awards for Montana residents in one of the areas listed above who are enrolled in any two- or four-year college. Must have a GPA of 3.0 or better. Write to the address below for more information.

National Tour Foundation
546 East Main St.
P.O. Box 3071
Lexington, KY 40596

3164
Montclair Art Museum Internship

Amount: $5,000 **Deadline:** Apr 15
Fields/Majors: Art History, Anthropology, Native American Studies

Internship program for Native American students in a program of art history, anthropology, or Native American studies. Based on resume, academics, and recommendations. Write to the address below for more information.

Montclair Art Museum, New Jersey State Council On The Arts
Twig Johnson, Curator Of Education
3 South Mountain Ave.
Montclair, NJ 07042

3165
Monticello College Foundation Fellowship For Women

Amount: $12,000 **Deadline:** Jan 20
Fields/Majors: History (Western And American), Women's Studies, Lit.

Open to women with Ph.D. degree. Preference will be given to applicants whose scholarship is particularly concerned with the study of women, but study may be proposed in any field appropriate to Newberry's collections. Must be a U.S. citizen. Fellowship is for 6 months work in residence at the Newberry Library. Write to the address below for complete details.

Newberry Library
Committee On Awards
60 W. Walton St.
Chicago, IL 60610

3166
Moody Scholars Program

Amount: Varies **Deadline:** Oct 1
Fields/Majors: All Areas Of Study

Scholarships available to seniors graduating from a Galveston, Texas County high school. Applicants must have a minimum GPA of 3.0 and plan to attend a college or university within the state of Texas. Student must need financial assistance to attend college. Write to the address below for further details.

Moody Foundation
2302 Postoffice St., Suite 704
Galveston, TX 77550

3167
Moorman's Scholarship Program

Amount: Varies **Amount:** Varies
Fields/Majors: Agriculture

Moorman sponsors this scholarship program at thirty agriculture colleges. Each school is responsible for selecting recipients of award which are based on leadership, scholastic achievement, financial need, and interest in agriculture. Contact individual schools of agriculture for more information or write to the address below for details. Application is made to your college or university.

Moorman Manufacturing Company Fund
1000 North 30th St., P.O. Box C1
Quincy, IL 62305

3168
MOPH Scholarship Program

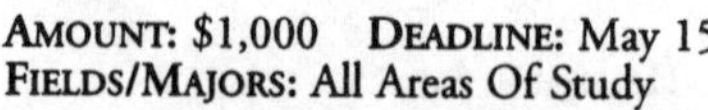

Amount: $1,000 **Deadline:** May 15
Fields/Majors: All Areas Of Study

Open to children and grandchildren of members of the order with a minimum 2.5 GPA, and attending an accredited college, university, professional school, vocational school, or junior or community college. Two- and four-year scholarships are available and renewable with maintained 2.5 GPA. Applicants must be U.S. citizens and enrolled full-time. Write to the address below for details. Applications will not be available until January of the year it is due.

Military Order of the Purple Heart
Adjutant General
5413-B Backlick Rd.
Springfield, VA 22151

3169

Morehead State University Award

AMOUNT: $1,200 **DEADLINE:** Mar 15
FIELDS/MAJORS: All Areas Of Study

Renewable $1,200 award given to freshmen entering MSU or transferring from another school and having an admissions index of 550. Write to the address listed below for information.

Morehead State University
Office of Admissions
301 Howell-McDowell
Morehead, KY 40351

3170

Morgan L. Fitch Scholarship

AMOUNT: $2,000 (min) **DEADLINE:** May 1
FIELDS/MAJORS: Real Estate

Scholarships for upperclassmen or graduate students at the University of Illinois, Champaign-Urbana. Based on career interests, grades, need, and references. A GPA of at least 3.5 on a 5.0 point scale (2.8 on a 4.0 scale) is required. Must be a resident of the state of Illinois. Write to the address below for details.

Illinois Real Estate Educational Foundation
3180 Adloff Ln.
P.O. Box 19451
Springfield, IL 62794

3171

Morris Doctoral Fellowship Program

AMOUNT: $12,000 **DEADLINE:** Jan 19
FIELDS/MAJORS: Most Areas Of Study

Fellowships are available at SIU for graduate students pursuing a doctorate in one of the areas listed above. Must have a GPA of at least 3.25. Write to the address listed below for information.

Southern Illinois University
Morris Doctoral Fellowship Program
Dean Of The Grad. School, Mailcode 4716
Carbondale, IL 62901

3172

Morris Hanauer And Irene Mack Scholarships

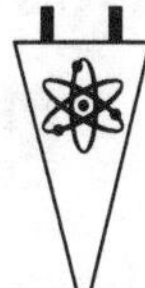

AMOUNT: $500-$600 **DEADLINE:** Nov 1
FIELDS/MAJORS: Gemology

Awards are available for students enrolled in a GIA distance education program. Must be a U.S. citizen or permanent resident. Write to the address below for more information.

Gemological Institute Of America
Office of Student Financial Assistance
1660 Stewart St.
Santa Monica, CA 90404

3173

Morris K. Udall Scholarship Program

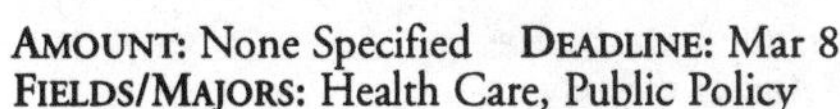

AMOUNT: None Specified **DEADLINE:** Mar 8
FIELDS/MAJORS: Health Care, Public Policy

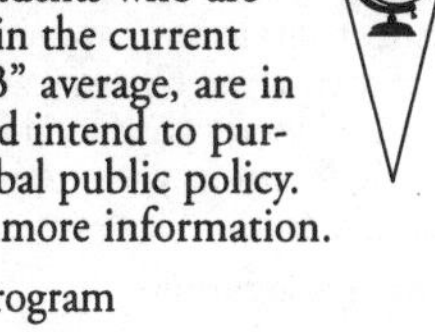

Awards scholarships to outstanding Native American and Alaska native students who are college sophomores or juniors in the current academic year, have a least a "B" average, are in the upper 1/4 of their class, and intend to pursue careers in health care or tribal public policy. Write to the address below for more information.

Morris K. Udall Scholarship Program
2201 North Dodge St.
Iowa City, IA 52243

3174

Morse Scholarships

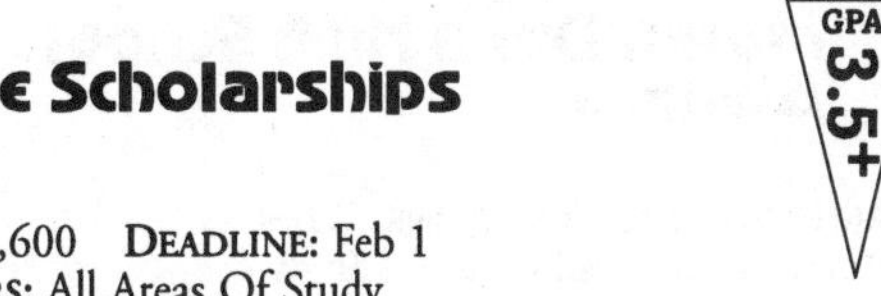

AMOUNT: $15,600 **DEADLINE:** Feb 1
FIELDS/MAJORS: All Areas Of Study

Awards for entering students based on academics. Must have a GPA of at least 3.8 and a minimum SAT score of 1370 or ACT score of 33. Renewable with continued academic achievement. Write to the address below for more information.

Rhodes College
Office of Admissions
2000 North Parkway
Memphis, TN 38112

3175

Morton B. Duggan, Jr. Memorial Scholarship

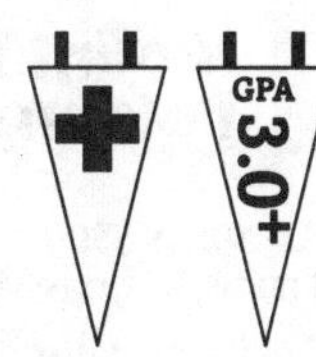

AMOUNT: $500 **DEADLINE:** Jun 30
FIELDS/MAJORS: Respiratory Therapy

One scholarship for a student who has completed at least one semester in an AMA-approved respiratory care program. Preference is given to students from Georgia or South Carolina, but applications from students in all other states will be accepted. Must have a GPA of at least 3.0. Write to the address below for details.

American Respiratory Care Foundation
11030 Ables Lane
Dallas, TX 75229

3176

Morton International, Morton Salt Division Scholarships

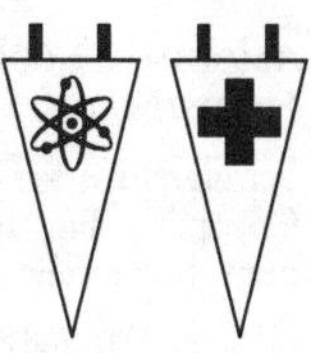

AMOUNT: $1,000 **DEADLINE:** Feb 15
FIELDS/MAJORS: Animal Science, Preveterinary Medicine

Scholarships are available for FFA members pursuing a four-year degree in animal science or preveterinary medicine. Preference will be given to students who demonstrate an interest in animal nutrition. Write to the address below for details.

National FFA Foundation
Scholarship Office
P.O. Box 15160
Alexandria, VA 22309

3177

Most Valuable Student Awards

AMOUNT: $1,000-$5,000 **DEADLINE:** Jan 18
FIELDS/MAJORS: All Areas Of Study

Awards are offered to graduating high school seniors who are U.S. citizens residing within the jurisdiction of a local order of the Elks Lodge. Membership is not required. Students should stand in the upper 5% of their class. Criteria: academic success/leadership & financial need. Contact your local BPO Elks Lodge for details. The address may be found in your telephone directory. Information may also be obtained on the Elks' website - http://www.elks.org/enf/.

Elks National Foundation
2750 N. Lakeview Ave.
Chicago, IL 60614

Mount Dora High School Awards

AMOUNT: Varies **DEADLINE:** Varies
FIELDS/MAJORS: All Areas Of Study

Scholarships are available for graduates of Mount Dora High School in Mount Dora, Florida. Includes the Liz Perrett Memorial, Anchor Club, Mike Olivenbaum Athletic Scholarships and many others. Individual award requirements will vary. Contact your guidance counselor for more information.

Mount Dora High School
Guidance Department
Mount Dora, FL 32757

Mount Ida College-Edith Folsom Hall Scholarship

AMOUNT: $500 **DEADLINE:** Mar 1
FIELDS/MAJORS: All Areas Of Study

Applicants must be young women high school graduates who have been accepted by Mount Ida College. Several scholarships available. Write to the address below for details.

General Federation Of Women's Clubs Of Massachusetts
777 Dedham St.
Newton Centre, MA 02159

Mountaineer Gas Company Scholarship Fund

AMOUNT: $1,000 **DEADLINE:** Mar 15
FIELDS/MAJORS: All Areas Of Study

Scholarships for dependents of employees of Mountaineer Gas Company. For undergraduate study. Awarded to entering freshmen, but renewable. Write to the address below for details.

Greater Kanawha Valley Foundation
Scholarship Committee
P.O. Box 3041
Charleston, WV 25331

Mr. & Mrs George D. Hall Jr. Memorial Athletic Scholarship

AMOUNT: Varies **DEADLINE:** Feb 1
FIELDS/MAJORS: All Areas Of Study

Scholarships are available at the University of Hawaii, Hilo for full-time students who participate in the intercollegiate athletics program. Write to the address listed below for information.

University Of Hawaii At Hilo
Financial Aid Office
200 West Kawili St.
Hilo, HI 96720

3182

Mr. & Mrs. Marl Motsenbocker Scholarship In Honor Of Dorothy L. Hanson

AMOUNT: $500 **DEADLINE:** Feb 1
FIELDS/MAJORS: Agricultural Business Management

Student must be a sophomore or above majoring in agricultural business management with an interest in food distribution. Must have a GPA of 2.5 or better. Write to the address below for more information.

California State Polytechnic University, Pomona
College Of Agriculture
Building 2, Room 215
Pomona, CA 91768

Mr. & Mrs. Sze Lee Scholarship Program

AMOUNT: $2,000 **DEADLINE:** Mar 29
FIELDS/MAJORS: All Areas Of Study

Scholarships are available for employees or dependents of the San Francisco International Airport, or airlines/businesses based at the airport. Write to the address listed below for additional information.

Peninsula Community Foundation
1700 South El Camino Real, Suite 300
San Mateo, CA 4402

Mr. And Mrs. A.E. Hunt Scholarship

AMOUNT: $150-$200 **DEADLINE:** Mar 1
FIELDS/MAJORS: Elementary Or Secondary Education

Award for juniors or seniors who are studying to be an elementary or high school level teacher. Must have a GPA of at least 3.0 and be a resident of New Mexico. Write to the address below for more information.

Eastern New Mexico University
College Of Education And Technology
Station 25
Portales, NM 88130

3185

Mr. And Mrs. James M. Kirk Endowment Scholarships

AMOUNT: $1,000 **DEADLINE:** Mar 1
FIELDS/MAJORS: All Areas Of Study

Three scholarships available to entering freshmen who are graduates of Lancaster County high schools. Renewable for three years. Contact the financial aid office at the address below for details.

Clemson University
Financial Aid Office
G01 Sikes Hall
Clemson, SC 29634

3186

Mr. And Mrs. Willis Doyle Nursing Scholarship

Amount: $3,000 **Deadline:** None Specified
Fields/Majors: Nursing

Awards given to students at St. Petersburg Junior College studying nursing with a strong desire to graduate from the program and strong determination to overcome all obstacles in pursuit of goals. You may write to the address below, but more information will appear in campus publications.

St. Petersburg Junior College
Office of Financial Aid
P.O. Box 13489
St. Petersburg, FL 33733

3187

MSSCSP Summer Research Fellowship

Amount: Varies **Deadline:** Mar 1
Fields/Majors: Biological Sciences

Eight to ten-week fellowship for a minority 2nd or 3rd year undergraduate planning to attend graduate school in the biological sciences. Must be a U.S. citizen or a permanent resident. Write to the address below for additional information.

American Society For Microbiology
Office of Education And Training
1325 Massachusettes Ave, N.W.
Washington, DC 20005

3188

Muddy Waters Scholarship

Amount: $2,000 **Deadline:** Mar 31
Fields/Majors: Music, Music Education, Journalism, Radio/TV/Film, Performing Arts

Awards for students at Chicago-area schools above the freshman level who are studying one of the fields listed. Write to the address below for more information.

Blues Heaven Foundation, Inc.
Scholarship Coordinator
249 N. Brand Blvd.
Glendale, CA 91203

3189

Multi-Cultural Scholarship

Amount: $500-$2,600 **Deadline:** Dec 15
Fields/Majors: All Areas Of Study

Scholarships for students who underrepresented on campus. This includes ethnicity or cultural experience. For undergraduate study. Must be U.S. citizens or permanent residents and show academic promise. Renewable upon good academic standing. Write to the address below for more details.

University Of Redlands
Office of Financial Aid
1200 East Colfax Ave, P.O. Box 3080
Redlands, CA 92373

3190

Multi-Ethnic Recruitment Scholarship Program

Amount: $1,000-$5,000
Deadline: None Specified
Fields/Majors: Library/Information Science

Graduate and continuing level scholarships for minorities underrepresented in California libraries - American Indian, Asian/Pacific Islander, Hispanic, and African American. For study in an accredited library school in California. Requires application directly to and nomination by a public, academic, or cooperative library or an accredited graduate library school. Contact your library or library school for details and application.

California State Library
Library Development Services Bureau
P.O. Box 942837
Sacramento, CA 94237

3191

Multicultural Achievement Award

Amount: $125 **Deadline:** March
Fields/Majors: All Areas Of Study

Award based on GPA (minimum 3.0), two letters of recommendation from faculty and academic staff, completed application form with personal statement and identification of leadership. Contact the division of academic support, UW Oshkosh for more details.

University Of Wisconsin, Oshkosh
Financial Aid Office, Dempsey 104
800 Algoma Blvd.
Oshkosh, WI 4901

3192

Multicultural Grants

Amount: $1,500 (max) **Deadline:** Feb 1
Fields/Majors: All Areas Of Study

Awards for African American, Native American, and Hispanic students who can demonstrate financial need. Write to the address below for more information.

Lewis And Clark College
Office of Admissions
Portland, OR 97219

3193

Multiple Sclerosis Society Research Grants

Amount: Varies **Deadline:** Varies
Fields/Majors: Biomedical Research: Multiple Sclerosis

The National Multiple Sclerosis Society provides funds for biomedical and postdoctoral fellowships specifically concerning the disease multiple sclerosis. Contact the Director of Research and Training Programs at the address below for details.

National Multiple Sclerosis Society
Research And Medical Programs
733 Third Ave.
New York, NY 10017

3194

Munich Fellowships

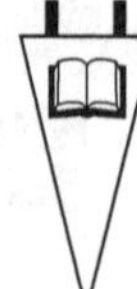

AMOUNT: None Specified **DEADLINE:** Apr 3
FIELDS/MAJORS: All Areas Of Study

Fellowships are available for Wayne State graduate students who have written and oral competence in the German language to study for 10 months at the University of Munich. Applicants must be U.S. citizens. Write to the address below for further details.

Wayne State University
Graduate School
Office of The Dean
Detroit, MI 48202

3195

Murphy Farms, Inc. Scholarship

AMOUNT: $3,000 **DEADLINE:** Mar 1
FIELDS/MAJORS: Animal Science, Agricultural Economics

Awards are available for freshmen at North Carolina State University who are studying in one of the fields above. Based on merit and financial need. Write to the address below for more information.

North Carolina State University
School Of Agriculture
Raleigh, NC 27695

3196

Murray Gellmann Scholarship, C.N. Yang Scholarship

AMOUNT: Varies **DEADLINE:** Feb 15
FIELDS/MAJORS: Physics

Scholarships are available at the University of Utah for full-time entering freshmen majoring in physics. Write to the address below for information.

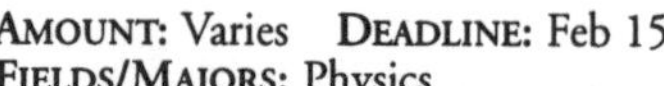

University Of Utah
Dr. Leslie Glaser
239 John A. Widtsoe Building
Salt Lake City, UT 84112

3197

Muscular Dystrophy Assoc. Research Fellowship Program

AMOUNT: Varies **DEADLINE:**
FIELDS/MAJORS: Medical Research, Neurology

Post-doctoral research fellowships for investigators (in U.S. or abroad) who hold a Ph.D., M.D., or equivalent. Most grants are for 2 years. Special consideration given to young investigators. Write to the address below for complete details.

Muscular Dystrophy Assoc., Inc.
Cindy Stein, Grants Program Manager
3300 E. Sunrise Dr.
Tucson, AZ 85718

3198

Muse-Moody-Holloway Scholarship

AMOUNT: Varies **DEADLINE:** None Specified
FIELDS/MAJORS: All Areas Of Study

Scholarship available at ETSU for outstanding graduates of Johnson County High School in Mountain City, Tennessee. Contact the Office of Financial Aid at the address below.

East Tennessee State University
Office of Financial Aid
Box 70722
Johnson City, TN 37614

3199

Music/Choral Scholarship

AMOUNT: Varies **DEADLINE:** None Specified
FIELDS/MAJORS: Music

Scholarships are available to John Brown College for full-time undergraduate students who are pursuing a degree in music. Write to the address below for details.

John Brown University
Office of Financial Aid
2000 West University Dr.
Siloam Springs, AR 72761

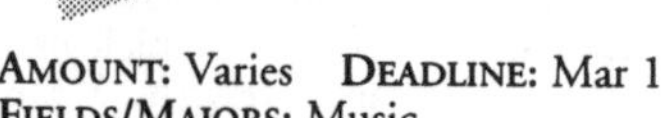

3200

Music Achievement Award

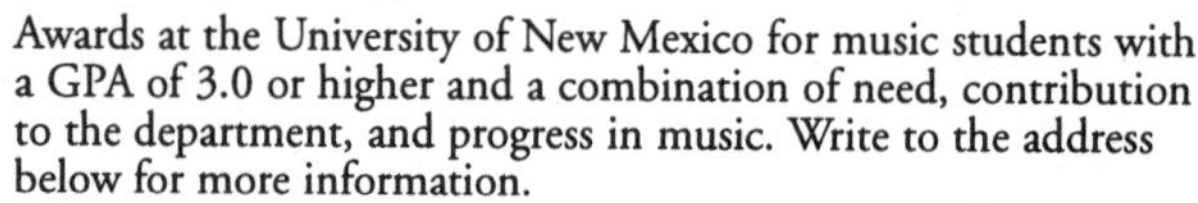

AMOUNT: Varies **DEADLINE:** Mar 1
FIELDS/MAJORS: Music

Awards at the University of New Mexico for music students with a GPA of 3.0 or higher and a combination of need, contribution to the department, and progress in music. Write to the address below for more information.

University Of New Mexico, Albuquerque
Office of Financial Aid
Albuquerque, NM 87131

3201

Music Assistance Fund Scholarships

AMOUNT: $2,500 (max) **DEADLINE:** Dec 15
FIELDS/MAJORS: Music, Instrumental

Scholarships for students of African American descent (and similar heritages such as African Caribbean, etc.) who are studying toward a career in this country's symphony orchestra. Must be a U.S. citizen. Based on auditions, recommendations, and need. Must be a student of orchestral instruments. (note: voice, piano, saxophone, composition and conducting are not included.) Write to the address below for details.

American Symphony Orchestra League
1156 15th St. NW, Suite 800
Washington, DC 20005

3202

Music Department Awards

AMOUNT: Varies **DEADLINE:** Jan 15
FIELDS/MAJORS: Music

Awards for music students at Valparaiso University. Must be a freshman or a transfer student and have a GPA of at least 2.0. Based on an audition and a recommendation from the department chairman. Renewable. Write to the address below for further details.

Valparaiso University
Office of Admissions And Financial Aid
Kretzmann Hall
Valparaiso, IN 46383

3203

Music Department Scholarships

Amount: $250-$1,000 **Deadline:** Jan 1
Fields/Majors: Music

Awards are available to music students based on demonstrated musical abilities on voice or instrument. Financial need is considered. Must have a GPA of at least 3.0. Write to the address below for more information.

Portland State University
Music Department
231 Lincoln Hall
Portland, OR 97207

3204

Music Department Tuition Remission Scholarships

Amount: In-State Tuition **Deadline:** May 1
Fields/Majors: Music

Awards are available to music majors with a GPA of at least 3.0. Applicants must demonstrate and continue to demonstrate outstanding music skill. Renewable. Write to the address below for more information.

Portland State University
Music Department
231 Lincoln Hall
Portland, OR 97207

3205

Music Departmental Scholarships

Amount: Varies **Deadline:** Jan 20
Fields/Majors: Music

Scholarships are available at the University of Utah for full-time music majors. Various scholarships are offered. Individual award requirements may vary. Write to the address below for details.

University Of Utah
Music Scholarship Committee
204 David P. Gardner Hall
Salt Lake City, UT 84112

3206

Music Endowed And Private Scholarships

Amount: Varies **Deadline:** Feb 15
Fields/Majors: Music

Scholarships are available at Evangel for full-time students pursuing a degree in music. Applicants must have a GPA of at least 3.0. Includes fifteen different awards. Requirements vary. Write to the address listed below for information.

Evangel College
Office of Enrollment
1111 N. Glenstone
Springfield, MO 65802

3207

Music Performance Scholarship

Amount: $1,000 **Deadline:** Apr 15
Fields/Majors: Music

Awards for students with talents or ability in music. Must be a full-time student and maintain a GPA of 2.5 or better. Renewable. Write to the address below for more information.

Bethel College
Office of Financial Planning
3900 Bethel Dr.
St. Paul, MN 55112

3208

Music Performance Scholarships

Amount: $100-$200 **Deadline:** None Specified
Fields/Majors: Music

Scholarships for students at COS who are performing artists, vocalists and/or instrumentalists. Applicants must perform in a minimum of three groups and be enrolled in music theory each semester, to qualify for the $200 scholarships. For the $100 scholarships, the student must perform at least twice each semester and is encouraged to enroll in music theory. Contact the music department for deadlines and other information or write to the address below for details.

College Of The Siskiyous
Financial Aid Office
800 College Ave
Weed, CA 6094

3209

Music Performance Scholarships

Amount: $5,000 (max) **Deadline:** None Specified
Fields/Majors: Music

Renewable scholarships for students at Eckerd College who excel in instrumental, vocal, or keyboard music performance. Contact the address below for details.

Eckerd College
Director of Financial Aid
P.O. Box 12560
St. Petersburg, FL 33733

3210

Music Program Scholarships

Amount: $750 (max) **Deadline:** May 1
Fields/Majors: Music

Scholarships for music students at Five Towns College. Awarded on the basis of performing ability, service to the college and economic need. Write to the address below for additional information.

Five Towns College
305 N. Service Road/Lie Exit 50
Dix Hills, NY 11746

3211

Music Scholarship

Amount: $1,500 (max) **Deadline:** Dec 1
Fields/Majors: Music

Scholarships available in amounts from $500 to $1,500 for students who are or will be attending Ripon College, and pursuing a degree in music. Write to the address below for details.

Ripon College
300 Seward St.
P.O. Box 248
Ripon, WI 54971

3212

Music Scholarship

Amount: Varies **Deadline:** Mar 1
Fields/Majors: Music

Scholarships are available at Kentucky Wesleyan College for undergraduate students who plan to pursue a career in music. Write to the address below for details.

Kentucky Wesleyan College
Financial Aid Office
3000 Frederica St.
Owensboro, KY 43202

3213

Music Scholarship

Amount: $200-$4,000 **Deadline:** Dec 15
Fields/Majors: Music

Scholarships for students majoring in or talented in some area of music. Must audition in person or on tape for award. Based on ability. Renewable with a 2.7 GPA. For undergraduate study. Write to the address below for more details.

University Of Redlands
Office of Financial Aid
1200 East Colfax Ave., P.O. Box 3080
Redlands, CA 92373

3214

Music Scholarship

Amount: $1,200 (max) **Deadline:** May 1
Fields/Majors: Music

Awards for freshmen who demonstrate ability or talent in the field of interior design. Based primarily on an audition. Renewable. Write to the Chair of the Department of Music at the address below for more information.

Winthrop University
Department of Music
119 Tillman Hall
Rock Hill, SC 29733

3215

Music Scholarship

Amount: Varies **Deadline:** Unspecified
Fields/Majors: Music

Awards to students recommended by the FIU Music Department after auditions. The Music Department will provide audition dates. Write to the address below for more information.

Florida International University
Music Department-DM 347
University Park
Miami, FL 33199

3216

Music Scholarships

Amount: $500 **Deadline:** Feb 15
Fields/Majors: Music-Piano Or Instrumental, Music Education, Music Therapy

Applicant must be a senior in a Massachusetts high school and present a letter of endorsement from sponsoring women's club in your community. Auditions will be held. Applicant's interest must be in piano, instrument, music education or music therapy. Write to the address below for details.

General Federation Of Women's Clubs Of Massachusetts
Chairman, Music Division
P.O. Box 679
Sudbury, MA 01776

3217

Music Scholarships

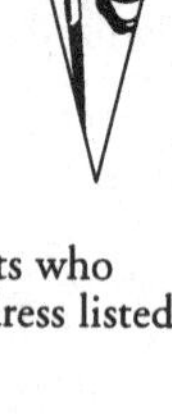

Amount: None Specified **Deadline:** Apr 1
Fields/Majors: Music

Scholarships are available at Evangel for full-time students who are or plan to pursue a degree in music. Write to the address listed below for information.

Evangel College
Chairperson
Music Department
Springfield, MO 65802

3218

Music Scholarships

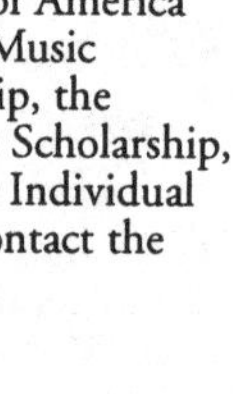

Amount: None Specified
Deadline: None Specified
Fields/Majors: Music

Scholarships are available at the Catholic University of America for students studying music. Includes the John Paul Music Scholarship, the David Burchuk Memorial Scholarship, the Clifford E. Brown Scholarship, the William Masselos Scholarship, and the Benjamin T. Rome Endowment Scholarship. Individual award requirements may vary. For graduate study. Contact the financial aid office at the address below for details.

The Catholic University Of America
Office of Admissions And Financial Aid
Washington, DC 20064

3219

Music Scholarships

Amount: Varies **Deadline:** None Specified
Fields/Majors: Music

Several scholarships are offered to the a cappella and show choirs, Marching Southerners, pep band, and voice students. Contact the head of the music department for more information.

Jacksonville State University
Financial Aid Office
Jacksonville, AL 36265

3220

Music Scholarships

Amount: $200-$600 **Deadline:** Apr 15
Fields/Majors: Music

Award for music students at Liberty or for those in any area of study who participate in music activities on campus. Contact the Fine Arts Department for more information.

Liberty University
Office of Student Financial Aid
Box 20,000
Lynchburg, VA 24506

3221

Music Scholarships

AMOUNT: $500-$2,500 **DEADLINE:** Feb 1
FIELDS/MAJORS: Music

Awards for Lewis and Clark students who have outstanding talent in music. Write to the address below for complete details.

Lewis And Clark College
Department of Music
0615 SW Palatine Hill Road
Portland, OR 97219

3222

Music Scholarships

AMOUNT: Varies **DEADLINE:** None Specified
FIELDS/MAJORS: Music

Awards for Furman students on the basis of auditions held in December and January. Contact the Department of Music for more information.

Furman University
Director. Of Financial Aid
3300 Poinsett Highway
Greenville, SC 29613

3223

Music Scholarships

AMOUNT: Varies **DEADLINE:** None Specified
FIELDS/MAJORS: Music

Scholarships awarded on the basis of performance ability, academic achievement and financial need. Write to the address below for more information.

University Of Miami
Office of Financial Assistance Services
P.O. Box 248187
Coral Gables, FL 33124

3224

Music Scholarships

AMOUNT: None Specified
DEADLINE: None Specified
FIELDS/MAJORS: Music

Scholarships are available at the Catholic University of America for students who have demonstrated musical proficiency. These awards are available from the Benjamin T. Rome School of Music. Contact the Office of the Dean, Benjamin T. Rome School of Music, the Catholic University of America, Washington, DC 20064 for more information.

Catholic University Of America
Office of Admissions And Financial Aid
Washington, DC 20064

3225

Music, Drama, Speech, And Visual Arts Scholarships

AMOUNT: Varies **AMOUNT:** Varies
FIELDS/MAJORS: Music, Art, Photography, Drama/theatre

Selection based on demonstrated talent. Available to freshmen students at Loyola University-New Orleans. Write to the address below for additional information.

Loyola University-New Orleans
Office of Admissions
6363 St. Charles Ave.
New Orleans, LA 70118

3226

Myasthenia Gravis Foundation Fellowships

AMOUNT: Varies **DEADLINE:** Nov 1
FIELDS/MAJORS: Neuromuscular Medicine

Fellowships are available for postdoctoral scholars involved in clinical research related to Myasthenia Gravis (MG). Write to the address listed below for information.

Myasthenia Gravis Foundation Of America
Fellowship Program
222 S. Riverside Plaza, Suite 1540
Chicago, IL 60606

3227

Myasthenia Gravis Foundation Nurses Research Fellowship

AMOUNT: Varies **DEADLINE:** Feb 1
FIELDS/MAJORS: Research Nursing

Award for currently licensed or registered professional nurses who are interested in research pertaining to problems faced by Myasthenia Gravis patients. Must be U.S. or Canadian citizens or permanent residents. Write to the address below for more information.

Myasthenia Gravis Foundation Of America
222 S. Riverside Plaza, Suite 1540
Chicago, IL 60606

3228

Myra Levick Scholarship Fund

AMOUNT: None Specified **DEADLINE:** Jun 15
FIELDS/MAJORS: Art Therapy

Scholarships for graduate students who have demonstrated academic excellence and are in an AATA approved art therapy program. Applicants must demonstrate financial need in order to complete their program of study and have an undergraduate GPA of at least a 3.0. Write to the address below for complete details.

The American Art Therapy Assoc., Inc.
Scholarship Committee
1202 Allanson Road
Mundelein, IL 60060

3229

Myron J. Walker Scholarships

AMOUNT: Varies **DEADLINE:** Feb 15
FIELDS/MAJORS: Religion

Scholarships are available at the University of Iowa for full-time students from Iowa who plan to pursue a career in the ministry or rabbinate. Write to the address listed below for information.

University Of Iowa
School Of Religion
314 Gilmore Hall
Iowa City, IA 52242

3230

Myrtle & Earl Walker Scholarship

AMOUNT: $500 **DEADLINE:** Mar 1
FIELDS/MAJORS: Manufacturing Engineering, Manufacturing Engineering Technology

Scholarships for full-time undergraduate students who have completed at least thirty credit hours and are seeking a career in manufacturing engineering or manufacturing engineering technology. Student must have a minimum grade point average of 3.5. Write to the address below for details. Information may also be available in your department office. If writing please specify what scholarship(s) you are interested in.

SME Manufacturing Engineering Education Foundation
One SME Drive
P.O. Box 930
Dearborn, MI 48121

3231

Myrtle Okey Scholarships

AMOUNT: Varies **DEADLINE:** Mar 1
FIELDS/MAJORS: All Areas Of Study

Awards are available at the University of New Mexico for American Indian students. Write to the address below for more information.

University Of New Mexico, Albuquerque
Office Of Financial Aid
Albuquerque, NM 87131

3232

Myrtle P. Teter Memorial Scholarship

AMOUNT: $400 **DEADLINE:** None Specified
FIELDS/MAJORS: Education

Student must be enrolled full-time in the College of Education with a GPA of 3.0 or better. Contact the Curriculum and Instruction Department for more information.

Southwest Missouri State University
Office Of Financial Aid
901 South National Ave.
Springfield, MO 65804

3233

N. Patricia Yarborough Scholarship

AMOUNT: Varies **DEADLINE:** Mar 15
FIELDS/MAJORS: All Areas Of Study

Awards open to TPU students who have completed sixty credit hours and who have a GPA of 3.25 or higher. Award is to be used for travel abroad. Write to the address below for more information.

Teikyo Post University
Office Of Financial Aid
800 Country Club Road
Waterbury, CT 06723

3234

NAACP Department of Energy Scholarship

AMOUNT: $10,000 **DEADLINE:** Apr 30
FIELDS/MAJORS: Engineering, Computer Science Science, Math, Environmental Studies

Applicants must be H. S. seniors, and NAACP members with a 3.0 GPA, studying for a career in one of the above areas. Applicant must be prepared to spend one summer prior to graduation as an intern at a DOE facility, participate in 120 hours of community service, and be employed by the DOE for at least two years after graduation. Renewable if 3.0 average is maintained. Write to the address below for details and include the scholarship name on the envelope.

NAACP Special Contribution Fund
Education Department
4805 Mount Hope Dr.
Baltimore, MD 21215

3235

NAACP Willems Scholarship-Graduate

AMOUNT: $3,000 **DEADLINE:** Apr 30
FIELDS/MAJORS: Engineering, Chemistry, Physics, Computer Science, Mathematics

Applicants must be graduate students who are members of the NAACP with at least a GPA of 3.0. Renewable. Write to the address below for details and include the scholarship name on the envelope.

NAACP Special Contribution Fund
Education Department
4805 Mount Hope Dr.
Baltimore, MD 21215

3236

NAACP Willems Scholarship-Undergraduate

AMOUNT: $2,000 (max) **DEADLINE:** Apr 30
FIELDS/MAJORS: Engineering, Chemistry Physics, Computer Science, Mathematics

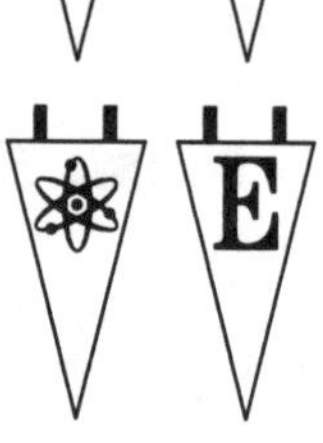

Applicants must be a member of NAACP with a 3.0 GPA in one of the fields of study listed above. Renewable. Write to address below for more details and include the scholarship name on the envelope.

NAACP Special Contribution Fund
Education Department
4805 Mount Hope Dr.
Baltimore, MD 21215

3237

NACM Student Scholarship

AMOUNT: Varies **DEADLINE:** None Specified
FIELDS/MAJORS: Judicial Administration, Court Management

Awards for graduate students currently enrolled in a master's degree program in judicial administration at the American University (Washington, DC), University of Denver, or the

University of Southern California. Write to the address below for more information.

National Assoc. Of Court Management
NACM Secretariat, Ctr. For State Courts
300 Newport Ave.
Williamsburg, VA 3185

3238

NACME-Incentive Grants Program (IGP)

Amount: $250-$2,000
Deadline: None Specified
Fields/Majors: Engineering

Open to American Indian, African American, or Hispanic students. Must demonstrate need or be designated to receive a merit award. For full-time enrollment in one of the participating colleges. Applicants must be U.S. citizens and have a GPA of at least 2.5. For freshman year of study. Write to the address below for details and a list of participating colleges.

National Action Council For Minorities In Engineering, Inc.
3 W. 35th St.
New York, NY 10001

3239

Nadine Blackburn Memorial Award

Amount: Varies **Deadline:** Mar 1
Fields/Majors: Theater And Dance

Awards are available at the University of New Mexico for students with a GPA of at least 2.5 and financial need. Students must have past involvement in department/production activities and demonstrate talent. Write to the address below for more information.

University Of New Mexico, Albuquerque
Office of Financial Aid
Albuquerque, NM 87131

3240

NAHJ Scholarships

Amount: $1,000-$2,000 **Deadline:** Jan 31
Fields/Majors: Journalism And Communications

For high school seniors, college undergraduates or graduate students majoring in journalism or mass communications. Scholarship recipients will be selected based on academic excellence, a demonstrated interest in journalism as a career, and financial need. Applications and materials may be submitted in either Spanish or English. Thirty-two awards per year. Students majoring in other fields must be able to demonstrate a strong interest in pursuing a career in journalism. Write to the address below for complete details.

National Assoc. Of Hispanic Journalists
529 14th St., NW
1193 National Press Bldg.
Washington, DC 20045

3241

NAHJ/Newhouse Scholarship/Internship Program

Amount: $5,000 **Deadline:** Jan 31
Fields/Majors: Journalism And Communications

Summer internship program for Hispanic college juniors and seniors majoring in journalism. Internship must be between the junior and senior year of study. Write to the address below for more information.

National Assoc. Of Hispanic Journalists
529 14th St., NW
1193 National Press Building
Washington, DC 20045

3242

NALF Grants

Amount: Varies **Deadline:** Dec 15
Fields/Majors: Ornithology-Loon Research

Grants to support specific research, management, and educational projects which may yield results useful to the NALF in furtherance of its goals and which will promote and enhance the conservation and management of loons in North America. Write to the address below for more information.

North American Loon Fund
Grant Committee
6 Lily Pond Road
Gilford, NH 03246

3243

NAMTA Scholarships

Amount: None Specified **Deadline:** Mar 15
Fields/Majors: All Areas Of Study

Applicants must be an employee or a relative of an employee of a NAMTA member firm. Award is based on GPA, financial need, extracurricular activities, career choice, and special interests. Write to the address below for details.

National Art Materials Trade Assoc.
178 Lakeview Ave.
Clifton, NJ 07011

3244

Nancy B. Woolridge Graduate Fellowship

Amount: $500-$1,000 **Deadline:** Feb 1
Fields/Majors: All Areas Of Study

Fellowships for members of Zeta Phi Beta sorority who have demonstrated ability in their areas of expertise. For full-time study at the undergraduate or graduate level. Renewable. Contact your chapter or send an SASE to the national headquarters at the address below before February 1 for further information.

Zeta Phi Beta Sorority
National Educational Foundation
1734 New Hampshire Ave., NW
Washington, DC 20009

3245

Nancy Jeanne Garner Scholarship

Amount: $2,000 **Deadline:** None Specified
Fields/Majors: All Areas Of Study

Scholarships are awarded to students who participate in the Cal Poly Pomona Youth Gospel Choir and to African American students. Must have a GPA of 2.0 or better. Write to the address below for more information.

California State Polytechnic University, Pomona
Office of Financial Aid
3801 West Temple Ave.
Pomona, CA 91768

3246

Napa Auto Parts Scholarships

AMOUNT: $1,000 **DEADLINE:** Mar 31
FIELDS/MAJORS: Agriculture

Awards for students in FFA, whose chapter is located within a 15 mile radius of a Napa store. Applicants must obtain the store manager's signature on the scholarship application. For undergraduate study. Write to the address below for more information.

National FFA Foundation
P.O. Box 15160
5632 Mt. Vernon Memorial Highway
Alexandria, VA 22309

3247

NAPHCC Educational Foundation Scholarship

AMOUNT: $2,500 **DEADLINE:** Apr 1
FIELDS/MAJORS: Plumbing And Related Fields

Applicants must be current high school seniors or college freshmen. Must be sponsored by an NAPHCC member. Renewable for up to four years. Must have knowledge of or experience in the heating-plumbing-cooling industry. Up to three awards per year. Not for apprenticeship programs. Write to the address below for details. Also, contact your local PHCC Assoc. for other scholarships.

National Assoc. Of Plumbing, Heating And Cooling Contractors
NAPHCC Educational Found. Scholarship
P.O. Box 6808
Falls Church, VA 22040

3248

Nard Foundation Student Loan Program

GPA 2.5+

AMOUNT: $1,000 (max) **AMOUNT:** Varies
FIELDS/MAJORS: Pharmacy

Awards are available for pharmacy students who are enrolled in their last 2 and a half years of a B.S. program. Must be a U.S. citizen with a GPA of at least 2.5. Write to the address below for more information.

Nard Foundation
205 Dangerfield Road
Alexandria, VA 22314

3249

Nard Student Achievement Award

AMOUNT: $200+Plaque Rolling
FIELDS/MAJORS: Pharmacy

Awards for students enrolled in a College of Pharmacy with at least one year of study left, who are interested in a career in independent pharmacy and the entrepreneurial spirit to achieve this goal. Write to the address below for more information.

Nard Foundation
Student Affairs
205 Daingerfield Road
Alexandria, VA 22314

3250

NASA Graduate Student Fellowships In Global Change Research

AMOUNT: Varies **DEADLINE:** Mar 15
FIELDS/MAJORS: Earth Related Sciences (Geology, Meteorology, Hydrology, Etc.)

Fellowships for students enrolled full-time in a graduate program at a U.S. university and in a field relevant to NASA's global change research efforts. Additional information is available electronically via the internet at: http://www.hq.nasa.gov/office/mtpe/ or via anonymous ftp at: ftp.hp.nasa.gov/pub/mtpe. Paper copies of information received on-line will only be available to those who do not have access to the internet.

NASA Global Change Fellowship Program
Code Ysp-44
Attn: Dr. Ghassem Asrar
Washington, DC 20546

3251

NASA Training Project

E GPA 3.0+ D

AMOUNT: Varies **DEADLINE:** Mar 1
FIELDS/MAJORS: Engineering, Mathematics, Physics

Awards are available at the University of New Mexico for undergraduates with a GPA of at least 3.0 in the fields above. Must be a minority student or a student who is physically challenged. Recipients must indicate a willingness to invest at least 10 hours per week for structured study and to work at a NASA sponsored facility in a co-op education program when eligible. Write to the address below for more information.

University Of New Mexico, Albuquerque
Office of Financial Aid
Albuquerque, NM 87131

3252

Nascher/Manning Memorial Award

AMOUNT: Expenses **DEADLINE:** Dec 5
FIELDS/MAJORS: Geriatrics

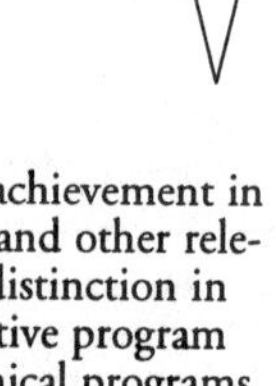

Open to individuals with distinguished, life-long achievement in clinical geriatrics, including medicine, psychiatry, and other relevant disciplines. The awardee may have achieved distinction in clinical geriatrics through activities such as innovative program development or administration of outstanding clinical programs. Write to the address below for more information.

American Geriatrics Society
770 Lexington Ave., Suite 300
New York, NY 10021

3253

Nat Moore Memorial Scholarship

GPA 3.5+

AMOUNT: Varies **DEADLINE:** Apr 1
FIELDS/MAJORS: Art-Painting

Scholarships are available at the University of New Mexico for full-time art undergraduates, with a concentration in painting, who are 25 years or older. Must have a GPA greater than 3.5. Write to the address listed below for information.

University Of New Mexico, Albuquerque
College Of Fine Arts
Office of The Dean
Albuquerque, NM 87131

3254

Nat Moore Memorial Scholarships

Amount: Varies **Deadline:** Mar 1
Fields/Majors: Art, Painting

Awards are available at the University of New Mexico for undergraduates studying art and concentrating in painting who are age 25 or older. Must demonstrate artistic excellence and financial need. Contact the Fine Arts Department for more information.

University Of New Mexico, Albuquerque
Office of Financial Aid
Albuquerque, NM 87131

3255

Nathalie Rutherford Scholarship

Amount: $1,000 **Deadline:** Apr 5
Fields/Majors: Music

Scholarships for graduating high school seniors interested in pursuing a career in music. Must be from Port Chester, Rye, Rye Brook (Westchester County, NY), Greenwich, Stamford, Darien, New Canaan, Norwalk, Westport, or Wilton (Fairfield County, CT). Based on "musical qualification." Write to the address below for details or call (203) 622-5136.

Greenwich Choral Society
Nathalie Rutherford Scholarship
P.O. Box 5
Greenwich, CT 06836

3256

Nathan Cummings Scholarship Program, Sara Lee Corporation

Amount: Varies **Deadline:** Jan 1
Fields/Majors: All Areas Of Study

Any full-time employee of Sara Lee Corporation or dependents of employees are eligible for participation in the program. Eligible employees and their dependents should contact their divisional human resources department for application procedures.

Sara Lee Corporation
Scholarship/Student Loan Administration
Three First National Plaza
Chicago, IL 60602

3257

Nation/I.F. Stone Award For Student Journalism

Amount: $1,000 **Deadline:** Jun 29
Fields/Majors: Journalism

This award recognizes excellence in student journalism. Entries should exhibit the uniquely independent journalistic tradition of I.F. Stone. A self-described "Jeffersonian Marxist," Stone combined progressive politics, investigative zeal and a compulsion to tell the truth with a commitment to human rights and justice. Open to all undergraduate journalism majors. Write to the address listed below for information.

Nation Institute
Nation/Stone Award
72 Fifth Ave.
New York, NY 10011

3258

Nation Internship Program

Amount: Varies **Amount:** Varies
Fields/Majors: Magazine Journalism

Internship program for college upperclassmen and recent graduates interested in magazine journalism and publishing. Based primarily on resume, writing sample, and interview. Write to the address below for more information.

Nation Magazine
Peter Meyer/Kio Stark
72 Fifth St.
New York, NY 10011

3259

National Achievement Scholarship

Amount: Half Tuition **Deadline:** None Specified
Fields/Majors: All Areas Of Study

Selection by National Merit Scholarship corporation. Freshmen will automatically be given the award. Applicant must have outstanding test performance. Four-year scholarship. To renew scholarship a GPA of 3.2 is required. Write to the address below for details.

Denison University
Financial Aid Office
Box M
Granville, OH 43023

3260

National Achievement Scholarships For Outstanding Negro Students

Amount: $2,000 **Deadline:** None Specified
Fields/Majors: Engineering

Awards for African American students who are National Merit finalists and intending to enroll in an accredited school to earn a degree in engineering. Award is given to high school seniors. Must be U.S. citizens. Write to the address below for more information.

National Merit Scholarship Corporation
One Rotary Center
1560 Sherman Ave.
Evanston, IL 60201

3261

National AgricultureCenter And Hall Of Fame Scholarships

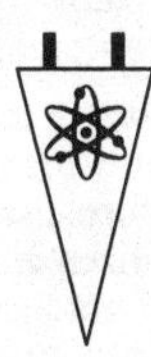

Amount: $2,000 **Deadline:** Feb 15
Fields/Majors: Agriculture

Scholarships are available for FFA members pursuing a two- or four-year degree in any area of agriculture who are in the top 50% of their class. Write to the address below for details.

National FFA Foundation
Scholarship Office
P.O. Box 15160
Alexandria, VA 22309

3262
National Alumni Fellowship

AMOUNT: $500 **DEADLINE:** Dec 15
FIELDS/MAJORS: Home Economics/Related Fields

Applicants must be members of Kappa Omicron Nu and a master's candidate. Write to the address below for details.

Kappa Omicron Nu Honor Society
4990 Northwind Dr., Suite 140
East Lansing, MI 48823

3263
National Assoc. Of Chain Drug Stores, Albert C. Wehrenberg Scholarship

AMOUNT: $500-$1,250 **DEADLINE:** Feb 1
FIELDS/MAJORS: Pharmacy

Scholarships are available at the University of Oklahoma, Norman, for full-time freshmen or sophomore pharmacy majors. Based on academic excellence. Write to the address listed below for information.

University Of Oklahoma, Norman
College Of Pharmacy
P.O. Box 26901
Oklahoma City, OK 73190

3264
National Assoc. For Hispanic Elderly Assoc. Scholarship

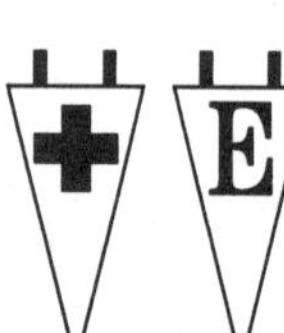

AMOUNT: Varies **DEADLINE:** None Specified
FIELDS/MAJORS: Physical Therapy, Human Service, Geriatrics, Social Service, Health

Scholarships are available at the University of Oklahoma, Norman, for full-time students majoring in the above areas. Write to the address listed below for information.

University Of Oklahoma, Norman
Department of Physical Therapy
OUHSC, P.O. Box 26901
Oklahoma City, OK 73190

3265
National Assoc. Of Black Journalists Scholarship Awards

AMOUNT: $2,500 **DEADLINE:** Mar 22
FIELDS/MAJORS: Journalism, Mass Communications, Photojournalism

Twelve scholarships awarded to African American college students majoring in or intending to pursue a career in journalism or mass communications. Must be U.S. citizen and have a GPA of at least 2.5. For undergraduate or graduate study at a four-year college or university. Previous NABJ winners ineligible. The NABJ also offers a large internship program. Must become member of NABJ. Nomination by school advisor, dean, or faculty member is required. Write to the address below for further information.

National Assoc. Of Black Journalists
Scholarship Program
11600 Sunrise Valley Drive
Reston, VA 22091

3266
National Assoc. Of Black Journalists Scholarships

AMOUNT: $2,500 **AMOUNT:** Varies
FIELDS/MAJORS: Journalism

Awards for African American undergraduate or graduate journalism majors enrolled in a four-year accredited college or university. Must write a 500 to 800 word essay on a black journalist and submit three samples of writing. Write to the address below or check with local NABJ chapters for more information.

National Assoc. Of Black Journalists
Scholarship Award
P.O. Box 17212
Washington, DC 20041

3267
National Assoc. Of Educational Office Personnel Awards

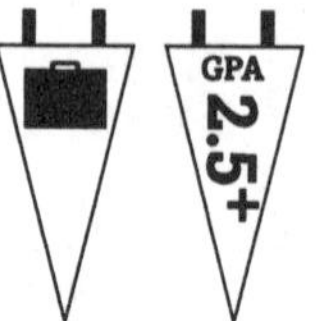

AMOUNT: Varies **DEADLINE:** Open
FIELDS/MAJORS: Business Secretarial

Award for minority high school graduate planning on or attending a two- or four-year college or vocational/occupational school to pursue a career in secretarial business. Must have taken two or more business courses and have a GPA of at least 2.8. Write to the address below for more information.

National Assoc. Of Educational Office Personnel
Scholarship Committee
7226 Lee Highway, Suite 301
Falls Church, VA 22046

3268
National Assoc. Of Purchasing Management Scholarship

AMOUNT: $250 **DEADLINE:** None Specified
FIELDS/MAJORS: Management

Student must be a management major interested in purchasing and materials management. Contact the COBA office for more information.

Southwest Missouri State University
Office of Financial Aid
901 South National Ave.
Springfield, MO 65804

3269
National Black Nurses Assoc. Scholarship Program

AMOUNT: $500-$2,000 **DEADLINE:** Apr 15
FIELDS/MAJORS: Nursing

Scholarships are available for African American nursing students who have at least one year remaining of study. Applicant must be a member of the NBNA, and demonstrate participation in African American community affairs. Write to the address listed below for information.

National Black Nurses Assoc.
NBNA Scholarship Program
P.O. Box 1823
Washington, DC 20013

3270

National Council Of Jewish Women, Rhode Island Section Scholarships

AMOUNT: None Specified **DEADLINE:** None Specified
FIELDS/MAJORS: All Areas Of Study

Scholarships available to Rhode Island students attending college in the fall. Scholarships will be awarded based on financial need, evidence of involvement in community service, and academic worthiness. Checks for this award are made out to the recipients to do with as they deem necessary for their education. Colleges are not informed. Write to the address below for details. The deadline for requesting applications is Mar 24.

National Council Of Jewish Women, Rhode Island Section
Attn: Seena Dittleman
93 Crestwood Rd
Cranston, RI 02920

3271

National Council Of State Garden Clubs Scholarships

AMOUNT: $1,000 **DEADLINE:** Mar 1
FIELDS/MAJORS: Horticulture, Forestry, Land Management, Botany & All Related Fields

Awards for college students who are Connecticut residents and have a good academic standing. Write to the address below for details.

The Federated Garden Clubs Of Connecticut, Inc.
Jo Rondestvedt, Scholarship Chairperson
P.O. Box 672
Wallingford, CT 06492

3272

National Distillers Distribution Foundation Merit Scholarships

AMOUNT: $500-$2,000 **DEADLINE:** None Specified
FIELDS/MAJORS: All Areas Of Study

Scholarships are available to graduating high school seniors who are National Merit finalists and children of employees of distributors who are members of the National Distillers Distributors Foundation. Up to twelve awards are offered annually. Write to the address listed below for information.

National Merit Scholarship Corporation/Nat. Distillers Dist. Foundation
1560 Sherman Ave., Suite 200
Evanston, IL 60201

3273

National Doctoral Fellowships In Business And Management

AMOUNT: $10,000 **DEADLINE:** Feb 8
FIELDS/MAJORS: Business Administration

Scholarships are available at the University of Oklahoma, Norman, for full-time Ph.D. candidates in business administration or management, who are citizens of the U.S. or Canada. Write to the address listed below for information.

University Of Oklahoma, Norman
College Of Business Administration
208 Adams Hall
Norman, OK 73019

3274

National Education Loan Fund

AMOUNT: $1,000 (max) **DEADLINE:** Mar 1
FIELDS/MAJORS: All Areas Of Study

Interest-free loans for children of full-paid life members of the Disabled American Veterans Auxiliary, children of full paid life members of the Disabled American Veterans (if mother is deceased), or full paid life members of the Disabled American Veterans Auxiliary. For full-time study in the U.S. Must have a GPA of 2.0 or better. Write to the address below for details.

Disabled American Veterans Auxiliary, National Headquarters
National Education Loan Fund Director
3725 Alexandria Pike
Cold Spring, KY 41076

3275

National Education Scholarship Awards

AMOUNT: None Specified **DEADLINE:** Apr 1
FIELDS/MAJORS: Fields Related To Materials Joining

Scholarships are available for students enrolled in programs related to materials joining at any college, university or vocational/technical school in the U.S. Write to the address listed below for information.

American Welding Society
National Education Scholarship Committee
550 NW Lejeune Road
Miami, FL 33126

3276

National Endowment For The Humanities Fellowships

AMOUNT: $30,000 (max) **DEADLINE:** Jan 20
FIELDS/MAJORS: History, Humanities, Linguistics

Six to eleven month fellowships are available for postdoctoral research in any subject relevant to the library materials. Applicants must be citizens of the U.S. or foreign nationals who have been resident in the U.S. for at least three years. Preference is given to applicants who have not held major fellowships or grants in the previous three years. Write to the address below for details.

Newberry Library
Committee On Awards
60 W. Walton St.
Chicago, IL 60610

3277

National Endowment For The Humanities Younger Scholars Program

AMOUNT: Varies **DEADLINE:** None Specified
FIELDS/MAJORS: All Areas Of Study

Scholarships are available at the University of Iowa for freshmen, sophomores and juniors who are U.S. citizens or legal residents. Write to the address listed below for information.

University Of Iowa
Shambaugh House Honors Center
Iowa City, IA 52242

3278

National Federation Of Press Women Minigrants

AMOUNT: $200 **DEADLINE:** May 1
FIELDS/MAJORS: Communication, Journalism

Small grants for members or student members to do research or attend a career-related course, seminar, or workshop. Must have been a member for at least two years. Paid after research or course. Write for mini-grant application at address below.

National Federation Of Press Women
Box 99
Blue Springs, MO 64013

3279

National Federation Of The Blind Humanities Scholarship

AMOUNT: $3,000 **DEADLINE:** Mar 31
FIELDS/MAJORS: Humanities

Award recipient must be legally blind students in any of the traditional humanities. Write to the address below for details.

National Federation Of The Blind
Mrs. Peggy Elliott, Chairman
814 Fourth Ave., Suite 200
Grinnell, IA 50112

3280

National Federation Of The Blind Scholarships

AMOUNT: $4,000 (max) **DEADLINE:** Mar 31
FIELDS/MAJORS: All Areas Of Study

Award recipient must be legally blind. There are no further restrictions on this award. Fourteen total scholarships available. Based on academics, community service, and financial need. Write to the address below for complete details.

National Federation Of The Blind
Mrs. Peggy Elliott, Chairman
814 Fourth Ave., Suite 200
Grinnell, IA 50112

3281

National Fellows Program

AMOUNT: None Specified
DEADLINE: None Specified
FIELDS/MAJORS: History, Sociology, Political Science, Economics, Law, Int'l. Relations

Post-doctoral fellowships provide particularly give gifted scholars the opportunity to spend one full year on unrestricted creative research and writing at the Hoover Institution. For study of eastern Europe and the Independent States of the former Soviet Union. Write to the address below for details.

Hoover Institution On War, Revolution And Peace
Stanford University
Stanford, CA 94305

3282

National Fellowship Loan Fund

AMOUNT: Varies **DEADLINE:** Open
FIELDS/MAJORS: All Areas Of Study

Loans for African Americans who are pursuing a degree in any area of graduate study. Write to the address below for more information.

National Fellowship Fund
Cn. 5281
Princeton, NJ 08543

3283

National FFA Alumni Scholarships

AMOUNT: $1,000 **DEADLINE:** Feb 15
FIELDS/MAJORS: Agricultural Education

Scholarships are available for FFA members pursuing a four-year degree in agricultural education. Write to the address below for details.

National FFA Foundation
Scholarship Office
P.O. Box 15160
Alexandria, VA 22309

3284

National Guard Educational Assistance Program

AMOUNT: $1,000 (max) **DEADLINE:** None Specified
FIELDS/MAJORS: All Areas Of Study

Grants for members of the Alabama National Guard. For undergraduate or graduate studies at Alabama institutions. Must be an Alabama resident and at least 17 years of age. Contact your Guard unit or write to the address below for details.

Alabama Commission On Higher Education
P.O. Box 30200
Montgomery, AL 36130

3285

National Health Service Corps Loan Repayment Program

AMOUNT: Varies **DEADLINE:** Ongoing
FIELDS/MAJORS: Medicine, Social Work, Nursing, Dentistry, Psychology, Family Therapy

Loan repayment program for students who agree to provide primary care services in a priority shortage area for at least two years. Applicants must be U.S. citizens with a valid, unrestricted state license. Program includes a competitive salary, a percentage of loans repaid and a stipend. Write to the address below for more information or call (800) 221-9393.

National Health Service Corps
2070 Chain Bridge Road
Suite 450
Vienna, VA 2182

3286

National Health Service Corps Scholarship Program

AMOUNT: Varies **DEADLINE:** None Specified
FIELDS/MAJORS: Medicine, Osteopathy, Nursing, Medical Assisting

Scholarship program for students in one of the areas listed above.

For each year of support, recipients are obligated to serve one year in full-time clinical practice of their profession, or employed by the National Health Service Corps, a component of the U.S. Public Health Service. Assignments will be in eligible health shortage manpower areas in the U.S. Applicants must be U.S. citizens. Programs includes payment of full-tuition as well as a monthly stipend. Write to the address below or call (301) 443-1650 for more information.

National Health Service Corps
Parklawn Bldg., Room 7-18
5600 Fishers Lane
Rockville, MD 20857

3287 National High School Oratorical Contest

Amount: $18,000 (max) **Deadline:** Dec 1
Fields/Majors: All Areas Of Study

Open to high school students. Undergraduate scholarships to the top four winning contestants of the competition. Participants at the regional level all receive $1,000 scholarships. For U.S. citizens. Oratory competition. Write to the American Legion State Headquarters in your state of residence for contest procedures. Write to the address below if you are unable to locate your local or state American Legion.

American Legion, National Headquarters
P.O. Box 1055
Indianapolis, IN 46206

3288 National Hispanic Scholarship Fund

Amount: $500-$1,000 **Deadline:** Oct 1
Fields/Majors: All Areas Of Study

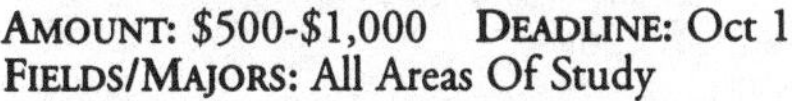

Scholarships for U.S. citizens or permanent residents of Hispanic background. Must be full-time students at a college or university in the U.S. or Puerto Rico and have completed a minimum of 15 hours of college work prior to submission of application. Write to the address below for details. Be certain to enclose an SASE.

National Hispanic Scholarship Fund
Selection Committee
P.O. Box 728
Novato, CA 94948

3289 National History Day Contest

Amount: Varies **Deadline:** None Specified
Fields/Majors: History

Scholarships are available to graduating high school seniors who are winners of the National History Day contest. Applicants must write a paper, prepare a project, compose a dramatic performance, or create a media presentation on the topic "taking a stand in history". Write to the address listed below for an information kit. The standard amount for an award ranges from $250-$1,000. Details are also available on the website http://www.inform.umd.edu/nhd.

University Of Maryland
0119 Cecil Hall
College Park, MD 20742

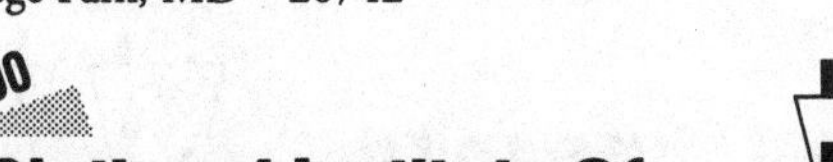

3290 National Institute Of Health Scholarships

Amount: $20,000 (max) **Amount:** Varies
Fields/Majors: Health Sciences, Biomedical Research

10 scholarships for students with disadvantaged backgrounds. Must demonstrate financial need or a statement indicating non-

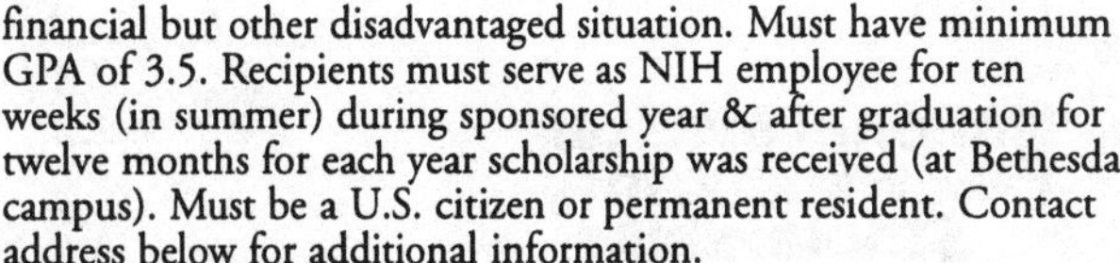

financial but other disadvantaged situation. Must have minimum GPA of 3.5. Recipients must serve as NIH employee for ten weeks (in summer) during sponsored year & after graduation for twelve months for each year scholarship was received (at Bethesda campus). Must be a U.S. citizen or permanent resident. Contact address below for additional information.

U.S. Department of Health & Human Services
Public Health Service Institutes
7550 Wisconsin Ave. #604
Bethesda, MD 20892

3291 National Institutes Of Health AIDS Research Loan Repayment Program

Amount: $20,000 (max) **Deadline:** None Specified
Fields/Majors: AIDS-Related Research

Special loans are available for research for individuals with Ph.D., M.D., D.O., D.D.S., D.M.D., D.V.M., A.D.N./B.S.N., or equivalent degrees. Research must be AIDS-related and applicants must be NIH employees for the length of the contracted service. Write to the address listed below for information.

National Institutes Of Health
Loan Repayment Programs
7550 Wisconsin Ave., Room 102
Bethesda, MD 20892

3292 National Insurance Enterprise Foundation Scholarships

Amount: $1,000 **Deadline:** Feb 15
Fields/Majors: Agriculture

Scholarships are available for FFA members pursuing a four-year degree in any area of agriculture. Three awards are offered annually. Write to the address below for details.

National FFA Foundation
Scholarship Office
P.O. Box 15160
Alexandria, VA 22309

3293 National Juice Products Assoc.

Amount: $1,500 **Deadline:** Apr 15
Fields/Majors: Fruit And Vegetable Industry

Open to students with a career interest in the fresh fruit and vegetable juice and products industry. Write to the address below for more information.

California State Polytechnic University, Pomona
College Of Agriculture
Building 7, Room 110
Pomona, CA 91768

3294 National Mastitis Council Scholarships

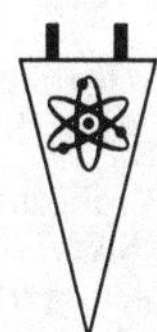

Amount: $500 **Deadline:** Feb 15
Fields/Majors: Dairy Science

Scholarships are available for FFA members pursuing a two- or four-year degree in dairy science. Write to the address below for details.

National FFA Foundation
Scholarship Office
P.O. Box 15160
Alexandria, VA 22309

3295

National Medical Fellowships, Inc., Scholarships

AMOUNT: $2,000 (max) **DEADLINE:** Aug 31
FIELDS/MAJORS: Medicine

Scholarships for minority medical students in the U.S. First-time applicants should be in their first or second year of medical school. Minorities are defined here as African American, Mexican American, mainland Puerto Rican, and American Indian. Must be a U.S. citizen. Write to the address listed below for additional information.

National Medical Fellowships, Inc.
Special Programs
110 West 32nd St.
New York, NY 10001

3296

National Merit & National Achievement Awards For Freshmen

AMOUNT: $4,000 **DEADLINE:** Jan 15
FIELDS/MAJORS: All Areas Of Study

All finalists of the National Merit or National Achievement Scholarship competitions who name Texas A&M as first choice are assured a scholarship in this program. This award can be combined with any other university scholarships earned. Payable in installments of $500 per semester for four years. Write to the address below for details.

Texas A & M University
University Honors Program
101 Academic Building
College Station, TX 7843

3297

National Merit And Achievement Scholarships

AMOUNT: $3,500 **DEADLINE:** None Specified
FIELDS/MAJORS: All Areas Of Study

Awards for high school seniors with a GPA of at least 3.0 or transfer students with a 3.25 GPA or better who were named National Merit finalists or semi-finalists. Write to the address below for more information.

Cedarville College
Financial Aid Office
P.O. Box 601
Cedarville, OH 45314

3298

National Merit Founders Scholarship

AMOUNT: Varies **DEADLINE:** Jan 1
FIELDS/MAJORS: All Areas Of Study

Applicant must show outstanding performance on college board PSAT/NMSQT. Selection by National Merit Scholarship Corp. National Merit finalists invited into the Denison Honors Program will automatically be given the award. Scholarship renewable for four-years. For entering freshman only. Write to the address below for details.

Denison University
Financial Aid Office
Box M
Granville, OH 43023

3299

National Merit Scholarships

AMOUNT: $2,000 **DEADLINE:** Feb 1
FIELDS/MAJORS: All Areas Of Study

Awards for National Merit finalists who indicate Furman as their first choice college. Write to the address below for more information.

Furman University
Director Of Financial Aid
3300 Poinsett Highway
Greenville, SC 29613

3300

National Merit Scholarships At Case Western

AMOUNT: $500-$2,000 **DEADLINE:** Feb 1
FIELDS/MAJORS: All Areas Of Study

At least 25 four-year scholarships for National Merit Scholarship Corporation finalists who have listed case Western Reserve University as their first-choice institution. Write to the address below for details.

Case Western Reserve University
Office of Financial Aid, 109 Pardee Hall
10900 Euclid Ave.
Cleveland, OH 44106

3301

National Merit/National Achievement Scholarships

AMOUNT: None Specified **DEADLINE:** Dec 1
FIELDS/MAJORS: All Areas Of Study

Scholarships are available at ut-austin for entering freshman students who are National Merit or National Achievement finalists. Write to the address below for details.

University Of Texas, Austin
Office of Student Financial Services
P.O. Box 7758
Austin, TX 78713

3302

National Minority Scholarship Program

AMOUNT: $1,500 **DEADLINE:** Apr 5
FIELDS/MAJORS: Public Relations, Communications

Applicants must be minority undergraduate students in public relations and attending four-year accredited schools. Must have a GPA of at least 3.0. Public Relations Student Society of America membership and a major or minor of public relations is preferred. Students should have obtained at least junior status by the time the scholarship will be used. Write to the address below for details.

Public Relations Society Of America
Director, Educational Affairs
33 Irving Place
New York, NY 10003

3303

National Museum Of American Art Intern Programs

AMOUNT: Varies **DEADLINE:** Mar 1
FIELDS/MAJORS: Art History, American Studies, Studio Art

Internships for graduate students seeking degrees in the above areas of study. Opportunity exists to earn course credits during internship. Write to the address below for details.

Smithsonian Institution-National Museum Of American Art
Intern Program Officer
Research And Scholars Center
Washington, DC 20560

3304

National Needs Graduate Fellowship Program

AMOUNT: $17,000 + Tuition
DEADLINE: None Specified
FIELDS/MAJORS: Materials/Wood Science; Civil/Mechanical/Chem. Engineering; Chemistry

Program for students pursuing a doctoral degree in one of the areas listed above. Applicants must be U.S. citizens and possess a strong technical background in the basic sciences and engineering, with appropriate bachelors and master's degrees. This is a three-year program beginning in Aug. or Jan. Write to Dr. Joseph Loferski, project director at the address below for more information.

Virginia Tech/U.S. Department of Agriculture
Dept. Of Wood Science & Forest Products
Brooks Forest Products Center, VA Tech
Blacksburg, VA 24061

3305

National Osteopathic Foundation Scholarships And Loan Fund

AMOUNT: $400-$2,000 **DEADLINE:** None Specified
FIELDS/MAJORS: Osteopathic Medicine

Open to third- or fourth-year medical students at an osteopathic college. Includes the McCaughan Scholarship, the William B. Strong Scholarship, and the Avallone Scholarship. Information should be available at the financial aid office of your school. If not, write to the address below for details.

National Osteopathic Foundation
5775-G. Peachtree-Dunwoody Road
Suite 500
Atlanta, GA 30342

3306

National Pork Fellowship

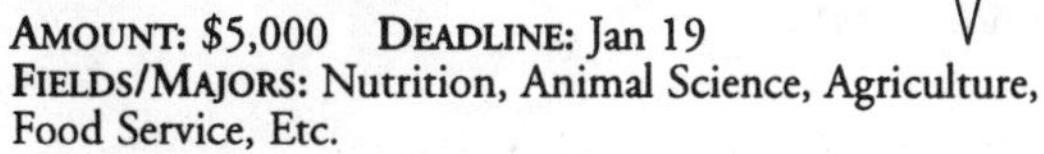

AMOUNT: $5,000 **DEADLINE:** Jan 19
FIELDS/MAJORS: Nutrition, Animal Science, Agriculture, Food Service, Etc.

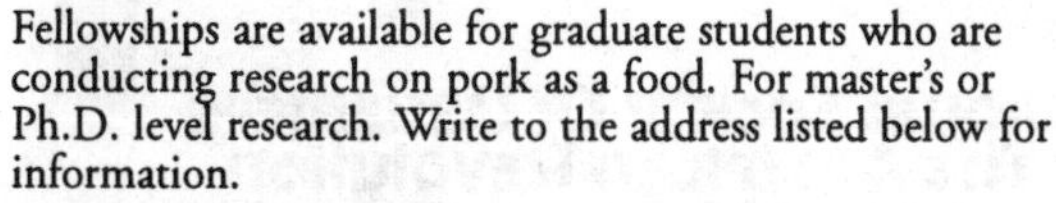

Fellowships are available for graduate students who are conducting research on pork as a food. For master's or Ph.D. level research. Write to the address listed below for information.

National Pork Fellowship
P.O. Box 10838
Des Moines, IA 50306

3307

National Presbyterian Church Scholarship

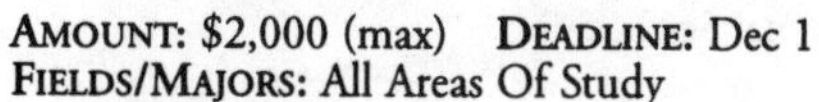

AMOUNT: $2,000 (max) **DEADLINE:** Dec 1
FIELDS/MAJORS: All Areas Of Study

Scholarships for St. Andrews students with demonstrated need who are members of the Presbyterian church. Write to the address

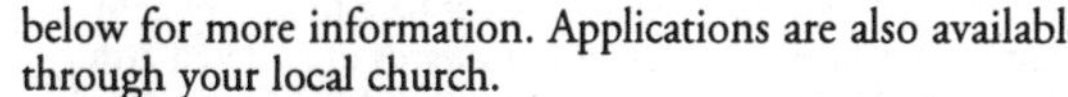

below for more information. Applications are also available through your local church.

St. Andrews College
Office of Financial Aid
1700 Dogwood Mile
Laurinburg, NC 28352

3308

National Presbyterian College Scholarship

AMOUNT: $500-$1,400 **DEADLINE:** Dec 1
FIELDS/MAJORS: All Areas Of Study

Scholarships for high school seniors who are members of the Presbyterian church (U.S.A.) and are U.S. citizens or permanent residents. Applicants must take the SAT/ACT prior to Dec 15 of their senior year. Write to the address listed below for information and an application.

Presbyterian Church (U.S.A.)
Office of Financial Aid For Studies
100 Witherspoon St., Room M042-A
Louisville, KY 40202

3309

National President's Scholarship

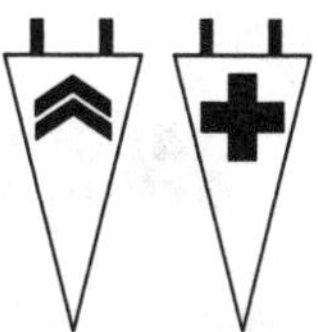

AMOUNT: $1,500-$2,000 **DEADLINE:** May 11
FIELDS/MAJORS: All Areas Of Study

Awards available for high school seniors who are children of U.S. Veterans of WWI, WWII, Korea, Vietnam, Grenada, Lebanon, Panama, or the Persian Gulf. Applicants must have completed at least 50 hours of community service. Must be interested in the health care field. Write to your local American Legion auxiliary unit president to get more information on the program in your area.

American Legion Auxiliary
Department of Arizona
4701 N. 19th Ave., Suite 100
Phoenix, AZ 85015

3310

National Restaurant Assoc. Undergraduate Scholarships In Foodservice

AMOUNT: $1,000-$5,000 **DEADLINE:** Mar 1
FIELDS/MAJORS: Foodservice/Hospitality

Scholarships for full-time foodservice and hospitality majors working toward an associate or bachelor degree. Must have food-service/hospitality work experience, a GPA of at least 3.0 and intend to be enrolled at a single school for the entire academic year. Applicants must have completed their first semester of study. Contact your school's program director for more information.

National Restaurant Assoc., Educational Foundation
Scholarship Department
250 South Wacker Drive, Suite 1400
Chicago, IL 60606

3311

National Restaurant Assoc. Graduate Degree Fellowships

AMOUNT: $2,000 **DEADLINE:** Feb 15
FIELDS/MAJORS: Foodservice/Hospitality

Scholarships for full-time foodservice and hospitality majors working toward postgraduate degrees. Must be a food service/hospitality educator or administrator. Seven awards are offered annually. Write to the address below or call (800) 765-2122 for details.

National Restaurant Assoc., Educational Foundation
Scholarship Department
250 South Wacker Drive, Suite 1400
Chicago, IL 60606

3312

National Scholarship Trust Fund

Amount: $500-$1,000
Deadline: Mar 1, Apr 1
Fields/Majors: Graphic Communications

Applicants must be interested in a graphic communications career and be a full-time freshman, sophomore, or junior. High school seniors are also eligible. 100 scholarships per year. Write to the address below for details. Deadline for college students is Apr 1, for high school students, Mar 1.

National Scholarship Trust Fund Of The Graphic Arts
4615 Forbes Ave.
Pittsburgh, PA 15213

3313

National Scholarships And Activity Grants

Amount: $2,500-$2,800 **Deadline:** Mar 15
Fields/Majors: All Areas Of Study

Awards for undergraduate students at Adams State. Must have a GPA of at least a 2.5. The National Scholarship is for residents of states other than Colorado. Write to the address below for more details.

Adams State College
Financial Aid Office
Alamosa, CO 81102

3314

National Science Scholars Program

Amount: $5,000 **Deadline:** None Specified
Fields/Majors: Physical, Life, Or Computer Science; Mathematics; Engineering

Scholarships open to high school seniors entering their freshmen year at a Minnesota college or university. Students must be planning to major in one of the fields above and be a Minnesota resident. Write to the address below for details.

Minnesota Higher Education Coordinating Board
Capitol Square, Suite 400
550 Cedar St.
Saint Paul, MN 55101

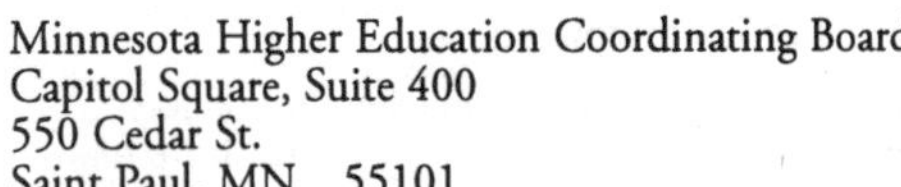

3315

National Sculpture Society Scholarship

Amount: Varies **Deadline:** May 31
Fields/Majors: Art-Sculpture

Scholarships are available for all levels of students enrolled in an art program with an emphasis in sculpture. Three 8 x 10 photos of works by the applicant must be sent with the application. For sculptors age 35 or less there is an annual competition with prizes of up to $1,000. Write to the address listed below for information.

National Sculpture Society
Attn: Scholarships
1177 Ave. Of The Americas
New York, NY 10036

3316

National Security Education Program Graduate Fellowships

Amount: $2,000-$10,000 **Amount** Varies
Fields/Majors: Foreign Cultures & Foreign Languages

The NSEP graduate fellowships are for U.S. citizens who study critical languages, cultures, and regions of the world (except Canada, Western Europe, Australia, New Zealand). All fellowships must include study of a language or culture other than English. Study outside the U.S is encouraged, but not required. Write to the address below for details.

Academy For Educational Development
1255 23rd St., NW, Suite 400
Washington, DC 20037

3317

National Security Education Undergraduate Scholarships

Amount: Varies **Deadline:** None Specified
Fields/Majors: Foreign Studies, Foreign Languages

Scholarships for undergraduate students majoring in foreign studies. Students must be planning to use the scholarship for study abroad. These scholarships are not for study in the U.S. Applicants must be U.S. citizens. Write to the address below for details.

National Security Education Program
1101 Wilson Boulevard, Suite 1210
Rosslyn, VA 22209

3318

National Sheriff's Assoc. Law Enforcement Scholarships

Amount: $1,000 **Deadline:** Apr 1
Fields/Majors: Criminal Justice

Awards for undergraduates in the field of criminal justice. Applicants must be employed by a sheriff's office or the son or daughter of an individual employed by a sheriff's office. Write to the address below for more information.

National Sheriff's Assoc.
The Scholarhship Fund
1450 Duke St.
Alexandria, VA 22314

3319

National Society Of Daughters Of The American Revolution Scholarship

Amount: $500-$1,000 **Amount:** Varies
Fields/Majors: Range Animal Science

Awards for Sul Ross undergraduates who are studying range animal science, are U.S. citizens, and have financial need. Must have a GPA of at least 2.0. Write to the address below for more information.

Sul Ross State University
Division Of Range Animal Science
Box C-110
Alpine ,TX 79832

3320

National Society Of Public Accountants Scholarship Foundation

AMOUNT: $500-$1,000 **DEADLINE:** Mar 10
FIELDS/MAJORS: Accounting

For undergraduate accounting majors enrolled in accredited business schools, junior colleges, and universities. Must have a GPA of at least a 3.0. Must be a full-time student (evening program considered full-time if pursuing a degree of accounting). An additional stipend is awarded to the outstanding student of the competition. Must be a U.S. or Canadian citizen. Applications and appraisal forms may be obtained from your school or by writing to the NSPA scholarship foundation at the address below. Students from a four-year school may apply for the 3rd and 4th year only.

National Society Of Public Accountants Scholarship Foundation
1010 N. Fairfax St.
Alexandria, VA 22314

3321

National Society To Prevent Blindness Grants-In-Aid

AMOUNT: $12,000 (max) **DEADLINE:** Mar 1
FIELDS/MAJORS: Ophthalmology

Grants are for the funding of studies that have limited or no research funding. They are used to help defray the costs of personnel, equipment, and supplies. Write to the address below for details.

Fight For Sight Research Division
National Society To Prevent Blindness
500 E. Remington Rd.
Schaumburg, IL 60173

3322

National Society To Prevent Blindness Postdoctoral Research Fellowship

AMOUNT: $28,000 (max) **DEADLINE:** Mar 1
FIELDS/MAJORS: Ophthalmology

Research fellowship for basic or clinical work at the early postdoctoral stage in ophthalmology, vision, or related sciences. Write to the address below for details.

Fight For Sight Research Division
National Society To Prevent Blindness
500 E. Remington Rd.
Schaumburg, IL 60173

3323

National Society To Prevent Blindness Student Fellowships

AMOUNT: $500 (monthly) **DEADLINE:** Mar 1
FIELDS/MAJORS: Ophthalmology

Fellowship is available to undergraduates, medical students, and graduate students interested in eye-related clinical or basic research. Award is given for up to three months of research. Write to the address below for details.

Fight For Sight Research Division
National Society To Prevent Blindness
500 E. Remington Rd.
Schaumburg, IL 60173

3324

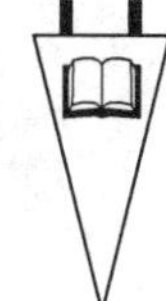

National Speakers Assoc. Scholarship Program

AMOUNT: $2,500 **DEADLINE:** Jun 1
FIELDS/MAJORS: Speech, Public Speaking

Awards for juniors, seniors, or graduate students studying in one of the fields above. For full-time study at any college or university. Write to the address below for more information.

National Speakers Assoc.
Attn: Scholarship Committee
1500 South Priest Drive
Tempe, AZ 85281

3325

National States Meat Assn. & Frank Debenedetti Scholarship

AMOUNT: $1,000 **DEADLINE:** May 1
FIELDS/MAJORS: Animal Science, Food Science, Poultry Science

Students must have a GPA of 3.0 or better majoring in animal and/or food sciences with orientation toward the science of red and/or poultry meats. Write to the address below for more information.

California State Polytechnic University, Pomona
College Of Agriculture
Building 2, Room 215
Pomona, CA 91768

3326

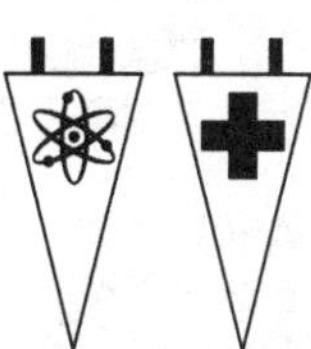

National States Meat Assn. & WMSA Undergraduate Scholarship

AMOUNT: $1,000 **DEADLINE:** May 1
FIELDS/MAJORS: Animal Science, Food Science, Poultry Science

Students must have a GPA of 3.0 or better majoring in animal and/or food sciences with orientation toward the science of red and/or poultry meats. Two awards are given yearly. Write to the address below for more information.

California State Polytechnic University, Pomona
College Of Agriculture
Building 2, Room 215
Pomona, CA 91768

3327

National States Meat Assn.& Edward Price Toby Mem. Scholarship

AMOUNT: $1,000 **DEADLINE:** May 1
FIELDS/MAJORS: Agricultural Engineering, Food Engineering, Meat Science, Food Science

Students must be majoring in agricultural engineering or food engineering with an orientation to meat science/food science. Write to the address below for more information.

California State Polytechnic University, Pomona
College Of Agriculture
Building 2, Room 215
Pomona, CA 91768

3328

National Telephone/Penn-Del Directory Scholarship Fund

AMOUNT: Varies **DEADLINE:** Mar 1
FIELDS/MAJORS: All Areas Of Study

Awards for students with one parent who is an employee of National Telephone Directory or Penn-Del Directory for at least three years. Student must be a current high school senior or graduate and have maintained a GPA of 3.0 through school. Must indicate financial need and be a New Jersey resident. Contact the address below for further information.

Yellow Pages
3 Executive Dr.
Somerset, NJ 08875

3329

National Testing Merit Scholarship

AMOUNT: Tuition **DEADLINE:** Mar 31
FIELDS/MAJORS: All Areas Of Study

Awards for students who performed above the 90th percentile in the ACT or SAT tests. Renewable if a GPA of 3.0 is maintained. Write to the address below for more information.

Columbia Union College
Financial Aid Office
7600 Flower Ave.
Takoma Park, MD 20912

3330

National Theate Conservatory Awards

AMOUNT: $7,750 + Stipend **DEADLINE:** Jan 31
FIELDS/MAJORS: Theater, Acting

Program for students interested in the area of theater. This is a three-year residential program for students who have completed at least 90 quarter or 60 semester hours. Write to the address below for more information.

National Theater Conservatory
1050 13th St.
Denver, CO 80204

3331

National University Scholarship Program

AMOUNT: $2,500 (max) **DEADLINE:** None Specified
FIELDS/MAJORS: All Areas Of Study

Grants for students at National University who have received recognition of achievement (such as letter of commendation, etc.) or demonstrate financial need. Contact the financial aid office at the address below for details.

National University
Financial Aid Office
4025 Camino Del Rio South
San Diego, CA 92108

3332

National Zoo Research Traineeship Program

AMOUNT: $2,400 **DEADLINE:** Jan 27
FIELDS/MAJORS: Zoology, Animal Behavior, Veterinary Pathology, Horticulture

Selection criteria focus on applicants statement of interest, scholastic achievement, relevant experience and letters of reference. Preference is given to advanced undergraduates and recent graduates. All programs are at the national zoological park in Washington DC. Contact the address below for complete information.

Friends Of The National Zoo
Office of Volunteer & Educational Servs.
National Zoological Park
Washington, DC 20008

3333

Nationsbank Scholarship Fund

AMOUNT: $750 **DEADLINE:** None Specified
FIELDS/MAJORS: Business

Scholarship available to El Paso County resident students at the University of Texas El Paso who are pursuing business administration, accounting, or finance degree. Write to the address listed below for information.

El Paso Community Foundation
201 East Main, Suite 1616
El Paso, TX 79901

3334

Nationwide Insurance Enterprise Foundation Scholarship

AMOUNT: $700 **DEADLINE:** Feb 9
FIELDS/MAJORS: Management, Marketing

Award for students majoring in management/marketing with a minimum of a 3.0 GPA. Must show financial need. One award reserved for a protected class member. Use Bloomsburg University scholarship application. Contact Mr. Gene Remoff, Dean, College of Business for further information.

Bloomsburg University
19 Ben Franklin Hall
400 E. Second St.
Bloomsburg, PA 17815

3335

Native American Education Grants

AMOUNT: $200-$1,500 **DEADLINE:** Jun 1
FIELDS/MAJORS: All Areas Of Study

Undergraduate grants for Alaska natives and Native Americans pursuing college educations. Must be U.S. citizens and have completed at least one semester of work at an accredited institution of higher education. Applicants must be members of the Presbyterian Church (U.S.A.) and demonstrate financial need. Write to address below for details. Specify Native American Education Grants (NAEG).

Presbyterian Church (U.S.A.)
Office of Financial Aid For Studies
100 Witherspoon St.
Louisville, KY 40202

3336

Native American Indian Scholarships

AMOUNT: Varies **DEADLINE:** None Specified
FIELDS/MAJORS: All Areas Of Study

Scholarships are available at NAU for full-time students who are Native American Indians. Includes the IMB scholarship, the Native American scholarship, the Peabody Coal Navajo Scholarship, and the Sally Fleming Memorial Scholarships.

Individual award requirements will vary. Write to the address listed below for information.

Northern Arizona University
Nau Scholarship Office
P.O. Box 4199
Flagstaff, AZ 86011

3337 Native American Student Aid

AMOUNT: $1,550 (max) **AMOUNT:** Varies
FIELDS/MAJORS: All Areas Of Study

Grants for Native Americans who are NY residents, on an official tribal roll of a NY state tribe (or children of), and attending an approved postsecondary institution in NY state. Renewable for up to four years. Write to the address below for complete details.

New York State Education Department
Attn: Native American Education Unit
Room 543, Education Building
Albany, NY 12234

3338 Native American Tuition Waivers

AMOUNT: Tuition **DEADLINE:** None Specified
FIELDS/MAJORS: All Areas Of Study

Awards for Native American students at UMass that are certified as such by the U.S. Bureau of Indian affairs and are permanent legal residents of Massachusetts. For more information, contact the commonwealth on Indian affairs, John W. McCormick Bldg., One Ashburton Place, Room 1004, Boston, MA 02108.

University Of Massachusetts-Amherst
Office of Financial Aid Services
255 Whitmore Admin. Bldg., Box 38230
Amherst, MA 01003

3339 Naturalist Intern Program

AMOUNT: Room + $100/week
DEADLINE: Varies
FIELDS/MAJORS: Environmental Education, Science Education, Natural Resources

Internship program for students who have completed at least two years of college study in one of the fields listed above. For students from or attending school in New York. Write to the address below for more information.

New York State Department of Environmental Conservation
Five Rivers Environmental Education Ctr.
Game Farm Road
Delmar, NY 12054

3340 Naval Academy Class Of 1963 And Class Of 1966 Foundation Scholarships

AMOUNT: $2,000-$2,500 **DEADLINE:** None
FIELDS/MAJORS: All Areas Of Study

Scholarships for sons and daughters of deceased persons who began schooling with the U.S. Naval Academy Class of 1963 or Class of 1966 or later entered the class. For study at any accredited two-year, four-year, or technical/vocational school. Renewable. Class of 1966 awards: write to U.S. Naval Academy, Class of 1966 Foundation, P.O. Box 6428, Annapolis, M.D., 21401-0428. Class of 1963 awards: write to the address below.

U.S. Naval Academy
Class Of 1963 Foundation
Alumni House
Annapolis, MD 21402

3341 Navy League Scholarship Program

AMOUNT: Varies **DEADLINE:** Apr 1
FIELDS/MAJORS: All Areas Of Study

Scholarships for dependents of U.S. Navy, U.S. Marine, U.S. Coast Guard, or U.S. Merchant Marine officers or enlisted personnel who are active, retired with pay, or deceased. Applicants must be U.S. citizens under the age of 25. Preference will be given to students studying math or science. Send an SASE to the address below for details.

Navy League Of The United States
Attn: Scholarship Program
2300 Wilson Boulevard
Arlington, VA 22201

3342 Navy Supply Corps Foundation Scholarships

AMOUNT: None Specified **DEADLINE:** Feb 15
FIELDS/MAJORS: All Areas Of Study

Sons/daughters of Navy Supply Corps officers (including warrant officers) and Supply Corps associated enlisted personnel on active duty, reserve, retired with pay, or deceased. For undergraduate study. Must have a GPA of at least 3.0. For two- or four-year college. Several scholarships available. Write to the address below for details.

Navy Supply Corps Foundation
Navy Supply Corps School
1425 Prince Ave.
Athens, GA 30606

3343 NAWE Women's Research Awards

AMOUNT: $750 **DEADLINE:** Oct 1
FIELDS/MAJORS: Women's Studies

Supports research on any topic about the education, personal, and professional development of women and girls. Two awards, one for graduate students, and one for persons at any career/professional level. Membership not required. Write to the address below for details. Please be certain to enclose an SASE with your request for information.

National Assoc. For Women In Education
Anna Roman-Koller, Ph.D.
Dept. Of Pathology, 701 Scaife Hall
Pittsburgh, PA 15261

3344 NAWIC Undergraduate Scholarships

AMOUNT: None Specified **DEADLINE:** Feb 1
FIELDS/MAJORS: Construction Related Fields

Scholarships are available for freshman, sophomore and junior students who are enrolled in a construction-related program on a full time basis. The applicant must desire a career in the construction industry. Write to the address listed below for information.

National Assoc. Of Women In Construction
NAWIC Founders' Scholarship Foundation
327 South Adams
Fort Worth, TX 76104

3345

Nazareth Scholars Program

AMOUNT: Half Tuition **DEADLINE:** Feb 15
FIELDS/MAJORS: All Areas Of Study

Scholarships are available to Nazareth College for full-time undergraduate students who demonstrate outstanding academic performance. Must be a U.S. citizen. Write to the address below for details.

Nazareth College
Office of Financial Aid
4245 East Ave.
Rochester, NY 14618

3346

Nazareth Scholarship

AMOUNT: $1,000 (max) **DEADLINE:** Feb 15
FIELDS/MAJORS: All Areas Of Study

Scholarships are available to Nazareth College for full-time undergraduate students who demonstrate financial need. Must be a U.S. citizen. Write to the address below for details.

Nazareth College
Office of Financial Aid
4245 East Ave.
Rochester, NY 14618

3347

NBAA Scholarship Program In Aviation

GPA 3.0+

AMOUNT: $1,000 **DEADLINE:** Oct 17
FIELDS/MAJORS: Aviation

Scholarships for students who will be sophomores or above at an NBAA member school and are planning a career in aviation. Applicants must have a minimum GPA of 3.0 and be U.S. citizens. Five awards per year. Write to the address below for details. Information may also be available in your department.

National Business Aircraft Assoc., Inc.
NBAA Scholarship Program
1200 Eighteenth St., NW, Suite 200
Washington, DC 20036

3348

NBC Fellowship Program

E

AMOUNT: $8,000 **AMOUNT:** Varies
FIELDS/MAJORS: Broadcasting, Communications

Open to minority graduate students who attend the University of Miami (School of Communications), University of Sou (Journalism), Howard University (Communications), Columbia (Journalism), or Northwestern (Kellogg). Must have had at least 2 years full-time business experience after graduation from undergraduate school and be a U.S. citizen or permanent resident. Contact your financial aid office for further details. The address below cannot respond to any requests for more information.

National Broadcasting Company, Inc.
NBC Fellowships, Employee Relations
30 Rockefeller Plaza, Room 1678
New York, NY 10112

3349

NC+Hybrids Scholarships

AMOUNT: $500-$1,000 **DEADLINE:** Feb 15
FIELDS/MAJORS: Agriculture

Scholarships are available for FFA members pursuing a two- or four-year degree in any area of agriculture, who reside in California, Colorado, Delaware, Kansas, Iowa, Illinois, Indiana, Maryland, Minnesota, Missouri, Montana, Idaho, Nebraska, New Mexico, Ohio, Pennsylvania, South Dakota, Texas, Oklahoma or Wyoming. Write to the address below for details.

National FFA Foundation
Scholarship Office
P.O. Box 15160
Alexandria, VA 22309

3350

NCAR Postdoctoral Appointments

AMOUNT: $33,415-$34,645 **DEADLINE:** Jan 3
FIELDS/MAJORS: Atmospheric Sciences or Any Related Area

Interested scientists just receiving the Ph.D. (or equivalent) and scientists with no more than four year's applicable experience past the Ph.D. are eligible to apply. Primary criteria for selection are the applicants scientific capability and potential, originality and independence and the ability to undertake research. U.S. or foreign applicants. Write to Barbara Hansford, Coordinator, at the address below for details. (e-mail address: barbm@asp2.ucar.edu)

National Center For Atmospheric Research
Advanced Study Program
P.O. Box 3,000
Boulder, CO 80307

3351

NCCER Scholarships

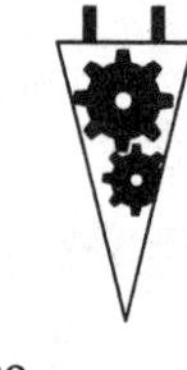

AMOUNT: $500-$2,000 **DEADLINE:** Dec 15
FIELDS/MAJORS: Construction

Awards are available for students currently enrolled, who have successfully completed at least one year in a baccalaureate degree program in construction. Students attending schools with an ABC student chapter, must be an active member of that chapter. Write to the address below for more information.

National Center For Construction Education & Research
Manager, College Relations
1300 North Seventeenth St.
Rosslyn, VA 22209

3352

NCOA Scholarship Grant Program

GPA 2.5+

AMOUNT: $750-$1,000 **DEADLINE:** Mar 31
FIELDS/MAJORS: All Areas Of Study

Scholarships for spouses, sons, and daughters of members. Sons and daughters must be under 25 years of age. Based primarily on academics. Renewable. 35 awards offered per year. For undergraduate study. Includes the Mary Barraco Scholarship, the William T. Green Scholarship, and the NCOA/Pentagon Federal Credit Union Grant. Write to the address below for details.

Non-Commissioned Officers Assoc.
Scholarship Administrator
P.O. Box 33610
San Antonio, TX 78265

3353

NCR Corporation Scholarship

AMOUNT: Varies **DEADLINE:** Feb 29
FIELDS/MAJORS: Finance

Awards for outstanding finance majors and for participants in the school's minority management education program. For students in their sophomore, junior, or senior year. Applications for School of Management Scholarships will be available in the SOM Development Office, room 206.

University Of Massachusetts, Amherst
School Of Management
SOM Development Office, Room 206
Amherst, MA 01003

3354

NCSU Merit Awards Program

AMOUNT: Varies **DEADLINE:** Nov 1
FIELDS/MAJORS: All Areas Of Study

Scholarships for entering students at North Carolina State University who are academically accomplished (generally in top 5% of class). Write to the address below for additional information.

North Carolina State University
Merit Awards Program
P.O. Box 7342
Raleigh, NC 27695

3355

NCTE Grants-In-Aid

AMOUNT: $12,500 **DEADLINE:** Feb 15
FIELDS/MAJORS: English/Education

The grant program is for research in the field of English/reading education and is open to graduate students and educators. Must be member of NCTE. Write to the address below for details.

National Council Of Teachers Of English Research Foundation
Project Assistant
1111 W. Kenyon Road
Urbana, IL 61801

3356

NDSEG Fellowships

AMOUNT: $16,500-$18,500
DEADLINE: Jan 17
FIELDS/MAJORS: Mathematics, Engineering, Physics, Marine And Biological Sciences

Research fellowships are available for students at the beginning of their graduate studies in one of the areas listed above. Applicants must be U.S. citizens. Minority, handicapped and female candidates are encouraged to apply. Write to the address listed below for information.

National Defense Science And Engineering Fellowship Program
Dr. George Outterson
200 Park Dr., Suite 211
P.O. Box 13444
Research Triangle, NC 27709

3357

Neal W. Munch & Marvin A. Clark Conservation Scholarship

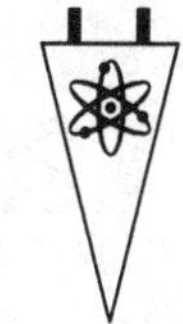

AMOUNT: $1,000 **DEADLINE:** Jun 7
FIELDS/MAJORS: Conservation, Forestry, Soil Science, Environmental Studies & Related

Two Scholarships are available for junior and senior students who reside in either Middlesex or Monmouth County, and are studying in a conservation-related field. Write to the address listed below for information

Freehold Soil Conservation District
Education Coordinator
211 Freehold Road
Manalapan, NJ 07726

3358

Near And Middle Eastern Fellowships

AMOUNT: None Specified **DEADLINE:** Nov 1
FIELDS/MAJORS: Middle Eastern Studies

Fellowships are available for scholars enrolled in a U.S. doctoral program. Applicants must have completed all the program requirements except for the dissertation. Research must be in near or Middle Eastern studies (defined as North Africa, Middle East, Afghanistan, Iran and Turkey.) Write to the address listed below for information.

Social Science Research Council
Fellowships And Grants
605 Third Ave.
New York, NY 10158

3359

Near And Middle Eastern Grants

AMOUNT: $10,000 (max) **DEADLINE:** Dec 1
FIELDS/MAJORS: Near And Middle Eastern Studies

Grants are available for postdoctoral scholars studying in the U.S., for research on all aspects of the societies and cultures of the near or Middle East. Applicants should be scholars whose competence for research in the area has been established and who intend to continue to make contributions to the field. Write to the address listed below for information.

Social Science Research Council
Fellowships And Grants
605 Third Ave.
New York, NY 10158

3360

Nebraska Library Assoc. Scholarships

AMOUNT: $750 **DEADLINE:** May 15
FIELDS/MAJORS: Library Science

Scholarships for students in a master's degree program in library science. Varying number of awards per year. Applicants must be members of the Nebraska Library Assoc. or employed in a library. Write to the address below for details.

Nebraska Library Assoc.
Peru State College Library
Peru, NE 68421

3361

Nebraska Scholarship Challenge Program

Amount: $500 **Deadline:** Mar 15
Fields/Majors: Travel And Tourism, Hotel/Motel Management

Awards for Nebraska residents in one of the areas listed above who are enrolled in any two- or four-year college. Must have a GPA of 3.0 or better. Write to the address below for more information.

National Tour Foundation
546 East Main St.
P.O. Box 3071
Lexington, KY 40596

3362

Neca Navajo Engineering And Construction Authority

Amount: Varies **Deadline:** Mar 1
Fields/Majors: Engineering

Awards are available at the University of New Mexico for American Indian engineering students. Contact the School of Engineering for more information.

University Of New Mexico, Albuquerque
Office of Financial Aid
Albuquerque, NM 87131

3363

Ned McWherter Scholars Program

Amount: $5,000 **Deadline:** None Specified
Fields/Majors: All Areas Of Study

Scholarship open to Tennessee high school seniors who plan to enroll in a Tennessee higher education institution. Applicant must have a 3.5 grade point average and have a 28 on the ACT or 1190 on the SAT. Write to the address below for details.

Tennessee Student Assistance Corporation
Suite 1950, Parkway Towers
404 James Robertson Parkway
Nashville, TN 37243

3364

Need-Based Scholarships

Amount: Varies **Deadline:** Feb 15
Fields/Majors: All Areas Of Study

The followingScholarships are available to students with financial need: the John Alden & Amelia Wright Bowers, F.S. Auerbach, George P. Bowers Memorial, Class of 1930, Amanda Brim Daugherty, Reader's Digest, Farmers Insurance Group, Samuel D. & Edith D. Green, Sarah Hammond, Sue Huntington, Rees & Eleanor Jensen, and Georgia Mather Scholarships. Individual award requirements vary. Write to the address below for information.

University Of Utah
Financial Aid And Scholarships Office
105 Student Services Building
Salt Lake City, UT 84112

3365

NEH Fellowship In Classical And Byzantine Studies

Amount: $30,000 **Deadline:** Nov 15
Fields/Majors: Classical And Byzantine Studies

Awards are available for postdoctoral scholars in the fields of classical and Byzantine studies. Must be a U.S. citizen or permanent resident. Write to the address below for more information.

American School Of Classical Studies At Athens
Committee On Admissions And Fellowships
993 Lenox Drive, Suite 101
Lawrenceville, NJ 08648

3366

NEHA Education/Scholarship Foundation Award

Amount: None Specified **Deadline:** Jan 10
Fields/Majors: All Areas Of Study

Scholarship offered to members of the NEHA who are enrolled in a program of study leading to an undergraduate or associate degree. Application involves submitting an original manuscript on housekeeping within any industry segment. Write to the address below for details.

National Executive Housekeepers Assoc.
Fields/Majors:
Educational Department
1001 Eastwind Drive, Suite 301
Westerville, OH 43081

3367

NEHA Scholarship Awards

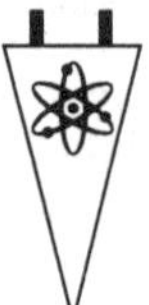

Amount: $1,000 **Deadline:** Feb 1
Fields/Majors: Environmental Health

Scholarships to be used toward tuition and fees of a student enrolled in an environmental health curriculum at an approved college or university in the U.S. Must be junior, senior, or graduate student. Renewable. Write to the address below for details.

National Environmental Health Assoc. Scholarship
Vicki Potter, Member Liaison
720 S. Colorado Blvd., Suite #970
Denver, CO 80222

3368

Nell A. Kimble Scholarship

Amount: Tuition **Deadline:** Apr 1
Fields/Majors: All Areas Of Study

Awards for entering freshmen who have demonstrated academic excellence. Applicants must have a GPA of at least 3.8 and SAT scores of 1260 or ACT scores of 30 or better. Also based on a scholarship competition held at the university. Renewable with a GPA of 3.5. Write to the address below for more information.

Baker University
Office of Financial Aid
P.O. Box 65
Baldwin City, KS 66006

3369

Nelle Gooch Travelstead Scholarship

Amount: Varies **Deadline:** Mar 1
Fields/Majors: Education

Awards are available at the University of New Mexico for students enrolled in the college of education with demonstrated merit and performance. Must have completed at least sixty hours of course work with a GPA of 3.0 or better.

University Of New Mexico, Albuquerque
Office of Financial Aid
Albuquerque, NM 87131

3370

Nellie Martin Carman Scholarship Trust

AMOUNT: $1,000 **DEADLINE:** Mar 15
FIELDS/MAJORS: Most Areas Of Study

Scholarship available to high school seniors in the counties of King, Pierce and Snohomish in the state of Washington. Candidates must be U.S. citizens with at least five years of domicile in the state of Washington and must plan to attend a college in the state of Washington. Criteria: financial need; academic record; college test scores; and a GPA of 3.0 or above. Write to the address below for details. Candidates for this scholarship must be nominated by their high schools each year, so application forms are not sent directly to students.

Nellie Martin Carman Scholarship Committee
c/o Barbara M. Scott Admin. Secretary
18223 73rd Ave., NE #B101
Bothell, WA 98011

3371

Nelson A. Miller Memorial Scholarship

AMOUNT: Varies **DEADLINE:** None Specified
FIELDS/MAJORS: All Areas Of Study

Award for student active in music performance through ensembles. Applicant will demonstrate leadership, musical proficiency and contributions to the department. Selection made by the music department faculty. Contact a member of the music department faculty for further information.

Bloomsburg University
19 Ben Franklin Hall
400 E. Second St.
Bloomsburg, PA 17815

3372

Nelson L. And Vera B. Lee Scholarship

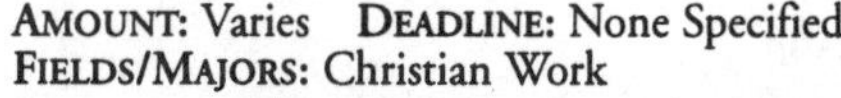

AMOUNT: Varies **DEADLINE:** None Specified
FIELDS/MAJORS: Christian Work

Awards are available for students at Cedarville College who are preparing for full-time vocational Christian work. Must have a GPA of at least 2.0. Write to the address below for more information.

Cedarville College
Financial Aid Office
P.O. Box 601
Cedarville, OH 45314

3373

Neo-Flight Annette Hein Memorial Scholarship

AMOUNT: None Specified **DEADLINE:** None Specified
FIELDS/MAJORS: Nursing

Scholarships are open to a part-time or full-time ASN or BSN student in the final year of study. Must have a life experience that influenced them to enter the nursing profession. Write to the address below for more information.

Indiana University Purdue University, Indianapolis
School Of Nursing
1111 Middle Dr., Nu 122
Indianapolis, IN 46202

3374

Neva Loving Memorial Scholarships

AMOUNT: $2,000 **DEADLINE:** Feb 3
FIELDS/MAJORS: Marketing

Scholarships are available at the University of Oklahoma, Norman for full-time junior or senior marketing majors, with demonstrated financial need. Write to the address listed below for information.

University Of Oklahoma, Norman
Director, Division Of Marketing
1 Adams Hall
Norman, OK 73019

3375

Nevada Student Incentive Grant Program

AMOUNT: $5,000 (max) **DEADLINE:** None Specified
FIELDS/MAJORS: All Areas Of Study

Only Nevada residents attending approved Nevada postsecondary schools are eligible for grants. Write to the address below for more information.

Nevada Department of Education
400 West King St., Capitol Complex
Carson City, NV 89710

3376

Neviaser Ahana Student Achievement Award

AMOUNT: $2,000 **DEADLINE:** Mar 15
FIELDS/MAJORS: All Areas Of Study

Awards for incoming freshmen who are African American, Asian, Hispanic, or Native American with a GPA of at least 2.5 and rank in the upper 50% of their graduating class. Preference will be given to Dane County residents. Renewable. Write to the address below for details.

Edgewood College
Office of Admissions
855 Woodrow St.
Madison, WI 53711

3377

New England Regional Scholarship

AMOUNT: $1,000 **DEADLINE:** May 31
FIELDS/MAJORS: All Areas Of Study

Scholarships for Italian American residents of the six New England states. For undergraduate study. Write to the address below for details.

National Italian American Foundation
Dr. Maria Lombardo, Education Director
1860 Nineteenth St., NW
Washington, DC 20009

3378

New England Sports Turf Managers Assoc. Scholarship

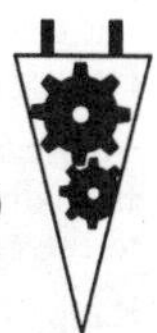

AMOUNT: Varies **DEADLINE:** Jun 1
FIELDS/MAJORS: Turfgrass Management

Awards for UMass students in the field of turfgrass management.

Contact the Director, Stockbridge School for more information.

University Of Massachusetts, Amherst
Director, Stockbridge School
Amherst, MA 01003

3379

New Focus Research Awards

AMOUNT: $23,000 **DEADLINE:** Apr 8
FIELDS/MAJORS: Lasers And Electro-optics

Research grants for doctoral candidates who are pursuing thesis projects in lasers and electro-optics or who are making technological advances in other fields through the application of lasers and electro-optics. Research must take place in the U.S. Write to the address below for more information.

New Focus Inc.
Optical Society Of America
2010 Massachusettes Ave., NW
Washington, DC 20036

3380

New Hampshire Science Center Internships

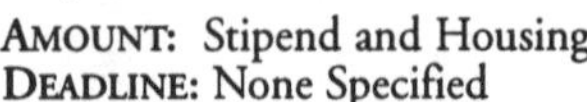

AMOUNT: Stipend and Housing
DEADLINE: None Specified
FIELDS/MAJORS: Natural Sciences, Environmental Studies Or Related Field

Internship program in New Hampshire for college juniors through graduate students interested in one of the areas listed above. Must demonstrate enthusiasm, motivation, and a desire to work with people and animals. Program offers a weekly stipend, free housing arrangements, and lasts a minimum of ten weeks. Write to the address below for more information.

Science Center Of New Hampshire
Intern Coordinator
P.O. Box 173
Holderness, NH 03245

3381

New Holland Scholarships

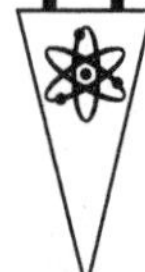

AMOUNT: $1,000 **DEADLINE:** Feb 15
FIELDS/MAJORS: All Areas Of Study

Scholarships are available for FFA members pursuing a degree in any area of study who participated in the chapter safety program. Write to the address below for details.

National FFA Foundation
Scholarship Office
P.O. Box 15160
Alexandria, VA 22309

3382

New Initiatives Grant

AMOUNT: $4,500 **DEADLINE:** Dec 15
FIELDS/MAJORS: Home Economics/Related Fields

Applicants must be Kappa Omicron Nu members. Awarded annually from the Kappa Omicron Nu new initiatives fund. Write to the address below for details.

Kappa Omicron Nu Honor Society
4990 Northwind Dr., Suite 140
East Lansing, MI 48823

3383

New Investigators Award

AMOUNT: $2,000 **DEADLINE:** Dec 5
FIELDS/MAJORS: Geriatrics

Awards are restricted to fellows-in-training and new and junior investigators holding an academic appointment not longer than 5 years postfellowship. Awards will be chosen based on originality, scientific merit, relevance of the research, and the overall academic accomplishments. Write to the address below for more information.

American Geriatrics Society
770 Lexington Ave., Suite 300
New York, NY 10021

3384

New Jersey Funeral Directors Assoc. Scholarships

AMOUNT: $1,000 **DEADLINE:** Jun 30
FIELDS/MAJORS: Mortuary Science

Awards for New Jersey students currently registered in a mortuary science program. Based on academic performance and commitment to funeral service. Write to the address below for more information.

New Jersey Funeral Directors Assoc.
P.O. Box L
Manasquan, NJ 08736

3385

New Jersey I Scholarship Challenge Program

AMOUNT: $1,500 **DEADLINE:** Mar 15
FIELDS/MAJORS: Travel And Tourism, Hotel/Motel Management

Awards for New Jersey residents in one of the areas listed above who are enrolled in any 4-year college. Must have a GPA of 3.0 or better and be in junior or senior year. Write to the address below for more information.

National Tour Foundation
546 East Main St.
P.O. Box 3071
Lexington, KY 40596

3386

New Jersey II Scholarship Challenge Program

AMOUNT: $500 **DEADLINE:** Mar 15
FIELDS/MAJORS: Travel And Tourism, Hotel/Motel Management

Awards for New Jersey residents in one of the areas listed above who are enrolled in any 2-year college. Must have a GPA of 3.0 or better. Write to the address below for more information.

National Tour Foundation
546 East Main St.
P.O. Box 3071
Lexington, KY 40596

3387

New Jersey Medical Society Medical Student Loans

AMOUNT: $3,000 (max) **DEADLINE:** Mar 31
FIELDS/MAJORS: Medicine

Loans at 7% interest for medical students. Must be U.S. citizens and residents of New Jersey for at least 5 years. Must be (or become) member of MSNJ-Student Assoc. and in the 3rd or 4th year of medical school. Write to the Chairman of the Committee on Medical Student Loan Fund at the address below for details.

Medical Society Of New Jersey
Committee On Medical Student Loan Fund
Two Princess Road
Lawrenceville, NJ 08648

3388 New Jersey Osteopathic Education Foundation Loans

AMOUNT: Varies **DEADLINE:** Sep 1
FIELDS/MAJORS: Osteopathic Medicine

Loans for second-, third-, or fourth-year students in osteopathic colleges. Must be residents of New Jersey. Recipients must agree to practice in new jersey for at least two years after completion of residency. Write to the address below for details.

New Jersey Osteopathic Education Foundation
1212 Stuyvesant Ave.
Trenton, NJ 08618

3389 New Jersey Osteopathic Education Foundation Scholarships

AMOUNT: None Specified **DEADLINE:** Apr 30
FIELDS/MAJORS: Osteopathic Medicine

Scholarships for New Jersey residents entering their first year of study at an osteopathic college. Must have an undergraduate GPA of at least 3.0. Based on grades, need, motivation, and professional promise. Recipients must agree to practice in New Jersey for two years after education and training is complete. Application forms may be obtained from your medical advisor or by writing to the administrator at the address below.

New Jersey Osteopathic Education Foundation
One Distribution Way
Monmouth Junction, NJ 08852

3390 New Mexico Access To Research Careers (NMARC) Scholarship

AMOUNT: Varies **DEADLINE:** Mar 1
FIELDS/MAJORS: Psychology, Sociology

Awards are available at the University of New Mexico for sophomores or juniors in the fields of psychology or sociology. Contact Dr. Judith Arroyo in psychology or Dr. Phillip May, Director of the Center on Alcoholism, Substance Abuse, and Addictions for more details.

University Of New Mexico, Albuquerque
Office of Financial Aid
Albuquerque, NM 87131

3391 New Mexico Adult Education Scholarships

AMOUNT: Varies **DEADLINE:** June 30
FIELDS/MAJORS: All Areas Of Study

Awards for freshman who have received the GED in a New Mexico ABE program during the same year of application to college. Provides tuition assistance and a textbook scholarship of $175. Write to the address below for more information.

Secretary NMAEA Board
UNM Gallup, 200 College Blvd.
Gallup, NM 87301

3392 New Mexico Claims Assoc. Endowed Scholarship

AMOUNT: $200 **DEADLINE:** Mar 1
FIELDS/MAJORS: Business

Award for a full-time undergraduate business student who has a GPA of at least 3.0 and has successfully completed sixty credit hours by the effective date of the award. Write to the address below for more information.

Eastern New Mexico University
ENMU College Of Business, Station 49
Portales, NM 88130

3393 New Mexico Folklore Scholars In English

AMOUNT: Varies **DEADLINE:** Mar 1
FIELDS/MAJORS: Folklore

Awards are available at the University of New Mexico for students studying creative research and writing in the area of New Mexico folklore.

University Of New Mexico, Albuquerque
Office Of Financial Aid
Albuquerque, NM 87131

3394 New Mexico Public Relations Society Of America Communications Fund

AMOUNT: Varies **DEADLINE:** Mar 1
FIELDS/MAJORS: Journalism Or Communication

Awards are available at the University of New Mexico for full-time students in the field of public relations with a GPA of at least 2.5. Must demonstrate financial need. Write to the address listed below for information.

University Of New Mexico, Albuquerque
Office of Financial Aid
Albuquerque, NM 87131

3395 New Mexico Scholar's Scholarship

AMOUNT: Tuition & Fees **DEADLINE:** Mar 1
FIELDS/MAJORS: All Areas Of Study

Scholarships for New Mexico residents entering their freshman year at New Mexico State University. Applicant's family adjusted income must be $30,000 or less for one student and $40,000 or less for more than one student. Applicants must be in the top 5% of their high school class and have an SAT score of 1060 or ACT of 25 or higher. Renewable with a GPA of 3.0 or better. Contact the financial aid office at the address below for more information.

New Mexico State University
Office of Student Financial Aid
Box 30001, Dept. 5100
Las Cruces, NM 88003

3396 New Mexico Scholars Program

AMOUNT: Varies **DEADLINE:** None Specified
FIELDS/MAJORS: All Areas Of Study

Full tuition and fees award given to New Mexico resident students who have graduated in the top 5% of their high school class and have scored at least 25 on the ACT or 1020 on the SAT tests. Must enter college/university in New Mexico in the same year as graduation from high school. Write to the address listed below for additional information.

New Mexico Commission On Higher Education
1068 Cerrillos Road
Santa Fe, NM 87501

3397 New Mexico Society Of Certified Public Accountants/Roswell Scholarship

AMOUNT: $500 **DEADLINE:** Mar 1
FIELDS/MAJORS: Accounting

Award for a full-time undergraduate accounting student who has a GPA of at least 3.0 and has successfully completed sixty credit hours (15 hours in accounting courses) by the effective date of the award. Write to the address below for more information.

Eastern New Mexico University
ENMU College Of Business, Station 49
Portales, NM 88130

3398 New Mexico Society Of Public Accountants, A.J. Groebner Scholarship

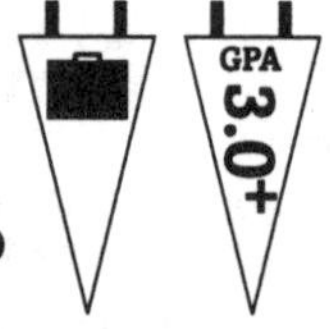

AMOUNT: $600 **DEADLINE:** Mar 1
FIELDS/MAJORS: Accounting

Award for a full-time undergraduate accounting student who has a GPA of at least 3.0, has successfully completed sixty credit hours and is a graduate of a New Mexico high school.

Eastern New Mexico University
ENMU College Of Business, Station 49
Portales, NM 88130

3399 New Mexico Soil And Water Conservation Scholarships

AMOUNT: Varies **DEADLINE:** Mar 1
FIELDS/MAJORS: Biology, Geography, Geology, Architecture

Awards are available at the University of New Mexico for juniors studying one of the fields above who have a GPA of at least 3.0.

University Of New Mexico, Albuquerque
Office of Financial Aid
Albuquerque, NM 87131

3400 New Mexico State Police Assoc. Scholarships

AMOUNT: Varies **DEADLINE:** Mar 1
FIELDS/MAJORS: All Areas Of Study

Awards are available at the University of New Mexico for dependents of a member of the New Mexico State Police. Must be enrolled in full-time study, and demonstrate financial need and a satisfactory GPA. Write to the address below for more information.

University Of New Mexico, Albuquerque
Office of Financial Aid
Albuquerque, NM 87131

3401 New Mexico Student Incentive Grant

AMOUNT: $2,500 (max) **DEADLINE:** None Specified
FIELDS/MAJORS: All Areas Of Study

Scholarships ($200 to $2,500) available to undergraduates enrolled at New Mexico schools with extreme financial need. Must be U.S. citizen and a resident of New Mexico. Contact the financial aid office at any New Mexico postsecondary institution.

New Mexico Commission On Higher Education
1068 Cerrillos Road
Santa Fe, NM 87501

3402 New Mexico Veterans' Service Commission Education Benefits

AMOUNT: Tuition Plus $300 **DEADLINE:** None Specified
FIELDS/MAJORS: All Areas Of Study

Must be son or daughter whose parent was Killed In Action or died as a result of military service in the U.S. Armed Forces during a period of armed conflict or died during active service on the New Mexico National Guard or State Police. Applicants must be between the ages of 16 and 26 and New Mexico residents attending New Mexico institutions. Write to the address below for complete details.

New Mexico Veterans' Service Commission
P.O. Box 2324
Santa Fe, NM 87503

3403 New York Farmers Scholarship

AMOUNT: Varies **DEADLINE:** Jun 1
FIELDS/MAJORS: Agriculture, Food Science

Awards for UMass students in the fields of agriculture or food science. Based on scholarship, need and participation in campus activities. For entering sophomores, juniors, or seniors. Contact the Associate Dean, College of Food and Natural Resources for more information.

University Of Massachusetts, Amherst
Associate Dean, College Of Food And Natural Resources
Amherst, MA 01003

3404 New York Life Foundation Scholarships For Women In Health Professions

AMOUNT: $500-$1,000 **DEADLINE:** Apr 15
FIELDS/MAJORS: Health Care

Undergraduate women, 25 or older, seeking the necessary education for a career in a health care field and within 24 months of graduation. Must demonstrate need. Must be a U.S. citizen. The preapplication screening form is only available between Oct 1 and Apr 1. Up to 100 scholarships are available. Not for graduate study correspondence programs, or non-degreed programs. Relatives of officers of New York Life Insurance Company are ineligible. Write to address below for details.

Business And Professional Women's Foundation Scholarships
2012 Massachusetts Ave., NW
Washington, DC 20036

3405 New York Scholarship Challenge Program

AMOUNT: $500 **DEADLINE:** Mar 15
FIELDS/MAJORS: Travel And Tourism, Hotel/Motel Management

Awards for New York residents in one of the areas listed above who are enrolled in any New York school. Must have a GPA of 3.0 or better and have completed at least 30 hours of study.

National Tour Foundation
546 East Main St.
P.O. Box 3071
Lexington, KY 40596

3406 New York State Assembly Session Internship

AMOUNT: $2,800 **DEADLINE:** Nov 1
FIELDS/MAJORS: State Government

Awards for students from New York or who attend school in New York who are interested in a career in state government. For undergraduate juniors and seniors. Up to 150 positions are available. Contact a NY Assembly Campus Liaison or the address below for more information.

The Assembly State Of New York, Albany
Assembly Intern Committee
Room 104A, Legislative Office Building
Albany, NY 12248

3407 New York State College Of Ceramics Grant

AMOUNT: Varies **DEADLINE:** Dec 15
FIELDS/MAJORS: Ceramics

For full-time undergraduate students entering the New York State College of Ceramics. Applicants must demonstrate financial need and be a U.S. citizen or permanent resident. Awards may be continued based on an annual determination of need, academic preformance, and a GPA of 2.0. Write to the address below for details.

Alfred University
Student Financial Aid Office
26 N. Main St.
Alfred, NY 14802

3408 New York State Grange Cornell Fund

AMOUNT: None Specified **DEADLINE:** None Specified
FIELDS/MAJORS: Agriculture/Life Sciences Related

Scholarships for students in the College of Agriculture and Life Sciences at Cornell University. Preference given to students from Grange families. Further preference given to students who transfer from a New York A&T College. Contact the financial aid office or write to the address below for details.

New York State Grange
Scholarship Coordinator
100 Grange Place
Cortland, NY 13045

3409 New York State Grange Student Loan Fund

AMOUNT: $1,000 (max) **DEADLINE:** None Specified
FIELDS/MAJORS: All Areas Of Study

Scholarships for members of a New York state subordinate Grange. Must have been a member for at least six months at time of application. Renewable up to $5,000. No repayment until after graduation. Interest: 5%.

New York State Grange
Scholarship Coordinator
100 Grange Place
Cortland, NY 13045

3410 New York Times Minority Scholarship

AMOUNT: $1,500-$3,000 **DEADLINE:** Mar 1
FIELDS/MAJORS: Journalism, Advertising

For junior and senior minority students planning careers in newspaper journalism or newspaper advertising. Must be attending the University of Florida. Renewable up to four years. Must have at least a 2.8 GPA.

University Of Florida
2070 Weimer Hall
Director, Minority Scholarship Program
Gainesville, FL 32611

3411 NEWH Chicago Chapter Scholarships

AMOUNT: $1,000 **DEADLINE:** Jun 1
FIELDS/MAJORS: Hospitality, Food Services

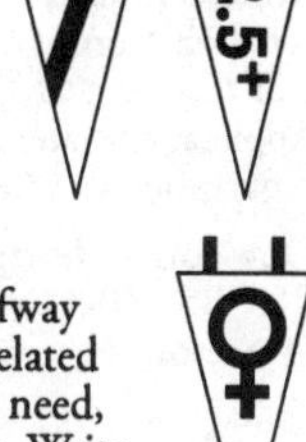

Awards are available for female students over halfway through an accredited hospitality/food services-related program. Applicants must demonstrate financial need, have good grades, and reside in the Chicago area. Write to the address below or e-mail jgoldsberry@tjbc.com for more information.

Network Of Executive Women In Hospitality, Chicago Chapter
Jill Goldsberry, c/o John Buck Company
233 S. Wacker Dr., Suite 4410
Chicago, IL 60606

3412 Newport Scholarship Fund Scholarships

AMOUNT: None Specified **DEADLINE:** May 10
FIELDS/MAJORS: All Areas Of Study

Scholarships for graduating seniors and alumni of Newport (NH) High School. Applications are available from the school's guidance office, or write to the address below for details.

Newport Scholarship Fund
P.O. Box 524
Newport, NH 03773

3413

News 4 Media Scholarship

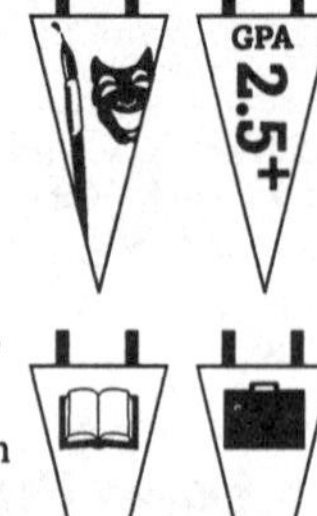

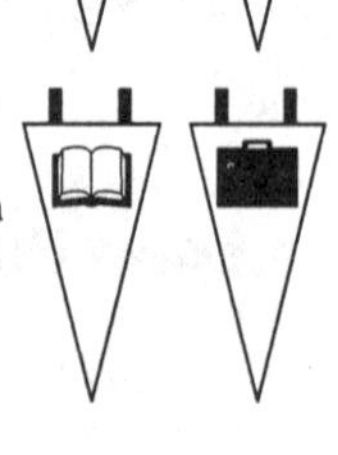

AMOUNT: None Specified **DEADLINE:** May 3
FIELDS/MAJORS: Communications, Journalism, Advertising, PR, Video, Film, Photography

Scholarships for Colorado residents majoring in communications. Must have a GPA of at least 2.5. Interview required. For graduating high school seniors or GED recipients. Write to the address below for details.

KCNC-TV Media Scholarship
P.O. Box 5012
Denver, CO 80217

3414

News Photographer Scholarships

AMOUNT: $1,000 **DEADLINE:** Apr 30
FIELDS/MAJORS: Photojournalism

Applicants must be a resident of New Jersey and attend a school of photography as an undergraduate. Recommendation required with application. Two awards per year. Write to the address below for details.

Bob Baxter Scholarship Foundation
New Jersey Newsphotos
Hemisphere Center, Route #1
Newark, NJ 07114

3415

Newspaper Editing Intern Program For Upperclassmen & Graduate Students

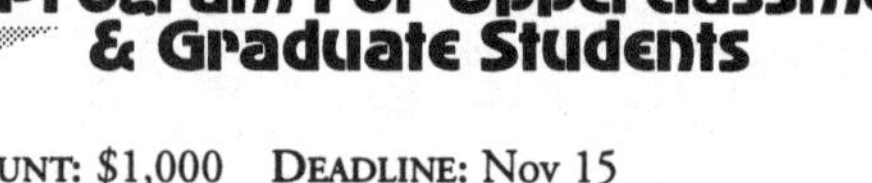

AMOUNT: $1,000 **DEADLINE:** Nov 15
FIELDS/MAJORS: Newspaper Journalism

Awards are available for juniors, seniors, or graduate students who work as interns to copy editors. Recipients are paid regular wages for their summer work and upon returning to school, the students will receive a $1,000 scholarship. Must be a U.S. citizen to apply. Applications are only available from September 1 through November 1. Write to the address below for more information.

Dow Jones Newspaper Fund
P.O. Box 300
Princeton, NJ 08543

3416

Newspaper Fund Reporter's Scholarship

AMOUNT: $1,000 **DEADLINE:** Nov 15
FIELDS/MAJORS: Journalism

Scholarships ($1,000) awarded to minority students who have completed a full-time reporting internship for at least eight weeks at a daily or weekly newspaper. Applicants must be a sophomore planning on continuing their education at four-year or community colleges. African American, Hispanic, Asian, Pacific Islander, American Indian and Alaskan Native students are encouraged to apply. Please write to the address listed below for further information and an application. Must be a U.S. citizen to apply.

Dow Jones Newspaper Fund
P.O. Box 300
Princeton, NJ 08543

3417

Newton Scholarship

AMOUNT: Varies **DEADLINE:** Jun 1
FIELDS/MAJORS: Agriculture

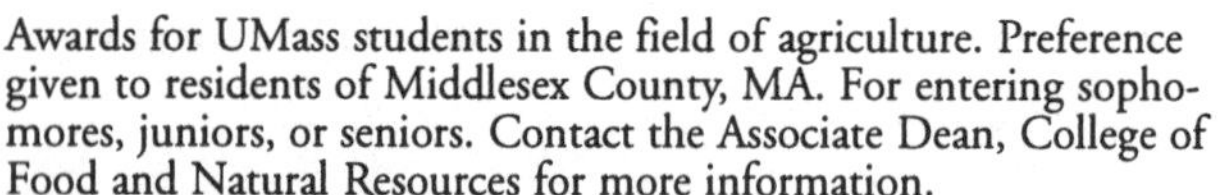

Awards for UMass students in the field of agriculture. Preference given to residents of Middlesex County, MA. For entering sophomores, juniors, or seniors. Contact the Associate Dean, College of Food and Natural Resources for more information.

University Of Massachusetts, Amherst
Associate Dean
College Of Food And Natural Resources
Amherst, MA 01003

3418

NHPRC/Andrew W. Mellon Foundation

AMOUNT: $40,000 (max) **DEADLINE:** Mar 1
FIELDS/MAJORS: Archival Administration

Open to students who have had two to five years of previous experience in archival work. This award includes $7,000 of benefits. Write to address below for details.

National Historical Publications And Records Commission (NP)
Archival Fellowship Program
National Archives Bldg.
Washington, DC 20408

3419

NIAF-Pavarotti Scholarship

AMOUNT: $1,000 **DEADLINE:** May 31
FIELDS/MAJORS: Music

Scholarship for an undergraduate or graduate student from southern CA who is studying music. Write to the address below for details.

National Italian American Foundation
Dr. Maria Lombardo, Education Director
1860 19th St., NW
Washington, DC 20009

3420

NIAF/Sacred Heart University Matching Scholarship

AMOUNT: $2,000 **DEADLINE:** May 31
FIELDS/MAJORS: All Areas Of Study

Fellowships are available for Italian American undergraduates enrolled at Sacred Heart University in Connecticut. Write to the address below for details.

National Italian American Foundation
Dr. Maria Lombardo, Education Director
1860 19th St., NW
Washington, DC 20009

3421

Nicaraguan And Haitian Scholarship Program

AMOUNT: $4,000-$5,000 **DEADLINE:** Jul 1
FIELDS/MAJORS: All Areas Of Study

Scholarships for residents of Florida who were born in Nicaragua or Haiti, or hold citizenship in either country. Applicant needs a cumulative high school GPA of 3.0 on a 4.0 scale, and have demonstrated community service. Write to the address below for details.

Florida Department of Education
Office of Student Financial Assistance
1344 Florida Education Center
Tallahassee, FL 32399

3422

Niccum Educational Trust Foundation Scholarships

AMOUNT: Varies **DEADLINE:** Mar 1
FIELDS/MAJORS: All Areas Of Study

Scholarships are available for residents of Elkhart, St. Joseph, Marshall, Noble, Kosciusko, and Lagrange County, IN. Write to the address listed below for information.

Niccum Educational Trust Foundation
NBD Bank, Trust Department
P.O. Box 27
Goshen, IN 46527

3423

Nicholas And Mary Agnes Trivillian Memorial Scholarship Fund

AMOUNT: None Specified **DEADLINE:** Mar 15
FIELDS/MAJORS: Medicine, Pharmacy

Scholarships for West Virginia residents in a course of study in medicine or pharmacy at any institution. Based on financial need. Renewable. Write to the address below for details.

Greater Kanawha Valley Foundation
Scholarship Committee
P.O. Box 3041
Charleston, WV 25331

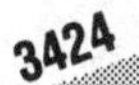

3424

Nicholas Boraski Scholarship

AMOUNT: Varies **DEADLINE:** Mar 1
FIELDS/MAJORS: Engineering

Awards for college juniors or seniors enrolled full-time in the College of Engineering. Financial need is a primary factor. Recipients must have a GPA of 3.0 or better and possess leadership qualities. Contact the Director of Recruitment, Marston Hall for more information.

University Of Massachusetts, Amherst
Director, Recruitment
Marston Hall
Amherst, MA 01003

3425

Nicholas Meyer Playwriting Scholarship

AMOUNT: Tuition **DEADLINE:** Mar 15
FIELDS/MAJORS: Playwriting

Scholarships are available at the University of Iowa for full-time students pursuing the study of dramatic writing. Based upon academic record and demonstrated ability. Write to the address listed below for information.

University Of Iowa
Department of Communication Studies
105 Communication Studies Building
Iowa City, IA 52245

3426

Nicholas Van Slyck Scholarship

AMOUNT: $400 **DEADLINE:** May 1
FIELDS/MAJORS: Music

Scholarship for Merrimack Valley area graduating high school seniors who intend to pursue a career in music. Write to the address below for details.

Merrimack Valley Philharmonic Society, Inc.
Attn: Scholarship
P.O. Box 512
Lawrence, MA 01842

3427

Nick & Helen Papanikolas Minority Student Scholarship

AMOUNT: $515 (min) **DEADLINE:** Feb 10
FIELDS/MAJORS: All Areas Of Study

Scholarships are available at the University of Utah for full-time students of African American, Asian/Pacific American, or Native American descent, who have completed at least thirty credit hours. Write to the address below for information.

University Of Utah
Scholarship Chairperson
112 Carlson Hall
Salt Lake City, UT 84112

3428

NIGMS Predoctoral Fellowships

AMOUNT: None Specified
DEADLINE: None Specified
FIELDS/MAJORS: Medical Science

Awards are available for minority graduate students working toward their Ph.D. in medical science. Must be a U.S. citizen. Write to the address below for additional information.

National Institute Of General Medical Sciences
National Institute Of Health
45 Center Dr. MSC 6200, Room 2AS.43
Bethesda, MD 20892

3429

NIH Research Grant And Contract Awards

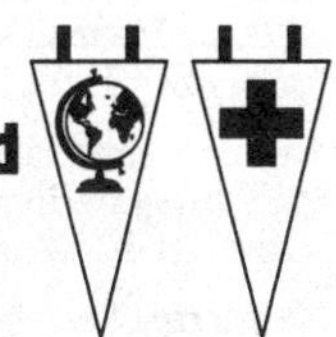

AMOUNT: Varies **DEADLINE:** None Specified
FIELDS/MAJORS: Biomedical And Behavioral Science Research

Awards for scientists to pursue research in any area of the biomedical and behavioral sciences within the scope of the NIH mission. U.S. and foreign scientists are both eligible for these awards. Write to the address below for more information.

National Institutes Of Health, Division Of Research Grants
Office of Grant Inquiries
Westwood Building, Room 449
Bethesda, MD 20892

3430

Nina Mae Kellogg Awards

AMOUNT: Varies **DEADLINE:** None Specified
FIELDS/MAJORS: English

Awards are available at Portland State University for sophomores or seniors who demonstrate excellence in the use of the English language. Based on GPA, and recommendations of faculty. Contact the English department at the address below for more information.

Portland State University
English Department
405 Neuburger Hall
Portland, OR 97207

3431

Nine-Month Internships

AMOUNT: $12,000 **DEADLINE:** Feb 2
FIELDS/MAJORS: Art History, Art Conservation, Art Education

Nine-month internships at the Museum for graduating seniors, graduates or graduate students who are studying art history or a related field. Program begins September 9 and runs through June 7. For residents of New York state. Write to the address listed below for additional information.

Metropolitan Museum Of Art
Office of Academic Programs
1000 Fifth Ave
New York, NY 10028

3432

NJLA Member Scholarship, George M. Lamonte, Sarah B. Askew Scholarship

AMOUNT: $1,000-$3,000 **DEADLINE:** Feb 15
FIELDS/MAJORS: Library Science

Scholarships for New Jersey residents admitted to an ALA-accredited, graduate-level library science program. Financial need is required. Write to Penny B. Page, Chair, NLJA Scholarship Committee, for information.

New Jersey Library Assoc.
Scholarship Committee
P.O. Box 969
Piscataway, NJ 08855

3433

NJSCLS Scholarships

AMOUNT: $500-$1,000 **DEADLINE:** Jun 15
FIELDS/MAJORS: Medical Technology, Medical Laboratory Technician

Awards are available for students who are enrolled in an ML or an MLT program in a New Jersey institution and entering their final year of study. Write to the address below for more information.

New Jersey Society For Clinical Laboratory Science
Mr. Edward J. Peterson, Jr.
34 Diamond Dr.
Egg Harbour Twp, NJ 08234

3434

NJSCPA Accounting Manuscript Contest

AMOUNT: $1,500 **DEADLINE:** Dec 15
FIELDS/MAJORS: Accounting

Scholarships for sophomores or juniors from New Jersey who are studying in the field of accounting at a New Jersey college or university. Based on the clarity, content, and ability to effectively communicate the relevance of accounting principles or practices to the topic, and ability to communicate information that is relevant to New Jersey businesses. Write to the address below for more information.

New Jersey Society Of Certified Public Accountants
Scholarship Awards Committee
425 Eagle Rock Ave.
Roseland, NJ 07068

3435

NJSCPA College Scholarship Program

AMOUNT: $1,000 **DEADLINE:** Jan 15
FIELDS/MAJORS: Accounting

Scholarships for juniors from New Jersey who are studying in the field of accounting at a New Jersey college or university. Contact your department chairperson for more information. Applicants must be nominated by the department chair for award consideration.

New Jersey Society Of Certified Public Accountants
Scholarship Awards Committee
425 Eagle Rock Ave.
Roseland, NJ 07068

3436

NJSCPA High School Scholarship Program

AMOUNT: $500-$2,500 **DEADLINE:** Oct 31
FIELDS/MAJORS: Accounting

Scholarships for New Jersey high school seniors who plan to enter the field of accounting and study at a New Jersey college or university. Contact your high school guidance counselor or write to the address below for more information.

New Jersey Society Of Certified Public Accountants
Scholarship Awards Committee
425 Eagle Rock Ave.
Roseland, NJ 07068

3437

NM Federation For The Council For Exceptional Children Scholarships

AMOUNT: $1,000 **DEADLINE:** Jan 7
FIELDS/MAJORS: Special Education

Awards for sophomores or juniors in college majoring in and planning a career in special education. Write to the address below for more information.

NMFCEC Scholarships
1609 Cedar Ridge, NE
Albuquerque, NM 87112

3438

NM Physician & Physician Assistant Student Loan For Service Program

AMOUNT: $12,000 (max) **DEADLINE:** None Specified
FIELDS/MAJORS: Medicine

$12,000 Annual Loan ($12,000) available to New Mexico resident graduate students in medicine. Loan may be repaid or forgiven by working in a medically underserved area of New Mexico. Must be U.S. citizen or legal resident who demonstrates financial need and attends a New Mexico school. Write to the address listed below for further information.

New Mexico Commission On Higher Education
1068 Cerrillos Road
Santa Fe, NM 87501

3439

NMSU Alumni Out-Of-State Scholarship

Amount: Varies **Deadline:** Mar 1
Fields/Majors: All Areas Of Study

Scholarships for students from out of state who will be attending New Mexico State University. Minimum GPA 3.0. Renewable. Contact the financial aid office at the address below for more information.

New Mexico State University
Office of Student Financial Aid
Box 30001, Dept. 5100
Las Cruces, NM 88003

3440

NMSU Minority Presidential Scholarship

Amount: $400 **Deadline:** Mar 1
Fields/Majors: All Areas Of Study

Scholarships for entering freshmen at New Mexico State University who are minority group members. 15 awards per year. Must have a high school GPA of at least 2.5. Renewable. Contact the financial aid office at the address below for more information.

New Mexico State University
Office of Student Financial Aid
Box 3,0001, Dept. 5100
Las Cruces, NM 88003

3441

NMSU Regents' Scholarship

Amount: $1,900 **Deadline:** Mar 1
Fields/Majors: All Areas Of Study

Scholarships for New Mexico residents entering their freshman year at New Mexico State University. Value of scholarship is tuition and fees (approximately $1,900). A 3.0 high school GPA is required. Renewable under certain conditions. Contact the financial aid office at the address below for more information.

New Mexico State University
Office of Student Financial Aid
Box 3,0001, Dept. 5100
Las Cruces, NM 88003

3442

NMSU Transfer Tuition Scholarships & Transfer $500 Scholarships

Amount: Varies **Deadline:** Mar 1
Fields/Majors: All Areas Of Study

Scholarships for students transferring to New Mexico State University from community or junior college. Must have at least 30 credit hours and a 3.5 GPA. Renewable for one additional year. Contact the financial aid office at the address below for more information.

New Mexico State University
Office of Student Financial Aid
Box 30001, Dept. 5100
Las Cruces, NM 88003

3443

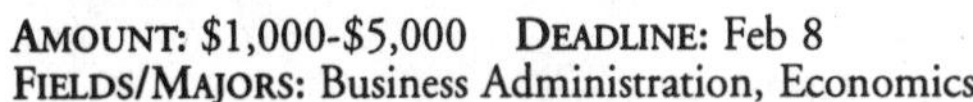

Noble Foundation Scholarships

Amount: $1,000-$5,000 **Deadline:** Feb 8
Fields/Majors: Business Administration, Economics

Scholarships are available at the University of Oklahoma, Norman, for full-time MBA and Ph.D. candidates in business administration, who are U.S. citizens. Write to the address listed below for information.

University Of Oklahoma, Norman
College Of Business Administration
208 Adams Hall
Norman, OK 73019

3444

Non-Resident Graduate Tuition Scholarships

Amount: Varies **Deadline:** Varies
Fields/Majors: All Areas Of Study

Awards for graduate students with a cumulative GPA of 3.0 for all previous academic work. Underrepresented minorities in graduate studies are also eligible. Write to the address below for more information.

University Of Nebraska, Omaha
Office of Admissions, Eab 103
60th And Dodge Streets
Omaha, NE 68182

3445

Non-Resident Tuition Waiver Scholarships For Graduate Assistants

Amount: $1,000 (approx) **Deadline:** Mar 1
Fields/Majors: All Areas Of Study

Scholarships are available at the University of Oklahoma, Norman for full-time students, who are residents of a state other than Oklahoma, and are graduate assistants or research assistants. Write to the address listed below for information.

University Of Oklahoma, Norman
Office of Financial Aid
Norman, OK 73019

3446

Non-Resident Tuition Waiver Scholarships For Minority Students

Amount: $1,000 (approx) **Deadline:** Mar 1
Fields/Majors: All Areas Of Study

Scholarships are available at the University of Oklahoma, Norman for full-time graduate minority students, who are residents of a state other than Oklahoma. Write to the address listed below for information.

University Of Oklahoma, Norman
Graduate College
1000 Asp Ave., Room 313
Norman, OK 73019

3447

Non-Resident Undergraduate Tuition Scholarships

AMOUNT: Varies **DEADLINE:** Varies
FIELDS/MAJORS: All Areas Of Study

Awards for entering freshmen who rank in the top 25% of their high school class, scored 23 or more on the ACT or 970 or higher on the SAT. Transfer students who have a cumulative GPA of 3.0 or better and underrepresented minorities or individuals with special talents are also eligible. Write to the address below for more information.

University Of Nebraska, Omaha
Office of Admissions, Eab 103
60th And Dodge Streets
Omaha, NE 68182

3448

Nonprofit Sector Research Fund Grants

AMOUNT: $20,000-$50,000 **DEADLINE:** Jan 1, Jun 1
FIELDS/MAJORS: Public Policy, Political Science

Grants are available to encourage graduate students and scholars in the early stages of their careers to conduct research to expand understanding of non-profit activities, including philanthropy and its underlying values. For dissertation and advanced research. Write to the address listed below for information.

Aspen Institute
Nonprofit Sector Research Fund
1333 New Hampshire Ave., Suite 1070
Washington, DC 20036

3449

Nontraditional Student Tuition Waivers And Scholarships

AMOUNT: Varies **DEADLINE:** Feb 15
FIELDS/MAJORS: All Areas Of Study

Scholarships are available at the University of Utah for full-time female students who have had at least a five-year interruption in their undergraduate education. Write to the address below for information.

University Of Utah
Women's Resource Center
293 Olpin Union
Salt Lake City, UT 84112

3450

Norbert Schimmel Fellowship For Mediterranean Art And Archaeology

AMOUNT: $21,000-$29,000 **DEADLINE:** Nov 9
FIELDS/MAJORS: Art History, Classical Studies, Art Conservation, Archaeology

Award is for graduate students that have been admitted to a doctoral program in the United States and are planning a thesis on ancient Near-Eastern art and archaeology or with Roman or Greek art. Write to "Fellowship Programs" at the address below for complete details.

Metropolitan Museum Of Art
Office of Academic Programs
1000 Fifth Ave.
New York, NY 10028

3451

Nordstrom Scholarships

AMOUNT: $2,000 **DEADLINE:** Apr 12
FIELDS/MAJORS: Business

Scholarships are available for undergraduate students with disabilities enrolled in or planning to enroll in a business program. Requires a four-part essay of not more than fifteen pages, and documentation of your handicap. Write to the address listed below for information.

President's Committee On Employment
Of People With Disabilities
Scholarship Program
1331 F St., NW
Washington, DC 20004

3452

Norfolk Southern Foundation Scholarships

AMOUNT: $1,000 **DEADLINE:** Feb 15
FIELDS/MAJORS: Agriculture, Agricultural Education

Scholarships are available for FFA members pursuing a four-year degree in agricultural education, or a two-year degree in any area of agriculture. Write to the address below for details.

National FFA Foundation
Scholarship Office
P.O. Box 15160
Alexandria, VA 22309

3453

Norma '54 And Saul '54 Feingold Award

AMOUNT: Varies **DEADLINE:** Feb 29
FIELDS/MAJORS: Management, Insurance

Scholarships are awarded to School of Management students on the basis of academic merit and financial need. Preference is given to students who demonstrate an interest in a career in the insurance industry and are natives of Worcester County, MA. For students in their sophomore, junior, or senior year. Applications for School of Management Scholarships will be available in the SOM Development Office, Room 206.

University Of Massachusetts, Amherst
School Of Management
SOM Development Office, Room 206
Amherst, MA 01003

3454

Norman Hilgar Scholarship

AMOUNT: $400 **DEADLINE:** Feb 9
FIELDS/MAJORS: Accounting

Award for a junior who is an accounting major. Outstanding academic achievement in accounting is required. Financial need considered only to break a tie between finalists. Use Bloomsburg University scholarship application. Contact Dr. Richard Baker, chairperson, accounting for further information.

Bloomsburg University
19 Ben Franklin Hall
400 E. Second St.
Bloomsburg, PA 17815

3455

Norman K. Dunn Memorial Scholarship

Amount: None Specified **Deadline:** Nov 1
Fields/Majors: Equine Studies

Open to full-time incoming freshmen with an interest in Arabian breed and/or the equine industry. Must have a minimum of twelve units and a GPA of 3.0 or better. Write to the address below for more information.

California State Polytechnic University, Pomona
College Of Agriculture
Building 29, Room 100
Pomona, CA 91768

3456

Norman V. Pearle Scholarship

Amount: $5,800 **Deadline:** Jan 15
Fields/Majors: All Areas Of Study

Awards for freshmen who have an ACT score of at least 25 and a GPA of at least 3.5. Based on a special scholarship competition. Renewable with a GPA of 3.0 or better. Write to the address below for more information.

Northwestern College
Financial Aid Office
101 7th St., SW
Orange City, IA 51041

3457

North American Limousin Foundation Scholarships

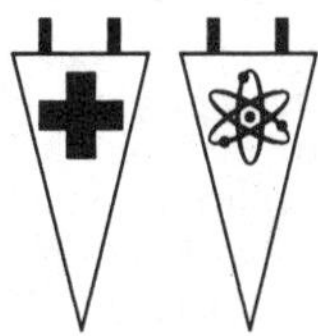

Amount: $1,000 **Deadline:** Feb 15
Fields/Majors: Animal Science, Pre-vet

Scholarships are available for FFA members pursuing a four-year degree in animal science or preveterinary medicine. Write to the address below for details.

National FFA Foundation
Scholarship Office
P.O. Box 15160
Alexandria, VA 22309

3458

North Carolina Contractual Scholarships

Amount: Varies **Deadline:** None Specified
Fields/Majors: All Areas Of Study

Need-based awards for students attending Meredith College who are legal residents of North Carolina. Write to the address below for more information.

Meredith College
Office of Admissions
3800 Hillborough St.
Raleigh, NC 27607

3459

North Carolina Legislative Tuition Grant

Amount: $1,250 (approx.) **Deadline:** Apr 1
Fields/Majors: All Areas Of Study

Every North Carolina resident who attends Elon College as a full-time student automatically receives a legislative tuition grant from the North Carolina General Assembly of approximately $1,250. Applicants must present proof of legal residency. Write to the address below for details.

Elon College
Office of Financial Planning
2700 Campus Box
Elon College, NC 27244

3460

North Carolina Library Assoc. Scholarships

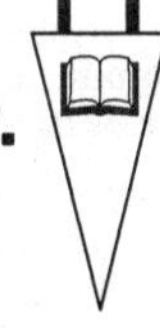

Amount: $300-$1,000 **Deadline:** Apr 25
Fields/Majors: Library Science

Scholarships at all levels of study for North Carolina residents who are studying library science. Query-long scholarships also available for persons who will work with children or young adults. Write to Sandra Smith, Chair, NCLA Scholarship Committee, at the address below for details.

North Carolina Library Assoc.
NCLA Scholarship Committee
1416 Hickory Woods Dr.
Monroe, NC 28112

3461

North Carolina Scholarship Challenge Program

Amount: $1,000 **Deadline:** Mar 15
Fields/Majors: Travel And Tourism, Hotel/motel Management

Awards for North Carolina residents in one of the areas listed above who are enrolled in any four-year college. Must have a GPA of 3.0 or better and be in junior or senior year. Write to the address below for more information.

National Tour Foundation
546 East Main St.
P.O. Box 3071
Lexington, KY 40596

3462

North Carolina Student Incentive Grant

Amount: $1,500 (max) **Deadline:** Mar 15
Fields/Majors: All Areas Of Study

Scholarships are available to North Carolina residents who are U.S. citizens with extreme financial need. For undergraduate study. Write to the address below for details.

North Carolina State Education Assistance Authority
P.O. Box 2688
Chapel Hill, NC 27515

3463

North Carolina Teaching Fellows Program

Amount: $5,000 **Deadline:** None Specified
Fields/Majors: Education

Scholarships are available for graduating high school seniors residing in North Carolina, who plan to pursue a career in teaching. Recipients must commit to teaching in a public or government school in North Carolina for four years after graduation. The typical recipient will have a GPA of 3.6 or above, and be in the top 10% of his/her class. Write to the address listed below for information.

Public School Forum Of North Carolina
3739 National Drive, Suite 210
Raleigh, NC 27612

3464

North Carolina Teaching Fellowships

AMOUNT: $10,000 **DEADLINE:** Apr 1
FIELDS/MAJORS: Education

Awards are available to full-time Elon College students who plan to pursue a career in teaching. Recipients must teach for four years in a North Carolina public school after graduation.

Elon College
Office of Financial Planning
2700 Campus Box
Elon College, NC 27244

3465

North Central Edward H. Rensi Regional Scholarships

AMOUNT: $1,000 **DEADLINE:** May 31
FIELDS/MAJORS: All Areas Of Study

Scholarships for Italian American residents of Ohio, Kentucky, Indiana, Illinois, Wisconsin, Michigan, Minnesota, North and South Dakota. For undergraduate study.

National Italian American Foundation
Dr. Maria Lombardo, Education Director
1860 19th St., NW
Washington, DC 20009

3466

North Dakota Board Of Nursing Education Loan Program

AMOUNT: $1,000 (max) **DEADLINE:** Jul 1
FIELDS/MAJORS: Nursing

Open to North Dakota residents who are United States citizens, have financial need, and have been accepted into a board-approved nursing program.

North Dakota Board Of Nursing
919 South 7th St., Suite 504
Bismarck, ND 58504

3467

North Dakota Department of Transportation Scholarship Program

AMOUNT: $1,000-$3,000 **DEADLINE:** None Specified
FIELDS/MAJORS: Civil Engineering, Construction, Industrial Drafting, Related Fields

Applicants must have completed one year of study at an accredited North Dakota school in the above fields. Recipients must agree to work for the department for a period of time at least equal to the time needed to complete the grant study period. Those who do not accept employment with the department, must repay grant on a pro-rated basis at 6 percent.

North Dakota Department of Transportation
Human Resources Division
608 E. Boulevard Ave.
Bismarck, ND 58505

3468

North Dakota Indian Scholarships

AMOUNT: $600-$2,000 **DEADLINE:** Jul 15
FIELDS/MAJORS: All Areas Of Study

Scholarships for North Dakota residents who are at least one-quarter Indian blood or an enrolled member of a tribe in North Dakota, accepted for admission as a full-time student at a school within North Dakota. Priority will be given to applicants with a GPA of 3.5 or above, but a GPA of 2.0 is required. Write to the address below for further information or an application.

North Dakota Indian Scholarship Program
State Capitol, 10th Floor
600 East Boulevard Ave.
Bismarck, ND 58505

3469

North Platte Jaycees Scholarship

AMOUNT: None Specified **DEADLINE:** Mar 1
FIELDS/MAJORS: All Areas Of Study

Scholarships are available to graduating seniors from a high school in North Platte with a GPA of at least 2.0. Write to the address listed below for information.

Mid-Nebraska Community Foundation
410 Rodeo Road
P.O. Box 1321
North Platte, NE 69103

3470

North Texas GIA Alumni Assoc. (NTGIAAA) Scholarship

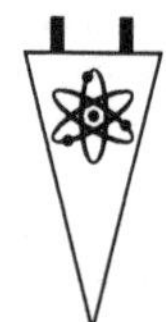

AMOUNT: $1,000 **DEADLINE:** Nov 1
FIELDS/MAJORS: Gemology

Awards are available for undergraduates enrolled in any GIA education program. Must be a U.S. citizen or permanent resident and live in the north Texas area. This area can be defined by the following first three numbers of the zip code areas: 750-757, 760-769, and 790-797. Write to the address below for more information.

Gemological Institute Of America
Office of Student Financial Assistance
1660 Stewart St.
Santa Monica, CA 90404

3471

Northeast Alabama Traffic Club

AMOUNT: $1,000 **DEADLINE:** None Specified
FIELDS/MAJORS: Nursing

Awards for Jacksonville State University students who are in the field of nursing. Must be from Etowah or Calhoun Counties in Alabama. Contact the College of Nursing for more information.

Jacksonville State University
Financial Aid Office
Jacksonville, AL 36265

3472

Northeast Printers And Pendell Family Scholarship

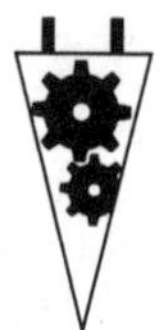

AMOUNT: $500-$1,000 **DEADLINE:** None Specified
FIELDS/MAJORS: Pulp & Paper Science, Graphic Arts

Scholarships reserved for juniors in the Department of Paper and Printing Science and Engineering at WMU. Based on academics and need. Pendell Award is renewable for senior year. Write to the address below for more information.

Western Michigan University
College Of Engineering & Applied Science
Dept. Of Paper & Printing Science & Eng.
Kalamazoo, MI 49008

3473

Northeastern Junior College Scholarships

Amount: Varies **Deadline:** Apr 1
Fields/Majors: All Areas Of Study

Northeastern Junior College administers approximately $225,000 per year in scholarships for students admitted to the college. Information on these awards can be found in a brochure from the financial aid office or in the general catalog. Criteria for these awards varies widely. One application will suffice to apply for most awards.

Northeastern Junior College
Coordinator Of Financial Aid
Sterling, CO 80751

3474

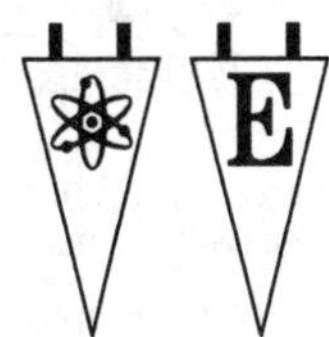

Northern Lake Huron Bioreserve Intern

Amount: None Specified
Deadline: None Specified
Fields/Majors: Biological Science, Environmental Science, Conservation Science

Enrollment in college program with intention to pursue biological, environmental, or conservation sciences. Good communication skills, familiarity with IBM computers and ability to work with diverse people. Experience handling boats preferred. For Michigan minority students only.

Nature Conservancy
Kent Gilges, UP Project Director
P.O. Box 567
Cedarville, MI 49719

3475

Northern NY Volunteer Firemen's Association Scholarship

Amount: None Specified **Deadline:** Apr 1
Fields/Majors: All Community Related Areas Of Study

Scholarships are available for members, or children of members of the Northern New York Volunteer Firemen's Association. Must be enrolled in a "community oriented" field of study

Northern NY Volunteer Firemen's Association
James Cayey, Secretary
P.O. Box 433
Colton, NY 13625

3476

Northrop Corporation Founders Scholarship

Amount: $1,000 **Deadline:** Feb 1
Fields/Majors: Engineering

Scholarship for a sophomore woman SWE Member. Must be an engineering major and a U.S. citizen. A GPA of at least 3.5 is required. Write to address below for details. Please be certain to enclose an SASE. Information and applications for the SWE awards are also available from the deans of engineering schools.

Society Of Women Engineers
120 Wall St., 11th Floor
New York, NY 10005

3477

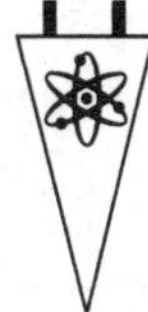

Northrup King Company Scholarships

Amount: $1,000 **Deadline:** Feb 15
Fields/Majors: Agriculture

Scholarships are available for FFA members pursuing a four-year degree in any area of agriculture, who reside in Illinois, Iowa, Minnesota, Nebraska, and Wisconsin.

National FFA Foundation
Scholarship Office
P.O. Box 15160
Alexandria, VA 22309

3478

Northwest Regional Scholarships

Amount: $1,000 **Deadline:** May 31
Fields/Majors: All Areas Of Study

Scholarships for Italian American residents of Washington state, Oregon, Idaho, Montana, Wyoming, and Alaska. For undergraduate study.

National Italian American Foundation
Dr. Maria Lombardo, Education Director
1860 19th St., NW
Washington, DC 20009

3479

Northwest Transport Scholarship

Amount: $1,000 **Deadline:** None Specified
Fields/Majors: Business

Awards for full-time Mesa State juniors or seniors majoring in a business field. Must have a GPA of at least 3.0..

Mesa State College
Office of Financial Aid
P.O. Box 2647
Grand Junction, CO 81501

3480

Northwestern Grants

Amount: $200-$2,500 **Deadline:** None Specified
Fields/Majors: All Areas Of Study

Awards for Northwestern students who show evidence of good character, leadership abilities, and financial need.

Northwestern College
Financial Aid Office
101 7th St., SW
Orange City, IA 51041

3481

NQA Grant And Scholarship Program

Amount: Varies **Deadline:** Aug 15
Fields/Majors: Quilting

Awards for individuals or groups who have committed artistic development and/or experimentation in the field of quilting, have conducted research into the historical documentation of quilts and quiltmakers, or are quiltmakers trying to further their education. Membership in the NQA is encouraged, but not required.

National Quilting Assoc., Inc.
NQA Grant And Scholarship Chairperson
P.O. Box 393
Elliot City, MD 21041

3482 NSA Undergraduate Training Program

Amount: Tuition and Fees **Deadline:** Nov 10
Fields/Majors: Computer Science, Electrical Or Computer Engineering, Languages, Math

Program for high school seniors who are interested in studying one of the fields above. Program offers full tuition, books, and a salary during the undergraduate years, as well as job in the summer. Applicants must have a minimum GPA of 3.0, an ACT score of 24 or SAT score of 1000, and be a U.S. citizen. Write to the address below for additional details.

National Security Agency
Manager, Undergraduate Training Program
Attn: M325 (UTP)
Ft. Meade, MD 20755

3483 NSF Graduate Research Fellowships

Amount: $14,400 **Deadline:** Nov 6
Fields/Majors: Mathematics, Life & Social Sciences, Engineering, And Related Fields

Fellowships for students in a wide area of studies leading toward M.A./M.S. or Ph.D. Must be U.S. citizen, national, or permanent resident. Fellows choose their own fellowship institution. Intended mainly for beginning graduate students. Not for clinical, business, medical, legal, or educational areas of study. Write to the address below for details. Information is also available from departmental offices at many colleges and universities. Programs are highly competitive. Special awards are also available for minority applicants.

National Science Foundation
Oak Ridge Associated Universities
P.O. Box 3010
Oak Ridge, TN 37831

3484 NSPE-Presidential Scholarship

Amount: $1,000 **Deadline:** None Specified
Fields/Majors: Engineering

Awards for engineering students from New Mexico attending New Mexico institutions. Applicants must attend an ABET-approved school of engineering, be U.S. citizens, and have a GPA of at least 3.0. Write to the address below for more information.

National Society Of Professional Engineers
1420 King St.
Alexandria, VA 22314

3485 NSPE-Professional Engineers In Industry Scholarship

Amount: $2,500 **Deadline:** None Specified
Fields/Majors: Industrial Engineering

Awards for juniors or seniors studying industrial engineering at an ABET-accredited engineering school. Applicants must be U.S. citizens with a GPA of at least 3.0. Preference is given to students affiliated to the NSPE. Write to the address below for more information.

National Society Of Professional Engineers
1420 King St.
Alexandria, VA 22314

3486 NSPE Student Chapter Member

Amount: $1,000 **Deadline:** None Specified
Fields/Majors: Engineering

Awards for sophomore, junior or senior NSPE student members who are in good standing. Applicants must be U.S. citizens, have a GPA of at least 3.0 and attend an ABET-accredited institution. Write to the address below for more information.

National Society Of Professional Engineers
1420 King St.
Alexandria, VA 22314

3487 NSPE/DOW Minority Scholarship

Amount: $3,000 **Deadline:** Nov 21
Fields/Majors: Chemical Engineering

Scholarship open to minority students living in Illinois, with a GPA of 3.0 or greater. Applicant must be attending an ABET-approved institution and be a U.S. citizen. Write to the address below for more information.

National Society Of Professional Engineers Education Foundation
1420 King St.
Alexandria, VA 22314

3488 Nursing Alumni Fund

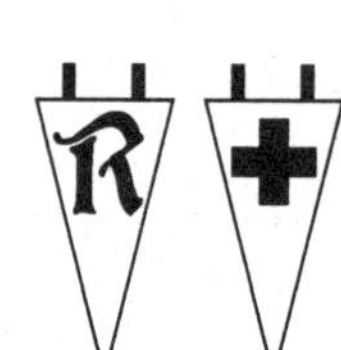

Amount: None Specified
Deadline: None Specified
Fields/Majors: Nursing

Loans are available at the Catholic University of America for full-time nursing students. Write to the address below for details.

The Catholic University Of America Alumni Assoc.
The Catholic University Of America
School Of Nursing
Washington, DC 20064

3489 Nursing Economics Foundation Scholarships

Amount: $5,000 **Deadline:** May 1
Fields/Majors: Nursing

Scholarships are available to master's and doctoral candidates in nursing science, with an emphasis on nursing administration or management. Write for complete details.

Nursing Economics Foundation
East Holly Ave., Box 56
Pitman, NJ 08701

3490 Nursing Endowed Scholarship Fund

Amount: Varies **Deadline:** None Specified
Fields/Majors: Nursing

Awards available for qualified nursing students at Cedarville College. Must have a GPA of at least 2.0, financial need, and potential for Christian leadership in nursing. Write to the address below for more information.

Cedarville College
Financial Aid Office
P.O. Box 601
Cedarville, OH 45314

3491

Nursing Grants For Persons Of Color

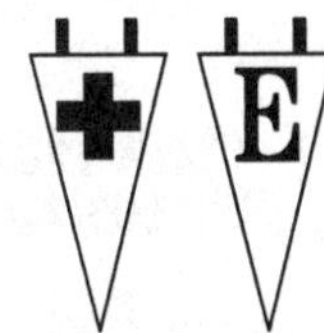

Amount: $2,000-$4,000
Deadline: None Specified
Fields/Majors: Nursing

Awards are available for African American Minnesota students in a nursing program in the state of Minnesota. Must be a U.S. citizen or permanent resident. Write to the address below for more information.

Minnesota Higher Education Services Office
400 Capital Square
550 Cedar St.
Saint Paul, MN 55101

3492

Nursing Incentive Scholarship Fund

Amount: $2,340 (max) **Deadline:** Jun 1
Fields/Majors: Nursing

Scholarships for Kentucky residents who have been admitted to a nursing school in Kentucky. Preference is given to applicants with financial need, and who have agreed to work in a sponsoring hospital. Write to the address below for more information.

Kentucky Board Of Nursing
Nursing Incentive Scholarship Fund
312 Whittington Parkway, Suite 300
Louisville, KY 40222

3493

Nursing Merit Scholarship

Amount: $1,000 **Deadline:** None Specified
Fields/Majors: Nursing

Student must be enrolled at least eight hours each semester as a senior in the bachelor of science in nursing program. Must have completed the first clinical course and maintain a GPA of 3.25 or better. Recipient must plan to remain in the local area and may not be awarded any other scholarship. Contact the Nursing Department for more information.

Southwest Missouri State University
Office of Financial Aid
901 South National Ave.
Springfield, MO 65804

3494

Nursing Scholarship

Amount: Varies **Deadline:** None Specified
Fields/Majors: Nursing

Award for Indiana students who have been admitted to attend an Indiana school as a full-time or part-time nursing student. Applicants must have a GPA of 2.0 or better and demonstrate financial need. Recipients are required to agree, in writing, to work in any type of health care setting in Indiana for at least 2 years after graduation. Write to the address below for more information.

Indiana Student Assistance Commission
150 W. Market St., Suite 500
Indianapolis, IN 46204

3495

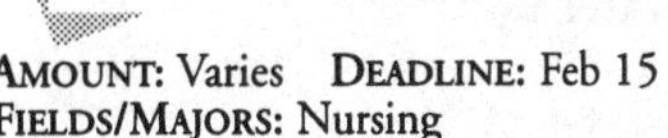

Nursing Scholarships

Amount: Varies **Deadline:** Feb 15
Fields/Majors: Nursing

Scholarships offered to freshman students attending or planning to attend Loyola University on a full-time basis. Applicants must rank in the top 25% of their graduating class, and have a composite ACT score of at least 26 or SAT score of 1000 or better. Renewable for one or two years if the recipient maintains a GPA of at least 3.2. Write to the address below for details.

Loyola University
Dean, Niehoff School Of Nursing
6525 North Sheridan Road
Chicago, IL 60626

3496

Nursing Scholarships

Amount: Varies **Deadline:** None Specified
Fields/Majors: Nursing

Awards for students who have attained the clinical level of their nursing education and are interested in continuing with their education. Applicants must attend a nursing school in Texas and be U.S. citizens or permanent residents. Write to the address below for more information.

Good Samaritan Foundation
Scholarship Coordinator
5615 Kirby Dr., Suite 308
Houston, TX 77005

3497

Nursing Scholastic Achievement Scholarships

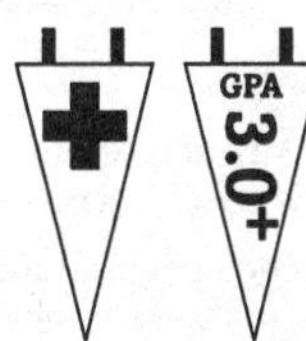

Amount: $1,000 **Deadline:** Mar 15
Fields/Majors: Nursing

Scholarships for communicant members of Lutheran congregations who are juniors or seniors in a school of nursing. Must have a GPA of at least 3.0 and be able to demonstrate past or present involvement in a community or church activity which benefits people who are mentally retarded. Write to the address below (or call 1-800-369-INFO, ext. 525) for details.

Bethesda Lutheran Home
National Christian Resource Center
700 Hoffmann Drive
Watertown, WI 53094

3498

Nursing, Physical Therapy Or Respiratory Therapy Scholarships

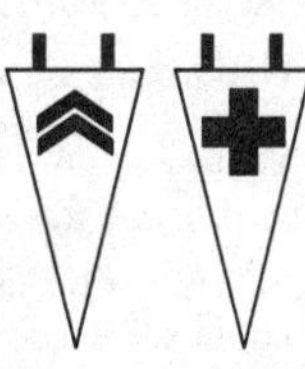

Amount: $500 **Deadline:** Mar 15
Fields/Majors: Nursing, Physical Or Respiratory Therapy

Scholarships available for Michigan residents who will be or are attending a college or university in Michigan. Applicants must be citizens of the U.S., and children of veterans, enrolled or accepted in one of the above programs. Write to the address listed below for additional information.

American Legion Auxiliary-Department of Michigan
212 North Verlinden
Lansing, MI 48915

3499

NWSA Graduate Scholarship In Lesbian Studies

Amount: $1,000 **Deadline:** Feb 15
Fields/Majors: Women's Studies-Lesbian Studies

Scholarship for graduate student researching for master's thesis or Ph.D. dissertation in lesbian studies. Write to the address listed below for information and an application.

National Women's Studies Assoc.
University Of Maryland
7100 Baltimore Ave., Suite 301
College Park, MD 20740

3500

NWSA Scholarship In Jewish Women's Studies

Amount: $500 **Deadline:** Feb 15
Fields/Majors: Jewish Women's Studies

Scholarship for graduate student whose area is Jewish women's studies. Write to the address below for details.

National Women's Studies Assoc.
University Of Maryland
7100 Baltimore Ave., Suite 301
College Park, MD 20740

3501

O'Meara Foundation Scholarships

Amount: $300-$1,500 **Deadline:** Jun 1
Fields/Majors: All Areas Of Study

Scholarship awards for worthy Hartford County (CT) residents who desire to obtain a college education but lack funds to do so on their own. There are approximately 100 awards given annually. Applications should be mailed to the address below during the months of January, February, or March.

O'Meara Foundation, Inc.
4 Grimes Rd.
Rocky Hill, CT 06067

3502

O.G.&E. Accounting Scholarship

Amount: $750 **Deadline:** Feb 3
Fields/Majors: Accounting

Scholarships are available at the University of Oklahoma, Norman for full-time undergraduate accounting majors, who reside in Oklahoma. Four awards are offered annually. Write to the address listed below for information.

University Of Oklahoma, Norman
School Of Accounting
200 Adams Hall
Norman, OK 73019

3503

O.H. Ammann Fellowship

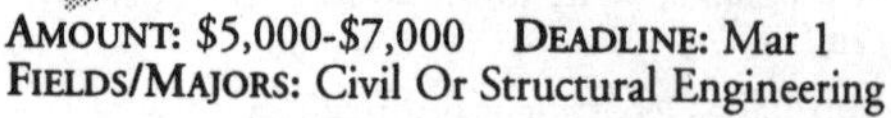

Amount: $5,000-$7,000 **Deadline:** Mar 1
Fields/Majors: Civil Or Structural Engineering

Applicant must be a national ASCE member in good standing in any grade. Award is used for purposes of encouraging the creation of new knowledge in the field of structural design and construction. Write to the address below for complete details.

American Society Of Civil Engineers
Member Scholarships And Awards
345 E. 47th St.
New York, NY 10017

3504

Oak Harbor Educational Foundation Scholarships

Amount: $500 **Deadline:** None Specified
Fields/Majors: All Areas Of Study

Scholarships offered to Oak Harbor High School graduates. Awards based on school performance, activities, written essays and interviews. Financial need and GPA not factors. Two scholarships will be awarded. Write to the address below for details.

Oak Harbor Educational Foundation
P.O. Box 1801
Oak Harbor, WA 98277

3505

Occupational Therapy Scholarships

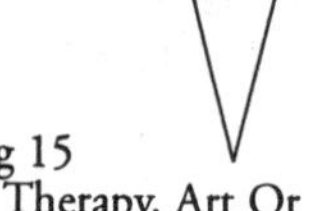

Amount: $500-$1,000 **Deadline:** Feb 15, Aug 15
Fields/Majors: Occupational Therapy, Physical Therapy, Art Or Music Therapy

Students must be enrolled in an accredited school of occupational, physical, art or music therapy. United States citizenship is required. For undergraduate study. Contact your local DAR chapter or write to the address below for complete details.

National Society Daughters Of The American Revolution
NSDAR Scholarship Committee
1776 D St., NW
Washington, DC 20006

3506

Office Technology Scholarship

Amount: $1,500 **Deadline:** None Specified
Fields/Majors: Business Technology

Scholarships for new students at Kent State who are majoring in business technology. Must have solid academic record. Contact the financial aid office for details.

Kent State University, Tuscarawas Campus
Financial Aid Office
University Dr., NE
New Philadelphia, OH 44663

3507

OH/PA Alumni Assoc. Scholarship

Amount: $500 **Deadline:** Apr 15
Fields/Majors: Horticulture, Park Administration

Open to students enrolled in horticulture or park administration. Write to the address below for more information.

California State Polytechnic University, Pomona
College Of Agriculture
Building 7, Room 110
Pomona, CA 91768

3508

Ohio Academic Scholarship Program

Amount: $1,000 **Deadline:** Feb 23
Fields/Majors: All Areas Of Study

Scholarships are available to graduating Ohio high school seniors who plan to attend a college or university in Ohio. Based upon GPA and ACT test scores. One award will be available for each high school. Write to the address listed below for information, or contact your school guidance counselor.

Ohio Student Aid Commission
Customer Service
P.O. Box 16610
Columbus, OH 43216

3509

Ohio Baptist Education Society Scholarship Program

Amount: None Specified **Deadline:** None Specified
Fields/Majors: All Areas Of Study

Scholarships for members of an American Baptist church in Ohio who intend to enter a field of Christian service, Christian ministry, or church music. Based on need and potential. For junior level of study and above. Write to the address below for details.

Ohio Baptist Education Society
Dr. Ralph K. Lamb, Executive Secretary
248 Pine Tree Dr., NE
Granville, OH 43023

3510

Ohio Instructional Grant, Ohio Student Choice Grant

Amount: $3,750 (max) **Deadline:** Oct 1
Fields/Majors: All Areas Of Study

Scholarships are available to full-time undergraduate students who are Ohio residents attending or planning to attend a college or university in Ohio. Write to the address listed below for information.

Ohio Student Aid Commission
Customer Service
P.O. Box 16610
Columbus, OH 43216

3511

Ohio League For Nursing Student Aid

Amount: Varies **Deadline:** Apr 15
Fields/Majors: Nursing

Grants, loans, and combination grant/loans for students pursuing initial RN or LPN licensure. Renewable. Must live and attend school in the greater Cleveland area. Expected to join OLN after graduation and work as a nurse in the Cleveland area after graduation (Cuyahoga, Geauga, Lake, Lorain, Medina, Portage, or Summit Counties). Write to the address below for details.

Ohio League For Nursing
Student Aid For Greater Cleveland Area
2800 Euclid Ave., Suite 235
Cleveland, OH 44115

3512

Ohio Nurse Education Assistance Loan Program

Amount: $3,000 **Deadline:** None Specified
Fields/Majors: Nursing

Loans are available to Ohio residents who are enrolled or plan to enroll in a LPN or RN program in an Ohio college, university, vocational school or hospital. Applicant must intend to practice nursing in the state of Ohio after graduation. Write to the address listed below for information.

Ohio Student Aid Commission
Customer Service
P.O. Box 16610
Columbus, OH 43216

3513

Ohio Pork Council Women Scholarship

Amount: $500 **Deadline:** Apr 16
Fields/Majors: All Areas Of Study

Scholarships for Ohio residents who are sons or daughters of members of a local and/or state pork producers council. For junior, senior, or graduate study. Must have a GPA of at least 2.5. Write to the address below for more information.

Ohio Pork Council Women Scholarship
Ohio Pork Producers Council
5930 Sharon Woods Blvd., Suite 101
Columbus, OH 43229

3514

Ohio River Valley Safety Council Scholarship

Amount: None Specified **Deadline:** Feb 1
Fields/Majors: Health And Occupational Safety

Scholarship awarded annually to a student pursuing a program of study in the occupational safety and health program at Murray State University. Write to the address below for details.

Murray State University
Office of University Scholarships
Ordway Hall, 1 Murray St.
Murra, KY 42071

3515

Ohio Safety Officers College Memorial Fund

Amount: Varies **Deadline:** None Specified
Fields/Majors: All Areas Of Study

Scholarships are available to undergraduate Ohio residents who are children of deceased peace officers or firefighters. Applicant must be under 26 years of age. Write to the address listed below for information, or your school financial aid office.

Ohio Student Aid Commission
Customer Service
P.O. Box 16610
Columbus, OH 43216

3516

Oklahoma Library Assoc. Scholarships

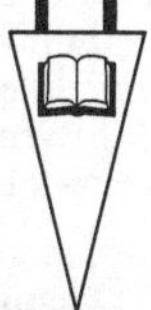

Amount: Varies **Deadline:** Feb 1
Fields/Majors: Library Science

Scholarships for Oklahoma students of library science at the any level of study. Write to the address below for details.

Oklahoma Library Assoc.
Kay Boies
300 Hardy Dr.
Edmond, OK 73013

3517

Oklahoma Memorial Union Board Of Trustees Scholarship

Amount: $1,000 **Deadline:** Apr 15
Fields/Majors: All Areas Of Study

Scholarships are available at the University of Oklahoma, Norman for juniors, seniors and graduate students. Undergraduate students must have a GPA of at least 3.0 and graduate students must have a GPA of at least 3.5. Write to the address listed below for information.

University Of Oklahoma, Norman
Union Business Office
900 ASP, Room MZ3
Norman, OK 73019

3518

Oklahoma Natural Gas Company Scholarships

Amount: $1,000 **Deadline:** Feb 15
Fields/Majors: Agriculture

Scholarships are available for FFA members pursuing a four-year degree in any area of agriculture at an Oklahoma institution, who reside in Oklahoma. Write to the address below for details.

National FFA Foundation
Scholarship Office
P.O. Box 15160
Alexandria, VA 22309

3519

Oklahoma State Garden Club Scholarship

Amount: $500 **Deadline:** Feb 15
Fields/Majors: Landscape Architecture, Horticulture, Botany, Zoology, Environmental

Scholarships are available for residents of Oklahoma or students enrolled in Oklahoma schools, pursuing a degree in one of the above fields. Write to the address listed below for information.

Oklahoma Garden Clubs, Inc.
Mrs. Frank Olney, State Chairman
1216 Cruce
Norman, OK 73069

3520

Oklahoma State Regents' Academic Scholars Program

Amount: $3,100-$5,000 **Deadline:** Aug 1
Fields/Majors: All Areas Of Study

This program was designed to retain top-ranked Oklahoma students and to attract high-caliber out-of-state students to Oklahoma institutions. For use at both public and private Oklahoma colleges and universities. Must have a GPA of 3.25 or greater and full-time enrollment. Must be National Merit finalist or scholar, National Achievement, Hispanic or Presidential scholar. Write to the address below or call (405) 524-9153 for further details.

Oklahoma State Regents For Higher Education
Academic Scholars Office
500 Education Building
Oklahoma City, OK 73105

3521

Oklahoma Tuition Aid Grant Program

Amount: $1,000 **Deadline:** May 1
Fields/Majors: All Areas Of Study

This is a need-based program that awards grants to students as partial reimbursements for student fees and tuition in both public and private institutions in Oklahoma. Applicants must be Oklahoma residents. Write to the address below for more information.

Oklahoma State Regents For Higher Education
State Capitol Complex
500 Education Building
Oklahoma City, OK 73101

3522

Olfactory Research Fund

Amount: Varies **Deadline:** Jan 1
Fields/Majors: Otolanyngology

Fund is to support research which seeks to integrate the study of olfaction with current issues in developmental, perceptual, social and cognitive psychology and related disciplines. For those who are currently specializing in olfaction or those who wish to redirect their research. Applicant must possess a doctoral degree in a related field. Contact the address below for additional information.

Olfactory Research Fund, Ltd.
145 E. 32nd St.
New York, NY 10016

3523

Olga V. Alexandria Logan Scholarship

Amount: Varies **Deadline:** Feb 1
Fields/Majors: All Areas Of Study

Scholarships are available at the University of Utah for full-time female students, who demonstrate extreme financial need and have a GPA of 3.5 or better. Write to the address below for details.

University Of Utah
Barbara Hamblin
116 Marriott Center For Dance
Salt Lake City, UT 84112

3524

Olin Fellowships

Amount: $1,000-$3,000 **Deadline:** Mar 15
Fields/Majors: Fisheries, Marine Biology, And Related Areas

ASF fellowships are offered annually to individuals seeking to improve their knowledge or skills in advanced fields related to Atlantic salmon (biology, management, or conservation). For use at any accredited university, research laboratory, or active management program. Must be U.S. or Canadian citizen. Application forms may be obtained from the Atlantic Salmon Federation, P.O. Box 429, St. Andrews, NB, E0G 2X0, Canada.

Atlantic Salmon Federation
P.O. Drawer C
Calais, ME 04619

3525

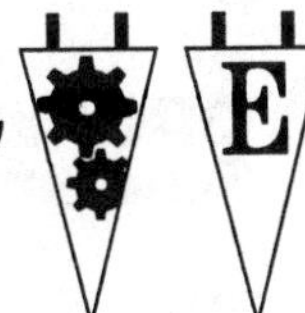

Olin Ordinance Minority Scholarship

AMOUNT: Varies **DEADLINE:** None Specified
FIELDS/MAJORS: All Areas Of Study

Awards for minority students at St. Petersburg Junior College in any field of study who are able to demonstrate financial need. Preference is given to students majoring in engineering. Write to the address below for more information.

St. Petersburg Junior College
Financial Aid Office
P.O. Box 13489
St. Petersburg, FL 33733

3526

Olive Lynn Salembier Scholarships

AMOUNT: $2,000 **DEADLINE:** May 15
FIELDS/MAJORS: Engineering

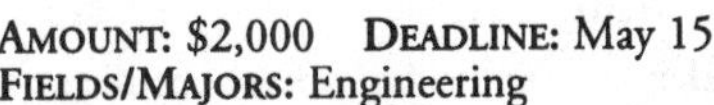

Scholarship for women who have not worked in the field of engineering for at least two-years, and who must acquire the credentials to return to the market as an engineer. Any year undergraduate or graduate student. Must have had a GPA of at least 3.5. Write to the address below for details. Please be certain to enclose an SASE. Information and application forms are also available from the deans of engineering schools.

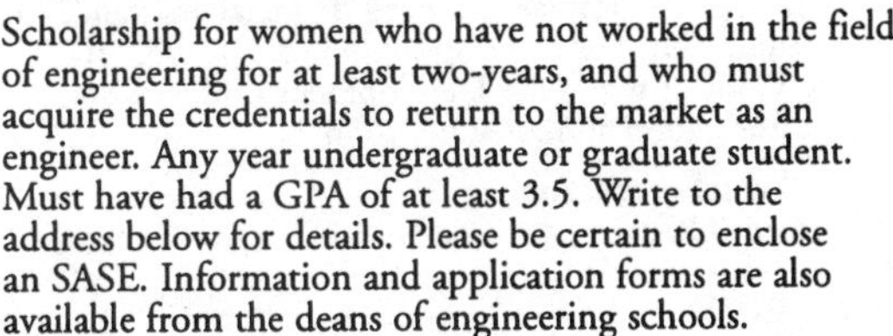

Society Of Women Engineers
120 Wall St., 11th Floor
New York, NY 10005

3527

Oliver H. Delchamps, Jr. Endowed Scholarship Amount:

AMOUNT: $1,000 **DEADLINE:** Feb 15
FIELDS/MAJORS: Communications

Renewable $1,000 award for undergraduate or graduate students enrolled in the College of Communication at the University of Alabama, whose current record and potential indicates a successful career as a communicator. Created in 1983 to honor the sesquicentennial of the university. Write to the address listed below for further information and an application.

University Of Alabama
College Of Communications
P.O. Box 870172
Tuscaloosa, AL 35487

3528

Olivia James Traveling Fellowship

AMOUNT: $15,000 **DEADLINE:** Nov 1
FIELDS/MAJORS: Classics, Sculpture, Architecture Archaeology, And History

Competition is open to students who are citizens or permanent residents of the United States. The award is to be used for travel and study in: Greece, the Aegean Islands, Sicily, southern Italy, Asia Minor or Mesopotamia. Preference will be given to individuals engaged in dissertation research or to recent recipients of the Ph.D. Write to the address below for details.

Archaeological Institute Of America
Boston University
656 Beacon St., 4th Floor
Boston, MA 02215

3529

Olsher Scholarship

AMOUNT: Varies **DEADLINE:** Feb 29
FIELDS/MAJORS: Management

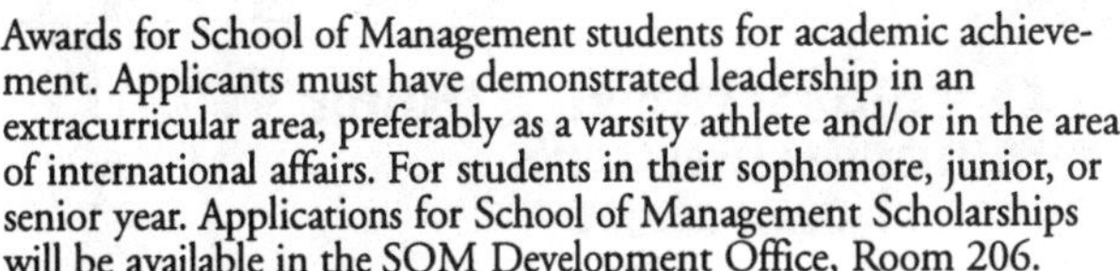

Awards for School of Management students for academic achievement. Applicants must have demonstrated leadership in an extracurricular area, preferably as a varsity athlete and/or in the area of international affairs. For students in their sophomore, junior, or senior year. Applications for School of Management Scholarships will be available in the SOM Development Office, Room 206.

University Of Massachusetts, Amherst
School Of Management
SOM Development Office, Room 206
Amherst, MA 01003

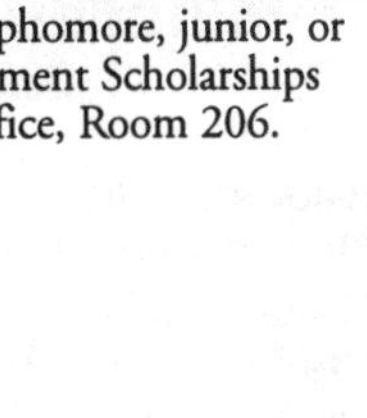

3530

Omicron Nu Research Fellowship

AMOUNT: $2,000 **DEADLINE:** Jan 15
FIELDS/MAJORS: Home Economics/Related Fields

Applicants must be members of Kappa Omicron Nu and enrolled in a Ph.D. program in home economics. Write to the address below for details.

Kappa Omicron Nu Honor Society
4990 Northwind Dr., Suite 140
East Lansing, MI 48823

3531

Oncology Nursing Bachelor's Scholarships

AMOUNT: $2,000 **DEADLINE:** Dec 1
FIELDS/MAJORS: Oncology Nursing

Grants available to bachelor's students in the field of oncology nursing. All applicants must be registered nurses. For full-time or part-time students in an NLN-accredited school of nursing. Write to the address below for more information.

Oncology Nursing Foundation
501 Holiday Dr.
Pittsburgh, PA 15220

3532

Oncology Nursing Certification Nursing Certification Scholarships

AMOUNT: $3,000 **DEADLINE:** Dec 1
FIELDS/MAJORS: Oncology Nursing

Grants available to master's students in the field of oncology nursing. All applicants must be registered nurses. For full-time or part-time students. Write to the address below for more information.

Oncology Nursing Foundation
501 Holiday Dr.
Pittsburgh, PA 15220

3533

Oncology Nursing Ethnic Minority Bachelor's Scholarships

AMOUNT: $2,000 **DEADLINE:** Dec 1
FIELDS/MAJORS: Oncology Nursing

Grants available to minority bachelor's students in the field of oncology nursing. All applicants must be registered nurses. For full- or part-time students in an NLN-accredited school of nursing. Write to the address below for more information.

Oncology Nursing Foundation
501 Holiday Dr.
Pittsburgh, PA 15220

3534

Oncology Nursing Ethnic Minority Master's Scholarships

AMOUNT: $3,000 **DEADLINE:** Dec 1
FIELDS/MAJORS: Oncology Nursing

Grants available to minority master's students in the field of oncology nursing. All applicants must be registered nurses. For full- or part-time students. Write to the address below for more information.

Oncology Nursing Foundation
501 Holiday Dr.
Pittsburgh, PA 15220

3535

Oncology Nursing Foundation Research Grants

AMOUNT: Varies **DEADLINE:** Dec 1
FIELDS/MAJORS: Oncology Nursing

Research grants available to students and scholars in the field of oncology nursing. Over 25 grants are available, and the individual criteria for each may vary. All applicants must be registered nurses. Write to the address below for more information.

Oncology Nursing Foundation
501 Holiday Dr.
Pittsburgh, PA 15220

3536

Oncology Nursing Master's Scholarships

AMOUNT: $3,000 **DEADLINE:** Dec 1
FIELDS/MAJORS: Oncology Nursing

Grants available to master's students in the field of oncology nursing. All applicants must be registered nurses. For full-time or part-time students. Write to the address below for more information.

Oncology Nursing Foundation
501 Holiday Dr.
Pittsburgh, PA 15220

3537

Opal Dancey Memorial Foundation

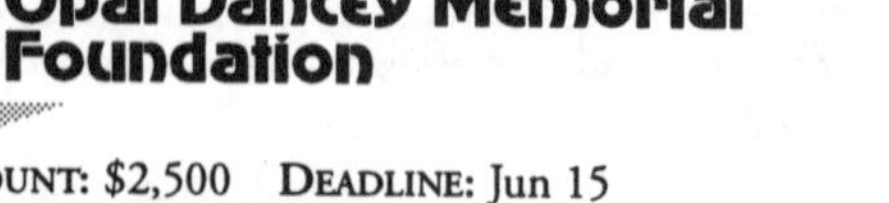

AMOUNT: $2,500 **DEADLINE:** Jun 15
FIELDS/MAJORS: Theology

Grants awarded primarily in the Midwest (U.S.). Preference given to McCormick, United, Garrett, Trinity, Asbury and Methodist theological schools in Ohio. Given to students seeking a master of divinity degree only from accredited theological schools and seminaries. Write to the address below for more information.

Opal Dancey Memorial Foundation
Rev. Gary R. Imms, Chairman
45 South St.
Croswell, MI 48422

3538

OPC Foundation Scholarships

AMOUNT: $1,000 **DEADLINE:** Dec 9
FIELDS/MAJORS: Foreign Affairs/Journalism

Awards are available for students in the U.S. who are planning careers as foreign correspondents. Based on essay and career objectives. Write to the address below for more information.

Overseas Press Club Of America
320 East 42nd
New York, NY 10017

3539

Operations Management Council Scholarship

AMOUNT: Varies **DEADLINE:** Feb 29
FIELDS/MAJORS: Operations Management

Awards for outstanding students in the field of operations management who show great promise and need financial assistance to complete their education. For entering sophomore, junior, or senior students. Contact the SOM Development Office, Room 206, for more information and an application.

University Of Massachusetts, Amherst
SOM Development Office
Room 206
Amherst, MA 01003

3540

Opportunity At Iowa Scholarships

AMOUNT: $3,000 **DEADLINE:** None Specified
FIELDS/MAJORS: All Areas Of Study

Scholarships are available at the University of Iowa for entering freshmen minority students who have a minimum GPA of at least 3.5. Write to the address listed below for information.

University Of Iowa
Office of Admissions
107 Calvin Hall
Iowa City, IA 52242

3541

Opportunity Awards For African American And Hispanic Students

AMOUNT: 50% Tuition **DEADLINE:** Mar 31
FIELDS/MAJORS: All Areas Of Study

Awards for Hispanic or African American students with academic potential or achievement and who have been accepted to Hood. Write to the address below for more information.

Hood College
Admissions Office
401 Rosemont Ave.
Frederick, MD 21701

3542

Opportunity Grant

AMOUNT: $1,000 **DEADLINE:** None Specified
FIELDS/MAJORS: All Areas Of Study

Award available to qualified students on the basis of academic performance. Renewable. Write to the address below for more information.

Carthage College
Financial Aid Office
Kenosha, WI 53140

3543

Oprah Winfrey Scholarship

AMOUNT: Varies **DEADLINE:** None Specified
FIELDS/MAJORS: All Areas Of Study

Awards for entering freshman at Morehouse College who have a GPA of at least 3.5 and an SAT score of 1000 or better. Recipients must maintain a GPA of at least 3.0 and work as peer tutors on campus. Write to the address below for more information.

Morehouse College
Office of Student Financial Aid
830 Westview Drive SW
Atlanta, GA 30314

3544

Optimist International Essay Contest

AMOUNT: Varies **DEADLINE:** None Specified
FIELDS/MAJORS: All Areas Of Study

Contest for students who are currently in their sophomore, junior, or senior years of high school. Based on 400-600 word essay. Write to the address below for more information.

Optimist International
Programs And Youth Clubs Department
4494 Lindell Blvd.
St. Louis, MO 63108

3545

Oral Hearing Impaired Section Scholarship Award

AMOUNT: Varies **DEADLINE:** Apr 15
FIELDS/MAJORS: All Areas Of Study

Applicants must be born deaf or became deaf before acquiring language. Must use speech/residual hearing or lip-reading as primary communication and be a student entering or attending a college or university program for hearing students. Two awards per year. Write to the address below for complete details.

Alexander Graham Bell Assoc. For The Deaf
3417 Volta Place, NW
Washington, DC 20007

3546

Orange County Wine Society, Inc. Scholarship

AMOUNT: $500 **DEADLINE:** None Specified
FIELDS/MAJORS: Hotel & Restaurant Management

Scholarships are available for full-time students majoring in hotel & restaurant management. Must have a GPA of 2.0 or better. Financial need must be demonstrated. Write to the address below for more information.

California State Polytechnic University, Pomona
Office of Financial Aid
3801 West Temple Ave.
Pomona, CA 91768

3547

Orchard Mesa Lion's Club Scholarship

GPA 3.0+

AMOUNT: $1,000 **DEADLINE:** None Specified
FIELDS/MAJORS: All Areas Of Study

Awards for Mesa State upperclassmen who are from Mesa County and have a GPA of at least 3.0. Write to the address below for more details.

Mesa State College
Office of Financial Aid
P.O. Box 2647
Grand Junction, CO 81501

3548

Order Of AHEPA Educational Scholarships

AMOUNT: Varies **DEADLINE:** May 1
FIELDS/MAJORS: All Areas Of Study

Scholarships are available for students of Hellenic heritage at the undergraduate or graduate levels. Individual criteria for these awards varies. Includes the George Leber, Sterios B. Milonas, Carlos Touris, Nick Cost, Sam Nakos, and Dr. John Yavis scholarships and trusts. Write to the address below for more information and for an application.

American Hellenic Educational Progressive Assoc.
1909 Q St., NW, Suite 500
Washington, DC 20009

3549

Order Of The Alhambra Scholarships In Special Education

AMOUNT: None Specified **DEADLINE:** None Specified
FIELDS/MAJORS: Special Education

Applicant must be entering the junior or senior year of college as a special education major. Write to the address below for more information.

International Order Of The Alhambra
Scholarship Committee
4200 Leeds Ave.
Baltimore, MD 21229

3550

OREF Research Grants

AMOUNT: $50,000 **DEADLINE:** Aug 1
FIELDS/MAJORS: Medicine: Orthopedics

Grants to support and encourage young investigators by providing seed money and start-up funding. Awards may be made for one or two years. Principal or co-principal must be an orthopedic surgeon working at an institution in the U.S. or Canada. Write to Katherine Walker, Director of Grants, at the address below for details.

Orthopedic Research And Education Foundation
6300 N. River Rd., Suite 700
Rosemont, IL 60018

3551

OREF Resident Research Awards

AMOUNT: $15,000 **DEADLINE:** Aug 1
FIELDS/MAJORS: Medicine: Orthopedics

Grants for one year are offered to residents in approved orthopedic programs to encourage the development of research interests. These grants provide funds for supplies and expenses but not for a resident's salary. Write to Katherine Walker, Director of Grants, at the address below for details.

Orthopedic Research And Education Foundation
6300 N. River Rd., Suite 700
Rosemont, IL 60018

3552

Oregon Associated Loggers (OAL) Scholarship Grant

AMOUNT: $1,000 **DEADLINE:** Apr 16
FIELDS/MAJORS: Forestry, Logging, And Related

Grant for Oregon high school seniors who intend to pursue a college education, and subsequently a career in, forest industries related fields. Based on application, transcripts and essay (less than two pages). Write to the address below for details.

Associated Oregon Loggers, Inc.
1127 25th St., SE
P.O. Box 12339
Salem, OR 97309

3553

Oregon Assoc. Of Chiefs Of Police Scholarships

GPA 3.0+

AMOUNT: $500 **DEADLINE:** Nov, Dec
FIELDS/MAJORS: Administration Of Justice

Awards are available to administration of justice majors who have completed 90 to 130 credits of college level course work while maintaining a minimum GPA of 3.0. Write to the address below for more information. No application is necessary, students meeting the basic requirements are placed on ballot and selected by faculty vote.

Portland State University
Financial Aid Office
176 Neuberger Hall
Portland, OR 97207

3554

Oregon Assoc. Of Public Accountants Scholarships

AMOUNT: $500-$1,000 **DEADLINE:** Apr 1
FIELDS/MAJORS: Accounting

Scholarships for Oregon residents who are attending school in Oregon and studying for a career in accounting. The sponsor urges applicants to pay close attention to the instructions on the application form (or else be disqualified). Mail your request for an application to the address below and enclose a business-size (no. 10) SASE.

Oregon Assoc. Of Public Accountants
Scholarship Foundation
1804 NE 43rd Ave.
Portland, OR 97213

3555

Oregon Laurels Graduate Tuition Remission Program

AMOUNT: Varies **DEADLINE:** Apr 15
FIELDS/MAJORS: All Areas Of Study

Merit-based awards are available at Portland State University for graduate students. Preference is given to Oregon residents. Contact the Office of Graduate Studies & Research for more information.

Portland State University
Office of Graduate Studies & Research
105 Neuberger Hall
Portland, OR 97207

3556

Oregon Laurels Scholarships

GPA 3.5+

AMOUNT: Varies **DEADLINE:** Mar 1
FIELDS/MAJORS: All Areas Of Study

Awards are available at Portland State University for high school seniors with a GPA of 3.5 or better or for current undergraduates with a minimum GPA of 3.25. Extracurricular activities and community service activities are also evaluated. Must be a resident of Oregon. Renewable. Write to the address below for more information.

Portland State University
Office of Academic Affairs
3349 Cramer Hall
Portland, OR 97207

3557

Oregon Laurels/Eastern Scholar

GPA 3.0+

AMOUNT: Varies **DEADLINE:** Mar 1
FIELDS/MAJORS: All Areas Of Study

Award for a student at eastern who is from Oregon and has a GPA of at least 3.0. Write to the address below for more information.

Eastern Oregon State College
Financial Aid Office
1041 L Ave.
La Grande, OR 97850

3558

Oregon Sheep Growers Assoc. Scholarship

AMOUNT: $1,000 **DEADLINE:** Jul 15
FIELDS/MAJORS: Animal Husbandry, Agriculture, Pre-veterinary Medicine, Animal Science

Two scholarships for students in the areas of animal husbandry and agriculture, with an interest in the sheep industry. For sophomore, junior, senior or graduate students. Applicant must be a resident of Oregon, but does not need to attend an Oregon school. Write to the address below for details.

Oregon Sheep Growers Assoc.
Scholarship Committee
1270 Chemeketa St., NE
Salem, OR 97301

3559

Oregon Sports Lottery Graduate Scholarships Program

AMOUNT: Varies **DEADLINE:** Apr 15
FIELDS/MAJORS: All Areas Of Study

Awards are available at Portland State University for full-time graduate students. Preference is given to doctoral students. Contact the Office of Graduate Studies & Research for more information.

Portland State University
Office of Graduate Studies & Research
105 Neuberger Hall
Portland, OR 97207

Oregon State Home Builders Scholarships

Amount: None Specified **Deadline:** Mar 1
Fields/Majors: Construction, Architectural Engineering, Real Estate Development.

Scholarships for students of construction engineering, housing studies, or interior merchandising at Oregon State University; building inspection at Chemeketa; construction technology at Lane College or Portland Community College; architectural engineering at Mt. Hood Community College; or building construction at Clackamas Community College. Contact the financial aid office at your college for details.

Oregon State Scholarship Commission
Attn: Grant Department
1500 Valley River Dr., #100
Eugene, OR 97401

Orentreich Foundation For The Advancement Of Science Inc.

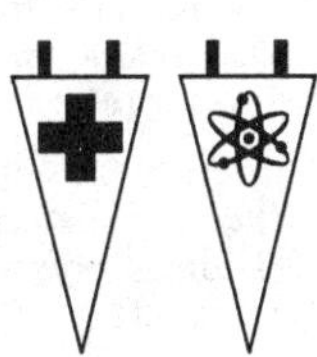

Amount: None Specified **Deadline:** None Specified
Fields/Majors: Science, Medicine

For recipients who are at or above postgraduate level in science or medicine at accredited universities or research institutions in the U.S. Write to the address below for more information.

Orentreich Foundation For The Advancement Of Science Inc.
Biomedical Research Station
Rd 2 Box 375, 855 Route 301
Cold Spring-On-Hudson, NY 10516

Orlando Sentinel/ Sun-Sentinel Of Ft. Lauderdale Minority Scholarship

Amount: $1,500-$3,000 **Deadline:** Mar 1
Fields/Majors: Newspaper Journalism, Newspaper Advertising

Awards for junior or senior minority students at the University of Florida who are planning careers in newspaper journalism or newspaper advertising. Preference to students from Orlando and Ft. Lauderdale areas. Renewable. Write to the address below for details.

University Of Florida
2070 Weimer Hall
Director, Minority Scholarship Program
Gainesville, FL 32611

Orton And Francis Keyes Scholarship

Amount: $300 **Deadline:** Feb 15
Fields/Majors: All Areas Of Study

Awards for UW Platteville continuing students who demonstrate academic excellence and participation in extracurricular activities. Write to the address below for more information.

University Of Wisconsin, Platteville
Office of Admissions And Enrollment
Platteville, WI 53818

3564

Orville Hitchcock Awards

Amount: $125 **Deadline:** None Specified
Fields/Majors: Communications, Broadcasting, Film

Scholarships are available at the University of Iowa for full-time freshmen, sophomores or juniors who have the highest GPA's in the department. Five awards are offered. Write to the address listed below for information.

University Of Iowa
Department of Communication Studies
105 Communication Studies Building
Iowa City, IA 52245

3565

Oscar W. Rittenhouse Memorial Scholarship

Amount: $2,500 **Deadline:** Jun 15
Fields/Majors: Law

Scholarship for New Jersey residents who are enrolled in or accepted into law school and who have an interest in pursuing a career in law enforcement. One year scholarship grant. Persons may reapply in succeeding years. Write to the address below for details.

County Prosecutors Assoc. Of New Jersey Foundation
Prosecutors Supervisory Section
25 Market St., Cn-085
Trenton, NJ 08625

3566

Oshkosh Foundation Grants

Amount: None Specified **Deadline:** None Specified
Fields/Majors: All Areas Of Study

Scholarships are offered by the Oshkosh Foundation for the benefit of residents of Oshkosh, WI. Must be graduating high school senior from one of the 6 schools in the Oshkosh School District and be a resident of Oshkosh or of Winnebago County. Write to the address below for further information.

Oshkosh Foundation
404 N. Main St.
P.O. Box 1726
Oshkosh, WI 54902

3567

Otis A. Barnes Scholarship

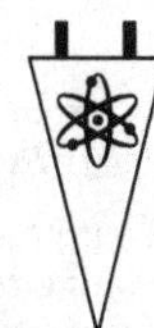

Amount: Tuition **Deadline:** Feb 15
Fields/Majors: Chemistry

Scholarships are available at Colorado College for new students majoring in chemistry. Renewable for three additional years. Contact the Chemistry Department or write to the address listed below for information.

Colorado College
Office of Financial Aid
14 East Cache La Poudre
Colorado Springs, CO 80903

3568
Otis Gossman Memorial Scholarship

AMOUNT: $1,000 **DEADLINE:** April 6
FIELDS/MAJORS: Print Journalism

Must be a junior or senior studying print journalism at the University of Florida. Must have at least a 3.0 GPA. Must be from the northwest Florida area. This scholarship is provided by the Daily News of Fort Walton Beach. Write for complete details.

University Of Florida
2070 Weimer Hall
Scholarship & Placement Director
Gainesville, FL 32611

3569
Otological Research Fellowships

AMOUNT: $13,500 (max) **DEADLINE:** Mar 15
FIELDS/MAJORS: Otological Research

Fellowships supporting otological research by third-year medical students (or students in other doctoral programs related to otology. Requires a leave of absence from studies. Write to the address listed below for additional information.

Deafness Research Foundation
The Deafness Research Foundation
9 East 38th St.
New York, NY 10016

3570
Ottis Lock Scholarships

AMOUNT: $500 **DEADLINE:** May 1
FIELDS/MAJORS: American History-East Texas

One scholarship for a student pursuing the study of history or social studies at a college or university in east Texas. The Association supports studies relating to east Texas. Award is not renewable. Research grants for study of east Texas history are also available. Write to the address below for details.

East Texas Historical Assoc.
Ottis Lock Scholarship
P.O. Box 6223, SFA Station
Nacogdoches, TX 75962

3571
Otto Klineberg Intercultural And International Relations Award

AMOUNT: $1,000 **DEADLINE:** Feb 1
FIELDS/MAJORS: Intercultural Or International Relations

Award for unpublished or recently published papers relating to intercultural or international relations. Papers may be theoretical or empirical. Membership in SPSSI is not required. Graduate students are especially urged to submit papers. Write to the address below for a description of this award. Information may also be available in the psychology departments of many universities.

Society For The Psychological Study Of Social Issues
Attn: Klineberg Award Committee
P.O. Box 1248
Ann Arbor, MI 48106

3572
Otto M. Stanfield Legal Scholarship

AMOUNT: Varies **DEADLINE:** Feb 15
FIELDS/MAJORS: Law

Open to active Unitarian Universalists who are entering law school and have financial need. Write to the address below for details.

Unitarian Universalist Assoc.
Publication Department
25 Beacon St.
Boston, MA 02108

3573
OU Alumni Club Of Cleveland County Scholarships

AMOUNT: $1,000 **DEADLINE:** Mar 31
FIELDS/MAJORS: All Areas Of Study

Scholarships are available at the University of Oklahoma, Norman, for students who are residents of Cleveland County in Oklahoma. Must be entering freshmen. Write to the address listed below for information.

University Of Oklahoma, Norman
Office of Financial Aid
731 Elm, Robertson Hall
Norman, OK 73019

3574
OU Alumni Club Of Dallas Scholarships

AMOUNT: $2,000 **DEADLINE:** Mar 15
FIELDS/MAJORS: All Areas Of Study

Scholarships are available at the University of Oklahoma, Norman, for students who are residents of the Dallas area. Must be entering freshmen. Write to the address listed below for information.

University Of Oklahoma, Norman
Mike Tuttle
P.O. Box 670753
Dallas, TX 75367

3575
OU Alumni Club Of Greater Oklahoma City Scholarships

AMOUNT: $1,000 **DEADLINE:** Mar 31
FIELDS/MAJORS: All Areas Of Study

Scholarships are available at the University of Oklahoma, Norman, for students who are residents of Oklahoma County. Must be entering freshmen. Write to the address listed below for information.

University Of Oklahoma, Norman
Marian Brown
900 ASP, Room MZL
Norman, OK 73019

3576

OU Institutional Loans

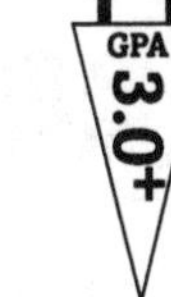

Amount: $2,000-$3,000 **Deadline:** Mar 1
Fields/Majors: All Areas Of Study

Loans are available at the University of Oklahoma, Norman, for students who do not qualify for need-based aid. Based on academic ability. Write to the address listed below for information.

University Of Oklahoma, Norman
Office of Financial Aid Services
731 Elm
Norman, OK 73019

3577

OU Music Awards

Amount: $50-$400 **Deadline:** None Specified
Fields/Majors: Music

Scholarships are available at the University of Oklahoma, Norman, for full-time music majors, of sophomore standing or above. Includes the Ellsworth Dungan, Eva Turner, Jewel Nelson Luccock, Joseph Benton, Maxine Appleman Fagin, Opera Guild, Mildred Carr Wolfard, Ritter, and Robert Tyler Logan awards. Individual award requirements will vary. At least thirteen awards offered annually. Write to the address listed below for information.

University Of Oklahoma, Norman
Director, School Of Music
560 Parrington Oval
Norman, OK 73019

3578

OU Music Scholarships

Amount: $200-$1,500 **Deadline:** None Specified
Fields/Majors: Music

Scholarships are available at the University of Oklahoma, Norman for full-time music majors. Includes the Ben Barnett, Holmberg, Holmes, Logan, Non-Resident Fee Waiver, Resident Fee Waiver and William Henry Brakebill Scholarships. Individual award requirements may vary, especially on residency requirements. About fifty awards are offered annually. Write to the address listed below for information.

University Of Oklahoma, Norman
Director, School Of Music
560 Parrington Oval
Norman, OK 73019

3579

OU Need-Based Scholarships

Amount: $200-$1,000 **Deadline:** Mar 1
Fields/Majors: All Areas Of Study

Scholarships are available at the University of Oklahoma, Norman, for students demonstrating financial need. Includes the C.J. Wrightsman, G.E. College Bowl, Ernest W. McFarland, Fern Brown Memorial, W. Dixon Morris Memorial, Willie Carter Memorial, and Otey B. Paschall scholarships. 31-35 awards are offered annually. Individual award requirements may vary. Requires a 3.25 GPA. Write to the address listed below for information.

University Of Oklahoma, Norman
Office of Financial Aid Services
731 Elm
Norman, OK 73019

3580

OU Pharmacy Scholarships

Amount: $250-$1,500 **Deadline:** Feb 1
Fields/Majors: Pharmacy

Scholarships are available at the University of Oklahoma, Norman for full-time pharmacy majors. Based on academic excellence and interest in community pharmacy. Includes the Oklahoma Society of Hospital Pharmacists Scholarship and the OPHA Auxiliary District 1 Scholarship. Individual award requirements may vary. Up to 37 awards offered annually. Write to the address listed below for information.

University Of Oklahoma, Norman
College Of Pharmacy
P.O. Box 26901
Oklahoma City, OK 73190

3581

Outcomes Research Training Award

Amount: $100,000 (max) **Deadline:** Apr 15
Fields/Majors: Gastroenterology Medicine

Applicants must be MD's who are committed to academic careers and who have completed the clinical training necessary for board eligibility in gastroenterology (12 months) at an accredited North American institution. Write to the address below for more information.

American Digestive Health Foundation
7910 Woodmont Ave., Suite 700
Bethesda, MD 20814

3582

Outdoor Writers Scholarship Award

Amount: $1,500-$3,000 **Deadline:** None Specified
Fields/Majors: Journalism And Mass Communications

Contest awarding scholarship for college juniors, seniors, or master's students with outdoor interests studying toward careers in outdoor writing, radio, TV, photography, art, video. Application is made through your school (each accredited school of journalism or mass communication may select no more than 1 applicant). Information may be available from your journalism/mass communications school.

Outdoor Writers Assoc. Of America, Inc.
Executive Director
2017 Cato Ave., Suite 101
State College, PA 16801

3583

Outstanding Art Student Scholarship

Amount: Tuition **Deadline:** Feb 1
Fields/Majors: Art

Scholarships are available at the University of Utah for full-time entering freshmen planning to enroll in an art program. Must have participated in the Utah High School Art Show or the Springville Art Show. Write to the address below for details.

University Of Utah
Mary Francey
156 Art And Architecture Center
Salt Lake City, UT 84112

3584

Outstanding Student Awards

Amount: $200 **Deadline:** None Specified
Fields/Majors: Computer Technology

Awards for outstanding computer technology students recommended by and voted upon by the faculty. Given to outstanding associate degree graduate, baccalaureate degree graduate, upperclassmen and underclassmen. Write to the address below for more information.

Indiana University Purdue University, Indianapolis
Purdue School Of Technology
799 West Michigan St.
Indianapolis, IN 46202

3585

Outstanding Transfer Scholarship

Amount: Half Tuition **Deadline:** Feb 23
Fields/Majors: All Areas Of Study

Students must have a cumulative GPA of 3.2 or higher for all course work completed prior to Feb 23 and plan to complete, prior to matriculation at RIT, an associate degree or equivalent credits in a field related to chosen major at RIT. Scholarships are renewable each year assuming that a cumulative GPA of "B" or higher is achieved. Write to the address below for details.

Rochester Institute Of Technology
Bausch & Lomb Center, Financial Aid Office
60 Lomb Memorial Drive
Rochester, NY 14623

3586

Owen Electric Cooperative Scholarship Program

GPA 3.0+

Amount: $2,000 (max) **Deadline:** Feb 1
Fields/Majors: All Areas Of Study

Scholarships are available for students living in Owen Electric's service area, who are U.S. citizens, juniors or seniors, with a GPA of at least 3.0. For full-time study. Service area covers Boone, Campbell, Carroll, Gallatin, Grant, Kenton, Owen, Pendleton and Scott Counties in Kentucky. Write to the address listed below for information.

Owen Electric Cooperative
Scholarship Program
510 South Main St.
Owenton, KY 40359

3587

P. Boyd Smith Scholarship

Amount: Varies **Deadline:** None Specified
Fields/Majors: Business

Awards for business majors at California Baptist College. Contact the division of business administration for more information.

California Baptist College
8432 Magnolia Ave.
Riverside, CA 92504

3588

P. Buckley Moss Scholarship

Amount: $500 **Deadline:** Apr 1
Fields/Majors: Post-secondary Education

Scholarships are awarded to qualified learning-disabled individuals who are pursuing postsecondary educational opportunities. Must have a GPA of 2.0 or better and an undergraduate at a school in Ohio. Write to the address below for more information.

Learning Disabilities Assoc. Of Ohio, Inc.
1380 Pearl Road, Suite 203
Brunswick, OH 44212

3589

P.F.I. Scholarship Program

Amount: Varies **Deadline:** Mar 10
Fields/Majors: All Areas Of Study

Awards are available for students of Portuguese ancestry who are enrolled in full-time study at the undergraduate level or full-or part-time study at the graduate level. Must be a resident of Connecticut and a U.S. citizen or permanent resident. Applicants cannot have previously received more than four foundation scholarships. Write to the address below for more details.

Portuguese Foundation, Connecticut
86 New Park Ave.
Hartford, CT 06106

3590

Pacesetter Leadership Scholarships

Amount: Tuition **Deadline:** Jan 15
Fields/Majors: All Areas Of Study

Awards for high school seniors from selected area Nebraska high schools to apply. GPA is considered as well as leadership experience/ability and potential for future leadership at UNO. Finalists will interview with a selection committee. Write to the address below for more information.

University Of Nebraska, Omaha
Office of Financial Aid, EAB 103
60th And Dodge Streets
Omaha, NE 68182

3591

Pacific Palisades Garden Club

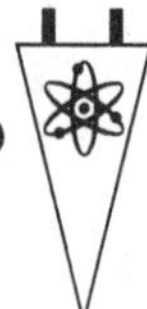

Amount: $1,500 **Deadline:** Apr 15
Fields/Majors: Horticulture

Open to students majoring in horticulture with an interest in landscape and/or nursery management. Two awards are given yearly. Write to the address below for more information.

California State Polytechnic University, Pomona
College Of Agriculture
Building 7, Room 110
Pomona, CA 91768

3592

Palm Aire Women's Club Scholarship

Amount: $1,200 **Deadline:** Apr 1
Fields/Majors: All Areas Of Study

Scholarships are available for female Sarasota or Manatee County residents who demonstrate academic excellence, participation in extracurricular activities, show financial need, and have a minimum GPA of at least 3.0. Applicants must have attended Manatee Community College for at least 60 hours. Write to the address listed below for information.

Palm Aire Women's Club
c/o Florence White, Co-chair
5849 Clubside Dr.
Sarasota, FL 34243

3593

Palm Beach Post Minority Scholarships

AMOUNT: $1,500-$3,000 **DEADLINE:** Mar 1
FIELDS/MAJORS: Journalism, Advertising

Awards for minority juniors or seniors at the studying journalism or advertising at the University of Florida. Must be from the West Palm Beach area. Write to the address below for details.

University Of Florida
2070 Weimer Hall
Director, Minority Scholarship Program
Gainesville, FL 32611

3594

Palmetto Fellows Scholarship

AMOUNT: $5,000 (max) **DEADLINE:** None Specified
FIELDS/MAJORS: All Areas Of Study

Scholarships for South Carolina residents who will be entering freshmen. Based on demonstrated academic ability and PSAT test scores. For use at a South Carolina institution. Write to the address listed below for additional information.

South Carolina Commission On Higher Education
1333 Main St., Suite 200
Columbia, SC 29201

3595

Panaewa Hawaiian Home Lands Community Assoc. Scholarship

AMOUNT: $150-$250 **DEADLINE:** Feb 1
FIELDS/MAJORS: All Areas Of Study

Scholarships are available at the University of Hawaii, Hilo, for full-time students who are children of members of the Panaewa Hawaiian Home Lands Community Assoc. Write to the address listed below for information.

University Of Hawaii At Hilo
Phhl Community Assoc. Scholarship
102 Paipai St.
Hilo, HI 96720

3596

Panasonic & Rosemary Kennedy International Young Soloists Award

AMOUNT: None Specified **DEADLINE:** Sep 15
FIELDS/MAJORS: Vocal Music, Instrumental Music

Scholarship is available to applicants who are vocalist or instrumentalist and are 25 years of age and under and disabled. Write to the address below for more information.

Very Special Arts
Education Office
J.F. Kennedy Ctr. For The Performing Art
Washington, DC 20566

3597

Panther Athletic Grants

AMOUNT: Varies **DEADLINE:** Mar 1
FIELDS/MAJORS: All Areas Of Study

Scholarships are available at Kentucky Wesleyan College for undergraduate students who plan to participate in the intercollegiate athletics program. Write to the address below for details.

Kentucky Wesleyan College
Financial Aid Office
3000 Frederica St.
Owensboro, KY 43202

3598

Paragano Scholarship

AMOUNT: $1,000 **DEADLINE:** May 31
FIELDS/MAJORS: Italian Language

Scholarship for Italian American residents of New Jersey studying Italian. Write to the address below for details.

National Italian American Foundation
Dr. Maria Lombardo, Education Director
1860 19th St., NW
Washington, DC 20001

3599

Parajon, HLA Scholarships

AMOUNT: Varies **DEADLINE:** None Specified
FIELDS/MAJORS: All Areas Of Study

Scholarships for Hispanic, Asian and Native American freshmen at Denison University. Strong academic performance and potential is required. Contact the Office of Admissions or the Financial Aid Office at the address below for details.

Denison University
Financial Aid Office, Box M
Granville, OH 43023

3600

Park National Bank Scholarship

AMOUNT: $2,000 **DEADLINE:** Jan 1
FIELDS/MAJORS: All Areas Of Study

Scholarships for freshmen at Denison University from Licking County (OH) who have superior academic records or potential. Renewable for up to four years. One or two awards per year. 3.0 GPA required. Write to the address below for details.

Denison University
Financial Aid Office, Box M
Granville, OH 43023

3601

Parker B. Francis Fellowship Grants

AMOUNT: $38,000 (max) **DEADLINE:** Oct 12
FIELDS/MAJORS: Medical Research-Pulmonary & Anesthesiology

Non-Residential fellowships providing stipends and modest incidental expenses in support of qualified postdoctoral candidates performing fundamental research in pulmonary medicine or anesthesiology at a U.S. or Canadian institution. Sponsorship by an established investigator required. Application is made on the candidate's behalf by the director of the program within an institution. Write to the address below for details.

The Francis Families Foundation
Ms. Linda K. French
800 W. 47th St., #604
Kansas City, MO 64112

3602

Parkinson's Disease Foundation Summer Fellowship

AMOUNT: $1,800-$2,200 **DEADLINE:** Apr 1
FIELDS/MAJORS: Medical Research (Parkinson's Disease)

Program for graduate students to participate in ten weeks of research and investigation in Parkinson's Disease. Write to the address below for more details.

Parkinson's Disease Foundation
William Black Medical Research Bldg.
650-710 West 168th St.
New York, NY 10032

3603

Parks Memorial Scholarship Fund

AMOUNT: Varies **DEADLINE:** Feb 17
FIELDS/MAJORS: Education

Scholarships are available at the University of Oklahoma, Norman, for full-time education majors, sophomore level or higher, who are descendents of Oklahoma pioneers. If no qualified candidate can be found, the award will go to a qualified second-generation Oklahoma resident. Write to the address listed below for information.

University Of Oklahoma, Norman
College Of Education, Student Services
Room 137, ECH
Norman, OK 73019

3604

Parliamentary Procedure Scholarships

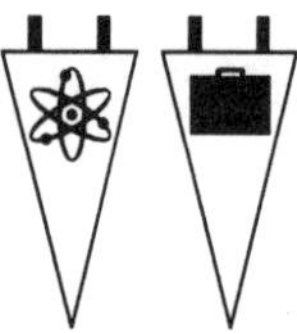

AMOUNT: $1,000 **DEADLINE:** Feb 15
FIELDS/MAJORS: Agriculture, Agribusiness

Scholarships are available for FFA members pursuing a four-year degree in any area of agriculture or agribusiness, who competed in the Parliamentary Procedure Contest above the local level. Write to the address below for details.

National FFA Foundation
Scholarship Office
P.O. Box 15160
Alexandria, VA 22309

3605

Parry Scholarship

AMOUNT: $500-$2,500 **DEADLINE:** May 15
FIELDS/MAJORS: Nursing

Scholarships are available at the University of Oklahoma, Norman, for full-time junior or senior nursing students, with GPA's of 3.5 (for juniors) or 3.25 (for seniors). Write to the address listed below for information.

University Of Oklahoma, Norman
College Of Nursing
P.O. Box 26901
Oklahoma City, OK 73190

3606

Participation Award

AMOUNT: Varies **DEADLINE:** Apr 1
FIELDS/MAJORS: All Areas Of Study

Awards for students who attend Baker and participate in an art, athletics, debate, forensics, communication, music, or theater. Must have a GPA of at least 2.3. Renewable with a GPA of at least 2.0. Contact the appropriate faculty sponsor or coach for more information.

Baker University
Office of Financial Aid
P.O. Box 65
Baldwin City, KS 66006

3607

Partnership Grant

AMOUNT: $500 (max) **DEADLINE:** Aug 1, Jan 1
FIELDS/MAJORS: All Areas Of Study

Dollar-for-dollar match of a church scholarship. The church must complete an agreement form and mail the check to Bethel. Applicants must be full-time students. Write to the address below for more information.

Bethel College
Office of Financial Planning
3900 Bethel Dr.
St. Paul, MN 55112

3608

Past President's Parley Nurses Scholarships

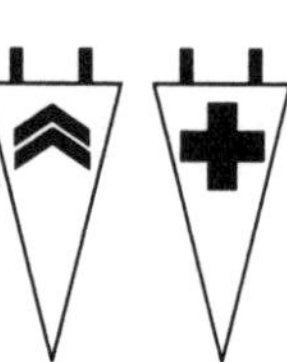

AMOUNT: $350 **DEADLINE:** May 15
FIELDS/MAJORS: Nursing

Scholarships are available for residents of North Dakota who graduated from a North Dakota high school. Applicants must be citizens of the U.S. and children of Legion or Auxiliary members. Write to the address listed below for additional information.

American Legion Auxiliary-Department of North Dakota
c/o Viola Vigen
804 1st St. S., #A2
Carrington, ND 58421

3609

Pastore Scholarship

AMOUNT: $1,000 **DEADLINE:** May 31
FIELDS/MAJORS: All Areas Of Study

Scholarship for an Italian American student who is a resident of or studying in Rhode Island. For undergraduate or graduate studies. Write to the address below for details.

National Italian American Foundation
Dr. Maria Lombardo, Education Director
1860 19th St., NW
Washington, DC 20009

3610

Pat And Ed Tooker Football Scholarship

AMOUNT: Tuition And Fees
DEADLINE: None Specified
FIELDS/MAJORS: All Areas Of Study

Awards for full-time Mesa State students who are active in the football program and are Colorado residents. Must have a GPA of at least 2.5. Contact the football coach for more details.

Mesa State College
Office of Financial Aid
P.O. Box 2647
Grand Junction, CO 81501

3611 Patricia Hudgins McMahan Memorial Art Foundation Scholarship

Amount: $1,000 **Deadline:** Apr 1
Fields/Majors: Drawing Or Painting Art

Applicant must be an Alabama resident with exceptional ability in drawing or painting and plan to enhance artistic ability in an advanced course of study. For high school seniors only. Write to the address below for more details.

Patricia Hudgins McMahan Memorial Art Foundation
Wayne McMahan
836 Washington Ave.
Montgomery, AL 36104

3612 Patricia L. Kurtzman Memorial Alumni Scholarship

Amount: $1,000 (max) **Deadline:** None Specified
Fields/Majors: All Areas Of Study

Awards for TTC students pursuing an associate degree who are Trident area residents and are enrolled in at least 12 credit hours. Must have a GPA of at least 2.5. Write to the address below for more information.

Trident Technical College
Financial Aid Office
P.O. Box 118067
Charleston, SC 29423

3613 Patricia L. Shannon Scholarship

Amount: $750-$2,000 **Deadline:** Mar 1
Fields/Majors: Public Relations

Must be a junior or senior studying public relations at the University of Florida. Must have at least a 2.8 GPA. Write to the address below for complete details.

University Of Florida
2070 Weimer Hall
Scholarship & Placement Director
Gainesville, FL 32611

3614 Patricia Roberts Harris Fellowship Program

Amount: $14,000 + Tuition
Deadline: None Specified
Fields/Majors: Selected Areas Of Study

Fellowships are available at the University of Oklahoma, Norman for full-time minority graduate students. Contact your department to see if your area of study is included in the selection criteria.

University Of Oklahoma, Norman
Graduate College
1000 Asp Ave., Room 313
Norman, OK 73019

3615 Patricia Roberts Harris Fellowship Program

Amount: None Specified **Deadline:** None Specified
Fields/Majors: All Areas Of Study

Program which provides assistance to graduate students who demonstrate great financial need. Applicants must be U.S. citizens. Write to the address below for further details.

Wayne State University Graduate School
Dr. Walter Edwards, Associate Dean
4300 Faculty/Administration Building
Detroit, MI 48202

3616 Paul & Mary Haas Foundation Scholarship Grant

Amount: $1,000 (max) **Deadline:** Nov 30
Fields/Majors: All Areas Of Study

Scholarships are available to graduating high school seniors who reside within 20 miles of Corpus Christi, have above-average grades, and can demonstrate financial need. Write to the address listed below for information.

Paul & Mary Haas Foundation
Scholarship Program
P.O. Box 2928
Corpus Christi, TX 78403

3617 Paul A. Funk Foundation Freshman, Sophomore, Junior Scholarship

Amount: $1,000 **Deadline:** Nov 17
Fields/Majors: Agriculture

Scholarships are available for sophomore, junior, or senior students with the best academic records in their freshman, sophomore, and junior years in agriculture. Sophomores must complete at least 60 total hours and at least 30 hours during the last academic year at ISU. Juniors must complete at least 90 total hours and at least 30 hours during the last academic year at ISU. Write to the address below for more information.

Illinois State University, Dept. Of Agriculture
Turner Hall 150
Campus Box 5020
Normal, IL 61761

3618 Paul A. Keehn Memorial Scholarships

Amount: $250 **Deadline:** Feb 15
Fields/Majors: Civil Engineering

Awards for sophomores, juniors, or seniors at UW Platteville studying civil engineering who show evidence of motivation, financial need, and achievement. Write to the address below for more information.

University Of Wisconsin, Platteville
Office of Enrollment And Admissions
Platteville, WI 53818

3619 Paul And Teeby Forcheimer Communication Scholarship

AMOUNT: $200-$400 **DEADLINE:** Varies
FIELDS/MAJORS: Communication

Awards for Sul Ross undergraduates studying communication who have good academic standing. Write to the address below for more information.

Sul Ross State University
Financial Aid Office
Box C-113
Alpine, TX 79832

3620 Paul B. Patterson Scholarship

AMOUNT: None Specified **DEADLINE:** Dec 15
FIELDS/MAJORS: Mathematics

Scholarships awarded to students at Appalachian State University who are mathematics majors. Write to the address listed below for information.

Appalachian State University
Department of Mathematics
Boone, NC 28608

3621 Paul Biller And Maude Eastwood Scholarship

AMOUNT: Varies **DEADLINE:** None Specified
FIELDS/MAJORS: All Areas Of Study

Awards available to female students who are in need of financial assistance. Write to the address below for more information.

Rockford College
Financial Aid Office
5050 East State St.
Rockford, IL 61108

3622 Paul Collins Scholarship

AMOUNT: $500-$2,500 **DEADLINE:** Apr 14
FIELDS/MAJORS: Fine Or Applied Arts

Scholarships for residents of Kent County who plan to pursue studies at one of the following schools: Aquinas College, Calvin College, Grand Valley State University, Grand Rapids Community College, Kendall College of Art & Design. For full-time undergraduate students. 2.5 GPA and artistic talent required. Write to the address below for details.

Grand Rapids Foundation
209-C Waters Bldg.
161 Ottawa Ave., NW
Grand Rapids, MI 49503

3623 Paul D. And Marian F. Minick Scholarship

AMOUNT: $1,500 **DEADLINE:** Mar 31
FIELDS/MAJORS: All Areas Of Study

Student must graduate in the top 15 percent of their high school class and a GPA of 3.0 or better. Write to the address below for more information.

Southwest Missouri State University
Office of Financial Aid
901 South National Ave.
Springfield, MO 65804

3624 Paul D. Scholz Award

AMOUNT: $1,500 **DEADLINE:** None Specified
FIELDS/MAJORS: Engineering

Scholarships are available at the University of Iowa for full-time undergraduate engineering students with high academic standing who plan to continue their education in graduate school. Write to the address listed below for information.

University Of Iowa
Student Services, College Of Engineering
3100 Engineering Building
Iowa City, IA 52242

3625 Paul Fowler Scholarship

AMOUNT: $2,830 **DEADLINE:** Jun 1
FIELDS/MAJORS: All Areas Of Study

Scholarship program for high school seniors in Washington state who are designated as Washington scholars. Non-renewable. Write to the address listed below for information.

Washington Higher Education Coordinating Board
917 Lakeridge Way
P.O. Box 43430
Olympia, WA 98504

3626 Paul H. Kutschenreuter Scholarship

AMOUNT: $5,000 **DEADLINE:** Jun 14
FIELDS/MAJORS: Metrology, Atmospheric Science

Scholarships for students entering their last year of study toward a degree in meteorology. Based on academics, need, and a personal statement. Must have a GPA of at least 3.0 and be a U.S. citizen or permanent resident. Application forms and further information may be obtained through the ams headquarters at the address below.

American Meteorological Society
45 Beacon St.
Boston, MA 02108

3627 Paul Jackson Memorial Scholarship, V.L. Peterson Scholarship

AMOUNT: Varies **DEADLINE:** Jul 1
FIELDS/MAJORS: All Areas Of Study

Scholarships available to members of the American Jersey Cattle Assoc. who are of sophomore standing or above. Write to the address below for details.

American Jersey Cattle Assoc.
Scholarship Committee
6486 East Main St.
Reynoldsburg, OH 43068

3628

Paul Kulka Memorial And Harry Leonard Scholarships

AMOUNT: Varies **DEADLINE:** Mar 1
FIELDS/MAJORS: Earth And Planetary Sciences

Awards are available at the University of New Mexico for students in the fields of earth and planetary sciences. Applicants must demonstrate financial need, scholastic ability, and be from New Mexico. Write to the address listed below for information.

University Of New Mexico, Albuquerque
Office of Financial Aid
Albuquerque, NM 87131

3629

Paul L. Fowler Memorial Scholarship

AMOUNT: $2,830 **DEADLINE:** Jan 31
FIELDS/MAJORS: All Areas Of Study

Scholarships are available for Idaho resident graduating high school seniors who demonstrate outstanding academic ability. For full-time undergraduate study at any accredited U.S. college or university. Two awards are offered annually. Write to the address listed below for information.

Idaho State Board Of Education
P.O. Box 83720
Boise, ID 83720

3630

Paul Muench Scholarship

AMOUNT: $500 **DEADLINE:** Mar 1
FIELDS/MAJORS: Piano Music

Awards for piano music majors at Eastern New Mexico University based on strength of musician and pianistic ability. Write to the address below for more information.

Eastern New Mexico University
College Of Fine Arts
Station 16
Portales, NM 88130

3631

Paul Powell Memorial AmVets Award & Amvets Auxiliary Scholarship

AMOUNT: $500 **DEADLINE:** Mar 1
FIELDS/MAJORS: All Areas Of Study

Awards for children of veterans who are unmarried high school seniors. Applicants must be from Illinois and have taken the ACT. Write to the address below for more information.

Illinois Amvets Scholarship Program
Illinois Amvets State Headquarters
2200 South Sixth St.
Springfield, IL 62703

3632

Paul V. Whalen Scholarship

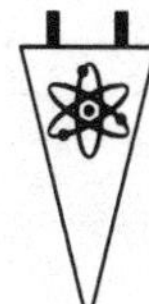

AMOUNT: $500 **DEADLINE:** Nov 17
FIELDS/MAJORS: Agriculture

Scholarship awarded to an incoming freshman enrolling in an agriculture curriculum at Illinois State University. Selection will be based upon demonstrated academic achievement and leadership abilities. Applicants must be residents of Colchester or the surrounding area. For more information contact your high school guidance counselor or write to the address below.

Illinois State University, Dept. Of Agriculture
Turner Hall 150
Campus Box 5020
Normal, IL 61761

3633

Paul Vouras, Robert D. Hodgson, And Otis Paul Starkey Funds

AMOUNT: $500 (generally) **DEADLINE:** Dec 31
FIELDS/MAJORS: Geography

Provides financial assistance for dissertation research or dissertation preparation to candidates is the field of geography. Must have been a member of AAG for at least one year. All course requirements must be completed in the academic term following the approval of the grant. Request application form from Elizabeth Beetschen at the address below.

Assoc. Of American Geographers
Aag Dissertation Research Grants
1710 16th St., NW
Washington, DC 20009

3634

Paul W. Guy Scholarship

AMOUNT: $1,000 **DEADLINE:** Nov 1
FIELDS/MAJORS: Human Resources Management, Industrial Relations, Business Admin.

Awards for Indiana residents who are juniors, seniors, or graduate students registered in an Indiana accredited college or university. For full- or part-time study. Write to the address below for more information.

Indiana Society Of Health Care Resources Administration
Wage & Benefits Mgr., Anderson Hospital
1515 N. Madison Ave.
Anderson, IN 46011

3635

Paul W. Ryan Scholarship

AMOUNT: None Specified
DEADLINE: None Specified
FIELDS/MAJORS: Landscape Architecture, Environmental Design

Scholarships are awarded to students within the division of landscape architecture and environmental design. Juniors and seniors in the field of natural resources are also eligible. Contact the Chair, Scholarship Committee, Landscape Architecture and Regional Planning for more information.

University Of Massachusetts, Amherst
Chair, Scholarship Committee
Landscape Architecture & Regional Planng
Amherst, MA 01003

3636

Paula Patton Grahame Scholarships

AMOUNT: $200-$1,000 **DEADLINE:** Feb 1
FIELDS/MAJORS: Art, Art History

Scholarships are available at the University of Iowa for full-time incoming freshman students majoring in art or art history. Write to the address listed below for information.

University Of Iowa
School Of Art And Art History
E100 Art Building
Iowa City, IA 52245

3637

Pauly D'Orlando Memorial Art Scholarship

AMOUNT: Varies **DEADLINE:** Mar 31
FIELDS/MAJORS: Enameling, Drawing, Painting, Or Printmaking

Award for members of a Unitarian Universalist congregation studying in the areas listed above. Write to the address below for more information.

Unitarian Universalist Assoc. Of Congregations
Worship Arts Department
25 Beacon St.
Boston, MA 02108

3638

Paumanauke Native American Indian Scholarship

AMOUNT: $500 **DEADLINE:** Dec 1, Jun 1
FIELDS/MAJORS: All Areas Of Study

Scholarships are available for full-time students who are of Native American Indian heritage. Six awards are offered annually. Write to the address listed below for information.

Paumanauke Pow-Wow & Native American Living Arts Festival, Inc.
333 Lagoon Drive South
Copiague, NY 11726

3639

Pawtucket East High School Class Of '42 Scholarship

AMOUNT: $500 **DEADLINE:** Apr 1
FIELDS/MAJORS: All Areas Of Study

Scholarships are available for graduating seniors of Tolman High School in Pawtucket, Rhode Island. Write to the address listed below for information.

Rhode Island Foundation
70 Elm St.
Providence, RI 02903

3640

Peabody College Graduate Scholarships And Assistantships

AMOUNT: $500-tuition **DEADLINE:** None Specified
FIELDS/MAJORS: All Areas Of Study (within Peabody College)

Scholarships, assistantships, and grants for students in the George Peabody College for teachers at Vanderbilt University. Some programs are based on need; some, on academics; and some, on career goals. Write to the address below for details.

Vanderbilt University
Admissions And Financial Assistance
Box 327 Peabody College
Nashville, TN 37203

3641

Peace And Social Justice Scholarships

AMOUNT: $100 **DEADLINE:** Dec 1
FIELDS/MAJORS: All Areas Of Study

This scholarship is offered to any student who is involved in peace and social justice issues. Applicants must be attending universities or colleges in the Northland region of Wisconsin or Minnesota. Write to the address below for the address of the chapter nearest you.

Grandmothers For Peace, Northlands Chapter
2614 N. 22nd St.
Superior, WI 54880

3642

Pearce, Bevil, Leesburg, And Moore, P.c. Scholarship

AMOUNT: $500 **DEADLINE:** None Specified
FIELDS/MAJORS: Accounting

Awards for Jacksonville State University students in the field of accounting. Contact the head of the accounting department for more details.

Jacksonville State University
Financial Aid Office
Jacksonville, AL 36265

3643

Pearce-Goodchild Scholarships

AMOUNT: $800-$1,000 **DEADLINE:** Mar 1
FIELDS/MAJORS: Journalism, Communications, Public Relations, Advertising

Awards for juniors and seniors in the college who have a GPA of 2.8 or better. Write to the address below for more information.

University Of Florida
Knight Scholarship & Placement Director
2070 Weimer Hall
Gainesville, FL 32611

3644

Pearl H. Falk Scholarships

AMOUNT: $400 **DEADLINE:** Mar 31
FIELDS/MAJORS: All Areas Of Study

Scholarships are available at the University of Iowa for undergraduate students who are Protestant. Preference is given to incoming freshmen. Applicants must be Iowa residents. Write to the address listed below for information.

University Of Iowa
Iowa State Bank & Trust, Trust Dept.
P.O. Box 1700
Iowa City, IA 52244

3645 Pearl Harbor-Honolulu Branch 46 Fleet Reserve Assoc. Scholarship

AMOUNT: None Specified **DEADLINE:** Apr 15
FIELDS/MAJORS: All Areas Of Study

Scholarships for sons, daughters, and spouses of members in good standing (alive or deceased) of the Pearl Harbor-Honolulu Branch 46 of the Fleet Reserve Assoc. Based on academics, character, leadership, and financial need. Write to the address below for additional information.

Fleet Reserve Assoc.
Pearl Harbor-Honolulu Branch 46
P.O. Box 6067
Honolulu, HI 96818

3646 Pearl Sue Lady Scholarship

GPA 3.5+

AMOUNT: $500 **DEADLINE:** None Specified
FIELDS/MAJORS: All Areas Of Study

Scholarships for the student at the Kingsport University Center (Sullivan Co.) with the highest GPA, given each fall and spring. Contact the office of financial aid for details.

East Tennessee State University
Office of Financial Aid
Box 70722
Johnson City, TN 37614

3647 Pearl V. Ramsey Memorial Nursing Scholarship

AMOUNT: $200 **DEADLINE:** Apr 20
FIELDS/MAJORS: Nursing, Allied Health Services

Awards for female Maine residents who are or have been accepted in any of the health fields of study. Must demonstrate financial need and be in good academic standing. Contact the address below for further information.

Business & Professional Women's Clubs-Maine
Myra Chaloult
P.O. Box 585
Waterville, ME 04903

3648 Pedrick Nursing Scholarship

GPA 2.5+

AMOUNT: Varies **DEADLINE:** Mar 1
FIELDS/MAJORS: Nursing

Awards are available at the University of New Mexico for full-time nursing students with financial need and a GPA of at least 2.5. Write to the address below or contact the school of nursing for more details.

University Of New Mexico, Albuquerque
Office of Financial Aid
Albuquerque, NM 87131

3649 Peer Mentor Scholarships

GPA 3.0+

AMOUNT: Varies **DEADLINE:** Mar 1
FIELDS/MAJORS: All Areas Of Study

Tuition remission program for sophomores and juniors to serve on faculty teams in the university studies program and assist freshmen and sophomores for 6 hours per week. Must be a full-time student with a GPA of 3.0 or better. Applicants must also be able to pursue research, communicate effectively, and work with people from a variety of contexts and backgrounds. Contact the Office of University Studies for more information.

Portland State University
Office of University Studies
445 Neuberger Hall
Portland, OR 97207

3650 Peggy Howard Fellowship In Economics

AMOUNT: Varies **DEADLINE:** Dec 15
FIELDS/MAJORS: Economics

Open to undergraduates and alumnae of Wellesley College both for postgraduate study and for special projects in economics. Write to the address below for details.

Wellesley College, Economics Department
Peggy Howard Fellowship
106 Central St.
Wellesley, MA 02181

3651 Pendleton Community Memorial Health Corporation Scholarships

AMOUNT: None Specified **DEADLINE:** Jun 20
FIELDS/MAJORS Health/Medicine, Dentistry

Scholarships for residents of the following areas: Pendleton, Pilot Rock, Athena, Weston, Adams, Helix, and Ukiah (Umatilla County, Oregon). For study in a healthcare-related field. For full time study. Applicants must maintain a 2.0 GPA. Write to the address below for details.

Pendleton Community Memorial Health Corporation
P.O. Box 786
Pendleton, OR 97801

3652 PenElec Scholarship

AMOUNT: None Specified **DEADLINE:** None Specified
FIELDS/MAJORS: All Areas Of Study

Scholarships are awarded to PenElec employee dependents awarded by the Pennsylvania electric company. Contact the chair of the Venango Campus Scholarship Committee for more information.

Clarion University
104 Egbert Hall
Office of Financial Aid
Clarion, PA 16214

3653

Penfield Fellowship

Amount: $1,800 (max)
Deadline: None Specified
Fields/Majors International Affairs, Diplomacy

Scholarships are available at the Catholic University of America for graduate students in their second year studying international affairs or diplomacy. Contact the financial aid office at the address below for details.

The Catholic University Of America
Office of Admissions And Financial Aid
Washington, DC 20064

3654

Pennsylvania Assoc. Of Conservation Districts Auxiliary Scholarships

Amount: $200 **Deadline:** Sep 1
Fields/Majors: Agriculture, Conservation, Environmental Studies

Scholarships for Pennsylvania residents studying in one of the above fields in Pennsylvania. For junior or senior students in four-year programs and second-year students in associate degree programs. Based on need. Write to "Scholarship" at the address below for details.

Pacd Auxiliary
Blair County Conservation District
1407 Blair St.
Holidaysburg, PA 16648

3655

Pennsylvania Farm Show Scholarship Foundation

Amount: $1,000 **Deadline:** Nov 21
Fields/Majors: All Areas Of Study

Scholarships are awarded to students representing Pennsylvania 4-H. Applicant must have exhibited a market steer, lamb, or hog at the Pennsylvania Farm Show. Based on scholarship, financial need, and service to 4-H or FFA and the community as determined from the application and letters of support. Write to the address below for more information.

Pennsylvania Farm Show Scholarship Foundation
4714 Orchard Rd.
Harrisburg, PA 17109

3656

Penny Thompson Barshied Scholarship

Amount: None Specified **Deadline:** None Specified
Fields/Majors: All Areas Of Study

Awards are available for all students at SUNY, Potsdam, based on achievement. Write to the address below for more information.

SUNY, Potsdam
Office of Admissions
44 Pierrepont Ave.
Potsdam, NY 13676

3657

Pennzoil Scholarship Endowment

Amount: None Specified **Deadline:** None Specified
Fields/Majors: All Areas Of Study

Scholarships are made available by the foundation through an endowment account established by Pennzoil. Based on academic achievement and financial need. Contact the chair of the Venango Campus Scholarship Committee for more information.

Clarion University
104 Egbert Hall
Office of Financial Aid
Clarion, PA 16214

3658

Pep Band/Cheerleader Grants

Amount: $2,000 **Deadline:** Feb 1
Fields/Majors: All Areas Of Study

Scholarships are available at Bellarmine College for full-time students who plan to participate in the band or cheerleader programs. For undergraduate study. Contact the financial aid office at the address below for details.

Bellarmine College
Financial Aid Office
2001 Newburg Road
Louisville, KY 40205

3659

Performing Arts Scholarships

Amount: Varies **Deadline:** Mar 1
Fields/Majors: Theater, Drama, Dance, Vocal Or Instrumental Music, Forensics

Scholarships available at Sterling for undergraduate full-time students who will be majoring in one of the above fields. Write to the address below for details.

Sterling College
Financial Aid Office
Sterling, KS 67579

3660

Pergamon-NWSA Graduate Scholarship In Women's Studies

Amount: $1,500 **Deadline:** Feb 15
Fields/Majors: Women's Studies

Award available for a woman researching for a master's thesis or Ph.D. dissertation in women's studies. Preference will be given to NWSA members and to those whose research projects focus on "color" or "class." Write to the address below for details.

National Women's Studies Assoc.
7100 Baltimore Ave., Suite 301
University Of Maryland
College Park, MD 20740

3661

Perozzi Scholarship

AMOUNT: None Specified **DEADLINE:** Oct 15
FIELDS/MAJORS: Food Science

Scholarships are awarded to food science majors who have completed two semesters at UMass with a GPA of 3.0 or higher. Based on need, campus contributions, past experience and future career in the food industry. Contact the Undergraduate Program Director, Food Science for more information.

University Of Massachusetts, Amherst
Undergraduate Program Director
Food Science
Amherst, MA 01003

3662

Perrota Scholarship

AMOUNT: $1,000 **DEADLINE:** May 31
FIELDS/MAJORS: Italian Studies

Scholarships for Italian American residents of Connecticut who are majoring in Italian studies. For graduate study. Write to the address below for details.

National Italian American Foundation
Dr. Maria Lombardo, Education Director
1860 Nineteenth St., NW
Washington, DC 20009

3663

Perry Persichilli Memorial Scholarship And Scalia Scholarship

AMOUNT: $1,000 **DEADLINE:** May 31
FIELDS/MAJORS: All Areas Of Study

Scholarships for Italian American undergraduate or graduate students who are residents of or studying in New York state. Write to the address below for details.

National Italian American Foundation
Dr. Maria Lombardo, Education Director
1860 19th St., NW
Washington, DC 20001

3664

Perry-White Charitable Scholarship Fund

AMOUNT: $1,000 **DEADLINE:** Mar 1
FIELDS/MAJORS: All Areas Of Study

Awards for worthy high school graduates of the Hopewell, Prince George, Petersburg, Colonial Heights, or Chesterfield areas. Based on scholarship, deportment, and need. Students must have also been admitted to one of the following: Coll. Of William & Mary, Longwood College, Randolph-Macon & Randolph-Macon Woman's College, School of Pharmacy, MCV/VCU or University of Virginia. Write to the address below for more information.

Community Foundation Serving Richmond And Central Virginia
1025 Boulders Parkway, Suite 405
Richmond, VA 23225

3665

Pet Incorporated Scholarships

AMOUNT: $2,500 **DEADLINE:** Feb 15
FIELDS/MAJORS: Food Science/Technology, Agribusiness

Scholarships are available for FFA members pursuing a four-year degree in food science/technology or agribusiness. Write to the address below for details.

National FFA Foundation
Scholarship Office
P.O. Box 15160
Alexandria, VA 22309

3666

Peter And Alice Koomruian Armenian Education Fund

AMOUNT: None Specified **DEADLINE:** None Specified
FIELDS/MAJORS: All Areas Of Study

Awards for undergraduate and graduate students of Armenian descent who are enrolled in an accredited U.S. college or university. Based on financial need and academic ability. Send an SASE to the address below for more information.

Peter And Alice Koomruian Fund
P.O. Box 0268
Moorpark, CA 93020

3667

Peter Barr Advertising Scholarships

AMOUNT: $500 **DEADLINE:** Mar 1
FIELDS/MAJORS: Advertising

Awards for juniors and seniors planning to enter the field of advertising. Must have a GPA of at least 2.8. Write to the address below for more information.

University Of Florida
Knight Scholarship & Placement Director
2070 Weimer Hall
Gainesville, FL 32611

3668

Peter Connacher Scholarships

AMOUNT: None Specified **DEADLINE:** Mar 1
FIELDS/MAJORS: All Areas Of Study

Scholarships for Oregon residents who were Prisoners of War or who are descendants of Prisoners of War. Must be able to provide documentation. Renewable. Contact your high school guidance department, your college financial aid office, or write to the address below for details.

Oregon State Scholarship Commission
Attn: Grant Department
1500 Valley River Dr., #100
Eugene, OR 97401

3669

Peter D. Courtois Concrete Construction Scholarships

Amount: $1,000 **Deadline:** Jan 15
Fields/Majors: Engineering, Construction, Material Science, Etc.

Two $1,000 scholarships for senior undergraduate students in engineering, architectural and/or material science programs in the area of concrete where design, materials, construction (or combination of these) are studied. Membership in the American Concrete Institute is not required. Write to the address below for details.

American Concrete Institute
Director Of Education
P.O. Box 19150
Detroit, MI 48219

Peter Damian Covich Memorial Scholarship

Amount: None Specified **Deadline:** None Specified
Fields/Majors: Flight Operations

Awards for seniors in the Flight Operations Program at Daniel Webster. Based on flight performance, academics, and financial need. Write to the address below for more details.

Daniel Webster College
Financial Assistance Office
20 University Dr.
Nashua, NH 03063

Peter V. Rovnianek

E

Amount: None Specified **Deadline:** May 1
Fields/Majors: All Areas Of Study

Scholarships for members of the National Slovak Society. Must have been a member for at least two years prior to application (non-members are not eligible) and be a high school senior. Renewable with GPA of at least 2.0. Write to the address below for details.

National Slovak Society
2325 E. Carson St.
Pittsburgh, PA 15203

Petroleum Accountant's Society Of New Mexico Scholarship

Amount: $500 **Deadline:** Mar 1
Fields/Majors: Accounting

Award for an accounting student with an interest in oil and gas accounting. Write to the address below for more information.

Eastern New Mexico University
ENMU College Of Business
Station 49
Portales, NM 88130

Petroleum And Geological Engineering Scholarships

Amount: $500-$3,000 **Deadline:** Mar 1
Fields/Majors: Petroleum And Geological Engineering

Scholarships are available at the University of Oklahoma, Norman, for full-time petroleum and geological engineering majors, with a minimum 3.0 GPA. Includes the Charlie Hughes Memorial, Lester B. Roberts Memorial, O.H. & Ruth Verne Davis Reaugh, PGE Keys to Success, and Robert H. Huston Jr. Memorial Endowment Scholarships. Individual award requirements may vary. Write to the address listed below for information.

University Of Oklahoma, Norman
Scholarship Coord., Pet. & Geol. Eng.
T301 Energy Center
Norman, OK 73019

Petroleum Land Management Scholarships

Amount: $500-$5,000 **Deadline:** Feb 3
Fields/Majors: Petroleum Land Management

Scholarships are available at the University of Oklahoma, Norman, for full-time petroleum land management majors. Includes the American Assoc. of Petroleum Landmen, Keown Memorial, Phillips Petroleum, and Rapp Memorial Scholarships. Individual award requirements may vary. Requires a minimum GPA of 3.0. Write to the address listed below for information.

University Of Oklahoma, Norman
Director., Division Of Petroleum Land Mgmt.
103 Adams Hall
Norman, OK 73019

Petry-Lomb Scholarship/ Research Grant

Amount: $1,000 (min) **Deadline:** Oct 15
Fields/Majors: Optometry, Opthomology

Scholarships and research grants for optometry students and for graduate students in schools of optometry. Based on need and desire to return to upstate New York after schooling. Must be a New York resident. Write to the address below for details.

Petry-Lomb Education Committee
Dr. David D'Amico, Chairman
3220 Chili Ave.
Rochester, NY 14624

3676

PG&E Career Scholarship Program-Cal Poly Tech, San Luis Obispo

Amount: $2,000 **Deadline:** Jan 16
Fields/Majors: Electrical, Mechanical, Or Industrial Engineering

Awards are available for sophomores or juniors at California Polytechnic State University in one of the fields of study listed above. Must be a U.S. citizen or permanent resident. Call Shirley Nelson at (800) 537-4180 or write to the address below for more information.

Pacific Gas And Electric Company
Mail Code P15C
P.O. Box 770000
San Francisco, CA 94177

PG&E Career Scholarship Program-California State University, Sacramento

Amount: $2,000 **Deadline:** Jan 16
Fields/Majors: Electrical Engineering, Computer Science

Awards are available for sophomores or juniors at California State University, Sacramento, in one of the fields of study listed above. Must be a U.S. citizen or permanent resident. Call Shirley Nelson at (800) 537-4180 or write to the address below for more information.

Pacific Gas And Electric Company
Mail Code P15C
P.O. Box 770000
San Francisco, CA 94177

PG&E Career Scholarship Program-California State University, Fresno

Amount: $2,000 **Deadline:** Jan 16
Fields/Majors: Electrical Engineering, Computer Science

Awards are available for sophomores or juniors at California State University, Fresno, in one of the fields of study listed above. Must be a U.S. citizen or permanent resident. Call Shirley Nelson at (800) 537-4180 or write to the address below for more information.

Pacific Gas And Electric Company
Mail Code P15C
P.O. Box 770000
San Francisco, CA 94177

PG&E Career Scholarship Program-California State University, Hayward

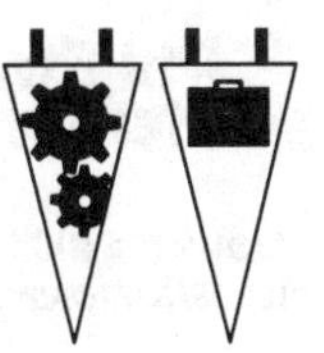

Amount: $2,000 **Deadline:** Jan 16
Fields/Majors: Business, Accounting, Computer Science, Mis

Awards are available for sophomores or juniors at California State University, Hayward, in one of the fields of study listed above. Must be a U.S. citizen or permanent resident. Call Shirley Nelson at (800) 537-4180 or write to the address below for more information.

Pacific Gas And Electric Company
Mail Code P15C
P.O. Box 770000
San Francisco, CA 94177

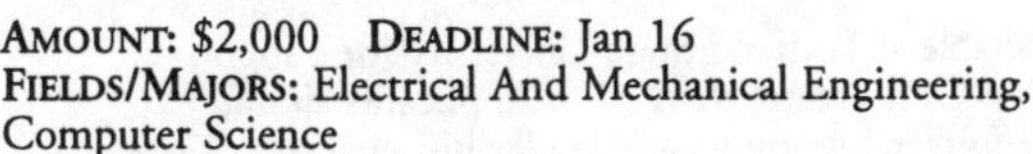

PG&E Career Scholarship Program-Georgia Tech

Amount: $2,000 **Deadline:** Jan 16
Fields/Majors: Electrical And Mechanical Engineering, Computer Science

Awards are available for sophomores or juniors studying at Georgia Tech University in one of the fields listed above. Applicants must be a U.S. citizen or permanent resident. Call Shirley Nelson at (800) 537-4180 or write to the address below for more information.

Pacific Gas And Electric Company
Mail Code P15C
P.O. Box 770000
San Francisco, CA 94177

PG&E Career Scholarship Program-New Mexico State University

Amount: $2,000 **Deadline:** Jan 16
Fields/Majors: Electrical And Mechanical Engineering

Awards are available for sophomores or juniors at New Mexico State University in one of the fields listed above. Applicants must be a U.S. citizen or permanent resident. Call Shirley Nelson at (800) 537-4180 or write to the address below for more information.

Pacific Gas And Electric Company
Mail Code P15C
P.O. Box 770000
San Francisco, CA 94177

3682

PG&E Career Scholarship Program-San Francisco State University

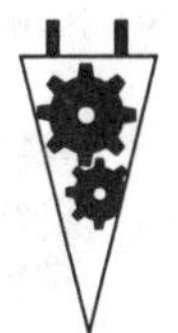

Amount: $2,000 **Deadline:** Jan 16
Fields/Majors Electrical Engineering, Computer Science, Mis, Computer Info. Systems

Awards are available for sophomores or juniors studying at San Francisco State University in one of the fields listed above. Applicants must be a U.S. citizen or permanent resident. Call Shirley Nelson at (800) 537-4180 or write to the address below for more information.

Pacific Gas And Electric Company
Mail Code P15C
P.O. Box 770000
San Francisco, CA 94177

3683

PG&E Career Scholarship Program-Stanford University

Amount: $2,000 **Deadline:** Jan 16
Fields/Majors Electrical, Mechanical, Industrial Eng., Computer Science, Economics

Awards are available for sophomores or juniors studying at Stanford University in one of the fields listed above. Applicants must be a U.S. citizen or permanent resident. Call Shirley Nelson at (800) 537-4180 or write to the address below for more information.

Pacific Gas And Electric Company
Mail Code P15C
P.O. Box 770000
San Francisco, CA 94177

3684

PG&E Career Scholarship Program-University Of California, Berkeley

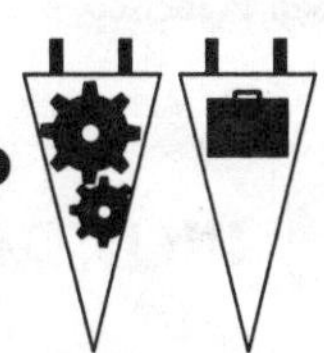

Amount: $2,000 **Deadline:** Jan 16
Fields/Majors: Elec., Mech., Nuclear Engineering, Computer Science, Business, Econ.

Awards are available for sophomores or juniors studying at the University of California, Berkeley, in one of the fields listed above. Applicants must be a U.S. citizen or permanent resident. Call Shirley Nelson at (800) 537-4180 or write to the address below for more information.

Pacific Gas And Electric Company
Mail Code P15C
P.O. Box 770000
San Francisco, CA 94177

3685

PG&E Career Scholarship Program-University Of California, Davis

AMOUNT: $2,000 **DEADLINE:** Jan 16
FIELDS/MAJORS: Electrical Or Mechanical Engineering, Computer Science

Awards are available for sophomores or juniors studying at the University of California, Davis, in one of the fields listed above. Applicants must be a U.S. citizen or permanent resident. Call Shirley Nelson at (800) 537-4180 or write to the address below for more information.

Pacific Gas And Electric Company
Mail Code P15C
P.O. Box 770000
San Francisco, CA 94177

3686

PG&E Career Scholarship Program-University Of Illinois, Urbana

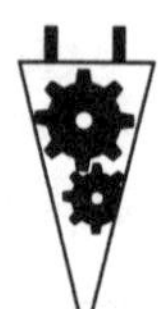

AMOUNT: $2,000 **DEADLINE:** Jan 16
FIELDS/MAJORS: Electrical Or Mechanical Engineering, Computer Science

Awards are available for sophomores or juniors studying at the University of Illinois in one of the fields listed above. Applicants must be a U.S. citizen or permanent resident. Call Shirley Nelson at (800) 537-4180 or write to the address below for more information.

Pacific Gas And Electric Company
Mail Code P15C
P.O. Box 770000
San Francisco, CA 94177

3687

PG&E Career Scholarship Program-Washington State University

AMOUNT: $2,000 **DEADLINE:** Jan 16
FIELDS/MAJORS: Electrical Or Mechanical Engineering

Awards are available for sophomores or juniors studying at Washington State University in one of the fields listed above. Applicants must be a U.S. citizen or permanent resident. Call Shirley Nelson at (800) 537-4180 or write to the address below for more information.

Pacific Gas And Electric Company
Mail Code P15C
P.O. Box 770000
San Francisco, CA 94177

3688

Ph.D. Research Grants

AMOUNT: Varies **DEADLINE:** Mar 1
FIELDS/MAJORS: American History-Historical Editing

Doctoral awards for applicants with at least an M.A. in American history or American civilization who demonstrate an interest in specialized training in historical editing. U.S. citizen or legal resident. Write to the address below for complete details.

National Historical Publications And Records Commission (NP)
Archival Fellowship Program
National Archives Bldg.
Washington, DC 20408

3689

Pharmaceutical Assoc. Of Bucks County Scholarships

AMOUNT: None Specified **DEADLINE:** Apr 1
FIELDS/MAJORS: Pharmacy, Pharmacology

Scholarships for Bucks County (PA) residents who are entering their last year of study in pharmacy. Write to the address below for details.

Bucks County Pharmaceutical Assoc., Inc.
Alan Vogenberg, R.Ph., Scholarship Chair
P.O. Box 747
Langhorne, PA 19047

3690

Phi Beta Kappa Scholarship

AMOUNT: Varies **DEADLINE:** None Specified
FIELDS/MAJORS: All Areas Of Study

Awards for Jacksonville State University juniors of top academic standing. Write to the address below for more details.

Jacksonville State University
Financial Aid Office
Jacksonville, AL 36265

3691

Phi Eta Sigma-Scott Mathis Memorial Scholarship

AMOUNT: $400 **DEADLINE:** None Specified
FIELDS/MAJORS: All Areas Of Study

Student must be a sophomore or above who is an active member of Phi Eta Sigma. Must have a GPA of 3.5 or better. Contact the Phi Eta Sigma advisor for more information.

Southwest Missouri State University
Office of Financial Aid
901 South National Ave.
Springfield, MO 65804

3692

Phi Kappa Phi Scholarships

AMOUNT: $800 **DEADLINE:** None Specified
FIELDS/MAJORS: All Areas Of Study

Award available at Portland State University for a sophomore with a GPA greater than 3.79. Applicants should emphasize university honors and leadership qualities. Write to the address below for more information.

Portland State University
Office of Academic Affairs
3349 Cramer Hall
Portland, OR 97207

3693

Phi Sigma Iota Member Scholarships

Amount: $500 **Deadline:** Mar 15
Fields/Majors: Foreign Languages

Open to active members of Phi Sigma Iota (foreign languages honor society) who meet standards of excellence in scholarship in any of the foreign languages. Eight award programs per year. Contact your faculty advisor or write to the address below for complete details.

Phi Sigma Iota
Office of The Executive Director
5211 Essen Lane, Suite 2
Baton Rouge, LA 70809

3694

Phi Theta Kappa Alumni Scholarship

Amount: $1,000 **Deadline:** Mar 1
Fields/Majors: All Areas Of Study

Scholarships are available at WMU for transfer students with a GPA of at least 3.5, who are members in good standing of Phi Theta Kappa. Contact your graduate college for further information about these programs.

Western Michigan University
Student Financial Aid
3306 Faunce Student Services Building
Kalamazoo, MI 49008

3695

Phi Theta Kappa Scholarship

Amount: Varies **Deadline:** None Specified
Fields/Majors: All Areas Of Study

Awards for full-time TTC students who have completed at least two semesters of college study and have a GPA of at least 3.75. Must have demonstrated service to trident. Write to the address below for more information.

Trident Technical College
Financial Aid Office
P.O. Box 118067
Charleston, SC 29423

3696

Philip L. Graham Minority Scholarship

Amount: $1,500 **Deadline:** Mar 1
Fields/Majors: Telecommunications

Must be a minority student majoring in telecommunications at the University of Florida. Must be a resident ofthe Jacksonville or Miami area (Florida). Must have at least a 2.8 GPA. Write to the address below for details.

University Of Florida
2070 Weimer Hall
Director, Minority Scholarship Program
Gainesville, FL 32611

3697

Philip Pearlman Scholarship Fund

Amount: $500 **Deadline:** May 15
Fields/Majors: Social Service, Rabbinics, Education, Jewish Studies

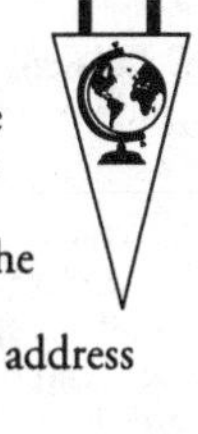

Scholarships for Jewish residents of New Jersey who are studying toward a career in the Jewish field, whether in the rabbinate, cantorate, education, administration or social work. For undergraduate or graduate studies in the U.S. or Israel. Recipients must be present at the Jewish festival (on June 9th) to accept the award. Write to the address below for details.

Jewish Festival Of The Arts
Ms. Simi Pearlman, Committee Chairman
34 Wellington Rd.
East Brunswick, NJ 08816

3698

Phillip D. Miller Memorial Scholarship

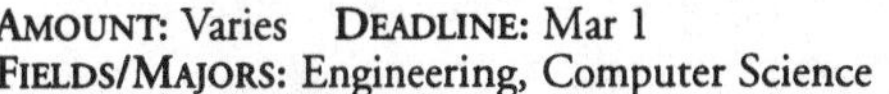

Amount: Varies **Deadline:** Mar 1
Fields/Majors: Engineering, Computer Science

Awards are available at the University of New Mexico for freshmen planning to enroll in an engineering or computer science program. Must exhibit a good academic background. Write to the address below for more information.

University Of New Mexico, Albuquerque
Office of Financial Aid
Albuquerque, NM 87131

3699

Phillips Petroleum Company Scholarship

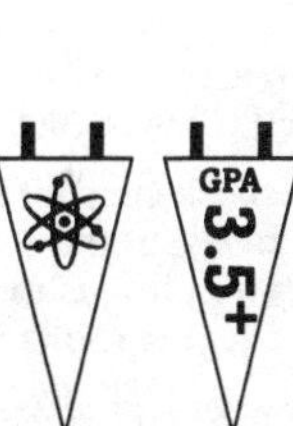

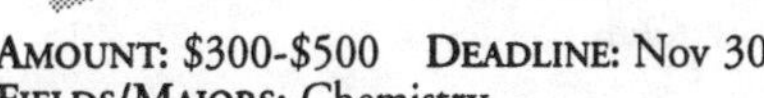

Amount: $300-$500 **Deadline:** Nov 30
Fields/Majors: Chemistry

Scholarships are available at the University of Oklahoma, Norman, for students majoring in chemistry, with high GPA's. Write to the address listed below for information.

University Of Oklahoma, Norman
Department of Chemistry & Biochemistry
620 Parrington Oval
Norman, OK 73019

3700

Philo Bennett Scholarship

Amount: Varies **Deadline:** Mar 1
Fields/Majors: All Areas Of Study

Awards are available at the University of New Mexico for freshmen women who are from New Mexico. Awards are only given in the spring. Write to the address below for more information.

University Of New Mexico, Albuquerque
Office of Financial Aid
Albuquerque, NM 87131

Philosophy Departmental Scholarships

AMOUNT: Varies **DEADLINE:** Feb 1
FIELDS/MAJORS: Philosophy

Scholarships are available at the University of Utah for full-time students majoring in philosophy. Write to the address below for details.

University Of Utah
Dr. Peter C. Appleby
338 Orson Spencer Hall
Salt Lake City, UT 84112

Philosophy Scholarships

AMOUNT: Varies **DEADLINE:** None Specified
FIELDS/MAJORS: Philosophy

Scholarships are available at the Catholic University of America for graduate philosophy majors. Includes the Anna Hope Hudson, the Most Reverend Francis M. Kelly, and the John K. Ryan Scholarships. Individual award requirements may vary. Contact the financial aid office at the address below for details.

The Catholic University Of America
Office of Admissions And Financial Aid
Washington, DC 20064

Phoenix Scholarship

AMOUNT: $1,000 (approx.) **DEADLINE:** Apr 26
FIELDS/MAJORS: Creative Arts

Scholarships for residents of Livingston County, who have an interest in the creative arts. Based on need and exceptional creativity. Applicants must be high school seniors, or first or second year college students. Write to the address below for more information.

Psychological Services For Youth
Dr. Patricia Carpenter
121 West North St.
Brighton, MI 48116

Phyllis And Tom Burnham Creative Writing Awards

AMOUNT: Varies **DEADLINE:** None Specified
FIELDS/MAJORS: Creative Writing

Awards are available at Portland State University for the students who write the best works of fiction in classes taught by faculty members in the PSU Department of English. Contact the English Department at the address below for more information.

Portland State University
English Department
405 Neuburger Hall
Portland, OR 97207

Phyllis Robideaux Wiener Memorial Scholarship

AMOUNT: $1,000 **DEADLINE:** Jun 15
FIELDS/MAJORS: Political Science

Awards are available for juniors or seniors who are studying political science and have at least 3 terms of full-time study remaining. Write to the address below for more information.

Portland State University
Political Science Department
117 Cramer Hall
Portland, OR 97207

Physical & Occupational Therapists And Assistants Program

AMOUNT: $2,000 **DEADLINE:** Jul 1
FIELDS/MAJORS: Physical Therapy, Occupational Therapy

Grants for Maryland residents working toward a degree in physical or occupational therapy or assisting at an institution within the state of Maryland. Write to the address below for additional information.

Maryland State Higher Education Commission
16 Francis St.
Annapolis, MD 21401

3707

Physical And Mathematical Sciences Scholarships

AMOUNT: $500-$2,500 **DEADLINE:** None Specified
FIELDS/MAJORS: Physical And Mathematical Sciences

Awards for undergraduates who are studying in the fields above at North Carolina State University. Write to the address below for more information.

North Carolina State University
College Of Physical/Mathematical Science
Robert G. Savage, Asst. Dean, Box 8201
Raleigh, NC 27695

3708

Physical Therapy Scholarship

AMOUNT: $4,000 **DEADLINE:** Ongoing
FIELDS/MAJORS: Physical Therapy, Occupational Therapy

Contractual scholarships available for physical therapy or occupational therapy majors entering their final year of study. Recipients must allow the Resource Group to place them in their first professional job after graduation. May apply before senior year (but funds are not disbursed until senior year.) Based on academics, leadership, and career potential. Call 1-800-217-7870 or write to the address below for details.

Allied Resource
810 Regal Drive, Suite H
Huntsville, AL 35801

3709

Physician Assistant Foundation Awards Program

AMOUNT: $2,000-$5,000 **DEADLINE:** Feb 1
FIELDS/MAJORS: Physician Assisting

Various scholarships to undergraduates and graduates in a physician assistant program. Based on academic record, activities, community involvement, and financial need. Applicants must be attending a CAAHEP-accredited program and be student members of the AAPA. Write to the address below for more information.

Physician Assistant Foundation Of American Academy Of Physician Assistants
Undergraduate Of Graduate Education Prog.
950 N. Washington St.
Alexandria, VA 22314

3710

Physician Loan Repayment Program

Amount: $20,000 **Deadline:** None Specified
Fields/Majors: Medicine

This program offers repayment of student loans for physicians who agree to practice in specialized areas in Ohio with limited access to medical care. Up to $20,000 per year for four years of student loan indebtedness may be cancelled. Write to the address listed below for information.

Ohio Student Aid Commission
Customer Service
P.O. Box 16610
Columbus, OH 43216

3711

Physics Merit Scholarships

Amount: None Specified **Deadline:** Dec 15
Fields/Majors: Physics

Scholarships awarded to students at Appalachian State University who are physics majors. Write to the address listed below for information.

Appalachian State University
Department of Physics
Boone, NC 28608

3712

Physics Scholarship At Case Western

Amount: $2,000 **Deadline:** Feb 1
Fields/Majors Physics

Four scholarships offered to entering freshmen at Case Western Reserve who intend to major in physics. Criteria for selection include high school grades, college entrance examination scores, and extracurricular activities. Scholarship is renewable for one additional year provided high academic achievement is maintained. May not be offered every year. Write to the address below for details.

Case Western Reserve University
Office of Financial Aid, 109 Pardee Hall
10900 Euclid Ave.
Cleveland, OH 44106

3713

Physics Student Support Fund And The William Reed Physics Scholarship

Amount: None Specified **Deadline:** Feb 1
Fields/Majors: Physics

Scholarships are awarded to students who plan to major in the field of physics at Murray State University. Write to the address below for details.

Murray State University
Office of University Scholarships
Ordway Hall, 1 Murray St.
Murray, KY 42071

3714

Pi Gamma Mu Scholarship

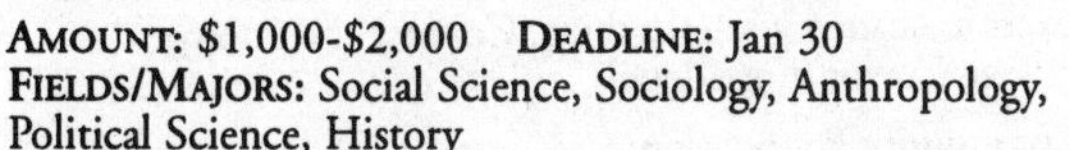

Amount: $1,000-$2,000 **Deadline:** Jan 30
Fields/Majors: Social Science, Sociology, Anthropology, Political Science, History

Open to Pi Gamma Mu members who are full-time graduate students with financial need. Letters of recommendation are required. Intended primarily for first-year graduate study. Write to the address below for details.

Pi Gamma Mu International Honor Society In Social Science
Executive Director
1001 Millington, Suite B
Winfield, KS 67156

3715

Piancone Family Agricultural Scholarship

Amount: $2,000 **Deadline:** May 31
Fields/Majors: Agriculture

Scholarships are available for Italian American agriculture majors residing in New Jersey, New York, Pennsylvania, Delaware, Virginia, Maryland, Washington, DC, and Massachusetts. Write to the address below for details.

National Italian American Foundation
Dr. Maria Lombardo, Education Director
1860 19th St., NW
Washington, DC 20009

3716

Pickens County Scholars Program

Amount: $7,500 **Deadline:** Mar 1
Fields/Majors: All Areas Of Study

Scholarships offered to freshmen who are graduated of Pickens County high schools. Renewable for three years. Contact the financial aid office at the address below for details.

Clemson University
Financial Aid Office
G01 Sikes Hall
Clemson, SC 29634

3717

Pickett And Hatcher Educational Fund Loans

Amount: $5,000 (max) **Deadline:** None Specified
Fields/Majors: All Areas Of Study

Open to undergraduate students who are residents of Alabama, Florida, Georgia, Kentucky, Mississippi, North Carolina, South Carolina, Tennessee, and Virginia. Interest rate is 2% per annum while in school. Renewable up to $16,000. No support for students planning to enter fields of medicine, law, or the ministry. For study in the states of Alabama, Florida, Georgia, Kentucky, Mississippi, North/South Carolina, Tennessee, or Virginia. Must be a U.S. citizen. Write to the address below for details.

Pickett And Hatcher Educational Fund, Inc.
P.O. Box 8169
Columbus, GA 31908

3718

PIF/Lifeline Scholarship Program

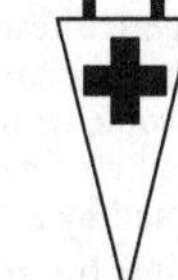

Amount: $1,000 (max) **Deadline:** Mar 15
Fields/Majors: See Listing Of Fields Below

Scholarships available for adult students who are enrolled in one of the following programs: physical therapy, occupational therapy, speech/hearing therapy, mental health, or rehabilitation. Recipients must be preparing for, or already involved in, careers working with people with disabilities/brain related disorders. Send an SASE to the address listed below for information. All applicants must be sponsored by a Pilot Club in their hometown or college/university town.

Pilot International Foundation
P.O. Box 5600
244 College St.
Macon, GA 31208

3719

Pillsbury Creative Writing Scholarship Program

Amount: None Specified **Deadline:** Oct 31
Fields/Majors: Creative Writing

Aid for students with potential in writing. Unrestricted age level/financial need. Must live or have lived in Santa Barbara County. Write to the address below for further information

Santa Barbara Foundation
Student Aid Director
15 East Carrillo St.
Santa Barbara, CA 93101

3720

Pillsbury Music Scholarship Program

Amount: None Specified **Deadline:** May 15
Fields/Majors: Music

Aid for students with potential in music. Unrestricted age level/financial need. Must live or have lived in Santa Barbara County. Based on interview and audition. Write to the address below for further information.

Santa Barbara Foundation
Student Aid Director
15 East Carrillo St.
Santa Barbara, CA 93101

3721

Pilot Club Of Tulsa Scholarship

Amount: $2,000 **Deadline:** Varies
Fields/Majors: Dentistry

Scholarships are available at the University of Oklahoma, Norman for full-time female graduate dentistry or dental hygiene students, who are in their fourth year of study. Write to the address listed below for information.

University Of Oklahoma, Norman
College Of Dentistry
1001 Stanton L. Young Blvd.
Oklahoma City, OK 73190

3722

Pilot International Foundation And Marie Newton Sepia Memorial Awards

Amount: $1,000 (max) **Deadline:** Mar 15
Fields/Majors: See Listing Of Fields Below

Scholarships for undergraduates or graduate students enrolled in one of the following programs: physical therapy, occupational therapy, speech/hearing therapy, mental health, or rehabilitation. Recipients must be preparing for, or already involved in, careers working with people with disabilities/brain related disorders. Send an SASE to the address listed below for information. All applicants must be sponsored by a Pilot Club in their hometown or college/university town.

Pilot International Foundation
P.O. Box 5600
244 College St.
Macon, GA 31208

3723

Pinellas County High School Scholarships

Amount: Varies **Deadline:** None Specified
Fields/Majors: All Areas Of Study

Scholarships for graduating high school seniors from high schools that are located in Pinellas County. Individual criteria for each award will vary. Includes the Kiwanis Clubs of Seminole & Clearwater, the Clarence Lightsey, Northeast H.S., Richard Ott, Lou & Lillian Padolf, Rotary Ann Club, and the Rotary Clubs of Pinellas Park & St. Petersburg West. Contact your high school guidance counselor for more information.

St. Petersburg Junior College
Financial Aid Office
P.O. Box 13489
St. Petersburg, FL 33733

3724

Pinellas-Seminole Woman'sClub

Amount: $400 **Deadline:** None Specified
Fields/Majors: All Areas Of Study

Awards for students at St. Petersburg Junior College. Preference is given to nursing students. Write to the address below for more information.

St. Petersburg Junior College
Financial Aid Office
P.O. Box 13489
St. Petersburg, FL 33733

3725

Pioneer Spirit Scholarships

Amount: $450 **Deadline:** Feb 15
Fields/Majors: All Areas Of Study

Awards for UW Platteville continuing students who have a GPA of at least 2.2 and whose special needs are not met by the student aid packages. Write to the address below for more information.

University Of Wisconsin, Platteville
Office of Admissions And Enrollment
Platteville, WI 53818

3726

Pioneers Of Flight Scholarship-Academic/Flight Training

Amount: $2,500 **Deadline:** Nov 15
Fields/Majors: Aviation-Related Fields

Grants for undergraduates who are at least 18 years old and are working toward a career in general aviation. Renewable one time. Nomination by member (regular or associate) of the National Air Transportation Assoc. is required. Based on academics, potential, leadership, etc. Write the address below or call (703) 845-9000 to obtain a National Air Transportation Assoc. member listing by state if you are unaware of members with whom you would pursue nomination.

National Air Transportation Foundation
Pioneers Of Flight Scholarship Programs
4226 King St.
Alexandria, VA 22302

3727

Piscataquis County Area Scholarships—Foxcroft Academy

Amount: Varies **Deadline:** Mar 18
Fields/Majors: All Areas Of Study

Awards for graduates of Foxcroft Academy in Piscataquis County, Maine. Includes the Walter H. and Eva L. Burgess, Harry M. and Lillian R. Bush, and Howard T. Clark Foxcroft Academy scholarships. Contact the Foxcroft Academy registrar for more details.

Maine Community Foundation
P.O. Box 148
Ellsworth, ME 04605

3728

Piton Foundation/Charter Fund Scholarships

AMOUNT: Varies **DEADLINE:** May 13
FIELDS/MAJORS: All Areas Of Study

Scholarships for graduating high school seniors from Colorado. Based upon financial need. Write to the address below, or call Cindy Kennedy at (303) 572-1727 for details.

Charter Fund
The Charter Fund
370 17th St., Suite 5300
Denver, CO 80202

3729

Pittsburgh Institute Of Mortuary Science Awards

AMOUNT: $1,000 **DEADLINE:** None Specified
FIELDS/MAJORS: Mortuary Science

Awards for students at the Pittsburgh Institute at any level of study. Write to the address below for more information.

Pittsburgh Institute Of Mortuary Science
Office Of Financial Aid
808 Baum Blvd.
Pittsburgh, PA 15206

3730

Plain Dealer Charities Scholarship

AMOUNT: $1,000 **DEADLINE:** Feb 1
FIELDS/MAJORS: Business Management, Print Journalism

Scholarships for entering freshmen at Case Western who are studying business management or print journalism. Must have graduated in the top 20% of high school class in Cuyahoga, Lake, Geauga, Portage, Summit, Medina, or Lorain Counties (OH). Applicants must have genuine financial need (to be determined by the CWRU Office of Financial Aid). Write to the address below for details.

Case Western Reserve University
Office of Financial Aid, 109 Pardee Hall
10900 Euclid Ave.
Cleveland, OH 44106

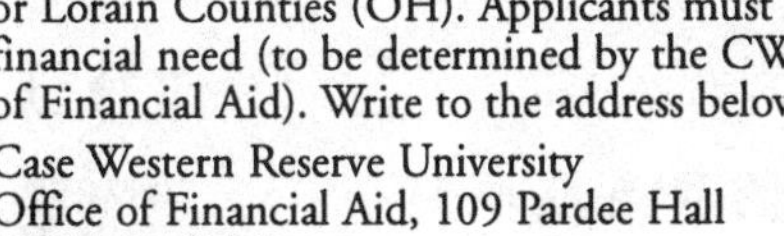

3731

Pleasant Hawaiian Holidays Scholarship

AMOUNT: $1,500 **DEADLINE:** Jun 23
FIELDS/MAJORS: Travel And Tourism

Awards are available for students from southern California whose parents are employed in the travel industry and who have career goals in the travel industry as well. Applicants must submit an essay explaining their future plans, have a GPA of 3.0 or greater, and be a U.S. citizen or legal resident. Write to the address below for more information.

American Society Of Travel Agents
Scholarship Committee
1101 King St., Suite 200
Alexandria, VA 22314

3732

Pleasant View Baptist Church Of Wren, OH Endowed Scholarship Fund

AMOUNT: Varies **DEADLINE:** None Specified
FIELDS/MAJORS: All Areas Of Study

Awards available for Baptist students at Cedarville College from the Pleasant View Church. Must have a GPA of at least 2.0 and demonstrated financial need. Write to the address below for more information.

Cedarville College
Financial Aid Office
P.O. Box 601
Cedarville, OH 45314

3733

Plenum Scholarship Program

AMOUNT: $1,000 **DEADLINE:** Oct 31
FIELDS/MAJORS: Library And Information Science

Scholarships for members of the Special Libraries Assoc. who have worked in special libraries. For doctoral study. Preference is given to persons who display an aptitude for special library work. One award per year. Based on academic achievement, evidence of financial need, and dissertation topic approval. Write to the address below for details.

Special Libraries Assoc.
SLA Scholarship Committee
1700 Eighteenth St., NW
Washington, DC 20009

3734

Plocieniak Scholarships

AMOUNT: Varies **DEADLINE:** Mar 1
FIELDS/MAJORS: All Areas Of Study

Scholarship offered to freshman students attending or planning to attend Loyola University on a full-time basis, who are of Polish descent and are fluent in the Polish language. Applicants must pass a language proficiency test. Renewable for up to three years. Write to the address below for details.

Loyola University
Undergraduate Admissions Office
820 North Michigan Ave.
Chicago, IL 60611

3735

PMI Food Equipment Group Merit Scholarships

AMOUNT: $500-$2,000 **DEADLINE:** None Specified
FIELDS/MAJORS: All Areas Of Study

Scholarships are available to graduating high school seniors who are National Merit Finalists and children of employees of PMI Food Equipment Group and its subsidiaries. Write to the address listed below for information, or contact the human resources department at PMI.

National Merit Scholarship Corporation/PMI Food Equipment Group
1560 Sherman Avenue, Suite 200
Evanston, IL 60201

3736

Poinsettia Mens Club Scholarships

AMOUNT: $1,000 **DEADLINE:** None Specified
FIELDS/MAJORS: Ballet Dance

Applicants must be incoming freshmen majoring in ballet dancing. Write to the address below for more information.

University Of Alabama, Birmingham
Department of Theatre And Dance
700 13th St. South, UAB Station
Birmingham, AL 35294

3737

Polaire Weissman Fund

Amount: $22,500 **Deadline:** Jan 5
Fields/Majors: Fine Arts, Costume History

Applicants should be graduate students in the fine arts or costume history and would like to pursue costume history in a museum, teaching, or other area related to the field of costume history. Award is available in alternate years. Write to "Fellowship Programs" at the address below for details.

Metropolitan Museum Of Art
Office Of Academic Programs
1000 Fifth Ave.
New York, NY 10028

3738

Police Officer/Fire Officer Survivor Grant Program

Amount: $3,500 (max) **Deadline:** Sep 1
Fields/Majors: All Areas Of Study

The Police Officer/Fire Officer Grant provides payment of tuition and mandatory fees for the spouse and children (ages 25 and under) of Illinois police/fire officers killed in the line of duty. Recipients must be enrolled on at least a half-time basis. Applicant must be a U.S. citizen and an Illinois resident. Write to the address below for details.

Illinois Student Assistance Commission
1755 Lake Cook Road
Deerfield, IL 60015

3739

Police Officers & Firefighters Survivors Educ. Assistance Program

Amount: Tuition And Fees **Deadline:** None Specified
Fields/Majors: All Areas Of Study

This program provides assistance to students who are dependents or spouses of police officers or firefighters killed in the line of duty in Alabama. Students must be enrolled in an undergraduate program at a public, postsecondary educational institution in Alabama. Other special criteria apply. There is no limit on the amount awarded to the recipients. Write to the address below for details.

Alabama Commission On Higher Education
P.O. Box 30200
Montgomery, AL 36130

3740

Polish National Alliance Scholarship Award Program

Amount: $500 **Deadline:** Apr 15
Fields/Majors: All Areas Of Study

Awards are available for sophomores, juniors, or seniors, who are members of the Polish National Alliance and have been so for at least five years prior to applying. Write to the address below for more information.

Polish National Alliance
Education Department
6100 N. Cicero Ave.
Chicago, IL 60646

3741

Political Science Department Scholarships

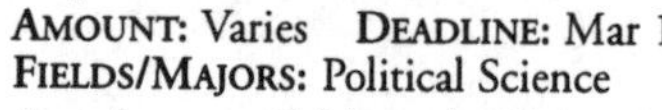

Amount: Varies **Deadline:** Mar 1
Fields/Majors: Political Science

Awards are available at the University of New Mexico for students majoring in political science. Financial need is given primary consideration. Write to the address below for more information.

University Of New Mexico, Albuquerque
Office of Financial Aid
Albuquerque, NM 87131

3742

Political Science Departmental Scholarships

Amount: Varies **Deadline:** Feb 15
Fields/Majors: Political Science

Scholarships are available at the University of Utah for full-time students majoring in political science. Write to the address below for information.

University Of Utah
Dr. Howard Lehman
252 Orson Spencer Hall
Salt Lake City, UT 84112

3743

Population Council Fellowships In The Social Sciences

Amount: Varies **Deadline:** None Specified
Fields/Majors: Population Studies And Related Fields

Doctoral, postdoctoral & midcareer research fellowships in population studies. Doctoral applicants should have made considerable progress toward their Ph.D. Or an equivalent degree. Selection criteria will stress academic excellence and prospective contribution to the population field. Write for complete details. Include a brief description of your academic qualifications and a description of your research plans.

Population Council
Manager, Fellowship Prog., Research Div.
One Dag Hammarskjold Plaza
New York, NY 10017

3744

Porter Ellifrit Award

Amount: $150-$350 **Deadline:** Feb 15
Fields/Majors: Music

Awards for students at UW Platteville who are in the area of music. Based on scholastic achievement and performance contribution. Write to the address below for more information.

University Of Wisconsin, Platteville
Office of Enrollment And Admissions
Platteville, WI 53818

3745

Porter McDonnell Memorial Award

Amount: $1,000 **Deadline:** Dec 15
Fields/Majors: Surveying, Cartography

Awards are available for female juniors or seniors enrolled in a surveying or mapping program in any accredited college or university in the U.S. Must be a U.S. citizen. Write to the address below for more information.

American Congress On Surveying And Mapping
5410 Grosvenor Lane, Suite 100
Bethesda, MD 20814

3746
Portia Irick Nursing Scholarship

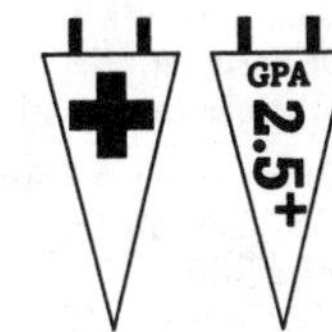

AMOUNT: Varies **DEADLINE:** Mar 1
FIELDS/MAJORS: Nursing

Awards are available at the University of New Mexico for full-time junior or senior nursing students with a minimum GPA of 2.5 and financial need. Write to the address below or contact the School of Nursing for more details.

University Of New Mexico, Albuquerque
Office of Financial Aid
Albuquerque, NM 87131

3747
Portland General Electric Scholarships

AMOUNT: $2,250 **DEADLINE:** Feb 1
FIELDS/MAJORS: All Areas Of Study

Awards for entering freshmen who are from Oregon and demonstrate academic excellence. Renewable with continued academic merit.

Lewis And Clark College
Office of Admissions
Portland, OR 97219

3748
Portland Seamen's Society Scholarship

AMOUNT: Varies **DEADLINE:** None Specified
FIELDS/MAJORS: All Areas Of Study

Awards restricted to seamen who reside in the state of Maine that demonstrate extreme financial need. Write to the address below for more information.

Portland Seamen's Friend Society
Mr. Louis Emery
14 Lewis St.
Westbrook, ME 04092

3749
Portland Teachers Program

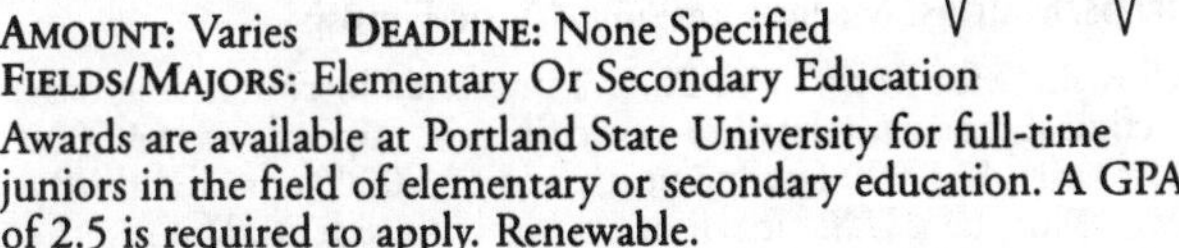

AMOUNT: Varies **DEADLINE:** None Specified
FIELDS/MAJORS: Elementary Or Secondary Education

Awards are available at Portland State University for full-time juniors in the field of elementary or secondary education. A GPA of 2.5 is required to apply. Renewable.

Portland State University
Educational Equity Programs And Services
120 Smith Memorial Center
Portland, OR 97207

3750
Portland Teachers Program

AMOUNT: Resident Tuition
DEADLINE: Ongoing
FIELDS/MAJORS: Education

Award for juniors or above in enrolled in an education program. Must be an Oregon resident with a GPA of 3.0 or better and be committed to teach in Portland public schools upon graduation. Contact the Dean's Office in the School of Education.

Portland State University
Student Services
608 School Of Education Building
Portland, OR 97207

3751
Portuguese Continental Union Scholarships

AMOUNT: Varies **DEADLINE:** Feb 15
FIELDS/MAJORS: All Areas Of Study

Scholarships for members of Portuguese Continental Union. Must have good character and meet entrance (or continuing) requirements for college or university of your choice. For full-time, undergraduate study. Scholarship is paid directly to your school. Write to the Union at the address below for details.

Portuguese Continental Union
Scholarship Committee
899 Boylston St.
Boston, MA 02115

3752
Post-Doctoral Fellowship

AMOUNT: $29,000 **DEADLINE:** Nov 1
FIELDS/MAJORS: Early American History And Culture

Post-doctoral residential fellowship. Must meet requirements for Ph.D. Before beginning fellowship (ABD). Must have potential for eventual publication. Residence is maintained at the college of William and Mary. Applicants may not have previously published a book. Ph.D. Holders who have begun careers in the field are welcome to apply. Tenure is for 2 years. Includes appointment as Asst. Professor. Write to the address below for more information.

Institute Of Early American History And Culture
Office of The Director
P.O. Box 8781
Williamsburg, VA 23187

3753
Post-Doctoral Fellowships

AMOUNT: Varies **DEADLINE:** None
FIELDS/MAJORS: Toxicology And Related Disciplines

Post-doctoral research fellowships for recent recipients of D.V.M., M.D., or Ph. D. (biochem., pharmacol., cell/molecular bio., genetics, immunol., chemistry, biophysics, mathematics, etc.). Supports original research related to chemical toxicity at CIIT's laboratory. Up to 25 awards per year. Write to the address below for details.

Chemical Industry Institute Of Toxicology
6 Davis Dr.
P.O. Box 12137
Research Triangle Park, NC 27709

3754
Post-Doctoral Fellowships At The Institute For Advanced Study

AMOUNT: Varies **DEADLINE:** Varies
FIELDS/MAJORS: Historical Studies, Social Sciences, Natural Sciences, Mathematics

The Institute has four separate schools as listed by field above. Competition is open and the major consideration is the expectation that each fellow's period of residence will result in work of significance and individuality. Write to the address below for details. Each school has different deadlines for application.

Institute For Advanced Study
Post-doctoral Fellowships
Olden Lane
Princeton, NJ 08540

3755

Post-Doctoral Grants

Amount: $20,000 **Deadline:** Jan 15
Fields/Majors Mammalian Reproductive Physiology

Grants are available for research in mammalian reproduction physiology and biochemistry for the advancement of contraception, pregnancy termination, and/or sterilization methods. Must hold Ph.D. or M.D. Write to address below for details.

Lalor Foundation
P.O. Box 2493
Providence, RI 02906

3756

Post-Doctoral Research Fellowships & Grants

Amount: $20,000 (max) **Deadline:** Sep 27
Fields/Majors: Social Sciences & Humanities

Applicants must be Ph.D. scholars who provide evidence of degree, field of specialization, research proposal, and project duration. U.S. citizenship or legal residency required. ACLS supports research in the humanities and the humanistic aspects of the social sciences. Write to the address below for complete details.

American Council Of Learned Societies
Office of Fellowships And Grants
228 E. 45th St.
New York, NY 10017

3757

Post-Doctoral Research Fellowships For Basic And Physician Scientists

Amount: $100,000 **Deadline:** Jul 1
Fields/Majors: Cancer Research (oncology)

Open to the following degree holders: M.D., Ph.D., D.D.S., or D.V.M. who are involved in cancer research. Sponsorship by a senior member of the research community is required. Write to the address below for details.

Damon Runyon-Walter Winchell Cancer Fund
131 E. 36th St.
New York, NY 10016

3758

Post-Doctoral Fellowship Program

Amount: $24,000-$30,000 **Deadline:** Sep 1
Fields/Majors: Biology, Medicine, Relevant To Cancer Research

Fellowships are available for postdoctoral research at California institutions in the biological or medical sciences relevant to cancer research. There are no citizenship requirements but the applicant must already hold the Ph.D. Write to the address listed below for information.

American Cancer Society, California Division
Research Fellowship Program
P.O. Box 2061
Oakland, CA 94604

3759

Post-Doctoral Fellowship Program

Amount: Varies **Deadline:** Jan 1
Fields/Majors: Sleep Disorders And Mechanisms

Research grants for postdoctoral scientists in the areas of study listed above. Must be a U.S. citizen or resident alien. Can be used for basic, applied, or clinical research. Write to the address below for more information.

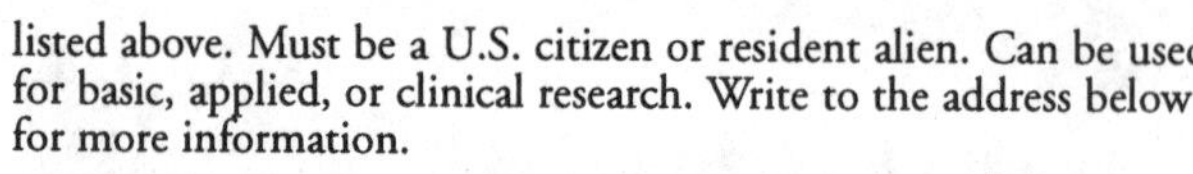

National Sleep Foundation
1367 Connecticut Ave., NW
Suite 200
Washington, DC 20036

3760

Post-Doctoral Fellowship, Physician Research Training, Scholar Awards

Amount: Varies **Deadline:** Mar 1
Fields/Majors: Cancer Research And Related Fields

The American Cancer Society provides support to new investigators to qualify for an independent career in cancer research. Both basic and applied research is supported. Must hold Ph.D. at the time application is made. Write to the address below or call 404-329-7558 for details and policies.

American Cancer Society, Inc.
Extramural Grants And Awards
1599 Clifton Road, NE
Atlanta, GA 30329

3761

Post-Doctoral Fellowships

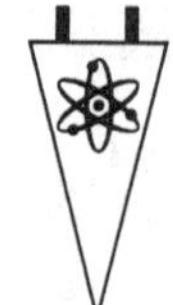

Amount: $36,000 **Deadline:** Jan 15
Fields/Majors: Ocean Science-Related Fields

Scientists with more than three to four years of postdoctoral experience are not eligible. Recipients of awards are selected on a competitive basis, with primary emphasis placed on research premise of the applicant. Awards are made to further the education and training of the recipient. Write to the address below for details.

Woods Hole Oceanographic Institution
Education Office, Clark Laboratory
Woods Hole, MA 02543

3762

Post-Doctoral Research Fellowships

Amount: $30,000-$33,000 **Deadline:** Sep 1
Fields/Majors: Medical Research-Cystic Fibrosis

Fellowships for M.D.'s and Ph.D.'s interested in conducting basic or clinical research related to cystic fibrosis. Stipends are $30,000 (first year), $31,000 (second year), and $33,000 (optional third year). Must be a U.S. citizen or permanent resident. Write to the address below for details.

Cystic Fibrosis Foundation
Office of Grants Management
6931 Arlington Rd.
Bethesda, MD 20814

3763

Post-Doctoral Research Fellowships

Amount: $30,000 **Deadline:** Nov 30
Fields/Majors: Mathematics

Awards for scholars who have earned their Ph.D. in the field of mathematics. Most fellowships last for a year, but a shorter period is possible, and in exceptional cases, two-year awards may be made. Write to the address below for more information.

Mathematical Sciences Research Institute
1000 Centennial Dr. #5070
Berkeley, CA 94720

3764

Post-Doctoral Research Fellowships For Physicians

Amount: $40,000-$57,500 **Deadline:** Early Jan
Fields/Majors: Medicine

Fellowships are available for scholars with the M.D., Ph.D., D.O., M.B.B.S., or equivalent degree who wish to further their education through research into basic biological processes and disease mechanisms. Applicant should have no more than two years of postdoctoral research training, and should have received first medical degree no more than ten years previously. Write to the address listed below for additional information.

Howard Hughes Medical Institute
Office of Grants And Special Programs
4,000 Jones Bridge Road
Chevy Chase, MD 20815

3765

Postgraduate Scholarship Program

Amount: $6,000 **Deadline:** Feb 15
Fields/Majors: All Areas Of Study

Must be nominated by the faculty athletic representative or director of athletics of an NCAA member institution. Eligibility is restricted to student athletes attending NCAA member institutions. 125 awards per year. Must be U.S. citizens and ethnic minorities. Selections are made in the academic year in which the student completes his or her final season of eligibility for intercollegiate athletics under NCAA legislation. Write to the address below for details.

National Collegiate Athletic Assoc.
6201 College Blvd.
Overland Park, KS 66211

3766

Potsdam Foundation Honors Scholarships

Amount: $1,000 **Deadline:** None Specified
Fields/Majors: All Areas Of Study

Awards are available for incoming freshmen who have demonstrated excellence in academic performance and/or extracurricular or community activities. Write to the address below for more information.

Suny, Potsdam
Office of Admissions
44 Pierrepont Ave.
Potsdam, NY 13676

3767

Poultry Science Scholarships

Amount: $500-$1,500 **Deadline:** None Specified
Fields/Majors: Poultry Science

Several scholarships for students at Virginia Tech who are studying poultry science. Programs include Poster, Wampler, VA Poultry Fed., Tyson, Gen'l Poultry Sci., Rocco, Poultry Science Club, VA broiler, Delmarva, Cherry, Wisman, SPEA, 4-H, Ag Career Awareness, and Rockingham scholarships. Write to Dr. Cindy Wood at the address below for details.

Virginia Tech College Of Agriculture And Life Sciences
Deptartment Of Poultry Science
3400 Litton Reaves Hall
Blacksburg, VA 24061

3768

Powell Scholarship

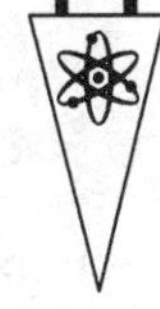

Amount: None Specified **Deadline:** Dec 15
Fields/Majors: Natural Resources, Wildlife, Fisheries Biology

Scholarships are awarded to students at UMass in the natural resource studies/wildlife and fisheries biology programs. For entering sophomores, juniors, or seniors. Contact the Department Head, Forestry and Wildlife Management, for more information.

University Of Massachusetts, Amherst
Department of Forestry And Wildlife Mgmt.
Amherst, MA 01003

3769

Practical Nurse Scholarships, Nurse Gift Tuition Scholarships

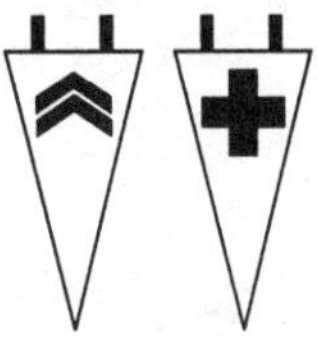

Amount: $400-$500 **Deadline:** Apr 12
Fields/Majors: Nursing

Scholarships are available for Nebraska students who are citizens of the U.S., children of veterans, and studying for a career in nursing. Write to the address listed below for additional information.

American Legion Auxiliary-Department of Nebraska
Department Headquarters
P.O. Box 5227
Lincoln, NE 68505

3770

Practicum Stipend In The Area Of Developmental Disability Services

Amount: $4,000 **Deadline:** Aug 1
Fields/Majors: Social Work

Awards are available at the University of Oklahoma, Norman, for full-time students in the school of social work and eligible to take the SWK 4325 practicum. Student must be willing to seek professional positions with the division of developmental disabilities of the Oklahoma Department of Human Services. Write to the address listed below for information.

University Of Oklahoma, Norman
School Of Social Work
217 Rhyn
Norman, OK 73019

3771

Pre-Dissertation Fellowship Program

Amount: $3,000 **Deadline:** Feb 1
Fields/Majors: History, Sociology, Poly Sci, Anthropology, Economics, Geography

Research grants are available to those studying in the above fields and specializing in European studies who have completed a minimum of two years of graduate study. These are non-residential fellowships. Must be a citizen or legal resident of the U.S. or Canada. Write to address below for details.

Council For European Studies
Columbia University
Box 44, Schermerhorn Hall
New York, NY 10027

3772

Pre-Paid Tuition Reimbursement Contract

AMOUNT: Varies **DEADLINE:** None Specified
FIELDS/MAJORS: Nursing

Open to full- or part-time Rush nursing students who are employed full-time in a division of nursing at Rush-Presbyterian-St. Luke's Medical Center or the Johnston R. Bowman Center. Amount of contract is approved and paid by the Department of Nursing Financial Affairs. Write to the address below or to the Office of Nursing Financial Affairs at Rush University, 435 Schweppe, Chicago, IL, 60612.

Rush University
Office of Student Financial Aid
1743 West Harrison St.
Chicago, IL 60612

3773

Pre-Veterinary Scholarships

AMOUNT: $250 **DEADLINE:** Apr 15
FIELDS/MAJORS: Veterinary Medicine

Awards for undergraduates enrolled in a preveterinary program. Must plan to attend a veterinary school. Applicants must be residents of New Mexico. Write to the address below for more information.

Albuquerque Veterinary Assoc.
Ms. Mary H. Hume, DVM
3601 Eubank NE
Albuquerque, NM 87111

3774

Precision Laboratories, Inc. Scholarships

AMOUNT: $1,000 **DEADLINE:** Feb 15
FIELDS/MAJORS: Agricultural Economics, Agribusiness

Scholarships are available for FFA members pursuing a four-year degree in agricultural economics or agribusiness, who reside in Illinois. Applicants must also attend an Illinois university. Write to the address below for details.

National FFA Foundation
Scholarship Office
P.O. Box 15160
Alexandria, VA 22309

3775

Predicanda Degeer Scholarship

AMOUNT: Varies **DEADLINE:** Mar 1
FIELD/MAJOR: All Areas of Study

Awards are available at the University of New Mexico for full-time students who have financial need. First preference is given to native New Mexican students of Hispanic descent.

University of New Mexico, Albuquerque
Office of Financial Aid
Albuquerque, NM 87131

3776

Predoctoral Fellowship, AHA California Affiliate

AMOUNT: $16,500 **DEADLINE:** Oct 1
FIELD/MAJOR: Cardiovascular Research

Predoctoral fellowships for California residents or students at California institutions to support doctoral dissertation projects in areas relating to cardiovascular research. Must be a U.S. citizen or hold a current visa. Deadline to request applications is Jul 1.

American Heart Association, California Affiliate
Research Department
1710 Gilbreth Road
Burlingame, CA 94010

3777

Predoctoral Minority Fellowship

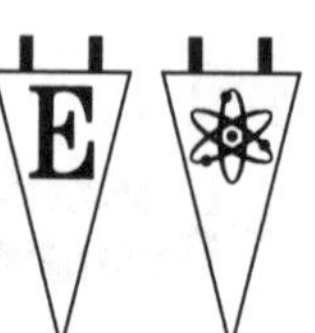

AMOUNT: $12,000 **DEADLINE:** May 1
FIELD/MAJOR: Microbiological Sciences

One year fellowship for a minority predoctoral student in the field of microbiological sciences. Must be a U.S. citizen or permanent resident and an ASM member.

American Society For Microbiology
Office of Education and Training
1325 Massachusettes Ave., NW
Washington, DC 20005

3778

Predoctoral Ortho-McNeil Fellowship

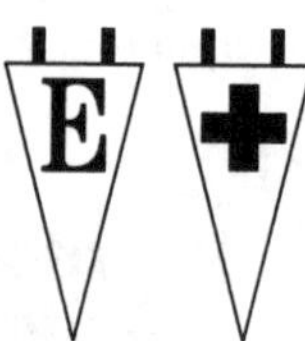

AMOUNT: $12,000 **DEADLINE:** May 1
FIELD/MAJOR: Antimicrobial Agents

Two year fellowship for a minority predoctoral student in the field of antimicrobial agents. Must be a U.S. citizen or permanent resident.

American Society For Microbiology
Office of Education and Training
1325 Massachusettes Ave., NW
Washington, DC 20005

3779

Prepharmacy Scholarship

AMOUNT: None Specified **DEADLINE:** May 1
FIELD/MAJOR: Pharmacy

Scholarship for African American students from the state of Washington who are studying to become a pharmacist. Based on academics, an essay, and an interview with the Coalition Scholarship Committee in the Seattle area. Write to the address below for more information.

Northwest Pharmacists Coalition
P.O. Box 22975
Seattle, WA 96122

3780

President's And Adams Scholarships

Amount: Varies **Deadline:** Mar 15
Field/Major: All Areas Of Study

Scholarships for incoming freshman or transfer students at Adams State. Must have a GPA of at least a 3.2. For President's Award must have an ACT score of at least 21 or an SAT score of 850. Write to the address below for more information.

Adams State College
Financial Aid Office
Alamosa, CO 81102

3781

President's And Plymouth Scholars

Amount: $1,000 **Deadline:** Mar 1
Field/Major: All Areas Of Study

Scholarships are available at Plymouth State for entering freshman students who demonstrate outstanding academic achievement and future potential. There are fifty awards offered each year. Additionally, twenty awards are given to currently enrolled students. Write to the address listed below for information.

Plymouth State College
Financial Aid Office
Speare Administration Bldg.
Plymouth, NH 03264

3782

President's Award

Amount: $4,000 (max) **Deadline:** Mar 15
Field/Major: All Areas Of Study

Scholarships are available at Wheaton College for undergraduate students who have a minimum GPA of 3.6, with a composite ACT score of 32 or an SAT score of 1400. Write to the address below for details.

Wheaton College
Financial Aid Office
Wheaton, IL 60187

3783

President's Council Scholars Program

Amount: $1,000 **Deadline:** Varies
Field/Major: Agriculture

Student must be a full-time junior or senior majoring in agriculture with a GPA of 3.5 or better. Must be a U.S. citizen. Write to the address below for more information.

California State Polytechnic University, Pomona
College of Agriculture
Building 2, Room 216
Pomona, CA 91768

3784

President's Endowed University Scholars Program

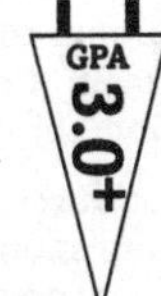

Amount: $2,000 **Deadline:** Apr 1
Field/Major: All Areas Of Study

Awards for freshmen at Sul Ross who have obtained an academic seal on their high school diploma and who have an ACT score of at least 25 or an SAT score of at least 1050. Renewable. Write to the address below for more information.

Sul Ross State University
Financial Aid Office
Box C-113
Alpine, TX 79832

3785

President's Leadership Class

Amount: $1,000 Fee Waiver **Deadline:** Feb 15
Field/Major: All Areas Of Study

Scholarships are available at the University of Oklahoma, Norman, for entering freshmen who are graduating high school seniors, and class officers or student council representatives. Write to the address listed below for information.

University of Oklahoma, Norman
Prospective Student Services
Boyd House, 407 W. Boyd Street
Norman, OK 73019

3786

President's Scholarship

Amount: $1,000 / Quarter **Deadline:** Feb 1
Field/Major: All Areas Of Study

Scholarships are available at the University of Utah for full-time students who will be entering freshmen who qualify for an "honors at entrance" scholarship. Up to fifty awards are offered annually. Write to the address below for details. Information is also available from your high school guidance counselor.

University Of Utah
Financial Aid And Scholarship Office
105 Student Services Building
Salt Lake City, UT 84112

3787

President's Scholarship

Amount: $2,000 **Deadline:** None Specified
Field/Major: All Areas Of Study

Awards for high school seniors or transfer students with a GPA of at least 3.0. High school seniors must also have an SAT score of 1310 or better or an ACT score of at least 30. Write to the address below for more information.

Cedarville College
Financial Aid Office
P.O. Box 601
Cedarville, OH 45314

3788

President's Scholarships

Amount: $10,000 (max) **Deadline:** Aug 1, Jan 1
Field/Major: All Areas Of Study

Award for freshmen at Liberty whose parent is employed full-time as pastor or church staff. Must have an SAT score of at least 800 or an ACT score of at least 15. Write to the address below for more information.

Liberty University
Office Of Student Financial Aid
Box 20000
Lynchburg, VA 24506

3789

President's Scholarships

Amount: $3,000-$5,000 **Deadline:** Feb 1
Field/Major: All Areas Of Study

Scholarships for entering freshmen who have demonstrated academic excellence in high school and who have the ability to become academic leaders at CBU or SJU. Applicants must have a GPA of at least 3.6 or be in the top 5% of their high school class. Renewed automatically with satisfactory academic progress. Write to the address below for more information.

College Of Saint Benedict And Saint John's University
Office of Financial Aid
37 South College Ave.
St. Joseph, MN 56374

3790

Presidential And Academic Scholarships

Amount: Tuition **Deadline:** Mar 15, Nov 15
Field/Major: All Areas Of Study

Awards for entering students with outstanding academic credentials. Freshmen must have SAT scores of 1100 or above and rank in the top 15% of their class. Transfers must have a GPA of at least 3.4. Applicants must have participated in extracurricular or community activities. Write to the address below for more information.

Gwynedd-Mercy College
Student Financial Aid
Sumneytown Pike
Gwynedd Valley, PA 19437

3791

Presidential And Minority Scholarships

Amount: None Specified **Deadline:** None Specified
Field/Major: All Areas Of Study

Scholarships for entering minority freshman who have demonstrated academic achievement or participation in extracurricular activities. Write to the address below for more information.

Trenton State College
Hillwood Lakes CN 4700
Trenton, NJ 08650

3792

Presidential And Salem Scholar Honor Awards

Amount: Varies **Deadline:** Mar 1, Apr 1
Field/Major: All Areas Of Study

Award given to incoming freshmen in recognition of academic achievement. Recipients must maintain full-time status and a cumulative GPA of 3.0 or better. Write to the address below for more information.

Salem College
Financial Aid Office
P.O. Box 10548
Winston-Salem, NC 27108

3793

Presidential Full-Tuition Scholar Award

Amount: Full-tuition **Deadline:** Feb 28
Field/Major: All Areas Of Study

Awards are available for entering freshmen at Abilene Christian University who have an ACT score of at least 31 or an SAT score of at least 1310. Applicants must have a GPA of 3.5 or better. Selection is also based on an interview, service activities, leadership, and good moral character. Write to the address below for more information. Partial tuition awards are also available for students who scored between 28-31 on the ACT or 1240-1380 on the R-SAT.

Abilene Christian University
Mr. Don King, Director Of Admissions
ACU Box 6000
Abilene, TX 79699

3794

Presidential Grants

Amount: $500 (min) **Deadline:** None Specified
Field/Major: All Areas Of Study

Tuition grants for students with special talent or potential for enriching the campus atmosphere. Must demonstrate financial need. Write to the address below for details.

Mercyhurst College
Glenwood Hills
Erie, PA 16546

3795

Presidential Opportunity Scholarships

Amount: $2,100 **Deadline:** Mar 1
Field/Major: All Areas Of Study

Awards for entering freshmen minorities with an ACT score of 29 or better and a GPA of at least 3.5. Renewable. Write to the address below for more information.

Auburn University
Office Of Student Financial Aid
203 Mary Martin Hall
Auburn University, AL 36849

3796

Presidential Scholar Awards Tuition And Fees

Amount: None Specified **Deadline:**
Field/Major: All Areas Of Study

Awards for African American or Hispanic H.S. seniors who rank in the top 10% of their class or have at least a 3.5 GPA. Applicants must score at least an 1100 on the SAT or a 25 on the ACT. Finalists will be invited to campus to interview and compete for the award in March. Renewable. Write to the address below for more information.

Southwestern University
Admissions Office
Georgetown, TX 78626

3797

Presidential Scholars

Amount: None Specified **Deadline:** Feb 20
Field/Major: All Areas Of Study

Scholarships are available at the University of San Diego for freshmen with a GPA of at least 3.5 and high SAT scores. Write to the address listed below for information.

University of San Diego
Office Of Financial Aid
5998 Alcala Park
San Diego, CA 92110

3798

Presidential Scholars

Amount: $2,311 **Deadline:** Dec 1
Field/Major: All Areas Of Study

Scholarships are available at the University of New Mexico for entering freshmen who are New Mexico residents with a high GPA and demonstrated leadership skills. Must maintain a GPA of at least 3.0 and maintain thirty semester hours per academic year. Write to the address listed below for information.

University Of New Mexico, Albuquerque
Student Financial Aid Office
Mesa Vista Hall North, Student Services
Albuquerque, NM 87131

3799

Presidential Scholars Program

Amount: Full Tuition **Deadline:** Feb 15
Field/Major: All Areas Of Study

Scholarships are available to Nazareth College for full-time undergraduate students who demonstrate outstanding academic performance. Must be a U.S. citizen. Write to the address below for details.

Nazareth College
Office Of Financial Aid
4245 East Avenue
Rochester, NY 14618

3800

Presidential Scholarship

Amount: Half Tuition **Deadline:** Mar 15
Field/Major: All Areas Of Study

Open to incoming freshmen with at least a 3.5 GPA, ACT minimum of 25 (SAT of 1100), and rank in the top 15% of their graduating class. Extracurricular activities are considered. Renewable. Write to the address below for details.

Edgewood College
Office Of Admissions
855 Woodrow St.
Madison, WI 53711

3801

Presidential Scholarship

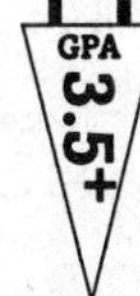

Amount: Varies **Deadline:** None Specified
Field/Major: All Areas Of Study

Available to full-time freshmen and transfer students who have a GPA of at least 3.6 and are in the top 10% of their class. The award amounts vary depending upon the applicant's academic credentials, financial need, and family circumstances. Renewal of awards requires full-time attendance and a 3.0 GPA. Write to the address below for details.

Alfred University
Student Financial Aid Office
26 N. Main St.
Alfred, NY 14802

3802

Presidential Scholarship

Amount: Varies **Deadline:** Jan 20
Field/Major: All Areas Of Study

Scholarships are available to John Brown College for full-time undergraduate students who demonstrate superior academic and leadership potential with a GPA of at least 3.9, who were in the top 5% of their graduating class. Write to the address below for details.

John Brown University
Office Of Financial Aid
2000 West University St.
Siloam Springs, AR 72761

3803

Presidential Scholarship

Amount: $5,000 **Deadline:** Apr 1
Field/Major: All Areas Of Study

Scholarships are available at Siena Heights College for full-time students who have a GPA of at least 3.70, and an ACT score of 25 or higher. Up to fourteen awards offered each year. Write to the address listed below for information.

Siena Heights College
Financial Aids Office
1247 East Siena Heights Drive
Adrian, MI 49221

3804

Presidential Scholarship

Amount: One-Half Tuition **Deadline:** Mar 2
Field/Major: All Areas Of Study

Scholarships are awarded to entering freshmen. Write to the address below for more information.

Dominican College Of San Rafael
Office Of Admissions
50 Acacia Avenue
San Rafael, CA 94901

3805

Presidential Scholarship

Amount: $500-$1,500 **Deadline:** None Specified
Field/Major: All Areas Of Study

Non-need based awards for students with a GPA of at least a 3.5 and an SAT score of at least 1000 or ACT of 23. For undergraduate study. Renewable upon maintaining a 3.0 GPA. Write to the address below for additional information.

University of Redlands
Office Of Financial Aid
1200 East Colton Ave., P.O. Box 3080
Redlands, CA 92373

3806

Presidential Scholarship

AMOUNT: Tuition and Fees **DEADLINE:** Jan 15
FIELD/MAJOR: All Areas Of Study

Awards for entering freshman who rank in the upper 10% of their class and have an ACT composite score of 30 or above or have been selected as national merit finalists. Renewable. Write to the address below for more details.

Southwest Missouri State University
Financial Aid Office
901 South National Ave.
Springfield, MO 65804

3807

Presidential Scholarship

AMOUNT: $750 **DEADLINE:** None Specified
FIELD/MAJOR: All Areas Of Study

Awards for full-time undergraduate transfer students and freshmen. Based on financial need, personal essay, and recommendation from high school faculty or administration. Renewable if a GPA of at least 2.75 is maintained. Write to the address below for more information.

Concordia College, Nebraska
Office Of Financial Aid
800 N. Columbia Ave.
Seward, NE 68434

3808

Presidential Scholarship

AMOUNT: $3,900-$4,800 **DEADLINE:** None Specified
FIELD/MAJOR: All Areas Of Study

Awards for freshmen who have an ACT score of at least 28 and are in the top 5% of their graduating class. Renewable with a GPA of 3.0 or better. Write to the address below for more information.

Northwestern College
Financial Aid Office
101 7th St., SW
Orange City, IA 51041

3809

Presidential Scholarship

AMOUNT: $2,700 **DEADLINE:** None Specified
FIELD/MAJOR: All Areas Of Study

Scholarships for entering freshmen who have a high school GPA of at least 3.0 and ACT scores of 27 or SAT scores of 1110. Must be a U.S. citizen and and enrolled in full-time study. Renewable. Write to the address below for more information.

New Mexico Tech
Admission Office
Soccorro, NM 87801

3810

Presidential Scholarship

AMOUNT: Varies **DEADLINE:** Mar 1
FIELD/MAJOR: All Areas Of Study

Awards for incoming freshmen with a GPA of at least 3.5. Renewable with continued academic excellence. Write to the address below for more information.

Lake Erie College
Financial Aid Office
391 W. Washington St.
Painesville, OH 44077

3811

Presidential Scholarship

AMOUNT: $5,000 **DEADLINE:** None Specified
FIELD/MAJOR: All Areas Of Study

Award available to students with the highest academic credentials. Write to the address below for more information.

Carthage College
Financial Aid Office
Kenosha, WI 53140

3812

Presidential Scholarship, James Graham Brown Scholarship

AMOUNT: Varies **DEADLINE:**Mar 1
FIELD/MAJOR: All Areas Of Study

Scholarships are available at Kentucky Wesleyan College for undergraduate students, based upon academic excellence and school and community service. Write to the address below for details.

Kentucky Wesleyan College
Financial Aid Office
3000 Frederica Street
Owensboro, KY 42303

3813

Presidential Scholarships

AMOUNT: $4,500 (max) **DEADLINE:** Feb 1
FIELD/MAJOR: All Areas Of Study

Applicants must be incoming freshmen ranked in the upper 5% of their graduating class and have scored at least 26 on the ACT or 1000 on the SAT. Renewable. Write to the address below for details.

Mount Mercy College
Office Of Admission
1330 Elmhurst Dr., NE
Cedar Rapids, IA 52402

3814

Presidential Scholarships

AMOUNT: $6,000-$8,000 **DEADLINE:** Feb 15
FIELD/MAJOR: All Areas Of Study

Scholarships for outstanding entering freshmen at Eckerd College. Based on academic achievement and demonstrated leadership and service. Twenty-five awards given per year. Write to the address below for details.

Eckerd College
Director Of Financial Aid
P.O. Box 12560
St. Petersburg, FL 33733

3815

Presidential Scholarships

AMOUNT: $26,000 (max) **DEADLINE:** Feb 1
FIELD/MAJOR: All Areas Of Study

Scholarships are renewable each year, contingent upon the student maintaining a 3.0 GPA. Winners for the scholarship will be chosen on the basis of high school record, test scores, recommendations, extracurricular activities, and scores on a scholarship examination administered during the competition. Write to the address below for details.

Rochester Institute of Technology
Bausch & Lomb Center
Financial Aid Office
60 Lomb Memorial Drive
Rochester, NY 14623

3816

Presidential Scholarships

AMOUNT: $2,000-$3,000 **DEADLINE:** None Specified
FIELD/MAJOR: All Areas Of Study

Scholarships available for students at Geneva College who demonstrate high academic achievement and financial need. Contact the Office of Admissions for further information.

Geneva College
Office Of Admissions
Beaver Falls, PA 15010

3817

Presidential Scholarships

AMOUNT: $5,000 **DEADLINE:** Mar 1
FIELD/MAJOR: All Areas Of Study

Scholarships available at Sterling for undergraduate full-time students who demonstrate a record of leadership in school, church, and community. Must have a minimum GPA of at least 3.75 and an ACT score of 29 or SAT score of at least 1210. Renewable. Write to the address below for details.

Sterling College
Financial Aid Office
Sterling, KS 67579

3818

Presidential Scholarships

AMOUNT: $3,000 To Tuition **DEADLINE:** Jan 15
Field/Major: All Areas Of Study

Freshman applicants with a 3.7 GPA, SAT score of 1300, and rank-in-class in the upper one-tenth will be considered on a competitive basis. Not need-based. Write to the address below for additional information.

Loyola College In Maryland
Director Of Financial Aid
4501 North Charles St.
Baltimore, MD 21210

3819

Presidential Scholarships

AMOUNT: $5,000 **DEADLINE:** Feb 1
FIELD/MAJOR: All Areas Of Study

Awards for entering students based on academics. Must have a GPA of at least 3.6 and a minimum SAT score of 1180 or ACT score of 28. Renewable with continued academic achievement. Write to the address below for more information.

Rhodes College
Office Of Admissions
2000 North Parkway
Memphis, TN 38112

3820

Presidential Scholarships

AMOUNT: Tuition and Fees **DEADLINE:** Mar 1
FIELD/MAJOR: All Areas Of Study

Awards are available at Portland State University for high school seniors with a GPA greater than 3.75 and SAT scores higher than 1150 (ACT 27) whose names are submitted by their high school counselor. Extracurricular activities and community service activities are also evaluated. Write to the address below for more information.

Portland State University
Office Of Academic Affairs
3349 Cramer Hall
Portland, OR 97207

3821

Presidential Scholarships, Dean's Honors Program Scholarships

AMOUNT: $1,000-$3,000 **DEADLINE:** None Specified
FIELD/MAJOR: All Areas Of Study

Scholarships are available at the University of Iowa for entering freshmen who rank in the top 5% of their class, and whose ACT composite score is 30 or higher (or SAT of 1270 or better.) Write to the address listed below for information.

University of Iowa
Office Of Admissions
107 Calvin Hall
Iowa City, IA 52242

3822

Presidential, Academic Achievement, College Honor Scholarships

AMOUNT: $1,000-$2,000 **DEADLINE:** Apr 1
FIELD/MAJOR: All Areas Of Study

Scholarships are available at Evangel for freshmen/transfer students who demonstrate academic achievement in high school. Based upon a combination of GPA and test scores. Write to the address listed below for information.

Evangel College
Office Of Enrollment
1111 N. Glenstone
Springfield, MO 65802

3823

Presidents Achievement Award For Freshmen And Aggie Spirit Awards

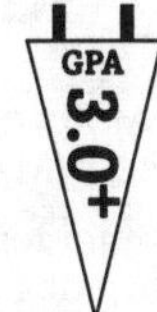

AMOUNT: $1,000-$3,000 **DEADLINE:** Jan 8
FIELD/MAJOR: All Areas Of Study

Four year scholarships are available for African American and Hispanic freshmen. Award is based on academic achievement, test scores, leadership skills, and class rank. Applicant must be a U.S.

citizen and have a GPA of at least 3.0. Write to the address below for details.

Texas A & M University
Department Of Student Financial Aid
College Station, TX 77843

3824

Presidents Research Fellowship

AMOUNT: $1,000 **DEADLINE:** Mar 1
FIELD/MAJOR: Home Economics

Open to Phi Upsilon Omicron members who are doing research at the master's or doctoral level. Research prospectus must accompany application. Based on use of funds, pertinence of research question, and personal qualifications. Write to the address below for details.

Phi Upsilon Omicron National Office
Ohio State University, 171 Mount Hall
1050 Carmack Road
Columbus, OH 43210

3825

Presidents Scholarships At Case Western

GPA 3.5+

AMOUNT: $12,600 **DEADLINE:** Feb 1
FIELD/MAJOR: All Areas Of Study

Scholarships are awarded to entering freshmen who rank in the top 10% of their high school graduating class and who have composite SAT scores of at least 1450 or a composite ACT score of 33. A cumulative GPA of 3.4 is required for renewal. Write to the address below for details.

Case Western Reserve University
Office Of Financial Aid, 109 Pardee Hall
10900 Euclid Avenue
Cleveland, OH 44106

3826

Press Club Of El Paso Scholarship

AMOUNT: $900 (max) **DEADLINE:** None Specified
FIELD/MAJOR: Journalism

Scholarship available for El Paso County resident juniors and seniors pursuing a career in journalism, preferably print media, print photography or electronic media at the University of Texas El Paso. Write to the address listed below for additional information.

Press Club Of El Paso Scholarship Fund
El Paso Community Foundation
201 East Main, Suite 1616
El Paso, TX 79901

3827

Presser Foundation Scholarship

AMOUNT: $2,250 **DEADLINE:** Mar 1
FIELD/MAJOR: Music

Award for a student at Eastern New Mexico University who is majoring in music and completing their junior year of study. Must have at least 1/3 of accumulated credit hours in subjects outside the field of music. Write to the address below for more information.

Eastern New Mexico University
College Of Fine Arts, Station 16
Portales, NM 88130

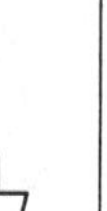

3828

Presser Scholarship

AMOUNT: Varies **DEADLINE:** Mar 1
FIELD/MAJOR: Music

Awards at the University of New Mexico for music students who have successfully completed their junior year. Write to the address below for more information.

University Of New Mexico, Albuquerque
Office Of Financial Aid
Albuquerque, NM 87131

3829

Principal Scholarships

GPA 3.0+

AMOUNT: Varies **DEADLINE:** Mar 1
FIELD/MAJOR: All Areas Of Study

Awards for incoming freshmen with a GPA between 3.25 and 3.5. Renewable with continued academic excellence and full-time enrollment. Write to the address below for more information.

Lake Erie College
Financial Aid Office
391 W. Washington St.
Painesville, OH 44077

3830

Printing Industries Of The Carolinas Scholarships

AMOUNT: None Specified **DEADLINE:** Dec 15
FIELD/MAJOR: Printing

Scholarships are available to students at Appalachian State University who are printing majors. Write to the address listed below for information.

Appalachian State University
Department Of Technology
Boone, NC 28608

3831

Printing, Publishing And Packaging Scholarships

AMOUNT: $500-$4,000 **DEADLINE:** Jan 10
FIELD/MAJOR: Printing, Publishing, and Packaging

Nation-wide competition open to students interested in a career in graphic communication. Student must submit application, transcripts, at least two letters of recommendation, and a copy of intended course of study. Number of awards: 100-150 ranging in value from $500 to $4,000. Scholarship renewable if recipient maintains a high scholastic average and continues approved program. Awards are given to college seniors planning to continue graduate study and students currently enrolled in a graduate program. Write to the address below for more information.

National Scholarship Trust Fund Of The Graphic Arts
4615 Forbes Avenue
Pittsburgh, PA 15213

3832

Priscilla Maxwell Endicott Scholarship Fund

AMOUNT: $500-$1,500 **DEADLINE:** Apr 20
FIELD/MAJOR: All Areas Of Study

Award for female high school seniors or women enrolled in college. Must have a standing as an amateur woman golfer, demonstrate financial need, scholastic achievement, and provide letters of recommendation from a teacher and a golf pro or coach. Must also be a resident of Connecticut. Contact your high school guidance counselor for further information and an application or write to the address below.

Connecticut Women's Golf Association
PME Scholarship Fund
1321 Whittemore Rd.
Middlebury, CT 06762

3833

Priscilla R. Morton Scholarship

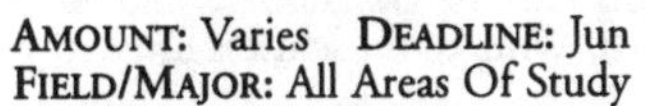

AMOUNT: Varies **DEADLINE:** Jun 1
FIELD/MAJOR: All Areas Of Study

Scholarships are available for Methodist students, who are U.S. citizens and enrolled in an accredited institution. Preference is given to students with a GPA of 3.5 or higher attending United Methodist schools. Write to the address listed below for information.

General Board Of Higher Education and Ministry
Office Of Loans And Scholarships
P.O. Box 871
Nashville, TN 37202

3834

Private Fellowships, Scholarships, Grants, and Assistantships

AMOUNT: Varies **DEADLINE:** Varies
FIELD/MAJOR: All Areas Of Study

Wide variety of scholarships available for students at SUNY-Syracuse. Criteria for these awards varies. Contact the financial aid office at the address below, the alumni office, and your major department to find out about these scholarships.

State University Of New York College At Cortland
Financial Aid Office
Bray Hall
Syracuse, NY 13210

3835

Pro Deo And Pro Patria Scholarships

AMOUNT: $1,500 **DEADLINE:** Mar 1
FIELD/MAJOR: All Areas Of Study

Scholarships for high school seniors planning on attending a Catholic college in the U.S. Must be a member of the Knights of Columbus or the child of an active or deceased knight. Twelve of the sixty-two awards are for use at the Catholic University of America, the remainder are for use at other Catholic colleges or universities. Renewable for up to four years. Write to the address below for details. Similar awards, Percy J. Johnson Scholarships and Canadian Scholarship Program (for study in Canada), are also offered by the K of C.

Knights Of Columbus
Director Of Scholarship Aid
P.O. Box 1670
New Haven, CT 06507

3836

Pro-Therapy Student Advance Program

AMOUNT: Varies **DEADLINE:** None Specified
FIELD/MAJOR: Physical Or Occupational Therapy

Awards for students in their final year of physical/occupational therapy school. In return for receiving the award, the student makes a commitment to become a member of the Pro-Therapy Traveling Team, upon graduation, for a period of one year. Write to the address below for more information.

Pro-Therapy Of America, Inc.
P.O. Box 1600
Birmingham, MI 48012

3837

Procter & Gamble Oral Health/ADHA Institute Scholarship Program

AMOUNT: $1,000 **DEADLINE:** June 15
FIELD/MAJOR: Dental Hygiene

Scholarships for full-time students studying toward a degree/certificate in dental hygiene. Must have a GPA of at least 3.0 and show evidence of community service, leadership, and/or extracurricular activities. Write to the address below for more information.

American Dental Hygienists' Association Institute For Oral Health
444 N. Michigan Ave., Suite 3400
Chigago, IL 60611

3838

Proctor & Gamble Oral Health/ADHA Institute Scholarship Program

AMOUNT: $1,000 **DEADLINE:** May 1
FIELD/MAJOR: Dental Hygiene

Applicants must have a minimum GPA of 3.0 and a 3.0 in natural science courses. Student must be planning to major in dental hygiene. Twenty-five awards of $1,000 each offered in nation-wide competition. Application will be available in guidance offices or students may write for an application packet. Write to Beatrice H. Pedersen, Associate Administrator, at the address below for more details.

ADHA Institute For Oral Health
444 N. Michigan Ave., Suite 3400
Chicago, IL 60611

3839

Proctor And Gamble Professional Opportunity & APS Student Awards

AMOUNT: $500 **DEADLINE:** None Specified
FIELD/MAJOR: Psychology

Awards are available for predoctoral students who are the first authors of an abstract submitted to the APS and are within 12-18 months of completing the Ph.D. degree. Applicants must be a member of or supported by a member of the APS and be a U.S. citizen or permanent resident. Write to the address below for more information.

American Psychology Society
9650 Rockville Pike
Bethesda, MD 20814

3840

Production Assistantships

AMOUNT: $1,000 **DEADLINE:** None Specified
FIELD/MAJOR: Design

Assistantships for students in the Department of Theatre and Dance at the University of Alabama at Birmingham. For production work on costumes and sets for the department. Write to the address below for information.

University Of Alabama, Birmingham
Department Of Theatre and Dance
700 13th Street South, UAB Station
Birmingham, AL 35294

3841
Professional Awards

AMOUNT: $1,000 **DEADLINE:** Mar 1
FIELD/MAJOR: Dentistry, Law, Medicine, Nursing, Pharmacy

Awards for Maryland residents studying in any of the areas above and who attend a Maryland institution. Applicants can be undergraduates or graduate students, but they must be enrolled full-time. Write to the address below for more information.

Maryland Commission On Higher Education
State Scholarship Administration
16 Francis St.
Annapolis, MD 21401

3842
Professional Church Work Grant

AMOUNT: $3,500 **DEADLINE:** None Specified
FIELD/MAJOR: Christian Service, Education, Social Work

Awards for students at Concordia University, Oregon who indicate an intent to serve the Lord Jesus Christ in a Lutheran Church Missouri Synod ministry (i.e. pastor teacher, director of Christian education or social worker). You will receive guaranteed $3,500 per year as part of your financial assistance. Write to the address below for more information.

Concordia University, Oregon
Office Of Admissions
2811 NE Holman St.
Portland, OR 97211

3843
Professional Churchwork Grant

AMOUNT: $750 **DEADLINE:** None Specified
FIELD/MAJOR: Religious Work

Awards for full-time undergraduates who are members of the Lutheran Church-Missouri Synod, who declare their intent and commitment to enter full-time professional church work. Renewable upon conditions set up by the dean. Write to the address below for more information.

Concordia College, Nebraska
Office Of Financial Aid
800 N. Columbia Ave.
Seward, NE 68434

3844
Professional Development Fellowship For Artists And Art Historians

AMOUNT: $5,000 **DEADLINE:** Jan 31
FIELD/MAJOR: Art, Art History

Fellowships are available for minority art and art history majors in the final year of graduate study. Applicants must be U.S. citizens or permanent residents and be able to demonstrate financial need. Write to the address listed below for information.

College Art Association Fellowship Program
275 Seventh Avenue
New York, NY 10001

3845
Professional Development Fellowship In American Art

AMOUNT: $5,000 **DEADLINE:** Jan 31
FIELD/MAJOR: American Art, Art History Or Conservation, Museum Studies

Fellowships are available for students in the fields above in their graduate years of study. Applicants must be U.S. citizens and be able to demonstrate financial need. Write to the address listed below for information.

College Art Association Fellowship Program
275 Seventh Avenue
New York, NY 10001

3846
Professional Education Scholarship For Graduate Study

AMOUNT: $1,000 **DEADLINE:** May 1
FIELD/MAJOR: Journalism

Must be a women member of NFPW with a B.A. or B.S. and two years' membership. Based on academic and professional performance, career potential, and financial need. Write to the address below for details.

National Federation Of Press Women
Box 99
Blue Springs, MO 64013

3847
Professional Engineers Of Oregon Scholarship

AMOUNT: $1,000 **DEADLINE:** Spring
FIELD/MAJOR: Engineering, Computer Science

Awards are available to students majoring in engineering or computer science with upper division standing. Must have graduated from an Oregon high school, be an Oregon resident, and a U.S. citizen. Contact the Dean's Office at the address below for more information.

Portland State University
Engineering And Applied Sciences
118 Science Building 2
Portland, OR 92707

3848
Professional Fellowship

AMOUNT: $8,000 **DEADLINE:** Mar 1
FIELD/MAJOR: Art, Fine Arts, Art History, Photography, Film Making, And Video

Fellowships are available to professional artists, to aid them in their careers. Must be a Virginia resident. Write to the address below for more information.

Virginia Museum Of Fine Arts
Office of Education And Outreach
2800 Grove Ave.
Richmond, VA 23221

3849

Professional Grounds Management Society Scholarship

AMOUNT: Varies **DEADLINE:** Jan 15
FIELD/MAJOR: Turfgrass Management, Landscape and Grounds Mgt., Irrigation Tech.

Awards for Stockbridge students in one of the fields listed above. Contact the Director, Stockbridge School, for more information.

University Of Massachusetts, Amherst
Director, Stockbridge School
Amherst, MA 01003

3850

Professional Growth Scholarship

AMOUNT: $500 **DEADLINE:** Apr 15
FIELD/MAJOR: Food Service/Management

For graduate students who must have a minimum 2.7 GPA, must be a member of the American School Food Service Association or a child of a member, and plan to have a career in food service. Renewable. Write to the address below for additional information.

American School Food Service Association
Scholarship Committee
1600 Duke Street, 7th Floor
Alexandria, VA 22314

3851

Professional Land Surveyors Of Oregon Scholarships

AMOUNT: None Specified **DEADLINE:** Mar 1
FIELD/MAJOR: Surveying

Scholarships for Oregon residents who are majoring in surveying. Must intend to pursue a career in land surveying. Must be entering junior or senior year in the fall at an Oregon college. Contact your financial aid office, or write to the address below for details.

Oregon State Scholarship Commission
Attn: Grant Department
1500 Valley River Dr., #100
Eugene, OR 97401

3852

Professional Nurse Traineeship

AMOUNT: $2,000-$6,000 **DEADLINE:** None Specified
FIELD/MAJOR: Nursing

Open to full-time graduate nursing students. Must be licensed registered nurse to apply. Funds are awarded based on availability and demonstrated need. Write to the address below for more details.

Rush University
Office Of Student Financial Aid
1743 West Harrison St.
Chicago, IL 60612

3853

Professional Secretaries Int'l Kohala Coast Chapter Scholarship

AMOUNT: $250-$500 **DEADLINE:** Feb 15
FIELD/MAJOR: Business Administration, Secretarial Science, Office Administration

Scholarships are available at the University of Hawaii, Hilo for full-time students who are big island residents enrolled in one of the areas listed above. Write to the address listed below for information.

University Of Hawaii At Hilo
Gail Watson, President, PSI
P.O. Box 383598
Waikoloa, HI 96738

3854

Professional Training Grant Program

AMOUNT: $1,000 **DEADLINE:** Apr 15
FIELD/MAJOR: Library Science

Part- and full-time grants are available to master's degree candidates in library science. Recipient must commit to work in an Alabama public library for two years after graduation. Write to the address listed below for complete details.

Alabama Public Library Service
Fred. D. Neighbors, Asst. Director
6030 Monticello Drive
Montgomery, AL 36130

3855

Professor Arnold D. Rhodes Scholarship

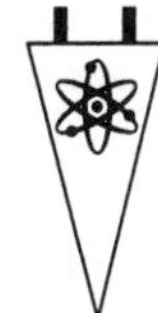

AMOUNT: None Specified **DEADLINE:** Dec 15
FIELD/MAJOR: Forestry

Scholarships are awarded to juniors or seniors who are majoring in forestry and demonstrate scholarship, need and leadership. Contact the Department Head, Forestry and Wildlife Management, for more information.

University of Massachusetts, Amherst
Department Of Forestry And Wildlife Mgmt
Amherst, MA 01003

3856

Program In Economic Policy Management

AMOUNT: Varies **DEADLINE:** Jan 15
FIELD/MAJOR: Economics, Business, Public Affairs

Graduate fellowships are available at Columbia to impart to young policy-makers the skills required to design and implement policy effectively in their home countries. Applicants must be nationals of a World Bank member country, with an undergraduate degree in economics and recent experience in a public agency or a non-governmental organization. Write to the address listed below for information.

Columbia University / World Bank
Program In Economic Policy Management
1013 International Affairs Building
New York, NY 10027

3857

Program On Nonviolent Sanctions, Pre And Postdoctoral Fellowships

AMOUNT: Varies **DEADLINE:** Jan 15
FIELD/MAJOR: Arms Control and Disarmament

Residential fellowships at the center for international affairs of Harvard for Ph.D. candidates (course work completed before beginning of fellowship) and postdoctoral scholars. Supports research on the degree to which, and how, nonviolent direct action provides an alternative to violence in resolving the problems of totalitarian rule, war, genocide, and oppression. Contact

Dr. Ted MacDonald at the address below for program details and application guidelines. Persons interested in applying should contact the program director to discuss research project before compiling application.

Harvard University, Center For International Affairs
CFIA Student Programs And Fellowships
1737 Cambridge St.
Cambridge, MA 02138

3858

Progressive Farmer Magazine Scholarships

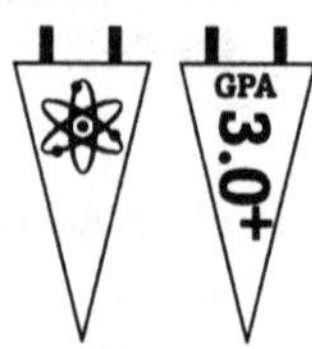

AMOUNT: $1,500 **DEADLINE:** Feb 15
FIELD/MAJOR: Agriculture, Agribusiness

Scholarships are available for FFA members pursuing a four-year degree in any area of agriculture or agribusiness. Must have a GPA of at least 3.0. Write to the address below for details.

National FFA Foundation
Scholarship Office
P.O. Box 15160
Alexandria, VA 22309

3859

Project 21 Poster And Essay Scholarship

AMOUNT: $1,000 **DEADLINE:** Jun 21
FIELD/MAJOR: Commercial Art, Creative Writing

Scholarships are available to the ten winners of the Project 21 Poster and Essay Contest. Applicants must submit a poster which must have been displayed in their school, or an essay, which must have been published in the school newspaper, on the issue of underage casino gambling. Must reside in New York, Connecticut, Delaware, D.C., Maryland, New Jersey, or Pennsylvania. Write to the address listed below for information. Students who are high school students as well as college undergraduates attending school in the states listed above are eligible.

Harrah's Casino Hotel
James E. Butler, Esquire, Legal Dept.
1725 Brigantine Blvd.
Atlantic City, NJ 08401

3860

Project Grants

AMOUNT: $3,000-$10,000 **DEADLINE:** Nov 1
FIELD/MAJOR: Byzantine Studies, Pre-Columbian Studies, Landscape Architecture

Grants available to assist with scholarly projects in the above fields. Projects supported are generally related to the study and or excavation of a site (byzantine, pre-columbian, or garden) but other relevant projects will be considered. Write to the address below for details.

Dumbarton Oaks
Office Of The Director
1703 32nd Street, NW
Washington, DC 20007

3861

Pronet Engineering Scholarship

AMOUNT: $2,500 **DEADLINE:** None Specified
FIELD/MAJOR: Engineering

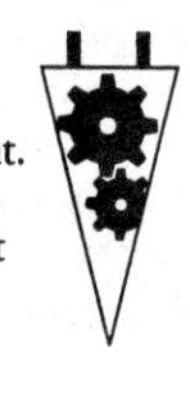

Awards for junior or senior engineering students who have a career objective in the field of business management. Applicants must attend an ABET approved school of engineering, be U.S. citizens, and have a GPA of at least 3.0. Write to the address below for more information.

National Society Of Professional Engineers
1420 King St.
Alexandria, VA 22314

3862

Prospective Teacher Research Initiative

AMOUNT: $2,703 **DEADLINE:** Varies
FIELD/MAJOR: Teaching

Research project open to minority students enrolled in a pre-service teacher education program at UW. Applicants should express interest in teaching life sciences at the K-12 level and demonstrate an interest in participating in a research program. Each perspective teacher will be paid $8.75 per hour, not to exceed $2,703 for a minimum eight-week summer experience. Write to the address below for more details.

University Of Wyoming
Div. Of Student Educational Opportunity
P.O. Box 3808
Laramie, WY 82071

3863

Prospective Teacher Scholarship Loan

AMOUNT: $2,000 (max) **DEADLINE:** None Specified
FIELD/MAJOR: Education

Any N.C. Resident enrolled in a education program at a North Carolina school is eligible to apply. Based on grades, standardized test scores, and recommendations. Must be a U.S. citizen and have a GPA of at least a 2.0. Renewable with a 2.5 GPA. You will be obligated to teach in a North Carolina public school one year for each year of assistance received after graduation. Write to the address below for complete details.

North Carolina Department Of Public Instruction
Division Of Teacher Education Services
301 North Wilmington Street
Raleigh, NC 27601

3864

Prospective Teacher Scholarship Loan

AMOUNT: None Specified **DEADLINE:** None Specified
FIELD/MAJOR: Education

Loans are available to students at Appalachian State University who plan to enter the teaching profession. Write to the address listed below for information.

Appalachian State University
Financial Aid Office
Scholarship Section
Boone, NC 28608

Proudfoot Scholarships

Amount: $200 **Deadline:** None Specified
Field/Major: Art

Scholarships are available at the University of Iowa for full-time undergraduate and graduate students majoring in art. Write to the address listed below for information.

University Of Iowa
School Of Art And Art History
E100 Art Building
Iowa City, IA 52245

Provident Scholarships

Amount: $5,000 (max) **Deadline:** Mar 28
Field/Major: All Areas Of Study

Scholarships are available for residents of Chattanooga, Tennessee, who graduated from Chattanooga public schools. Preference is given to African American students. Requires a minimum GPA of 2.5 and financial need. Write to the address listed below for information.

Community Foundation Of Greater Chattanooga, Inc.
1701 American Bank Building
736 Market Street
Chattanooga, TN 37402

Provost Scholars

Amount: None Specified **Deadline:** Feb 20
Field/Major: All Areas Of Study

Scholarships are available at the University of San Diego for handicapped or minority students with a GPA of at least 3.0 who have financial need. Write to the address listed below for information.

University Of San Diego
Office Of Financial Aid
5998 Alcala Park
San Diego, CA 92110

Provost Scholars

Amount: $2,500 **Deadline:** Mar 1
Field/Major: All Areas Of Study

Selected from applicants of African American, Hispanic, or Native American backgrounds. Must be ranked in the top 15% of your class and have an SAT score of at least 1019 or an ACT of 24. Write to the address below for more information.

Bradley University
Office Of Financial Assistance
Bradley University
Peoria, IL 61625

Provost's Scholarships At Case Western

Amount: $10,300 (max) **Deadline:** Feb 1
Field/Major: All Areas Of Study

Provost's scholarships are awarded to entering freshmen who rank in the top 15% percent of their high school graduating class and who have composite SAT scores of 1300 or a composite ACT score of 31. Student must maintain a 3.2 GPA to renew scholarship. Write to the address below for details.

Case Western Reserve University
Office Of Financial Aid, 109 Pardee Hall
10900 Euclid Avenue
Cleveland, OH 44106

3870

Psychology Departmental Scholarships

Amount: Varies **Deadline:** Feb 15
Field/Major: Psychology

Scholarships are available at the University of Utah for full-time students majoring in psychology. Write to the address below for information.

University Of Utah
Sally Ozonoff
502 Behavioral Science Building
Salt Lake City, UT 84112

PTC Research Prizes

Amount: $2,000 **Deadline:** Jun 30
Field/Major: Telecommunications Research

Awards are available for the authors of the best research papers concerning telecommunications concerns of the Pacific region. Must hold at least a bachelor's degree. Write to the address below for more information.

Pacific Telecommunications Council
2454 Beretania Street, Suite 302
Honolulu, HI 96826

3872

Public Accounting Scholarships

Amount: Varies **Deadline:** Mar 1
Field/Major: Accounting

Scholarship offered to freshman students attending or planning to attend Loyola University on a full-time basis, who will be majoring in accounting. Awards are offered on a competitive basis without regard to financial need and are renewable for up to three years. Write to the address below for details.

Loyola University Chairperson, Accounting Dept.
820 N. Michigan Avenue
Chicago, IL 60611

3873

Public Education And Citizenship Statewide Essay Contest

Amount: $500 **Deadline:** Feb 15
Field/Major: All Areas Of Study

Contest open to all graduating high school seniors in the state of Florida who will be attending a state-supported school in Florida. Recipients must enter the school within one quarter/semester (excluding summer) after they are awarded the scholarship. Write to the address below for more information.

Masons Of Florida Grand Lodge Of Florida
P.O. Box 1020
Jacksonville, FL 32201

3874

Public Health Student Recognition Award

AMOUNT: Varies **DEADLINE:** None Specified
FIELD/MAJOR: Public Health

Awards for students entering their sophomore, junior, or senior year in the field of public health. Based on GPA and service to the school and university. Contact the Dean, School of Public Health, for more information.

University Of Massachusetts, Amherst
Dean School Of Public Health
Amherst, MA 01003

3875

Public Interest Law Graduate Fellow/Staff Attorney Fellowships

AMOUNT: $29,900 **DEADLINE:** Nov 15
FIELD/MAJOR: Law (Public Policy, Communications)

Two-year postgraduate (i.e., post-JD/LLB) residential fellowships for law students. Provides extensive training and experience in public interest advocacy in the federal courts, administrative agencies, and legislative bodies. Fellows receive an LLM in advocacy at the end of the fellowship term. Four fellowships per year (2-3 were available for the 1993-95 term). Write to the address below for details.

Georgetown University Law Center
Institute For Public Representation
600 New Jersey Ave., NW, Suite 312
Washington, DC 20001

3876

Public Investor Scholarship

AMOUNT: $3,000 **DEADLINE:** Feb 18
FIELD/MAJOR: Public Or Business Administration, Finance, Social Sciences

Scholarship for graduate students in the above areas of study who are planning to pursue a career in state or local government finance. For full- or part-time study. Must have superior academic record. One award per year. For U.S. or Canadian citizens or permanent residents. Information may be available from the head of your accounting department. If not, write to the address below. Applications are available in November for awards in the following spring.

Government Finance Officers Association
Scholarship Committee
180 N. Michigan Avenue, Suite 800
Chicago, IL 60601

3877

Public Library Section Scholarship

AMOUNT: $200 **DEADLINE:** Mar 1
FIELD/MAJOR: Library Sciences

Grants for students of library sciences who have been employed in a Kentucky library for at least one year. Approximately three awards per year. Write to the address below for details.

Kentucky Library Association
Mr. Tom Underwood, KLA 1501
Twilight Trail
Frankfort, KY 40601

3878

Public Service War Orphans Scholarship Program

AMOUNT: Varies **DEADLINE:** None Specified
FIELD/MAJOR: All Areas Of Study

For residents of Massachusetts who are enrolled in any postsecondary institution. Student must be between the ages of 16 and 24 years, and the dependent child of a veteran who died during service. Write to the address below for details.

Massachusetts Board Of Regents Of Higher Education
State Scholarship Office
330 Stuart St.
Boston, MA 02116

3879

Pullman Foundation Scholarship

AMOUNT: Varies **DEADLINE:** None Specified
FIELD/MAJOR: All Areas Of Study

Scholarships are available at the University of Illinois for Illinois residents who are graduating high school seniors. Nominated by high school. Based on grades, financial need, and extracurricular activities. Also available to descendents of graduates of the Pullman Free School of manual training. Must be Cook County residents. Contact your high school guidance counselor or the address below for more information.

George M. Pullman Educational Foundation
5020 South Lake Shore Drive
Chicago, IL 60615

3880

Pulp And Paper Foundation Scholarships

AMOUNT: $1,000 **DEADLINE:** Feb 1
FIELD/MAJOR: Pulp and Paper Related, Engineering

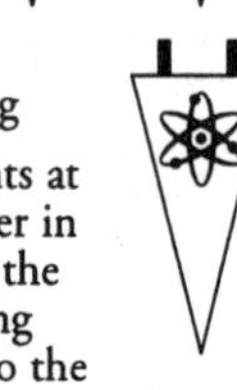

Scholarships are available for undergraduate students at the University of Maine who wish to pursue a career in the pulp and paper industry. Freshmen must be in the upper 10% of their high school class and continuing students must have a GPA of 2.6 or better. Write to the address listed below for information.

University Of Maine Pulp And Paper Foundation
5737 Jenness Hall
Orono, ME 04469

3881

Pulp And Paper Merit Scholarships

AMOUNT: Varies **DEADLINE:** Jan 15
FIELD/MAJOR: Pulp and Paper Industry

Scholarships for high school seniors who are going to major in a curriculum which could lead to the study of the pulp and paper industry. Must have a GPA of at least a 3.0 and be accepted into North Carolina state university. Based primarily on merit. Write to the address below for more information.

North Carolina State University
Pulp And Paper Foundation, Inc.
P.O. Box 8005
Raleigh, NC 27695

3882

Purina Mills Research Fellowship

Amount: $12,500 **Deadline:** Feb 6
Field/Major: Animal Science and Nutrition

Fellowships for graduate students conducting research relating to the field of nutrition and companion animal sciences. For full-time study. Based on application, transcripts, grade reports, recommendations, and research proposal. Write to the address below to request an application packet.

Purina Mills, Inc.
Purina Research Awards Committee
P.O. Box 66812,
c/o Joan Roslauski-2E
St. Louis, MO 63166

3883

Purina Mills, Inc. Scholarships

Amount: $1,000 **Deadline:** Feb 15
Field/Major: Animal Science, Agribusiness

Scholarships are available for FFA members pursuing a degree in animal science or agribusiness. Applicant must have competed in the livestock contest above the local level. Write to the address below for details.

National FFA Foundation
Scholarship Office
P.O. Box 15160
Alexandria, VA 22309

3884

PWP International Scholarship Program

Amount: None Specified **Deadline:** Mar 15
Field/Major: All Areas Of Study

Scholarships for children, under the age of 25, of members of Parents Without Partners. For undergraduate study. Number of awards is up to six throughout the organization; one for every 4,000 members in each zone. Information can be obtained from your parent's chapter (in the chapter newsletter, or from the chapter president).

Parents Without Partners
International Scholarship Program
401 North Michigan Ave.
Chicago, IL 60611

3885

Quaker Chemical Foundation Scholarship Grants

Amount: None Specified **Deadline:** None Specified
Field/Major: All Areas Of Study

Applicants must be undergraduate children of Quaker Chemical employees. Write to the address below for details.

Quaker Chemical Foundation
Mary Lou Mcclain, Foundation Secretary
P.O. Box 809
Conshohocken, PA 19428

3886

Quality Stores, Inc. Scholarships

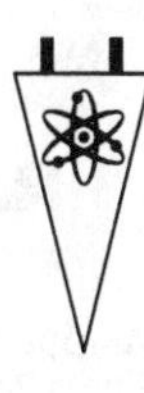

Amount: $1,000 **Deadline:** Feb 15
Field/Major: Agribusiness

Scholarships are available for FFA members pursuing a four-year degree in agribusiness, who reside in Indiana, Michigan, or Ohio. Write to the address below for details.

National FFA Foundation
Scholarship Office
P.O. Box 15160
Alexandria, VA 22309

3887

Queen Elizabeth Of Belgium Scholarship

Amount: Varies **Deadline:** Mar 1
Field/Major: Music

Awards at the University of New Mexico for music students with talent and financial need. Must be recommended by a faculty member. Write to the address below for more information.

University Of New Mexico, Albuquerque
Office Of Financial Aid
Albuquerque, NM 87131

3888

Questar Scholarship

Amount: $1,000 (max) **Deadline:** Feb 1
Field/Major: Engineering

Scholarships are available at the University of Utah for full-time students enrolled in an engineering program who demonstrate financial need. Write to the address below for details.

University Of Utah Dean's Office, College Of Engineering
2202 Merrill Engineering Building
Salt Lake City, UT 84112

3889

R. Boyd Gunning Scholarship

GPA 3.5+

Amount: $2,000 **Deadline:** May 4
Field/Major: All Areas Of Study

Scholarships are available at the University of Oklahoma, Norman, for entering freshmen with a 3.75 or better GPA. Write to the address listed below for information.

University Of Oklahoma, Norman
Honors Program
347 Cate Center
Norman, OK 73019

3890

R. Gordon Kennedy Criminal Justice Scholarship

Amount: Varies **Deadline:** None Specified
Field/Major: Criminal And Social Justice

Award for students at Mercyhurst who are pursuing a career in the field of criminal and social justice. Write to the address below for more information.

Mercyhurst College
Financial Aid Office
Glenwood Hills
Erie, PA 16546

3891

R. Ray Singleton Memorial Fund

AMOUNT: None Specified **DEADLINE:** Mar 15
FIELD/MAJOR: All Areas Of Study

Scholarships for greater Kanawha Valley residents who are attending a college or university in the state of West Virginia. For undergraduate and graduate studies. Based on need. Write to the address below for details.

Greater Kanawha Valley Foundation
Scholarship Committee
P.O. Box 3041
Charleston, WV 25331

3892

R.B. Pamplin Corporation Scholarships

AMOUNT: $2,500 **DEADLINE:** Feb 1
FIELD/MAJOR: All Areas Of Study

Awards for sophomores who have demonstrated academic achievement as well as community and college service. Renewable with continued academic merit. Write to the address below for complete details.

Lewis And Clark College
Office of Admissions
Portland, OR 97219

3893

R.C. Rogers, Sr. Memorial Scholarships

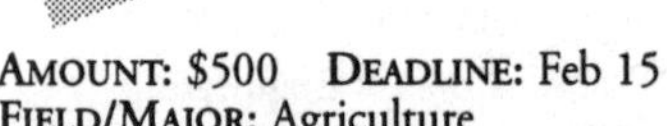

AMOUNT: $500 **DEADLINE:** Feb 15
FIELD/MAJOR: Agriculture

Scholarships are available for FFA members pursuing a two- or four-year degree in any area of agriculture, who reside in South Carolina. Preference will be given to students from Dillon County. Write to the address below for details.

National FFA Foundation
Scholarship Office
P.O. Box 15160
Alexandria, VA 22309

3894

R.L. Gillette Scholarship

AMOUNT: $1,000 **DEADLINE:** Apr 1
FIELD/MAJOR: Music, Literature

Must be legally blind woman enrolled in an four-year baccalaureate degree program in literature or music. Student must submit a sample performance tape (not to exceed thirty minutes) or a creative writing sample. Applicant must be a U.S. citizen. Two awards are offered annually. Write to the address below for complete details.

American Foundation For The Blind
Scholarship Coordinator
11 Penn Plaza, Suite 300
New York, NY 10011

3895

R.N. Baccalaureate Program-State Of Maine

AMOUNT: None Specified **DEADLINE:** Apr 15
FIELD/MAJOR: Registered Nursing

Scholarships for Maine residents in a four-year nursing program in the state of Maine. Write to the address below for details.

Odd Fellows and Rebekahs Nursing Scholarship Program
Ms. Ellen F. Washburn
22 Munsey Ave.
Livermore Falls, ME 04254

3896

R.W. Bob Holden Scholarship

AMOUNT: $250-$1,000 **DEADLINE:** Jun 30
FIELD/MAJOR: Hotel Management

Scholarships for Hawaii residents studying hotel management. Must have a GPA of at least 2.8.

Hawaii Hotel Association
Ms. Susan Haramoto
2270 Kalakaua Ave., Suite 1103
Honolulu, HI 96815

3897

Radcliffe Research Support Program

AMOUNT: $5,000 (max)
DEADLINE: Oct 15, Apr 15
FIELD/MAJOR: History Of Women, Human Development

This program offers grants to postdoctoral investigators for research drawing on the Center's data resources. The center is a national repository for social science data on human development and social change, particularly the changing life experience of American women.

Radcliffe College
Henry A. Murray Research Center
10 Garden Street
Cambridge, MA 02138

3898

Radford University Foundation Scholarships And Awards

AMOUNT: Varies **DEADLINE:** Mar 1
FIELD/MAJOR: All Areas Of Study

Awards and scholarships are available for students at Radford University. There are many different awards available with varying criteria.

Radford University
Office Of Financial Aid
Radford, VA 24142

3899

Radford University Grant

AMOUNT: Varies **DEADLINE:** Mar 1
FIELD/MAJOR: All Areas Of Study

Awards for legal residents of Virginia who attend Radford University. Must demonstrate financial need.

Radford University
Office Of Financial Aid
Radford, VA 24142

3900

Ragan-Thieme Scholarship

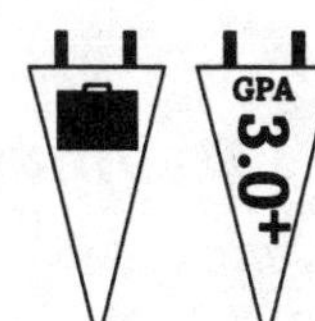

AMOUNT: $250-$500
DEADLINE: None Specified
FIELD/MAJOR: Business

Student must be a full-time sophomore or above COBA major from a southwest Missouri high school with a minimum 3.0 GPA. Contact the COBA office for more information.

Southwest Missouri State University
Office Of Financial Aid
901 South National Ave.
Springfield, MO 65804

3901

Rain Bird Company Scholarship

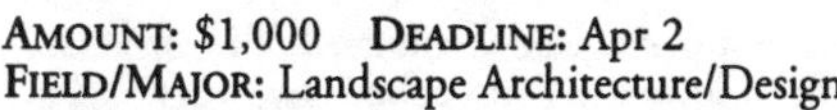

AMOUNT: $1,000 **DEADLINE:** Apr 2
FIELD/MAJOR: Landscape Architecture/Design

Applicants must be in their third, fourth, or fifth year of study and demonstrate financial need.

Landscape Architecture Foundation
4401 Connecticut Ave., NW, Suite 500
Washington, DC 20008

3902

Rainy River Scholarships

AMOUNT: Varies **DEADLINE:** None
FIELD/MAJOR: All Areas Of Study

Scholarships for students at Rainy River Community College. Several different awards are available. Criteria vary.

Rainy River Community College
Highway 11 and 71
International Falls, MN 56649

3903

Ralph And Carol Williams Management Scholarship

AMOUNT: $700 **DEADLINE:** None Specified
FIELDS/MAJORS: Management

Student must be a full-time junior or senior management major with a GPA of 3.1 or better. Preference is given to members of Delta Sigma Pi. Contact the COBA office for more information.

Southwest Missouri State University
Office Of Financial Aid
901 South National Ave
Springfield, MO 65804

3904

Ralph W. Stone Award

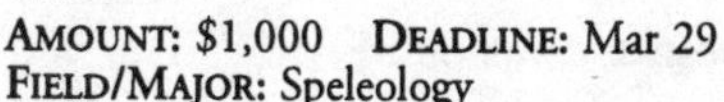

AMOUNT: $1,000 **DEADLINE:** Mar 29
FIELD/MAJOR: Speleology

Scholarship for cave-related thesis research in the biological, social, or earth sciences. The applicant must submit a proposal and be member of the National Speleological Society.

National Speleological Society
Dr. Carol M. Wicks
University of Missouri, 101 Geology Bldg.
Columbia, MO 65211

3905

Rand Institute College Scholarship Essay Contest

AMOUNT: $5,000 (max) **DEADLINE:** Apr 15
FIELD/MAJOR: All Areas Of Study

Essay contest for high school juniors and seniors. Based on 2-4 page paper on a topic relating to Ayn Rand's novel, "The Fountainhead." ten-3rd place, five-2nd place, and one first place award. See your literature/English teacher for details.

Ayn Rand Institute
The Fountainhead Essay Contest
P.O. Box 6004 Ef
Inglewood, CA 90312

3906

Rand Institute College Scholarship Essay Contest

AMOUNT: $100, $200, $1,000 **DEADLINE:** Apr 1
FIELD/MAJOR: All Areas Of Study

Essay contest for high school juniors and seniors. Based on 2-3 page paper on a topic relating to Ayn Rand's novelette, "Anthem." Twenty-3rd place, ten-2nd place, and one first place award. See your literature/English teacher for details.

Ayn Rand Institute
Anthem Essay Contest
P.O. Box 6099
Inglewood, CA 90312

3907

Randy Wilt Memorial Scholarship

AMOUNT: Varies **DEADLINE:** Mar 1
FIELD/MAJOR: Engineering

Awards are available at the University of New Mexico for full-time junior or senior engineering students.

University of New Mexico, Albuquerque
Office Of Financial Aid
Albuquerque, NM 87131

3908

Rawley Silver Scholarship Fund

AMOUNT: None Specified **DEADLINE:** Jun 15
FIELD/MAJOR: Art Therapy

Scholarships for graduate students who have demonstrated academic excellence and are in an AATA-approved art therapy program. Applicants must demonstrate financial need in order to complete their program of study.

The American Art Therapy Association, Inc.
Scholarship Committee
1202 Allanson Road
Mundelein, IL 60060

3909

Ray Allen Billington Award

Amount: $400 **Deadline:** Jul 1
Field/Major: Western History

A cash award of $300 is given to the author and $100 to the publisher annually for the best article on western history. Write to the address listed below for information.

Western History Association
University Of New Mexico
1080 Mesa Vista Hall
Albuquerque, NM 87131

3910

Ray and Susie Forsythe Scholarship

Amount: $1,750 **Deadline:** None Specified
Field/Major: Business

Student must be a junior or senior COBA major with leadership characteristics and a GPA of 3.3 or better. Preference is given to SMSU varsity athletes, one being a graduate of Springfield public schools. Contact the COBA office for more information.

Southwest Missouri State University
Office Of Financial Aid
901 South National Ave.
Springfield, MO 65804

3911

Ray Glynn Scholarship

Amount: $500 **Deadline:** Nov 1
Field/Major: Gemology

Awards are available for students enrolled in a GIA Distance Education program. Recipient must be a legal resident of the state of Alaska, Idaho, Oregon, Montana, or Washington. For use in a GIA course of diamonds, colored stones, or gem identification. Must be a U.S. citizen or permanent resident. Write to the address below for more information.

Gemological Institute Of America
Office Of Student Financial Assistance
1660 Stewart St.
Santa Monica, CA 90404

3912

Ray Woodham And Nellie Huntsinger Scholarships

Amount: Varies **Deadline:** Mar 1
Field/Major: Nursing

Awards are available at the University of New Mexico for full-time nursing students with a minimum GPA of 2.5 and financial need. Write to the address below or contact the school of nursing for more details.

University of New Mexico, Albuquerque
Office of Financial Aid
Albuquerque, NM 87131

3913

Raymond Davis Scholarship

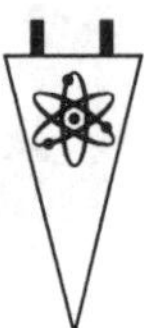

Amount: $1,000 (min) **Deadline:** Dec 15
Field/Major: Imaging Science/Photogrammetry

Scholarships for undergraduate juniors or seniors or graduate students for full-time continuing studies in imaging technology sciences. Write to the address below for complete details.

Society For Imaging Science And Technology
Membership Office
7003 Kilworth Lane
Springfield, VA 22151

3914

Raymond E. Page Scholarship Fund

Amount: $500 **Deadline:** Apr 2
Field/Major: Landscape Architecture/Design

These awards are for any students who are in need of financial assistance regardless of scholastic ability. Must submit two-page explanation describing financial need and how the money is to be used. One scholarship is given to an undergraduate. One scholarship is given to a graduate student. Write to the address below for details.

Landscape Architecture Foundation
4401 Connecticut Ave., NW, Suite 500
Washington, DC 20008

3915

Raymond H. Trott Scholarship Fund

Amount: $500 **Deadline:** May 1
Field/Major: Banking

Scholarships are available for residents of Rhode Island who preparing for a career in banking. Write to the address listed below for information.

Rhode Island Foundation
70 Elm Street
Providence, RI 02903

3916

Raymond Shoemaker Scholarship Program

Amount: Varies **Deadline:** Mar 1
Field/Major: All Areas Of Study

Awards are available at the University of New Mexico for students who are single parents and residents of New Mexico. Must be a U.S. citizen. Write to the address below for more information.

University Of New Mexico, Albuquerque
Office Of Financial Aid
Albuquerque, NM 87131

3917

Real Estate And Land Use Institute Scholarships

Amount: $935 (max) **Deadline:** Apr 30
Field/Major: Real Estate

Scholarships for minority undergraduate or graduate students studying toward a career in real estate at any campus of California State University. Undergraduate students must have a GPA of at least 2.25; graduate students, a GPA of at least 3.0. Renewable. $60,300 total available to be awarded. Write to the address below for details.

California State University—Real Estate and Land Use Institute
Scholarship Selection Committee
7750 College Town Drive, Suite 102
Sacramento, CA 95826

3918

Real-time Information Program For Upperclassmen & Graduate Students

AMOUNT: $1,000 **DEADLINE:** Nov 15
FIELD/MAJOR: Electronic Media (Not Including Broadcasting)

Awards are available for juniors, seniors, or graduate students who work as interns in electronic media. Recipients are paid regular wages for their summer work and upon returning to school, the students will receive a $1,000 scholarship. Must be a U.S. citizen to apply. Applications are only available from September 1 through November 1. Write to the address below for more information.

Dow Jones Newspaper Fund
P.O. Box 300
Princeton, NJ 08543

3919

Recognition Awards

AMOUNT: $2,500 **DEADLINE:** Apr 15
FIELD/MAJOR: All Areas Of Study

Awards available at Loras College to high school seniors who rank in the top 20% of their class and have a GPA of at least 3.5 with an ACT score of 24 or SAT score of 1050. Write to the address below for details.

Loras College
Office Of Financial Planning
1450 Alta Vista St., P.O. Box 178
Dubuque, IA 52004

3920

Recreation And Leisure Departmental Scholarships

AMOUNT: Varies **DEADLINE:** Feb 15
FIELD/MAJOR: Recreation And Leisure Studies

Scholarships are available at the University of Utah for full-time students enrolled in a recreation and leisure program. Write to the address below for details.

University Of Utah
Dr. John Crossley
226 Hpern
Salt Lake City, UT 84112

3921

Red "Kiwanis" Crawford Scholarship

AMOUNT: $1,250 **DEADLINE:** None Specified
Field/Major: Electronics Technology

Awards for students at Mesa State College who are Colorado residents and are in the electronics technology program. Contact the United Technical Educational Center (UTEC) on campus for further details.

Mesa State College
Financial Aid Office
P.O. Box 2684
Grand Junction, CO 81501

3922

Red Barker Radio Scholarships

AMOUNT: $300 **DEADLINE:** Mar 1
FIELD/MAJOR: Telecommunications

Awards for juniors and seniors majoring in telecommunications who plan to pursue a career in sports broadcasting Must have a GPA of at least 2.8 and have demonstrated financial need. Write to the address below for more information.

University Of Florida
Knight Scholarship And Placement Director
2070 Weimer Hall
Gainesville, FL 32611

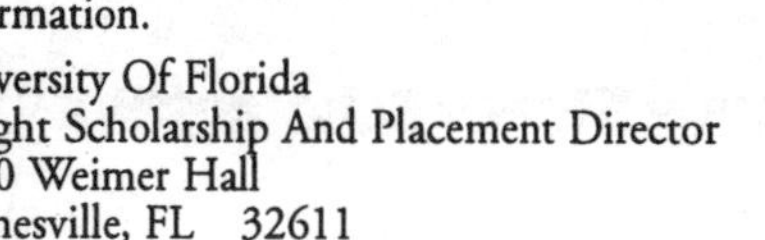

3923

Red Crawford Tennis Awards

AMOUNT: $1,000 **DEADLINE:** None Specified
FIELD/MAJOR: All Areas Of Study

Awards for students at Mesa State College who are active in the tennis program. Must have and maintain a GPA of at least 2.0 and be full-time students. Contact the physical education department/tennis coach for further details.

Mesa State College
Financial Aid Office
P.O. Box 2684
Grand Junction, CO 81501

3924

Reed Scholarship

AMOUNT: $1,000 **DEADLINE:** None Specified
FIELD/MAJOR: Engineering

Scholarships are available at the University of Iowa for full-time sophomore engineering students from Iowa, with preference given to residents of Tama County. Applicant must have a GPA of at least 2.7. Write to the address listed below for information.

University Of Iowa
Student Services, College Of Engineering
3100 Engineering Building
Iowa City, IA 52242

3925

Reference Service Press Fellowship

AMOUNT: $2,000 **DEADLINE:** May 31
FIELD/MAJOR: Library Science

Awards for college seniors or graduates who have been accepted into an accredited MLS program. Must be a California resident or attending a school in California. Request an application form and further information from the address below.

California Library Association
Scholarship Committee
717 K St., Suite 300
Sacremento, CA 95814

3926

Reforma Scholarship Program

AMOUNT: $1,000 (min) **DEADLINE:** May 15
FIELD/MAJOR: Library Science

Awards are available for college seniors or graduate level students

accepted into an ALA-accredited graduate program. Applicants must speak Spanish and be U.S. citizens or permanent residents. Must also show evidence of commitment and desire to serve the Spanish-speaking community. Write to the address below for more information.

National Association To Promote Library Services To The Spanish Speaking
Yolanda Marino Fonseca, Chair
2407 Ridgeway
Evanston, IL 60201

3927

Regent Drug Stores Scholarship

AMOUNT: Varies **DEADLINE:** Mar 1
FIELD/MAJOR: Pharmacy

Awards are available at the University of New Mexico for pharmacy students graduating from New Mexico high schools. Must show promise for the practice of the pharmacy profession and financial need. Write to the address below for more information.

University Of New Mexico, Albuquerque
Office Of Financial Aid
Albuquerque, NM 87131

3928

Regent's Scholars

AMOUNT: $5,400 **DEADLINE:** Dec 1
FIELD/MAJOR: All Areas Of Study

Scholarships are available at the University of New Mexico for entering freshmen who are National Merit, National Achievement, or National Hispanic finalists; valedictorians; or who have a GPA of at least a 3.9. Renewable for up to three more years. Fifteen awards are offered annually. Write to the address listed below for information.

University Of New Mexico, Albuquerque
Student Financial Aid Office
Mesa Vista Hall North, Student Services
Albuquerque, NM 87131

3929

Regents Graduate/Professional Fellowships

AMOUNT: $3,500 (max) **DEADLINE:** Mar 1
FIELD/MAJOR: All Areas Of Study

Scholarships are available to Ohio resident graduate students who continue their education in an Ohio school. Based upon academic ability. Write to the address listed below for information, or your school financial aid office.

Ohio Student Aid Commission
Customer Service
P.O. Box 16610
Columbus, OH 43216

3930

Regents Health Care Scholarships For Medicine Or Dentistry

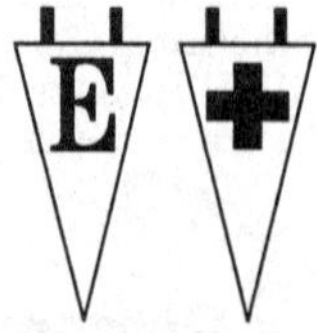

AMOUNT: $1,000-$10,000 **DEADLINE:** Mar 1
FIELD/MAJOR: Medicine/Dentistry

Program for minority residents of New York for at least one year preceding date of award. Students must be enrolled in/accepted to approved medical/dental school in NY. Must agree to practice in a designated shortage area for at least twenty-four months. Renewable. Must be a U.S. citizen or legal resident. Write to the address below for complete details.

New York State Education Department
Bureau Of Postsecondary Grants Admin.
Cultural Education Center
Albany, NY 12230

3931

Regents Physician Loan Forgiveness Program

AMOUNT: $10,000 (max) **DEADLINE:** Apr 1
FIELD/MAJOR: Medicine

Must agree to practice medicine in an area of New York state for a period of 24 months for each award received. Must have completed residency training in medicine within the five years immediately preceding the period for which the award is granted. Be licensed to practice medicine in New York prior to beginning the service commitment. Must be a legal resident of New York. May not have ever received a regents physician shortage scholarship. Preference will be given to applicants who have completed a residency in family practice or primary care. Eighty awards per year.

New York State Education Department
Bureau Of Postsecondary Grants Admin.
Cultural Education Center
Albany, NY 12230

3932

Regents Professional Opportunity Scholarships

AMOUNT: $1,000-$5,000 **DEADLINE:** May 1
FIELD/MAJOR: All Areas Of Approved Study

Minority U.S. citizen or legal resident. NY resident (at least one yr.) enrolled in a NY institution in program requiring state license. Typical fields are vet. medicine, medicine, pharmacy, engineering, dental hygiene, physical therapy, etc. For undergraduate or graduate-level study. Must agree to practice in New York state for at least one year. Write to the address below for details.

New York State Education Department
Bureau Of Postsecondary Grants Admin.
Cultural Education Center
Albany, NY 12230

3933

Regents Scholarship Program

AMOUNT: Tuition And Fees **DEADLINE:** Dec 1
FIELD/MAJOR: All Areas Of Study

Scholarships at UM College Park for excellent high school seniors. Recipients receive full financial support for 4 years, admission to the University Honors Program, eligibility for honors housing, and a $1,000 stipend. Based on GPA, SAT scores, and the rigor of their academic program. Write to the address below for details.

University Of Maryland, College Park
Office Of Student Financial Aid
0102 Lee Building
College Park, MD 20742

3934

Regents Scholarships

AMOUNT: $1,000 To Tuition **DEADLINE:** Jan 15
FIELD/MAJOR: All Areas Of Study

Scholarships for outstanding freshmen at UNL. Must be a graduate of a Nebraska high school with a GPA of at least a 3.0. For full-time study only. Renewable with a minimum undergraduate GPA of 3.5. Write to address below for more information.

University Of Nebraska, Lincoln
Office Of Scholarships And Financial Aid
16 Administration Bldg., P.O. Box 880411
Lincoln, NE 68588

3935

Regents Scholarships

GPA 3.5+

AMOUNT: $500-$14,968 **DEADLINE:** Nov 30
FIELD/MAJOR: All Areas Of Study

Scholarships are available at UCSD for entering freshman who have demonstrated high scholastic aptitude and exceptional test scores. Applicants must have a minimum GPA of 3.86. Eligible applicants are automatically considered for this scholarship upon applying to UCSD.

University Of California, San Diego
Student Financial Services
9500 Gilman Drive
La Jolla, CA 92093

3936

Regents Scholarships In Cornell University

GPA 3.0+

AMOUNT: $1,000 (max) **DEADLINE:** Apr 1
FIELD/MAJOR: All Areas Of Study

Scholarships for New York state residents who are or will be studying at Cornell University. Based upon academic ability and ACT/SAT scores. Over 61 awards per year. Write to the address listed below for additional information.

New York State Education Department
Bureau of Postsecondary Grants Admin.
Cultural Education Center
Albany, NY 12230

3937

Regents' Scholars Program For Transfer Students

GPA 3.5+

AMOUNT: $5,400 **DEADLINE:** Dec 1
FIELD/MAJOR: All Areas Of Study

Scholarships are available at the University of New Mexico for transfer students with a GPA of at least 3.90. Write to the address listed below for information.

University Of New Mexico, Albuquerque
Student Financial Aid Office
Mesa Vista Hall North, Room 1044
Albuquerque, NM 87131

3938

Regents' Scholarships, Chancellor's Scholarships

GPA 3.5+

AMOUNT: $500 **DEADLINE:** Mar 2
FIELD/MAJOR: All Areas Of Study

Scholarships are available at the University of California, Berkeley for entering freshmen and transfer students with a GPA of at least 3.8, demonstrated academic ability, and future potential. Write to the address below for complete details.

University Of California, Berkeley
Office Of Financial Aid
Room 211, Sproul Hall
Berkeley, CA 94720

3939

Regents'/Trustees' Scholarships

AMOUNT: $6,500 Per Year **DEADLINE:** Feb 1
FIELD/MAJOR: All Areas Of Study

Scholarships for entering freshmen who have demonstrated superior academic achievement in high school and who have the ability to become leaders at CBU or SJU. Applicants must have a GPA of at least 3.6 or be in the top 5% of their high school class and have an ACT score of 30 or SAT score of 1340 or better. Also based on faculty interviews conducted in early and mid-February. Renewed automatically with satisfactory academic progress. Write to the address below for more information.

College Of Saint Benedict And Saint John's University
Office Of Financial Aid
37 South College Ave.
St. Joseph, MN 56374

3940

Regional Scholarships

GPA 3.0+

AMOUNT: $5,000 **DEADLINE:** Feb 15
FIELD/MAJOR: All Areas Of Study

Awards for entering freshwomen who have demonstrated superior scholastic achievement and distinguished themselves in their extracurricular activities or personal interests. Must have a GPA of 3.2 from high school and an SAT score of at least 1100. Write to the address below for additional information.

Mills College
Office Of Financial Aid
5000 MacArthur Blvd.
Oakland, CA 94613

3941

Regular Membership Fellowships

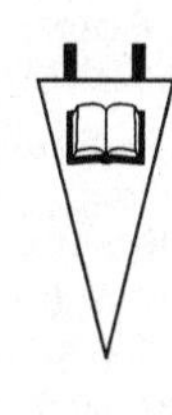

AMOUNT: $6,640 and Fees **DEADLINE:** Jan 5
FIELD/MAJOR: Classical Studies

Awards are available for graduate students in classical studies in the U.S. or Canada. Based on transcripts, recommendations, and examinations. Write to the address below for more information.

American School Of Classical Studies At Athens
Committee On Admissions And Fellowships
993 Lenox Drive, Suite 101
Lawrenceville, NJ 08648

3942

Reimbursement of Fire Fighters

AMOUNT: $2,620 (max) **DEADLINE:** Jul 1
FIELD/MAJOR: Fire Science, Paramedical

Applicants must be pursuing a degree in fire fighting or other safety majors at a Maryland school and agree to serve in Maryland as fire fighter or rescue squad member.

Maryland residency is also required. Write to the address below for details.

Maryland State Higher Education Commission
16 Francis Street
Annapolis, MD 21401

3943

Religious Service Award

AMOUNT: $500 **DEADLINE:** None Specified
FIELD/MAJOR: All Areas Of Study

Students must be full-time currently volunteering their services in church-related activities. Renewable. Write to the address below for more information.

Silver Lake College
Student Financial Aid Office
2406 South Alverno Rd.
Manitowoc, WI 54220

3944

Renal Physiology Section Award For Excellence In Renal Research

AMOUNT: $200 **DEADLINE:** None Specified
FIELD/MAJOR: Renal Physiology

Awards are available to students interested in renal physiology. The recipient must be the first author on the abstract presented at the APS annual meeting. Selection based on abstract, as well as oral presentation. Write to the address below for more information.

American Psychology Society
Membership Services Office
9560 Rockville Pike
Bethesda, MD 20814

3945

Research And Education Grant

AMOUNT: $5,000 (max) **DEADLINE:** Jan 31
FIELD/MAJOR: Science, Horticulture

Graduate and postdoctoral grants are available for scholars with a proposed program of scientific, academic, or artistic investigation of herbal plants. Write to the address listed below for information.

Herb Society of America, Inc.
Research And Education Grants
9019 Kirtland Chardon Road
Kirtland, OH 44094

3946

Research Assistance

AMOUNT: $500 (max) **DEADLINE:** Nov 1, Mar 1
FIELD/MAJOR: Japanese Studies

Small grants are available for a variety of scholarly needs that are not covered by other funding sources, such as research assistance and manuscript typing. Applicants must clearly explain what the funds would be used for. Write to the address below for more information.

Northeast Asia Council Association For Asian Studies
1 Lane Hall
University Of Michigan
Ann Arbor, MI 48109

3947

Research Awards And Grants Program

AMOUNT: Varies **DEADLINE:** Varies
FIELD/MAJOR: Respiratory Disease, Medical Research, Epidemiology

Awards for scholars with two years of research experience or for doctoral candidates. Programs for funding include research training, pediatric pulmonary research, nursing research, Dalsemer Scholar, Career Investigator Research Grant, and Behavioral Science Dissertation Grant. Must be a Canadian citizen or a U.S. citizen or permanent resident. Write to the address below for information.

American Lung Association
Medical Affairs Division
1740 Broadway
New York, NY 10019

3948

Research Awards At The Huntington Library

AMOUNT: $1,800/month **DEADLINE:** Dec 15
FIELD/MAJOR: American and British Literature, Art, Science, and Culture

For doctoral and postdoctoral students. Awards are for work which will sufficiently utilize the Huntington collections. Applications should include a project outline, the period of proposed residence at the library, personal data, previous scholarly work and references. For scholars of high merit. Write to the address below for complete details.

Huntington Library, Art Collections, And Botanical Gardens
Committee On Awards
1151 Oxford Road
San Marino, CA 91108

3949

Research Fellowship And Grant Awards

AMOUNT: $10,000 (max) **DEADLINE:** Oct 2
FIELD/MAJOR: Dermatology Research

Awards are to initiate research projects in dermatology. Applicant must designate a preceptor who holds, or hold him/herself, an appointment in a division or department of dermatology. Research must be performed in the U.S. or Canada. Only one grant application or two fellowship applications will be accepted from any one institution. Please write to the address below for complete details.

Dermatology Foundation
Medical And Scientific Committee
1560 Sherman Ave.
Evanston, IL 60201

3950

Research Fellowships And Grants (HDSA)

AMOUNT: $35,500 (max) **DEADLINE:** None Specified
FIELD/MAJOR: Medical Research

Neuromuscular Grants and Fellowships for current Ph.D. or M.D. Holders. Supports basic and applied research into causes and treatments of Huntington's Disease. Must be affiliated with a medical school, university, or research institution. Write to the society at the address below for details.

Huntington's Disease Society Of America
140 W. 22nd Street
New York, NY 10011

3951

Research Fellowships In American History And Culture

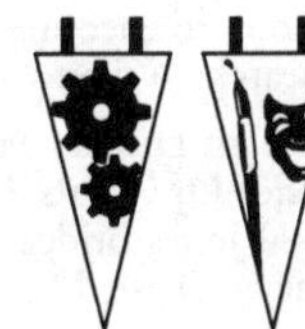

AMOUNT: $1,350/month **DEADLINE:** Feb 1
FIELD/MAJOR: American History And Culture, Architectural History, Art History, Etc.

Fellowships are available for pre- and postdoctoral scholars to support research at the Library Company of Philadelphia in one of the areas listed above. Applicants are urged to inquire about the appropriateness of the research topic prior to applying. Call 215-546-3181 for information and to discuss your proposed research topic or write to the address below.

Library Company Of Philadelphia
James Green, Assistant Librarian
1314 Locust Street
Philadelphia, PA 19107

3952

Research Fellowships In Marine Policy and Ocean Management

AMOUNT: $36,600 **DEADLINE:** Jan 15
FIELD/MAJOR: Marine Policy, Ocean Management, Etc.

Recent doctorates and persons having similar qualifications through work experience in social and natural sciences are eligible for this fellowship. Fellows from many different disciplines utilize their skills to examine economic, political, legal, and environmental effects from uses of the world's oceans. Some programs are held in conjunction with M.I.T. Write to the Dean of Graduate studies at the address below for details.

Woods Hole Oceanographic Institution
Dean of Grad. Studies, Education Office
Clark Laboratories
Woods Hole, MA 02543

3953

Research Fellowships In New England History And Culture

AMOUNT: $750 / Month **DEADLINE:** Jan 31
FIELD/MAJOR: History-New England

Research fellowships are available for graduate and postgraduate scholars conducting research into the history of New England, at the Peabody Essex Museum. Stipends will be awarded for up to two months. Write to the address listed below for information.

Peabody Essex Museum
Fellowship Program
East India Square
Salem, MA 01970

3954

Research Grant Competition For New Investigators

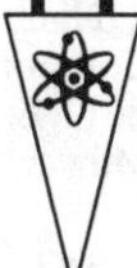

AMOUNT: $4,000 **DEADLINE:** Jul 12
FIELD/MAJOR: Speech Science, Audiology

Research grant for scholarly research by students who have received his/her master's or doctoral degree in the fields of study above. Based on academic abilities and proposed project. Students enrolled in a degree program or who have received prior funding for research are ineligible for this award. Write to the address below for more information.

American Speech-Language-Hearing Foundation
10801 Rockville Pike
Rockville, MD 20852

3955

Research Grants

AMOUNT: $1,465 (avg.) **DEADLINE:** Feb 15
FIELD/MAJOR: Geology

Open to any master's or doctoral student at universities in the USA, Canada, Mexico, or Central America. Award is intended to help support thesis research. GSA membership is not required. Approximately 250 awards per year. Write for complete details. Application forms should be available from your department or from the campus GSA representative. If necessary, write to the Research Grants Administrator, at the address below.

Geological Society Of America
3300 Penrose Place, P.O. Box 9140
Boulder, CO 80301

3956

Research Grants

AMOUNT: $400-$2,000 **DEADLINE:** None Specified
FIELD/MAJOR: U.S. Military And Naval History

Awards are available for graduate students who are researching some aspect of military history relevant to the Marine Corps. Students are expected to do some portion of their research in the Marine Corps Historical Center and in the other federal archival centers in Washington DC. Write to the address listed below for information

Marine Corps Historical Center
Building 58, Washington Navy Yard
Washington, DC 20374

3957

Research Grants/New Investigator Grants

AMOUNT: $30,000 (max) **DEADLINE:** Sep 1
FIELD/MAJOR: Medical Research-Cystic Fibrosis

Grants are available for developing and initially testing new hypotheses and methods (or those being applied to CF for the first time) intended to enable the investigator to collect sufficient data to compete successfully for long-term support from the NIH. Awards of up to $30,000 per year for two years may be requested. Write to the address below for details.

Cystic Fibrosis Foundation
Office Of Grants Management
6931 Arlington Rd.
Bethesda, MD 20814

3958

Research Grants Program

AMOUNT: $2,500 (max) **DEADLINE:** Oct 1
FIELD/MAJOR: Librarianship

Students must be attending a participating ALISE member school. Awards are given to support specific research projects or for outstanding Ph.D. dissertations. Applicants must be members of ALISE as of the Oct 1 deadline. Write to the address below for details.

Association For Library And Information Science Education-ALISE
4101 Lake Boone Trail, Suite 201
Raleigh, NC 27607

3959
Research In The Biology of Aging

Amount: $1,500-$5,500 **Deadline:** Feb 26
Field/Major: Geriatrics

Open to Ph.D. and medical students at any level to undertake a three-month research project on any subject related to the basic science of aging. Write to the address below for more information.

AFAR/Glenn Foundation
1414 Avenue Of The Americas
New York, NY 10019

3960
Research Professorships

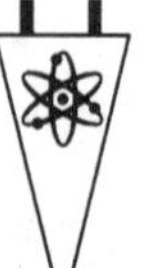

Amount: $40,000 (max) **Deadline:** Sep 30
Field/Major: Mathematics

Awards for scholars who have earned their Ph.D. in the field of mathematics. The award is limited to a ceiling of $40,000 and normally will not exceed half of the applicant's salary. Write to the address below for more information.

Mathematical Sciences Research Institute
1000 Centennial Dr. #5070
Berkeley, CA 94720

3961
Research Seed Grants

Amount: $25,500 (avg) **Deadline:** Nov 1
Field/Major: Engineering

Graduate and postgraduate grants for research projects in the general field of engineering to qualified individuals, organizations, and technical societies. Ten awards per year. Usually, these serve as seed grants for research that is unlikely to be funded by other organizations. Most recipients are new faculty and new investigators. Write to the address below for complete details.

Engineering Foundation
United Engineering Center
345 E. 47th St.
New York, NY 10017

3962
Research Support Grants

Amount: $18,000-$22,000 **Deadline:** Dec 1
Field/Major: Humanities And Certain Related Fields

Fellowships are available at the Getty Center to support scholars and advanced students who are unaffiliated with the center to pursue short-term research projects using the resources of the Center's collections. Write to the address listed below for information.

Getty Center For The History Of Art And The Humanities
The Scholars And Seminars Program
401 Wilshire Blvd., Suite 1000
Santa Monica, CA 90401

3963
Research Training Fellowships For Medical Students

Amount: $15,000 **Deadline:** Varies
Field/Major: Medicine

Fellowships for doctoral candidate students enrolled in medical school, to encourage more M.D.s to pursue a career in biological research. Write to address below for further information.

Howard Hughes Medical Institute
Office Of Grants And Special Programs
4000 Jones Bridge Road
Chevy Chase, MD 20815

3964
Research Travel Within The U.S.A.

Amount: $1,500 (max) **Deadline:** Nov 1, Mar 1
Field/Major: Japanese Studies

Awards for graduate students who are engaged in scholarly research on Japan and wish to use museum, library, or other archival materials located in the U.S.A. Applicants must be U.S. citizens or permanent residents. Though primarily to support postdoctoral research on Japan, Ph.D. candidates may also apply. Write to the address below for more information.

Northeast Asia Council Association For Asian Studies
1 Lane Hall
University of Michigan
Ann Arbor, MI 48109

3965
Resident Fellowships For Unaffiliated Scholars

Amount: $250 Per Quarter **Deadline:** Jan 20
Field/Major: History, Humanities, Linguistics

Fellowships are available for postdoctoral research for scholars who are not employed as such, and who have held a Ph.D. for at least two years. Applicants must be working on a research project in a field appropriate to the Newberry's Collections. Write to the address below for details.

Newberry Library
Committee On Awards
60 W. Walton St.
Chicago, IL 60610

3966
Respiratory Diseases Research Award

Amount: $25,000 **Deadline:** Feb 15
Field/Major: Allergy/Immunology Medical Research

Grants for members of the American Academy of Allergy and Immunology (or persons who are awaiting acceptance into the academy) who are M.D.s or Ph.D.s, associated with an approved allergy and immunology or clinical and laboratory immunology training program. Write to the address below for details.

American Academy Of Allergy And Immunology / Allen And Hanburys
Committee Chair To Grant Research Awards
E611 E. Wells Street
Milwaukee, WI 53202

3967
Retired Officers Association Student Loans

Amount: $2,500 (max) **Deadline:** Mar 1
Field/Major: All Areas Of Study

Loans for dependent sons and daughters (under 24 years old) of members of the Retired Officers Association. For undergraduate study. Renewable. Applicants must never have been married and have a GPA of at least 3.0. Write to the address below for details. Persons applying for these loans are automatically considered for special grant programs.

Retired Officers Association
Administrator, Scholarship Loan Program
201 N. Washington St.
Alexandria, VA 22314

3968

Rev. And Mrs. Earl V. Willett Endowed Grant Fund

Amount: Varies **Deadline:** None Specified
Field/Major: All Areas Of Study

Awards are available for full-time students at Cedarville College who have a GPA of at least 2.0. Write to the address below for more information.

Cedarville College
Financial Aid Office
P.O. Box 601
Cedarville, OH 45314

3969

Rev. James Anderson/ American Chemical Society Award

Amount: $1,000 **Deadline:** None Specified
Field/Major: Chemistry

Awards are available at Portland State University for students who intend to pursue a career in chemistry. Academic excellence is a primary consideration. Contact the Chemistry Department at the address below for more information.

Portland State University
Chemistry Department
262 Science Building 2
Portland, OR 97207

3970

Reverend Ernest F. Smith Scholarship

Amount: None Specified **Deadline:** None
Field/Major: All Areas Of Study

Awards for students at Mercyhurst College, based on academic promise and financial need. Write to the address below for details.

Mercyhurst College
Glenwood Hills
Erie, PA 16546

3971

Reverend Uvaldo Martinez Memorial Scholarship

Amount: Varies **Deadline:** Mar 1
Field/Major: Nursing

Awards are available at the University of New Mexico for full-time female nursing students with a minimum GPA of 2.5 and financial need. Applicants must be Spanish-speaking and desire to enter the field of public health nursing in New Mexico. Write to the address below or contact the school of nursing for more details.

University Of New Mexico, Albuquerque
Office Of Financial Aid
Albuquerque, NM 87131

3972

Revolution Masonic Lodge Scholarship

Amount: None Specified **Deadline:** None Specified
Field/Major: All Areas Of Study

Scholarships are available for members and their families of the Revolution Masonic Lodge in Greensboro, North Carolina. Write to the address below for details.

Tannenbaum-Sternberger Foundation
Robert O. Klepfer, Jr.
P.O. Box 3112
Greensboro, NC 27402

3973

Rex L. Inman Memorial Scholarship

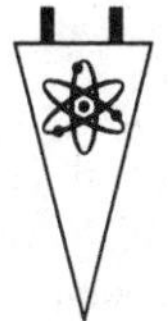

Amount: Varies **Deadline:** Apr 1
Field/Major: Meteorology

Scholarships are available at the University of Oklahoma, Norman, for full-time meteorology majors, who are incoming freshmen. Write to the address listed below for information.

University of Oklahoma, Norman
Director, School Of Meteorology
Energy Center Tower, Room 1310
Norman, OK 73019

3974

Rex T. Roberts Scholarship

Amount: $1,000 **Deadline:** Apr 15
Field/Major: Advertising, Consumer-Related Communications Field

Scholarships are for a junior or senior college student, permanent resident of the U.S., and a record of high academic achievement. Contact IPCC Scholarship Chairperson, 535 S. Illinois St., Indianapolis, IN 46225-1192 for more details.

Indiana University Purdue University, Indianapolis
Purdue School Of Technology
799 West Michigan St.
Indianapolis, IN 46202

3975

Rho Chi/AFPE/Merck First Year Graduate Scholarship

Amount: $7,500 **Deadline:** Jan 15
Field/Major: Pharmaceutical Sciences

Open to graduate students accepted to/enrolled in accredited school of pharmacy. Must be a U.S. citizen or permanent resident. Applications available through your local chapter of Rho Chi Society, or write to the address below.

Rho Chi Pharmacy Honor Society
Robert D. Sinedelar, Ph.D.; Sec., Rho Chi
University Of Mississippi, Pharmacy School
University, MS 38677

3976

Rhode Island Higher Education Assistance Authority Scholarships

Amount: $250-$700 **Deadline:** Mar 1
Field/Major: All Areas Of Study

Rhode Island resident who is enrolled or plans to enroll at least 1/2 time at an eligible postsecondary institution. Must demonstrate financial need. For study at a vocational-technical school, community college, or 4-year college. U.S. citizen, national or permanent resident. Renewable. Write to the address below for complete details.

Rhode Island Higher Education Assistance Authority
560 Jefferson Blvd.
Warwick, RI 02886

3977

Rhode Island Polonia Undergraduate Scholarships

AMOUNT: $500 **DEADLINE:** Feb 15
FIELD/MAJOR: All Areas Of Study

Awards for Rhode Island students of Polish-American descent who are planning to enroll in an accredited postsecondary institution of either two- or four-year study. Write to the address below or call (401) 831-7177 for more information.

Rhode Island Polonia Scholarship Foundation
Foundation Office
866 Atwells Ave.
Providence, RI 02909

3978

Rhode Island Summer Government Internship Program

AMOUNT: Varies **DEADLINE:** May 15
FIELD/MAJOR: All Areas Of Study

Internship program for Rhode Island residents who attend an out of state college or university. Applicants must have completed the sophomore year and have a 2.5 GPA or higher. Interns are able to work in a variety of local and state agencies. Write to the address below for more information.

State Of Rhode Island
Mr. Robert Gemma, Executive Director
State Capitol, Room 8AA
Providence, RI 02903

3979

Rhodes Awards

AMOUNT: $1,000-$4,000 **DEADLINE:** Feb 1
FIELD/MAJOR: All Areas Of Study

Awards for entering students based on academics. Must have a GPA of at least 3.0 and a minimum SAT score of 1140 or ACT score of 27. Renewable with continued academic achievement. Write to the address below for more information.

Rhodes College
Office Of Admissions
2000 North Parkway
Memphis, TN 38112

3980

Rice Scholarship

AMOUNT: Varies **DEADLINE:** Mid-Oct
FIELD/MAJOR: Animal Science, Equine Industries

Awards for UMass sophomores, juniors, or seniors in one of the fields listed above. Contact the Chair, Scholarship Committee, Veterinary and Animal Sciences for more information.

University Of Massachusetts, Amherst
Chair, Scholarship Committee
Veterinary And Animal Sciences
Amherst, MA 01003

3981

Rice-Cullimore Scholarship

AMOUNT: $2,000 **DEADLINE:** Feb 15
FIELD/MAJOR: Mechanical Engineering

Grants for foreign students studying mechanical engineering at a U.S. school on the graduate level. Applications are made through the Institute of International Education. Write to the address below for details.

American Society Of Mechanical Engineers Auxiliary, Inc.
345 E. 47th Street
New York, NY 10017

3982

Richard A. Benefield Scholarship

AMOUNT: $1,000 **DEADLINE:** Feb 9
FIELD/MAJOR: Business Management

Award for management majors who are seniors. Must have minimum GPA of 3.5 and be enthusiastic and dynamic. Use Bloomsburg University scholarship application. Contact Dr. Mark Larson, Associate Professor, Management Department, for any additional information.

Bloomsburg University
19 Ben Franklin Hall
400 E. Second St.
Bloomsburg, PA 17815

3983

Richard and Mary Olson Scholarship Fund

AMOUNT: Varies **DEADLINE:** None Specified
FIELD/MAJOR: All Areas Of Study

Awards available for junior or senior students at Cedarville College. Must have a GPA of at least 3.0 and demonstrated financial need. Write to the address below for more information.

Cedarville College
Financial Aid Office
P.O. Box 601
Cedarville, OH 45314

3984

Richard B. Combs Scholarships

AMOUNT: $750 **DEADLINE:** Mar 22
FIELD/MAJOR: Tourism

Applicant must be a graduating senior or have graduated from a Connecticut high school. Student must demonstrate financial need and provide a short essay. Contact the address below for further information and an application.

Connecticut Tourism Industry Committee
University Of New Haven-Dr. E.S. Van Dyke
300 Orange Ave.
New Haven, CT 06516

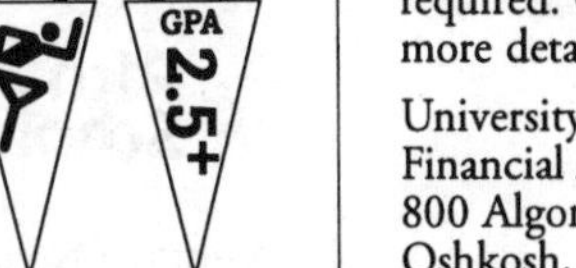

3985

Richard B. Williams

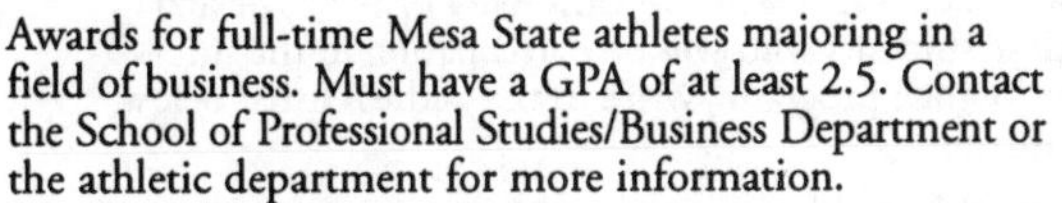

AMOUNT: Tuition And Fees
DEADLINE: None Specified
FIELD/MAJOR: Business

Awards for full-time Mesa State athletes majoring in a field of business. Must have a GPA of at least 2.5. Contact the School of Professional Studies/Business Department or the athletic department for more information.

Mesa State College
Office Of Financial Aid
P.O. Box 2647
Grand Junction, CO 81501

3986

Richard C. Flint Scholarship Fund

AMOUNT: None Specified **DEADLINE:** Apr 15
FIELD/MAJOR: Health Services, Industrial Relations, Human Resources, Public Service

Scholarships for West Virginia residents enrolled in the Health Services Administration Program or related programs at the West Virginia Institute of Technology. Four awards are offered. Write to the address below for details.

Greater Kanawha Valley Foundation
Scholarship Committee
P.O. Box 3041
Charleston, WV 25331

3987

Richard C. Maguire Scholarship

AMOUNT: $1,000 **DEADLINE:** Apr 15
FIELD/MAJOR: History And Related Fields

Scholarships for U.S. citizens doing postgraduate study in history or any related field. Must be pursuing a master's degree or higher. Based on grades career goals, recommendations, transcripts and extracurriculars. Write to the address below for details.

Rock Island Arsenal Museum
Richard C. Maguire Scholarship Committee
Atn: SIORI-CFM, Rock Island Arsenal
Rock Island, IL 61299

3988

Richard D. Irwin Doctoral Fellowships

AMOUNT: $2,000-$2,500 **DEADLINE:** Feb 15
FIELD/MAJOR: Business/Economics

Open to Ph.D. candidates in business or economics who have completed all work except the dissertation. Applicants must be nominated by the dean of their department. Write to the address below for details.

Richard D. Irwin Foundation
1333 Burr Ridge Parkway
Burr Ridge, IL 60521

3989

Richard Dale Buckley Scholarship

AMOUNT: $180 **DEADLINE:** Mar 1
FIELD/MAJOR: Elementary Education

Awards are available to senior elementary education majors with a minor in elementary social science. Minimum GPA of 3.0 is required. Contact Curriculum and Instruction, UW Oshkosh for more details.

University Of Wisconsin, Oshkosh
Financial Aid Office, Dempsey 104
800 Algoma Blvd.
Oshkosh, WI 54901

3990

Richard E. Bangert Business Award

AMOUNT: $1,000 **DEADLINE:** None Specified
FIELD/MAJOR: Business

Scholarships are available for junior business majors who are residents of Washington, who demonstrate exceptional academic ability. Award can be used at one of eight Washington colleges and universities. Contact the financial aid office of the school of your choice for details.

First Interstate Bank Of Washington Foundation
Administration
P.O. Box 160
Seattle, WA 98111

3991

Richard E. Merwin Scholarship

AMOUNT: $3,000 **DEADLINE:** May 31
FIELD/MAJOR: Engineering, Computer Science and Engineering, Design Automation

Scholarship open to at least junior level students in the fields listed above who are active members of the Computer Society student branch chapter at their institution. Applicants must have a minimum overall GPA of 2.5 for all undergraduate course work and be enrolled as a full-time student as defined by his or her academic institution during the course of the award. Write to the address below for details.

Institute of Electrical And Electronics Engineers, Inc.
IEEE Computer Society
1730 Massachusettes Avenue, NW
Washington, DC 20036

3992

Richard Epping Scholarships

AMOUNT: $2,000 **DEADLINE:** Jul 26
FIELD/MAJOR: Travel And Tourism

Awards for permanent residents of northern California/northern Nevada who are studying travel and tourism. Applicants must be enrolled in a travel and tourism curriculum in northern California/northern Nevada. Based on a 500-word essay. Write to the address below or contact your local chapter for more information.

American Society Of Travel Agents, Northern California Chapter
Scholarship Committee
1101 King St., Suite 200
Alexandria, VA 22314

3993

Richard F. Gilmore Sr., DDS Award

AMOUNT: $300 **DEADLINE:** None Specified
FIELD/MAJOR: Dentistry

Award for Mesa State College senior who is pursuing a career in dentistry. Applicant must have and maintain a GPA of at least 2.75 and be enrolled in the School of Natural Sciences and

Mathematics or Professional Studies/Nursing Area. Contact the School of Natural Sciences and Mathematics or Professional Studies/Nursing Area for more information.

Mesa State College
Office Of Financial Aid
P.O. Box 2647
Grand Junction, CO 81501

3994 Richard F. Walsh Foundation Scholarship

AMOUNT: $1,750 **DEADLINE:** Dec 31
FIELD/MAJOR: All Areas Of Study

Scholarship for sons and daughters of members in good standing of the International Alliance of Theatrical Stage Employees and Moving Picture Machine Operators of the U.S. and Canada (IATSE). Applicant must be a high school senior planning to enroll in a full-time program at any accredited college or university. Renewable. Write to the address below for complete details.

Richard F. Walsh Foundation
Foundation Office
1515 Broadway, Suite 601
New York, NY 10036

3995 Richard Fessenden Award

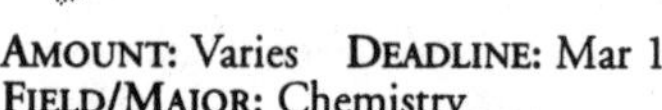

AMOUNT: Varies **DEADLINE:** Mar 1
FIELD/MAJOR: Chemistry

Awards for sophomores, juniors, or seniors in the Department of Chemistry. Contact the Chemistry Department for more information.

University Of Massachusetts, Amherst
Chemistry Department
Amherst, MA 01003

3996 Richard H. Plock Jr. Memorial Fund

AMOUNT: Varies **DEADLINE:** None Specified
FIELD/MAJOR: Political Science

Awards for full-time Mesa State juniors or seniors majoring in political science with an interest in state government. Must have a GPA of at least 2.5. Contact the Humanities or Social Science Department for more information.

Mesa State College
Office Of Financial Aid
P.O. Box 2647
Grand Junction, CO 81501

3997 Richard Klutznick Scholarship Fund

AMOUNT: $2,500 (max)
DEADLINE: None Specified
FIELD/MAJOR: Social Work

Applicants must be Jewish graduate students attending accredited schools of social work and have a record of good scholarship. Award recipients must agree to accept a two-year position with BBYO upon graduation. Write to the address below for details.

B'nai B'rith Youth Organization
1640 Rhode Island Ave., NW
Washington, DC 20036

3998 Richard L. Pribble Athletic Scholarship Fund

AMOUNT: None Specified **DEADLINE:** Mar 1
FIELD/MAJOR: All Areas Of Study

Scholarships are available at the University of New Mexico for full-time students who will be participating in the intercollegiate football program. Write to the address listed below for information.

University Of New Mexico, Albuquerque
Department Of Student Financial Aid
Mesa Vista Hall North
Albuquerque, NM 87131

3999 Richard M. Morrison Scholarship

AMOUNT: $1,000 **DEADLINE:** Apr 1
FIELD/MAJOR: Medicine, Nursing

Scholarship open to students from the Venice Hospital servicing area who are pursuing a degree of doctor of medicine or a bachelor's degree of nursing. Recipients must have an avowed interest to return to Venice, Florida, to practice and work upon graduation. Preference will be given to students attending institutions in Florida. Write to the address below for details.

Venice Hospital Foundation Women's Board
601 Tamiami Trail South, Suite A
Venice, FL 34285

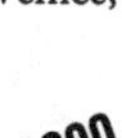

4000 Richard M. Weaver Fellowship and Salvatori Fellowship Awards Programs

AMOUNT: Varies **DEADLINE:** Jan 15
FIELD/MAJOR: Teaching-College Level

One year fellowship to encourage graduate work in preparation for college teaching. Must be U.S. citizen and ISI member. For study at any school in the U.S. or abroad. Write to the address below for complete details.

Intercollegiate Studies Institute
Fellowship Awards Programs
3901 Centerville Rd., P.O. Box 4431
Wilmington, DE 19807

4001 Richard Muller Art Scholarships

AMOUNT: Varies **DEADLINE:** Apr 1
FIELD/MAJOR: Art (Drawing, Painting, Printmaking)

Awards are available to art majors with a special focus in drawing, painting, or printmaking. Write to the address below for more information.

Portland State University
Art Department
239 Neuberger Hall
Portland, OR 97207

4002

Richard R. and Ruth F. Evans Petroleum Engineering Scholarship

AMOUNT: $500-$1,500 **DEADLINE:** Mar 1
FIELD/MAJOR: Petroleum Engineering

Scholarships are available at the University of Oklahoma, Norman, for full-time petroleum engineering majors, with a minimum GPA of at least 3.0. Write to the address listed below for information.

University Of Oklahoma, Norman
Scholarship Coord., Pet. And Geol. Eng.
T301 Energy Center
Norman, OK 73019

4003

Richard S. Milstone Psychology Scholarship

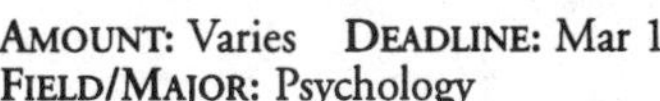

AMOUNT: Varies **DEADLINE:** Mar 1
FIELD/MAJOR: Psychology

Awards for students studying psychology with demonstrated financial need. For entering sophomores, juniors, or seniors. Contact the Chair, Psychology Department, for more information.

University Of Massachusetts, Amherst
Chair, Psychology Department
Amherst, MA 01003

4004

Richard Savage Poetry Awards

AMOUNT: $1,000 **DEADLINE:** None Specified
FIELD/MAJOR: Poetry

First, second, and third prizes will be awarded for individual poems by Bloomsburg undergraduates. Information available in the English department.

Bloomsburg University
19 Ben Franklin Hall
400 E. Second St.
Bloomsburg, PA 17815

4005

Richard West Fund

AMOUNT: Varies **DEADLINE:** None Specified
FIELD/MAJOR: Education

Award for academically qualified Mercyhurst students who are studying education. Write to the address below for more information.

Mercyhurst College
Financial Aid Office
Glenwood Hills
Erie, PA 16546

4006

Richard Wlodarczyk Scholarship

AMOUNT: Varies **DEADLINE:** None Specified
FIELD/MAJOR: Hotel, Restaurant, Institutional Management

Award for Mercyhurst students studying hotel, restaurant, and

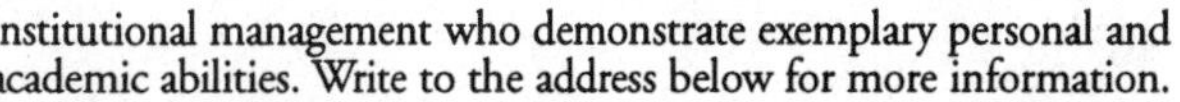

institutional management who demonstrate exemplary personal and academic abilities. Write to the address below for more information.

Mercyhurst College
Financial Aid Office
Glenwood Hills
Erie, PA 16546

4007

Richard, Lee, Rowley, Cobb And Hall Partners In Education Scholarship

AMOUNT: $1,000 **DEADLINE:** None Specified
FIELD/MAJOR: All Areas Of Study

Scholarships available to graduates of public high schools in El Paso and Ysleta school districts. One award each year to a graduate of each school. Write to the address listed below for additional information.

El Paso Community Foundation
201 East Main, Suite 1616
El Paso, TX 79901

4008

Richardson Scholarship

AMOUNT: Varies **DEADLINE:** Mar 1
FIELD/MAJOR: Women's Studies

Awards for sophomores, juniors, or seniors in the women's studies program at UMass. Contact the Director, Women's Studies for more information.

University of Massachusetts, Amherst
Director, Women's Studies Program
Amherst, MA 01003

4009

Ricky J. Parisian Scholarship

AMOUNT: $500 **DEADLINE:** None Specified
FIELD/MAJOR: All Areas Of Study

Award available for a graduating high school senior from Oneonta High School who exemplifies the following qualities: respect, integrity, honesty, responsibility, loyalty, reliability, fairness, kindness, caring, and is a good citizen. Write to the address below for more information.

Ricky J. Parisian Scholarship Foundation
P.O. Box 1201
Oneonta, NY 13820

4010

Ridley Scholarships

AMOUNT: Varies **DEADLINE:** Varies
FIELD/MAJOR: All Areas Of Study

Scholarships for physically disabled students at the University of Michigan. Based on financial need. Must be a legal U.S. resident. Ridley scholarships are renewable with re-application. Contact the SSD office at the address below for details.

University Of Michigan
Services For Students With Disabilities
G625 Haven Hall
Ann Arbor, MI 48109

4011
Rife Endowed Scholarship Fund

AMOUNT: Varies **DEADLINE:** None Specified
FIELD/MAJOR: All Areas Of Study

Awards are available for full-time students at Cedarville College who have financial need. Must have a GPA of at least 2.0. Write to the address below for more information.

Cedarville College
Financial Aid Office
P.O. Box 601
Cedarville, OH 45314

4012
Ripon Alumni Grant

AMOUNT: $2,000 **DEADLINE:** None Specified
FIELD/MAJOR: All Areas Of Study

Scholarships for children of Ripon alumni who are or will be attending Ripon College. Write to the address below for details.

Ripon College
300 Seward Street
P.O. Box 248
Ripon, WI 54971

4013
Rita G. Rudel Award

AMOUNT: $20,000 **DEADLINE:** May 31
FIELD/MAJOR: Behavioral Neurology, Developmental Neuropsychology

Applicants must hold a Ph. D. or M.D. degree and should be in the early to middle stage of their postdoctoral careers. Must be doing research in the field of developmental neuropsychology or developmental behavioral neurology. Write to the address below for more information.

Rita G. Rudel Foundation
P.O. Box 674
Chappaqua, NY 10514

4014
Rita G. Sanchez Scholarships

AMOUNT: Varies **DEADLINE:** Mar 1
FIELD/MAJOR: All Areas Of Study

Awards are available at the University of New Mexico for full-time Hispanic undergraduates with academic ability and financial need. Must be a resident of New Mexico. Write to the address below for more information.

University Of New Mexico, Albuquerque
Office Of Financial Aid
Albuquerque, NM 87131

4015
Rita M. Guerrieri Memorial Scholarship

AMOUNT: $500 **DEADLINE:** Feb 9
FIELD/MAJOR: All Areas Of Study

Award for Sigma Sigma Sigma sorority member who has as least one complete semester remaining before graduation. Applicant needs to emulate Rita's nature, provide service to, and be active in the sorority. Use the Bloomsburg University scholarship application. Contact Dr. John Maittlen-Harris, advisor, Sigma Sigma Sigma sorority for further information.

Bloomsburg University
19 Ben Franklin Hall
400 E. Second St.
Bloomsburg, PA 17815

4016
Ritchie Industries, Inc. Scholarships

AMOUNT: $1,000 **DEADLINE:** Feb 15
FIELD/MAJOR: Agriculture

Scholarships are available for FFA members pursuing a four-year degree in any area of agriculture, who reside in Iowa. Write to the address below for details.

National FFA Foundation
Scholarship Office
P.O. Box 15160
Alexandria, VA 22309

4017
RMCMI Scholarships

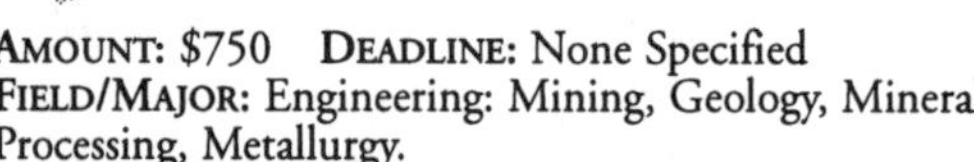

AMOUNT: $750 **DEADLINE:** None Specified
FIELD/MAJOR: Engineering: Mining, Geology, Mineral Processing, Metallurgy.

Scholarships for sophomores in the above areas of study who are U.S. citizens and legal residents of either AZ, CO, MT, NM, ND, or WY. For full-time study. For students who are pursuing a degree in a mining related field or an engineering discipline. Applications are available in the offices of department heads at many universities or from the address below.

Rocky Mountain Coal Mining Institute
3000 Youngfield St., Suite 324
Lakewood, CO 80215

4018
Roanoke Valley Horseman's Association Scholarships

AMOUNT: $500 **DEADLINE:** May 1
FIELD/MAJOR: Pre-Vet, Related

Two scholarships for students at Virginia Tech who are studying a pre-vet course or will go into a related area. Based on need and grades. Write to the address below for details.

Virginia Tech College Of Agriculture And Life Sciences
Dr. John M. White, Assoc. Dean
1060 Litton Reaves Hall
Blacksburg, VA 24061

4019
Robbin E.L. Washington Scholarship

AMOUNT: $500 **DEADLINE:** None Specified
FIELD/MAJOR: All Areas Of Study

Scholarship available to African American El Paso County resident freshmen who graduated from either El Paso or Ysleta high school districts. Write to the address listed below for additional information.

El Paso Community Foundation
201 East Main, Suite 1616
El Paso, TX 79901

4020

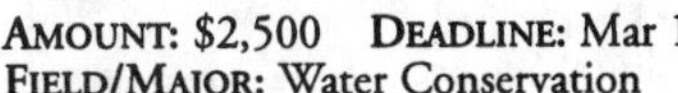

Robert A. Canham Scholarship

AMOUNT: $2,500 **DEADLINE:** Mar 1
FIELD/MAJOR: Water Conservation

Scholarship (1) for postbaccalaureate student in the water conservation field. Based on statement of degree objectives, career goals, and recommendation. Write to the Water Environment Federation at the address below for details.

Water Environment Federation
Student Programs, Attn: Liza Clark
601 Wythe St.
Alexandria, VA 22314

4021

Robert and Charlotte Bitter Graduate Scholarship

AMOUNT: $900 **DEADLINE:** None Specified
FIELD/MAJOR: Accounting

Student must be admitted to the MBA or master of accountancy program, with a combined GMAT and GPA admission score of 1100 or higher. Must be enrolled in twelve hours each semester and have a GPA of 3.33 or better. Contact the COBA office for more information.

Southwest Missouri State University
Office Of Financial Aid
901 South National Ave.
Springfield, MO 65804

4022

Robert and Rosemary Low Scholarships

AMOUNT: $250-$1,000 **DEADLINE:** Jan 1
FIELD/MAJOR: Music

Awards are available to undergraduate music majors based on financial need. Write to the address below for more information.

Portland State University
Music Department
231 Lincoln Hall
Portland, OR 97207

4023

Robert Atkinson Memorial Scholarships

AMOUNT: Varies **DEADLINE:** None Specified
FIELD/MAJOR: Political Science, History, Music

Awards are available for juniors at Cedarville College majoring political science, history, or music. Must have a GPA of at least 2.0. Preference is given to members of Licking County Grace Brethren, Trinity Grace Brethren Church in Columbus, or to children of current missionaries. Write to the address below for more information.

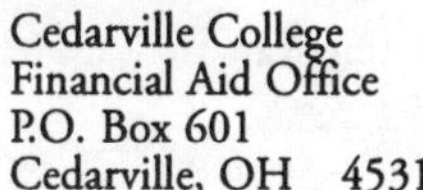

Cedarville College
Financial Aid Office
P.O. Box 601
Cedarville, OH 45314

4024

Robert B. Bailey III Minority Student Scholarships

AMOUNT: $250-$1,000 **DEADLINE:** Apr 1, Nov 1
FIELD/MAJOR: Foreign Studies

Awards are available for minority students interested in study abroad. The stipend is intended for use in the cost of travel or the program fee. Must be a U.S. citizen. For undergraduate study. Write to the address below for more information.

Council On International Educational Exchange
Scholarship Committee
205 East 42nd St.
New York, NY 10017

4025

Robert B. Noble Excellence In Advertising Award

AMOUNT: $300 **DEADLINE:** None Specified
FIELD/MAJOR: Advertising

Student must demonstrate superior academic performance, potential, and involvement in advertising club activities. Contact the COBA office for more information.

Southwest Missouri State University
Office Of Financial Aid
901 South National Ave.
Springfield, MO 65804

4026

Robert B. Noble Scholarship

AMOUNT: $425 **DEADLINE:** Mar 31
FIELD/MAJOR: Advertising, Culinary, Visual, Performing Arts, Communications

First preference is given to a dependent of a Noble Communications employee. Preference is also given to a student majoring in the following areas; advertising, culinary arts, visual arts, performing arts, or communications. Must have a GPA of 2.5 or better. Write to the address below for more information.

Southwest Missouri State University
Office Of Financial Aid
901 South National Ave.
Springfield, MO 65804

4027

Robert Bosch Foundation Fellowship

AMOUNT: Varies **DEADLINE:** Oct 15
FIELD/MAJOR: All Areas Of Study

Fellowships are available for postdoctoral scholars to study in Germany. Applicant must be fluent in German, and be available to work in a government assignment for nine months, and in the private sector for four months. Write to the address listed below for information.

CDS International, Inc.
330 7th Avenue, 19th Floor
New York, NY 10001

4028

Robert C. Thomas Memorial Scholarship Loan Fund

Amount: $1,000 **Deadline:** Mar 15
Field/Major: Education, Public Administration

No-interest loans for Alaska residents for studies related to education or public administration. Recipients shall receive forgiveness of 20% of the loan amount for every year he/she is employed full-time in Alaska in a public administration or education field. Write to the address listed below for information.

Alaska Commission On Postsecondary Education
Department Of Education
801 West 10th St.
Juneau, AK 99801

4029

Robert Chin Memorial Award

Amount: $1,000 **Deadline:** Sep 30
Field/Major: Psychology, Social-Intergroup Relations

The award is offered each year for the best paper or article on scholarly contributions to research, knowledge, application, or policy on child abuse or an investigator who is conducting research in this area. Graduate students and postdoctoral scholars are encouraged to enter. Write to the address below for details.

Society For The Psychological Study Of Social Issues
P.O. Box 1248
Ann Arbor, MI 48106

4030

Robert Crowley Scholarship

Amount: Varies **Deadline:** Mar 1
Field/Major: Newspaper Writing

Awards for students entering their sophomore, junior, or senior at UMass based on excellence in newspaper column writing. Contact the Dean, Humanities and Fine Arts, not the address below for more information.

University Of Massachusetts, Amherst
255 Whitmore Administration Building
Box 38230
Amherst, MA 01003

4031

Robert D. Ashworth Fund

Amount: None Specified **Deadline:** Mar 15
Field/Major: All Areas Of Study

Scholarships for members of the Mount Calvary Baptist Church in Charleston (WV). For undergraduate study. Write to the address below for details.

Greater Kanawha Valley Foundation
Scholarship Committee
P.O. Box 3041
Charleston, WV 25331

4032

Robert Dean Bass Scholarship

Amount: Varies **Deadline:** Unspecified
Field/Major: Economics, Political Science, History, Classics

Scholarships are available at the University of Oklahoma, Norman for students majoring in one of the above fields. Student must be a sophomore or junior with a GPA of 3.65 or better. Must be pursuing a career in some type of government agency. Write to the address listed below for information.

University Of Oklahoma, Norman
College Of Arts And Sciences
601 Elm, Room 429
Norman, OK 73019

4033

Robert E. And Evelyn Mckee Foundation Scholarship

Amount: Varies **Deadline:** Mar 1
Field/Major: Nursing

Awards are available at the University of New Mexico for nursing students with financial need. Must be a U.S. citizen. Write to the address below or contact the school of nursing for more details.

University Of New Mexico, Albuquerque
Office Of Financial Aid
Albuquerque, NM 87131

4034

Robert E. Guiles Leadership Scholarship

Amount: Varies **Deadline:** Feb 23
Field/Major: All Areas Of Study

Awards for second semester sophomores at UW Oshkosh who are nominated by students, faculty, or staff. Must show ability to work within the system as well as leadership in attracting other students to become positively involved in campus-wide activities. Scholarship achievement considered. Contact the Dean of Students Office, UW Oshkosh, for more details.

University of Wisconsin, Oshkosh
Financial Aid Office, Dempsey 104
800 Algoma Blvd.
Oshkosh, WI 54901

4035

Robert E. Thunen Memorial Educational Scholarships

Amount: $2,500 **Deadline:** Mar 1
Field/Major: Architecture, Electrical Engineering, Interior Decorating And Design

Scholarships are available to those in the above fields who wish to study illumination as a career. Applicants must be undergraduate juniors or seniors or graduate students who are enrolled in a four-year school located in one of the following areas: northern California, Nevada, Oregon, or Washington state. Letters of recommendation are required. Write to the address below for details.

Illuminating Engineering Society Of North America
460 Brannen St., P.O. Box 77527
San Francisco, CA 94107

4036

Robert F. Hardin Scholarships

AMOUNT: None Specified **DEADLINE:** None Specified
FIELD/MAJOR: All Areas Of Study

Scholarships for students from Unaka, Elizabethton, or Hampton (one at each) high schools (Carter County, TN) who have the highest GPA in their graduating class. Contact the principal's office at your high school for details.

East Tennessee State University
Office Of Financial Aid
Box 70722
Johnson City, TN 37614

4037

Robert F. Kearson Scholarship Program

AMOUNT: $250 **DEADLINE:** Mar 1
FIELD/MAJOR: All Areas Of Study

Award for a Broward County high school senior who is planning to enroll in an accredited four-year program at any Florida college or university. Preference will be given to applicants planning to major in industrial safety. Write to the address below for more information.

National Safety Council, South Florida Chapter
2099 West Prospect Rd.
Fort Lauderdale, FL 33309

4038

Robert F. Thomson, Jr. Memorial Scholarship

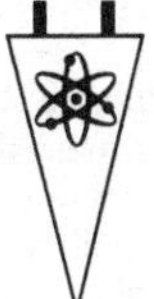

AMOUNT: $150 **DEADLINE:** None Specified
FIELD/MAJOR: Agriculture

Student must be an agriculture major who demonstrates leadership, character and financial need. Contact the Agriculture Department for more information.

Southwest Missouri State University
Office Of Financial Aid
901 South National Ave.
Springfield, MO 65804

4039

Robert G. and Dorothy P. Tilden Scholarship

AMOUNT: None Specified **DEADLINE:** Jun 1
FIELD/MAJOR: Food, Resources, Agriculture, Crop Sci., Nutrition, Horti/Floriculture

Scholarships are awarded to Stockbridge students based on financial need. For students in their sophomore, junior, or senior year at UMass. Contact the Director, Stockbridge School, for more information.

University Of Massachusetts, Amherst
Director, Stockbridge School
Amherst, MA 01003

4040

Robert H. And Cynthia B. Cutter Scholarship

AMOUNT: $1,000 **DEADLINE:** None Specified
FIELD/MAJOR: Theater

Awards for students at Mesa State College who are active in the theater program. Must have and maintain a GPA of at least 2.0 and be full-time students. Contact the theater department for further details.

Mesa State College
Financial Aid Office
P.O. Box 2684
Grand Junction, CO 81501

4041

Robert H. Weitbrecht Scholarship, David Von Hagen Scholarship

AMOUNT: $250-$1,000 **DEADLINE:** Apr 15
FIELD/MAJOR: Engineering, Science

Applicants must be born deaf or became deaf before acquiring language, and must use speech/residual hearing or lip-reading as primary communication. Also, must be a student entering or attending a college or university program for hearing students. A student of engineering or science is preferred. Two awards per year under each program. Write to the address below for complete details.

Alexander Graham Bell Association For The Deaf
3417 Volta Place, NW
Washington, DC 20007

4042

Robert Hardie Memorial Scholarship

AMOUNT: $400 **DEADLINE:** None Specified
FIELD/MAJOR: Economics

Student must be a full-time economics major with a GPA of 3.0 or better. Contact the Economics Department for more information.

Southwest Missouri State University
Office Of Financial Aid
901 South National Ave.
Springfield, MO 65804

4043

Robert J. DiPetro Scholarship

AMOUNT: $1,000 **DEADLINE:** May 31
FIELD/MAJOR: All Areas Of Study

Scholarships for Italian American students who are age 25 or less. Based on essay on Italian heritage and how applicant intends to preserve it throughout his or her lifetime (400-600) words. Write to the address below for details.

National Italian American Foundation
Dr. Maria Lombardo, Education Director
1860 Nineteenth Street, NW
Washington, DC 20009

4044

Robert Kaufman Memorial Scholarship Fund

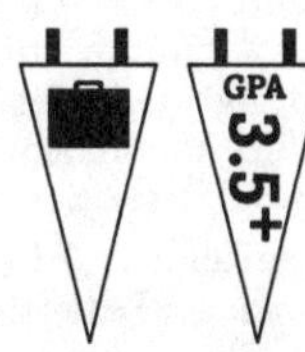

AMOUNT: $250-$5,000 **DEADLINE:** Mar 1
FIELD/MAJOR: Accounting

Scholarships are available for students who are pursuing or planning to pursue an education in accounting at an accredited college or university in the U.S. Applicants must be third year students or above and have a 3.5 GPA or equivalent in accounting. Write to the address listed below for an application, and enclose an SASE.

Independent Accountants International Educational Foundation, Inc.
9200 South Dadeland Boulevard, Suite 510
Miami, FL 33156

4045
Robert L. Farris, Sr. Scholarship

AMOUNT: $1,000 **DEADLINE:** Apr 15
FIELD/MAJOR: Advertising, Consumer-Related Communications Field

Scholarships are for a junior or senior college student, permanent resident of the U.S., and a record of high academic achievement. Contact IPCC Scholarship Chairperson, 535 S. Illinois St., Indianapolis, IN 46225-1192, for more details.

Indiana University/Purdue University, Indianapolis
Purdue School Of Technology
799 West Michigan St.
Indianapolis, IN 46202

4046
Robert L. Quimby Memorial Fund

AMOUNT: $100 **DEADLINE:** None Specified
FIELD/MAJOR: All Areas Of Study

Awards for female athletes at Mesa State College. Must be enrolled full-time and have a GPA of at least 3.5. Contact the Athletic Department for more details.

Mesa State College
Office Of Financial Aid
P.O. Box 3692
Grand Junction, CO 81501

4047
Robert Lee Scott Memorial Scholarship

AMOUNT: $500 **DEADLINE:** Mar 31
FIELD/MAJOR: All Areas Of Study

Students must be upperclassmen with academic promise and financial need. Write to the address below for more information.

Southwest Missouri State University
Office Of Financial Aid
901 South National Ave.
Springfield, MO 65804

4048
Robert M. Burger Fellowship

AMOUNT: Tuition And Fees **DEADLINE:** Feb 1
FIELD/MAJOR: Microelectronics

Fellowships are available at Duke University, North Carolina State University, and the University of North Carolina for graduate students pursuing a doctoral degree in areas related to microelectronics. Awards pay tuition and fees as well as a monthly stipend of $1,400, and a $2,000 gift to the university department with which the student is associated. Must be a U.S. citizen. Write to the address below for complete details and an application.

Semiconductor Research Corporation Education Alliance
Graduate Fellowship Program
P.O. Box 12053
Research Triangle Park, NC 27709

4049
Robert M. Lawrence, MD Scholarship

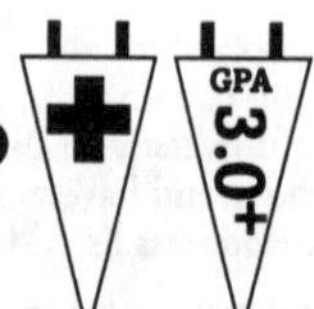

AMOUNT: $2,500 **DEADLINE:** Jun 30
FIELD/MAJOR: Respiratory Therapy

Award for a third- or fourth-year student in an accredited respiratory therapy program. Must have a GPA of at least 3.0. Also based on recommendations and an essay. Write to the address below for more information.

American Respiratory Care Foundation
Scholarship Committee
11030 Ables Lane
Dallas, TX 75229

4050
Robert O. Miller Scholarships

AMOUNT: None Specified **DEADLINE:** Feb 1
FIELD/MAJOR: Law, Medicine

Scholarships will be awarded to residents of Calloway County, Kentucky, pursuing a degree in law or medicine at Murray State University. Financial need shall be considered. Write to the address below for details.

Murray State University
Office Of University Scholarships
Ordway Hall, 1 Murray St.
Murray, KY 42071

4051
Robert P. Scripps Graphic Arts Grants

AMOUNT: $1,000-$3,000 **DEADLINE:** Feb 25
FIELD/MAJOR: Graphic Arts (Newspaper Industry)

Awards for full-time undergraduate students majoring in graphic arts as applied to newspaper industry. Must demonstrate high academic achievement, interest in journalism and graphic arts, and financial need. Renewable. Applicants must be U.S. citizens. Write to the address below for details. Include a self-addressed mailing label showing the words "Scholarship Application." Also, please state your major and your career goals. Deadline to request an application is Dec 20.

Scripps Howard Foundation
Scholarships Coordinator
P.O. Box 5380
Cincinnati, OH 45201

4052
Robert P. Stack Memorial Scholarship

AMOUNT: $1,000 (max) **DEADLINE:** None Specified
FIELD/MAJOR: All Areas Of Study

Scholarships are available at the University of Iowa for entering freshmen from Iowa City high schools. Based upon academic ability and financial need. Contact your school guidance counselor for information.

University Of Iowa
Office Of Student Financial Aid
208 Calvin Hall
Iowa City, IA 52242

4053
Robert R. Robinson Memorial Scholarship

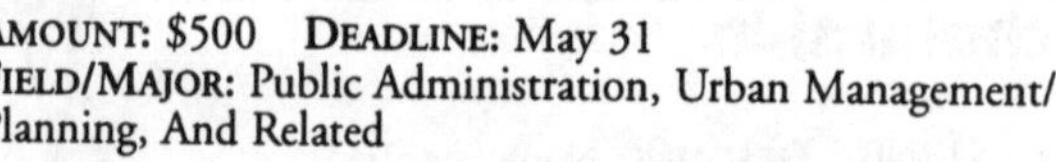

AMOUNT: $500 **DEADLINE:** May 31
FIELD/MAJOR: Public Administration, Urban Management/Planning, And Related

Scholarships for students enrolled in Michigan colleges and universities as a junior, senior, or graduate student. Competitively awarded based on academics, community involvement, and a commitment to a career in local government administration. Write to the address below for details.

Michigan Townships Associaiton
P.O. Box 80078
Lansing, MI 48909

4054

Robert Redman Scholarship

AMOUNT: $650 **DEADLINE:** None Specified
FIELD/MAJOR: All Areas Of Study

Athletic award for football team member. Recipient will be selected by the head football coach. Contact the football coach for additional information.

Bloomsburg University
19 Ben Franklin Hall
400 E. Second St.
Bloomsburg, PA 17815

4055

Robert S. Morison Fellowship

AMOUNT: $40,000 Stipend **DEADLINE:** Nov 1
FIELD/MAJOR: Neurology, Neurosurgery

Fellowships for medical doctors who have been accepted into or completed residence in neurology or neurosurgery and in need of two years of intensive research or training preparation for a career in academic neurology or neurosurgery. Write to the address below for complete details.

Grass Foundation
77 Reservoir Road
Quincy, MA 02170

4056

Robert Schmaeff Scholarship

AMOUNT: Varies **DEADLINE:** Mar 1
FIELD/MAJOR: Pharmacy

Awards are available at the University of New Mexico for full-time pharmacy students demonstrating excellent scholastic achievement and financial need. Write to the address below for more information.

University Of New Mexico, Albuquerque
Office Of Financial Aid
Albuquerque, NM 87131

4057

Robert T. Ghattas Scholarship

AMOUNT: Varies **DEADLINE:** Mar 1
FIELD/MAJOR: Pharmacy

Awards are available at the University of New Mexico for pharmacy students demonstrating academic excellence and financial need. Write to the address below for more information.

University Of New Mexico, Albuquerque
Office Of Financial Aid
Albuquerque, NM 87131

4058

Robert Trathen Memorial Scholarship

AMOUNT: Varies **DEADLINE:** None Specified
FIELD/MAJOR: Accounting

Awards for Jacksonville State University students in the field of accounting. Contact the head of the accounting department for more details.

Jacksonville State University
Financial Aid Office
Jacksonville, AL 36265

4059

Robert V. Peterson Scholarship

AMOUNT: $1,200 **DEADLINE:** Feb 15
FIELD/MAJOR: News Journalism

Scholarships are available at the University of Oklahoma, Norman, for senior news journalism majors, who anticipate a career in community journalism. Write to the address listed below for information.

University Of Oklahoma, Norman
School Of Journalism And Mass Comm.
860 Van Vleet Oval
Norman, OK 73019

4060

Robert W. Tuveson Memorial Scholarship

AMOUNT: None Specified
DEADLINE: None Specified
FIELD/MAJOR: Biological Science

Scholarships are for entering or currently enrolled students majoring in biological science. Additional consideration will be given to an African American student. Write to the address below for more information.

Indiana University Purdue University, Indianapolis
Purdue School Of Technology
799 West Michigan St.
Indianapolis, IN 46202

4061

Robert W. Woodruff Fellowship

AMOUNT: $15,000 (max) **DEADLINE:** May 31
FIELD/MAJOR: Public Or Business Administration, Social Work, Recreation And Leisure

This graduate fellowship program has two options for master's degree candidates and for those hold a master's. All applicants must be currently involved with the Boys and Girls Clubs and must make a commitment to a minimum of two years full-time employment at a Boys and Girls Club after completion of the program. Write to the address below for details.

Boys And Girls Clubs Of America
Human Resource Group
1230 W. Peachtree St., NW
Atlanta, GA 30309

4062

Robin Armell And Brodmerkel-brown Memorial Scholarship Awards

AMOUNT: Varies **DEADLINE:** Mar 1
FIELD/MAJOR: Nursing

Awards are available at the University of New Mexico for full-time nursing students with a minimum GPA of 2.5 and financial need.

Write to the address below or contact the school of nursing for more details.

University Of New Mexico, Albuquerque
Office Of Financial Aid
Albuquerque, NM 87131

4063

Rock Sleyster Memorial Scholarship

AMOUNT: $2,500 **DEADLINE:** May 1
FIELD/MAJOR: Psychiatry

Candidates must be a high-achieving senior with demonstrated interest and financial need. Nomination by medical school is required. For U.S. or Canadian citizens. Approximately twenty scholarships will be given annually. Write to the address below for complete details.

American Medical Association
Division Of Undergraduate Medical Educ.
515 North State Street
Chicago, IL 60610

4064

Rockefeller Foundation Fellowships In Legal Humanities

AMOUNT: $30,000 **DEADLINE:** Nov 15
FIELD/MAJOR: Law, Humanities, Social Science

Postdoctoral fellowships are available at Stanford to support research on theories of interpretation, intention, narrative, and human agency in law and the humanities, especially as these affect subordinated populations. Write to the address listed below for information.

Stanford University
Stanford Humanities Center
Mariposa House
Stanford, CA 94305

4065

Rockefeller State Wildlife Scholarship

GPA 2.5+

AMOUNT: $1,000 **DEADLINE:** None Specified
FIELD/MAJOR: Forestry, Wildlife Studies, Marine Science

Scholarships offered to Louisiana residents who are or will be full-time students at a college or university in Louisiana. Applicants must be U.S. citizens and undergraduate students with a GPA of at least 2.5. Write to the address below for details.

Louisiana Office Of Financial Assistance
P.O. Box 91202
Baton Rouge, LA 70821

4066

Rockford Health Careers Foundation

AMOUNT: Varies **DEADLINE:** None Specified
FIELD/MAJOR: Nursing

Awards available to nursing students at Rockford College. Write to the address below for more information.

Rockford College
Financial Aid Office
5050 East State St.
Rockford, IL 61108

4067

Rockford Memorial Scholars Program

AMOUNT: Varies **DEADLINE:** None Specified
FIELD/MAJOR: Nursing

Awards available to students pursuing a bachelor of science in nursing degree. Write to the address below for more information.

Rockford College
Financial Aid Office
5050 East State St.
Rockford, IL 61108

4068

Rockwell International Scholarships

AMOUNT: Varies **DEADLINE:** Mar 1
FIELD/MAJOR: Engineering

Awards are available at the University of New Mexico for undergraduate female or minority students in electrical or mechanical engineering. Selection based on academic achievement. Must be a U.S. citizen. Write to the address below for more information.

University Of New Mexico, Albuquerque
Office Of Financial Aid
Albuquerque, NM 87131

4069

Rocky Mountain Chapter National Security Industrial Assoc. Scholarship

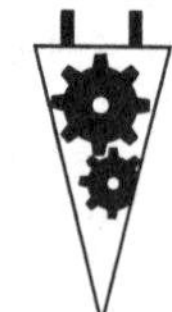

AMOUNT: None Specified **DEADLINE:** Apr 12
FIELD/MAJOR: Aeronautical/Aerospace, Space Science, And Related Fields

Scholarships for students seeking a career in space operations or a related field. Based on need, academics, motivation, and moral fiber. Write to the address below for details.

National Security Industrial Association
Scholarship Committee
P.O. Box 15200
Colorado Springs, CO 80935

4070

Rocky Mountain Farmers Union Scholarship

AMOUNT: $500 **DEADLINE:** Apr 1
FIELD/MAJOR: All Areas Of Study

Scholarship available to current regular or associate members of the Rocky Mountain Farmers Union who plan to attend any college or vocational school that conform to the GI Bill qualifications. One award given per year. Write to the address listed below for further information and an application.

Rocky Mountain Farmers Union Scholarship Program
10800 E. Bethany Drive, 4th Floor
Aurora, CO 80014

4071

Rodney C. Rhodes Memorial Scholarship

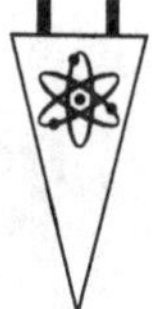

AMOUNT: Varies **DEADLINE:** Mar 1
FIELD/MAJOR: Earth And Planetary Sciences, Geology

Awards are available at the University of New Mexico for juniors

or seniors studying geology or students pursuing a graduate degree the fields of earth and planetary science. Write to the address listed below for information.

University of New Mexico, Albuquerque
Office of Financial Aid
Albuquerque, NM 87131

4072 Roemisch Scholarships

AMOUNT: Varies **DEADLINE:** Mar 1
FIELD/MAJOR: Business

Awards for junior or senior business students at Lake Erie College with potential and initiative. Write to the address below for more information.

Lake Erie College
Financial Aid Office
391 W. Washington St.
Painesville, OH 44077

4073 Roesel Award

AMOUNT: None Specified
DEADLINE: None Specified
FIELD/MAJOR: Mathematics, Physics, Chemistry, Biology, Computer Science

Scholarships for students at East Tennessee State University majoring in one of the above areas of study. Must be junior year students. Two awards per year. Contact your department for details.

East Tennessee State University
Office Of Financial Aid
Box 70722
Johnson City, TN 37614

4074 Roger Hospital Fellowship

AMOUNT: Varies **DEADLINE:** None Specified
FIELD/MAJOR: Nursing

Awards for full-time TTC students in the nursing program who can submit two letters of recommendation (1 from director of nursing) and have a GPA of at least 3.0. Recipient must sign a letter of intent to work at Roper Hospital for 15 to 21 months after graduation. Write to the address below for more information.

Trident Technical College
Financial Aid Office
P.O. Box 118067
Charleston, SC 29423

4075 Roger L. Davies Scholarships

AMOUNT: $175 **DEADLINE:** None Specified
FIELD/MAJOR: Astronomy, Biology, Chemistry, Geography, Physics

Awards for continuing students at UW Platteville who demonstrate financial need and have a GPA of 3.0 or greater. Primary major must be in one of the fields listed above. Write to the address below or contact the office at (608) 342-1125 for more information.

University Of Wisconsin, Platteville
Office Of Admissions And Enrollment Mgt.
Platteville, WI 53818

4076 Romeo B. Garrett Scholarship

AMOUNT: Varies **DEADLINE:** Mar 1
FIELD/MAJOR: All Areas Of Study

Selected from applicants of African American heritage. Based on financial need, ACT/SAT scores, and class rank. Write to the address below for more information.

Bradley University
Office Of Financial Assistance
Bradley University
Peoria, IL 61625

4077 Ronald E. Lincoln Scholarships

AMOUNT: $1,000 **DEADLINE:** May 30
FIELD/MAJOR: Metallurgy, Metallurgical Engineering, Materials Science

Awards are available for students entering their final undergraduate year in any of the fields listed above. Only one candidate will be considered per school. Students must apply in their junior year. Write to the address below for more details.

Iron And Steel Society
Kathryn E. Kost
410 Commonwealth Dr.
Warrendale, PA 15086

4078 Ronald K. Krinsky Memorial Scholarship

AMOUNT: $250 **DEADLINE:** None Specified
FIELD/MAJOR: Political Science

Student must be a full-time political science major with demonstrated aptitude and financial need. Contact the political science department for more information.

Southwest Missouri State University
Office Of Financial Aid
901 South National Ave.
Springfield, MO 65804

4079 Ronald K. Payne/KPMG Peat Marwick Scholarship Fund

AMOUNT: $500 **DEADLINE:** Mar 1
FIELD/MAJOR: Accounting

Award for a full-time undergraduate accounting student who has a GPA of at least 3.0. Write to the address below for more information.

Eastern New Mexico University
Enmu College of Business
Station 49
Portales, NM 88130

4080

Ronald L. Coulter Outstanding Marketing Research Student Award

AMOUNT: $100 **DEADLINE:** None Specified
FIELD/MAJOR: Marketing

Student must be a junior, senior, or graduate marketing major with an emphasis in marketing research and a GPA of 3.0 or better. Must participate in a professional business student organization. Contact the COBA office for more information.

Southwest Missouri State University
Office Of Financial Aid
901 South National Ave.
Springfield, MO 65804

4081

Ronald McDonald Children's Charities Health And Medical Scholars Program

AMOUNT: $1,000-Tuition **DEADLINE:** Jan 31
FIELD/MAJOR: Pre-Medical Or Health Care

Awards for African American college sophomores in one of the fields above. Applicants must have a GPA of at least 3.0, have unmet financial need and be involved in community service in the area of health care. Write to the address below for more information.

United Negro Scholarship Fund
8260 Willow Oaks Corporate Drive
P.O. Box 10444
Fairfax, VA 22031

4082

Ronald McNair Program

AMOUNT: $2,400 **DEADLINE:** Feb 10
FIELD/MAJOR: Most Areas Of Study

Open to highly motivated, disciplined, and hard-working individuals who are citizens and/or permanent, legal residents of the U.S.A. and college-level rising juniors, seniors, and graduates. Applicants must be a member of a numerically underrepresented group in good academic standing who have been traditionally underrepresented. For UT Knoxville students. Write to the address below for more information.

U.S. Department Of Education-Trio Program
University Of Tennessee, Knoxville
900 1/2 Volunteer Blvd.
Knoxville, TN 37996

4083

Ronald Reagan Leadership Award

AMOUNT: $1,000 **DEADLINE:** Jun 1
FIELD/MAJOR: All Areas Of Study

Leadership awards for Tau Kappa Epsilon members given in recognition of outstanding leadership as demonstrated by activities and accomplishments on campus, in the community, and within the chapter. All initiated undergraduate members of Tau Kappa Epsilon are eligible. Contact the address below for complete information.

TKE Educational Foundation
8645 Founders Rd.
Indianapolis, IN 46268

4084

Rooke Soccer Scholarship Fund

AMOUNT: Varies **DEADLINE:** None Specified
FIELD/MAJOR: All Areas Of Study

Awards are available for full-time students at Cedarville College who have talent and ability in soccer. Must have a GPA of at least 2.0. Write to the athletic department for more information.

Cedarville College
Financial Aid Office
P.O. Box 601
Cedarville, OH 45314

4085

Root Tilden Snow Scholarship Program

AMOUNT: Varies **DEADLINE:** None Specify
FIELD/MAJOR: Law

Scholarships for entering or first year students at the New York University School of Law who are committed to using their legal education in the service of the public. Contact the school for details on these and other scholarship programs available to students in the School of Law.

New York University, School Of Law
D'agostino Hall
110 West Third St., 2nd Floor
New York, NY 10012

4086

Rosann S. Berry Annual Meeting Fellowship

AMOUNT: $500 **DEADLINE:** Dec 15
FIELD/MAJOR: Architectural History

Awards are available for architectural history students engaged in advanced graduate study to attend the annual meeting of the society of architectural historians. Write to the address below for more information.

Society Of Architectural Historians
1365 North Astor St.
Chicago, IL 60610

4087

Rose And Joseph Sokol Scholarship Fund

AMOUNT: $500 **DEADLINE:** None Specified
FIELD/MAJOR: All Areas Of Study

The Rose and Joseph Sokol Scholarship Fund was established in memory of Rose and Joseph Sokol by their children. It is dedicated to helping South Carolina students of the Jewish faith in need of financial aid to attend any college of their choosing. Write to the address below between September 1 and November 1 for details.

Rose And Joseph Sokol Scholarship Fund
Mrs. Dorothy S. Kipnis
118 Chadwick Dr.
Charleston, SC 29407

4088

Rose And Edwin Daniels Nursing Scholarship, Professional Nurse Award

AMOUNT: $3,000 **DEADLINE:** Dec 15, Jun 15
FIELD/MAJOR: Nursing

Awards are available to full-time nursing students enrolled in Practicum I or II. Outstanding GPA and financial need are required. Contact the College of Nursing at UW Oshkosh for more details.

University Of Wisconsin, Oshkosh
Financial Aid Office, Dempsey 104
800 Algoma Blvd.
Oshkosh, WI 54901

4089

Rose And Edwin Daniels Nursing Scholarship, Pre-Nursing Award

AMOUNT: $1,500 **DEADLINE:** Dec 15, Jun 15
FIELD/MAJOR: Nursing

Awards are available to full-time pre-nursing students accepted into the clinical portion of nursing major. Outstanding GPA and financial need are required. Contact the College of Nursing at UW Oshkosh for more details.

University Of Wisconsin, Oshkosh
Financial Aid Office, Dempsey 104
800 Algoma Blvd.
Oshkosh, WI 54901

4090

Rose Basile Green Scholarship

AMOUNT: $1,000 **DEADLINE:** May 31
FIELD/MAJOR: Italian-American Studies

Scholarship for Italian undergraduates studying in areas relating to Italian American studies. Write to the address below for details.

National Italian American Foundation
Dr. Maria Lombardo, Education Director
1860 19th Street, NW
Washington, DC 20009

4091

Rose Rudin Roosa Scholarship

AMOUNT: Varies **DEADLINE:** Mar 1
FIELD/MAJOR: Political Science

Awards are available at the University of New Mexico for students majoring in political science. GPA is given primary consideration and financial need is a secondary factor. Write to the address below for more information.

University Of New Mexico, Albuquerque
Office Of Financial Aid
Albuquerque, NM 87131

4092

Rose Traurig Scholarship

AMOUNT: Varies **DEADLINE:** Mar 15
FIELD/MAJOR: All Areas Of Study

Awards open to continuing TPU students who have a GPA of at least 3.0 and contribute to university activities. Write to the address below for more information.

Teikyo Post University
Office Of Financial Aid
800 Country Club Road
Waterbury, CT 06723

4093

Rosemarie Zaro Scholarship

AMOUNT: Varies **DEADLINE:** Mar 15, Nov 15
FIELD/MAJOR: All Areas Of Study

Award for women based on academic capability, financial need and career goals. Preference is given to women with children or unique family responsibilities. Write to the address below for more information.

Gwynedd-Mercy College
Student Financial Aid
Sumneytown Pike
Gwynedd Valley, PA 19437

4094

Roswell Artist-in-Residence Program

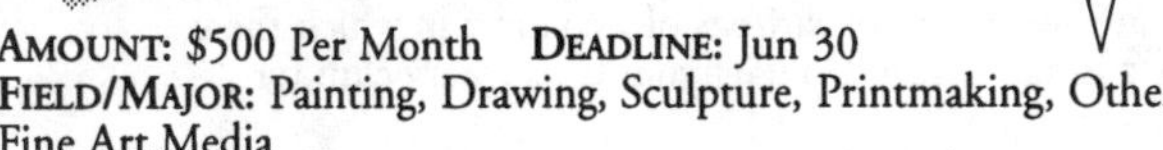

AMOUNT: $500 Per Month **DEADLINE:** Jun 30
FIELD/MAJOR: Painting, Drawing, Sculpture, Printmaking, Other Fine Art Media

Residence program for professional studio artists to provide the unique opportunity to concentrate on their work in a supportive, communal environment for periods of six months to one year. Write to the address below for more information.

Roswell Museum And Art Center Foundation
100 West 11th St.
Roswell, NM 88201

4095

Rotary Club Of Johnson City Scholarship

AMOUNT: None Specified **DEADLINE:** None Specified
FIELD/MAJOR: All Areas Of Study

Scholarships at ETSU for residents of Johnson City or Washington County. Must be an incoming freshman and have a GPA of at least 3.5 and an ACT score of 28 or greater. Contact the Office of Financial Aid at the address below.

East Tennessee State University
Office Of Financial Aid
Box 70722
Johnson City, TN 37614

4096

Rotary Club Of South Hilo Scholarship

AMOUNT: $500 **DEADLINE:** Feb 1
FIELD/MAJOR: Ecology, Environmental Studies

Scholarships are available at the University of Hawaii, Hilo for full-time students enrolled in ecology or environmental studies programs. Write to the address listed below for information.

University Of Hawaii At Hilo
Financial Aid Office
200 West Kawili Street
Hilo, HI 96720

4097

Rotary Club Scholarship

AMOUNT: $1,000 **DEADLINE:** None Specified
FIELD/MAJOR: All Areas Of Study

Awards for Mesa State continuing students with financial need and with special circumstances (major change in life, disadvantaged, etc.). Must have and maintain a GPA of at least 3.0. Write to the address below for more details.

Mesa State College
Office Of Financial Aid
P.O. Box 2647
Grand Junction, CO 81501

4098

Rotary International Foundation Scholarships

AMOUNT: $10,000-$22,200 **DEADLINE:** Varies
FIELD/MAJOR: International And Cultural Studies

Scholarships are available for students interested in a period of study abroad. Scholarship terms are for the academic year, 2-3 full years, or 3-6 months. Applicants must have completed at least two years of university or college coursework and be citizens of a country in which there is a Rotary Club. Contact your local rotary club for information.

Rotary International Foundation
One Rotary Center
1560 Sherman Avenue
Evanston, IL 60201

4099

ROTC Scholarships

AMOUNT: Varies **DEADLINE:** Varies
FIELD/MAJOR: All Areas Of Study

A variety of ROTC scholarships are awarded to students each year. Two-, three-, and four-year scholarships are offered to undergraduates on a competitive basis. Each of these scholarships provides for tuition, textbooks, fees, and other purely academic expenses, in addition to $100 per month subsistence allowance. Special benefits for "qualified" Army ROTC recipients. Write to the address below for details.

Loyola University-New Orleans
Attn: Coordinator Of Scholarship Programs
6363 St. Charles Ave Campus Box 18
New Orleans, LA 70118

4100

ROTC Scholarships

AMOUNT: Varies **DEADLINE:** Mar 15
FIELD/MAJOR: All Areas Of Study

Scholarships are available at Wheaton College for undergraduate students who will be participating in the ROTC program. Write to the address below for details.

Wheaton College
Financial Aid Office
Wheaton, IL 60187

4101

ROTC Scholarships

AMOUNT: Tuition and Fees **DEADLINE:** None Specified
FIELD/MAJOR: All Areas Of Study

Scholarships are available at the University of Iowa for full-time undergraduate students who plan to participate in the Air Force or Army ROTC program. Write to the address listed below for information.

University Of Iowa
Department Of Aerospace Military Studies
126 South Quadrangle
Iowa City, IA 52242

4102

ROTC Scholarships

AMOUNT: Tuition **DEADLINE:** None Specified
FIELD/MAJOR: All Areas Of Study

Scholarships are available at the University of Illinois for students enrolled in the campus ROTC program. For Illinois residents. Contact your university ROTC unit or the address listed below for additional information.

University Of Illinois At Urbana-Champaign
Office Of Student Financial Aid
610 East John Street, 4th Floor
Champaign, IL 61820

4103

ROTC Scholarships

AMOUNT: Varies **DEADLINE:** Dec 1
FIELD/MAJOR: All Areas Of Study

Scholarships are available at the University of New Mexico for entering freshmen who will be participating in the campus ROTC program. For the Air Force Program, write to AFROTC, Aerospace Studies Building or for the Army ROTC program, write to Army ROTC, Military Science Building at the same city, state, and zip listed below.

University Of New Mexico, Albuquerque
Student Financial Aid Office
Mesa Vista Hall North, Student Services
Albuquerque, NM 87131

4104

Roth Journalism Fellowship

AMOUNT: $22,575 **DEADLINE:** None Specified
FIELD/MAJOR: Journalism

Applicants must be graduate students pursuing a journalism career, a New York state citizen, or a student at a New York state college or university. This is a fellowship program in the New York state legislature, not an on-campus aid program. Up to fourteen awards per year. For U.S. citizens only. Write to Dr. Russell J. Williams, director, at the address below for details.

New York State Senate
Senate Student Programs
90 South Swan Street, Room 401
Albany, NY 12247

4105

Rowley/Ministerial Education Scholarship

Amount: Varies **Deadline:** Mar 15
Field/Major: Theology

Applicants must be members of the Christian Church (Disciples of Christ) who are preparing for the ordained ministry as a full-time student. Financial need is considered. Write to the address below for details.

Christian Church (Disciples Of Christ)
Attn: Scholarships
P.O. Box 1986
Indianapolis, IN 46206

4106

Roy A. Wilson And Ruth A. Wilson Memorial Fund Award

Amount: None Specified **Deadline:** Apr 1
Field/Major: All Areas Of Study

Scholarships for students at Kent State who were residents of the Claymont School district when they graduated from high school. Preference is given to freshmen. Applicants must demonstrate financial need. Contact the financial aid office at your campus for details.

Kent State University, Tuscarawas Campus
Financial Aid Office
University Drive, NE
New Philadelphia, OH 44663

4107

Roy Hickman Family Fund

Amount: Varies **Deadline:** Mar 1
Field/Major: Sports Administration Program

Awards are available at the University of New Mexico for graduate students in a sports administration program who are seeking an assistantship. Contact the Health Education Department for more information.

University Of New Mexico, Albuquerque
Office Of Financial Aid
Albuquerque, NM 87131

4108

Roy Martin Scholarship For Outdoor Communicators

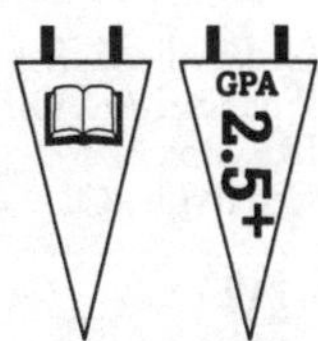

Amount: $1,000 **Deadline:** Mar 1
Field/Major: Journalism

For a student who has a career goal communicating to the public an appreciation for the outdoor experience. Must have at least a 2.8 GPA and attend the University of Florida. Student should be able to demonstrate interest through previous internships, jobs or news clippings. Write to the address below for complete details.

University of Florida
Scholarship and Placement Director
2070 Weimer Hall
Gainesville, FL 32611

4109

Roy Wilkins Scholarship

Amount: $1,000 **Deadline:** Apr 30
Field/Major: All Areas Of Study

Applicant must be an African American high school senior and be a member of the NAACP. Student must have a GPA of 2.5. Write to the address below for more details.

NAACP Special Contribution Fund
Education Department
4805 Mount Hope Drive
Baltimore, MD 21215

4110

Royal A. And Mildred D. Eddy And Louise I. Latshaw Student Loans

Amount: $4,000 (max) **Deadline:** Varies
Field/Major: All Areas Of Study

Loans are available for U.S. citizens who have completed a minimum of two years at an accredited college or university. These loans are also granted to graduate students. Contact the address below for further information.

Royal A. And Mildred E. Eddy And Louise I. Latshaw Trust Funds
NBD Bank
8585 Broadway #396
Merrillville, IN 46410

4111

Royal Neighbors Of America Fraternal Scholarships

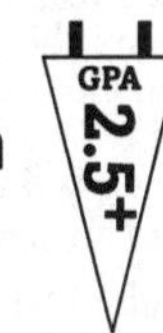

Amount: $2,000 **Deadline:** Dec 1
Field/Major: All Areas Of Study

Applicants must be high school seniors who have been beneficial members of the Royal Neighbors for at least two years preceding the date of the application and be in the upper third of graduating class. Write to the address below for details.

Royal Neighbors Of America
Fraternal Scholarship Committee
230 16th Steet
Rock Island, IL 61201

4112

RPCNA Grants At Geneva

Amount: Varies **Deadline:** None Specified
Field/Major: All Areas Of Study

Renewable scholarships for students at Geneva College who are communicant members of the Reformed Presbyterian Church of North America (RPCNA). For full-time study. Contact the Office of Admissions for further information.

Geneva College
Office Of Admissions
Beaver Falls, PA 15010

4113

RTNDR Summer And Entry Level Internships

Amount: $1,000-$1,300/month
Deadline: Mar 1
Field/Major: News Management, Electronic Journalism

Internship program juniors, seniors, or graduate minority students who are interested in news management or electronic journalism. Write to the address below for more information.

Radio And Television News Directors Foundation
1000 Connecticut Ave., NW, Suite 615
Washington, DC 20036

4114

RTNDF Undergraduate And Graduate Scholarship Programs

Amount: Varies **Deadline:** Mar 1
Field/Major: Broadcast Or Electronic Journalism

Must be a sophomore, junior, or senior seeking a career in broadcast journalism. Based on examples of reporting and/or photographic skills. Thirteen awards are offered per year. Write to the address below for details.

Radio And Television News Directors Foundation, Inc.
RTNDF Scholarships
1000 Connecticut Ave., NW, Suite 615
Washington, DC 20036

4115

Ruby Marsh Eldred Scholarship Fund

Amount: None Specified **Deadline:** Mar 1
Field/Major: All Areas Of Study

As a memorial to Ruby Marsh Eldred, a scholarship has been established in her name for students who reside in central or western Crawford County, who plan to enroll in a regionally accredited two- or four-year college, and rank in the top 25% of their class. Write to the address listed below for further information and an application.

Ruby Marsh Eldred Scholarship Fund
c/o Mary Ann Kirkpatrick, Esquire
Old Post Bldg., 941 Federal Court
Meadville, PA 16335

4116

Ruby Newhall Memorial Scholarship Program

Amount: $1,000 (max) **Deadline:** Mar 15
Field/Major: See Listing Of Fields Below

Scholarships available for international students enrolled in one of following programs: physical therapy, occupational therapy, speech/hearing therapy, mental health, or rehabilitation. Recipients must be preparing for, or already involved in, careers working with people with disabilities/brain-related disorders or in human health fields. For study in the U.S. or Canada. Send an SASE to the address listed below for information. All applicants must be sponsored by a Pilot Club in their hometown or college/university town.

Pilot International Foundation
P.O. Box 5600
244 College Street
Macon, GA 31208

4117

Rudolph And Fannie Susman Scholarship

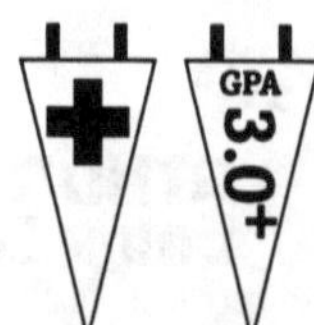

Amount: Tuition And Fees
Deadline: None Specified
Field/Major: Nursing

Awards for Mesa State sophomores, juniors, or seniors majoring in the field of nursing. Must have a GPA of at least 3.0. Contact the school of professional studies/nursing area for more details.

Mesa State College
Financial Aid Office
P.O. Box 2647
Grand Junction, CO 81501

4118

Rudolph Dillman Memorial Scholarship

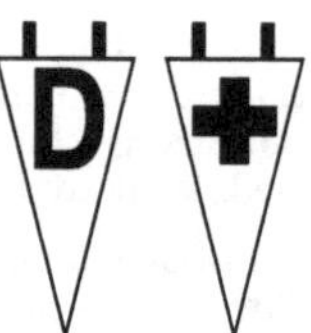

Amount: $2,500 **Deadline:** Apr 1
Field/Major: Rehabilitation: Education Of Visually Impaired And Blind Persons

Must be legally blind graduate student who is studying in the field of rehabilitation and/or education of visually impaired and blind persons. Must be a U.S. citizen. Write to the address below for complete details.

American Foundation For The Blind
Scholarship Committee
11 Penn Plaza, Suite 300
New York, NY 10001

4119

Rudy Bedford Endowed Memorial Scholarships

Amount: Varies **Deadline:** None Specified
Field/Major: Business

Awards are available for students at Cedarville College majoring in business. Must have a GPA of at least 2.0. Write to the address below for more information.

Cedarville College
Financial Aid Office
P.O. Box 601
Cedarville, OH 45314

4120

Rudy E. Booher Bontrager Memorial Endowed Grant Fund

Amount: Varies **Deadline:** None Specified
Field/Major: All Areas Of Study

Awards are available for students at Cedarville College who have demonstrated financial need. Must have a GPA of at least 2.0. Write to the address below for more information.

Cedarville College
Financial Aid Office
P.O. Box 601
Cedarville, OH 45314

4121

Rueben Cowles Scholarship

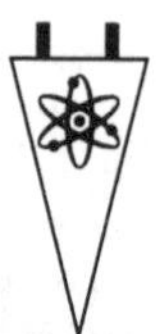

Amount: Varies **Deadline:** Jul 1
Field/Major: Dairy Science

Scholarships are available to students who reside in North Carolina, Georgia, South Carolina, Virginia, and Tennessee. Applicants must be enrolled in a dairy-related field of study and be less than age 31. Write to the address below for details.

American Jersey Cattle Association
Scholarship Committee
6486 East Main Street
Reynoldsburg, OH 43068

4122

Ruetgers-Nease Corporation Scholarships

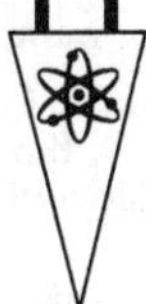

AMOUNT: $1,000 **DEADLINE:** Feb 15
FIELD/MAJOR: Agriculture

Scholarships are available for FFA members pursuing a four-year degree in any area of agriculture at Penn State University. Write to the address below for details.

National FFA Foundation
Scholarship Office
P.O. Box 15160
Alexandria, VA 22309

4123

Ruppert Educational Grant Program

AMOUNT: $800 **DEADLINE:** Mar 29
FIELD/MAJOR: All Areas Of Study

Scholarships are available for undergraduate study to graduating high school seniors from San Mateo County. Not based upon academics. Up to twenty awards offered each year. Write to the address listed below for additional information.

Peninsula Community Foundation
1700 South El Camino Real, Suite 300
San Mateo, CA 94402

4124

Rural Kentucky Medical Scholarship Fund

AMOUNT: $12,000 (max) **DEADLINE:** Apr 1
FIELD/MAJOR: Medicine

Loans for Kentucky residents who have been admitted to one of the two accredited medical schools in Kentucky. Recipients must agree to practice twelve months in an approved rural Kentucky county for each loan received. Write to the address below for more information.

Kentucky Medical Association
301 N. Hurstbourne Parkway, Suite 200
Louisville, KY 40222

4125

Ruritan National Foundation Awards

AMOUNT: $700 **DEADLINE:** Apr 1
FIELD/MAJOR: All Areas Of Study

Educational grants and loans are offered by Ruritan. Requires reference of two Ruritan members. Grades and need are considered. Re-application is permitted to continue the award into subsequent years of study. Some degree of preference is given to freshmen and sophomores. Write to the address below for details.

Ruritan National Foundation
P.O. Box 487
Dublin, VA 24084

4126

Rush University Grants And Endowment Funds

AMOUNT: Varies **DEADLINE:** None Specified
FIELD/MAJOR: All Areas Of Study

Awards for full-time graduate and undergraduate students. Based mainly on financial need. Write to the address below for details.

Rush University
Office Of Student Financial Aid
1743 West Harrison St.
Chicago, IL 60612

4127

Russell Ashby Memorial Scholarship

AMOUNT: Varies **DEADLINE:** Mar 1
FIELD/MAJOR: Nursing

Awards are available at the University of New Mexico for full-time nursing students who have completed at least sixty hours of study. Must have a minimum GPA of 2.5 and financial need. Write to the address below or contact the School of Nursing for more details.

University Of New Mexico, Albuquerque
Office Of Financial Aid
Albuquerque, NM 87131

4128

Russell Brines Memorial Scholarship

AMOUNT: $1,000 **DEADLINE:** Mar 1
FIELD/MAJOR: Journalism

Must be a junior or senior seeking a career in reporting in areas of international politics, foreign affairs, or national politics. Must be attending the University of Florida and have at least a 2.8 GPA. Write to the address below for complete details.

University of Florida
Scholarship And Placement Director
2070 Weimer Hall
Gainesville, FL 32611

4129

Russell K. Sims Scholarship, Chemistry Alumni Awards

AMOUNT: Varies **DEADLINE:** None Specified
FIELD/MAJOR: Chemistry

Scholarships are available at the University of Iowa for full-time sophomore, junior, or senior chemistry majors. Write to the address listed below for information.

University Of Iowa
Department Of Chemistry
305 Chemistry Building
Iowa City, IA 52245

4130

Russell Peters Endowed Scholarships

AMOUNT: Varies **DEADLINE:** Mar 1
FIELD/MAJOR: Business

Awards for entering freshman with the intended majors in the Foster College of Business. Competitive awards based mainly on test scores and class rank. Write to the address below for more information.

Bradley University
Office Of Financial Assistance
Bradley University
Peoria, IL 61625

4131

Russian Fellowships

Amount: None Specified **Deadline:** Varies
Field/Major: Russian Studies

Fellowships are available for scholars enrolled in a U.S. Doctoral program. Applicants must have completed all the program requirements except for the dissertation. Research must be in Russian or Soviet studies. Write to the address listed below for information.

Social Science Research Council
Fellowships And Grants
605 Third Avenue
New York, NY 10158

4132

Ruth Burgess Memorial Scholarship

Amount: Varies **Deadline:** None Specified
Field/Major: All Areas Of Study

Awards available to female students who are in need of financial assistance. Write to the address below for more information.

Rockford College
Financial Aid Office
5050 East State St.
Rockford, IL 61108

4133

Ruth Corpening Adams Scholarship, Holly Adams Memorial Scholarship

Amount: None Specified **Deadline:** None Specified
Field/Major: Art

Scholarships for art majors at East Tennessee State University who are or will be art majors. Contact the financial aid office at the address below for details, or direct inquiries to the Department of Art Chairman.

East Tennessee State University
Office Of Financial Aid
Box 70722
Johnson City, TN 37614

4134

Ruth E. Black Scholarship

Amount: $200 (min) **Deadline:** Feb 1
Field/Major: Engineering, Architecture And Construction-Related Fields

Scholarships are available to the University of Hawaii, Hilo, for full-time students enrolled in a construction-related program. Write to the address listed below for information.

University Of Hawaii At Hilo
Financial Aid Office
200 West Kawili Street
Hilo, HI 96720

4135

Ruth Good And Louis C. Stearns III Scholarship Fund

Amount: Varies **Deadline:** None Specified
Field/Major: All Areas Of Study

Awards for graduating seniors from Hampden Academy in Bangor, Maine. Contact the Hampden Academy guidance office for more information.

Maine Community Fund
P.O. Box 148
Ellsworth, ME 04605

4136

Ruth Gulden Holsteen And Charles Sophus Holsteen Memorial Scholarship

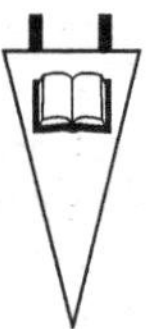

Amount: Varies **Deadline:** Mar 1
Field/Major: English

Scholarships are available at the University of Iowa for full-time junior or senior English majors who are U.S. citizens, and who excel in the field of English literature and composition. Write to the address listed below for information.

University Of Iowa
Department Of English
308 English-Philosophy Building
Iowa City, IA 52242

4137

Ruth Hinckley Willes Scholarship

Amount: $600 **Deadline:** April 15
Field/Major: English

Scholarships are available at the University of Utah for full-time students enrolled in an English program. Must have completed English 351, 352, and one additional English course, and be a Utah resident. Write to the address below for details.

University of Utah
Scholarship Chairperson
3500 Lnco
Salt Lake City, UT 84112

4138

Ruth Satter Memorial Award

Amount: None Specified **Deadline:** Jan 15
Field/Major: All Areas Of Study

Scholarship for women pursuing their doctorate who have taken at least three years off to raise children. Write to the address below for more details.

Association For Women In Science Educational Foundation
National Headquarters
1522 K St., NW, Suite 820
Washington, DC 20005

4139

Ruth Taylor Scholarship

Amount: Varies **Deadline:** Jun 15
Field/Major: Medicine, Social Work (And Related)

Scholarships for Westchester County (NY) graduate students in social work or medicine. Write to the commissioner's office at the address below for details.

Westchester County Department Of Social Services
Ruth Taylor Award Fund Committee
112 E. Post Road
White Plains, NY 10601

4140

S. California Institute Of Food Technologists

Amount: $250-$1,500 **Deadline:** Mar 15
Field/Major: Food Science, Nutrition

Students must be full-time at Cal Poly Pomona with a career goal in food science and/or nutrition. Must be a resident of California. Six awards are given yearly. Write to the address below for more information.

California State Polytechnic University, Pomona
College Of Agriculture
Building 7, Room 110
Pomona, CA 91768

4141

S. Evelyn Lewis Memorial Scholarship In Medical Health Sciences

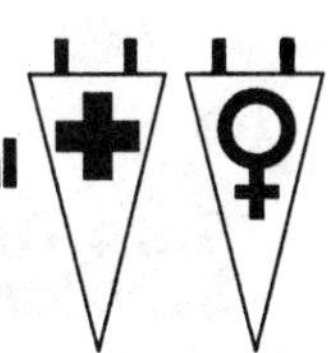

Amount: $500-$1,000 **Deadline:** Feb 1
Field/Major: Medicine, Health Sciences

Scholarships for undergraduate or graduate women currently enrolled in a degree-granting program in medicine or health sciences. For one year, full-time study. No affiliation with Zeta Phi Beta is required. Send an SASE to the national headquarters at the address below for further information.

Zeta Phi Beta Sorority
National Educational Foundation
1734 New Hampshire Ave., NW
Washington, DC 20009

4142

S. John and Elizabeth Trudeau Scholarships

Amount: $600 **Deadline:** Spring
Field/Major: Fine Arts

Awards are available to full-time majors in the school of Fine and Performing Arts, who have a GPA of 3.0 or higher (3.5 or better in their major). Contact your major department chairperson for more information.

Portland State University
Music Department
231 Lincoln Hall
Portland, OR 97207

4143

S. Ralph Edmonds Young Scholars Competition

Amount: $100-$250 **Deadline:** Feb 15
Field/Major: Drama, Theater

Contest for the best papers written on an aspect of African American theater in the U.S. or throughout the world. Paper should be ten pages in length, including endnotes and bibliography. Winners will also be invited to deliver their papers at the Black Theater Network Conference in New York City. Write to the address below for more information. Papers will be returned only if accompanied by an SASE.

Black Theater Network
Dr. Harry Elam, Department of Drama
Stanford University
Stanford, CA 94305

4144

Saccomanno Higher Education Foundation Scholarship

Amount: Varies **Deadline:** None Specified
Field/Major: All Areas Of Study

Awards for Mesa State students who are residents of Mesa County, CO, or Carbon County, UT. Must demonstrate financial need. Contact the Saccomanno Higher Education Foundation or the financial aid office at the address below for more information.

Mesa State College
Office Of Financial Aid
P.O. Box 3692
Grand Junction, CO 81501

4145

Sachs Foundation Scholarship

Amount: $3,000-$4,000 **Deadline:** Mar 1
Field/Major: All Areas Of Study

Scholarships are available for African American students who are residents of Colorado. Applicant must demonstrate financial need. Undergraduates must have a GPA of at least 3.5 and graduate students must have a GPA of at least 3.8. Community involvement is also an important aspect of evaluation. Write to the address listed below for information.

Sachs Foundation
90 S. Cascade Avenue, Suite 1410
Colorado Springs, CO 80903

4146

SAE Undesignated Engineering Scholarships

Amount: $1,000-$1,500 **Deadline:** Dec 1
Field/Major: Engineering

Scholarships for engineering students. For study at any accredited school in the U.S. Must have a GPA of at least 3.5 (and 90th percentile SAT scores). Renewable for four years. Three awards per year. Programs include BMW, Fred Young Sr., and Hendrickson Scholarships. Must be current high school senior, a U.S. citizen, and plan to earn a degree in engineering. Write to the address below for details.

Society of Automotive Engineers
Engineering Education Scholarships
400 Commonwealth Dr.
Warrendale, PA 15096

4147

Sage Scholarships

Amount: $500-$1,000 **Deadline:** Apr 8
Field/Major: All Areas Of Study

Awards for graduating high school seniors from Ventura County who have shown initiative and improvement in his/her academic accomplishments. Must show financial need with maximum parent income of no more than $65,000 per year and be intending to enroll as a degree candidate at a vocational or trade school, community or accredited college or university. Write to the address below or contact your high school counselor for more information.

Ventura County Community Fund
1355 Del Norte Road
Camarillo, CA 93010

4148

Salk Scholarship Award

AMOUNT: $4,000 (max) **DEADLINE:** None Specified
FIELD/MAJOR: Medicine

Scholarships are available for undergraduates and graduates of the senior colleges of the City University of New York who have received an acceptance for admission in an American medical school in pursuit of the M.D., Ph.D., D.O., or the D.Sc. Write to the address below for more information.

City University Of New York
Medgar Evers College
1650 Bedford Ave.
Brooklyn, NY 11225

4149

Sallie And Beulah Alexander Scholarship

AMOUNT: $1,000 **DEADLINE:** Apr 1
FIELD/MAJOR: All Areas Of Study

Scholarships are available at the University of Oklahoma, Norman for students who are of Commanche Indian heritage. Three or four awards offered annually. Write to the address listed below for information.

University Of Oklahoma, Norman
Office Of Financial Aid Services
731 Elm
Norman, OK 73019

4150

Sally Kress Tompkins Fellowship

AMOUNT: $7,500 **DEADLINE:** Dec 15
FIELD/MAJOR: Architectural History

Awards are available for students studying architectural history to work as an intern on a historic American buildings survey summer project. Based primarily on academic records and recommendations. Write to the address below for more information.

Society Of Architectural Historians
1365 North Astor St.
Chicago, IL 60610

4151

Salzer Foundation Physician Assistant Awards

AMOUNT: $1,000-$2,000 **DEADLINE:** None Specified
FIELD/MAJOR: Physician Assisting

Awards are available for physician assisting students. There are no mandatory criteria. Candidates with special needs and situations (non-eligible for Pell Grants, veterans, extraordinary family obligation, etc.) are favored. Write to the address below for more information.

Salzer Foundation
Thomas Salzer
5 Averstone Dr., East
Washington Crossing, PA 18977

4152

Sam S. Kuwahara Memorial Scholarship

AMOUNT: Varies **DEADLINE:** Apr 1
FIELD/MAJOR: Agriculture

Awards for undergraduate students of Japanese ancestry who are studying agriculture. Write to the address below for more details. Please be sure to include an SASE with your request.

Japanese American Citizens League
National Headquarters
1765 Sutter St.
San Francisco, CA 94115

4153

Sam Turk Memorial Scholarship In Music

AMOUNT: $1,000 **DEADLINE:** May 1
FIELD/MAJOR: Performing Music

Awarded annually to a performing music student at Five Towns College who demonstrates academic potential and/or economic need. Write to the address below for more details.

Five Towns College
305 N. Service Road/Lie Exit 50
Dix Hills, NY 11746

4154

Samuel And Jetty Whitehead Scholarship

AMOUNT: Varies **DEADLINE:** Mar 1
FIELD/MAJOR: Music

Awards at the University of New Mexico for music students enrolled in the College of Fine Arts. Write to the address below for more information.

University Of New Mexico, Albuquerque
Office Of Financial Aid
Albuquerque, NM 87131

4155

Samuel Fletcher Tapman Student Chapter Scholarships

AMOUNT: $1,500 **DEADLINE:** Mar 1
FIELD/MAJOR: Civil Engineering

Must be member in good standing of an American Society of Civil Engineers student chapter. No more than one applicant from each chapter. Must continue undergraduate education in a recognized educational institution, and be a freshman, sophomore, or junior. Write to the address below for more details.

American Society Of Civil Engineers
Member Scholarships And Awards
345 E. 47th St.
New York, NY 10017

4156

Samuel H. Kress Joint Athens-Jerusalem Fellowship

Amount: $5,500 and Fees **Deadline:** Nov 15
Field/Major: Classical Studies, Art History, Architecture, Archaeology

Awards are available for Ph.D. candidates in the areas of study above. Must be a U.S. citizen. Write to the address below for more information.

American School Of Classical Studies At Athens
Committee On Admissions And Fellowships
993 Lenox Drive, Suite 101
Lawrenceville, NJ 08648

4157

Samuel H. Winston Memorial Scholarship

Amount: $400 **Deadline:** Apr 1
Field/Major: Sciences

Scholarships for students at Kent State University who graduated from Tuscarawas High School and studying any of the sciences. Must have a GPA of at least 3.0. Contact the financial aid office for details.

Kent State University, Tuscarawas Campus
Financial Aid Office
330 University Drive, NE
New Philadelphia, OH 44663

4158

Samuel Huntington Public Service Award

Amount: $10,000 **Deadline:** Feb 15
Field/Major: Public Service

Awards are available to graduating seniors from accredited colleges who would like to pursue public service anywhere in the world. The stipend allows students to engage in a meaningful public service activity for up to one year before proceeding on to graduate school or a career. Write to the address below for more information.

Samuel Huntington Fund
Attn: D.F. Goodwin
25 Research Dr.
Westborough, MA 01582

Samuel Robinson Award

Amount: $1,000 **Deadline:** Apr 1
Field/Major: All Areas Of Study

Scholarships for juniors or seniors at a Presbyterian college. Applicants must be U.S. citizens and members of the Presbyterian Church (U.S.A.). Must be a full-time student. Write to the address listed below for information and an application.

Presbyterian Church (U.S.A.)
Office Of Financial Aid For Studies
100 Witherspoon Street
Louisville, KY 40202

4160

San Joaquin Medical Society Scholarship Loan Program

Amount: $8,000-$40,000 **Deadline:** Dec 1, Jun 1
Field/Major: Medicine, Nursing

Applicants must be residents of San Joaquin, Amador, or Calaveras Counties and enrolled in a full-time program in either medicine or nursing. Write to the address below for details.

San Joaquin Medical Society
P.O. Box 230
Stockton, CA 95201

4161

San Pedro Peninsula Hospital Auxiliary Health Grants

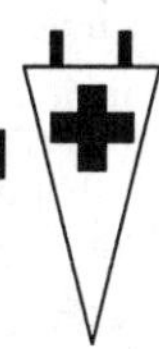

Amount: $600-$1,000 **Deadline:** Nov 15
Field/Major: Healthcare Related

Scholarships for students who reside in the San Pedro Peninsula hospital service area who plan to enter a health-care profession. Renewable once. For two- or four- year study. Must have completed at least one semester of study. Service area includes cities of San Pedro, Palos Verdes Peninsula, Lomita, Harbor City, and Wilmington. Write to the address below for details.

San Pedro Peninsula Hospital Auxiliary
Health Careers Committee
1300 W. Seventh Street
San Pedro, CA 90732

4162

Sandoz Agro, Inc. Scholarships

Amount: $2,000 **Deadline:** Feb 15
Field/Major: Agriculture

Scholarships are available for FFA members pursuing a four-year degree in any area of agriculture, enrolled at the University of Illinois, Purdue University, Cornell University, Iowa State, University of Minnesota, Michigan State, Texas A&M, University of Wisconsin (Madison), Virginia Polytechnic, Florida A&M, or University of California (Davis). Write to the address below for details.

National FFA Foundation
Scholarship Office
P.O. Box 15160
Alexandria, VA 22309

4163

Sandoz Animal Health Scholarships

Amount: $2,000 **Deadline:** Feb 15
Field/Major: Veterinary Medicine

Scholarships are available for FFA members pursuing a four-year degree in the above area, and enrolled in the school of veterinary medicine at Texas A &M, University of California (Davis), University of Florida (Gainesville), University of Georgia (Athens), Oklahoma State University (Stillwater), or Tuskegee University. Write to the address below for details.

National FFA Foundation
Scholarship Office
P.O. Box 15160
Alexandria, VA 22309

4164

Santa Fe Pacific Foundation Scholarships

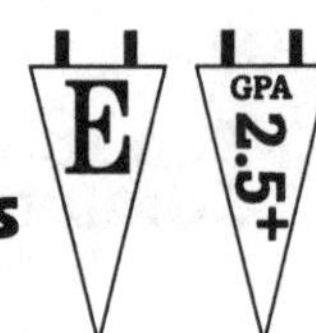

AMOUNT: $2,500 **DEADLINE:** None Specified
FIELD/MAJOR: All Areas Of Study

Five scholarships for high school seniors who are of Indian descent (1/4). No relationship to Santa Fe Pacific is required. Two of the awards are given to Navajo tribe members. For any school in the U.S. Preference given to sciences-medicine, engineering, and natural/physical, business, education, and health administration. Must live in Arizona; Colorado; Kansas; New Mexico; Oklahoma; or San Bernardino County, CA. Applications may be obtained by writing to the address below. Please specify that you are interested in the Santa Fe Pacific Awards.

American Indian Science And Engineering Society
Scholarship Coordinator
1630 30th Street, Suite 301
Boulder, CO 80301

4165

Santa Fe Pacific Scholarships

AMOUNT: $1,000 **DEADLINE:** Feb 15
FIELD/MAJOR: Agriculture And Related

Scholarships for FFA members in Arizona, California, Colorado, Illinois, Kansas, Missouri, New Mexico, Oklahoma, and Texas. Nonrenewable. A trip to the annual national FFA convention is included. Must be senior in high school who will be majoring in an agriculture-related field of study at a land grant college in their home state. Eighteen scholarships annually. Write to the address below for details. Contact your local FFA for applications.

National FFA Foundation
Scholarship Office
P.O. Box 15160
Alexandria, VA 22309

4166

Sara Jackson Award

AMOUNT: $500 **DEADLINE:** Jul 1
FIELD/MAJOR: Western History

Scholarships are awarded to a graduate student research award of $500 given annually for research support. Preference is given to African American or other minority students. Write to the address listed below for information.

Western History Association
University Of New Mexico
1080 Mesa Vista Hall
Albuquerque, NM 87131

4167

Sara Thorniley Phillips Awards

AMOUNT: $300 **DEADLINE:** Mar 1
FIELD/MAJOR: Collegiate And Community Service

Awarded to undergraduates for outstanding leadership and participation in collegiate and community programs. Must be a member of Phi Upsilon Omicron. Two awards are given yearly. Write to California Home Economics Association, 3040 Dwight Way, Stockton, CA 95204, for more information.

California State Polytechnic University, Pomona
College Of Agriculture
Building 7, Room 110
Pomona, CA 91768

4168

Sarah Bradley Tyson Memorial Fellowships

AMOUNT: $500 **DEADLINE:** Apr 15
FIELD/MAJOR: Agriculture, Horticulture, And Related

Fellowships for advanced study at an educational institution of recognized standing in the U.S. Awards have been made in recognition of leadership in cooperative extension work and initiative in scientific research. Write to the address below for complete details.

Woman's National Farm And Garden Association
Mrs. Elmer Braun
13 Davis Drive
Saginaw, MI 48602

4169

Sarah Rebecca Reed Scholarship

AMOUNT: Varies **DEADLINE:** Mar 15
FIELD/MAJOR: Library And Information Science

Applicants must have been admitted to a graduate program in library science accredited by the ALA. For master's level study. Write to the Executive Secretary at the address below for details.

Beta Phi Mu International Library Science Honor Society
Executive Secretary, Beta Phi Mu
SLIS-Florida State University
Tallahassee, FL 32306

4170

Sarasota Jazz Club Scholarships

AMOUNT: $500-$1,000 **DEADLINE:** Feb 1
FIELD/MAJOR: All Areas Of Study

Scholarships for residents of Sarasota or Manatee Counties (FL). Based on musical (jazz) audition. Four-$1,000 scholarships, two-$500 scholarships, and two-$500 merit awards are given. Write to the address below for details.

Jazz Club Of Sarasota
Scholarship Committee
290 Cocoanut Ave., Bldg. 3
Sarasota, FL 34236

4171

Sato Memorial Scholarship

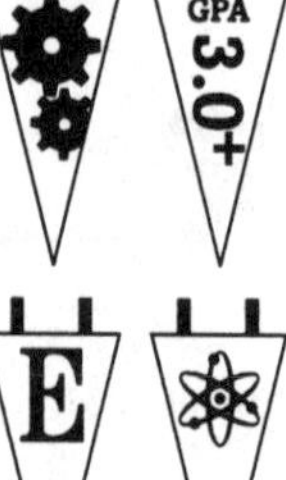

AMOUNT: $500 **DEADLINE:** None Specified
FIELD/MAJOR: Engineering, Mathematics, Natural Sciences

Awards are available at Portland State University for Asian students in the fields of math, engineering, or natural science. A GPA of 3.0, as well as enrollment in at least 12 credits is required to apply. Renewable. Write to the address below for more information.

Portland State University
Educational Equity Programs And Services
120 Smith Memorial Center
Portland, OR 97207

4172

SCA/Interior Americorps Program

AMOUNT: $2,363 **DEADLINE:** None Specified
FIELD/MAJOR: Ecology, Environmental Studies, Fisheries, Wildlife Studies, Hydrology

Awards are available for students over the age of 17 to work for a 900- to 1700-hour term on a program site in Texas, New Mexico, or Florida. This program is done in conjunction with the U.S. Department of the Interior. Must be a U.S. citizen or permanent resident. Write to the address below for more information. Recipients also receive free medical insurance and a subscription to Earth Work magazine.

Student Conservation Association, Inc.
P.O. Box 550
Charlestown, NH 03603

4173

SCE&G Minority Achievement Scholarship

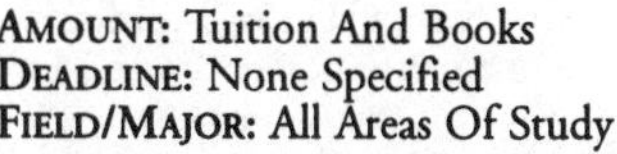

AMOUNT: Tuition And Books
DEADLINE: None Specified
FIELD/MAJOR: All Areas Of Study

Awards for minority Trident area students in financial need that are enrolled full-time in an associate degree program. Must have demonstrated achievement in academic, extracurricular, and community activities. A GPA of at least 2.5 is required. Write to the address below for more information.

Trident Technical College
Financial Aid Office
P.O. Box 118067
Charleston, SC 29423

4174

Schechter Foundation Grants

AMOUNT: Varies **DEADLINE:** None Specified
FIELD/MAJOR: Physical, Occupational Therapy

Grants for students enrolled in one of the above programs at New York, Columbia, or Hahnemann universities. Contact the address below for further information.

Schechter Foundation
535 Madison Ave., 28th Floor
New York, NY 10022

4175

Schering-Plough Museum Internship

AMOUNT: $4,000 **DEADLINE:** May 15
FIELD/MAJOR: Museum Studies, Art History

Internship program for students in a program of art history or museum studies. Based on resume, work experience, and interview. Write to the address below for more information.

Schering-Plough Corporation, Montclair Art Museum
Curator Of Education
3 South Mountain Ave.
Montclair, NJ 07042

4176

Schinnerer/Pepp Management Study Fellowship

AMOUNT: $3,000 **DEADLINE:** Feb 1
FIELD/MAJOR: Engineering

One $3,000 fellowship is available to an engineer pursuing advanced studies in management. Must be a registered P.E., have a GPA of at least 3.0 and be enrolled in an accredited MBA, master's in management, or master's in engineering management program. Write to the address below for details.

National Society Of Professional Engineers
Office Of Student Services
1420 King St.
Alexandria, VA 22314

4177

Schizophrenia Research Program Dissertation Fellowships

AMOUNT: $12,2000 **DEADLINE:** Feb 1
FIELD/MAJOR: Psychology, Psychiatry (Relating To Schizophrenia Research)

Dissertation fellowships for Ph.D. candidates (ABD) in areas of study which will add to the corpus of knowledge of schizophrenia. Candidates in other fields (epidemiology, neuroscience, e-physiology, etc.) may be considered. The council appears to support mostly non-clinical research. Application must be initiated by a letter from a sponsoring scientist which includes evidence of the candidate's distinction in grad. performance and outline of the research protocol to be pursued. Letter should be addressed to the research director before Feb 1. Write for brochure/instructions if needed. Include investigators' names, mail address, and phone/fax numbers.

Supreme Council 33rd Degree, A.A. Scottish Rite
Schizpohrenia Research Program, NMJ, USA
33 Marrett Road, P.O. Box 519
Lexington, MA 02173

4178

Schizophrenia Research Program Research Grants

AMOUNT: $30,000 (max) **DEADLINE:** Dec 15
FIELD/MAJOR: Psychology, Psychiatry (Relating To Schizophrenia Research)

Grants supporting research into nature and causes of schizophrenia. Typically therapeutic aspects not supported. Preference given to pilot and basic research. Based on relevance to foundation goals, scientific merit, and relevance to progress in understanding the causes of schizophrenia. Application must be initiated by a letter to Steven Matthysse, Ph.D., Research Director. Max: 2-3 single space pages incl refs, supporting materials. Describe specific aims and significance of project (not details/methodology). No cv or reprints necess. Incl. investigators' names (in order of appearance), mail address, phone/fax, and project title. Write for brochure/instructions if needed.

Supreme Council 33rd Degree, A.A. Scottish Rite Schizpohrenia Research Program, NMJ, USA
33 Marrett Road, P.O. Box 519
Lexington, MA 02173

4179

Schneider-Emanuel Scholarships

AMOUNT: $500 **DEADLINE:** None Specified
FIELD/MAJOR: All Areas Of Study

Scholarships are available for residents of Wisconsin who are children of American Legion or Auxiliary members, and who participate in American Legion or Auxiliary youth programs. Must be U.S. citizens. Write to the address listed below for additional information.

American Legion,-Department Of Wisconsin
Department Headquarters
812 East State Street
Milwaukee, WI 53202

4180

Scholars In Residence Program Fellowships

AMOUNT: $30,000 (max) **DEADLINE:** Jan 15
FIELD/MAJOR: Black Culture, History, Museum Administration

To assist scholars and professionals whose research in the black experience will benefit from extended access to the center's collections. Allows fellows to spend six months to a year in residence and includes seminars, forums and conferences. Candidates for advanced degrees must have received the degree or completed all the requirements for it by the center's deadline. Contact the address below for further information and application.

Schomburg Center For Research In Black Culture
515 Malcolm X Boulevard
New York, NY 10037

4181

Scholarship Awards And Achievement Awards

AMOUNT: $100 To $1,000 **DEADLINE:** May 14
FIELD/MAJOR: All Areas Of Study

The prospective candidate must have been a member of the Sons of Poland for at least two years and be insured by the association. You must be entering an accredited college in September of the year of graduation from high school. Write to the address below for complete details.

Association Of The Sons Of Poland
Scholarship Committee
333 Hackensack St.
Carlstadt, NJ 07072

4182

Scholarship Awards Of Excellence

AMOUNT: $1,000 **DEADLINE:** Mar 1
FIELD/MAJOR: Agriculture

Awards are available to freshmen at Purdue University who enroll in the school of agriculture. Write to the address below for more information.

Purdue Agricultural Alumni Association And Ag Businesses
Purdue University, Associate Dean
Director of Academic Programs
West Lafayette, IN 47907

4183

Scholarship Grants For Prospective Educators

AMOUNT: $1,000-$2,000 **DEADLINE:** Jan 31
FIELD/MAJOR: Education

Candidates must be high school seniors who are planning to pursue careers in education. The criteria involved in the selection include academic records, recommendations, school and community activities, and written expression. Forty-three awards are offered annually. Write to Attn: Chapter Programs at the address below for details.

Phi Delta Kappa
International Headquarters
P.O. Box 789
Bloomington, IN 47402

4184

Scholarship Program

AMOUNT: $250-$2,000 **DEADLINE:** Jun 30
FIELD/MAJOR: Automotive Technology

Students must be active in automotive curricula in two- or four-year schools, or interested in pursuing an automotive career. Must be at the sophomore level of study the year the scholarship is granted. Write to the address below for complete details. The Hall of Fame also has a resume bank to help graduates locate jobs.

Automotive Hall Of Fame
3225 Cook Road
P.O. Box 1727
Midland, MI 48641

4185

Scholarship Program For Dependents of Seafarers

AMOUNT: $15,000 **DEADLINE:** Apr 15
FIELD/MAJOR: All Areas Of Study

Renewable four-year scholarships for dependents of members of the Seafarers International Union. Children must be unmarried and under 25 years of age. Parent must have worked for at least three years for an employer who contributes to the Seafarers Welfare Plan. Write to the address below for details.

Seafarers' Welfare Plan
Scholarship Program
5201 Auth Way
Camp Springs, MD 20746

4186

Scholarship Program For Seamen

AMOUNT: $6,000-$15,000 **DEADLINE:** Apr 15
FIELD/MAJOR: All Areas Of Study

Open to seamen who have credit for two years of employment with an employer who is obligated to make contributions to the Seafarers' Welfare Plan on the employer's behalf prior to the date of application. Must have at least 120 days of employment with some days from the previous calendar year. Applicant must be a high school graduate or its equivalent. Contact the address below for complete details.

Seafarers' Welfare Plan
Scholarship Program
5201 Auth Way
Camp Springs, MD 20746

4187

Scholarships For Achievement In Specific Fields of Study

AMOUNT: Varies **DEADLINE:** Mar 2
FIELD/MAJOR: Most Areas Of Study

Departmental awards for Holy Names students. Individual criteria for each award may vary. Write to the address below for more information.

Holy Names College
Financial Aid Office
3500 Mountain Blvd.
Oakland, CA 94619

4188

Scholarships For Aspiring Financial Writers

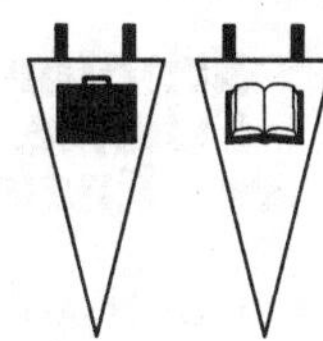

AMOUNT: $2,000 **DEADLINE:** Dec 22
FIELD/MAJOR: Business Or Financial Journalism

Awards are available for students in the metropolitan New York area who are seriously interested in pursuing a career as business and financial journalists. Write to the address below for more information.

New York Financial Writers Association, Inc.
Scholarship Committee
P.O. Box 21
Syosset, NY 11791

4189

Scholarships For Children Of Deceased Or Disabled Veterans

AMOUNT: Tuition and Fees **DEADLINE:** Apr 1
FIELD/MAJOR: All Areas Of Study

U.S. citizen and Florida resident. Enrolled full-time in Florida public institution. Children of deceased or 100% disabled veterans, or children of servicemen classified as POW or MIA. Parent must have entered military from Florida and have served during one of the defined conflict periods included on application. Information is available at the school you plan to attend, or write to the Department of Veterans' Affairs or to the address below for details.

Florida Department Of Education
Office Of Student Financial Assistance
1344 Florida Education Center
Tallahassee, FL 32399

4190

Scholarships For Children Of Missionaries

AMOUNT: Varies **DEADLINE:** Jun 1
FIELD/MAJOR: All Areas Of Study

Scholarships for children of missionaries (active, retired, or deceased) from the Episcopal Church. Available for undergraduate or graduate level study. Write to the address below for more details.

Episcopal Church Center
815 Second Ave.
New York, NY 10017

4191

Scholarships For Dependents of Blind Parents

AMOUNT: Tuition And Fees **DEADLINE:** None Specified
FIELD/MAJOR: All Areas Of Study

Scholarship is designed to cover instructional fees and tuition at any Alabama state institution of higher learning for children from families in which the head of the family is blind and whose family income is insufficient to provide educational benefits. The program is restricted to students who are Alabama residents. Students must apply within two years of high school graduation. Write to the address below for details.

Alabama Commission On Higher Education
P.O. Box 30200
Montgomery, AL 36130

4192

Scholarships For Disadvantaged Students (SDS)

AMOUNT: Varies **DEADLINE:** Mar 1
FIELD/MAJOR: Nursing

Awards are available at the University of New Mexico for full-time nursing students who come from a disadvantaged background and have financial need. Must be a U.S. citizen or permanent resident. Write to the address below or contact the school of nursing for more details.

University Of New Mexico, Albuquerque
Office Of Financial Aid
Albuquerque, NM 87131

4193

Scholarships For Disadvantaged Students (SDS)

AMOUNT: Varies **DEADLINE:** Mar 1
FIELD/MAJOR: Pharmacy

Awards are available at the University of New Mexico for full-time pharmacy students with a disadvantaged background and financial need. Must be a U.S. citizen or permanent resident. Write to the address below for more information.

University Of New Mexico, Albuquerque
Office Of Financial Aid
Albuquerque, NM 87131

4194

Scholarships For Foreign Students

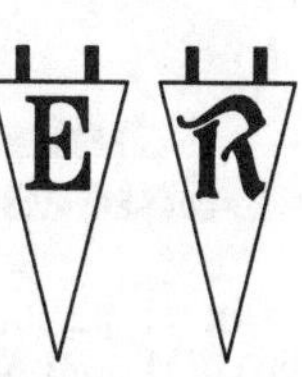

AMOUNT: Varies **DEADLINE:** Jun 1
FIELD/MAJOR: Church-Related Studies, Theology

Scholarships for students from developing countries who are in some type of theological training within the Anglican Communion. Preference is given to students pursuing a master's degree but it is open for all levels of study. Write to the address below for more details. Applications must be authorized or approved by the Diocesan Bishop, the Archbishop, or another provincial authority.

Episcopal Church Center
815 Second Ave.
New York, NY 10017

4195

Scholarships For Freshmen

AMOUNT: $800-$1,000 **DEADLINE:** May 1
FIELD/MAJOR: Agriculture, Life Sciences

Scholarships for entering freshmen at Virginia Tech. Approximately fifty awards per year. Criteria varies by award. Write to the address below for details.

Virginia Tech College Of Agriculture And Life Sciences
Dr. John M. White, Assoc. Dean
1060 Litton Reaves Hall
Blacksburg, VA 24061

4196

Scholarships For Graduate Study In Scotland

AMOUNT: $13,300 **DEADLINE:** Dec 15
FIELD/MAJOR: All Areas Of Study

Graduate scholarship for a year-study in Scotland is available for seniors of Scottish descent, who demonstrate academic excellence, leadership skills, and participation in extracurricular activities. Applicants must be endorsed by the president of the institution as the student most qualified in terms of character and indications of probable future development. Write to the address listed below for information.

St. Andrew's Society Of The State Of New York
Chairman, Scholarship Committee
71 West 23rd Street
New York, NY 10010

4197

Scholarships For Minority Ministries

AMOUNT: Varies **DEADLINE:** Jun 1
FIELD/MAJOR: Church-Related Studies, Theology

Scholarships for Asian American, African American, Hispanic, and Native American students for assistance in pursuing theological education or a graduate-level degree at a church approved seminary or in an Episcopal studies program. Write to the address below for more details.

Episcopal Church Center
815 Second Ave.
New York, NY 10017

4198

Scholarships For Minority Students

AMOUNT: $2,500 **DEADLINE:** Feb 15
FIELD/MAJOR: All Areas Of Study

RIT has developed several scholarship programs designed to assist qualified African American, Hispanic and Native American students in financing their education. Scholarships are awarded based on academic qualifications, leadership potential, and demonstrated financial need. Contact the Coordinator of Minority Student Admissions, at the address below, for details.

Rochester Institute Of Technology
Bausch & Lomb Center, Financial Aid Office
60 Lomb Memorial Drive
Rochester, NY 14623

4199

Scholarships For Returning Students

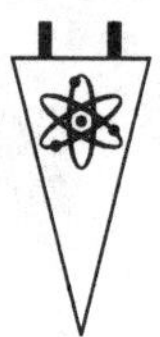

AMOUNT: $500-$1,500 **DEADLINE:** May 1
FIELD/MAJOR: Agriculture, Life Sciences

Scholarships for returning students at Virginia Tech. Approximately nineteen awards per year. Criteria vary by award. Write to the address below for details.

Virginia Tech College Of Agriculture And Life Sciences
Dr. John M. White, Assoc. Dean
1060 Litton Reaves Hall
Blacksburg, VA 24061

4200

Scholarships For Science, Math And Engineering Research

AMOUNT: $1,000-$40,000 **DEADLINE:** Dec 1
FIELD/MAJOR: Math, Science, Engineering

Open to senior high school students. Based on an independent research project and high school record. Forty awards per year. (all awards larger than $1,000 are four-year awards). Request official rules and entry form from your high school. If they are not available there, write to the address below.

Westinghouse Science Talent Search
c/o Science Service
1719 N Street, NW
Washington, DC 20036

4201

Scholarships For Study In Japan

AMOUNT: $1,500-$8,000 **DEADLINE:** Mar 1
FIELD/MAJOR: Japanese Studies

Scholarships for undergraduate or graduate students enrolled full-time in an accredited school in the District of Columbia, Maryland, Virginia, or West Virginia. Must have started a program of Japanese study and have completed one year of college-level study. Must be a U.S. citizen or permanent resident. Write to the address below for additional information.

The Japan-American Society Of Washington
1020 Nineteenth St., NW
Washington, DC 20036

4202

Scholarships For Women

AMOUNT: $1,000-$3,500 **DEADLINE:** Jan 15
FIELD/MAJOR: All Areas Of Study

Thirty scholarships for women whose education has been interrupted after more than 1 1/2 years and are in academic or professional programs at any University of Michigan campus. Women in business, chemistry, engineering, mathematics, and other less traditional areas are especially encouraged to apply. Write to the address below for details.

University Of Michigan
Center For The Education Of Women
330 E. Liberty Street
Ann Arbor, MI 48104

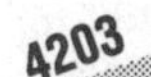
4203

Scholarships In Preparation For Positions In Jewish Community Centers

AMOUNT: $15,500 (max) **DEADLINE:** Feb 1
FIELD/MAJOR: Education, Social Work, Jewish Studies

Should have a strong desire to enter and work in the Jewish center field. For graduate study. Must have GPA of at least 3.0. Renewable for two years. Write to the address below for details.

Jewish Community Centers Association
Attn: Scholarship Program Coordinator
15 E. 26th St.
New York, NY 10010

4204

Scholastic Arts Awards/ Colorado Institute Of Art Scholarship

AMOUNT: $500 **DEADLINE:** None Specified

FIELD/MAJOR: Visual Communications, Photography

Art Institute annually awards two full-tuition scholarships in visual communications to a winner of the Scholastic Arts Awards competition as awarded by the national jury. Entry requirements are listed with eligible high school art departments. Open to high school seniors. Contact your high school art teacher for more information.

Colorado Institute Of Art
Financial Aid Office
200 E. 9th Ave.
Denver, CO 80203

4205

Scholastic Sports America Scholarship

AMOUNT: $2,500 **DEADLINE:** Mar 15
FIELD/MAJOR: All Areas Of Study

Grants for graduating high school seniors (graduating in this school year. eight awards per year; half to males, half to females). Based on academics and school/community service. Not based on athletics (but they may be considered toward school service). Must be U.S. citizen or legal resident. These are one-time grants. Competitive. Write to the address below for complete details and application (information may also be available in your high school guidance office). Applications are only accepted until March 17. Employees (and their immediate family members) of ESPN, Inc., Capital Cities/ABC Inc., the Hearst Corporation or their subsidiaries are not eligible.

ESPN Scholarship
ESPN Plaza
P.O. Box 986
Bristol, CT 06011

4206

School Academic Scholarship

GPA 3.0+

AMOUNT: $700 **DEADLINE:** None Specified
FIELD/MAJOR: All Areas Of Study

Awards for Mesa State students from Colorado who have a GPA of at least 3.0. Applicants must be enrolled in at least twelve hours of study. Contact the chairman of your academic or vocational division at Mesa State.

Mesa State College
Office Of Financial Aid
P.O. Box 2647
Grand Junction, CO 81501

4207

School Administration Scholarships At Peabody College

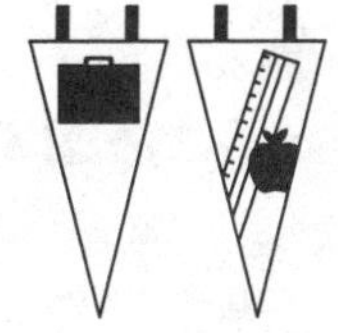

AMOUNT: None Specified **DEADLINE:** None Specified
FIELD/MAJOR: School Administration

Scholarships for graduate students in Peabody College at Vanderbilt who are majoring in school administration. Write to the address below for more information.

Vanderbilt University
Admissions And Financial Assistance
Box 327 Peabody College
Nashville, TN 37203

4208

School Librarians Workshop Scholarship

AMOUNT: $2,500 **DEADLINE:** Feb 1
FIELD/MAJOR: Library Science, Children's Or Young Adult

Applicants must be entering an ALA-accredited master's program or a school library media program that meets ala curriculum guidelines for an NCATE-accredited unit. Based on interest in working with children or young adults in a school library setting. Write to the address shown for details.

American Library Association
American Assn. Of School Librarians
50 E. Huron Street
Chicago, IL 60611

4209

School Of Extended Studies Scholarship

AMOUNT: $250 (max) **DEADLINE:** Varies
FIELD/MAJOR: All Areas Of Study

Awards are available for nontraditional students who demonstrate a commitment to life-long learning, do not qualify for other scholarships offered through PSU, and are not receiving other educational subsides from academic, private, or corporate sources. Write to the address below for more information.

Portland State University
Financial Aid Office
176 Neuberger Hall
Portland, OR 97207

4210

School Of Geology And Geophysics Awards

AMOUNT: $500-$3,000 **DEADLINE:** Mar 1
FIELD/MAJOR: Geology, Geophysics

Scholarships are available at the University of Oklahoma, Norman, for full-time geology or geophysics majors. Includes the Conoco Scholarship Award, the George G. Huffman scholarship, and the Heston Scholarship. Write to the address listed below for information.

University Of Oklahoma, Norman
Director, School of Geology And Geophysics
100 East Boyd Street, Room 810
Norman, OK 73019

4211

School Of Music Scholarships

AMOUNT: Varies **DEADLINE:** None Specified
FIELD/MAJOR: Music

Scholarships ranging from $500 to full tuition and fees are available to undergraduate students at Florida State University pursuing a degree in music—all instruments, voice, and composition. Write to the address below for details.

Florida State University
School Of Music
Tallahassee, FL 32306

4212

School Of Music Scholarships

AMOUNT: Varies **DEADLINE:** Mar 1
FIELD/MAJOR: Music

Scholarships are available to students at Appalachian State University who are music majors. Includes the Cratis Williams Scholarship, Dorothy Frazee Thomas Scholarship in Strings, Elsie Erneston Music Scholarship in Voice, Music Talent Awards, Pedrigo Music Scholarship in Voice, and A.J. Fletcher Scholarships. Write to the address listed below for information.

Appalachian State University
School Of Music
Boone, NC 28608

4213

School Of Nursing Scholarships

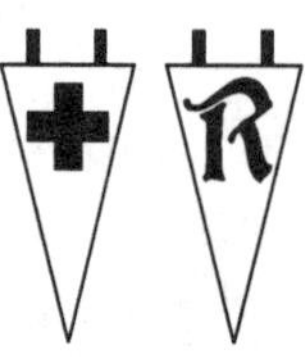

AMOUNT: None Specified
DEADLINE: None Specified
FIELD/MAJOR: Nursing

Scholarships are available at the Catholic University of America for full-time nursing scholarships. Write to the address below for details.

The Catholic University of America
School of Nursing
Washington, DC 20064

4214

School Of Public Health Financial Assistance Programs

AMOUNT: Varies **DEADLINE:** Varies
FIELD/MAJOR: Public Health And Related

Graduate fellowships and scholarships, nonresident tuition/fee scholarships, and the graduate minority program, are available to graduate students in the school of public health. Descriptions and instructions about these and other programs are available in the current program announcement. Request it from the address below.

University of California, Berkeley
Graduate School of Public Health
19 Earl Warren Hall, #7360
Berkeley, CA 94720

4215

Schreiner Academic Scholarship For Freshmen

AMOUNT: $3,000-$6,000 **DEADLINE:** Mar 31
FIELD/MAJOR: All Areas Of Study

Grant for freshmen accepted for full-time admission who scored a 25 on the ACT or 1100 on the SAT or better. Must be in the top 25% of graduating high school class and be entering college for the first time. Renewable. Write to the address below for more information.

Schreiner College
Financial Aid Office
Kerrville, TX 78028

4216

Schreiner Academic Scholarship For Returning Or Transfer Students

AMOUNT: $3,000-$6,000 **DEADLINE:** Mar 31
FIELD/MAJOR: All Areas Of Study

Grant for students accepted for full-time admission who have established a college GPA of at least 3.25. Must demonstrate good citizenship and academic standing. Write to the address below for more information.

Schreiner College
Financial Aid Office
Kerrville, TX 78028

4217

Schreiner Campus Ministry Grant-in-Aid

AMOUNT: $500 (max) **DEADLINE:** None Specified
FIELD/MAJOR: All Areas Of Study

Awards for students who are willing to work with campus ministry or with the church. Write to the address below for more information.

Schreiner College
Financial Aid Office
Kerrville, TX 78028

4218

Schreiner College Honors Scholarship

AMOUNT: $9,000 **DEADLINE:** Mar 15
FIELD/MAJOR: All Areas Of Study

Grant for freshmen accepted for full-time admission who scored a 27 on the ACT or 1170 on the SAT or better. Must be in the top 10% of graduating high school class. Transfer students are also eligible if they have a GPA of at least 3.6. Write to the address below for more information.

Schreiner College
Financial Aid Office
Kerrville, TX 78028

4219

Schreiner Merit Scholarship

AMOUNT: $1,000 **DEADLINE:** Mar 15
FIELD/MAJOR: All Areas Of Study

Grant for students accepted for full-time admission who have ACT scores of 23-24 or SAT scores of 1000-1100 and have a GPA from 3.0 to 3.24. Must demonstrate good citizenship and academic standing. Write to the address below for more information.

Schreiner College
Financial Aid Office
Kerrville, TX 78028

4220

Schuyler M. Meyer, Jr. Scholarship Fund

Amount: $1,000 **Deadline:** Jun 15
Field/Major: All Areas Of Study

Scholarships are available for Native American Indians who demonstrate financial need, academic ability, and potential for success. Applicants must be single parents, full-time students and have a GPA of 2.0 or better. Write to the address listed below for information.

George Bird Grinnell American Indian Children's Education Foundation
1111 Osage St., Bldg. B
Suite 205-A
Denver, CO 80204

4221

Schweinburg Merit Scholarships

Amount: $500-$2,000 **Deadline:** None Specified
Field/Major: All Areas Of Study

Scholarships are available to graduating high school seniors who are National Merit Finalists and graduates of New York City high schools. Write to the address listed below for information.

National Merit Scholarship Corporation
1560 Sherman Avenue, Suite 200
Evanston, IL 60201

4222

Science And Engineering Research Semester

Amount: $225 Per Week
Deadline: Mar 15, Oct 20
Field/Major: Physical And Life Sciences, Mathematics, Computer Sciences, Engineering

Research internship program provides students with an opportunity to work in above areas in relation to energy development. Open to full-time college juniors and seniors. U.S. citizen or legal resident. Must have at least a 3.0 GPA. Program is available at Argonne only. Academic term is September-December or January-May. Write to the Science and Engineering Research Semester Program at the address below for details.

Argonne National Laboratory
Div. Of Educational Student Programs
9700 S. Cass Ave.
Argonne, IL 60439

4223

Science Fellows Scholarship Program

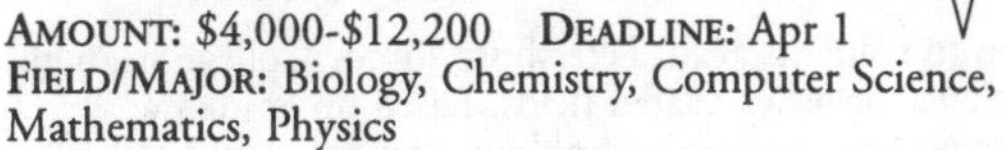

Amount: $4,000-$12,200 **Deadline:** Apr 1
Field/Major: Biology, Chemistry, Computer Science, Mathematics, Physics

Awards are available for incoming freshmen in the areas of study listed above. Based on academics, recommendations, and an on-campus interview. Renewable. Write to the address below for details.

Elon College
Office Of Financial Aid
2700 Campus Box
Elon College, NC 27244

4224

Science Scholars Fellowship Program

Amount: $37,7200 **Deadline:** Oct 15
Field/Major: See Listing Of Fields Below

Residential fellowship for women who have held a Ph.D. For at least two years.

Scholars perform research in a laboratory or with a research group in the Boston area. For study in astronomy, biochemistry, chemistry, computer science, electrical, aerospace, and mechanical engineering, geology, materials science, math, physics, ecology, and evolutionary biology. Must be U.S. citizen. Also for study in molecular and cellular biology, cognitive and neural science, naval architecture, and all fields that relate to the study of oceans. Write to the address below for complete details.

Radcliffe College
Mary Ingraham Bunting Institute
34 Concord Avenue
Cambridge, MA 02138

4225

Science Scholarship Program

Amount: Varies **Deadline:** Jan 15
Field/Major: Science

Scholarship program awarding high school juniors or seniors medals and the opportunity to receive scholarships at the University of Rochester. Information should be available from your science teacher or guidance counselor. If not, write to the address below for details.

Bausch & Lomb
P.O. Box 54
Rochester, NY 14601

4226

Science-Math Scholarship

Amount: Tuition **Deadline:** None Specified
Field/Major: Science, Math

Award available to students in the fields of science or math. Awarded to the winner of science-math competition held in December. Write to the address below for more information.

Carthage College
Financial Aid Office
Kenosha, WI 53140

4227

Scientist Development Grant

Amount: $65,5000 **Deadline:** None Specified
Field/Major: Medical Research (Cardiovascular And Other Related Areas)

Awards for beginning investigators in the areas of cardiovascular research. Applications may be submitted in the final year of a postdoctoral fellowship or within the first four years of a faculty appointment. Based on originality and scientific merit of proposed project, prior productivity of the applicant, and evidence that the award will promote independent status for the applicant. Write to the address below for more information.

American Heart Association
National Center
7272 Greenville Ave.
Dallas, TX 75231

4228

Scott Wilkinson Awards

Amount: Varies **Deadline:** Mar 1
Field/Major: Music Theory Or Composition

Awards at the University of New Mexico for music students with an emphasis on music theory or composition. Recipient will be determined by the College of Music. Contact the College of Music for more information.

University Of New Mexico, Albuquerque
Office Of Financial Aid
Albuquerque, NM 87131

4229

Scottish Gardening Scholarship

Amount: Varies **Deadline:** Dec 31
Field/Major: Horticulture

Awards for students who are have a high school diploma and are between the ages of 18 and 21. Applicants must have demonstrated good academic standing and have previous work in ornamental horticulture (at least one summer). This is a work/study award at Castle Douglas, Scotland for one year. The program pays for transportation, food, tuition, and a monthly stipend. Write to the address below for more information.

National Junior Horticulture Association
Project Chairperson, Mr. Tom Clark
224 River Drive
Hadley, MA 01035

4230

SCPA Scholarship Fund

Amount: None Specified **Deadline:** Mar 1
Field/Major: All Areas Of Study

Scholarships for West Virginia residents from a number of the southern counties in West Virginia who are/were employed by a coal mining/processing company or whose parents were so employed. Write to the address below for details.

Greater Kanawha Valley Foundation
Scholarship Committee
P.O. Box 3041
Charleston, WV 25331

4231

SCPA Scholarship Fund

Amount: None Specified **Deadline:** Mar 15
Field/Major: All Areas Of Study

Scholarships for West Virginia residents from a number of the southern counties in West Virginia who are/were employed by a coal mining/processing company or whose parents were so employed. Three awards per year. Write to the address below for details.

Greater Kanawha Valley Foundation
Scholarship Committee
P.O. Box 3041
Charleston, WV 25331

4232

Scripps Howard Foundation Scholarships

Amount: $1,000-$3,000 **Deadline:** Feb 25
Field/Major: Print And Broadcast Communications

Applicants must be undergraduate students pursuing a career or majoring in print or broadcast communications. Based on grades and need. Must be a U.S. citizen. For full-time study. Write to address below for details. Include a self-addressed mailing label showing the words "scholarship application." Please also indicate your major and your career goals. Deadline to request an application is Dec 20.

Scripps Howard Foundation
Scholarships Coordinator
P.O. Box 5380
Cincinnati, OH 45201

4233

SeaBee Memorial Association Scholarship

Amount: $1,350 **Deadline:** Apr 15
Field/Major: All Areas Of Study

Scholarships for sons or daughters of regular, reserve, retired, or deceased officers or enlisted members who have served or who are now serving with the Naval Construction Force (SeaBees) or the Naval Civil Engineer Corps. Renewable. Write to the chairman at the address below for details.

SeaBee Memorial Scholarship Association, Inc.
P.O. Box 6574
Silver Spring, MD 20916

4234

SEAC Small Grants For Isolated Scholars

Amount: $5,000 (max) **Deadline:** Mar 8, Oct 15
Field/Major: Japanese Studies

Grants are available for scholars that are not affiliated with institutions that have major centers or programs in Southeast Asia. The grant can be used for research in Southeast Asia, for a language refresher course, or for any other scholarly project. Write to the address below for more information.

Southeast Asia Council Association For Asian Studies
1 Lane Hall
University Of Michigan
Ann Arbor, MI 48109

4235

Sean W. Corrao Endowed Memorial Scholarship

Amount: Varies **Deadline:** None Specified
Field/Major: Computer Science Or Related Technology

Awards given to students at St. Petersburg Junior College studying computer science or other related fields. Based on academic promise, interest in computer technology, and financial need. Contact the Office of the Director of Scholarships and Student Financial Assistance at the campus you attend or write to the address below.

St. Petersburg Junior College
Office Of Financial Aid
P.O. Box 13489
St. Petersburg, FL 33733

4236

Seaspace Scholarship Program

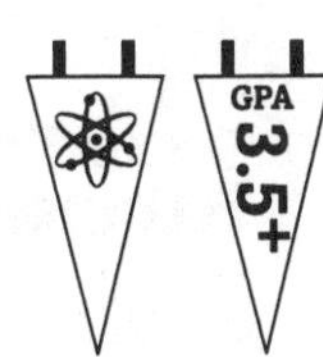

AMOUNT: Varies **DEADLINE:** Mar 1
FIELD/MAJOR: Marine And Aquatic Sciences

Awards for juniors, seniors, and graduate students studying in the field listed above. Juniors and seniors must have GPA of 3.5 or better and graduate students must have at least a 3.0 GPA. For study in the U.S. Must demonstrate financial need. Write to the address below for more information.

Houston Underwater Club, Inc.
Seaspace Scholarship Committee
P.O. Box 3753
Houston, TX 77253

4237

Seby Jones Scholarships

AMOUNT: None Specified **DEADLINE:** Dec 15
FIELD/MAJOR: All Areas Of Study

Scholarships awarded to students at Appalachian State University who reside in Wake County, North Carolina. Contact the Office of Admissions for details.

Appalachian State University
Office Of Financial Aid
Scholarship Section
Boone, NC 28608

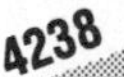

4238

Second Century Awards, Franklin And Henrietta Dickman Memorial Awards

AMOUNT: $250-$1,000 **DEADLINE:** Apr 15
FIELD/MAJOR: All Areas Of Study

Applicants must be born deaf or became deaf before acquiring language. Must use speech/residual hearing or lip-reading as primary communication and be a student entering or attending a college or university program for hearing students. 20-30 awards per year. Write to the address below for complete details.

Alexander Graham Bell Association For The Deaf
3417 Volta Place, NW
Washington, DC 20007

4239

Second Century Scholarship

AMOUNT: Tuition and Fees **DEADLINE:** None Specified
FIELD/MAJOR: All Areas Of Study

Awards for Mesa State freshmen, or current Colorado high school graduates who have a GPA of at least 3.25 and an ACT score of 22 or SAT score of 940. Write to the address below for more information.

Mesa State College
Office Of Financial Aid
P.O. Box 3692
Grand Junction, CO 81501

4240

Second Effort Scholarship

AMOUNT: $1,000 **DEADLINE:** None Specified
FIELD/MAJOR: All Areas Of Study

Applicants must be Arkansas residents who achieved a high score on their GED. The GED test must have been taken in Arkansas. For approved Arkansas two- or four-year public or private school. Write to the address below for details.

Arkansas Department Of Higher Education
Financial Aid Division
114 East Capitol
Little Rock, AR 72201

4241

Second Marine Division Association Memorial Scholarship

AMOUNT: Varies **DEADLINE:** Apr 1
FIELD/MAJOR: All Areas Of Study

Scholarships for children of current or former 2nd Marine Division officers or enlisted men. Based on need (yearly family earnings must be less than $30,000). Renewable. Applicants must be unmarried, in the undergraduate years. Write to the address below for details. Requests for applications must be in the form of a handwritten letter by the applicant with an SASE to the address below.

Second Marine Division Association
Memorial Scholarship Fund
P.O. Box 8180
Camp Lejeune, NC 28542

4242

Secretary Of State/Illinois State Library Scholarships

AMOUNT: $7,500 **DEADLINE:** May 1
FIELD/MAJOR: Library Science, Information Science

Up to ten scholarships for Illinois residents who are or will be attending an Illinois graduate school and pursuing a master's degree in library or information science. Must be a U.S. citizen and agree to work in an Illinois library after graduation. For full-time or part-time study. Write to the address below for details.

Illinois State Library Scholarship Program
300 South Second Street
Springfield, IL 62701

4243

SEG Foundation Scholarship Program

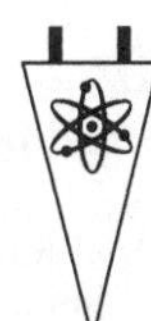

AMOUNT: $500-$3,000 **DEADLINE:** Mar 1
FIELD/MAJOR: Geophysics

Scholarships are available for students who intend to pursue careers in exploration geophysics. For undergraduate or graduate study. Based on academic ability. Write to the address below for complete details.

Society of Exploration Geophysicists Foundation
Scholarship Committee
P.O. Box 702740
Tulsa, OK 74170

4244

SEIU Scholarship Program

AMOUNT: $1,000-$3,000 **DEADLINE:** Mar 15
FIELD/MAJOR: All Areas Of Study

Applicants must be union members or the children of members in good standing and have not completed more than one year of college. Automatically renewable for up to four years. Eleven awards per year. Contact your parent's local SEIU, or write to the address below for details.

Service Employees International Union
Scholarship Committee
1313 L St., NW
Washington, DC 20005

4245 Selby Foundation High School Science/Math Awards

AMOUNT: $1,000 **DEADLINE:** None Specified
FIELD/MAJOR: Mathematics, Science

One award to the top math or science senior at each high school in Sarasota County, based entirely on academic achievement. Write to the address below for further information or see your counselor.

Selby Foundation
Robert E. Perkins, Executive Director
1800 Second St., #905
Sarasota, FL 34236

4246 Selby Foundation Minority Scholarships

AMOUNT: Varies **DEADLINE:** None Specified
FIELD/MAJOR: All Areas Of Study

Awards for minority students who will be attending Bethune-Cookman College full time. Must be a resident of Sarasota County before entering college and have a minimum GPA of 2.5. Write to address below for further information.

Selby Foundation
Bethune-Cookman-Financial Aid Officer
640 Second St.
Daytona Beach, FL 32015

4247 Selby Foundation Minority Scholarships

AMOUNT: Varies **DEADLINE:** None Specified
FIELD/MAJOR: All Areas Of Study

Awards for minority students who are/will be attending Florida A&M full time. Must be a resident of Sarasota County and have a minimum GPA of 2.5. Write to the address below for further information.

Selby Foundation
Florida A&M-Financial Aid Officer
Florida A&M
Tallahassee, FL 32306

4248 Selby Foundation Minority Teacher Training Scholarships

AMOUNT: Varies **DEADLINE:** None Specified
FIELD/MAJOR: Teaching

Awards for minority students with a career goal of teaching and an interest in teaching in the Sarasota County school system. Write to the address below for further information.

Selby Foundation
School Board Of Sarasota Co.-Personnel
1960 Landings Blvd.
Sarasota, FL 34231

4249 Selby Foundation Sarasota Technical Institute Scholarships

AMOUNT: Varies **DEADLINE:** None Specified
FIELDS/MAJORS: All Areas Of Study

Awards for students who can demonstrate financial need and be accepted into specific selected programs at Sarasota County Technical Institute. Contact the Financial Aid Officer at the address below for further information.

Selby Foundation
Sarasota County Technical Institute
4748 S. Beneva Rd.
Sarasota, FL 34233

4250 Selby Foundation Undergraduate Scholarship Program

AMOUNT: Varies **DEADLINE:** None Specified
FIELD/MAJOR: All Areas Of Study

Awards for undergraduate students from Sarasota or Manatee Counties planning to attend a qualified Florida postsecondary institution. Applicants must have a GPA of 3.0 or greater and have financial need, as determined by the school. Contact the financial aid office at your college/university for more information.

Selby Foundation
1800 Second St., Suite 905
Sarasota, FL 34236

4251 Seminars On Teaching About Japan

AMOUNT: $2,500 (max) **DEADLINE:** Nov 1, Mar 1
FIELD/MAJOR: Japanese Studies

Grants are available for scholars to design seminars or courses to improve the teaching of the Japanese studies at the college or pre-college level. Applicants should be prepared to explain the character or rationale of their seminar and be able to prepare a budget estimate. Write to the address below for more information.

Northeast Asia Council Association For Asian Studies
1 Lane Hall
University of Michigan
Ann Arbor, MI 48109

4252 Seminole Ridge Business And Professional Women's Association

AMOUNT: Varies **DEADLINE:** Varies
FIELD/MAJOR: All Areas Of Study

Award for a student at St. Petersburg Junior College who has demonstrated financial need and academic achievement. Write to the address below for more details.

St. Petersburg Junior College
Financial Aid Office
P.O. Box 13489
St. Petersburg, FL 33733

4253

Seminole/Miccosukee Indian Scholarships

AMOUNT: Varies **DEADLINE:** None Specified
FIELD/MAJOR: All Areas Of Study

Resident of Florida. Member of Seminole or Miccosukee Indian tribe. Enrolled as full-time or part-time undergraduate or graduate student at an eligible Florida institution. Must demonstrate financial need. Write for further information. Details and application forms are available from your tribal office.

Florida Department Of Education
Office Of Student Financial Assistance
1344 Florida Education Center
Tallahassee, FL 32399

4254

Senator George J. Mitchell Scholarship Fund

AMOUNT: Varies **DEADLINE:** Apr 26
FIELD/MAJOR: All Areas Of Study

Awards for Maine high school graduates who plan to attend a college or university in Maine. Based on academics, financial need, community service, and public service. Scholarships are awards on a rotational basis. No high school will qualify for a second scholarship until each high school in Maine has received one scholarship. Write to the address below for more details.

Maine Community Foundation
P.O. Box 148
Ellsworth, ME 04605

4255

Senator Robert J. Noell And Randolph A. Noell Scholarships

AMOUNT: $1,000 **DEADLINE:** May 1
FIELD/MAJOR: Agriculture, Life Sciences

Scholarships for incoming freshmen and returning undergraduates in the fields of agriculture and life sciences. Must be residents of Virginia, with preference given to residents west of Lynchburg. Based on a combination of merit and need. Write to the address below for more information.

Virginia Tech College Of Agriculture And Life Sciences
Dr. John M. White, Associate Dean
1060 Litton Reaves Hall
Blacksburg, VA 24061

4256

Senior Adult Scholarship Program

AMOUNT: Full Tuition **DEADLINE:** None Specified
FIELD/MAJOR: All Areas Of Study

Scholarships for Alabama residents 60 years old or older who are attending an accredited two-year college in Alabama. Contact the financial aid office at your college for details.

Alabama Commission On Higher Education
P.O. Box 30200
Montgomery, AL 36130

4257

Senior Challenge Scholarships

AMOUNT: Varies **DEADLINE:** Feb 1
FIELD/MAJOR: All Areas Of Study

Awards for current sophomores or juniors to use in the following academic year. Based on academic excellence, community and college service, and financial need. Write to the address below for complete details.

Lewis And Clark College
Office Of Admissions
Portland, OR 97219

4258

Senior Comprehensive Exam Award

AMOUNT: $100 **DEADLINE:** Feb 15
FIELD/MAJOR: Chemistry

Scholarships are available at the University of Utah for full-time senior chemistry majors who demonstrate exceptional performance in the departmental senior comprehensive exams. Write to the address below for information.

University Of Utah
Dr. Fred Montague
135 Building 44
Salt Lake City, UT 84112

4259

Senior Health Scholarship For Students In The Greater St. Louis Area

AMOUNT: $1,500 **DEADLINE:** Apr 10
FIELD/MAJOR: Health, Medicine

Awards are available for high school seniors in the St. Louis metropolitan area who intend to enter a four-year college in the field of health studies. Must demonstrate financial need. Contact your guidance counseling office for applications and information. The foundation does not send out any information.

Combined Health Appeal Of Greater St. Louis
9440 Manchester, Suite 106
St. Louis, MO 63119

4260

Senior International Fellowships

AMOUNT: $45,500 **DEADLINE:** Varies
FIELD/MAJOR: Biomedical And Behavioral Science Research

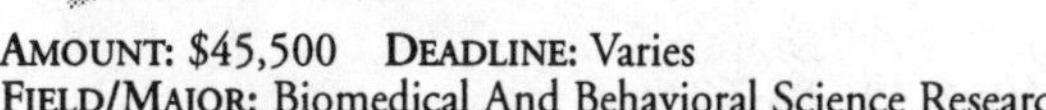

Awards for scientists in the fields of biomedical or behavioral science research who have been invited to study at a nonprofit foreign institution. Applicants must be U.S. citizens. Write to the address below for more information.

National Institutes Of Health, Fogarty International Center
Building 31, Room B2C39
31 Center Drive MSC 2220
Bethesda, MD 20892

4261

Senior Merit Awards

AMOUNT: Varies **DEADLINE:** Aug 31
FIELD/MAJOR: Medicine

Awards given to senior medical students in recognition of outstanding academic achievement, leadership, and community service. Includes the Irving Graef Memorial Scholarship, the William and Charlotte Cadbury Award, the Franklin C. McLean Award, and the James H. Robinson Memorial Prize. Send an SASE (.55), to the address below for additional information.

National Medical Fellowships, Inc.
110 West 32nd Street
New York, NY 10001

4262

Senior Performing Arts Fellowships

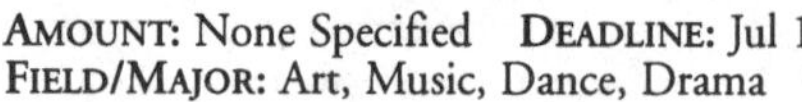

AMOUNT: None Specified **DEADLINE:** Jul 1
FIELD/MAJOR: Art, Music, Dance, Drama

Fellowships are available for undergraduate students who demonstrate that studying in India will enhance their skills in the area of the performing arts of India. Write to the address listed below for and application.

American Institute Of Indian Studies
1130 East 59th Street
Chicago, IL 60637

4263

Sentry Insurance Leadership Scholarship

AMOUNT: $2,000 **DEADLINE:** Mar 15
FIELD/MAJOR: Business, Math, Computer Science

Awards for entering freshmen who rank in the top 15% of their class and demonstrate outstanding leadership potential. Contact the Office of Admissions, UW Oshkosh, for more information.

University Of Wisconsin, Oshkosh
Financial Aid Office, Dempsey 104
800 Algoma Blvd.
Oshkosh, WI 54901

4264

Sequoyah Fellowship Program

AMOUNT: $1,500 **DEADLINE:** Oct 1
FIELD/MAJOR: All Areas Of Study

Fellowships are available for American Indian or Alaskan Indian graduate students. Ten awards are offered for study in all areas. Write to the address below for details.

Association On American Indian Affairs, Inc.
Box 268
Sisseton, SD 57262

4265

Sequoyah Heritage Award

AMOUNT: Varies **DEADLINE:** Unspecified
FIELD/MAJOR: Arts And Sciences

University of Oklahoma, Norman offers the Sequoyah Heritage Award to full-time American Indian students with (60-90 hrs.) completed. Applicant must show potential for significant contributions to the Indian community and all majors may apply. Write to the address listed below for information.

University Of Oklahoma, Norman
College Of Arts And Sciences
601 Elm, Room 429
Norman, OK 73019

4266

Sergeant Major Douglas R. Drum Memorial Scholarship Program

AMOUNT: Varies **DEADLINE:** Apr 28
FIELD/MAJOR: All Areas Of Study

Scholarships for current members or dependents (spouses, children, grandchildren) of current members of the American Military Retirees Association. For use in a degree seeking program. Based on scholarship, leadership, character, citizenship, and financial need. Write to the address below for details.

American Military Retirees Association, Inc.
Administrative Office, Drum Scholarship
68 Clinton Street
Plattsburgh, NY 12901

4267

Sergio Franchi Music Scholarship In Voice Performance

AMOUNT: $1,000 **DEADLINE:** May 31
FIELD/MAJOR: Music-Voice

Scholarship for Italian American students (undergraduate or graduate) who are, or will be, studying voice music. Write to the address below for details.

National Italian American Foundation
Dr. Maria Lombardo, Education Director
1860 19th Street, NW
Washington, DC 20009

4268

Sertoma Communicative Disorders Scholarship Program

AMOUNT: $2,500 **DEADLINE:** Apr 1
FIELD/MAJOR: Audiology, Speech Pathology

Scholarships for students in master's level programs in audiology or in speech pathology. Must be a citizen of the U.S., Mexico, or Canada enrolled in full-time study. Information is available from the address below or from NSSLHA chapters, universities, Sertoma affiliates, speech and hearing organizations, etc.

Sertoma International
Sertoma Scholarship
1912 East Meyer Blvd.
Kansas City, MO 64132

4269

Sertoma Scholarships For Students With Hearing Loss

AMOUNT: $1,000 **DEADLINE:** May 3
FIELD/MAJOR: All Areas Of Study

Scholarships are available for full time students enrolled in or planning to enroll in any accredited four-year program. Applicants must have a documented hearing loss, and a GPA of at least 3.2. Based on academic ability. Write to the address listed below for information.

Sertoma International
Sertoma Scholarship
1912 East Meyer Blvd.
Kansas City, MO 64132

4270

Servco Foundation Scholarship

AMOUNT: $1,500-$2,000 **DEADLINE:** Apr 15
FIELD/MAJOR: All Areas Of Study

Scholarships are awarded to applicants whose parents or spouse are employed by Servco. Must pursue a higher education at one the campuses at the University of Hawaii or at any accredited college. Must have a GPA of 3.0 or higher. Write to the address below for more information.

Servco Foundation
Scholarship Selection Committee
P.O. Box 2788
Honolulu, HI 96803

4271

Service Loan

AMOUNT: $1,500 **DEADLINE:** Apr 1
FIELD/MAJOR: All Areas Of Study

Provides undergraduate students with an opportunity to pay a portion of their educational debt through service in various school, church and community projects. Applicant must be full-time sophomore or junior students, and must serve 300 hours in a campus-related project, church-related project, community organization, or as a volunteer in mission. Contact financial aid office at your school for information and forms. If those are not available there, write to address below.

Presbyterian Church (U.S.A.)
Office Of Financial Aid For Studies
100 Witherspoon Street
Louisville, KY 40202

4272

Service Merchandise Scholarship Program

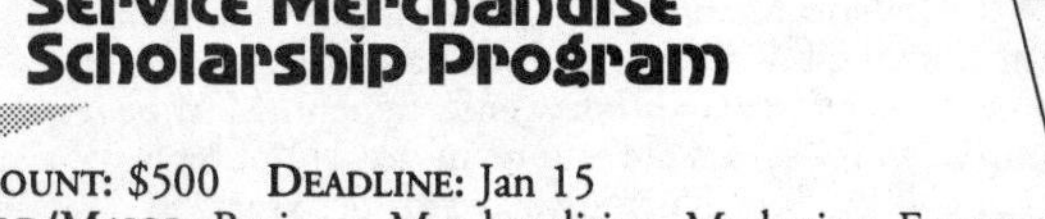

AMOUNT: $500 **DEADLINE:** Jan 15
FIELD/MAJOR: Business, Merchandising, Marketing, Economics, and Accounting

Applicant must be a current high school senior or graduate planning to attend a four-year college on a full-time basis. Please stop by your local Service Merchandise store after October 15 to pick up an application/brochure.

Service Merchandise Company, Inc.
Scholarship Program
P.O. Box 2810
Cherry Hill, NJ 08034

4273

Sesame Street Scholarship (Athletic)

AMOUNT: $250 **DEADLINE:** None Specified
FIELD/MAJOR: All Areas Of Study

For residents of Sesame Street who are members of one of the following teams: women's soccer, field hockey, softball; men's basketball and football. If there is no resident on an identified team, coaches may select a resident who is a member of another bu athletic team. Contact a member of the coaching staff for additional information.

Bloomsburg University
19 Ben Franklin Hall
400 E. Second St.
Bloomsburg, PA 17815

4274

SETAC Program For Minority Students And Mentors In Environmental Chem.

AMOUNT: Varies **DEADLINE:** Sep 8
FIELD/MAJOR: Environmental Chemistry And Toxicology

Awards are available for minority students and faculty mentors in the areas of environmental chemistry or toxicology. Selected individuals will receive a one-year membership to the Society of Environmental Toxicology and Chemistry and funds to travel and attend the SETAC World Conference in Canada. Write to the address below for more information.

Society of Environmental Toxicology And Chemistry
Mr. Rodney Parrish, Executive Director
1010 North 12th Avenue
Pensacola, FL 32501

4275

Seth P. Gavason Memorial Scholarship

AMOUNT: $300 **DEADLINE:** Feb 9
FIELD/MAJOR: All Areas Of Study

For students with sensory, physical, or learning disabilities. Must demonstrate financial need and academic good standing. Use Bloomsburg University scholarship application. Attach a list of BU Tutorial/504 Office Services you have used and a copy of documentation describing your disability. For further information contact Mr. Peter Walter, Coordinator Tutorial/504 Services, 12 Ben Franklin Hall.

Bloomsburg University
19 Ben Franklin Hall
400 E. Second St.
Bloomsburg, PA 17815

4276

Seventy-Fifth Anniversary Alumni Scholarships

AMOUNT: Varies **DEADLINE:** Mar 1
FIELD/MAJOR: All Areas Of Study

Awards for juniors at Lake Erie College for academic achievement, leadership, and loyalty to their school. Write to the address below for more information.

Lake Erie College
Financial Aid Office
391 W. Washington St.
Painesville, OH 44077

4277

Seville Flowers Scholarship, Stephen D. Durrant Scholarship

Amount: Varies **Deadline:** Feb 15
Field/Major: Biology

Scholarships are available at the University of Utah for full-time entering freshmen biology majors. Durrant Scholarship is awarded every four years, with the next award offered in 1996. Write to the address below for details.

University Of Utah
Dr. Fred Montague
135 Building 44
Salt Lake City, UT 84112

4278

Sharon Christa McAuliffe Scholarship

Amount: $8,600 (max) **Deadline:** Jul 1
Field/Major: Teaching-Education

Maryland residents who are majoring in education or special education. For study at a Maryland institution. Must agree to teach in Maryland for one year for each year of award. McAuliffe Award requires GPA of at least 3.0 and sixty credit hours. Paul Douglas Teacher Scholarship (federal) information is also available through this agency. Write to the address below for complete details.

Maryland State Higher Education Commission
16 Francis Street
Annapolis, MD 21401

4279

Shaw-Worth Scholarship Award

Amount: $1,000 **Deadline:** Apr 1
Field/Major: Animal Rights

Awards for New England high school seniors who have a meaningful contribution to animal protection over a significant period of time. Contact Heidi Lawrence at the address below for more information.

Humane Society Of The United States
New England Regional Office
P.O. Box 619
Jacksonville, VT 05342

4280

Sheet Metal Workers' International Scholarship Fund

Amount: $2,500 (max) **Deadline:** Mar 1
Field/Major: All Areas Of Study

Scholarships for members or immediate family of members of the Sheet Metal Workers International Association. For full-time undergraduate study. Write to the address below for more information.

Sheet Metal Workers International Association
1750 New York Avenue, NW, 6th Floor
Washington, DC 20006

4281

Sheldon Peterson Award

Amount: $500 **Deadline:** Apr 5
Field/Major: Broadcast Journalism

Awards for sophomore or junior undergraduates studying broadcast journalism at any state college or university. Write to the address below for more details.

Society Of Professional Journalists
Rose Beetem And Bob Boczkiewicz, Co-Chairs
3225 W. 29th Ave.
Denver, CO 80211

4282

Shell Companies/Shell Oil Products Marketing Merit Scholarships

Amount: $500-$2,000 **Deadline:** None Specified
Field/Major: All Areas Of Study

Scholarships are available to graduating high school seniors who are National Merit Finalists and children of employees of Shell Oil Company and its dealers and jobbers. Fifty-five awards are offered annually. Write to the address listed below for information, or contact the Human Resources Department at Shell Oil.

National Merit Scholarship Corporation/Shell Oil Company
1560 Sherman Avenue, Suite 200
Evanston, IL 60201

4283

Shelley Coldeway Memorial Scholarship

Amount: $200 **Deadline:** Varies
Field/Major: Range Animal Science

Awards for Sul Ross undergraduates who are studying range animal science, have a GPA of at least 2.0, and are NIRA eligible. Write to the address below for more information.

Sul Ross State University
Division Of Range Animal Science
Box C-110
Alpine, TX 79832

4284

Sheriffs' Association of Indiana Scholarships

Amount: None Specified **Deadline:** Apr 1
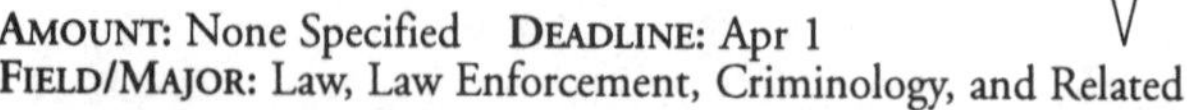
Field/Major: Law, Law Enforcement, Criminology, and Related

Scholarships for members and sons and daughters of members of the Indiana Sheriffs' Association. Must be Indiana resident studying full-time at an Indiana college or university toward a career related to law enforcement. Must be between 17 and 23 years old and be in top 1/2 of high school or college class. Thirty-two awards per year. Applications are available through your local sheriff's office; the financial aid, counselors, or admissions office at your college; or the guidance office of your high school. Please obtain application from one of those sources.

Indiana Sheriffs' Association, Inc.
P.O. Box 19127
Indianapolis, IN 46219

4285

Sheryl A. Horak Law Enforcement Explorer Memorial Scholarship

AMOUNT: $1,000 **DEADLINE:** Mar 31
FIELD/MAJOR: Law Enforcement

Any law enforcement explorer who is at least in the twelfth grade may apply. Candidates will be evaluated according to their academic record, leadership ability, extracurricular activities, and their personal statement on "Why I Want To Pursue A Career In Law Enforcement." Write to the address below for more information.

Boy Scouts Of America
Exploring Division, S210
1325 West Walnut Hill Ln., P.O. Box 152079
Irving, TX 75015

4286

Shipton's Big R Scholarships

AMOUNT: $1,000 **DEADLINE:** Feb 15
FIELD/MAJOR: Agriculture

Scholarships are available for FFA members pursuing a degree in any area of agriculture, residing in Campbell, Johnson, or Sheridan County, WY, or in Big Horn, Carbon, Custer, Fergus, Garfield, Golden Valley, Meagher, Prairie, Petroleum, Musselshell, Rosebud, Stillwater, Sweetgrass, Treasure, Wheatland, or Yellowstone County in Montana. Write to the address below for details.

National FFA Foundation
Scholarship Office
P.O. Box 15160
Alexandria, VA 22309

4287

Shirley A. Hamilton Memorial Music Award

AMOUNT: Varies **DEADLINE:** Mar 1
FIELD/MAJOR: Music

Award for students at Eastern New Mexico University who are majoring in music and can demonstrate financial need. Write to the address below for more information.

Eastern New Mexico University
College Of Fine Arts, Station 16
Portales, NM 88130

4288

Shirley Burgin Memorial Scholarship Fund

AMOUNT: None Specified **DEADLINE:** Apr 15
FIELD/MAJOR: Health Service

Scholarships available to residents of Johnson County, MO, who show intent to pursue a career in the health services industry. Applicant must be in school or planning to start next semester and have financial need. Write to the address below for details.

Johnson County Community Health Services
c/o Barbara Williams, R.N.
429 Burkarth Road, Innes Medical Plaza
Warrensburg, MO 64093

4289

Shirley N. And Frank B. Gilliam Scholarship

AMOUNT: Varies **DEADLINE:** Mar 1
FIELD/MAJOR: Nursing

Awards are available at the University of New Mexico for full-time junior or senior nursing students with a minimum GPA of 2.8 and financial need. Preference is given to a resident of New Mexico. Write to the address below or contact the school of nursing for more details.

University Of New Mexico, Albuquerque
Office Of Financial Aid
Albuquerque, NM 87131

4290

Shirley N. And Frank B. Gilliam Scholarships

AMOUNT: Varies **DEADLINE:** Mar 1
FIELD/MAJOR: Medicine

Awards are available at the University of New Mexico for full-time medical students who have completed at least one year of study at UNM Medical Center. Must demonstrate financial need and satisfactory academic standing. Write to the address below for more information.

University Of New Mexico, Albuquerque
Office Of Financial Aid
Albuquerque, NM 87131

4291

Short-Term Fellowships

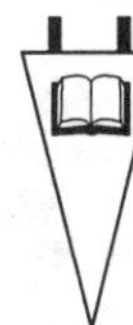

AMOUNT: $1,000 **DEADLINE:** Jan 31
FIELD/MAJOR: Bibliography, History of Printing and Publishing

Graduate research fellowships for one or two months. Supports inquiry into research focusing on books or manuscripts (the physical objects themselves). Approximately seven awards per year. Three letters of recommendation are required. Award amount is per month. Write to the address below for details.

Bibliographical Society Of America
BSA Executive Secretary
P.O. Box 397, Grand Central Station
New York, NY 10163

4292

Short-Term Resident Fellowships For Individual Research

AMOUNT: $800 Per Month **DEADLINE:** Mar 1, Oct 15
FIELD/MAJOR: History (American and Western), Humanities, Literature

Scholars who hold a Ph.D may apply. Applicants must be working on a specific research project in a field appropriate to the Newberry's collection. Doctoral candidates who have completed all requirements except the dissertation are also invited to apply. For study and research involving the collections of the Newberry. Preference given to scholars from outside the Chicago area. Write to the address below for details.

Newberry Library
Committee On Awards
60 W. Walton St.
Chicago, IL 60610

4293

Short-Term Travel To Japan For Professional Purposes

AMOUNT: Varies **DEADLINE:** Nov 1, Mar 1
FIELD/MAJOR: Japanese Studies

Awards for doctoral students who need time in Japan to complete their work. These grants are intended for short-term research trips by scholars who are already familiar with Japan and with their topic. Write to the address below for more information.

Northeast Asia Council Association For Asian Studies
1 Lane Hall
University Of Michigan
Ann Arbor, MI 48109

4294

SHPE Engineering and Science Scholarships

AMOUNT: \$500-\$7,000 **DEADLINE:** Apr 15
FIELD/MAJOR: Engineering, Science

Scholarships for Hispanic students seeking careers in science or engineering. For undergraduate or graduate study. Based on potential, character, need, involvement, and scholastic aptitude. Write to the address below for details.

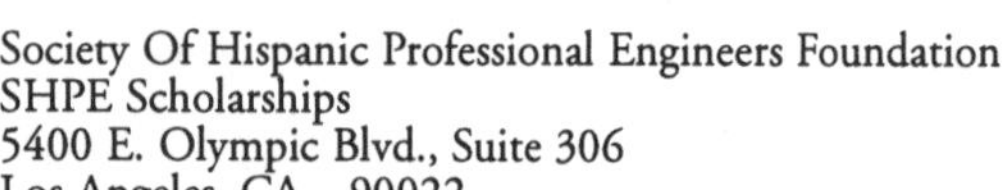

Society Of Hispanic Professional Engineers Foundation
SHPE Scholarships
5400 E. Olympic Blvd., Suite 306
Los Angeles, CA 90022

4295

Sid Richardson Memorial Fund Grants

AMOUNT: None Specified **DEADLINE:** Mar 30
FIELD/MAJOR: All Areas Of Study

Grants for children of persons who are or were employed by one of these Sid Richardson companies: Sid Richardson Carbon and Gas, Richardson Aviation, Bass Enterprises Production Co., Bass Brothers Enterprises, Richardson Oils, Perry R. Bass, Richardson Foundation, San Jose Cattle Co., or City Center Development Company. Write to address below for details. Please include the name, social security number, and dates of employment of the qualifying employee.

Sid Richardson Memorial Fund
Ms. Jo Helen Rosacker
309 Main Street
Fort Worth, TX 76102

4296

Siena Heights Academic Scholarship

AMOUNT: \$1,000-\$3,000 **DEADLINE:** Apr 1
FIELD/MAJOR: All Areas Of Study

Scholarships are available at Siena Heights College for full-time freshmen who have a GPA of at least 3.20, and a composite ACT score of 21 or more. Write to the address listed below for information.

Siena Heights College
Financial Aid Office
1247 East Siena Heights Drive
Adrian, MI 49221

4297

Siena Heights Grant

AMOUNT: Varies **DEADLINE:** Apr 1
FIELD/MAJOR: All Areas Of Study

Scholarships are available at Siena Heights College for full-time students who demonstrate financial need and academic excellence. Write to the address listed below for information.

Siena Heights College
Financial Aid Office
1247 East Siena Heights Drive
Adrian, MI 49221

4298

Sigma Phi Alpha Undergraduate Scholarship

AMOUNT: None Specified **DEADLINE:** Apr 1
FIELD/MAJOR: Dental Hygiene

Awarded to an outstanding candidate who is pursuing an associate/certificate or baccalaureate degree at an accredited dental hygiene school with an active chapter of the Sigma Phi Alpha dental hygiene honor society. Write to the address below for more information.

American Dental Hygienists' Association Institute For Oral Health
444 North Michigan Ave., Suite 3400
Chicago, IL 60611

4299

Sigma Phi Epsilon Scholarship

AMOUNT: \$750 **DEADLINE:** Feb 15
FIELD/MAJOR: All Areas Of Study

Scholarships are available at the University of Utah for full-time entering freshmen who are males with a high GPA. Write to the address below for information.

University Of Utah-Lewis A. Kingsley Foundation
Financial Aid And Scholarships Office
105 Student Services Building
Salt Lake City, UT 84112

4300

Sigma Theta Tau Int'l/ American Association Of Diabetes Educators Grant

AMOUNT: \$6,000 (max) **DEADLINE:** Oct 1
FIELD/MAJOR: Nursing

Grant for nurses who have completed master's degree study, to encourage them to contribute to the enhancement of quality and increase the availability of diabetes education and care research. One grant is offered annually. Request application forms for the AADE Grant Program from the address below.

Sigma Theta Tau International Honor Society of Nursing
AADE Education And Research Foundation
444 North Michigan Avenue, Suite 1240
Chicago, IL 60611

4301

Sigma Theta Tau Int'l/ Emergency Nursing Foundation Grant

AMOUNT: $6,000 (max) **DEADLINE:** Mar 1
FIELD/MAJOR: Nursing

Grant for nurses who have completed master's degree study, which will advance the specialized practice of emergency nursing. One grant is offered annually. Request application forms for the AADE Grant Program from the address below.

Sigma Theta Tau International
Emergency Nursing Foundation
216 Higgins Road
Park Ridge, IL 60068

4302

Sigma Theta Tau Int'l/Mead Johnson Nutritionals Perinatal Grants

AMOUNT: $10000 (max) **DEADLINE:** Jun 1
FIELD/MAJOR: Nursing

Grant for nurses who have completed master's degree study. Supports research relating to perinatal issues (up to 1 year old). One award per year. Must be a U.S. citizen. Request application forms for the Mead Johnson Grant Program from the below address.

Sigma Theta Tau International Honor Society Of Nursing
Program Department
550 West North Street
Indianapolis, IN 46202

4303

Sigma Theta Tau International/Glaxo Wellcome Research Grant

AMOUNT: $5,000 (max) **DEADLINE:** Oct 1
FIELD/MAJOR: Nursing

Grant for nurses who have completed master's degree study. Supports research relating to the prescribing practices of advanced practicing nurses. One award is offered annually. Request application forms for the Glaxo Grant Program from the address below.

Sigma Theta Tau International Honor Society Of Nursing/
GlaxoWellcome, Inc.
Program Department
550 West North Street
Indianapolis, IN 46202

4304

Sigma Theta Tau International Small Research Grants

AMOUNT: $3,000 (max) **DEADLINE:** Mar 1
FIELD/MAJOR: Nursing

Grants for nurses who have completed master's degree study. No specific focus of this program; but pilot, multidisciplinary and international research is encouraged. 10-15 awards per year. Request application forms for the Small Grants Program from the address below.

Sigma Theta Tau International Honor Society Of Nursing
Program Department
550 West North Street
Indianapolis, IN 46202

4305

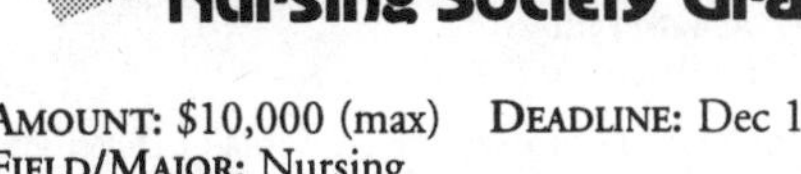

Sigma Theta Tau International/Oncology Nursing Society Grant

AMOUNT: $10,000 (max) **DEADLINE:** Dec 1
FIELD/MAJOR: Nursing

Grant for nurses who have completed master's degree study. Supports research of an oncology clinically-oriented topic. One award per year. Request application forms for the ONS Grant Program from the address below.

Sigma Theta Tau International Honor Society Of Nursing
Oncology Nursing Foundation
501 Holiday Drive
Pittsburgh, PA 15220

4306

Sigwald Thompson Composition Award Competition

AMOUNT: None Specified **DEADLINE:** None Specified
FIELD/MAJOR: Music Composition

This award was established to biennially select American composers for the commissioning of a work to be premiered by the Fargo-Moorhead Symphony Orchestra during its concert season. Must be a U.S. citizen. Write to the address below for complete details.

Fargo-Moorhead Orchestral Association
Sigwald Thompson Composition Competition
P.O. Box 1753
Fargo, ND 58107

4307

Silgan Containers Corporation Scholarships

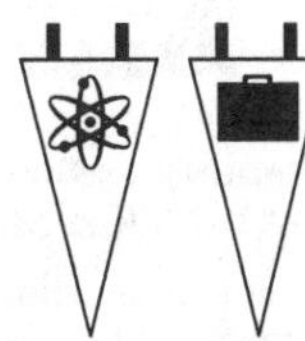

AMOUNT: $1,000 **DEADLINE:** Feb 15
FIELD/MAJOR: Agribusiness, Food Science/Technology

Scholarships are available for FFA members pursuing a four-year degree in agribusiness or food science, who reside in California, Illinois, Iowa, Texas, Pennsylvania, Missouri, Oregon, Utah, Washington, or Wisconsin. Write to the address below for details.

National FFA Foundation
Scholarship Office
P.O. Box 15160
Alexandria, VA 22309

4308

Silver Scholar Scholarship

AMOUNT: $4,000 **DEADLINE:** None Specified
FIELD/MAJOR: All Areas Of Study

Scholarships for entering freshmen who have a high school GPA of at least 3.5 and ACT scores of 30 or SAT scores of 1240. Must be a U.S. citizen and and enrolled in full-time study. Renewable. Write to the address below for more information.

New Mexico Tech
Admission Office
Soccorro, NM 87801

4309

Simmons Scholarships

Amount: $2,000 **Deadline:** Jul 26
Field/Major: Travel and Tourism

Awards are available for master's or doctoral students of travel and tourism at a recognized college, university, or proprietary travel school. Must be U.S. citizens or legal residents and have a GPA of at least 2.5. Two awards per year are given. Write to the address below for more information.

American Society Of Travel Agents
Scholarship Committee
1101 King St., Suite 200
Alexandria, VA 22314

4310

Simon And Satenig Ermonian Memorial Scholarship

Amount: Varies **Deadline:** Mar 1
Field/Major: Engineering

Awards for sophomores, juniors or seniors enrolled full-time. Based on financial need, academic merit, and potential leadership in engineering. Contact the Director of Recruitment, Marston Hall for more information.

University Of Massachusetts, Amherst
Director, Recruitment
Marston Hall
Amherst, MA 01003

4311

Sinfonia Foundation Research Assistance Grants

Amount: $1,000 (max) **Deadline:** Apr 1
Field/Major: Music Research

Grants supporting research on American music or music in America. Must show history of scholarly writing in music or show unusual knowledge in area to be researched. Write to the address below for details.

Sinfonia Foundation
10600 Old State Rd.
Evansville, IN 47711

4312

Single Parent Scholarship Fund

Amount: $1,000 **Deadline:** Mar 1
Field/Major: All Areas Of Study

Awards for undergraduate students who are single parents, heads of household, and who have a total income of less than $10,000 a year. Contact the Financial Aid Office, UW Oshkosh for more details.

University Of Wisconsin, Oshkosh
Financial Aid Office, Dempsey 104
800 Algoma Blvd.
Oshkosh, WI 54901

4313

Sister Angela Cummings Art Scholarship

Amount: Varies **Deadline:** None Specified
Field/Major: Art

Award given to students showing exceptional promise and talent in art. Write to the address below for more information.

Mercyhurst College
Financial Aid Office
Glenwood Hills
Erie, PA 16546

4314

Sister Irene Kohne Scholarship

Amount: $700 **Deadline:** Feb 20
Field/Major: All Areas Of Study

Award for full- or part-time students. Must have completed a minimum of 30 credits. Must be Fond Du Lac County residents involved in community service and extracurricular activities. Contact the Financial Aid Office, UW Oshkosh for more information.

University Of Wisconsin, Oshkosh
Financial Aid Office, Dempsey 104
800 Algoma Blvd.
Oshkosh, WI 54901

4315

Sister Marie Denise Scholarships

Amount: $2,000-$8,000 **Deadline:** Mar 15, Nov 15
Field/Major: All Areas Of Study

Awards for students based on achievement and financial need. The recipient of this award must provide 70 service hours for each year he/she holds the scholarship. Renewable with a GPA of at least 3.0. Write to the address below for more information.

Gwynedd-Mercy College
Student Financial Aid
Sumneytown Pike
Gwynedd Valley, PA 19437

4316

Sister Mary Carmelia O'Connor Scholarship

Amount: $1,600 (max) **Deadline:** Apr 1
Field/Major: All Areas Of Study

Scholarships are available at Siena Heights College for full-time students who are actively involved in community service projects and have a minimum GPA of at least 3.0. Write to the address listed below for information.

Siena Heights College
Financial Aids Office
1247 East Siena Heights Drive
Adrian, MI 49221

4317

SIU College Of Technical Careers-MC6615 Scholarships

Amount: $250-$750 **Deadline:** None Specified
Field/Major: Mortuary Science

Awards for full-time students at SIUC who are enrolled in the mortuary science program. All but one of the awards are restricted to students in second-year sequence. Must be in good academic standing. Write to the address below for more information.

Southern Illinois University At Carbondale
Mortuary Science And Funeral Service
Carbondale, IL 62901

4318

Six Month Internships

Amount: $8,000 **Deadline:** Feb 2
Field/Major: Art History, Art Conservation

Internships for African American, Hispanic or other minority students who are studying art history or a related field. For seniors, recent graduates or graduate students. For study at the Museum. Write to the address listed below for additional information.

Metropolitan Museum Of Art
Office of Academic Programs
1000 Fifth Ave.
New York, NY 10028

4319

SJU Merrill Lynch Scholarships

Amount: $2,000 **Deadline:** Feb 1
Field/Major: All Areas Of Study

Scholarships for Saint John's University freshmen who demonstrate exceptional leadership in their high school and community. Renewed automatically with satisfactory academic progress. Write to the address below for more information.

College Of Saint Benedict And Saint John's University
Office Of Financial Aid
37 South College Ave.
St. Joseph, MN 56374

4320

Skeggs Scholarship

Amount: Varies **Deadline:** Mar 1
Field/Major: Natural Science

Awards for students at Lake Erie College pursuing a degree in the natural sciences. Write to the address below for more information.

Lake Erie College
Financial Aid Office
391 W. Washington St.
Painesville, OH 44077

4321

SLA Scholarship Program

Amount: $6,000 **Deadline:** Oct 31
Field/Major: Library/information Science

For study in librarianship leading to a master's degree at a recognized school of library or information science. Preference will be given to those who display an aptitude for and interest in special library work. Up to three awards given per year. Write to the address below for complete details.

Special Libraries Association
SLA Scholarship Committee
1700 Eighteenth St., NW
Washington, DC 20009

4322

Sloan Doctoral Dissertation Fellowships

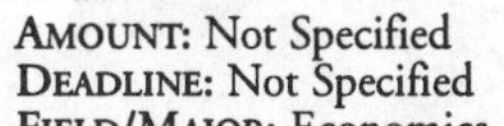

Amount: Not Specified
Deadline: Not Specified
Field/Major: Economics, Mathematics

Dissertation fellowships for candidates in areas of traditional interest to the Sloan Foundation. 50 awards per year. Request information on the Dissertation Fellowships Program from the below address.

Alfred P. Sloan Foundation
Sloan Foundation Fellowship Programs
630 Fifth Ave.
New York, NY 10111

4323

Sloan Research Fellowships

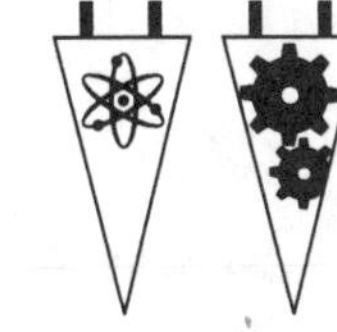

Amount: $30,000 (max)
Deadline: None Specified
Field/Major: Chemistry, Computer Science, Economics, Math, Neuroscience, Physics

Post-doctoral fellowships for promising researchers early in their careers. Fellowships are for 2 years. The Foundation also directly supports research in areas it feels are not sufficiently covered by agencies such as NSF and NIH. Request the brochure "Sloan Research Fellowships" from the address below.

Alfred P. Sloan Foundation
Sloan Foundation Fellowship Programs
630 Fifth Ave.
New York, NY 10111

4324

Smithkline Beecham Animal Health Scholarships

Amount: $1,000 **Deadline:** Feb 15
Field/Major: Pre-Vet

Scholarships are available for FFA members enrolled in a pre-veterinary program at a land grant university or a private institution. Four awards are offered annually. For undergraduate study. Write to the address below for details.

National FFA Foundation
Scholarship Office
P.O. Box 15160
Alexandria, VA 22309

4325

Smithsonian Fellowship Program

Amount: $3,000-$25,000
Deadline: Jan 15
Field/Major: Humanities, Art Studies, Anthropology, Astrophysics, Biology, History

Fellowships are available to graduate students, pre- and postdoctoral scholars for research in one of the above fields, or any field of interest to the Smithsonian. Write to the address below for details. Request the publication "Smithsonian Opportunities for Research and Study." those interested in environmental research may wish to write to Work/Learn Program, Smithsonian Environmental Research Center, P.O. Box 28, Edgewater, MD 21037.

Smithsonian Institution
Office Of Fellowships And Grants
955 L'enfant Plaza, Suite 7000
Washington, DC 20560

4326

Smithsonian Marine Station At Link Port Fellowships

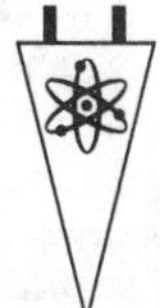

Amount: Varies **Deadline:** Feb 15
Field/Major: Marine Sciences

Fellowships are available for pre- and postdoctoral scholars to support research in marine science at Link Port. Three levels of fellowships are offered-ten week periods for graduate students, two- to twelve-month periods for recent Ph.D.'s, and also for senior scholars who have held the Ph.D. for more than seven years. Write to the address listed below for information.

Smithsonian Institution
Smithsonian Marine Station At Link Port
Old Dixie Highway
Fort Pierce, FL 34946

4327

Snow-Angleman Scholarship

AMOUNT: Varies **DEADLINE:** Feb 1
FIELD/MAJOR: English

Scholarships are available at the University of Utah for full-time entering freshmen enrolled in an English program. Write to the address below for details.

University Of Utah
Scholarship Chairperson
3500 Lnco
Salt Lake City, UT 84112

4328

SNPA Foundation Adopt-A-Student Minority Scholarship Program

AMOUNT: $1,000-$2,000 **DEADLINE:** Apr 1
FIELD/MAJOR: Journalism, Business, Advertising, Graphics, Computer Science

Open to high school seniors or graduates who are racial minorities, have at least a "C" average and have been nominated by SNPA members. Contact a member newspaper of the SNPA foundation for more information on nomination procedures and application

Southern Newspaper Publishers Association
P.O. Box 28875
Atlanta, GA 30358

4329

Social Issues Dissertation Award

AMOUNT: $200-$300 **DEADLINE:** Mar 1
FIELD/MAJOR: Psychology

Awards for psychological dissertations with application to social problems. Write to the address below for details on this and other awards offered by the SPSSI. Information may also be available in the psychology departments of many universities.

Society For The Psychological Study Of Social Issues
Attn: Dissertation Award Committee
P.O. Box 1248
Ann Arbor, MI 48106

4330

Social Science Endowed And Private Scholarships

AMOUNT: Varies **DEADLINE:** Feb 15
FIELD/MAJOR: Social Sciences

Scholarships are available at Evangel for full-time students pursuing a degree in the social sciences. Applicants must have a GPA of at least 3.0. Includes eleven different awards. Requirements vary. Write to the address listed below for information.

Evangel College
Office Of Enrollment
1111 N. Glenstone
Springfield, MO 65802

4331

Social Service Scholarships

AMOUNT: Varies **DEADLINE:** None Specified
FIELD/MAJOR: Social Service

Scholarships are available at the Catholic University of America for graduate students in the School of Social Service. Contact the financial aid office at the address below for details.

The Catholic University of America
Office of Admissions And Financial Aid
Washington, DC 20064

4332

Society For Cardiac Angiography And Interventions Fellowship Award

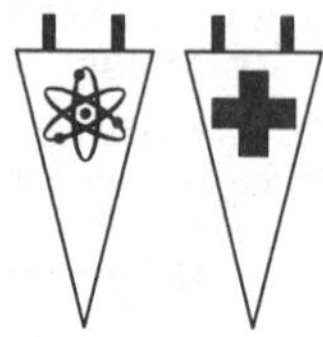

AMOUNT: $25,5000 (max) **DEADLINE:** Jan 16
FIELD/MAJOR: Medicine-Cardiology, Imaging Science

Grants supporting research focused on the advancement of cv imaging. Based on scientific value and on potential diagnostic advances, improvement in patient care, and successful completions of objectives. For persons currently serving in cardiology or radiology fellowship training program. Must be sponsored by member of the Society for Cardiac Angiography and Interventions. Application forms are available from the director of your institution's fellowship training program or the Society for Cardiac Angiography and Interventions at the address below (or (303)453-1773).

Bracco Diagnostics, Inc./SCA & I
Justine J. Parker
P.O. Box 7849
Breckenridge, CO 80424

4333

Society For The Humanities Postdoctoral Fellowships

AMOUNT: None Specified **DEADLINE:** Oct 21
FIELD/MAJOR: Humanities

Six fellowships for Ph.D. applicants with at least 1 year of college teaching experience. Ph.D. must have been awarded before applying for this fellowship. Program seeks to bring scholars from a wide variety of disciplines in the study of one topic. Write to the address below for details. Must have Ph.D. in hand at time of application.

Cornell University
Agnes Sirrine, Program Administrator
27 East Ave.
Ithaca, NY 14853

4334

Society Of Automotive Engineers Award

AMOUNT: $100 **DEADLINE:** None Specified
FIELD/MAJOR: Mechanical Engineering

Scholarships are available at the University of Iowa for full-time undergraduates majoring in mechanical engineering. Write to the address listed below for information.

University of Iowa
Department of Mechanical Engineering
2202 Engineering Building
Iowa City, IA 52245

4335

Society Of Consumer Affairs/ Professionals In Business

AMOUNT: $600 **DEADLINE:** Apr 30
FIELD/MAJOR: Consumer Affairs Professional Or Related Fields

Students must be anticipating careers as consumer affairs professional in areas such as consumer education, customer service, community relations, consumer economics, or family financial counseling. Three awards are given yearly. Write to the address below for more information.

California State Polytechnic University, Pomona
College Of Agriculture
Building 1, Room 308
Pomona, CA 91768

4336

Society Of Naval Architects and Marine Engineers Awards

AMOUNT: Varies **DEADLINE:** None Specified
FIELD/MAJOR: Naval Architecture, Marine Engineering

Undergraduate and graduate scholarships for students studying naval architecture, marine engineering, or ocean engineering. Applicants must be U.S. Or Canadian citizens and be members of the Society of Naval Architects and Marine Engineers. Write to the address below for further information.

Society of Naval Architects And Marine Engineers
Executive Director Of The Society
601 Pavonia Ave.
Jersey City, NJ 07306

4337

Society Of Plastics Engineers Scholarship Fund

AMOUNT: $4,000 (max) **DEADLINE:** Dec 15
FIELD/MAJOR: Plastics Engineering

Awards are available for full-time students in a four-year college or two-year technical program in engineering with a focus on plastics. Preference is given to upperclass students who are members or whose parents are members of the SPE. Applicants must be graduates of public or private high schools. Write to the address below for more information.

Society Of Plastics Engineers
14 Fairfield Dr.
Brookfield, CT 06804

4338

Society Of Satellite Professionals International Scholarships

AMOUNT: $1,000-$1,500 **DEADLINE:** Nov 15
FIELD/MAJOR: Aeronautical/Aerospace Engineering, Communications, Related Fields

Scholarships for undergraduate or graduate students in the above areas of study who are committed to the field of satellite communications. Includes the SSPI Scholarship, the A.W. Perigard Scholarship, the Phillips Publishing Inc. Scholarship, and the Hughes Communications Scholarships. Recipients must provide their own transportation to the awards ceremony in Washington D.C. Applications should be available from your department. If they do not have current information and application forms, please have them write to the society for more information.

Society Of Satellite Professionals International
Educational Award Programs
2200 Wilson Blvd., Suite 102-248
Arlington, VA 22201

4339

Sociology Departmental Scholarships

AMOUNT: Varies **DEADLINE:** Feb 15
FIELD/MAJOR: Sociology

Scholarships are available at the University of Utah for full-time students majoring in sociology. Write to the address below for information.

University Of Utah
Scholarship Chairperson
Behavioral Science Building
Salt Lake City, UT 84112

4340

Solid Waste Processing Division Scholarship

AMOUNT: $5,000 (max) **DEADLINE:** Feb 1
FIELD/MAJOR: Mechanical Engineering

Five scholarships for ASME student members who are majoring in mechanical engineering and specializing in solid waste management. For additional information, call or write the ASME Foundation.

American Society Of Mechanical Engineers
Education Services Department
345 E. 47th Street
New York, NY 10017

4341

SOM Foundation Traveling Fellowship Awards

AMOUNT: $10,000 **DEADLINE:** None Specified
FIELD/MAJOR: Architecture

Fellowship program for students receiving bachelor's or master's degrees in the field of architecture. Must be a U.S. citizen. Awards are to fund a proposed travel/study plan. Based initially on portfolio review. Finalists are judged on final proposal and interview. Write to the address below for more information.

Skidmore, Owings, & Merrill Foundation
224 South Michigan Ave., Suite 1000
Chicago, IL 60604

4342

Sophie Anderson Educational Trust

AMOUNT: Varies **DEADLINE:** None Specified
FIELD/MAJOR: All Areas Of Study

Awards for Washington residents with financial need, who attend Seattle Pacific University, the University of Puget Sound or Whitworth College. Also based on GPA. Preference is given to students majoring in nursing, pre-med, education, history, or liberal arts. Contact the Financial Aid Office at one of the above mentioned colleges for more information.

Seafirst Charitable Investment Services
701 Fifth Ave.
P.O. Box 24565
Seattle, WA 98124

4343

South Asian Fellowships, Southeast Asian Fellowships

AMOUNT: None Specified **DEADLINE:** Nov 1
FIELD/MAJOR: Asian Studies

Fellowships are available for scholars enrolled in a U.S. doctoral program. Applicants must have completed all the program requirements except for the dissertation. Research must be in Asian studies (including Sri Lanka, Nepal, Bangladesh, India, Pakistan, Brunei, Burma, Indonesia, Kampuchea, Laos, Malaysia, Singapore, Philippines, Thailand, and Vietnam). Write to the address listed below for information.

Social Science Research Council
Fellowships And Grants
605 Third Avenue
New York, NY 10158

4344

South Asian Grants, Southeast Asian Grants

AMOUNT: Varies **DEADLINE:** Nov 1, Dec 1
FIELD/MAJOR: Asian Studies

Grants are available for postdoctoral scholars who are U.S. citizens, for research on all aspects of the societies and cultures of Southern or Southeast Asia (as defined by Bangladesh, India, Nepal, Pakistan, Dri Lanka, Brunei, Burma, Indonesia, Kampuchea, Laos, Malaysia, Philippines, Thailand, Singapore, and Vietnam). Write to the address listed below for information.

Social Science Research Council
Fellowships And Grants
605 Third Avenue
New York, NY 10158

4345

South Carolina "Other Race" Program

AMOUNT: $1,000 (max) **DEADLINE:** None Specified
FIELD/MAJOR: All Areas Of Study

Scholarships for South Carolina residents who are members of a minority group attending a South Carolina public college or university. Write to the address listed below for additional information.

South Carolina Commission On Higher Education
1333 Main Street, Suite 200
Columbia, SC 29201

4346

South Carolina Graduate Incentive Fellowship Program

AMOUNT: $10,000 (max) **DEADLINE:** None Specified
FIELD/MAJOR: All Areas Of Study

Fellowships for South Carolina residents who are members of a minority group attending a South Carolina public college or university. For graduate and doctoral study. Write to the address listed below for additional information.

South Carolina Commission On Higher Education
1333 Main Street, Suite 200
Columbia, SC 29201

4347

South Carolina Higher Education Tuition Grants

AMOUNT: $2,100 (avg) **DEADLINE:** Jun 30
FIELD/MAJOR: All Areas Of Study

Tuition grants program established for student residing in South Carolina who wish to pursue studies at an independent South Carolina school on a full-time basis. Requirements are an SAT score of 900 or more, or an equivalent ACT score, and a class rank in the upper 75% of your graduating class. For further information, a list of participating schools and an application, please write to the address listed below.

South Carolina Education Tuition Grants Commission
1310 Lady Street, P.O. Box 12159
Columbia, SC 29211

4348

South Carolina National Guard Tuition Assistance

AMOUNT: $500 (max) **DEADLINE:** Mar 1
FIELD/MAJOR: All Areas Of Study

Scholarships for South Carolina National Guard or Air National Guard who are attending an in-state school in a program approved by the Veterans Education Division. Renewable. Write to the local national guard or to Adjutant General of SC, 1 National Guard Road, Columbia, SC, 29201, for more information.

South Carolina Commission On Higher Education
1333 Main Street, Suite 200
Columbia, SC 29201

4349

South Carolina Press Association Foundation Scholarships

AMOUNT: $2,000 **DEADLINE:** Jun 1
FIELD/MAJOR: Newspaper Related

Scholarships for students entering their junior year in a South Carolina college or university program and preparing for a career in the newspaper industry. Must agree to work in the newspaper field in the U.S. for at least two years. Renewable. Write to the address below for details.

South Carolina Press Association Foundation, Inc.
William C. Rogers, Secretary
P.O. Box 11429
Columbia, SC 29211

4350

South Carolina State Library Scholarships

AMOUNT: Varies **DEADLINE:** Varies
FIELD/MAJOR: Library Science

Scholarships for continuing education in library science. Must work or have worked in a public or institutional library. Write to Mr. James B. Johnson, Director, at the address below for details.

South Carolina State Library
Career Education Program
P.O. Box 11469, 1500 Senate St.
Columbia, SC 29211

4351 South Carolina Tuition Grants

AMOUNT: $3,320 (max) **DEADLINE:** None Specified
FIELD/MAJOR: All Areas Of Study

Scholarship are available a to undergraduate students who are residents of South Carolina attending a private in-state institution. Based primarily on financial need. Contact your financial aid office or the following address for more information: Tuition Grants Commission, 1310 Lady St., Suite 811, Keenan Bldg., P.O. Box 12159, Columbia, SC 29211.

South Carolina Commission On Higher Education
1333 Main Street, Suite 200
Columbia, SC 29201

4352 South Central Modern Languages Association Fellowships

AMOUNT: $800 **DEADLINE:** Mar 1
FIELD/MAJOR: History (American and European), Humanities, Literature

Fellowships are available for work in residence by a member of the South Central Modern Language Association. Applicants must be postdoctoral scholars. Contact the address below for more details.

Newberry Library
Committee On Awards
60 W. Walton St.
Chicago, IL 60610

4353 South Central Regional Scholarships

AMOUNT: $1,000 **DEADLINE:** May 31
FIELD/MAJOR: All Areas Of Study

Scholarships for Italian American residents of Alabama, Mississippi, Texas, Tennessee and Louisiana. For undergraduate study. Write to the address listed below for information.

National Italian American Foundation
Dr. Maria Lombardo, Education Director
1860 19th Street, NW
Washington, DC 20009

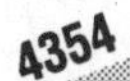

4354 South Dakota Retailers Association

AMOUNT: $1,000 **DEADLINE:** May 13
FIELD/MAJOR: Retail

Scholarships are available for students enrolled in a retail-related course of study at a university, college or vocational school located in South Dakota. Applicant must intend to pursue a career in a retail field. Write to the address below for more information.

South Dakota Retailers Association
P.O. Box 638
Pierre, SD 57501

4355 South Dakota Tuition Equalization Grant Program

AMOUNT: Varies **DEADLINE:** None Specified
FIELD/MAJOR: All Areas Of Study

Grants available to residents of South Dakota who are enrolled at a SD private college as a full-time undergraduate student. Student must not be enrolled in a course of study leading to a degree in theology or religious education, or receiving an athletic scholarship. Applicant must have completed a federally-approved needs analysis which indicates a financial need of $100 or more. Payment of awards is made directly to the student and sent to the institution in equal installments at the beginning of each academic term upon evidence that the student is officially enrolled in the institution. Write to the address below for details.

South Dakota Department Of Education And Cultural Affairs
Office Of The Secretary
700 Governors Drive
Pierre, SD 57501

4356 Southampton Campus Art Scholarships

AMOUNT: $1,000-$3,000 **DEADLINE:** Jun 1
FIELD/MAJOR: Art

Awards for freshmen or transfer students on the basis of an art portfolio review. Students must major in art. Portfolio reviews are normally done in March. Write to the address below for more information.

Long Island University
Financial Aid Office
Southampton, NY 11968

4357 Southampton Campus Writing Scholarships

AMOUNT: $500-$2,500 **DEADLINE:** Jun 1
FIELD/MAJOR: English

Awards for freshmen or transfer students on the basis of a writing competition. Students must major in English. Write to the address below for more information.

Long Island University
Financial Aid Office
Southampton, NY 11968

4358 Southeast Regional Scholarships

AMOUNT: $1,000 **DEADLINE:** May 31
FIELD/MAJOR: All Areas Of Study

Scholarships for Italian American residents of north or South Carolina, Georgia or Florida. For undergraduate study. Write to the address listed below for information.

National Italian American Foundation
Dr. Maria Lombardo, Education Director
1860 19th Street, NW
Washington, DC 20009

4359

Southern Building Code Congress International Education Fund

AMOUNT: Varies **DEADLINE:** May 31
FIELD/MAJOR: All Areas Of Study

Awards for dependents of members of the Southern Building Code Congress International. Based on financial need, character, integrity, and scholastic ability. Write to the address below for more information.

Southern Building Code Congress International
Educational Services
900 Montclair Road
Birmingham, AL 35213

4360

Southern California Food Brokers Association Scholarship

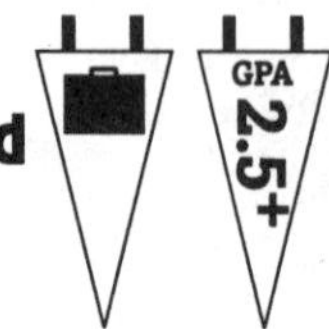

AMOUNT: $1,000 **DEADLINE:** Feb 1
FIELD/MAJOR: Agricultural Business Mgmt, Agricultural Ed., International Agric.

Student must be a full-time sophomore or above majoring in agricultural business management, agricultural education or international agriculture with an interest in food distribution. Must have a GPA of 2.5 or better. Write to the address below for more information.

California State Polytechnic University, Pomona
College Of Agriculture
Building 2, Room 215
Pomona, CA 91768

4361

Southern California Frozen Food Council

AMOUNT: Varies **DEADLINE:** Feb 1
FIELD/MAJOR: Business

Student must be a junior, senior, or graduate majoring in business with an interest in food distribution. Must have a GPA of 2.5 or better. Write to the address below for more information.

California State Polytechnic University, Pomona
College Of Agriculture
Building 2, Room 215
Pomona, CA 91768

4362

Southern California Grocers Association In Memory Of Denise Martinez

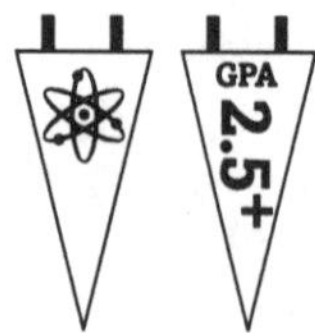

AMOUNT: $500 **DEADLINE:** Feb 1
FIELD/MAJOR: Agricultural Business Mgmt, Agricultural Ed., International Agric.

Student must be a junior or senior majoring in agricultural business management, agricultural education or international agriculture with an interest in food distribution. Must have a GPA of 2.5 or better. Write to the address below for more information.

California State Polytechnic University, Pomona
College Of Agriculture
Building 2, Room 215
Pomona, CA 91768

4363

Southern California Pub Links Scholarship

AMOUNT: $5,000 **DEADLINE:** Feb 1
FIELD/MAJOR: All Areas Of Study

Award for a high school senior from southern California who is sponsored by a golf club that is a member of the Southern California Public Links Golf Association. Applicants must have a GPA of at least 3.0 and a 750 or better on the SAT or 18 or higher on the ACT. Contact your local golf club to obtain more information.

Southern California Public Links Golf Association
7035 E. Orangethorpe, #E
Buena Park, CA 90621

4364

Southern Scholarship Foundation Scholars

AMOUNT: $4,800 (avg) **DEADLINE:** Mar 1, Nov 1
FIELD/MAJOR: All Areas Of Study

Need-based awards for students at FSU, University of Florida, Bethune-Cookman College or Florida A&M University which provides housing at no cost. Must maintain a GPA of least 2.85. Based on need, academic promise, and character. Write to the address below for details.

Southern Scholarship Foundation
322 Stadium Drive
Tallahassee, FL 32304

4365

Southern States Cooperative, Inc. Scholarships

AMOUNT: $600-$800 **DEADLINE:** None Specified
FIELD/MAJOR: All Areas Of Study

Awards are available for children of farmers at North Carolina State University. Based on merit. Write to the address below for more information.

North Carolina State University
School Of Agriculture And Life Sciences
Box 7601
Raleigh, NC 27695

4366

Southwest Regional Scholarships

AMOUNT: $1,000 **DEADLINE:** May 31
FIELD/MAJOR: All Areas Of Study

Scholarships for Italian American residents of Arizona, New Mexico, southern California, and southern Nevada. Write to the address listed below for information.

National Italian American Foundation
Dr. Maria Lombardo, Education Director
1860 19th Street, NW
Washington, DC 20009

4367

Southwest Texas Gas Corporation Scholarship

AMOUNT: $1,000 **DEADLINE:** Apr 1
FIELD/MAJOR: All Areas Of Study

Awards for all Sul Ross students who are from Alpine, Balmorhea,

Ft. Davis, or Marfa, TX. Must demonstrate financial need. Write to the address below for more information.

Sul Ross State University
Financial Aid Office
Box C-113
Alpine, TX 79832

4368

Southwestern Scholar

Amount: $1,000 **Deadline:** Mar 1
Field/Major: All Areas Of Study

Applicant must be a first-time entering freshman residing in Oklahoma. Write to the address below for more information.

Southwestern Oklahoma State University
Student Financial Services Office
100 Campus Drive
Weatherford, OK 73096

4369

Souvenir Shirts Etc. Scholarships

Amount: $2,000 **Deadline:** Feb 15
Field/Major: Agriculture

Scholarships are available for FFA members pursuing an undergraduate degree in any area of agriculture. Two awards are offered annually. Write to the address below for details.

National FFA Foundation
Scholarship Office
P.O. Box 15160
Alexandria, VA 22309

4370

Spalding Award For Scholastic Excellence

GPA 3.0+

Amount: $500 **Deadline:** Mar 1
Field/Major: All Areas Of Study

Awards for Spalding undergraduates. Must have a GPA of at least 3.0 and have an ACT score of 21. Write to the address below for more details.

Spalding University
Financial Aid Office
851 S. Fourth St.
Louisville, KY 40203

4371

Sparks Companies, Inc. Scholarships

Amount: $2,000 **Deadline:** Feb 15
Field/Major: Animal Science

Scholarships are available for FFA members pursuing a four-year degree in animal science at Oklahoma State University. Write to the address below for details.

National FFA Foundation
Scholarship Office
P.O. Box 15160
Alexandria, VA 22309

4372

Special Achievement Award In Music

Amount: $1,000-$2,500 **Deadline:** Mar 15
Field/Major: Music

Scholarships are available at Wheaton College for undergraduate students who are enrolled in the music conservatory. Write to the address below for details.

Wheaton College
Financial Aid Office
Wheaton, IL 60187

4373

Special Achievement Awards

Amount: $500-$1,000 **Deadline:** Mar 1
Field/Major: All Areas Of Study

Awards for Muskingum students with the potential to make outstanding contributions relating to a particular academic area. Write to the address below for more information.

Muskingum College
Office of Admission
New Concord, OH 43762

4374

Special Awards

Amount: $100-$1,500 **Deadline:** None Specified
Field/Major: All Areas Of Study

Awards for current Bethel students upon the recommendation of Bethel faculty members. Both need and non-need based scholarships are available. Write to the address below for more information.

Bethel College
Office of Financial Planning
3900 Bethel Dr.
St. Paul, MN 55112

4375

Special Departmental Scholarship

Amount: Varies **Deadline:** Apr 15
Field/Major: Education

Scholarships are available at the University of Utah for full-time entering freshmen and transfer students who have a GPA of at least 3.5 who intend to pursue a career in teaching. Must be a Utah resident. Write to the address below for details.

University Of Utah
Financial Aid And Scholarship Office
105 Student Services Building
Salt Lake City, UT 84112

4376

Special Education Teacher Scholarship

Amount: Varies **Deadline:** Jun 1
Field/Major: Education, Special Education

Scholarships for Illinois high school seniors and undergraduates majoring in special education who will be attending one of the Illinois state colleges and universities. Must agree to teach in

Illinois after graduation. Contact your high school guidance counselor, principal or the address below for more information.

Superintendent Of Local Education Services Region
Illinois Student Assistance Commission
1755 Lake Cook Rd.
Deerfield, IL 60015

4377 Special Education Teacher Services Scholarship

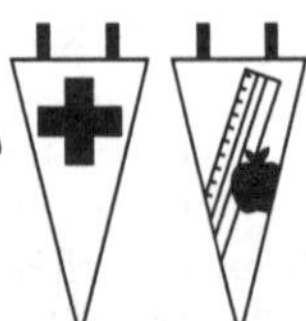

AMOUNT: Varies **DEADLINE:** None Specified
FIELD/MAJOR: Special Education (Includes Occupational Or Physical Therapy)

This scholarship program is open to Indiana students planning to pursue a course of study that will lead to a career in special education. Applicants must be full-time students with a GPA of 2.0 or better. Recipients are required to study at an Indiana institution and teach in an accredited Indiana elementary or secondary school. Write to the address below for details.

Indiana Student Assistance Commission
ISTA Center Building
150 West Market Street, Suite 500
Indianapolis, IN 46204

4378 Special Honors Scholarships

AMOUNT: $15,975 **DEADLINE:** Feb 15
FIELD/MAJOR: All Areas Of Study

Scholarships for freshman at Eckerd College who have been named finalists or semifinalists in the National Merit Scholarship, the National Achievement and the National Hispanic Scholarship Programs. 15 awards per year. Contact the address below for details.

Eckerd College
Director Of Financial Aid
P.O. Box 12560
St. Petersburg, FL 33733

4379 Special Merit Scholarships At Peace College

AMOUNT: $1,500-$3,000
DEADLINE: None Specified
FIELD/MAJOR: All Areas Of Study

Scholarships for above-average women who are or will be attending peace college. Must have a GPA of at least 3.0, SAT scores of at least 1010, and rank in the top 25% of their high school graduating class. Renewable. Contact the director of financial aid at the address below for details.

Peace College
Director Of Financial Aid
15 East Peace Street
Raleigh, NC 27604

4380 Special Talent Scholarships

AMOUNT: $5,000 (max) **DEADLINE:** None Specified
FIELD/MAJOR: All Areas Of Study

Renewable scholarships for students at Eckerd College who have shown a remarkable talent in a curricular or extra-curricular activity (math, science, English, sports, music, theater, art, leadership, community service, etc.). Amount partially depends upon financial need. Contact the Director of Financial Aid at the address below for details.

Eckerd College
Director Of Financial Aid
P.O. Box 12560
St. Petersburg, FL 33733

4381 Specialist Chad Delos Santos Memorial Scholarship

AMOUNT: $1,000 **DEADLINE:** Feb 1
FIELD/MAJOR: All Areas Of Study

Scholarships are available at the University of Hawaii, Hilo, for full-time students who are members or children of members of the Hawaii Army or Air Force National Guard. Write to the address listed below for information.

University Of Hawaii At Hilo
Financial Aid Office
200 West Kawili Street
Hilo, HI 96720

4382 Spencer Dissertation Year Fellowships For Research In Education

AMOUNT: $1,000-$12,000 **DEADLINE:** Nov 2
FIELD/MAJOR: Education

Fellowships are available for doctoral students who have completed all program requirements except the dissertation to encourage research relevant to the improvement of education. Write to the address listed below for information.

Spencer Educational Foundation, Inc.
900 North Michigan Avenue, Suite 2800
Chicago, IL 60611

4383 Spencer Educational Scholarships

AMOUNT: Varies **DEADLINE:** Feb 1
FIELD/MAJOR: Risk Management and Insurance

Scholarships for juniors, seniors, or graduate students who are enrolled full-time in a risk management, actuarial science, or insurance field. Based primarily on merit. Write to the address below for complete details. Information will be available in October of the previous year the scholarship is awarded.

Spencer Educational Foundation, Inc.
655 Third Ave.
New York, NY 10017

4384 Spencer Post Doctoral Fellowship Program

AMOUNT: $40,000 **DEADLINE:** Dec 21
FIELD/MAJOR: Education, Humanities, Social Science, Behavioral Sciences

Post-doctoral fellowships for persons in education, the humanities, or the social and behavioral sciences. They must describe research whose relevance to education is apparent. Must have Ph.D or Ed.D within last 5 years. Up to 30 fellowships per year. Amount shown may be for one- or two-year award. This is a non-residential fellowship. Write to the address below for complete details.

National Academy Of Education
Stanford University, School of Education
Ceras-108
Stanford, CA 94305

4385

Spencer T. Olin Fellowships For Women In Graduate Study

Amount: $20,000-$33,000
Deadline: Feb 1
Field/Major: See Listing Of Fields Below

Fellowships are available at Washington University for female scholars in one of the following fields: biology, biomedicine, humanities, physics, math, social science, behavioral science, architecture, business administration, engineering, fine arts, law, medicine, and social work. For master's and doctoral level study. Write to the address listed below for information.

Monticello College Foundation/Washington University
Margaret Watkins, Olin Fellowship Prog.
Campus Box 1187, One Brookings Drive
St. Louis, MO 63130

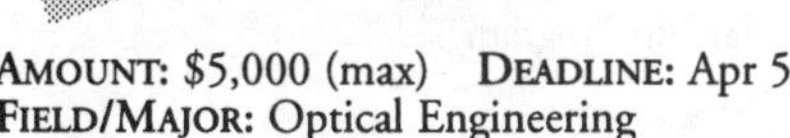

4386

Spie Educational Scholarship/ Grant Program

Amount: $5,000 (max) **Deadline:** Apr 5
Field/Major: Optical Engineering

Award is based on the student's potential contributions to optical or optoelectronic applied science and engineering. In addition, institutions may make grant applications under this program. Awards will not be made on the basis of need. Write to the address listed below for details.

International Society For Optical Engineering
Spie Scholarship Committee
P.O. Box 10
Bellingham, WA 98227

4387

Spiva-Timmons Scholarships

Amount: Tuition **Deadline:** Mar 1
Field/Major: All Areas Of Study

Awards for students at Pittsburg State University who demonstrate financial need. Renewable with a GPA of at least 3.0. Write to the address below for more information.

Pittsburg State University
Office Of Academic Affairs
203 Russ Hall
Pittsburg, KS 66762

4388

SPJST Scholarship Program

Amount: $500 **Deadline:** Feb 1
Field/Major: All Areas Of Study

Scholarships for current members of the Slavonic Benevolent Order of the State of Texas (SPJST). Must hold active insurance certificate for one year before application. Application is made in senior year of high school or while in undergraduate years (for the following year). Based on test scores, academic records, recommendations, and SPJST involvement. Write to the address listed below for additional information.

Slavonic Benevolent Order Of The State Of Texas
Supreme Lodge SPJST
c/o Scholarships
P.O. Box 100
Temple, TX 76503

4389

Sponsored Research Funding

Amount: None Specified **Deadline:** None Specified
Field/Major: All Areas Of Study

Graduate students at the University of Dayton are eligible for sponsored research or external sources of funding for their research. Contact the academic research information services, located in Kettering Laboratories, Rm. 505 or call (513) 229-3173.

University of Dayton
Office Of Scholarships And Financial Aid
300 College Park
Dayton, OH 45469

4390

Spraying Systems Company Scholarships

Amount: $1,000 **Deadline:** Feb 15
Field/Major: Agronomy, Ag Engineering/Mechanization, Turf Management, Horticulture

Scholarships are available for FFA members pursuing a four-year degree in one of the areas listed above. Write to the address below for details.

National FFA Foundation
Scholarship Office
P.O. Box 15160
Alexandria, VA 22309

4391

Springfield Business And Professional Women's Club Scholarship

Amount: $350 **Deadline:** Mar 31
Field/Major: All Areas Of Study

Student must be a full-time junior or senior with a GPA of 3.0 or better. Preference is given to women who demonstrate financial need. Write to the address below for more information.

Southwest Missouri State University
Office Of Financial Aid
901 South National Ave.
Springfield, MO 65804

4392

Springfield Regional Stockyards and LCF Scholarship

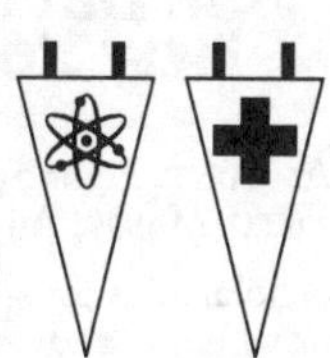

Amount: $300 **Deadline:** None Specified
Field/Major: Agriculture

Student must be a junior animal science major who demonstrates scholarship, leadership and character. Contact the agriculture department for more information.

Southwest Missouri State University
Office of Financial Aid
901 South National Ave.
Springfield, MO 65804

4393

Square D Foundation Merit Scholarships

AMOUNT: $500-$2,000 **DEADLINE:** None Specified
FIELD/MAJOR: All Areas Of Study

Scholarships are available to graduating high school seniors who are National Merit finalists and children of employees of the Square D Company. Up to five awards are offered annually. Write to the address listed below for information, or contact the human resources department at Square D.

National Merit Scholarship Corporation/Square D Company
1560 Sherman Avenue, Suite 200
Evanston, IL 60201

4394

SRC Education Alliance Graduate Fellowship

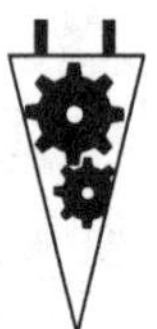

AMOUNT: Tuition and Fees **DEADLINE:** Feb 1
FIELD/MAJOR: Microelectronics

Must be U.S. or Canadian citizen or permanent resident and pursuing a Ph.D program in areas relevant to microelectronics and is or will be performing research under the guidance of an SRC-designated faculty member. Should be interested in the possibility of an academic career in areas relevant to microelectronics at a U.S. university or employment with an SRC member. Write to the address below for complete details.

Semiconductor Research Corporation Education Alliance
Graduate Fellowship Program
P.O. Box 12053
Research Triangle Park, NC 27709

4395

St. Catherine Moran Foreign Language Scholarship

AMOUNT: $500-$1,500 **DEADLINE:** Mar 15
FIELD/MAJOR: Foreign Languages: French Or Spanish

Applicants must be incoming freshmen who are interested in majoring in a foreign language. Applicants will arrange for an oral audition and submit a written essay. Edgewood offers majors in French and Spanish. Write to the address below for details.

Edgewood College
Office of Admissions
855 Woodrow Street
Madison, WI 53711

4396

St. David's Society Of New York Scholarships

AMOUNT: None Specified **DEADLINE:** May 30
FIELD/MAJOR: All Areas Of Study-Or-Welsh Studies

Scholarships for students who are either of Welsh descent or who are studying Welsh (or perhaps Celtic) language, literature, culture, or music. For any study beyond high school. Write to the address below for details.

St. David's Society Of New York
Scholarship Committee
71 W. 23rd St., Room 1006
New York, NY 10010

4397

St. Petersburg General Hospital Auxiliary Scholarship

AMOUNT: Varies **DEADLINE:** Varies
FIELD/MAJOR: Nursing

Award for a student in the field of nursing who have a GPA of at least 2.0. Applicant must demonstrate financial need. Contact St. Petersburg General Hospital one month before your session begins for further details.

St. Petersburg Junior College
Financial Aid Office
P.O. Box 13489
St. Petersburg, FL 33733

4398

St. Petersburg Times Minority Scholarships

AMOUNT: $1,500-$3,000 **DEADLINE:** Mar 1
FIELD/MAJOR: Newspaper Journalism, Newspaper Advertising

Must be a minority student. Must be a junior or senior at the University of Florida and planning for a career in newspaper journalism or advertising. Preference will be given to students from the St. Petersburg, FL area. Must have at least a 2.8 GPA. Renewable. Summer internships available to winners. Write to the address below for details.

University Of Florida
2070 Weimer Hall
Director, Minority Scholarship Program
Gainesville, FL 32611

4399

St. Vincent Pallotti Fellowship

AMOUNT: Varies **DEADLINE:** None Specified
FIELD/MAJOR: All Fields of Study

Fellowships are available at the Catholic University of America for graduate students who agree to serve the mission of the church for two years after completion of their degree program. Awards open to the laity as well as the clergy. Contact the financial aid office at the address below for details.

The Catholic University Of America
Office Of Admissions And Financial Aid
Washington, DC 20064

4400

Stackpole-Hall Foundation Scholarship

AMOUNT: Varies **DEADLINE:** None Specified
FIELD/MAJOR: All Areas Of Study

Award for students at Mercyhurst who are from Elk County, Pennsylvania and who have a record of academic achievement or demonstrated leadership ability. Write to the address below for more information.

Mercyhurst College
Financial Aid Office
Glenwood Hills
Erie, PA 16546

4401
Stamps Foundation Ministerial Fund

AMOUNT: Varies **DEADLINE:** None Specified
FIELD/MAJOR: Christian Ministry

Awards for CHC students who are pursuing a career in Christian ministry. Applicants must be from southern California (North Los Angeles and southward) and demonstrate financial need. Write to the address below for more information.

Christian Heritage College
Financial Aid Office
2100 Greenfield Dr.
El Cajon, CA 92019

4402
Stanislaus County Legal Secretaries Association Scholarship

AMOUNT: Varies **DEADLINE:** Apr 1
FIELD/MAJOR: Legal Secretary, Paralegal, Court Reporting

Scholarships are available for graduating high school seniors, undergraduates, and individuals who wish to re-enter the work force. Applicant must have career goal of working in the legal field. Write to the address listed below for information.

Legal Secretaries, Inc.
Cassandra A. Sove
P.O. Box 3465
Modesto, CA 95353

4403
Stanley Drama Award

AMOUNT: $2,000 **DEADLINE:** Sep 1
FIELD/MAJOR: Playwriting

Annual award for the best play or musical submitted to the competition. Script must not be commercially produced or published. Plays must be recommended by a theatre professional. Previous winners ineligible. Application must be submitted with script. Write for complete details and application.

Wagner College
Department Of Humanities
631 Howard Ave.
Staten Island, NY 10301

4404
Stanley E. Jackson Scholarship

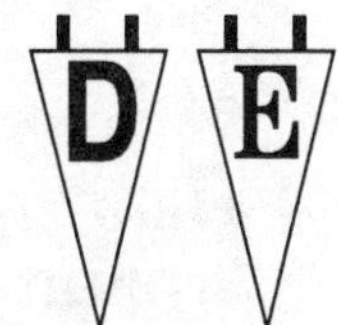

AMOUNT: $1,000 **DEADLINE:** Feb 1
FIELD/MAJOR: All Areas Of Study

Scholarships for entering freshmen who are disabled. Special awards are also available for minority students who are disabled and for gifted students. Applicants must be considered 100% disabled. Write to the address below for details.

Foundation For Exceptional Children
Stanley E. Jackson Scholarship
1920 Association Dr.
Reston, VA 22091

4405
Stanley-University of Iowa Summer Language Study Scholarships

AMOUNT: $2,100 **DEADLINE:** Apr 1
FIELD/MAJOR: Foreign Languages-Chinese, Japanese, Hindi

Scholarships are available at the University of Iowa for full-time students majoring in Japanese, Chinese or Hindi languages. Write to the address listed below for information.

University of Iowa
Department of Asian Languages
314 Gilmore Hall
Iowa City, IA 52245

4406
Star Supporter Scholarship/Loan

AMOUNT: Varies **DEADLINE:** Mar 15
FIELD/MAJOR: Theology, Church Related Studies

Applicants must be African American members of the Christian Church who are preparing to enter the ordained ministry and can demonstrate financial need. Full-time enrollment is mandatory. Write to the address below for details.

Christian Church (Disciples of Christ)
Attn: Scholarships
P.O. Box 1986
Indianapolis, IN 46206

4407
State Board Of Governors Scholarships

AMOUNT: Varies **DEADLINE:** None Specified
FIELD/MAJOR: All Areas Of Study

Scholarships are available to minority students at Clarion with a minimum GPA of 2.5. Amount varies based on the student's financial need. Contact the Admissions Office for further information.

Clarion University
104 Egbert Hall
Office of Financial Aid
Clarion, PA 16214

4408
State Department Federal Credit Union Scholarship Fund

AMOUNT: Varies **DEADLINE:** Apr 12
FIELD/MAJOR: All Fields of Study

Scholarships for members of SDFCU. Must be currently enrolled in a degree program and have completed 12 credit hours. Must have a GPA of at least 2.5. Write to address below for details. Please note: you must be a member of the State Department Federal Credit Union. Members of the credit unions of other agencies are not eligible.

State Department Federal Credit Union
Marketing Department
1630 King Street
Alexandria, VA 22314

4409

State Farm Companies Foundation Scholarships

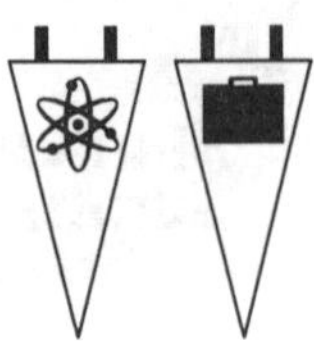

AMOUNT: $1,000 **DEADLINE:** Feb 15
FIELD/MAJOR: Agriculture, Agribusiness

Scholarships are available for FFA members pursuing a four-year degree in any area of agriculture, who reside in Illinois. Four awards are offered annually. Write to the address below for details.

National FFA Foundation
Scholarship Office
P.O. Box 15160
Alexandria, VA 22309

4410

State Graduate Deans' Fellowship Program

AMOUNT: Varies **DEADLINE:** Late Feb
FIELD/MAJOR: All Areas Of Study

Awards are available for Virginia residents who are enrolled in graduate or professional programs in one of the following universities: George Mason, Old Dominion, Virginia, Virginia Polytechnic Institute and State, Virginia Commonwealth, and The College of William and Mary. Must be a U.S. citizen. Write to the address below for more information.

Virginia Council Of Higher Education
James Monroe Building
101 North 14th St.
Richmond, VA 23219

4411

State Medical Board of Georgia Scholarships

AMOUNT: $8,000 **DEADLINE:** May 15
FIELD/MAJOR: Medicine

Scholarships are available for Georgia resident medical students who plan to practice medicine in a rural area of Georgia upon graduation. Write to the address listed below for information.

State Medical Board Of Georgia
244 Washington Street, SW
Room 574
Atlanta, GA 30334

4412

State Need Grant

AMOUNT: $1,350 (avg) **DEADLINE:** Jun 1
FIELD/MAJOR: All Areas Of Study

Scholarship program for undergraduate students in Washington state supported schools. Based on financial need. Students with dependents may be eligible for dependent care allowance. Write to the address listed below for information.

Washington Higher Education Coordinating Board
917 Lakeridge Way
P.O. Box 43430
Olympia, WA 98504

4413

State Of Idaho Scholarship Program

AMOUNT: $2,650 **DEADLINE:** Jan 31
FIELD/MAJOR: All Areas Of Study

Scholarships are available for Idaho resident graduating high school seniors who are planning to enroll at an Idaho college or university. Twenty-five awards are offered annually, with one quarter of these awards going to vocational students. Write to the address listed below or contact your high school counselor for more information.

Idaho State Board Of Education
Ms. Caryl Smith
P.O. Box 83720
Boise, ID 83720

4414

State of Illinois Director of Agriculture Scholarship

AMOUNT: $1,000 **DEADLINE:** Nov 17
FIELD/MAJOR: Agriculture Or Agribusiness

Scholarship awarded to an incoming freshman or transfer student enrolling in an agricultural curriculum at Illinois State University. Selection will be based upon demonstrated academic achievement and leadership abilities. Financial need will be considered. Applicants must be Illinois farmers or children of Illinois farmers. Five awards per year. For more information contact your high school guidance counselor or write to the address below.

Illinois State University, Dept. Of Agriculture
Turner Hall 150
Campus Box 5020
Normal, IL 61761

4415

State of Virginia Diversity Enhancement Scholarships

AMOUNT: $2,500-$5,000 **DEADLINE:** May 1
FIELD/MAJOR: Agriculture, Life Sciences

Scholarships for underrepresented incoming freshmen and returning undergraduates in the fields of agriculture and life sciences. Priority is given to residents of Virginia. Write to the address below for more information.

Virginia Tech College Of Agriculture And Life Sciences
Dr. John M. White, Associate Dean
1060 Litton Reaves Hall
Blacksburg, VA 24061

4416

State Student Incentive and Schreiner Need-Based Grants

AMOUNT: $2,434 (max) **DEADLINE:** None Specified
FIELD/MAJOR: All Areas Of Study

Grant for students enrolled at least half-time at Schreiner who can demonstrate financial need. Applicants for the State Student Incentive Grant must be recipients of the Tuition Equalization Grant. Write to the address below for more information.

Schreiner College
Financial Aid Office
Kerrville, TX 78028

4417

State University System Farm Family Scholarship

AMOUNT: Varies **DEADLINE:** Varies
FIELD/MAJOR: All Areas Of Study

Awards are available for Minnesota students who are from farm families and demonstrate severe financial need resulting from farm foreclosure, repossession or debt restructuring. Must be recommended by your county extension office and be enrolled in one of the Minnesota state universities. Contact your school's financial aid office for more information.

Minnesota State University Campuses
Office Of Financial Aid
Minneapolis, MN 55455

4418

Statler Foundation Scholarships

AMOUNT: $500 **DEADLINE:** Apr 15
FIELD/MAJOR: Culinary Arts, Hotel/Motel Management

Scholarships for full-time students in the fields of hotel/motel management or the culinary arts. Renewable. Write to the address below for details.

Statler Foundation
107 Delaware Ave., Suite 508
Buffalo, NY 14202

4419

STC Scholarships In Technical Communication

AMOUNT: $2,000 **DEADLINE:** Feb 15
FIELD/MAJOR: Technical Communication

Scholarships for students in established degree programs studying some area of technical communication. Must be full-time student and either have upper class standing in a 2- or 4-year program (including students who will be sophomores) or be a full-time master's or doctoral student. Fourteen awards given per year (7 undergrad, 7 grad). Write to the address below or contact your department of study for application forms or additional information.

Society For Technical Communication
901 N. Stuart St., Suite 904
Arlington, VA 22203

4420

Stefano Frigo Mental Health Grant

AMOUNT: $750 **DEADLINE:** Apr 30
FIELD/MAJOR: Mental Health

Award for undergrad or graduate student who is a Connecticut resident. Scholastic achievement is considered. See your high school guidance counselor or write to the address below for further information.

Mental Health Association Of Connecticut
20-30 Beaver Rd.
Wethersfield, CT 06109

4421

Steffensen Cannon Scholarship

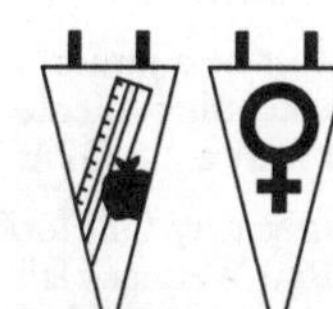

AMOUNT: $8,500-$12,000 **DEADLINE:** Feb 15
FIELD/MAJOR: Education

Scholarships are available at the University of Utah for full-time entering freshmen with a 3.0 GPA or better, continuing students with a 2.75 GPA or higher, or graduate students with a GPA of at least 3.0. Must be committed to a teaching career. Write to the address below for details.

University Of Utah
Education Advising Center
226 Milton Bennion Hall
Salt Lake City, UT 84112

4422

Stephanie Papanikola Scholarship, Virginia Zamboukas Scholarship

AMOUNT: Varies **DEADLINE:** Feb 15
FIELD/MAJOR: All Areas Of Study

Scholarships are available at the University of Utah for full-time students of Greek Orthodox descent. Write to the address below for information.

University Of Utah
Financial Aid And Scholarships Office
105 Student Services Building
Salt Lake City, UT 84112

4423

Stephen C. And Cynthia E. Mitchell Endowed Scholarship

AMOUNT: Varies **DEADLINE:** Mar 1
FIELD/MAJOR: Civil Engineering

Awards are available at the University of New Mexico for full-time civil engineering students with academic achievement and financial need. Must be born, raised, and educated in New Mexico. Write to the address below for more information.

University Of New Mexico, Albuquerque
Office Of Financial Aid
Albuquerque, NM 87131

4424

Stephen Kearney Scholarship

AMOUNT: $100 **DEADLINE:** Apr 1
FIELD/MAJOR: Human Services

Awards for full-time students in the human services program. Must demonstrate financial need. Contact the College of Education and Human Services, UW Oshkosh for more information.

University Of Wisconsin, Oshkosh
Financial Aid Office, Dempsey 104
800 Algoma Blvd.
Oshkosh, WI 54901

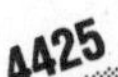

4425

Steve Reynolds Memorial Scholarship

AMOUNT: Varies **DEADLINE:** Mar 1
FIELD/MAJOR: Water Resources, Civil Engineering

Awards are available at the University of New Mexico for water resource or civil engineering majors with demonstrated academic achievement. Write to the address below for more information.

University Of New Mexico, Albuquerque
Office of Financial Aid
Albuquerque, NM 87131

4426

Steven Becker Memorial Scholarship

Amount: $1,000 **Deadline:** May 1
Field/Major: Accounting

Awarded annually to a Five Towns student studying accounting who demonstrates academic potential and/or economic need. Write to the address below for more information.

Five Towns College
305 N. Service Road/Lie Exit 50
Dix Hills, NY 11746

4427

Stevenson Family Scholarship

Amount: $1,000 **Deadline:** None Specified
Field/Major: All Areas Of Study

Scholarship available for El Paso County resident students at the University of Texas El Paso, who graduated from either Montwood or Burgess High School with at least a "B" average. Student must maintain a GPA of 2.7. Write to the address listed below for additional information.

Stevenson Family Fund
El Paso Community Foundation
201 East Main, Suite 1616
El Paso, TX 79901

4428

Stone & Webster Merit Scholarships

Amount: $500-$2,000 **Deadline:** None Specified
Field/Major: All Areas Of Study

Scholarships are available to graduating high school seniors who are National Merit Finalists and children of employees of Stone & Webster, Inc., and its subsidiaries. Write to the address listed below for information, or contact the human resources department at Stone & Webster.

National Merit Scholarship Corporation / Stone & Webster, Inc.
1560 Sherman Avenue, Suite 200
Evanston, IL 60201

4429

Stone Bridge Volunteer Fire Dept. Scholarship Fund

Amount: $500 **Deadline:** Apr 20
Field/Major: All Areas Of Study

Scholarships are available for residents of Tiverton, Rhode Island. Write to the address listed below for information.

Stone Bridge Fire Department
Advisory Committee Chair
48 Leonard Drive
Tiverton, RI 02878

4430

Stoody-West Fellowship

Amount: $6,000 **Deadline:** Feb 15
Field/Major: Journalism (religious)

Awards for Christian graduate students enrolled in journalism at accredited schools who plan a career in religious journalism. Write to the fellowship committee at the address below for details.

United Methodist Communications
Fellowship Committee, Public Media Div.
P.O. Box 320
Nashville, TN 37202

4431

Storer Scholarships

Amount: Tuition and Fees
Deadline: None Specified
Field/Major: All Areas Of Study

Scholarships covering tuition and fees are offered to African American students attending WVU. Based on academic achievement. State residency not required. Must have a high school GPA of at least 3.0. 20 awards per year. Contact the financial aid office at the address below for details.

West Virginia University
Financial Aid Office
P.O. Box 6004
Morgantown, WV 26506

4432

Street Tree Seminar

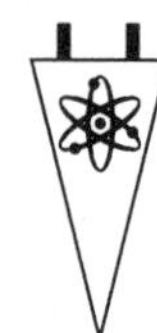

Amount: $500 **Deadline:** Nov 3
Field/Major: Horticulture

Open to full-time students majoring in horticulture with an interest in urban forestry or aboriculture. Write to the address below for more information.

California State Polytechnic University, Pomona
College Of Agriculture
Building 7, Room 110
Pomona, CA 91768

4433

Strnad Nursing Fund

Amount: $300 **Deadline:** None Specified
Field/Major: Nursing

Awards for Mesa State nursing students who have a GPA of at least 2.5. Contact the school of professional studies/nursing area for more details.

Mesa State College
Financial Aid Office
P.O. Box 2647
Grand Junction, CO 81501

4434

Stuart G. Newman Public Relations Scholarship

Amount: $1,000 **Deadline:** Mar 1
Field/Major: Public Relations

Must be a junior or senior at the University of Florida who is planning to enter the field of public relations. Must have at least a 2.8 GPA. Write to the address below for details.

University Of Florida
2070 Weimer Hall
Scholarship and Placement Director
Gainesville, FL 32611

4435

Stuck Memorial Endowed Grant Fund

AMOUNT: Varies **DEADLINE:** None Specified
FIELD/MAJOR: All Areas Of Study

Awards are available for full-time students at Cedarville College who have a GPA of at least 2.0. Write to the address below for more information.

Cedarville College
Financial Aid Office
P.O. Box 601
Cedarville, OH 45314

4436

Student Aid Award For Physically Disabled Students

AMOUNT: $2,500 (max) **DEADLINE:** Dec 1
FIELD/MAJOR: All Areas Of Study

Scholarships for physically handicapped students. Must be between 15 and 35 years old. Contact your local Venture Club or write to the address below for details.

Venture Clubs Of The Americas
Two Penn Center Plaza, Suite 100
Philadelphia, PA 19102

4437

Student Assistance Grant

AMOUNT: $624 **DEADLINE:** Apr 15
FIELD/MAJOR: All Areas Of Study

Applicants must be Arkansas residents who are full-time undergraduates or high school seniors. Awarded on a first come, first served basis by financial need. Student must be attending or planning to attend an approved Arkansas public or private postsecondary institution. Write to the address below for details.

Arkansas Department Of Higher Education
Financial Aid Division
114 East Capitol
Little Rock, AR 72201

4438

Student Associate Membership Fellowships

AMOUNT: None Specified **DEADLINE:** Jan 31
FIELD/MAJOR: Classical Studies, Anthropology, Art History

Awards are available for graduate students in the areas of study above. Based on transcripts, recommendations, and project descriptions. Write to the address below for more information.

American School Of Classical Studies At Athens
Committee On Admissions And Fellowships
993 Lenox Drive, Suite 101
Lawrenceville, NJ 08648

4439

Student Award Program

AMOUNT: $3,000 **DEADLINE:** Apr 30
FIELD/MAJOR: Medicine (M.D./Ph.D.)

Stipends for doctoral (M.D. and Ph.D.) students interested in the improvement of health and medical care in the state of Michigan. Supports a wide range of activities including research, pilot projects, intervention/demonstration projects, feasibility studies, proposal development, and critical literature reviews. Projects must address quality of care, cost containment, healthcare access or a major public health/medical issue. Must focus (geographically) on the state of Michigan. Proposal required. Program announcement may be found in your department office or financial aid office. If unavailable, write to the address below.

Blue Cross Blue Shield Of Michigan Foundation
Susan Van Der Maas, Program Officer
600 Lafayette East, B243
Detroit, MI 48226

4440

Student Body Loan And Grant Fund

AMOUNT: Varies **DEADLINE:** None Specified
FIELD/MAJOR: All Areas Of Study

Awards are available for full-time students at Cedarville College who have a GPA of at least 2.0 and financial need. Write to the address below for more information.

Cedarville College
Financial Aid Office
P.O. Box 601
Cedarville, OH 45314

4441

Student Choice Grants

AMOUNT: Varies **DEADLINE:** None Specified
FIELD/MAJOR: All Areas Of Study

Awards for undergraduates who have completed at least six credit hours at one the following; College of Santa Fe, St. Johns College in Santa Fe, or the College of the Southwest in Hobbs. Applicant must be a resident of New Mexico. Contact the financial aid office at one of the schools listed above for more information.

New Mexico Commission On Higher Education
1068 Cerrillos Road
Santa Fe, NM 87501

4442

Student Deposit Scholarship

AMOUNT: $1,000 **DEADLINE:** Apr 1
FIELD/MAJOR: All Areas Of Study

Awards for all Sul Ross undergraduates who are from Texas and have a GPA of at least 2.5. Write to the address below for more information.

Sul Ross State University
Financial Aid Office
Box C-113
Alpine, TX 79832

4443

Student Film Awards Competition

AMOUNT: $1,000-$2,000 **DEADLINE:** Apr 1
FIELD/MAJOR: Filmmaking

The purpose of the academy's student film awards competition is to support and encourage filmmakers without previous professional experience who are enrolled in accredited colleges and universities. Award may be used for any purpose. Please write for complete information. Please note that this is an award for completed films, rather than a scholarship program.

Academy Of Motion Picture Arts And Sciences
8949 Wilshire Blvd.
Beverly Hills, CA 90211

4444

Student Internship Program

AMOUNT: Varies **DEADLINE:** Mar 31
FIELD/MAJOR: Television and Film Related Fields

Summer internships for full-time students pursuing degrees at a college or university in the U.S.. Those who have graduated 15 months prior to the deadline to apply are also eligible. Twenty-eight positions are available. Write to the address below for more details. Information is also available on-line at http://www.emmys.org or through e-mail at academy-info@emmys.org.

Academy Of Television Arts And Sciences
5220 Lankershim Blvd.
North Hollywood, CA 91601

4445

Student Loan Fund

AMOUNT: $2,500 (max) **DEADLINE:** Apr 15, Oct 7
FIELD/MAJOR: Mechanical Engineering

You must be a junior, senior, or graduate mechanical engineering student enrolled in a U.S. school with an accredited mechanical engineering or engineering technology curricula. Must be a member of ASME and a U.S. citizen. Write to the address below for details.

American Society Of Mechanical Engineers Auxiliary, Inc.
Mrs. Robert B. Watson, Chairman
623 N. Valley Forge Rd.
Devon, PA 19333

4446

Student Loan-for-Nursing Program

AMOUNT: $2,500 **DEADLINE:** Jul 1
FIELD/MAJOR: Nursing

$2,500 annual loan (not to exceed $10,000) for students pursuing a nursing profession in New Mexico. Must be a resident of New Mexico and a U.S. citizen or a legal resident. Loan can be forgiven by serving as a nurse in an underserved area of New Mexico for at least one year. Write to the address listed below for additional information.

New Mexico Commission On Higher Education
1068 Cerrillos Road
Santa Fe, NM 87501

4447

Student Opportunity Scholarships

AMOUNT: $100-$1,400 **DEADLINE:** Apr 1
FIELD/MAJOR: All Areas Of Study

Scholarships for minority groups (African American, Hispanic, Asian, or Native American). Must be Presbyterian Church members and U.S. citizens or permanent residents. For high school seniors entering college full-time as incoming freshmen. Renewable. Write to address below for details. Specify Student Opportunity Scholarships (SOS).

Presbyterian Church (U.S.A.)
Office Of Financial Aid For Students
100 Witherspoon Street
Louisville, KY 40202

4448

Student Paper Competition

AMOUNT: $250-$1,000 **DEADLINE:** Jan 1
FIELD/MAJOR: Water Conservation

Twelve awards given for best papers on water pollution control, water quality problems, water-related concerns, or hazardous wastes. Semi-finalists will present papers at the annual WPCF conference. Categories are 1) operations students, 2) bachelor's students, 3) master's students, 4) Ph.D. students. Initial judging is based on 500-1,000 word abstract. Write to the address below for details.

Water Environment Federation
Student Programs, Attn: Liza Clark
601 Wythe St.
Alexandria, VA 22314

4449

Student Research Award

AMOUNT: None Specified **DEADLINE:** Dec 5
FIELD/MAJOR: Geriatrics

Awards will be given to the student presenting the most outstanding paper at the AGS annual meeting. Awardee will be chosen based on originality, scientific merit and relevance or the research. All students who submit abstracts to the AGS annual meeting will be considered for this award. Write to the address below for more information.

American Geriatrics Society
770 Lexington Ave., Suite 300
New York, NY 10021

4450

Student Research Fellowships

AMOUNT: $2,400 **DEADLINE:** Jan 15
FIELD/MAJOR: Dental Research

For dental students at an accredited dental school within the U.S. Must be sponsored by a faculty member at that school. Should not be due to receive their degree in the year the award is given. Applicants may have an advanced degree in a basic science subject. Contact the address below for complete information.

American Association For Dental Research
Patricia J. Lewis
1111 Fourteenth Street, NW, Suite 1000
Washington, DC 20005

4451

Student Research Fellowships In Liver/Hepatic Research

AMOUNT: $2,500 **DEADLINE:** Dec 15
FIELD/MAJOR: Medicine, Medically Related Fields

Fellowships for M.D. and Ph.D. students to encourage them to gain exposure in the research laboratory, and possibly consider liver research as a career option. Fellowships are for 3 months. Must be full-time student at a graduate or medical school. Not for terminal Ph.D. funding. Write to the Foundation at the address below for details.

American Liver Foundation
Student Research Fellowships
1425 Pompton Ave.
Cedar Grove, NJ 07009

4452

Student Research Program, AHA California Affiliate

AMOUNT: $2,500 **DEADLINE:** Jan 16
FIELD/MAJOR: Heart Or Stroke Research

Program for California students or students at California institutions to work in an assigned laboratory in California under the direction and supervision of experienced scientists. Must be a junior or senior and have completed one year of organic chemistry and biological sciences and one quarter of physics or calculus. Write to the address below for more information. Deadline to request applications is Dec 15.

American Heart Association, California Affiliate
Research Department
1710 Gilbreth Road
Burlingame, CA 94010

4453

Student Traineeship Research Grants

AMOUNT: $1,500 **DEADLINE:** Ongoing
FIELD/MAJOR: Cystic Fibrosis Research

Doctoral (M.D. or Ph.D.) research grants for students that plan a career in research and have a lab project that can be completed in less than 1 year. Award intended to interest student in cystic fibrosis research and offset costs of the project. Seniors planning to enter graduate training may also apply. Contact the foundation for further information on application procedure.

Cystic Fibrosis Foundation
Medical/Research Programs
6931 Arlington Rd.
Bethesda, MD 20814

4454

Study Awards

AMOUNT: $200-$4,000 **DEADLINE:** Jun 1
FIELD/MAJOR: All Areas Of Study

Awards are available for students who demonstrate financial need. Write to the address below for more information.

Long Island University
Financial Aid Office
Southampton, NY 11968

4455

Sub-Saharan Africa Dissertation Internship Awards

AMOUNT: $20,000 **DEADLINE:** Oct 1, Mar 1
FIELD/MAJOR: All Areas Of Study

Fellowships are available to African scholars who have completed all the Ph.D. requirements except the dissertation. Award is to increase the quality of overseas advanced studies for outstanding African scholars and to enhance the relevance of their training to the process of economic development in Africa. Priority is given to agricultural and environmental majors. Write to the address listed below for information.

Rockefeller Foundation
African Dissertation Internships
420 Fifth Avenue
New York, NY 10018

4456

Suburban Cable Scholars Program

AMOUNT: $1,000-$3,500 **DEADLINE:** Mar 4
FIELD/MAJOR: All Areas Of Study

Awards are available for high school seniors who reside in the suburban cable servicing area. Based on academic achievement, leadership, community service and communication skills. Relatives of employees of Suburban Cable and the Lenfest Group are not eligible to apply. The suburban servicing area consists of counties in eastern PA and western NJ. Write to the address below for more information.

Suburban Cable
1332 Enterprise Drive, Suite 100
West Chester, PA 19380

4457

Suburban Hospital Scholarship Program

AMOUNT: $5,000 (max) **DEADLINE:** Apr 30
FIELD/MAJOR: Nursing, Medical Technology, Medical Therapy, Physician Assistant

Program for juniors or seniors in the fields of study listed above who are from the Washington, D.C. metropolitan area. Applicants must have a GPA of at least a 2.5. Write to the address below for more details.

Suburban Hospital
Department Of Human Resources
8600 Old Georgetown Rd.
Bethesda, MD 20814

4458

Successful Farming Scholarship

AMOUNT: $1,000 **DEADLINE:** None Specified
FIELD/MAJOR: Agriculture

Scholarships for graduating high school seniors from farming families (parents or guardians derive majority of income from farming) who will be studying agriculture in an approved curriculum at a four-year college. Must be in the top 50% of high school class and in test scores. Strong consideration given to extracurricular activities and work. Twenty awards offered per year. Write to the address below for details.

Successful Farming
1716 Locust Street
Des Moines, IA 50309

4459

Sudden Opportunities Awards

AMOUNT: $1,000 **DEADLINE:** Varies
FIELD/MAJOR: Art, Dance, Music

Awards to fund unique professional opportunities for improved ability and growth that are only available during a limited time period. Must be an Idaho resident who is over the age of 18 as well as a U.S. citizen or permanent resident. Write to the address below for additional details.

Idaho Commission On The Arts
P.O. Box 83720
Boise, ID 83720

4460

Sul Ross Scholars And Leadership Programs

AMOUNT: $1,000 **DEADLINE:** Apr 1
FIELD/MAJOR: All Areas Of Study

Awards for freshmen at Sul Ross who have demonstrated academic excellence or leadership. Write to the address below for more information.

Sul Ross State University
Financial Aid Office
Box C-113
Alpine, TX 79832

4461

Sumitomo Bank Of California Scholarships

AMOUNT: Varies **DEADLINE:** Apr 1
FIELD/MAJOR: Business, Banking, Accounting, Economics, International Trade

Applicants must be of Japanese ancestry, California residents attending California schools, and majoring in the above fields. Applications and information may be obtained from local JACL chapters, district offices, and the national headquarters at the address below. Please indicate your level of study and be certain to include a legal-sized SASE.

Japanese American Citizens League
National Scholarship And Award Program
1765 Sutter St.
San Francisco, CA 94115

4462

Summer Archival Internships

AMOUNT: $2,572 **DEADLINE:** Apr 1
FIELD/MAJOR: History, Archival Science, Library Science

Internships for students who are from Maryland or who attend school in Maryland who are studying one of the areas above. For juniors, seniors, or graduate students who have demonstrated academic achievement. Write to the address below for more details.

Maryland State Archives
Internship Program, Maryland State Arch.
350 Rowe Boulevard
Annapolis, MD 21401

4463

Summer Fellowship Grants

AMOUNT: $1,500 **DEADLINE:** Apr 1
FIELD/MAJOR: Medical Research (Allergy/Immunology)

Grants for medical students pursuing a career in the fields of allergy and immunology. Grants support research during summers. Write to the address below for details.

American Academy Of Allergy And Immunology
Jerome Schultz, Continuing Med. Educ. Mgr.
611 E. Wells St.
Milwaukee, WI 53202

4464

Summer Fellowship Program

AMOUNT: $125 Per Week **DEADLINE:** Mar 31
FIELD/MAJOR: Economics and Related (Banking, Finance)

Summer fellowships in economic science at the institute open to undergraduates who have completed their junior year and are applying to doctoral programs or to graduate students already enrolled in a doctoral program. Write to the address below for complete details.

American Institute For Economic Research
Pamela P. Allard, Asst. To The Director
Division Street
Great Barrington, MA 01230

4465

Summer Fellowship Program

AMOUNT: Varies **DEADLINE:** Nov 20
FIELD/MAJOR: Communications, Radio, Television

Awards are available for juniors or seniors in a four-year college or university who are interested in the fields of communication, radio, or television. Write to the address below for more information.

International Radio And Television Society Foundation
420 Lexington Ave., Suite 1714
New York, NY 10170

4466

Summer Fellowships

AMOUNT: Varies **DEADLINE:** Nov 1
FIELD/MAJOR: Byzantine Studies (And Related), Pre-Columbian Studies

Fellowships are available for a period of four to nine weeks and are open to all scholars at any graduate level. Resident fellowships. Write to the address below for details.

Dumbarton Oaks
Office Of The Director
1703 32nd St., NW
Washington, DC 20007

4467

Summer Fellowships Of The Electrochemical Society, Inc.

AMOUNT: $9,000 **DEADLINE:** Jan 1
FIELD/MAJOR: Electrochemistry and Related Fields

Awards are available for graduate students enrolled in a college or university in the U.S. or Canada. Applicants must be studying a field related to the objectives of the electrochemical society. Renewable. Write to the address below for more information.

Electrochemical Society, Inc.
10 South Main St.
Pennington, NJ 08534

4468

Summer Internship Program

Amount: Varies **Deadline:** Apr 1
Field/Major: All Areas Of Study

Ten-week summer internship program to provide valuable work experience for a blind postsecondary student. Duties include activities in the areas of public information and education, membership assistance, communications, legislative monitoring and publications. Write to the address below for details.

American Council Of The Blind
Oral Miller, Executive Director
1155 15th St., NW, Suite 720
Washington, DC 20005

4469

Summer Internships

Amount: $2,250 **Deadline:** Feb 2
Field/Major: Art History, Art Conservation

Summer internships at the museum for undergraduate junior, seniors or graduate students who are studying art history or a related field. Program begins on June 17 and runs through August 16. Write to the address listed below for additional information.

Metropolitan Museum Of Art
Attn: Internship Programs
1000 Fifth Ave.
New York, NY 10028

4470

Summer Medical Student Fellowship

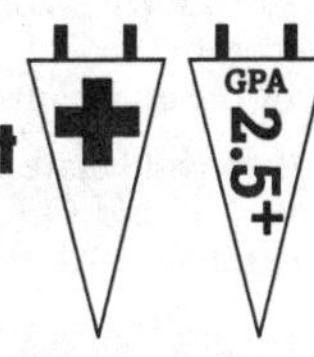

Amount: $2,000 **Deadline:** Apr 15
Field/Major: Urology

Fellowships allowing highly qualified medical students to work in urology research laboratories for two months in the summer. Write to the address listed below for additional information.

American Foundation For Urologic Disease, Inc.
Research Scholar Division
300 West Pratt Street, Suite 401
Baltimore, MD 21201

4471

Summer Programs In Poland

Amount: $650-$1,100 **Deadline:** None Specified
Field/Major: Polish Culture

Open to high school graduates, undergraduate and graduate students studying Polish cultures in Poland and Rome. Write to the address below for more information.

Kosciuszko Foundation
15 East 65th St.
New York, NY 10021

4472

Summer Research Fellowships In Law And Social Science

Amount: $3,300 **Deadline:** Mar 1
Field/Major: Social Science, Humanities

Fellowships are available for minority sophomores or juniors pursuing a degree in humanities or social sciences. Applicants must have a minimum GPA of 3.0. Recipients will be assigned to an American Bar Foundation Research Fellow who will involve the student in his or her research project. Recipient will work at the abf offices for 35 hours per week for 10 weeks. Write to the address listed below for information.

American Bar Foundation
Assistant Director
750 N. Lake Shore Drive
Chicago, IL 60611

4473

Summer Research Participation Program

Amount: $225 Per Week **Deadline:** Feb 1
Field/Major: Physical And Life Sciences, Mathematics, Computer Sciences, Engineering

Research internship program provides students with an opportunity to work in above areas in relation to energy development. Open to full-time undergrad juniors/ seniors or first-year grad students. U.S. citizen or legal resident. Must have at least a 3.0 GPA. Program is available at Argonne only. Term is 11 weeks (June-August). Write to the summer research participation program at the address below for details.

Argonne National Laboratory
Div. Of Educational Student Programs
9700 S. Cass Ave.
Argonne, IL 60439

4474

Summer Research Program For Minorities & Women

Amount: Varies **Deadline:** Dec 1
Field/Major: Engineering, Math, Science, Physics

Program offers minority and women students technical employment experience at Bell Laboratories. Students should have completed their third year of college. 60-100 awards per year. Write to the address below or call (908) 582-6461 for complete details.

AT&T Bell Laboratories
University Relations, SRP Manager
101 Crawfords Corner Rd, Rm. 1B-222
Holmdel, NJ 07733

4475

Summer Scholarships In Epidemiology

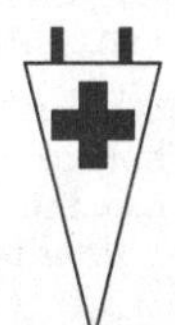

Amount: $2,000 (max) **Deadline:** Apr 1
Field/Major: Medical Research-Cystic Fibrosis

Scholarships are available for M.D.'s currently working in cystic fibrosis to increase skills in epidemiology. Awards cover tuition and expenses of up to $2,000 for selected summer epidemiology programs. Coursework should include biostatics and epidemiology, particularly clinical epidemiology and/or clinical trials. Write to the address below for details.

Cystic Fibrosis Foundation
Office Of Grants Management
6931 Arlington Rd.
Bethesda, MD 20814

4476 Summer Session Scholarships

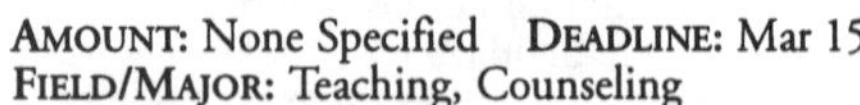

AMOUNT: None Specified **DEADLINE:** Mar 15
FIELD/MAJOR: Teaching, Counseling

Open to credentialed classroom teachers and counselors. Send a legal-size SASE to the address below for an application.

California Congress Of Parents, Teachers, And Students, Inc.
930 Georgia St., P.O. Box 15015
Los Angeles, CA 90015

4477 Summer Student Fellowship

AMOUNT: $3,900 **DEADLINE:** Mar 1
FIELD/MAJOR: Oceanography and Related Fields

Summer fellowships to study oceanography and related fields for undergraduate seniors or beginning graduate students in any of the fields of science or engineering. Write to the address below for complete details.

Woods Hole Oceanographic Institution
Education Office Fellowship Committee
W.H.O.I.
Woods Hole, MA 02543

4478 Sun Bay Business And Professional Women's Club Of St. Petersburg Awards

AMOUNT: Varies **DEADLINE:** Varies
FIELD/MAJOR: All Areas Of Study

Award for a student at St. Petersburg Junior College who has dependent children and financial need. Write to the address below for more details.

St. Petersburg Junior College
Financial Aid Office
P.O. Box 13489
St. Petersburg, FL 33733

4479 Sun Company, Inc., Scholarships

AMOUNT: $1,000 **DEADLINE:** Feb 15
FIELD/MAJOR: Horticulture, Floriculture

Scholarships are available for FFA members pursuing a degree in horticulture or floriculture at a four-year institution, who participated in the floriculture contest above the local level. Write to the address below for details.

National FFA Foundation
Scholarship Office
P.O. Box 15160
Alexandria, VA 22309

4480 Sunkist Growers, Inc., Scholarship

AMOUNT: $2,000 **DEADLINE:** Apr 15
FIELD/MAJOR: Fruit Industry

Open to fruit industries majors or others with a demonstrated interest in pursuing careers in the citrus fruit industry. Write to the address below for more information.

California State Polytechnic University, Pomona
College Of Agriculture
Building 7, Room 110
Pomona, CA 91768

4481 Sunny King Memorial Scholarship

AMOUNT: $1,000 **DEADLINE:** Mar 15
FIELD/MAJOR: All Areas Of Study

Awards for Jacksonville State University students who are in any field of study. Write to the address below for more information.

Jacksonville State University
Financial Aid Office
Jacksonville, AL 36265

4482 Sunny King Toyota Entrepreneurial Scholarship

AMOUNT: $1,000 **DEADLINE:** Mar 15
FIELD/MAJOR: Commerce, Business

Awards for Jacksonville State University seniors who are majoring in commerce or business. Based primarily on entrepreneurial spirit of the applicants. Write to the address below for more details.

Jacksonville State University
Financial Aid Office
Jacksonville, AL 36265

4483 SurfLant Scholarship

AMOUNT: None Specified **DEADLINE:** Apr 15
FIELD/MAJOR: All Areas Of Study

Scholarships for children of active duty or retired personnel who are, or who have been for at least 3 years between 1975 and the present, serving in a unit under the command of Naval Surface Force, U.S. Atlantic Fleet. Undergraduate study only. Write for more info and an application form (you will be asked to specify parent's duty station in Atlantic Surface Fleet and dates served). Information may also be found in the American Legion publication "Need a Lift?" which can be found in many guidance offices/financial aid offices.

Surflant Scholarship Foundation
Michigan House
1531 Dillingham Blvd., Naval Station
Norfolk, VA 23511

4484 Susan James McDonald Memorial Scholarship

AMOUNT: $1,000 **DEADLINE:** Feb 29
FIELD/MAJOR: Management

Awards for juniors in the School of Management. Recipient will be selected on the basis of scholarship, financial need, and commitment to the highest ideals of the management profession. Female students will be given preference. Applications for School of Management Scholarships will be available in the SOM Development Office, Room 206.

University Of Massachusetts, Amherst
School Of Management
SOM Development Office, Room 206
Amherst, MA 01003

4485

Sutton Education Scholarship

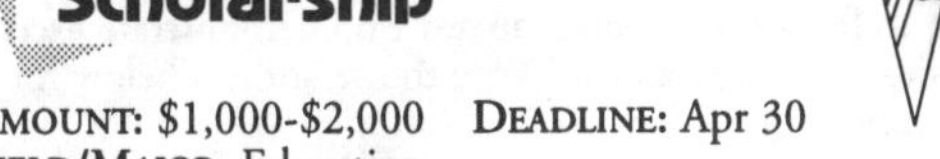

AMOUNT: $1,000-$2,000 **DEADLINE:** Apr 30
FIELD/MAJOR: Education

Applicants must be full-time students and NAACP memb studying for a career in education. Undergraduates must have a GPA of at least 2.5 and graduate students must have a cumulative 3.0 GPA or better. Write to the address below for details and include the scholarship name on the envelope.

NAACP Special Contribution Fund
Education Department
4805 Mount Hope Dr.
Baltimore, MD 21215

4486

Swedish Community Scholarships

AMOUNT: $1,250 (max) **DEADLINE:** Apr 1
FIELD/MAJOR: All Areas Of Study

Scholarships for graduating high school seniors residing in King County (WA). Based on academics and need. Interview required. Write to the address below for details.

Seattle Swedish Community Scholarships
1416 N. 55th St.
Seattle, WA 98103

4487

Swiss Benevolent Society Of Chicago Scholarships

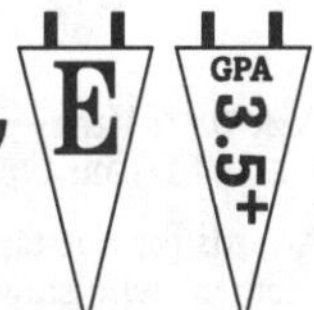

AMOUNT: $2,500 (max) **DEADLINE:** Mar 5
FIELD/MAJOR: All Areas Of Study

Scholarships for residents of Illinois and southern Wisconsin who are Swiss nationals or of Swiss descent. Applicants must be prospective college freshmen or college students with less than 125 semester hours of completed college courses and have a GPA of 3.5 or greater. Swiss students studying in the U.S. on a student or visitor's visa are not eligible. Write to the address below for details.

Swiss Benevolent Society Of Chicago
Scholarship Committee
6440 N. Bosworth Avenue
Chicago, IL 60626

4488

Sy Kogan Memorial Award

AMOUNT: $500 **DEADLINE:** May 1
FIELD/MAJOR: Jazz/Commercial Music

Award given annually to a jazz/commercial music student at Five Towns College. Write to the address below for more information.

Five Towns College
305 N. Service Road/Lie Exit 50
Dix Hills, NY 11746

4489

Sybil Weaver Scholarship

AMOUNT: $1,000 **DEADLINE:** Mar 1
FIELD/MAJOR: All Areas Of Study

Scholarships are available at the University of Oklahoma, Norman, for female students who have a GPA of 3.25 or above. Write to the address listed below for information.

University Of Oklahoma, Norman
Office Of Financial Aid Services
731 Elm
Norman, OK 73019

4490

Sylvia H. Cronin Memorial Music Scholarship

AMOUNT: Varies **DEADLINE:** None Specified
FIELD/MAJOR: Elementary Education

Award for elementary education major with a strong interest in music, as a piano student in the department of music or with a music minor. Selection is made by the Music Department faculty. Contact a member of the Music Department faculty for further information.

Bloomsburg University
19 Ben Franklin Hall
400 E. Second St.
Bloomsburg, PA 17815

4491

Sylvia Lewis General Scholarship Fund Award

AMOUNT: $1,000 **DEADLINE:** Mar 1
FIELD/MAJOR: All Areas Of Study

Scholarships are available at the University of Oklahoma, Norman, for full-time minority students, who have a GPA of at least 2.0 (undergraduate) or 3.0 (graduate). Based on academic, leadership and citizenship qualities. Write to the address listed below for information.

University Of Oklahoma, Norman
Assoc. Director, Student Support Service
Hester Hall, Room 200
Norman, OK 73019

4492

Sylvia W. Farny Scholarship

AMOUNT: $1,500 **DEADLINE:** Feb 15
FIELD/MAJOR: Mechanical Engineering

Scholarships for mechanical engineering students entering their final year of undergraduate study. Application must be made in junior year (students enrolled in a five-year program would apply in the 4th year). Must be a student member of ASME. Information sheets are forwarded to the colleges and universities in the fall of each year. If necessary to write for more details, please be certain to enclose an SASE.

American Society Of Mechanical Engineers Auxiliary, Inc.
ASME Foundation
345 East 47th Street
New York, NY 10017

4493
T.H. Harris State Academic Scholarship

Amount: $400 **Deadline:** None Specified
Field/Major: All Areas Of Study

Scholarships offered to Louisiana residents who will be enrolling as full-time freshman students at a public university in Louisiana. Applicants must be U.S. citizens with a GPA of at least 3.0. Write to the address below for details.

Louisiana Office Of Financial Assistance
P.O. Box 91202
Baton Rouge, LA 70821

4494
THANKS Agricultural Student Scholarship Program

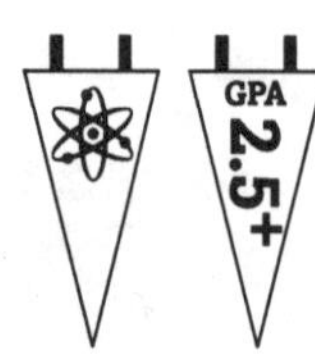

Amount: Varies **Deadline:** May 1
Field/Major: Agriculture

Awards for students at the junior level or above who are studying in the field of agriculture at Fresno State, Cal Poly San Luis Obispo, or UC Davis. Must have a GPA of at least 2.5 and be a U.S. citizen. Write to the address below for more details.

Together Helping Americans Nationwide Keep Strong, Inc.
P.O. Box 1864
Watsonville, CA 95077

4495
T.J. Myers Memorial Scholarship Fund

Amount: Varies **Deadline:** None Specified
Field/Major: Dance

Scholarships are available at the University of Iowa for full-time male undergraduates majoring in dance, who show exceptional talent and potential. Write to the address listed below for information.

University Of Iowa
Department of Dance
E114 Halsey Hall
Iowa City, IA 52245

4496
Ta Liang Memorial Award

Amount: $500 **Deadline:** Jan 5
Field/Major: Photogrammetry, Remote Sensing

Applicants must be a student member of the Society who is currently pursuing graduate-level studies. Based on scholastic record, research plans, recommendations, and community service activities. Write to the address below for more information.

American Society For Photogrammetry And Remote Sensing
ASPRS Awards Program
5410 Grosvenor Lane, Suite 210
Bethesda, MD 20814

4497
Taco Bell Tennis Club Scholarship

Amount: Varies **Deadline:** None Specified
Field/Major: All Areas Of Study

Scholarships for Mesa State students who are active in the tennis program. Contact the tennis coach for more details.

Mesa State College
Office Of Financial Aid
P.O. Box 2647
Grand Junction, CO 81501

4498
Talent Awards

Amount: Varies **Deadline:** None Specified
Field/Major: Art, Music, Speech/Drama

Awards given to full-time undergraduates who demonstrate excellence in the fields of study above. Write to the address below for more information.

Concordia College, Nebraska
Office Of Financial Aid
800 N. Columbia Ave.
Seward, NE 68434

4499
Talented Minority Scholarship Program

Amount: $5,000 **Deadline:** None Specified
Field/Major: All Areas Of Study

Incoming students are considered for this award during the admissions process; no separate application needed. Returning UMass students must complete an application during February to be considered. Returning UMass students can receive additional information from the office of enrollment services at the University of Massachusetts-Amherst.

University Of Massachusetts-Amherst
Office Of Financial Aid Services
255 Whitmore Admin. Bldg., Box 38230
Amherst, MA 01003

4500
Tambrands, Inc. Scholarship

Amount: Varies **Deadline:** Feb 29
Field/Major: Operations Management

Awards for outstanding students in the field of operations management who show great promise and need financial assistance to complete their education. For entering sophomore, junior, or senior students. Contact the SOM Development Office, Room 206, for more information and an application.

University Of Massachusetts, Amherst
SOM Development Office, Room 206
Amherst, MA 01003

4501
Tammy Hrusovsky Scholarship

Amount: $100 **Deadline:** Feb 9
Field/Major: Special Education-Communication Disorders

Award for special education/communication disorders majors with a disability and a minimum of 35 earned credit hours. Must demonstrate financial need. Use Bloomsburg University scholarship application and attach a description of the disability. Contact Dr. Carroll Redfern, Chairperson, Department of Communication Disorders and Special Education for further information.

Bloomsburg University
19 Ben Franklin Hall
400 E. Second St.
Bloomsburg, PA 17815

4502

Tampa Bay Police Chiefs Association Scholarship

AMOUNT: $250 **DEADLINE:** Varies
FIELD/MAJOR: Criminal Justice Technology

Award for a student at St. Petersburg Junior College studying criminal justice technology who has completed at least one semester with high academic standing and leadership qualities. Contact the criminal justice technology program at SPJC for details.

St. Petersburg Junior College
Financial Aid Office
P.O. Box 13489
St. Petersburg, FL 33733

4503

Tandy Technology Scholars

AMOUNT: $1,000 **DEADLINE:** Oct 15
FIELD/MAJOR: Mathematics, Science, Computer Science

Scholarships are available for graduating high school seniors who plan to enroll in a full-time four-year program in one of the above fields. Based on grades, test scores, and extracurricular and community service activities. Approximately 100 awards given per year. Write to the address listed below for information.

Tandy Corporation
Tandy Technology Scholars Program
P.O. Box 32897, TCU Station
Fort Worth, TX 76129

4504

Taraknath Das Grants

AMOUNT: $3,500 **DEADLINE:** Aug 1
FIELD/MAJOR: All Areas Of Study

Grants for Indian nationals (holding Indian passports) who are enrolled in graduate studies in the U.S. Applicants must have completed at least one year of graduate study. Write to the address below for more information.

Taraknath Das Foundation, Southern Asian Institute
Columbia University
420 West 118th St.
New York, NY 10027

4505

Tau Beta Pi Fellowships

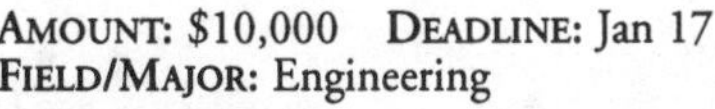

AMOUNT: $10,000 **DEADLINE:** Jan 17
FIELD/MAJOR: Engineering

Open to all Tau Beta Pi members for full-time graduate study. Slight preference given to students who are just beginning graduate study. Approximately 35-40 awards per year. Write to the address below for details.

Tau Beta Pi Association, Inc.
P.O. Box 2697
University Station
Knoxville, TN 37901

4506

Teacher Cadet Scholarship

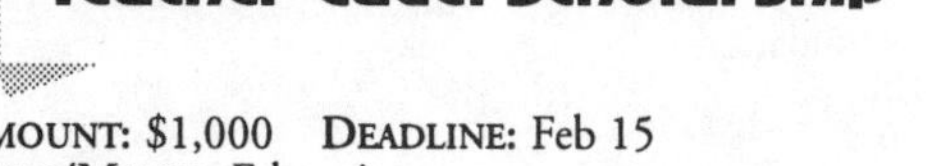

AMOUNT: $1,000 **DEADLINE:** Feb 15
FIELD/MAJOR: Education

Awards for freshmen who demonstrate a commitment to teaching, leadership, and high academic achievement. Write to the address below for more information.

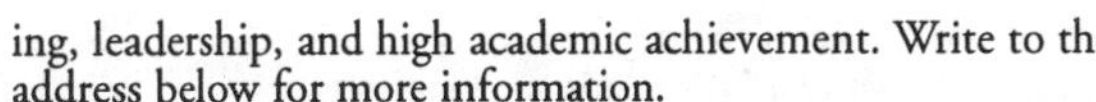

Winthrop University, School Of Education
Office Of Student Services
119 Tillman Hall
Rock Hill, SC 29733

4507

Teachers Choice Service Award

AMOUNT: $500 **DEADLINE:** Mar 1
FIELD/MAJOR: All Areas Of Study

Awards for Spalding undergraduates. Must have a GPA of at least 2.8 and have an ACT score of 18. Write to the address below for more details.

Spalding University
Financial Aid Office
851 S. Fourth St.
Louisville, KY 40203

4508

Teachers' Loan-For-Service Program

AMOUNT: $4,000 (max) **DEADLINE:** Jul 1
FIELD/MAJOR: Education

Awards for minority or physically disabled students from New Mexico who attend a New Mexico institution and are studying to be teachers of grades K to 12. Open to undergrads or graduate students. Loan will be forgiven if recipient agrees to serve at a public institution in Lea, Otero, Eddy, Chaves, or Roosevelt Counties in New Mexico following graduation. Write to the address below for more information.

New Mexico Commission On Higher Education
1068 Cerrillos Rd.
Santa Fe, NM 87501

4509

Teaching Fellows Scholarship

AMOUNT: None Specified **DEADLINE:** None Specified
FIELD/MAJOR: Education

Scholarships are available to students at Appalachian State University who plan to enter the teaching profession. Applicant must be a resident of North Carolina. Write to the address listed below for information.

Appalachian State University
Financial Aid Office
Scholarship Section
Boone, NC 28608

4510

Teamsters Scholarship Fund

AMOUNT: $1,000-$1,500 **DEADLINE:** Dec 15
FIELD/MAJOR: All Areas Of Study

Must be H.S. senior and dependent child of Teamster member. Must be in top 15% of senior class with excellent SAT/ACT scores. Must attend an accredited college or university and demonstrate financial need. Twenty-five awards per year (10 are renewable). Contact your Teamster office, write to address below, or send in the order form in the August through October "International Teamster" Magazine for further details and application form.

International Brotherhood Of Teamsters
Scholarship Fund
25 Louisiana Ave., NW
Washington, DC 20001

4511

Technical Vocational Grants

AMOUNT: None Specified **DEADLINE:** Apr 1
FIELD/MAJOR: Aerospace Studies (vocational/technical)

Candidates must be CAP cadets and seniors who are qualified and want to continue their education in special aerospace courses at an accredited trade, technical, or vocational school. Write to the address below for details.

Civil Air Patrol
National Headquarters CAP(TT)
Maxwell AFB, AL 36112

4512

Technology Scholarship Program For Alabama Teachers

AMOUNT: Tuition And Fees **DEADLINE:** None Specified
FIELD/MAJOR: Teaching

A State Scholarship Loan not to exceed the graduate tuition and fees for attendance at a public college or university. Students who are full-time, regularly certified Alabama public school teachers enrolled in approved courses or programs that incorporate new technologies in the curriculum. Write to the address below for details.

Alabama Commission On Higher Education
P.O. Box 30200
Montgomery, AL 36130

4513

Ted And Nora Anderson Scholarship Fund

AMOUNT: $500 **DEADLINE:** Feb 15
FIELD/MAJOR: All Areas Of Study

Scholarships for Kansas residents who are or will be attending a college or university in Kansas. Applicant must be a U.S. citizen, a child of a Legion or Auxiliary member, and a high school senior or a freshman or sophomore in college. Write to the address listed below for additional information or application.

American Legion, Department Of Kansas
1314 SW Topeka Blvd.
Topeka, KS 66612

4514

Ted Russell Memorial Scholarship

AMOUNT: None Specified **DEADLINE:** Mar 1
FIELD/MAJOR: Business

Scholarships are available at the University of New Mexico for full-time undergraduate business majors. Write to the address listed below for information.

University Of New Mexico, Albuquerque
Department Of Student Financial Aid
Mesa Vista Hall North
Albuquerque, NM 87131

4515

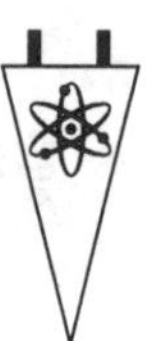

Ted Simms Memorial Scholarship/American Society Horticulture Science

AMOUNT: $1,000 **DEADLINE:** Feb 1
FIELD/MAJOR: Horticulture, Floriculture

Open to a full-time student with interests in horticultural specialization, gardens, nursery, pomology, floriculture, and vegetables. Write to the address below for more information.

California State Polytechnic University, Pomona
College Of Agriculture
Building 7, Room 110
Pomona, CA 91768

4516

Telesensory Scholarship-American Foundation Of The Blind

AMOUNT: $1,000 **DEADLINE:** Apr 1
FIELD/MAJOR: All Areas Of Study

To be eligible, the applicant must be a U.S. citizen and submit evidence of legal blindness; transcripts of grades; three letters of recommendation; a typed-written statement up to three pages including educational and career goals, work history, information on college financial assistance received, and how scholarship monies will be used. Write to the Foundation at the address below to receive information on this award and other programs they administer.

American Foundation For The Blind
Scholarship Coordinator
11 Penn Plaza, Suite 300
New York, NY 10001

4517

Telesensory Scholarship And William And Dorothy Ferrell Scholarship

AMOUNT: None Specified **DEADLINE:** Apr 15
FIELD/MAJOR: All Areas Of Study

Scholarships for persons who are legally blind and members of the Association for Education and Rehabilitation of the Blind and Visually Impaired. Awarded in even-numbered years. Write to the address below for details.

Assoc. For Educ. And Rehab. Of The Blind And Visually Impaired
206 N. Washington St., Suite 320
Alexandria, VA 22314

4518

Tennessee Farmers Cooperative Scholarships

AMOUNT: $500 **DEADLINE:** Feb 15
FIELD/MAJOR: Agriculture, Agribusiness

Scholarships are available for FFA members pursuing a four-year degree in any area of agriculture, enrolled at the University of Tennessee at Martin or Knoxville, Middle Tennessee State University (Murfreesboro), or Tennessee Technological University at Cookville. Applicant must be a Tennessee resident. Write to the address below for details.

National FFA Foundation
Scholarship Office
P.O. Box 15160
Alexandria, VA 22309

4519

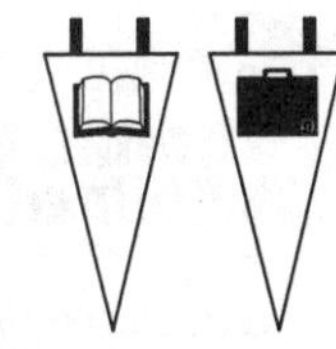

Teresa A'Hearn Brown Scholarship

AMOUNT: Varies **DEADLINE:** None Specified
FIELD/MAJOR: Business Education Or Liberal Arts

Award given to a student who exemplifies the spirit of "Carpe Diem" (seize the day), is majoring in business education or liberal arts, and is from Pennsylvania or New Jersey. Write to the address below for more information.

Mercyhurst College
Financial Aid Office
Glenwood Hills
Erie, PA 16546

4520

Teresa Bowers Scholarship

AMOUNT: None Specified **DEADLINE:** None Specified
FIELD/MAJOR: Vocal Music

Awards are available for ETSU students majoring in vocal music. Contact the Chairman of the Department of Music for more information.

East Tennessee State University
Office Of Financial Aid
Box 70722
Johnson City, TN 37614

4521

Terra Avionics Collegiate Scholarship

AMOUNT: $2,500 **DEADLINE:** Apr 8
FIELD/MAJOR: All Areas Of Study

Scholarship for a high school senior who is a child or grandchild of an employee of an Aircraft Electronics Association regular member. For students planning to attend an accredited school or college in any area of study. Based on essay (2,500 word max) 1993 topic: how to prosper in today's general aviation market. Min GPA: 2.5. Write to Terra Scholarship essay at the address below for information.

Aircraft Electronics Association Educational Foundation
P.O. Box 1981
Independence, MO 64055

4522

Terra International, Inc. Scholarships

AMOUNT: $1,500 **DEADLINE:** Feb 15
FIELD/MAJOR: Agriculture

Scholarships are available for FFA members pursuing a four-year degree in any area of agriculture. Write to the address below for details.

National FFA Foundation
Scholarship Office
P.O. Box 15160
Alexandria, VA 22309

4523

Tessie Agan Award Competition

AMOUNT: $200-$500 **DEADLINE:** May 15
FIELD/MAJOR: Housing-Related Areas

Award for a research or position paper on some aspect or current issue in housing. Winner will present it at the Amer. Assn. of Housing Educators annual conference (conference fees waived). Twenty-five page (max) work based on significance or timeliness of topic, contribution to field, recognition of previous work, methodology, depth, and mechanics (readability, etc). Write to the address below for details. The cash award is intended to fund students presentations at the AAHE conference.

American Association Of Housing Educators
AAHE Awards Committee Chair
Queens College, Dept. Of Home Economics
Flushing, NY 11367

4524

Tetra Corporation Scholarship

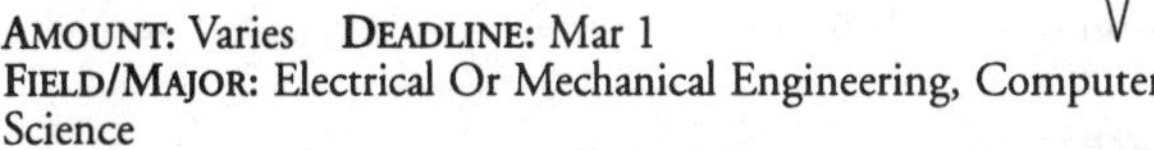

AMOUNT: Varies **DEADLINE:** Mar 1
FIELD/MAJOR: Electrical Or Mechanical Engineering, Computer Science

Awards are available at the University of New Mexico for sophomores, juniors or seniors in the areas of study listed above. Write to the address below for more information.

University Of New Mexico, Albuquerque
Office Of Financial Aid
Albuquerque, NM 87131

4525

Tetra Pak Scholarships

AMOUNT: $500-$1,000 **DEADLINE:** Feb 15
FIELD/MAJOR: Food Science/technology

Scholarships are available for FFA members pursuing a two- or four-year degree in food science/technology. Write to the address below for details.

National FFA Foundation
Scholarship Office
P.O. Box 15160
Alexandria, VA 22309

4526

Texaco Foundation Scholarships

AMOUNT: $2,000 **DEADLINE:** Feb 1
FIELD/MAJOR: Engineering: Chemical, Mechanical

Two scholarships for Society of Women Engineers student members who will be juniors in the top 20% of her class in one of the above areas of engineering. Must be a U.S. citizen. Information and applications for the SWE awards are available from the deans of engineering schools, or write to the address below. Please be certain to enclose an SASE.

Society Of Women Engineers
120 Wall Street
New York, NY 10005

4527

Texas Library Association Research Grant

AMOUNT: Varies **DEADLINE:** Feb 1
FIELD/MAJOR: Library Science

Grants for Texas students to support research involving library use, resource sharing, administrative study, etc. Pilot studies are encouraged. Write to the address below for more information.

Texas Library Association
3355 Bee Cave Rd., Suite 401
Austin, TX 78746

4528

Texas Library Association Scholarships

AMOUNT: $500-$2,000 **DEADLINE:** Feb 1
FIELD/MAJOR: Library Science

Awards are for Texas graduate students to study at an ALA-accredited school in Texas leading to a library science degree. Write to the address below for more information.

Texas Library Association
3355 Bee Cave Rd., Suite 401
Austin, TX 78746

4529

Texas Sheep And Goat Raisers Auxiliary Letter Writing Contest

AMOUNT: $100-$1,000 **DEADLINE:** Dec 31
FIELD/MAJOR: Property Rights

Contest open to Texas high school students who write a letter to the state's national Senators or U.S. Representatives discussing why property rights are important to the state. Applicants must be U.S. citizens. Write to the address below or contact Mr. Ben Love, P.O. Box 387, Marathon, TX 79842, for more information.

American Sheep Industry Women's Auxiliary
Ms. Doris Haby
P.O. Box 1496
Brackettville, TX 78832

4530

Texas Transportation Scholarship

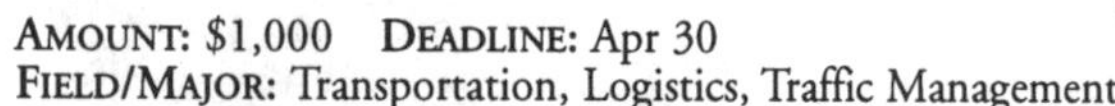

AMOUNT: $1,000 **DEADLINE:** Apr 30
FIELD/MAJOR: Transportation, Logistics, Traffic Management

Open to students enrolled in an educational program in an accredited institution of higher learning, offering courses in transportation, logistics, traffic management, or related fields, who intends to prepare for a career in these areas. Must be enrolled in a school in Texas at some phase of their education. Write to the address below for more information.

Transportation Clubs International Scholarships
1275 Kamus Dr., Suite 101
Fox Island, WA 98333

4531

Textiles Scholarships

AMOUNT: $1,000-$4,000 **DEADLINE:** Mar 1
FIELD/MAJOR: Textiles

Awards for undergraduates in the field of textiles at North Carolina State University. Must be a U.S. citizen. Write to the address below for more information.

North Carolina State University
Kent Hester, Assoc. Director-Stdt. Serv.
College of Textiles, Box 8301
Raleigh, NC 27695

4532

Thanks Be To Grandmother Winifred Foundation

AMOUNT: $5,000 (max) **DEADLINE:** Mar 21, Sep 21
FIELD/MAJOR: All Areas Of Study

Grants are available to women who are least 54 years of age and U.S. citizens with a social security number. Applicants must submit a grant proposal that benefits a specific group of women. Write to the address below for more information.

Thanks Be To Grandmother Winifred Foundation
P.O. Box 1449
Wainscott, NY 11975

4533

Tharold Dorn Scholarships

AMOUNT: $200 **DEADLINE:** None Specified
FIELD/MAJOR: All Areas Of Study

Awards for continuing students at UW Platteville who demonstrate scholastic achievement, participation in extracurricular activities, and character. Write to the address below or contact the office at (608) 342-1125 for more information.

University Of Wisconsin, Platteville
Office Of Admissions And Enrollment Mgt.
Platteville, WI 53818

4534

Thatcher Foundation

AMOUNT: None Specified **DEADLINE:** None Specified
FIELD/MAJOR: All Areas Of Study

Funding is limited to Pueblo County and Pueblo County residents only. Write to the address below for more information.

Thatcher Foundation
P.O. Box 1401
Pueblo, CO 81002

4535

The 40's Alumni Scholarship

AMOUNT: $500 **DEADLINE:** None Specified
FIELD/MAJOR: All Areas Of Study

Award for full-time Mesa State college juniors and seniors. Must have a GPA of at least 2.5. Write to the address below for more information.

Mesa State College
Office Of Financial Aid
P.O. Box 2647
Grand Junction, CO 81501

4536

The AEJ Summer Internship For Minorities

AMOUNT: $200 Per Week **DEADLINE:** Oct 30
FIELD/MAJOR: Journalism

Internships for minority sophomores, juniors, or seniors who are majoring in or interested in journalism. The programs lasts 10 weeks, beginning in mid-June. Write to the address below for more information.

The Association For Education In Journalism
269 Mercer St., Suite 601
New York, NY 10003

The ASCAP Dreyfus/Warner-Chappell, City College Scholarship

Amount: None Specified **Deadline:** None Specified
Field/Major: Music Or Lyrics

Awards to music or lyrics students at the City College of New York. Contact the Office of Financial Aid at the school for more details.

American Society Of Composers, Authors, And Publishers
One Lincoln Plaza
New York, NY 10023

The ASCAP Foundation Frederick Loewe Scholarship

Amount: None Specified **Deadline:** None Specified
Field/Major: Musical Theater Composition

Awards to musical theater composition students at the Tisch School of Arts at New York University. Contact the Office of Financial Aid at New York University for more details.

American Society Of Composers, Authors, And Publishers
One Lincoln Plaza
New York, NY 10023

The ASCAP Raymond Hubbell Music Scholarship Awards

Amount: None Specified **Deadline:** None Specified
Field/Major: Music Composition

Awards to music composition students at various colleges, universities, or conservatories across the country. Contact the office of financial aid at your school for more details.

American Society Of Composers, Authors, And Publishers
One Lincoln Plaza
New York, NY 10023

The David And Dovetta Wilson Scholarship

Amount: $1,000 (max) **Deadline:** Mar 24
Fields/Majors: All Areas Of Study

Award for college-bound high school seniors with at least a GPA of 3.0. Applicants must be actively involved in community and religious service and demonstrate financial need. Send a SASE to the address below for more information.

The David And Dovetta Wilson Scholarship Fund
P.O. Box 038-321
Alden Manor
Elmont, NY 11003

4541

The Helen Pearson Scholarship

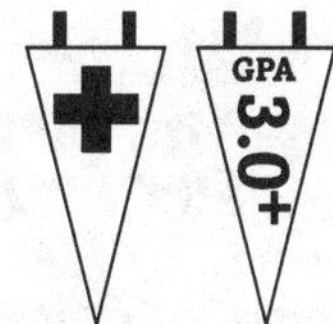

Amount: $1,500 **Deadline:** Feb 15
Fields/Majors: Nurse Midwifery, Physical & Respiratory Therapy, Pre-Med, Pre-Osteopathy

Award for students from Texas studying any field above to achieve a career in the perinatal field. Applicants must be graduating high school seniors with a minimum GPA of 3.0. Write to the address below for more information.

Texas State Council/March Of Dimes Birth Defects Foundation
8131 LBJ Fwy., Suite 115
Dallas, TX 75251"

4542

The Iowa Short Fiction And John Simmons Short Fiction Awards

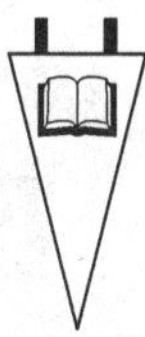

Amount: Varies **Deadline:** Sep 30
Fields/Majors: Creative Writing

Competition for creative writers who have never written any previously published prose fiction. Open to all level students at the University of Iowa. Write to the address below for more information.

University Of Iowa
The Program In Creative Writing
436 English Philosophy Bldg.
Iowa City, IA 52242"

4543

The Leadership/Performance Scholarship

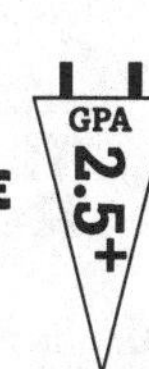

Amount: Varies **Deadline:** Mar 15
Fields/Majors: All Areas Of Study

Scholarships for incoming freshman based on their achievements in academics, extracurricular activities, and leadership. Renewable with a 2.8 GPA. Write to the address below for more information.

Middle Tennessee State University
Office Of. Student Financial Aid
Murfreesboro, TN 37132

4544

The Matching Scholarship Program

Amount: Varies **Deadline:** Mar 15
Fields/Majors: All Areas Of Study

Awards for African American students who are qualified for admission to or are currently enrolled in Middle Tennessee State University. Based on academic potential, area of specialization, and economic status. Applicant must be a U.S. citizen. Write to the address below for more information.

Middle Tennessee State University
Office Of. Student Financial Aid
Murfreesboro, TN 37132

4545

The Mellon Collaborative Program

AMOUNT: Varies **DEADLINE:** None Specified
FIELDS/MAJORS: Education

Merit based fellowships for minority students planning to enter the field of education. The fellowship is available to students studying at Cornell University, Harvard University, Stanford University or Columbia University. Write to the address below for more information.

Andrew W. Mellon Foundation, Box 4
Teachers College, Columbia Univ.
525 120th St.
New York, NY 10027

4546

The Michael M. Assarian Scholarship

AMOUNT: Varies **DEADLINE:** Jun 1
FIELDS/MAJORS: All Areas Of Study

Awards for full-time students of Armenian descent. Based on academic achievement, extracurricular activities, and financial need. Write to the address below for more information.

Wayne State University Scholarship Officer
Office Of Scholarships And Financial Aid
Detroit, MI 48202

4547

The Orth Graduate Student Research Award

AMOUNT: Varies **DEADLINE:** Apr 30
FIELDS/MAJORS: Clinical Laboratory Science

Awards to directly fund proposed investigation in the field of clinical laboratory science. Applicants must be graduate students doing research in the field. Write to the address below for more information.

American Society For Clinical Laboratory Science
Director Of Education
7910 Woodmont Ave., Suite 1301
Bethesda, MD 20814

4548

The Otis L. Floyd Academic Excellence Scholarship

AMOUNT: Varies **DEADLINE:** Mar 15
FIELDS/MAJORS: All Areas Of Study

Awards for African American incoming freshman who have a GPA of at least 3.2 and an ACT score of at least 25. Renewable with a GPA of 3.0. Write to the address below for more details.

Middle Tennessee State University
Office Of Student Financial Aid
Murfreesboro, TN 37132

4549

The Presidential Scholarship

AMOUNT: $3,275 **DEADLINE:** Mar 15
FIELDS/MAJORS: All Areas Of Study

Scholarships guaranteed to incoming freshman who have a GPA of at least 3.5 and an SAT score of 1100 or an ACT score of 28. Renewable with a GPA of 3.0. There is no application form, but freshman need to submit a transcript and SAT or ACT score report to the admissions office. Write to the address below for more complete information.

Middle Tennessee State University
Office Of Student Financial Aid
Murfreesboro, TN 37132

4550

The Renato Poggioli Translation Award

AMOUNT: $3,000 **DEADLINE:** Dec 31
FIELDS/MAJORS: Italian Language

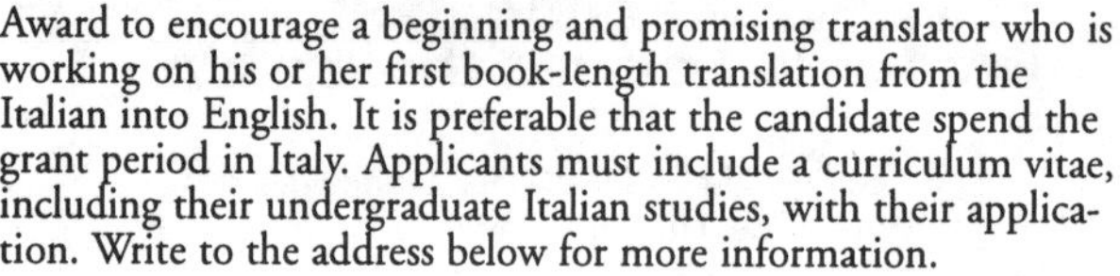

Award to encourage a beginning and promising translator who is working on his or her first book-length translation from the Italian into English. It is preferable that the candidate spend the grant period in Italy. Applicants must include a curriculum vitae, including their undergraduate Italian studies, with their application. Write to the address below for more information.

The Italian Academy For Advanced Studies In America
Pen American Center
568 Broadway
New York, NY 10012

4551

Theater And Dance Activity Scholarship

AMOUNT: $1,850 **DEADLINE:** None Specified
FIELDS/MAJORS: Acting, Theater Technician, Dance, Performance. Studies

Scholarships are for full-time students with an outstanding ability to demonstrate acting, performance studies, technical theater, and dance. Must have a GPA of 2.5 or better. Contact the Theater and Dance Department for more information.

Southwest Missouri State University
Office Of Financial Aid
901 South National Ave.
Springfield, MO 65804

4552

Theater Assistantships, College Teaching Fellowship

AMOUNT: $6,600 + Tuition **DEADLINE:** None Specified
FIELDS/MAJORS: Drama/theater, Fine Arts, Costume Design

Assistantships and fellowships for students in the MFA program in the School of Theater at the Florida State University. Awarded competitively. Must have a minimum GPA of 3.2 and a GRE score of 1150 or better. Contact Vinette Wilson, Graduate Coordinator, at the address below for details.

Florida State University School Of Theater
Graduate Fellowships Coordinator
School Of Theater
Tallahassee, FL 32306

4553

Theater Department Scholarships, Victor Jory Scholarship

AMOUNT: Varies **DEADLINE:** Feb 1
FIELDS/MAJORS: Drama

Scholarships are available at the University of Utah for full-time drama majors. Jory award is usually offered in the areas of acting or directing. Write to the address below for details.

University Of Utah
Dr. William C. Siska
206 Performing Arts Building
Salt Lake City, UT 84112

4554

Theater Faculty Freshman Scholarship, Talent/Participation Award

AMOUNT: None Specified **DEADLINE:** Mar 15
FIELDS/MAJORS: Drama

Scholarships are available to students at Appalachian State University who are drama majors. Write to the address listed below for information.

Appalachian State University
Department Of Theater And Dance
Boone, NC 28608

4555

Theater First Nighter Scholarship

AMOUNT: $1,000 (max) **DEADLINE:** May 1
FIELDS/MAJORS: Theater

Awards for freshmen who demonstrate ability or talent in the field of theater. Based primarily on an audition. Renewable. Write to the chair of the department of theater and dance at the address below for more information.

Winthrop University
Department Of Theater And Dance
119 Tillman Hall
Rock Hill, SC 29733

4556

Theater Scholarships

AMOUNT: Varies **DEADLINE:** Feb 15
FIELDS/MAJORS: Theater

Scholarship offered to students attending or planning to attend Loyola University on a full time basis, who plan to major in theater. Based upon interviews, auditions, academic ability, and recommendations. Scholarships are available in acting, directing, design, theater history, criticism, and literature. Write to the address below for details.

Loyola University
Chairperson, Theater Department
6525 North Sheridan Road
Chicago, IL 60626

4557

Theater Scholarships

AMOUNT: Varies **DEADLINE:** None Specified
FIELDS/MAJORS: Theater

Scholarships are available to students who participate in the university theater. Selections are based on attitude, dependability, dedication to theater, talent, and performance. Contact the director of theater for more information.

Clarion University
104 Egbert Hall
Office Of Financial Aid
Clarion, PA 16214

4558

Theo Dykes Memorial Scholarship

AMOUNT: $3,000 **DEADLINE:** Jun 1
FIELDS/MAJORS: All Areas Of Study

Award for an African American male with demonstrated economic need, as verified by parent's tax return for prior year or other suitable documents. Must be a graduating high school senior or college student with a GPA of 2.5 or better. Also based upon three letters of reference, an essay on the challenge to American families today, and involvement in school and community activities. Contact Nylcare Customer Service at (800) 635-3121 for more information.

Nylcare/Mid-Atlantic Scholarship Foundation, Inc.
7617 Ora Glen Drive
Greenbelt, MD 20770

4559

Theodore C. Sorensen Fellowship

AMOUNT: $3,600 **DEADLINE:** Mar 15
FIELDS/MAJORS: Domestic Policy, Political Journalism, Polling, Press Relations

Preference is given in this fellowship to research on domestic policy, press relations, political journalism, or polling. One award per year. Write to the address below for more information.

John F. Kennedy Library Foundation
William Johnson, Chief Archivist
Columbia Point
Boston, MA 02125

4560

Theodore Roosevelt Memorial Fund

AMOUNT: $200-$1,000 **DEADLINE:** Feb 15
FIELDS/MAJORS: Natural History

Grants for study of North American fauna including field research, study of the collections at the American Museum of Natural History, or for work at any of the museum's field stations. Write to the address below for complete information.

American Museum Of Natural History
Central Park West At 79th St.
New York, NY 10024

4561

Theresa Wezwick Memorial Scholarship

AMOUNT: $100 **DEADLINE:** None Specified
FIELDS/MAJORS: Nursing

Awards for Mesa State students majoring in the field of nursing.

Contact the school of professional studies/nursing area for more details.

Mesa State College
Financial Aid Office
P.O. Box 2647
Grand Junction, CO 81501

4562
Thirty-Seventh Infantry Division Scholarship Grant

AMOUNT: None Specified **DEADLINE:** Apr 1
FIELDS/MAJORS: All Areas Of Study

Scholarships for sons and daughters of 37th Infantry Division veterans of WWI, WWII, or Korea. May be high school senior or already enrolled in postsecondary school (college, university, or vocational/trade program). Write to the address below for details. Please include the name, address, and unit in which your father served. Also, if father deceased, list date of demise, if known.

Thirty-Seventh Division Veterans Association
183 E. Mound St., Ste. 103
Columbus, OH 43215

4563
Thoburn Foundation For Education

AMOUNT: None Specified **DEADLINE:** None Specified
FIELDS/MAJORS: All Areas Of Study

Scholarships are available to assist individuals attending institutions of higher learning, including, but not limited to, colleges, universities, and vocational or technical schools. Must be in the Ligonier Valley of western Pennsylvania to be eligible for the scholarship. Write to the address below for more information.

Thoburn Foundation For Education
Rd. 4, Box 8
Ligonier, PA 15658

4564
Thomas B. Curtis Scholarship

AMOUNT: None Specified **DEADLINE:** Nov 30
FIELDS/MAJORS: Biology, Chemistry, Physics

Scholarships are available at UCSD for undergraduate students who plan to or who are majoring in chemistry, biology or physics. Write to the address listed below for information.

University Of California, San Diego
Student Financial Services
9500 Gilman Drive
La Jolla, CA 92093

4565
Thomas C. Rumble University Graduate Fellowship

AMOUNT: $5,500 **DEADLINE:** Feb 1
FIELDS/MAJORS: All Areas Of Study

Recipients must be enrolled in a Ph.D., M.M., or M.F.A. Program at WSU during the semesters for which the award is given. Recipients may not hold other fellowships, scholarships, assistantships, or internships or hold full-time employment during fellowship period. Only full-time students are eligible. The fellowships are awarded primarily on the basis of academic qualifications to eligible graduate students with clearly defined objectives in their field of specialization and demonstrated capacity for independent study; financial need is also a consideration. Write to the address below for details.

Wayne State University
4302 Faculty/Administration Building
Detroit, MI 48202

4566
Thomas E. Cook Memorial Scholarship For Humanities

AMOUNT: $500 **DEADLINE:** Feb 1
FIELDS/MAJORS: Humanities

Scholarships are available at the University of Hawaii, Hilo for full-time students enrolled in a humanities program. Applicants must be big island residents, with preference given to applicants of Hawaiian ancestry. Write to the address listed below for information.

University Of Hawaii At Hilo
Financial Aid Office
200 West Kawili St.
Hilo, HI 96720

4567
Thomas Edison/Max McGraw Scholarship Program

AMOUNT: $1,500-$5,000 **DEADLINE:** Dec 15
FIELDS/MAJORS: Science And Engineering

Competition for students in grades 9-12 who have an interest in science, engineering, or both. Based on proposal or experiment or project idea. Your chemistry or physics teacher may have details on this program. Write to the address below if necessary.

National Science Education Leadership Association
P.O. Box 5556
Arlington, VA 22205

4568
Thomas F. Seay Scholarship

AMOUNT: $2,000 (min) **DEADLINE:** May 1
FIELDS/MAJORS: Real Estate

Scholarship for Illinois residents enrolled in a degree program with an emphasis on real estate. Based on career interest, GPA, and need. Must have a GPA of at least 3.5 on a 5.0 point scale (2.8 on a 4.0 scale) and have completed thirty college credit hours. Write to the address below for details.

Illinois Real Estate Educational Foundation
3180 Adloff Ln.
P.O. Box 19451
Springfield, IL 62794

4569
Thomas J. Watson Fellowship Program

AMOUNT: $16,000-$22,500 **DEADLINE:** Nov 6
FIELDS/MAJORS: All Areas Of Study

Fellowships are available for graduating college seniors to engage in a year of independent study and travel abroad following graduation. The award is given to individuals who demonstrate integrity, strong ethical character, intelligence, capacity for vision and leadership, and the potential for humane and effective participation in the world community. Write to the address below or contact your department chairperson for details. Must be a student at one of fifty private schools in the U.S. who is nominated by a foundation representative from the school. Students who receive this award on their printout are from member institutions.

Thomas J. Watson Foundation
Fellowship Coordinator
217 Angell St.
Providence, RI 02906

4570 Thomas Jordan Doctoral Scholarships

Amount: $3,000 **Deadline:** Dec 1
Fields/Majors: Oncology Nursing

Grants available to doctoral students in the field of oncology nursing. All applicants must be registered nurses. Write to the address below for more information.

Oncology Nursing Foundation
501 Holiday Dr.
Pittsburgh, PA 15220

4571 Thomas M. Conner Scholarship

Amount: $500-$750 **Deadline:** Apr 1
Fields/Majors: All Areas Of Study

Awards for all Sul Ross juniors and seniors who have GPA of at least 2.0. Write to the address below for more information.

Sul Ross State University
Financial Aid Office
Box C-113
Alpine, TX 79832

4572 Thomas M. Hunter Endowed Scholars Program

Amount: $2,000 **Deadline:** Mar 1
Fields/Majors: Engineering

Scholarship for an entering freshmen with outstanding potential in engineering. Renewable for three years. Contact the financial aid office at the address below for details.

Clemson University
Financial Aid Office
G01 Sikes Hall
Clemson, SC 29634

4573 Thomas R. Camp Scholarship

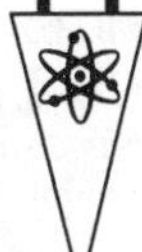

Amount: $5,000 **Deadline:** Jan 15
Fields/Majors: Drinking Water Research

Award for master's or doctoral students who are doing applied research in the drinking water field. Based on excellence of academic record and potential to provide leadership in research activities. Write to the address below for more information.

American Water Works Association
Scholarship Coordinator
6666 W. Quincy Ave
Denver, CO 80235

4574 Thomas Wilkerson Scholarships

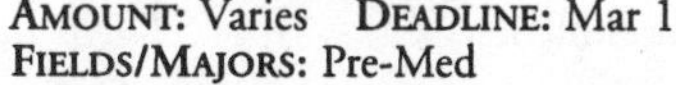

Amount: Varies **Deadline:** Mar 1
Fields/Majors: Pre-Med

Awards are available at the University of New Mexico for pre-med juniors or seniors with academic achievement. Write to the address below for more information.

University Of New Mexico, Albuquerque
Office Of Financial Aid
Albuquerque, NM 87131

4575 Three Percent Scholarship Program

Amount: Varies **Deadline:** None Specified
Fields/Majors: All Areas Of Study

Scholarships available to New Mexico resident students who possess good moral character, satisfactory initiative, and good scholastic standing. 1/3 of awards based upon financial need. Applicants must attend a New Mexico postsecondary institution. Contact the financial aid office at any New Mexico public institution.

New Mexico Commission On Higher Education
1068 Cerrillos Road
Santa Fe, NM 87501

4576 Thunderbird Scholarships

Amount: $1,000-$5,700 **Deadline:** Mar 1, Oct 1
Fields/Majors: All Areas Of Study

Scholarships for students at Thunderbird. Based on merit. Programs include FMC, Honeywell, Johnson & Higgins, Amalio M. Suarez Memorial Scholarships, Presidential, Whirlpool, & Thunderbird Scholarships. Some require work be performed for your department. Write to the address below for additional information.

Thunderbird American Graduate School Of International Management
15249 N. 59th Ave
Glendale, AZ 85306

4577 Thurgood Marshall Scholarships

Amount: Varies **Deadline:** None Specified
Fields/Majors: All Areas Of Study

Awards for entering freshman who are pursuing a bachelor's degree full-time at one of the 37 historically African American public colleges and universities. Applicants must be U.S. citizens, have a GPA of at least 3.0, and have a score of 1000 or more on the SAT or 24 or higher on the ACT. Renewable for four years. Write to the address below or contact the on-campus TMSF coordinator for more information.

Thurgood Marshall Scholarship Fund
Scholarship Coordinator
100 Park Ave
New York, NY 10017

4578 Tilles Charity Fund

Amount: None Specified **Deadline:** None Specified
Fields/Majors: All Areas Of Study

Open to residents of St. Louis City or St. Louis County who are attending colleges and universities in Missouri. Write to the address below for more information.

Rosalie Tilles Non-Sectarian Charity Fund
c/o Mercantile Bank NA
P.O. Box 387
St. Louis, MO 63166

4579

Tim Grubbs Memorial Scholarship

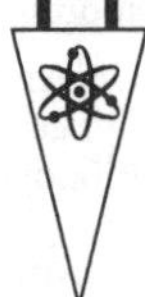

AMOUNT: $150 **DEADLINE:** Varies
FIELDS/MAJORS: Range Animal Science

Awards for Sul Ross undergraduates who are studying range animal science, have a GPA of at least 2.0, and are NIRA eligible. Write to the address below for more information.

Sul Ross State University
Division Of Range Animal Science
Box C-110
Alpine, TX 79832

4580

Timken Company Educational Fund

AMOUNT: None Specified **DEADLINE:** Nov 10
FIELDS/MAJORS: All Areas Of Study

Must be sons or daughters of Timken Company employee who are currently in their senior year of high school. Write to the address below for details.

Timken Company Educational Fund, Inc.
1835 Dueber Ave., SW
P.O. Box 6927
Canton, OH 44706

4581

Tindall Scholarship Fund

AMOUNT: Varies **DEADLINE:** None Specified
FIELDS/MAJORS: All Areas Of Study

Awards are available for full-time students at Cedarville College who have a GPA of at least 2.0 and extreme and urgent needs. Write to the address below for more information.

Cedarville College
Financial Aid Office
P.O. Box 601
Cedarville, OH 45314

4582

TMS Undergraduate Scholarships

AMOUNT: $4,000 **DEADLINE:** Jun 30
FIELDS/MAJORS: Metallurgy, Material Sciences

Scholarships for undergraduates enrolled full-time in a metallurgy engineering and materials science and engineering, or minerals processing/extraction program at a college or university. Write to the address below for details.

Minerals, Metals, And Materials Society
TMS Scholarship Committee
420 Commonwealth Dr.
Warrendale, PA 15086

4583

Todd Wehr Edgedome Grant

AMOUNT: $250-$1,500 **DEADLINE:** Mar 15
FIELDS/MAJORS: All Areas Of Study

Awards for freshmen, particularly those with an interest in intercollegiate athletics. Grant recipients will be required to spend two to three hours a week doing a service project for the athletic department. Applicant need not be on a team for consideration. Write to the address below for details.

Edgewood College
Office Of Admissions
855 Woodrow St.
Madison, WI 53711

4584

Tolbert Grant

AMOUNT: $1,500 **DEADLINE:** Varies
FIELDS/MAJORS: Vocational And Technical Programs

Scholarships for Maryland residents who are or will be attending a private career school in Maryland for full-time study. Application will be made through the financial aid office at your school. Contact that office or write to the address below for details.

Maryland State Higher Education Commission
16 Francis St.
Annapolis, MD 21401

4585

Tom A. Stombaugh Premedical Scholarship

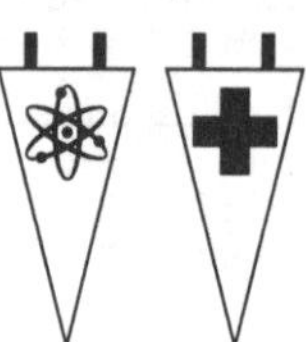

AMOUNT: $500 **DEADLINE:** None Specified
FIELDS/MAJORS: Biology

Student must be a full-time junior or senior biology major with a GPA of 3.0 or better. Must have completed fifteen hours of biology, including BIO 235, with a 3.0 GPA. Preference is given to a student planning a career in medicine. Contact the biology department for more information.

Southwest Missouri State University
Office Of Financial Aid
901 South National Ave
Springfield, MO 65804

4586

Tom Matherly Eagle Scout Scholarship

AMOUNT: $500 **DEADLINE:** Dec 1
FIELDS/MAJORS: All Areas Of Study

Scholarships area available to an Eagle Scout registered in the Suwannee River Area Council, Boy Scouts of America. For high school seniors. Write to the address below for more information.

Suwannee River Area Council, BSA
2729 West Pensacola St.
Tallahassee, FL 32304

4587

Tom Phillips Memorial Endowment

AMOUNT: Varies **DEADLINE:** Mar 1
FIELDS/MAJORS: All Areas Of Study

Varying amount each year to a student with a 3.0 GPA. Student must be attending NMSU and involved in swimming, tennis, or golf. Apply to athletic department. Write to the address below for details.

New Mexico State University
Department Of Intercollegiate Athletics
Box 30001, Dept 3145
Las Cruces, NM 88003

4588

Tony Oliver Memorial Scholarships

Amount: Varies **Deadline:** Mar 1
Fields/Majors: All Areas Of Study

Awards are available at the University of New Mexico for returning students age 35 or older. Contact the Dean of Continuing Education for more information.

University Of New Mexico, Albuquerque
Office Of Financial Aid
Albuquerque, NM 87131

4589

Tony's Food Service Scholarship

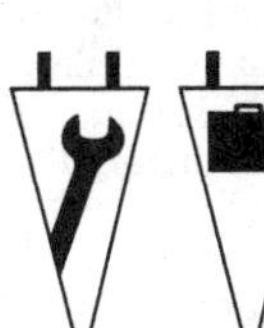

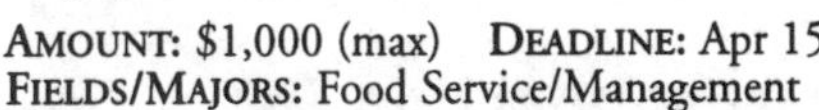

Amount: $1,000 (max) **Deadline:** Apr 15
Fields/Majors: Food Service/Management

Grants to support improved food service and food service careers. Must be ASFSA member or son/daughter of member. Based on satisfactory academics and financial need. Renewable. Write to the address below for details.

American School Food Service Association
SFS Foundation Scholarship Committee
1600 Duke St., 7th Floor
Alexandria, VA 22314

4590

Touch The Face Of God Scholarship

Amount: Varies **Deadline:** May 30
Fields/Majors: Aviation

Award for young female pilots, at least 18 years of age, who demonstrate a true love for flying and the field of aviation. Applicants must have a GPA of 3.0 or greater and submit a letter describing her feelings about aviation and her motives for desiring to become a professional pilot. Write to the address below for more information.

Nancy Horton Scholarship Fund, Inc.
234 Jay Hakes Road
Cropseyville, NY 12052

4591

Tourette Syndrome Association Research & Training Grants

Amount: $5,000-$25,000 **Deadline:** Dec 21
Fields/Majors: Tourette Syndrome Related (Biochem, Epidemiology, Psychology, Etc.)

Post-doctoral training fellowships and basic or clinical research grants for researchers whose areas of study are specifically relevant to Gilles de la Tourette Syndrome. To receive an application packet and a review of TSA literature (including areas of interest to TSA), interested persons should call (718) 224-2999 or fax (718) 279-9596. Preliminary screening based on letter of intent: brief description scientific basis of proposed project and approximate level of funding sought.

Tourette Syndrome Association, Inc.
Research And Training Grants
42-40 Bell Blvd.
Bayside, NY 11361

4592

Tower Hill Botanic Garden Scholarship

Amount: $500-$2,000 **Deadline:** May 1
Fields/Majors: Horticulture Or Related Field

Scholarship available to junior or senior undergraduate or graduate students studying horticulture or a related field. Applicant must be a resident of New England, or enrolled in a college or university in New England. Based upon academic ability and financial need. Write to the address listed below for information.

Worcester County Horticultural Society
Tower Hill Botanic Garden
P.O. Box 598
Boylston, MA 01505

4593

Tower Scholarship

Amount: Varies **Deadline:** None Specified
Fields/Majors: All Areas Of Study

Awards for undergraduate transfer students. Amount of award depends on GPA (must be over 3.0) and if the applicant was a National Merit Finalist. Renewable if applicant maintains a GPA of at least 3.0. Write to the address below for more information.

Concordia College, Nebraska
Office Of Financial Aid
800 N. Columbia Ave
Seward, NE 68434

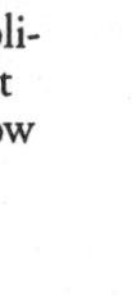

4594

Township Officials Of Illinois Scholarship

Amount: None Specified **Deadline:** Jun 1
Fields/Majors: History, Government And Related

Scholarship for graduating seniors from Illinois high schools who have maintained at least a 3.0 GPA and will be attending an Illinois college, majoring in history or government related areas. Based on school and community activities and a 500-word essay. Write to the address below for details.

Township Officials Of Illinois
Scholarship Program
P.O. Box 455
Astoria, IL 61501

4595

Toyota Motor Sales, USA, Inc. Scholarships

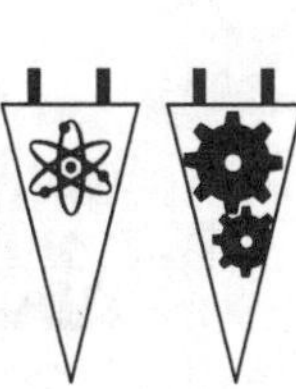

Amount: $5,000 **Deadline:** Feb 15
Fields/Majors: All Areas Of Study

Scholarships for FFA members in any area of study. Preference given to those studying agricultural science or engineering. Based on academic ability, financial need, and participation in extracurricular activities. Two awards will be offered to Iowa FFA members, and three other awards will be offered nationally. For undergraduate study. Write to the address below for details.

National FFA Foundation
Scholarship Office
P.O. Box 15160
Alexandria, VA 22309

4596

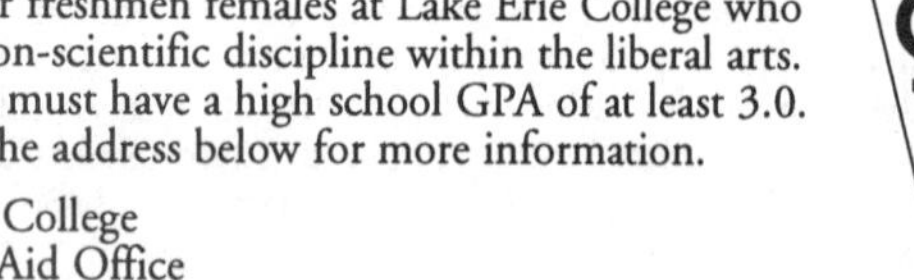

Tracy Harrington Dickinson Scholarship

AMOUNT: Varies **DEADLINE:** Mar 1
FIELDS/MAJORS: Liberal Arts

Awards for freshmen females at Lake Erie College who are in a non-scientific discipline within the liberal arts. Applicant must have a high school GPA of at least 3.0. Write to the address below for more information.

Lake Erie College
Financial Aid Office
391 W. Washington St.
Painesville, OH 44077

4597

Tracy Lee Maker Scholarship

AMOUNT: Varies **DEADLINE:** Mar 1
FIELDS/MAJORS: Political Science

Awards for full-time undergraduate students studying political science who demonstrate financial need and exceptional scholarship. For entering sophomores, juniors, or seniors. Contact the Head, Political Science Department, for more information.

University Of Massachusetts, Amherst
255 Whitmore Administration Building
Box 38230
Amherst, MA 01003

4598

Training Awards Program

AMOUNT: Varies **DEADLINE:** Dec 15
FIELDS/MAJORS: All Areas Of Study

Scholarships for mature women. For technical or vocational training or for completion of undergraduate degree. Regional and national awards are also available ($3,000-regional, $10,000-national). Applicants must be considered the head of household. Application is made through participating soroptimist clubs. Club addresses can be found in your local telephone directory, chamber of commerce, or city hall.

Soroptimist International Of The Americas, Inc.
Two Penn Center Plaza
Suite 1000
Philadelphia, PA 19102

4599

Training Fellowship For Minorities In Substance Abuse Research

AMOUNT: $5,000 **DEADLINE:** None Specified
FIELDS/MAJORS: Substance Abuse And Treatment, Epidemiology, Health Policy

Awards for minority students in the second or third year of study an any of the fields listed above. Must be a U.S. citizen. Send an SASE (.55) to the address below for more information.

National Medical Fellowships, Inc.
110 West 32nd
8th Floor
New York, NY 10001

4600

Training In The Neurosciences For Minorities

AMOUNT: Varies **DEADLINE:** Jan 15
FIELDS/MAJORS: Neurosciences

Fellowships for ethnic minority students pursuing doctoral degrees in APA accredited doctoral programs in psychology or neuroscience. Must be a U.S. citizen or permanent resident. Write to the address below or call (202) 336-6027 for more information.

American Psychological Association
Minority Fellowship Program/Neuroscience
750 First St., NE
Washington, DC 20002

4601

Training Personnel For The Education Of The Handicapped

AMOUNT: Varies **DEADLINE:** Sept 1
FIELDS/MAJORS: Special Education

Many scholarships are available for students of 2 or 4 year undergraduate, graduate, or professional schools. Students must be preparing to work with disabled children and youth. Write to the address below for more information.

U.S. Department Of Education
Room 2177, Mail Stop 6267
400 Maryland Ave, SW
Washington, DC 20202

4602

Transammonia Scholarships

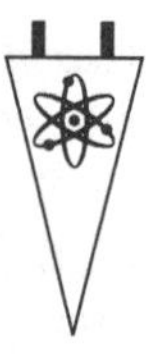

AMOUNT: $1,000 **DEADLINE:** Feb 15
FIELDS/MAJORS: Agriculture

Scholarships are available for FFA members pursuing a four-year degree in any area of agriculture. Five awards are offered annually. Write to the address below for details.

National FFA Foundation
Scholarship Office
P.O. Box 15160
Alexandria, VA 22309

4603

Transfer Academic Scholarships

AMOUNT: $1,000-$2,000
DEADLINE: None Specified
FIELDS/MAJORS: All Areas Of Study

Awards for transfers who have been admitted to CHC and have a GPA of 3.0 or better and over thirty hours of credit. The amount of the award varies depends mainly on GPA. Renewable with a GPA of at least 3.4. Write to the address below for more information.

Christian Heritage College
Financial Aid Office
2100 Greenfield Dr.
El Cajon, CA 92019

4604

Transfer Excellence Award

GPA 3.5+

Amount: $2,500 **Deadline:** Jun 1
Fields/Majors: All Areas Of Study

Awards for transfer students with at least thirty-two credits at an accredited college or university and a GPA of at least 3.5. Write to the address below for more information.

Long Island University
Financial Aid Office
Southampton, NY 11968

4605

Transfer Honor Scholarship

GPA 3.0+

Amount: $500-$1,500 **Deadline:** Dec 1, Aug 1
Fields/Majors: All Areas Of Study

Applicants must be transferring to Edgewood from another school with a minimum of fifteen credits and a minimum 3.0 GPA. Renewable. For undergraduate study. Write to the address below for details.

Edgewood College
Office Of Admissions
855 Woodrow St.
Madison, WI 53711

4606

Transfer Merit Scholarship

GPA 3.5+

Amount: Varies **Deadline:** Mar 16
Fields/Majors: All Areas Of Study

Awards for exceptional students transferring to the University of Maryland from a Maryland community college with a GPA greater than 3.5. Applicants must have completed their associate's degree prior to applying. Contact the address below or call (301) 314-8758 for more information.

University Of Maryland, College Park
Mary Kilmeyer, Assistant Director
Undergraduate Admissions, 0102 Lee Bldg.
College Park, MD 20742

4607

Transfer Scholarship

Amount: Varies **Deadline:** Mar 1
Fields/Majors: All Areas Of Study

Scholarships are available at Kentucky Wesleyan College for undergraduate students who transfer from another college. Write to the address below for details.

Kentucky Wesleyan College
Financial Aid Office
36000 Frederica St.
Owensboro, KY 43202

4608

Transfer Scholarship

GPA 3.0+

Amount: $3,500 **Deadline:** Mar 15
Fields/Majors: All Areas Of Study

Awards open to full-time transfer students with a GPA of at least 3.0 and thirty credits transferred in. Renewable. Write to the address below for more information.

Teikyo Post University
Office Of Financial Aid
800 Country Club Road
Waterbury, CT 06723

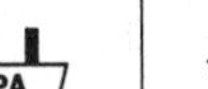

4609

Transfer Scholarship

GPA 3.0+

Amount: $1,800 **Deadline:** Jun 1
Fields/Majors: All Areas Of Study

Awards for transfer students with at least thirty credits at an accredited college or university and a GPA of 3.0 or better. Write to the address below for more information.

Long Island University
Financial Aid Office
Southampton, NY 11968

4610

Transfer Scholarships

GPA 3.0+

Amount: $1,000 (max) **Deadline:** Varies
Fields/Majors: All Areas Of Study

Scholarships are available at the University of New Mexico for transfer students with a GPA of at least 3.25. Write to the address listed below for information.

University Of New Mexico, Albuquerque
Student Financial Aid Office
Mesa Vista Hall North, Room 1044
Albuquerque, NM 87131

4611

Transfer Scholarships

GPA 3.0+

Amount: $5,000 (max) **Deadline:** Apr 1
Fields/Majors: All Areas Of Study

Awards for transfer students who have demonstrated superior scholastic achievement, leadership ability, and/or have contributed significantly to their previous educational institution. Renewable with a 3.2 GPA and full time enrollment. Write to the address below for more details.

Mills College
Office Of Financial Aid
5000 MacArthur Blvd.
Oakland, CA 94613

4612

Transfer Student Honors At Entrance Scholarship

Amount: Tuition **Deadline:** Feb 1
Fields/Majors: All Areas Of Study

Scholarships are available at the University of Utah for full-time students who are transfer students with a minimum GPA of 3.8, with an associate degree or equivalent. Write to the address below for details. Information is also available from your high school guidance counselor.

University Of Utah
Financial Aid And Scholarship Office
105 Student Services Building
Salt Lake City, UT 84112

4613

Transportation Planning Division Minority Scholarship

Amount: $2,500 **Deadline:** May 15
Fields/Majors: Planning-Traffic/Transportation

Scholarships for minority (African American, Hispanic, Asian American, and Native American) undergraduate or graduate students specializing in transportation planning. Applications may be available planning departments (or programs). If not available there, details and forms may be obtained by writing to "Planning Division Minority Scholarship in Transportation Planning" at the below address.

American Planning Association
Celia McAdams, Butte County Govts.
479 Oro Dam Blvd., E, #A
Oroville, CA 95965

4614

Travel Grants To Visit The Gerald R. Ford Library

Amount: $2,000 (max) **Deadline:** Mar 15, Sep 15
Fields/Majors: U.S. Government Domestic, Economic, Foreign And National Policies

Grants are available to assist graduate researchers in traveling to the Gerald R. Ford Library in Ann Arbor, Michigan. These grants are to give researchers in the fields listed above access to the archival collections of the library. Write to the address below or e-mail to library@fordlib.nara.gov for more information.

Gerald R. Ford Library
Mr. William McNitt
1000 Beal Ave
Ann Arbor, MI 48109

4615

Travel Womens Hawaii-Hilo Chapter Scholarship

Amount: $500 **Deadline:** Feb 1
Fields/Majors: Travel And Tourism

Scholarships are available at the University of Hawaii, Hilo for full-time sophomores planning to pursue a career in the travel industry on the island of Hawaii. Must be a Hawaii resident. Write to the address listed below for information.

University Of Hawaii At Hilo
Financial Aid Office
200 West Kawili St.
Hilo, HI 96720

4616

Traveling Fellowships In Architectural Design And Technology

Amount: None Specified **Deadline:** Mar 1
Fields/Majors: Architecture, Architectural Engineering

Participants must be United States citizens who have/or anticipate receiving their first professional degrees in architecture by December. Write to the address below for details.

Van Alen Institute
Design Competitions
30 W. 22nd St.
New York, NY 10010

4617

Traveling Men's Booster Club Scholarship

Amount: $100 **Deadline:** Mar 31
Fields/Majors: All Areas Of Study

Student must demonstrate satisfactory scholarship and financial need. Write to the address below for more information.

Southwest Missouri State University
Office Of Financial Aid
901 South National Ave
Springfield, MO 65804

4618

Treadwell Scholarship

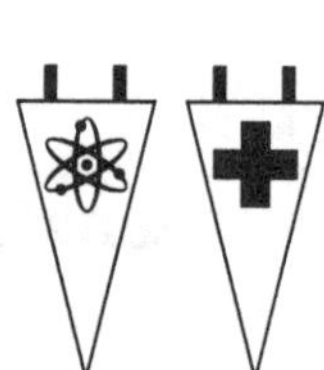

Amount: Varies **Deadline:** Mid-Oct
Fields/Majors: Animal Science And Agriculture

Awards for UMass students in one of the fields listed above. Must have good academic standing, financial need, Massachusetts residency, and a desire to have a career in poultry husbandry. For entering sophomores, juniors, or seniors. Contact the Chair, Scholarship Committee, Veterinary and Animal Sciences, for more information.

University Of Massachusetts, Amherst
Chair, Scholarship Committee
Veterinary And Animal Sciences
Amherst, MA 01003

4619

Treasure Islettes Scholarships

Amount: Tuition & Books **Deadline:** Varies
Fields/Majors: All Areas Of Study

Award for a student at St. Petersburg junior college student who is from Treasure Island, FL. Based on financial need and recommendations. Contact the Treasure Islettes Club president or the address below for more information.

St. Petersburg Junior College
Financial Aid Office
P.O. Box 13489
St. Petersburg, FL 33733

4620

Treasury Management Association Of Indiana Scholarship

Amount: $1,000 **Deadline:** Mar 27
Fields/Majors: Finance

Scholarships are for a junior level student. The student must have completed at least six credit hours of finance courses by the end of the academic year. Contact Margaret Kluesener, First of America Bank, 5300 Crawfordsville Rd., Indianapolis, IN 46222, for more information.

Indiana University/Purdue University, Indianapolis
Purdue School Of Technology
799 West Michigan St.
Indianapolis, IN 46202

4621

Trent R. Dames & William W. Moore Fellowships

Amount: Varies **Deadline:** Feb 15
Fields/Majors: Civil Engineering

Awards for practicing engineers or earth scientists, professors, or graduate students. To be used for post graduate research to aid in the creation of new knowledge for the benefit and advancement of the profession of civil engineering. Contact your local ASCE chapter or write to the address below for details.

American Society Of Civil Engineers
ASCE Student Services
345 E. 47th St.
New York, NY 10017

4622

Treva C. Kintner Scholarship

Amount: $650 **Deadline:** Mar 1
Fields/Majors: Home Economics

Applicants must be Phi Upsilon Omicron members who are over thirty years of age and has completed half of the requirements toward a bachelors degree in home economics. Two awards per year. Write to the address below for details.

Phi Upsilon Omicron National Office
Ohio State University, 171 Mount Hall
1050 Carmack Road
Columbus, OH 43210

4623

Tri-County Grant

Amount: $500 **Deadline:** None Specified
Fields/Majors: All Areas Of Study

Award available to students from Kenosha, Racine, or Walworth counties in Wisconsin. Renewable. Write to the address below for more information.

Carthage College
Financial Aid Office
Kenosha, WI 53140

4624

Tribal Priority Scholarship

Amount: Varies
Deadline: Varies
Fields/Majors: Law, Natural Resources, Education, Med/Health, Engineering, Business

Award for college juniors, seniors, or graduate students pursuing baccalaureate or graduate degrees in the fields above. Recipients are encouraged to apply their training and expertise to tribal goals and objectives. Must be a member of the Hopi tribe. Write to the address below for more information.

Hopi Tribe Grants And Scholarship Program
Scholarship Committee
P.O. Box 123
Kykotsmovi, AZ 86039

4625

Trident Technical Coll. Alumni Scholarship For Newly Enrolled Students

GPA 3.0+

Amount: $1,000 (max) **Deadline:** None Specified
Fields/Majors: All Areas Of Study

Awards for graduating high school seniors from Berkeley, Charleston, or Dorchester counties in South Carolina. Must be active in high school activities or employment and have a GPA of at least 3.0. Also based on recommendations from high school faculty. Write to the address below for more information.

Trident Technical College
Financial Aid Office
P.O. Box 118067
Charleston, SC 29423

4626

Trident Technical College Alumni Scholarship For Continuing Students

Amount: $1,000 (max) **Deadline:** None Specified
Fields/Majors: All Areas Of Study

Awards for continuing TTC students in financial need with a GPA of at least 2.5. Write to the address below for more information.

Trident Technical College
Financial Aid Office
P.O. Box 118067
Charleston, SC 29423

4627

Trillion Diamond Company Endowed Scholarship

Amount: $500 **Deadline:** Nov 1
Fields/Majors: Gemology

Awards are available for students enrolled in a GIA distance education program. Recipient must be a legal resident of the state of New York, New Jersey, or Connecticut. Must be a U.S. citizen or permanent resident. Write to the address below for more information.

Gemological Institute Of America
Office Of Student Financial Assistance
1660 Stewart St.
Santa Monica, CA 90404

4628

Troll-Dickinson Scholarship

Amount: None Specified **Deadline:** Dec 1
Fields/Majors: Food, Resources, Agriculture, Crop Science, Nutrition, Horti/Floriculture

Scholarships are awarded to Stockbridge seniors. Contact the Director, Stockbridge School for more information.

University Of Massachusetts, Amherst
Director
Stockbridge School
Amherst, MA 01003

4629

Trout Unlimited Conservation Scholarships

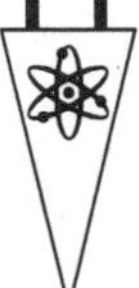

Amount: $1,000 **Deadline:** None Specified
Fields/Majors: Conservation, Aquatic Sciences

Scholarships are available to senior students who display keen interest in the conservation natural aquatic resources, especially cold-water. The award will be based first on a written statement of the student's conservation goals and second their academic record. Contact Dr. Terry Morrow, Department of Biology, for further information.

Clarion University
104 Egbert Hall
Office Of Financial Aid
Clarion, PA 16214

4630

Trout Unlimited Scholarship, Sebago Lake Chapter

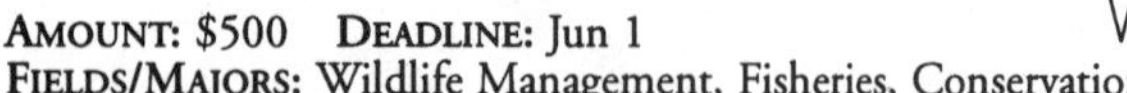

Amount: $500 **Deadline:** Jun 1
Fields/Majors: Wildlife Management, Fisheries, Conservation

Awards for Maine residents who are currently enrolled in a post-secondary institution and will be entering their junior or senior college year. The declared major must be in fisheries, wildlife management, conservation, or a related field. Not available to graduating high school students. Write to the address below for more information.

Sebago Lake Chapter Of Trout Unlimited
P.O. Box 3862
Portland, ME 04104

4631

Truelson Senior Scholarship

Amount: $600 **Deadline:** April 15
Fields/Majors: English

Scholarships are available at the University of Utah for full-time seniors enrolled in an English program. Must apply in the junior year and have at least 125 credit hours at that time. Write to the address below for details.

University Of Utah
Scholarship Chairperson
3500 Lnco
Salt Lake City, UT 84112

4632

Truman Scholarships

Amount: $3,000-$27,000 **Deadline:** Nov 1
Fields/Majors: Public Service, Government Service

Scholarships are available at the University of Iowa for juniors planning careers in government-related public service. Ninety awards offered nationally per year. Three University of Iowa nominees compete for national awards. Write to the address listed below for information.

University Of Iowa
Shamburgh House Honors Center
Iowa City, IA 52242

4633

Trustee And Presidential Scholarships

Amount: None Specified **Deadline:** None Specified
Fields/Majors: All Areas Of Study

Awards given to students who will attend St. Petersburg junior college who are graduates of Pinellas County high schools. Based on academic qualifications. Contact the Office the Director of Scholarships and Student Financial Assistance at the campus you attend or write to the address below.

St. Petersburg Junior College
Office Of Financial Aid
P.O. Box 13489
St. Petersburg, FL 33733

4634

Trustee Grants

Amount: Varies **Deadline:** Dec 15
Fields/Majors: All Areas Of Study

Scholarships for undergraduate students enrolled full-time at Alfred. Many awards are given annually. Must be U.S. citizen or permanent resident. For information on these and other scholarships administered by Alfred University, contact the address below.

Alfred University
Student Financial Aid Office
26 N. Main St.
Alfred, NY 14802

4635

Trustee Scholars

Amount: None Specified **Deadline:** Feb 20
Fields/Majors: All Areas Of Study

Scholarships are available at the University of San Diego for freshmen with an incoming GPA of at least 3.8 and high test scores. Renewable with a 3.45 GPA or better. Write to the address listed below for information.

University Of San Diego
Office Of Financial Aid
5998 Alcala Park
San Diego, CA 92110

4636

Trustee Scholarship

Amount: $5,000 **Deadline:** Mar 31
Fields/Majors: All Areas Of Study

Awards for students with outstanding academic records who have a score of 1050 on the SAT or 25 on the ACT or higher. These awards are not based on need. Write to the address below for more information.

Hood College
Admissions Office
401 Rosemont Ave.
Frederick, MD 21701

4637

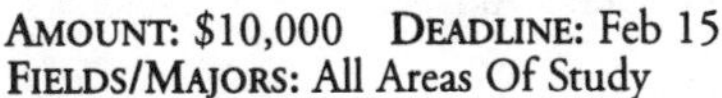

Trustee Scholarships

AMOUNT: $10,000 **DEADLINE:** Feb 15
FIELDS/MAJORS: All Areas Of Study

Awards for entering female freshmen who have demonstrated superior scholastic achievement and distinguished themselves in their extracurricular activities or personal interests. Must have a GPA of 3.5 from high school and an SAT score of at least 1200. Write to the address below for additional information.

Mills College
Office Of Financial Aid
5000 MacArthur Blvd.
Oakland, CA 94613

4638

Trustee Scholarships

AMOUNT: $2,000 -$18,000 **DEADLINE:** Feb 15
FIELDS/MAJORS: All Areas Of Study

Scholarships are for new students with 24 or less credit hours who score 22 on the ACT or 1020 on the SAT. Must be enrolled at least 12 hours per semester. Write to the address below for more information.

Abilene Christian University
Office Of Admissions
Box 6000
Abilene, TX 79699

4639

Trustee's Award For Outstanding Scholar/Evelyn D. Armer Memorial

AMOUNT: $2,500 **DEADLINE:** None Specified
FIELDS/MAJORS: All Areas Of Study

Scholarships are awarded to full-time students enrolled in CSU. Students must demonstrate financial need, academic performance, community service, and personal achievements. Write to the address below for more information.

California State Polytechnic University, Pomona
Office Of Financial Aid
3801 West Temple Ave.
Pomona, CA 91768

4640

Trustee, TSC Scholars, & Alumni Scholarships

AMOUNT: None Specified **DEADLINE:** None Specified
FIELDS/MAJORS: All Areas Of Study

Scholarships for entering freshman who have demonstrated academic achievement or participation in extracurricular activities. Write to the address below for more information.

Trenton State College
Hillwood Lakes
CN 4700
Trenton, NJ 08650

4641

Trustees' And Founder's Scholarships

AMOUNT: Tuition And Fees **DEADLINE:** May 1
FIELDS/MAJORS: All Areas Of Study

Awards for freshmen who rank in the top 10% of their class and have a minimum SAT score of 1300 (ACT 31). Renewable for three years. Write to the address below for more information.

Winthrop University
Financial Resource Center
119 Tillman Hall
Rock Hill, SC 29733

4642

Trustees' Award

AMOUNT: Varies **DEADLINE:** Varies
FIELDS/MAJORS: All Areas Of Study

Awards for Concordia students from underrepresented ethnic backgrounds. Must have a GPA of at least 2.5 and be a U.S. citizen. Write to the address below for more information.

Concordia University, Irvine
Financial Aid Office
1530 Concordia West
Irvine, CA 92715

4643

Trustees' Leadership Grants

AMOUNT: $1,500 (max) **DEADLINE:** Feb 1
FIELDS/MAJORS: All Areas Of Study

Awarded to students at Mount Mercy College to reward academic excellence and student leadership. Recipients are expected to participate in the college's emerging leaders program and to become actively involved in the leadership of the campus. Write to the address below for details.

Mount Mercy College
Office Of Admission
1330 Elmhurst Dr., NE
Cedar Rapids, IA 52402

4644

TRW Scholarships

AMOUNT: $2,500 **DEADLINE:** May 15
FIELDS/MAJORS: Engineering

Scholarships to encourage freshman women to choose engineering as their major. Must have a GPA of at least a 3.5. Write to address below for details. Please be certain to enclose an SASE. Information and application forms are also available from the deans of engineering schools.

Society Of Women Engineers
120 Wall St., 11th Floor
New York, NY 10005

4645

TSC Scholl]arships

AMOUNT: $3,330 **DEADLINE:** Feb 15
FIELDS/MAJORS: Agriculture

Three scholarships, renewable for four years, for FFA members in a TSC region. Must maintain a GPA of 2.0. Need is heavily considered. Must be high school seniors entering first year of college at the time of application. Applications are available from your area TSC store and from the National FFA Center at the address below.

National FFA Foundation
Scholarship Office
P.O. Box 15160
Alexandria, VA 22309

4646 TTRA Travel Research Award

Amount: $2,000 **Deadline:** Mar 1
Fields/Majors: Travel And Tourism

Awards for individuals or organizations performing research which benefits the travel and tourism industry. Write to the address below for details.

Travel And Tourism Research Association
TTRA Awards Committee
10200 W. 44th Ave, Suite 304
Wheat Ridge, CO 80033

4647 Tuition Equalization Grant

Amount: $2,434 (max) **Deadline:** None Specified
Fields/Majors: All Areas Of Study

Grant for students enrolled at least half-time at Schreiner who can demonstrate financial need. Recipients of athletic grants or those pursuing theology or vocational nursing degrees are not eligible. Must be a resident of Texas. Write to the address below for more information.

Schreiner College
Financial Aid Office
Kerrville, TX 78028

4648 Tuition Incentive Program

Amount: Tuition And Fees **Deadline:** None Specified
Fields/Majors: All Areas Of Study

Tuition incentive program for students who have graduated high school or obtained a GED certificate within the last four years. Applicant must be a Michigan. Resident and be a member of a family who has income at or below poverty level at the time of application and for the calendar year prior to application. Student must be under the age of 20 at the time high school graduation or GED completion. Student must be enrolled at least half time in an associate degree or certificate program at any Michigan public community college, federal tribally controlled community college, independent/nonprofit associate degree-granting college/university, or public university which offers associate degree or certificate programs. Write to the address below for details.

Michigan Department Of Social Services
Suite 1318
P.O. Box 30037
Lansing, MI 48909

4649 Tuition Remission For Seminarians

Amount: 1/3 Tuition **Deadline:** None Specified
Fields/Majors: Theology

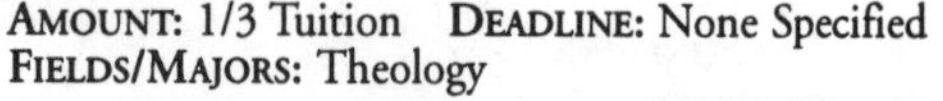

Remission of 1/3 of tuition is granted to Diocesan Seminarians and members of religious institutes preparing for ordination to the Roman Catholic priesthood. Applicant must have been admitted into a graduate program in either the school of philosophy or the school of religious studies. Contact the financial aid office at the address below for details.

The Catholic University Of America
Office Of Admissions And Financial Aid
Washington, DC 20064

4650 Tuition Scholarships

Amount: $300-$500 **Deadline:** Mar 15
Fields/Majors: All Areas Of Study

Open to any Catholic Aid Association member of at least two years who is a high school graduate and is now entering their freshman or sophomore year in a college, university, or technical school. Write to the address below for complete details.

Catholic Aid Association
3499 N. Lexington Ave
Saint Paul, MN 55126

4651 Tuition Scholarships For Children Of Veterans

Amount: Tuition Waiver **Deadline:** None
Fields/Majors: All Areas Of Study

Must be children of war veterans who were legal residents of South Carolina at time of entry into military service and who during service: were killed in action, died of diseases, disability, or from other causes resulting from service. Applicants must be U.S. citizens pursuing undergraduate degrees at South Carolina institutions and age 26 or under. Write to the address below for details.

South Carolina, Office Of The Governor
Division Of Veterans Affairs
1205 Pendleton St., Brown Bldg.
Columbia, SC 29201

4652 Tuition Waiver Awards

Amount: Varies
Deadline: Feb 1
Fields/Majors: All Areas Of Study

Tuition waivers are available at the University of Hawaii, Hilo for full-time students in athletics, in the College of Arts & Sciences, in the College of Agriculture, graduates of Big Island high schools, in Asian-Pacific studies, in the teacher-education program, of Hawaiian ancestry, veterans or dependents of deceased veterans, senior citizens, or blind. Individual award requirements may vary. Write to the address listed below for information.

University Of Hawaii At Hilo
Financial Aid Office
200 West Kawili St.
Hilo, HI 96720

4653 Tuition Waiver For Children Of Deceased Or Disabled Law Officers

Amount: In-State Tuition **Deadline:** None Specified
Fields/Majors: All Areas Of Study

Tuition waivers are available for South Carolina dependents of deceased or disabled firemen, law officers, and members of civil air patrol or organized rescue squad. Students must attend public institutions located in South Carolina. Children of deceased or totally disabled veterans are also eligible. Contact your school's financial aid office or the address below for more information.

South Carolina Commission On Higher Education
1333 Main St.
Suite 200
Columbia, SC 29201

4654

Tuition Waiver For Senior Citizens

Amount: In-State Tuition **Deadline:** None Specified
Fields/Majors: All Areas Of Study

Tuition waivers are available for South Carolina residents, age sixty and over, attending South Carolina public colleges. Contact your school's financial aid office or the address below for more information.

South Carolina Commission On Higher Education
1333 Main St.
Suite 200
Columbia, SC 29201

4655

Tuition Waivers At Curtis Institute

Amount: Full Tuition **Deadline:** Feb 16
Fields/Majors: All Areas Of Study Offered At Curtis

Renewable scholarships, covering full tuition, at the Curtis Institute of Music. Based on merit and financial need. Write to the address below for complete details.

Curtis Institute Of Music
1726 Locust St.
Philadelphia, PA 19103

4656

Tuition/Book Or Standardized Test Fee Scholarship

E

Amount: Varies **Deadline:** Varies
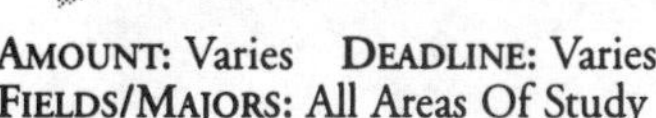
Fields/Majors: All Areas Of Study

Tuition/book award is for Hopi tribe members who are attending school for reasons of personal growth, career enhancement, or career change. The standardized test award is to assist Hopi students in paying for the ACT, SAT, GRE, GMAT, LSAT, or any other standardized test. Write to the address below for more information.

Hopi Tribe Grants And Scholarship Program
Scholarship Committee
P.O. Box 123
Kykotsmovi, AZ 86039

4657

Tulsa Legacy Scholarships

GPA 3.0+

Amount: $500 **Deadline:** Mar 15
Fields/Majors: Travel And Tourism, Hotel/Motel Management

Awards for Oklahoma juniors or seniors in one of the areas listed above who are enrolled in a four-year college in Oklahoma. Must have a GPA of 3.0 or better. Write to the address below for more information.

National Tour Foundation
546 East Main St.
P.O. Box 3071
Lexington, KY 40596

4658

Turf & Ornamental Communication Association

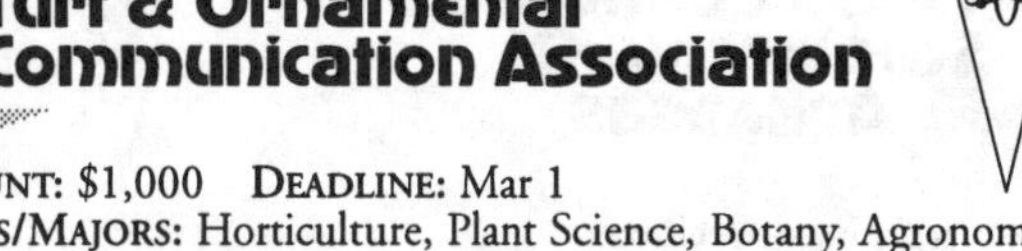

Amount: $1,000 **Deadline:** Mar 1
Fields/Majors: Horticulture, Plant Science, Botany, Agronomy

Open to students majoring in horticulture, plant science, botany, or agronomy with an interest in green industry communications. Two awards per year. Write to the address below for more information.

California State Polytechnic University, Pomona
College Of Agriculture
Building 7, Room 110
Pomona, CA 91768

4659

Two-Year College Academic Scholarship Program

Amount: Tuition **Deadline:** None Specified
Fields/Majors: All Areas Of Study

This program is limited to students who are accepted for enrollment at public, two-year, postsecondary educational institutions in Alabama. Awards are based on academic merit as determined by the Institutional Scholarship Committee. Not based on financial need and may be renewed if students demonstrate academic excellence. Priorities given to in-state residents. Apply through the financial aid office at any public, two-year, postsecondary educational institution, rather than address listed below.

Alabama Commission On Higher Education
P.O. Box 30200
Montgomery, AL 36130

4660

Two/Ten International Footwear Foundation Scholarship Program

Amount: $200-$2,000 **Deadline:** Jan 15
Fields/Majors: All Areas Of Study

Applicants must be worker or a dependent of a worker whose work is related to the footwear, leather, or allied industries. Based on need. Two-hundred fifty awards per year. Must have been graduated from high school within the last four years. Write to the address below for details and a preliminary application form.

Two/Ten International Footwear Foundation
56 Main St.
Watertown, MA 02172

4661

Tylenol Scholarship

Amount: $1,000-$10,000 **Deadline:** Nov 15
Fields/Majors: All Areas Of Study

Must be a freshman, sophomore, or junior attending any college or vocational or technical school. Over five-hundred awards are available. Information and applications will be available throughout the month of October in stores where Tylenol products are sold.

McNeilab, Inc.
Scholarship Office
Fort Washington, PA 19034

4662

Tyson Foundation Scholarship Of Arkansas

Amount: None Specified
Deadline: Apr 20, Dec 15
Fields/Majors: Business, Agriculture, Engineering, Computer Science, Nursing

Applicant must be a U.S. citizen and a permanent resident living in the vicinity of a Tyson operating facility in Alaska. Applicants should be majoring in one of the areas listed above and be enrolled full-time in an accredited institution. Write to the address below for more information.

Tyson Foundation, Inc.
2210 West Oaklawn
Springdale, AR 72762

4663

Tyson Foundation Scholarship Of China

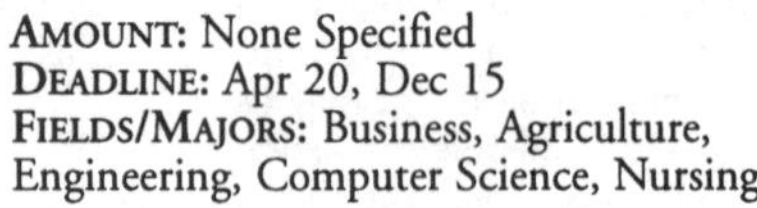

Amount: None Specified
Deadline: Apr 20, Dec 15
Fields/Majors: Business, Agriculture, Engineering, Computer Science, Nursing

Applicant must be a U.S. citizen and a permanent resident living in the vicinity of a Tyson operating facility in Alaska. Applicants should be majoring in one of the areas listed above and be enrolled full-time in an accredited institution. Write to the address below for more information.

Tyson Foundation, Inc.
2210 West Oaklawn
Springdale, AR 72762

4664

Tyson Foundation Scholarship Of Florida

Amount: None Specified
Deadline: Apr 20, Dec 15
Fields/Majors: Business, Agriculture, Engineering, Computer Science, Nursing

Applicant must be a U.S. citizen and a permanent resident living in the vicinity of a Tyson operating facility in Alaska. Applicants should be majoring in one of the areas listed above and be enrolled full-time in an accredited institution. Write to the address below for more information.

Tyson Foundation, Inc.
2210 West Oaklawn
Springdale, AR 72762

4665

Tyson Foundation Scholarship Of Illinois

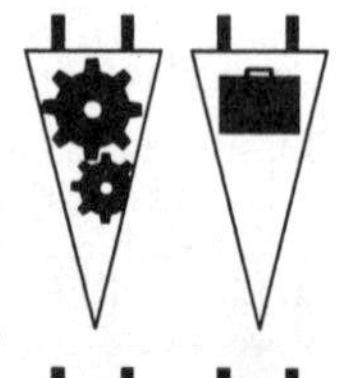

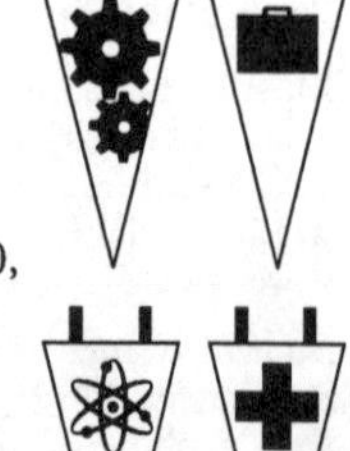

Amount: None Specified **Deadline:** Apr 20, Dec 15
Fields/Majors: Business, Agriculture, Engineering, Computer Science, Nursing

Applicant must be a U.S. citizen and a permanent resident living in the vicinity of a Tyson operating facility in Alaska. Applicants should be majoring in one of the areas listed above and be enrolled full-time in an accredited institution. Write to the address below for more information.

Tyson Foundation, Inc.
2210 West Oaklawn
Springdale, AR 72762

4666

Tyson Foundation Scholarship Of Michigan

Amount: None Specified
Deadline: Apr 20, Dec 15
Fields/Majors: Business, Agriculture, Engineering, Computer Science, Nursing

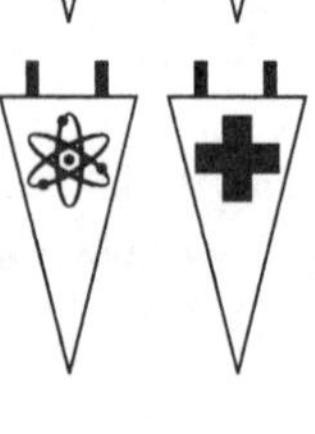

Applicant must be a U.S. citizen and a permanent resident living in the vicinity of a Tyson operating facility in Alaska. Applicants should be majoring in one of the areas listed above and be enrolled full-time in an accredited institution. Write to the address below for more information.

Tyson Foundation, Inc.
2210 West Oaklawn
Springdale, AR 72762

4667

Tyson Foundation Scholarship Of Minnesota

Amount: None Specified
Deadline: Apr 20, Dec 15
Fields/Majors: Business, Agriculture, Engineering, Computer Science, Nursing

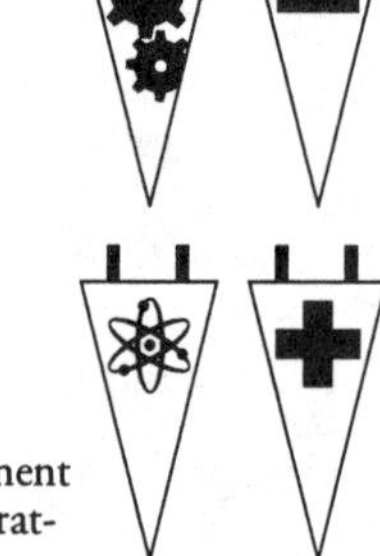

Applicant must be a U.S. citizen and a permanent resident living in the vicinity of a Tyson operating facility in Alaska. Applicants should be majoring in one of the areas listed above and be enrolled full-time in an accredited institution. Write to the address below for more information.

Tyson Foundation, Inc.
2210 West Oaklawn
Springdale, AR 72762

4668

Tyson Foundation Scholarship Of Pennsylvania

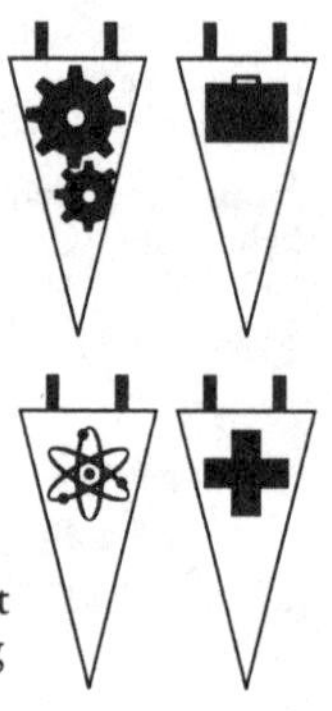

Amount: None Specified
Deadline: Apr 20, Dec 15
Fields/Majors: Business, Agriculture, Engineering, Computer Science, Nursing

Applicant must be a U.S. citizen and a permanent resident living in the vicinity of a Tyson operating facility in Alaska. Applicants should be majoring in one of the areas listed above and be enrolled full-time in an accredited institution. Write to the address below for more information.

Tyson Foundation, Inc.
2210 West Oaklawn
Springdale, AR 72762

4669

Tyson Foundation Scholarship Of Washington

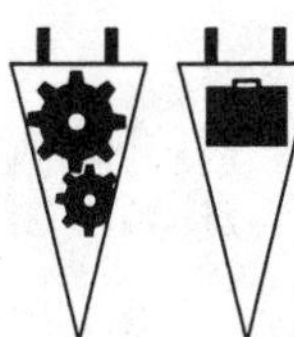
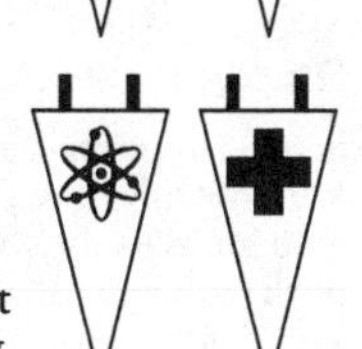
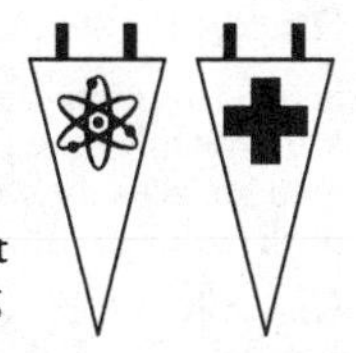

AMOUNT: None Specified
DEADLINE: Apr 20, Dec 15
FIELDS/MAJORS: Business, Agriculture, Engineering, Computer Science, Nursing

Applicant must be a U.S. citizen and a permanent resident living in the vicinity of a Tyson operating facility in Alaska. Applicants should be majoring in one of the areas listed above and be enrolled full-time in an accredited institution. Write to the address below for more information.

Tyson Foundation, Inc.
2210 West Oaklawn
Springdale, AR 72762

4670

U.P. Hedrick Awards

AMOUNT: $300, $100 **DEADLINE:** May 1
FIELDS/MAJORS: Horticulture

Awards are available for the best research paper and best library review paper relating to cultivars of deciduous, tropical, or subtropical fruits as related to climate, soil, rootstocks, a specific experiment, a breeding project, history and performance of new or old cultivars, a library review pertinent to pomology, or a personal experience with a particular fruit cultivar. Write to the address listed below for information.

American Pomological Society
103 Tyson Building
University Park, PA 16802

4671

U.S. Environmental Protection Agency Scholarship

AMOUNT: $4,000 **DEADLINE:** Jun 15
FIELDS/MAJORS: Chemistry, Chemical Engininneering, Environmental Sciences, Biology, And Related

Scholarship for students with junior status or higher. Must agree to work at the environmental protection agency, a tribal location, or an environmental facility during the summers, if a job is offered. Write to the address below for details.

American Indian Science And Engineering Society
Scholarship Coordinator
1630 30th St., Suite 301
Boulder, CO 80301

4672

U.S. Institute Of Peace Fellows

AMOUNT: $14,000 **DEADLINE:** Dec 1
FIELDS/MAJORS: Areas Related To International Peace And Conflict Management

Fellowships are available for doctoral candidates who have demonstrated a clear interest in issues of international peace and conflict management, who have completed all required work except the dissertation. Dissertation study must reflect a topic that advances the state of knowledge about international peace and conflict management. Write to the address listed below for information.

U.S. Institute Of Peace
Jennings Randolph Fellowship Program
1550 M St., NW, Suite 700
Washington, DC 20005

4673

U.S. National Arboretum Internships

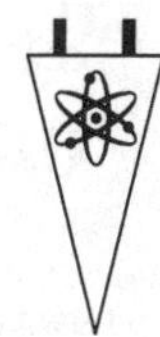

AMOUNT: $8.00 Per Hour **DEADLINE:** Varies
FIELDS/MAJORS: Horticulture, Floriculture, Plant Related, Entomology

Internship program for students in any field or related field to those listed above. All applicants must have completed course work or practical experience in these fields as well as have the ability to work independently. Individual requirements for each specific internship may vary. Write to the address below for more information on the programs offered.

Friends Of The National Arboretum
Internship Coordinator
3501 New York Ave, NE
Washington, DC 20002

4674

U.S. Submarine Veterans Of WWII Scholarship

AMOUNT: $1,750 **DEADLINE:** Apr 15
FIELDS/MAJORS: All Areas Of Study

For sons/daughters of paid-up regular members of the U.S. Submarine veterans of World War II. Applicants must be unmarried, and high school seniors or graduates from high school no more than four years prior to applying. Based on a combination of academics and need. For undergraduate study at any accredited institution. Must be under the age of 24. Write to the address below for details.

U.S. Submarine Veterans Of WWII Scholarship Program
Norfolk Naval station
405 Dillingham Boulevard
Norfolk, VA 23511

4675

U.S. Tobacco (Copenhagen-Skoal) Rodeo Scholarship

AMOUNT: $200-$500 **AMOUNT:** Varies
FIELDS/MAJORS: Range Animal Science

Awards for Sul Ross undergraduates who are studying range animal science, have a GPA of at least 2.0, and are NIRA eligible. Write to the address below for more information.

Sul Ross State University
Division Of Range Animal Science
Box C-110
Alpine, TX 79832

4676

U.S. West Veterans Scholarship

AMOUNT: Varies **DEADLINE:** Feb 15
FIELDS/MAJORS: All Areas Of Study

Scholarships are available at the University of Utah for full-time students who are veterans. Based on GPA and financial need. Write to the address below for information.

University Of Utah
Financial Aid And Scholarships Office
105 Student Services Building
Salt Lake City, UT 84112

4677

UAB Deans Scholarship

AMOUNT: $1,000 **DEADLINE:** None Specified
FIELDS/MAJORS: Theater, Dance

Applicants must be incoming freshmen who have a minimum ACT of 22. Renewable. For study at the University of Alabama at Birmingham. Contact the office of student financial aid for details.

University Of Alabama, Birmingham
Student Financial Aid, Univ. Ctr, 250
700 13th St. South, UAB Station
Birmingham, AL 35294

4678

UCSD Foundation Undergraduate Scholarship

AMOUNT: None Specified **DEADLINE:** Nov 30
FIELDS/MAJORS: All Areas Of Study

Scholarships are available at UCSD for minority undergraduate students who exhibit academic excellence and leadership abilities. Write to the address listed below for information.

University Of California, San Diego
Student Financial Services
9500 Gilman Drive
La Jolla, CA 92093

4679

UCT Retarded Citizens Teacher Scholarship

AMOUNT: $750 **DEADLINE:** None Specified
FIELDS/MAJORS: Special Education, Mentally Handicapped

Scholarships for juniors, seniors, and graduate students in special education, or current teachers who require continuing education in special education. Prime consideration is given to UCT members. Recipients must plan to be of service in the U.S. or Canada. When requesting an application, list a brief history of your experience with the mentally handicapped, an indication of your current standing in college, and a statement of your educational or career plans. Application is made through the local uct contact person, whose name may be received from the home office at the address below.

United Commercial Travelers Of America
Scholarship Coordinator
632 N. Park St., P.O. Box 159019
Columbus, OH 43215

4680

UFCW Scholarship Program

AMOUNT: $4,000 (total) **DEADLINE:** Dec 31
FIELDS/MAJORS: All Areas Of Study

Applicants must be members or children of members of the UFCW who are high school seniors and will be enrolling in a college or university as a full-time student. Automatically renewable for four years, at $1,000 per year. Applicants must be less than age 20. Seven awards offered each year. Write to the address below for details. Information is also available in editions of "UFCW Action," the bi-monthly magazine of the union.

United Food And Commercial Workers International Union
Education Office
1775 K St., NW
Washington, DC 20006

4681

UHHSA Student Association Motivated Student Scholarship

AMOUNT: $600 **DEADLINE:** Feb 1
FIELDS/MAJORS: All Areas Of Study

Scholarships are available at the University of Hawaii, Hilo for full-time students with a GPA of 3.0 or more who are actively involved in co-curricular activities. Write to the address listed below for information.

University Of Hawaii At Hilo
Financial Aid Office
200 West Kawili St.
Hilo, HI 96720

4682

UI Alumni Association Iowa Club Scholarships

AMOUNT: $500 **DEADLINE:** Mar 1
FIELDS/MAJORS: All Areas Of Study

Scholarships are available at the University of Iowa for entering freshmen who exhibit a strong background of academic accomplishment and participation in high school and community activities. Up to twenty awards offered each year. Write to the address listed below for information.

University Of Iowa
Scholarship Committee, UI Alumni Association
Alumni Center
Iowa City, IA 52242

4683

UK Community College Transfer Scholarship

AMOUNT: Varies **DEADLINE:** Mar 1
FIELDS/MAJORS: All Areas Of Study

Scholarships are available at Kentucky Wesleyan College for undergraduate students who transfer from a Kentucky community college. Write to the address below for details.

Kentucky Wesleyan College
Financial Aid Office
3000 Frederica St.
Owensboro, KY 43202

4684

Undergraduate & Graduate Grants, Loans, And Employment

AMOUNT: Varies **DEADLINE:** None Specified
FIELDS/MAJORS: All Areas Of Study

Grants, loans, and employment opportunities are available for MIT students. Most awards are based on financial aid or academic ability or both. Financial aid forms are available with the admissions applications. Write to the address below for more information. Continuing students may contact the financial aid office for more details.

Massachusetts Institute Of Technology
Office Of Admissions
Room 3-108, 77 Massachusettes Ave.
Cambridge, MA 02139

4685

Undergraduate/Graduate Loans

AMOUNT: $200-$1,000 **DEADLINE:** None Specified
FIELDS/MAJORS: All Areas Of Study

Loans for full-time undergraduate or graduate students who are U.S. citizens and members of the Presbyterian church (USA). Based upon academic ability and demonstrated financial need. Write to the address below for details.

Presbyterian Church (USA)
Office For Financial Aid For studies
100 Witherspoon St.
Louisville, KY 40202

4686

Undergraduate And Graduate Scholarships

AMOUNT: $500-$1,000 **DEADLINE:** Apr 1
FIELDS/MAJORS: All Areas Of Study

Applicants must be students of Armenian ancestry enrolled at an accredited college or university. Based on financial need. Involvement with the Armenian community is considered. Renewable once. Write to the address below for details.

Armenian Relief Society Of North America, Inc.
Ms. Seda Aghamianz
80 Bigelow Ave.
Watertown, MA 02172

4687

Undergraduate Award For Excellence In Chemistry

AMOUNT: $300 **DEADLINE:** Feb 16
FIELDS/MAJORS: Chemistry

Awards for senior, female chemistry students in any accredited school. Applicants need not be members of Iota Sigma Pi. Based on academic excellence. Write to Dr. Barbara A. Sawrey, Ph.D., at the address below for more details.

Iota Sigma Pi
UCSD, Dept. Of Chemistry And Biochemistry
9500 Gilman Dr., Dept. 0303
La Jolla, CA 92093

4688

Undergraduate Awards

AMOUNT: Varies **DEADLINE:** Apr 1
FIELDS/MAJORS: All Areas Of Study

Applicants must be of Japanese ancestry and undergraduates who are currently enrolled or returning to school. Several award programs are available. Applications and information may be obtained from local JACL chapters, district offices and national headquarters at the address below. Please indicate your level of study and be certain to include a legal sized SASE. (Offices are in San Francisco, Seattle, LA, Chicago, and Fresno.)

Japanese American Citizens League
National Scholarship And Award Program
1765 Sutter St.
San Francisco, CA 94115

4689

Undergraduate College Scholarships

AMOUNT: None Specified **DEADLINE:** Apr 1
FIELDS/MAJORS: All Disciplines

Applicants must be CAP cadets or senior members who have received the Billy Mitchell Award or the senior rating in Level II of the senior training program scholarship will be offered in each of the four disciplines (engineering, science, education, humanities). Write to the address below for details.

Civil Air Patrol
National Headquarters Cap(tt)
Maxwell AFB, AL 36112

4690

Undergraduate Disabled Student Scholarship Program

AMOUNT: $1,000-$2,000 **DEADLINE:** Mar 15
FIELDS/MAJORS: All Areas Of Study

Scholarships are offered to disabled students who are U.S. citizens and residents of California or Hawaii. Scholarships are for undergraduate work at an accredited community college, university, or licensed vocational school only. Individuals applying must be in second semester of senior year in high school, or have completed high school or passed the GED. Write to the address below for more information.

California-Hawaii Elks Major Project, Inc.
Scholarship Committee
5450 East Lamona Ave
Fresno, CA 93727

4691

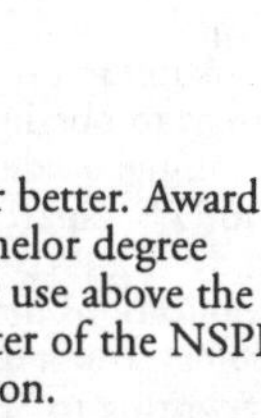

Undergraduate Engineering Scholarships For Enrolled College Students

AMOUNT: $1,000 **DEADLINE:** Feb 1
FIELDS/MAJORS: Engineering

Requires continuous undergraduate GPA of 3.0 or better. Award available to students enrolled in an accredited bachelor degree program in engineering. Must be U.S. citizen. For use above the freshman level of studies. Contact your state chapter of the NSPE or write to the address below for further information.

National Society Of Professional Engineers Education Foundation
1420 King St.
Alexandria, VA 22314

4692

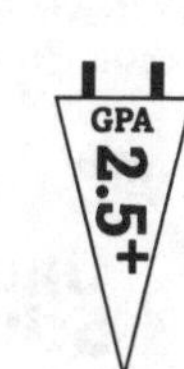

Undergraduate Fellowships

AMOUNT: $1,000 **DEADLINE:** Mar 1
FIELDS/MAJORS: All Areas Of Study

Awards are available at Plymouth State for junior or seniors who have maintained a 2.5 GPA or above. Twenty awards are offered each year. Write to the address listed below for information.

Plymouth State College
Financial Aid Office
Speare Administration Building
Plymouth, NH 03264

4693

Undergraduate Fellowships And Graduate Fellowships

AMOUNT: $4,000-$5,000 **DEADLINE:** Mar 1
FIELDS/MAJORS: Art, Fine Arts, Art History, Photography, Film Making, And Video

Fellowships are available to those who are enrolled, or are planning to be enrolled, full-time for the entire academic year at an accredited school of arts, college, or university. Must be a Virginia resident. Write to the address below for more information.

Virginia Museum Of Fine Arts
Office Of Education And Outreach
2800 Grove Ave.
Richmond, VA 23221

4694

Undergraduate Geology Departmental Scholarships

AMOUNT: Varies **DEADLINE:** Feb 1
FIELDS/MAJORS: Geology

Scholarships are available at the University of Utah for full-time undergraduate geology majors. Includes the Amax, R.V. Brown Memorial, Chevron, and Mineralogical Society of Utah Memorial scholarships. Individual award requirements may vary. Write to the address below for details.

University Of Utah
Kim Atwater
714 William C. Browning Building
Salt Lake City, UT 84112

4695

Undergraduate Minority Scholarship Program

AMOUNT: $2,500 **DEADLINE:** May 15
FIELDS/MAJORS: Planning & Urban Development, Public Admin., Environmental Science

Scholarships for minority (African American, Hispanic, and Native American) undergraduates in planning programs in the U.S. Based on intent to obtain an undergraduate degree in planning, academic merit, leadership potential, and U.S. citizenship are primary criteria. Brief essay required. For study at a PAB-accredited school beyond the freshman year. Applications may be available planning departments (or programs). If not available there, details and forms may be obtained by writing to "Planning and the African American Community Division Scholarship" in care of the address below.

American Planning Association
Fellowships And Scholarships In Planning
1776 Massachusetts Ave., NW
Washington, DC 20036

4696

Undergraduate Minority Scholarships

AMOUNT: $300-$2,000 **DEADLINE:** None Specified
FIELDS/MAJORS: All Areas Of Study

Awards for minorities at Moorhead State University based on academic achievement, special talents, or leadership. Write to the address below for more specific details.

Moorhead State University
Financial Aid Office
107 Owens
Moorhead MN 56563

4697

Undergraduate Program

AMOUNT: None Specified **DEADLINE:** None Specified
FIELDS/MAJORS: All Areas Of Study

Scholarships for residents of Guilford County, North Carolina, attending one of these local colleges. Colleges include UNC (Greensboro & Chapel Hill), Greensboro College, Guilford College, NC A&T, Bennett, Elon College, High Point, Guilford Tech College, Wake Forest, Duke, NC State, and NC School of the Arts. Contact the financial aid office at your college for details.

Tannenbaum-Sternberger Foundation
Robert O. Klepfer, Jr.
P.O. Box 3112
Greensboro, NC 27402

4698

Undergraduate Research Fellowship

AMOUNT: $4,000 (max) **DEADLINE:** Feb 1
FIELDS/MAJORS: Microbiological Sciences

Three to six month fellowship available to second or third year undergraduates planning to attend graduate school and study the microbiological sciences. Must be a U.S. citizen or permanent resident. Write to the address below for complete details.

American Society For Microbiology
Office Of Education And Training
1325 Massachusettes Ave, NW
Washington, DC 20005

4699

Undergraduate Research Scholarship Program In Microscopy

AMOUNT: $2,500 **DEADLINE:** Dec 30
FIELDS/MAJORS: Microscopy

Applicants must be full-time undergraduate students pursuing microscopy as a career or major research tool. Write to the address below for details.

Microscopy Society Of America
Undergraduate Scholarship Program
4 Barlows Landing Road, Suite 8
Pocasset, MA 02559

4700

Undergraduate Scholarship Program

AMOUNT: Varies **DEADLINE:** Jun 15
FIELDS/MAJORS: All Areas Of Study

Applicants must be Georgia residents who have completed their first year as an undergraduate. A minimum 3.0 GPA and financial need is required. Write to the address below for details.

Ty Cobb Educational Foundation
P.O. Box 725
Forest Park, GA 30051

4701

Undergraduate Scholarships

AMOUNT: $1,000 **DEADLINE:** Jun 15
FIELDS/MAJORS: Agriculture

Four awards given for outstanding essays on topics concerned with issues affecting the operations of American agricultural cooperatives. Must be a sophomore, junior or senior (first semester only if senior), and have a GPA of at least 3.0. Each entry must be accompanied by a registration form which is available from ncfc. Write to "undergraduate scholarship" at the address below for information and an application.

National Council Of Farmer Cooperatives Education Foundation
50 F St., NW, Suite 900
Washington, DC 20001

4702

Undergraduate Scholarships

AMOUNT: $750-$2,000 **DEADLINE:** Feb 1
FIELDS/MAJORS: Food Science And Technology

Undergraduate scholarships open to students enrolled in or planning to enroll in a food service and technology curriculum. Applicant must have a GPA of at least 2.5. Seventy-five awards per year. Write to the address below for details. Please specify your year in school.

Institute Of Food Technologists
Scholarship Department
221 North LaSalle St.
Chicago, IL 60601

4703

Undergraduate Scholarships

AMOUNT: $650 **DEADLINE:** Mar 1
FIELDS/MAJORS: Home Economics

Applicants must be Phi Upsilon Omicron undergraduate members who are working toward a bachelors degree. Award is based on scholastic record and Phi U and AHEA activities. Ten awards per year. Write to the address below for details.

Phi Upsilon Omicron National Office
Ohio State University, 171 Mount Hall
1050 Carmack Road
Columbus, OH 43210

4704

Undergraduate Scholarships

AMOUNT: None Specified **DEADLINE:** Feb 15
FIELDS/MAJORS: All Areas Of Study

Scholarship applicant's permanent residence or high school must be located within thirty miles of a Potlatch Corp. Facility. The majority of scholarships are awarded to students residing near company facilities in Idaho, Minnesota, and Arkansas. Write to the address below for further information. A return envelope is not necessary. Applications must be requested between Oct 1-Dec 15.

Potlatch Foundation For Higher Education
Corporate Programs Administrator
P.O. Box 193591
San Francisco, CA 94119

4705

Undergraduate Scholarships

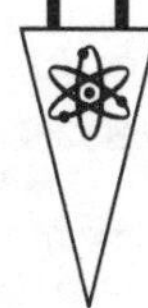

AMOUNT: Varies **DEADLINE:** Jun 15
FIELDS/MAJORS: Metallurgy, Materials Science

Scholarships are for undergraduates. Selection is based on interest in metallurgy and materials science, motivation, achievement, potential, and scholarship. 34-$500 awards. 3-$2,000 awards. 1-full tuition award. Must be sophomore, junior, or senior (jr. or sr. for full tuition award). Must be U.S., Canadian, or Mexican citizen. Application forms are available in the offices of the university departments of metallurgy/materials, from faculty advisors of ASM student chapters, from local ASM chapters, or by writing to the address below.

Asm Foundation For Education And Research
Scholarship Program
Materials Park, OH 44073

4706

Undergraduate Scholarships

AMOUNT: $2,500 **DEADLINE:** None Specified
FIELDS/MAJORS: All Areas Of Study

Must be Indiana high school senior in good standing who has never attended college. Must have faith in a divine being, and a firm belief in the free enterprise system and the American way of life. Must exhibit outstanding scholastic achievement and leadership potential. Awards are limited to certain Indiana colleges. Financial need not a factor. Unspecified number of scholarships. Renewable. Write to the address below for complete details.

Eisenhower Memorial Scholarship Foundation, Inc.
223 South Pete Ellis Dr., Suite 27
Bloomington, IN 47408

4707

Undergraduate Scholarships

AMOUNT: $1,000-$5,000 **DEADLINE:** Jul 1
FIELDS/MAJORS: Health Information Management, Health Information Technology

Scholarships for undergraduates currently enrolled in health information management or technology programs at a committee on allied health education and accreditation accredited school. Includes the FORE, Smart Corporation, Barbara Thomas Enterprises, Inc., Transcriptions, Ltd., and St. Anthony Publishing, Inc. Scholarships. Write to the address listed below for information.

Foundation Of Research And Education Of AHIMA
American Health Information Management Association
919 N. Michigan Ave., Suite 1400
Chicago, IL 60611

4708

Undergraduate Scholarships

AMOUNT: Varies **DEADLINE:** Feb 1
FIELDS/MAJORS: All Areas Of Study

Scholarships for undergraduates at California State University at Fresno who have a minimum GPA of 3.0 (exception of 2.5 GPA is made for special grants). Involvement in campus and community activities is required. Students studying for a second baccalaureate or master's degree are not eligible. Write to the address below for more information.

California State University At Fresno
Financial Aid Office
5150 North Maple Ave.
Fresno, CA 93740

4709

Undergraduate Scholarships

AMOUNT: $500-$1,500 **DEADLINE:** Mar 1
FIELDS/MAJORS: Graphic Communications

Open to high school seniors who are planning to study graphic communications at a post-secondary institution. Based on academic records, class rank, recommendations, honors, and extracurricular activities. Renewable with a GPA of at least 3.0. Write to the address below for details.

National Scholarship Trust Fund Of The Graphic Arts
4615 Forbes Ave.
Pittsburgh, PA 15213

4710
Undergraduate Session Assistants Program

AMOUNT: $2,500 **DEADLINE:** None Specified
FIELDS/MAJORS: Political Science, Government, Public Service

This program is intended to provide talented undergraduate students with first-hand experience in New York state government as part of their home campus academic curricula. Must have good academic record. Must be at least a sophomore. Must be a New York state resident and be enrolled on an accredited campus located in New York state. Up to sixty-one awards per year. Write to Dr. Russell J. Williams, Director, at the address below for details. Applications and information should also be available each fall on your college campus financial aid office.

New York State Senate
Senate Student Programs
90 South Swan St., Room 401
Albany, NY 12247

4711
Undergraduate University Scholarships

AMOUNT: $100-$750 **DEADLINE:** None Specified
FIELDS/MAJORS: All Areas Of Study

Awards for undergraduates at Moorhead State University based on academic achievement, special talents, or leadership. Write to the address below for more specific details.

Moorhead State University
Financial Aid Office
107 Owens
Moorhead, MN 56563

4712
Undergraduate Work Grant

AMOUNT: $1,000 **DEADLINE:** None Specified
FIELDS/MAJORS: Science

Student must demonstrate scholarship and an interest in science through projects or presentations. Contact the physics and astronomy department for more information.

Southwest Missouri State University
Office Of Financial Aid
901 South National Ave.
Springfield, MO 65804

4713
Undergraduate, Curriculum, And Post-Graduate Scholarships

AMOUNT: None Specified **DEADLINE:** Feb 1
FIELDS/MAJORS: Athletic Trainer

For student members of National Athletic Trainers Association. Must be an upperclassman undergraduate or graduate student pursuing an academic program leading to a career in athletic training. A GPA of at least 3.0 is expected. Write to the address below for details.

National Athletic Trainers' Association
Grants And Scholarship Foundation, Inc.
2952 Stemmons Freeway
Dallas, TX 75247

4714
Undergraduate, President's Fellowships

AMOUNT: None Specified **DEADLINE:** Nov 30
FIELDS/MAJORS: All Areas Of Study

Fellowships are available at UCSD for undergraduate students involved in special studies and projects under faculty supervision. This award is for enrolled undergraduates only, not entering freshmen. Write to the address listed below for information.

University Of California, San Diego
Student Financial Services
9500 Gilman Drive
La Jolla, CA 92093

4715
Undergraduate/Graduate Rehabilitation Scholarships

AMOUNT: $750-$1,000 **DEADLINE:** Feb 15
FIELDS/MAJORS: Physical/Occupational/Speech/Hearing Therapy, Mental Health, Rehabilitation

Scholarships for female junior, senior, and graduate students enrolled in one of the programs listed above, who are on a campus with a KKG chapter. Must be a U.S. or Canadian citizen. Write to the address listed below for information.

Kappa Kappa Gamma
Mrs. L.A. Williams
4720 Pickett Road
Fairfax, VA 22032

4716
Underrepresented Minority Achievement Scholarships For Freshmen

AMOUNT: Varies **DEADLINE:** Mar 1
FIELDS/MAJORS: All Areas Of Study

Awards are available at Portland State University for African American, Hispanic, or Native American freshmen. Must maintain a GPA of at least 2.5 and be enrolled in at least twelve credits per term. Renewable for five years or fifteen terms. Write to the address below for more information.

Portland State University
Office Of Admissions
104 Neuberger Hall
Portland, OR 97207

4717
Underrepresented Minority Investigators In Asthma And Allergy Award

AMOUNT: $30,000 **DEADLINE:** Apr 14
FIELDS/MAJORS: Medical Research (Allergy/Immunology)

Research grants for minority scholars holding an M.D. or Ph.D. who are U.S. citizens or permanent residents. For research in the areas of asthma, allergy, infectious lung diseases. Write to the address below for details.

American Academy Of Allergy And Immunology
Jerome Schultz
611 East Wells St., 4th Floor
Milwaukee, WI 53202

4718

Underwood-Smith Teacher Scholarships

Amount: $5,000 **Deadline:** Apr 1
Fields/Majors: Education

Undergraduate and graduate students from West Virginia having outstanding academic credentials. Applicant's academic performance must be in the top 10% of their class. The intention is for a recipient to obtain a teaching certificate and to commit to an elementary or secondary teaching career in West Virginia. Must have a GPA of 3.25 and attend a school in West Virginia. Write to the address below for details.

State College And University Systems Of West Virginia
University Systems
P.O. Box 4007
Charleston, WV 25364

4719

Unico Scholarships

Amount: $500-$1,000 **Deadline:** None Specified
Fields/Majors: All Fields Of study.

Scholarship offered to high school senior who are residents of Madison. Two awards given. Write to the address below for details.

Unico Civic Organization
A.J. Donato
P.O. Box 3
Madison, NJ 07940

4720

Union Bank Scholarships

Amount: Varies **Deadline:** Apr 1
Fields/Majors: Business, Accounting, Economics, International Trade

Applicants must be of Japanese ancestry and California residents majoring in the above fields. Applications and information may be obtained from local JACL chapters, district offices, and the national headquarters at the address below. Please indicate your level of study and be certain to include a legal sized SASE.

Japanese American Citizens League
National Scholarship And Award Program
1765 Sutter St.
San Francisco, CA 94115

4721

Union Pacific Foundation Scholarship

Amount: $1,000 **Deadline:** Mar 1
Fields/Majors: Accounting

Scholarships are available at the University of Iowa for full-time seniors majoring in accounting. Write to the address listed below for information.

University Of Iowa
College Of Business Admin., Suite W160
108 Pappajohn Business Admin. Bldg.
Iowa City, IA 52245

4722

Union Pacific Foundation Scholarships

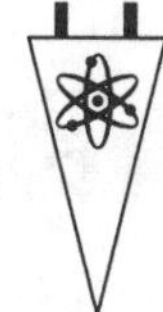

Amount: $1,000 **Deadline:** Feb 15
Fields/Majors: Agriculture

Scholarships for FFA members who are pursuing four-year degrees in any area of agriculture. Applicants must reside in Arkansas, California, Colorado, Idaho, Illinois, Iowa, Kansas, Louisiana, Missouri, Nebraska, Nevada, Oregon, Oklahoma, Texas, Utah, Washington, or Wyoming. Sixteen awards will be offered annually. Write to the address below for details.

National FFA Foundation
Scholarship Office
P.O. Box 15160
Alexandria, VA 22309

4723

Union Pacific Railroad Employee Dependent Scholarship Program

Amount: None Specified **Deadline:** Feb 1
Fields/Majors: All Areas Of Study

Scholarships for sons and daughters of employees of the Union Pacific Railroad (for at least one year by Sep 1 of year scholarship starts). Must be senior in high school, rank in upper 1/4th of class, and meet entrance requirements of the college you will be attending. Renewable. Sons and daughters of elected railroad officers are not eligible. No student may receive both an employee dependent and PU Corp Merit Scholarship. Dependents of retired or deceased employees are eligible. Write to the address below for details.

Union Pacific Railroad
Scholarship Administrator
1416 Dodge St., Room 320
Omaha, NE 68179

4724

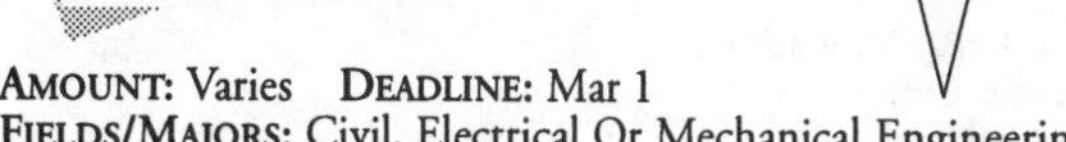

Union Pacific Railroad Scholarship

Amount: Varies **Deadline:** Mar 1
Fields/Majors: Civil, Electrical Or Mechanical Engineering

Awards are available at the University of New Mexico for minority or female juniors in the areas of study listed above. Must have a GPA of at least 3.0. Write to the address below for more information.

University Of New Mexico, Albuquerque
Office Of Financial Aid
Albuquerque, NM 87131

4725

United Daughters Of The Confederacy Scholarships

Amount: None Specified **Deadline:** None Specified
Fields/Majors: Nursing

Scholarships for lineal descendents of worthy confederates or collateral descendents who are members of the children of the confederacy or the United Daughters of the Confederacy. The ship island award is reserved for graduate studies. Includes the Phoebe Pember Memorial Scholarship, and Ship Island-Mrs. J.O. Jones Memorial Scholarship. Write to the UDC chapter nearest you. If address is not known, write to the address below for further information and the address.

United Daughters Of The Confederacy
Scholarship Coordinator
328 North Boulevard
Richmond, VA 23220

4726 United States Senate Youth Program

Amount: $2,000 **Deadline:** Oct 1
Fields/Majors: All Areas Of Study

Scholarships are available for graduating high school seniors who are class officers (president, vice president, secretary, treasurer) or student council representatives. Recipients will receive one week, all expenses paid, in Washington, DC, as a guest of the U.S. Senate. Two delegates will be chosen from each state and from the District of Columbia. Write to the address listed below for information.

William Randolph Hearst Foundation
90 New Montgomery St., Suite 1212
San Francisco, CA 94105

4727 United Students Of UAS-Juneau Full-Time Scholarships

GPA 3.0+

Amount: $1,000 **Deadline:** None Specified
Fields/Majors: All Areas Of Study

Scholarships are available at the University of Alaska, Juneau for full-time students. Based on academic achievement, leadership potential, and goal-oriented motivation. Undergraduate students must have a 3.0 GPA, and graduate students must have a GPA of at least 3.5. Write to the address listed below for information.

University Of Alaska-Southeast (Juneau)
Financial Aid Office
11120 Glacier Highway
Juneau, AK 99801

4728 Universal Leaf Tobacco Company Scholarships

Amount: $500 **Deadline:** Feb 15
Fields/Majors: Agribusiness

Scholarships are available for FFA members pursuing a two-year degree in agribusiness, who reside in North Carolina. Write to the address below for details.

National FFA Foundation
Scholarship Office
P.O. Box 15160
Alexandria, VA 22309

4729 University Achievement Class Award

GPA 2.5+

Amount: $1,000 Fee Waiver **Deadline:** Feb 15
Fields/Majors: All Areas Of Study

Scholarships are available at the University of Oklahoma, Norman for full-time minority students, who are graduating high school seniors of exceptional academic ability. Seventy-six awards offered annually. Write to the address listed below for information.

University Of Oklahoma, Norman
Prospective Student Services
Boyd House, 407 West Boyd St.
Norman, OK 73019

4730 University And Departmental Scholarships

Amount: Varies **Deadline:** None Specified
Fields/Majors: All Areas Of Study

Scholarships are available at Grand Canyon for full-time students. Based on academic ability, financial need, or both. Individual award requirements will vary. Write to the address listed below for information.

Grand Canyon University
Director Of Financial Aid
3300 W. Camelback Road, P.O. Box 11097
Phoenix, AZ 85601

4731 University Competitive Academic Scholarship Program

Amount: $200 **Deadline:** Apr 1
Fields/Majors: All Areas Of Study

Awards for freshmen or transfers at Sul Ross who have demonstrated academic excellence. Write to the address below for more information.

Sul Ross State University
Financial Aid Office
Box C-113
Alpine, TX 79832

4732 University Endowed Scholarships/Fellowships

GPA 3.5+

Amount: $2,000-$3,000 **Deadline:** Jan 8
Fields/Majors: All Areas Of Study

Applicants must be incoming freshmen who are ranked in the top 10% of their class and scored at least 1300 on the SAT (30 ACT). Semifinalists of the National Merit Scholarship competition are also eligible. Includes the Lechner Fellowship, McFadden Scholarship, and President's Endowed Scholarships. Recipients from outside of Texas qualify for a non-resident tuition waiver. Write to the address below for details.

Texas A & M University
University Honors Program
101 Academic Bldg.
College Station, TX 77843

4733 University Fellowships, And Assistantships

Amount: Varies **Deadline:** Feb 1
Fields/Majors: Any Area Of Study

University fellowships, university minority fellowship, teaching assistantship, and research assistantships offered to graduate students. Almost all of the graduate students receive university support for their studies. For more information write to the address below.

University Of Texas, Austin
Director Of Graduate Admissions
2608 Whittis
Austin, TX 78713

4734 University Fellowships, Teaching And Research Assistantships

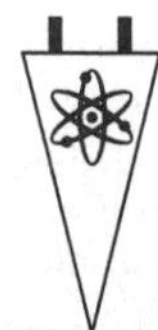

Amount: $9,000-$11,000 **Deadline:** Jan 5
Fields/Majors: Zoology, Biology, Ecology And Evolutionary Biology, And Related Fields

Fellowships and assistantships for graduate students in the department of zoology at University of Texas at Austin. Write to the address below for details.

University Of Texas, Austin
Graduate Coordinator
Department Of Zoology
Austin, TX 78712

4735

University Foundation & College/ Academic Dept. Awards (Upperclassmen)

AMOUNT: None Specified **DEADLINE:** Feb 1
FIELDS/MAJORS: All Areas Of Study

Scholarships are available to sophomore, junior, and senior students at unl. Based on various criteria, such as college, major, or financial need. Application is made by filing the "Application for Upperclass Scholarships," available from the deans of the colleges and from the address below.

University Of Nebraska, Lincoln
Office Of Scholarships And Financial Aid
16 Administration Bldg., P.O. Box 880411
Lincoln, NE 68588

4736

University Foundation & College/ Academic Dept. Scholarships (Freshmen)

AMOUNT: Varies **DEADLINE:** Jan 15
FIELDS/MAJORS: All Areas Of Study

Scholarships are available for UNL freshman. Based on various criteria, such as college, major, or financial need. Write to the address below for more information and to obtain an application for freshman scholarships.

University Of Nebraska, Lincoln
Office Of Scholarships And Financial Aid
16 Administration Bldg., P.O. Box 880411
Lincoln, NE 68588

4737

University Grants-In-Aid, University Loans (At CWRU)

AMOUNT: $100-$4,000 **DEADLINE:** Apr 30
FIELDS/MAJORS: All Areas Of Study

A Case Western Reserve University grant-in-aid is a tuition allowance awarded to a student who exhibits a combination of academic success and financial need. A university loan is a low-interest (8%) long-term loan to a student to assist with educational expenses. Grants-in-aid grants range from $100-$1,700. University loans grants range from $200-$4,000. Write to the address below for details.

Case Western Reserve University
Office Of Financial Aid, 109 Pardee Hall
10900 Euclid Ave.
Cleveland, OH 44106

4738

University Honors Program Scholarship

AMOUNT: $500 **DEADLINE:** None Specified
FIELDS/MAJORS: All Areas Of Study

Student must be enrolled in the honors program and have a good social standing. Five awards given with at least one recipient from each college (arts and sciences, business, professional studies). One award to a student who has completed the scholars program. Contact Dr. Jeanette Keith, Director of Scholars Program, Room 7 Bakeless Center. Phone (717) 389-4713.

Bloomsburg University
19 Ben Franklin Hall
400 E. Second St.
Blomsburg, PA 17815

4739

University Ladies Club Centennial Endowed Scholarship

AMOUNT: None Specified **DEADLINE:** Dec 1
FIELDS/MAJORS: All Areas Of Study

Two scholarships (one male and one female recipient) for graduates of an Austin high school. Not for recipients of other major awards. Must have a GPA of at least 3.25. Write to the address below for details.

University Of Texas, Austin
Office Of Student Financial Services
P.O. Box 7758
Austin, TX 78713

4740

University Of Alaska Scholarships

AMOUNT: Varies **DEADLINE:** None Specified
FIELDS/MAJORS: All Areas Of Study

Scholarships are available at the University of Alaska, Fairbanks for full-time students. Individual award requirements will vary. Fifteen new awards each year are given to Alaska Native and Native American students. Write to the address listed below for information.

University Of Alaska, Fairbanks
Financial Aid Office
P.O. Box 756360
Fairbanks, AK 99775

4741

University Of Central Oklahoma Funeral Service Scholarships

AMOUNT: $250-$400 **DEADLINE:** None Specified
FIELDS/MAJORS: Mortuary Science

Awards for students enrolled in the funeral service program at the University of Central Oklahoma. Write to the address below for more information.

University Of Central Oklahoma
Office Of Financial Aid
Edmond, OK 73034

4742

University Of Guam Scholarships, Grants, And Loans

AMOUNT: Varies **DEADLINE:** Varies
FIELDS/MAJORS: All Areas Of Study

Scholarships, grants, and loans offered to students enrolled or planning to enroll in the University of Guam. Other requirements may be necessary for eligibility. Write to the university at the address below for details.

University Of Guam
Financial Aid Office
303 University Dr.
Mangilao, GU 96923

4743
University Of Iowa National Merit Scholarship

Amount: $750-$2,000 **Deadline:** None Specified
Fields/Majors: All Areas Of Study

Scholarships for students who were named finalists in the National Merit Scholarship Contest, and chose U of I as their first school of choice. Contact the office of student financial aid for details.

University Of Iowa
Office Of Student Financial Aid
208 Calvin Hall
Iowa City, IA 52242

4744
University Of Iowa Tuition Scholarships

GPA 3.0+

Amount: $200-Tuition **Deadline:** None Specified
Fields/Majors: All Areas Of Study

Scholarships are available at the University of Iowa for undergraduates who demonstrate financial need and academic merit. Entering freshmen must have an ACT score of 28 or more and be in the top 10% of their class. Returning students must have a GPA of at least 3.0. Write to the address listed below for information.

University Of Iowa
Office Of Student Financial Aid
208 Calvin Hall
Iowa City, IA 52242

4745
University Of Michigan Club Of Downriver

Amount: $500 **Deadline:** Jun 17
Fields/Majors: All Areas Of Study

Scholarships are available to Downriver students attending the University of Michigan at Ann Arbor, Dearborn or Flint. Candidates must be at a full-time sophomore with a "C" plus grade average of better and working towards an undergraduate degree. Write to the address below for more information. Applications must be requested by May 6.

U-M Club Of Downriver
Scholarship Committee
P.O. Box 294
Trenton, MI 48183

4746
University Of Redlands Achievement Award

Amount: $5,000 (max) **Deadline:** Dec 15
Fields/Majors: All Areas Of Study

Awarded to students who have demonstrated an unusual degree of leadership and accomplishment in school or community activities. Renewable with a GPA of at least a 3.0. For undergraduate study. Write to the address below for more details.

University Of Redlands
Office Of Financial Aid
1200 East Colton Ave., P.O. Box 3080
Redlands, CA 92373

4747
University Of San Diego Scholarships/Grants

Amount: Varies **Deadline:** Feb 20
Fields/Majors: All Areas Of Study

Scholarships are available at the University of San Diego for students who demonstrate academic excellence, potential for success, and financial need. Write to the address listed below for information.

University Of San Diego
Office Of Financial Aid
5998 Alcala Park
San Diego, CA 92110

4748
University Of Toledo Scholarships

Amount: $100-$5,000 **Deadline:** Jan 26
Fields/Majors: All Areas Of Study

Over 300 freshmen scholarships, as well as scholarships for continuing and transfer students, are administered by the UT financial aid office. Renewable based on continued academic success at UT. "The freshman academic scholarship application is required for all general scholarships." Contact the financial aid office for details.

University Of Toledo
Office Of Student Financial Aid
4023 Gillham Hall, 2801 W. Bancroft St.
Toledo, OH 43606

4749
University Of Utah General Scholarships

Amount: Varies **Deadline:** Feb 15
Fields/Majors: All Areas Of Study

The following scholarships are available to students with financial need: the Katherine J. McClellan, George and Suzanne Nebeker, Peggy Lundquist Olson, Jack M. and Freda T. Pringle, Seimens, George Thomas, and Mark Weiss scholarships. Individual award requirements may vary. Write to the address below for information.

University Of Utah
Financial Aid And Scholarships Office
105 Student Services Building
Salt Lake City, UT 84112

4750
University Of Utah Merit Scholarship

Amount: $500 **Deadline:** Feb 1
Fields/Majors: All Areas Of Study

Scholarships are available at the University of Utah for full-time students who are National Merit Scholarship Finalists. Write to the address below for details. Information is also available from your high school guidance counselor.

University Of Utah
Financial Aid And Scholarship Office
105 Student Services Building
Salt Lake City, UT 84112

4751

University Of Utah Merit Scholarship With Presidential Honors

AMOUNT: $1,250 **DEADLINE:** Feb 1
FIELDS/MAJORS: All Areas Of Study

Scholarships are available at the University of Utah for full-time students who are National Merit Scholarship Finalists, and who meet the criteria for the president's scholarship. Write to the address below for details. Information is also available from your high school guidance counselor.

University Of Utah
Financial Aid And Scholarship Office
105 Student Services Building
Salt Lake City, UT 84112

4752

University Of Utah Young Alumni Scholarship

AMOUNT: Varies **DEADLINE:** Mar 17
FIELDS/MAJORS: All Areas Of Study

Scholarships are available at the University of Utah for full-time senior students who demonstrate significant extracurricular activities and community involvement. Write to the address below for information.

University Of Utah
Alumni House
155 S. Central Campus Drive
Salt Lake City, UT 84112

4753

University Opportunity Scholarships

AMOUNT: $2,100 **DEADLINE:** Mar 1
FIELDS/MAJORS: All Areas Of Study

Awards for high school seniors with an ACT score of 29 or better and a GPA of at least 3.5. Renewable with a GPA of 3.0 or higher. Write to the address below for more information.

Auburn University
Office Of Student Financial Aid
203 Mary Martin Hall
Auburn University, AL 36849

4754

University Scholar Award

AMOUNT: Tuition & Fees **DEADLINE:** Mar 1
FIELDS/MAJORS: All Areas Of Study

Scholarships are available at Northern Illinois University for full-time entering freshmen in the top 5% of their high school graduating class, with high ACT scores or transfer students from a community college with a GPA of at least 3.5. Write to the address listed below for information.

Northern Illinois University
University Scholarship Committee
DeKalb, IL 60115

4755

University Scholarship

AMOUNT: Tuition And Fees **DEADLINE:** Jan 15
FIELDS/MAJORS: All Areas Of Study

Awards for entering freshman who rank in the upper 10% of their class and have an ACT composite score of 30 or above or have been selected as National Merit Finalists. Renewable with a GPA of at least 3.5. Write to the address below for more details.

Southwest Missouri State University
Financial Aid Office
901 South National Ave.
Springfield, MO 65804

4756

University Scholarship, Centennial Scholarship

AMOUNT: Half Tuition
DEADLINE: None Specified
FIELDS/MAJORS: Architecture And Planning, Arts And Sciences, Engineering, Library And Information Science, Music, Nursing, Social Services, Philosophy, Religious Studies

Scholarships are available at the Catholic University of America for graduate students enrolled in the above schools. Contact the financial aid office at the address below for details.

The Catholic University Of America
Office Of Admissions And Financial Aid
Washington, DC 20064

4757

University Scholarships

AMOUNT: $6,000 (max) **DEADLINE:** Jan 15
FIELDS/MAJORS: All Areas Of Study

Scholarships of $500 to $6,000 are available to undergraduate students at the University of Pittsburgh who maintain at least a 3.0 GPA. Renewable. Write to the address below for details.

University Of Pittsburgh
Office Of Admissions And Financial Aid
Bruce Hall, Second Floor
Pittsburgh, PA 15260

4758

University Scholarships

AMOUNT: $7,800 **DEADLINE:** Feb 1
FIELDS/MAJORS: All Areas Of Study

Awards for entering students based on academics. Must have a GPA of at least 3.8 and a minimum SAT score of 1300 or ACT score of 30. Renewable with continued academic achievement. Write to the address below for more information.

Rhodes College
Office Of Admissions
2000 North Parkway
Memphis, TN 38112

4759

University Scholarships

AMOUNT: $10,000 **DEADLINE:** Jun 1
FIELDS/MAJORS: All Areas Of Study

Awards for entering freshmen who have a high school GPA of 3.7 or better and an ACT score of at least 31 or SAT score of 1350. Scholarships can be pro-rated for part-time attendance. Ten given per year. Write to the address below for more information.

Long Island University
Financial Aid Office
Southampton, NY 11968

4760

University Scholarships

AMOUNT: $5,000 **DEADLINE:** Apr 1
FIELDS/MAJORS: All Areas Of Study

Awards for entering freshmen who have demonstrated academic excellence. Applicants must have a GPA of at least 3.6 and SAT scores of 1170 or ACT scores of 28 or better. Also based on a scholarship competition held at the university. Renewable with a GPA of 3.25. Write to the address below for more information.

Baker University
Office Of Financial Aid
P.O. Box 65
Baldwin City, KS 66006

4761

University Scholarships, Fellowships, Merit Awards And Assistantships

AMOUNT: Varies **DEADLINE:** None Specified
FIELDS/MAJORS: All Areas Of Study

Merit-based and need-based scholarships are available for students studying at the graduate level at the University of Maryland, Baltimore (and UMD-Baltimore County). Special graduate fellowships are reserved for African American students. Contact the graduate admissions office or the financial aid office for details.

University Of Maryland, Baltimore
Graduate School
5401 Wilkens Ave.
Baltimore, MD 21228

4762

University Symphony League Scholarship

AMOUNT: $400-$600 **DEADLINE:** Mar 1
FIELDS/MAJORS: All Areas Of Study

Award for a student at Eastern New Mexico University who is active in the university symphony orchestra in the string section. Must be recommended by the orchestra director and approved by the members of the University symphony league board. Write to the address below for more information.

Eastern New Mexico University
College Of Fine Arts
Station 16
Portales, NM 88130

4763

University Women's Association Scholarship

AMOUNT: $1,000 **DEADLINE:** Mar 1
FIELDS/MAJORS: All Areas Of Study

Scholarships are available at the University of Oklahoma, Norman for junior or senior students who are Oklahoma residents, with a GPA of at least 3.5. Write to the address listed below for information.

University Of Oklahoma, Norman
Office Of Financial Aid Services
731 Elm
Norman, OK 73019

4764

UNM Architecture Scholarships

AMOUNT: Varies **DEADLINE:** Mar 1
FIELDS/MAJORS: Architecture

Scholarships are available at the University of New Mexico for full-time architecture students. Includes the Friends of the School of Architecture and Planning, Albuquerque Chapter American Institute of Architects, and the Blankman Foundation Scholarships. Individual award requirements may vary. Write to the address listed below for information.

University Of New Mexico, Albuquerque
School Of Architecture
Office Of The Dean
Albuquerque, NM 87131

4765

UNM Engineering Alumni Club Scholarship

AMOUNT: Varies **DEADLINE:** Mar 1
FIELDS/MAJORS: Engineering

Awards are available at the University of New Mexico for junior level and above engineering students with academic potential and financial need. Juniors and seniors must have a GPA of at least 2.0 and graduate students must have a GPA of at least 3.0. Write to the address below for more information.

University Of New Mexico, Albuquerque
Office Of Financial Aid
Albuquerque, NM 87131

4766

UNM Golf Scholarships

AMOUNT: None Specified **DEADLINE:** Mar 1
FIELDS/MAJORS: All Areas Of Study

Scholarships are available at the University of New Mexico for full-time students who will be participating in the Intercollegiate Golf Program. Includes the J.R. "Bob" Carriveau Memorial Golf Scholarship, the Urrea Golf Scholarship, and the University Golfers' Association Scholarship (requires New Mexico residency.) Write to the address listed below for information.

University Of New Mexico, Albuquerque
Department Of Student Financial Aid
Mesa Vista Hall North
Albuquerque, NM 87131

4767

UNM Management Scholarships

AMOUNT: None Specified **DEADLINE:** Mar 1
FIELDS/MAJORS: Business

Scholarships are available at the University of New Mexico for full-time business majors. Includes the Clinton P. Anderson Memorial Scholarship, the Nat F. De Palma Scholarship, the Ben Lomond Roberts Memorial Scholarships, and the J.C. Penney Scholarship. Individual award requirements may vary. Write to the address listed below for information.

University Of New Mexico, Albuquerque
Department Of Student Financial Aid
Mesa Vista Hall North
Albuquerque, NM 87131

4768

UNM Scholars Program

AMOUNT: Tuition **DEADLINE:** Feb 1
FIELDS/MAJORS: All Areas Of Study

Scholarships are available at the University of New Mexico for entering freshmen who graduated in the top 20% of their class, have above average SAT/ACT scores, and leadership skills. Renewable for up to seven more semesters. Up to 300 awards are offered annually. Write to the address listed below for information.

University Of New Mexico, Albuquerque
Student Financial Aid Office
Mesa Vista Hall North, Student Services
Albuquerque, NM 87131

4769

UNO Scholarships

GPA 2.5+

AMOUNT: $250-$3,000 **DEADLINE:** Feb 15
FIELDS/MAJORS: All Areas Of Study

Scholarships are available at the University of New Orleans for full-time students. Includes the UNO Alumni Association Scholarships, Chancellor's Scholarships, Decennial Honor Awards, Bienville Scholarships for campus housing, Founders' Scholarships, and Freshman Honor Awards. Individual award requirements will vary. Write to the address below for details.

University Of New Orleans
Student Financial Aid Office
1005 Administration Building, Lake Front
New Orleans, LA 70148

4770

Unocal 76 Scholarships

AMOUNT: $1,000 **DEADLINE:** Feb 15
FIELDS/MAJORS: All Areas Of Study

Scholarships are available for FFA members pursuing a four-year degree in any area of study, who reside in California or Washington. Write to the address below for details.

National FFA Foundation
Scholarship Office
P.O. Box 15160
Alexandria, VA 22309

4771

Upper Iowa Programs

AMOUNT: Varies **DEADLINE:** None Specified
FIELDS/MAJORS: All Areas Of Study

Awards are available for students at Upper Iowa University. Various criteria such as academic record, major field of study, or religious affiliation will determine eligibility for different awards. Write to the address below for more information.

Upper Iowa University
Office Of Enrollment Management
605 Washington St.
Fayette, IA 52142

4772

Upper Mid-Atlantic Regional Scholarship In Memory Of John Basilone

AMOUNT: $1,000 **DEADLINE:** May 31
FIELDS/MAJORS: All Areas Of Study

Scholarships for Italian American residents of New York and northern New Jersey (north of Trenton). For undergraduate study. Write to the address listed below for information.

National Italian American Foundation
Dr. Maria Lombardo, Education Director
1860 19th St., NW
Washington, DC 20009

4773

Upperclass Finance Scholarships

AMOUNT: $500-$1,000 **DEADLINE:** Feb 3
FIELDS/MAJORS: Finance

Scholarships are available at the University of Oklahoma, Norman for full-time junior or senior finance majors. Write to the address listed below for information.

University Of Oklahoma, Norman
Director, Division Of Finance
205-A Adams Hall
Norman, OK 73019

4774

Upperclass Merit Scholarships

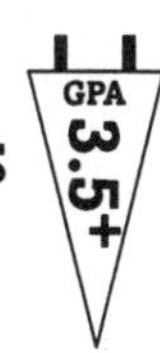

AMOUNT: $500 **DEADLINE:** May 15
FIELDS/MAJORS: All Areas Of Study

Awards are available for upperclass students with at least twenty-four credit hours and a GPA of 3.75 or better. Write to the address below for more information.

University Of Pittsburgh
Office Of Admissions And Financial Aid
Bruce Hall, Second Floor
Pittsburgh, PA 15260

4775

Upperclass Minority Scholarship

AMOUNT: None Specified **DEADLINE:** Apr 30
FIELDS/MAJORS: All Areas Of Study

Applicants must be currently enrolled MSU minority students with a GPA of 2.5 or better. Write to the address below for more information.

Moorhead State University
Office Of Scholarship And Financial Aid
107 Owens Hall, Campus Box 327
Moorhead, MN 56563

4776

Upperclassman Fee Waiver

AMOUNT: Tuition **DEADLINE:** May 1
FIELDS/MAJORS: All Areas Of Study

Applicants can be full time or part time undergraduate or graduate students. Must have a GPA of 2.7 or better and be an active member of a university club or organization. Transfer students are welcome to apply. Write to the address below for more information.

Southwestern Oklahoma State University
Student Financial Services Office
100 Campus Dr
Weatherford, OK 73096

4777

Urban And Public Affairs Memorial Award

Amount: $500 **Deadline:** Mar 15
Fields/Majors: Urban And Public Affairs

Awards are available to outstanding students in the urban and public affairs department who are recommended by their department and chosen by a faculty committee. The award rotates among the four academic departments of the school. Write to the address below for more information.

Portland State University
Dean's Office
101 School Of Urban And Public Affairs
Portland, OR 97207

4778

Urban And Rural Teacher Loan Forgiveness Program

Amount: $10,000 (max) **Deadline:** Nov 1
Fields/Majors: Teaching

Applicant must be a first-year full-time permanent teacher, have a Pennsylvania teaching certificate that entitles you to teach in Pennsylvania, and be employed on a full-time, permanent basis at a commonwealth-designated urban or rural public district or at a nonprofit, nonpublic school. Up to $2,500 of loan debts are forgiven per year of employment. Write to the address below for more information.

Pennsylvania Higher Education Assistance Agency
1200 N. 7th St.
P.O. Box 8114
Harrisburg, PA 17102

4779

Urban Fellows Program

Amount: $18,000 **Deadline:** Jan 20
Fields/Majors: Urban Government, Public Administration, Planning, Public Service

Full-time program lasting nine months that combines work in mayoral offices and city agencies with an intensive seminar component that explores key issues facing New York city government. For recent bachelor's degree holder (must have received degree within past two years). For New York residents. Write to the address below for complete details.

New York City Department Of Personnel
Urban Fellows Program
2 Washington St., 15th Floor
New York, NY 10004

4780

Urban Studies Awards

Amount: None Specified **Deadline:** None Specified
Fields/Majors: Urban studies

Internships for graduate students in the school of urban studies at Wayne State University. Write to the address below for details.

Wayne State University
Center For Urban Studies
3049 Faculty Adminitration Bldg.
Detroit, MI 48202

4781

USC Fellowships

Amount: Varies **Deadline:** Varies
Fields/Majors: All Areas Of Study

For graduate students. Based on academics, leadership, and need. Includes the Norman Topping Student Aid Fund (student must perform 20 hours of community service), the All-University Predoctoral Merit Fellowship, graduate assistantships, and department fellowships. Write to the graduate school for information on the All-University awards, the Director of the Norman Topping Fund for the Topping award, and to your department for other awards.

University Of Southern California
Office Of Graduate Admissions, University Park
Los Angeles, CA 90089

4782

USL Capital Scholarships

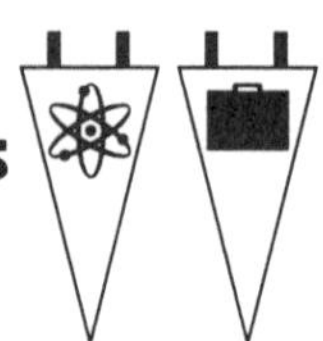

Amount: $1,000 **Deadline:** Feb 15
Fields/Majors: Agriculture, Agribusiness, Animal Science

Scholarships are available for FFA members pursuing a four-year degree in any area of study, who reside in northern California. Write to the address below for details.

National FFA Foundation
Scholarship Office
P.O. Box 15160
Alexandria, VA 22309

4783

Utah Achievement Award

Amount: Varies **Deadline:** Feb 1
Fields/Majors: All Areas Of Study

Scholarships are available at the University of Utah for full-time entering freshmen or transfer students with a GPA of at least 3.5. Write to the address below for information.

University Of Utah
Suzanne Espinoza
80 Olpin Union
Salt Lake City, UT 84112

4784

Utah Career Teaching Scholarship

Amount: $1,000 **Deadline:** Mar 30, Apr 15
Fields/Majors: Education

Scholarships are available at the University of Utah for full-time students planning to become teachers in Utah. Must have a 2.7 or better GPA. Transfer and continuing student deadline is Apr 15 and the freshman deadline is Mar 30. Write to the address below for details.

University Of Utah
Education Advising Center
226 Milton Bennion Hall
Salt Lake City, UT 84112

4785 Utah State Student Incentive Grant

Amount: $2,500 (max) **Deadline:** Feb 15
Fields/Majors: All Areas Of Study

Scholarships for residents of Utah who demonstrate financial need. For undergraduate study in a Utah college or university. Write to the address below for details. Information is also available from your high school guidance counselor.

Utah State Board Of Regents
355 W. North Temple
3 Triad Center, Suite 550
Salt Lake City, UT 84180

4786 UTE Chapter Of Professional Engineers Of Colorado Scholarship

Amount: $500 **Deadline:** None Specified
Fields/Majors: Engineering

Award for Mesa State students entering their sophomore year of an associate engineering program who have the intention of completing their baccalaureate in an engineering program. Must have a GPA of at least 2.5. Preference given to Western Slope residents. Contact the school of natural science and math for more details.

Mesa State College
Office Of Financial Aid
P.O. Box 2647
Grand Junction, CO 81501

4787 Utility Workers Union Of America Merit Scholarships Program

Amount: $500-$2,000 **Deadline:** Dec 31
Fields/Majors: All Areas Of Study

Must be a child of a member of the utility workers union of America, AFL-CIO. Winners are juniors who took the National Merit Scholarship exams. Criteria: high school academic records, test scores, qualities of leadership, etc. Two four-year scholarships awarded annually. Write to the address below for details.

Utility Workers Union Of America, AFL-CIO
Merit Scholarships Program
815 16th St., NW, #605
Washington, DC 20006

4788 UTUIA Scholarships

Amount: $500 **Deadline:** Mar 31
Fields/Majors: All Areas Of Study

For U.S. citizens who are high school graduates under 25 years of age. Must be UTU members; or children/grandchildren of UTU members. Must maintain satisfactory academic record. For full-time study at a community college, vocational-technical school, or four-year college/university. Fifty awards offered each year. Renewable for up to three more years. Write to the address listed below for additional information.

United Transportation Union Insurance Association
Utuia Scholarship Program
14600 Detroit Ave.
Cleveland, OH 44107

4789 UWO Accounting Club Scholarship

Amount: $150 **Deadline:** Early Spring
Fields/Majors: Accounting

Awards for accounting majors who are graduating within two years. Must show a high level of achievement through academic and extracurricular activities. Extracurricular activities will be broadly viewed to include employment activity that aided in the financing of the student's education. Contact the Department of Accounting, UW Oshkosh, for more details.

University Of Wisconsin, Oshkosh
Financial Aid Office, Dempsey 104
800 Algoma Blvd.
Oshkosh, WI 54901

4790 UWP License Plate Scholarship

Amount: $300 **Deadline:** Feb 1
Fields/Majors: All Areas Of Study

Awards for incoming freshmen at UW Platteville who are Wisconsin residents. Must show participation in co-curricular activities, outstanding leadership abilities, strong character, campus involvement, and academic achievement. Write to the address below or contact the office at (608) 342-1125 for more information.

University Of Wisconsin, Platteville
Office Of Admissions And Enrollment Mgt.
Platteville, WI 53818

4791 Valmont Irrigation Scholarships

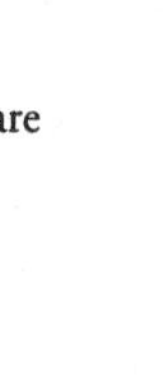

Amount: $1,000 **Deadline:** Feb 15
Fields/Majors: Agriculture

Scholarships are available for FFA members pursuing a four-year degree in any area of agriculture. Five awards are offered annually. Write to the address below for details.

National FFA Foundation
Scholarship Office
P.O. Box 15160
Alexandria, VA 22309

4792 Van Alen Fellowship In Public Architecture

Amount: Varies **Deadline:** May 6
Fields/Majors: Architecture, Architectural Engineering

Open to architecture and architectural engineering students around the world. Should be currently enrolled in a degree granting program. Write to the institute at the address below for information on this and other award programs. Information must be requested in January of the year you are applying.

Van Alen Institute
Design Competitions
30 W. 22nd St.
New York, NY 10010

4793

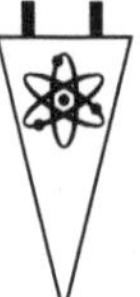

Van Bloem Gardens Horticultural Scholarship

AMOUNT: $1,500 **DEADLINE:** Mar 1
FIELDS/MAJORS: Horticulture

Open to juniors in horticulture who has demonstrated academic excellence and commitment to the horticulture industry. Write to the address below for more information.

California State Polytechnic University, Pomona
College Of Agriculture
Building 7, Room 110
Pomona, CA 91768

4794

Van Harreveld Memorial Award

AMOUNT: $250 **DEADLINE:** None Specified
FIELDS/MAJORS: Neuroscience

Awards are available to students interested in neuroscience. The recipient must be the first author on the abstract presented at the APS annual meeting. Write to the address below for more information.

American Psychology Society
Membership Services Office
9560 Rockville Pike
Bethesda, MD 20814

4795

Velma P. Foster Memorial Scholarship

AMOUNT: $400 **DEADLINE:** None Specified
FIELDS/MAJORS: Elementary Education

Award available to juniors, seniors or graduate students in elementary education degree programs at the University of Texas, El Paso. Must be an El Paso County resident. Write to the address listed below for further information.

El Paso Community Foundation
201 East Main
Suite 1616
El Paso, TX 79901

4796

Venango Campus Scholarship

AMOUNT: None Specified **DEADLINE:** None Specified
FIELDS/MAJORS: All Areas Of Study

Scholarships for students are based on academic record, participation in extracurricular activities, and financial aid. Contact the administrative office, Venango campus for more information.

Clarion University
104 Egbert Hall
Office Of Financial Aid
Clarion, PA 16214

4797

Ventura County Minority Business Group Scholarships

AMOUNT: $4,000 **DEADLINE:** Apr 8
FIELDS/MAJORS: Business

Applicants must be high school graduating seniors in the spring of the year of application. They must be a minority student who is enrolled, or intending to enroll, as a candidate for a business-related degree at a fully accredited college, university, vocation, trade or business school. Must have a GPA of 3.0 or better. Write to the address below for more information.

Ventura County Community Foundation
1355 Del Norte Rd.
Camarillo, CA 93010

4798

Vermont American Legion Scholarship Program

AMOUNT: $500-$1,000 **DEADLINE:** Apr 15
FIELDS/MAJORS: All Areas Of Study

Scholarships for graduating high school seniors from Vermont high schools. Contact your school guidance counselor or principal or write to the address below for details.

American Legion, Department Of Vermont
Education And Scholarship Committee
P.O. Box 396
Montpelier, VT 05602

4799

Vermont Scholarship Program

AMOUNT: $250 Per Year **DEADLINE:** None Specified
FIELDS/MAJORS: All Areas Of Study

Scholarships available to residents of Vermont who will be enrolling in college as entering freshmen. Applicant must be a U.S. citizen and be able to demonstrate financial need and academic excellence. Renewable for two or four years. Write to the address listed below for additional information.

American Legion, Department Of Vermont
Education And Scholarship Committee
P.O. Box 396
Montpelier, VT 05601

4800

Verne Catt McDowell Corporation Scholarship

AMOUNT: None Specified **DEADLINE:** None
FIELDS/MAJORS: Theology/Religion

Applicants must be members of the Christian church (Disciples of Christ) and accepted into a professional degree program in theology leading to service in the ministry. Preference given to members of First Christian Church, Albany, Oregon. Four to six students are supported on a monthly basis. Write to the address shown below for details.

Verne Catt McDowell Corporation
P.O. Box 1336
Albany, OR 97321

4801

Vernon And Mary Jane Shepherd Scholarship Fund

Amount: None Specified **Deadline:** None Specified
Fields/Majors: Nursing

Scholarships are open to ASN students in their first, second, or third semester of study who are 30 or older, have family responsibilities with dependent children, and maintain a GPA of 3.0 or higher. Write to the address below for more information.

Indiana University/Purdue University, Indianapolis
School Of Nursing
1111 Middle Dr., Nu 122
Indianapolis, IN 46202

4802

Vernon E. Goedken Scholarships

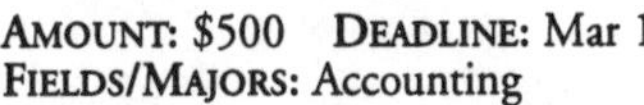

Amount: $500 **Deadline:** Mar 1
Fields/Majors: Accounting

Scholarships are available at the University of Iowa for full-time undergraduates majoring in accounting. Financial need is considered. Write to the address listed below for information.

University Of Iowa
College Of Business Admin., Suite W160
108 Pappajohn Business Admin. Bldg.
Iowa City, IA 52245

4803

Vernon E. Goedken Scholarships

Amount: $1,000 **Deadline:** Mar 1
Fields/Majors: Accounting

Scholarships are available at the University of Iowa for full-time undergraduates majoring in accounting. Write to the address listed below for information.

University Of Iowa
College Of Business Admin., Suite W160
108 Pappajohn Business Admin. Bldg.
Iowa City, IA 52245

4804

Vernon Rochester Award

Amount: $1,000 **Deadline:** None Specified
Fields/Majors: All Areas Of Study

Football award for player(s) who have shown the most courage during football season. Recipient chosen by the coaches and physical therapist. If student is graduating senior, scholarship may be used for graduate school. Send requests for information to the director of athletics at address below.

Bloomsburg University
19 Ben Franklin Hall
400 E. Second St.
Bloomsburg, PA 17815

4805

Vertical Flight Foundation Scholarships

Amount: $2,000 (max) **Deadline:** Feb 1
Fields/Majors: Aerospace Engineering, Helicopter/Vertical Flight

Annual scholarships to undergraduate or graduate students who

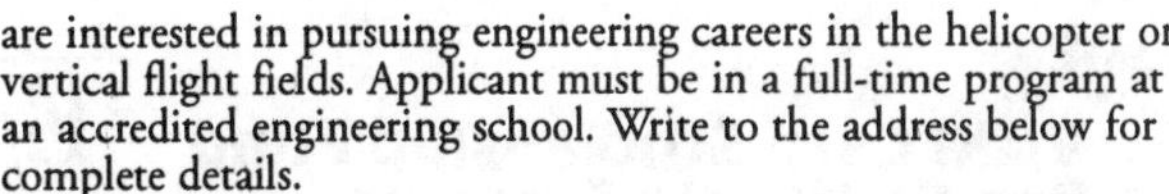

are interested in pursuing engineering careers in the helicopter or vertical flight fields. Applicant must be in a full-time program at an accredited engineering school. Write to the address below for complete details.

Vertical Flight Foundation
217 N. Washington St.
Alexandria, VA 22314

4806

Very Reverend Walter J. Schmitz, Johannes Quasten Scholarships

Amount: Varies **Deadline:** None Specified
Fields/Majors: Religious Studies

Scholarships are available at the Catholic University of America for graduate religious studies students. Contact the financial aid office at the address below for details.

The Catholic University Of America
Office Of Admissions And Financial Aid
Washington, DC 20064

4807

Veterans Dependents Educational Assistance Program

Amount: $7,000 **Deadline:** None Specified
Fields/Majors: All Areas Of Study

Applicants must be surviving children, widows, or spouses of California veterans who are service connected disabled or died of service related causes. Award must be used at California state-supported schools only. Write to the address below for details.

California Department Of Veterans Affairs
Division Of Veterans Services
P.O. Box 942895
Sacramento, CA 94295

4808

Veterans Dependents Educational Benefits

Amount: Varies **Deadline:** None Specified
Fields/Majors: All Areas Of Study

Open to undergraduate Maine residents who are children or spouses of veterans who are totally disabled due to service or who died in service. Write to the address below for details.

Maine Bureau Of Veteran Services
State House Station, #117
Augusta, ME 04333

4809

Vice Admiral E.P. Travers Scholarship And Loan

Amount: $2,000-$3,000 **Deadline:** None Specified
Fields/Majors: All Areas Of Study

Grants for sons and daughters of active duty servicemembers (USN, USMC, USGC). Based primarily on need, with academic progress also considered. Must have a GPA of at least 2.0. Write to the address below for information. Please indicate the name of the award program when requesting information.

Navy-Marine Corps Relief Society
Education Programs
801 N. Randolph St., Ste 1228
Arlington, VA 22203

4810

Vicki Carr Scholarship Fund For California Students

AMOUNT: None Specified **DEADLINE:** Apr 15
FIELDS/MAJORS: All Areas Of Study

Awards for California residents of Latino heritage. Must be between the ages of 17 and 22. Must be a legal U.S. Resident. Send a #10 SASE to the address below for an official application. Applications will only be accepted between Feb 1 and Apr 15.

Vikki Carr Scholarship Foundation
P.O. Box 5126
Beverly Hills, CA 90210

4811

Vicki Carr Scholarship Fund For Texas Students

AMOUNT: None Specified **DEADLINE:** Mar 1
FIELDS/MAJORS: All Areas Of Study

Awards for Texas residents of Latino heritage. Must be between the ages of 17 and 22. Must be a legal U.S. Resident. Send a #10 SASE to the address below for an official application. Applications will only be accepted between Jan 1 and Mar 1.

Vikki Carr Scholarship Foundation
P.O. Box 780968
San Antonio, TX 78278

4812

Vicki Howard Community Service Award

AMOUNT: $500 **DEADLINE:** Apr 8
FIELDS/MAJORS: All Areas Of Study

Awards for graduating high school seniors from the Simi Valley/Moorpark area who have shown outstanding dedication to his/her community through community service. Applicants must have a GPA of 3.0 or greater and be enrolled or intending to enroll as a degree candidate at a fully accredited college, vocation, trade, or business school. Write to the address below or contact your high school counselor for more information.

Ventura County Community Fund
1355 Del Norte Road
Camarillo, CA 93010

4813

Vietnam Veteran's Scholarship Program

AMOUNT: Varies **DEADLINE:** None Specified
FIELDS/MAJORS: All Areas Of Study

Vietnam veterans are eligible for scholarships to attend New Mexico schools. Must be a resident of New Mexico and eligibility must be certified by the New Mexico Veteran's Service Commission. Write to the address listed below or contact the financial aid office at the New Mexico school of your choice.

New Mexico Veterans' Service Commission
P.O. Box 2324
Santa Fe, NM 87503

4814

Vin Gupta, And Richard H. Larsen Scholarships

AMOUNT: Varies **DEADLINE:** Jan 15
FIELDS/MAJORS: All Areas Of Study

Scholarships for promising minority students entering UNL as freshmen. Based on grades, leadership, and extracurricular activities. Gupta scholarship is for students of engineering and the physical sciences. Write to the address below for details.

University Of Nebraska, Lincoln
Office Of Scholarships And Financial Aid
16 Administration Bldg., P.O. Box 880411
Lincoln, NE 68588

4815

Vincent & Anna Visceglia Fellowship

AMOUNT: $1,000 **DEADLINE:** May 31
FIELDS/MAJORS: Italian Studies

Fellowships are available for Italian American students working on their master's degree or doctorate in Italian studies. Write to the address below for details.

National Italian American Foundation
Dr. Maria Lombardo, Education Director
1860 19th St., NW
Washington, DC 20009

4816

Vincent Astor Memorial Foundation Award

AMOUNT: $500-$1,500 **DEADLINE:** Feb 15
FIELDS/MAJORS: All Areas Of Study

Award for best essay on a topic that relates to leadership in the Navy, Marines, or Coast Guard. For junior officers and officer trainees in the USN, USMC, and USGC. Write to the address below for details.

U.S. Naval Institute
Naval Institute Essay And Photo Contests
118 Maryland Ave.
Annapolis, MD 21402

4817

Vincent K. Derscheid Scholarship Fund

AMOUNT: $2,500 **DEADLINE:** Nov 30
FIELDS/MAJORS: Accounting

Scholarships are available for junior accounting majors enrolled in a regionally accredited accounting program at a Wisconsin college or university. Based on academic achievement, extracurricular activities, community service, and recommendations from educators. Write to the address listed below for information.

WICPA Educational Foundation, Inc.
180 N. Executive Drive
P.O. Box 1010
Brookfield, WI 53008

4818

Violet C. Moore Memorial Award

Amount: Varies **Deadline:** Mar 1
Fields/Majors: Theater And Drama

Awards are available at the University of New Mexico for full-time theater students at the senior level of study who exhibit excellence in performance. Write to the address below for more information.

University Of New Mexico, Albuquerque
Office Of Financial Aid
Albuquerque, NM 87131

4819

Virgil C. Self Scholarship

Amount: Varies **Deadline:** None Specified
Fields/Majors: Music

Annual award given to an ETSU sophomore, junior, or senior music major who is concentrating in keyboard or voice, with first preference given to organ. Applicant must have a GPA of at least 3.0. Contact the department of music or the office of financial aid for details.

East Tennessee State University
Office Of Financial Aid
Box 70722
Johnson City, TN 37614

4820

Virgil Cheek Memorial Scholarship

Amount: $300 **Deadline:** None Specified
Fields/Majors: Business

Student must be a junior or senior COBA major with leadership potential, scholastic achievement and financial need. Contact the COBA office for more information.

Southwest Missouri State University
Office Of Financial Aid
901 South National Ave.
Springfield, MO 65804

4821

Virgil M. Hancher Award, William & Elizabeth Penningroth Award

Amount: $500 **Deadline:** None Specified
Fields/Majors: All Areas Of Study

Scholarships are available at the University of Iowa to seniors who demonstrate academic excellence and leadership. Penningroth award of $350 is given to the runner-up for the Hancher award. Students must be nominated by their college.

University Of Iowa
Office Of Student Financial Aid
208 Calvin Hall
Iowa City, IA 52242

4822

Virginia Ag Chemicals & Soil Fertility Society Scholarships

Amount: $1,000 **Deadline:** May 1
Fields/Majors: Horticulture, Crop And Soil Environmental Sciences

Two scholarships for students at Virginia Tech who are studying in either of the above areas. Based on academics, extracurriculars, career plans, and need. Must be a resident of Virginia to apply. Write to the address below for details.

Virginia Tech College Of Agriculture And Life Sciences
Dr. John M. White, Assoc. Dean
1060 Litton Reaves Hall
Blacksburg, VA 24061

4823

Virginia Pearson Ransburg Delta Kappa Gamma Scholarship

Amount: Tuition **Deadline:** Feb 1
Fields/Majors: Education

Scholarships are available at the University of Hawaii, Hilo for full-time students enrolled in the teacher education program. Applicants must be from the Federated States of Micronesia, the Republic of Palau, the Marshall Islands, or the Commonwealth of the North Marianas Islands. Preference is given to female applicants. Write to the address listed below for information.

University Of Hawaii At Hilo
Financial Aid Office
200 West Kawili St.
Hilo, HI 96720

4824

Virginia Student Financial Aid Program

Amount: Varies **Deadline:** None Specified
Fields/Majors: All Areas Of Study

Awards are available for Virginia residents who have demonstrated financial need. For the VGAP awards, applicants must have a GPA of at least 2.5 and rank in the top 20% of financially needy first time freshman. All other awards are for any level of study in a Virginia institution. Write to the address below for more information.

Virginia Council Of Higher Education
James Monroe Building
101 North 14th St.
Richmond, VA 23219

4825

Virginia Transfer Grant Program

Amount: Tuition & Fees **Deadline:** Varies
Fields/Majors: All Areas Of Study

For a minority Virginia resident in undergraduate study at a public Virginia college or university. Transferring GPA must be at least a 2.0. All students who transfer to Virginia State University or Norfolk State University are eligible. Write to the address below for complete details.

Virginia Council Of Higher Education
James Monroe Bldg.
101 N. 14th St.
Richmond, VA 23219

4826

Virginia Volkwein, Katherine Siphers, Gladys Stone Wright Scholarships

AMOUNT: $300 **DEADLINE:** Nov 15
FIELDS/MAJORS: Music Education

Scholarships for young women entering the field of music education and intending a career in band directing. For juniors and seniors. Write to the address listed below for additional information.

Women Band Directors National Association
Ms. Susan D. Creasap
4401 West Woodway Drive
Muncie, IN 47304

4827

Viscosity Oil Company Scholarships

AMOUNT: $2,000-$8,000 **DEADLINE:** Feb 15
FIELDS/MAJORS: All Areas Of Study

Scholarships for FFA members who are pursuing two or four-year degrees in any field. Financial need will be considered. Write to the address below for details.

National FFA Foundation
Scholarship Office
P.O. Box 15160
Alexandria, VA 22309

4828

Visiting Fellowships

AMOUNT: Varies **DEADLINE:** Dec 16
FIELDS/MAJORS: Law Enforcement, Criminal Justice, Criminology

Two or three fellowships for research related to criminal justice. Applicants must have received bachelor's degree. Researchers and practitioners (criminal justice system employees) are encouraged to apply. Fellowships support full-time academic research. For program information, write to the address below.

National Institute Of Justice
Graduate Research Fellowship Program
633 Indiana Ave., NW
Washington, DC 20531

4829

Vocational/Technical Scholarships

AMOUNT: $200-$300 **DEADLINE:** Apr 12
FIELDS/MAJORS: Vocational/Technical Fields

Scholarships are available for Nebraska students who are U.S. citizens and veterans, or children of veterans. Write to the address listed below for additional information.

American Legion Auxiliary, Department Of Nebraska
Department Headquarters
P.O. Box 5227
Lincoln, NE 68505

4830

Vocational Gold Seal Endorsement Scholarship Program

AMOUNT: $2,000 (max) **DEADLINE:** Apr 1
FIELDS/MAJORS: Vocational And Technical Fields

Grants for Florida residents (for at least one year) who will be pursuing postsecondary vocational or technical education. Award is given to students who have been awarded the gold seal. Vocational achievement award requires nomination from school district. Contact your public high school guidance office for details.

Florida Department Of Education
Office Of Student Financial Assistance
1344 Florida Education Center
Tallahassee, FL 32399

4831

Vocational Horticulture Scholarships

AMOUNT: $500-$1,000 **DEADLINE:** Apr 1
FIELDS/MAJORS: Horticulture, Floriculture

Scholarships for students enrolled in one or two year vocational or technical horticulture or floriculture programs. Up to four awards per year. Minimum GPA of 3.0 required. Must be U.S. or Canadian citizen. Write to the address below for details. Please specify your interest in the vocational scholarships program.

Bedding Plants Foundation, Inc.
Scholarship Program
P.O. Box 27241
Lansing, MI 48909

4832

Vocational Rehabilitation Benefits

AMOUNT: $2,000 (max) **DEADLINE:** None Specified
FIELDS/MAJORS: All Areas Of Study

Grants for physically or mentally handicapped South Carolina residents who are attending a South Carolina college or university. Based on financial need. Contact the nearest vocational rehabilitation office or the Vocational Rehabilitation Dept., 1410 Boston Ave., P.O. Box 15, W. Columbia, SC 29171.

South Carolina Commission On Higher Education
1333 Main St., Suite 200
Columbia, SC 29201

4833

Vocational Rehabilitation Program

AMOUNT: Varies **DEADLINE:** None
FIELDS/MAJORS: All Areas Of Study

Open to North Carolina residents with mental or physical disabilities. Write to the address below for details.

North Carolina Division Of Vocational Rehabilitation Services
P.O. Box 26053
Raleigh, NC 27611

4834 Vocational/Technical School Scholarship Program

Amount: $500 **Deadline:** Nov 30
Fields/Majors: Vocational/Technical Programs

Competition is open to AAL members of any age who are enrolled or who plan to enroll in an accredited vocational/technical institute or two-year college. Students can attend on a full or half-time basis and must pursue an associate degree or vocational diploma. 100 scholarships. 50 renewable scholarships will be awarded to graduating high school seniors. An additional 50 renewable scholarships will be awarded to those members who have graduated from high school in previous years. Write to the address below for more information.

Aid Association For Lutherans
Attn: AAL Scholarships
4321 N. Ballard Rd.
Appleton, WI 54915

4835 Volta Scholarship Awards

Amount: $250-$1,000 **Deadline:** Apr 15
Fields/Majors: All Areas Of Study

Applicants must be born deaf or became deaf before acquiring language. Must use speech/residual hearing or lip-reading as primary communication and be a student entering or attending a college or university program for hearing students. One award per year. Write to the address below for complete details.

Alexander Graham Bell Association For The Deaf
3417 Volta Place, NW
Washington, DC 20007

4836 Vulcan Materials Company Presidential Honors Scholarships

Amount: $4,000 **Deadline:** Mar 1
Fields/Majors: All Areas Of Study

Awards for entering freshmen with an ACT score of 29 or better and a GPA of at least 3.5. Renewable with a GPA of 3.0 or higher. Also based on applicant's character and integrity, promise for leadership, and likelihood of significant achievement in the chosen field of endeavor. Write to the address below for more information.

Auburn University
Office Of Student Financial Aid
203 Mary Martin Hall
Auburn University, AL 36849

4837 W. Burghardt Turner Fellowship Program

Amount: Tuition + Stipend
Deadline: None Specified
Fields/Majors: Most Areas Of Study

Fellowship program for candidates of African American, Native American, or Latino descent. Applicants must hold a bachelor's degree from an accredited college or university and be admitted to a master's or doctoral program at one of the SUNY campuses. For U.S. citizens or permanent residents. Program requires nomination by the department in which you are studying. Contact Dr. Pedro Gonzalez, Assistant Vice Provost for Graduate Studies, at the address below for more information.

State University Of New York
The Graduate School, SUNY Stony Brook
Computer Science Bldg.
Stony Brook, NY 11794

4838 W. Harold Dalgliesh, Brigham D. Madsen Scholarships

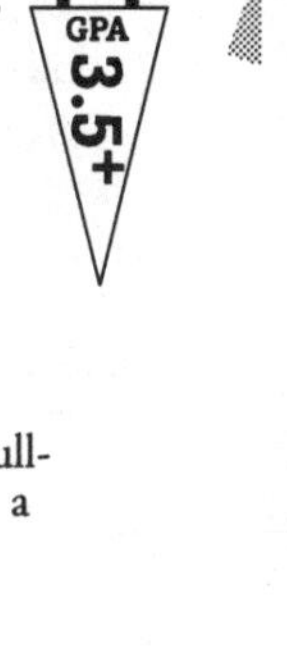

Amount: Varies **Deadline:** Feb 15
Fields/Majors: History

Scholarships are available at the University of Utah for full-time entering freshmen and transfer students enrolled in a history program. Continuing students with a GPA of at least 3.5 are also eligible. Write to the address below for details.

University Of Utah
Dr. Jeanne A. Ojala
211 Carlson Hall
Salt Lake City, UT 84112

4839 W.H. "Howie" McClennan Scholarship

Amount: $2,500 **Deadline:** Jul 1
Fields/Majors: All Areas Of Study

Awards for high school seniors or undergraduates with a parent who was a fire fighter and died in the line of duty. Students must have a minimum GPA of 2.0 and be able to demonstrate financial need. Contact the address below for further information.

International Association Of Fire Fighters
Office Of The General President
1750 New York Ave., NW
Washington, DC 20006

4840 W.H. Plemmons Leadership Fellows Program

Amount: $1,000 **Deadline:** Dec 15
Fields/Majors: All Areas Of Study

Scholarships awarded to students at Appalachian State University who have demonstrated outstanding academic ability and participation in community service activities. Contact the office of admissions for details.

Appalachian State University
Office Of Admissions
Scholarship Section
Boone, NC 28608

4841 W.K. Kellogg Foundation Fellowship

Amount: Varies **Deadline:** Dec 31
Fields/Majors: Human Services

Awards for a three-year period will be made in behalf of as many as fifty individuals of exceptional merit and competence. During the program the fellow maintains his/her present employment while pursuing fellowship activities. Must be U.S. citizen. Must be professional in the earlier years of career who shows leadership potential. Not for basic research. Write to the address below for further information.

W.K. Kellogg Foundation
Fellowship Program Assistant
One Michigan Ave. E
Battle Creek, MI 49017

4842

W.P. & H.B. White Foundation Merit Scholarships

Amount: $500-$2,000 **Deadline:** None Specified
Fields/Majors: All Areas Of Study

Scholarships are available to graduating high school seniors who are National Merit Finalists and residents of the Chicago area. Five awards are offered each year. Write to the address listed below for information.

National Merit Scholarship Corporation
1560 Sherman Ave., Suite 200
Evanston, IL 60201

4843

W.P. Black Scholarship Fund

Amount: $500 **Deadline:** Mar 15
Fields/Majors: All Areas Of Study

Scholarships for West Virginia residents. For use at any undergraduate school in the U.S. or abroad. Based on need and merit. Average recipient has had an ACT score of 25 (composite) and a GPA of 3.81. Write to the address below for details.

Greater Kanawha Valley Foundation
Scholarship Committee
P.O. Box 3041
Charlestown, WV 25331

4844

W.S. Tippen Scholarships

Amount: None Specified **Deadline:** None Specified
Fields/Majors: Athletics

Scholarships are awarded to both men and women who compete on intercollegiate teams at Clarion. Contact the respective coach at Clarion for more information.

Clarion University
104 Egbert Hall
Office Of Financial Aid
Clarion, PA 16214

4845

W.T. Goodloe Rutland Endowed Scholarship

Amount: $1,500 **Deadline:** Mar 1
Fields/Majors: Speech Communication

Renewable $1,500 award for full time students at the University of Alabama whose academic records, leadership abilities, test scores, and recommendations indicate potential in the study of speech communications and a keen interest in the art of debate, discussion, and persuasion. Priority is given to freshmen. Write to the address listed below for further information.

University Of Alabama
College Of Communications
P.O. Box 870172
Tuscaloosa, AL 35487

4846

W.W. Smith Charitable Trust Scholarships

Amount: $2,000 **Deadline:** Mar 15, Nov 15
Fields/Majors: All Areas Of Study

Awards for students with outstanding academic credentials and involvement in community and extracurricular activities. Must demonstrate financial need. Renewable. Write to the address below for more information.

Gwynedd-Mercy College
Student Financial Aid
Sumneytown Pike
Gwynedd Valley, PA 19437

4847

Wagner And Martha Love Athletic Scholarship

Amount: None Specified **Deadline:** None Specified
Fields/Majors: Men's Sports

Student must be full-time and a member of a men's athletic team. Contact the Men's Athletics Office for more information.

Southwest Missouri State University
Office Of Financial Aid
901 South National Ave.
Springfield, MO 65804

4848

Wakefield Citizens' Scholarship

Amount: Varies **Deadline:** None Specified
Fields/Majors: All Areas Of Study

Scholarships for graduating high school seniors who reside in Wakefield, MA. For full-time study. Financial need is a primary consideration. Write to the address below for details. Information may also be available from you high school guidance office.

Citizens Scholarship Foundation Of Wakefield, Inc.
P.O. Box 321
Wakefield, MA 01880

4849

Wal-Mart Competitive Edge Scholarship

Amount: Varies **Deadline:** Dec 1
Fields/Majors: Mathematics, Engineering, Science

Scholarships are available at the University of New Mexico for entering freshmen enrolled in or planning to enroll in one of the areas listed above. Must be U.S. citizens with a GPA of at least 3.5 and have demonstrated community service and leadership. Write to the address listed below for information.

University Of New Mexico, Albuquerque
Student Financial Aid Office
Mesa Vista Hall North, Room 1044
Albuquerque, NM 87131

4850

Wal-Mart Scholarship

Amount: $1,000 **Deadline:** Feb 1
Fields/Majors: Pharmacy

Scholarships are available at the University of Utah for full-time junior pharmacy majors, with financial need, leadership qualities, and a desire to enter community pharmacy practice. Write to the address below for details.

University Of Utah
College Of Pharmacy
Office Of Student Affairs
Salt Lake City, UT 84112

4851

Walco International, Inc. Scholarships

Amount: $1,000 **Deadline:** Feb 15
Fields/Majors: Animal Science

Scholarships are available for FFA members pursuing a four-year degree in animal science. Three awards are offered annually. Write to the address below for details.

National FFA Foundation
Scholarship Office
P.O. Box 15160
Alexandria, VA 22309

4852

Waldo E. Rennie Student Loan Program

Amount: $2,000 (max) **Deadline:** Varies
Fields/Majors: Engineering, Geology, Physics

Awards for undergraduate students between the ages of 18 and 26 in one of the areas of study listed above. Applicants must attend a college or university supported principally by the state of Colorado. Write to the address below for more information.

First Interstate Bank Of Denver, N.A.
Yvonne J. Baca, Senior Vice-President
P.O. Box 5825
Denver, CO 80217

4853

Walker College Scholarships

Amount: None Specified **Deadline:** May 1
Fields/Majors: All Areas Of Study

Many scholarship programs are administered by Walker College for students who have been admitted to the college. One application will suffice to apply for all scholarships. Programs include awards based on academics, area of study, descendents of specific families (Monteith, Hulsey, Ferguson, or Edgil), or other criteria. A complete listing of scholarships, as well as application forms are available from the address below.

Walker College
Scholarships/Financial Aid Office
Jasper, AL 35501

4854

Wall St. Council Scholarships

Amount: $1,000 **Deadline:** May 31
Fields/Majors: Banking & Finance

Scholarships for Italian American residents of New York, New Jersey, or Connecticut. For undergraduate study. Write to the address below for details.

National Italian American Foundation
Dr. Maria Lombardo, Education Director
1860 19th St., NW
Washington, DC 20009

4855

Walter And Louise Keller Memorial Music Scholarship Endowment

Amount: Varies **Deadline:** Mar 1
Fields/Majors: Music

Awards are available at the University of New Mexico for full-time students majoring in music. Must have financial need and a minimum GPA of 3.0. Recipients are selected by the music department. Contact the music department for more information.

University Of New Mexico, Albuquerque
Office Of Financial Aid
Albuquerque, NM 87131

4856

Walter And Virginia Nord Scholarships

Amount: $1,000 **Deadline:** Feb 15
Fields/Majors: All Areas Of Study

Awards for high school seniors from Lorain County, OH, with financial need and academic achievement. Write to the address below for more information.

Community Foundation Of Greater Lorain County
1865 N. Ridge Road, East
Suite A
Lorain, OH 44055

4857

Walter Cronkite Scholarship

Amount: None Specified **Deadline:** Apr 21
Fields/Majors: Broadcasting

Scholarship for an undergraduate or graduate student in the area of broadcasting and studying at a school, within 150 miles of St. Louis, which has student or faculty membership in the Saint Louis Chapter of the National Academy of Television Arts and Sciences. Contact your department or a broadcasting faculty member to find out if your school has such membership. If so, write to the address below for further information.

National Academy Of Television Arts & Sciences
St Louis Chapter KETC-TV Channel 9, Ms. B. Larose
6996 Millbrook
St. Louis, MO 63130

4858

Walter D. & Grace Bonner Memorial Award

Amount: $150 **Deadline:** Feb 15
Fields/Majors: Chemistry

Scholarships are available at the University of Utah for full-time senior chemistry majors who demonstrate an outstanding academic record. Write to the address below for information.

University Of Utah
Dr. Fred Montague
135 Building 44
Salt Lake City, UT 84112

4859

Walter O. Mason Jr. Scholarship

AMOUNT: $1,000 **DEADLINE:** May 1
FIELDS/MAJORS: Health Science

Scholarships are available at the University of Oklahoma, Norman for full-time minority health science majors. Write to the address listed below for information.

University Of Oklahoma, Norman
Director, Office Of Financial Aid
Ouhsc, P.O. Box 26901
Oklahoma City, OK 73190

4860

Walter Reed Smith Scholarship

AMOUNT: None Specified
DEADLINE: None Specified
FIELDS/MAJORS: Home Economics, Nutrition, Nursing

Scholarships for students in home economics who are direct descendents of worthy confederates. Must be able to prove lineage. For women over the age of 30. Contact the UDC nearest you. If the address is not known, write to the below address for further information and address.

United Daughters Of The Confederacy
Scholarship Coordinator
328 North Boulevard
Richmond, VA 23220

4861

Walter Rumminger Tradesman Scholarship

AMOUNT: Varies **DEADLINE:** None Specified
FIELDS/MAJORS: Vocational Studies

Applicants must be second-year students in a trade program in the division of trades and technology. Other criteria include: demonstrated ability to work in trade of choice, financial need, and spiritual leadership. Write to the address below for details.

Bob Jones University
Attn: Director Of Student Financial Aid
Greenville, SC 29614

4862

Walter S. Barr Graduate Fellowships

AMOUNT: None Specified **DEADLINE:** Feb 1
FIELDS/MAJORS: All Areas Of Study

Fellowships available to Hampden County residents who are furthering their education into full-time graduate studies. Write to the executive secretary at the address below for details.

Horace Smith Fund
Executive Secretary
P.O. Box 3034
Springfield, MA 01101

4863

Walter S. Barr Scholarships & Horace Smith Fund Loans

AMOUNT: Varies **DEADLINE:** None Specified
FIELDS/MAJORS: All Areas Of Study

Scholarships and loans for residents of Hampden County, MA. Awards are given to high school seniors and renewed each year. If repayment is made on loans one year after the student completes his formal education, no interest is charged. Write to address below for further details.

Horace Smith Fund
P.O. Box 3034
Springfield, MA 01101

4864

Walter S. Rygiel Scholarship

AMOUNT: $300 **DEADLINE:** Feb 9
FIELDS/MAJORS: Education (Business)

Award for business education major. Must demonstrate financial need, academic achievement, and activities. Use Bloomsburg University scholarship application. Contact Dr. Roger Ellis, Chairperson, Business Education Department, for further details.

Bloomsburg University
19 Ben Franklin Hall
400 E. Second St.
Bloomsburg, PA 17815

4865

Walter Schoenknect Tourism Scholarship

AMOUNT: $750 **DEADLINE:** Mar 22
FIELDS/MAJORS: Tourism

Awards for Connecticut residents who are high school seniors or college students who graduated from a Connecticut high school. Must be in good academic standing. A short essay will be required. Contact the address below for further information.

Connecticut Tourism Industry Committee
Dr. Elisabeth S. Van Dyke
300 Orange Ave.
West Haven, CT 06516

4866

Walter T. Cox Presidential Scholarship

AMOUNT: $6,000 **DEADLINE:** Mar 1
FIELDS/MAJORS: All Areas Of Study

Scholarship offered to the most promising entering freshman. Renewable for three years. Contact the financial aid office at the address below for details.

Clemson University
Financial Aid Office
G01 Sikes Hall
Clemson, SC 29634

4867

Wanda And Donald Atkinson Scholarship

AMOUNT: Varies **DEADLINE:** Mar 1
FIELDS/MAJORS: Medicine

Awards are available at the University of New Mexico for medical students who demonstrate academic ability and financial need. Write to the address below for more information.

University Of New Mexico, Albuquerque
Office Of Financial Aid
Albuquerque, NM 87131

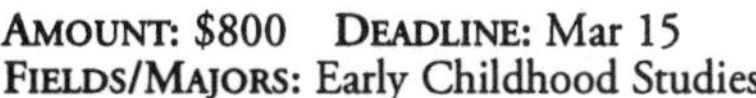

4868

Wanda White Memorial Scholarship

AMOUNT: $800 **DEADLINE:** Mar 15
FIELDS/MAJORS: Early Childhood Studies

Awards for Jacksonville State University students who are in the field of early childhood studies. Based on character, academics, and extracurricular activities. Write to the address below for more information.

Jacksonville State University
Financial Aid Office
Jacksonville, AL 36265

4869

War Orphans Educational Aid

AMOUNT: $3,000 (max) **DEADLINE:** None Specified
FIELDS/MAJORS: All Areas Of Study

Resident of Iowa for at least two years prior to application. Child of parent who died in, or as a result of, military service. Must attend a college or university in Iowa. Write to the address below for complete details.

Iowa Division Of Veteran Affairs
Camp Dodge
7700 NW Beaver Drive
Johnston, IA 50131

4870

Ware Scholarship

AMOUNT: $500 **DEADLINE:** None Specified
FIELDS/MAJORS: Engineering

Scholarships are available at the University of Iowa for full-time junior or senior engineering students with high academic standing. Write to the address listed below for information.

University Of Iowa
Student Services, College Of Engineering
3100 Engineering Building
Iowa City, IA 52242

4871

Warner-Hall, Presbytery Women Of The Church, & P.I.E. Scholarships

AMOUNT: $1,000-$2,000 **DEADLINE:** Mar 15
FIELDS/MAJORS: All Areas Of Study

Scholarships for St. Andrew's students who are members of the Presbyterian church. Must be nominated by your pastor or youth minister for Warner-Hall Award or by the women of the church for the Presbytery Award. The P.I.E. Award is a matching contribution for students from a local congregation. Write to the address below or contact your local church for more complete details.

St. Andrews College
Office Of Financial Aid
1700 Dogwood Mile
Laurinburg, NC 28352

4872

Warren T. Mithoff Memorial Scholarship

AMOUNT: $750 **DEADLINE:** None Specified
FIELDS/MAJORS: Mass Communications

Scholarship available to El Paso County resident students who are pursuing a mass communications career at the University of Texas at El Paso. Write to the address listed below for additional information.

Warren T. Mithoff Memorial Scholarship Fund
El Paso Community Foundation
201 East Main, Suite 1616
El Paso, TX 79901

4873

Warren W. Brainerd, Jr. Memorial Scholarship

AMOUNT: None Specified
DEADLINE: None Specified
FIELDS/MAJORS: Science, Pre-Med, Pre-Engineering, Pre-Math, Pre-Elementary Education

Awards given to students who attend St. Petersburg Junior College and are seeking a degree in one of the fields above. Applicants must be a graduate of a Pinellas County high school and entering their second year at SPJC. Contact the Affice of the Director of Scholarships and student financial assistance at the campus you attend or write to the address below. Notification of this award will also appear in the campus newsletters.

St. Petersburg Junior College
Office Of Financial Aid
P.O. Box 13489
St. Petersburg, FL 33733

4874

Washington And Lee Scholarships

AMOUNT: None Specified **DEADLINE:** None Specified
FIELDS/MAJORS: All Areas Of Study

Scholarships for students at Washington and Lee University who are direct descendents of confederate soldiers. Must be able to prove lineage. Write to the UDC chapter nearest you. If address is not known, write to the address below for further information and address.

United Daughters Of The Confederacy
Scholarship Coordinator
328 North Boulevard
Richmond, VA 23220

4875

Washington Apple Commission Farmworker Education Program

AMOUNT: Varies **DEADLINE:** July 1
FIELDS/MAJORS: All Areas Of Study

Scholarships available for farmworkers, spouses, or children of farmworkers who have worked as laborers in the apple orchards of Washington state. Applicants must be or will be full time students in an accredited school. Write to the address listed below for additional information.

Washington Apple Commission
P.O. Box 18
Wenatchee, WA 98807

4876

Washington Crossing Foundation Scholarship

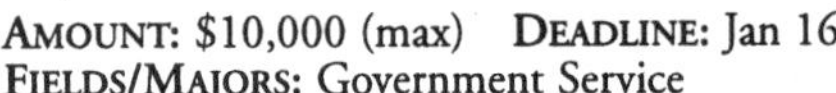

AMOUNT: $10,000 (max) **DEADLINE:** Jan 16
FIELDS/MAJORS: Government Service

Applicants must be high school seniors and U.S. citizens who are planning careers of government service at the local, state, or federal level. Award is based on essay, scholarship, and recommendation of high school principal. Write to the address below for details.

Washington Crossing Foundation
1280 General Defermoy Road
P.O. Box 17
Washington Crossing, PA 18977

4877

Washington International Competition For Young Musicians

AMOUNT: Varies **DEADLINE:** Jan 10
FIELDS/MAJORS: Music-Voice, Opera, String, Piano

Cash awards are available for young artists, under the age of 33, who are preparing for a professional singing career, with preference given to those choosing an opera career. Finalists will compete in Washington, DC, for eleven prizes. Write to the address listed below for information.

Friday Morning Music Club Foundation, Inc.
c/o Rosemarie Houghton, Chairman
4925 MacArthur Blvd. NW
Washington, DC 20007

4878

Washington Library Association Scholarships

AMOUNT: Varies **DEADLINE:** Mar 16
FIELDS/MAJORS: Library Science

Scholarships for master's level students who have completed at least two quarters of graduate school in library science at the University of Washington. Must be a member of the Washington Library Association. Write to the address below for details.

Washington Library Association
Corresponding Secretary
4016-1st Ave., NE
Seattle, WA 98105

4879

Washington Printing Guild

AMOUNT: Varies **DEADLINE:** Feb 28
FIELDS/MAJORS: Graphic Arts Education

Awards for students accepted into a graphic arts education program who are from the Washington, DC, Metropolitan area. Must be U.S. citizens and have demonstrated financial need. Write to the address below for more information. Candidates must be recommended by his/her supervisor, employer, or department chairperson.

Printing And Graphic Communications Association
Scholarship Coordinator
7 West Tower, 1333 H St., NW
Washington, DC 20005

4880

Washington Pulp And Paper Foundation Scholarships

AMOUNT: None Specified **DEADLINE:** Feb 1
FIELDS/MAJORS: Chemical, Computer, Industrial Engineering

Scholarships for entering freshman, college or community college transfer students with an interest in process, chemical, computer, or industrial engineering. Contact the college of forest resources at the address below for details.

University Of Washington, College Of Forest Resources
Washington Pulp And Paper Foundation
Bloedel Hall, Ar-10
Seattle, WA 98195

4881

Washington Scholars Program

AMOUNT: $3,021 (max) **DEADLINE:** Jun 1
FIELDS/MAJORS: All Areas Of Study

Scholarship program for outstanding students in Washington state high schools. Must be nominated by high school principal. Supports study at public or private colleges. Based on academic achievements, leadership, and community service activities. Contact your counselor or principal for details.

Washington Higher Education Coordinating Board
917 Lakeridge Way
P.O. Box 43430
Olympia, WA 98504

4882

Washington University Scholarships

AMOUNT: Varies **DEADLINE:** None Specified
FIELDS/MAJORS: All Areas Of Study

Scholarships for undergraduates at Washington University in St. Louis. Based on financial need. Contact the financial aid office at the address below for details.

Washington University
Office Of Financial Aid
Campus Box 1041
St. Louis, MO 63130

4883

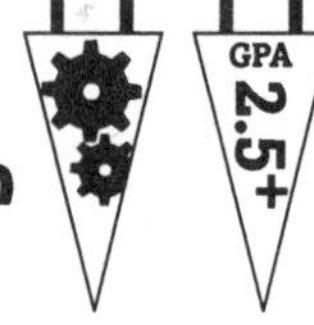

Waste Management Education And Research Consortium

AMOUNT: Varies **DEADLINE:** Mar 1
FIELDS/MAJORS: Engineering, Computer Science Related To Waste Management

Awards are available at the University of New Mexico for undergraduate engineering or computer science students with a minimum GPA of 2.5. Must be a U.S. citizen or permanent resident and be enrolled in the WERC certificate program. Write to the address below for more information.

University Of New Mexico, Albuquerque
Office Of Financial Aid
Albuquerque, NM 87131

4884

Water & Electrolyte Homeostasis Young Investigator Award In Physiology

Amount: $500 **Deadline:** None Specified
Fields/Majors: Integrative Physiology

Awards are available to students interested in integrative physiology. The recipient must be the first author on the abstract presented at the APS annual meeting. Applicants must be under the age of 40. Write to the address below for more information.

American Psychology Society
Membership Services Office
9560 Rockville Pike
Bethesda, MD 20814

4885

Watson Jewelers Scholarship

Amount: $250 **Deadline:** Varies
Fields/Majors: All Areas Of Study

Awards for Sul Ross students from the Alpine, TX, area who have financial need and a GPA of 2.0 or greater. Write to the address below for more information.

Sul Ross State University
Financial Aid Office
Box C-113
Alpine, TX 79832

4886

Wayne Kay Graduate Fellowship

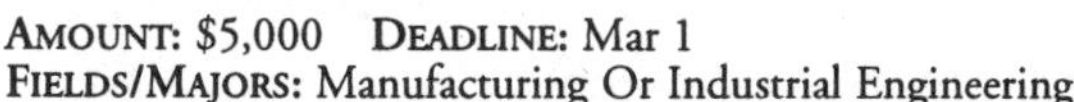

Amount: $5,000 **Deadline:** Mar 1
Fields/Majors: Manufacturing Or Industrial Engineering

Scholarships for graduate students who are enrolled in a graduate program in manufacturing or industrial engineering. Write to the address below for details. Information may also be available in your department office. If writing please specify what scholarship(s) you are interested in.

SME Manufacturing Engineering Education Foundation
One SME Drive
P.O. Box 930
Dearborn, MI 48121

4887

Wayne Kay Scholarship

Amount: $2,500 **Deadline:** Mar 1
Fields/Majors: Manufacturing Engineering & Technology

Scholarships for full-time undergraduate students who have completed at least thirty credit hours. Student must have a minimum GPA of 3.5. Write to the address below for details. Information may also be available in the college blue book. If writing please specify what scholarship(s) you are interested in.

SME Manufacturing Engineering Education Foundation
One SME Drive
P.O. Box 930
Dearborn, MI 48121

4888

Waynesburg College Grants And Scholarships

Amount: $1,000-$4,000 **Deadline:** Mar 15
Fields/Majors: All Areas Of Study

Awards are available for students at Waynesburg College based on academics, extracurricular activities, and leadership. Includes the Presidential Honor, Waynesburg Honor, and Waynesburg Achievement Scholarships. To apply for these awards, simply submit the free application for federal student aid which can be obtained from your high school guidance office or from Waynesburg College.

Waynesburg College Financial Aid Office
51 West College St.
Waynesburg, PA 15370

4889

Waynesburg College Merit Awards

Amount: Varies **Deadline:** Mar 1
Fields/Majors: All Areas Of Study

Awards are available for students at Waynesburg College based on academics, extracurricular activities, and leadership. Applicants may have to interview for these awards. Includes the Outstanding Scholars Program, Waynesburg Leadership Program, Bonner Scholars Program, and other awards. Write to the address below for more information.

Waynesburg College
Financial Aid Office
51 West College St.
Waynesburg, PA 15370

4890

Weinberg Regents Scholarship

Amount: Varies **Deadline:** Jun 15
Fields/Majors: All Areas Of Study

Awards for exceptional students transferring to the University of Maryland from a Maryland community college with a GPA of 4.0. Applicants must have completed their associate's degree prior to applying. Contact the address below for more information.

University Of Maryland, College Park
Systems Administration
3300 Mertzerott Road
Adelphi, MD 20783

4891

Wells Scholarship In Science

Amount: Tuition **Deadline:** Jan 1
Fields/Majors: Math And Science

For freshman math and science major. Applicant must apply for both admission and scholarship; must meet the criteria for the honors program; must have interview or attend campus visitation program. Four year renewable scholarship. Write to the address below for details.

Denison University
Financial Aid Office
Box M
Granville, OH 43023

4892

Welsh Pony And Cob Foundation Scholarship

Amount: $500 **Deadline:** Sep 15
Fields/Majors: All Areas Of Study

Scholarship for students who have been active in horse shows or related events. Based on academics, extracurricular activities, broad background in the horse field, and general well-roundedness. Write to the address below for details (information may be available at your local horse club).

Welsh Pony And Cob Foundation, Inc.
P.O. Box 2977
Winchester, VA 22604

4893

Werc Scholarships And Research Programs

Amount: Varies **Deadline:** Mar 15
Fields/Majors: Environmental Sciences, Biology, Engineering, Water/Waste Management

Awards for students at New Mexico State University, University of New Mexico, New Mexico Institute of Mining and Technology, or Navajo Community College. Applicants must be interested in enrolling in a program related to waste environmental studies. Write to the address below for more information.

Waste-Management Education And Research Consortium
WERC Administrative Office
Box 30001, Dept. WERC
Las Cruces, NM 88003

4894

Werts Scholarship

Amount: $500 **Deadline:** Feb 15
Fields/Majors: Education

Awards for freshmen who participate in the teacher cadet program. Write to the address below for more information.

Winthrop University, School Of Education
Office Of Student Services
119 Tillman Hall
Rock Hill, SC 29733

4895

West Scholarship

Amount: None Specified **Deadline:** Dec 15
Fields/Majors: Forestry

Scholarships are awarded to juniors or seniors who are majoring in forestry and demonstrate scholarship, need and leadership. Contact the Department Head, Forestry and Wildlife Management, for more information.

University Of Massachusetts, Amherst
Department Of Forestry And Wildlife Mgmt
Amherst, MA 01003

4896

West Virginia Broadcasters Association Fund

Amount: None Specified **Deadline:** Mar 16
Fields/Majors: Communications And Related Fields

Scholarships are available for residents of West Virginia who are pursuing a degree in communications or a related field (including but not limited to: broadcasting, speech, journalism, film, advertising, and broadcasting technology). Renewable. Write to the address listed below for information and an application.

Greater Kanawha Valley Foundation
Scholarship Committee
P.O. Box 3041
Charleston, WV 25331

4897

West Virginia Higher Education Grant Program

Amount: $350-$2,136 **Deadline:** Mar 1
Fields/Majors: All Areas Of Study

Applicant must be a U.S. citizen and a resident of West Virginia for 1 year prior to application. Recipient must enroll as a full-time undergraduate in an approved educational institution in West Virginia or Pennsylvania. Contact your high school guidance counselor, your college financial aid office, or the address below for details.

West Virginia Higher Education Grant Program
State College And University Systems Of WV
P.O. Box 4007
Charleston, WV 25364

4898

West Virginia Italian Heritage Festival Scholarships

Amount: $2,000 (max) **Deadline:** May 31
Fields/Majors: All Areas Of Study

Scholarships for Italian American students from West Virginia entering or enrolled at any college or university. For undergraduates only. Write to the address below for details.

National Italian American Foundation
Dr. Maria Lombardo, Education Director
1860 19th St., NW
Washington, DC 20009

4899

Western Auto And Cato Knight Memorial Scholarships

Amount: Varies **Deadline:** Apr 15
Fields/Majors: All Areas Of Study

Scholarships available for entering freshmen at ABAC who have a high school GPA of at least 2.5 and a minimum SAT score of 750. Applicants must be from Tift County, GA, and be enrolled in full-time study. Write to the address below for additional information.

Abraham Baldwin Agricultural College
Office Of Admissions
2802 Moore Highway
Tifton, GA 31794

4900

Western Colorado Chapter (WCC) Of The Retired Officers Scholarship

Amount: $250 **Deadline:** None Specified
Fields/Majors: All Areas Of Study

Scholarships for Mesa State sophomores who are the children of active or retired military personnel who have a GPA of at least 2.5. Write to the address below for more information.

Mesa State College
Office Of Financial Aid
P.O. Box 2647
Grand Junction, CO 81501

4901

Western Dairymen-John Elway-Melba Scholarships

AMOUNT: $500 **DEADLINE:** Feb 15
FIELDS/MAJORS: Agriculture, Agribusiness

Scholarships are available for FFA members pursuing a degree in any area of agriculture or agribusiness, who reside in Idaho and have a GPA of at least 3.0. Preference will be given to students from the Melba chapter. For undergraduate study. Write to the address below for details.

National FFA Foundation
Scholarship Office
P.O. Box 15160
Alexandria, VA 22309

4902

Western European Fellowships

AMOUNT: None Specified **DEADLINE:** Varies
FIELDS/MAJORS: European Studies

Fellowships are available for scholars enrolled in a U.S. doctoral program. Applicants must have completed all the program requirements except for the dissertation. Research must be in European studies. Write to the address listed below for information.

Social Science Research Council
Fellowships And Grants
605 Third Ave.
New York, NY 10158

4903

Western Sunbathing Association Scholarship Program

AMOUNT: $1,000 **DEADLINE:** Apr 1
FIELDS/MAJORS: All Areas Of Study

Scholarships for children of members (for at least 3 years) of the Western Sunbathing Association. Must be less than 27 years old and have a GPA of at least 2.5. Part-time students will be considered. Two awards per year. Write to the address below for details.

Western Sunbathing Association, Inc.
WSA Scholarship Committee
P.O. Box 1168-107
Studio City, CA 91604

4904

Western Undergraduate Exchange Program For Alaska Students

AMOUNT: Varies **DEADLINE:** None Specified
FIELDS/MAJORS: All Areas Of Study

Program which allows students from western states to attend any school not in their state of residence that is part of the western exchange program for reduced tuition. Participating states include: Alaska, Colorado, Hawaii, Idaho, Montana, Nevada, New Mexico, North Dakota, Oregon, South Dakota, Utah, and Wyoming. Write to the address listed below or look on the web site http://www.wiche.edu for more information.

Western Interstate Commission For Higher Education
Student Exchange Programs
P.O. Box Drawer P
Boulder, CO 80301

4905

Western Undergraduate Exchange Program For Colorado Students

AMOUNT: Varies **DEADLINE:** None Specified
FIELDS/MAJORS: All Areas Of Study

Program which allows students from western states to attend any school not in their state of residence that is part of the western exchange program for reduced tuition. Participating states include: Alaska, Colorado, Hawaii, Idaho, Montana, Nevada, New Mexico, North Dakota, Oregon, South Dakota, Utah, and Wyoming. Write to the address listed below or look on the web site http://www.wiche.edu for more information.

Western Interstate Commission For Higher Education
Student Exchange Programs
P.O. Box Drawer P
Boulder, CO 80301

4906

Western Undergraduate Exchange Program For Nevada Students

AMOUNT: Varies **DEADLINE:** None Specified
FIELDS/MAJORS: All Areas Of Study

Program which allows students from western states to attend any school not in their state of residence that is part of the western exchange program for reduced tuition. Participating states include: Alaska, Colorado, Hawaii, Idaho, Montana, Nevada, New Mexico, North Dakota, Oregon, South Dakota, Utah, and Wyoming. Write to the address listed below or look on the web site http://www.wiche.edu for more information.

Western Interstate Commission For Higher Education
Student Exchange Programs
P.O. Box Drawer P
Boulder, CO 80301

4907

Western Undergraduate Exchange Program For Oregon Students

AMOUNT: Varies **DEADLINE:** None Specified
FIELDS/MAJORS: All Areas Of Study

Program which allows students from western states to attend any school not in their state of residence that is part of the western exchange program for reduced tuition. Participating states include: Alaska, Colorado, Hawaii, Idaho, Montana, Nevada, New Mexico, North Dakota, Oregon, South Dakota, Utah, and Wyoming. Write to the address listed below or look on the web site http://www.wiche.edu for more information.

Western Interstate Commission For Higher Education
Student Exchange Programs
P.O. Box Drawer P
Boulder, CO 80301

4908

Westhaysen Scholarship

AMOUNT: Varies **DEADLINE:** Jun 15
FIELDS/MAJORS: Medicine, Nursing

Awards for students from Lake County, IN, who are enrolled in a full-time program in the health and medical areas. Applicants must show outstanding scholastic ability and demonstrate financial need. Write to the address below for more information. Application forms will not be sent out until Mar 1.

Calumet National Bank
5231 Hohman Ave.
Hammond, IN 46320

4909
Westinghouse Bertha Lamme Scholarship

AMOUNT: $1,000 **DEADLINE:** May 15
FIELDS/MAJORS: Engineering

Applicants must be incoming female freshmen who are pursuing an engineering degree. Three awards per year. Mustbe a U.S. citizen or permanent resident and have a GPA of at least 3.5. Request information on the Westinghouse Bertha Lamme Scholarship from the address below. Please be certain to enclose an SASE. Information and applications for the SWE awards are also available from the deans of engineering schools.

Society Of Women Engineers
120 Wall St., 11th Floor
New York, NY 10005

4910
Wexner Graduate Fellowship Program

AMOUNT: Varies **DEADLINE:** Feb 15
FIELDS/MAJORS: Jewish Studies

Awards for North American students who are college graduates and plan to enter a graduate program in preparation for a career in Jewish education, communal service, the rabbinate, the cantorate, or Jewish studies. Write to the address below for more information.

Wexner Foundation
158 W. Main St.
P.O. Box 668
New Albany, OH 43054

4911
Wharton Doctoral Fellowships In Risk & Insurance

AMOUNT: $36,000 (approx.) **DEADLINE:** Feb 1
FIELDS/MAJORS: Insurance/Actuarial Science, Risk Management

Doctoral fellowships available at the Wharton School of Business. Must be a U.S. or Canadian citizen. Postdoctoral fellowships also available. Write to the address below for complete details.

S.S. Huebner Foundation For Insurance Education
Univ. Of Pennsylvania
3733 Spruce St., 430 Vance Hall
Philadelphia, PA 19104

4912
Wheaton College Restricted Scholarships, Wheaton Grants

AMOUNT: $10,000 (max) **DEADLINE:** Mar 15
FIELDS/MAJORS: All Areas Of Study

Scholarships and other awards are available at Wheaton College for undergraduate students who demonstrate academic excellence or financial need or both. Write to the address below for details.

Wheaton College
Financial Aid Office
Wheaton, IL 60187

4913
Wheaton College Revolving Loan

AMOUNT: $1,600 (max) **DEADLINE:** Mar 15
FIELDS/MAJORS: All Areas Of Study

Low cost loan available for Wheaton College students. 5% interest rate with repayment beginning after graduation, with ten years to pay back loan. Write to the address below for details.

Wheaton College
Financial Aid Office
Wheaton, IL 60187

4914
Whirly-Girls Scholarships

AMOUNT: $4,500 **DEADLINE:** Nov 30
FIELDS/MAJORS: Helicopter Flight Training

Scholarships are available to women for helicopter flight training. Two awards per year: one for initial helicopter rating, and one for advanced rating. Write to the address below for details.

International Women Helicopter Pilots
Office Of The Executive Director
P.O. Box 74416
Menlo Park, CA 94026

4915
Whitlock, Selim & Keehn Scholarship

AMOUNT: $500 **DEADLINE:** None Specified
FIELDS/MAJORS: Accounting

Student must be a full-time junior or senior accounting major who has completed Intermediate Accounting I with a minimum 3.0 GPA. Contact the COBA office for more information.

Southwest Missouri State University
Office Of Financial Aid
901 South National Ave.
Springfield, MO 65804

4916
Whitney M. Young Memorial Scholarship

AMOUNT: $2,000 (max)
DEADLINE: None Specified
FIELDS/MAJORS: All Areas Of Study

Available for male or female minority students who are currently enrolled in a postsecondary institution. Students must maintain a GPA of 2.5 or better. Must demonstrate financial need and live in the Chicago area. Write to the address below for more information.

Chicago Urban League
Gina Blake, Scholarship Specialist
4510 South Michigan Ave.
Chicago, IL 60653

4917
Whittier Home Economists In Homemaking Scholarship

AMOUNT: $400 **DEADLINE:** Apr 15
FIELDS/MAJORS: Home Economics

Students must be attending a California college and majoring in home economics in one of the following areas: child development, clothing and textiles, consumer education-family finance, food and nutrition, housing-interior design. Write to the address below for more information.

California State Polytechnic University, Pomona
College Of Agriculture
Building 7, Room 110
Pomona, CA 91768

4918

Who's Who Among American High School Students Scholarships

AMOUNT: $500-$1,000 **DEADLINE:** Feb 15
FIELDS/MAJORS: All Areas Of Study

Scholarships are available for FFA members pursuing a four-year degree in any area of study. Write to the address below for details.

National FFA Foundation
Scholarship Office
P.O. Box 15160
Alexandria, VA 22309

4919

Wiche Doctoral Scholars Program

AMOUNT: $17,000 **DEADLINE:** None Specified
FIELDS/MAJORS: All Areas Of Study

Awards are available for the purpose of encouraging ethnic minority students to pursue doctoral degrees and become college level teachers. Preference is given to science, engineering, and mathematics students. For residents of Alaska, Arizona, Colorado, Hawaii, Idaho, Montana, Nevada, Oregon, Utah, North/South Dakota, New Mexico, Washington, and Wyoming. Write to the address listed below for information.

Western Interstate Commission For Higher Education
P.O. Drawer P
Boulder, CO 80301

4920

Wiche Professional Student Exchange Program

AMOUNT: Varies **DEADLINE:** None Specified
FIELDS/MAJORS: Dentistry, Medicine, Occupational Therapy, Optometry, Podiatry, Osteopathy, Physical Therapy, Veterinary Medicine

The student exchange program helps Alaska residents obtain access to eight fields of graduate education not available in Alaska, but made available at participating institutions in other western states at reduced tuition rate. Write to the address listed below for information.

Alaska Commission On Postsecondary Education
Wiche Certifying Office
3030 Vintage Blvd.
Juneau, AK 99801

4921

WICI, Seattle Professional Chapter Communications Scholarships

AMOUNT: $600-$1,000 **DEADLINE:** Mar 2
FIELDS/MAJORS: Communications

Awards for Washington residents and/or students at a four-year institution in the state of Washington. For female juniors, seniors, or graduate students. Applications are available at many financial aid offices and schools or departments of communication, or write to the address below for details and an application.

Women In Communications, Inc., Seattle Professional Chapter
WICI Scholarship Chair
8310 SE 61st St.
Mercer Island, WA 98040

4922

Wickerham Memorial Endowed Grant Fund

AMOUNT: Varies **DEADLINE:** None Specified
FIELDS/MAJORS: All Areas Of Study

Awards are available for full-time students at Cedarville College who have a GPA of at least 2.0 and demonstrated financial need. Write to the address below for more information.

Cedarville College
Financial Aid Office
P.O. Box 601
Cedarville, OH 45314

4923

WICPA Accounting Scholarships

AMOUNT: $4,000 Over Four Years
DEADLINE: Nov 30
FIELDS/MAJORS: Accounting

Scholarships are available for graduating high school seniors who reside in Wisconsin and are planning to enroll in an accredited accounting program at an accredited Wisconsin college or university. Applicant must have a GPA of at least 3.0. Write to the address listed below for information.

WICPA Educational Foundation, Inc.
180 N. Executive Drive
P.O. Box 1010
Brookfield, WI 53008

4924

WICPA Minority Accounting Program

AMOUNT: $4,000 Over Four Years
DEADLINE: Nov 30
FIELDS/MAJORS: Accounting

Scholarships are available for graduating high school seniors who reside in Wisconsin and are planning to enroll in an accredited accounting program at an accredited Wisconsin college or university. Applicant must have a GPA of at least 3.0, and be of Hispanic, African American, Native American, or Asian descent. Write to the address listed below for information.

WICPA Educational Foundation, Inc.
180 N. Executive Drive
P.O. Box 1010
Brookfield, WI 53008

4925

Wiebe Public Service Fellowship

AMOUNT: $22,575 **DEADLINE:** None Specified
FIELDS/MAJORS: Public Service

Applicants must be full-time graduate students who are residents of New York or students attending New York schools. This is a fellowship in the New York state government, not on-campus financial aid. Applicants should be exceptionally well-suited for placement in a high level leadership office. Write to Dr. Russell J. Williams, Director, at the address below for details.

New York State Senate
Senate Student Programs
90 South Swan St., Room 401
Albany, NY 12247

4926

Wilbur Shank Memorial Scholarship

AMOUNT: $300 **DEADLINE:** None Specified
FIELDS/MAJORS: Industrial Management

Student must be a senior industrial management major who demonstrates scholarship, leadership, and financial need. Contact the technology department for more information.

Southwest Missouri State University
Office Of Financial Aid
901 South National Ave.
Springfield, MO 65804

4927

Wildlife Leadership Awards

AMOUNT: $1,500 **DEADLINE:** Mar 1
FIELDS/MAJORS: Wildlife Science

Awards for full-time undergraduate juniors or seniors enrolled in a wildlife science program. Recipients must have at least one semester or two quarters remaining in their degree program. Previous winners of this award are ineligible to reapply. Write to the address below for more information.

Rocky Mountain Elk Foundation
Rmef Conservation Education Department
P.O. Box 8249
Missoula, MT 59807

4928

Wildlife Scholarship

AMOUNT: $500 **DEADLINE:** None Specified
FIELDS/MAJORS: Biology

Student must be a full-time junior or senior biology major with a GPA of 3.0 or better. Must have completed 15 hours in biology with a 3.0 GPA. Contact the biology department for more information.

Southwest Missouri State University
Office Of Financial Aid
901 South National Ave.
Springfield, MO 65804

4929

Wilfred Galbraith Endowed Scholarship

AMOUNT: $1,000 **DEADLINE:** Feb 15
FIELDS/MAJORS: Journalism

Renewable $1,000 award given to freshman through master's students pursuing a journalism degree at the University of Alabama. Priority will be given to students with a demonstrated financial need. Write to the address listed below for further information and an application.

University Of Alabama
College Of Communications
P.O. Box 870172
Tuscaloosa, AL 35487

4930

Willard D. Keim Memorial Scholarship

AMOUNT: $500 **DEADLINE:** Feb 1
FIELDS/MAJORS: Political Science

Scholarships are available at the University of Hawaii, Hilo for full-time political science majors with a 3.0 or better GPA. Write to the address listed below for information.

University Of Hawaii At Hilo
Financial Aid Office
200 West Kawili St.
Hilo, HI 96720

4931

Willard H. Erwin, Jr. Memorial Scholarship Fund

AMOUNT: $500 (max) **DEADLINE:** Mar 15
FIELDS/MAJORS: Business, Healthcare Finance

Scholarships for West Virginia residents in at least their junior year of undergraduate study in a state school in WV. Renewable for one additional year. For full- or part-time study. Write to the address below for details.

Greater Kanawha Valley Foundation
Scholarship Committee
P.O. Box 3041
Charleston, WV 25331

4932

Willcockson Art Scholarship

AMOUNT: Varies **DEADLINE:** Apr 1
FIELDS/MAJORS: Art

Awards for entering freshmen who demonstrate talent in art. Must rank in the top 25% of class. Contact the Office of Admissions, UW Oshkosh for more details.

University Of Wisconsin, Oshkosh
Financial Aid Office, Dempsey 104
800 Algoma Blvd.
Oshkosh, WI 54901

4933

Willcockson Nursing Scholarship

AMOUNT: Varies **DEADLINE:** Feb 15
FIELDS/MAJORS: Nursing

Awards for full-time nursing students who have completed at least one semester of the professional major. Must have a GPA of 3.0 or better. Contact the College of Nursing, UW Oshkosh, for more details.

University Of Wisconsin, Oshkosh
Financial Aid Office, Dempsey 104
800 Algoma Blvd.
Oshkosh, WI 54901

4934

William & Anna Speiss Memorial Scholarship

AMOUNT: $1,000 (max) **DEADLINE:** Feb 15
FIELDS/MAJORS: Art

Scholarships are available at the University of Utah for full-time students enrolled in an art program, who are worthy scholars with financial need. Write to the address below for details.

University Of Utah
Delores Simons
161 Art And Architecture Center
Salt Lake City, UT 84112

4935

William & Ruth Julin Scholarships

AMOUNT: $300-$2,000 **DEADLINE:** None Specified
FIELDS/MAJORS: Printmaking, Art History

Scholarships are available at the University of Iowa for full-time undergraduate students majoring in printmaking, or art history majors studying the history of printmaking. Write to the address listed below for information.

University Of Iowa
School Of Art And Art History
E100 Art Building
Iowa City, IA 52245

4936

William A. Chessall Memorial Scholarship

AMOUNT: Varies **DEADLINE:** None Specified
FIELDS/MAJORS: All Areas Of Study

Awards for graduating high school seniors of the Ukiah High School in Ukiah, California. Contact the guidance counselor or the address below for more information.

William A. Chessall Memorial Scholarship Fund
200 North School St.
P.O. Box 419
Ukiah, CA 95482

4937

William A. Fischer Memorial Scholarship

AMOUNT: $2,000 **DEADLINE:** Jan 5
FIELDS/MAJORS: Remote Sensing

Award is to facilitate graduate-level studies and career goals adjudged to address new and innovative uses of remote sensing data/techniques that relate to natural, cultural, or agricultural resources. Awards are restricted to members of ASPRS. Write to the address below for more information.

American Society For Photogrammetry & Remote Sensing
ASPRS Awards Program
5410 Grosvenor Lane, Suite 210
Bethesda, MD 20814

4938

William A. Kenyon Scholarships

GPA 2.5+

AMOUNT: $2,500 **DEADLINE:** Mar 1
FIELDS/MAJORS: All Areas Of Study

Seven scholarships available to entering freshmen with outstanding academic potential. Renewable for three years. Contact the financial aid office at the address below for details.

Clemson University
Financial Aid Office
G01 Sikes Hall
Clemson, SC 29634

4939

William A. Lank Memorial Scholarship

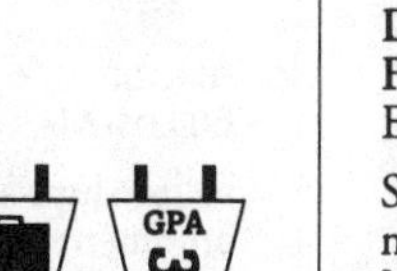

AMOUNT: $1,000 **DEADLINE:** Feb 9
FIELDS/MAJORS: Finance

Award for finance major who must have a minimum GPA of 3.0. Use Bloomsburg University scholarship application. Contact Dr. David Heskel, Chairperson, Finance & Business Law, for information.

Bloomsburg University
19 Ben Franklin Hall
400 E. Second St.
Bloomsburg, PA 17815

4940

William A. Russell Scholarship

AMOUNT: Varies **DEADLINE:** Jul 1
FIELDS/MAJORS: All Areas Of Study

Scholarships available to members of the American Jersey Cattle Association. Write to the address below for details.

American Jersey Cattle Association
Scholarship Committee
6486 East Main St.
Reynoldsburg, OH 43068

4941

William And Cora Norman Henry Endowed Memorial Scholarship

AMOUNT: Varies **DEADLINE:** None Specified
FIELDS/MAJORS: All Areas Of Study

Awards are available for full-time students at Cedarville College who have financial need. Must have a GPA of at least 2.0. Write to the address below for more information.

Cedarville College
Financial Aid Office
P.O. Box 601
Cedarville, OH 45314

4942

William And Edith Rockie Geography Scholarships

AMOUNT: Varies **DEADLINE:** Early Spring
FIELDS/MAJORS: Geography

Awards are available at Portland State University for juniors, seniors, or graduate students studying geography. Undergraduate applicants must have completed a minimum of eighteen credits in geography. Contact the geography department office for more details.

Portland State University
Geography Department Office
424 Cramer Hall
Portland, OR 97207

4943

William And Elizabeth Hart Scholarship

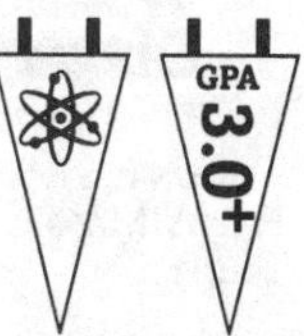

AMOUNT: None Specified
DEADLINE: Late Feb
FIELDS/MAJORS: Mathematics, Physics, Chemistry, Geography, Earth Science, Biology

Scholarships are available to Clarion students majoring mathematics, physics, chemistry, geography, earth science, or biology. Must have a GPA of 3.0 overall, GPA of 3.3 in math and science and completed 45 credits. Contact the Scholarship Committee Chair, Dr. Wollaston, for more information.

Clarion University
104 Egbert Hall
Office Of Financial Aid
Clarion, PA 16214

4944

William And Margaret Nutting Award

AMOUNT: Varies **DEADLINE:** Mar 1
FIELDS/MAJORS: Pre-Med

Awards for UMass sophomores, juniors, or seniors enrolled in a pre-med program. Contact the Chair, Pre-Medical Advisory Committee, for more information.

University Of Massachusetts, Amherst
Chairperson
Pre-Medical Advisory Committee
Amherst, MA 01003

4945

William And Margaret Nutting Scholarship

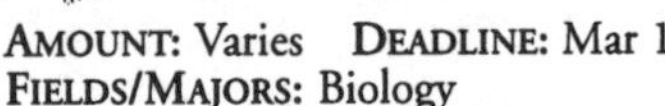

AMOUNT: Varies **DEADLINE:** Mar 1
FIELDS/MAJORS: Biology

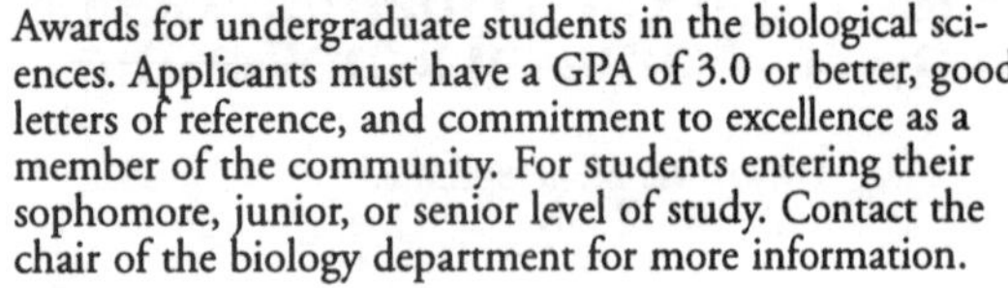

Awards for undergraduate students in the biological sciences. Applicants must have a GPA of 3.0 or better, good letters of reference, and commitment to excellence as a member of the community. For students entering their sophomore, junior, or senior level of study. Contact the chair of the biology department for more information.

University Of Massachusetts, Amherst
Chairperson
Biology Department
Amherst, MA 01003

4946

William And Mary Reed Memorial Scholarship

AMOUNT: Varies **DEADLINE:** Mar 1
FIELDS/MAJORS: Civil Engineering

Awards are available at the University of New Mexico for civil engineering undergraduates with a GPA of at least 2.5 and genuine financial need. Write to the address below for more information.

University Of New Mexico, Albuquerque
Office Of Financial Aid
Albuquerque, NM 87131

4947

William B. Keeling DissertationAward

AMOUNT: $1,500 **DEADLINE:** Mar 1
FIELDS/MAJORS: Hotel-Restaurant Administration, Travel & Tourism

Graduate students who have completed or are about to complete doctoral dissertation in a travel/tourism related area are eligible for this award. Applicants are asked to submit abstract. Finalists will be judged on final dissertation. Write to the address below for details.

Travel And Tourism Research Association
10200 W. 44th Ave.
Suite 304
Wheat Ridge, CO 80033

4948

William B. Ruggles Right To Work Scholarship

AMOUNT: $2,000 **DEADLINE:** Mar 31
FIELDS/MAJORS: Journalism, Communications, Advertising, Broadcasting

Scholarships are available for students majoring in communications or mass media/mass communications. Applicants must submit an 500-word essay which demonstrates understanding of the "right to work" principle. Write to the address below for complete details.

National Right To Work Committee
Attn: William B. Ruggles Scholarship
8001 Braddock Road
Springfield, VA 22160

4949

William C. Browning Scholarship

AMOUNT: Varies **DEADLINE:** Feb 15
FIELDS/MAJORS: Mining Engineering

Scholarships are available at the University of Utah for full-time students who are mining engineering majors. Must have a GPA of at least 3.0. Up to fifteen awards are available to entering freshmen, and a variable number is available to transfer or continuing students. Write to the address below for details.

University Of Utah
Dr. M.K. McCarter
313 William C. Browning Building
Salt Lake City, UT 84112

4950

William C. Doherty Scholarship

AMOUNT: $800 **DEADLINE:** Dec 31
FIELDS/MAJORS: All Areas Of Study

Must be natural or legally adopted child of a letter carrier. Parent must have been a member of the Nat'l Association of Letter Carriers for at least one year. Applicant must be a high school senior. Fifteen awards per year. Renewable. Applications and information are available only through "The Postal Record" (periodical).

National Association Of Letter Carriers
Scholarship Committee
100 Indiana Ave., NW
Washington, DC 20001

4951

William C. Ezell Fellowship

AMOUNT: $6,000 (max) **DEADLINE:** May 1
FIELDS/MAJORS: Optometry

Fellowships are available for masters or doctoral candidates in optometry who are pursuing a degree on a full-time basis. Write to the address listed below or contact your department of optometry for information.

American Optometric Foundation
4330 East West Highway, Suite 1117
Bethesda, MD 20814

4952

William C. Foster Fellows Visiting Scholars Program

AMOUNT: None Specified **DEADLINE:** Jan 31
FIELDS/MAJORS: Physics, Arms Control, Chem., Biology, Foreign Affairs, Math, Engineering.

Program for scholars in the fields listed above to work for different bureaus in the U.S. Arms Control and Disarmament Agency. Applicants must be U.S. citizens and tenured or on the tenure track of a recognized institution of higher learning. Write to the address below for additional information.

United States Arms Control And Disarmament Agency
Office Of Oper. Analysis And Info. Mgt.
320 21st St., NW, Room 5726
Washington, DC 20451

4953

William C. Stokoe Scholarship

AMOUNT: $1,000 **DEADLINE:** Mar 15
FIELDS/MAJORS: Deaf Education, Sign Language

Must be a deaf student who is pursuing part-time or full-time graduate studies in a field related to sign language or the deaf community, or a graduate student who is developing a special project on one of these topics. Write to the address below for details.

National Association Of The Deaf
Stokoe Scholarship Secretary
814 Thayer Ave.
Silver Spring, MD 20910

4954

William D. Kent Scholarship

AMOUNT: $500 **DEADLINE:** Feb 1
FIELDS/MAJORS: Engineering

Awards for incoming freshmen or sophomores at UW Platteville who are studying engineering. Must demonstrate financial need and a GPA of 2.0 or better. Write to the address below or contact the office at (608) 342-1125 for more information.

University Of Wisconsin, Platteville
Office Of Admissions And Enrollment Mgt.
Platteville, WI 53818

4955

William D. Kent Scholarships

AMOUNT: $500 **DEADLINE:** Feb 15
FIELDS/MAJORS: Engineering

Awards are available for at UW Platteville for freshmen or sophomore engineering students with a GPA of 2.0 or better. Four awards are available. Write to the address below for more information.

University Of Wisconsin, Platteville
Office Of Enrollment And Admissions
Platteville, WI 53818

4956

William Dennis Scholarships

AMOUNT: $100-$350 **DEADLINE:** Feb 15
FIELDS/MAJORS: Music

Awards for sophomores at UW Platteville who are in the area of music. Based on scholastic achievement and performance contribution. Write to the address below for more information.

University Of Wisconsin, Platteville
Office Of Enrollment And Admissions
Platteville, WI 53818

4957

William E. Jackson Award

AMOUNT: $2,000 **DEADLINE:** Jun 30
FIELDS/MAJORS: Aviation Electronics, Telecommunications

Award for a graduate students' theses, project papers, technical journal articles, or work completed within the last three years in the areas of aviation electronics or telecommunications. Write to the address below for details.

RTCA-Requirements And Technical Concepts For Aviation
William E. Jackson Award
1140 Connecticut Ave., NW, Suite 1020
Washington, DC 20036

4958

William E. Weisel Scholarship

AMOUNT: $1,000 **DEADLINE:** Mar 1
FIELDS/MAJORS: Manufacturing Engineering/Technology: Robotics/Automated Systems

Scholarships for full-time undergraduate students who have completed at least thirty credit hours and are planning a career in robotics/automated systems. Must have a GPA of at least 3.5 and be a U.S. or Canadian citizen. Number of awards varies. Write to the address below for details. If writing, please specify what scholarship(s) you are interested in.

SME Manufacturing Engineering Education Foundation
One SME Drive
P.O. Box 930
Dearborn, MI 48121

4959

William Eiler Memorial Scholarship

AMOUNT: $400 **DEADLINE:** Feb 1
FIELDS/MAJORS: Engineering

Awards for incoming freshmen at UW Platteville who are studying engineering. Write to the address below or contact the office at (608) 342-1125 for more information.

University Of Wisconsin, Platteville
Office Of Admissions And Enrollment Mgt.
Platteville, WI 53818

4960

William F. Bolger Scholarship

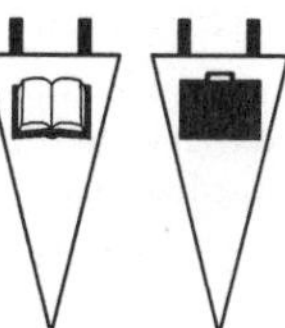

AMOUNT: $1,000 **DEADLINE:** Apr 15
FIELDS/MAJORS: Advertising, Consumer-Related Communications Field

Scholarships are for a junior or senior college student, permanent resident of the U.S., and a record of high academic achievement. Contact IPCC Scholarship Chairperson, 535 S. Illinois St., Indianapolis, IN 46225-1192, for more details.

Indiana University/Purdue University, Indianapolis
Purdue School Of Technology
799 West Michigan St.
Indianapolis, IN 46202

4961

William F. Christensen Scholarship

Amount: Tuition **Deadline:** Mar 15
Fields/Majors: Dance-Ballet

Scholarships are available at the University of Utah for full-time entering freshmen enrolled in a ballet program. Must have a GPA of at least 3.0. Write to the address below for details.

University Of Utah
Barbara Hamblin
116 Marriott Center For Dance
Salt Lake City, UT 84112

4962

William F. Miller, M.D., Post Graduate Scholarship

Amount: $1,000 **Deadline:** Jun 30
Fields/Majors: Respiratory Therapy

Scholarship for a respiratory care practitioner who is pursuing a degree beyond the bachelor's level. GPA of at least 3.0 is required. Renewable. 1200-word essay required. Write to the address below for details.

American Respiratory Care Foundation
11030 Ables Lane
Dallas, TX 75229

4963

William Fairburn, Jr. And Cynthia Fairburn Memorial Scholarships

Amount: $2,000 **Deadline:** Apr 8
Fields/Majors: Liberal Arts, Humanities

Applicants must be graduating high school seniors in Ventura County who intend to pursue studies in liberal arts/humanities at an accredited college or university. Must have a GPA of 3.0 or better. Based on letters of recommendation, essay, and a possible personal interview. Write to the address below for more information.

Ventura County Community Foundation
1355 Del Norte Road
Camarillo, CA 93010

4964

William Flinn Rogers Award

Amount: None Specified **Deadline:** None Specified
Fields/Majors: History

Awards are available for ETSU students demonstrating academic excellence in history. Contact the department of history for more information.

East Tennessee State University
Office Of Financial Aid
Box 70722
Johnson City, TN 37614

4965

William G. Corey Memorial Scholarship

Amount: $2,500 **Deadline:** Mar 1
Fields/Majors: All Areas Of Study

Scholarship awarded to the top applicant from Pennsylvania. Must be legally blind. Write to the address below for details.

American Council Of The Blind
Scholarship Coordinator
1155 15th St., NW, Suite 720
Washington, DC 20005

4966

William J. And Marijane E. Adams, Jr. Scholarship

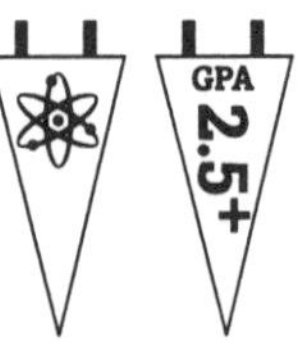

Amount: $1,000 **Deadline:** Apr 15
Fields/Majors: Agricultural And Biological Engineering

Awards available for undergraduates in the areas of agricultural or biological engineering. Must be in at least their second year of study and have a GPA of 2.5 or higher. Must demonstrate financial need. Write to the address below for more information.

American Society For Engineering In Agriculture, Food And Biological Systems
2950 Niles Road
St. Joseph, MI 49085

4967

William J. And Marijane E. Adams, Jr. Scholarship

Amount: $1,000 **Deadline:** Apr 15
Fields/Majors: Biological Engineering, Agricultural Engineering

Scholarships are available for undergraduates majoring in biological engineering or agricultural engineering accredited by ABET or CEAB with a GPA of 2.5 or better. Write to the address below for more information.

Adams Scholarship Fund
ASAE Foundation
2950 Niles Rd.
St. Joseph, MI 49085

4968

William J. And Mary Jane E. Adams, Jr., Scholarship

Amount: $1,000 **Deadline:** Apr 15
Fields/Majors: Mechanical Engineering

Scholarship for an ASME student member attending a college in ASME Region IX (CA, HI, and NV). For additional information, call or write the ASME foundation.

American Society Of Mechanical Engineers
Education Services Department
345 E. 47th St.
New York, NY 10017

4969

William J. Cook Scholarship

Amount: Varies **Deadline:** Feb 15
Fields/Majors: All Areas Of Study

Scholarships are available at the University of Illinois for students who reside in Cook County. Based on academic ability, financial need, and participation in extracurricular activities. For undergraduate study. Write to the address listed below for information.

Cook Scholarship Foundation
5020 South Lake Shore Drive
Suite 307
Chicago, IL 60615

4970 William J. Locklin Scholarship

Amount: $500 **Deadline:** Apr 2
Fields/Majors: Landscape Architecture/Design

Award was initiated to stress the importance of 24-hour lighting in landscape designs. Applicants must submit an essay and visual samples. Write to the address below for details.

Landscape Architecture Foundation
4401 Connecticut Ave., NW, Suite 500
Washington, DC 20008

4971 William James Erwin Scholarships

Amount: $2,500 **Deadline:** Mar 1
Fields/Majors: All Areas Of Study

Scholarship for entering freshmen with outstanding academic potential. Renewable for three years. Provides two scholarships. Contact the financial aid office at the address below for details.

Clemson University
Financial Aid Office
G01 Sikes Hall
Clemson, SC 29634

4972 William M. And Ruth Ann Lewis Endowed Assistance Fund

Amount: Varies **Deadline:** None Specified
Fields/Majors: All Areas Of Study

Awards are available for full-time students at Cedarville College who have financial need. Must have a GPA of at least 2.0. Write to the address below for more information.

Cedarville College
Financial Aid Office
P.O. Box 601
Cedarville, OH 45314

4973 William M. Junk And Frances William Smith Junk Endowed Grant

Amount: Varies **Deadline:** None Specified
Fields/Majors: All Areas Of Study

Awards are available for freshmen students at Cedarville College who have demonstrated academic prowess and financial need. Must have a GPA of at least 2.0. Write to the address below for more information.

Cedarville College
Financial Aid Office
P.O. Box 601
Cedarville, OH 45314

4974 William P. "Red" Curtin Scholarship

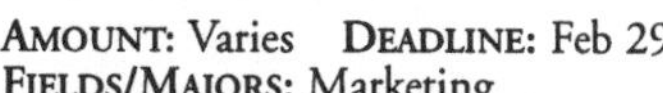

Amount: Varies **Deadline:** Feb 29
Fields/Majors: Marketing

Awards for students in the field of marketing with financial need and good academic standing. For entering sophomore, junior, or senior students. Contact the SOM Development Office, Room 206, for more information and an application.

University Of Massachusetts, Amherst
Som Development Office
Room 206
Amherst, MA 01003

4975 William P. Red Curtin Scholarship

Amount: Varies **Deadline:** Mar 1
Fields/Majors: Journalism

Awards for journalism students entering their sophomore, junior, or senior year at UMass. Contact the Dean, Humanities and Fine Arts, not the address below for more information.

University Of Massachusetts, Amherst
255 Whitmore Administration Building
Box 38230
Amherst, MA 01003

4976 William P. Willis Scholarship

Amount: $2,600 **Deadline:** May 1
Fields/Majors: All Areas Of Study

Scholarships are available for Oklahoma residents attending public Oklahoma schools. Based on financial need. One award per public institution. Requires nomination by university president. Write to the address listed below for information.

Oklahoma State Regents For Higher Education
State Capitol Complex
500 Education Building
Oklahoma City, OK 73105

4977 William Powers Sadler Scholarships

Amount: $1,000 **Deadline:** May 1
Fields/Majors: Agriculture, Life Sciences

Scholarships for incoming freshmen and returning undergraduates in the fields of agriculture and life sciences. Based on academic merit and financial need. Write to the address below for more information.

Virginia Tech College Of Agriculture And Life Sciences
Dr. John M. White, Associate Dean
1060 Litton Reaves Hall
Blacksburg, VA 24061

4978 William R. Biggs Scholarships

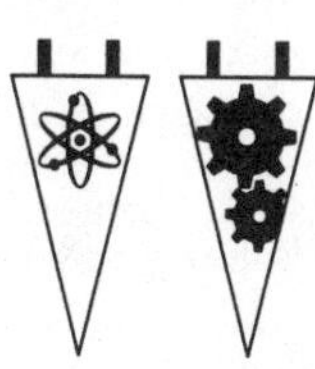

Amount: Varies **Deadline:** None Specified
Fields/Majors: Agricultural Communications

Awards for agricultural communications majors at Iowa State,

Michigan State, Texas Tech, University of Illinois, Ohio State, or the graduate school at the University of Wisconsin. Write to the address below for more information.

Gilmore Associates
National FFA Foundation
310 North Midvale Blvd., P.O. Box 5117
Madison, WI 53705

4979

William Toto Scholarship

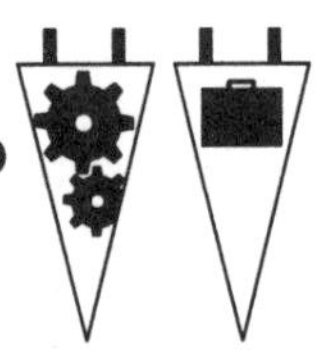

AMOUNT: $1,000 **DEADLINE:** May 31
FIELDS/MAJORS: Business, Engineering

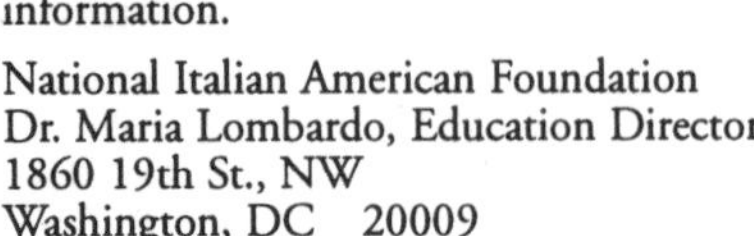

Awards for Italian American students who have successfully completed their sophomore year in engineering or business management. Write to the address below for more information.

National Italian American Foundation
Dr. Maria Lombardo, Education Director
1860 19th St., NW
Washington, DC 20009

4980

William W. Burgin, Jr., M.D. Scholarship

AMOUNT: $2,500 **DEADLINE:** Jun 30
FIELDS/MAJORS: Respiratory Therapy

Award for a second-year student in an accredited respiratory therapy program. Must have a GPA of at least 3.0. Also based on recommendations and an essay. Write to the address below for more information.

American Respiratory Care Foundation
Scholarship Committee
11030 Ables Lane
Dallas, TX 75229

4981

William, Betty Jane, And Elizabeth Boyd Scholarship Fund

AMOUNT: $250 Per Session **DEADLINE:** None Specified
FIELDS/MAJORS: Music

Awards for students studying for a career in music at St. Petersburg Junior College. Contact the Office of the Director of Scholarships and Student Financial Assistance at the St. Petersburg/Gibbs campus.

St. Petersburg Junior College
Office Of Financial Aid
P.O. Box 13489
St. Petersburg, FL 33733

4982

Williams Pipe Line Company Scholarships

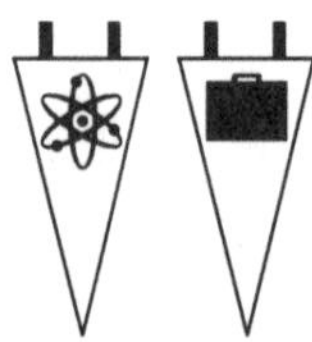

AMOUNT: $1,000 **DEADLINE:** Feb 15
FIELDS/MAJORS: Agribusiness

Scholarships are available for FFA members pursuing a four-year degree in agribusiness, who reside or attend school in Illinois, Iowa, Kansas, Minnesota, Missouri, North or South Dakota, Nebraska, Oklahoma, or Wisconsin. Write to the address below for details.

National FFA Foundation
Scholarship Office
P.O. Box 15160
Alexandria, VA 22309

4983

Willis S. Barnes Memorial Fund

AMOUNT: None Specified **DEADLINE:** Mar 1
FIELDS/MAJORS: All Areas Of Study

Scholarships are available at the University of New Mexico for full-time students who will be participating in the intercollegiate athletics program. Write to the address listed below for information.

University Of New Mexico, Albuquerque
Department Of Student Financial Aid
Mesa Vista Hall North
Albuquerque, NM 87131

4984

Willy Korf Memorial Fund Scholarships

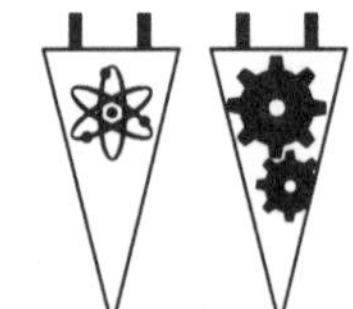

AMOUNT: $1,000 **DEADLINE:** May 30
FIELDS/MAJORS: Metallurgy, Metallurgical Engineering, Materials Science

Awards are available for students entering their final undergraduate year in any of the fields listed above. Only one candidate will be considered per school. Students must apply in their junior year. Write to the address below for more details.

Iron And Steel Society
Kathryn E. Kost
410 Commonwealth Dr.
Warrendale, PA 15086

4985

Wilma Sheridan Scholarship For Fine And Performing Arts

AMOUNT: $1,000 **DEADLINE:** Spring
FIELDS/MAJORS: Fine And Performing Arts

Awards are available to upper-division, full-time majors in the school of fine arts, who have a GPA of 3.0 or higher (3.5 or better in their major). Contact your major department chairperson for more information.

Portland State University
Music Department
231 Lincoln Hall
Portland, OR 97207

4986

Wilson-Hartsell Scholarship

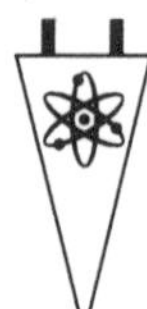

AMOUNT: None Specified **DEADLINE:** None Specified
FIELDS/MAJORS: Mathematics

Scholarship available to ETSU students majoring in mathematics. Write to the address below for details or contact the ETSU Department of Mathematics.

East Tennessee State University
Office Of Financial Aid
Box 70722
Johnson City, TN 37614

4987

Wilson Ornithological Society Awards

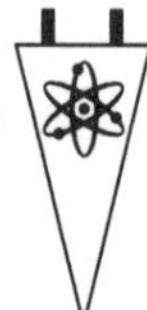

AMOUNT: $200-$600 **DEADLINE:** Jan 15
FIELDS/MAJORS: Ornithology

Applicants must submit a project outline for avian studies. The three awards are given for different types of ornithological research. Includes the Louis Agassiz Fuertes, Margaret Morse Nice, and Paul A. Stewart Awards. Write to the address below for details.

Wilson Ornithological Society
Dr. Dan Klem
Dept. Of Biology, Muhlenburg College
Allentown, PA 18104

4988 Winnebago County Bar Foundation Scholarship

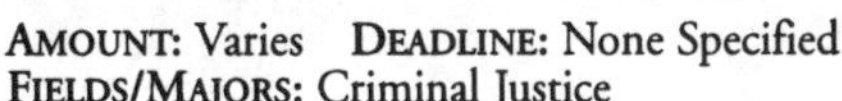

AMOUNT: Varies **DEADLINE:** None Specified
FIELDS/MAJORS: Criminal Justice

Awards available to outstanding students pursuing a career in the field of criminal justice. Write to the address below for more information.

Rockford College
Financial Aid Office
5050 East State St.
Rockford, IL 61108

4989 Winnie C. Davis-Children Of The Confederacy Scholarship

AMOUNT: Varies **DEADLINE:** None Specified
FIELDS/MAJORS: All Areas Of Study

Scholarships for members of the Children of the Confederacy. Must be approved by the Third Vice President General. Write to the UDC chapter nearest you. If address is not known, write to the address below for further information and the address.

United Daughters Of The Confederacy
Scholarship Coordinator
328 North Boulevard
Richmond, VA 23220

4990 Winston Cox Memorial Scholarships

AMOUNT: Varies **DEADLINE:** Apr 1
FIELDS/MAJORS: Business

Awards available to entering or returning students who have a GPA of at least 3.5 and enroll in at least one business administration course each semester. Based also on recommendations regarding the applicant's potential in business and on an essay on their career objectives in economics/business administration. Write to the address below for more information.

Rocky Mountain College
Office Of Financial Assistance
1511 Poly Drive
Billings, MT 59102

4991 Winston E. Parker Scholarship

AMOUNT: Varies **DEADLINE:** May 1
FIELDS/MAJORS: Forestry, Arboriculture, Ornamental Horticultural, Or Related Fields

Scholarships available to college students in their junior, senior or graduate years of study in one of the fields listed above. Applicant must reside in central or southern New Jersey. Write to the address below for details.

Moorestown Rotary Charities Inc.
Winston E. Parker Scholarship Committee
P.O. Box 105
Moorestown, NJ 08057

4992 Winterthur Museum Fellowships

AMOUNT: $2,000 Max/month **DEADLINE:** Dec 1
FIELDS/MAJORS: See Listing Below

Fellowships are available for doctoral and postdoctoral research at the Winterthur Museum and Library in African American history, cultural history, historic preservation, folklore, anthropology, archaeology, art history, decorative arts, material culture, preindustrial technology, women's history, architectural history, and urban studies. Write to the address listed below for information.

Winterthur Museum And Library
Advanced Studies Office
Research Fellowship Program
Winterthur, DE 19735

4993 Winthrop Scholars Award

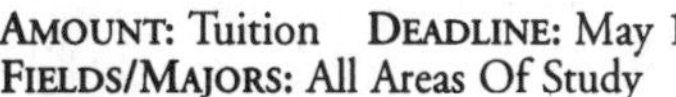

AMOUNT: Tuition **DEADLINE:** May 1
FIELDS/MAJORS: All Areas Of Study

Awards for freshmen who are in one of the following categories: rank in the top 10% of their high school class and have and SAT score of at least 1200, are National Merit Semifinalists and have an SAT of at least 1100, or are minority students with an SAT of 950 or better. Renewable. Write to the address below for more information.

Winthrop University
Financial Resource Center
119 Tillman Hall
Rock Hill, SC 29733

4994 Wisconsin Association Of Milk And Food Santiarians, Inc.

AMOUNT: $1,000 **DEADLINE:** Jul 1
FIELDS/MAJORS: All Areas Of Study

Applicant must be a Wisconsin resident full-time student accepted or enrolled in a Wisconsin or Minnesota college. Must display an interest in dairy food science environmental health or allied areas of life sciences. Includes the E.H. Marth Food and Environmental Sciences. Write to the address below for more information.

University Of Wisconsin, Oshkosh
Financial Aid Office, Dempsey 104
800 Algoma Blvd.
Oshkosh, WI 54901

4995 Wisconsin Higher Education Grant (WHEG)

AMOUNT: None Specified **DEADLINE:** None Specified
FIELDS/MAJORS: All Areas Of Study

Funds are available to residents of Wisconsin attending the University of Wisconsin system, Wisconsin technical college system, or private Wisconsin colleges. Write to the address below for details.

State Of Wisconsin Higher Educational Aids Board
P.O. Box 7885
Madison, WI 53707

4996

Wisconsin Native American Student Grant

Amount: $2,200 **Deadline:** None Specified
Fields/Majors: All Areas Of Study

Funds are available to residents of Wisconsin who are of Native American origin (at least 25% Native American). Applicant must attend a college or university in Wisconsin and demonstrate financial need. Write to the address below for details.

State Of Wisconsin Higher Educational Aids Board
P.O. Box 7885
Madison, WI 53707

4997

Wix Corporation Scholarships

Amount: $1,000 **Deadline:** Feb 15
Fields/Majors: Agricultural Mechanics, Agricultural Engineering

Scholarships are available for FFA members pursuing a four-year degree in agricultural mechanics or agricultural engineering. Write to the address below for details.

National FFA Foundation
Scholarship Office
P.O. Box 15160
Alexandria, VA 22309

4998

Wolcott Foundation Fellowships

Amount: $1,800 **Deadline:** Feb 1
Fields/Majors: Business Administration, Public Management, International Affairs

Fellowships for master's degree students at George Washington University. Award is considered a grant if for four years after graduation, recipients work in federal, state or local government or in select private international business. Some preference given to persons active in Masonic activities (Demolay, Job's Daughters, Rainbow, etc.). Must be a U.S. citizen. Information is available from the address below.

High Twelve International
Wolcott Foundation Fellowships At GWU
402 Beasley St.
Monroe, LA 71203

4999

Wolves Club Of Erie Scholarship Fund

Amount: Varies **Deadline:** None Specified
Fields/Majors: All Areas Of Study

Awards for Erie County, PA, residents who graduated in the top 25% of their high school class and enrolled in any undergraduate degree program. Write to the address below for more information.

Mercyhurst College
Financial Aid Office
Glenwood Hills
Erie, PA 16546

5000

Woman's Seamen's Friend Society Of Connecticut

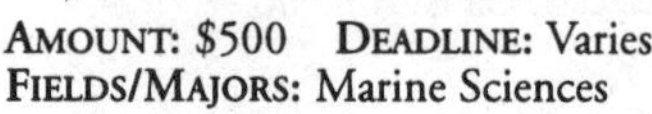

Amount: $500 **Deadline:** Varies
Fields/Majors: Marine Sciences

Scholarships are available to students who are majoring in marine science at any college in Connecticut or for Connecticut residents who are studying marine sciences at any institution in the U.S. Connecticut residents who are or are dependents of merchant seafarers are also eligible. For graduate level research only. Write to the address below for details.

Woman's Seamen's Friend Society Of Connecticut, Inc.
Attn: Scholarships
74 Forbes Ave.
New Haven, CT 06512

5001

Women In Engineering Program

Amount: $500 **Deadline:** Jan 15
Fields/Majors: Engineering

Scholarships for women who are either freshmen or transfer students at the University of Missouri, Rolla pursuing an engineering degree. Approximately thirty awards per year. Not renewable. Contact Mr. Floyd Harris, Director, Women in Engineering Program, at the below address for details.

University Of Missouri, Rolla
107 Norwood Hall
Rolla, MO 65401

5002

Women In Science & Engineering Scholarship Program

Amount: Varies **Deadline:** None Specified
Fields/Majors: Science, Mathematics, Computer Science

Merit-based scholarships are available for full-time juniors and seniors at Spelman College. Applicant must have a GPA of at least 3.0. Write to the address listed below for additional information.

Spelman College
Office Of Admission And Orientation
350 Spelman Lane, SW, Box 277
Atlanta, GA 30314

5003

Women Of Wayne Alumni Association Scholarships

Amount: Varies **Deadline:** None Specified
Fields/Majors: All Areas Of Study

Scholarships for women students at Wayne State University studying part-time on the undergraduate, graduate, or postgraduate level. Write to the address below for details.

Wayne State University
Women's Resource Center
573 Student Center Bldg.
Detroit, MI 48202

5004

Women's Auxiliary Scholarship Loan Fund

Amount: Varies **Deadline:** Mar 15
Fields/Majors: Mining, Metallurgy, Material Science

Awards for full-time junior or senior college or university students and and graduate students for a degree in earth sciences or related fields. Other fields recognized include mining, geology, metallurgy, petroleum, mineral sciences, materials science, mining economics, and other related fields. Contact the chapter of WAAIME at your college or university for details. If necessary to find out the address of your local scholarship loan fund chairman, write to the address below. Application forms are not sent until after the interview.

WAAIME Headquarters
Scholarship Loan Fund
345 E. 47th St., 14th Floor
New York, NY 10017

5005

Women's Auxiliary To Greater Albuquerque Medical Assoc. Scholarship

Amount: Varies **Deadline:** Mar 1
Fields/Majors: Medicine

Awards are available at the University of New Mexico for medical students with demonstrated merit and qualities of heart and mind that indicate humanitarian principles dedicated to high ideals of medical practice. Write to the address below for more information.

University Of New Mexico, Albuquerque
Office Of Financial Aid
Albuquerque, NM 87131

5006

Women's Club Of Albuquerque Scholarship

Amount: Varies **Deadline:** Mar 1
Fields/Majors: Medicine

Awards are available at the University of New Mexico for medical students with demonstrated scholastic ability and financial need. Write to the address below for more information.

University Of New Mexico, Albuquerque
Office Of Financial Aid
Albuquerque, NM 87131

5007

Women's Club Scholarship

Amount: $500-$1,000 **Deadline:** None Specified
Fields/Majors: All Areas Of Study

Scholarships are available for full-time juniors or seniors. Must have a GPA of 3.0 or better. Financial need must be demonstrated. Write to the address below for more information.

California State Polytechnic University, Pomona
Office Of Financial Aid
3801 West Temple Ave.
Pomona, CA 91768

5008

Women's Club/Clare Smith Memorial Scholarship

Amount: $500 **Deadline:** None Specified
Fields/Majors: All Areas Of Study

Scholarships are available for full-time juniors, seniors or graduate students. Must have a GPA of 3.0 or better. Financial need must be demonstrated. Write to the address below for more information.

California State Polytechnic University, Pomona
Office Of Financial Aid
3801 West Temple Ave.
Pomona, CA 91768

5009

Women's Club/Gwen La Bounty Scholarship

GPA 3.0+

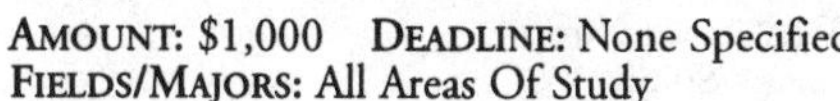

Amount: $1,000 **Deadline:** None Specified
Fields/Majors: All Areas Of Study

Scholarships are available for full-time juniors, seniors, or graduate students. Must have a GPA of 3.0 or better. Financial need must be demonstrated. Write to the address below for more information.

California State Polytechnic University, Pomona
Office Of Financial Aid
3801 West Temple Ave.
Pomona, CA 91768

5010

Women's Club/Kay Kramer Scholarship

Amount: $500 **Deadline:** None Specified
Fields/Majors: All Areas Of Study

Scholarships are available for full-time juniors, seniors, or graduate students. Must have a GPA of 3.0 or better. Financial need must be demonstrated. Write to the address below for more information.

California State Polytechnic University, Pomona
Office Of Financial Aid
3801 West Temple Ave.
Pomona, CA 91768

5011

Women's Jewelry Association, Inc. Scholarship

Amount: $750-$1,000 **Deadline:** May 30
Fields/Majors: Jewelry

Awards available for women students enrolled in jewelry programs who are in need of financial assistance. Write to the address below for more information.

Women's Jewelry Association, Inc.
Scholarship Committee
333B Rte. #46 West
Fairfield, NY 07004

5012

Women's Research And Education Institute Congressional Fellowship

Amount: $9,000 **Deadline:** Feb 19
Fields/Majors: Women And Public Policy Issues

Annual fellowship program that places women graduate students in congressional offices and on strategic committee staffs. Encouraging more effective participation by women in the formation of policy at all levels. Must be currently enrolled in a graduate degree program. Award also pays $1,500 per month for tuition expenses. Write to the address below for details.

Women's Research And Education Institute
Alison Dineen, Fellowships Director
1700 18th St., NW, Suite 400
Washington, DC 20009

5013

Women's Studies Research Grants

AMOUNT: $1,500 **DEADLINE:** Nov 5
FIELDS/MAJORS: Women's Studies

For doctoral candidates in the above fields who will soon complete all doctoral requirements except the dissertation. These grants are to be used for research expenses connected with the dissertation. The purpose is to encourage original and significant research on topics about women. Approximately twenty grants per year. Write to the attention of women's studies department for further information. Application request deadline is Oct 20.

Woodrow Wilson National Fellowship Foundation
Women's Studies Research Grants
CN 5281
Princeton, NJ 08543

5014

Womens Ballet Committee Scholarship, Ballet UAB Alumni Scholarship

AMOUNT: $1,000 **DEADLINE:** None Specified
FIELDS/MAJORS: Ballet Dancing

Applicants must be incoming freshmen who are majoring in ballet dancing. Write to the address below for more information.

University Of Alabama, Birmingham
Department Of Theater And Dance
700 13th St. South, UAB Station
Birmingham, AL 35294

5015

Woodard Memorial Scholarship Program

AMOUNT: $3,400 (approx) **DEADLINE:** Mar 15
FIELDS/MAJORS: All Areas Of Study

Scholarships for students at Adams State College. For full-time study. Thirty awards offered annually. Based on leadership, academics, and character. "Must not have appeared on any list published indicating. membership in any organization that is subversive to the interest of the United States of America." Contact the Woodward Scholarship Committee through the financial aid office for complete details.

Adams State College
Financial Aid Office
Alamosa, CO 81102

5016

Woodrow Wilson Fellowships

AMOUNT: Varies **DEADLINE:** Oct 1
FIELDS/MAJORS: Humanities, Social Sciences, Public And International Affairs

Fellowships for postdoctoral scholars in the fields above. Selection primarily based on scholarly promise, importance and originality of project proposal, and the likelihood that the work will advance basic understanding of the topic of study. Write to the address below for more information.

Woodrow Wilson International Center
Fellowships Office
100 Jefferson Dr., SW SI Mrc 022
Washington, DC 20560

5017

Woodrow Wilson Program In Public Policy And International Affairs

AMOUNT: Varies **DEADLINE:** Varies
FIELDS/MAJORS: Public Policy/International Affairs

Minority program for juniors, seniors, and graduate students interested in careers in public policy and international affairs. Must be a U.S. citizen or permanent resident. Write to the address below for details.

Woodrow Wilson National Fellowship Foundation
Dr. Richard O. Hope, VP, WWNFF
CN 5281
Princeton, NJ 08543

5018

Woomer Scholarship

AMOUNT: Varies **DEADLINE:** None Specified
FIELDS/MAJORS: All Areas Of Study

Awards for students at WJC based on academic performance and leadership. Write to the address below for more information.

Wheeling Jesuit College
Student Financial Planning
316 Washington Ave.
Wheeling, WV 26003

5019

Workshops And Courses To Improve Language Teaching And Pedagogy

AMOUNT: $5,000 (max) **DEADLINE:** Nov 1, Mar 1
FIELDS/MAJORS: Japanese Language

Grants are available for scholars to design workshops or courses to improve the teaching of the Japanese language at the college or pre-college level. Applicants should be prepared to explain the character or rationale of their project and be able to prepare a budget estimate. Write to the address below for more information.

Northeast Asia Council Association For Asian Studies
1 Lane Hall
University Of Michigan
Ann Arbor, MI 48109

5020

World Book, Inc. Award

AMOUNT: $1,500 (max) **DEADLINE:** Mar 15
FIELDS/MAJORS: Library Science

Must be member of Catholic Library Association. Purpose of award is to add expertise in the field of children's or school librarianship. For graduate study and research only. One award is given per year. Write to the address below for more information.

Catholic Library Association
Scholarship Committee
461 West Lancaster Ave.
Haverford, PA 19041

5021

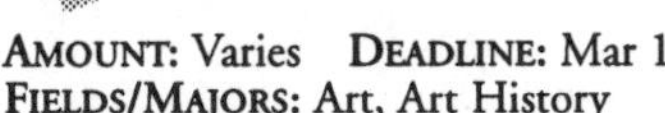

Wortham Akin Memorial Scholarship

AMOUNT: Varies **DEADLINE:** Mar 1
FIELDS/MAJORS: Art, Art History

Scholarships are available at the University of New Mexico for full-time junior or senior art or art history majors. Write to the address listed below for information.

University Of New Mexico, Albuquerque
College Of Fine Arts
Office Of The Dean
Albuquerque, NM 87131

5022

Writers Of The Future Contest

AMOUNT: $500-$4,000 **DEADLINE:** Varies
FIELDS/MAJORS: Science Fiction Or Fantasy Writing

Contest for amateur science fiction writers. Entries must be works of prose (short stories or novels) that have not been previously published. Write to the address below for more details.

L. Ron Hubbard
P.O. Box 1630
Los Angeles, CA 90078

5023

Writing Scholarships

AMOUNT: Tuition **DEADLINE:** Mar 15
FIELDS/MAJORS: Writing

Awards for Jacksonville State University students who are in the field of writing. Contact the head of the English department for more information.

Jacksonville State University
Financial Aid Office
Jacksonville, AL 36265

5024

WTS Undergraduate Scholarship

AMOUNT: $2,000 **DEADLINE:** Feb 27
FIELDS/MAJORS: Transportation Related

Scholarship for a student expressing interest in transportation as an academic and career goal. Must be a female and have a GPA of at least 3.0. Applicants must be enrolled in an accredited degree program in Indiana or Illinois. Write to Ms. Karen M. George at the address below for details.

Women's Transportation Seminar Scholarship Committee Chair
c/o Barton-Aschman Associates, Inc.
820 Davis St., Suite 300
Evanston, IL 60201

5025

Wuenschel/Gerboth Teaching Scholarship

AMOUNT: Varies **DEADLINE:** None Specified
FIELDS/MAJORS: Education

Award for students who are studying education and exhibit financial need. Write to the address below for more information.

Mercyhurst College
Financial Aid Office
Glenwood Hills
Erie, PA 16546

5026

WVU National Merit Scholarship

AMOUNT: $2,000 (max) **DEADLINE:** None Specified
FIELDS/MAJORS: All Areas Of Study

Scholarships for National Merit Scholarship finalists who select WVU as their college of choice. Winners of other NMSC scholarships are not eligible. Preference is given to West Virginia residents. Write to the address below for details.

West Virginia University
Financial Aid Office
P.O. Box 6004
Morgantown, WV 26506

5027

WVU Scholarships

AMOUNT: $250-$2,000 **DEADLINE:** Varies
FIELDS/MAJORS: All Areas Of Study

Scholarships for students at WVU. Criteria vary for different awards. Programs include WVU foundation, presidential, high school leadership, designated, and departmental scholarships. Contact the financial aid office at the address below for details.

West Virginia University
Financial Aid Office
Mountainlair, 2nd Floor
Morgantown, WV 26506

5028

Wyeth Fellowship

AMOUNT: $13,000 **DEADLINE:** Nov 15
FIELDS/MAJORS: American Art

Two year fellowships are available for doctoral scholars researching for the dissertation. One year will be spent on research, and one year will be spent at the National Gallery of Art. Applicants must know two foreign languages related to the topic of the dissertation and be U.S. citizens or legal residents. Write to the address listed below for information.

National Gallery Of Art
Center For Advanced Study In Visual Arts
Predoctoral Fellowship Program
Washington, DC 20565

5029

Wylie Math Scholarships

AMOUNT: Varies **DEADLINE:** Feb 1
FIELDS/MAJORS: All Areas Of Study

Awards for entering freshmen who have outstanding mathematical ability and a combined SAT score of at least 1300. Write to the address below for more information.

Furman University
Director Of Financial Aid
3300 Poinsett Highway
Greenville, SC 29613

5030

Xeric Foundation Grants

AMOUNT: $5,000 (max) **DEADLINE:** Jan 31, Jul 31
FIELDS/MAJORS: Comic Book Art

Grants for students interested in comic book art or writing. Funds are to be used to assist with the physical production and distribution of your book. Write to the address below for more information.

Xeric Foundation
351 Pleasant St., #214
Northhampton, MA 01060

5031

Xerox Technical Minority Scholarship Program

AMOUNT: None Specified **DEADLINE:** Sep 15
FIELDS/MAJORS: Engineering And Science

Scholarships for full-time minority students enrolled in one of the following fields: chemical, computer, electrical, materials, mechanical, optical or civil engineering, computer science, physics, and imaging. Write to Eleanor J. Krieger, College Relations Manager, at the address below for details.

Xerox Corporation, Staffing Strategies And Solutions
Technical Minority Scholarship Fund
800 Phillips Road-205-99E
Webster, NY 14580

5032

Yetter Manufacturing Company Scholarships

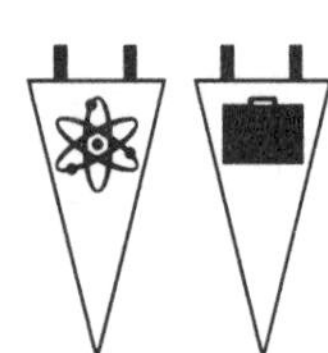

AMOUNT: $500 **DEADLINE:** Feb 15
FIELDS/MAJORS: Agriculture, Agribusiness

Scholarships are available for FFA members pursuing a two-year degree in any area of agriculture or agribusiness. Write to the address below for details.

National FFA Foundation
Scholarship Office
P.O. Box 15160
Alexandria, VA 22309

5033

Yoshiko Tanaka Memorial Scholarship

AMOUNT: Varies **DEADLINE:** Apr 1
FIELDS/MAJORS: Japanese Language And Culture

Awards for undergraduate students of Japanese ancestry who have an interest in Japanese language, culture, or enhancing U.S.-Japan relations. Write to the address below for more details. Please be sure to include an SASE with your request.

Japanese American Citizens League
National Headquarters
1765 Sutter St.
San Francisco, CA 94115

5034

Yoshiyama Award For Exemplary Service To The Community

AMOUNT: $5,000 **DEADLINE:** Apr 1
FIELDS/MAJORS: All Areas Of Study

Awards are available for graduating and rising high school seniors in the United States and territories engaged in extraordinary community service. Submit nomination packages to the Yoshiyama Award, P.O. Box 19247, Washington, DC 20036-9247.

Hitachi Foundation
1509 22nd St., NW
Washington, DC 20037

5035

Young American Creative Patriotic Art Program

AMOUNT: $500-$3,000 **DEADLINE:** May 1
FIELDS/MAJORS: All Areas Of Study

Awards are available for graduating senior high school students who submit one of five winning entries in this contest. Artwork must express a patriotic theme. Applicant must be sponsored by a local VFW Auxiliary. Contact your local VFW Auxiliary chapter or write to the address listed below for further information.

Ladies Auxiliary To The Veterans Of Foreign Wars Of The United States, National Headquarters
406 West 34th St.
Kansas City, MO 64111

5036

Young Composers Awards

AMOUNT: $250-$1,000 **DEADLINE:** May 1
FIELDS/MAJORS: Music Composition

Awards from a competition open to students who are citizens of the United States or Canada, age 18 or less, for composing an original work of music. Student must be enrolled in a recognized musical institution, a music curriculum, or be engaged in the private study of music with an established teacher.

National Guild Of Community Schools Of The Arts
Kate Brackett, Executive Assistant
40 N. Van Brunt St., P.O. Box 8018
Englewood, NJ 07631

5037

Young Lawyers Program

AMOUNT: Varies **DEADLINE:** Mar 15
FIELDS/MAJORS: Law

Grants to lawyers who hold the JD or LLB degree, have passed the bar exam, and who are under the age of 32. This program offers young lawyers the chance to gain unique insight into the structure and function of German law through ten months of taking legal courses and interning in Germany. Applicants must be fluent in German and be U.S. or Canadian citizens. Write to the address below for more details.

Daad German Academic Exchange Service, New York Office
950 Third Ave., 19th Floor
New York, NY 10022

5038

Young Playwrights, Inc., Playwriting Contest

AMOUNT: None Specified **DEADLINE:** Oct 15
FIELDS/MAJORS: Playwriting

The festival is a national playwriting contest for writers aged 18 and younger. Winning playwrights receive a full production of their plays and a royalty. Musicals and screenplays are not accepted. Must have been 18 or younger as of July 1 of the contest year.

Young Playwrights Festival
National Playwriting Contest
321 W. 44th St., Suite 906
New York, NY 10036

5039

Youth Activity Grant Fund

AMOUNT: None Specified **DEADLINE:** Apr 30
FIELDS/MAJORS: Natural Sciences

Youth activity grant is for high school and undergraduate students, to help them participate in field research in the natural sciences anywhere in the world. Applicants must be U.S. citizens. Write to the address below for complete details.

Explorers Club
Youth Activity Fund
46 East 70th St.
New York, NY 10021

5040

Youth Citizenship Award Program

AMOUNT: $1,250 **DEADLINE:** None Specified
FIELDS/MAJORS: All Areas Of Study

Awards for graduating high school seniors who have demonstrated service to their community, home, and school. Not based on academic achievement. Fifty-four awards are given regionally, and one $2,000 national award is given to the finalist. Application is made through participating soroptimist clubs. Addresses can be found in your local telephone directory, chamber of commerce, or city hall.

Soroptimist International Of The Americas, Inc.
1616 Walnut St.
Philadelphia, PA 19103

5041

Yutaka Nakazawa Memorial Scholarship

AMOUNT: Varies **DEADLINE:** Apr 1
FIELDS/MAJORS: Judo

Applicants must be of Japanese ancestry and studying Judo at the college level. Applications and information may be obtained from local JACL chapters, district offices, and the national headquarters at the address below. Please indicate your level of study and be certain to include a legal-sized SASE.

Japanese American Citizens League
National Scholarship And Award Program
1765 Sutter St.
San Francisco, CA 94115

5042

YWCA Women On The Awards Move

AMOUNT: Varies **DEADLINE:** Mar 1
FIELDS/MAJORS: All Areas Of Study

Awards are available at the University of New Mexico for full-time juniors or seniors with a GPA of at least 2.5.

University Of New Mexico, Albuquerque
Office Of Financial Aid
Albuquerque, NM 87131

5043

Zachary And Elizabeth M. Fisher Armed Services Foundation Scholarship

AMOUNT: Varies **DEADLINE:** Feb 1
FIELDS/MAJORS: All Areas Of Study

Scholarships for sons/daughters of active duty/reserve U.S. Service member in good standing, discharged (honorably or medically), or deceased. For undergraduate, vocational, or technical study. Students whose family income exceeds $37,000 per year are ineligible. Write to the attention of Ms. Roseanne Raczko at the address below for further information. Please include a stamped, self-addressed postcard with your requests.

Zachary And Elizabeth M. Fisher Armed Services Foundation
Intrepid Sea, Air, Space Museum
12th Ave. And W. 46th St.
New York, NY 10036

5044

Zeneca Pharmaceuticals Underserved Healthcare Grant

AMOUNT: $5,000 (min) **DEADLINE:** None Specified
FIELDS/MAJORS: Osteopathic Medicine

Grants for third-year students committed to practice in underserved minority populations. Grant is intended to encourage the participation of minority students in this field. Write to the address below for more information. Applications are available from the foundation office after Jan 1.

National Osteopathic Foundation
5775G Peachtree-Dunwoody Road, Suite 500
Atlanta, GA 30342

5045

Zia Activity Scholarships

AMOUNT: None Specified **DEADLINE:** Feb 1
FIELDS/MAJORS: All Areas Of Study

Scholarships are available at the University of New Mexico for entering freshmen who were not selected for a Regent's, Presidential, or UNM Scholars award, but who have demonstrated outstanding leadership and involvement in school or community activities. Write to the address listed below for information.

University Of New Mexico, Albuquerque
Student Financial Aid Office
Mesa Vista Hall North, Student Services
Albuquerque, NM 87131

5046

Zia Scholarships

AMOUNT: None Specified **DEADLINE:** Feb 1
FIELDS/MAJORS: All Areas Of Study

Scholarships are available at the University of New Mexico for entering minority freshmen who have demonstrated outstanding leadership and involvement in high school or community activities. Write to the address listed below for information.

University Of New Mexico, Albuquerque
Student Financial Aid Office
Mesa Vista Hall North, Student Services
Albuquerque, NM 87131

5047

Zia Transfer Scholarships

AMOUNT: $1,000 (max) **DEADLINE:** Varies
FIELDS/MAJORS: All Areas Of Study

Scholarships are available at the University of New Mexico for minority transfer students with a GPA of at least 3.25.

University Of New Mexico, Albuquerque
Student Financial Aid Office
Mesa Vista Hall North, Room 1044
Albuquerque, NM 87131

Major/Career Objective Index

BUSINESS

EDUCATION

Engineering

Fine Arts

HUMANITIES

MEDICINE

SCIENCE

SOCIAL SCIENCES

Vocational

Special Criteria Index

Athletics

Disability

Ethnic Background

Gender

Grade Point Average

Heritage

Marital Status

Military Service

Religion

School Index